MW00757925

A devotional written for teen girls and young women

LINDA KREH

WestBow Press books may be ordered through booksellers or by contacting:

WestBow Press
A Division of Thomas Nelson & Zondervan
1663 Liberty Drive
Bloomington, IN 47403
www.westbowpress.com
1 (866) 928-1240

ISBN: 978-1-5127-4443-9 (sc)
ISBN: 978-1-5127-4444-6 (hc)
ISBN: 978-1-5127-4442-2 (e)

Library of Congress Control Number: 2016908896

Print information available on the last page.

WestBow Press rev. date: 7/11/2016

Shout for joy to the Lord, all the earth.
Worship the Lord with gladness;
come before him with joyful songs.
Know that the Lord is God.
It is he who made us, and we are his;
we are his people, the sheep of his pasture.

Enter his gates with thanksgiving
and his courts with praise;
give thanks to him and praise his name.
For the Lord is good and his love
endures forever;
his faithfulness continues
through all generations.

Psalm 100

To my nieces:
Melissa
Danielle
Nicole
Krista
The Lord has blessed me.
Each of you, in your own special way, has brought me great joy.
Continue to keep your eyes focused on Jesus, and in ***all things****,*
allow Him to lead.

And to my beautiful mother, Alberta, who is loving and giving and prays without ceasing.

Ackowledgements

Stephanie Hogan- Thank you for your enthusiasm, for your encouragement and for your prayers when this devotional was just a newly planted seed.

Emily, Hannah, and Madison- I appreciate your input and your suggestions.

Kelly Piatek- My sister in faith, who spent hours upon hours editing page after page of my mistakes. I am so glad your red pen did not run out of ink! I can't thank you enough. It had to be a labor of love!

My niece, Melissa Koehler- Thanks, Melis, for coming to my rescue with technical assistance.

With appreciation to my family and friends for all of their prayers and support.

TO GOD BE THE GLORY!

The inspiration for this devotional started in 2010, when a dear friend gave me the journal version of S***treams In the Desert*** for my birthday. *Streams In the Desert* is my most treasured devotional. Even though I had read this several times in the past, I was very excited as I anticipated reading through it once again.

As I started writing responses in the journal each day, it soon became evident that it was not only about my daily devotions. My focus became two-fold. Above all, I wanted to be open and obedient to God's direction with each response. I wanted the pages to be filled with His words, not my words. I tried very hard to stay out of His way.

Secondly, my thoughts were on my four precious nieces. As never having children of my own, you can only imagine how special they are to me. Each one of them has a spiritual foundation that allows them, even at a young age, to be a light in this dark and fallen world.

I wanted to give them something that would inspire them, comfort them, and in some ways, prepare them for whatever they encountered in life. I also wanted to leave room on each page for them to add their own thoughts.

Even as I continued to write keeping my nieces in mind, God was speaking to my heart, as well. It seems that, what I intended as a gift for "my girls", also became a gift to me.

A few years later, I felt the Lord prompting me to write a devotional for teenage girls and young adults. This devotional contains many of the original entries that were written for my nieces in 2010.

Introduction

When you think of "royalty", what comes to mind? Kings and queens from ages past that fill history books? The British royals such as Queen Elizabeth and Prince Charles? And let's not forget the two handsome sons, Prince William and Prince Harry.

Or, do you picture a lush, lavish palace with all "the upgrades"?

If you are like me, you probably don't often think of yourself as royalty. After all, that would mean that your parents are the king and queen "of something." And that would make you a princess, with all of the influence, privileges, and opportunities that come with being the daughter of a king.

Chances are, no one who will be reading this book lives in a palace. And I think it's safe to say, at this moment, no one is bowing down at your feet.

However, dear ones, it is my hope that these pages will remind you of, who you are in Christ, and that you will seriously consider how much the King loves you as His precious daughter.

Our Father in Heaven is the King of kings and the Lord of lords. You are His child, His daughter. And yes, that makes you royalty!

I know that it is not easy to live in a world that does not value the things of God. I pray that as you read the pages and entries for each day, you will be encouraged, uplifted, comforted, and filled with Truth.

Daughters of the King

I am a daughter of the King.

My Father is King of all nations.
He has all things at His disposal and
the ends of the earth are at His feet.

His wisdom defies human understanding
and His power and authority cannot be contained.

I am a daughter of the King.

My Father is mighty enough to conquer kingdoms,
yet tender enough to cradle me in His arms.

The problems of this world are on His shoulders,
yet He is never too busy to hear my cries.
I do not wait in line to have an audience with the King.

He has been with me from the beginning,
and He will be with me to the end.

I am a daughter of the King.

I was born into royalty
and blessed with an inheritance that this world cannot conceive.

I have a past that has been wiped clean,
and a future that has been bought and paid for.

I am a daughter of the King, but...
I am not an only child,
for, my sisters are many.

Let us rejoice together as
DAUGHTERS OF THE KING!
Linda Kreh, 2010

Contents

January

The Heart of Our King

A new year is upon us, ready or not! Let us step into this new year with hope and with excitement as we anticipate all that the Lord has in store for us.

Let us not be fearful of any uncertainty that a new year might bring, but let us walk with confidence and trust that our futures are secure because the Lord goes with us.

Put ***it all*** in His hands: every moment, every day, and every situation.

Let's get excited about what the Lord has in store for us in the days, the weeks, and the months ahead.

> The Lord himself goes before you and will be with you;
> he will never leave you nor forsake you. Do not be afraid;
> do not be discouraged. Deuteronomy 31:8

As you think about this new year, would you rather walk through it with Jesus or walk it alone? Explain.

____

____

____

____

____

____

____

January 2nd

As this new year unfolds, help us, Lord, to choose what is **best**, to choose the way of eternity, not the way of the world.

Even as there are temptations all around you and negativity that consumes your thoughts at times, ask Jesus to help you stay focused on what's really important and make that a priority.

Don't settle for what is good, or what is better, but allow God to lead you toward what is **best**.

To know the Father's heart is to love Him and trust Him.

> Choose for yourselves this day whom you will serve.
> Joshua 24:15

What is the difference between "the way of eternity" and "the way of the world"? Why do you think the majority of people choose "the way of the world"?

____

____

____

____

____

____

____

God's ways are not our ways and our ways are not His ways. There is quite a lot we do not understand about God. But, even as our knowledge of His ways is limited, we can trust His perfect will for our lives.

His ways will never be fully known to us, but they can be fully trusted. Our God is faithful and loving. He loves you as His beautiful daughter…

And that will never change!

> See I lay a stone in Zion, a tested stone, a precious cornerstone for a sure foundation; the one who trusts will never be dismayed. Isaiah 28:16

What comes to mind when you think of yourself as a beautiful daughter of the King of kings? Do you believe that He has a specific plan for your life? Do you believe that Christ will provide all that you need in order to accomplish that plan?

January 4th

The Lord knows those who are His. Those who belong to Him (2 Timothy 2: 19).

There is nothing this world can throw at us, that we cannot rise above.

He is our Shield.

There is nothing we cannot face with confidence.

He is our Strength.

There is nothing to fear. We belong to the King of kings! And no one can snatch us out of His hand (John 10:28).

> No one is like you, O Lord; you are great, and your name is mighty in power. Jeremiah 10:6

What does it mean to you to know that the Creator of the universe knows you by name?

____

____

____

____

____

____

____

January 5th

Several years ago during a trip to France, I saw Mont Blanc for the very first time. This massive mountain has snow-covered peaks that extend high up into the heavens. What a magnificent sight, even from a distance!

Standing in the valley and looking up, the mountain is awesome in its size and in its beauty. Standing at the top and looking down, I stood amazed at the Lord's beautiful creation.

To me, Mont Blanc is a visual reminder of God's faithfulness. It shall not be moved. It stands strong, unwavering, in all of its splendor.

> Your love, O Lord, reaches to the heavens, your faithfulness to the skies. Your righteousness is like the mighty mountains.
>
> Psalm 36:5,6

What crosses your mind when you get a beautiful glimpse of the Lord's creation? Can you think of a time when God's creation took your breath away?

January 6th

The Lord of lords, the King of kings.

He is the Lord of the impossible. Never predictable. Always incredible!

His power cannot be contained, nor can it be understood. Nothing is beyond His reach.

His ways exceed all expectation. He holds nothing back.

Our Father mightily and lovingly opens the floodgates of heaven and pours out His blessings on all who put their hope in Him.

> He performs wonders that cannot be fathomed, and miracles that cannot be counted. Job 5:9

Do you believe that "nothing is impossible" with God? Have you ever witnessed His power and His love in an impossible situation?

January 7th

When we lean on God, we are acknowledging that we **cannot** bear the burden alone. We are also expressing that we **do not want to** bear it alone.

Throughout the Bible, the Lord repeats, "I will be with you." This is a promise that I find great comfort in. Just knowing that the Lord is **always** with me gives me strength and hope.

Be assured! You are never alone! The Lord and Savior is with you, and regardless of your situation, that will never change!

> And surely I am with you always, to the very end of the age.
> Matthew 28:20

As the Lord invites you into a relationship with Him, are you hesitant in any way to accept the invitation? Explain.

I believe that God is active and involved in every detail of our lives. Even if we might not "feel" His presence, we know that He is with us.

Psalm 121 is one of my favorite chapters in the Bible and it is one that I have leaned on many times. It tells about the watchfulness of God. He watches us day and night. Nothing is hidden from Him.

He is the Maker and Creator of all. The Maker and Creator of ***us***!

He is our Helper and our Protector. Even as we are at rest, God is at work.

> The Lord watches over you- the Lord is your shade at your right hand; the sun will not harm you by day, nor the moon by night. Psalm 121:5,6

What do you think is meant by "the watchful eye of God"?

Let the things that you ***know*** overshadow the things that you ***feel.***

-**Know** that the Lord is always with you.
-**Know** that He is all that you need.
-**Know** that His grace is sufficient for you.
-**Know** that He only wants what is best for you.

Don't allow your feelings to interfere with the <u>Truth</u>.
Stay focused on what you know… and on Who you know.

> I consider everything a loss compared to the surpassing greatness of knowing Christ Jesus my Lord.
>
> Philippians 3:8

Can you remember a time when your feelings overshadowed the Truth? Why is it important to know the TRUTH?

January 10th

Does your view of God change when you are facing trials and hardships? Do you think that maybe He has "fallen asleep at the wheel"? Do you wonder if the Lord has forgotten all about you?

Honestly, I am sure that we can all relate to these questions at some point in our lives. But, the truth is…

Even as we are questioning, "Lord, where are You?" God is right there beside us. He is faithful. He does not leave us alone to fend for ourselves. He wants us to trust Him in all situations.

Believe in His faithfulness. He will never leave you!

> But I trust in you, O Lord; I say, "You are my God." My times are in your hands. Psalm 31:14,15

Have you ever asked God, "Where are you?" Do you know the answer to that question?

____

____

____

____

____

____

____

When you give your cares to Jesus, you no longer have to carry them around. What good does it do for you to carry all of that weight on your own?

You can have complete confidence that the One Who hears your prayer, will answer your prayer. The One Who sees you struggling under all of that weight, is the One Who will help you carry your load.

Our Lord is loving and gracious. He lightens your load and works on your behalf. How awesome it is that He is so willing to bear your burdens!

> For great is your love, higher than the heavens; your faithfulness reaches to the skies. Psalm 108:4

When the world is weighing you down, are you quick to seek the Lord for help, or are you reluctant to seek Him out? Explain.

January 12th

Only the Lord can redeem what sinfulness has set out to destroy. His forgiveness is complete with no strings attached.

I am so thankful that we have a Heavenly Father Who so freely forgives and seeks to restore what has been lost.

There is nothing that we have ever done and nothing that we will ever do, that the Lord God cannot redeem. He will lovingly heal, mightily transform, and gently redirect.

He is the Lord of restoration and is the only One Who can put the pieces back together.

> But you are a forgiving God, gracious and compassionate,
> slow to anger and abounding in love. Nehemiah 9:17

Is there something going on with you right now that needs to be healed or restored? Do you believe that the Lord is willing and able to redeem any situation that has been affected by sin?

____

____

____

____

____

____

January 13th

What would you be willing to trade?

Would you be willing to trade <u>your</u> riches for <u>Godly</u> riches?

Would you be willing to give up <u>your</u> strength, in order to live in <u>God's</u> strength?

Would you be willing to trade in <u>your</u> agenda for <u>God's</u> agenda?

With God, there are no even exchanges. What He wants to give us far outweighs any sacrifice we could ever make.

> Taste and see that the Lord is good; blessed is the man who takes refuge in him. Psalm 34:8

How do earthy riches compare to God's abundance?

____

____

____

____

____

____

____

____

January 14th

Adversity is inevitable. It shows up when we least expect it. But, as unpredictable as life is, we can always count on the faithfulness of our Lord and Savior.

We can stand on the certainty that we are never alone. We can count His promises as Truth and daily experience the love that He has for each one of us.

We do not serve a "wishy washy" God. His promises are in stone and they are unconditional!

The promises that the Lord makes to us are always punctuated with periods, not question marks.

> Your word, O Lord, is eternal; it stands firm in the heavens.
> Your faithfulness continues through all generations.
>
> Psalm 119:89,90

What do you think about the fact that God does not change His mind? Is that a good thing?

____

____

____

____

____

____

January 15th

Christ left the gates of heaven to show us the way. He died on the cross and paid the price for our sins. He gave up everything for us................. ***TWICE.***

Jesus did not come to earth "divinely insulated" from evil. He was tempted, mocked, slandered, rejected, tortured, and misunderstood. He endured much!

There is nothing that you could ever experience, nothing that you could ever feel, that Christ has not already felt. He understands all that you are going through and He can relate!

When you weep… He weeps.
When you rejoice… He is rejoicing with you.
When you are in pain… He feels it too.

> He was despised and rejected by men, a man of sorrows, and familiar with suffering. Isaiah 53:3

Do you think that Jesus can identify with anything and everything you might have to deal with in life? Can you think of a situation that Jesus faced that you too have experienced?

____

____

____

____

____

January 16th

Mountains are often symbolic of obstacles and challenges. And the image of God melting away any mountain that we could ever face is an awesome reminder of Who He is, in all of His power and might.

However, I do not want you to expect all mountains to melt! The Lord has His purposes, and if the mountain has been placed in your path by the Lord, there is certainly a good reason for it, and He will use it for your benefit.

I would rather climb the steepest mountain with my Lord, than never to have encountered the mountain at all.

Mountains also remind me that Christ is my rock and my refuge. His greatness cannot be contained, nor can it be understood with the human mind.

But... even in His greatness, He takes the time to reach down and take hold of us and love us like no other.

> The mountains melt like wax before the Lord, before the Lord of all the earth. Psalm 97:5

What purposes might there be for the mountains that God puts in your way?

____

____

____

____

____

January 17th

Even as the Lord is filled with power, might, and wisdom, there is a tenderness about Him that seems almost contrary to an Almighty God, Creator of the Universe. He is gentle, loving, and understands us better than we understand ourselves.

Sometimes I wonder, "Who am I, that You care so much for me? Who am I, that You reached down and took hold of me? Who am I, to be blessed so abundantly?" And then His sweet loving voice says to me, "You are mine."

Never forget who you are and Who you belong to...

Loving Father, Gentle Shepherd, Creator of the Universe.

> O great and powerful God, whose name is the Lord Almighty, great are your purposes and mighty are your deeds. Jeremiah 32:18,19

What image of God comes to mind when you think of Him? Are you more inclined to picture His tenderness or His power?

____

____

____

____

____

____

January 18th

What more could we want than to know that we belong to the King! He is our Comforter and our Encourager, our Light and our Hope, and He has a purpose and a specific plan for each one of us.

Can you even fathom the fact that the King of kings watches over you like a hawk? Lovingly. Wanting only to love you, to protect you, to teach you, and to guide you. Wanting only the best for you.

The Lord of All, the Creator of the Universe, delights in you!

> He shielded him and cared for him; he guarded him as the apple of his eye, like an eagle that stirs up its nest and hovers over its young, that spreads its wings to catch them and carries them on its pinions.
>
> Deuteronomy 32:10,11

Do you sleep better at night knowing that The King is watching over you? Do you walk more boldly knowing that He "has your back"?

____

____

____

____

____

____

____

January 19th

We are so transparent to the Lord. He can see right through us, like no one else can. He sees our scars, our wounds, our half-hearted efforts, and our misplaced priorities… and still, He loves us.

There is no one who loves like Jesus does. His love is so universal, yet so personal. There is nothing that could ever change or erase His love for you.

How awesome it is to be loved unconditionally by your Heavenly Father! Even when you mess up, He loves you.

He will never turn His back on you when you fall. But, He will pick you up, brush you off, then take your hand, lovingly.

> May your unfailing love be my comfort.
>
> Psalm 119:76

How would you "quantify" the Father's love for you? Try to put into words how much He loves you.

For example… He loves you to the moon and back.

____

____

____

____

____

____

January 20th

The eye-opening, jaw dropping realities of this world are very troubling. My mind would be on "overload" if it was not for the safe haven that the Lord provides. He is my Refuge, where I can find peace and refreshment.

I know, without a doubt, that I do not have what it takes to face tomorrow. Thankfully, I do not have to face it alone, and I do not have to rely on my own strength... and neither do you!

Jesus is more than enough, even when all seems lost. He provides for your every need, sustaining you day after day.

Always, in our weaknesses, the Lord's strength becomes so evident.

> The Spirit of God has made me; the breath of the Almighty gives me life. Job 33:4

What are some things in this world that are troubling to you? Why is it important to have a loving Heavenly Father who wants to be your Refuge?

____

____

____

____

____

____

____

January 21st

Oh, how I need the Peace that passes all understanding! The Peace that only Jesus can provide. It is so obvious, when the day gets ahead of me, and I have not taken the time to be filled with His Presence. My peace is easily disturbed; my strength has not been renewed and soon becomes depleted. It is not a pretty picture!

Christ is the Source, the Provider, of all that we need. I encourage you to take the time to recharge and to be filled in His Presence. It is here that you will find things that cannot be acquired anywhere else.

Ask Him to fill you with all that He has for you: peace, love, strength, patience, and understanding. Enjoy spending time in His Presence. Whenever we seek His face, we are blessed beyond measure!

> Where the Spirit of the Lord is, there is freedom. And we, who with unveiled faces all reflect the Lord's glory, are being transformed into his likeness.
>
> 2 Corinthians 3:17,18

What are some ways that you can prevent yourself (your spirit) from "running out of gas"?

January 22nd

When we are able to rest in Christ, the troubles of this world fade into the distance. He saturates us with His Love and with His Peace and pours into us, all that we have been lacking.

His Peace is a precious gift. Let us not fail to see the blessing of resting in His Presence. Jesus is the only One Who can provide the inner peace that will shelter us from the stress and pressures of the world.

When you get discouraged, He will lift your head. Please rest, dear one, in the knowledge that the Lord goes before you and will provide safe havens along the way.

> But those who hope in the Lord will renew their strength. They will soar on wings like eagles; they will run and not grow weary, they will walk and not be faint.
>
> Isaiah 40:31

What are the outward signs of inward peace?

____

____

____

____

____

____

____

January 23rd

I used to "pride" myself on my independence. I never wanted to ask for help. I did not want to inconvenience anyone, which then might have led to disappointment or rejection. It was always safer to be self-reliant.

However, my independence also spilled over into my relationship with the Lord. I often had the "I can do it myself" attitude of a three year old child. Wow, that really left God out of the picture!

Did I think that I could do it better? Did I not want to bother Him with such small matters? Or, did I think that the Lord would not be there for me when I needed Him?

Well, somewhere along the way, Jesus showed me otherwise. He showed me how much I need to depend on Him, knowing that I will never be disappointed or rejected. He showed me that He wants to be included in the details, as well as the big picture.

I hope you can learn to rely on the Lord, whatever the circumstances. He is just waiting for you to ask.

> Surely God is my help; the Lord is the one who sustains me. Psalm 54:4

Are you comfortable relying and depending on God, or are you afraid that He is going to let you down?

____

____

____

January 24th

Some days I just want to be able to rest in the loving arms of Jesus, knowing that I am protected, and hear Him say, "All is well." I wonder if you've ever felt this way.

Most of us have such a great need to be loved and accepted. Whether you've experienced love and acceptance or have felt sorely lacking in these areas, Jesus is ready to embrace you with His everlasting arms.

He is the One Who will calm all of your fears. He is the One Who will quiet all that is stirred up within you. He is the One Who will hold you close and provide you with comfort and hope.

> How priceless is your unfailing love! Both high and low among men find refuge in the shadow of your wings.
> Psalm 36:7

What words do you most need to hear from Jesus today? Words of encouragement? Words of love? Words of comfort? Words of reassurance? Or something else?

____

____

____

____

____

____

January 25th

There is a picture, a painting, that depicts Jesus knocking on a door. The walkway leading to the house is lined with flowers. The door is a large wooden door that leads into a house made of stone.

The most interesting part of this picture is that there is no doorknob on the outside of the door. The only way to get in is for someone to answer and open the door.

I love this image of Jesus knocking. The strong stone house reminds me of our hearts. Sometimes our hearts are so hard that we have closed Jesus out, for whatever reason. Then there are hearts that do not know Him yet.

Whatever the circumstance, Jesus does not give up. He knocks and knocks and waits for us to open the door. He will not enter until He is invited and welcomed in.

> Here I am! I stand at the door and knock. If anyone hears my voice and opens the door, I will come in and eat with him, and he with me. Revelation 3:20

Is Jesus knocking on the door of your heart or have you already let Him in? Explain.

____

____

____

____

____

January 26th

When I think of world leaders, whether they are kings, queens, presidents, emperors, or prime ministers, they all seem to have one thing in common. They are all usually far removed from the people living within their countries.

These leaders do not often mix with "commoners", and are unlikely willing to accept an invitation to someone's house for dinner. They are pretty much unavailable, unreachable, and unapproachable.

Not so when describing the Lord of All, the Creator of the Universe, Almighty God, our Lord and Savior. He wants nothing more than to be with us! He wants to be actively involved in our lives and seeks to have daily communication with us. It seems as though He just can't get enough of us!

Oh, what a personal Savior! What an intimate friend!

> O Lord God Almighty, who is like you? You are mighty,
> O Lord, and your faithfulness surrounds you.
>
> Psalm 89:8

Why is it such a blessing that our Lord is so accessible?

____

____

____

____

____

The Love of Christ far exceeds anything that we could possibly imagine. His love looks beyond the present, beyond our blemishes, our failures, and our weaknesses, and sees what we will become. He can see the finished product, and He will love us all the way through.

He loves us so much that He will not rest, while there is still work to be done ***in*** us. We are all a work in progress. We're still under construction. His Word says that if anyone is in Christ, he is a new creation.

Let us allow the Love of Christ to transform us, to help us to grow beyond where we are right now. I believe that the Lord truly sees the condition of our hearts and that change can, and will, take place if we open our hearts to Him.

> Create in me a clean heart, O God, and renew a steadfast spirit within me. Psalm 51:10

If you saw the true condition of your heart, what would it look like? Don't take this opportunity to be critical about yourself, but take an honest look at what the Lord needs to transform.

____

____

____

____

____

____

January 28th

The Bible tells us to enter His gates with thanksgiving and His courts with praise... for the Lord is good and His love endures ***forever*** (Psalm 100:4,5).

Wow, "forever" is a long time! That means that we will never be without the love of Christ. What assurance we have that His love is everlasting and nothing, and no one, can take that away from us! He cares so much for us.

When we are down, He lifts us up.

When we have nowhere to turn, He is there for us.

When we are empty, He fills us with His love.

Oh, how blessed we are to have a Heavenly Father Who is so attentive and loving and Who spares no expense when it comes to His loved ones.

> But from everlasting to everlasting the Lord's love is with those who fear him. Psalm 103:17

What does it mean to "spare no expense"? Does that mean you get everything that you want?

____

____

____

____

____

Have you ever given any thought to the fact that the Lord has an unending supply of all that we need? His love will never run out. His mercies will never cease. His compassion for us is without limit.

The Lord will supply us with all that we need. And… I believe, the greatest thing of all, is that He knows exactly what we need.

I stand amazed that the God of the Universe is just waiting to step in and provide for each one of us and bless us in ways that we never would have expected.

Only He can satisfy your deepest longings and desires, and He will gladly provide all that His beloved daughter needs.

> They will tell of the power of your awesome works, and I will proclaim your great deeds. They will celebrate your abundant goodness and joyfully sing of your righteousness.
>
> Psalm 145:6,7

Have you ever experienced a blessing from God that you did not expect? Explain.

January 30th

Are there days when you feel like you are "running on empty"? Maybe you have been overwhelmed with commitments and have been too busy to take the time to recharge. Or, maybe there has been so much on "your plate" that you just don't know how it will all get done.

The Lord does not want you to run yourself into the ground, even if it is done with an attitude of service. He knows that you are human, even if you forget that from time to time.

It is under these circumstances that we need to take our "superhero cape" off and ask the Lord for His help and for His guidance. Turn to Him and allow Him to fill you up and recharge your battery. He is our greatest Source of Strength.

When you just want to fall into His lap and hide for awhile, His arms are wide open.

> He who dwells in the shelter of the Most High will rest in the shadow of the Almighty. Psalm 91:1

How much "battery life" do you usually have left before you turn to the Lord for help?

____

____

____

____

____

January 31st

Where do we look to find relief? Where can we find refuge for our weary souls?

When we turn to "what feels good", it only provides us with temporary relief. So let us instead turn to "what we know", or should I say, "Who we know."

Let us go directly to the Father, Who is waiting to embrace us and provide us with a restful place.

In your despair, look to Him, and you will be comforted. In your hour of need, reach for Him and He will always be there. In your emptiness, cry out to Him, and He will hold you tight.

> I will refresh the weary and satisfy the faint.
>
> Jeremiah 31:25

Describe, in detail, what a beautiful restful place would look like to you. Use all of your senses; don't forget to include Jesus.

____

____

____

____

____

____

February

The Language of Love

February 1st

As a daughter of the King of kings, do you really know how much you are loved? Can you even begin to understand the depth of His love for you?

His love is… from everlasting to everlasting.

His love is… as high as the heavens are above the earth.

His love is… beyond understanding.

His love is stubborn, relentless, and unconditional. It is not random and does not come with strings attached. It is not based on performance or status.

AND… **no one** can take it away!

> How great is the love the Father has lavished on us, that we should be called children of God! I John 3:1

What are some of the blessings that come from being dearly loved by your Heavenly Father?

____

____

____

____

____

____

February 2nd

It has always been hard for me to grasp the concept of unconditional love. My experience as a child had been, "I will love you if"…, or "I will love you when..."

The love that I so desperately longed for seemed always to be tied to how well I did in school, my accomplishments, and of course, if I was well behaved. So you can see how unconditional love really took some getting used to for me.

No one loves as Jesus loves. He knows our whole story, yet He still loves us. He accepts us as we are! We do not have to be perfect. We do not have to be at the top of our class, and His love is not based on our performance.

I still sometimes forget and have to remind myself that our Heavenly Father's love has no strings attached.

How awesome it is to be one of **His** children!

Chosen! Valued! Cherished! Blessed!

> Keep me as the apple of your eye; hide me in the shadow of your wings. Psalm 17:8

Have you experienced anything in your life that makes it hard for you to accept unconditional love?

____

____

____

February 3rd

Who can understand the vastness of God?

Who can explain the goodness of God?

Can we even put into words, or grasp, how wide and long, and how high and deep the love of Christ is for each one of us?

We will only know the *LOVE* that surpasses all knowledge, as we allow Him to draw us unto Himself.

My hope and prayer for you is that you will experience the great love that Jesus has for you throughout your life, and that you will understand just how special you are to Him.

> But you, O Lord, are a compassionate and gracious God,
> slow to anger, abounding in love and faithfulness.
>
> Psalm 86:15

In the space below, try to put into words just how much Jesus loves you.

____

____

____

____

____

____

February 4th

Think for a moment about one of your friends. How is it that you connected with this person? How did you maintain this friendship? What are some of the things that you enjoy doing together?

Friendship, as we know, is a two way street. It is a relationship that needs to be cultivated and nurtured. It is not born overnight, but it grows as two people spend time together, developing a strong bond of trust and writing their own personal history together.

As with any friendship, our relationship with Christ will only grow and strengthen as we spend time with Him. I truly believe that He cherishes the time that we spend with Him.

> Blessed are those you choose and bring near to live in your courts! We are filled with the good things of your house, of your holy temple. Psalm 65:4

How have your personal friendships developed and strengthened throughout the years? How can you relate this to your relationship with Christ?

____

____

____

____

____

____

February 5th

Years ago, I remember seeing a beautiful painting that showed little children sitting on the ground listening to Jesus. As He spoke, they intently listened. There was such joy on each little face! And, it was plain to see the love that He had for each one of them.

I wonder what Jesus was telling these little children. Was He teaching them about life? Was He telling them stories? Was He reminding each one that they are deeply loved? Regardless of what He was sharing with the little kids, He certainly must have been relating to them in a way in which they would understand.

No matter how old (or young) we are, Jesus speaks our language.

May we never outgrow the joy of sitting at Jesus' feet.

> "Let the children come to me, and do not hinder them, for the kingdom of God belongs to such as these." And he took the children in his arms, put his hands on them and blessed them. Mark 10:14,16

Think once again about the painting that I described above. Why do you think the little children were so attracted to Jesus?

____

____

____

____

____

February 6th

Oh, what an awesome God we serve that He would open the floodgates of heaven.
For you! For me!

Our Heavenly Father does not love us sparingly,
but lavishly.
He does not care for us conditionally, but tenderly.
He does not bless us occasionally, but abundantly.

It is impossible to measure the love that the Lord has for you. His love is relentless. His love can be trusted. His love never ends.

No one can "out love" God. It doesn't get any better than that!

> For great is his love toward us, and the faithfulness of the Lord endures forever. Psalm 117:2

If someone told you that you were not worthy of God's love, how would you respond with the Truth?

____

____

____

____

____

____

February 7th

The Lord is our constant Companion. Even when we don't feel His presence, He is right there with us. He walks with us through the darkness and lights our way. He steadies us with His strong arm as we stumble over rocky roads. He is our anchor when life is unpredictable.

Many times, the circumstances that surround us are so overwhelming that we cannot see past them. Our short-sightedness causes confusion, and we begin to doubt God's love for us.

We must remember that we **do** have a loving God and His love **will never fail.** He is our refuge when we are afraid. He is our rest when we are weary.

Is there any other, so loving and so faithful?

> But I trust in your unfailing love, my heart rejoices in your salvation. I will sing to the Lord, for he has been good to me.
>
> Psalm 13:5,6

Knowing that the Lord is your constant Companion, how does that give you hope and strength as you navigate through your life?

____

____

____

____

____

____

February 8th

Jesus did not come to earth divinely insulated from evil. He walked this earth and experienced every kind of situation and circumstance that was common to man. He was tempted, slandered, rejected, tortured and misunderstood.

Onlookers mocked Him. They insulted Him. They challenged His holiness. There was no greater darkness than the darkness that Christ experienced on the cross. Oh, how much love it took for Him to stay on that cross!

Christ abandoned everything for us. He submitted to the will of His Father and suffered a humiliating and painful death. Through this ultimate sacrifice, He paid the ransom for our sins. Greater love has no man than this.

> This is love: not that we loved God, but that he loved us
> and sent his Son as an atoning sacrifice for our sins.
>
> I John 4:10

What are your personal thoughts regarding the sacrifice that Jesus made for you? How does this impact your life?

___

___

___

___

___

___

___

February 9th

How awesome it is to know that we have a Good and Loving Shepherd, who tenderly cares for His sheep, that not even one of them should be lost.

We are under His watchful eye at all times. Whenever we start to drift or wander off, He leads us back to the fold.

The Lord is relentless in caring for those who belong to Him. He knows that the best place for us to be is within the sound of His voice.

Stay close, dear sisters, so that you will be able to follow wherever He leads. If His voice becomes distant, it is probably time to turn around.

> My sheep listen to my voice; I know them, and they follow me. I give them eternal life, and they shall never perish; no one can snatch them out of my hand.
>
> John 10:27,28

Why do you think that Jesus is so relentless in rescuing His lost sheep?

February 10th

Discipline, correction, and punishment are never pleasant, and I'm sure that you, at times, have received more than you felt that you deserved. But, just think about where you would be if you were never disciplined, redirected, or humbled. You would probably be out of control, self centered, with little regard for others.

The Lord expresses His love for us in so many ways. Yes, even in ways that are not so warm and fuzzy.

Love is …
When He disciplines and when He comforts.
When He leads and when He redirects.
When He encourages and when He humbles us.

Regardless of your situation, whether laughter or tears,
His love shines through.

> No discipline seems pleasant at the time, but painful. Later on, however, it produces a harvest of righteousness and peace for those who have been trained by it.
>
> Hebrews 12:11

How can you relate the love of Jesus to the act of discipline?

____

____

____

____

February 11th

When I was young, I used to think that God's love for me was based on how much I did for Him. I thought it was conditional upon my service and my efforts. The more I did, the more He loved me. Right? Wasn't I supposed to earn His love?

It took me awhile to realize that God's love does not come with a price tag. Part of me thought that this was too good to be true!

However, little by little, the Lord showed me that His love is not something that I had to work for.

His love does not depend on our circumstances, or our accomplishments, or our service. I believe that the effort that we put into things on His behalf are for His glory. We do not need to win His love. He could never love us more or less.

> I have loved you with an everlasting love; I have drawn you with loving-kindness. Jeremiah 31:3

Do you, or have you ever, thought that you had to earn God's love? Where do you think these thoughts come from?

____

____

____

____

____

February 12th

We will never ever be able to comprehend how much our Father in heaven loves us. His love is not based on what we do or how we look. It is not tarnished by our past, or by the sins we have committed.

Because of His love, Christ seeks to transform us by lovingly molding and shaping us. It's not that He does not love us the way we are, but He has something better in mind for each one of us.

Allow Him full access into all of the places of your heart. Ask Him to change what needs to be changed, to fix what needs to be fixed, and to make your heart more like His.

Only the eyes of the Lord can see the finished product. Even as you are still a work in progress, His grace will cover you as the process continues.

> He reveals deep and hidden things; he knows what lies in darkness and light dwells with him.
>
> Daniel 2:22

Why do you think that God's grace is an important part of the transformation process?

____

____

____

____

____

February 13th

Transparency can be very frightening and intimidating. Can you imagine if your friends knew every single detail about you? How would they react if they learned about things that you would rather keep private? Even your closest friend does not know everything about you.

We are so transparent to the Lord. There is nothing hidden from Him. He sees our wounds, our scars, our weaknesses and our sins, and yet He loves us anyway.

We have a loving and gracious Lord. He uses all that He knows about us for our benefit, without holding it against us, in order to cleanse us, heal us, and make us whole.

So, let us not fear transparency, but be thankful that we have a loving, gentle Father who knows our every need, inside and out.

> Search me, O God, and know my heart; test me and know my anxious thoughts. See if there is any offensive way in me, and lead me in the way everlasting.
>
> Psalm 139:23,24

Describe two aspects of transparency. Why does it make you feel a bit uneasy, and why it is necessary to be transparent to the Lord?

____

____

____

____

February 14th

Our Father in heaven knows us better than anyone. He loves us so much that He will not sit by while there's work to be done. A work **in** us. He will use trials and challenges in His refining process. He will restore and rebuild us in ways that would otherwise have not been possible. We are all a work in progress.

Allow the Lord to shine His light into your heart, exposing all the things that need to be uprooted and cleansed. All the work that is being done in you has an eternal purpose.

The Lord makes all things possible. Through His transformation, He will open the way and set you on a path that you never would have expected or dreamed.

Never hesitate to follow where He leads. He will never let you down.

> For our light and momentary troubles are achieving for us
> and eternal glory that far outweighs them all.
>
> 2 Corinthians 4:17

What does it mean that "beauty is only skin deep"? What concerns the Lord more than your outward appearance?

____

____

____

____

____

February 15th

What does it take for someone to be loved by the world? They are probably pleasing to look at, popular because of their talents, financially well off, or in a high position of authority.

Well... that leaves me out! I am certainly **NOT** loved by the world!

I do not want to seek superficial, temporary approval from a worldly point of view, but I'd much rather be pleasing in His sight.

There is no one who loves you like Jesus. His love is so universal, yet so personal. There is nothing that will ever change His love for you.

So reassuring!

He sees it "all" and knows it "all", and He will never stop loving you.

> If anyone acknowledges that Jesus is the Son of God, God lives in him and he in God. And so we know and rely on the love God has for us. I John 4:15,16

What else do you think God wants you to remember about His love for you?

____

____

____

____

____

February 16th

Let Jesus be your daily refreshment. Sit at His feet surrounded by His love. True love that never fails. True love that never wavers.

As a Loving Father, His everlasting arms are always there to catch you. He will pick you up and set you back on your feet. He will be your greatest comfort and refuge when times are tough. He will also rejoice with you and celebrate your victories. HE is your BIGGEST FAN!

So, whatever the day may bring, whether you are struggling or celebrating, seek Him first. Jesus is there to, not only lift you up, but also to laugh and sing and celebrate with you.

> I was filled with delight day after day, rejoicing always in his presence. Proverbs 8:30

Knowing that Christ is your biggest fan, what image comes to your mind?

February 17th

What do you think that the Lord wants us to do with His continuous abundance of love? I believe that the Lord does not want us to keep it all to ourselves, but that He wants us to share His love with others.

There are several ways that we can share the love of Christ. One way is by telling others about the love of Jesus and sharing with them the magnitude of His love. Another way is by reflecting His love through random acts of kindness and thoughtfulness.

One thing that I think we all need to remember is to also share His love with those who are neglected, hopeless, and with those who do not have a whole lot to smile about.

The more love we shower on others, and the more love that we give away, the more the love in our heart grows.

> Whoever loves his brother lives in the light, and there is nothing in him to make him stumble. I John 2:10

Why is it important to go the extra mile and not only share God's love with those around you, but share it with someone outside of your familiar circle?

____

____

____

____

____

February 18th

I'm sure you know how "contagious" some things are, like laughter, for one example. Have you ever been in class, trying to pay attention and someone says something under her breath? All of a sudden the two of you cannot stop laughing. And, the more you try to stop laughing, the more it cannot be contained.

Love can also be contagious. It can spread like wildfire, from person to person if we let it.

So, let us not only **share** the love of Christ, but let us **spread** the love of Christ. Remember the beginning of "contagious" starts with one person. We all have an opportunity to be that person.

Jesus is love. Spread it around!

> Dear friends, let us love one another, for love comes from God. Everyone who loves has been born of God and knows God. I John 4:7

How might this world be different if more people could experience the love of Christ?

February 19th

God's love is so vital in the process of transformation. As He molds and shapes us, as He teaches and directs us, His love continues to shine through. His gentle words of correction are in such contrast to the voices of shame and criticism that come from the enemy.

Our hands are not always clean and our minds are not always pure, but the love of Christ continues to fill us in all the right places. His gentle, loving transformation introduces us to the Truth and allows us to gradually grow in our faith.

Praise God that He knows what lessons we need to learn and as He teaches, He continues to love and care for us. He gives us so much of Himself. He is the Author of our love story.

> Send forth your light and your truth, let them guide me; let them bring me to your holy mountain, to the place where you dwell. Psalm 43:3

How can you distinguish between the correction of the Lord and the condemnation of the enemy?

____

____

____

____

____

____

February 20th

The Lord's love will warm our hearts at unexpected times. When this happens, it is unmistakable. To me, these special times are gifts of love from my Father in Heaven.

There are so many ways that Christ reminds us of His matchless love. We never have to look very far. The beauty of His creation. His still small voice. The Light on our path, the simple nudging of our heart, and the blessings that are all around us.

The more we realize just how much He loves us, the more of Him we crave.

I pray that the Lord will continue to reveal Himself to you. That your knowledge of Him will continue to grow, and you will experience the love He has for you everyday.

> But the eyes of the Lord are on those who fear him, on those whose hope is in his unfailing love.
>
> Psalm 33:18

In what ways has God revealed Himself to you?

____

____

____

____

____

____

February 21st

There are many paths to choose from as we walk through life. Some paths are obviously the wrong path, and it's easy to see that this road will only lead to destruction. There are also other well traveled paths that might look very attractive and innocent, but as you walk this path, it only becomes darker and darker.

Then there is the narrow road. The narrow road is not well traveled. This is the road that leads to life.

Jesus reminds us in John 14, "I am the way and the truth and the life."

Jesus knows that the way of Truth is not an easy road to travel. It is not the most popular road, and there will be many distractions and people who try to get you off course.

But because of His great love, Christ will always be by your side, helping you to walk in His Truth.

> "Enter through the narrow gate. For wide is the gate and broad is the road that leads to destruction, and many enter through it. But small is the gate and narrow the road that leads to life, and only a few find it." Matthew 7:13,14

Why do you think so many people prefer to take the "broad" road?

____

____

____

____

February 22nd

When people look at us, do they see the love of Jesus in us? Do our actions demonstrate just how much He loves us?

As Christ pours His love into us, let us be a reflection of His love to others. Let us glorify Him by being an example of kindness, gentleness, patience, and love.

There are so many lost souls in this world. Let us come along side those who are searching and show them what His love is all about.

When you see a need, view it as an opportunity to reflect His love to others. Make it obvious that you have the love of Jesus in your heart. Make it evident to all that you belong to Him.

> Live as children of light (for the fruit of the light consists
> in all goodness, righteousness and truth).
>
> Ephesians 5:8,9

In what way can you reflect the love of Christ to someone in the next few days?

____

____

____

____

____

____

February 23rd

There are so many examples of love in the Bible. In the New Testament, we find the love of Jesus pretty much everywhere. There were so many ways that Jesus expressed His love for others, even to those who did not know Him.

Jesus displayed His love for His friends and for His disciples. The love that He had for Mary, Martha, and Lazarus was very evident as He wept when he was told that Lazarus had died. But, that was not the end for Lazarus because Jesus then raised him from the dead (see John, Chapter 11).

One touching expression of Jesus' love for His disciples was when He humbled Himself and washed their feet in the Upper Room. He even washed the feet of Judas who He knew was about to betray Him.

Jesus' love was not only showered on those He knew intimately, but it was also was poured out on those who crossed His path. Jesus healed the sick, restored sight to the blind, and spent time with the rich, as well as the poor. His love was not exclusive, but inclusive.

"My command is this: Love each other as I have loved you."
John 15:12

How has the love of Christ made a difference in your life?

____

____

____

____

____

February 24th

The price that Jesus paid for us on the cross was a humbling, sacrificial expression of His love for us. His sacrifice went beyond physical pain. He suffered emotionally as His Father's plan unfolded right before His eyes.

As He prayed in the garden, as they hauled Him away, as He carried His cross… such emotional torment!

The Father asked His Son to give Himself up for the sake of all mankind, and He did. Our sin was on His shoulders. He took our place. He endured so much for us. Let us never take that "love offering" for granted.

The price He paid, was **all that He could give.**

> "Greater love has no one than this, that he lay down his life for his friends." John 15:13

How might you explain the love of Jesus to others?

____

____

____

____

____

____

____

February 25th

I want us to think today about sacrificial love and what this means to us and to others. This is the kind of love that comes with a cost. The cost could be time, energy, inconvenience, or even a financial sacrifice.

Sacrificial love is shown when you really don't have the time, but you take the time. It is giving, even when you don't have much yourself. It might also include rearranging your day so that you can be available for someone.

I had an Uncle Jim who was always looking to help others. The Bible tells us that God loves a cheerful giver and that describes my uncle perfectly. Everyone said, "Yeh, Jim would give you the shirt off his back." (Please don't go that far!!) His love for others was so obvious.

This kind of love is very rare. Jesus tells us to put others first. We are our brother's (*sister's*) keeper.

> "I tell you the truth," he said, "this poor widow has put in more than all the others. All these people gave their gifts out of their wealth; but she out of her poverty put in all she had to live on. Luke 21:3,4

What do you think is the biggest stumbling block associated with putting others first?

____

____

____

____

February 26th

Have you ever heard of the term "laundry list"? As we use this phrase today, it has very little to do with laundry. A laundry list is a very long list of things such as assignments, complaints, items, or things that need to get done. My laundry list often comes into play when I have so much to do and very little time to get it all finished.

The inference is that "the list" is overwhelming. As time goes by, things on a laundry list tend to pile up (hey, just like dirty clothes) and the list just keeps growing.

I realized the other day while I was praying that so many times my prayers just reflect a laundry list of wants and needs. Then I thought to myself, what about changing things up and presenting a laundry list of PRAISE to my loving Father.

Our Father certainly cares about our wants and our needs, but let us not stop there. Let us be thankful and praise Him for all of the ways that He loving blesses us. I think that PRAISE is music to His ears.

> I will praise you, O Lord, with all my heart; I will tell of all your wonders. I will be glad and rejoice in you; I will sing praise to your name, O Most High. Psalm 9:1,2

Write down at least 3 things in your life that you can praise God for. Try this each day for a week and watch your laundry list of praise keep growing.

February 27th

I am wondering what others might see if they had the opportunity to observe me for a day. What kind of impression would I make on them? Would they know that I am a Christian by how I treat others?

If we are to set an example of love, we need our words, our actions, and our deeds to reflect the definition of love which can be found in I Corinthians 13. This is one example that Jesus provided for us.

Our words, our actions and our behavior display what is really in our hearts. If we really have a heart for helping others and serving the Lord, but also display rudeness and disrespect as we go through our day, then there's something wrong with this picture.

Let the love in your heart be reflected in all that you say and in all that you do. Be a loving example for others to follow.

> Love must be sincere. Hate what is evil; cling to what is good. Romans 12:9

Do you think that your words and actions are consistent with a loving heart?

____

____

____

____

____

____

February 28th

How much time do we spend each day thinking about our own needs and our own situations? Serving others is a wonderful way of getting the focus off of ourselves.

When we fix our eyes on Jesus, and take the focus off of ourselves, we are better able to extend love to others. When we are confident that the Lord is able to meet all of our needs, we have a greater ability to see the needs of others.

Jesus tells us that the first must be last. He tells us to put others before ourselves. This is the opposite of what we see in the competitive world that we live in.

Ask the Lord for His help so that you will be able to put others first, with the hope that in time, you will even be able to ***joyfully*** go to the back of the line.

> Be imitators of God, therefore, as dearly loved children and live a life of love, just as Christ loved us and gave himself up for us as a fragrant offering and sacrifice to God.
>
> Ephesians 5:1,2

How can getting the focus off of yourself and focusing more on the needs of others be a "win-win" situation?

____

____

____

____

February 29th

When we truly love someone, what does that look like? Is true love contingent upon someone loving us back? Is love a feeling or an action? Do we give love freely or are there certain requirements?

Love is an action, not a feeling.
Love is a commitment, not a fantasy.
Love is not based on popularity, appearance, or status.

True love is patient.
True love does not keep score, and it does not expect anything in return.
True love does not hold grudges, but it is forgiving.
True love does not tear down, but it builds up.
True love perseveres through the roughest of times.
True love endures.

> "A new command I give you: Love one another. As I have loved you, so you must love one another. By this all men will know that you are my disciples, if you love one another."
>
> John 13:34,35

How do the above descriptions of love apply to the love that Christ has for you?

____

____

____

____

____

March

Be Still: Learn to Listen

March 1st

Settle your mind; quiet your thoughts, that you may hear the reassuring voice of Jesus.

Be still ~ let Him speak words of Truth to you.

Be still ~ allow Him to restore a weary soul.

Be still ~ while He reveals Himself to you.

Be still ~ and drink the Living Water.

> Come to me, all you who are weary and burdened, and I will give you rest. Matthew 11:28

How easy, or hard, is it for you to be still? Why does God want us to be still?

March 2nd

How often does God have our undivided attention? We are so busy, busy, busy! We are never still enough, for long enough.

In the quiet moments that we spend with Him, we will be refreshed and strengthened. As long as we are face to face with Him, there is a Peace that nothing can shatter.

The precious time that we spend with our King reminds us who we are in Christ. We are cherished children of the One True God!

Allow Him to reenergize you and refill you with all the strength that you need.

> The Lord gives strength to his people; the Lord blesses his people with peace. Psalm 29:11

What does it mean to you to know that you are a cherished child of the One True God?

March 3rd

Many people, including myself, find it very difficult to just sit and be still. We seem to be trained and taught to accomplish, to be productive, to get things done.

However, there is nothing like the ability to achieve quietness so the Holy Spirit can warm our hearts. We all need to be recharged, refreshed, and renewed. Only the Lord can provide the daily renewal that we need.

Whenever we seek Him, we will find Him. Christ makes Himself known to all who come to Him.

The Lord is always ready to greet you with His love. In the stillness, you will experience the sweetness of His Presence. Only in the quietness, can you hear the whispers of His voice.

> Be still and know that I am God. Psalm 46:10

What are some things that distract your thoughts and interrupt your ability to focus? What can you do in order to really be able to "be still" and focus on Christ?

March 4th

Teach us, Lord, how to be still. As the Light of Your Presence shines on us, our hearts are filled with peace. When we are with You, we lack nothing; we have all that we need.

You, Lord, are our Light, our Hope, our Refuge. Fill us with all that You have for us; the things of You that cannot be acquired anywhere else. The things of You that overshadow all of our weaknesses and shortcomings.

As we open our hands, our mind, and our heart to You, may we always be ready to receive all that You have to offer.

Reign in us, O Lord!

> Blessed are those who hunger and thirst for righteousness,
> for they will be filled. Matthew 5:6

Is there anyone who has more to offer you than Jesus? What kinds of things does our Heavenly Father want to give you? Do you believe that when you are with Him, you lack nothing?

____

____

____

____

____

____

March 5th

Take time out to be alone with God.
Get quiet.

Give Him your undivided attention.
Just you and Him.

Meditate on His word.
Listen to His voice.

Be embraced by the King in these quiet moments.

His Peace is priceless. It will still your stirred up mind and melt away your fears. As you refocus your thoughts on Him, He will cover you with His love and strengthen you so that you can confidently walk in His ways.

> Let the beloved of the Lord rest secure in him, for he shields him all day long, and the one the Lord loves rests between his shoulders. Deuteronomy 33:12

How can quiet time with Jesus prepare you for your day?

____

____

____

____

____

____

March 6th

All that we seek and desire can be found in the Presence of Jesus. We need not look any further.

Even in the busyness of life as we are surrounded by distractions and worldliness, the Lord calls us to look **UP** and set our minds on things above. It is there that we will find all that we need… love, peace, comfort, security, and hope.

Let us not frantically rush into His Presence or hastily rush out of His Presence. Instead, let us intentionally seek to protect our time with Jesus, without allowing the constraints of time to interfere.

Ask Him to free your mind, so you can focus on Him. Clear away the clutter, so you can enjoy His Presence.

> Enter his gates with thanksgiving and his courts with praise; give thanks to him and praise his name. For the Lord is good and his love endures forever.
>
> Psalm 100:4,5

Is there something that is cluttering your mind right now? Is there "stuff" in your heart that might be preventing you from being completely comfortable in His Presence?

____

____

____

____

March 7th

Be still.

Listen to the peace that Jesus is offering.

Rest in His love.

Bask in His light.

Allow Him to breathe new life into you.

> How lovely is your dwelling place, O Lord Almighty! My soul yearns, even faints, for the courts of the Lord; my heart and my flesh cry out for the living God.
>
> Psalm 84:1,2

What does it mean to you to be able to rest in His love and to bask in His light?

March 8th

How blessed we are that we can come into the Presence of the King of kings! It is here, in these quiet moments, that we can shut out the world and experience the Light of His Presence. It is here that we find peace and rest from the craziness of life.

There is nothing like His Peace that passes all understanding. His Peace is like a tiny taste of heaven. Nothing is sweeter, nothing more reassuring!

> You will go out in joy and be led forth in peace; the mountains and hills will burst into song before you, and all the trees of the field will clap their hands.
>
> Isaiah 55:12

Describe your "craziness of life." How comforting is it to know and experience the Peace of Christ?

March 9th

Lasting, unshakable peace comes only from the Lord. His Peace is not illusive but can be found when we earnestly seek it. It is a gift just waiting to be received.

Peace is the place where Christ resides. It is accessible to all who seek His face.

Only as we release the grip that we have on worldly things, are we free to experience all that He has for us. As we empty ourselves, there is a greater capacity for His Living Water to flow through us.

When you are able to rest in Him, His Spirit will fill your soul as you empty yourself in His Presence.

It is my hope that as this year moves on, your ability to rest in Him will increase and your mind will be strengthened by His Spirit, Who lives in you.

For he himself is our peace. Ephesians 2:14

What kinds of things have you received that you would consider very special gifts? What kind of gifts does the Lord have in store for you?

March 10th

The Lord calls us to a secret place.

A place of rest.

A place of peace.

It is here that we can shut out the world and hear only one Voice.

The secret place.

The Voice of Truth.

Alone with God.

> Surely you have granted him eternal blessings and made him glad with the joy of your presence. Psalm 21:6

Do you have a secret, quiet place where you can go to be alone with God? Why do you think it is important (or not) to have such a place?

March 11th

In order to hear His gentle whisper, we must be in tune with His voice. Sometimes, a gentle whisper can feel like a small tugging of the heart. Gentle enough to know that it is from God, but just loud enough to get our attention.

A gentle whisper from God might serve to get us back on track, or possibly, lead us to a less traveled road where the Lord alone... will *LIGHT* the way.

Out of all of the possible paths that you might encounter, He will help you to choose the best way. The path that is paved with Love and with Understanding. The path that Jesus Himself has designed for you.

> Listen to his voice and hold fast to him.
>
> Deuteronomy 30:20

How do you usually know when you are not "on track"? How do you know which road is the one that God wants you to take?

____

____

____

____

____

____

____

March 12th

Usually, the hardest thing for me to do, is to do nothing; to be **still**. I admit, I am more "Martha" (all about **doing**) than "Mary" (always content to sit at the feet of Jesus). See Luke 10:38-42.

I often think to myself, "How can I be still when there's work to be done?"

Then, the Lord's sweet voice whispers to my heart, "I know there's work to be done; that's why I need you to be still."

I guess the best choice is to be Mary and Martha. Choose first to sit at the feet of Jesus, so He will strengthen you and encourage you for the work that needs to be done.

> Come let us bow down in worship, let us kneel before the Lord our Maker. Psalm 95:6

Are you more like Mary or more like Martha? Explain.

____

____

____

____

____

____

____

March 13th

When the Lord is silent,

Wait!

When you can't see,

Believe!

When you do not understand,

Trust!

Fill me up, Lord. Fill every corner of my heart with Your Presence. My need for You is so great. Your Glory is ever magnified by my weakness.

> O God, you are my God, earnestly I seek you; my soul thirsts for you, my body longs for you in a dry and weary land where there is no water. Psalm 63:1

At what times in your life have you really needed to lean on the Lord? What does it mean that His Glory is magnified by your weakness?

____

____

____

____

____

March 14th

In your troubles

-talk to God.

Through your disappointment

-talk to God.

When your heart is breaking

-talk to God.

Bring it *all* and lay it at His feet. He is always ready to listen and to wrap His loving arms around you.

> The Lord is a refuge for the oppressed, a stronghold in times of trouble. Those who know your name will trust in you, for you, Lord, have never forsaken those who seek you. Psalm 9:9,10

How much do you think that God cares about the troubling times you have experienced? What do you think He wants you to know? What do you think He wants to do for you?

____

____

____

____

March 15th

Lord, help me to be more intentional in seeking You throughout each day. Let not my communications and encounters be limited to the quiet moments, but help me to be consciously aware of You throughout the day as You reveal Yourself to me in so many ways.

The beauty of Your creation.
The kindness of others.
A hug or a smile from a friend.
A "redirection" of my day that leads to a blessing.
An unexpected opportunity to serve.
The sweet sound of the birds as the sun begins to set.

Thank You, Lord, for the "Holy hugs" that come from You every day.

> Your ways, O God, are holy. What god is so great as our God? You are the God who performs miracles; you display your power among the peoples. Psalm 77:13,14

Describe any "Holy hugs" or God sightings that you have experienced recently?

____

____

____

____

____

____

March 16th

Ask the Lord to help you to be still. As the Light of His Presence shines on you, you will be filled with peace. When you are able to be still in His Presence, nothing can disturb your Peace. As you focus on Him… the world fades away.

With open arms, welcome the transformation that Jesus can provide. He will mold you, shape you, and cleanse you.

Being renewed in the Spirit will enable you to face the challenges of the day. Walk confidently and securely with the knowledge… that you do not walk alone.

> I love the house where you live, O Lord, the place where your glory dwells. Psalm 26:8

What specific parts of you need to be transformed? Do you think that transformation needs to be painful? What are some ways that God uses His transforming power to change us from the inside-out?

March 17th

Taken aside by Jesus,

To sit quietly at His feet.

One on one with the Father,

How wonderful, peaceful, and sweet!

> You have make known to me the path of life; you will fill me with joy in your presence, with eternal pleasures at your right hand. Psalm 16:11

When you are one on one with the Father, what is it that you want Him to know? What is it that you want to hear?

March 18th

There is no fear in His Presence. His Light dispels the darkness. Let us live in the Light, so close to Him, that even in the worst of circumstances, we will have no fear. Even when everything seems to be falling apart around us, we will be safe in His arms.

Regardless of how we feel and what we think about our present situation, we must stay connected to Our Hope. Spending time with our loving Father gives us hope and strength, and reminds us that we do not face anything on our own. For, we are in His loving care at all times.

> I have set the Lord always before me. Because he is at my right hand, I will not be shaken. Therefore, my heart is glad and my tongue rejoices; my body also will rest secure.
>
> Psalm 16:8,9

What can you experience in the presence of the Lord that you cannot experience anywhere else?

____

____

____

____

____

____

____

March 19th

Thank You, Lord, for the "sacred space" that surrounds me when I am in Your Presence. I am saturated with Your love and infused with Your peace. You are my refuge and my safe haven. My time with You is precious.

Lord, I want "our time" to be a priority. I don't want to keep You waiting, and I do not want to be neglectful of our relationship. I want to come to You with the reverence and awe that You truly deserve.

> Ascribe to the Lord the glory due his name; worship the Lord in the splendor of his holiness.
>
> Psalm 29:2

What are some ways that you keep the relationship you have with your friends alive and well? Do you think that your relationship with Jesus is alive and well? When you look to spend time with Jesus do you think that He has a smile on His face? Are His arms wide open?

___

___

___

___

___

___

___

___

March 20th

I must confess, when problems arise, my first instinct had always been to try to handle things myself. Then when all else fails, I would turn to the Lord for help. However, I have learned over the years that He is just waiting for me to come to Him. And… the longer I wait and try to figure things out on my own… the larger the problem becomes.

Ask the Lord to cleanse you, so that your thoughts and motives are pure. Seek Him above all else. Let your first instinct be to look UP.

Allow yourself to be pliable, like clay, as He molds and reshapes your heart.

Our thoughts and actions indicate the condition of our hearts. In my case, I knew that God had a lot of work to do!

> Then you will call upon me and come and pray to me, and I will listen to you. You will seek me and find me when you seek me with all your heart. Jeremiah 29:12,13

What is it that makes us think that we can handle things on our own? Why is this not the best approach?

____

____

____

____

____

____

March 21st

How awesome is Your Presence, O Lord! There is no darkness, only Light. There is no fear, only Rest.

Lord, heighten our awareness of You, that we would see You in all things, at all times. As we go through each day, we are so blessed to have a constant companion.

Let Christ be the center of your world. Allow Him to fill every part of you… And you will "want" no more.

> "Come, let us go up to the mountain of the Lord, to the house of the God of Jacob. He will teach us his ways, so that we may walk in his paths." Isaiah 2:3

If you were to spend a day with Jesus, what would that be like?

March 22nd

To sit with Him,

is to know Him.

To know Him,

is to love Him.

To love Him,

is to long for Him.

As the deer pants for streams of water, so my soul pants for you, O God. My soul thirsts for God, for the living God.
Psalm 42:1,2

Have you ever been so thirsty that you could hardly wait to be refreshed? What does it take to acquire an intense thirst for God?

March 23rd

Worry is not from God. Worry is from the enemy who tries to weigh us down. He tries to throw us off course any way that he can. He knows how prone we are to be consumed by the simplest things.

Even before we wake, the enemy is ready and waiting to pounce. In the Presence of the Lord, we are never vulnerable. In the Light of His Presence we are safe and protected. As we are filled with His Peace, we are strengthened.

Ask God to strengthen your mind so that even Satan's greatest attempt to get you stirred up, will be in vain.

> Be self-controlled and alert. Your enemy the devil prowls
> around like a roaring lion looking for someone to devour.
> Resist him, standing firm in the faith. I Peter 5:8,9

What are some ways that the enemy tries to stir you up? What are some ways that you can shut him up?

March 24th

Spending time in the Spirit does much for one's soul. Quiet time with the Lord is uplifting and refreshing. But, oh, how much we forfeit when we do not seek Him out.

How many blessings do we miss out on because we stop short of accessing all that God has for us?

How many prayers are said in haste?

How often do we intend to spend time with God and then we just get too busy?

If hurts me when I think about, how many times I've put God "on hold."

We all have an opportunity to capture a little piece of heaven everyday.

> Glory in his holy name; let the hearts of those who seek the Lord rejoice. Psalm 105:3

How are we affected when we put God "on hold"?

____

____

____

____

____

____

March 25th

So many people have crossed my path throughout the years. Some are more inclined to reach out for God in tough times. Others are more connected to Him when things are going well. I have to admit that I have sought the Lord more often when facing trials and challenges than when I have been joyful.

Let our search for Jesus not be conditional upon our circumstances. Let us seek Him in all things, at all times.

The Lord wants to comfort us, but He also wants to rejoice with us.

Whether we are laughing or crying, victorious or defeated, we know that He is with us, and we can trust in the One Who never fails us.

> But may all who seek you rejoice and be glad in you;may those who love your salvation always say, "Let God be exalted!" Psalm 70:4

What are some things that bring you joy? What are some ways that you can include Jesus when you are joyful?

____

____

____

____

____

____

March 26th

Nothing can penetrate the peace that we have in the Presence of our King. It is like a wall of protection for our hearts and minds. It is here that we find rest from our weariness.

We are so blessed *in* His Presence. We are so blessed *with* His Presence.

It is my hope for you that the Lord will continue to open your eyes to the wonder of His Presence and your ears to His sweet loving voice. The Voice of Comfort, the Voice of Peace, the Voice of Encouragement. The Voice that says, "I love you; you are mine; I will never leave your side."

> For great is your love, reaching to the heavens; your faithfulness reaches to the skies. Psalm 57:10

What happens to your weariness when you are in the presence of your King?

March 27th

In our quiet moments with You, Lord, we pray that You will clean us out and cleanse us from everything that is hindering our walk with You.

Replace the "clutter" with Your Spirit. Show us areas in our lives that we have not yet completely turned over to You. Help us to loosen our grip and give You full access to those places in our hearts that need to be cleaned out, healed, and restored.

We trust that You will continue to do a work in each one of us, as we open our hearts to You and allow You to enter those dark places that we have been concealing for so long.

> I will sprinkle clean water on you, and you will be clean; I will cleanse you from all your impurities and from all your idols. I will give you a new heart and put a new spirit in you; I will remove from you your heart of stone and give you a heart of flesh. Ezekiel 36:25,26

Are there some places in your life or in your heart that are "off limits" to God? If so, why?

____

____

____

____

____

____

March 28th

Sitting still, contradicts all that the world teaches. A worldly view has us always on the move, achieving, striving, accomplishing, BUSY!

The emphasis is on **doing** rather than **being**.

I believe that the Lord wants us to slow down! To sit with Him. Still. In His Presence.

Quiet. Allowing only the sound of His voice.

He will strengthen us for whatever lies ahead, as we spend time sitting at His feet.

> The Lord is my shepherd, I shall not be in want. He makes me lie down in green pastures, he leads me beside quiet waters, he restores my soul. Psalm 23:1-3

How do the values of this world differ from the values of Christ?

March 29th

When we make a decision to follow Christ, we also must make a conscious decision to change our ways, which involves crucifying "the old self."

Some people think that they are beyond redemption and so far gone that nothing could make a difference in their lives. Not so!

No one is so hopeless and so "scarred" that the Lord cannot transform her. It is usually a process which requires patience, as well as, perseverance.

If someone desires to make changes and is ready to trade in her old ways for "His ways", it is necessary to spend time with the Master. It is here that the transformation will begin. It is here that the Lord will start to rebuild from the ground, up and from the inside, out.

Old ways… new ways.
Sinful… forgiven.
Hopeless… hopeful.
Defeated… victorious!

> My lips will shout for joy when I sing praise to you-I, whom you have redeemed. Psalm 71:23

Why do you think it is necessary to give up "the old self"? What would that look like for you?

____

____

____

____

March 30th

I have many friends who have loved and supported me through the darkest of times. When it comes to friends, I am so very blessed!

However, even as well as my friends know me, it is only Jesus Who completely knows exactly what I am going through and can hear the groans of my heart.

It is only Jesus Who will uplift us in ways that no one else can. In His Presence, He provides comfort and healing. He will breathe new life into us. He will "love away" our hurts.

In His Presence we take refuge and surround ourselves with Someone Who loves us and knows how we feel.

> He heals the brokenhearted and binds up their wounds. He determines the number of stars and calls them each by name. Great is our Lord and mighty in power; his understanding has no limit. Psalm 147:3-5

What are some of the benefits of friendship? What are some of the limitations of friendship? What can Christ do for you that your friends cannot?

____

____

____

____

____

March 31st

Slow down. Simplify.
Be still.
Renewed. Refreshed. Restored.
The Fruit of His Presence.

He will teach us a new way.
There is so much waiting for us,
In His Presence.

> Whoever is thirsty, let him come; and whoever wishes, let him take the free gift of the water of life.
>
> Revelation 22:17

Is "being still" something that you do well or something that's going to take some practice? As we close this chapter, think about what we gain when we have the ability to "be still" in the presence of Jesus.

____

____

____

____

____

____

____

____

April

Life is Hard, God is Faithful

God knew that, at some point in our lives we would face painful situations, trials, and temptations. However, He has not left us without a lifeline. During these trying times, we have God's promises to hold onto.

I will never leave you, nor forsake you.
I am with you always.
Come to me and I will give you rest.
I will turn the darkness into light and make the rough
places smooth.
Those who hope in me will not be disappointed.

> The Lord is faithful to all his promises and loving toward all he has made. Psalm 145:13

Why do you think Christians are not excluded from pain and suffering?

When in the midst of suffering, it is understandable that we might tend to question, "Why?"
The "rough road" surely would not have been the one that we would have chosen.

Without the trials, the measure of our faith would never change. God knows what is best for us and will not waste even one ounce of suffering. His desire is for us to have opportunities to exercise our faith and to be strengthened in the process.

When life seems unfair, uncertain, confusing, or painful, make sure to stay connected to the Source of all Strength.

> In my anguish I cried out to the Lord, and he answered by setting me free. The Lord is with me; I will not be afraid.
> Psalm 118:5,6

If you did not ever have to face tough times and rocky roads, how might that affect your character, your values, your future and your relationship with God?

____

____

____

____

____

____

We have all experienced circumstances that seem too big to overcome. It seems that "life" has thrown us a curve ball. Something that we never would have expected.

These are the times when we most need to cling to the Truth. The times when we need to hold on tight to our God.

The enemy is always out to seek and destroy. He would like nothing more than to weigh you down with a spirit of hopelessness and despair. Don't allow him to make you think that there is no hope!

You have an awesome Almighty Hope!

> For in the day of trouble he will keep me safe in his dwelling; he will hide me in the shelter of his tabernacle and set me high upon the rock. Psalm 27:5

What do you think is important to remember about the hope you have in Christ?

____

____

____

____

____

____

April 4th

Human difficulties-
    Divine guidance.
Human weakness-
    Divine power and strength.

Only God can make…
    the impossible ~ possible.

    the rough places ~ smooth.

    the desperate ~ restored.

    the rivers ~ passable.

    the broken ~ whole.

> I sought the Lord, and he answered me; he delivered me from all my fears. Psalm 34:4

Do you think that a person's level of hope also reflects their level of faith and trust?

____

____

____

____

____

Looking up from the valley, the mountain may appear impossible to climb. Many will find the climb too tough soon after they begin, and return to the valley.

But, those who stay the course and continue to set their sights on what is above, will reach the mountaintop and set their feet on higher ground.

Keep your eyes on the Prize. Don't be overwhelmed by the size of the mountain. Take one step at a time and remember, you are not climbing alone.

> It is God who arms me with strength and makes my way perfect. He makes my feet like the feet of a deer; he enables me to stand on the heights. Psalm 18:32,33

When facing a specific challenge, why do you think it is so easy to get overwhelmed?

The uncertainty of the world and the anxiety that it produces within us, can be so unsettling at times that we become stuck in a cycle of fear. We may then find ourselves fearful of making decisions or unable to move forward. Stuck!

Anxiety and uncertainty dwell in the "what ifs" of our thoughts. The Lord does not want us to be fearful. He tells us over and over in His Word, "Fear not!"

We can overcome our fears, first by giving them to the Lord, and then by clinging to the Rock, Who is our Strong Tower, our Refuge, our Deliverer.

> The name of the Lord is a strong tower; the righteous run to it and are safe. Proverbs 18:10

How might anxiety and fear affect God's plan and purpose for your life?

Whatever this day brings, we will not face it alone. There might be joy and laughter. There could be pain and tears. Only the Lord knows what lies ahead. This day may have many twists and turns; ups and downs, but we will walk through it, moment by moment, with Him.

Whether…

-temptation

-hardship

-illness

-disappointment

-or uncertainty,

let us anchor ourselves to the Rock. We are not left to fight the battle alone.

> My soul finds rest in God alone; my salvation comes from him. He alone is my rock and my salvation; he is my fortress, I will never be shaken. Psalm 62:1,2

What image comes to mind when you think of an anchor? Why is it important to stay anchored to the Rock at all times?

____

____

____

In 2 Corinthians, Paul pleaded with the Lord for Him to take away a specific affliction that Paul referred to as a "thorn in the flesh." The Lord's reply was, in effect, "No." He told Paul, "My grace is sufficient for you."

To some extent, we are all given a thorn, or two. God allows these circumstances in order that we would rely on Him without trying to accomplish things in our own strength. For, He knows what it looks like when we leave Him out of the picture.

> Not that we are competent in ourselves to claim anything for ourselves, but our competence comes from God.
>
> 2 Corinthians 3:5

How do you think Paul felt when his request was denied?

Three times, Paul asked God to remove something from him that was very difficult for him to bear. We do not know what Paul's "thorn" was, but it was obviously a significant burden for him to carry. Something he wanted the Lord to heal or maybe restore.

God did not grant Paul's request, so Paul pressed on trusting in his Lord and allowing God to be glorified through his own weaknesses and difficulties.

Honestly, it never occurred to me to actually be thankful for the thorns in my life. But, even as the thorns have been painful, I have no doubt that they have been necessary. They are a constant reminder of just how much I need the Lord.

The thorns will teach us to live in God's strength and will remind us that Jesus is more than enough to carry us through.

> Look to the Lord and his strength; seek his face always.
> Psalm 105:4

How do you think God can use "thorns" in the transformation process?

____

____

____

____

____

____

Life is full of ups and downs. Trials, temptations, and challenges all have a way of getting the best of us.

When you find "LIFE" staring you in the face, try not to be discouraged or fearful. Your tough situations and overwhelming circumstances are no match for your God!

The bigger your problem.......

the **bigger** your God.

The greater the odds...........

the **greater** the glory!

> Can you fathom the mysteries of God? Can you probe the limits of the Almighty? Job 11:7

Is there something that you are facing right now that seems overwhelming?

____

____

____

____

____

____

Whether we are on the mountaintop, in the valley, or somewhere in between. Let us not get distracted or tempted by an easier route, but follow Christ regardless of the conditions of the course. Whatever we are facing, we have the assurance that He is right there with us.

He is so faithful in taking our hand and walking us through each day. When our eyes are fixed on Christ, nothing is insurmountable.

Stay focused and go where He leads, even as the world seeks to pull you in a different direction.

Walk the narrow path; the one less traveled. Hand in hand, there is nothing to fear. Side by side, rely on the One Who has a perfect plan for each one of us.

> Yet I am always with you; you hold me by my right hand.
> You guide me with your counsel.
>
> Psalm 73:23,24

What do you think is meant by "the narrow path"?

____

____

____

____

____

____

We cannot fight the battle against sin on our own. When we are confronted with evil, it is most always a spiritual battle. Even our greatest efforts will fail time and time again if we do not ask the Mighty One to fight along with us.

In Ephesians 6, we are told to be strong in the Lord and to put on the full armor of God, so that when the day of evil comes, we will be able to stand our ground.

We need not run. We need not hide.
The Lord is our Strength, our Shield,
ever-present on the battlefield.

> I have set the Lord always before me. Because he is at my right hand, I will not be shaken. Psalm 16:8

How do you feel about the fact that the Lord is with you as you face your battles?

The Lord's way might not be the "easy way", but it is the "best way." It is the way that leads to Life.

He tells us in His word that, in this world, we will have trouble. Oh, how easy it would be for us to stray from the path because there might be trouble ahead.

We need not fear for the Lord surrounds us with His Arms of Protection. He goes before us and prepares the way.

I encourage you to stay on track regardless of what you might encounter. Be strong and courageous. Choose the way of Life, knowing that the Lord is always with you on that path.

> When my spirit grows faint within me, it is you who know my way. Psalm 142:3

What difference does it make to you to know that the Lord goes before you and is with you in the battle?

____

____

____

____

____

____

April 14th

Anxiety and worry will squeeze the joy out of life.

Restless heart...

trust

love

pray

rest

hope.

Thank the Lord, for lifting you up and for reminding you that you belong to Him.

> Fear not, for I have redeemed you; I have summoned you
> by name; you are mine. Isaiah 43:1

Explain how anxiety and fear can interfere with even the happiest of occasions.

____

____

____

____

____

Nothing is more comforting...
Nothing is more uplifting...
Nothing is more desirable...
Nothing is more reassuring... than to be able to trust that the Lord is always more than enough.

His love, His wisdom, His grace, and His goodness are more than enough for whatever we face and for whatever challenges lie ahead.

So, stand firm in His strength. There is no one as faithful as our Lord and Savior.

> We wait in hope for the Lord; he is our help and our shield. In him our hearts rejoice, for we trust in his holy name. May your unfailing love rest upon us, O Lord, even as we put our hope in you. Psalm 33:20-22

Complete this sentence.
The Lord is more than enough ...

____

____

____

____

____

____

The prophet, Isaiah, writes, "when we pass through the waters", not if we pass through the waters. The assumption is that the floodwaters will certainly rise. We can surely count on the fact that in this life there will be trouble. But thankfully, we can also count on the fact that God is bigger than our troubles. He is with us and understands all that we are going through.

The love Christ has for you will never fail. So even when you are "holding on for dear life", be assured that the Lord has not left your side. Not even for a minute! His grace will see you through.

> The Lord is good, a refuge in times of trouble. He cares for those who trust in him. Nahum 1:7

Just a short time before His death, Jesus told His disciples, "In this world you will have trouble." Why do you think Jesus wanted His disciples to know this?

Life is hard. **Trust** in Him.

T̲o follow where He leads.

R̲esign your will for His.

U̲nder His hand of protection.

S̲imple childlike faith.

T̲ackling life together!

We have an Almighty Father Who loves and cares about us. Trust!

> Blessed is the man who trusts in the Lord, whose confidence is in him. He will be like a tree planted by the water that sends out its roots by the stream. It does not fear when heat comes; its leaves are always green. Jeremiah 17:7,8

Write your own acrostic for the word **T R U S T**.

____

____

____

____

____

____

Many times, it is only when we come to the end of our own strength and acknowledge that we are not wise enough, or strong enough, that God will have our undivided attention.

This is the point where He will lift us up, and we will begin to live in His strength alone.

In Him, we will go from strength to strength, not from fear to fear. In Him, uncertainty gives way to assurance, and fear gives way to confidence as we allow Him, Who is more than able, to carry us through.

> Look to the Lord and his strength; seek his face always.
> I Chronicles 16:11

Why do you think that it is so hard, at times, for God to get your attention?

Continue to trust, even as the clouds get darker and darker. Even when everything around you seems to be crumbling. Even when the world says otherwise.

The ability to ***trust*** results in the ability to ***endure.***
The ability to ***endure*** leads to ***victory.***

Continue to trust in the Lord. He has a watchful eye on you, and He will lead you through the storm. Trust in His unfailing love.

Only He can keep you on solid ground, and with Jesus by your side, you will be able to move forward with confidence.

> I am he, I am he who will sustain you. I have made you and
> I will carry you; I will sustain you and I will rescue you.
> Isaiah 46:4

What is so hard about enduring?

____

____

____

____

____

____

____

Sometimes, when we get so discouraged by our circumstances, we seem to forget that our Father is the King of kings and the Lord of lords. How blessed we are to belong to Him. To be loved and cared for by the Lord of All!

You can be sure that whatever you are facing, He is with you. He will never let you down.

He will speak Words of comfort, Words of wisdom, and Words of love and encouragement to your heart.

Turn to Him. Run to Him. And rest in the knowledge that He is greater than your circumstances.

> The Lord is near to all who call on him, to all who call on him in truth. Psalm 145:18

When you are discouraged and feeling exhausted by your situation, what words do you need to hear from your loving Father?

As I look back, I suppose the greatest lessons that I have learned have come to me in the darkest times. Those times when it felt like I was walking in the desert all alone.

It is not easy for any of us to persevere and endure the trials that God allows in our life. We might question why our loving God does not swoop down and pluck us out of painful situations.

I believe that Our Father is constantly confounding the enemy on our behalf. But, the storms that He permits, He uses to make us more like Christ.

The Potter does His best work in stormy weather.

> Be strong and take heart, all you who hope in the Lord.
>
> Psalm 31:24

How do you think God is molding and shaping you at this time of your life?

April 22nd

In this chaotic, fast paced world, is there anything more precious than peace?

There is a kind of peace when the circumstances around you settle down, and all is well, once again. But, there is also a deeper kind of peace. A peace that is not easily shaken or disturbed by situations, circumstances, or the actions of others. An unshakable peace. An unmistakable peace that only the Lord can provide.

In the quiet moments that you spend with Jesus, you will be refreshed and strengthened. It is here that you will find the rest and the peace that you crave.

When you sit at His feet, you can also rest in His arms.

> You will keep in perfect peace him whose mind is steadfast,
> because he trusts in you. Isaiah 26:3

What is the one thing that can really disturb your peace? What can you do about it?

____

____

____

____

____

____

We might not have a choice about many of the situations and circumstances in our lives, but we do have a choice about how we respond. The enemy does his best to magnify our troubles and attempts to make us feel crushed and hopeless.

We can choose to retreat and allow "crushed" and "hopeless" to drag us down, or we can choose to walk with confidence and courage, allowing God to be victorious in the battle we are facing.

Lay your burdens down at His feet. The weight is surely too much for you to bear on your own. Even as you are no match for the problems that surround you, the enemy is no match for Almighty God!

> But the Lord is with me like a mighty warrior.
>
> Jeremiah 20:11

What can you tell yourself when the enemy starts to drag you down?

The Lord blesses us in so many ways. But, when we find ourselves in desperate times, the blessings are often hidden from view. It is in these troubling times that God does His best work. Many of God's richest blessings have been poured out during tough times.

When we feel as though we cannot put one foot in front of the other, that is just the time we must move forward.

Persevere. Do not be afraid to follow in His footsteps.

Ask the Lord to lead the way.

WALK BY FAITH.

> For I am the Lord, your God, who takes hold of your right hand and says to you, Do not fear; I will help you.
>
> Isaiah 41:13

Why are blessings often invisible to you when you are going through rough times?

____

____

____

____

____

____

The sun will rise; the sun will set. The rain will come and the wind will blow. Even when we can't see with our eyes, or understand with our mind, the Lord is at work. Even when we can't see beyond our overwhelming situation, the Lord is at work.

Let us remember that <u>feelings</u> are not <u>Truth</u>. Do not let your feelings overshadow the Truth.

Even though we might not see Him in the storm, we **know** that He is with us. When the wind is blowing and the waves are crashing, cling to the Lord.

He is your Rock and your Refuge, your Loving God. There is nothing to fear because you know Who walks with you.

> The rain came down, the streams rose, and the winds blew and beat against that house; yet it did not fall, because it had its foundation on the rock. Matthew 7:25

Why is it important to have a strong spiritual foundation?

____

____

____

____

____

____

Faith cannot be developed during days of smooth sailing and ideal conditions. It is in the rough seas that we are stretched and our faith grows.

When it might seem as if all is lost, cry out to the Lord. As the waves are about to wash over you, anchor yourself to the faithfulness of God and ride out the storm with Him.

Facing the wind will bring you to higher heights. God sends the wind to teach and to strengthen. Without the wind, you will never have the ability or opportunity to soar.

Do not resent that which God has allowed. He always has a higher purpose.

> Then they cried out to the Lord in their trouble, and he brought them out of their distress. He stilled the storm to a whisper; the waves of the sea were hushed.
>
> Psalm 107:28,29

Would you rather be sailing in calm waters alone or facing the waves with Christ?

____

____

____

____

____

____

Let us be <u>thankful</u> that we serve a Mighty God.

Let us be <u>confident</u> that our Lord knows best.

Let us be <u>hopeful</u> even in the midst of sorrow,
that the sun will shine again.

Let us <u>rest</u> in the knowledge that our God is faithful.

Stay the course. Do not skip over or fast forward through any of it. Be patient with the journey. Persevere, for the path will be filled with blessings, as well as, teachable moments.

Ask the Lord to give you confidence to go wherever He leads and ask Him to give you 20/20 vision in order to see His footsteps clearly. Be assured that He will provide all that you need along the way.

> "Then you will know that I am the Lord; those who hope in me will not be disappointed." Isaiah 49:23

Has there ever been a time in your life when you would have liked to use the "fast forward" button?

____

____

____

____

____

You will be able to move forward through challenges, because your Comforter and Friend is with you. He will provide all that you need to take the next step.

Stay firmly connected to Him every step of the way, being content to live moment by moment at His side, never running ahead or lagging behind.

When the Lord walks with you, anything is possible, and you need not be afraid of what lies ahead.

The Lord is trustworthy and faithful. Trust Him at all times and with all things. Let the fingerprints of God be evident in all situations as you trust the One from Whom all blessings flow.

> And when Daniel was lifted from the den, no wound was found on him, because he trusted in his God.
>
> Daniel 6:23

What do you think is meant by the **fingerprints** of God?

____

____

____

____

____

____

I recently was working on a 1,000 piece puzzle. It took many hours and many days to complete. However, when I was finished, I noticed that there was one piece missing. That one missing piece really messed up the whole picture. As you can imagine, I was really annoyed because the puzzle would never be complete. All that work, and all I could focus on was the piece that was not there.

I see so many people who try to navigate this world on their own. People who are obviously searching for that "missing piece." They have gained much success but they are still searching. They might have tried any number of temporary "fixes", but they are still not satisfied. They walk around looking for ways to complete their puzzle yet nothing is fitting into that empty space.

Jesus Christ is the Missing Piece. He is the Piece that holds everything together. He is the Piece that fills the "holes in our souls." There is nothing in this world that will satisfy those who are searching, like the love of Christ.

> Never again will they hunger; never again will they thirst... For the Lamb at the center of the throne will be their shepherd; he will lead them to springs of living water.
>
> Revelation 7:16,17

What happens when people try to substitute other things for the True Missing Piece?

____

____

____

Though the darkness is all around me…
Yet I will rejoice in the Lord!

Though everything seems like an uphill climb…
Yet I will rejoice in the Lord!

Though the waves are closing in on me…
Yet I will rejoice in the Lord!

Though my situation seems to have gone from bad to worse…
Yet I will rejoice in the Lord!

Though I am weary and my strength is gone…
Yet I will rejoice in the Lord!

> Though I have fallen, I will rise. Though I sit in darkness, the Lord will be my light. Micah 7:8

What reasons do you have to rejoice in the Lord?

____

____

____

____

____

____

May

Arms Wide Open

I am so thankful that the Lord accepts me as I am. Even when I am not so pleased with myself, His arms are open wide. He loves me even when I am not feeling all that loveable. How about you? Have you ever had any of those unlovable times?

The Word of the Lord tells us that He delights in us. We do not have to be perfect. We do not have to have all the answers and we do not have to earn His love.

The arms of Jesus are always open wide. They draw us in as He welcomes us into His love. To me, the image of Jesus waiting for us to run into His arms is priceless!

Even in our most unlovable moments, *HE DELIGHTS IN US.*

> For the Lord takes delight in his people; he crowns the humble with salvation. Psalm 149:4

Is there any reason why you might think that you are unlovable at times?

____

____

____

____

____

____

Jesus does not discriminate. He calls the young, as well as, the old. He calls the poor, as well as the wealthy. He calls the pastor, as well as the prostitute.

The Lord makes Himself known to all who seek Him. In the Light of His love there is no condemnation. It is there that we find unconditional love. It is there that we will find safety and security… in His arms.

In His arms we have freedom from pressure, freedom from expectations, and freedom from daily concerns. It is a "worry-free" zone. A place where we can let our guard down and surrender all to Him. A place where we can feel free to come as we are.

Jesus is always waiting to embrace you!

> "If anyone is thirsty, let him come to me and drink. Whoever believes in me, as the Scripture has said, streams of living water will flow from within him."
>
> John 7:37,38

What thoughts do you have regarding the fact that Jesus' arms are always open wide for you?

____

____

____

____

____

I truly believe that God loves us as we are, but I also believe that He loves us far too much to allow us to stay that way. He opens His loving arms in a welcoming embrace. He knows where we've been, and yes, He still loves us!

However, even as God loves us unconditionally, His vision for us goes beyond who we are. He sees who we can become. He will purge the things that are a hindrance, the things that hold us back and weigh us down. He will fill us with all that we are lacking.

As He cleans out and cleans up our hearts and our lives, He is transitioning us from where we were, to where we are, to where we are headed. And, He knows just how much rain it will take to make the flowers grow.

> For God who said, "Let light shine out of darkness," made his light shine in our hearts to give us the light of the knowledge of the glory of God in the face of Christ.
>
> 2 Corinthians 4:6

What obstacles might possibly get in the way as Christ seeks to transform your heart?

____

____

____

____

____

____

When I think of the morning, the sunrise, a new day, it reminds me of how the Lord makes everything new. Springtime is also a good example of new life, new beginnings.

How awesome it is to think that Christ has the same desire for us, to make us new! A new heart, a new mind, a new direction.

Imagine for a moment, looking at the buds on a tree, the birds singing on the branches, and feeling the warm breezes that have replaced the brisk winter wind. Let these images remind you that the Lord wants to do something new in each one of us.

Open arms are calling, drawing you to Jesus. He makes all things new.

> He saved us through the washing of rebirth and renewal by the Holy Spirit, whom he poured out on us generously through Jesus Christ our Savior, so that, having been justified by grace, we might become heirs having the hope of eternal life. Titus 3:5-7

What is so important about new beginnings?

____

____

____

____

____

May 5th

The Lord is so gracious and loving. Some days we simply rely on Him, and some days we lean heavily on Him. Then there are the days when it's hard to put one foot in front of the other. These are the days that He tenderly carries us and holds us close. Regardless of the circumstances, we are never alone.

When our own strength is depleted, and we are at the end of ourselves, that is just the time when the Lord's strength takes over. We can do all things, even the impossible, in His strength.

His shoulders bear our burdens. His arms hold us tight. Just when we think that we cannot take one more step, He makes it possible. Jesus is more than enough!

> In your unfailing love you will lead the people you have redeemed. In your strength you will guide them to your holy dwelling. Exodus 15:13

Would you rather be carried by the Lord or able to do things in your own strength?

____

____

____

____

____

____

Trust Him, though you cannot see Him. Trust Him in the storms. Trust Him through the challenges. Trust Him as you wait for His timing in all things.

Don't allow your trust in Jesus to be shaken by emotions, mood, or circumstances. His everlasting arms are always there to catch you. You need not be afraid.

The same arms that gently hold you, also command armies on your behalf. The loving arms that comfort you, are the same arms that were nailed to the cross.

Jesus holds the whole world in His hands. The hands that hold the world, are the same hands that hold you and me.

Praise the Lord for His arms of love, His arms of protection, and for His arms of strength!

> It is God who arms me with strength and makes my way perfect. 2 Samuel 22:33

What would you say to someone who tells you that they cannot believe in a God they cannot see?

____

____

____

____

May 7th

The Lord is my Shepherd,
what more could I want!

He walks with me
and understands all that I am going through.

With His gentle touch,
He reminds me of His love.

Just to know that He is near,
brings me comfort and joy.

Your righteousness reaches to the skies, O God, you who have done great things. Psalm 71:19

Why do you think the first line is punctuated with an exclamation mark instead of a question mark?

If we look intently to the Lord and seek Him in all circumstances we will always find Him.

When you are at your wit's end…
When you cannot see past your pain…
When all of your strength is gone…
When no one else understands…

That is just the time that the faithfulness of the Lord is most evident. He will step into the middle of your troubles and take the weight off of your shoulders and lift you up, as only He can.

Daughters of the King, do not be discouraged. Do not loose heart. Unburden yourselves. Let the King Who loves and cares for you carry your load.

> He will cover you with his feathers, and under his wings you will find refuge; his faithfulness will be your shield and rampart. Psalm 91:4

Why do you think we are so determined to carry our own burdens when the Lord is just waiting to share the load?

We have all, at one time or another, found ourselves in a hurtful situation. Maybe we have been insulted, misunderstood, unappreciated, or falsely accused. When we feel hurt, we tend to want to even the score, and often times, our mouths shift into autopilot.

In these times, show restraint! Take a step back. Do not plot evil against evil.

Give all your hurt and pain to the Lord. Ask Him to settle you down. He clearly sees the situation and all that is going on.

Be patient and allow Him to work in the situation. Only Christ can provide the relief that you seek and healing to your heart. Let Him settle the score, His way.

> The Lord redeems his servants; no one will be condemned
> who takes refuge in him. Psalm 34:22

Why is it better to show restraint and turn everything over to God, even when everything within you is screaming revenge?

____

____

____

____

____

____

Many times when we feel as if we've been treated unfairly, we continue to replay the situation in our mind, over and over, to the point that we get all stirred up inside. We end up causing more pain to ourselves than to the person who offended us. The more we dwell on the situation, the bigger the problem becomes.

In my experience, whenever I bring these hurtful wounds to the Lord, His love immediately begins to heal those sore spots.

Look to Jesus for healing. He is a Refuge for the hurting. He will not only heal your mind and your heart, but He will also bring healing and resolution to your circumstances.

The "rewind button" will only create more bitterness. Hit the pause button instead! Pause. Pray. Give your hurts to God.

> Do not say, "I'll pay you back for this wrong!" Wait for the Lord, and he will deliver you. Proverbs 20:22

What happens to you when you continue to dwell on a situation?

____

____

____

____

____

____

Sometimes, when facing rejection, it is hard not to look inward and view ourselves as "less than." Jesus knows all about rejection. Throughout His life, Jesus was rejected time and again. Luke, Chapter 4, tells about Jesus even being rejected in His hometown of Nazareth.

In this situation, Jesus shook it off and moved on. He did not allow the insults of others to throw Him off track. He did not change His message or His words because He was rejected. He remained true to Himself and to His Father. He continued to speak the Truth to all who would listen.

In this life, you will not be loved and appreciated by everyone you meet, but rejection does not mean that you are "less than." Don't change who you are to suit those around you. As long as the Lord is pleased with you, shake it off and keep walking. For He thinks that you are something special!

> There is now no condemnation for those who are in Christ Jesus. Romans 8:1

In the face of rejection, what can you tell yourself about the love of Christ?

____

____

____

____

____

____

May 12th

What does it take for us to fall into the arms of Jesus?

Pain?
Pressure?
Suffering?
Circumstances?
Desperation?

When you are all stirred up on the inside, that is just the right time to quiet yourself before the Lord. In the holy quietness, the Lord will make His presence known.

Allow Him to soothe your spirit and calm your fears. He will help you climb above your current situation. He will lift your spirit as you rest in His arms.

During difficult times, there's no place I'd rather be than in His arms. He is our Rock, our Comforter, our Loving Father. He will hold us close until the storm has passed.

> He tends his flock like a shepherd: He gathers the lambs in his arms and carries them close to his heart.
>
> Isaiah 40:11

How does the Shepherd and the lamb symbolize your relationship with Jesus?

____

____

____

There have been many ups and downs throughout my life. During the tough times, the Lord has never failed to be with me in my hour of need. Whether comfort, guidance, security, or healing, He always knows what I need, and He lovingly provides it.

The Lord is never too late in coming to our rescue. But usually, He is just late enough.

Just late enough so that we must exercise our faith while we wait.
Just late enough so we will trust a little bit more next time.
Just late enough that when the world starts to question our hope...

Our Hope intervenes in a Mighty Way!

> He brought me out into a spacious place; he rescued me because he delighted in me. 2 Samuel 22:20

When you think that God is late in showing up, how hard is it for you to continue to trust Him?

____

____

____

____

____

____

May 14th

Just as we would trust our bridegroom:

... in sickness and in health,

... in good times and in bad,

... in joy and in sorrow,

... with all things, and in all things,

We can count on the Lord to see us through.

The love of Christ is constant. When we are going through tough times or pain and suffering, it is not because He has stopped loving us.

Let us not harden our hearts during these times, but open them up and allow Jesus to come in and minister to the hurting, wounded places deep within us.

> God's solid foundation stands firm, sealed with this inscription: "The Lord knows those who are his."
>
> 2 Timothy 2:19

Have you ever felt abandoned by God during tough times? What is the **truth** about these feelings?

____

____

____

May 15th

Help me, Lord, to break the chains of doubt and to be able to stand strong in my faith. Help me to keep my mind saturated with Your Truth and protected from the schemes and deception of the evil one.

Thank You, Lord, for not rejecting me when doubts creep into my thoughts. Instead, You seek to strengthen my faith by revealing more and more of Yourself to me.

Jesus, Your patience with me must be an indication of Your love. Thank You for not giving up on me. Thank You for being with me through "thick and thin."

Please help me to keep my eyes fixed on You as You replace any doubts or confusion in my mind with Your Truth.

> Have faith in the Lord your God and you will be upheld.
>
> 2 Chronicles 20:20

Why do you think the enemy is pleased when you have doubts about the Kingdom of God?

____

____

____

____

____

____

I cannot imagine meeting Jesus face to face. Our minds are so limited to our earthly experiences that we couldn't possibly fathom what this would be like. His Majesty and Splendor will far exceed anything that we could ever conceive.

I really do think that Jesus will have a smile on His face when He meets us. Of course, I picture His arms open wide, ready to receive us, and I am sure that He will call us by name.

I am so thankful that we have the promise of eternity; the promise of one day meeting Jesus face to face. But, until then, we must walk the path that He has designed for each one of us.

Even the most beautiful place on earth will not compare to the beauty that will be revealed in heaven, and I have no doubt that when the time comes, He will take our breath away.

> Praise be to the God and Father of our Lord Jesus Christ! In his great mercy he has given us new birth into a living hope through the resurrection of Jesus Christ from the dead, and into an inheritance that can never perish, spoil or fade- kept in heaven for you. I Peter 1:3,4

What do you think you will say to Jesus upon your first face to face encounter with Him? What do you hope He will say to you?

____

____

____

There will be times in your life when God will take you out of comfortable, familiar surroundings and lead you in a new direction. These changes will bring new opportunities, as well as, provide you with circumstances that will "stretch" you and help to strengthen your faith.

During these times it will be necessary for you to rely on God and trust in His provision, His plan, and His goodness.

Changing direction has always been a bit intimidating for me, and yes, there have certainly been many opportunities for me to stretch my faith. However, the Lord has never sent me in a direction where He did not go with me, always providing all that I needed.

Trust in Him. Our hope and strength is not in ourselves. It is not in the world, and it is not in others. Our only hope is in our God!

> And my God will meet all your needs according to his glorious riches in Christ Jesus. Philippians 4:19

Are you someone who likes change or do you prefer the familiar and the predictable?

____

____

____

____

____

There are going to be times when you will find yourself at a crossroad with many options.

God will show the way.

Other times, you will seem to be on the right path, but you will end up at a dead end.

God can make a way.

It only takes one open door even if you've had so many that have been closed.

God will lead the way.

When you have more options than answers, take it to Jesus and allow Him to narrow things down, and eventually He will lead you through the right door.

> "I am the light of the world. Whoever follows me will never walk in darkness, but will have the light of life."
>
> John 8:12

Have you ever been at a crossroad and not sure which way to go? How did you decide which road to follow? How did it turn out?

____

____

____

____

May 19th

Trust in the Lord. Don't be apprehensive in moving forward. Follow wherever He leads no matter what the cost. Trust that His way is best. Be assured that the One Who is directing your paths is always right beside you.

As you allow the Lord to lead, ask for His protection from the evil that surrounds you. Day after day, the enemy looms and will seek to lead you astray. He will try with all his might to shake your foundation and get you off course. The enemy will also make other paths look so much more attractive than the one you are on.

Don't be deceived. Stay focused on Jesus. Your God is mightier than the schemes and deceptions of the evil one. Stick close to Him and His power, and His purposes will prevail!

> Let your eyes look straight ahead, fix your gaze directly before you. Make level paths for your feet and take only ways that are firm. Proverbs 4:25,26

What are some ways that the enemy might try to distract you from following Jesus?

____

____

____

____

____

____

May 20th

Without You, Lord, we would be drowning in our sin. We would be unclean and unworthy. Only because of Your love and Your grace we are made new *(clean)*. It is nothing that ***we*** have done. We are only worthy because of what ***You*** have done.

You cancel all of our debt so that we are free. You set us on a different path, a narrow path, one that leads to life.

The poverty of our soul, that we ourselves have created, is washed clean because of Your love for us.

Fill me up, Lord. Fill every corner of my heart with Your Presence. My need for You is so great. Your Glory is ever magnified in my weakness.

Let the praises of my heart reach Your ears. You are my All in All, my Bread of Life, my Gentle Shepherd, my Loving Father, my Deliverer.

> Cleanse me with hyssop, and I will be clean; wash me, and
> I will be whiter than snow. Psalm 51:7

Why do you think the Lord is in the "cleaning" business?

____

____

____

____

____

May 21st

Jesus is the Source of rest and refreshment. Only He can renew your mind and your spirit. Only He can strengthen you from top to bottom, and from inside-out. He will always brighten your day regardless of your circumstances.

Jesus will never minimize what you are going through. Instead, He will embrace you and love you through it.

The Light of His Presence overshadows fear and doubt and will provide you with hope for each new day. In Him, you have the promise of eternal riches. With Him, you have all that you need.

Surround yourself with the Light of Jesus. Continue to grow in Him. Continue to work with Him to build a strong foundation that will not be shaken by the challenges of life.

> You, O Lord, keep my lamp burning; my God turns my darkness into light. Psalm 18:28

What do you think is needed for a strong foundation in Christ? How does this foundation get built?

When adversity strikes, we need not fear, for the Lord is already there with us in the midst of our pain. He has promised to never leave us, and I truly have experienced His faithfulness!

Regardless of how you feel, Jesus is there. I want you to know this and get to the point that you can accept this as Truth.

Even though you do not **see** Him and you might not **feel** His Presence, rest assured that the King has His eyes on His precious princess. And if that weren't enough...

He's not only watching, but He is holding you close and whispering in your ear, "I love you. We will get through this together."

> I will say of the Lord, "He is my refuge and my fortress,
> my God, in whom I trust." Psalm 91:2

What are some ways that you can overshadow your feelings with the Truth?

____

____

____

____

____

____

____

When you come into His Presence, there might be so many things that are stirring you up. You might have concerns about relationships, worries about the future, or even decisions that are weighing heavy on your mind.

When you are in the arms of Jesus, nothing can penetrate the Peace that you have in His Presence. His Peace is like a wall of protection for your heart and mind. His Peace keeps the world at a distance and allows Him to minister to your heart.

As you leave His Presence, you will find that you have been loved and strengthened, and you will be able to deal with whatever had been stirring in your mind.

Whenever you have so much on your mind, ask the Lord to settle you down and to give you clarity regarding specific concerns. Get caught up in the Peace that only He can provide.

> I pray that out of his glorious riches he may strengthen you with power through his Spirit in your inner being, so that Christ may dwell in your hearts through faith.
>
> Ephesians 3:16,17

Why do you think that the Lord does not want you to have a cluttered mind?

___

___

___

___

May 24th

Worry is something that we all deal with at times in our lives. It is a condition of the mind that could also affect the rest of our body, as well. It can be short-lived or have lasting affects. Sometimes it seems that the more we try to stop worrying, the more we worry.

Worrying about the future robs us of joy in the present. If we trust that our future is in the Lord's hands, we can have confidence that whatever the future brings, He is right there with us and He is faithful.

When you go to Lord on a regular basis, the things that you would normally worry about do not seem to be as urgent. The Lord takes your worry and reminds you that He will provide. He provided for you in the past. He is providing for you now, and He will continue to provide for you tomorrow.

Claim the assurance that the Lord goes with you.

> No, in all these things we are more than conquerors through him who love us. Romans 8:37

What comes to mind when you think of yourself as a conqueror?

____

____

____

____

____

____

We all have different wounds and things that need the Lord's attention, as well as, His healing touch.

While in the arms of Jesus, receive His goodness. Allow Him to warm your heart. Allow Him to heal your brokenness.

Where there is shame, He provides **acceptance.**
When you are confused, He provides **clarity.**
When you are afraid, He provides **courage** and **strength.**
Where there is anxiety, He provides **peace.**
Where there is desperation, He provides **hope.**
When you are guilty, He provides **forgiveness.**
Where there is sin, He provides **salvation.**

Only Jesus can provide it all!

> How great is your goodness, which you have stored up for those who fear you, which you bestow in the sight of men on those who take refuge in you. Psalm 31:19

What wounds do you have that need the Lord's healing touch?

____

____

____

____

____

Have you ever heard the story of the prodigal son? It is a story about two brothers. The older one was obedient and hard working, and the younger brother just wanted his share of his father's inheritance, even though it seemed that he did very little to deserve it.

The father agreed and split his estate between his two sons. Upon getting his share, the younger son left home and squandered all of his money on a wild lifestyle.

When the son returned home, hungry and penniless, the father welcomed him with open arms and threw a party in his honor. This made the dutiful, older son quite angry!

I see the father's reaction to his wayward son's return as loving and forgiving. He was excited about the fact that his son had come to his senses and acknowledged his sinfulness.

I believe that Christ would have that same response to one of His own who was lost and who now wanted to be forgiven. "Open arms. You are forgiven."

> "But while he was still a long way off, his father saw him
> and was filled with compassion for him; he ran to his son,
> threw his arms around him and kissed him."
>
> Luke 15:20

What do you think about the younger brother getting so much attention from his father upon his return?

____

____

When Jesus wraps His loving arms around you, what do you think He is trying to communicate to you? I suppose there would be a variety of answers to that question depending on who you asked.

I believe that just as Jesus opens His arms in a loving welcoming way to us, we should also open our arms to others.

Have you ever been given a hug when you ***really*** needed one? How awesome was that? No words were even needed. The hug communicated love, caring, and kindness.

Let us never be afraid of showing someone just how much we care. I am sure that when we are welcoming and comforting to others, Jesus is smiling and probably thinking, "You go, girl!"

> Praise be to the God and Father of our Lord Jesus Christ, the Father of compassion and the God of all comfort, who comforts us in all our troubles, so that we can comfort those in any trouble with the comfort we ourselves have received from God. 2 Corinthians 1:3,4

How would you answer the initial question above? What would Jesus be trying to communicate to you as He wraps His arms around you?

____

____

____

____

May 28th

Have you ever felt abandoned or betrayed by someone: a friend, a parent, or family member? Obviously our lives are not perfect and neither are the people in our lives. We've all probably felt left out or neglected at some point.

Jesus will never turn His back on you. He is always available, and He cherishes the relationship that He has with you.

Only Jesus can satisfy your deepest longings. Only He can fill the empty places in your heart.

So, whenever you start to feel alone, or whenever you get mistreated by someone that was supposed to love you, turn to your King for comfort and reassurance. He will not disappoint you, for you are His beloved daughter.

> The eyes of the Lord are on the righteous and his ears are attentive to their cry. Psalm 34:15

How is your relationship with Jesus different from any other relationship?

____

____

____

____

____

____

I think the biggest indication that we are in need of our Loving Father is when we run to Him on any given day. When we seek His strength and His comfort, we are basically saying that we can't do this thing called "life" alone. We are expressing the need for our Lord to shelter us, protect us, and hold us close.

When you declare that you do not want to walk alone, Jesus is always there to take your hand. He will walk you through one day at a time as you learn to trust Him.

Seek Him. Run to Him. Jump into His arms and allow Him to shower you with love and understanding.

So, when you feel like your heart is in pieces, or you feel like you are falling apart, Jesus will lovingly put the pieces back together again.

> I long to dwell in your tent forever and take refuge in the shelter of your wings. Psalm 61:4

Why do you think so many people are bound and determined to walk through life "on their own"?

____

____

____

____

____

May 30th

As we get close to the end of this month, I want to encourage you to be strong in the Lord. Stay in the Light, where darkness cannot find you. Trust Him for whatever lies ahead. We are all called to persevere. Don't quit. Don't ever give up!

Allow Jesus to be the Author of your next chapter. He is the Source of "new beginnings." He will lead you in the right direction and be with you through any challenges you might face. Trust in His love for you and trust in His ability to provide for you.

Seek Jesus in all situations. Seek Him on sunny days, as well as, on cloudy and rainy days. Stay rooted in the Truth and saturate yourself with His Word. Allow the love of Jesus to guide your heart and your mind in this often troubling and confusing world.

> The Lord is righteous in all his ways and loving toward all he has made. Psalm 145:17

If you and the Lord started to write a new chapter in your life, what would be a good title for this chapter?

____

____

____

____

____

____

I hope you always remember that the arms of Jesus are always open wide. If you've been gone for awhile, He is ready to welcome you home. If you have been feeling a bit incomplete, He is ready to make you whole. If you have been lost in the world, He is ready to help you find a new direction.

Run to the waiting arms of Jesus. He has so much that He wants to share with you. There's so much that He has been waiting to tell you.

Draw strength and find hope in His embrace. Allow Him to uplift you and encourage you. Know beyond a shadow of a doubt that you are precious to Him. You are His princess, and He is your King!

And, there really is... "no place like home."

> For he has rescued us from the dominion of darkness and brought us into the kingdom of the Son he loves, in whom we have redemption, the forgiveness of sins.
>
> Colossians 1:13,14

How is being "at home" in the arms of Jesus different from what you have experienced in your current or childhood home?

____

____

____

____

____

June

Our God Reigns

June 1st

OUR GOD REIGNS!

God's power is evident throughout the Bible and beyond. His power cannot be contained. It has no limit, and it has no end. There is no way that we can fathom the magnitude of His power and might.

God demonstrated His power at creation. His power was displayed at the cross and then again at the tomb. There are endless examples of the Almighty using His power on behalf of His people.

The Old Testament is filled with situations where God used His power to intervene for the Israelites. The New Testament reveals His power and His love when He sent His Son to be the Light of the World for each of us.

And, even after Christ died, God did not leave us to figure things out on our own. He gave us the Holy Spirit to keep us connected to Him and to help guide us in the Truth. The Holy Spirit lives in us and empowers us to live for Christ.

> The Lord reigns, he is robed in majesty; the Lord is robed in majesty and is armed with strength. Psalm 93:1

List a few examples which describe the power of the Lord that can be found in the Old Testament.

____

____

____

____

Our God is the God of the Universe!! There is nothing that is beyond His power! The Lord wants so much to bless us. He wants to give us more than we could ever imagine. I am wondering how many times I have prayed, and God thinks, "Is that it? Is that all you want? I had so much more in mind."

God has a great vision for each one of us. His goodness and grace have no limit. He is the Giver of life, the Giver of gifts, and the Author of salvation.

Oh, how the Lord wants to bless us! He has so much in store for us.

By faith and obedience, and through prayer, let us start to access all that God has to offer. Our God reigns!

> Ask and it will be given to you; seek and you will find; knock and the door will be opened to you. For everyone who asks receives; he who seeks finds; and to him who knocks, the door will be opened. Matthew 7:7,8

What are some of the blessings that you might receive through prayer?

____

____

____

____

____

____

Have you ever wondered what the Lord sees when He looks at you? I think He sees someone beautiful, someone He created. His lovely princess!

There are many days when we do not feel lovely or all that beautiful. Understandably, our view of ourselves often depends on our circumstances.

Good news, princess!! The Lord's view of you never changes. He always sees you through His eyes of love.

Remember, He delights in you. You are beautiful. You are His!

> But I am like an olive tree flourishing in the house of God;
> I trust in God's unfailing love for ever and ever.
>
> Psalm 52:8

Is there anything that is preventing you from believing that the God of All Creation delights in you?

____

____

____

____

____

____

____

June 4th

I wonder if we will ever realize the magnitude of God's blessings. There are blessings in our lives that are so evident, and yet there are others that are not so obvious.

Still, there are countless ways that God works on our behalf that we are not even aware of. We are always on His mind. How awesome is that!

Let us not take God's blessings for granted, but praise Him continuously for Who He is, for what He has done, and for what He will continue to do in our lives. He is a "Giving God" Who seeks to bless His children. His blessings are more numerous than the stars in the sky.

> Come and see what God has done, how awesome his works
> in man's behalf! Psalm 66:5

In what ways has God blessed you within the past week?

____

____

____

____

____

____

____

____

Sing for joy, O daughters of the King.
Sing for joy and praise His Holy Name!

You have been chosen; you have been set apart.
Not because of anything that you have done, but because of His love and because of His grace.

Sing for joy with a thankful heart and rejoice, for the King of kings knows you by name.

Sing for joy, O daughters of the King.
Sing for joy and praise His Holy Name!

> Worship the Lord with gladness; come before him with joyful songs. Know that the Lord is God. It is he who made us, and we are his; we are his people, the sheep of his pasture. Psalm 100:2,3

What does being the daughter of the King of kings mean to you?

Our faith is not based on feeling, but on Truth. Truth is our solid foundation. It is an anchor that we hold onto when things don't make sense. It is a shield that keeps us grounded when everything else is spinning out of control.

Faith believes, even when it does not see.
Faith trusts, even when the world says otherwise.
Faith is confident that the Lord is at work.
Faith is our anchor that secures us to the Rock.

> "If you have faith as small as a mustard seed, you can say to this mountain, 'Move from here to there' and it will move. Nothing will be impossible for you." Matthew 17:20

How easy or hard is it for you to rest on the Truth when your emotions are leading you down a different path?

____

____

____

____

____

____

____

____

June 7th

The enemy is always throwing stones onto our path. They are meant to hurt us, distract us, discourage us, and wear us down. However, the stones that are meant to block our way, God uses as stepping stones that will serve to lead us right into heaven.

Even as the enemy will try to discourage us, he will not defeat us. He can distract us, but he cannot take away our hope. He can try to deceive us, but he cannot overshadow the Truth. What the enemy intends for destruction, the Lord uses to promote us.

The Lord is **with you**; you need not fear.
The Lord is **in you**; the devil will not have his way.
The Lord **goes before you**; trust Him for all that lies ahead.

> But as for me, I will always have hope; I will praise you more and more. My mouth will tell of your righteousness, of your salvation all day long, though I know not its measure. Psalm 71:14,15

What are some things that you can do when evil is thrown onto your path?

____

____

____

____

____

____

One thing that has never changed throughout the years is the desire to "fit in." We put so much pressure on ourselves to impress others; wear the right clothes, listen to the most popular music, make sure you are up to date on all of the celebrity news. And, of course, make sure you do not go out of the house with "bad hair"!

When it comes to your Heavenly Father, you are under no such pressure. He is already impressed with you and calls you to "come as you are."

Come with your faults. Come with your imperfections. Come with your weaknesses. And yes, even come with your "bad hair"!

The Lord welcomes us... as we are. He accepts us... as we are. He loves us... as we are.

You have nothing to prove to your Heavenly Father. After all, He already knows it all. He knows where you've been. He knows where you are, and He knows where you're headed. AND... He has never, not even for a second, stopped loving you!

> The Lord your God is with you, he is mighty to save. He will take great delight in you, he will quiet you with his love, he will rejoice over you with singing.
>
> Zephaniah 3:17

How important is it for you to "fit in" with others?

___

___

___

It is truly amazing as I reflect on all the ways the Lord has provided for me. How about you? Have you tasted the goodness of the Lord?

When we stop and look back, we will surely see His hand of blessing in our lives. He takes pleasure in blessing us and providing for us.

He knows our every need. He provided for us yesterday, He continues to provide for us today, and we can be sure that more of His goodness awaits us tomorrow.

How awesome is our God! He has designed a very unique path for each one of us. May we always be aware of where He is leading, ready and willing, as He shows us the next step. As the Lord leads, let us fearlessly take His hand.

> How great is your goodness, which you have stored up for those who fear you, which you bestow in the sight of men on those who take refuge in you. Psalm 31:19

What are some reasons why you might be hesitant in taking the Lord's hand and going where He leads?

June 10th

Patience is a virtue. To me, that means it is not easily acquired and it is not easily learned. Honestly, for me, patience has always been one of my weaknesses. I do not ***wait*** well! I certainly have, at times, learned "the hard way."

Impatience undoubtedly steers us away from God's plan and leads us away from the will of God. It involves a lack of trust, and we end up thinking that our way is best. Have patience! Patience will not disappoint, and God will not let us down.

God's way is always the best way. He has a plan for us, and sometimes that plan includes waiting for His timing. Let us learn to wait on the Lord, knowing and trusting that He's got everything under control!

> Therefore, as God's chosen people, holy and dearly loved, clothe yourselves with compassion, kindness, humility, gentleness and patience. Colossians 3:12

How can having patience lead to blessings?

How vulnerable we are to the enemy as we wait on God's timing! Satan knows how much we hate to wait. He is the master of putting doubts in our mind as he tries to bring us to the point of anxiety, worry, and frustration. He wants nothing more than to see us step out of God's will and try to take care of everything in our own strength.

Why are we so tempted to step in and jump ahead of God? I can't even count the times when I got impatient and took matters into my own hands. It always ended up that I made a mess out of the situation.

Have faith that God will reveal your next move when it's time. And even as the enemy tries to get you off track, stand firm and wait on God.

Don't be deceived. And, while you're at it… remind him **Who** he's messing with!

> Because of the Lord's great love we are not consumed, for his compassions never fail. They are new every morning; great is your faithfulness. I say to myself, "The Lord is my portion; therefore I will wait for him."
>
> Lamentations 3:22-24

Have you ever made a mess of a situation or made a wrong choice because you did not seek God first?

____

____

____

____

June 12th

Sometimes, it is obvious that I need a complete transfusion. A transfusion of the Peace of Christ; a transfusion that will allow me to refocus on His Presence, and rest with Him in the heavenly realms.

Life can get us so stirred up! Sometimes we can make little things seem bigger than they really are. And sometimes we might be in the middle of a situation that we cannot see past.

Either way, when we are able to step back and "**look up**", we find that the Lord will fill us with all that we need and give us a brand new perspective.

When our focus is **up,** our spirit will be lifted, and it will be much harder for life to drag us down.

> Praise be to the God and Father of our Lord Jesus Christ, who has blessed us in the heavenly realms with every spiritual blessing in Christ. Ephesians 1:3

What are some things that you can do when a difficult situation starts to get the best of you?

June 13th

Oh, the constant refrain of troubled times.
The words to the song, I cannot begin to know.
But, I persevere- I trust- I do not lose hope.

God is in the midst of writing a new song that will proclaim power, victory, and deliverance.
A song that never would have been written, if not for the refrain of troubled times.

As Christians, we are not guaranteed a life free from suffering and pain. On the contrary, Jesus said, "In this world, you will have trouble," which suggests to us that it will not always be smooth sailing.

God is preparing us for heaven! Our circumstances are not by chance and neither is our inheritance!

> I consider that our present sufferings are not worth comparing with the glory that will be revealed in us.
>
> Romans 8:18

Why do you think that God does not shelter us from all pain and suffering?

____

____

____

____

____

It is only after enduring the dark cold days of winter that we get to feel the warm sunshine of spring on our face. God has perfectly designed the seasons of our lives in order to mold us and shape us internally, from the inside out.

What we think might be tearing us down is actually building us up.

God will not allow pain without a plan. Every ounce of suffering is used for a greater purpose.

Often we do not understand. We might question, "Why?" Even then, God is at work.

Every time the Holy Spirit restores us by breathing new life into us, we are forever changed.

> Now it is God who makes both us and you stand firm in Christ. He anointed us, set his seal of ownership on us, and put his Spirit in our hearts as a deposit, guaranteeing what is to come. 2 Corinthians 1:21,22

Is it only in the tough times that God is shaping and molding you? Explain.

____

____

____

____

____

June 15th

When God brings a storm, His blessings are not far behind. Many times it takes a storm in order for God to have an opportunity to shower us with His blessings… the blessings of perseverance, patience, hope, and peace. Blessings that will shine even brighter after the storm has passed.

The Lord does not leave us defenseless in times of trouble. When the clouds roll in, He wants us to hold on tight. He wants to love us and comfort us, as He uses our circumstances as a catalyst for change.

Even as the world seeks to beat us down, the Lord seeks to raise us up!

> And the God of all grace, who called you to his eternal glory in Christ, after you have suffered a little while, will himself restore you and make you strong, firm and steadfast. I Peter 5:10

Can you recall a lesson that you have learned through hardship or tough circumstances?

___

___

___

___

___

___

___

Because God has given all of us free will, we always have choices. We can choose to follow the One and Only King of kings, or we can gravitate toward the ways of the world.

We can choose to turn our backs on God at the first sign of trouble, or we can choose to "stay put" and learn the lessons that He is trying to teach us.

We can choose to retreat when life gets too hard, or we can trust that Christ will see us through.

There is a certain beauty that comes from "choosing" to endure because we have allowed God to be God. When we trust Him enough to allow Him to choose the colors in our life, a beautiful painting will start to emerge.

> Being confident of this, that he who began a good work in you will carry it on to completion until the day of Christ Jesus. Philippians 1:6

What do you think about the "free will" that God has given to you? How can free will bring you closer to God and how could it also lead you astray?

Jesus, Name above all names. No one could ever measure the depths of His love for us or completely understand the magnitude of His mercy and grace.

When we are weak, He is our Strength.
When we are broken, His arms will embrace us.
When we are empty, He will fill us up.
When we feel defeated, He is our Hope.

When we are down and out, He lifts us up.
When we are misunderstood, He can relate.
When we are frustrated, He is our Peace.
When we are fearful, He is our Rock.

And… when we are filled with questions, and don't know where to turn… He is the Answer!

> I will sing of the Lord's great love forever; with my mouth I will make your faithfulness known through all generations.
>
> Psalm 89:1

At what times in your life have you needed the love of Jesus most of all?

___

___

___

___

___

It has been said that when God closes a door, He opens a window. It can be frustrating when we think we know where we are headed, and God closes that door. It can also be quite confusing when we are motivated to serve, and God might have something different in mind for us.

I have learned to be thankful for closed doors. It is a sure redirection from God and He surely has a purpose for closing a door.

-God might have something else in mind for you.
-That specific door might have someone else's name on it.
-God might be leading you into a season of rest and renewal.
-Or, you might already have enough on your plate, and be spreading yourself too thin.

Only God knows what's on the other side of the door. He alone knows what is best.

> For we are God's workmanship, created in Christ Jesus to do good works, which God prepared in advance for us to do. Ephesians 2:10

What might happen if you decided to bust down the doors that God has already closed?

____

____

____

____

The promises of God are many. Every fear, every worry, every concern that we have can be redirected, countered, and conquered when we are able to claim those promises for ourselves.

Recite the promises in your mind and carry them in your heart.

If you turn each promise into a personal truth, you will have a stronger foundation on which to stand.

One way that I claim these Truths for myself is to personalize scripture and pray through it.
For instance: let's look at 2 Corinthians 1:21.
I will use ( ) to indicate where the personalization takes place.

Now it is God who makes (me) stand firm in Christ. He anointed (me), set his seal of ownership on (me), and put his Spirit in (my) heart as a deposit, guaranteeing what is to come.

The promises of our Father will encourage us, strengthen us, and give us hope.

> Let us hold unswervingly to the hope we profess, for he who promised is faithful. Hebrews 10:23

Look up 1 Corinthians 2:12. In the space below personalize this scripture and claim it for yourself.

____

____

____

What comes to mind when you think of "clouds"? Do you think that rain is sure to follow? Do clouds represent a trying time in your life? Do you think that the only purpose for clouds is to obscure a bright sunny day?

God used clouds to guide the Israelites and many times in His Word, clouds are used to reveal His mighty power.

I do a lot of walking. Lately I have been looking to the sky as I walk and trying to pick out the most beautiful colors of the daytime sky. Some days I see a color of blue that is so brilliant. Some days I choose a beautiful shade of gray.

As I look at the clouds along my way, sometimes they look like a big white blanket. This reminds me of God's comfort and protection. Other times, I see rays of light shining through the clouds that signify to me God's love shining down on me. And there have been days when the whole sky is filled with clouds, except for one little spot of blue. I call this my little tiny slice of heaven.

Clouds serve a purpose and are designed by God. The most colorful, beautiful sunsets cannot be painted without the clouds.

> At that time men will see the Son of Man coming in the clouds with great power and glory. Mark 13:26

Describe the most beautiful sky you have ever seen. If you have never experienced such beauty, start looking!

Maybe you've heard the story of Shadrach, Meshach, and Abednego. They were friends of the prophet Daniel.

At that time, Nebuchadnezzar, was king of Babylon and requested young, smart, handsome men to serve in the king's palace. Daniel and his three friends were chosen to serve the king.

At some point the king had an image of gold made that was ninety feet tall. Each day, all the people in the kingdom and all who served the king were to bow down and worship this golden image, and if anyone did not worship the idol, they would be thrown into a blazing furnace.

It was reported to the king that Shadrach, Meshach, and Abednego refused to bow down to the idol. Even when facing a fiery furnace and certain death, the three men stayed true to their God. They told the king that whether or not God saw fit to rescue them, they would never bow down to his image of gold!

In the end, the Lord did indeed save the men and not even a hair on their heads was burned. Such power!
Such faith!

> Some trust in chariots and some in horses, but we trust in the name of the Lord our God. Psalm 20:7

How would you describe the faith of these three men?

____

____

____

When trouble strikes and hardship falls, it is sometimes hard to see that God's hand is still in everything. We are quick to forget how He had delivered us so many times before.

I believe that it is through trials and challenges that we learn our best lessons. These are usually the times when the Lord has our undivided attention.

I can speak from experience and tell you that I was not quick to learn some of God's lessons. Sometimes I even wonder how many times I have tried His patience!

The Lord knows exactly what we still need to learn, and He will use our challenges as "teachable moments." Through each tough lesson, He does not leave us to figure things out on our own. He continues to teach, to mold, and to shape. His objective is not pain, but change.

> Teach me your way, O Lord, and I will walk in your truth.
> Psalm 86:11

Can you think of a specific lesson that the Lord has taught you through a challenge that you had been facing?

The enemy can try to discourage us, but he will not defeat us. He can try to distract us, but he cannot take away our vision. He can try to deceive us, but he cannot overshadow the Truth. All the ways of the enemy are known and used by God.

As we go through life, we will encounter many "giants" along the way. Their mission will be to consume and destroy us. In our own strength, the possibility of victory does not exist. Thankfully, we are not left to fight the battles alone.

The odds were not in David's favor. However, even as other men were terrified and ran away, and even as King Saul told him that he was not fit for the fight, David marched forward to confront the giant.

As fierce as Goliath was, he was no match for David and his God!

> David said to the Philistine, "You come against me with sword and spear and javelin, but I come against you in the name of the Lord Almighty. I Samuel 17:45

How did God use David in this situation to display His awesome power?

____

____

____

____

____

June 24th

Many times, it is easy for us to become overwhelmed and discouraged by our circumstances. Life drags us down, and we know that we do not have what it takes to overcome the situation.

In acknowledging that we are not strong enough or wise enough, we will come to the end of ourselves and begin to seek the guidance and the strength that only the Lord can provide. This is the point where He will lift us up, and we will begin to walk in His strength alone.

Let us not allow our circumstances to break our spirit. Though the outcome might still be a mystery, walk in the strength of the Lord and trust in the One Who delivers.

> My flesh and my heart may fail, but God is the strength of my heart and my portion forever. Psalm 73:26

What can you do the next time that you encounter a situation that seems impossible to overcome?

Have you ever wondered why some people appear to "have it all", yet others seem to struggle just to survive? There are those who are popular and those who seem to have been forgotten. There are those who have no financial worries and others who cannot afford their next meal. Does it seem that God is playing favorites?

I believe that God loves each and every one He created. And, each and every person has the opportunity to seek and find a relationship with Him.

Outer appearances and external conditions do not define us. The Lord is more concerned with the condition of our heart than what kind of car we drive. He wants us to get to know Him better. He wants us to focus on who we are, as opposed to what we have.

The happiest children that I have ever met lived in an orphanage in Jamaica. They had no shoes on their feet and nothing of material value to speak of, but their smile could light up a room, and their enthusiasm for God was contagious.

Let us remember that wherever we are, and whatever our circumstances, OUR GOD REIGNS!

> The Lord does not look at the things man looks at.Man looks at the outward appearance, but the Lord looks at the heart. I Samuel 16:7

What do you think was the reason for the joyful hearts of the orphans?

____

____

Sometimes, I get so absorbed in the plans "that I have for me", that I miss the plans "that God has for me." It's like I am determined to stay on my own path, with blinders on, instead of willfully allowing the Lord to lead.

I suppose there are many possible outcomes when we do not yield to the Lord's will. There are possibilities of getting way off course, and we might be left just "spinning our wheels" needlessly. Or maybe, we will get so wrapped up in our own self-will that we miss the opportunities that the Lord has put in front of us.

When we hold things loosely (such as plans) and soften our grip on our own agenda, the Lord has a much easier time directing our steps and guiding our way.

> Teach me to do your will, for you are my God; may your good Spirit lead me on level ground. Psalm 143:10

Can you recall a time when you had such a tight grip on something that you could not see the alternatives or hear God's voice?

____

____

____

____

____

____

June 27th

Your Almighty Father is with you in all of your circumstances. Turn to Him, lean on Him, trust in Him.

Learn to rely on the One Who created you, the One Who loves you, the One from Whom all blessings flow.

Even when we are confused and not sure which path to take, He is with us. What a difference His Presence makes! What a blessing to know that He is with us and will supply all that we need!

When all else fails… God does not. Always remember to bring all of your concerns to Him, with the confidence and faith knowing that the Lord's purposes and timing are perfect. Allow Him to be your ever-present Source of strength and comfort.

> Cast your cares on the Lord and he will sustain you;he will never let the righteous fall. Psalm 55:22

Do you have any hesitation about bringing your concerns to the Lord? Do you exhaust all other options before turning to Him?

____

____

____

____

____

____

In retrospect, I can see how the Lord has used trials and setbacks to mold me and shape me. He has used so many situations and life events as opportunities for spiritual growth.

Without His grace, I would continue to be wandering around in the desert. But because of His grace, the transformation continues.

Be intentional in putting off the "old self" and in desiring the "new self." I pray that you will be determined not to blend in with your surroundings, but that you will allow the Lord to make changes in your life. So many changes, that others will notice that something is different about you.

Open your spirit as the Lord of lords leads you, teaches you, and shapes you. Let the day to day encounters be a source of change.

> For it is God who works in you to will and to act according to his good purpose. Philippians 2:13

Can you think of a way that you have put off your "old self" and allowed God's transformation to take place?

____

____

____

____

____

____

History is filled with accounts of kings and kingdoms. If we take a look back, we can read about kings who ruled with an iron fist and kings who governed with fear and terror. There were also kings who removed themselves from the every day life of their people while allowing those in command to carry out their orders.

Our King, however, reigns with ***LOVE***. What a contrast! Even with all the power that our Creator possesses, He reigns with mercy and grace, and has compassion for everyone.

Our King does not dictate. He does not force or coerce. He opens His arms and invites us to taste the love that He has for each one of us.

Our King does not sit from afar, removed and distant. He is present with us. He is as involved in our lives as we want Him to be.

> The Lord is good to all; he has compassion on all he has made. All you have made will praise you, O Lord; your saints will extol you. They will tell of the glory of your kingdom and speak of your might, so that all men may know of your mighty acts and the glorious splendor of your kingdom. Psalm 145:9-12

Describe some other fine qualities of your King. If someone were to ask you about Him, what would you say?

___

___

___

June 30th

Yes, it is true that the Lord reigns! However, His Kingdom is not of this world; it is a Kingdom that is reserved for those who accept His invitation to "come follow me." It is an eternal Kingdom that will never fade away.

Just as we know that the Lord reigns over all the earth, He will also reign in our hearts, if we let Him.

Ask the Lord to dispel all of your doubts. Ask Him to teach you about His love. Ask Him to show you more about Himself.

When Christ lives in us, we draw from His strength. We learn to rely on Him and to trust Him, and to live in His Truth.

Be filled with the Holy Spirit. Allow the King of kings to reign in your heart!

> I keep asking that the God of our Lord Jesus Christ, the glorious Father, may give you the Spirit of wisdom and revelation, so that you may know him better. I pray also that the eyes of your heart may be enlightened in order that you may know the hope to which he has called you.
>
> Ephesians 1:17,18

What do you think might be a sign to others that the Holy Spirit is living in you?

____

____

____

July

Following the Father

To follow the Father is a calling from the Lord. He invites us to walk the path with Him, to learn as we go and to deepen our relationship with Him. It is His invitation, but we must be willing to accept it.

If the Lord points us in a certain direction, He will then also open the door that will allow us to pass through.

It might only start out as a small seed that the Lord plants in our heart. But as it grows, He will continue to reveal more and more to us as He confirms the path that He has prepared.

We need not fear when God puts something new and different in our hearts. He has a purpose and will provide all that we need along the way.

> And we know that in all things God works for the good of those who love him, who have been called according to his purpose. Romans 8:28

Are you fearful of new directions or are you energized by change?

July 2nd

Hand in hand
we go where He leads
Whether mountaintop or valley,
He's all that we need.

On our way up
or on our way down,
we'll find He is with us
and His mercies abound.

If I rise on the wings of the dawn, if I settle on the far side of the sea, even there your hand will guide me, your right hand will hold me fast. Psalm 139:9,10

Imagine Jesus standing on the top of a mountain. Would you rather be on your way up or on your way down?

"No matter what!"
Are we able to say this with confidence?
Let us not only say it, but believe it.

I will trust the Lord, no matter what.
I will seek Him, no matter what.
I will follow where He leads, no matter what.
We will weather the storms together, no matter what.

And… no matter what… He is faithful!

> Surely God is my salvation; I will trust and not be afraid. The Lord, the Lord, is my strength and my song; he has become my salvation. Isaiah 12:2

What does the faithfulness of God mean to you?

The July 4th holiday celebrates our country's independence from British rule. I wonder what the Founding Fathers would think if they could see what their "one nation under God" has become.

Would they be content and satisfied with the progression of things? Or, would they be appalled and saddened that our nation has turned so far away from the Lord?

We seem to have become an "anything goes" country. Old values have been replaced by new ideas that contradict Biblical teaching. So, what are we to do?

I would encourage that, as hard as it is at times, we need to stand up for what we know to be right without compromising our beliefs. The Lord does not call us to blend in, but to stand out!

> And proclaim liberty throughout the land to all its inhabitants. (inscription on the Liberty Bell in Philadelphia)
> Leviticus 25:10

What are some ways that you see our country turning away from the Lord? How easy, or hard, is it for you to stand up for the Truth?

____

____

____

____

____

Jesus and I ~
We cannot be defeated as long as we stick together. There is nothing too hard, no battle too great, with Jesus at my side.

He never gives in, and I will never give up.
I will go where He leads, regardless of the cost.

When people ask about the confidence that I have, my only reply is…

Jesus and I.

> Be strong and courageous. Do not be terrified; do not be discouraged, for the Lord your God will be with you wherever you go. Joshua 1:9

When Jesus says, "Come, take my hand", is your first instinct to reach out with relief, or is it to reach out with reluctance?

____

____

____

____

____

____

____

Toward the end of the book of Genesis we read about Joseph and his brothers. Joseph was highly favored by his father and did not let his brothers forget it. So, his brothers proceeded to try to get rid of him. First, by plotting to kill him, then by selling him into slavery.

In the years that followed, Joseph faced many challenges but never stopped relying on his God. The end result… deliverance.

We must remember that God's timing is perfect, and He wants so much to bless us. Even when the days are long and the nights are dark, God continues to work out our deliverance.

He hears our groans, our cries, and our petitions. As we wait, we trust. As we trust, we have confidence that God has a plan and He has not forgotten us.

In His timing… He will deliver.

> You are my hiding place; you will protect me from trouble
> and surround me with songs of deliverance.
>
> Psalm 32:7

Why do you think that God did not intervene immediately when Joseph's life was getting tough?

Out in the desert with the Lord.
Away, but not alone.

He bids us, "Come as you are."
There are no conditions.

He will provide the Bread of Life and the Living Water.
You will find rest for your weary soul. You will be refreshed as you spend time with the Master.

> Blessed are those who have learned to acclaim you, who walk in the light of your presence, O Lord.
>
> Psalm 89:15

Explain how the Bread of Life and the Living Water can refresh you from the inside-out?

The Lord is the true Source of Strength. As long as we stay connected to Him, we are plugged into the Power. Only in His strength can we climb the mountain, reach the top, and enjoy the view. And... He is there with us, loving us and encouraging us all the way up.

Be assured that you do not climb alone, nor do you stand on the mountaintop by yourself.

Then when the Lord is ready, He will send you back down into the valley to be an encouragement for those who have yet to climb.

> Come, let us go up to the mountain of the Lord, to the house of the God of Jacob. He will teach us his ways, so that we may walk in his paths. Micah 4:2

What lessons can be learned as you make the steep climb up the mountain? What do you think the Lord will say to you when you reach the top? Why is "the descent" just as important as "the climb"?

There are times when we come up against challenges and obstacles that get in our way. It might seem so overwhelming that our first response is to run in the other direction or find an alternate route.

It is not God's intention that we become discouraged and immobilized with fear. He wants us to meet the problem, head on, with a holy boldness and with the confidence that comes from knowing that He is right beside us.

After all, even as He is the Creator of All and holds the entire universe in His hands, He knows each one of us by name.

> But we are not of those who shrink back and are destroyed,
> but of those who believe and are saved.
>
> Hebrews 10:39

What would happen if you took a detour around every challenge that you faced?

____

____

____

____

____

____

____

How often do we find ourselves "sweating the small stuff", worrying about the little things that most of the time are beyond our control? We spend valuable time and energy getting frustrated and allowing the "inconveniences" to snowball into "boulders."

Wow! If we could only learn to "go with the flow" more often and not allow those minor irritations to steal our joy and our peace. If we stay focused on Christ, He will help us to shrug off the daily frustrations and give us a new perspective.

> Set your minds on things above, not on earthly things.
>
> Colossians 3:2

What can you do so that life's inconveniences do not ruin your day?

There are times in our lives when the Lord starts to lead us in a new direction. Usually, He will reveal His plan a little at a time because He knows how uncomfortable most of us are with change.

The new direction is often unexpected and, in our limited view, hard to comprehend. If God would lay it all out at once, we would probably have many questions about how He was going to get us there.

Don't get ahead of God trying to figure it all out. Have patience as His plan unfolds. Lean on Him. **Trust**.

> The Lord will guide you always; he will satisfy your needs in a sun-scorched land and will strengthen your frame. You will be like a well-watered garden, like a spring whose waters never fail. Isaiah 58:11

How do you know when a new direction is the route that God wants you to take?

____

____

____

____

____

____

____

As we look for clear and definite answers from the Lord, sometimes we find ourselves in a season of waiting. For some reason, the Lord in His infinite wisdom, has put on the brakes and we are left waiting, wondering: "Why? When? How?"

It is not for us to try to figure out God's ways but to trust in His ways.

Hang onto His faithfulness. Cling to His promises and never be without hope… even in His delays.

> May the God of hope fill you with all joy and peace as you trust in him, so that you may overflow with hope by the power of the Holy Spirit. Romans 15:13

When God "puts on the brakes", how do you respond?

In the Old Testament, in the book of Exodus, we read about the Israelites being led through the desert by God. A "cloud" was the symbol of His Presence. It was a visible sign that God was among His people and was providing Divine guidance.

As long as the cloud stayed above the tabernacle, the Israelites were to remain in camp. Even if the cloud did not move for days, months, or even a year, the Israelites were to stay where they were. Only when the cloud lifted would they start to travel once again.

I wonder what might have been going through their minds as they waited for God's timing? Were they content to wait, or did they question what God had in mind?

There is always a reason when the Lord keeps us waiting. Most of the time we will not understand the delay, but we must trust that even when God's voice is silent; even when "the cloud" has not moved, the Lord is at work accomplishing His purposes and preparing the way for us.

Better to remain under the cloud, than to rush ahead of God into uncharted waters.

> By day the Lord went ahead of them in a pillar of cloud to guide them on their way. Exodus 13:21

What are some of the consequences that might be an outcome of "running ahead of God"?

____

____

The "season of waiting" has never been my favorite season. I'd much rather be "doing." I'd rather be busy, than still. Sometimes when I say, "Ok, let's go," God says, "Not yet."

Burning the candle at both ends will quickly burn us out! We all need to be recharged from time to time. The season of waiting allows us, not only to exercise our trust in Him, but allows us to be still and hear God's voice.

He will surely tell us when it's time to move on.

> Let the morning bring me word of your unfailing love, for I have put my trust in you. Show me the way I should go, for to you I lift my soul. Psalm 143:8

What is the hardest part about being called to "wait" when God is just not moving fast enough for you?

When we follow in the Lord's footsteps, do we follow without hesitation, or are we apprehensive about what lies ahead? Are we able to walk with confidence, or do we start to ask ourselves, "What if…?"

When we begin to have "what if" moments, we are usually thinking uncomfortable thoughts about the future. Then worry starts to creep in and maybe we even start to question the plan that God has started to reveal to us.

"What ifs" are not very productive and many times it is the enemy's attempt to get us off track. If we trust God in the "present", we must also trust that He will take care of the future.

Give all of your hesitation to the Lord, and ask Him to give you the courage to move forward.

> "Who of you by worrying can add a single hour to his life? Therefore do not worry about tomorrow, for tomorrow will worry about itself. Each day has enough trouble of its own." Matthew 6:27,34

How can "what if" thoughts get a person off track?

____

____

____

____

____

When the enemy comes calling, it is probably because he is feeling threatened. The enemy seeks to destroy and discredit the things of God.

Since we belong to the Lord, we can expect to come up against some resistance. But, what the enemy intends for our downfall, the Lord uses for our benefit and for His glory. 2 Timothy 2:19, reminds us that "the Lord knows those who are his."

So, when the enemy tries to discourage you, remind him who your Daddy is!

> Let the heavens rejoice, let the earth be glad; let them say among the nations, "The Lord reigns!"
>
> I Chronicles 16:31

If you were to design a tee shirt that would remind the enemy of who you are, what would it say? What would it look like?

There are so many things in this world that try to get our attention and attempt to get us off track. Temptations are all around us. Some of them are very obvious, yet others are much more subtle. But, nevertheless, they are there, enticing us and pulling our focus away from the path that the Lord has laid out for us.

The solution for temptation is to stay closely connected to the Father. Use your spiritual weapons such as prayer, scripture, and worship. Put on the full Armor of God!

Ask Him to help you stay on track. Keep your eyes on Him, and He will steer you away from the pits and keep you from falling.

> But when you are tempted, he will also provide a way out
> so that you can stand up under it.
>
> I Corinthians 10:13

Can you think of other things that can help you stay on track and help you avoid giving in to temptation?

____

____

____

____

____

____

The Lord is the Way, the Truth, and the Life (Matthew 14:6). There are many in this world who claim to be wise, who claim to hold the truth in their hands, and who are also very convincing.

Don't be fooled by imposters and deceivers! There is no other Way, and no other Truth. Christ is the One and Only. His Way leads to Life!

When you are not sure of the path to take or are fearful of getting off course, keep your eyes fixed on Jesus and allow Him to lead.

Always seek the Truth. And, at times, when you do not understand, put your trust in the One Who will walk with you. The One Who died for you.

> For he guards the course of the just and protects the way of his faithful ones. Proverbs 2:8

How can you tell when someone is not speaking the Truth? What are some clues that help you to know that they are not the "real deal"?

____

____

____

____

____

____

____

There are so many roads that I have traveled throughout my life. Some roads were obviously ordained by God and some I found myself on because I had gotten off course.

In your life, you will be faced with many choices: a variety of roads all leading in different directions.

Whenever you find yourself at a crossroad, look to the Lord to light your way. There are many roads, but only one **true path**.

> Whether you turn to the right or to the left, your ears will hear a voice behind you, saying, "This is the way; walk in it."
> Isaiah 30:21

As children of God, we are called to take the "narrow path." What do you think this means? Why do you think the path is so narrow?

Whenever you look for the Lord or look to the Lord, He will always be there. When you seek His face, He is always ready and waiting to hear from you.

Sometimes I find it hard to believe that the Lord of All, the King of kings, finds so much pleasure in my relationship with Him. But… I know it's true! The Bible tells us that He delights in us.

You are His precious princess, and He wants nothing more than to spend time with you.

Keeping your eyes on Jesus will help you to stay on track. Focusing on the One Who knows the way will help you put off many distractions and temptations that attempt to get you off course.

> Great peace have they who love your law, and nothing can make them stumble. Psalm 119:165

What happened to Peter when he took his eyes off of Jesus? For more information read Matthew 14:22-30.

The Lord can accomplish so much more in us, and through us, when we put our complete trust in Him. Trust breaks through the obstacles of fear and worry, and allows us to walk courageously without second guessing the route that He has prepared for us.

Challenges are opportunities to live in His strength by moving forward with eager anticipation to see His power at work.

I believe that our roots grow deeper every time we trust in Him. The deeper our roots, the stronger our faith. The stronger our faith, the harder it is for "life" to shake our foundation.

> Those who trust in the Lord are like Mount Zion, which cannot be shaken but endures forever. Psalm 125:1

How can fear and worry interfere with your ability to trust your Heavenly Father?

___

___

___

___

___

___

___

There is no way that we can prepare ourselves for what lies ahead. Only the Lord knows what each day will bring, and only He can prepare us and strengthen us for whatever we will encounter.

So stay connected to the Power Source, the Source of your Strength. Abide in Him.

Christ is the Source of all that is good. Allow Him to walk with you and pour His goodness into you.

Learn to depend and rely on the Lord to show you the way. He will never let you down. He is the reason for your hope.

> When I am afraid I will trust in you. In God, whose word I praise, in God I trust; I will not be afraid.
>
> Psalm 56:3,4

What are some outward signs that someone might be disconnected from the Power Source?

____

____

____

____

____

____

In Mark 8:34, we hear Jesus speaking to a crowd which also included his disciples and saying, "If anyone would come after me, he must deny himself and take up his cross and follow me."

If we break down this verse, we can see three distinct parts.

Deny yourself. In other words, "Not my will, but Yours, O Lord."

Take up your cross. Your cross can be a powerful witness, depending on how you carry it. Are you carrying it with resentment, grumbling and complaining? Or, are you carrying it with dignity, humility, and perseverance?

Follow me. Let your focus be on Christ, not on your cross.

I have no doubt that if we are "willing", Christ will make us "able."

> But in your hearts set apart Christ as Lord. Always be prepared to give an answer to everyone who asks you to give the reason for the hope that you have.
>
> I Peter 3:15

What will happen if you focus too much on your cross, and not enough on Jesus?

____

____

____

____

July 24th

I am wondering how many of you are somewhat like me? There have been times when things had gotten tough and I cried out to the Lord but then only gave Him a little "piece" of the problem. And times when I had sincerely cried out to Him and soon became inpatient enough to take matters into my own hands.

Whenever there is a matter of great concern, I have learned that the best thing to do is to give it ALL to God without conditions and without interference, without holding anything back. Be totally dependent on Him for the outcome. Trust!

The Lord is not looking for us to be selective in what we bring to Him. He wants it all! He sees the big picture and knows exactly what we need.

God already has the route mapped out. He is just waiting for us to give Him the reins.

> Trust at all times, O People; pour out your hearts to him,
> for God is our refuge. Psalm 62:8

How would your life be different if you could learn to trust the Lord in **all** circumstances?

____

____

____

____

____

If we take steps that are not ordered by God, there are always consequences. In order for God to move us forward, He will first prepare the way and will also prepare our hearts.

If we are standing at a crossroad, there are several paths we can choose and a variety of possible choices we could make. We stop and we look, weighing our options, it is then that we need to seek the Lord for guidance, for only He knows what's down the road. In His perfect timing, the uncertainty in our hearts will change into peaceful confidence as His plan is just about ready.

It is then that we hear the Lord saying, "Move on" as He shows us the way. His way... the best way.

> Stand at the crossroads and look; ask for the ancient paths, ask where the good way is, and walk in it, and you will find rest for your souls. Jeremiah 6:16

What is the difference between the ordinary road that most people take and the extraordinary road that Christ maps out for you?

____

____

____

____

____

____

As hard as we sometimes try, it would be futile to search for security in this world. It seems as though there is always something that is ready to "rock our boat" and shake our foundation.

True and lasting security comes from Above. It is found in the One Who created us, the One Who died for us, the One with Whom we will spend eternity.

Ask Jesus, Precious Lord, to help you to walk the path of life with confidence, knowing full well that together you can overcome any challenges that lie ahead. Ask Him to help you to stay on the path with Him, close to Him, safe and secure, relying on Him for all things.

> But the Lord has become my fortress, and my God the rock in whom I take refuge. Psalm 94:22

Why can long lasting security only be found in Jesus Christ?

____

____

____

____

____

____

____

Do not dwell on the past or worry about tomorrow. But instead, let us keep our eyes on the Shepherd, wherever He leads. Let us follow in each footprint with a childlike faith, completely trusting in the One Who leads.

No need to look back. No desire to run ahead. Content to remain with Him, our constant Companion.

Jesus will brighten our days regardless of our circumstances. He never minimizes what we are going through, but He continues to walk with us, bearing our load and giving us hope.

How awesome that the footsteps we follow eventually lead right into heaven!

> Surely God is my help; the Lord is the one who sustains me. Psalm 54:4

Knowing that Jesus is always there to lovingly carry your load, how heavy does your load need to be before you ask Him for help?

____

____

____

____

____

____

____

The enemy will stop at nothing to make us think that God has abandoned us. Even in times of waiting for our prayers to be answered, the "great deceiver" puts doubts in our head. He wants us to think that God has not heard us, nor does He care about us.

Don't fall for his lies. Stay grounded in the Truth. As long as we keep our eyes fixed on Christ and stand firm in Him, Satan's efforts are in vain!

Do not be deceived!
Walk in victory, clothed with the Armor of God!
Remind yourself "Who" you belong to!

> But the Lord is faithful, and he will strengthen and protect you from the evil one. 2 Thessalonians 3:3

What are some things you can do that can help you stay grounded in the Truth?

____

____

____

____

____

____

____

When we trust in the Living God, are we secure enough to trust Him **in** all things, **with** all things, and trust Him **through** all things? Do we trust Him when we have more questions than answers? Do we trust Him even on the darkest of days?

If we trust, there is no need for fear. No need for restlessness.

There is no way that any of us can predict or adequately prepare ourselves for whatever comes our way. Only the Lord knows what each day will bring, and only He can prepare and strengthen us for whatever we will encounter.

We need not fear, for He is, and ever will be, with us.

When your thoughts start to get the best of you… hold them up to the *LIGHT.*

> Let him who walks in the dark, who has no light, trust in the name of the Lord and rely on his God.
>
> Isaiah 50:10

How can staying close to the Lord today, prepare you for tomorrow?

___

___

___

___

___

Have Your Way in us, O Lord. Not our will, but Your will be done. Help us, Lord, so that our "trusting" thoughts can overpower our "fearful" thoughts. Only with Your help can we walk in victory and freedom. Not as the world defines it, but victory and freedom that result from complete trust in You.

UNSHAKABLE TRUST!
Trust that will never fade or waiver.
Trust that allows us to walk by faith, not by sight.
Trust... without hesitation, no shrinking back.

Let the unfailing love of your Lord and Savior be your anchor and your refuge.

> So do not fear, for I am with you; do not be dismayed, for I am your God. I will strengthen you and help you; I will uphold you with my righteous right hand.
>
> Isaiah 41:10

What would it look like for you to walk in victory and freedom?

____

____

____

____

____

____

F ather

A nd

I

T ogether

H and in hand.

"Don't be afraid; just believe." Mark 5:36

What is the greatest blessing for you as you walk hand and hand with the Father?

August

Approaching the Throne of Grace

I don't know about you, but when I think of a king sitting on his throne, I picture someone who is far removed from those in his kingdom. Someone who gives orders from afar, with no clue about what his people want or what they need, nor does he care. Only with a wave of his royal scepter, or with permission, does anyone dare enter the king's presence.

Our King is such a contrast! Our King knows us by name! He knows all about our wants and our needs. We do not need permission to approach His throne. He is always waiting to hear from us.

There need not be any fear or apprehension in approaching the Throne of Grace. Approach His throne with reverence and with assurance. With the reverence deserving of our Lord and Savior and with the assurance that He calls us to come as we are.

What a King!
What a Savior!

> Let us then approach the throne of grace with confidence, so that we may receive mercy and find grace to help us in our time of need. Hebrews 4:16

Is there anything that prevents you from approaching the Throne of Grace with confidence?

August 2nd

Having 24/7 access to the Lord is a priceless gift that we all have been blessed with. We are told to pray in all circumstances. God wants to rejoice with us, comfort us, lead us, and strengthen us.

There is no right or wrong way to pray. There are no perfect words. In fact, I have a precious little nephew who prays with his mom before bed every night and lifts up the names of everyone in his immediate family, and he ends by praying for Cheyenne the dog, and for "Batman."

The simplest words lifted up to the Lord from a humble heart will certainly put a smile on His face.

> But God has surely listened and heard my voice in prayer.
> Psalm 66:19

Why do you think that even the prayer of a young child is so precious to the Lord?

When the challenges of the day seem overwhelming and you become so exhausted just thinking about all that needs to be done, turn to the Lord and ask Him for help.

LOOK UP! Pray for strength and guidance.

It might not be a "huge" prayer request, but the Lord is just waiting for an invitation into the details of your day.

He wants nothing more than to walk you through it.

Hand in hand, side by side, you will find that everything just falls into place.

Rely on the Lord. Allow Him to be your Constant Companion. No need to ever walk alone.

> Praise be the Lord, to God our Savior, who daily bears our burdens. Psalm 68:19

Do you think that there would ever be a prayer request that would not be worth God's time and attention? Explain.

____

____

____

____

____

When you pray, are you confident that God is listening? Do you pray with an expectant heart, assured that God will answer? Do you let God be God, or do you want "your way" in "your timing"?

God is always attentive to our prayers and to our needs. He stands ready, willing, and "more than" able to hear our requests and to answer our prayers.

Lift up your voice to the Lord. Tell Him what's on your mind. Let Him know what is possibly weighing you down. He will always be there to help you carry your burdens and to lead you to the Truth.

Pray with confidence, with assurance, and with expectation, but remember to leave room and allow for God to do things HIS WAY.

> This is the confidence we have in approaching God: that if we ask anything according to His will, he hears us.
>
> I John 5:14

Honestly, what are your concerns or fears in letting God answer your prayers His way?

____

____

____

____

____

____

When you are able to turn everything over to the Lord including your worries, your challenges, and your struggles, then your mind and your heart can freely focus on Him. Nothing will interfere or distract you from the sound of His voice.

Just you and your Creator. The Loving Father, the Voice of Truth, Who wants you to lean on Him and to trust Him.

When you are truly able to cast all your cares on Him, the weight of the burden is lifted. It is then out of your hands, and you do not have to continue to try to "figure it all out."

God will work it all out. Turn it **all** over to Him.
Let God ~ be God.

> Do not be afraid or discouraged… For the battle is not yours, but God's. 2 Chronicles 20:15

What are the benefits of giving your burden to the Lord?

____

____

____

____

____

____

August 6th

Whenever you pray, you can be confident that God has heard your prayer. You have His complete, undivided attention.

Dear daughters of the One True King, always expect that your prayer has been heard, that it will be answered, and that every heartfelt word has reached the ears of the Father Who loves you.

Allow Him to lighten your load and to brighten your day!

Let every "Amen" open your eyes in watchfulness, being confident that the Lord is at work on your behalf. He knows what's best, and He only wants the best for you.

> Those who know your name will trust in you, for you, Lord, have never forsaken those who seek you.
>
> Psalm 9:10

Are you content to leave your cares in His care?

When our resources dry up, or our current circumstances change, our first response might be one of worry or panic.

I tend to be a creature of habit, very content with the familiar. Change is something that is quite unsettling for many people. Suddenly, we are not as secure or self sufficient as we used to be. We just want things to be as they always were... comfortable and predictable. And as good as that might sound, the absence of change will do nothing to equip us for this ever-changing world.

From time to time, I need to remind myself that **God does not want me to be self sufficient!** He wants me to rely on Him and to find my security in Him.

The end of our resources is the beginning of God's grace.

> And God raised us up with Christ and seated us with him in the heavenly realms in Christ Jesus, in order that in the coming ages he might show the incomparable riches of his grace. Ephesians 2:6,7

Why do you think it is better for you to rely on God and not on yourself?

____

____

____

____

____

In Your Presence, Lord...

Renew my spirit. Refresh my mind. Restore my peace.

Help me to focus on the blessings and not on the troubles. Help me to be sensitive to the sound of Your Voice and willing to go where You lead.

Give me a new perspective that will allow me to leave yesterday behind and walk with You through this day with confidence.

I am so thankful that I do not have to walk alone. You are always there to guide me, to strengthen me, and to lift me up. Thank you for loving me as You do.

> To bestow on them a crown of beauty instead of ashes, the oil of gladness instead of mourning, and a garment of praise instead of despair. They will be called oaks of righteousness, a planting of the Lord for the display of his splendor. Isaiah 61:3

What can be found in the presence of the Lord that cannot be found anywhere else?

____

____

____

____

____

Often times, there are things in our lives and in our hearts that need to be uprooted. Sometimes we are not even aware of the weeds that are beginning to grow until our garden starts to deteriorate.

Some weeds might be obvious as they are out of control and consuming the garden. Some might have been hiding under the flowers and growing a little at a time, but we still know that they are there. While others might be a result of just trying to blend in with the rest of the world.

Ask God to help you to get rid of the weeds, and allow Him to plant new seeds that will make the garden even more beautiful.

> Since we have these promises, dear friends, let us purify ourselves from everything that contaminates body and spirit, perfecting holiness out of reverence for God.
>
> 2 Corinthians 7:1

Look real close. Can you identify any weeds in your garden that need to be uprooted?

____

____

____

____

____

____

God's grace was, is, and always will be sufficient for us. No matter what we face, we will never face it alone.

I can honestly say that there was never a moment when God's grace was not present in my life. But, I am sure there were times when I did not acknowledge His grace, times when I did not appreciate His grace, and times when I might have taken His grace for granted.

The Lord continues to walk with us, and He will provide all that we need, every step of the way. The more we need, the more that He provides.

In our greatest moment of weakness, God's grace is more than enough to get us through.

> "My grace is sufficient for you, for my power is made perfect in weakness." 2 Corinthians 12:9

Do you have any doubts or questions about God's grace?

Our strength, our faith, our courage. They are all tested at one time or another throughout our lives. It is in these times that we need to rely on the One Who has an infinite supply of all that we need.

Turn to Him.

Lean on Him.

Rest in Him.

Trust Him.

Let us throw away all of the "what ifs", all of our self reliance, and all of our doubts and focus instead on God's sustaining grace.

> The eternal God is your refuge, and underneath are the everlasting arms. Deuteronomy 33:27

How do you think "self reliance" gets in the way of God's grace?

There are times throughout "our walk" when each of us will need to be recharged. We might feel dried up, burned out, disconnected, or just plain exhausted. Life might be simply wearing us out!

We do not need to continue to walk aimlessly in this condition, searching for relief and rarely finding it. We serve a God Who calls us to come to Him, so He can give us rest.

This is when we need to take our weary selves, approach the Throne of Grace, and spend time in the Lord's presence.

When we thirst for Living Water and turn to the Lord, He will open the floodgates and give us our own personal revival.

> "Come, all you who are thirsty, come to the waters."
> Isaiah 55:1

What are some of the effects of being exhausted? How can spending time in God's presence help you to recharge?

____

____

____

____

____

____

How much time and energy is wasted when we are in need of answers, and we do not go directly to the Source!

Do we not want to bother God? Do we think that God only gets involved in the "big things"? Do we try to handle the situation on our own or turn to those around us?

Even seeking counsel and advice from Godly people, before bringing our needs to Christ, delays the deliverance that He is ready to give.

So many times we attempt to figure it all out on our own...
And God is still waiting for us to "look up."

The Lord wants to be involved in it **all**.

> Find rest, O my soul, in God alone; my hope comes from him. Psalm 62:5

Why is seeking God the best choice when you are trying to figure things out?

____

____

____

____

____

____

August 14th

What happens when you get discouraged or when you've had one disappointment after another? Understandably, you probably get down in the dumps. Your mood gets low and your steps become heavy. Then you might start to feel sorry for yourself (been there, done that).

I have learned from experience that the Lord is the Source of all comfort and healing. When I had neglected to seek him in times of discouragement and hurt, I started to sink lower and lower. But when I chose to give Him my hurts and pain, my outlook brightened and I was comforted.

We will never see a rainbow unless we look "up." When faced with discouragement, look "up" and seek the face of Christ.

> Praise be to the God and Father of our Lord Jesus Christ, the Father of compassion and the God of all comfort, who comforts us in all our troubles. 2 Corinthians 1:3,4

Are there any hurts, discouragements, or uncertainties in your life right now that you need to share with Jesus?

____

____

____

____

____

____

So often, I allow my day to day annoyances and inconveniences to tie me into knots. Frustration turns to irritation, and irritation leads to anger. Can you relate?

Let us pray for the Lord to give us perspective in all things, so that the little things do not snowball into bigger things.

With trust and confidence turn it ALL over to Him, placing all matters into His hands without holding anything back.

Let the Light of His perspective shine in all of your circumstances.

> The Lord is my strength and my shield, my heart trusts in him, and I am helped. My heart leaps for joy and I will give thanks to him in song. Psalm 28:7,8

Why do you think people are so easily frustrated? What are some things you can do so that daily frustrations and inconveniences do not ruin your day?

Quiet yourself before the Lord. Bring all of your cares to Him. When you give God the little concerns, worries, and irritations of your day, He will prevent them from accumulating.

Accumulating concerns and worries will only weigh you down. They will dull the beauty around you. They will dampen your spirit and allow negative thoughts to creep into your mind.

Seek the Lord. Ask Him to help you refocus. Allow Him to transform your heart and your mind.

May God always be your first thought and not your last resort.

> I lift up my eyes to the hills- where does my help come from? My help comes from the Lord, the Maker of heaven and earth. Psalm 121:1,2

What is the first sign that "life" is weighing you down?

The Lord has a divine plan for each one of us. It is never limited to what we can accomplish in our own strength. As a matter of fact, I believe that God's plan for us is purposely designed so that we **cannot** do it on our own.

In order to walk the path that the Lord lays out for us, we will need to rely on Him. We will need to stay connected to Him and allow our challenges to be met with His strength.

When the Holy Spirit puts a desire in your heart, He will also provide all that you need in order for you to move forward in faith.

The possibilities are endless when you trust that His grace is sufficient.

> Mightier than the thunder of the great waters, mightier than the breakers of the sea- the Lord on high is mighty.
>
> Psalm 93:4

How will the wisdom, the power, and the strength of the Almighty help you to accomplish the plans He has for you?

___

___

___

___

___

___

Do you know people who always seem to be grumbling and complaining? How do you feel, and what are your thoughts as they approach you? Do you want to run in another direction? Do you find it difficult to listen to their list of complaints?

How often do we come into the Holy Presence of the Lord grumbling and complaining? I wonder what He thinks when He sees us coming?

The Lord is not blind to what we are going through. He already knows our circumstances. However, I believe that praising Him with a thankful heart opens the door for us to be renewed and uplifted in His Presence.

Let us acknowledge all the ways that our Loving Heavenly Father has blessed us, rather than allowing ourselves to get caught up in an attitude of negativity.

> From the rising of the sun to the place where it sets, the name of the Lord is to be praised. Psalm 113:3

How can having a more positive attitude open the door to better communication?

____

____

____

____

____

Whenever we come into the Presence of the Lord, there are many distractions that we might bring with us. Sometimes our minds are already on "overload" because of the demands of the day. Sometimes our thoughts are dominated by fears and concerns.

Ask Jesus to help you settle your thoughts and quiet your mind. Ask Him to help you focus on Him alone. He is just waiting to breathe new life into you and to fill those empty places.

When you are resting in His arms, there is no need to try to figure everything out. There is no need to keep pace with the rest of the world.

Let Jesus hold you. Let Him surround you with His love. Only He can melt away your hurts and soothe your soul.

> Be at rest once more, O my soul, for the Lord has been good to you. Psalm 116:7

What are some of the things that have been consuming your mind recently?

____

____

____

____

____

____

August 20th

There is nothing hidden from the Lord. He sees our faults, our sins, our weaknesses and our fears. He sees it all, and yet He still loves us. What a relief to know that we can come into His Presence just as we are!

The "masks" that we might wear day after day that suggest to those around us that everything is fine are not necessary with God. He already knows how we are feeling and what we've been through. It's time to lay it all at His feet.

Allow Him to minister to you, to comfort you, and to shower you with His love. His Presence is a place of complete unconditional acceptance. It is a place where you can find peace and rest.

> You know when I sit and when I rise; you perceive my thoughts from afar. You discern my going out and my lying down; you are familiar with all my ways.
>
> Psalm 139:2,3

Why is it so comforting that you can "be yourself" when you are spending time with Christ?

____

____

____

____

____

____

When we spend time with Jesus we are reenergized and strengthened for whatever the day brings. We get a clearer picture of what needs to be done and the best way to spend our time and energy.

The Lord already knows what you will encounter as the day unfolds. He knows exactly what you will need and when you will need it. He will not only prepare the way, but He will be with you throughout the day.

As you go through your day, be aware of His continued Presence. Listen for His Voice. Trust Him with each step you take. With Him, you will surely have all that you need!

> The Lord is my strength and my shield; my hearttrusts in him, and I am helped. Psalm 28:7

How can spending time with the Lord prepare you for your day?

If an athlete does not practice, she will soon be out of shape and off her game. Likewise, when we do not exercise the practice of prayer, we become spiritually out of shape and out of touch, disconnected from the One Who loves us so much.

I realize that it is very easy for me to allow things to get in the way of my prayer time. Sometimes I put it off intending to "fit it in" later and it never happens. Then, one day will turn into two, and two turns into three, and before I know it, I am out of touch with my Master.

It is obvious to me when my prayer time starts to suffer, and it might be just as obvious to those around me.

I do not want to just squeeze Jesus into my schedule. I want Him to have the first fruits of my day. I want to start the day in His Presence and in prayer.

Don't allow your spiritual muscles to get out of shape. Begin your day with the Lord.

> Blessed are they who keep his statutes and seek him with all their heart. Psalm 119:2

What are some of the effects and signs of being spiritually out of shape?

When you approach the Throne of Grace, what is it that you expect? Do you expect that your prayers have been heard? Do you expect God to give you clarity? Do you expect immediate answers and solutions?

I would imagine that each of us have different expectations depending on our circumstances.

It is by faith that we know that our prayers have been received. However, the answer to our prayers might not be as quickly evident. If we trust in the Lord's plan, we must also trust in His timing.

Sometimes God's silence is just a "divine delay" as He works on our behalf. In waiting and believing God for an answer, we are given opportunities to grow in faith. God usually makes it worth the wait.

> I wait for the Lord, my soul waits, and in his word I put my hope. Psalm 130:5

What is the first thing that comes to your mind when your prayer encounters a "divine delay"?

____

____

____

____

____

____

August 24th

The scriptures tell us that all we have to do is "ask." Jesus tells us specifically that if we ask anything in His name He will do it.

The Lord knows our hearts, and He knows the motive behind every request. He knows if we are sincere, and He knows if our intentions are self serving. He not only knows what is beneficial to us, but He knows what is best for us.

I believe that the prayers of a humble heart put a smile on the face of our Lord. He is a generous and gracious Lord, Who wants to give us so much.

Don't be afraid to ask. God is waiting to do exceedingly more than you could ever imagine!

> Until now you have not asked for anything in my name.
> Ask and you will receive, and your joy will be complete.
> John 16:24

Is there something that you have been hesitant to bring before the Lord in prayer?

____

____

____

____

____

____

Anything that is disturbing your peace is worthy of prayer. God does not want us to live in a constant state of fear and chaos.

In Ephesians 4, Paul tells us to "not be anxious" and he goes on in the verses that follow and gives us more information.

Why we do not need to be anxious…
v.5 The Lord is near.
How we can feel more at ease…
v.6 You are to give it **all** to God.
Outcome?
v.7 You will have peace.

If something concerns you… it concerns Him! Let Him replace your anxiety with His Peace.

> Do not be anxious about anything, but in everything, by prayer and petition, with thanksgiving, present your requests to God. And the peace of God, which transcends all understanding, will guard your hearts and your minds in Christ Jesus. Philippians 4:6,7

What happens when you do not give it **all** to God?

August 26th

Childlike faith means trusting God to work out the things that are most troubling to us. Those things that are unfair. Those hurtful things that we do not deserve. And the things that catch us off guard that we never would have expected.

Jesus knows just "where it hurts."

Childlike faith lets us rest in His loving arms, knowing that He understands why we are hurting. In His arms we are held close, we are comforted, and we are lifted up.

Jesus will heal the hurts.

What a blessing to be comforted and understood by the King of kings and the Lord of lords!

> The Lord is close to the brokenhearted and saves those who are crushed in spirit. Psalm 34:18

Can you recall a hurtful situation in which you needed someone to listen and understand all that you were going through?

___

___

___

___

___

As I look back to a time when I was **so much** younger, there were so many situations and circumstances that were affecting my life. Without the grace of God and a prayerful mother, I am sure things would have turned out much differently for me.

It was hardly ever smooth sailing, but it is obvious that the Lord was watching over me. It seems that He had a plan for me that would be fulfilled regardless of my circumstances.

Only the Lord can release us from the shackles that bind us. Only He can transform a wounded soul and set it free!

Let nothing hold you back from seeking Him and walking in freedom.

> He brought them out of darkness and the deepest gloom and broke away their chains. Let them give thanks to the Lord for his unfailing love. Psalm 107:14,15

Are there any "shackles" in your life that seem to be holding you back?

____

____

____

____

____

____

What is your attitude toward prayer? What is it that you expect as you pray? What is it that you expect after you say, "Amen"?

Do you approach the Throne of Grace with confidence, or is there an attitude of "wishful thinking"?

A faithful prayer throws wishful thinking right out the window. A faithful prayer comes from a trusting and humble heart. It comes from a heart that confidently approaches the Lord and then walks away assured.

Let us always pray with prayers of faith, remembering that the One Who sits on the throne is ready and waiting to act on our behalf.

> In him and through faith in him we may approach God with freedom and confidence. Ephesians 3:12

What is the difference between wishful thinking and a prayer offered up with confidence?

Are there really any prayers that are left unanswered? Even a firm, "No" is an answer. But, "No" is often easier to accept than when we are in a process of waiting and our hour of need is great. No one likes to be put on hold.

God's silence does not mean that He has not heard our prayer. At the proper time, His perfect time, we will see His plan unfold.

I believe that all prayers are answered. Sometimes our timing is off. Sometimes God has something else in mind and sometimes whatever we pray for might not be in our best interest or part of His plan.

Cling to His promises in times of uncertainty and confusion. Stay rooted and grounded in Him. Allow the Lord to pour His Living Water into you as you continue to wait and as you grow in the knowledge of Him.

> But I trust in your unfailing love; my heart rejoices in your salvation. I will sing to the Lord, for he has been good to me. Psalm 13:5,6

If the Lord told you that something you prayed for was not in your best interest, would you still want it?

____

____

____

____

____

When we go into the Presence of the Lord let us have open hearts ready to receive all that He has to give. An open heart lays aside our own agendas. An open heart is willing to trust in His plan.

I have found out through experience that it is so much better to accept God's will and timing, than it is to be so stuck to our own desires that nothing else matters.

Hold your plans loosely allowing room for God to change your course. Listen closely for His voice above all else. Whether you are sailing on rough seas or smooth seas, you have a Savior Who will direct your life just as He directs the wind.

When there is a need for change, the wind will blow and fill your sails. When you are called to be still, the wind will cease, and you will hear His voice.

"**YIELD**" to His will. Allow Him to be in the driver's seat.

> God's voice thunders in marvelous ways; he does great things beyond our understanding. Job 37:5

What might happen when you hold on too tight to your own desires without allowing the Lord to guide you?

Why is it that so many times when we think we have given all of our concerns to the Lord, we continue to worry and allow those concerns to consume us? I'm sure there are many different answers to that question.

I think that most of us just like to be in control. When we are in control, there is a sense of security. Truthfully, a false sense of security.

If we are praying to the One Who created the universe, the One Who put each star in its place, then why can't we trust that He can take care of our situation?

When you give your cares to the One Who cares, leave them there. This is the one time that you won't be disappointed when you leave empty handed.

> Lift your eyes and look to the heavens: Who created all these? He who brings out the starry host one by one, and calls them each by name. Because of his great power and mighty strength, not one of them is missing.
>
> Isaiah 40:26

How is keeping things within your control a false sense of security?

____

____

____

____

____

September

Treasures Awaiting

September 1st

When you think of "treasure", what comes to mind? You might imagine gold, jewels, wealth, or fortune: things that would make you rich.

God's treasures are quite different. He does not intend for us to value the things of this world. He wants us to be rich in other ways. Rich in the kingdom of heaven. Rich in the ways of Christ. Rich in the knowledge of Him. A richness that would never have been found if we had followed the wide, broad path.

The "broad road" is traveled by many. Even as this road is probably the most popular route, it is the road that really leads to no where. The "narrow road", however, is the road that is traveled by those who choose to follow Christ. This is the road where treasures will be found.

I encourage you to walk the narrow path, even if it is not the path that your friends are choosing. The narrow path is paved with truth, with love, and with hope. Treasures that cannot be found anywhere else.

> My purpose is that they may be encouraged in heart and united in love, so that they may have the full riches of complete understanding, in order that they may know the mystery of God, namely, Christ, in whom are hidden all the treasures of wisdom and knowledge.
>
> Colossians 2:2,3

In what ways might the "narrow road" be challenging?

____

____

____

September 2nd

We seldom appreciate the things that are handed to us on a "silver platter." It is those things that come with a cost; those things that come through hard work, determination, and perseverance that we will treasure the most.

Should we pray for smooth seas… or for the Lord to be with us in the storm?

Should we seek to travel the easy road… or the road that leads to Christ?

So, when you see a storm up ahead, stay the course. Do not veer off the path because of what you see in the distance, for the Lord will see you through every circumstance.

Those who persist will be blessed.
Be strong. Be courageous. Allow Jesus to lead the way.

> But let all who take refuge in you be glad; let them ever sing for joy. Spread your protection over them, that those who love your name may rejoice in you. Psalm 5:11

What are some reasons why you might have a greater appreciation for something that you worked very hard for rather than something that was easily handed to you and required little to no effort on your part?

The Lord knows what our day will bring before we even set our feet on the floor.

I am quite sure that many times I have gotten in the way of what the Lord had prepared for me for that day. Whether I was wasting time, or I was not sensitive to His direction, or I might have put my agenda above His plan for that day.

We all can become our own obstacle to the blessings that God has in store for us.

Stay tuned in to His voice as He keeps you moving in the right direction. Keep your eyes focused on Him, so you do not miss out on the things that He has planned for you today.

> Many, O Lord my God, are the wonders you have done.
> The things you planned for us no one can recount to you;
> were I to speak and tell of them, they would be too many
> to declare. Psalm 40:5

What kinds of things might you miss out on if you are not tuned in to the voice of the Lord?

____

____

____

____

____

September 4th

I once had a dream. The main scene in the dream...
I was riding in a convertible on a highway with the top down. It was a warm sunny day, and my hair was blowing in the wind. God was driving!

You're probably wondering, "What did He look like?" Well, I was in the back seat and only saw the back of His head.

As simple as this dream sounds, it came at a time in my life when I needed to get out of the driver's seat and let God take the wheel.

Obviously, the dream had a profound impact on me, as it happened several years ago and I still remember it.

Sometimes, it is so hard to give God the wheel. Are you willing to take a back seat and leave the driving to Him?

> "For I know the plans I have for you," declares the Lord, "plans to prosper you and not to harm you, plans to give you hope and a future." Jeremiah 29:11

What concerns do you have about allowing God to take the wheel?

___

___

___

___

___

September 5th

When we give the Lord "the wheel" and allow Him to lead, it takes a lot of pressure off of ourselves. We don't need to worry about where we are headed; we just need to trust in the One Who is driving.

Just think… when Christ is at the wheel, we have no fear of getting lost, running out of gas, or getting off course.

So, let us take our hands off the wheel and be content to enjoy the ride with Christ in the driver's seat.

If we trust in Him, He will take us to places that we never could have imagined.

> "No eye has seen,
> no ear has heard,
> no mind has conceived
> what God has prepared for those who love him."
>
> I Corinthians 2: 9

Why do you think that it is better to give the keys to Christ and let Him do the driving?

____

____

____

____

____

September 6th

I can only imagine what Abraham must have been thinking when at the age of 99, the Lord told him that he would be the father of all nations. When Sarah, his wife, heard that she would be conceiving a child in her old age, she laughed.

God's reply… "Is anything too hard for the Lord?"

God is not limited to what is humanly possible. He is the God of the Universe. He created all that we see. He is not confined to what we can explain or understand.

Let us not have any doubts that God can do more than we could ever imagine. Let us hope for the impossible and believe in His ability to exceed all expectations!

> Now to him who is able to do immeasurably more than all we ask or imagine, according to his power that is at work within us, to him be glory in the church and in Christ Jesus throughout all generations, for ever and ever!
>
> Ephesians 3:20

Why do you think that "the world" always tries to find an explanation for the things of God that cannot be explained?

____

____

____

____

September 7th

The hills and mountains that we climb throughout our lifetime have been specifically placed in our path by God. Each one has a unique purpose.

So many times the road gets rough, and we become overwhelmed. It is so tempting to look for an easier way. But... we are not to give up or turn back!

Keep climbing! There are treasures waiting to be collected along the way. Treasures that cannot be found anywhere else but along the rocky cliffs. And remember, you are not climbing alone.

> As you know, we consider blessed those who have persevered. You have heard of Job's perseverance and have seen what the Lord finally brought about. The Lord is full of compassion and mercy. James 5:11

What are some of the character traits that can be developed as a result of climbing the mountains that God puts in your path?

____

____

____

____

____

____

____

September 8th

One day, while I was walking along a rugged path in the French Alps, I noticed a most beautiful flower, the color of periwinkle, growing out of the side of the mountain. The first thing I thought was, "How could something so beautiful grow out of such a hard place?"

Now, as I think about that flower, I realize that only such a hard place could have produced something so beautiful!

When we are willing to persevere and when we allow the Lord to see us through those hard places, we too, will become like the flower, ever so beautiful.

> I have fought the good fight, I have finished the race, I have kept the faith. 2 Timothy 4:7

What were some of the harsh conditions that the periwinkle flower had to endure? How can you relate this to your own life?

Even when we don't know… Why?… How?… What?… or When?…, the Lord is preparing us step by step for the things that are down the road, the things that lie ahead.

Usually these "things" are not revealed to us right away or all at once, but little by little in His timing.

Our trust in Jesus will lead us to experience more than we could ever expect.

Follow Him, even when you do not understand. Ask Him to help you to stay on the path that He has laid out for you. Even if He only reveals one step at a time, trust that you are moving in the right direction.

> I guide you in the way of wisdom and lead you along straight paths. When you walk, your steps will not be hampered; when you run, you will not stumble.
>
> Proverbs 4:11,12

Why do you think God only reveals His plan for you one step at a time?

September 10th

So often, in our prayers, we ask God to help us. We bring to Him our petitions, our concerns, and our desires. The hardest thing for us to do after we pray is **wait**. When God is not working at our speed, there is a great temptation to take matters into our own hands.

Perhaps one of the reasons that our answers are delayed is because we have a tendency to get in God's way. We are not patient enough or trusting enough to "let God, be God."

When God is silent, it is not because He does not see and it is not because He does not care. All of His ways are perfect and that includes His PERFECT TIMING.

Even in the silence, God is working out "your stuff." Silence does not indicate that He is inactive. It is only an indication that He is not finished yet. The Lord will never intervene prematurely, but He will step in just at the right time.

> In the morning, O Lord, you hear my voice; in the morning
> I lay my requests before you and wait in expectation.
>
> Psalm 5:3

What is the hardest part, for you, regarding God's perfect timing?

____

____

____

____

September 11th

Faith is:
...**believing** without evidence.
...**trusting** without the need for signs and wonders.
...**standing firm** when all that you "feel" says otherwise.

Faith believes that God "can do" the impossible.
Faith trusts that God "will do" the impossible.
Faith is willing to walk where He leads, in order to experience the One Who makes the ...

impossible... possible.

With faith, any one of us could walk on water!

> Now faith is being sure of what we hope for and certain of what we do not see. Hebrews 11:1

What are some important things to remember when your faith begins to weaken and your trust level is low?

____

____

____

____

____

____

____

September 12th

Dive deep into the Word of God. You will find that it provides all that you need and is relevant for any situation. The Word is filled with Truth and is rich in instruction.

Scripture provides words of comfort, guidance, and hope. It teaches us about God's design and plan for His creation and traces out the steps of Jesus.

There is so much that is contained within the pages. It seems as if each time I read a familiar section, God reveals something new to me that had not occurred to me before.

Soak up the Word. Store it in your heart. Walk in Truth!

> For the word of the Lord is right and true; he is faithful in all he does. Psalm 33:4

Do you think that it is important to read through the whole Bible, both new and old testaments, or is it enough just to focus on selective readings? What can you find in God's Word that cannot be found anywhere else?

____

____

____

____

____

____

"Life" is often compared to the running of a race. A starting point, a finish line, and all that is in between. However, it is not a race requiring speed, but endurance.

Immerse yourself in the Living Water. Be strengthened for the journey. Feed on the Word of God. Search, learn, grow.

Allow the Lord to stretch you beyond your comfort zone as He takes you to places you never would have imagined.

Only by faith are you able to leave the security of the shallow water and venture out into greater depths. There are treasures waiting to be found.

> However, I consider my life worth nothing to me, if only I may finish the race and complete the task the Lord Jesus has given me. Acts 20:24

What do you think God would say about your comfort zones?

September 14th

The Lord has designed a very unique path of life for each one of us. May we always be aware of, and sensitive to, His leading, ready and willing, as He shows us the next step.

As He lights the way, take His hand fearlessly. He will prepare the way and set you on paths that you never would have expected or dreamed.

The Lord demonstrates His power best by using ordinary people like us. We are not famous; we are not powerful. But… we are children of the Most High God!

Our human impossibilities are the Lord's opportunities. When we believe and trust in the power of God, the possibilities are endless.

> Great is the Lord and most worthy of praise; his greatness no one can fathom. Psalm 145:3

Would you rather be rich and famous or a child of the Most High God?

September 15th

The only limitation we have in knowing more of God and deepening our relationship with Him is- ourselves. Ouch! Did that sound harsh? It was not meant to be.

Truthfully, we are all probably in the same "boat" when it comes to accessing all that the Lord has for us and wants for us. Are we too busy? Are we fearful? Do our priorities get in the way of the One Who should be at the top of our list? Ouch! There I go again.

Yes, and about that "boat"… you and I will never be able to walk on water unless we get out of the boat.

Jesus is ready and waiting to show you all of the possibilities that are available to you as you take His hand, spend time with Him, and walk with Him. How blessed you are to have the opportunity to walk and talk with the King of kings!

> Delight yourself in the Lord and he will give you the desires of your heart. Psalm 37:4

What is it that keeps most people "**in** the boat"?

____

____

____

____

____

September 16th

We never need to look very far to find evidence of the Almighty, the Creator. He reveals Himself through the beauty of creation, His still small voice, His light on our path, or the simple nudging of our heart.

Everywhere we look, as far as the eye can see, His beauty is all around. Whether we are on top of the mountain looking down or down in the valley looking up, we are embraced by all that the Lord has created.

My favorite place is the beach, but not when it is so hot that my feet are melting in the sand and not when it is so crowded that the noise drowns out the music of the waves. But, when it is just Jesus and I enjoying His creation together.

> The heavens declare the glory of God; the skies proclaim the work of his hands. Psalm 19:1

What beauty have you seen recently that displays the wonder of God's creation?

____

____

____

____

____

____

____

Seasons come and seasons go. Each one is unique, never the same, yet each one is filled with blessings.

The varied seasons of life provide us with opportunities to learn more about God, to experience more of His grace, and to always depend on His faithfulness.

So often, when we are not content with our circumstances, it is natural for us to want "this season" to come to an end quickly. Let us not wish it away, but allow God to use it to reveal more of Himself to us.

And… just when we can't wait for winter to end and spring to bloom, He surrounds us with goodness and love and fills us with peace and joy. His peace is like a tiny taste of heaven. There is nothing sweeter, nothing more reassuring.

> Don't be impatient for the Lord to act! Keep traveling steadily along his pathway and in due season he will honor you with every blessing. Psalm 37:34 (TLB)

Has there ever been a particular "season" in your life that has been a challenge to endure?

____

____

____

____

____

September 18th

Oh, how hard it is for us, at times, to just "let God, be God." To completely leave our matters in His care. He knows our situation and the circumstances surrounding it better than we do. Sometimes, the best thing we can do is *NOTHING.*

The road up ahead might be paved with blessings, but if we are impatient and decide to take a different path, we will undoubtedly miss all of the treasure that awaits us.

So because we serve a "hands on" God, we can trust that He will take care of any and every situation if we let Him. His silence does not mean His absence.

Let the fingerprints of God be evident in all situations as you trust in the One from Whom all blessings flow.

> Hallelujah! For our Lord God Almighty reigns. Let us rejoice and be glad and give him glory!
>
> Revelation 19:6,7

What do you think is meant by "the fingerprints of God", and what does this have to do with *trust*?

____

____

____

____

____

September 19th

A steadfast faith proclaims victory in the midst of battle. Even, and especially, with the odds stacked against us, we know that we serve a God Who delights in the impossible.

He will defend us and bless us at just the right time. Many around us will be watching and having their doubts that the Lord will intervene on our behalf. Then in the blink of an eye, our Father will not only intervene, but He will do the impossible.

An unshakable faith stands firm even when there is no evidence on which to stand. Trust in the Unseen until the Lord brings everything into plain sight.

> So we fix our eyes not on what is seen, but on what is unseen. For what is seen is temporary, but what is unseen is eternal. 2 Corinthians 4:18

What do you think is meant by, "what is seen is temporary"?

____

____

____

____

____

____

____

September 20th

Each of us is given unique gifts and talents. I am wondering if you question that fact. Do you ask yourself, "What talents do I have?"

I can truthfully say that when I was "much" younger, I asked myself that same question. As I look back, I can see that my gifts and talents were not always obvious at a young age, but as I matured, the Lord was showing me what my gifts ***were*** and what my gifts ***were not.***

Several years ago I went on a variety of mission trips. God was quick to reveal to me that "this was not my calling"! However, I continued to sign up for more trips and travel to other countries. I guess I was either slow to catch on or a glutton for punishment.

God works in each of us in different ways. He wants us to do good works and equips us to do just that. He blesses us abundantly in so many ways and gives us opportunities to be a blessing to others.

> Let your light shine before men, that they may see your good deeds and praise your Father in heaven.
>
> Matthew 5:16

What gifts/talents has God given you that might be used to do good works?

September 21st

We have had so much rain this summer. Much more than usual. But, the grass has never been greener! The yard has never been more lush and colorful!

It is plain to see that even clouds serve a purpose. The rains are like blessings pouring down upon the plants and flowers.

And so it is with the "clouds" that we experience from time to time. They tend to block out the sun and could make things seem very dark. The clouds might stay a short while or seem to linger far longer than we would like.

But remember, the Lord uses every cloud for a specific purpose, even if we do not understand. And behind every cloud is a brilliant blue sky!

The true blessing is the beauty that blooms… after the storm.

> See! The winter is past; the rains are over and gone. Flowers appear on the earth; the season of singing has come.
>
> Song of Songs 2:11,12

How might you be different if you never had encountered any "clouds" in your life?

___

___

___

___

___

September 22nd

Sometimes God puts something on our heart that seems like such an impossibility that we quickly dismiss it. By all human standards it would be impossible.

If the Lord is putting something in our lap, the Holy Spirit will continue to stir within us. He is trying to get our attention.

I confess that many times when opportunities have come my way, my first thought is that I am not qualified. My next thoughts usually contain all the reasons (*excuses*) that I cannot take on this responsibility.

Let us not forfeit blessings because we did not respond when called. All God wants is for us to step out in faith and obedience and leave the rest to Him.

> By faith Abraham, when called to go to a place he would later receive as his inheritance, obeyed and went, even though he did not know where he was going.
>
> Hebrews 11:8

What might some of the consequences be (for us and for others) when we dismiss the nudging of the Holy Spirit?

____

____

____

____

____

September 23rd

Diamonds are precious, valuable jewels that can only be formed by high temperatures and high pressure deep within the earth. However, in their natural state, diamonds are not the beautiful gems that you will find at the jewelry counter. There is no glitter, shimmer, or brilliance to them yet. They must go through a process of preparation, cutting, and polishing in order to display their beauty.

So, you see, the diamond did not become beautiful overnight, nor did it acquire its shine and brilliance on its own. It needed a bit of help to become such a treasure!

Just as the sculptor prepares his work of art, God continues to chip away at our jagged edges and sand away our rough spots. This is a process that takes time, instruction, and sometimes, exposure to the elements (aka: the ups and downs of life).

The end result is a brilliant masterpiece that could only have been created, shaped, and polished by the Master.

> He has made everything beautiful in its time.
>
> Ecclesiastes 3:11

Why do you think that a "sculpting process" is necessary for everyone?

____

____

____

____

September 24th

In 2 Corinthians 6:10, Paul writes about being poor, yet being rich. Having nothing, yet possessing everything. I believe he is referring to external circumstances compared to internal riches. It seems as if he was using contrasting opposites to point out what is really important.

So in contrast, the poorest people in the world might be the richest people in the eyes of God. Those who possess nothing, might just have more than meets the eye.

Regardless of what is in our bank account or our measure of success as defined by the "world", if we are rich in Christ, then we are rich. As long as Christ is with us, we have all that we need.

Having nothing and yet possessing everything!
CHRIST IS SURELY ENOUGH!!!

> Listen, my dear brothers: Has not God chosen those who are poor in the eyes of the world to be rich in faith and to inherit the kingdom he promised those who love him?
> James 2:5

What is your own personal definition of "rich"? How does your description line up with God's economy?

____

____

____

____

September 25th

I wholeheartedly believe that the spiritual riches that we possess as followers of Christ are treasures that need to be shared. I do not think that the Lord teaches us, blesses us, and reveals Himself to us just for our own benefit, but He wants us to be inspired to share ***what*** we know and ***Who*** we know with others.

There is a dying world in need of a Savior. Every day we come across people who are dying inside and who have little or no direction in their lives. There is no joy. They seem to be just going through the motions of life.

There is no way for us to know if those who cross our path are searching for something better or searching for something/someone to believe in. Might they be looking for that significant relationship that will change their lives forever?

We do not have to quote scripture all day long at school or in our workplace to get the attention of others. Through our actions, we can be an example of one who has an inheritance, one who belongs to the family of Jesus. Let your riches be evident for all to see.

> I pray that you may be active in sharing your faith, so that you will have a full understanding of every good thing we have in Christ. Philemon 1:6

What are some obvious signs that we live in a dying world?

____

____

____

Our Lord, Our King, Our Father in Heaven, wants us to continue to grow in the knowledge of Him. He does not want us to become stagnant and ineffective. He wants us to add to the foundation that we have and to strengthen our relationship with Him as we continue to grow spiritually.

The more we dive into His Word, the more time we spend with the King of Our Hearts, the more growth will take place. We will begin to change on "the inside."

When you change on the inside, your behavior and actions change on the outside. If those around you start to notice that you are different, don't interpret that as a "put down" or a sign of weakness, but use the comments to motivate further change.

When we measure ourselves by the opinions of others, we will always fall short. When we hold ourselves to a Higher Standard... the Lord has a smile on His face.

> For this very reason, make every effort to add to your faith goodness; and to goodness, knowledge; and to knowledge, self control; and to self control, perseverance; and to perseverance, godliness; and to godliness, brotherly kindness; and to brotherly kindness, love. 2 Peter 1:5-7

Why is it unhealthy to automatically accept the opinion of others as Truth?

____

____

____

The story of the Good Samaritan can be found in the tenth chapter of Luke. As documented in these verses, there was a man lying in the road, left for dead, after he was beaten and robbed. Two men, who were known as religious leaders in the community, saw the man in distress and just kept on walking.

A third man who came upon the injured man was a foreigner from Samaria, a region that was highly despised by the Jewish people. The Samaritan took pity on the man and did all that he could to care for the badly beaten man.

Jesus tells us to, "love your neighbor as yourself." To me that means even to the point of self sacrifice, as was the case with the Samaritan man.

Believe it or not, treasures can be found in helping others. Opportunities that the Lord puts in your path are never a coincidence.

> "I tell you the truth, whatever you did for one of the least of these brothers of mine, you did for me."
>
> Matthew 25:40

What should be your main motivation in helping others?

____

____

____

____

____

September 28th

The busier I am, the more I crave the Peace that only Jesus can provide. Only He can renew and refresh my spirit. Only He can lead me beside still waters and restore my soul.

So many times there is nothing I need more, nothing that I treasure more, than the Peace that passes all understanding. The challenge that I have is in holding on to that Peace.

Christ does not want to see us tied up in knots or all stirred up inside. A daily dose of peace is always available. It will provide day to day renewal and strength for whatever lies ahead. And… to find this treasure, you do not need a shovel or a map, you just have to take the time to sit in His Presence.

> He will stand and shepherd his flock… and they will live securely, for then his greatness will reach to the ends of the earth. And he will be their peace. Micah 5:4,5

How might a daily dose of peace help you throughout your day?

____

____

____

____

____

____

____

How awesome is our God! He loves us all through life, from beginning to end. He walks the rugged road with us and promises never to leave us.

Each and every day the Lord continues to teach and to transform us by showing us the things in life that are truly important, the things that are priceless and of great value in the Kingdom of God.

I find great comfort and hope in the promise that Christ will never leave us nor forsake us, and also in the truth that nothing can separate us from His love. He **was** with us in the past, He **is** with us now, and He **will be** with us through all of our tomorrows.

Jesus is the Way, the Truth, and the Life. There is no other Way, and no other Truth. Stay on the narrow road and don't be afraid to go where He leads. His love will guide you as there are treasures waiting to be found.

> For I am convinced that neither death nor life, neither angels nor demons, neither the present nor the future, nor any powers, neither height nor depth, nor anything else in all creation, will be able to separate us from the love of God that is in Christ Jesus our Lord. Romans 8:38,39

List some things in your life that you think are "priceless."

____

____

____

____

September 30th

F̲ear not!

A̲lways expect the unexpected.

I̲n all things give thanks.

T̲rust in the Lord.

H̲e is faithful.

> I will sing of the Lord's great love forever; with my mouth I will make your faithfulness known through all generations.
> Psalm 89:1

What do you treasure most about your relationship with the Lord?

____

____

____

____

____

____

____

____

October

Keys to the Kingdom

October 1st

I believe that there are specific "keys" that help each one of us to unlock the mystery of the Kingdom of God. These keys that I will identify throughout the month of October are certainly not a complete list, and as we go through the month, you will probably think of some others that are just as important to you which I have not included.

I invite you to make your own list and look up scripture verses that help to clarify each additional "key" to the Kingdom.

As you search… you learn, as you learn… you grow, as you grow… you strengthen your relationship with Christ and allow Him to reign in you.

> Yours, O Lord, is the greatness and the power, and the glory and the majesty and the splendor, for everything in heaven and earth is yours. Yours, O Lord, is the kingdom; you are exalted as head over all. I Chronicles 29:11

What is the purpose of a key? How does this relate to the kingdom of God?

____

____

____

____

____

____

____

October 2nd

Abide

The word "**abide**" means to remain, to dwell, to reside. There are many things that interfere with our ability to abide in Christ. Our thoughts become clouded and our vision is impaired; it becomes hard to maintain our focus especially when times get tough.

Through the tears… abide.
Through the heartache… abide.
Through the temptation… abide.
Through the pain… abide.
Through the disappointments… abide.
Through the loss… abide.
Through the storms… abide.

He will: comfort
soothe
strengthen
restore
encourage
deliver.

Abide *in* all things.
Abide *through* all things.

> "As the Father has loved me, so have I loved you. Now remain in my love." John 15:9

Why is it important to abide in Christ?

Growth

God uses our external circumstances to improve and strengthen our internal condition and help us to **grow** in Him. He wants to cleanse us from the inside-out. He is more concerned about "cleaning us up" on the inside, than keeping us happy and comfortable on the outside.

There are many paths that lead to spiritual growth such as spending time in the Word, attending small groups or Bible studies, fellowshipping with other believers, and allowing God to use you to help others.

Another more painful path that leads to growth is the path of trials and suffering. Ouch! Yes, we would gladly leave this one off of the list, but it is true that when we find ourselves in trying situations, we are certainly stretched.

The fruit of the Spirit does not arrive at our door in pretty gift wrapped packages. It is developed over time, as we allow the Holy Spirit to work "in us."

> But the fruit of the Spirit is love, joy, peace, patience, kindness, goodness, faithfulness, gentleness, and self control. Galatians 5:22

Has the Lord ever encouraged you to step outside of your comfort zone? How can this also lead to growth?

____

____

____

October 4th

Contentment

The world leads us to believe that our ultimate goal should be *happiness.* Yes, and maybe that's how some people would define "the American dream."

As believers, we are not necessarily called to be happy, but instead we are taught about *blessings* that can be found through sacrifice, obedience, suffering, service, and perseverance. It is through these experiences that we learn what it means to be **content.**

Happiness is fleeting and lasts only until someone "ruins your day." Blessings are from the Lord, and no one can take them away from you!

> For I have learned to be content whatever the circumstances. I know what it is to be in need, and I know what it is to have plenty. I have learned the secret of being content in any and every situation. Philippians 4:11,12

What is the difference between happiness and contentment? What things do you need in order to be content?

____

____

____

____

____

____

October 5th

Perseverance

When we find ourselves in the wilderness, our first response is usually, "Get me out of here!" The quicker, the better!

If we are asked, "Do we want God to prevent our trails and challenges? Do we want to be rescued from our suffering?" How easy would it be to answer both questions with a resounding "YES!"

As hard as it is when we are going through trying times to see the greater picture, these times of pain are also times of teaching and preparation. God will not waste one ounce of suffering without a greater purpose. We must **persevere.**

The pruning of the Gardener yields a harvest of fruit.

> Blessed is the man who perseveres under trial, because when he has stood the test, he will receive the crown of life that God has promised to those who love him. James 1:12

What is the definition of perseverance? What would any tough situation look like if you did not have any perseverance at all? Why is this **not** an option for you?

___

___

___

___

October 6th

Truth

It is so hard for us, at times, to put our feelings aside and go with "what we know" rather than "what we feel." Let us not allow our feelings to cast a shadow over what we know to be the **Truth.**

The enemy is so good at deceiving us into thinking that what we feel and what we know are one and the same. Not true!

Feelings are unpredictable, ever-changing, and unreliable. What we can count on is the everlasting Truth and the rock solid promises of God.

Trust in the Lord, even when you don't understand your circumstances. Even when there seems to be more questions than answers. Trust completely, without a doubt. He's got everything under control.

> In you they trusted and were not disappointed.
>
> Psalm 22:5

When is the last time you let your feelings get the best of you? Why is it better to stand on the **truth** rather than to trust your feelings instead?

____

____

____

____

____

October 7th

The Word of God

In Matthew 6:25-34, Jesus tells us NOT TO WORRY. Throughout the Old and New Testaments, we are told to "be anxious for nothing, and do not fear." The Bible is full of verses that tell us to "fear not."

God knew that we would be prone to worry and anxiety. He gives us encouragement and reassurance in His Word.

The **Word of God** is rich with instruction, with Truth, and with guidance. It contains all that we need to stay on track, even in this modern, fast paced world.

So saturate yourself in His Word, and you will find all that you need.

> Your word is a lamp to my feet and a light for my path.
> Psalm 119:105

How does the Word of God keep you connected to your Father, the King? Why is this so important?

____

____

____

____

____

____

October 8th

Stay "rooted" and grounded

Satan uses his deception to try to pull us in the wrong direction, and he makes bad choices seem very attractive. With his lies and schemes, he interrupts and corrupts our thoughts when we least expect it, often times, sending our minds into a tailspin. He would like nothing more than to start causing cracks in our foundation.

Every time we are able to resist the temptation and the distraction of the enemy, we become more **rooted** in Christ and He is glorified.

Be thankful for His arm of protection. The evil one knows that you belong to the Lord, and I am certain that just one glance from the Father in the enemy's direction is more than enough to send him packing!

> Because the one who is in you is greater than the one who is in the world. I John 4:4

Why are roots important to a tree? What purpose do they serve? How does this relate to being rooted in Christ?

____

____

____

____

____

____

October 9th

Surrender

One of the hardest things for many of us to do is to **surrender** our will and allow God to have His way. We tend to have such a tight grip on our own agenda that we do not leave room for God to redirect us as He tries to show us a better way.

If we continue to stay chained to our own plan, we will surely miss the many blessings that the Lord has in store for us.

Let us hold things loosely, allowing the Lord to direct our steps. Letting go of our own will frees us up to take His hand and go where He leads.

> "I am the Lord your God, who teaches you what is best for you, who directs you in the way you should go."
>
> Isaiah 48:17

When it comes to "your will" versus "God's will", who usually wins? How easy (or not) is it for you to trade your path, for God's path?

____

____

____

____

____

____

October 10th

Faith

Wouldn't it be nice if we were born with a measure of unwavering faith that could withstand even the greatest test? But the truth is faith is not "given"; faith is "developed."

The path that leads to unshakable faith has many lessons along the way. Without these opportunities to grow, we would never learn to trust the One Who loves us unconditionally.

Faith allows us to believe the impossible. Faith gives us Someone to hold on to when the road starts to get bumpy. Faith makes it possible to have hope, even in the fiery furnace.

> "O Nebuchadnezzar, we do not need to defend ourselves before you in this matter. If we are thrown into the blazing furnace, the God we serve is able to save us from it, and he will rescue us from your hand, O king." Daniel 3:16,17

What kind of circumstances have you experienced that have really shaken your faith? Why do you think having faith is such a "big deal"?

____

____

____

____

____

October 11th

Strength and Courage

Be **strong** and **courageous** in the Lord. The battles are never fought alone.
Persevere.
Press on.
Claim for yourself the promises of God and believe them with all of your heart.

I will never leave you, nor forsake you.
(Deuteronomy 31:6)
Whoever follows me will never walk in darkness.
(John 8:12)
Call to me and I will answer you.
(Jeremiah 33:3)
Do not fear for I am with you.
(Isaiah 41:10)

> But you are a shield around me, O Lord; you bestow glory on me and lift up my head. Psalm 3:3

What do the promises of God have to do with your ability to be strong and courageous?

____

____

____

____

____

October 12th

<u>*Hope*</u>

Our **hope** in Christ gives us strength. The strength that comes from Him gives us hope.

Hope diverts our attention away from the bumps in the road and allows us to set our sights on Him.

Without the Lord, we would have no hope. Our hope comes from the knowledge that our lives are in His hands. We have hope because He is always with us. We have hope in His promise of eternity.

Ask the Lord to help you, to live each day rooted and secure in His Promises and in His faithfulness. To replace worry with praise. To help you to replace fear with confidence. Confidence that can, and will, be realized because of the promises that you hold on to, for He alone is your Hope.

> And hope does not disappoint us, because God has poured out his love into our hearts by the Holy Spirit, whom he has given us. Romans 5:5

Why is hope such an important key to the kingdom? Do you know anyone who needs a bit of hope right now? What can you do that would encourage this person?

____

____

____

____

October 13th

Assurance

Blessed **assurance**! Knowing that Christ always has hold of our hand. He will love us and never leave us. He has a special plan for each one of us, and He will be there with us, every step of the way.

Faith like a little child allows us to take hold of the Father's hand without question or hesitation, eager and excited to see what He has in store for us.

We belong to Him! No need to keep up with the rest of the world.

Take hold of the hand of Jesus and allow Him to lead. There are blessings waiting for you. You will never be disappointed! He will surely show you the things in life that have true value.

> I will instruct you and teach you in the way you should go;
> I will counsel you and watch over you. Psalm 32:8

Do you have any concerns when it comes to taking Jesus by the hand and going where He leads? Are you confident that He will always be with you every step of the way?

October 14th

Prayer

How often when we pray, do we only scratch the surface of what God wants to do for us and in us? There is so much to be accessed through prayer. We pray to a loving Father Who wants to give us more than we could ever expect or imagine.

Prayer keeps us connected to our King. Prayer gives us an opportunity to sit at His feet and get renewed and refreshed while we receive instruction from the One Who knows us best.

The closer we are to Him, the better we will be able to face this unpredictable world.

If we are "prayed up" each day, the enemy will certainly be at a disadvantage!

> Yet the Lord longs to be gracious to you; he rises to show you compassion. Isaiah 30:18

Do you think that the Lord looks forward to hearing from you each day? How does staying connected with Him give you strength?

___

___

___

___

___

October 15th

Glorify Him

"The tomb." This was expected to be Christ's final resting place. We can only imagine what His followers were thinking as they laid Him in the tomb.

"This is it."

"It's over."

"Our Master is gone."

"What hope do we have now?"

Then just a few days after they laid Him there, the stone was rolled away and the tomb was empty! Jesus overcame the grave, and there was victory over darkness! Christ proved to all the skeptics that He truly is the King of kings!

Is this just a really nice new testament story, or do you really believe it? And if you really believe it, what do you do with it?

Well, I surely would encourage you to share it. Share the good news of Jesus. Share it by telling others. Share it by living for Christ. **Glorify** Him so that others will want what you already have.

> My soul will boast in the Lord; let the afflicted hear and rejoice. Glorify the Lord with me; let us exalt his name together. Psalm 34:2,3

What are some ways that you can share Jesus with others?

___

___

___

October 16th

Trust

The lessons of faith are learned in the valleys, in the low points of our lives, our desert moments. As our faith grows, we learn to **trust**.

As we experience the Lord's faithfulness, trust comes a bit easier. As we see, (much of the time in hindsight), how the Lord has intervened, how He has rescued us from trouble, and how He has always provided for us, we can rest assured that He is a Loving God, Who can always be trusted. We will know, without a doubt, that the Lord has never let us down.

When we trust completely, not in ourselves, but in the Lord, we will not only be able to climb mountains, we will be able to move them.

> Trust in the Lord with all your heart and lean not on your own understanding; in all your ways acknowledge him, and he will make your paths straight. Proverbs 3:5,6

How can your trust in the Lord give you the confidence and the strength you need to get through tough times?

____

____

____

____

____

____

October 17th

Patience

Patience is the evidence of trust and faith. **Patience** keeps us from taking matters into our own hands and interfering with God's plan. It allows God time to accomplish His purposes... His way.

Patience expresses, "I trust that the answer will come, and I am content to wait."

Many times when you are at a "standstill", friends will give you well-intended advice. They will try to help you fix the problem or encourage you to move on. I believe that this is the hardest time to be patient.

Sometimes "inaction" appears to be "no action", but when you exercise patience, and remain in prayer about what you are facing, you are a bold witness for Christ.

Don't run ahead of God, but wait on Him and watch as His plan unfolds, and remember that His timing is PERFECT.

> The Lord will fulfill his purpose for me; your love, O Lord, endures forever. Psalm 138:8

Can you think of a time when you were not very patient? How did that turn out for you?

____

____

____

October 18th

Rest

When we worry and continue to allow ourselves to be all stirred up, we are expending a great deal of energy that could be put to better use.

Just think about how much time and energy you put into worrying about situations that are completely out of your control anyway. How often do you tie yourself up in knots before you seek the comfort and peace of Jesus?

It is unrealistic for us to expect to be completely worry-free, but we can choose to not let worry consume us. Instead of worrying, exercise those "trust muscles" and **rest** securely in the palm of His hand.

> Because I know whom I have believed, and am convinced that he is able to guard what I have entrusted to him for that day. 2 Timothy 1:12

What are some signs that you are getting all stirred up inside? What can you do so that the worry and negative thoughts do not take control?

____

____

____

____

____

____

October 19th

Obedience

How often does God put something on our heart or in our mind, and instead of taking action, we just add "it" to our "to do" list? Or maybe, we waste time trying to figure out all of the details ahead of time, instead of being obedient in the moment.

There are many ways that we can choose to be **obedient** or not. When the Lord gives us a gentle nudge, or when we hear His voice encouraging us to step out of our comfort zone, are we inclined to take action, or do we find ourselves making many excuses which either delays His assignment or hinders His desired outcome?

If we wait until we are better prepared or wait for a more convenient time, the opportunity probably will have already come and gone.

Obedience, without questioning and without strings, is a sure sign of spiritual growth. Many times God invites us to work with Him. All He asks us to do is to show up and leave the rest to Him.

> He guides the humble in what is right and teaches them his way. Psalm 25:9

Why is it important to take advantage of the opportunities that God puts in your path?

___

___

___

October 20th

Obedience

Yes, I know that I wrote about obedience yesterday. However, this "key" is just too important to confine to just one day.

Yesterday's reading related to the children of the King being ready for action and being **obedient** when called upon. Today, I would like to reflect on the day to day obedience that it takes in order to walk the "narrow" road, the road that leads to holiness.

We live in a world that is so destructive and sinful. A world that, most of the time, contradicts what we know to be true. A world where wrong seems right and right seems wrong. We are bombarded every day with evil that tries to derail us. It is a day to day battle to live a life that is congruent with our Christian values.

When the temptations to "conform" start to get into your head, ask the Lord for help. Put your focus back on Him, and He will provide you with the strength that you need.

> We demolish arguments and every pretension that sets itself up against the knowledge of God, and we take captive every thought to make it obedient to Christ.
>
> 2 Corinthians 10:5

In what areas do you struggle the most with being obedient?

____

____

____

October 21st

Guard your words

I wonder if you've ever stopped to think about the impact that **words** have on you and on those around you. Words can be used to build up or to tear down. I am sure that we have all experienced a situation when the words of someone were used as a weapon against us. The flip side of that is when we use our words to intentionally hurt someone else.

Words are powerful! Once they are said, they are out. There is no rewind button. We all have a choice about how we will use our words.

Because we claim to be a child of God, other people are always watching and LISTENING. They are noticing what kinds of words we are using. What kind of example are we setting for others?

I truly believe that you can tell the condition of a person's heart by the words that they use, words that are used in public, as well as, words that are used behind closed doors.

Be an encourager! Use your words to love, to heal, and to glorify God.

> Therefore encourage one another and build each other up.
> I Thessalonians 5:11

What are some ways that you can use your words in a positive way today?

____

____

____

Rejoice

I admit, sometimes my circumstances get the best of me, and I find it hard to rejoice. Can you relate?

Why is it that, so often, we gravitate toward negativity? Why is it easier for us to focus on what's going wrong in our lives, than it is to be positive and thankful for all that the Lord has done for us?

Joy is not the same as happiness. Joy comes from within. It does not depend on our current circumstances. The ability to rejoice, and the intentional action of rejoicing, is something that we (I) need to do more often.

I believe that we are blessed every day and always have something to rejoice about. I have realized that the more I have to complain about, the more I need to **rejoice.**

Rejoicing shifts the focus from "all that is wrong" to "all the ways the Lord has blessed us." Rejoicing is music to His ears!

> You turned my wailing into dancing; you removed my sackcloth and clothed me with joy, that my heart may sing to you and not be silent. My Lord my God, I will give you thanks forever. Psalm 30:11,12

List at least 3 reasons that you have to rejoice today.

____

____

____

October 23rd

Receive

Our Father is the God of the Universe! All that we have and all that we see is His. He is Creator, Protector, and Provider, and He wants so much to bless us.

Over the years, there have been many times when my stubborn spirit has gotten in the way of allowing the Lord to bless me. Times, when I have been holding onto something so tightly that my knuckles have turned white from the pressure of my grip.

Had I just released my grip, I would have been able to open up my hand and **receive** all that the Lord was trying to give me.

Christ is so generous and loving, and He has so much in store for us. With open hands and an open heart, let us gratefully be ready to receive all that He desires to give us.

> "And see if I will not throw open the floodgates of heaven and pour out so much blessing that you will not have room enough for it." Malachi: 3:10

What are some things that might be getting in the way and preventing you from receiving all that Christ has for you?

____

____

____

____

October 24th

Identify your idols

There are things in life that all of us worship whether we want to admit it or not. Such things could be: activities, friends, money, clothing, jewelry, the gym, celebrities, social media, or even "ourselves."

An **idol** can be defined as something that receives excessive devotion. In other words, things that take up an enormous amount of time, things that we are obsessive about, things that we think we can't live without, and things that interfere with spending time with God.

"Worship" should be reserved for The Lord Jesus Christ alone. He is the Only One that deserves this high place of honor in our lives.

The first thing that we need to do is to identify those things that have become idols in our lives. We might also ask God to help us with this, as sometimes we are not even aware of things that have gotten out of control. Then continue to ask Him to help you rid yourself of anything that "needs to go" and to help you get your focus back on Him.

> "This is what the Lord says- Israel's King and Redeemer, the Lord Almighty: I am the first and I am the last; apart from me there is no God." Isaiah 44:6

Is there anything in your life that you would classify as an idol?

____

____

____

October 25th

Cultivate a generous heart

I do not believe that God blesses us, so we can accumulate all that He gives us in great storehouses here on earth. Locked away. Stockpiled for a rainy day. No, I believe that our blessings are to be shared with others.

Blessings come in many forms. Some people might be blessed financially, while others have been blessed with unique gifts and talents. We all have something to give.

A **generous heart** will lead by example. It freely gives without expecting anything in return. A generous heart does not discriminate but is willing to help all who are in need.

The Bible tells us that God loves a cheerful giver. So as the Lord is generous to us, let us also be generous to others.

Sometimes I wonder if the Lord blesses us and then waits and watches to see what we're going to do with it.

> Command them to do good, to be rich in good deeds, and to be generous and willing to share. In this way they will lay up treasure for themselves as a firm foundation for the coming age. I Timothy 6:18,19

When you give to someone, is it freely given or is there an expectation of getting something in return?

____

____

October 26th

Be the clay

I believe that the Lord desires us to be pliable so that He can continue to shape and mold us into His likeness. However, I know there have been times when I have not been the moldable **clay** in His hands.

There are many things that interfere with our ability to be cooperative with His transformation. One of those things is our pride. You know… when we think we know what's best. When we have such a tight grip on our own ways that we do not see that the Lord has something much better in mind.

I encourage you to allow your Heavenly Father, the Potter, to smooth out your rough edges as He molds and reshapes you into His masterpiece.

> Yet, O Lord, you are our Father. We are the clay, you are the potter; we are all the work of your hand.
>
> Isaiah 64:8

How might your attitudes and actions get in the way while the Lord is in the process of your transformation?

____

____

____

____

____

____

October 27th

Humility

I believe that developing a **humble** heart starts with our relationship with Christ. It begins with an attitude of reverence as we bow down to Him and acknowledge Him as Lord. Lord of "us", and Lord of all.

Humility is the opposite of pride. It recognizes that we are all sinners and that God loves us all equally. We have all been created by God, and He has a purpose for each and every one of us.

Humility is an inward quality that is evidenced in our outward behavior toward others. It is inclusive, not exclusive. It sends a message to others that they are important and accepted.

A child of God with a humble heart does not pretend to be better than she really is or better than those around her. She is willing to put others first, and at times, to even take a "backseat" so that others can shine.

> All of you, clothe yourselves with humility toward one another, because, "God opposes the proud but gives grace to the humble." I Peter 5:5

Have you ever experienced being "left out"? How did that feel? What can you do to be more inclusive to those around you?

____

____

____

____

October 28th

Walk in freedom

The Bible tells us that we all have sinned and fallen short of the glory of God. We all have made mistakes, and each of us has done things that we have come to regret. We all have a past, and as each one of us looks back, we can probably recognize ways that we have fallen short, in addition to ways that the sinful behavior of others might also have impacted us.

I truly believe that even though the situations of our past cannot be changed, we do not need to "live in the past" and continue to allow it to affect our present and our future. I am not trying to minimize the struggles that some of you have faced, but I do know from experience that if you carry the weight of the past around with you, it does slow you down and prevents you from **walking in freedom**.

The Lord wants you to be *FREE!* He can redeem situations and restore lives. I encourage you to allow "the Love of your life" to lead you to freedom and help you to live for today.

> I have seen his ways, but I will heal him; I will guide him and restore comfort to him. Isaiah 57:18

Is there anything from your past that is currently preventing you from walking in freedom?

____

____

____

____

October 29th

Forgiveness

I believe that one of the greatest gifts we can ever give to someone is **forgiveness**. In addition to that, I also believe that to be true about forgiving ourselves.

We have all at some time been offended, insulted, and hurt. And… we probably at some time have offended, insulted, and hurt others. As we walk through life, we have choices to make regarding forgiveness.

Offering forgiveness does not mean that you were not offended. It does not minimize what was done to you or the hurt that you felt.

But, when we live with a spirit of unforgiveness it then becomes another burden that we carry around. It is like a wound that will never heal, and it keeps "us" in bondage to the hurt and the pain of the past.

Forgiveness is a choice that you make with your heart. It does not necessarily mean that you have to come face to face with the one who hurt you.

With forgiveness, comes freedom. Jesus wants you to forgive and leave the rest to Him.

> Let the peace of Christ rule in your hearts.
>
> Colossians 3:15

What does forgiveness do for the one who forgives?

____

____

October 30th

A repentant heart

Sometimes as children of God, we might have a tendency to compare ourselves with the depraved sinfulness that we see all around us. And... when we do that, we probably look pretty good!

Let us never forget that we, too, are sinners. Sin is not relative to one's situation. Sin is sin, and we all need to be washed clean.

When we come to the Lord with **a repentant heart**, we willingly confess our thoughts and our actions that were not pleasing to our Lord and Savior. When we get honest with God it is not to fill Him in about our misdeeds... He is already well aware of the condition of our hearts. What we are seeking is forgiveness and cleansing from the Lord.

A repentant heart "does more for us" as we examine our hearts and consider our ways. When we think that we are getting honest with God, we are really just getting honest with ourselves.

> You are forgiving and good, O Lord, abounding in love to all who call to you. Psalm 86:5

What impact does a repentant heart have on your relationship with Jesus?

____

____

____

____

October 31st

Love

Jesus calls us to **love** others. He even tells us to love our enemies.

What? Love people who don't care about us? Love those who are hurtful toward us?

Yes, and guess what? He not only tells us to love them but also to pray for them!

Wow, it is so much easier to love those who love us back! It is so much easier to love the "loveable."

So, I challenge you to start "loving." Love when you don't feel like it. Love when they don't deserve it. Love without exception. Surely this is something that we ALL need to work on.

LOVE IS CONTAGIOUS! Let it start with us!

> And now these three remain: faith, hope and love. But the greatest of these is love. I Corinthians 13:13

Have you ever met someone who was really hard to love? What do you think Christ would tell you about loving that person?

____

____

____

____

November

Worship the King

November 1st

The Lord, the Almighty, Our Heavenly Father, He alone is God. There is no other. He showers His blessings on us daily. He reaches down and blesses us in ways that we cannot comprehend or explain. His giving goes above and beyond our expectations. His love is beyond measure. There are no words to describe it.

Let us walk with an "attitude of gratitude." Let us be thankful for all of the blessings that we see around us. Let us also realize that the Lord is blessing us every day in ways that we cannot see. Ways that we are not yet aware of that would make us shake our heads in awe of Him.

With a thankful heart, receive all that He freely gives.

> Sing and make music in your heart to the Lord, always giving thanks to God the Father for everything, in the name of our Lord Jesus Christ. Ephesians 5:19,20

What does it mean to have an "attitude of gratitude"?

____

____

____

____

____

____

____

November 2nd

Who is like our God? He is the Creator of all, the Giver of life, and the Source of all goodness. Let us sing with the angels in praise and thanksgiving to our Lord!

Praise Him with all of your heart. There is always cause to rejoice! Regardless of your circumstances, there is always cause to rejoice!

Rejoice and be thankful because you know that the Lord is always with you.
Rejoice and be thankful because you belong to Him.
Rejoice and be thankful that you are deeply loved.
Rejoice and be thankful because there will come a day when you will see Him face to face!

...And He will take your breath away!

> Let them praise the name of the Lord, for his name alone
> is exalted; his splendor is above the earth and the heavens.
>
> Psalm 148:13

In what kind of circumstances do you find it most difficult to rejoice and be thankful?

November 3rd

The Jewish people of Moses' time frequently witnessed provision and deliverance by the hand of God, yet they so quickly turned their backs on Him when things did not go their way. Their faith was conditional. Conditional upon fair weather and smooth sailing.

We are so blessed! Why do we allow ourselves to focus our thoughts on the darkness rather than the Light? Every day can be a beautiful day regardless of our situation.

Let us not be like the Israelites who were so quick to grumble and complain. Let us not have circumstantial trust that wavers from day to day. Instead, let us ask the Lord to help us to see through the clouds and give us a "kingdom" perspective. He would be glorified more often if *thankfulness* prevailed over grumbling and complaining.

> I will praise God's name in song and glorify him with thanksgiving. Psalm 69:30

What can you tell yourself when grumbling and complaining start to creep into your thoughts?

____

____

____

____

____

____

November 4th

Only Christ can satisfy our deepest needs. Instead of being attracted to the things of this world, let us stay focused on Him and be thankful and content with everything that He so graciously provides.

Praise God with thanksgiving for what **He has done.**
Praise Him continually for what **He is doing.**
Praise Him with confidence, for what **He has yet to do.**

You can rest secure knowing that your times are in His hands. Be thankful that your life is not random. He is in the details of your life as well as the bigger picture. He will provide strength for today and hope for tomorrow.

He has a purpose and a unique plan just for you.

> Praise the Lord. Sing to the Lord a new song, his praise in the assembly of the saints. Let Israel rejoice in their Maker; let the people of Zion be glad in their King.
>
> Psalm 149:1,2

Where do you think "life" would take you if you allowed the attractions and temptations of the world to draw your attention away from Christ?

____

____

____

____

____

November 5th

Thank You, Lord, for being a "hands on" God and not One who stands from afar expecting me to fend for myself. Thank You for the guidance of the Holy Spirit. It is only because of You that I can even begin to navigate through this broken world.

Thank You for the gentle nudging of my heart. You bring me back when I start to stray. You know, Lord, just how to get my attention. Thank You for the love that binds us together and for Your Spirit that keeps me in check.

Lord Jesus, let me never become complacent by taking Your goodness for granted, but let me praise You for Who You are with a humble and a thankful heart.

You are the Ultimate Giver and Provider. My Faithful Father.

> It is good to praise the Lord and make music to your name, O Most High, to proclaim your love in the morning and your faithfulness at night. Psalm 92:1,2

Can you think of an example of a time when you started to stray from the Truth and the Lord got your attention?

____

____

____

____

____

November 6th

In Mark, Chapter 4, we find the disciples facing a fierce storm on the Sea of Galilee. As Jesus was sleeping on a cushion in the rear of the boat, the waves got larger and the storm got more intense. The disciples were terrified and woke Jesus from His sleep.

Jesus got up and He rebuked the wind and said to the waves, "Quiet! Be still!" All of a sudden the waves died down and the sea was calm.

I'm sure at this point in their walk with Jesus, the disciples did not yet really know Who they were traveling with. They did not realize that their Companion was more powerful than the storm.

Regardless of how we "feel", the Lord is never absent and, thankfully, He never takes a day off. We are never forgotten or neglected.

He may be silent, but He is always with us. Even in the silence, we continue to be surrounded with His love.

> Praise the Lord, all you nations; extol him, all you peoples. For great is his love toward us, and the faithfulness of the Lord endures forever. Psalm 117:1,2

How is it possible to continue to have an attitude of thankfulness even in the midst of a storm?

____

____

____

____

November 7th

Lord, help me to cling tightly to You! I am thankful that You are never out of reach. Truthfully, I know that I am not up to the challenges that life brings.

Without You, Lord, I would probably fall flat on my face or fall into a pit of fearfulness. Without You, I would be drowning in my own sin, overcome with guilt and with no hope at all.

Thank You, Lord, for Your guidance, for Your forgiveness, and for Your unconditional love. Thank You that I do not have to rely on my own strength. Thank You for being my Constant Companion and for graciously providing all that I need.

I want to learn to praise You even on the toughest of days, for my blessings far outweigh my ever-changing circumstances.

> And my God will meet all of your needs according to his glorious riches in Christ Jesus. Philippians 4:19

If you made a list of things that you are thankful for, what would be at the top of that list?

____

____

____

____

____

November 8th

The Lord's abundance has no limit.

Abundant love.

Abundant grace.

Abundant blessings.

Day after day, we are the recipients of His abundance.

Let our hearts and minds overflow with Hallelujahs, and our thoughts be filled with thankfulness and praise. Considering all the ways that we have been blessed, we should be exhausted from singing and dancing.

> The grace of our Lord was poured out on me abundantly,
> along with the faith and love that are in Christ Jesus.
>
> I Timothy 1:14

How would you finish this sentence?
"If my heart and mind were filled with thanksgiving and praise, there would not be any room left for …"

____

____

____

____

____

November 9th

Why do you think that we are more prone to moan and groan than we are to having an attitude of thankfulness? Why do we seem to never be content?

I think that our natural thought processes tend to focus on what we are lacking instead of what we are blessed with. Think about the last time someone greeted you with, "Hey, how are you?" You probably gave the usual, "I'm fine." Then immediately your thoughts turned to all of the things that were ***not fine***.

The attitude of discontent is contrary to the attitude of gratitude. I believe that discontent stems from negative thought patterns that can be turned around as we focus more intentionally on positive thoughts and thankfulness.

We need to "retrain the brain" in order to have a more positive outlook as we seek to glorify God for all of the ways that He has blessed us.

> Because your love is better than life, my lips will glorify you. I will praise you as long as I live, and in your name I will lift up my hands. Psalm 63:3,4

What are some things that you can do in order to promote more positive thoughts throughout your day?

____

____

____

____

November 10th

God's power in our lives will be evident if we let it. But how do we handle God's power in our lives? Do we hide it so that it's not so obvious to our friends? Do we deny it because we want to do a better job at fitting in with the popular crowd? Or do we embrace the fact that God's power is active and working in us? Maybe for you it's a little bit of all of the above; I know that was the case for me when I was young.

I think the older we get, and the more that God's transforming power takes hold, the more we are ready and willing to display His power for all to see.

We don't need to conceal the love that the Father has for us. Let it shine for all to see!

Let's get excited about the fact that God is doing a work in us. Let us acknowledge that we belong to Him, and that we are embraced by the King of kings!

> His divine power has given us everything we need for life and godliness through our knowledge of him who called us by his own glory and goodness. 2 Peter 1:3

Can you think of one specific way that the Lord is working in your life?

___

___

___

___

___

November 11th

Each one of us has different wants and needs depending on a variety of factors, such as our home environments, educational opportunities, geographic locations, social support, physical health and wellbeing, and spiritual growth.

Even as each one of us is extremely different, we have one thing in common. We have a powerful and loving God, Who personally cares for His children. His tender loving care watches over us and provides for us.

How awesome it is that the Lord clothes us with all that we need! Every royal garment is made by Divine design. No alterations necessary. No two are the same.

How blessed we are to have a Heavenly Father Who takes such a personal interest in us and Who wants only to clothe us with the best.

> I delight greatly in the Lord; my soul rejoices in my God. For he has clothed me with garments of salvation and arrayed me in a robe of righteousness. Isaiah 61:10

Do you think that your robe of righteousness should fit you perfectly right now or is it something that you have to grow into?

____

____

____

____

____

November 12th

The Lord Almighty is an Awesome God. His power cannot be contained nor can it be measured by human standards. He is watchful, faithful, powerful, and victorious.

The Lord protects us; He clarifies the Truth; He is the Light of Life. Let us be thankful that our God is even more powerful and relentless than the enemy. Evil is no match for our God!

In the end, Satan and the evil ones that he has enlisted will have to give an account and bow down to the Sovereign Lord.

Oh, what a day that will be!

> To him who is able to keep you from falling and to present you before his glorious presence without fault and with great joy- to the only God our Savior be glory, majesty, power and authority, through Jesus Christ our Lord, before all ages, now and forevermore! Jude 24

What is so exciting about belonging to a victorious God?

____

____

____

____

____

____

November 13th

Worship the Lord with awe and wonder. Celebrate His holiness and His mighty works.

How blessed we are to belong to Christ. The Lord, in all His glory, reached down, took hold of us, and gave us LIFE.

He knows our every thought and our every circumstance. Nothing is hidden from Him.

He is with us on the mountaintop and He is with us in the valley. How amazing to be chosen and loved by the Lord of All and to be able to walk through life hand in hand!

> Ascribe to the Lord the glory due his name. Bring an offering before him; worship the Lord in the splendor of his holiness. I Chronicles 16:29

Do you ever find yourself having doubts about the love that the Lord has for you? Do you ever question His love?

November 14th

We are called to give God glory in all circumstances. I realize that this is sometimes quite hard to do.

Whether in need or abundance, in sickness or health, in victory or defeat... seek the face of Jesus. Be thankful for His grace and for His goodness. He provides, He delivers, He redeems, He comforts and He protects.

Learn to trust in His faithfulness, having confidence in His promises. Even when you have to really look hard for the blessings... remember that Jesus will never let you down.

> Be joyful always; pray continually; give thanks in all circumstances, for this is God's will for you in Christ Jesus. I Thessalonians 5:16-18

Do you feel more confident knowing that Jesus is with you everyday? Explain.

November 15th

A thankful heart is not developed out of busyness. Thankfulness takes time. It requires a pace that allows you time to enjoy the blessings that surround you. Blessings from the Creator that will surely be missed if you rush from one place to another.

As you go from day to day, slow down and appreciate the beauty of creation. Make time to take in a sunset. Go outside after the rain in search of a rainbow. Pick up your phone and call a grandparent. Show them that they are appreciated. Be thankful for the beauty that you see around you and for the encouragers that God puts in your life.

As the Lord continues to change your heart, ask Him for an extra measure of thankfulness to be sown inside.

> May they sing of the ways of the Lord, for the glory of the Lord is great. Psalm 138:5

What blessings might you miss out on if your busyness gets the best of you?

____

____

____

____

____

____

____

November 16th

There are many ways to worship the Lord. We can worship Him with our words, with our actions, with our mind, and with our time. In addition to these ways, I believe that we are also supposed to honor and worship Him with our bodies.

In I Corinthians, Chapter 6, Paul tells us that our body is a temple of the Holy Spirit Who is in us, and he goes on to say that we should honor God with our body.

So, what does it mean to honor God with our body? First, we should keep our "temple" clean regarding the things that we put into our body. Secondly, we should honor God by what we do with our body. Simply put, we should take care of our body in every way possible.

Paul also writes in Romans, Chapter 6, that we should not offer any parts of our bodies to sin, as instruments of wickedness, but rather offer ourselves to God.

Our body is a temple and also a gift from God. We are called to take care of this gift.

> Offer your bodies as living sacrifices, holy and pleasing to God- this is your spiritual act of worship.
>
> Romans 12:1

What part of your "temple" needs a bit of Tender Loving Care?

____

____

____

November 17th

Even as we are reminded to honor God with our bodies, temptation is all around us in various forms. No matter what your age, or season of life, we seem to be drawn to things that are not good for us.

It seems that young people today have so many more temptations than those of previous generations. You are living in a much more liberal, "anything goes" society which does not always embrace Christian values. Therefore, you are constantly being bombarded with temptation from so many directions.

Even Jesus was faced with temptation during His time on earth. Can you imagine spending 40 days alone in a desert with constant temptation from the devil?

It is so important to avoid and resist temptation as we seek to worship God with our lives. Ask Him for help when you are being tempted. He will give you the strength that you need.

> Because he himself suffered when he was tempted, he is able to help those who are being tempted. Hebrews 2:18

What is the biggest temptation that you have faced recently?

____

____

____

____

____

November 18th

Have you ever wondered what Jesus really looks like? Even as we have seen Him portrayed in movies, we all probably have a very specific image of Him in our minds. But what does He really look like?

I don't think that our minds could ever conceive the beauty and splendor of our Lord. Even the most beautiful things on earth could not compare to the beauty of our Savior.

I'm not sure about any of the physical features or appearance of Jesus, but one thing I do know, when you look into His eyes, you will see LOVE.

How will we even begin to take it all in when we meet Him face to face?

> Splendor and majesty are before him; strength and glory are in his sanctuary. Psalm 96:6

What do you think Jesus sees when He looks at you through His eyes of love?

November 19th

Thank you, Lord, for a new day. A day filled with promise. A day filled with opportunity. A chance to leave yesterday behind and start anew.

Thank you, Lord, for new beginnings. I know that You make all things new and that applies to me as well. Help me to focus on You and to follow where You are leading, without dwelling on the past.

As I walk through this day, I will walk in confidence because of Your grace.

We will take one step at a time.
One day at a time.
You and me together.
Always.

> Forgetting what is behind and straining toward what is ahead, I press on toward the goal to win the prize for which God has called me heavenward in Christ Jesus.
>
> Philippians 3:13,14

Is there anything from your past that seems to be interfering with your ability to move forward?

____

____

____

____

____

November 20th

I cannot imagine going through life without Christ by my side. Someone I can talk to. Someone Who will make a way for me and then lead the way. Someone I can always count on.

Our God does not show up only when it is convenient for Him. He does not pick and choose to only get involved in certain situations. He does not abandon us in our time of need. He is constantly with us... ***at all times.*** This is something that we can all get excited about!

We never have to go it alone.
We always have a Constant Companion by our side.
We are never out of His reach.
The Lord loves, protects, and provides.
We are always on His mind.

> There is no one holy like the Lord; there is no one besides you; there is no Rock like our God. I Samuel 2:2

How is the Lord even more loving and faithful than your best friends?

____

____

____

____

____

____

November 21st

Our Lord and Savior is gracious in all that He does and in all that He provides.

If we only knew how many times He intervened in our day to day lives...
If we only knew how protective He is regarding His precious children...
If we only knew how many ways He has redeemed our circumstances...
If we only knew how often He saves us from ourselves...

We would surely be amazed!

Worship the Lord. Praise His name. Stand amazed at His love for you!

> "Great and marvelous are your deeds, Lord God Almighty.
> Just and true are your ways, King of the ages."
>
> Revelation 15:3

Can you think of an example or situation when it was obvious to you that God intervened in your life in a loving or protective way?

November 22nd

I hear a lot these days about a new generation of kids being raised in an environment of "entitlement." I am sure that this does not apply to everyone who is being brought up in today's society. Thankfully, there are still parents who teach a solid work ethic to their children. If you have had this experience, you will one day be thankful, too.

Entitlement is an attitude where people believe they deserve everything handed to them on a silver platter. No need to work for it, no need to put any effort into anything, no need to focus on others. It's all about **ME**!

I can only imagine how this attitude must make God cringe. He does not want us to be self centered and unappreciative. He wants us to be God centered and thankful.

I believe that if our hearts are in the right place, our focus will be on God and not "what's in it for me."

> See to it that no one takes you captive through hollow and deceptive philosophy, which depends on human tradition and the basic principles of this world rather than on Christ.
> Colossians 2:8

Do you see any "entitlement" going on around you? If so, what are your thoughts about it?

____

____

____

____

November 23rd

In all circumstances we have reason to be thankful. Challenges do not indicate an absence of blessings or the absence of His Presence. The Lord is near to all Who call on His name. He is not a distant God Who is physically and emotionally removed from His people. He is ready and waiting to help in any situation.

Even as this ever-changing world around us spins out of control, He is our Constant, our Rock. The Unchanging One Who will endure with us to the finish line. Our Lord pours out His blessings on us everyday as He supplies all of our needs.

When you seek Him, you will find Him. Keep Christ in the forefront of your mind. Listen for His voice. Be in constant communion with Him, never forsaking your First Love. What a blessing to have unlimited access to the Prince of Peace!

> Though you have not seen him, you love him; and even though you do not see him now, you believe in him and are filled with an inexpressible and glorious joy. I Peter I:8

Is there anything right now that is getting in the way of the relationship that you have with your First Love?

____

____

____

____

____

November 24th

When you have a decision to make or when you come to a fork in the road, where do you look for help and guidance?

When we keep our eyes on the Lord and look to Him in all things, we will be able to make the right choice and choose the right path. For it is only by His grace and in His strength that we are able to go where He leads and accomplish His purposes.

As the Lord works on our behalf, let us not get in His way but wait patiently as His plan unfolds. Let us please Him with our choices and with our thoughts, our words, and our actions.

Ask the Lord to help you to be attentive to His voice and sensitive to His direction. Be open to all that He has for you. If you are *ready* and *willing*, God will make you *able*.

> Commit to the Lord whatever you do, and your plans will succeed. Proverbs 16:3

What do you think your responsibility is when it comes to making a specific decision or choosing the right path?

____

____

____

____

____

November 25th

It seems to me that in my prayer life the one thing that I do not do enough of is repent. The act of confessing to God and asking for forgiveness has never been at the top of my list. It's not that I think I am perfect because I am far from perfect! It's not that I think that I do not need forgiveness because I certainly do! I think that when I am in prayer, I tend to spend more time *asking* than I do *confessing.* This is something that I need to work on.

I believe that when we do not seek continual cleansing from the Lord, which includes acts of repentance, there will naturally be an accumulation of debris that will be weighing us down. I also believe that repentance is a form of worship because we are humbling ourselves before the Lord.

Let us be thankful that we have a loving, forgiving God. When we acknowledge our sins before God, our hearts get all cleaned out. With forgiveness comes freedom.

> If we confess our sins, he is faithful and just and will forgive us our sins and purify us from all unrighteousness.
>
> I John I:9

Is there anything that is weighing you down right now because you have not confessed and asked God for forgiveness?

____

____

____

____

____

November 26th

I've heard people comment on how much we, as Christians, have to sacrifice and how much we have to give up in order to follow Christ. How could any sacrifice that we could possibly make ever compare to the sacrifice of the cross?

Our Lord, our Awesome God, is the only One Who can truly offer and Who can realistically provide the freedom that we crave. Anything else would just be a counterfeit, a fake, or a poor imitation.

The freedom that Christ offers is not temporary, but eternal. It does not discriminate. It is a gift that needs only to be unwrapped.

By faith and with perseverance, you will find freedom. Keep your eyes on Him. Choose the "real thing", the Truth, the authentic One and Only. There is no substitute.

> "I am the way and the truth and the life. No one comesto the Father except through me." John 14:6

What does freedom in Christ mean to you?

____

____

____

____

____

____

November 27th

You, Lord, are more than enough! You are bigger than my circumstances and more powerful than any GIANT that I could possibly face.

Thank You, Lord, for all of the ways that You have rescued me in the past and for always drawing me back to You.

When I see those GIANTS up ahead, I know that I do not have to fear. I have the King of kings by my side, and we will crush them together!

There is no fear when You are near. There is no mountain that I cannot climb and no river I cannot cross. I stand amazed at Your Power and find comfort that You are always with me.

So I will not turn and run. I will not live in fear. I will continue to walk on with confidence, knowing that You are my Strength and my Shield.

> The Lord is my light and my salvation- whom shall I fear? The Lord is the stronghold of my life- of whom shall I be afraid? Psalm 27:1

Why is there no need for you to fear when Christ is with you?

____

____

____

____

____

November 28th

After Jesus was arrested in the garden of Gethsemane, Peter, one of His disciples, denied ever knowing Him to three different people. Jesus was his Friend, his Mentor, his Teacher. Why did he deny knowing Jesus? Probably because of fear.

We might be rather critical of Peter, but none of us knows how we would have responded if we were faced with the same situation.

I hope and pray that if I was in the company of unbelievers and someone mentioned the name of Christ, I would not hesitate to speak up and say, "Yes, I know Him."

Let us never fear associating ourselves with Jesus. No hesitation. No denial. No excuses.

> Immediately a rooster crowed. Then Peter remembered the word Jesus had spoken: "Before the rooster crows, you will disown me three times." And he went outside and wept bitterly. Matthew 26:75

Have you ever been in a situation where you downplayed your Christian faith and beliefs?

____

____

____

____

____

November 29th

The Lord is our Shepherd… do we really want to be self-sufficient? Do we want our independence or are we glad that we have a loving, faithful Father Who watches over us like a hawk?

We have the Creator of the Universe looking out for us and even in our indifference, our disobedience, and our stubborn self-will, He continues to love and provide for us.

Where would we be without the love of Christ? I am quite sure that any goodness that is in us is there because of the transforming power of the Lord. He will take hold of us, deal with us accordingly, and show us a better way.

Appreciate His love. Be glad that He knows just the right time to intervene.

> Good and upright is the Lord; therefore he instructs sinners in his ways. Psalm 25:8

What would happen if you allowed self-sufficiency and self-will to get the best of you?

____

____

____

____

____

____

November 30th

Worship the Lord with a thankful heart.

Worship the Almighty One True God.

Worship the Creator of the Universe.

Worship the Lord, the Lover of my soul.

Worship the Lord, my faithful Provider and my Strength.

Worship the Lord, my Hope, my Deliverer, Who died so that I can live.

> I will bow down toward your holy temple and will praise your name for your love and your faithfulness.
>
> Psalm 138:2

The praises above would not be complete without your input. In the space below, add some of your own words.

____

____

____

____

____

____

____

December

Wearing the Crown

December 1st

Knowing that you belong to the Father, that you have a royal inheritance and are the daughter of the King comes with privileges, as well as, responsibilities.

Even as we are given a crown, I believe the real issue is how do we wear that crown? We could wear it in such a way as to stick our nose in the air and elevate ourselves above and beyond everyone else around us. We could wear it for all to see, never getting our hands dirty, or we can wear it as we reach out to help those in need.

Yes, being the daughter of the Almighty Creator of the Universe has royal implications, but the King of kings does not want us to sit back in our royal robes while there is work to be done. I believe that our crowns give us unlimited possibilities to reach the lost, to get involved in helping others, and to live for Christ.

> And we pray this in order that you may live a life worthy of the Lord and may please him in every way; bearing fruit in every good work, growing in the knowledge of God.
>
> Colossians 1:10

What do you think it means that "with privileges, come responsibilities"?

____

____

____

____

____

December 2nd

So often we crave the things of this world: a pricey new car, the latest technology, a big house, fancy designer clothes, a high paying job, a vacation that we really cannot afford. If we buy into what the advertising tells us, "we simply cannot live without these things", and of course, "we always deserve the best."

If we really stop and think, are these the priorities that God places on our lives? He, Himself, gives us gifts that far outweigh the things that the world tells us we need.

Sometimes it is good for us to take a closer look at what we value in life. It is the "finer things", the things that are unseen, the things of His kingdom that are most valuable. "Things" like healing, restoration, transformation, forgiveness, peace, deliverance, hope, His love, I could go on and on.

The most precious things cannot be bought, they are given. They are gifts from our Heavenly Father.

> Do not store up for yourselves treasures on earth... But store up for yourselves treasures in heaven... For where your treasure is, there your heart will be also.
>
> Matthew 6:19-21

What are some of the things that you value? How do your values influence your priorities?

____

____

____

December 3rd

The Lord has shown me through the years that we should not feel compelled to blend in with the rest of the world. He has called us by name and called us to be different.

I don't know about you, but I want to become all that He has made me to be. Nothing more, nothing less.

The journey of "becoming" does not include impressing others but is filled with growing more and more into His Likeness. I lovingly encourage you to care less about what others think of you and care more about what pleases Christ.

> But you are a chosen people, a royal priesthood, a holy nation, a people belonging to God, that you may declare the praises of him who called you out of darkness into his wonderful light. I Peter 2:9

How much do you care about what others think of you? What is one thing that can help you care more about what pleases Christ and care less about being included in the popular crowd?

____

____

____

____

____

____

December 4th

Our society (*the world*) values the intelligent, the attractive, the wealthy, the popular, and the powerful. God values the broken, the simple, the humble, the weak, and the poor.

We come to Christ under no such pressure to be the prettiest, the most popular, or the smartest. He calls us, "Come as you are." He wants "broken vessels" that He can transform into "beautiful vases."

So remember that God has a purpose for each and every one of us. If we allow Him to, He will continue to teach us, equip us, transform us, and make us beautiful from the inside - out.

> "Let not the wise man boast of his wisdom or the strong man boast of his strength or the rich man boast of his riches, but let him who boasts boast about this: that he understands and knows me, that I am the Lord who exercises kindness, justice and righteousness on earth, for in these I delight," declares the Lord.
>
> Jeremiah 9:23,24

Why do you think God is looking for "broken vessels" instead of "beautiful vases"?

____

____

____

____

____

December 5th

The ways of God are a stark contrast to the ways of the world in today's society.

When we empty ourselves, we shall be filled.
The first must be last.
The meek will inherit the earth.
When I am weak, then I am strong.

The Lord's way is not the easy way. And even as our understanding is limited, we are called to persevere. There are always unexpected outcomes and blessings when we are able to endure.

> So do not throw away your confidence; it will be richly rewarded. You need to persevere so that when you have done the will of God, you will receive what he has promised.
>
> Hebrews 10:35,36

What does it mean to you that "the first must be last"? Can you think of a way that Jesus was an example of this?

____

____

____

____

____

____

December 6th

When God chooses our course and our direction, He will also prepare the way. He needs foot soldiers, as well as generals.

The Lord needs people who are willing to work behind the scenes. People who are not interested in gaining worldly recognition, but who know where their reward lies.

The Lord sees it all. He sees those who are working "backstage", as well as, those who are front and center and standing in the spotlight.

Be content to bloom where God plants you, even if you do not clearly or immediately see His purposes.

> Whatever you do, work at it with all your heart, as working for the Lord, not for men, since you know that you will receive an inheritance from the Lord as a reward. It is the Lord Christ you are serving. Colossians 3:23,24

Are you more of a "behind the scenes" person or are you more of a "spotlight" person? How much does it mean to you to have worldly recognition?

December 7th

Even when we are on the right path, there are distractions that try to derail us. Things that compete for our time, our energy, and our attention. When we get distracted, it is so easy to get off course.

My hope is that you will be able to hear the voice of the Lord above and beyond the noise that surrounds you, and that you will always be able to recognize the Voice of Truth when you hear it.

Stay focused and grounded in Christ as He guides your steps in the way that will fulfill His purpose for your life and bring glory and honor to His name.

> So then, just as you received Christ Jesus as Lord, continue to live in him, rooted and built up in him, strengthened in the faith as you were taught, and overflowing with thankfulness. Colossians 2:6

What kind of distraction tends to take your focus off of the road ahead? What are some things that you can do to minimize the effects of these distractions?

December 8th

Be careful about admiring the life that someone else leads. You do not know what really goes on deep down inside a person's heart or behind closed doors. Rarely is the "grass greener" somewhere else!

The life that God has given each of us and the crosses that each one of us has to bear are specifically designed for us. But…

God does not leave us to carry them alone. He gives us just the right amount of support and grace to help ease the load.

The Lord does not just stand back and watch us carry our crosses. He is right there with us, with His mighty arms, helping us to bear the burdens that are weighing us down.

> Let us run with perseverance the race marked out for us.
>
> Hebrews 12:1

Is there something in your life right now that is weighing you down? What do you think the Lord wants you to know about this?

____

____

____

____

____

____

December 9th

I encourage you, sisters of mine, to stay on the High Way; the path that the Lord has uniquely designed for you. However, you will need His help along the way.

Stay focused on Him so that you do not get thrown off course and find yourself giving in to the worldly temptations that surround you.

Stay focused, also, on the Truth so that you do not become vulnerable to the deception of the enemy.

Let your strength, your confidence, and your hope come from the One Who walks beside you as He continues to cover you with His love.

> For we are the temple of the living God. As God has said: "I will live with them and walk among them, and I will be their God, and they will be my people".
>
> 2 Corinthians 6:16

How does the Truth help you to stay on course?

____

____

____

____

____

____

December 10th

Our purpose in life may never be understood this side of heaven. But, let us be faithful to the will of God. Even as we might have questions such as...

"What do you have in mind, Lord? Why me? Are You sure that You don't have me mixed us with somebody else?"

Let us not ignore God's marching orders, but let us move forward with the mission. Most of the time, we might just be a link in the chain that leads to greater things. However, our efforts are never in vain and God will reward our obedience.

Each link is crucial. Without each link, the chain would be broken.

> Great are your purposes and mighty are your deeds.
> Jeremiah 32:19

Do you think that just being a link in the chain of greater things is disappointing or empowering? Do you think that God has an important purpose for your life?

December 11th

We might wonder, maybe even doubt, that anything we might do could ever make a difference for the kingdom of God. However, there is something called "the ripple effect."

A single drop of water on the smooth surface of a pond. Ripples. One after another. Extending from one to the next. Outward. Never knowing where it will end.

The same can be said for the things that we do for others. A single good deed can have far reaching effects. Effects that we might never be aware of.

God can use even a single drop of water in a Mighty Way!

> Let us not become weary in doing good, for at the proper time we will reap a harvest if we do not give up. Therefore, as we have opportunity, let us do good.
>
> Galatians 6:9,10

What have you done lately or what kinds of things can you do to start the "ripple effect"?

____

____

____

____

____

____

December 12th

God calls us to service to use our gifts to help others and to further His Kingdom. Not everyone is called to a far away mission field. Some of us are led to serve right in our own community.

Whatever the case, the Lord has ordered our steps and will equip us to do the work that He has prepared for us. I believe that He has specifically designed the opportunities that we will have in our lives based on our gifts, our talents, and also our faith.

If you are unsure about serving or do not know where the Lord is leading you, ask Him for clarity.

You just need to bring your willing heart to the One Who is able.

> And God is able to make all grace abound to you, so that in all things at all times, having all that you need, you will abound in every good work. 2 Corinthians 9:8

What are some of your gifts and talents that you can use to help others? Why is it important to use these talents and not let them "collect dust"?

___

___

___

___

___

___

December 13th

Are we just talking the talk, or are we walking the walk? Walking the walk requires trust, courage, and the willingness to put aside our agenda and yield to the will of God.

Walking the walk will attract attention. Some will look at you and say, "Hey, you know there's an easier route to take." Others will encourage you to stay the course. And some will seem to be unaffected while the Holy Spirit starts to stir their hearts.

So, let us not be "all talk", but "walk" in a way that makes others stop and take notice.

> We are therefore Christ's ambassadors.
>
> 2 Corinthians 5:20

How hard is it for you to walk the path that Christ has laid out for you? What makes it so difficult?

December 14th

How would you define true satisfaction? There are those who seem to have all that life has to offer. Others might be highly successful in the eyes of the world.

To those outside of our immediate circle, we might even appear as if we've "got it all together." So, why are we restless? Why do we keep searching for a peace that seems to elude us?

There is no substitute for the "real thing." There is nothing so satisfying as the love of Christ, our King, our Father.

Until we know Christ and allow Him to shine His Light on those dark and empty places in our hearts, we will continue to search. There is nothing that quenches our thirst better than the Living Water that only He can provide.

> For he satisfies the thirsty and fills the hungry with good things. Psalm 107:9

Is there something in your life that is preventing you from being satisfied and content? Do you think that satisfaction is situational or a "state of mind"?

___

___

___

___

___

December 15th

We are called to be content in all circumstances. God has a unique purpose for each one of us. Let us not think that our purpose is any less important than someone else's.

Each piece of the puzzle is both unique and essential in completing the larger picture. There is no one else who can fill your shoes. No one else who can accomplish God's plan for you.

You might be filled with questions and might not understand what God is up to. But be assured that God knows what He's doing.

Trust Him. Rely on Him. Have confidence in Him. Only God can see the larger picture.

> Show me your ways, O Lord, and teach me your paths; guide me in your truth and teach me, for you are God my Savior, and my hope is in you all day long.
>
> Psalm 25:4,5

Do you think that God has a purpose and a plan for you, right here and right now? Do you think that you can make a difference in this world now or is there an "age requirement"?

December 16th

Gentleness and patience are two of the character traits included in the Fruit of the Spirit. The rest of the list can be found in Galatians 5:22-23.

In order for the Fruit of the Spirit to be developed in us, we must decide to live a life crucified to self and alive in Christ. We must be willing to sacrifice the things of this world, for the things of His Kingdom.

We are called to give up self will, for His Will. To trade our ways, for His Ways while allowing Him to mold us, shape us, and refine us, transforming us into a new creation.

> Therefore, if anyone is in Christ, he is a new creation; the old has gone, the new has come. 2 Corinthians 5:17

In what ways are you sacrificing the things of this world in order to stay true to God's Kingdom? How does that feel?

December 17th

Most of the time, the development of Christian character and Christ-like qualities requires "on the job" training. The Lord knows what we are lacking and where our weaknesses lie.

Jesus is in the reconstruction business. His desire is that we become the best that we can be. Many times this means being pruned so that new growth is possible or being sanded to smooth out the rough edges.

So when Satan does all that he can to bring you to your knees, that's just where you need to be… **on your knees.**
And that's just the time when God will use your circumstances for further training.

> Therefore, holy brothers *(and sisters)*, who share in the heavenly calling, fix your thoughts on Jesus.
>
> Hebrews 3:1

What qualities or characteristics in you need reconstruction? How do you think the process works?

____

____

____

____

____

____

December 18th

Even though some things seem so random that we fail to see any reason for our circumstances, rest secure in the fact that the Almighty has a purpose and a plan.

During these times, it is such a comfort and a blessing to me to know that He walks with me. I am never alone!

Wherever you go, He is already there and has never left your side. So walk with confidence and rest in His Peace. He will surround you with His Love through it all.

Our humanness cannot fully comprehend His Ways, but we can trust Him in ALL THINGS.

> As the mountains surround Jerusalem, so the Lord surrounds his people both now and forevermore.
>
> Psalm 125:2

What does it mean to you to know that your Loving Heavenly Father will never leave your side?

____

____

____

____

____

____

December 19th

Things are not always as they first appear. Our interpretation of events is based only on our limited view of the situation. Just when we think we cannot take one more step, the Lord reveals something to us that changes our course and renews our hope.

He reminds us in His Word, "My thoughts are not your thoughts, neither are your ways my ways," declares the Lord. "As the heavens are higher than the earth, so are my ways higher than your ways" (Isaiah 55:8,9).

How awesome are the ways of the Lord! There are reasons that He allows us to be tossed about by the waves and pounded by the rough surf. Reasons we might only realize once the seas are calm.

His ways are not our ways but He wants us to be all that He intended for us to be, a rare and precious jewel that will shine brightly for Him.

> He reached down from on high and took hold of me; he drew me out of the deep waters. Psalm 18:16

What are some things that can only be learned during tough times?

December 20th

Most of the time, when "dark clouds" seem to follow us everywhere we go, we would much rather fast forward through it or take a detour around it.

Endurance can be defined as the ability to bear pain and also includes the ability to continue on.

Let us not turn and run from the things that God will ultimately use to teach us and strengthen us.

The load that you carry was never meant for you alone. The burden was not designed for one- but for two. The Lord will help you carry your load and whenever necessary, He will lovingly carry you as well.

> I will lead the blind by ways they have not known, along unfamiliar paths I will guide them; I will turn the darkness into light before them and make the rough places smooth.
> Isaiah 42:16

Is there a particular "load" that you are carrying now that you need help with?

____

____

____

____

____

____

December 21st

Faith is not something to be attained; it is something to be developed. It is not something that we can acquire on our own but only with the help of the Holy Spirit.

We should never compare the measure of our faith with anyone else. Nor should we be quick to pass judgment on others. Our faith is a personal issue between God and ourselves.

Only God knows the true condition of our faith and knows just how much work still needs to be done.

> Yet he (*Abraham*) did not waiver through unbelief regarding the promise of God, but was strengthened in his faith and gave glory to God. Romans 4:20

Has anyone ever judged you based on your actions, your appearance, or what they thought was the level of your faith? Explain. Does that make you less likely to judge others?

____

____

____

____

____

____

____

December 22nd

When I look at stained glass, I realize that it only becomes beautiful when the light shines through. Such is the heart. Stained with sin, filled with darkness, until the Light of Life starts to shine through.

Let us not hold back in allowing Christ to shine His Light into our hearts so that we can become all that He intended for us to be.

We know that there is work to be done, but as long as we stay in the Light, our colors will continue to be revealed.

> Great are the works of the Lord; they are pondered by all who delight in them. Psalm 111:2

Do you think that you are a "work in progress"? What does this mean to you?

December 23rd

How easy it is for us to get lost in the shopping, the wrapping, and the endless busyness during the holiday season and miss the blessings of Christmas.
"Do this! Do that! Go here! Go there!"
Too busy to be blessed. Too busy to be a blessing.

Slow down. Refocus. Give thanks for the gifts that will never be found under the tree.

Love, Joy, Peace......................Jesus.

> Therefore God exalted him to highest place and gave him the name that is above every name, that at the name of Jesus every knee should bow, in heaven and on earth and under the earth, and every tongue confess that Jesus Christ is Lord, to the glory of God the Father.
>
> Philippians 2:9-11

What are some ways that you and/or your family prepare for Christmas? In what ways can you prepare your heart as well?

____

____

____

____

____

____

December 24th

How often do we attach our self-worth to how much we can accomplish in one day? How often do we feel guilty when we put something on hold, in order to break away from our "busyness"?

The world says, "Do, do, do!"
The Lord just wants us to "be."
He doesn't say, "Do for me." He says, "Be with me."

The hustle and bustle in preparation for Christmas is a good example. We spend more time getting ready for Christmas, than we do enjoying Christmas.

Slow down!!
Let us get all "wrapped up" **in Him** at this beautiful time of year.

Let us shift our focus from "doing" to "being."
MERRY CHRISTMAS!

> For to us a child is born, to us a son is given, and the government will be on his shoulders. And he will be called Wonderful Counselor, Mighty God, Everlasting Father, Prince of Peace. Isaiah 9:6

In what ways do you celebrate the birth of Jesus?

____

____

____

____

December 25th

Without Christmas… there would be no Easter.
The manger and the baby Jesus were the beginning of a journey that led to a cross.

It was God's glorious Gift, to all who would receive Him.

A perfect Gift from above.

Joy to the world!

> But the angel said to them, "Do not be afraid. I bring you good news of great joy that will be for all the people. Today in the town of David a Savior has been born to you; he is Christ the Lord." Luke 2:10,11

Do you consider Jesus to be the greatest gift of all? Explain.

December 26th

The Light of the World so graciously pours His Light into each one of us. Let us not be content just to have the Light, but let us get excited about sharing the Light.

So let us take the Light wherever we go and be an encouragement to others. Where there is darkness, let there be Light. Where there is hatred and resentment, let there be Love. Where there is turmoil and strife, let there be Peace.

Let us make the most of every opportunity to shine for Him!

> How beautiful on the mountains are the feet of those who bring good news, who proclaim peace, who bring good tidings, who proclaim salvation, who say to Zion, "Your God reigns!" Isaiah 52:7

Can you think of any specific places where the Light of the World is so obviously missing? What are some ways that you can share the Light with others?

____

____

____

____

____

____

December 27th

Have you ever heard of the "starfish story"? Well, it goes something like this.

There was a young girl who was walking on the beach one day. As she walked, she noticed that so many starfish had washed up on the shore. She realized that most of these starfish would not survive because the tide was still going out.

As the girl started to throw the starfish, one after another, back into the water, an older man came along and said to her, "Why are you bothering with the starfish? Don't you see how many there are? You couldn't possibly save them all. What difference does it make?"

Just then, the girl stooped down and picked up yet another starfish and replied, "Well, sir. It made a difference to this one!"

I believe that the Lord is counting on us. Counting on us to make a difference. Never think that your efforts are in vain. God can use each one of us.

> "The harvest is plentiful, but the workers are few."
>
> Luke 10:2

Do you think that making a difference for the Lord is only possible for adults or can young people also make a difference?

____

____

____

____

December 28th

As we focus this month on "wearing the crown", I am wondering what you might envision your crown to look like. Maybe it is adorned with precious jewels, probably filled with your favorite color, or it could be something quite simple, more of symbol that shows that you belong to the One True Christ.

Either way, the design, the colors, or the appearance of your crown is not what's most important. The crown that is given to you by your King comes with responsibility. With privilege comes responsibility. You have a responsibility to Christ and to others to "wear it well."

Wear your crown with dignity, with humility, and with an attitude of service, just as your King came to serve. Be a blessing to those who cross your path, and reflect the love that Christ so graciously pours into you.

> I urge you to live a life worthy of the calling you have received. Be completely humble and gentle; be patient bearing with one another in love. Ephesians 4:1,2

Why is it so important to wear your crown in a way that reflects the grace, the love, and the compassion of Christ?

___

___

___

___

___

December 29th

The privilege of the crown, and the fact that we belong to the Almighty King should remind us that we are, in many ways, setting an example. But... what kind of example do others see in us?

People are watching at all times. They might be looking to see if our behavior and our actions are congruent with the faith that we profess. Others might be observing a different way of life that propels them to make positive changes in their own lives.

My prayer for you is that your crown will enable you to become a light for others, and that you will use your gifts and talents in mighty ways. Serve. Give. Encourage. Love.

> For I testify that they gave as much as they were able, and even beyond their ability. 2 Corinthians 8:3

In what ways can you be a positive example for others? How might living out your Christian worldview impact those who cross your path?

____

____

____

____

____

____

____

December 30th

The Lord Almighty is the Author of our days. Each chapter that He writes prepares us for the next. Only He knows what the future holds. And even though our situations and circumstances vary, His love and faithfulness never change.

You can climb any mountain, as long as He is with you. The "highs" and the "lows", you will experience together.

In Him… you are well prepared and you will be well equipped.

> Your eyes saw my unformed body. All the days ordained for me were written in your book before one of them came to be. Psalm 139:16

Are there any concerns that you have about the future? Why do you think God prepares you for what lies ahead, one step at a time?

December 31st

The end of the year is a good time to look back. Not to look back with thoughts of "what if" or "if only", but to look back with thoughts of thankfulness for God's continued faithfulness.

Whenever we retrace our steps, we will clearly see the hand of God at work.

So with the New Year upon us

let us trust in the Almighty,

walk with confidence,

and always be ready to tell others the reason for our

HOPE.

> I will praise you, O Lord my God, with all my heart; I will glorify your name forever. Psalm 86:12

Make a list of the things that you have been blessed with during the past year. In what ways has God been faithful to you throughout the year?

____

____

____

____

____

Printed in the United States
By Bookmasters

MW00757264

RISK FACTORS FOR CEREBROVASCULAR DISEASE AND STROKE

Risk Factors for Cerebrovascular Disease and Stroke

Edited by Sudha Seshadri, MD
DEPARTMENT OF NEUROLOGY
BOSTON UNIVERSITY SCHOOL OF MEDICINE
INVESTIGATOR, THE FRAMINGHAM HEART STUDY
BOSTON, MA

and

Stéphanie Debette, MD, PhD
DEPARTMENT OF NEUROLOGY AND INSERM CENTER U897, EPIDEMIOLOGY
BORDEAUX UNIVERSITY HOSPITAL AND UNIVERSITY OF BORDEAUX
BORDEAUX, FRANCE

Oxford University Press is a department of the University of Oxford. It furthers the University's objective of excellence in research, scholarship, and education by publishing worldwide.

Oxford New York
Auckland Cape Town Dar es Salaam Hong Kong Karachi
Kuala Lumpur Madrid Melbourne Mexico City Nairobi
New Delhi Shanghai Taipei Toronto

With offices in
Argentina Austria Brazil Chile Czech Republic France Greece
Guatemala Hungary Italy Japan Poland Portugal Singapore
South Korea Switzerland Thailand Turkey Ukraine Vietnam

Published in the United States of America by
Oxford University Press
198 Madison Avenue, New York, NY 10016

Library of Congress Cataloging-in-Publication Data
Risk factors for cerebrovascular disease and stroke / edited by Sudha Seshadri and Stéphanie Debette.
p. ; cm.
Includes bibliographical references.
ISBN 978–0–19–989584–7 (alk. paper)
I. Seshadri, Sudha, editor. II. Debette, Stéphanie, editor.
[DNLM: 1. Cerebrovascular Disorders—etiology. 2. Stroke—epidemiology. 3. Cerebrovascular Disorders—genetics. WL 355]
RC388.5
616.8′1—dc23
2014025003

The science of medicine is a rapidly changing field. As new research and clinical experience broaden our knowledge, changes in treatment and drug therapy occur. The author and publisher of this work have checked with sources believed to be reliable in their efforts to provide information that is accurate and complete, and in accordance with the standards accepted at the time of publication. However, in light of the possibility of human error or changes in the practice of medicine, neither the author, nor the publisher, nor any other party who has been involved in the preparation or publication of this work warrants that the information contained herein is in every respect accurate or complete. Readers are encouraged to confirm the information contained herein with other reliable sources, and are strongly advised to check the product information sheet provided by the pharmaceutical company for each drug they plan to administer.

9 8 7 6 5 4 3 2 1
Printed in the United States of America
on acid-free paper

Contents

Foreword

THE DEVASTATING CONSEQUENCES of a stroke for the individual and for society are only too well known to the medical community. The Global Burden of Disease Stroke Experts Group recently reported in *The Lancet* that in 2010 there were 16.9 million people worldwide with a first stroke, 33 million stroke survivors, and about 6 million stroke-related deaths; in addition, 102 million disability-affected life years were lost. Of note, the global burden of stroke has increased substantially during the past two decades, with more than 75% of the burden being experienced in developing countries. Equally striking is the 3- to 10-fold variation in stroke burden across geographic regions. These are sobering figures that underscore the likelihood that the burden of stroke will likely escalate, given the aging of the world population. These data also point to the need for understanding the reasons for the geographic heterogeneity and varying burden of stroke worldwide.

Although these global trends seem alarming, they have to be juxtaposed against the major advances the medical community has made in the diagnosis of stroke and its prompt treatment and prevention during the past 50 years. During this time, stroke mortality has declined substantially. The decline can be attributed to an improved understanding of key stroke risk factors (from epidemiological studies), a changing landscape of the evidentiary basis for treating the condition (as a result of large, randomized, controlled clinical trials), and as a result of the major advances in the clinical care of stroke patients in intensive care stroke units. Indeed, one important related concept that is worth highlighting is that the day we make a clinical diagnosis of stroke in the emergency room is not when the disease process began. Indeed, the conventional starting point of medical treatment of a patient with an acute stroke represents medical failure—a failure of preventing the disease. The disease process itself begins with an inborn genetic susceptibility to the disease at birth, and continues to evolve throughout the entire adult life course, with continuous accrual of and exposure to key risk factors for stroke and the development of subclinical cerebrovascular disease that culminates in a clinical event one fine (or not so fine) day when a threshold is crossed. Several of these key risk factors are lifestyle related. Thus, stroke is a life course and lifestyle-related disease condition that is eminently preventable.

To that end, this book is an outstanding attempt to elucidate carefully the panoply of risk factors for stroke, their synergistic interactions, and the spectrum of disease conditions encompassed by the simple term *stroke*, including variations with age and sex. The editors have compiled a comprehensive and exhaustive set of chapters that trace the evolution of disease propensity throughout the life course under the combinatorial influence of environmental and genetic risk factors. Each of the major sections, authored by experts in their respective domains, is complete by itself, provides state-of-the-art information on the subject matter, and integrates nicely with the other sections to offer a holistic view of how the disease condition evolves and how best we can predict, prevent, and treat stroke and its subtypes. The chapter on integrative approaches to disease prevention is consistent with the need of the hour—a combinatorial approach to disease risk prediction and prevention. Overall, the book is a goldmine of key information for a wide spectrum of readership—from medical students to residents and fellows to academic and practicing clinicians and neurologists. I congratulate the authors and editors on this landmark achievement.

Vasan S. Ramachandran, MD, DM, FACC, FAHA
Professor of Medicine and Epidemiology,
Chief, Section of Preventive Medicine & Epidemiology, Dept. of Medicine
Boston University Schools of Medicine & Public Health,
Editor, *Circulation Cardiovascular Genetics*, Associate Editor, *Circulation*
Principal Investigator, Framingham Heart Study

Contributors

Yannick Béjot, MD, PhD
Dijon Stroke Registry
Medical School of Dijon
University of Burgundy
and
Department of Neurology
University Hospital
Dijon, France

Anna Bersano, MD, PhD
UO Malattie Cerebrovascolari
Fondazione IRCCS Istituto Neurologico C. Besta
Milan, Italy

Steve Bevan, PhD
Neurology Unit
Clinical Neuroscience
Cambridge University
Cambridge, UK

Cheryl D. Bushnell, MD
Associate Professor of Neurology
Director, Wake Forest Baptist Stroke Center
Winston-Salem, NC

Erica C. S. Camargo, MD, PhD
Assistant in Neurology
Massachusetts General Hospital
and
Instructor in Neurology
Harvard Medical School
Boston, MA

Raphael A. Carandang, MD
Assistant Professor of Neurology, Anesthesiology and Surgery
University of Massachusetts Medical School
Amherst, MA

Ganesh Chauhan, PhD
Inserm Centre U897, Epidemiology
University of Bordeaux
Bordeaux, France

Jennifer L. Dearborn, MD
Department of Neurology
Johns Hopkins University School of Medicine
Baltimore, MD

Stéphanie Debette, MD, PhD
Department of Neurology
and Inserm Center U897,
Epidemiology
Bordeaux University Hospital and
University of Bordeaux
Bordeaux, France
and
Department of Neurology
Boston University School of
Medicine
Framingham Heart Study
Boston, MA

David Della-Morte, MD, PhD
Department of Neurology
Miller School of Medicine
University of Miami
Miami, FL
and
Department of Laboratory Medicine
& Advanced Biotechnologies
IRCCS San Raffaele
Rome, Italy

Martin Dichgans, MD
Institute for Stroke and Dementia
Research
Klinikum der Universität Müchen
Ludwig-Maximilians-Universität
and
Munich Cluster for Systems
Neurology (SyNergy)
Munich, Germany

Guido J. Falcone, MD
Department of Neurology and Center
for Human Genetic Research
Massachusetts General Hospital
Boston, MA

Rebecca F. Gottesman, MD, PhD
Department of Neurology
Johns Hopkins University
School of Medicine
Baltimore, MD

Terttu Heikinheimo-Connell, MD
Department of Neurology
Helsinki University Central Hospital
Helsinki, Finland

Thomas Jeerakathil, MD
Associate Professor
Division of Neurology
University of Alberta
Edmonton, Alberta, Canada

Christina Jern, MD, PhD
Department of Clinical Genetics
Sahlgrenska University Hospital
Gothenburg, Sweden

Lenore J. Launer, PhD
Chief, Neuroepidemiology Section
Intramural Research Program,
National Institute on Aging
Bethesda, MD

Didier Leys, MD, PhD
Department of Neurology
Lille University Hospital, University
of Lille Nord de France
Lille, France

Svetlana Lorenzano, MD, PhD
J. Philip Kistler Stroke Research
Center and Stroke Service
Department of Neurology
Massachusetts General Hospital
Harvard Medical School
Boston, MA
and
Department of Neurology and
Psychiatry
Policlinico Umberto I Hospital
Sapienza University
Rome, Italy

Rainer Malik, PhD
Institute for Stroke and Dementia
Research,
Klinikum der Universität Müchen
Ludwig-Maximilians-Universität
Munich, Germany

Herbert A. Manosalva, MD
Stroke and Genetics Fellow
Division of Neurology
Department of Medicine
University of Alberta
Edmonton, Alberta, Canada

Thomas Marjot, MBBS
Imperial College Cerebrovascular Research Unit
Imperial College London and Hammersmith Hospitals
London, UK

Hugh S. Markus (DM)
St George's Hospital and Atkinson Morley Neuroscience Centre
London, UK

Annie Pedersén, MD
Department of Clinical Genetics
Sahlgrenska University Hospital
Gothenburg, Sweden

Alessandro Pezzini, MD
Department of Clinical and Experimental Sciences
Neurology Clinic
University of Brescia
Brescia, Italy

Aleksandra Pikula, MD
Attending Physician
Boston Medical Center
Assistant Professor of Neurology
Boston University School of Medicine
Boston, MA

Jukka Putaala, MD, PhD
Department of Neurology
Helsinki University Central Hospital
Helsinki, Finland

Jonathan Rosand, MD, MSc
Program in Medical and Population Genetics
Broad Institute
Cambridge, MA

Natalia S. Rost, MD
J. Philip Kistler Stroke Research Center and Stroke Service
Department of Neurology
Massachusetts General Hospital
Harvard Medical School
Boston, MA

Tatjana Rundek, MD, PhD
Department of Neurology
Miller School of Medicine
University of Miami
Miami, FL

Claudia L. Satizabal, PhD
Postdoctoral Fellow in Neuroepidemiology
Department of Neurology and The Framingham Heart Study
Boston University School of Medicine
Boston, MA

Sabrina Schilling, MS
Inserm Centre U897, Epidemiology
University of Bordeaux
Bordeaux, France

Pankaj Sharma, MD, PhD
Imperial College Cerebrovascular Research Unit
Imperial College London and Hammersmith Hospitals
London, UK

Turgut Tatlisumak, MD, PhD
Department of Neurology
Helsinki University Central Hospital
Helsinki, Finland

Emmanuel Touzé, MD, PhD
Université Caen Basse Normandie
Caen, France

Christophe Tzourio, MD, PhD
University Hospital of Bordeaux and
Inserm Centre U897, Epidemiology
University of Bordeaux
Bordeaux, France

Starla M. Wise, DO
Fellow in Neurology
Wake Forest University
Winston-Salem, NC

Bradford B. Worrall, MD, MSc
Harrison Distinguished Teaching Professor and Vice-Chair for Clinical Research of Neurology and Professor of Public Health Sciences
University of Virginia Health Systems
Charlottesville, VA

I

Introduction

1

EPIDEMIOLOGY OF CEREBROVASCULAR DISEASE AND STROKE

Yannick Béjot and Emmanuel Touzé

Introduction

Evaluating the epidemiology of cerebrovascular disease and stroke is of major interest because it will help us to identify risk factors, will establish needs with regard to the implementation of dedicated services, and will guide and evaluate future prevention priorities.

This chapter provides methodological key points to understand the epidemiology of cerebrovascular disease and stroke, and presents updated data about the incidence, recurrence, mortality, and prevalence of the disease.

Methodological Issues in Epidemiological Studies of Cerebrovascular Disease and Stroke

DEFINITION OF STROKE AND TRANSIENT ISCHEMIC ATTACK

The use of a universally accepted definition of stroke is an essential requirement for the study of epidemiology. Stroke is defined classically using the World Health Organization (WHO) diagnostic criteria as "rapidly developing clinical signs of focal (at times, global) disturbances of cerebral function, lasting more than 24 hours or leading to death with no apparent cause other than that of vascular origin."[1] Despite its apparently clear formulation, this definition raises some issues. First, if applied strictly, it would exclude patients with isolated symptoms, such as headache or paresthesia, but without neurological signs on examination, although some patients may have actually had a stroke. Consequently, it has been proposed that "symptoms" be substituted for "signs,"[2] and this somewhat modified definition is in fact applied in stroke epidemiological studies. Second, this definition excludes transient ischemic attack (TIA), which refers to patients with an acute focal loss of brain or monocular function with symptoms lasting less than 24 hours.[3] Recently, however, this arbitrary 24-hour time limit has been challenged because a large majority of TIAs have a shorter duration (usually less than 1 hour) and are sometimes associated with ischemic lesions on brain imaging (especially diffusion-weighted magnetic resonance imaging), all the more so when symptom duration is long.[4,5] In 2002, these observations led to the redefinition of TIA as a "brief episode of neurologic dysfunction caused by focal brain or retinal ischemia, with clinical symptoms typically lasting less than 1 h, and without evidence of acute infarction."[6] Although the new definition emphasizes that TIA is not a benign event, it is difficult to apply in epidemiological studies because the categorization of a cerebrovascular event as TIA or stroke is influenced considerably by access to diagnostic resources—the proportion of brain magnetic resonance imaging performed in patients with transient neurological symptoms, and also the sensitivity of diagnostic techniques, both of which are highly inconsistent among studied populations.[7] Consequently, the use of the classic definition of TIA and stroke appears to be more reliable for epidemiological studies.

WHAT IS MEASURED BY EPIDEMIOLOGICAL STUDIES?

Stroke epidemiological studies provide data on the incidence, prevalence, case fatality, and mortality rates of stroke (Box 1.1), all of which contribute to our understanding of the disease in different but complementary ways.

Hence, ascertaining stroke incidence is useful to establish the need for acute stroke services in a given area. Geographic comparisons of stroke incidence help to identify individual and environmental vascular risk factors, and determining temporal trends can reveal the efficacy of prevention strategies in reducing stroke occurrence. Case fatality rates reflect the severity of the disease and the efficacy of care management of patients with stroke; mortality rates identify the global burden of stroke in a population and thus allow comparisons with other diseases. As for incidence, geographic and temporal comparisons of case fatality rates are of a great interest. Stroke prevalence, which is the most difficult parameter to evaluate in epidemiological studies, is useful as it can be used to determine the need for poststroke facilities and to reveal the long-term complications of stroke, such as functional impairment, depression, and dementia.

More recently, the concept of disability-adjusted life years (DALYs) has been developed from the WHO Global Burden of Disease Project to measure the global burden of the disease and its consequences in terms of premature mortality and living with disability.[8,9] DALYs lost corresponds to the sum of years lost as a result of premature death, and years of healthy life lost because of disability. DALY is derived from population-based data on stroke incidence, prevalence, fatality, and disability levels. This measurement reflects explicitly the adverse consequences of stroke in a population and is useful for worldwide comparisons.[10]

HOW DOES ONE STUDY STROKE EPIDEMIOLOGY?

Prospective population-based stroke registries are the most reliable tools to provide accurate information on stroke epidemiology. Contrary to hospital-based studies, which are prone to referral bias, population-based registries contain an unbiased sample of incident cases. This makes it possible not only to calculate incidence rates, but also to obtain other important information, such as early and long-term case fatality rates, poststroke morbidity (handicap, epilepsy, depression, dementia), and recurrent events. They can also be used to assess and improve stroke management, measure the usefulness of investigations and the place of care, and provide a setting for case–control studies of risk

BOX 1.1

DEFINITION OF THE MAIN PARAMETERS MEASURED BY STROKE EPIDEMIOLOGICAL STUDIES

Incidence rate: the number of new cases of stroke in a given population in a given time period, usually expressed as the number of new cases per 100,000 population at risk per year. Because crude incidence rates are influenced by the structure of the studied population in terms of age and sex, standardization by applying age- and sex-specific rates to a "standard" population is necessary to allow reliable comparisons among studies.

Case fatality rate: the proportion of patients with stroke who die within a certain period of time. Early case fatality rates are usually expressed as the percentage of patients with stroke who die within the first 28 days or 1 month after a stroke occurrence.

Mortality rate: the number of deaths resulting from stroke in a given population in a given time period, usually expressed in units of deaths per 1000 individuals per year. To make the results of studies comparable with those in populations with different age and sex structures, the standardized mortality ratio represents a proportional comparison with the numbers of deaths that would have been expected if the population had been of a standard composition in terms of age and gender.

Prevalence rate: the number of people with a history of stroke in a given population at a given time, usually expressed in units per 1000 individuals per year. Prevalence is influenced largely by both the incidence and the case fatality of stroke—the greater the incidence, the greater the prevalence; and, inversely, the greater the case fatality, the lower the prevalence.

factors.[11] Several criteria for running "ideal" stroke incidence studies have been defined to make their findings comparable (Box 1.2).[2,11,12]

However, such studies are time-consuming and expensive, which explains why only 56 of these studies conducted by 47 centers were found in a recent review of published data on incidence and early case fatality from 1970 to 2008.[13] In addition, population-based registries are limited by the relatively small population covered, which may not reflect the composition of the entire population of a country. Indeed, differences among the various regions of a country, in terms of socioeconomic level of the population or access to medical services, including primary prevention of cerebrovascular diseases, may be considerable. In addition, population-based studies are conducted principally within urban areas, and it has been clearly established that the incidence rates of stroke differ between urban and rural populations, in part as a result of variations in the distribution of vascular risk factors.[14,15] Last, only limited data from population-based registries are available for low- to middle-income countries, where stroke incidence rates are high.[13] For this last reason, a stepwise approach for the development of stroke registers (STEP Stroke) has recently been implemented by the WHO.[16] This stroke surveillance system begins with patients with stroke admitted to the hospital (step 1) and is completed, whenever possible, by the addition of stroke events identified outside the hospital. Events can be either fatal (step 2) or nonfatal (step 3). The feasibility of such a program has been demonstrated, and it will be helpful in obtaining reliable epidemiological data on stroke in low- to middle-income countries.[17]

BOX 1.2

CRITERIA FOR RUNNING HIGH-QUALITY INCIDENCE STROKE STUDIES

Use of standard definitions

- World Health Organization definition of stroke
- Classification into ischaemic stroke, intracerebral hemorrhage, and subarachnoid hemorrhage with at least 80% verification of diagnosis by computed tomography or magnetic resonance imaging.
- Classification of ischaemic stroke into subtypes (e.g., large-artery disease, small-artery disease, cardioembolic, other) if possible
- First-ever-in-a-lifetime only (for incidence calculations) and recurrent stroke

Standard methods for case ascertainment

- Complete population-based case ascertainment based on multiple overlapping sources of information: hospitals (including admissions for acute vascular problems and cerebrovascular imaging studies and/or interventions), outpatient clinics (including regular checking of general practitioners' databases), and death certificates
- Prospective study design, ideally with "hot pursuit" of cases
- Large, well-defined stable population
- Follow-up of patients' vital status for at least 1 month
- Reliable method for estimating denominators (census data not more than 5 years old)

Standard data presentation of the findings for comparisons among studies

- Complete calendar years of data to avoid the influence of seasonal fluctuations, and not more than 5 years of data averaged together
- Men and women presented separately
- Recommended reporting of age-specific estimates within standard mid-decade age bands (e.g., 45–54 years), including oldest age group (≥85 years)

Incidence of Stroke and TIA

CURRENT INCIDENCE OF STROKE WORLDWIDE

In 2005, the WHO estimated that, worldwide, approximately 16 million people sustained a first-ever stroke annually.[18] Data from population-based studies conducted at the beginning of the 21st century revealed considerable geographic variations in the incidence of first-ever stroke (Figure 1.1).[19–35]

Standardized incidence currently ranges from 66 to 220/100,000/year, and the highest rates are observed in low- to middle-income countries, although the data available in these areas are rather limited. Older studies also observed this excess in stroke incidence in Eastern Europe; it was 238/100,000/year in Uzhhorod, West Ukraine, in 1999 to 2000,[36] and 155/100,000/year in Novosibirsk, Russia, in 1992.[37] Of note, no studies that meet the quality criteria for the estimation of incidence have been conducted in Africa. Nonetheless, estimates suggest that 8% of all first-ever strokes occur on this continent,[18] and incidence rates were estimated to be, respectively, 109/100,000/year and 316/100,000/year in two rural area in Tanzania in a survey done between 2003 and 2006.[38]

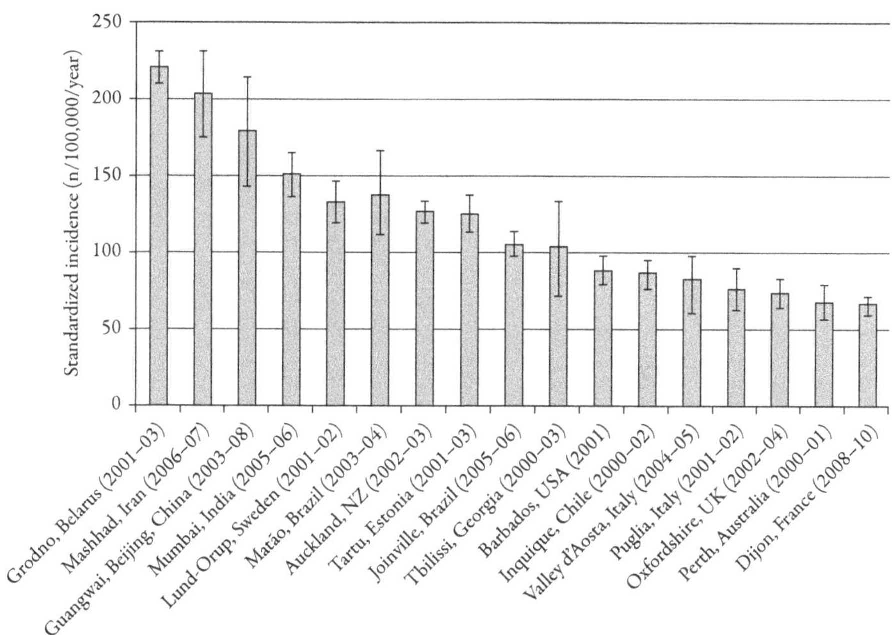

FIGURE 1.1 Worldwide stroke incidence according to contemporary, high-quality population-based registries. Incidence is age adjusted using the world population as the standard.

Sex differences in stroke incidence have been noted. Age-adjusted incidence rates are 1.5 times greater in men than in women in European registries (Figure 1.2).[19,32,39–41]

Similar results are found outside Europe.[42] However, the greater life expectancy of women, together with the increasing incidence rates with age, explain why more women sustain stroke in terms of absolute number. Of note, this excess in stroke incidence in men is particularly marked in people age 55 to 75 years old, whereas an inverse trend has been reported in older people.[43]

DISTRIBUTION OF STROKE SUBTYPES

Although ischemic stroke is the most frequent subtype, accounting for 55% to 90% of all cases, some worldwide variations in subtype distribution are observed (Figure 1.3).[19–25,27–35,39–41]

In contemporary population-based registries, the proportion of intracerebral hemorrhage reaches 22%. Older studies reported a greater proportion of hemorrhagic stroke in Asia, where they account for up to 35% of all strokes,[44,45] than in western countries. This disparity was attributed initially to a different distribution of genetic, environmental, sociocultural, and vascular risk factors. However, recent reliable data from a population-based study conducted in Beijing did not indicate an excess of intracerebral hemorrhage, and previous findings may, in part, have been distorted by poor methodology applied in these studies and/or changes in vascular risk factors over time.[21] Interestingly, in low- to middle-income countries, incidence rates of intracerebral hemorrhage and subarachnoid hemorrhage are almost twice those in high-income countries.[13]

Ischemic stroke itself is also a heterogeneous disease with different etiologic subtypes, usually classified according to the Trial of Org 10172 in Acute Stroke Treatment (TOAST) classification.[46] Population-based studies have demonstrated large differences in the distribution of these subtypes among ischemic patients with stroke, which may be the result of a number of reasons (Figure 1.4).[47–54]

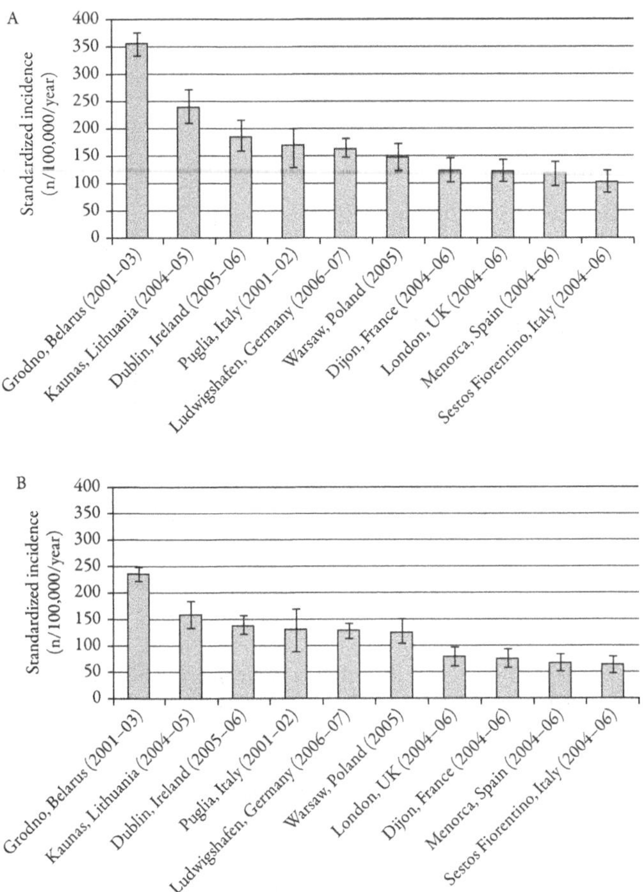

FIGURE 1.2 (A, B) Standardized incidence of stroke in men (A) and women (B) in contemporary European population-based registries. The European population is used as the standard.

First, the age structure of the study population is of major importance because the frequency of ischemic subtypes differs according to age. For example, the proportion of cardioembolic stroke increases sharply with age because of the rise in the prevalence of atrial fibrillation in elderly people.[55] Conversely, the category "other cause" is more frequent in young people, given the high proportion of cervical dissection at this age.[56] Second, race/ethnic discrepancies may also account for variations among studies in ischemic stroke subtype distribution, which can be explained by differences in the prevalence of vascular risk factors, and in both socioeconomic status and environmental status.[48,49,53] Last, because the TOAST classification requires the use of diagnostic procedures, discrepancies in access to medical resources can account for differences in the findings of studies. Consistent with this remark, the proportion of ischemic stroke of undetermined cause ranges from 22% to 52%. This category includes patients with insufficient diagnostic investigation.

TEMPORAL TRENDS IN STROKE INCIDENCE AND PROJECTIONS

In recent decades, few studies have evaluated temporal trends in stroke incidence. Stable incidence was observed in Dijon, France (1985–2006)[57]; and Rochester, Minnesota (1970–1989)[58]; whereas

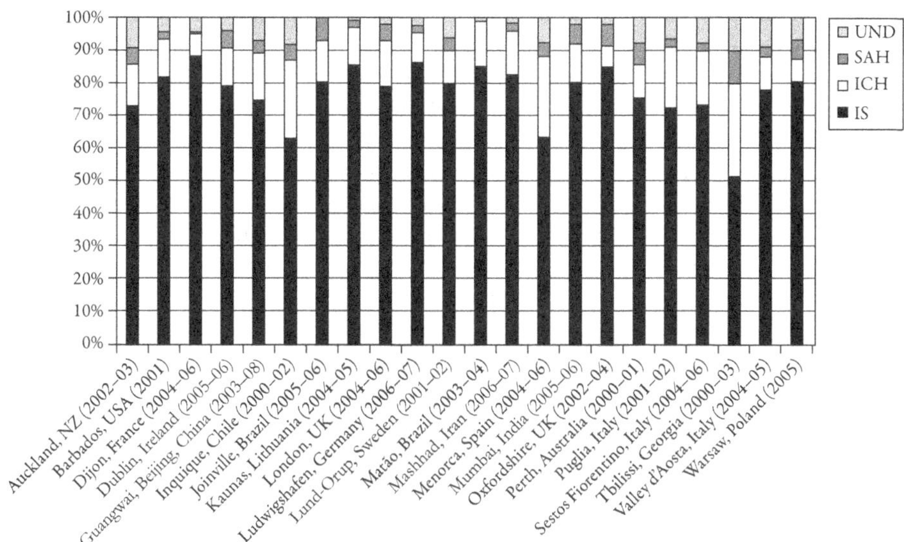

FIGURE 1.3 Distribution of stroke subtypes in contemporary stroke incidence studies. ICH, intracerebral hemorrhage; IS, ischemic stroke; SAH, subarachnoid hemorrhage; UND, undetermined stroke.

decreasing rates were noted in Oxfordshire, UK (between 1981–1984 and 2002–2004)[33]; Tartu, Estonia (between 1991–1992 and 2001–2003)[26]; Perth, Australia (between 1989–1990, 1995–1996, and 2000–2001)[34]; Auckland, New Zealand (between 1981–1982, 1991–1992, and 2002–2003)[25]; Val d'Aosta, Italy (between 1989 and 2004–2005)[31]; Joinville, Brazil (between 1995 and 2006)[59]; and Novosibirsk, Russia (from 1982–1992).[60] Conversely, stroke incidence increased in Lund-Orup, Sweden (between 1983–1985, 1993–1995, and 2001–2002).[23]

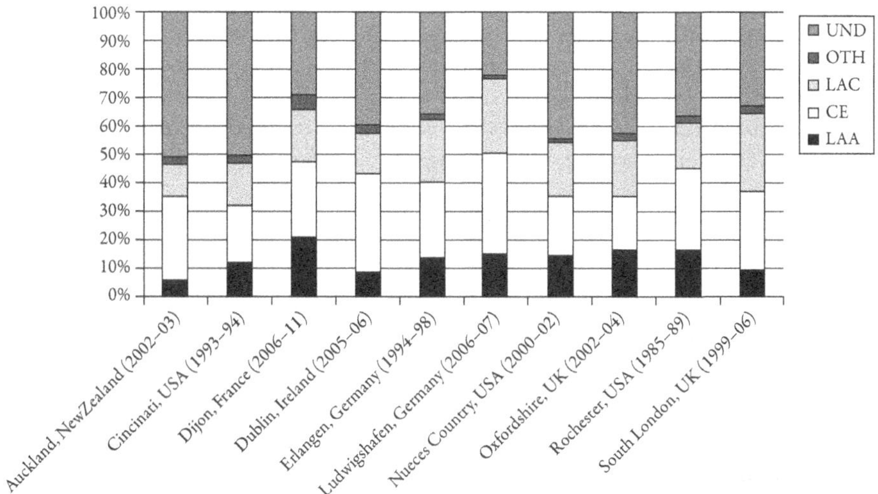

FIGURE 1.4 Distribution of etiologic subtypes of ischemic stroke in population-based studies. CE, cardioembolic; LAA, large-artery atherosclerosis; LAC, lacunar; OTH, other cause; UND, undetermined cause.

A meta-analysis of available data concluded there was a 42% decrease in stroke incidence in high-income countries from 1970 to 2008, whereas stroke incidence in low- to middle-income countries more than doubled during the same time.[13] Of note, these divergent trends were evident in both younger (<75 years) and older (≥75 years) individuals, although they were more pronounced in the older group. Improvements in preventive treatment and reductions in risk factors at the population level account for the reduction in stroke incidence in high-income countries, whereas the increase in stroke incidence observed in low- to middle-income countries could reflect the health and demographic transitions in these countries, and underlines the urgent need for the implementation of preventive strategies in these regions. Concomitant with these temporal trends in incidence, the mean age at stroke onset has increased over time in high-income countries, which may reflect the aging population and improvements in primary prevention leading to an increase in stroke-free life expectancy.[61]

Last, the WHO estimates indicate that the total number of first-ever strokes is expected to rise to 23 million annually by 2030 in the absence of additional populationwide interventions.[62]

INCIDENCE OF TIA

Only limited data about the incidence of TIA are available in the literature, probably because of the difficulty to investigate this disease reliably, resulting from the fact that diagnosis is sometimes difficult, and that a high proportion of patients with TIA do not seek medical attention, making it hard to obtain exhaustive case ascertainment. Recent population-based studies have estimated that age adjusted to the European population TIA incidence ranges from 28 to 59/100,000/year.[33,63–65]

Stroke Recurrence

After a first-ever stroke, the cumulative risk of recurrence ranges from 1% to 4% at 1 month, from 7% to 13% at 1 year, and reaches almost 40% at 10 years (Table 1.1).[66–70]

However, this risk may be underestimated, because studies excluded from the definition of stroke recurrence any stroke that occurred within 7 or 21 days in the same territory as the first event. Hence, when these patients with early recurrence were taken into account, the 3-month recurrence rate was substantially greater—about 15%—in the Oxford Vascular Study.[71]

Similar recurrence rates are observed for ischemic stroke and intracerebral hemorrhage, whereas patients with subarachnoid hemorrhage have a lower risk of stroke recurrence (<10% at 10 years).[66] The ischemic stroke etiologic subtype is associated strongly with recurrence. A meta-analysis of population-based studies revealed that 3-month recurrences were more frequent in ischemic stroke from large-artery atherosclerosis (14.3%) than in cardioembolic stroke (7.7%), lacunar stroke (2%), and ischemic stroke from undetermined cause (5.6%).[72] Patients presenting with a TIA are also at a high risk of subsequent stroke. The recurrence rates have been estimated at 5% at 7 days, and population-based studies demonstrated an annual risk ranging from 2% to 5% (although very early recurrences were excluded in these studies).[73]

Besides the risk of subsequent stroke, patients with stroke may also have other vascular diseases. The risk of myocardial infarction is 2.2%, and that of nonstroke vascular death is 2.1% (95% confidence interval, 1.9–2.4).[74] Very similar numbers are observed in patients with TIA.[73]

TABLE 1.1

Recurrence after first-ever stroke in population-based studies using a similar definition

Study place	Study period	Type of stroke included	Recurrence rates (%)					
			1 Month	6 Months	1 Year	2 Years	5 Years	10 Years
Erlangen, Germany	1994–1998	Ischemic stroke				10		
Northern Manhattan, New York	1990–1997	Ischemic stroke	2		8		18	
Oxfordshire, UK	1981–1986	Overall stroke		9	13		30	
Perth, Australia	1995–1996	Overall stroke	1	6	9		23	
Rochester, Minnesota	1975–1989	Ischemic stroke	4	9	12	17	29	39
South London, UK	1995–2004	Overall stroke			7		16	25

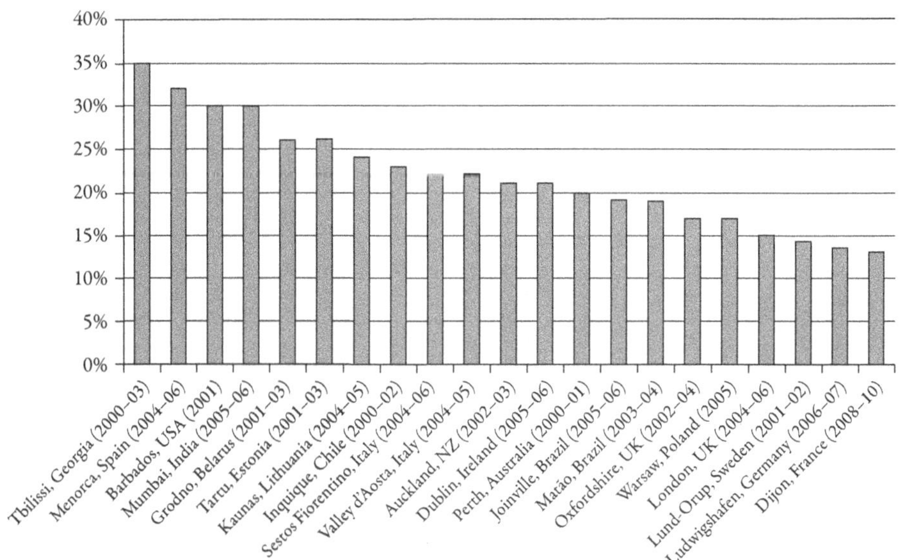

FIGURE 1.5 One-month case fatality rates of stroke in contemporary population-based registries.

Stroke Mortality

One-month case fatality rates of stroke range from 13% to 35% (Figure 1.5) in contemporary population-based registries.[19,22–24,26–32,33,34,40,41,75,76]

Rates are the highest for intracerebral hemorrhage (25%–61%) and subarachnoid hemorrhage (26%–48%), and the lowest for ischemic stroke (9%–19%). In addition, a poorer outcome is noted in low- to middle-income countries than in high-income countries. Less data are available for long-term mortality. Rates range from 25% to 38% at 1 year, 50% to 60% at 5 years, and up to 75% at 10 years.[24,75,77–84]

The prognosis of patients with ischemic stroke is heterogeneous and depends greatly on the underlying etiologic subtype. Worse survival is observed in patients with cardioembolic stroke (range, 40%–55% at 2 years) and, to a lesser degree, in those with stroke from large-artery atherosclerosis (range, 58%–80% at 2 years) compared with patients with lacunar stroke (range, 80%–90% at 2 years).[84–88]

Stroke is responsible for approximately 6 million deaths each year worldwide, and 85% of stroke deaths occur in low- to middle-income countries.[62] Age- and sex-adjusted mortality rates for stroke varies from 24 to 251/100,000/year.[10] The highest rates are observed in North Asia, Eastern Europe, Central Africa, and the South Pacific. According to WHO projections, 7.8 million stroke deaths per year are expected by 2030.[62]

Prevalence and Burden of Stroke

Scarce information exists on the prevalence of stroke. Studies revealed that age-standardized prevalence for people age 65 years or older ranges from 36 to 73/1000 population.[89–91] On the basis of a review of available data, Hankey and Warlow[92] estimated that, in a population of 1 million in a developed country, 12,000 individuals have had a previous cerebrovascular event: TIA

(n = 3000), stroke (n = 8000), or both (n = 1000). As for incidence, stroke prevalence is 40% greater among men than women. The male-to-female ratio peaks in the age range of 65 to 74 years, whereas it tends to decrease drop in the 75- to 84-year age range, and significantly so in the a range of 85 years or older.[42] From WHO data, the worldwide prevalence of stroke survivors was estimated at 62 million globally in 2005, and projections indicate that it will increase to 77 million by 2030.[62]

Besides its deleterious consequences on survival, stroke resulted in more than 50 million lost DALYs worldwide in 2005, accounting for 13% of the global burden of disease in the population older than 60 years, and 38% of the burden of cardiovascular diseases in the same age group.[62] DALY loss rates are almost four times greater in low-income countries than in middle-income and high-income countries, and a greater burden is observed in several areas such as Asia, Eastern Europe, Central Africa, and the South Pacific.[10]

Conclusion

Stroke and cerebrovascular diseases are very frequent and are associated with adverse consequences in terms of death and disability. Although recent improvements have been observed in high-income countries, stroke incidence is increasing dramatically in developing countries. Furthermore, the worldwide aging population will lead to an increase in the absolute number of patients experiencing a cerebrovascular event. These data clearly indicate the urgent need for a better identification and understanding of risk factors to improve both primary and secondary prevention.

References

1. World Health Organization. The world health report 2000: health systems improving performance. Geneva: World Health Organization, 2000.
2. Malmgren R, Warlow C, Bamford J, Sandercock P. Geographical and secular trends in stroke incidence. *Lancet.* 1987;2:1196–1200.
3. Hatano S. Experience from a multicenter register: a preliminary report. *Bull WHO.* 1976;54:541–553.
4. Kidwell CS, Alger JR, Di Salle F, et al. Diffusion MRI in patients with transient ischemic attacks. *Stroke.* 1999;30:1174–1180.
5. Engelter ST, Provenzale JM, Petrella JR, Alberts MJ. Diffusion MR imaging and transient ischemic attacks. *Stroke.* 1999;30:2762–2763.
6. Albers GW, Caplan LR, Easton JD, et al. Transient ischemic attack: proposal for a new definition. *N Engl J Med.* 2002;347:1713–1716.
7. Béjot Y, Giroud M. Epidemiological implications of the new definition of transient ischemic attack. *Neuroepidemiology.* 2009;33:358.
8. Murray CJL. Rethinking DALYs. In: Murray CJL, Lopez AD, eds. *The global burden of disease.* Vol. 1. Cambridge, MA: Harvard School of Public Health, 1996:1–98.
9. Hong KS. Disability-adjusted life years analysis: implications for stroke research. *J Clin Neurol.* 2011;7:109–114.
10. Johnston SC, Mendis S, Mathers CD. Global variation in stroke burden and mortality: estimates from monitoring, surveillance, and modelling. *Lancet Neurol.* 2009;8:345–354.
11. Sudlow CL, Warlow CP. Comparing stroke incidence worldwide: what makes studies comparable? *Stroke.* 1996;27:550–558.
12. Feigin V, Hoorn SV. How to study stroke incidence. *Lancet.* 2004;363:1920.

13. Feigin VL, Lawes CM, Bennett DA, Barker-Collo SL, Parag V. Worldwide stroke incidence and early case fatality reported in 56 population-based studies: a systematic review. *Lancet Neurol.* 2009;8:355–369.
14. Correia M, Silva MR, Matos I, et al. Prospective community-based study of stroke in northern Portugal: incidence and case fatality in rural and urban populations. *Stroke.* 2004;35:2048–2053.
15. Giroud M, Lemesle M, Quantin C, et al. A hospital-based and a population-based stroke registry yield different results: the experience in Dijon, France. *Neuroepidemiology.* 1997;16:15–21.
16. World Health Organization. WHO STEPS stroke manual: the WHO STEPwise approach to stroke surveillance. Geneva: World Health Organization, 2006. Available at: http://www.who.int/chp/steps/Manual.pdf (accessed July 18, 2012).
17. Truelsen T, Heuschmann PU, Bonita R, et al. Standard method for developing stroke registers in low-income and middle-income countries: experiences from a feasibility study of a stepwise approach to stroke surveillance (STEPS Stroke). *Lancet Neurol.* 2007;6:134–139.
18. World Health Organization. Burden of diseases statistics. Geneva, Switzerland: World Health Organization. Available at: http://www.who.int/healthinfo/bod/en/index.html (accessed July 18, 2012).
19. Kulesh SD, Filina NA, Frantava NM, et al. Incidence and case-fatality of stroke on the east border of the European Union: the Grodno Stroke Study. *Stroke.* 2010;41:2726–2730.
20. Azarpazhooh MR, Etemadi MM, Donnan GA, et al. Excessive incidence of stroke in Iran: evidence from the Mashhad Stroke Incidence Study (MSIS), a population-based study of stroke in the Middle East. *Stroke.* 2010;41:e3–e10.
21. Fang XH, Wang WH, Zhang XQ, et al. Incidence and survival of symptomatic lacunar infarction in a Beijing population: a 6-year prospective study. *Eur J Neurol.* 2012;19:1114–1120.
22. Dalal PM, Malik S, Bhattacharjee M, et al. Population-based stroke survey in Mumbai, India: incidence and 28-day case fatality. *Neuroepidemiology.* 2008;31:254–261.
23. Hallstrom B, Jonsson A-C, Nerbrand C, Norrving B, Lindgren A. Stroke incidence and survival in the beginning of the 21st century in southern Sweden: comparisons with the late 20th century and projections into the future. *Stroke.* 2008;39:10–15.
24. Minelli C, Fen LF, Minelli DPC. Stroke incidence, prognosis, 30-day, and 1-year case fatality rates in Matao, Brazil: a population-based prospective study. *Stroke.* 2007;38:2906–2911.
25. Anderson C, Carter KN, Hackett ML, et al. Trends in stroke incidence in Auckland, New Zealand, during 1981 to 2003. *Stroke.* 2005;36:2087–2093.
26. Vibo R, Korv J, Roose M. The third stroke registry in Tartu, Estonia: decline of stroke incidence and 28-day case-fatality rate since 1991. *Stroke.* 2005;36:2544–2548.
27. Cabral NL, Gonçalves AR, Longo AL, et al. Incidence of stroke subtypes, prognosis and prevalence of risk factors in Joinville, Brazil: a 2 year community based study. *J Neurol Neurosurg Psychiatry.* 2009;80:755–761.
28. Tsiskaridze A, Djibuti M, van Melle G, et al. Stroke incidence and 30-day case-fatality in a suburb of Tbilisi: results of the first prospective population-based study in Georgia. *Stroke.* 2004;35:2523–2528.
29. Corbin DOC, Poddar V, Hennis A, et al. Incidence and case fatality rates of first-ever stroke in a black Caribbean population: the Barbados Register of Strokes. *Stroke.* 2004;35:1254–1258.
30. Lavados PM, Sacks C, Prina L, et al. Incidence, 30-day case-fatality rate, and prognosis of stroke in Iquique, Chile: a 2-year community-based prospective study (PISCIS project). *Lancet.* 2005;365:2206–2215.
31. Corso GBE, Giardini G. Community-base study of stroke incidence in the Aosta Valley, Italy: CARe–Cerebrovascular Aosta Registry: years 2004–2005. *Neuroepidemiology.* 2009;32:186–195.

32. Manobianca G, Zoccolella S, Petruzzellis A, Miccoli A, Logroscino G. The incidence of major stroke subtypes in southern Italy: a population-based study. *Eur J Neurol.* 2010;17:1148–1155.
33. Rothwell PM, Coull AJ, Giles MF, et al. Change in stroke incidence, mortality, case-fatality, severity, and risk factors in Oxfordshire, UK from 1981 to 2004 (Oxford Vascular Study). *Lancet.* 2004;363:1925–1933.
34. Islam MS, Anderson CS, Hankey GJ, et al. Trends in incidence and outcome of stroke in Perth, Western Australia during 1989 to 2001: the Perth Community Stroke Study. *Stroke.* 2008;39:776–782.
35. Béjot Y, Aboa-Eboulé C, Durier J. Prevalence of early dementia after first-ever stroke: a 24-year population-based study. *Stroke.* 2011;42:607–612.
36. Mihalka L, Smolanka V, Bulecza B, Mulesa S, Bereczki D. A population study of stroke in West Ukraine: incidence, stroke services, and 30-day case fatality. *Stroke.* 2001;32:2227–2231.
37. Feigin VL, Wiebers DO, Nikitin YP, O'Fallon WM, Whisnant JP. Stroke epidemiology in Novosibirsk, Russia: a population-based study. *Mayo Clin Proc.* 1995;70:847–852.
38. Walker R, Whiting D, Unwin N, et al. Stroke incidence in rural and urban Tanzania: a prospective, community-based study. *Lancet Neurol.* 2010;9:786–792.
39. Heuschmann PU, Di Carlo A, Béjot Y, et al. Incidence of stroke in Europe at the beginning of the 21st century. *Stroke.* 2009;40:1557–1563.
40. Kelly PJ, Crispino G, Sheehan O, et al. Incidence, event rates, and early outcome of stroke in Dublin, Ireland: the North Dublin Population Stroke Study. *Stroke.* 2012;43:2042–2047.
41. Palm F, Urbanek C, Rose S, et al. Stroke incidence and survival in Ludwigshafen am Rhein, Germany: the Ludwigshafen Stroke Study (LuSSt). *Stroke.* 2010;41:1865–1870.
42. Appelros P, Stegmayr B, Terént A. Sex differences in stroke epidemiology: a systematic review. *Stroke.* 2009;40:1082–1090.
43. Reeves MJ, Bushnell CD, Howard G, et al. Sex differences in stroke: epidemiology, clinical presentation, medical care, and outcomes. *Lancet Neurol.* 2008;7:915–926.
44. Morikawa Y, Nakagawa H, Naruse Y, et al. Trends in stroke incidence and acute case fatality in a Japanese rural area: the Oyabe Study. *Stroke.* 2000;31:1583–1587.
45. Liu M, Wu B, Wang WZ, Lee LM, Zhang SH, Kong LZ. Stroke in China: epidemiology, prevention, and management strategies. *Lancet Neurol.* 2007;6:456–464.
46. Adams HP Jr, Bendixen BH, Kappelle LJ, et al Classification of subtype of acute ischemic stroke: definitions for use in a multicenter clinical trial. TOAST: Trial of Org 10172 in Acute Stroke Treatment. *Stroke.* 1993;24:35–41.
47. Schulz UG, Rothwell PM. Differences in vascular risk factors between etiological subtypes of ischemic stroke: importance of population-based studies. *Stroke.* 2003;34:2050–2059.
48. Feigin V, Carter K, Hackett M, et al. Ethnic disparities in incidence of stroke subtypes: Auckland Regional Community Stroke Study, 2002–2003. *Lancet Neurol.* 2006;5:130–139.
49. Schneider AT, Kissela B, Woo D, et al. Ischemic stroke subtypes: a population-based study of incidence rates among blacks and whites. *Stroke.* 2004;35:1552–1556.
50. Palm F, Urbanek C, Wolf J, et al. Etiology, risk factors and sex differences in ischemic stroke in the Ludwigshafen Stroke Study, a population-based stroke registry. *Cerebrovasc Dis.* 2012;33:69–75.
51. Marnane M, Duggan CA, Sheehan OC, et al. Stroke subtype classification to mechanism-specific and undetermined categories by TOAST, A-S-C-O, and causative classification system: direct comparison in the North Dublin Population Stroke Study. *Stroke.* 2010;41:1579–1586.
52. Uchino K, Risser JM, Smith MA, Moyé LA, Morgenstern LB. Ischemic stroke subtypes among Mexican Americans and non-Hispanic whites: the BASIC Project. *Neurology.* 2004;63:574–576.

53. Hajat C, Heuschmann PU, Coshall C, et al. Incidence of aetiological subtypes of stroke in a multi-ethnic population based study: the South London Stroke Register. *J Neurol Neurosurg Psychiatry.* 2011;82:527–533.
54. Béjot Y, Caillier M, Ben Salem D, Couvreur G, Rouaud O, Osseby GV, et al. Ischaemic stroke subtypes and associated risk factors: a French population based study. *J Neurol Neurosurg Psychiatry.* 2008;79:1344–1348.
55. Go AS, Hylek EM, Phillips KA, et al. Prevalence of diagnosed atrial fibrillation in adults: national implications for rhythm management and stroke prevention: the AnTicoagulation and Risk Factors in Atrial Fibrillation (ATRIA) Study. *JAMA.* 2001;285:2370–2375.
56. Debette S, Leys D. Cervical-artery dissections: predisposing factors, diagnosis, and outcome. *Lancet Neurol.* 2009;8:668–678.
57. Béjot Y, Osseby GV, Aboa-Eboulé C, et al. Dijon's vanishing lead with regard to low incidence of stroke. *Eur J Neurol.* 2009;16:324–329.
58. Brown RD, Whisnant JP, Sicks JD, O'Fallon WM, Wiebers DO. Stroke incidence, prevalence, and survival: secular trends in Rochester, Minnesota, through 1989. *Stroke.* 1996;27:373–380.
59. Cabral NL, Gonçalves AR, Longo AL, et al. Trends in stroke incidence, mortality and case fatality rates in Joinville, Brazil: 1995–2006. *J Neurol Neurosurg Psychiatry.* 2009;80:749–754.
60. Feigin VL, Wiebers DO, Whisnant JP, O'Fallon WM. Stroke incidence and 30-day case-fatality rates in Novosibirsk, Russia, 1982 through 1992. *Stroke.* 1995;26:924–929.
61. Béjot Y, Giroud M. Mean age at stroke onset: an instructive tool from epidemiological studies. *Eur J Neurol.* 2009;16:e3.
62. Strong K, Mathers C, Bonita R. Preventing stroke: saving lives around the world. *Lancet Neurol.* 2007;6:182–187.
63. Béjot Y, Rouaud O, Benatru I, et al. Trends in the incidence of transient ischemic attacks, premorbid risk factors and the use of preventive treatments in the population of Dijon, France from 1985 to 2004. *Cerebrovasc Dis.* 2007;23:126–131.
64. Fonseca PG, Weiss PA, Harger R, et al. Transient ischemic attack incidence in joinville, Brazil, 2010: a population-based study. *Stroke.* 2012;43:1159–1162.
65. Cancelli I, Janes F, Gigli GL, et al. Incidence of transient ischemic attack and early stroke risk: validation of the ABCD2 score in an Italian population-based study. *Stroke.* 2011;42:2751–2757.
66. Mohan KM, Crichton SL, Grieve AP, Rudd AG, Wolfe CD, Heuschmann PU. Frequency and predictors for the risk of stroke recurrence up to 10 years after stroke: the South London Stroke Register. *J Neurol Neurosurg Psychiatry.* 2009;80:1012–1018.
67. Petty GW, Brown RD Jr, Whisnant JP, Sicks JD, O'Fallon WM, Wiebers DO. Survival and recurrence after first cerebral infarction: a population-based study in Rochester, Minnesota, 1975 through 1989. *Neurology.* 1998;50:208–216.
68. Hardie K, Jamrozik K, Hankey GJ, Broadhurst RJ, Anderson C. Trends in five-year survival and risk of recurrent stroke after first-ever stroke in the Perth Community Stroke Study. *Cerebrovasc Dis.* 2005;19:179–185.
69. Hartmann A, Rundek T, Mast H, et al. Mortality and causes of death after first ischemic stroke: the Northern Manhattan Stroke Study. *Neurology.* 2001;57:2000–2005.
70. Burn J, Dennis M, Bamford J, Sandercock P, Wade D, Warlow C. Long-term risk of recurrent stroke after a first-ever stroke: the Oxfordshire Community Stroke Project. *Stroke.* 1994;25:333–337.
71. Coull AJ, Rothwell PM. Underestimation of the early risk of recurrent stroke: evidence of the need for a standard definition. *Stroke.* 2004;35:1925–1929.
72. Lovett JK, Coull AJ, Rothwell PM. Early risk of recurrence by subtype of ischemic stroke in population-based incidence studies. *Neurology.* 2004;62:569–573.

73. Pendlebury ST, Rothwell PM. Risk of recurrent stroke, other vascular events and dementia after transient ischaemic attack and stroke. *Cerebrovasc Dis.* 2009;27(Suppl 3):1–11.
74. Touzé E, Varenne O, Chatellier G, Peyrard S, Rothwell PM, Mas JL. Risk of myocardial infarction and vascular death after transient ischemic attack and ischemic stroke: a systematic review and meta-analysis. *Stroke.* 2005;36:2748–2755.
75. Feigin VL, Barker-Collo S, Parag V, et al. Auckland Stroke Outcomes Study. Part 1: gender, stroke types, ethnicity, and functional outcomes 5 years poststroke. *Neurology.* 2010;75:1597–1607.
76. Heuschmann PU, Wiedmann S, Wellwood I, et al. Three-month stroke outcome: the European Registers of Stroke (EROS) investigators. *Neurology.* 2011;76:159–165.
77. Chausson N, Olindo S, Cabre P, Saint-Vil M, Smadja D. Five-year outcome of a stroke cohort in Martinique, French West Indies: etude realisee en Martinique et centree sur l'incidence des accidents vasculaires cerebraux, part 2. *Stroke.* 2010;41:594–599.
78. Dennis MS, Burn JP, Sandercock PA, Bamford JM, Wade DT, Warlow CP. Long-term survival after first-ever stroke: the Oxfordshire Community Stroke Project. *Stroke.* 1993;24:796–800.
79. Ikebe T, Ozawa H, Lida M, Shimamoto T, Handa K, Komachi Y. Long-term prognosis after stroke: a community-based study in Japan. *J Epidemiol.* 2001;11:8–15.
80. Dombovy M, Basford J, Whisnant J, Bergstrahl E. Disability and use of rehabilitation services following stroke in Rochester, Minnesota, 1975–1979. *Stroke.* 1987;18:830–836.
81. Hankey GJ, Jamrozik K, Broadhurst RJ, et al. Five-year survival after first-ever stroke and related prognostic factors in the Perth Community Stroke Study. *Stroke.* 2000;31:2080–2086.
82. Kulesh SD, Kastsinevich TM, Kliatskova LA, et al. Long-term outcome after stroke in Belarus: the Grodno Stroke Study. *Stroke.* 2011;42:3274–3276.
83. Wolfe CD, Crichton SL, Heuschmann PU, et al. Estimates of outcomes up to ten years after stroke: analysis from the prospective South London Stroke Register. *PLoS Med.* 2011;8:e1001033.
84. Béjot Y, Jacquin A, Rouaud O, et al. One-year survival of demented stroke patients: data from the Dijon Stroke Registry, France (1985–2008). *Eur J Neurol.* 2012;19:712–717.
85. Kolominsky-Rabas PL, Weber M, Gefeller O, Neundoerfer B, Heuschmann PU. Epidemiology of ischemic stroke subtypes according to TOAST criteria: incidence, recurrence, and long-term survival in ischemic stroke subtypes: a population-based study. *Stroke.* 2001;32:2735–2740.
86. Petty GW, Brown RD Jr, Whisnant JP, Sicks JD, O'Fallon WM, Wiebers DO. Ischemic stroke subtypes: a population-based study of functional outcome, survival, and recurrence. *Stroke.* 2000;31:1062–1068.
87. Béjot Y, Catteau A, Caillier M, et al. Trends in incidence, risk factors, and survival in symptomatic lacunar stroke in Dijon, France, from 1989 to 2006: a population-based study. *Stroke.* 2008;39:1945–1951.
88. Béjot Y, Ben Salem D, Osseby GV, et al. Epidemiology of ischemic stroke from atrial fibrillation in Dijon, France, from 1985 to 2006. *Neurology.* 2009;72:346–353.
89. Feigin VL, Lawes CMM, Bennett DA, Anderson CS. Stroke epidemiology: a review of population-based studies of incidence, prevalence and case-fatality in the late 20th century. *Lancet Neurol* 2003;2:43–53.
90. Venketasubramanian N, Tan LC, Sahadevan S, et al. Prevalence of stroke among Chinese, Malay, and Indian Singaporeans: a community-based tri-racial cross-sectional survey. *Stroke.* 2005;36:551–556.
91. Orlandi G, Gelli A, Fanucchi S, Tognoni G, Acerbi G, Murri L. Prevalence of stroke and transient ischaemic attack in the elderly population of an Italian rural community. *Eur J Epidemiol.* 2003;18:879–882.
92. Hankey GJ, Warlow CP. Treatment and secondary prevention of stroke: evidence, costs, and effects on individuals and populations. *Lancet.* 1999;354:1457–1463.

II

Genetic Risk Factors

2

INTRODUCTION TO GENETIC RISK FACTORS FOR CEREBROVASCULAR DISEASE

Bradford B. Worrall

Introduction

Reports of familial occurrence of cerebrovascular disease date to antiquity. During the seventh century BCE, two brothers who were successive Elamite kings appear to have had strokes that ended their reigns, and these familial strokes likely contributed to the Assyrian ascension and ultimate domination at the time.[1] Stroke remains a devastating personal and public health burden. Understanding the genetic contributors to stroke risk provides information on individual or population risk that may allow targeted intervention, prevention, or treatment. Perhaps more important, the investigation of genetic risk in cerebrovascular disease can provide insights into the fundamental biology and pathophysiology of these diseases, and this improved mechanistic knowledge can lead to new and better targeted therapies. Stroke and cerebrovascular disease present a classic "lumper" versus "splitter" conundrum. Ultimately, genetics may prove that lumping or splitting or both are appropriate, but for now this phenotypic heterogeneity presents a challenge for researchers and clinicians.[2]

Genetic conditions such as sickle cell and Fabry disease have long been recognized as having increased risk for stroke as part of these diseases.[3] In addition, specific monogenic stroke conditions such as cerebral autosomal dominant arteriopathy with subcortical infarcts and leukoencephalopathy, cerebral autosomal recessive arteriopathy with subcortical infarcts and leukoencephalopathy, and retinal vasculopathy with cerebral leukodystrophy (also known as hereditary endotheliopathy retinopathy nephropathy and stroke) manifest as ischemic stroke.[4] Genetic forms of intracerebral hemorrhage (familial amyloid angiopathies) and vascular malformations (cerebral cavernous malformations, Osler-Weber-Rendu, and so on) that include cerebral vascular malformations as a primary or secondary phenotypic component are also often monogenic or single-gene conditions.[5,6] Intracranial aneurysm can occur in syndromic connective tissue diseases (adult polycystic kidney disease, vascular Ehlers-Danlos, Loeys-Dietz syndrome, COL4A1 syndrome, or Marfan disease).[7] Newly described genetic disorders such as aortic aneurysm/Moyamoya disease associated with mutations of the *ACTA2* gene have challenged our conceptualization of nonatherosclerotic arteriopathies, demonstrating a clear overlap among these phenotypes.[8] These monogenic conditions are rare individually; collectively, however, they account for an important clinical population and furthermore provide insight into the mechanisms and pathophysiologies of the corresponding common forms of cerebrovascular disease.[6]

The contributions of genetic variation to more common forms of cerebrovascular disease fall under the category of "complex genetics," in which genetic variants play a probabilistic rather than a deterministic role in risk for stroke. These genetic risks often interact with environmental exposures or other genetic or nongenetic heritable factors. Indeed, genetics may influence any complex phenotype through multiple mechanisms (Table 2.1). Genetic factors may directly alter the risk for a disease. Genetics may alter the severity of a disease (i.e., if you get the disease, you are affected more severely). Similarly, genetics may alter people's susceptibility to or severity of key risk factors such as hypertension or dyslipidemia. Gene-by-environment interactions can influence risk in the presence of an exposure such as cigarette smoking. Last, genetics may alter recovery from injury. Given that cerebrovascular disease represents multiple distinct and overlapping pathophysiological processes, the complexity quickly increases. Furthermore, as genetic researchers begin to identify novel mechanisms, the putative mechanism of genetic influence may change. For example, something thought to have a direct effect on risk may be discovered to mediate through a previously unrecognized interaction with a risk factor.

To date we have a handful of established or highly promising stroke genes for ischemic stroke[9] and ischemic stroke subtypes,[10–14] as well as intracerebral hemorrhage[15] and intracranial aneurysms.[16,17] Recent and ongoing efforts strive to amass an adequate number of stroke cases to have adequate

TABLE 2.1

Mechanisms by which genetic factors may influence complex phenotypes

General	Cerebrovascular specific	Example
Directly influence stroke risk	Harboring a particular genetic variant raises or lowers risk of stroke phenotype.	HDAC9
Influence severity	Harboring a particular genetic variant modifies the severity of the stroke phenotype if experienced.	Ischemic tolerance/ vulnerability
Influence likelihood of risk factor	Harboring a particular genetic variant raises or lowers the risk of a risk factor for a stroke phenotype.	Genetic determinants of T2DM
Influence response to risk factor	Harboring a particular genetic variant influences the likelihood of a cerebrovascular phenotype in the presence of a risk factor.	GWAS of CVD in T2DM
Influence response to an environmental exposure	Harboring a particular genetic variant influences the likelihood of a cerebrovascular phenotype in the presence of an environmental exposure.	Interaction of smoking and genetic burden in intracranial aneurysm
Influence recovery	Harboring a particular genetic variant influences recovery.	Neural plasticity

CVD, cerebrovascular disease; GWAS, genomewide association study; HDAC9, histone deacetylase 9; T2DM, type 2 diabetes mellitus.

power for discovery, as has been applied successfully to other complex genetic diseases and conditions using tens to hundreds of thousands of cases with substantial increases in yield with the successively larger data sets. The heterogeneity of mechanistic phenotypes included under stroke or even ischemic stroke rapidly partition even these larger samples into modest numbers at best. All of this occurs against a backdrop of waning enthusiasm for genomewide association studies (GWASs) as an approach. Next-generation genomics, gene expression, and epigenetics hold promise to help explain the "missing heritability" for stroke and other phenotypes.[18] Nevertheless, GWASs remain important and incompletely explored approaches for diseases such as stroke. Moving forward, GWASs will likely contribute in parallel to these and other newer approaches.

International efforts such as the International Stroke Genetics Consortium (ISGC) and METASTROKE provide venues for this important collaborative effort that bridge and supplement funded efforts such as the Wellcome Trust Case Control Consortium II—Stroke, the Australian Genetics Stroke Collaboration, and the Cohorts for Heart and Aging Research in Genomic Epidemiology (CHARGE) Consortium in ischemic stroke and related phenotypes. We anticipate the first results from the National Institute of Neurological Disorders and Stroke–funded Stroke Genetics Network in fall 2015, with cross-consortial meta-analyses and replication planned. Working groups in the ISGC focused on intracerebral hemorrhage and intracranial aneurysm genetic risk. This book represents a great deal of recent and ongoing work that is hot off the presses. It is an exciting but daunting time in stroke genetics.

REFERENCES

1. Ashrafian H. Familial stroke 2700 years ago. *Stroke.* 2010;41:e187; author reply, e8.
2. Falcone GJ, Malik R, Dichgans M, Rosand J. Current concepts and clinical applications of stroke genetics. *Lancet Neurol.* 2014;13:405–418.
3. Meschia JF, Worrall BB, Rich SS. Genetic susceptibility to ischemic stroke. *Nat Rev Neurol.* 2011;7:369–378.
4. Bersano A, Borellini L, Motto C, et al. Molecular basis of young ischemic stroke. *Curr Med Chem* 2013;20:3818–3839.
5. Lanfranconi S, Franco G, Borellini L, et al. Genetics of cerebral hemorrhage and microbleeds. *Panminerva Med.* 2013;55:11–28.
6. Leblanc GG, Golanov E, Awad IA, Young WL. Biology of vascular malformations of the brain. *Stroke.* 2009;40:e694–e702.
7. Debette S, Germain DP. Neurologic manifestations of inherited disorders of connective tissue. *Handbook Clin Neurol.* 2014;119:565–576.
8. Southerland AM, Meschia JF, Worrall BB. Shared associations of nonatherosclerotic, large-vessel, cerebrovascular arteriopathies: considering intracranial aneurysms, cervical artery dissection, Moyamoya disease and fibromuscular dysplasia. *Curr Opin Neurol.* 2013;26:13–28.
9. Kilarski LL, Achterberg S, Devan W, et al. Meta-analysis in over 17,900 cases of ischaemic stroke reveals a novel association at 12q24.12. *Neurology.* 2014;83:678–685.
10. Holliday EG, Maguire JM, Evans TJ, et al. Common variants at 6p21.1 are associated with large artery atherosclerotic stroke. *Nat Genet.* 2012;44:1147–1151.
11. International Stroke Genetics Consortium, Wellcome Trust Case Control Consortium, Bellenguez C, Bevan S, Gschwendtner A, et al. Genome-wide association study identifies a variant in HDAC9 associated with large vessel ischemic stroke. *Nature Genet.* 2012;44:328–333.

12. Traylor M, Farrall M, Holliday EG, et al. Genetic risk factors for ischaemic stroke and its subtypes (the METASTROKE collaboration): a meta-analysis of genome-wide association studies. *Lancet Neurol.* 2012;11:951–962.
13. Gudbjartsson DF, Holm H, Gretarsdottir S, et al. A sequence variant in *ZFHX3* on 16q22 associates with atrial fibrillation and ischemic stroke. *Nat. Genet.* 2009;41:876–878.
14. Gretarsdottir S, Thorleifsson G, Manolescu A, et al. Risk variants for atrial fibrillation on chromosome 4q25 associate with ischemic stroke. *Ann Neurol.* 2008;64:402–409.
15. Woo D, Falcone GJ, Devan WJ, et al. Meta-analysis of genome-wide association studies identifies 1q22 as a susceptibility locus for intracerebral hemorrhage. *Am J Hum Genet.* 2014;94:511–521.
16. Yasuno K, Bilguvar K, Bijlenga P, et al. Genome-wide association study of intracranial aneurysm identifies three new risk loci. *Nat Genet.* 2010;42:420–425.
17. Foroud T, Koller DL, Lai D, et al. Genome-wide association study of intracranial aneurysms confirms role of Anril and SOX17 in disease risk. *Stroke.* 2012;43:2846–2852.
18. Zeller T, Blankenberg S, Diemert P. Genomewide association studies in cardiovascular disease: an update 2011. *Clin Chem.* 2012;58:92–103.

3

MONOGENIC DISEASES CAUSING CEREBROVASCULAR DISEASE AND STROKE

Anna Bersano

Introduction

Stroke represents a leading cause of mortality and long-term disability in developed countries.[1] Conventional and modifiable risk factors such as hypertension, atrial fibrillation, and smoking explain only a part of stroke risk, supporting the idea that risk factors not yet identified could contribute to stroke pathogenesis.[2,3] Evidence from epidemiological and twin studies support the contribution of genetic factors to stroke occurrence and outcome, although the extent of genetic predisposition is uncertain.[4–6] However, it is expected that the identification of such factors provides insights in understanding the pathophysiology of stroke aimed at developing new prevention strategies and drug therapies. The genetic contribution to common stroke is believed to be polygenic, and a monogenic basis is recognized in a small percentage of cases. However, although considered rare and believed to account for about only 1% to 5% of all strokes, monogenic diseases are probably underrecognized.[4,5] Despite some elements such as young age at onset, positive familial history, presence of specific associated clinical features, and absence of conventional vascular risk factors, which may support a suspicion of monogenic disease, the latter can be underdiagnosed simply because physicians may not include them in the differential diagnoses. Also, there may be a pleiomorphic phenotypic spectrum, in which stroke may be only one part of a systemic disorder.[7] Although rare, the diagnosis of monogenic conditions causing stroke is important for the implementation of correct management, including genetic counseling, preventive measures, and therapeutic decisions, because they are often either life-threatening or complex chronically debilitating diseases with difficult management.[8–10] Moreover, understanding the pathophysiology of these disorders may provide insight into the mechanisms underlying multifactorial ischemic stroke.

A large number of single-gene disorders have been described so far as well-known causes of stroke. However, in the literature they are not classified in a standardized and homogeneous way as a result of the phenotype variability and the association with different stroke types and subtypes (hemorrhagic or ischemic, cardioembolic, small-vessel disease, and large-vessel disease).[8] Other than the most common monogenic diseases associated with stroke—such as cerebral autosomal dominant arteriopathy with subcortical infarcts and leukoencephalopathy (CADASIL); Fabry disease; mitochondrial myopathy, encephalopathy, lactic acidosis, and stroke-like episodes (MELAS); and Marfan syndrome—other rarer single-gene diseases, associated particularly with the cerebral small-vessel disease feature, such as collagen 4A1 (COL4A1) syndrome, cerebral autosomal recessive arteriopathy with subcortical infarcts and leukoencephalopathy (CARASIL), and hereditary endotheliopathy, retinopathy, nephropathy, and stroke, have been identified more recently.

In this chapter, we provide an updated review of monogenic stroke disorders associated with ischemic and hemorrhagic stroke, including a detailed description of their epidemiology, clinical and neuroradiological presentation, genetic and pathophysiological aspects, diagnostic features and therapeutic measures. We do not discuss in detail inherited connective disorders such as vascular Ehlers–Danlos syndrome (type IV), arterial tortuosity syndrome, Marfan syndrome, *Pseudoxanthoma elasticum*, and about Moyamoya disease, which are quite rare diseases that can also lead to ischemic stroke but are associated more frequently with cervical artery dissection (with or without ischemic stroke), carotid–cavernous fistula, intracranial dissections, and aneurysms potentially causing subarachnoid or intracerebral hemorrhage.

Table 3.1 summarizes the main clinical features of monogenic disorders associated with stroke.

Small-Vessel Diseases

CEREBRAL AUTOSOMAL DOMINANT ARTERIOPATHY WITH SUBCORTICAL INFARCTS AND LEUKOENCEPHALOPATHY

CADASIL (Online Mendelian Inheritance in Man [OMIM] 125310-600276) is an autosomal dominant disease involving small cerebral arteries, and it affects middle-age adults.[11,12] It is the most common Mendelian cause of stroke.

Epidemiology

CADASIL has been reported in more than 500 families worldwide, but its overall prevalence remains uncertain probably as a result of underrecognition of the variable phenotypic expressions. The estimated prevalence in populations of European descent varies from 2 to 4/100,000.[13–15]

Clinical Presentation

Although clinical presentation of CADASIL varies substantially among and within families, the disease is characterized by four main clinical features: migraine with aura, subcortical ischemic events, mood disorders, and cognitive impairment. These symptoms vary with patient age and disease duration.[16,17] Migraine with aura, which has been observed in 20% to 40% of patients, is often the presenting clinical manifestation (onset around 30 years; range, 6–48 years). The most frequent manifestations in CADASIL are recurrent, subcortical ischemic events (transient ischemic attack [TIA] or stroke) and have been reported in 60% to 85% of patients (mean age at onset, 49 years; range, 20–70 years).[18] Ischemic events are almost invariably subcortical and occur typically in the absence of common cerebrovascular risk factors, although the concomitant presence of such risk factors (e.g., smoking and high cholesterol levels) may condition for an earlier stroke onset.[19,20] Ischemic events are generally recurrent (range, 2–5 events) and lead progressively to gait difficulty, urinary urgency, and pseudobulbar palsy.[16,21] The secondmost frequent clinical manifestation is cognitive impairment, which was observed in nearly all patients by the age of 50 years[22] and involves mostly executive

TABLE 3.1

Monogenic Disorders Associated with Stroke: Mode of Inheritance, and Clinical and Neuroradiological Features

Disease	CADASIL	CARASIL	HERNS	*COL4A1*	Fabry's disease	SCD	NF1	MELAS
Incidence	4–15:100,000	Exceptionally rare (50 cases)	Exceptionally rare	Rare	1:40,000–117,000	1:2500	1:3500	18.4 per 100,000
Pattern of inheritance	AD	AR	AD	AD	X-linked recessive	AR	AD	Maternal inheritance
Gene	*NOTCH3* (600276)	*HTRA1* (602194)	*TREX1* (606609)	*COL4A1* (605595)	α-GAL A gene (GLA; 300644)	β globin	NF1	80% tRNA Leu (UUR), (*MTTL1*)
Chromosome	19	10q25	3p21.3-p21.2	13q34	Xq22	11p15.5	17q11.2	mtDNA
OMIM	125310	60142	192315	120130	301500	603903	162200	540000
Clinical manifestations								
Stroke	60–85%	50%	Yes	17.3%	24–48% (M), 7–32% (F)	Yes, 25% by 45 years	Yes, rare	Yes, strokelike
Age at onset, y	49 (range, 20–70)	32 (range, 20–44)	40–50	36.1 (range, 14–49)	33–46 (M), 40–52 (F)	Childhood	Childhood	<40 years
Stroke subtype								
Small-vessel disease	Yes	Yes	Yes	Yes	Yes	Yes	No	No
Large-vessel disease	1 report	No	No	No	Yes	Yes	Yes	Yes
Cardioembolic	No	No	No	No	Yes	No	No	Yes
Hemorrhagic	Rare	Rare	No	Yes	Yes	Yes	Yes	No
Other neurological manifestations								
Psychiatric disturbance	20%	Yes	Yes	Yes; depression, 4%	Yes, depression	Yes	No	Depression, 31%
Migraine with aura	20%–40%	Yes	Yes (70%)	Yes (19%)	No	No	Yes	Headache, 77%–91%
Seizures	5%–10%	No	Yes	Yes, 21%	Yes	Yes	Yes	Yes

(*continued*)

TABLE 3.1

Continued

Disease	CADASIL	CARASIL	HERNS	*COL4A1*	Fabry's disease	SCD	NF1	MELAS
Cognitive impairment	Vascular dementia	Vascular dementia	Yes	Yes, 4%; developmental delay	Yes, learning and growth delay	Yes	Yes, learning disabilities	Yes; memory problems, 71%–90%; learning deficits
Acute encephalopathy	Yes	Yes	Yes	No	Yes	Yes	No	Yes
Extraneurological manifestations								
Neuropathy	No	No	No	No	Yes, small-fiber neuropathy	No	Yes; neurofibroma, schwannoma	Yes
Dysautonomic features	No	No	No	No	No	No	No	No
Myopathy	No	No	No	Yes	No		No	Yes; weakness, 89%; exercise intolerance, 93%
Renal disease	No	No	Yes	Yes	Yes	Yes	No	Occasionally reported
Skin involvement	No	No	Yes	No	Yes, angiokeratoma	No	Yes, neurofibroma	Vitiligo pigmentary changes
Ocular involvement	No	No	Retinopathy with progressive visual loss; later stages of the disease, occlusion of branches of large retinal arteries	Yes, 47.6%; cataracts, retinal vessels tortuosity, retinal hemorrhages	Yes, cornea verticillata	No	Yes, ocular glioma, Lisch nodules	Yes, rare optic atrophy, pigmentary retinopathy

Gastrointestinal involvement	No	No	Yes	No	Yes, 19%–52%	No	No	Yes, 64%
Cardiac involvement	No	No	No	No	Yes; MI, valvular diseases, HCM, rhythm disturbances	No	No	Heart disease, 21%; conduction defects
Others	No	Alopecia, pseudobulbar palsy, spondylosis deformans, and acute lumbago with lumbar disc herniation, less common ataxia, ophthalmoplegia	Raynaud's phenomenon, 80%			Pain vaso-occlusive crises, acute chest syndrome, asthma, pulmonary artery hypertension, cholelithiasis priapism	Skeletal abnormalities, endocrine system (pheochromocytomas), CNS tumors, or malignant peripheral nerve sheath tumors	Hearing loss, 50%–77%; short stature, 33%; diabetes, 33%
Instrumental findings								
Cerebral MRI								
Stroke	Lacunar	Lacunar	Lacunar	Lacunar	Lacunar, subcortical, cortical	Lacunar and large vessel	Large vessel	Cortical
White matter lesions	Yes	Often relatively spared	Yes	Yes; white matter lesions, 63.5%; microbleeds, 52.9%; lacunar infarction, 13.5%; enlarged perivascular spaces, 19.2%	Yes, periventricular hyperintensities, multiple hyperintensities on T2- and FLAIR-weighted images affecting deep white matter	Yes, frontal and parietal lobes	UBOs	Yes
Aneurysms	No	No	No	Yes, 44.4%	Yes, basilar artery dolichoectasia	Yes, vertebrobasilar	Yes	No

(*continued*)

TABLE 3.1

Continued

Dise-ase	CADASIL	CARASIL	HERNS	COL4A1	Fabry's disease	SCD	NF1	MELAS
Age (complete expression), y	35	20–40	40–50	Perinatal/adults	54	20–49	—	20–40
Peculiar findings	Temporal lobe hyperintensities, external capsule involvement	Diffuse white matter abnormalities with small foci of lacunae similar to that observed in classic Binswanger encephalopathy	Subcortical contrast-enhancing lesions with surrounding edema	Porencephaly, 46.1%	Pulvinar hyperintensities on T1-weighted-images, 24%	Moyamoya disease	Moyamoya disease, UBOs, or "T2 hyperintensities" in at least 60% of children with NF1; neurofibromas, carotid artery stenosis	No classical vascular distribution, asymmetric cortical involvement (temporal, parietal, and occipital lobes), peculiar fluctuation of lesions over time
Laboratory findings								
Proteinuria	No	No	Yes	Yes	Yes	No	No	Yes
Lactic acidosis	No	No	No	Yes	no	No	No	Yes
Skin biopsy	GOM on electron microscopy (Sn, 85%–95%; Sp, 95%–100%	No GOM	Multilayer basement membranes beneath endothelial cells of capillaries, arterioles, and venules	Interruption and thickening of basement membrane	Typical cytoplasmic lipid inclusions	No	No	No

Brain biopsy	Diffuse demyelination of the cerebral white matter/small-vessel pathology	Diffuse demyelination of the cerebral white matter with some preservation of U fibers (consistent with small- vessel disease)	Subpial and subcortical white matter gliosis in the absence of inflammation or vasculitis	No	Deep matter lesions that may include lacunar infarctions or may be associated with small-arteriole narrowing	Stenosing arteriopathy and vasculopathy hypertrophy of the intima and media layers of large arteries	Neurofibroma usually consisting of a mixture of cell types including Schwann cells, fibroblasts, endothelial cells, pericytes, mast cells, and perineural cells; abnormal proliferation of spindle cells and of intima with fibrous thickening and mesodermal dysplasia or fibromuscular hyperplasia; micronodular formations of smooth muscle aggregates on the walls of vessels	No
Muscle biopsy	No	No	No	Normal	No	No	No	Ragged red fibers; cytochrome *c* oxidase activity (complex IV) only partially reduced

AD, autosomal dominant; AR, autosomal recessive; CADASIL, cerebral autosomal dominant arteriopathy with subcortical infarcts and leukoencephalopathy; CARASIL, cerebral autosomal recessive arteriopathy with subcortical infarcts and leukoencephalopathy; CNS, central nervous system; F, female; FLAIR, fluid-attenuated inversion recovery; GOM, granular osmiophilic material; HERNS, hereditary endotheliopathy retinopathy nephropathy and stroke; M, male; *MELAS*, Mitochondrial myopathy, encephalopathy, lactic acidosis and strokelike episodes; MI, myocardial infarction; MRI, magnetic resonance imaging; mtDNA, mitochondrial DNA; NF1, neurofibromatosis type 1; SCD, sickle cell disease; tRNA, transfer RNA; UBO, unidentified bright object.

functions and processing speed,[23] but may be associated with deficits in memory and attention. Cognitive decline is commonly progressive and worsens with recurrent stroke. Mood disorders are reported in 20% to 31% of patients and are characterized primarily by severe depression and apathy, which are the onset clinical symptoms in 1.2% to 9% of cases.[16,24,25] The origin of these disturbances is still unknown, although vascular damage of cortical–subcortical circuits has been suggested.[26] Other less common clinical manifestations are seizures, which have been reported in 5% to 10% of patients, intracerebral heamorrhage,[27,28] deafness and parkinsonism.[22]

Brain Imaging

Magnetic resonance imaging (MRI) changes, characterized mostly by leukoencephalopathy and lacunar infarcts, can be detected in all patients with CADASIL after the age of 35 years and generally precede symptom onset by 10 to 15 years. The earliest changes are diffuse hyperintense lesions on T2-weighted or fluid-attenuated inversion recovery (FLAIR) images affecting the periventricular areas and centrum semiovale. Lacunar infarcts are located mostly in subcortical white matter, basal ganglia, thalamus, internal capsule, and brainstem. These lesions were found in 75% of patients age 30 to 40 years, and their appearance increased with age.[29] Cortical microinfarcts have also been observed with high-resolution MRI in postmortem cerebral tissues.[30] Involvement of the anterior temporal lobe and external capsule is highly suggestive of CADASIL,[31,32] with a sensitivity and specificity of 90% and 100%, respectively. Lesional patterns become more severely diffuse with disease progression, and confluent hyperintensities on FLAIR images in the thalamus have been observed in about 12% of patients with CADASIL that were found to be associated significantly with age and related independently to the volume of white matter hyperintensities.[25,33] Other radiological features reported in CADASIL are subcortical microbleeds and cerebral atrophy.[34] Lacunar infarcts, but also microbleeds and ventricular volume, have been identified as the most important MRI parameters associated with cognitive disfunction,[26,35] whereas the association between cerebral atrophy and cognitive impairment in CADASIL is controversial.[34,36]

Genetics, Pathogenesis, and Pathological Aspects

CADASIL is an autosomal dominant disease caused by a mutation in the *NOTCH3* gene on chromosome 19q12 encoding a 2321-amino acid single-pass transmembrane receptor with an extracellular domain containing 34 epidermal growth factor repeats (EGFRs) with six cysteine residues, three Notch/Lin12 repeats, a single transmembrane domain, and an intracellular domain.[37,38] CADASIL results from mutations in exons encoding EGFRs (exons 2–24), with clustering in exons 3 and 4. However, a variation in mutational spectrum among CADASIL populations has been described.[39–41] Missense mutations account for 95% of cases, but small in-frame deletions or splice-site mutations have also been reported, all leading to a gain or a loss of a cysteine residue within the EGFR, thus altering the number of cysteine residues and leaving one unpaired.[22,42–45] Cysteine-sparing mutations of uncertain pathogenic significance associated with a CADASIL-like phenotype have been reported in a few patients.[46–49] The exact function of the *NOTCH3* gene is unknown. *NOTCH3* is expressed predominantly in vascular smooth cells of small arteries and pericytes of the brain,[50] as confirmed by microscopic and ultrastructural investigations, and *NOTCH3* knockout mice have been shown to have structural defects of small arteries resulting from altered differentiation of smooth cells and impaired autoregulation of cerebral blood flow.[51,52]

The Notch3 signaling pathway has been shown to be crucial to the structural and functional integrity of small arteries, and *NOTCH3* knockout mice have abnormally enlarged brain arteries with a thinner muscular coat and smaller smooth muscle cells.[51] It has been hypothesized that CADASIL mutated *NOTCH3* may interact with adjacent mutant receptors or other proteins by anomalous disulfide bond formation, leading to spontaneously forming oligomers and higher multimeric complexes. This may lead to a selective accumulation of extracellular domain of Notch3 within the small artery in the proximity of vascular smooth muscle cells, ultimately resulting in vascular smooth muscle cell degeneration.[53] Microscopic and ultrastructural examination show an arteriopathy that affects mainly penetrating cerebral and leptomeningeal arteries, but also other organs such as spleen, kidney, muscle, aorta, and skin, although clinical manifestations are only cerebral. The arteriopathy is characterized by thickening of the arterial wall, leading to lumen stenosis, and by the presence of nonamyloid granular osmiophilic material within the media extending into the adventitia.[22,54]

Diagnosis

Although migraine, a familial history of stroke before the age of 60 years, the presence of diffuse white matter changes with anterior temporal lobe involvement and external capsule involvement, and lacunar infarcts were shown to be strong predictors of *NOTCH3* gene mutations in subjects with a clinical suspicion of CADASIL, the extremely variable phenotype hampers the identification of standardized, pregenetic screening clinical criteria.[31]

Skin biopsy showing, on electron microscopy, the presence of granular osmiophilic material within the vascular smooth cells is a highly specific diagnostic tool, but the sensitivity of this test is variable.[55–58] Immunostaining of skin samples with a NOTCH3 monoclonal antibody, which can detect accumulation of Notch3 in the vessel wall, seems to improve sensitivity up to 95%.[58] However, DNA sequencing of exons 2 to 24 of *NOTCH3* remains the gold standard for the diagnosis of CADASIL, with a 100% specificity in detecting a mutation that changes the number of cysteine residues in an EGFR. Genetic testing is indicated in patients presenting with a characteristic clinical syndrome, in combination with characteristic neuroimaging features and a positive familial history.

Treatment

Currently, there are no specific treatments of proven efficacy for patients with CADASIL. General therapeutic measures to relieve symptoms can be administered, whereas some drugs or proceedings should be avoided or used carefully because of their side effects.[59] Prophylactic drugs for migraine attack prevention such as beta blockers, flunarizine, amitryptiline, and topiramate should be used carefully, considering their potential side effects on cognition and mood, whereas sodium valproate can be used if there is coexisting epilepsy. Acetazolamide was proposed as a promising prophylactic treatment, probably providing an increase in cerebral perfusion, although it needs to be tested formally in a randomized controlled trial (RCT).[60,61] Because there is no specific drug for acute stroke in CADASIL, patients have to be treated similarly to other stroke patients. Common treatments for vascular risk factors and stroke prevention are recommended, given the possible role of risk factors in accelerating disease progression. Tissue plasminogen activator should be administered when patients meet clinical criteria. Conversely, it is unknown whether antiplatelet agents are effective in secondary stroke prevention, and their administration should be individualized based on patient risk factor profile and tolerance; antiplatelet use has been related to intracerebral hemorrhage in patients with CADASIL.[62] Posada et al.[63] conducted an open pivot trial on galantamine in four patients with CADASIL, without conclusive results. The first (and so far only) RCT of CADASIL randomized 168 patients with cognitive impairment to receive either 10 mg donepezil per day or placebo. Donepezil had no effect on the primary end point—the Alzheimer's Disease Assessment Scale cognitive subscale. Improvements were noted on measures of executive function, but the very short follow-up limits the clinical relevance of these findings.[64] Although the efficacy of selective serotonin reuptake inhibitors in relieving depression or pseudobulbar syndrome have been demonstrated, there are no available studies that have tested drugs related mood disorders in patients with CADASIL.[59]

Last, supportive care and proper genetic counseling are necessary for patients with CADASIL and their family to help them in making informed medical and personal decisions, and minimizing potential psychological distress related to symptomatic or presymptomatic genetic testing.[59,65]

CEREBRAL AUTOSOMAL RECESSIVE ARTERIOPATHY WITH SUBCORTICAL INFARCTS AND LEUKOENCEPHALOPATHY

CARASIL (OMIM 192315) is an autosomal recessive single-gene disorder affecting cerebral small arteries.

Epidemiology

The exact prevalence of CARASIL is unknown. To date, approximately 50 cases have been reported, mainly in Asian populations,[66,67] with the exception of one recently reported white (Spanish) patient.[68] Genetically, no founder haplotype has been identified, and thus CARASIL is expected to be underdiagnosed.[69]

Clinical Presentation

CARASIL was reported originally in two brothers who presented with juvenile onset of progressive encephalopathy with pyramidal and extrapyramidal signs, dementia, and alopecia.[70] In 1995, Fukutake and Hirayama[71] reviewed 17 patients with CARASIL. Alopecia was the first clinical symptom, present in approximately 90% of patients during adolescence. Hair loss is confined to the head and is diffuse. The second most common and early manifestation is a progressive encephalopathy, with onset from 20 to 44 years (mean, 32 years). Acute ischemic stroke, typically lacunar, mainly in the basal ganglia or brainstem, is reported in about half the patients. One patient developed a cerebral hemorrhage during an advanced course of the disease.[69] Severe back pain attacks with lumbar disc herniation were also reported to occur in the same time frame as the onset of encephalopathy.[71] Dementia is another common clinical feature, developed by age 30 to 40 years, and is characterized by memory impairment followed by disorientation in time, calculation deficits, and emotional lability up to severe memory deficits and abulia.[69]

Additional manifestations are pseudobulbar palsy, personality changes, pyramidal signs, gait disturbance, and spondylosis deformans; less commonly, patients presented with ophthalmoplegia, ataxia, and brainstem signs. The disease affects males predominantly (3:1) and the average illness duration is 20 to 30 years, although most patients became bedridden within 10 years from onset.[71,72]

Brain Imaging

T2-weighted cerebral MRI shows, by age 20 years, diffuse and symmetric high-signal intensity lesions more often in the periventricular and deep white matter with lacunar lesions in the basal ganglia and thalamus, which usually precede symptom onset.[71] Lesions extend during the disease course into the basal ganglia, thalami, brainstem, and cerebellum, and sometimes involve temporal lobes and external capsules as CADASIL. Atherosclerosis has been described in about half the patients on cerebral angiography.

Genetics, Pathogenesis, and Pathological Aspects

In 2009, Hara et al.[72] reported mutations in the *HTRA1* gene on chromosome 10q25 as causative of CARASIL. *HTRA1* encodes a 480-amino acid serine protease belonging to the chymotrypsin family, conserved from prokaryotes to humans. Its structural complexity reflects its ability to act as chaperone and protease in various processes, including breakdown of the extracellular matrix, cancer, modulation of signaling pathways, osteoarthritis, age-related macular degeneration, and spinal disc degeneration. HTRA1 represses signaling by transforming growth factor (TGF)-β family members, with the protease domain located in exons 3 to 6. Mutations described in patients with CARASIL are mostly homozygous mutations in *HTRA1* exons 3 and 4, thought to cause dysregulation of TGF-β signaling.[72] Indeed, mutant proteins appeared unable to suppress TGF-β activity, leading to increased expression of *TGFB1* in the tunica media of affected small arteries. Increased expression of fibronectin, induced by TGF-β signaling, was found in the intima of patients with CARASIL.[67] Neuropathological examination revealed focal and diffuse demyelination with sparing of U fibers and severe arteriosclerotic changes in the small penetrating and leptomeningeal arteries, with fibrous intimal proliferation, hyalinosis, and intima splitting with concentric narrowing of the lumen.[70] Oide et al.[73] found sclerotic changes, with almost a complete disappearance of medial Smooth muscle cells (SMCs) in many arteries, thinning of adventitia, and increasing fragility of arterial walls, leading to collapse of arterial structure. No granular osmiophilic material or amyloid deposition were found.

Diagnosis

Although some clinical features of CARASIL are similar to CADASIL, early disease onset, mode of inheritance, presence of alopecia, and absence of migraine and mood disorders support the suspicion of CARASIL. Given the low involvement of extracerebral small arteries, genetic testing is the only diagnostic tool.

Treatment

No effective treatment is currently available. The efficacy of antiplatelet agents or anticoagulants for secondary stroke prevention is unclear. Genetic counseling and supportive care, as well as symptomatic drugs for dementia and cerebrovascular risk factors are suggested.[69]

AUTOSOMAL DOMINANT RETINAL VASCULOPATHY WITH CEREBRAL LEUKODYSTROPHY

Hereditary endotheliopathy with retinopathy, nephropathy, and stroke; cerebroretinal vasculopathy (CRV); and hereditary vascular retinopathy (HVR), originally reported as distinct disorders, have recently been found to be allelic variants of the same spectrum of disorders grouped under the name *retinal vasculopathy with cerebral leukodystrophy* (RVCL; OMIM 192315).[74–76]

Epidemiology

First described in 1988,[77] currently only a few patients and families have been described with RVCL.[74–83] Moreover, although RVCL is actually a known, heritable small-vessel disease, no epidemiological studies or systematic screening have been conducted so far.

Clinical Presentation

RVCL is a rare, adult-onset autosomal dominant disorder involving the small vessels and is associated with cerebral, ocular, and, less frequently, systemic vascular involvement. The clinical phenotype consists of progressive visual loss resulting from retinopathy followed by neurological involvement occurring during the third or fourth decade of life and consisting of stroke (mostly lacunar), seizures, migrainelike headache, psychiatric disturbances (personality disorders, depression, and anxiety), or cognitive decline.[74,75,77–83] Typical clinical hallmarks are ophthalmologic findings characterized by retinopathy early during the course of the disease, with capillary dropouts and microaneurisms (particularly in the macular region and detectable on retinal fluorescein angiograms), leading to loss of central vision, prominent juxtafoveolar capillary obliteration, and telangiectasias.[83–85] Systemic vascular involvement manifests as mild liver dysfunction, with autopsy report of nodular regenerative hyperplasia and renal dysfunction of glomerular origin, with proteinuria and elevation of creatinine and renal histopathology suggestive of accelerated arteriolonephrosclerosis. Raynaud's phenomena, chronic anemia, and gastrointestinal symptoms, but also small-vessel bleeds, were also seen. Disease onset is during the fourth or fifth decade and there is 100% mortality over a 5- to 10-year period secondary to progressive neurological decline.[83]

Genetics, Pathogenesis, and Pathological Aspects

RVCL is an autosomal dominant disorder resulting from a *TREX1* gene mutation on chromosome 3p21.1-21.3. The *TREX 1* gene encodes a 314-amino acid 3′-5′ exonuclease DNAase III, which is part of the SET complex, a reticulum-associated complex translocating to the nucleus in response to superoxide generation by granzyme A. The latter is an activator of a caspase-independent pathway leading to apoptosis. TREX 1 and the endonuclease NM23-H1 are involved in DNA degradation.[86] A heterozygous 1-bp insertion (3688_3689insG) leading to a premature stop codon causes CRV and HVR, whereas a heterozygous 4-bp insertion (3727_3730dupGTCA) resulting in a frameshift has been shown to cause hereditary endotheliopathy with retinopathy, nephropathy, and stroke. Frameshift mutations affecting the C terminus of *TREX1* were found in families with RVCL, and in three of them the alteration was the same as that found in the CRV and HVR pedigrees.[87] Homozygous mutations in the *TREX1* gene have also been reported to cause Aicardi-Goutières syndrome, a rare, familial, early-onset, progressive encephalopathy with basal ganglia calcifications and cerebrospinal fluid lymphocytosis. Mutations associated with Aicardi-Goutières syndrome result in disruption of the enzymatic sites in TREX1 with loss of exonuclease function, which is likely to cause accumulation of altered DNA, triggering a destructive autoimmune response.[88] Heterozygous mutations observed in RVCL spare the region coding the catalytic function without altering the exonuclease function. Histopathology demonstrates coagulative necrosis secondary to an obliterative vasculopathy and minimal inflammatory infiltrate. Ultrastructural examination of the brain and other tissues including the kidney, gastrointestinal tract, and skin, showed multilayer basement membranes beneath endothelial cells of capillaries, arterioles, and venules.[74]

Brain Imaging

Computed tomography (CT) scans often show tumorlike lesions with displacement of the surrounding structures, and central contrast enhancement commonly in the frontoparietal region. Cerebral MRI findings usually consist of multiple subcortical hyperintense lesions on T2-weighted sequences involving the periventricular and deep white matter and corpus callosum, as well as contrast-enhancing tumorlike lesions with surrounding edema that may change over time and occur even in the absence of a neurological deficit.[74] Multiple cerebral calcifications on brain CT and MRI were also found.

Diagnosis

Currently, genetic testing is the only diagnostic tool, because clear, standardized clinical criteria have not been established.

Treatment

Given the few cases identified, no disease-specific treatment is available. Genetic counseling and secondary preventive measures such as antiplatelet agent use can be suggested based on empirical arguments.

COL4A1 SYNDROME

Mutations in the *COL4A1* gene have been identified recently as a cause of autosomal dominant hereditary cerebrovascular disease (COL4A1 syndrome [OMIM 605595-120130]). In addition, a broad range of systemic injuries affecting the eyes, kidneys, and muscles has been related to *COL4A1* gene mutations.

Epidemiology

Reports of a total of 65 patients and 13 families with an identified mutation have been published to date.[89,90] However, given its recent identification and its variable clinical expression, COL4A1 syndrome is probably largely underestimated.

Clinical Presentation

Pediatric forms of *COL4A1* gene mutations include children of all ages, with onset starting as early as during the prenatal period. One of the most frequent disease phenotypes is infantile hemiparesis or congenital porencephaly, which is probably a result of perinatal intracerebral hemorrhage (as reported in two preterm siblings with *COL4A1* mutation born after an uneventful pregnancy and delivery except for mild antenatal trauma in one,[91]) but is also seen in childhood. Intracerebral hemorrhage has also been described in adults, in the absence of any perinatal events or infantile hemiparesis or porencephaly.[92] Systematic exploration of mutation carriers, both children and adults, in families with porencephaly or infantile hemiparesis or perinatal intracerebral hemorrhage, showed a variable cerebrovascular phenotype including asymptomatic porencephaly, diffuse brain white matter lesions, intracerebral hemorrhage, TIA, and, rarely, brain infarction.[91–99] Asymptomatic cerebral aneurysms, often multiple, were observed in 44% of subjects submitted to appropriate investigations. Clinical features of cerebral small-vessel disease are quite common findings in *COL4A1* mutation carriers. Stroke occurred in 17.3% of subjects, with a mean age at onset of 36.1 years (range, 14–40 years). All ischemic strokes were small subcortical infarcts (33%) and the other strokes were hemorrhagic (67%). Mental retardation, migraine with and without aura, and epilepsy are the other neurological manifestations of COL4A1 syndrome, sometimes even in the absence of any history of vascular clinical events.[95,99,100]

Extraneurological symptoms include retinal arteriolar tortuosity,[101] venule tortuosities, retinal ischemic changes, or visual loss, but also hereditary angiopathy with nephropathy, aneurysms, and muscle cramps.[102–104] Retinal vascular lesions are inconstant within families with mutations and, when present, they are either asymptomatic or responsible for retinal hemorrhage and transient visual loss. *COL4A1* mutations have also been associated with other ocular manifestations such as cataract formation and anterior segment dysgenesis (Axenfeld-Rieger anomaly), microcornea, congenital cataract, retinal detachment, high intraocular pressure, and optic nerve atrophy or excavation.[89,101] Kidney involvement includes frequent microscopic hematuria with, sometimes, episodes of severe hematuria, small or large bilateral renal cysts, and mild renal failure in some older patients. Muscular symptoms consist of painful cramps, with onset during early childhood, that are spontaneous or provoked by exercise. Patients have persistent elevated serum creatine kinase levels of usually moderate intensity, and electromyography and muscular biopsy are negative.[104] Less common findings are Raynaud's phenomenon, supraventricular arrhythmias, and mitral valve prolapse.[92]

Genetics, Pathogenesis, and Pathological Aspects

Type IV collagen is a major component of basement membranes and it consists of six homologous, but genetically distinct, α chains that are expressed selectively in different membranes and at different stages of embryonic development.[105] Three different networks have so far been identified. The $\alpha1-\alpha2$ network is widely expressed, whereas the $\alpha3-\alpha4-\alpha5$ and the $\alpha5-\alpha5-\alpha6$ networks show tissue-specific expression.[105–108] Collagen type IV, $\alpha3$, $\alpha4$, and $\alpha5$ has been reported to be associated with Alport's syndrome and benign familial hematuria.[109–111] Collagen IV, $\alpha1$ (COL4A1 [OMIM 120130]), is an essential component of basal membrane stability. All the reported mutations, except for the one described by Bilguvar et al.,[97] cause a glycine substitution, resulting in a destabilization of the triple helical domain, which is essential for macromolecular structure integrity. Mutations in the collagen IV genes are associated with reduced stability and defects of the basement membrane that, according to the different patterns of distribution of the different chains, may result in a tissue-restricted pathology when chains $\alpha3$ to $\alpha6$ are involved, and in a more diffuse disease when mutations occur in the $\alpha1$ gene.

Brain Imaging

The wide spectrum of MRI findings associated with *COL4A1* gene mutations, including diffuse leukoencephalopathy (63.5%), lacunar infarcts (16.5%), microbleeds (52.8% with gradient echo sequences), dilated perivascular spaces (19.2%), and deep cerebral hemorrhages, suggest an underlying cerebral small-vessel disease. The leukoencephalopathy, which is the most common neuroradiological finding, is usually bilateral and symmetric, and of variable severity. It involves mainly supratentorial regions, predominantly the frontal and parietal lobes, the periventricular regions, and the centrum semiovale, sparing the temporal and occipital lobes and arcuate fibers.[90,95,106] Brainstem, especially the pons, and cerebellar deep white matter may also be affected. Silent microbleeds are located mainly in the basal ganglia, supratentorial white matter, and cerebellum. Small, deep lacunar infarcts and dilated perivascular spaces have also been observed, as well as multiple microcalcifications in the basal ganglia. MRI may show recent or old intracranial hemorrhages, especially in the basal ganglia, centrum semiovale, and pons.[89,91,92] Asymptomatic carotid intracranial aneurysms, usually multiple and located on the extra- or intradural carotid siphon, are particularly frequent in the *COL4A1* phenotype.[92]

Diagnosis

Genetic testing is currently the only diagnostic tool. Although only a few cases have been described, some combinations of neurological and/or extraneurological symptoms have been recognized as highly suggestive and should support genetic testing in clinical practice: (a) any deep intracerebral hemorrhage of unknown cause in association with diffuse white matter abnormalities on brain MRI suggestive of diffuse small vessel disease or with one of the cardinal extraneurological symptoms of the disorder in the patient or in a family member, (b) any bilateral and symmetric leukoencephalopathy of unknown cause in the presence of one of the cardinal extraneurological symptoms of the disorder in the patient or a family member, (c) any intracranial aneurysm if associated with diffuse small vessel disease of the brain in the absence of hypertension and particularly in younger patients, and (d) any infantile hemiparesis and/or porencephaly of unknown cause.[89] The diagnostic pathway should include a comprehensive multisystemic exploration including neurological, extraneurological (ophthalmologic and renal, especially), vascular, and extravascular investigations, and a careful family history collection.

Treatment

No specific therapeutic measure has yet proved to be effective in this disorder. However, all patients with this mutation should be monitored systematically. Risk factors of hemorrhagic stroke are head trauma, intensive exercise, and the use of anticoagulants. Classic vascular risk factors such as hypertension should be prevented and treated carefully. Prophylactic interventions for sporadic, unruptured intracranial aneurysm should be discussed individually by a specialized multidisciplinary team. As in other autosomal dominant neurological disorders, genetic counseling of symptomatic and asymptomatic patients, and their close relatives is needed. Any at-risk pregnancy requires specific follow-up with repeated ultrasound evaluation of the fetus, and cesarean delivery may be the best option to decrease the risk of perinatal hemorrhagic events.[89]

Small-Vessel and Large-Artery Diseases

FABRY DISEASE

Fabry disease (FD; Anderson-Fabry disease, OMIM 301500) is a multisystem X-linked lysosomal storage disorder resulting in lysosomal glycosphingolipid (globotriaosylceramide [Gb3]) deposition from α-galactosidase A enzyme (α-Gal A) absence or deficiency caused by a mutation in the *GLA* gene.[112,113]

Epidemiology

The estimated prevalence ranges from 1:40,000 to 1:117,000, or 1:476,000 live male births worldwide.[114,115,116–122] In Portugal (population, approximately 10,000,000), it is estimated that as many as 3000 cases of FD are diagnosed every year in a population age 18 to 55 years.[123–125] Screening of 37,104 newborn males for deficient α-Gal A activity in Italy identified FD in 1:3100 subjects.[126] A high frequency of FD in newborn males was also found in Taiwan (approximately 1:1500).[127]

In a prospective study of 721 stroke patients (age, between 18 years and 55 years), the prevalence of FD was 4.9% among males and 2.4% among females.[128] The PORTYSTROKE study reported a 2.4% incidence of FD in 493 young Portuguese stroke patients, independent of age and sex.[129] Recently, researchers engaged in the Belgian Fabry Study screened 1000 patients with ischemic stroke, TIA or intracranial hemorrhage, unexplained white matter lesions, or vertebrobasilar dolichoectasia for FD. In that study, Gal A deficiency was demonstrated to play a role in up to 1% of young patients presenting with cerebrovascular disease.[130] Similar results were reported in the Zurich Fabry study, in which the genetic screening of 150 patients, age 18 to 55 years with stroke or TIA of undetermined origin, was negative.[131] In both studies, the results were incongruous with enzymatic activity, which was reduced respectively in 3.5% and 9% of cases, suggesting that this analysis may be false positive in some patients. Recently, the Stroke in Young Fabry Patients, or SIFAP1, study assessed a diagnosis of FD in 0.5% in a cohort of 5023 young stroke patients, supporting the idea that FD is not a frequent cause of young stroke.[131]

Clinical Presentation

Although Gb3 storage begins prenatally, clinical symptoms do not manifest until childhood. Burning pain in the extremities, gastrointestinal disorders, and hypohidrosis are the most common presenting features. Learning and growth delay have been reported as well.[132] In general, progressive renal involvement—mostly proteinuria, leading to renal failure—and cardiac and cerebrovascular disease develop after age 20 years. Neurological manifestations other than cerebrovascular accidents (TIA or ischemic and hemorrhagic stroke) include small-fiber neuropathy and dysautonomic disorders. In general, cerebrovascular complications, which are not uncommon in FD, develop after the age of 20 years, with a mean age at onset of 33 to 46 years in males and 40 to 52 years in females.[133–135] The reported prevalence ranges from 24% to 48% in affected males and from 7% to 32% in affected females.[133–136] Ischemic episodes (stroke or TIA), resulting from damage to small and large blood vessels, but also from cardiogenic embolism, occur mainly in the posterior circulation.[136] The reason for this distribution is unclear. Rolfs et al.,[137] in 2005, reported a new phenotype characterized only by cryptogenic stroke, primarily in the posterior circulation, and proteinuria. Mitsias and Levine[136] also described cerebral hemorrhage resulting from aneurysmal deformity of blood vessels. Stroke is associated with a more severe disease progression, with reported stroke recurrence and mortality rates as high as 76% and 55%, respectively.[133–138] The disease has a progressive clinical course, characterized by recurrent cerebrovascular episodes and an accumulation of cerebral lesions, increasing with age. Neurological manifestations other than cerebrovascular accidents include small-fiber neuropathy and dysautonomic disorders. Neuropathic involvement, which can be as high as 80% in FD,[138–140] is characterized by painful, distal, small-fiber sensory peripheral neuropathy conditioning acroparesthesia; burning dysesthesia; sensory loss (primarily temperature); and tenderness. Symptoms can manifest as a constant, burning neuropathic pain or, alternatively, as episodes of severe and disabling paroxysmal pain in the hands and feet with dysautonomic features, lasting from hours to several days. Stress, physical exercise, fever, or temperature variation can act as pain triggers. Multisystemic manifestations include kidney involvement, which often begins with microalbuminuria and proteinuria during the second and third decade of life. It is characterized first by alterations in tubular reabsorption, secretion, and excretion, and is masked initially by glomerular hyperfiltration; from third to fifth decade it is dominated by tubular fibrosis and sclerosis.[141] Cardiac symptoms including left ventricular hypertrophy, arrhythmia, valvular structural abnormalities, conduction disturbances, and coronary artery disease are reported in 40% to 60% of patients.[142] Other frequent manifestations include characteristic skin lesions (angiokeratomas), which are typically small, reddish, raised skin lesions; corneal opacity—which usually does not affect vision and is detectable by slit-lamp examination (cornea verticillata), occurring almost in all hemizygous males—gastrointestinal disorders; and hypohidrosis. Learning and growth delay have been reported as well.[143]

Brain Imaging

Accumulation of cerebral lesions, increasing with age, is detectable on neuroimaging.[135,143] T2- and FLAIR-weighted images typically show multiple hyperintensities affecting the deep hemispheric white matter and brainstem, often preceding the occurrence of neurological symptoms.[144,145] Cerebral involvement is usually widespread, although a predominant posterior involvement has been reported; however, the anterior circulation, particularly the parietal and frontal lobes, may also be affected.[137,145] In recent studies, some patients with FD who experienced stroke presented brain hemorrhages. Bleeding occurred in the anterior circulation territory and frequently affected patients with hypertension.[138] Microbleeds but also intracerebral hemorrhage, in association with classic mutations have also been detected in patients with FD.[146,147] Additional radiological findings are tortuosity and abnormal ectasia of large vessels (dolichoectasia). Pulvinar hyperintensities on T1-weighted images, detectable in 23% of patients with FD by the third decade of life, is the only specific radiological feature of this disease. Because they appear as hyperdensities on cerebral CT, it has been supposed that they may represent calcification and mineralization induced by increased blood flow in the posterior circulation rather than local accumulation of Gb3.[148,149]

Genetics, Pathogenesis, and Pathological Aspects

FD is an X-linked trait resulting from a mutation in the lysosomal *alfa-galactosidase A* (*GLA*) gene, located on chromosome Xq22. The disease occurs primarily among hemizygous males. However, a significant proportion of heterozygous (carrier) females also develop symptoms and signs of classic FD, usually at an older age.[150,151] Although an X inactivation mechanism has been involved, it cannot fully explain the presence of symptomatic heterozygous females[152]; therefore, the clinical variability is probably a result of other genetic or environmental factors. More than 585 mutations, mainly missense and nonsense point mutations, but also splicing mutations and small and large deletions, have been identified in the *GLA* gene.[153–155] The majority of these mutations lead to a loss of function of the enzyme. Although most families share unique mutations, there is an important intrafamilial variability in residual enzyme activity and disease course, which are strongly related. Although a clear genotype–phenotype correlation has not been demonstrated, mutations leading to a complete loss of function are generally associated with the classic phenotype. Although most clinical manifestations can be explained by the deposition of glycosphingolipids, particularly Gb3, in different tissues and organs, with predominant involvement of the vascular endothelium and smooth muscle cells, the pathophysiology of some clinical aspects such as cerebral vasculopathy is still poorly understood. The prevailing hypothesis is that a cardioembolic pathogenesis underlies only a small proportion of strokes in patients with FD, and that most cerebrovascular accidents derive from a more complex, multifactorial systemic vascular dysfunction, probably involving changes in vessel wall angioarchitecture, endothelial dysfunction, and abnormalities in blood constituents. Supporting this theory, increased markers of endothelial activation levels such as soluble vascular cell adhesion molecule, soluble intercellular adhesion molecule, P-selectin, E-selectin, and plasminogen activator inhibitor, as well as nitric oxide pathway dysfunction, have been reported in several studies to be associated with FD.[156–159] Polymorphisms of genes encoding proteins involved in the inflammatory response, vascular wall pathophysiology, and coagulation cascade (e.g., interleukin 6, endothelial nitric oxide synthase, factor V Leiden, and protein Z) have been shown to act as genetic modifiers of cerebral lesions.[160,161]

Diagnosis

Small- and large-vessel cerebrovascular disease and/or cardiovascular involvement with cerebral embolism and small-fiber neuropathies with specific associated signs and symptoms, such as angiokeratoma, proteinuria, cornea verticillata, and echocardiographic alterations suggestive of hypertrophic myocardiopathy, often not reported spontaneously by the patient, should alert physicians to the possibility of FD. However, the heterogeneous disease presentation and the similarity of some signs and symptoms to other common diseases make it challenging to recognize early manifestations of FD in clinical practice.[155] Thus, a diagnosis of FD may be delayed by as long as 15 years, if not overlooked.[162] Diagnostic guidelines suggesting a standardized clinical workup have been published.[163,164] However, given the availability of a specific treatment, early diagnosis of FD is necessary to prevent complications and disease progression, improve patients' quality of life, and avoid unnecessary additional investigations to detect the origin of stroke or neuropathies.[162,165]

Enzymatic assays demonstrating reduced alfa-galactosidase activity in plasma or leukocytes have been suggested to screen affected males systematically. However, plasma assays may occasionally lead to a false-positive diagnosis[166,167] or may fail to detect all cases of FD. Direct molecular analysis allows one to confirm the diagnosis and to identify the precise mutation. It should always be performed in females, given the high frequency of false-negative enzymatic activity assays. Plasma and urinary Gb3 dose have been also proposed, but the validity of this test is still uncertain.[168] Skin biopsy observed by electron microscopy may be a useful diagnostic tool when interpreted by an expert pathologist.[169]

Treatment

Enzyme replacement therapy (ERT) has revolutionized the care of patients with FD. In Europe, where this therapy was approved for clinical use in 2001, two different preparations of the α-Gal A enzyme are available (REPLAGAL® [agalsidase alfa], Shire Human Genetic Therapies, Boston, MA; and Fabrazyme [agalsidase beta], Genzyme Corporation, Cambridge, MA). Agalsidase-α is produced from a human fibroblast cell line, and agalsidase-β from a Chinese hamster ovary host cell line. Theoretically, replacing the missing enzyme and reducing the abnormal systemic accumulation of Gb3 should lead to clinical improvement. The treatment is safe except for some adverse effects that may occur especially during the first 3 months of treatment, consisting mainly of allergic reactions. Both preparations are administered as infusions. Differences also exist with respect to dosage (0.2 mg/kg for agalsidase-α and 1.0 mg/kg for agalsidase-β) and infusion time (40 minutes independent of body weight for agalsidase-α and 15 mg/hour for agalsidase-β). Although the two proteins differ in the glycosylation pattern, which depends on the originating cell line, and provide different reduction in Gb3 storage (agalsidase-α at a dose of 0.2 mg/kg and agalsidase-β at a dose of 1.0 mg/kg), currently there are no convincing data supporting substantial differences between the two preparations. Given their similar biological properties, any reported difference is likely a result of different dosing. The response to ERT is heterogeneous and not predictable.[170] Studies with both agalsidase-α and -β reported decreased cardiac mass, and clearance of storage in skin and kidneys, which improved renal dysfunction and delayed heart disease, and also relief of painful neuropathy, hearing loss, vestibular dysfunction and hypo-/anhidrosis. The greatest benefit has been shown when treatment is started during an early disease stage, before myocardial fibrosis has developed, thereby allowing the achievement of long-term improvement.[162] However, despite expectations, ERT has not been shown to affect the progression of white matter disease significantly,[171] nor to reduce the frequency of cerebrovascular events significantly,[172–174] and many questions on the effectiveness of this therapy still need to be answered, some of which stem from the fact that most of the studies conducted were observational and/or uncontrolled. There is a need for further studies of higher quality with more adequate outcome selection and follow-up duration.[162]

The results of the Stroke in Young Fabry Patients, or SIFAP2 study, involving a 36-month follow-up of stroke patients with proven FD treated with different prophylactic therapeutic approaches, will help to provide clearer information for the management of patients with FD.[132]

Currently, other therapeutic options such as gene therapies and restriction of Gb3 synthesis are under investigation.[175,176] Recent experimental results have highlighted the role of chaperone therapy. Chaperones are small molecules that are supposed to cross the blood–brain barrier (unlike ERT); these molecules have been shown to increase residual enzyme activity in FD animal models and in cultured cells from patients with FD. Chaperone therapies offer the advantage of oral administration, reducing the negative impact on quality of life caused by biweekly infusions of ERT. Migalastat (1-deoxygalactonojirimycin) was shown to be safe and well tolerated in a trial of 27 patients treated for 2 years, and seemed to improve α-Gal A activity in 24 patients.[177,178]

Other preventive measures, including administration of antithrombotic agents and control of vascular risk factors in patients with cerebrovascular manifestations, are indicated. However, given the still unclear pathogenetic mechanism, currently it is not known whether pharmacological treatments such as antiplatelet, anticoagulant, antihypertensive, or lipid-lowering agents may provide concrete benefits for patients with FD.[179]

SICKLE CELL DISEASE

Sickle cell disease (SCD; OMIM 603903) refers to a group of heterogeneous disorders that are unified by the presence of at least one β globin gene affected by the sickle mutation. Homozygotes for the sickle mutation have sickle cell anemia or hemoglobin (Hgb) synonym of sickle cell anemia (SS) disease, which accounts for 60% to 65% of cases of SCD. Heterozygous sickle mutations associated with other β globin gene mutations lead to distinct forms of SCD. The most common associated mutation is HgbC, which leads to sickle HgbC disease, accounting for 25% to 30% of all cases of SCD. Coinheritance of a β-thalassemia mutation with the sickle mutation leads to sickle β thalassemia (Sbo or sickle bþ, in relation to no or diminished β globin production), which accounts for 5% to 10% of all cases of SCD.[180]

Epidemiology

In the United States, sickle cell trait is carried by 7% to 8% of people of African ancestry, and the sickle hemoglobinopathies are estimated to affect 90,000 to 100,000 people. U.S. newborn screening data suggest that 1 in 2500 newborns is affected by SCD.[181]

Clinical Presentation

SCD can affect every organ or tissue in the body. Stroke is one of the most severe complications of SCD and it affects the pediatric population (ischemic subtype) and young adults (hemorrhagic subtype) primarily. The incidence of stroke in children with sickle cell anemia is roughly 1% per year.[182] However, in individuals with increased velocities in the distal internal carotid artery or middle cerebral artery, identified by transcranial Doppler imaging, the annual risk of stroke increases to 10%.[183] The risk of stroke increases with age in young adults: 11% by age 20 years, 15% by age 30 years, and 25% by age 45 years. Ischemic stroke accounts for approximately 75% of cases and hemorrhagic stroke for the remaining 25%.[184] The presenting symptoms of acute stroke in SCD include hemiparesis, facial droop, aphasia, and more generalized symptoms, including stupor and, rarely, seizures. The acute event is most often precipitated by severe anemia resulting from exacerbation of the steady-state values. Recurrence is frequent and 20% of acute stroke victims will experience a second acute stroke. The long-term outcome of acute stroke is variable; many patients lack significant motor impairment but may demonstrate impaired executive functioning. Moreover, 10% to 30% of patients with SCD have silent brain infarcts and diffuse white matter disease associated with cognitive deficiencies.[184–187] Neurocognitive impairment, including deficits in general intelligence, attention and executive functioning, memory, language, and visual–motor performance, have been also detected by neuropsychiatric and neurobehavioral testing in SCD and are associated with anemia and age.[188,189] Other frequent clinical manifestations are hematologic abnormalities, infections, and episodic pain crises. Anemia is the primary hematologic manifestation of SCD. After the transition to adult β globin expression, which occurs during the first year of life, children with SCD typically maintain stable baseline Hgb levels, with significant fluctuations occurring usually during acute disease complications. Leukocytosis and mild thrombocytosis were observed, too. Infections, mostly by *Streptococcus pneumoniae*, resulting from functional asplenia, have long been recognized in children with SCD, particularly before the introduction of vaccination and antibiotic prophylactic measures.[181] Severe, episodic pain crisis are another clinical hallmark of SCD. They are commonly referred to as *vaso-occlusive crises*, probably as a result of bone marrow ischemia with resulting infarction. Other clinical manifestations include acute chest syndrome characterized by fever, tachypnea, dyspnea, hypoxia, and chest pain, but also asthma, pulmonary artery hypertension, cholelithiasis, and priapism.

Brain Imaging

The distribution of infarctions seen on CT, MRI, and pathological examination seems to support the pathogenetic role of large-vessel disease of the internal carotid artery, middle cerebral artery, and anterior cerebral artery in symptomatic stroke. However, the location of silent infarcts suggests that these strokes are the result of occlusion of smaller, penetrating arteries. These lesions are typically small (85% are <1.5 cm) and are distributed mainly in the white matter of the frontal and parietal lobes.[190] Fewer are present in the basal ganglia or thalamus; none has been reported in the brainstem or cerebellum.[190,191,192] Attributed to small-vessel disease, these lesions have been designated as lacunes by some authors.[191] However, their spatial distribution is clearly distinct from lacunes seen in adult hypertensive patients, and classic lacunar syndromes have not been described in children with SCD. When multiple, small, adjacent white matter lesions in the centrum semiovale are seen on MRI, this may be the result of proximal large-artery occlusive disease and not primarily the result of penetrating artery disease. Intracranial hemorrhage is not uncommon in adult patients with SCD. The pattern of cerebral infarction in childhood and hemorrhage in adulthood mimics that of Moyamoya disease, and is probably the result of the bursting of fragile collateral vessels. There have been various reports of subarachnoid hemorrhage in patients with SCD. Intracranial aneurysms in these patients are often multiple and occur in greater frequency in the vertebrobasilar system.[193–195]

Genetics, Pathogenesis, and Pathological Aspects

SCD is an autosomal recessive condition caused by a point mutation in exon 1 of the *β globin* gene (codon GAG changes to codon GTG) on chromosome 11p15.5, resulting in the substitution of glutamic acid by valine at position 6 of the β globin polypeptide chain.[180] This single-point mutation renders the sickle gene pleiotropic in nature, with multiple phenotypic expressions associated with complex genetic interactions and modifiers that are not well understood. The point mutation leads to its pathological polymerization, red cell rigidity, hemolytic anemia, and poor microvascular blood flow with consequent tissue ischemia and infarction.[196] When it is deoxygenated, HgbS polymerizes reversibly to form a network of fibrous polymers that stiffen the erythrocyte membrane, increase viscosity, and cause dehydration resulting from potassium leakage and calcium influx. These changes also produce the characteristic sickle shape of the red cells, which lose the pliability required to traverse small capillaries successfully. Reticulocytes have altered expression of adhesion molecules and adhere abnormally to the endothelium of small vessels.[197] These phenomena cause episodes of microvascular occlusion and premature red blood cell destruction, which leads to chronic, severe hemolytic anemia and vascular occlusion.[197,198] Other pathophysiological mechanisms in patients with SCD have been observed, including activation of the vascular endothelium, leukocytosis, leukocyte activation, platelet activation, and oxidative stress from tissue reperfusion. The pathogenesis of acute stroke is not completely understood, but it includes a noninflammatory stenosing arteriopathy of the intracranial vessels, particularly those forming the circle of Willis, and a vasculopathy characterized by hypertrophy of the intima and media layers of large arteries mostly in the anterior cerebral circulation (primarily the middle cerebral arteries) and decreased cerebral blood flow. An elevated production of thrombin, platelet activation, and proinflammatory mediators as well as low levels of protein C and protein S have been described in SCD, suggesting the presence of an underlying procoaguable state.[199] An increased production of angiogenic factors occurs in response to severe stenoses, which promotes the development of newly formed collateral vessels (Moyamoya disease). These new collaterals are fragile and prone to rupture, causing intracerebral hemorrhage. Patients with SCD may also experience cerebral sinus venous thrombosis and cardioembolism.

Diagnosis

Before newborn screening, the diagnosis of SCD was made only after a potentially devastating complication prompted medical attention. Universal newborn screening with Hgb electrophoresis or other methods has become the standard in the United States. The confirmation of SCD is given by

DNA sequencing. As with most genetic conditions, prenatal diagnosis of a fetus with SCD is possible during the first trimester through chorionic villus sampling or during the second trimester through amniocentesis.[180]

Treatment

The suppression of endogenous red blood cell production by regular transfusion of donor red blood cells has the longest therapeutic history. The clearest indications for chronic transfusions are for both primary and secondary stroke prevention.[200] Blood transfusion improves oxygen saturation via increasing arterial oxygen pressure and Hgb–oxygen affinity, thereby reducing red cell sickling. There is an immediate hemodynamic effect and increase in hematocrit,[201] with reductions in middle cerebral artery velocities. The progression of large-vessel stenoses can also be curtailed by transfusion therapy, as proved with angiography.[202] With a periodic transfusion regimen, a significant reduction of stroke risk has been shown when compared with the natural history of close to 70%.[203] However, the optimum duration of transfusion therapy has not been established. Several potential complications are associated with chronic transfusion therapy, including transmission of viral infection and hemosiderosis. Iron loading occurs primarily in the liver, heart, and endocrine glands, and prevention with parenteral desferrioxamine is expensive and associated with visual and acoustic neurotoxic effects and growth retardation. Hydroxyurea (HU) is the only medication approved by the Food and Drug Administration for the treatment of SCD. HU was recognized to increase expression of fetal Hgb and thereby inhibit the polymerization of HgbS. A recently completed RCT of HU for infants with SCD (BABY-HUG) demonstrated that HU reduces rates of hospitalization, blood transfusion, and vascular occlusive crises.[204] Thus, HU has been proposed as an alternative option to periodic transfusion for stroke prevention. The Stroke with Transfusions Changing to Hydroxyurea trial was a noninferiority study designed to compare standard treatment (transfusions plus chelation) with HU plus phlebotomy in children with SCD and iron overload, with a composite primary end point allowing an increased risk of stroke but requiring superiority for removing iron. This study was terminated prematurely after interim analysis revealed equivalent liver iron content, indicating that transfusions and chelation remain a better way to manage children with SCA, stroke, and iron overload.[205] American Heart Association/American Stroke Association stroke prevention guidelines recommend the use of antiplatelet agents and vascular risk factor control along with regular blood transfusion, with the goal of reducing HgbS to 30% to 50% for adults with SCD and a history of stroke.[206] Bone marrow transplantation is the only potentially curative treatment currently available for SCD; however, this option is currently restricted to individuals with human leukocyte antigen-matched siblings, and its efficacy in stroke prevention has not been demonstrated.[207]

Large-Artery Diseases

NEUROFIBROMATOSIS TYPE 1

Neurofibromatosis type 1 (NF1; OMIM 162200), also called *von Recklinghausen disease* or *peripheral neurofibromatosis*, is an autosomal dominant multisystem disorder involving tissue of mesodermal and ectodermal origin.[208]

Epidemiology

The incidence of NF1 was estimated to be approximately 1/3500 individuals.[208–213]

Clinical Presentation

NF1 can affect nearly every organ system, and the complications vary among individuals, even within a single family but also even within a single person at different times in life. Various manifestations of NF1 have different characteristic times of appearance. However, the average life expectancy of individuals with NF1 is reduced by about 15 years, and the most important causes of early death in individuals with NF1 are malignant peripheral nerve sheath tumors and vasculopathy.[214–216]

The most frequent clinical manifestations are alterations of skin—in particular, café-au-lait spots, neurofibromas, and intertriginous freckling. Café-au-lait spots are usually the first manifestation of NF1. They are often present at birth and increase in number during the first years of life. They are most common in the skin but may affect virtually any organ in the body. Neurofibromas are benign tumors arising from the Schwann cells that surround peripheral nerves of all sizes. They can occur anywhere in the peripheral nervous system. Additional features include Lische nodules in the eye iris, but people with NF1 also frequently have learning disabilities, headache, and hydrocephalus or seizures and may develop skeletal abnormalities (scoliosis, dysplasia), endocrine system tumors (pheochromocytomas), central nervous system tumors, or malignant peripheral nerve sheath tumors. Stroke in patients with NF1 is rare. In a series of 158 patients with NF1,[215] neurological manifestations were observed in 55% of these patients, and only one had a history of stroke. However, the vascular manifestations are underestimated among patients with NF1, because the affected individuals are often asymptomatic. Cerebrovascular abnormalities may present in children with NF1 as stenoses or occlusions of the internal carotid, middle cerebral, or anterior cerebral arteries. Small telangiectasic vessels form around the stenotic area and appear as a "puff of smoke" (Moyamoya) on cerebral angiograph.[218,219] One recent study of 419 children with confirmed NF1, of whom 266 (63%) received neuroimaging, cerebral arteriopathy (including Moyamoya) and supraclinoid internal carotid artery stenosis were seen in at least 6% and were associated with young age and optic glioma.[217] Ectatic vessels and intracranial aneurysms also occur more frequently in individuals with NF1 than in the general population.[221]

Brain Imaging

The "target sign" in plexiform neurofibroma, resulting from a central fibrocollagenous core (T2 hypointense) surrounded by myxomatous tissue (T2 hyperintense), is an important diagnostic sign for NF1. MRI and magnetic resonance angiography sequences, but also cerebral angiography, are used to identify cerebrovascular abnormalities such as vessel stenosis or occlusion, ectasiae, and aneurysms. Unidentified bright objects (UBOs), which are sometimes called *T2 hyperintensities* or *focal areas of signal intensity*, can be visualized on T2-weighted MRI of the brain in at least 60% of children with NF1, but the clinical significance is uncertain. UBOs show no evidence of a mass effect and are not seen on T1-weighted MRI or on CT. They may disappear with age. Some studies have suggested that the presence, number, volume, or location of UBOs correlate with learning disabilities in children with NF1, but the findings have not been replicated consistently.[220] The value of performing routine brain MRI in individuals with NF1 at the time of diagnosis is controversial.[221]

Genetics, Pathogenesis, and Pathological Aspects

NF1 is an autosomal dominant disorder with complete penetrance but variable expression. It results from mutations in the *NF1* gene on chromosome 17q11.2. The gene spans more than 350 kb of genomic DNA and encodes a messenger RNA of 11 to 13 kb containing 57 constitutive exons and four alternatively spliced exons.[222] One hundred sixty-eight *NF1* pseudogenes occur on chromosomes 2q21.1,

14q11.1, 14q11.2, 15q11.2, 18p11.21, 21q11.2–q21.1, and 22q11.1, complicating the design of molecular assays for *NF1* mutations. The inheritance of NF1 follows an autosomal dominant trait, and all affected individuals are apparently heterozygous for an *NF1* mutation because persons with constitutive inactivation of both alleles of the *NF1* gene have not been found. More than 500 different mutations of the *NF1* gene have been identified; most are unique and are related to a particular family. Many mutations have been observed repeatedly, but none has been found in more than a few percent of families studied. However, the large size of the *NF1* gene alone does not explain the high frequency of de novo mutations. Nonsense mutations, amino acid substitutions, deletions (which may involve only one or a few base pairs, multiple exons, or the entire gene), insertions, intronic changes affecting splicing, alterations of the 3′ untranslated region of the gene, and gross chromosomal rearrangements have been detected. NF1 is presumed to result from loss-of-function mutations, because 80% of germline mutations described cause truncation of the gene product. In addition, deletion of the entire gene causes typical, although often severe, NF1.[223,224] The *NF1* gene product is termed *neurofibromin*. Its function is not fully understood, although it is known to activate ras-guanosine triphosphate-ase, which promotes the hydrolysis of active ras-guanosine triphosphate to inactive ras-guanosine diphosphate.[225] Histological features of affected blood vessels are an abnormal proliferation of spindle cells, and intima with fibrous thickening and mesodermal dysplasia or fibromuscular hyperplasia. Micronodular formations of smooth muscle aggregates appear on the walls of vessels. The vascular abnormalities involve both small and large vessels and lead to stenosis, occlusion, or rupture of the blood vessels.[227]

Diagnosis

The National Institutes of Health (NIH) diagnostic criteria for NF1, developed at a consensus conference in 1987, are met in an individual who has two or more of the following features in the absence of another diagnosis: (a) six or more café-au-lait macules larger than 5 mm in greatest diameter in prepubertal individuals and larger than 15 mm in greatest diameter in postpubertal individuals, (b) two or more neurofibromas of any type or one plexiform neurofibroma, (c) freckling in the axillary or inguinal regions, (d) optic glioma, (e) two or more Lisch nodules (iris hamartomas) or a distinctive osseous lesion such as sphenoid dysplasia or tibial pseudoarthrosis, or (f) a first-degree relative with NF1 as defined by the previous criteria.[226,228,229] It has been suggested that a pathogenic mutation in the *NF1* gene be added to the list of diagnostic criteria. A comprehensive *NF1* mutation screen can detect gene mutations in more than 92% of tested patients, fulfilling NIH diagnostic criteria.

Mutation analysis is especially important in very young children with a negative family history and who fulfill the NIH diagnostic criteria only in part. Molecular testing for NF1 is also useful for diagnostic confirmation in the case when an adult patient with café-au-lait macules and axillary freckles has no neurofibromas. A multistep mutation detection protocol that identifies more than 95% of pathogenic *NF1* mutations in individuals fulfilling the NIH diagnostic criteria is available. This protocol, which involves analysis of both messenger RNA and genomic DNA, includes real-time polymerase chain reaction, direct sequencing, microsatellite marker analysis, multiplex ligation-dependent probe amplification, and interphase fluorescence in situ hybridization. Because of the frequency of splicing mutations, and the variety and rarity of individual mutations found in people with NF1, methods based solely on analysis of genomic DNA have lower detection rates. Prenatal diagnosis for pregnancies at increased risk for NF1 is available by analysis of DNA extracted from fetal cells obtained by amniocentesis or chorionic villus sampling.[230,231]

Treatment

No medical treatment is available to prevent the characteristic lesions, and surgery, chemotherapy, and radiotherapy are currently the only treatment options for cutaneous or subcutaneous neurofibromas that are disfiguring or in inconvenient locations.[221,232] There is no specific therapy for the cerebrovascular complications. A phase I trial of Lovastatin showed improvement in memory, recall, and recognition.[233] Several drugs are currently at different stages of clinical evaluations. A majority of the trials, including Pirfenidone, Peg-Interferon Alpha-2b, Imatinib, Sirolimus, Vinblastine with Methotrexate, and photodynamic therapy are aiming for patients with plexiform neurofibroma.[233]

Mitochondrial Disorders

MITOCHONDRIAL MYOPATHY, ENCEPHALOPATHY, LACTIC ACIDOSIS, AND STROKELIKE EPISODES

MELAS (OMIM 540000) is a phenotypically and genetically heterogeneous mitochondrial disorder.

Epidemiology

MELAS is the most prevalent inherited mitochondrial disorder. The estimated prevalence of a 3243A>G mutation in mitochondrial DNA (mtDNA), which is responsible for 80% of MELAS cases, ranges from 5 to 236 per 100,000 in the white population.[234,235] One study, however, quantified the prevalence of this mutation in northern Finland as high as 1/9800 individuals in the adult population.[236,237]

Clinical Presentation

Hirano and Palavkis[238] first described the MELAS clinical spectrum, which allowed distinguishing MELAS from two other similar mitochondrial diseases: Kearns–Sayre syndrome and myoclonic epilepsy with ragged red fibers. The age of onset of initial symptoms is usually between 2 years and 20 years.[239] Strokelike episodes (usually characterized by aphasia, cortical blindness, hemianopia, and hemiparesis), which are usually transient, fluctuating, and not disabling, are the clinical disease hallmark. The strokelike lesions can evolve over weeks, resembling the spreading pattern of a cardioembolic or thrombotic stroke.[240] They are usually misdiagnosed as stroke, vasculitis, or encephalitis.[238] Multiple strokelike events may contribute to progressive disability and dementia.[241,242] Additional features, including seizures, normal early development followed by cognitive decline, short stature, hearing loss, psychosis, lactic acidosis, migraine, visual impairment, diabetes, and myopathy are also found in myoclonic epilepsy with ragged red fibers and Kearns–Sayre syndrome. Patients with MELAS often present acutely with a febrile illness and/or focal neurological deficits and/or seizure with a history of cataract and sensorineural deafness. Focal and generalized seizures are reported in 85% to 100% of patients with MELAS, often originating from the occipital lobe and during the strokelike episodes. They are initially infrequent and easy to treat, and during the disease course became more frequent and untreatable, probably contributing to disease progression.[242,243] Migraine is another common feature described in 77% of patients, and in 15% of cases may be the initial symptom.[238] Cognitive deficits include learning disability, decreased language and memory capabilities, and sometimes executive function impairment. Patients are, however, able to perform daily living activities until the later stages of disease.[244] Cardiomyopathy, conduction defects, or chronic heart failure, as well as diabetes mellitus and gastrointestinal disturbance, are also frequent complications of MELAS. Other nonspecific manifestations such as myopathy with easy fatigability and exercise intolerance, ophthalmic complications (ophthalmoplegia, pigmentary retinopathy, optic atrophy), and renal disturbances have been observed.[238] However, the presentation is variable as a result, at least in part, of the heteroplasmy phenomenon, with different levels of mutant and wild-type mtDNA in different tissues.[239]

One recent study with 10 years of follow-up of patients with MELAS showed neuropsychological decline and worsening of MRI abnormalities in patients with MELAS but not in carrier relatives (with the m.3243A>G mutation). Patients also had a greater risk of death than carrier relatives.[249]

Brain Imaging

Cerebral CT has revealed aspecific areas of cerebral infarction or bilateral basal ganglia calcifications.[238] However, infarction areas do not correspond to a definite vascular territory. In general, the posterior territories, particularly the temporoparieto-occipital lobes, are affected more frequently than the anterior regions.[244] MRI features are now the cornerstone of diagnosis, along with genetic studies and muscle biopsy.[243] Although there are no specific neuroradiological diagnostic features, hyperintensities on T2- and diffusion weighted imaging-weighted sequences that are not restricted to distinct arterial territories and migrate over time are highly suggestive of a metabolic disorders. The deep gray matter such as the thalamus may be involved, whereas cortical lesions generally spare the deeper white matter, reflecting the high metabolic demand of these regions. Some authors have reported an increased apparent diffusion coefficient (ADC) on MRI,[246] but these findings are controversial and the recent consensus is probably that there is restricted diffusion and therefore reduced ADC, as in ischemic stroke. The discrepancy in ADC findings is probably related to different time intervals between strokelike episodes and MRI[247]; longer time intervals are associated with greater ADC values related to the development of intracellular edema after the cytotoxic edema of the acute phase. ^{1}H magnetic resonance spectroscopy shows a decrease in N-acetylaspartate and an increase in lactate within strokelike lesions, whereas single proton emission computed tomography is characterized by a trend of hyperperfusion in acute, and hypoperfusion in chronic, disease phases.[247]

Genetics, Pathogenesis, and Pathological Aspects

MELAS is caused mostly by a point mutation in mtDNA, which is—in 80% of cases—a mutation (m.3243A>G) of the tRNALeu gene[248] Sato et al.,[249] in 1992, demonstrated the maternal pattern of inheritance of the mutation in a number of pedigrees. It should be emphasized that only a minor portion of subjects with the m.3243A>G mutation have clinical symptoms because, for the heteroplasmia phenomenon, each mitochondria has many copies of mtDNA, but the number of mutated mtDNA is variable. Thus, cell types and tissues within an individual have different amounts of abnormal mtDNA and it differs over time, explaining variable penetrance and clinical expression differences. Another important concept is the threshold effect: a threshold level, variable among individuals and based on the balance of oxygen supply and demand of mutated mtDNA, triggers the expression of disease symptoms. Given these peculiar aspects of mitochondrial heritability, a negative genetic test and muscle biopsy does not rule out the diagnosis definitively.

Other mtDNA mutations in *MTTL1* and other transfer RNA genes (*MTTF, MTTv, MTTQ*), as well as mutations in other subunits of complex 1, such as *MTND1, MTND5*, and *MTND6*, have also been identified as causing MELAS.[250] The mutations in MELAS most commonly disrupt mitochondrial protein synthesis, leading to decreased activity of respiratory chain elements and, finally, to an imbalance between energy requirements and the available energy of the cell. Dysfunction of complex I (43% of patients), II (29% of patients), and IV (23% of patients) has been mostly detected.[240] Mitochondrial mass increases inside the cells to compensate for respiratory chain failure, appearing on muscle biopsy as ragged red fibers.

Other mechanisms, including increased production or reactive oxygen species that are converted in toxic compounds or abnormal calcium and nitric oxide levels, have been described to play a role in the pathogenesis of MELAS.[240] Two theories have been hypothesized to explain the pathogenesis of strokelike episodes: the mitochondrial cytopathy theory and the mitochondrial angiopathy theory. According to the mitochondrial cytopathy theory, the leucine transfer RNA mutation decreases protein synthesis and causes oxidative phosphorylation failure, leading, ultimately, to adenosine triphosphate (ATP) depletion and energy failure. The mitochondrial angiopathy theory proposes that the accumulation of abnormal mitochondria in the endothelium and smooth muscle leads to cerebral small-vessel dysfunction. In addition, it has been recently proposed that the strokelike episodes in MELAS result from neuronal hyperexcitability, which increases the energy demand in a neuronal population with mitochondrial dysfunction. This, along with the increased capillary permeability, causes vasogenic edema involving the cerebral cortex primarily.

Diagnosis

Although clinical criteria for MELAS diagnosis are available in the literature, the diagnosis of MELAS is one of exclusion.[238,241] The diagnostic workup includes a combination of clinical and radiological findings in association with laboratory and genetic testing, which should include mtDNA sequencing. The latter may be performed by using tissues other than peripheral blood, such as skeletal muscle, hair follicles, buccal mucosa, or urine sediment, and may include the screening of other nuclear, possibly involved genes. Lactate levels, pyruvate levels, and the lactate-to-pyruvate ratio are elevated in serum and cerebrospinal fluid of patients with MELAS. Serum lactate levels can be normal during the early disease stages but increase during the disease course (particularly during strokelike episodes). Elevated lactate levels were found in more than 90% of patients sera whereas in 50% to 100% of patients, high lactate levels were detected in the cerebrospinal fluid.[237,241,242]

On skeletal muscle biopsy, patients with MELAS typically present ragged red fibers (80%–100% of specimens) that show positive staining for modified Gomori trichrome but also cytochrome *c* oxidase-negative fibers, succinate dehydrogenase hyperreactivity, and, at a ultrastructural level, abnormally shaped mitochondria with paracrystalline inclusions.[242]

Treatment

Although many treatment options for MELAS, which include lifestyle modifications and pharmacological options, have been proposed, there is no U.S. Food and Drug Administration–approved drug or protocol therapy for this disease. The rarity of MELAS makes clinical trials and large-scale drug studies challenging. Thus, most of the therapeutic strategies used in MELAS have been adopted from case reports and/or studies with heterogeneous populations. A variety of pharmacological options, mostly nutritional supplements and vitamins, used alone or in different combinations, have been tried with different level of success but without consistent benefits. Treatment focuses on increasing respiratory chain activity by administering antioxidants, respiratory chain substrates, and cofactors that augment the production or use of ATP.[241] Coenzyme Q10 (CoQ) is the most widely used treatment in patients with mitochondrial disorders. CoQ is a mitochondrial substrate with antioxidant properties and may provide benefits through multiple mechanisms, including enhancement of the activity of respiratory chain or increase of ATP production, or by antioxidant activity.[241] In small trials and case reports, CoQ used alone or in combination with creatine and lipoic acid decreased the level of lactic acid, improved cardiac conduction defects, reduced muscle weakness, and improved neurological function.[251] In the only RCT that reached level II status, only 16 patients completed the treatment with daily 120 mg Coq 10, 300 mg lipoic acid, and 3 g creatine for 2 months. Patients had low levels of serum lactate, and neuromuscular deficits improved modestly. However, the long-term clinical effects remain to be proved.[251,252,253] Idebenone, which is a synthetic analog of CoQ and has better central nervous system penetration, has been used to improve cerebral mitochondrial metabolism and decrease the frequency of strokelike episodes in patients with MELAS.[254] However, the drug use has been approved in Japan, but not in the United States, for the treatment of MELAS.

L-arginine (L-Arg) is a semiessential amino acid and a substrate of nitric oxide synthase involved in growth, urea detoxification, and nitric oxide synthesis. L-Arg also plays an important role in endothelial-dependent vascular relaxation. Several anecdotal reports have suggested L-Arg may enhance vascular reactivity in patients with MELAS.[255] The early infusion of L-Arg in the acute phase of strokelike episodes was associated with decreased severity and duration of strokelike events, reduced ischemic injury, and improved microcirculation, as evidenced on single proton emission computed tomography.[255,256] In addition, Koga et al.[255] reported that the oral supplementation of L-Arg (2–24 g/day or 150–300 mg/kg/day) decreases significantly the frequency and severity of strokelike episodes without major adverse effects.

Vitamins of complex B (thiamine B1, riboflavin B2, and nicotinamide B3) are considered a first-line treatment for MELAS. The active form of thiamine—thiamine pyrophosphate—is a coenzyme that increases acetyl coenzyme A, a substrate need for the proper functioning of the respiratory chain. A dosage ranging from 50 to 300 mg/day can be administered both to adult and pediatric patients. Riboflavin is a cofactor for electron transport in complexes I and II, finally enhancing ATP production. Last, nicotinamide, by increasing the supply of nicotinamide adenine dinucleotide in the respiratory chain, has also been shown to be somewhat beneficial.[240]

Dichloroacetate (DCA) is an indirect activator of the pyruvate dehydrogenase, a key enzyme complex that participates in the aerobic metabolism of pyruvic acid. By enhancing the activity of this complex, DCA increases the consumption of pyruvate and decreases the levels of lactic acid.

A randomized, placebo-controlled trial using DCA in patients with MELAS did not show treatment benefits and was terminated prematurely because of peripheral nerve toxicity.[257] Other treatments, including corticosteroids, carnitine, creatine, and antioxidants, such as vitamin E and C, have been proposed, but their beneficial effects have not been established.[237,240]

REFERENCES

1. Roger VL, Go AS, Lloyd-Jones DM, et al. Heart disease and stroke statistics: 2012 update: a report from the American Heart Association. *Circulation.* 2012;125:e2–e220.
2. Dichgans M. Genetics of ischaemic stroke. *Lancet Neurol.* 2007;6:149–161.
3. Sacco RL, Ellenberg JH, Mohr JP, et al. Infarcts of undetermined cause: the NINCDS Stroke Data Bank. *Ann Neurol.* 1989;25:382–390.
4. Hassan A, Markus HS. Genetics and ischaemic stroke. *Brain.* 2000;123:1784–1812.
5. Rubattu S, Giliberti R, Volpe M. Etiology and pathophysiology of stroke as a complex trait. *Am J Hypertens.* 2000;13:1139–1148.
6. Jerrard-Dunne P, Cloud G, Hassan A, Markus HS. Evaluating the genetic component of ischemic stroke subtypes: a family history study. *Stroke.* 2003;34:1364–1369.
7. Meschia JF, Worrall BB, Rich SS. Genetic susceptibility to ischemic stroke. *Nat Rev Neurol.* 2011;7:369–378.
8. Ballabio E, Bersano A, Bresolin N, Candelise L. Monogenic vessel diseases related to ischemic stroke: a clinical approach. *J Cereb Blood Flow Metab.* 2007;27:1649–1662.
9. Razvi SS, Bone I. Single gene disorders causing ischaemic stroke. *J Neurol.* 2006;253:685–700.
10. Markus HS. Stroke genetics. *Hum Mol Genet.* 2011;20:R124–R131.
11. Tournier-Lasserve E, Joutel A, Melki J, et al. Cerebral autosomal dominant arteriopathy with subcortical infarcts and leukoencephalopathy maps to chromosome 19q12. *Nat Genet.* 1993;3:256–259.
12. Bousser MG, Tournier-Lasserve E. Summary of the proceedings of the First International Workshop on CADASIL: Paris, May 19–21, 1993. *Stroke.* 1994;25:704–707.
13. Razvi SS, Davidson R, Bone I, Muir KW. The prevalence of cerebral autosomal dominant arteriopathy with subcortical infarcts and leucoencephalopathy (CADASIL) in the west of Scotland. *J Neurol Neurosurg Psychiatry.* 2005;76:739–741.

14. Kalimo H, Ruchoux MM, Viitanen M, Kalaria RN. CADASIL: a common form of hereditary arteriopathy causing brain infarcts and dementia. *Brain Pathol.* 2002;12:371–384.
15. Narayan SK, Gorman G, Kalaria RN, Ford GA, Chinnery PF. The minimum prevalence of CADASIL in Northeast England. *Neurology.* 2012;78:1025–1027.
16. Dichgans M, Mayer M, Uttner I, et al. The phenotypic spectrum of CADASIL: clinical findings in 102 cases. *Ann Neurol.* 1998;44:731–739.
17. Desmond DW, Moroney JT, Lynch T, Chan S, Chin SS, Mohr JP. The natural history of CADASIL: a pooled analysis of previously published cases. *Stroke.* 1999;30:1230–1233.
18. Bousser M, Tournier-Lasserve E. Cerebral autosomal dominant arteriopathy with subcortical infarcts and leukoencephalopathy: from stroke to vessel wall physiology. *J Neurol Neurosurg Psychiatry.* 2001;70:285–287.
19. Singhal S, Bevan S, Barrick T, Rich P, Markus HS. The influence of genetic and cardiovascular risk factors on the CADASIL phenotype. *Brain.* 2004;127:2031–2038
20. Adib-Samii P, Brice G, Martin RJ, Markus HS. Clinical spectrum of CADASIL and the effect of cardiovascular risk factors on phenotype: study in 200 consecutively recruited individuals. Stroke 2010; 41:630–634.
21. Opherk C, Peters N, Herzog J, Luedtke R, Dichgans M. Long-term prognosis and causes of death in CADASIL: a retrospective study in 411 patients. *Brain.* 2004;127:2533–2539
22. Chabriat H, Joutel A, Dichgans M, Tournier-Lasserve E, Bousser MG. CADASIL. *Lancet Neurol.* 2009;8:643–653.
23. Dichgans M. Cognition in CADASIL. *Stroke.* 2009;40:S45–S47.
24. Chabriat H, Vahedi K, Iba-Zizen MT, et al. Clinical spectrum of CADASIL: a study of 7 families: cerebral autosomal dominant arteriopathy with subcortical infarcts and leukoencephalopathy. *Lancet.* 1995;346:934–939.
25. Singhal S, Rich P, Markus HS. The spatial distribution of MR imaging abnormalities in cerebral autosomal dominant arteriopathy with subcortical infarcts and leukoencephalopathy and their relationship to age and clinical features. *AJNR Am J Neuroradiol.* 2005;26:2481–2487.
26. Valenti R, Poggesi A, Pescini F, Inzitari D, Pantoni L. Psychiatric disturbances in CADASIL: a brief review. *Acta Neurol Scand.* 2008;118:291–295.
27. Choi JC, Kang SY, Kang JH Park JK. Intracerebral hemorrhages in CADASIL. *Neurology.* 2006;67:2042–2044.
28. Lee YC, Liu CS, Chang MH, et al. Population-specific spectrum of *NOTCH3* mutations, MRI features and founder effect of CADASIL in Chinese. *J Neurol.* 2009;256:249–255.
29. Choi JC. Cerebral autosomal dominant arteriopathy with subcortical infarcts and leukoencephalopathy: a genetic cause of cerebral small vessel disease. *J Clin Neurol.* 2010;6:1–9.
30. Jouvent E, Poupon C, Gray F, et al. Intracortical infarcts in small vessel disease: a combined 7-T postmortem MRI and neuropathological case study in cerebral autosomal-dominant arteriopathy with subcortical infarcts and leukoencephalopathy. *Stroke.* 2011;42:e27–e30.
31. Pantoni L, Pescini F, Nannucci S, et al. Comparison of clinical, familial, and MRI features of CADASIL and *NOTCH3*-negative patients. *Neurology.* 2010;74:57–63.
32. Jacqmin M, Hervé, D, Viswanathan A, et al. Confluent thalamic hyperintensities in CADASIL. *Cerebrovasc Dis.* 2010;30:308–313.
33. Liem MK, Lesnik Oberstein SA, Haan J, et al. Cerebral autosomal dominant arteriopathy with subcortical infarcts and leukoencephalopathy: progression of MR abnormalities in prospective 7-year follow-up study. *Radiology.* 2008;249:964–971.
34. Peters N, Holtmannspötter M, Opherk C, et al. Brain volume changes in CADASIL: a serial MRI study in pure subcortical ischemic vascular disease. *Neurology.* 2006;66:1517–1522.
35. Liem MK, van der Grond J, Haan J, et al. Lacunar infarcts are the main correlate with cognitive dysfunction in CADASIL. *Stroke.* 2007;38:923–928.

36. Liem MK, Lesnik Oberstein SA, Haan J, et al. MRI correlates of cognitive decline in CADASIL: a 7-year follow-up study. *Neurology.* 2009;72:143–148.
37. Joutel A, Corpechot C, Ducros A, et al. *Notch3* mutations in CADASIL, a hereditary adult-onset condition causing stroke and dementia. *Nature.* 1996;383:707–710.
38. Joutel A, Corpechot C, Ducros A, et al. *Notch3* mutations in cerebral autosomal dominant arteriopathy with subcortical infarcts and leukoencephalopathy (CADASIL), a Mendelian condition causing stroke and vascular dementia. *Ann N Y Acad Sci.* 1997;826:213–217.
39. Dotti MT, Federico A, Mazzei R, et al. The spectrum of *Notch3* mutations in 28 Italian CADASIL families. *J Neurol Neurosurg Psychiatry.* 2005;76:736–738.
40. Cappelli A, Ragno M, Cacchiò G, Scarcella M, Staffolani P, Pianese L. High recurrence of the R1006C *NOTCH3* mutation in central Italian patients with cerebral autosomal dominant arteriopathy with subcortical infarcts and leukoencephalopathy (CADASIL). *Neurosci Lett.* 2009;462:176–178.
41. Bianchi S, Rufa A, Ragno M, et al. High frequency of exon 10 mutations in the *NOTCH3* gene in Italian CADASIL families: phenotypic peculiarities. *J Neurol.* 2010;257:1039–1042.
42. Dichgans M, Ludwig H, Muller-Hocker J, Messerschmidt A, Gasser T. Small in-frame deletions and missense mutations in CADASIL: 3D models predict misfolding of *Notch3* EGF-like repeat domains. *Eur J Hum Genet.* 2000;8:280–285.
43. Dotti MT, De Stefano N, Bianchi S, et al. A novel *NOTCH3* frameshift deletion and mitochondrial abnormalities in a patient with CADASIL. *Arch Neurol.* 2004;61:942–945.
44. Joutel A, Chabriat H, Vahedi K, et al. Splice site mutation causing a seven amino acid *Notch3* in-frame deletion in CADASIL *Neurology.* 2000;54:1874–1875.
45. Peters N, Opherk C, Bergmann T, Castro M, Herzog J, Dichgans M. Spectrum of mutations in biopsy-proven CADASIL: implications for diagnostic strategies. *Arch Neurol.* 2005;62:1091–1094.
46. Scheid R, Heinritz W, Leyhe T, et al. Cysteine-sparing *Notch3* mutations: CADASIL or CADASIL variants? *Neurology.* 2008;71:774–776.
47. Kim Y, Choi EJ, Choi CG, et al. Characteristics of CADASIL in Korea: a novel cysteine-sparing *Notch3* mutation. *Neurology.* 2006;66:1511–1516.
48. Santa Y, Uyama E, Chui DH, et al. Genetic clinical and pathological studies of CADASIL in Japan: a partial contribution on *Notch3* mutations and implications of smooth muscle cell degeneration for the pathogenesis. *J Neurol Sci.* 2003;212:79–84.
49. Uchino M, Hirano T, Uyama E, Hashimoto Y. Cerebral autosomal dominant arteriopathy with subcortical infarcts and leukoencephalopathy (CADASIL) and CADASIL-like disorders in Japan. *Ann N Y Acad Sci.* 2002;977: 273–278.
50. Joutel A, Monet-Leprêtre M, Gosele C, et al. Cerebrovascular dysfunction and microcirculation rarefaction precede white matter lesions in a mouse genetic model of cerebral ischemic small vessel disease. *J Clin Invest.* 2010;120:433–445.
51. Domenga V, Fardoux P, Lacombe P, et al. *Notch3* is required for arterial identity and maturation of vascular smooth muscle cells. *Genes Dev.* 2004;18:2730–2735.
52. Belin de Chantemele EJ, Retailleau K, Pinaud F, et al. Notch3 is a major regulator of vascular tone in cerebral and tail resistance arteries. *Arterioscler Thromb Vasc Biol.* 2008;28:2216–2224.
53. Opherk C, Duering M, Peters N, et al. CADASIL mutations enhance spontaneous multimerization of *NOTCH3*. *Hum Mol Genet.* 2009;18:2761–2767.
54. Miao Q, Paloneva T, Tuominen S, et al. Fibrosis and stenosis of the long penetrating cerebral arteries: the cause of the white matter pathology in cerebral autosomal dominant arteriopathy with subcortical infarcts and leukoencephalopathy. *Brain Pathol.* 2004;14:358–364.
55. Markus HS, Martin RJ, Simpson MA, et al. Diagnostic strategies in CADASIL. *Neurology.* 2002;59:1134–1138.

56. Ruchoux MM, Chabriat H, Bousser MG, Baudrimont M, Tournier-Lasserve E. Presence of ultrastructural arterial lesions in muscle and skin vessels of patients with CADASIL. *Stroke.* 1994;25:2291–2292.
57. Tikka S, Mykkänen K, Ruchoux MM, et al. Congruence between *NOTCH3* mutations and GOM in 131 patients with CADASIL. *Brain.* 2009;132:933–939.
58. Lesnik Oberstein SA, van Duinen SG, van den Boom R, et al. Evaluation of diagnostic *NOTCH3* immunostaining in CADASIL. *J Cereb Blood Flow Metab.* 2003;23:599–604.
59. del Río-Espínola A, Mendióroz M, Domingues-Montanari S, et al. CADASIL management or what to do when there is little one can do. *Exp Rev Neurother.* 2009;9:197–210.
60. Huang L, Yang Q, Zhang L, Chen X, Huang Q, Wang H. Acetazolamide improves cerebral hemodynamics in CADASIL. *J Neurol Sci.* 2010;292:77–80.
61. Donnini I, Nannucci S, Valenti R, et al. Acetazolamide for the prophylaxis of migraine in CADASIL: a preliminary experience. *J Headache Pain.* 2012;13:299–302.
62. Oh JH, Lee JS, Kang SY, Kang JH, Choi JC. Aspirin-associated intracerebral hemorrhage in a patient with CADASIL. *Clin Neurol Neurosurg.* 2008;110:384–386.
63. Posada IJ, Ferrero M, Lopez-Valdes E, Goni-Imzcoz M. Galantamine therapy in dementia associated with CADASIL. *Rev Neurol.* 2008;47:299–300.
64. Dichgans M, Markus HS, Salloway S, et al. Donepezil in patients with subcortical vascular cognitive impairment: a randomised double-blind trial in CADASIL. *Lancet Neurol.* 2008;7:310–318.
65. Reyes S, Kurtz A, Hervé D, Tournier-Lasserve E, Chabriat H. Presymptomatic genetic testing in CADASIL. *J Neurol.* 2012;25:2131–2136.
66. Zheng DM, Xu FF, Gao Y, Zhang H, Han SC, Bi GR. A Chinese pedigree of cerebral autosomal recessive arteriopathy with subcortical infarcts and leukoencephalopathy (CARASIL): clinical and radiological features. *J Clin Neurosci.* 2009;16:847–849.
67. Yanagawa S, Ito N, Arima K, Ikeda S. Cerebral autosomal recessive arteriopathy with subcortical infarcts and leukoencephalopathy. *Neurology.* 2002;58:817–820.
68. Mendioroz M, Fernández-Cadenas I, Del Río-Espinola A, et al. A missense *HTRA1* mutation expands CARASIL syndrome to the Caucasian population. *Neurology.* 2010;75:2033–2035.
69. Fukutake T. Cerebral autosomal recessive arteriopathy with subcortical infarcts and leukoencephalopathy (CARASIL): from discovery to gene identification. *J Stroke Cerebrovasc Dis.* 2011;20:85–93.
70. Maeda S, Nakayama H, Isaka K, Aihara Y, Nemoto S. Familial unusual encephalopathy of Binswanger's type without hypertension. *Folia Psychiatr Neurol Jpn.* 1976;30:165–177.
71. Fukutake T, Hirayama K. Familial young-adult-onset arteriosclerotic leukoencephalopathy with alopecia and lumbago without arterial hypertension. *Eur Neurol.* 1995;35:69–79.
72. Hara K, Shiga A, Fukutake T, et al. Association of *HTRA1* mutations and familial ischemic cerebral small-vessel disease. *N Engl J Med.* 2009;360:1729–1739.
73. Oide T, Nakayama H, Yanagawa S, Ito N, Ikeda S, Arima K. Extensive loss of arterial medial smooth muscle cells and mural extracellular matrix in cerebral autosomal recessive arteriopathy with subcortical infarcts and leukoencephalopathy (CARASIL). *Neuropathology.* 2008;28:132–142.
74. Jen J, Cohen AH, Yue Q, et al. Hereditary Endotheliopathy with Retinopathy Nephropathy and Stroke (HERNS). *Neurology.* 1997;49:1322–1330.
75. Terwindt GM, Haan J, Ophoff RA, et al. Clinical and genetic analysis of a large Dutch family with autosomal dominant vascular retinopathy migraine and Raynaud's phenomenon. *Brain.* 1998;121:303–316.
76. Ophoff RA, DeYoung J, Service SK, et al. Hereditary vascular retinopathy cerebroretinal vasculopathy and hereditary endotheliopathy with retinopathy nephropathy and stroke map to a single locus on chromosome 3p211-p213. *Am J Hum Genet.* 2001;69:447–453.

77. Grand MG, Kaine J, Fulling K, et al Cerebroretinal vasculopathy: a new hereditary syndrome. *Ophthalmology.* 1988;95:649–659.
78. Gutmann DH, Fischbeck KH, Sergott RC. Hereditary retinal vasculopathy with cerebral white matter lesions. *Am J Med Genet.* 1989;34:217–220.
79. Weil S, Reifenberger G, Dudel C, Yousry TA, Schriever S, Noachtar S. Cerebroretinal vasculopathy mimicking a brain tumor: a case of a rare hereditary syndrome *Neurology.* 1999;53:629–631.
80. Niedermayer I, Graf N, Schmidbauer J, Reiche W. Cerebroretinal vasculopathy mimicking a brain tumor. *Neurology.* 2000;54:1878–1879.
81. Storimans CW, Oosterhuis JA, van Schooneveld MJ, Bos PJ, Maaswinkel-Mooy PD. Familial vascular retinopathy: a preliminary report. *Doc Ophthalmol.* 1990;75:259–261. Cohn AC, Kotschet K, Veitch A, Delatycki MB, McCombe MF. Novel ophthalmological features in hereditary endotheliopathy with retinopathy nephropathy and stroke syndrome. *Clin Exp Ophthalmol.* 2005;33:181–183.
82. Winkler DT, Lyrer P, Probst A, et al. Hereditary systemic angiopathy (HSA) with cerebral calcifications, retinopathy, progressive nephropathy, and hepatopathy. *J Neurol.* 2008;255:77–88.
83. Kavanagh D, Spitzer D, Kothari PH, et al. New roles for the major human 3′-5′ exonuclease *TREX1* in human disease. *Cell Cycle.* 2008;7:1718–1725.
84. Federico A, Di Donato I, Bianchi S, Di Palma C, Taglia I, Dotti MT. Hereditary cerebral small vessel diseases: a review. *J Neurol Sci.* 2012;322:25–30.
85. Chowdhury D, Beresford PJ, Zhu P, et al. The exonuclease TREX1 is in the SET complex and acts in concert with NM23-H1 to degrade DNA during granzyme A-mediated cell death. *Mol Cell.* 2006;23:133–142.
86. Richards A, van den Maagdenberg AM, Jen JC, et al. C-terminal truncations in human 3′-5′ DNA exonuclease TREX1 cause autosomal dominant retinal vasculopathy with cerebral leukodystrophy. *Nat Genet.* 2007;39:1068–1070.
87. Crow YJ, Leitch A, Hayward BE, et al. Mutations in genes encoding ribonuclease H2 subunits cause Aicardi-Goutières syndrome and mimic congenital viral brain infection. *Nat Genet.* 2006;38:910–916.
88. Mateen FJ, Krecke K, Younge BR, et al. Evolution of a tumor-like lesion in cerebroretinal vasculopathy and *TREX1* mutation. *Neurology.* 2010;28:1211–1213.
89. Vahedi K, Alamowitch S. Clinical spectrum of type IV collagen (*COL4A1*) mutations: a novel genetic multisystem disease. *Curr Opin Neurol.* 2011;24:63–68.
90. Lanfranconi S, Markus HS. *COL4A1* mutations as a monogenic cause of cerebral small vessel disease: a systematic review. *Stroke.* 2010;41:e513–e518.
91. de Vries LS, Koopman C, Groenendaal F, et al. *COL4A1* mutation in two preterm siblings with antenatal onset of parenchymal hemorrhage. *Ann Neurol.* 2009;65:12–18.
92. Shah S, Kumar Y, McLean B, et al. A dominantly inherited mutation in collagen IV A1 (*COL4A1*) causing childhood onset stroke without porencephaly. *Eur J Paediatr Neurol.* 2010;14:182–187.
93. Breedveld G, de Coo IF, Lequin MH, et al. Novel mutations in three families confirm a major role of COL4A1 in hereditary porencephaly. *J Med Genet.* 2006;43:490–495.
94. Gould DB, Phalan FC, Breedveld GJ, et al. Mutations in *COL4A1* cause perinatal cerebral hemorrhage and porencephaly. *Science.* 2005;308:1167–1171.
95. Vahedi K, Massin P, Guichard JP, et al. Hereditary infantile hemiparesis retinal arteriolar tortuosity and leukoencephalopathy. *Neurology.* 2003;60:57–63.
96. Vahedi K, Kubis N, Boukobza M, et al. *COL4A1* mutation in a patient with sporadic recurrent intracerebral hemorrhage. *Stroke.* 2007;38: 461–1464.
97. Bilguvar K, DiLuna ML, Bizzarro MJ, et al. *COL4A1* mutation in preterm intraventricular hemorrhage. *J Pediatr.* 2009;155:743–745.

98. Emanuel BS, Sellinger BT, Gudas LJ, Myers JC. Localization of the human procollagen alpha-1(IV) gene to chromosome 13q34 by in situ hybridization. *Am J Hum Genet.* 1986;38:38–44.
99. Gould DB, Phalan FC, van Mil SE, et al. Role of COL4A1 in small-vessel disease and hemorrhagic stroke. *N Engl J Med.* 2006;354:1489–1496.
100. van der Knaap MS, Smit LM, Barkhof F, et al. Neonatal porencephaly and adult stroke related to mutations in collagen IV A1. *Ann Neurol.* 2006;59:504–511.
101. Sibon I, Coupry I, Menegon P, et al. *COL4A1* mutation in Axenfeld-Rieger anomaly with leukoencephalopathy and stroke. *Ann Neurol.* 2007;62:177–184.
102. Vahedi K, Boukobza M, Massin P, et al. Clinical and brain MRI follow-up study of a family with *COL4A1* mutation. *Neurology.* 2007;69:1564–1568.
103. Alamowitch S, Plaisier E, Favrole P, et al Cerebrovascular disease related to *COL4A1* mutations in HANAC syndrome. *Neurology.* 2009;73:1873–1882.
104. Plaisier E, Alamowitch S, Gribouval O, et al. Autosomal-dominant familial hematuria with retinal arterial tortuosity and contractures: a novel syndrome. *Kidney Int.* 2005;67:2354–2360.
105. Boutaud A, Borza DB, Bondar O, et al. Type IV collagen of the glomerular basement membrane: evidence that the chain specificity of network assembly is encoded by the noncollagenous NC1 domains. *J Biol Chem.* 2000;275:30716–30724.
106. Plaisier E, Gribouval O, Alamowitch S, et al. Mutations and hereditary angiopathy with nephropathy aneurysms and cramps (HANAC) syndrome. *N Engl J Med.* 2007;357:2687–2695.
107. Plaisier E, Chen Z, Gekeler F, et al. Novel *COL4A1* mutations associated with HANAC syndrome: a role for the triple helical CB3 [IV] domain. *Am J Med Genet.* 2010;152:2550–2555.
108. Gupta MC, Graham PL, Kramer JM. Characterization of alpha1(IV) collagen mutations in *Caenorhabditis elegans* and the effects of alpha1 and alpha2(IV) mutations on type IV collagen distribution. *J Cell Biol.* 1997;137:1185–1196.
109. Hudson BG, Tryggvason K, Sundaramoorthy M, Neilson EG. Alport's syndrome, Goodpasture's syndrome and type IV collagen. *N Engl J Med.* 2003;348:2543–2556.
110. Rouaud T, Labauge P, Tournier-Lasserve Mine M, Coustans M, Deburghgraeve V, Edan G. Acute urinary retention due to a novel collagen *COL4A1* mutation. *Neurology.* 2010;75:747–749.
111. Solomon E, Hiorns LR, Spurr N, et al. Chromosomal assignments of the genes coding for human types II, III, and IV collagen: a dispersed gene family. *Proc Natl Acad Sci U S A.* 1985;82:3330–3334.
112. Brady RO. Enzymatic abnormalities in diseases of sphingolipid metabolism. *Clin Chem.* 1967;13:7565–7577.
113. Brady RO, Gal AE, Bradley RM, Martensson E, Warshaw AL, Laster L. Enzymatic defect in Fabry disease ceramidetrihexosidase deficiency. *N Engl J Med.* 1967;276:1163–1167.
114. Hoffmann B, Mayatepek E. Fabry disease: often seen rarely diagnosed. *Dtsch Arztebl Int.* 2009;106:440–447.
115. Meikle PJ, Hopwood JJ, Clague AE, Carey WF. Prevalence of lysosomal storage disorders. *JAMA.* 1999;281:249–254.
116. Kotanko P, Kramar R, Devrnja D, et al. Results of a nationwide screening for Anderson-Fabry disease among dialysis patients. *J Am Soc Nephrol.* 2004;15:1323–1329.
117. Terryn W, Poppe B, Wuyts B, et al. Two-tier approach for the detection of β-galactosidase A deficiency in a predominantly female haemodialysis population. *Nephrol Dial Transplant.* 2008;23:294–300.
118. Nakao S, Kodama C, Takenaka T, et al. Fabry disease: detection of undiagnosed hemodialysis patients and identification of a "renal variant" phenotype. *Kidney Int.* 2003;64:801–807.
119. Kleinert J, Kotanko P, Spada M, et al. Anderson-Fabry disease: a case-finding study among male kidney transplant recipients in Austria. *Transplant Int.* 2009;22:287–292.

120. Sachdev B, Takenaka T, Teraguchi H, et al. Prevalence of Anderson-Fabry disease in male patients with late onset hypertrophic cardiomyopathy. *Circulation.* 2002;105:1407–1411.
121. Nakao S, Takenaka T, Maeda M, et al. An atypical variant of Fabry's disease in men with left ventricular hypertrophy. *N Engl J Med.* 1995;333:288–293.
122. Monserrat L, Gimeno-Blanes JR, Marin F, et al. Prevalence of Fabry disease in a cohort of 508 unrelated patients with hypertrophic cardiomyopathy. *J Am Coll Cardiol.* 2007;50:2399–2403.
123. Mehta A, Ricci R, Widmer U, et al. Fabry disease defined: baseline clinical manifestations of 366 patients in the Fabry Outcome Survey. *Eur J Clin Invest.* 2004;34:236–242.
124. Correia M, Silva MR, Matos I, et al. Prospective community-based study of stroke in northern Portugal: incidence and case fatality in rural and urban populations. *Stroke.* 2004;35:2048–2053.
125. Poorthuis BJ, Wevers RA, Kleijer WJ, et al. The frequency of lysosomal storage diseases in the Netherlands. *Hum Genet.* 1999;105:151–156.
126. Spada M, Pagliardini S, Yasuda M, et al. High incidence of later onset Fabry disease revealed by newborn screening. *Am J Hum Genet.* 2006;79:31–40.
127. Hwu WL, Chien YH, Lee NC, et al. Newborn screening for Fabry disease in Taiwan reveals a high incidence of the later-onset GLA mutation c.936+919G>A (IVS4+919G>A). *Hum Mutat.* 2009;30:1397–1405.
128. Baptista MV, Ferreira S, Pinho-e-Melo T, et al. Mutations of the *GLA* gene in young patients with stroke: the PORTYSTROKE study: screening genetic conditions in Portuguese young stroke patients. *Stroke.* 2010;41:431–436.
129. Brouns R, Sheorajpanday R, Braxel E, et al. Middelheim Fabry Study (MiFaS): a retrospective Belgian study on the prevalence of Fabry disease in young patients with cryptogenic stroke. *Clin Neurol Neurosurg.* 2007;109:479–484.
130. Sarikaya H, Yilmaz M, Michael N, Miserez AR, Steinmann B, Baumgartner RW. Zurich Fabry study: prevalence of Fabry disease in young patients with first cryptogenic ischaemic stroke or TIA. *Eur J Neurol.* 2012;19:1421–1426.
131. Rolfs A, Fazekas F, Grittner U, et al. Acute cerebrovascular disease in the young: the Stroke in Young Fabry Patients study. *Stroke.* 2013;44:340–349.
132. Zarate YA, Hopkin RJ. Fabry's disease. *Lancet.* 2008;372:1427–1435.
133. Gupta S, Ries M, Kotsopoulos S, Schiffmann R. The relationship of vascular glycolipid storage to clinical manifestations of Fabry disease: a cross-sectional study of a large cohort of clinically affected heterozygous women. *Medicine (Baltimore).* 2005;84:261–266.
134. Kolodny EH, Pastores GM. Anderson–Fabry disease: extrarenal neurologic manifestations. *J Am Soc Nephrol.* 2002;13:S3–S150.
135. Sims K, Politei J, Banikazemi M, Lee P. Stroke in Fabry disease frequently occurs before diagnosis and in the absence of other clinical events: natural history data from the Fabry Registry. *Stroke.* 2009;40:788–794.
136. Mitsias P, Levine SR. Cerebrovascular complications of Fabry disease. *Ann Neurol.* 1996;40:8–17.
137. Rolfs A, Böttcher T, Zschiesche M, et al. Prevalence of Fabry disease in patients with cryptogenic stroke: a prospective study. *Lancet.* 2005;366:1794–1796.
138. Schiffmann R. Natural history of Fabry disease in males: preliminary observations. *J Inherit Metab Dis.* 2001;24:15–17.
139. Kocen RS, Thomas PK. Peripheral nerve involvement in Fabry's disease. *Arch Neurol.* 1970;22:81–88.
140. Ramaswami U, Whybra C, Parini R, et al. Clinical manifestations of Fabry disease in children: data from the Fabry Outcome Survey. *Acta Paediatr.* 2006;95:86–92.
141. Schiffmann R, Warnock DG, Banikazemi M, et al. Fabry disease: progression of nephropathy, and prevalence of cardiac and cerebrovascular events before enzyme replacement therapy. *Nephrol Dial Transplant.* 2009;24:2102–2011.

142. Crutchfield KE, Patronas NJ, Dambrosia JM, et al. Quantitative analysis of cerebral vasculopathy in patients with Fabry disease. *Neurology.* 1998;50:1746–1749.
143. Fellgiebel A, Muller MJ, Ginsberg L. CNS manifestations of Fabry disease. *Lancet Neurol.* 2005;5:791–795.
144. Jardim L, Vedolin L, Schwartz IV, et al. CNS involvement in Fabry disease: clinical and imaging studies before and after 12 months of enzyme replacement therapy. *J Inherit Metab Dis.* 2004;27:229–240.
145. Reisin RC, Romero C, Marchesoni C, et al. Brain MRI findings in patients with Fabry disease. *J Neurol Sci.* 2011;305:41–44.
146. Nakamura K. Cerebral hemorrhage in Fabry's disease. *J Hum Genet.* 2010;55:259–261.
147. Moore DF, Scott LT, Gladwin MT, et al. Regional cerebral hyperperfusion and nitric oxide pathway dysregulation in Fabry disease: reversal by enzyme replacement therapy. *Circulation.* 2001;104:1506–1512.
148. MacDermot KD, Holmes A, Miners AH. Anderson-Fabry disease: clinical manifestations and impact of disease in a cohort of 60 obligate carrier females. *J Med Genet.* 2001;38:769–771.
149. Takanashi J, Barkovich AJ, Dillon WP, Sherr EH, Hart KA, Packman S. T1 hyperintensity in the pulvinar: key imaging feature for diagnosis of Fabry disease. *AJNR Am J Neuroradiol.* 2003;24:916–921.
150. Wendrich K, Whybra C, Ries M, Gal A, Beck M. Neurological manifestation of Fabry disease in females. *Contrib Nephrol.* 2001;136:241–244.
151. Wendrich K, Whybra C, Ries M, Gal A, Beck M. Neurological manifestation of Fabry disease in females. *Contrib Nephrol.* 2001;136:241–244.
152. Elstein D, Schachamorov E, Beeri R, Altarescu G. X-inactivation in Fabry disease. *Gene.* 2012;505:266–268.
153. Pastores GM, Lien YH. Biochemical and molecular genetic basis of Fabry disease. *J Am Soc Nephrol.* 2002;13;S130–S133.
154. Schäfer E, Baron K, Widmer U, et al. Thirty-four novel mutations of the *GLA* gene in 121 patients with Fabry disease. *Hum Mutat.* 2005;25:412.
155. Germain DP. Fabry disease. *Orphanet J Rare Disord.* 2010;5:30.
156. Shen Y, Bodary PF, Vargas FB, et al. Alpha-galactosidase A deficiency leads to increased tissue fibrin deposition and thrombosis in mice homozygous for the factor V Leiden mutation. *Stroke.* 2006;37:1106–1108.
157. De Graeba T, Azhar S, Dignat-George F, et al. Profile of endothelial and leukocyte activation in Fabry patients. *Ann Neurol.* 2000;47:229–233.
158. Moore DF, Scott LT, Gladwin MT, et al. Regional cerebral hyperperfusion and nitric oxide pathway dysregulation in Fabry disease: reversal by enzyme replacement therapy. *Circulation.* 2001;104:1506–1512.
159. Demuth K, Germain DP. Endothelial markers and homocysteine in patients with classic Fabry disease. *Acta Paediatr Suppl.* 2002;91:57–61.
160. Altarescu G, Moore DF, Schiffmann R. Effect of genetic modifiers on cerebral lesions in Fabry disease. *Neurology.* 2005;64:2148–2150.
161. Kaye EM, Kolodny EH, Logigian EL, Ullman MD. Nervous system involvement in Fabry's disease: clinicopathological and biochemical correlation. *Ann Neurol.* 1988;23:505–509.
162. Bersano A, Lanfranconi S, Valcarenghi C, Bresolin N, Micieli G, Baron P. Neurological features of Fabry disease: clinical, pathophysiological aspects and therapy. *Acta Neurol Scand.* 2012;126:77–97.
163. Eng CM, Germain DP, Banikazemi M, et al. Fabry disease: guidelines for the evaluation and management of multi-organ system involvement. *Genet Med.* 2006;8:539–548.

164. Salviati A, Burlina AP, Borsini W. Nervous system and Fabry disease, from symptoms to diagnosis: damage evaluation and follow-up in adult patients, enzyme replacement, and support therapy. *Neurol Sci.* 2010;31:299–306.
165. Lidove O, Kaminsky P, Hachulla E, et al. Fabry disease: "The New Great Imposter": results of the French Observatoire in Internal Medicine Departments (FIMeD). *Clin Genet.* 2012;81:571–577.
166. Hoffmann B, Georg Koch H, Schweitzer-Krantz S, Wendel U, Mayatepek E. Deficient alpha-galactosidase A activity in plasma but no Fabry disease: a pitfall in diagnosis. *Clin Chem Lab Med.* 2005;43:1276–1277.
167. Brouns R, Thijs V, Eyskens F, et al. Belgian Fabry study: prevalence of Fabry disease in a cohort of 1000 young patients with cerebrovascular disease. *Stroke.* 2010;41:863–868.
168. Young E, Mills K, Morris P, et al. Is globotriaosylceramide a useful biomarker in Fabry disease? *Acta Paediatr Suppl.* 2005;94:51–54.
169. Navarro C, Teijeira S, Dominguez C, et al. Fabry disease: an ultrastructural comparative study of skin in hemizygous and heterozygous patients. *Acta Neuropathol.* 2006;111:178–185.
170. Schaefer RM, Tylki-Szymanska A, Hilz MJ. Enzyme replacement therapy for Fabry disease: a systematic review of available evidence. *Drugs.* 2009;69:2179–2205.
171. Vedder AC, Linthorst GE, Van Breemen MJ, et al. The Dutch Fabry cohort: diversity of clinical manifestations and Gb3 levels. *J Inherit Metab Dis.* 2007;30:68–78.
172. Schiffmann R, Murray GJ, Treco D, et al. Infusion of alphagalactosidase A reduces tissue globotriaosylceramide storage in patients with Fabry disease. *Proc Natl Acad Sci USA.* 2000;97:365–370.
173. Banikazemi M, Bultas J, Waldek S, et al. Agalsidase-beta therapy for advanced Fabry disease: a randomized trial. *Ann Intern Med.* 2007;146:77–86.
174. Wilcox WR, Banikazemi M, Guffon N, et al. Long-term safety and efficacy of enzyme replacement therapy for Fabry disease. *Am J Hum Genet.* 2004;75:65–74.
175. Jung SC, Han IP, Limaye A, et al. Adeno-associated viral vector-mediated gene transfer results in long-term enzymatic and functional correction in multiple organs of Fabry mice. *Proc Natl Acad Sci U S A.* 2001;98:2676–2681.
176. Park J, Murray GJ, Limaye A, et al. Long-term correction of globotriaosylceramide storage in Fabry mice by recombinant adeno-associated virus-mediated gene transfer. *Proc Natl Acad Sci U S A.* 2003;100б:3450–3454.
177. Parenti G. Treating lysosomal storage diseases with pharmacological chaperones: from concept to clinics. *EMBO Mol Med.* 2009;1:268–279.
178. Yam GH, Bosshard N, Zuber C, Steinmann B, Roth J. Pharmacological chaperone corrects lysosomal storage in Fabry disease caused by trafficking competent variants. *Am J Physiol Cell Physiol.* 2006;290:C1076–C1082.
179. Politei JM. Can we use statins to prevent stroke in Fabry disease? *J Inherit Metab Dis.* 2009;32:481–487.
180. McCavit T. Sickle cell disease. *Pediatr Rev.* 2012;33:195–204.
181. Hassell KL. Population estimates of sickle cell disease in the U.S. *Am J Prev Med.* 2010;38:S512–S521.
182. Ohene-Frempong K, Weiner SJ, Sleeper LA, et al. Cerebrovascular accidents in sickle cell disease: rates and risk factors. *Blood.* 1998;91:288–294.
183. Adams R, McKie V, Nichols F, et al. The use of transcranial ultrasonography to predict stroke in sickle cell disease. *N Engl J Med.* 1992;326:605–610.
184. Moser FG, Miller ST, Bello JA, et al. The spectrum of brain MR abnormalities in sickle-cell disease: a report from the Cooperative Study of Sickle Cell Disease. *AJNR Am J Neuroradiol.* 1996;17:965–972.

185. Pavlakis SG, Bello J, Prohovnik I, et al. Brain infarction in sickle cell anemia: magnetic resonance imaging correlates. *Ann Neurol.* 1988;23:125–130.
186. Armstrong FD, Thompson RJ Jr, Wang W, et al. Cognitive functioning and brain magnetic resonance imaging in children with sickle cell disease: Neuropsychology Committee of the Cooperative Study of Sickle Cell Disease. *Pediatrics.* 1996;97:864–870.
187. Kinney TR, Sleeper LA, Wang WC, et al. Silent cerebral infarcts in sickle cell anemia: a risk factor analysis: the Cooperative Study of Sickle Cell Disease. *Pediatrics.* 1999;103:640–645.
188. Ballas SK, Lieff S, Benjamin LJ, et al. Definitions of the phenotypic manifestations of sickle cell disease. *Am J Hematol.* 2010;85:6–13.
189. Vichinsky EP, Neumayr LD, Gold JI, et al. Neuropsychological dysfunction and neuroimaging abnormalities in neurologically intact adults with sickle cell anemia. *JAMA.* 2010;303:1823–1831.
190. Pegelow CH, Macklin EA, Moser FG, et al. Longitudinal changes in brain magnetic resonance imaging findings in children with sickle cell disease. *Blood.* 2002;99:3014–3018.
191. Steen RG, Xiong X, Langston JW, Helton KJ. Brain injury in children with sickle cell disease: prevalence and etiology. *Ann Neurol.* 2003;54:564–572.
192. Switzer JA, Hes DCs, Nichols FT, Adams RJ. Pathophysiology and treatment of stroke in sickle-cell disease: present and future. *Lancet Neurol.* 2006;5:501–512.
193. Powars D, Adams RJ, Nichols FT, et al. Delayed intracranial hemorrhage following cerebral infarction in sickle cell anemia. *J Assoc Acad Minor Phys.* 1990;1:79–82.
194. Diggs LW, Brookoff D. Multiple cerebral aneurysms in patients with sickle cell disease. *South Med J.* 1993;86:377–379.
195. Anson JA, Koshy M, Ferguson L, Crowell RM. Subarachnoid hemorrhage in sickle-cell disease. *J Neurosurg.* 1991;75:552–558.
196. Bunn HF. Pathogenesis and treatment of sickle cell disease. *N Engl J Med.* 1997;337:762–769.
197. Voskaridou E, Christoulas D, Terpos E. Sickle-cell disease and the heart: review of the current literature. *Br J Haematol.* 2012;157:664–673.
198. Williams TN, Gladwin MT. Sickle-cell disease. *Lancet.* 2010;376:2018–2031.
199. Liesner R, Mackie I, Cookson J, et al. Prothrombotic changes in children with sickle cell disease: relationships to cerebrovascular disease and transfusion. *Br J Haematol.* 1998;103:1037–1044.
200. Russell MO, Goldberg H, Reis L, et al. Transfusion therapy for cerebrovascular abnormalities in sickle cell disease. *J Pediatr.* 1976;88:382–387.
201. Venketasubramanian N, Prohovnik I, Hurlet A, Mohr JP, Piomelli S. Middle cerebral artery velocity changes during transfusion in sickle cell anemia. *Stroke.* 1994;25:2153–2158.
202. Russell MO, Goldberg HI, Hodson A, et al. Effect of transfusion therapy on arteriographic abnormalities and on recurrence of stroke in sickle cell disease. *Blood.* 1984;63:162–69.
203. Powars D, Wilson B, Imbus C, Pegelow C, Allen J. The natural history of stroke in sickle cell disease. *Am J Med.* 1978;65:461–471.
204. Wang WC, Ware RE, Miller ST, et al. Hydroxycarbamide in very young children with sickle-cell anaemia: a multicentre, randomised, controlled trial (BABY HUG). *Lancet.* 2011;377:1663–1672.
205. Ware RE, Helms RW, SWiTCH Investigators. Stroke With Transfusions Changing to Hydroxyurea (SWiTCH). *Blood.* 2012;119:3925–3932.
206. Furie KL, Kasner SE, Adams RJ, et al. Guidelines for the prevention of stroke in patients with stroke or transient ischemic attack: a guideline for healthcare professionals from the American Heart Association/American Stroke Association. *Stroke.* 2011;42:227–276.
207. Walters MC, Hardy K, Edwards S, Adamkiewicz T, et al.: pulmonary, gonadal, and central nervous system status after bone marrow transplantation for sickle cell disease. *Biol Blood Marrow Transplant.* 2010;16:263–272.

208. Friedman JM. Epidemiology of neurofibromatosis type 1. *Am J Med Genet.* 1999;89:1–6.
209. Huson S, Compston D, Clark P, Harper P. A genetic study of von Recklinghausen neurofibromatosis in south east Wales: I. Prevalence, fitness, mutation rate, and effect of parental transmission on severity. *J Med Genet.* 1989; 26:704–711.
210. Lammert M, Friedman J, Kluwe L, Mautner V. Prevalence of neurofibromatosis 1 in German children at elementary school enrollment. *Arch Dermatol.* 2005;141:71–74.
211. DeBella K, Szudek J, Friedman JM. Use of the National Institutes of Health criteria for diagnosis of neurofibromatosis 1 in children. *Pediatrics.* 2000;105:608–614.
212. Boulanger JM, Larbrisseau A. Neurofibromatosis type 1 in a pediatric population: Ste-Justine's experience. *Can J Neurol Sci.* 2005;32:225–231.
213. Williams VC, Lucas J, Babcock MA, Gutmann DH, Korf B, Maria BL. Neurofibromatosis type 1 revisited. *Pediatrics.* 2009;123:124–133.
214. Zoller M, Rembeck B, Akesson HO, Angervall L. Life expectancy, mortality and prognostic factors in neurofibromatosis type 1: a twelve-year follow-up of an epidemiological study in Goteborg, Sweden. *Acta Dermatol Venereol.* 1995;75:136–140.
215. Creange A, Zeller J, Rostaing-Rigattieri S, et al. Neurological complications of neurofibromatosis type 1 in adulthood. *Brain.* 1999;122:473–481.
216. Norton KK, Xu J, Gutmann DH. Expression of the neurofibromatosis I gene product, neurofibromin, in blood vessel endothelial cells and smooth muscle. *Neurobiol Dis.* 1995;2:13–21.
217. Rea D, Brandsema JF, Armstrong D, et al. Cerebral arteriopathy in children with neurofibromatosis type 1. *Pediatrics.* 2009;124:e476–e483.
218. Rosser TL, Vezina G, Packer RJ. Cerebrovascular abnormalities in a population of children with neurofibromatosis type 1. *Neurology.* 2005;64:553–555.
219. Schievink WI, Riedinger M, Maya MM. Frequency of incidental intracranial aneurysms in neurofibromatosis type 1. *Am J Med Genet.* 2005;134:45–48.
220. Goh WH, Khong PL, Leung CS, Wong VC. T2-weighted hyperintensities (unidentified bright objects) in children with neurofibromatosis 1: their impact on cognitive function. *J Child Neurol.* 2004;19:853–858.
221. Jett K, Friedman JM. Clinical and genetic aspects of neurofibromatosis. *Genet Med.* 2010;12:1–11.
222. Shen MH, Harper PS, Upadhyaya M. Molecular genetics of neurofibromatosis type 1 (NF1). *J Med Genet.* 1996;33:2–17.
223. Ars E, Kruyer H, Morell M, et al. Recurrent mutations in the NF1 gene are common among neurofibromatosis type 1 patients. *J Med Genet.* 2003;40:e82.
224. Ars E, Serra E, Garcia J, et al. Mutations affecting mRNA splicing are the most common molecular defects in patients with neurofibromatosis type 1. *Hum Mol Genet.* 2000;9:237–247.
225. Trovo-Marqui AB, Tajara EH. Neurofibromin: a general outlook. *Clin Genet.* 2006;70:1–13.
226. Ward BA, Gutmann DH. Neurofibromatosis 1: from lab bench to clinic. *Pediatr Neurol.* 2005;32:221–228.
227. Hamilton SJ, Friedman JM. Insights into the pathogenesis of neurofibromatosis 1 vasculopathy. *Clin Genet.* 2000;58:341–344.
228. Williams VC, Lucas J, Babcock MA, Gutmann DH, Korf B, Maria BL. Neurofibromatosis type 1 revisited. *Pediatrics.* 2009;123:124–133.
229. Ferner RE, Huson SM, Thomas N, et al. Guidelines for the diagnosis and management of individuals with neurofibromatosis 1 (NF1). *J Med Genet.* 2007;44:81–88.

230. Yohay KH. The genetic and molecular pathogenesis of NF1 and NF2. *Semin Pediatr Neurol.* 2006;13:21–26.
231. Pros E, Gómez C, Martín T, Fabregas P, Serra E, Lazaro C. Nature and mRNA effect of 282 different NF1 point mutations: focus on splicing alterations. *Hum Mutat.* 2008;29:E173–E193.
232. Baujat B, Krastinova-Lolov D, Blumen M, Baglin AC, Coquille F, Chabolle F. Radiofrequency in the treatment of craniofacial plexiform neurofibromatosis: a pilot study. *Plast Reconstr Surg.* 2006;117:1261–1268.
233. Huson SM, Acosta MT, Belzberg AJ, et al. Back to the future: proceedings from the 2010 NF conference. *Am J Med Genet.* 2011;155A:307–321.
234. Testai FD, Gorelick PB. Inherited metabolic disorders and stroke part 1: Fabry and mitochondrial myopathy, encephalopathy, lactic acidosis, and stroke like episodes. *Arch Neurol.* 2010;67:19–24.
235. Manwaring N, Jones MM, Wang JJ, et al. Population prevalence of the MELAS A3243G mutation. *Mitochondrion.* 2007;7:230–233.
236. Majamaa K, Moilanen JS, Uimonen S, et al. Epidemiology of A3243G, the mutation for mitochondrial encephalomyopathy, lactic acidosis, and strokelike episodes: prevalence of the mutation in an adult population. *Am J Hum Genet.* 1998;63:447–454.
237. Scaglia F, Nortrop JL. The mitochondrial myopathy encephalopathy, lactic acidosis with stroke-like episodes (MELAS) syndrome: a review of treatment options. *CNS Drugs.* 2006;20:443–464.
238. Hirano M, Pavlakis SG. Mitochondrial, myopathy encephalopathy, lactic acidosis with stroke-like episodes (MELAS): current concepts. *J Child Neurol.* 1994;9:4–13.
239. Muqtadaar H, Testai FD. Single gene disorders associated with stroke: a review and update on treatment options. *Curr Treat Options Cardiovasc Med.* 2012;14:288–297.
240. Santa KM. Treatment options for mitochondrial myopathy, encephalopathy, lactic acidosis, and stroke-like episodes (MELAS) syndrome. *Pharmacotherapy.* 2010;30:1179–1196.
241. Sproule DM, Kaufmann P. Mitochondrial myopathy, encephalopathy, lactic acidosis and stroke-like episodes: basic concepts, clinical phenotype, and therapeutic management of MELAS syndrome. *Ann N Y Acad Sci.* 2008;1142:133–158.
242. Thambisetty M, Newman NJ, Glas JD, Frankel MR. A practical approach to the diagnosis and management of MELAS: case report and review. *Neurologist.* 2002;8:302–312.
243. Goodfellow JA, Dani K, Stewart W, et al. Mitochondrial myopathy, encephalopathy, lactic acidosis and stroke-like episodes: an important cause of stroke in young people. *Postgrad Med J.* 2012;88:326–334.
244. Neargarder SA, Murtagh MP, Wong B, Hill EK. The neuropsychologic deficits of MELAS: evidence of global impairment. *Cog Behav Neurol.* 2007;20:83–92.
245. Kaufmann P, Engelstad K, Wei Y, et al. Natural history of MELAS associated with mitochondrial DNA m.3243A>G genotype. *Neurology.* 2011;77:1965–1971.
246. Yoneda M, Maeda M, Kimura H, Fujii A, Katayama K, Kuriyama M. Vasogenic edema on MELAS: a serial study with diffusion-weighted MR imaging. *Neurology.* 1999;53:2182–2184.
247. Ito H, Mori K, Kagami S. Neuroimaging of stroke-like episodes in MELAS. *Brain Dev.* 2011;33:283–288.
248. Pavlakis SG, Phillips PC, DiMauro S, De Vivo DC, Rowland LP. Mitochondrial myopathy, encephalopathy, lactic acidosis and stroke-like episodes: a distinctive clinical syndrome. *Acta Neurol.* 1984;16:481–488.
249. Sato W, Hayasaka K, Komatsu K, et al. Genetic analysis of three pedigrees of mitochondrial myopathy, encephalopathy, lactic acidosis, and strokelike episodes (MELAS). *Am J Hum Genet.* 1992;50:655–657.
250. Kirby DM, McFarland R, Ohtake A, et al. Mutations of the mitochondrial *ND1* gene as a cause of MELAS. *J Med Genet.* 2004;41:784–789.

251. Rodriguez MC, MacDonald JR, Mahoney DJ, et al. Beneficial effects of creatine, CoQ10, and lipoic acid in mitochondrial disorders. *Muscle Nerve.* 2007;35:235–242.
252. Matthews PM, Ford B, Dandurand RJ, et al. Coenzyme Q10 with multiple vitamins is generally ineffective in treatment of mitochondrial disease. *Neurology.* 1993;43:884–890.
253. Peterson PL. The treatment of mitochondrial myopathies and encephalomyopathies. *Biochim Biophys Acta.* 1995;1271:275–280.
254. Napolitano A, Salvetti S, Vista M, Lombardi V, Siciliano G, Giraldi C. Long-term treatment with idebenone and riboflavin in a patient with MELAS. *Neurol Sci.* 2000;21:S981–S982.
255. Koga Y, Povalko N, Nishioka J, Katayama K, Kakimoto N, Matsuishi T. MELAS and L-arginine therapy: pathophysiology of stroke-like episodes. *Ann N Y Acad Sci.* 2010;1201:104–110.
256. Kubota M, Sakakihara Y, Mori M, Yamagata T, Momoi-Yoshida M. Beneficial effect of L-arginine for stroke-like episode in MELAS. *Brain Dev.* 2004;26:481–483.
257. Kaufmann P, Engelstad K, Wei Y, et al. Dichloroacetate causes toxic neuropathy in MELAS: a randomized, controlled clinical trial. *Neurology.* 2006;66:324–330.

4

HERITABILITY OF ISCHEMIC STROKE AND INTRACEREBRAL HEMORRHAGE

Annie Pedersén and Christina Jern

Introduction

The extent of hereditary influence on the pathophysiology of stroke has been investigated for several decades, and conflicting results have been presented throughout the years. Today, there is compelling evidence for a hereditary component to stroke risk, although compared with other complex vascular diseases such as coronary heart disease, it appears to be weaker.[1]

When investigating the heritability of a trait, the questions to be answered are: To what extent are differences in incidence the result of genetic variation? And to what extent are they the result of environmental differences? The genetic contribution could be the result of a single-gene mutation, as in monogenic or Mendelian disorders, or a combined action of a large number of genetic factors, each of which makes only a small contribution (i.e., a polygenic inheritance). In most instances, stroke is a so-called *multifactorial* or *complex disease* caused by a polygenic inheritance interplaying with different environmental factors. A number of monogenic forms of stroke exist; however, these uncommon conditions account collectively for only a small percentage of all stroke patients and are not addressed in this chapter.

Traditionally, investigation of heritability has been done in two principle ways: twin studies and family history studies. In twin studies, monozygotic (MZ) and dizygotic (DZ) twins are compared to determine how often affected twins have a cotwin that is affected by the same disease. Because MZ twins share all their genes and DZ twin share, on average, half their genes, a greater concordance among MZ twins means evidence for a genetic contribution. Twin studies have the advantage over family history studies in that they are better suited to separate genetic influences from environmental ones. A problem, however, is the difficulty in recruiting enough twin pairs with a late-onset disease such as stroke. Accordingly, the number of reported twin studies in stroke is very limited. Using data from a twin registry of U.S. veterans, Brass et al.[2] found a relatively strong genetic contribution to stroke risk, with a 17.7% concordance rate for MZ twins compared with 3.6% in DZ twins.

However, less convincing results have also been presented.[3,4] In 2005, Flossmann et al.[5] summarized these results in a meta-analysis. Overall, a genetic contribution to stroke risk was seen, with MZ twins being 1.65 times more likely to be concordant compared with DZ twins.[5]

In family history studies, the relatives of affected probands are compared with unrelated persons to determine whether they are more likely also to be affected. As opposed to twin studies, the number of published family history studies on stroke is quite numerous. In the systematic review and meta-analysis by Flossmann et al.[5] from 2005, results from family history studies, both case–control and cohort studies, supporting a genetic contribution to stroke risk were presented. However, the reliability of these results was questioned by the authors because of heterogeneity between studies and several methodological issues. More recent data supporting the heritability of ischemic stroke were presented from the Framingham study in 2010 and in a large, register-based Swedish study from 2012.[6,7]

Several aspects have to be taken into account when studying heritability and interpreting results from family history studies on stroke. These factors could probably explain a lot of the contradictory results seen throughout the years, and even if most people today agree that there is a hereditary component to stroke risk, there remain several gaps in our understanding of the hereditary patterns. First, associations seen in family history studies could be the result of genetic factors, familial shared environmental factors, or both. Similarly, interactions between genes and environmental factors could occur at various levels. There might be differences resulting from ethnicity, age, and sex. Not only does the risk of stroke have to be considered, but hereditary factors could also cause differences in a person's response to stroke therapy and the individual's capacity to recover after injury, as well as the brain's ability to withstand ischemia and the resulting severity of the stroke event. In addition, the inheritance patterns are likely to differ among the main stroke types—ischemic stroke, intracerebral hemorrhage, and subarachnoid hemorrhage—a fact that has been disregarded in many family history studies in which where stroke has been handled as one entity. Moreover, within each stroke type, different etiologic subtypes might further show different inheritance patterns. Last, rather than influence stroke risk directly, the genetic contribution could be mediated through intermediate phenotypes or risk factors, such as elevated blood pressure or diabetes. In the following sections, these matters are discussed further.

Ethnicity

Genetic susceptibility factors in complex diseases such as stroke are low pathogenic variants that have been able to segregate over generations in different populations. As a consequence, these factors are more likely to be shared by people of common ancestry. Therefore, ethnicity is fundamental in genetic epidemiological research. What is valid for one ethnic group is not necessarily true for another, and data from one ethnic group are not sufficient to draw conclusions in other groups. Furthermore, when it comes to family history and heritability, we have to be even more cautious, because not only genes, but also environmental and cultural factors might differ among ethnic groups.

There is a relative lack of family history studies on stroke patients with other than European or North American origin. There are a few studies from China and Taiwan supporting a relation between family history and stroke risk.[8–10] Likewise, one study from Russia and one from Korea have found associations.[11,12] In Japan, the results have been more diverse, with results contradicting a relation between family history and stroke,[13,14] as well as supporting a role for family history in cerebral hemorrhage, but not ischemic stroke.[15,16] There is also one study from Japan that reported that family history of stroke is an independent predictor of stroke recurrence after first-ever ischemic stroke.[17] A study from Pakistan also found that in patients with hypertension, diabetes, and obesity, a positive family history resulted in an increased stroke risk, with most strokes in this study being ischemic.[18]

On the other hand, a study from India did not detect any association between family history and *hemorrhagic* stroke.[19]

There are also a few studies that have made comparisons among different ethnic or regional groups. Lisabeth et al.[20,21] have observed a stronger familial influence on stroke risk in Mexican American stroke patients compared with white ischemic stroke or transient ischemic attack patients in Texas. A study from Singapore found that ethnic South Asian ischemic stroke patients had a greater frequency of positive family history compared with Chinese patients.[22] In a European multicenter study on ischemic stroke patients, no regional differences were seen when comparing southern, central, and northern European centers.[23] Last, American family history studies with mixed study populations including both white and black patients have found no racial differences in their results.[24,25]

To conclude, ethnic differences in the heritability of stroke are not unlikely. However, current knowledge is insufficient to permit any comprehensive conclusion.

Age

It has been suggested frequently that age influences the heritability of stroke, and there is some evidence that genetic factors are more important in stroke that occurs earlier in life.

When examining the age influence on familial aggregation of stroke there is a possibility of either looking into the age of onset in the affected relatives or in the patients themselves. A couple studies have found that an early age of onset in relatives increases the risk of stroke or death from coronary or cerebrovascular disease in probands.[7,26] In line with this, one of the most powerful studies supporting an association between family history and stroke risk has restricted a positive family history to that occurring before the age of 65 years.[6] Several studies have found a stronger familial aggregation of stroke in patients of younger age. This has been the case in European,[27–30] American,[24,31] and Asian[32,33] populations. These results are in line with results in studies including only younger subjects.[23,34]

To conclude, although there are a small number of studies suggesting the opposite,[35,36] the predominant evidence today points toward a stronger familial component in stroke occurring at younger ages.

Sex

As is the case with age, sex differences have likewise been suggested frequently to influence the hereditary pattern of stroke risk. However, here the results are more inconsistent.

In 2007, evidence for a greater heritability of ischemic stroke in women compared with men was presented from the Oxford Vascular Study (OXVASC) study.[37] The following year, the authors published a meta-analysis supporting their results. This study, which was not on ischemic stroke exclusively, showed that women with stroke were more likely than men to have a parental history of stroke, which was accounted for by an excess maternal history.[38] However, there is heterogeneity in design among the studies supporting a stronger female contribution to stroke risk, with some putting emphasis on the influence of relatives' sex, some on patients' sex, and some on both. There are also several studies that observed a stronger paternal as opposed to maternal influence on stroke risk or no sex differences at all.[7,22,39]

As in all family history studies on stroke, there is a risk of missing the true relations when mixing different stroke types because hereditary patterns might differ depending on etiology. This circumstance was observed in a small Asian study in which lifetime risk of stroke was increased significantly in parents and siblings of both ischemic and hemorrhagic stroke, except for fathers of ischemic stroke patients and sisters of hemorrhagic stroke patients, although limited power could also explain these differences in part.[8] Thus, to sort out clearly the influence of sex on stroke hereditary patterns, further studies accounting for both relative and proband sex, as well as stroke subtypes, are warranted.

Stroke Severity and Outcome

The familial contribution to stroke might not only influence stroke incidence, but also possibly the brain's ability to withstand ischemia and an individual's capacity to recover from a stroke event. However, only a few studies have investigated family history in relation to stroke severity or outcome.

With regard to stroke severity, an American study found that a sibling history of stroke was associated with more severe strokes (as assessed by the Barthel index, Oxford Handicap Scale, and Glasgow Outcome Scale, but not the National Institutes of Health Stroke Scale), but no such association was found for parental or offspring history of stroke.[40] Another study found that a parental history of stroke was associated with subclinical, but not clinical, stroke.[41] In addition, a study conducted on middle-age British men found an association with nonfatal, but not fatal, stroke.[42] Some investigators found a lack of association between family history of stroke and stroke severity[12,26,35] or stroke volume.[43]

With respect to stroke outcome, the results presented to date have been diverse. One study measuring outcome at discharge found that a positive family history of stroke was associated with a poor functional outcome measured by the modified Rankin Scale.[35] Family history of stroke has also been shown to increase the risk of stroke recurrence.[17,44] In contrast, another study measuring outcome at discharge suggested an association between family history and an increased frequency of discharge to home care, as well as increased ability to ambulate independently at discharge in patients with a positive family history.[31] Moreover, a Swedish study measuring outcome 3 months after stroke found that a family history of stroke was associated with a favorable outcome, as assessed by the modified Rankin Scale.[34] Last, a study from Korea, also measuring outcome 3 months after stroke using the modified Rankin Scale, found no association with family history.[12]

In summary, the number of studies investigating hereditary influence on stroke severity and outcome are limited to date, and there is clearly a need for further research in this field.

Ischemic Stroke and Etiologic Subtypes

Stroke is a heterogeneous disease and could, in fact, be regarded as a syndrome rather than a single disease. Despite this, a large proportion of family history studies, and all published twin studies to date, have handled the two main causes of stroke—ischemia and bleeding—as one. Ischemic stroke is the most common stroke type, accounting for approximately 85% of stroke cases, which makes it the stroke type to which the results from mixed studies are most applicable. It is also the stroke type that has been studied most extensively. As for overall stroke, today there is predominant evidence for a hereditary component in ischemic stroke risk, which has been demonstrated in studies from Europe,[7,34] the United States,[6] and Asia.[12] Interestingly, new support for a hereditary component to ischemic stroke was demonstrated by using genomewide association study data, which provide genotyped single nucleotide polymorphisms (SNPs) over the whole genome. Heritability can then be approximated by assessing the proportion of variation in case–control status explained by those SNPs simultaneously.[45] Using this approach, and the so-called applied genomewide complex trait analysis, the "heritability" (or phenotypic variance explained by SNPs) of overall ischemic stroke was estimated to be 38%.[46]

Even within the group of ischemic stroke, disease etiology shows heterogeneity, and there is, likewise, a lack of studies that have taken this into account. The most frequently used subtype classification systems for ischemic stroke is the Trial of Org. 10172 in Acute Stroke Treatment, which includes the following etiologic subtypes: large-vessel disease, cardioembolism stroke, small-vessel disease, other determined etiology (a mix of specified unusual causes), and undetermined etiology.[47] Because the etiology and, consequently, the spectrum of risk factors differ among the different subtypes of ischemic stroke, it is likely that different genetic and environmental factors are involved. Accordingly, family history studies that have looked into ischemic stroke subtypes have found subtype-specific differences. A pattern of stronger familial aggregation in large-vessel and small-vessel disease compared with cardioembolic and undetermined stroke has been observed in European and American studies,[34,39,48] as well as in Asian studies.[8,49] Similar results were shown in a meta-analysis in which the results from some of the previously mentioned studies were added to results from the OXVASC and Oxford Community Stroke Project (OCSP) samples.[27] Other studies have also found a quite strong familial aggregation in large-vessel disease, whereas the association for small-vessel disease was weaker or even absent.[12,50] In contrast, a study with a mixed study population of whites and Mexican Americans found that family history was most frequent in small-vessel disease and least frequent in large-vessel disease.[35] In one study that specified a group of cryptogenic stroke (i.e., when the etiology remains unknown despite extensive workup), an association with family history was also found for this subtype.[34] Interestingly, the study described earlier that estimated the "heritability" of overall ischemic stroke from genomewide association data also confirmed that this "heritability" varies by ischemic stroke subtype.[46] It was estimated to be 40% for large-vessel disease stroke, 33% for cardioembolic stroke, and only 16% for small-vessel disease stroke.[46]

A problem when collecting family history data is that the stroke subtype among affected family members is very difficult to ascertain, and therefore most studies have made no attempt to do so. This fact could mask stronger associations of less frequent stroke subtypes. However, one study that looked into stroke subtypes in probands and affected siblings found that the occurrence of one subtype in a proband was not associated with a greater likelihood of the same subtype in the sibling.[51] The sample size of this study was very small, though. Larger studies are warranted and, although challenging to reach adequate sample sizes, twin studies would also be of great interest.

Many studies not only included family history of stroke, but also history of myocardial infarction. Associations between a positive family history of myocardial infarction and the subtype of large-vessel disease have been observed, which could reflect a shared genetic susceptibility for atherosclerotic disease in coronary arteries and large arteries supplying the brain.[27,34]

To conclude, ischemic stroke is the most common and best-studied stroke type with regard to family history. There is convincing evidence for a familial contribution to the risk of overall ischemic stroke, but this contribution seems to vary depending on etiologic subtype.

Hemorrhagic Stroke

As mentioned in the previous section, many studies on family history of stroke have combined hemorrhagic and ischemic stroke, and among those that have not, the majority have been on ischemic stroke alone. However, there is evidence that the genetic influences on ischemic and hemorrhagic stroke differ.[52]

With regard to the most common type of hemorrhagic stroke—intracerebral hemorrhage—there are studies that show an association between a positive family history and stroke risk,[16,39] but contradicting results exist.[19,53] It has been reported that family history of overall stroke is a predictor of ischemic stroke versus intracerebral hemorrhage,[50] and that family history of overall stroke is more frequent in ischemic stroke compared with intracerebral hemorrhage.[54] In contrast, another study did not observe any difference in offspring risk of death from coronary or cerebrovascular disease in patients with ischemic stroke compared with patients with intracerebral hemorrhage.[26]

Noteworthy, in the abovementioned studies, a family history of stroke was considered positive, independent of stroke type. This might lead to underestimations of the familial influence on patients with intracerebral hemorrhage because ischemic stroke accounts for 85% of all stroke cases. The studies that have taken this into account have found mainly positive results,[15,52,55] except for one older study that found no association between cerebral hemorrhage and siblings' risk of death from cerebral hemorrhage, with the exception of the brothers of female patients.[56] Another fact that might cause difficulties in the interpretation of these studies is that a few did not separate distinctly intracerebral hemorrhage from subarachnoid hemorrhage.[26,50,56] Subarachnoid hemorrhage is a topic beyond the scope of this chapter. However, it should be noted that genetic factors clearly have a role in subarachnoid hemorrhage as well, which accounts for approximately 5% of all strokes. Aneurysms are the main cause of subarachnoid hemorrhage. In brief, first-degree relatives of patients with aneurysmal subarachnoid hemorrhage are at an approximately fourfold increased risk of ruptured intracranial aneurysms compared with the general population.[57] It has also been shown that the prevalence of asymptomatic intracranial aneurysms is approximately 10 times greater in subjects with a family history of intracranial aneurysms than in the average population,[58,59] and genomewide association studies have identified some loci associated with intracranial aneurysms.[60,61] Increased knowledge in this field will ultimately contribute to a better identification of persons at an increased risk of subarachnoid hemorrhage, and thus to a better selection of persons who may benefit from intracranial aneurysm screening.

Subtypes of intracerebral hemorrhage have been even less studied. However, Woo et al.[55] investigated family history and the risk of lobar and nonlobar intracerebral hemorrhage. A positive family history was found to be an independent risk factor for both subtypes; but, among cases of nonlobar intracerebral hemorrhage, this risk was seen predominantly in subjects younger than 70 years. No such age difference was seen among patients with lobar intracerebral hemorrhage.[55]

Intermediate Phenotypes

After the familial aggregation of a trait has been stated, the next question is: What does this aggregation stand for? Its content and nature need to be explored. It appears that the heritability of stroke is accounted for, to a certain degree, by the inheritance of intermediate phenotypes and risk factors, such as hypertension and atherosclerosis. This concept is in line with the fact that both the heritability patterns and the specific risk factors differ among stroke types and subtypes. Furthermore, coexistence between stroke and myocardial infarction, and the family history of these diseases have been observed frequently,[34,62–65] which could be explained by the inheritance of etiologic factors, common to both diseases, such as a genetic predisposition to arterial atherosclerosis in the case of large-vessel disease, or hypertension in the case of small-vessel disease. In line with this, family history of ischemic heart disease, stroke, diabetes mellitus, and hypertension have been shown to be associated significantly with each other in a large American population.[66]

The most commonly observed risk factor that has been shown to aggregate in families affected by stroke is hypertension. An association between hypertension and family history of stroke has been reported in many studies.[30,31,67,68] These results suggest that familial susceptibility to stroke is, in part, attributable to a predisposition to hypertension. Accordingly, associations between heritability of stroke and hypertension were found in a systematic review on family history of ischemic stroke and potential confounders.[69] It was further noted that family history of ischemic heart disease was associated mainly with stroke as a result of large-vessel atherosclerosis.[34] In contrast, family history of diabetes was not associated with stroke.[69,70] Other risk factors that have been pointed out as possibly related to family history of stroke are atrial fibrillation,[71] left ventricular hypertrophy,[71,72] congestive heart failure,[70] and the level of C-reactive protein.[73]

As demonstrated by the previously mentioned studies, some of the familial contribution to stroke risk seems to be accounted for by the inheritance of risk factors. On the other hand, a common inherited risk factor such as hypertension often leads to differential pathological manifestations, such as ischemic versus hemorrhagic stroke, that appear to aggregate in different families. Furthermore, family history has frequently been shown to associate with stroke independent of risk factors. Thus, it seems that disease-specific factors are clearly at play. There is probably an interplay between genetic and environmental factors, some disease specific and others shared. To what extent needs further clarification.

Future and Clinical Applicability

As illustrated in the previous sections, current knowledge supports a familial component in both ischemic and hemorrhagic stroke risk, although many details need to be elucidated further. For this knowledge to be useful in a clinical setting, one way would be to incorporate it in a readily available and practical tool. An illustrative example of this approach is the Systematic COronary Risk Evaluation (SCORE) algorithm, originating from the Framingham risk score, including age, sex, systolic blood pressure, smoking status, and cholesterol levels to predict vascular death.[74] Stroke-specific risk scores for clinical use have likewise been constructed, such as concerning stroke risk after transient ischemic attack, the ABCD2 score; and in patients with atrial fibrillation, the CHADS2 score.[75,76] The Framingham stroke-specific score is widely used for overall stroke risk prediction.[77] Interestingly, a recent Framingham study on family history suggests that parental stroke status and age of parent at stroke might be worth incorporating into future revisions of the Framingham and other stroke risk prediction algorithms.[6] In fact, a couple Asian studies attempting to construct stroke prediction scores have already included family history in their models.[9,10] To evaluate and, possibly, to incorporate family history in a risk score could make up a future way to achieve clinical benefits from the results of this research field. In addition, it is worth noting that obtaining a family history is recommended to help identify persons at increased risk of stroke based on the American Heart Association's guidelines for primary prevention of stroke from 2011.[78]

REFERENCES

1. Banerjee A, Silver LE, Heneghan C, et al. Relative familial clustering of cerebral versus coronary ischemic events. *Circulation.* 2011;4:390–396.
2. Brass LM, Isaacsohn JL, Merikangas KR, Robinette CD. A study of twins and stroke. *Stroke.* 1992;23:221–223.
3. De Faire U, Friberg L, Lundman T. Concordance for mortality with special reference to ischaemic heart disease and cerebrovascular disease: a study on the Swedish twin registry. *Prev Med.* 1975;4:509–517.
4. Bak S, Gaist D, Sindrup SH, Skytthe A, Christensen K. Genetic liability in stroke: a long-term follow-up study of Danish twins. *Stroke.* 2002;33:769–774.
5. Flossmann E, Schulz UG, Rothwell PM. Systematic review of methods and results of studies of the genetic epidemiology of ischemic stroke. *Stroke.* 2004;35:212–227.
6. Seshadri S, Beiser A, Pikula A, et al. Parental occurrence of stroke and risk of stroke in their children: the Framingham study. *Circulation.* 2010;121:1304–1312.
7. Kasiman K, Lundholm C, Sandin S, Malki N, Sparén P, Ingelsson E. Familial effects on ischemic stroke the role of sibling kinship, sex, and age of onset. *Circulation.* 2012;5:226–233.

8. Hsu WC, Chen ST, Wu YR, Chang HS, Lyu RK, Lo LS. The association of stroke and family history of stroke depends on its subtypes and gender: a family history study in Taiwan. *Acta Neurol Taiwan.* 2009;18:161–169.
9. Chien KL, Su TC, Hsu HC, et al. Constructing the prediction model for the risk of stroke in a Chinese population: report from a cohort study in Taiwan. *Stroke.* 2010;41:1858–1864.
10. Wu Y, Zhang L, Yuan X, Yi D. Quantifying links between stroke and risk factors: a study on individual health risk appraisal of stroke in a community of Chongqing. *Neurol Sci.* 2011;32:211–219.
11. Feigin VL, Wiebers DO, Nikitin YP, O'Fallon WM, Whisnant JP. Risk factors for ischemic stroke in a Russian community: a population-based case–control study. *Stroke.* 1998;29:34–39.
12. Choi JC, Lee JS, Kang SY, Kang JH, Bae JM. Family history and risk for ischemic stroke: sibling history is more strongly correlated with the disease than parental history. *J Neurol Sci.* 2009;284:29–32.
13. Shintani S, Kikuchi S, Hamaguchi H, Shiigai T. High serum lipoprotein(a) levels are an independent risk factor for cerebral infarction. *Stroke.* 1993;24:965–969.
14. Kadota A, Okamura T, Hozawa A, et al. Relationships between family histories of stroke and of hypertension and stroke mortality: Nippon data80, 1980–1999. *Hypertens Res.* 2008;31:1525–1531.
15. Kubota M, Yamaura A, Ono JI, et al. Is family history an independent risk factor for stroke? *J Neurol Neurosurg Psychiatry.* 1997;62:66–70.
16. Okada H, Horibe H, Ohno Y. A prospective study of cerebrovascular disease in Japanese rural communities, Akabane and Asahi. Part 1: Evaluation of risk factors in the occurrence of cerebral hemorrhage and thrombosis. *Stroke.* 1976;7:599–607.
17. Omori T, Kawagoe M, Moriyama M, et al. Multifactorial analysis of factors affecting recurrence of stroke in Japan. *Asia Pac J Public Health* 2012 Apr 11. [Epub ahead of print].
18. Itrat A, Ahmed B, Khan M, et al. Risk factor profiles of South Asians with cerebrovascular disease. *Int J Stroke.* 2011;6:346–348.
19. Zodpey SP, Tiwari RR. A risk scoring system for prediction of haemorrhagic stroke. *Indian J Public Health.* 2005;49:218–222.
20. Lisabeth LD, Kardia SL, Smith MA, Fornage M, Morgenstern LB. Family history of stroke among Mexican-American and non-Hispanic white patients with stroke and TIA: implications for the feasibility and design of stroke genetics research. *Neuroepidemiology.* 2005;24:96–102.
21. Lisabeth LD, Peyser PA, Long JC, Majerisk JJ, Smith MA, Morgenstern LB. Stroke among siblings in a biethnic community. *Neuroepidemiology.* 2008;31:33–38.
22. De Silva DA, Woon FP, Chen CLH, Chang HM, Wong MC. Ethnic South Asian ischaemic stroke patients have a higher prevalence of a family history of vascular disease compared with age, gender and diabetes-matched ethnic Chinese subjects. *J Neurol Sci.* 2009;285:118–120.
23. Putaala J, Yesilot N, Waje-Andreassen U, et al. Demographic and geographic vascular risk factor differences in european young adults with ischemic stroke: the 15 Cities Young Stroke Study. *Stroke.* 2012;43:2624–2630.
24. MacClellan LR, Mitchell BD, Cole JW, et al. Familial aggregation of ischemic stroke in young women: the Stroke Prevention in Young Women study. *Gen Epidemiol.* 2006;30:602–608.
25. Alberts MJ, McCarron MO, Hoffmann KL, Graffagnino C. Familial clustering of intracerebral hemorrhage: a prospective study in North Carolina. *Neuroepidemiology.* 2002;21:18–21.
26. Howard G, Evans GW, Toole JF, et al. Characteristics of stroke victims associated with early cardiovascular mortality in their children. *J Clin Epidemiol.* 1990;43:49–54.
27. Schulz UGR, Flossmann E, Rothwell PM. Heritability of ischemic stroke in relation to age, vascular risk factors, and subtypes of incident stroke in population-based studies. *Stroke.* 2004;35:819–824.
28. Jousilahti P, Rastenyte D, Tuomilehto J, Sarti C, Vartiainen E. Parental history of cardiovascular disease and risk of stroke: a prospective follow-up of 14,371 middle-aged men and women in Finland. *Stroke.* 1997;28:1361–1366.

29. Carrieri PB, Orefice G, Maiorino A, Provitera V, Balzano G, Lucariello A. Age-related risk factors for ischemic stroke in Italian men. *Neuroepidemiology.* 1994;13:28–33.
30. Lindgren A, Lovkvist H, Hallstrom B, et al. Prevalence of stroke and vascular risk factors among first-degree relatives of stroke patients and control subjects: a prospective consecutive study. *Cerebrovasc Dis.* 2005;20:381–387.
31. Hertzberg VS, Weiss P, Stern BJ, Frankel MR. Family history associated with improved functional outcome following ischemic stroke. *Neuroepidemiology.* 2006;27:74–80.
32. Yao XY, Lin Y, Geng JL, et al. Age- and gender-specific prevalence of risk factors in patients with first-ever ischemic stroke in China. *Stroke Res Treat.* 2012;2012:136398.
33. Lee YS, Chen DY, Chen YM, et al. First-ever ischemic stroke in Taiwanese elderly patients: predicting functional independence after a 6-month follow-up. *Arch Gerontol Geriatr.* 2009;49:S26–S31.
34. Jood K, Ladenvall C, Rosengren A, Blomstrand C, Jern C. Family history in ischemic stroke before 70 years of age: the Sahlgrenska Academy Study on Ischemic Stroke. *Stroke.* 2005;36:1383–1387.
35. Lisabeth LD, Smith MA, Brown DL, Uchino K, Morgenstern LB. Family history and stroke outcome in a bi-ethnic, population-based stroke surveillance study. *BMC Neurol.* 2005;5:20.
36. Brass LM, Shaker LA. Family history in patients with transient ischemic attacks. *Stroke.* 1991;22:837–841.
37. Touze E, Rothwell PM. Heritability of ischaemic stroke in women compared with men: a genetic epidemiological study. *Lancet Neurol.* 2007;6:125–133.
38. Touze E, Rothwell PM. Sex differences in heritability of ischemic stroke: a systematic review and meta-analysis. *Stroke.* 2008;39:16–23.
39. Polychronopoulos P, Gioldasis G, Ellul J, et al. Family history of stroke in stroke types and subtypes. *J Neurol Sci.* 2002;195:117–122.
40. Meschia JF, Case LD, Worrall BB, et al. Family history of stroke and severity of neurologic deficit after stroke. *Neurology.* 2006;67:1396–1402.
41. Morrison AC, Fornage M, Liao D, Boerwinkle E. Parental history of stroke predicts subclinical but not clinical stroke: the Atherosclerosis Risk in Communities Study. *Stroke.* 2000;31:2098–2102.
42. Wannamethee SG, Shaper AG, Ebrahim S. History of parental death from stroke or heart trouble and the risk of stroke in middle-aged men. *Stroke.* 1996;27:1492–1498.
43. Reed T, Kirkwood SC, DeCarli C, et al. Relationship of family history scores for stroke and hypertension to quantitative measures of white-matter hyperintensities and stroke volume in elderly males. *Neuroepidemiology.* 2000;19:76–86.
44. Zhang W, Chen Y, Liu P, et al. Variants on chromosome 9p21.3 correlated with anril expression contribute to stroke risk and recurrence in a large prospective stroke population. *Stroke.* 2012;43:14–21.
45. Yang J, Lee SH, Goddard ME, Visscher PM. Genome-wide complex trait analysis (GCTA): methods, data analyses, and interpretations. *Methods Mol Biol.* 2013;1019:215–236
46. Bevan S, Traylor M, Adib-Samii P, et al. Genetic heritability of ischemic stroke and the contribution of previously reported candidate gene and genomewide associations. *Stroke.* 2012;43:3161–3167.
47. Adams HP Jr, Bendixen BH, Kappelle LJ, et al. Classification of subtype of acute ischemic stroke: definitions for use in a multicenter clinical trial: TOAST: Trial of Org 10172 in Acute Stroke Treatment. *Stroke.* 1993;24:35–41.
48. Jerrard-Dunne P, Cloud G, Hassan A, Markus HS. Evaluating the genetic component of ischemic stroke subtypes: a family history study. *Stroke.* 2003;34:1364–1369.
49. Lee TH, Hsu WC, Chen CJ, Chen ST. Etiologic study of young ischemic stroke in Taiwan. *Stroke.* 2002;33:1950–1955.
50. Bogousslavsky J, Castillo V, Kumral E, Henriques I, Van Melle G. Stroke subtypes and hypertension: primary hemorrhage vs infarction, large- vs small-artery disease. *Arch Neurol.* 1996;53:265–269.

51. Wiklund PG, Brown WM, Brott TG, et al. Lack of aggregation of ischemic stroke subtypes within affected sibling pairs. *Neurology.* 2007;68:427–431.
52. Sundquist K, Li X, Hemminki K. Familial risk of ischemic and hemorrhagic stroke: a large-scale study of the Swedish population. *Stroke.* 2006;37:1668–1673.
53. Caicoya M, Corrales C, Rodriguez T. Family history and stroke: a community case–control study in Asturias, Spain. *J Epidemiol Biostat.* 1999;4:313–320.
54. Liu XF, Van Melle G, Bogousslavsky J. Analysis of risk factors in 3901 patients with stroke. *Chin Med Sci J.* 2005;20:35–39.
55. Woo D, Sekar P, Chakraborty R, et al. Genetic epidemiology of intracerebral hemorrhage. *J Stroke Cerebrovasc Dis.* 2005;14:239–243.
56. Marshall J. Familial incidence of cerebral hemorrhage. *Stroke.* 1973;4:38–41.
57. Schievink WI. Genetics of intracranial aneurysms. *Neurosurgery.* 1997;40:651–662; discussion, 662–653.
58. Ronkainen A, Hernesniemi J, Ryynanen M, Puranen M, Kuivaniemi H. A ten percent prevalence of asymptomatic familial intracranial aneurysms: preliminary report on 110 magnetic resonance angiography studies in members of 21 Finnish familial intracranial aneurysm families. *Neurosurgery.* 1994;35:208–212; discussion, 212–203.
59. Ronkainen A, Hernesniemi J, Puranen M, et al. Familial intracranial aneurysms. *Lancet.* 1997;349:380–384.
60. Ruigrok YM, Rinkel GJ. From GWAS to the clinic: risk factors for intracranial aneurysms. *Genome Med.* 2010;2:61.
61. Caranci F, Briganti F, Cirillo L, Leonardi M, Muto M. Epidemiology and genetics of intracranial aneurysms. *Eur J Radiol.* 2013;82:1598–1605.
62. Vitullo F, Marchioli R, Di Mascio R, Cavasinni L, Di Pasquale A, Tognoni G. Family history and socioeconomic factors as predictors of myocardial infarction, unstable angina and stroke in an Italian population. *Eur J Epidemiol.* 1996;12:177–185.
63. Yanez ND, Burke GL, Manolio T, Gardin JM, Polak J. Sibling history of myocardial infarction or stroke and risk of cardiovascular disease in the elderly: the Cardiovascular Health Study. *Ann Epidemiol.* 2009;19:858–866.
64. Banerjee A, Lim CCS, Silver LE, Welch SJV, Banning AP, Rothwell PM. Familial history of stroke is associated with acute coronary syndromes in women. *Circulation.* 2011;4:9–15.
65. Siegerink B, Rosendaal FR, Algra A. Family history differs between young women with myocardial infarction and ischemic stroke: results from the Ratio Case–Control Study. *Atherosclerosis.* 2012;223:235–238.
66. Williams RR, Hunt SC, Heiss G, et al. Usefulness of cardiovascular family history data for population-based preventive medicine and medical research (the Health Family Tree Study and the NHLBI Family Heart Study). *Am J Cardiol.* 2001;87:129–135.
67. Nicolaou M, DeStefano AL, Gavras I, et al. Genetic predisposition to stroke in relatives of hypertensives. *Stroke.* 2000;31:487–492.
68. Flossmann E, Rothwell PM. Family history of stroke in patients with transient ischemic attack in relation to hypertension and other intermediate phenotypes. *Stroke.* 2005;36:830–835.
69. Flossmann E, Schulz UGR, Rothwell PM. Potential confounding by intermediate phenotypes in studies of the genetics of ischaemic stroke. *Cerebrovasc Dis.* 2005;19:1–10.
70. Mvundura M, McGruder H, Khoury MJ, Valdez R, Yoon PW. Family history as a risk factor for early-onset stroke/transient ischemic attack among adults in the United States. *Public Health Genomics.* 2010;13:13–20.
71. Kennedy RE, Howard G, Go RC, et al. Association between family risk of stroke and myocardial infarction with prevalent risk factors and coexisting diseases. *Stroke.* 2012;43:974–979.
72. Tentschert S, Greisenegger S, Wimmer R, Lang W, Lalouschek W. Association of parental history of stroke with clinical parameters in patients with ischemic stroke or transient ischemic attack. *Stroke.* 2003;34:2114–2119.

73. Hamer M, Chida Y, Stamatakis E. The role of conventional and novel mechanisms in explaining increased risk of cardiovascular events in offspring with positive parental history. *J Hypertens.* 2009;27:1966–1971.
74. Conroy RM, Pyörälä K, Fitzgerald AP, et al. Estimation of ten-year risk of fatal cardiovascular disease in Europe: the Score Project. *Eur Heart J.* 2003;24:987–1003.
75. Johnston SC, Rothwell PM, Nguyen-Huynh MN, et al. Validation and refinement of scores to predict very early stroke risk after transient ischaemic attack. *Lancet.* 2007;369:283–292.
75, Diabetes Mellitus, and Prior Stroke or Transient Ischemic Attack (CHADS2) risk stratification scheme" journalName="Am Heart J" vol="156"> 76. Rietbrock S, Heeley E, Plumb J, van Staa T. Chronic atrial fibrillation: incidence, prevalence, and prediction of stroke using the Congestive Heart Failure, Hypertension, Age>75, Diabetes Mellitus, and Prior Stroke or Transient Ischemic Attack (CHADS2) risk stratification scheme. *Am Heart J.* 2008;156:57–64.
77. D'Agostino RB, Wolf PA, Belanger AJ, Kannel WB. Stroke risk profile: adjustment for antihypertensive medication: the Framingham study. *Stroke.* 1994;25:40–43.
78. Goldstein LB, Bushnell CD, Adams RJ, et al. Guidelines for the primary prevention of stroke: a guideline for healthcare professionals from the American Heart Association/American Stroke Association. *Stroke.* 2011;42:517–584.

5

GENETIC DETERMINANTS OF ISCHEMIC STROKE

Steve Bevan and Hugh S. Markus

Introduction

The term *stroke* is used to represent a clinical syndrome rather than a single disease and can be defined as "a focal neurological loss of function, usually of sudden onset, resulting from disturbance in the blood supply to the brain." In 80% to 85% of cases, stroke results from the occlusion of a cerebral vessel (called an *ischemic stroke*), whereas the remaining 15% to 20% result from vessel hemorrhage (called *hemorrhagic stroke*). Each of these phenotypes can be divided further into subtypes depending on the causative pathology determined by investigations, including brain and vascular imaging, and cardiac evaluation.

Stroke is a major health burden in the developed world, currently ranked as the third most common cause of death and single largest cause of adult chronic disability. Every year in the United States, almost 800,000 people experience an incident or recurrent stroke; mortality data from 2008 shows that 1 in 18 deaths are the result of this condition.[1] Data from the Framingham study showed that one in five women and one in six men age 55 to 75 years of age will experience a stroke sometime during their life.[2] Stroke mortality is also expected to double worldwide by 2020 as a result of the aging population and increasing incidence in developing countries. Cerebrovascular disease also causes vascular dementia and appears to act synergistically with Alzheimer's disease pathology, increasing the chance of resulting clinical dementia.[3] This is of particular significance given the high prevalence of both cerebrovascular and Alzheimer's pathology in the aging population. Any treatment that could reduce the incidence of stroke or subsequent pathologies, including vascular dementia, would therefore have significant patient and economic benefits.

Evidence for Genetic Risk of Stroke

Conventional risk factors for stroke are well known and include factors such as hypertension, diabetes, smoking, and high cholesterol, among others. Together, however, these conventional risk factors account for only 50% to 60% of stroke risk,[4] with the rest thought to be the result of genetic predisposition. The clearest evidence for this genetic predisposition comes from known forms of monogenic stroke—conditions resulting from a single gene that displays Mendelian patterns of inheritance and has a high penetrance. The most well studied of these is the condition known as cerebral autosomal dominant arteriopathy with subcortical infarcts and leukoencephalopathy. This phenotype is the result of specific mutations within cysteine residues of the *NOTCH3* gene, leading to aberrant binding of the gene product as a homodimer and causing small-artery stroke and small-vessel disease vascular dementia.[5] Stroke is also known to be a secondary presenting feature of other Mendelian single-gene disorders, such as Fabry disease (resulting from mutations in the α-galactosidase gene) and sickle cell disease (resulting from mutations in genes coding for hemoglobin). Although important to the individual patient, monogenic cases account for only a small percentage of overall stroke incidence and, to date, common variants in the same genes have not been associated with sporadic common polygenic stroke.[6]

Additional evidence in support of genetic risks for stroke come from both twin and family history studies.[7] Monozygotic twins share 100% of their DNA whereas dizygotic twins share 50%. An increased incidence of stroke in monozygotic twins therefore strongly implicates a genetic contribution to disease. Similarly, an increased risk in first-degree relatives over the general population risk implicates a genetic basis to stroke incidence. There is also evidence that the risks of the three main ischemic stroke subtypes—large-artery stroke, cardioembolic stroke, and small-vessel disease—have differing familial risks and hence discrete genetic risk profiles.[8] There is also evidence in support of genetic predisposition to stroke from the study of animal models of disease, with the stroke-prone, spontaneously hypertensive rat having been studied extensively. A number of loci have been proposed to harbor causative genes, although no specific mutation has yet been identified.[9]

As the end result of a progressive etiology, ischemic stroke can also be examined in terms of intermediate risk factors, the presence of which increases the likelihood of an ischemic stroke event in the future. Two such examples are the thickness of the carotid artery wall, known as *carotid artery intima media thickness* (IMT), and white matter abnormalities observable on magnetic resonance imaging of the brain and known as *white matter hyperintensities* (WMHs). Increased IMT and WMH are both associated with increased risk of future stroke, and both show significant heritability (the proportion of risk attributable to genetic risk factors). These estimates range from 55% to 75% for IMT[10–12] and 30% to 68% for WMH.[13–15] Identification of genetic risks for these intermediate phenotypes may allow intervention prior to more serious ischemic events occurring, as well as identify an at-risk population that would benefit from increased monitoring and lifestyle intervention to reduce later disease incidence.

Identification of Genetic Risk Variants in Ischemic Stroke

The human genome comprises some 3 billion base pairs and contains approximately 20,000 genes, many of which are alternatively spliced. Therefore, identification of, potentially, a single base change within the genome is not a trivial task. Until recently, the mainstay of stroke genetics was the candidate gene approach. Given the size and complexity of the genome, only small portions of it could be examined in a single experiment. Genetic variants (usually single nucleotide polymorphisms [SNPs]) were identified in a "candidate gene" that was hypothesized to be involved in stroke risk. The frequency of the SNP was then compared in stroke patients and stroke-free control subjects, with increased incidence in cases taken as evidence of a genetic risk.[16] Many hundreds of candidate gene studies have been performed in stroke with rather disappointing results. This picture is similar to many other complex diseases, and the underlying reasons for lack of success have been explored in detail.[17] In stroke in particular, important factors have included small sample sizes, a failure to replicate positive findings within the same study, a positive publication bias, and a lack of accurate phenotypic subtyping. An additional problem with candidate gene studies is that associations can be identified only in genes already discovered and implicated in stroke pathology; completely novel genes cannot be identified. Although meta-analysis can overcome some of these limitations, and results in considerable cohort sizes for meaningful investigation,[18] candidate gene studies have now been largely superseded by alternative investigative techniques such as genomewide association studies (GWASs).

The other mainstay of genetic investigation, the linkage study, is not typically applicable to stroke given the late age of onset of an ischemic event. The only documented linkage studies in common polygenic ischemic stroke have come from Iceland, where samples collected for genealogical purposes can be combined with phenotypic data for retrospective analysis. These studies identified the only linkage-defined gene for ischemic stroke—phosphodiesterase 4D, or *PDE4D*[19]—although subsequent meta-analyses and replication have failed to confirm this finding outside the Icelandic population.[20]

Although a candidate gene study is a hypothesis-driven approach to genetic investigation, a GWAS can be considered to be nonhypothesis driven. A GWAS allows up to 1 million or more SNPs, which provide coverage of the whole genome to be genotyped in a single individual. Using a case–control methodology similar to a candidate gene study, but with rigorous statistical methods to account for the multiple comparisons made, associations between novel chromosomal loci and disease can be identified. The close proximity of genotyped SNPs also allows nongenotyped SNPs to be inferred or "imputed" with a high degree of accuracy, providing further access to genomic regions not targeted originally. GWASs can be considered as 1 million candidate gene studies in a single experiment, which can then be examined as a whole to provide additional information about intervening loci as a consequence of linkage equilibrium. This is an approach that has revolutionized complex disease genetics and is now being applied to ischemic stroke.

First reported in 2005 examining the complement factor H gene in macular degeneration,[21] the technique really gained prominence when applied to seven common diseases as part of the Wellcome Trust Case Control Consortium Study.[22] Since then, more than 1600 GWASs identifying more than 10,000 genetic loci in excess of 1×10^{-5} have been published, with GWASs becoming the current mainstay of genetic investigation in complex disease (www.genome.gov/gwastudies).

GWASs and Stroke

The GWAS as a technique was applied to other cardiovascular diseases before it was applied to ischemic stroke. As a consequence, the first GWAS findings for stroke came either via replication of variants associated with other cardiovascular phenotypes in a stroke cohort or as part of larger analyses looking for shared genetic determinants of cardiovascular and cerebrovascular risk. The 9p21 locus across *CDKN2A* and *CDKN2B* identified in coronary artery disease was the first GWAS-identified region to be replicated in large-artery stroke,[23,24] followed closely by replication in cardioembolic stroke of the atrial fibrillation-associated gene *PITX2*.[25,26] Another locus on 16q22 around *ZFHX3* was identified subsequently in a joint analysis of atrial fibrillation and cardioembolic stroke.[27]

The first reported study investigating the genetic basis of ischemic stroke directly via GWAS was performed in 2007 in 249 ischemic stroke patients and 268 control subjects, although we now realize this was underpowered.[28] A GWAS in 2009 from the Cohorts for Heart and Aging Research in Genomic Epidemiology consortium investigated incident stroke in 1164 patients from a prospective community population, and associated the *NINJ2* gene on chromosome 12 with ischemic stroke risk.[29] This cohort examined ischemic stroke as a whole, without subphenotyping however, and a subsequent large replication study using a cross-sectional case–control cohort design in 8763 patients and 8733 control subjects failed to confirm the association.[30]

Experience from other diseases has shown that although a GWAS is a powerful technique, it requires very large and, most important, well-phenotyped cases series—usually in the thousands of samples—to be successful. Even then, typically identified odds ratios have been in the region of 1.2 to 1.5 for single GWASs. More recent studies have relied on meta-analysis of multiple GWAS data sets of a common phenotype to identify smaller risks.

The collection of large, well-phenotyped case series is challenging in stroke, given the late age of onset of the condition. In particular, the detailed phenotyping that we now realize is essential is both expensive and time-consuming. As in other complex diseases, the collection of sufficient case numbers for meaningful study requires international collaboration. The GWAS has led the field of genetics into a collaborative research model in a way that has not been seen before—not just in stroke, but in a wide range of phenotypes. Within stroke itself, the formation of the International Stroke Genetics Consortium (www.strokegenetics.com) in 2007 was for the express purpose of furthering our understanding of the genetic basis of stroke through large, well-powered GWASs.

This consortium reported the first large GWAS in ischemic stroke, including subtypes, in 2011, identifying histone deacetylase 9, or *HDAC9*, on 7p21.1 as a risk factor for large-artery stroke, with the association being specific to this stroke subtype.[31] This finding was well powered, with a discovery cohort of, overall, 3548 ischemic stroke patients and 5972 control subjects, and replication totaling 9856 patients and 40,344 control subjects. A second GWAS from the same consortium in 2012 further identified a locus on 6p21.1 in a discovery analysis of, overall, 1162 ischemic stroke patients and 1244 control subjects, and replication in 1715 patients and 52,695 control subjects.[32] This association was again with the large-artery subtype of ischemic stroke. Both of these findings were within the expected odds ratios for GWAS—1.42 and 1.62, respectively—and both were replicated robustly in larger sample cohorts than the discovery analysis. Despite the impressive cohort sizes in these studies, both associations have been identified with subtypes of ischemic stroke rather than with ischemic stroke as a whole, and the sample sizes in these subgroups were smaller. Although lending strength to the argument that specific stroke subtypes have distinct genetic risks, it is likely that with larger numbers of each subtype, additional genetic risks will be identified. A number of other GWASs in ischemic stroke are ongoing at the time of writing.

In addition to internal replication of GWAS findings, meta-analysis of GWASs can be a useful tool in confirming postulated genetic risks. Validation of GWAS-identified hits in ischemic stroke and its subtypes has been performed via the meta-analysis of GWAS cohorts in the METASTROKE study comprising 12,389 patients and 62,004 control subjects.[33] This study confirmed the previously reported associations with *HDAC9, PITX2*, and *ZFHX3*, as well as identified an additional 12 potentially novel loci that require further efforts to replicate. As has been shown in other complex diseases, it is likely that, as sample sizes increase, additional associations will be identified, although the effect size of these new loci tends to decrease as larger sample sizes are required to identify them. It should also be noted that the effects of genetic risk variants in stroke, and a number of other complex diseases, tend to be smaller than individual conventional risk factors such as family history or hypertension. The real challenge is how to translate these genetic discoveries into patient benefit through functional biology.

Functional Investigation of GWAS Findings in Ischemic Stroke

Identification of genetic risks does little for patient benefit alone. Although isolation of risk variants can identify at-risk patients for targeted screening, increased surveillance, and early intervention, the current variants account for only a small proportion of total genetic risk and are, therefore, not useful for risk prediction. A more tangible benefit to identifying genetic risk comes from novel insights into disease pathogenesis that may allow the development of better treatments. In general, this requires an understanding of the altered pathological mechanism of disease such that therapeutic intervention may be applied.

The genes *PITX2* and *ZFHX3* have been shown to regulate normal heart rhythm, with *PITX2* null +/− knockout mice shown to develop atrial arrhythmias and atrial flutter.[34] This abnormal heartbeat leads to altered blood flow, coagulation, and cardiac emboli formation, with these emboli circulating and blocking arteries within the brain, resulting in ischemia.

The 9p21 region, associated with coronary artery disease and subsequently large-artery stroke, has been associated with vascular smooth muscle cell (VSMC) proliferation, reduced expression of genes within the 9p21 region, and greater VSMC content within atherosclerotic plaques.[35] This altered plaque morphology is the source of large-artery stroke, during which plaque rupture leads to thrombus and formation of circulating emboli that block blood vessels within the brain and cause ischemia.

How variants within *HDAC9* may cause large-artery stroke exclusively is not yet known. Initial studies have shown that the *HDAC9* protein is expressed in both intracranial and systemic large arteries, including the carotid and middle cerebral arteries, with abundant staining found in both endothelial cells and VSMCs.[36] *HDAC9* messenger RNA expression was also shown to be upregulated in carotid atherosclerotic tissue. The *HDAC9* genetic variant associated with large-artery stroke has also been associated with both carotid artery IMT and asymptomatic carotid plaque in large-community populations.[36] The commonly used antiepileptic drug sodium valproate has been shown to have an *HDAC* inhibitory action. It has been shown to inhibit atherosclerosis in animal models.[37] Although its lack of specificity for *HDAC9* may make its use in stroke therapy less attractive, in a large-community study, sodium valproate was associated with lower stroke and myocardial infarction incidence when compared with other antiepileptic drugs.[38] Thus, although functional studies are required to determine exactly how *HDAC9* variants result in increased stroke risk, initial evidence suggests that *HDAC9* might offer a novel approach to stroke prevention.

How Has the GWAS Altered Our Understanding of Stroke Genetics?

The GWAS was devised initially to address the assumption that common variants in the human genome contribute to common disease. This common variant common disease theory informed the design of GWAS technology and chip design, as well as informed methods of data analysis. It is becoming increasingly clear, however, that the contribution of common, high-penetrance alleles to disease risk is less than originally envisaged, and that, in reality, most common diseases have been associated with a small number of loci contributing modest disease risk. As sample sizes have increased, smaller effect sizes have been detected; but, for most complex diseases, the overall genetic contribution to disease identified by GWASs is significantly less than that suggested from epidemiological studies.

GWASs result in the accumulation of vast amounts of genetic information, which with imputation can run to more than 10 million individual variants. Each of these is typically investigated as an individual risk factor with high stringency for multiple testing, but techniques have now evolved to examine global variance in this data, treating the data set as a whole. In this way, estimates of "global" genetic heritability can be made reflecting more accurately the totality of available genetic data, rather than focusing on single point estimates. It should be noted that these estimates are still restricted to the genetic information that can be genotyped or imputed directly based on the GWAS chip used, rather than all possible genetic information, however. Genomewide complex trait analysis provides such a tool to investigate the heritability of complex phenotypes[39] and has been applied to ischemic stroke.[40] This has shown the heritability of ischemic stroke when considering available

GWAS data was 37%, close to the 40% heritability figure estimated when considering the contribution of conventional risk factors. Intriguingly, the heritability of ischemic stroke subtypes showed considerable variability, being as high as 40% for large-vessel disease and as low as 16% for small-vessel disease. Cardioembolic stroke showed an intermediate genetic heritability of 32%.[40] Whether this variation reflects the underlying genetic architecture of these phenotypes or the certainty with which the phenotypes can be determined accurately is currently unclear, with the tighter the phenotype, the greater the underlying genetic contribution is likely to be when comparing patients and control subjects. One explanation for the lower heritability for small-vessel disease, which is at odds with the significant associations found in epidemiological family history data,[8] is that this subtype is heterogeneous and has more than one underlying pathology. These pathologies themselves have different genetic risks, diluting the phenotypic definition of small-vessel disease. Whichever is the true cause for differences in heritability, these heritability estimates add weight to the suggestion that individual ischemic stroke subtypes have different underlying genetic risk profiles.

The finding that the common-variant-common-disease hypothesis is not entirely accurate has led to a renewed interest in rare variants and their contribution to disease. It has been hypothesized that disease risk could be composed of a pool of common low-risk alleles together with a smaller number of rarer but high-risk alleles that are private to an individual or restricted to family members. In this manner, multiple risk alleles combine to produce the final phenotype, but the rare, highly penetrant alleles account for the observed familial aggregation of cases and increased incidence in related individuals. Such an occurrence would not lend itself to traditional linkage analysis because such genetic risks are not monogenic and would not be expected to display Mendelian patterns of inheritance, but nor would this disease model lend itself to a GWAS in which individual high-risk alleles would not be common enough in the general population to be detectable on currently used GWAS arrays. Identification of these high-risk alleles is best served by taking a sequencing approach to gene identification.

The Future of Gene Identification in Stroke

It is entirely feasible to sequence the entire genome. Currently, the limiting factor is primarily financial rather than technological. So-called *next-generation sequencing* originally referred to sequencing of the whole genome, but has recently become synonymous with the sequencing of the exome—the 1% of the genome that codes for protein. It is argued that a large proportion of disease-causing mutations is likely to affect protein-coding regions. Exome sequencing is viable financially, although the extent of the disease-relevant sequence outside the exome cannot yet be estimated in the absence of large-scale, whole-genome sequencing. Despite this, exome sequencing is growing in popularity, particularly in smaller cohorts, such as in the search for modifiers of disease presentation in familial clusters or in the search for known mutations in suspected carriers.[41] This latter approach is particularly attractive in that it enables areas of known or suspected relevance to be sequenced preferentially—a form of candidate gene sequencing. Such targeted sequencing approaches capture all the genetic variability within a genetic region but present a number of technological issues that must be overcome, including depth of coverage (how many times a region should be sequenced to be certain the sequence is accurate), the frequency a variant should have in a population to be defined as pathogenic or simply rare, and whether pooling of samples represents a viable method of reducing cost without reducing scientific robustness.

At the time of writing, published exome sequencing studies in stroke are limited, encompassing a study on intracranial aneurysm[42] and an exome pilot study identifying rare variants in ischemic stroke[43] using the search terms *stroke, exome,* and *sequencing* in PubMed. The evidence from other diseases, however, suggests that exome sequencing is increasing in importance. Whether this is related to familial aggregation and stroke will suffer from a late age of onset in the same way linkage studies bypass the condition is possible, although the applicability of exome sequencing to cohort studies being constrained by financial rather than technical limitations suggests that, as costs decrease, the popularity of next-generation sequencing is likely to increase. Sequencing studies of stroke and stroke-related endophenotypes have been undertaken as part of the National Heart, Lung and Blood Institute's Grand Opportunities Exome Sequencing Project http://www.ncbi.nlm.nih.gov/projects/gap/cgi- bin/study.cgi?study_id=phs000546.v1.p1), which sequenced select sib pairs and community samples of ischemic stroke patients and control subjects, and the Cohorts for Heart and Aging Research in Genomic Epidemiology consortium; these results are expected during the next 1 to 2 years.

Beyond the Genome

The central dogma of DNA leading to RNA leading to protein has been challenged in recent years, largely through efforts such as the human genome sequencing project and our increased understanding of genomic regulation. Although DNA is still the template in which an organism is encoded, control of expression of this DNA sequence through transcriptional, translational, and posttranslational regulation is providing an additional dimension to both normal and disease processes. Although still in their infancy compared with our understanding of DNA sequence, techniques such as transcriptional profiling, RNA sequencing, and proteomic analysis are beginning to be examined to further our understanding of genetic regulation and biological process.

Biomarkers of disease have long been examined as indicators of disease pathogenesis, with varying degrees of success. In ischemic stroke, the search for acute biomarkers of ischemia has been extensive but with little successful clinical utility.[44] More recent searches for panels of biomarkers are ongoing, but the major limitation of biomarkers remains the time lag to define a physiologically relevant pathology when compared with techniques such as imaging. As such, biomarkers are likely to be an adjunct to acute clinical care, but may be useful outside the acute setting, such as predicting recovery or secondary events.

One class of biomarkers receiving increased attention currently are microRNAs (miRNAs)—a class of small, noncoding RNAs typically 22 to 25 bp in length that regulate protein expression by binding to complementary messenger RNA sequences. These miRNAs were detected originally in intracellular locations, but have also been shown to circulate in the blood stream and to be remarkably resistant to degradation by exonucleases. This ability to circulate, and the implied stability of miRNAs, have led to their examination as biomarkers of disease, including cardiovascular disease[45] and stroke.[46] Although not a focus of this review, it is worth noting that DNA sequence changes that are often associated with disease do not explain the mechanism by which these associations manifest disease. The role of transcriptional, translational, and posttranslational regulation may yet prove to be of more relevance than DNA sequence change itself.

Conclusion

There is considerable epidemiological evidence that genetics plays an important role in stroke risk. Initial candidate gene studies failed to identify robust associations, in part as a result of small sample sizes, lack of power, failure to replicate, and inappropriate or limited phenotyping. Although meta-analysis of candidate gene studies identified some robust associations, these studies are very prone to positive publication bias. The advent of GWASs is beginning to transform our understanding of stroke genetics and, for the first time, are being used identify robust genetic risks of ischemic stroke directly. GWASs have also identified novel candidates for therapeutic investigation. There remains an ongoing role for additional GWASs, particularly in specific stroke subtypes and nonwhite populations, and identification of further risk loci is likely. Despite the success of GWASs, a large proportion of genetic risk could still be considered to be unaccounted for in terms of individual risk alleles. The contribution of rare variants is currently the focus of renewed investigation through techniques such as next-generation sequencing, but this type of study is not yet fully developed and is costly. When combined with additional biological processes such as examination of transcriptional and translational processing and control, our understanding of the molecular basis of disease risk is improving all the time. The key will be to translate these advances into patient benefit.

REFERENCES

1. Roger V, Go A, Lloyd-Jones DM, et al. Heart disease and stroke statistics: 2012 update: a report from the American Heart Association. *Circulation.* 2012;125:e2–e220.
2. Seshadri S, Beiser A, Kelly-Hayes M, et al. The lifetime risk of stroke: estimates from the Framingham study. *Stroke.* 2006;37:345–350.
3. Viswanathan A, Rocca WA, Tzourio C. Vascular risk factors and dementia: how to move forward? *Neurology.* 2009;72:368–374.
4. Sacco R, Ellenberg J, Mohr J, et al. Infarcts of undetermined cause: the NINDS Stroke Data Bank. *Ann Neurol.* 1989;25:382–390.
5. Joutel A, Corpechot C, Ducros A, et al. *Notch3* mutations in CADASIL, a hereditary adult-onset condition causing stroke and dementia. *Nature.* 1996;383:707–710.
6. Hassan A, Markus HS. Genetics and ischaemic stroke. *Brain.* 2000;123:1784–1812.
7. Flossmann E, Schulz U, Rothwell P. Systematic review of methods and results of studies of the genetic epidemiology of ischaemic stroke. *Stroke.* 2004;35:212–227.
8. Jerrard-Dunne P, Cloud G, Hassan A, Markus HS. Evaluating the genetic component of ischaemic stroke subtypes: a family history study. *Stroke.* 2003;34:1364–1369.
9. Rubattu S, Volpe M, Kreutz R, Ganten U, Lindpaintner K. Chromosomal mapping of quantitative trait loci contributing to stroke in a rat model of complex human disease. *Nat Genet.* 1996;13:429–434.
10. Duggirala R, Gonzalez Villalpando C, O'Leary DH, Stern MP, Blangero J. Genetic basis of variation in carotid artery wall thickness. *Stroke.* 1996;27:833–837.
11. Jartti L, Ronnemaa T, Kaprio J, et al. Population-based twin study of the effects of migration from Finland to Sweeden on endothelial functrion and intima-media thickness. *Arterioscler Thromb Vasc Biol.* 2002;22:832–837.
12. Moskau S, Golla A, Grothe C, Boes M, Pohl C, Klockgether T. Heritability of carotid artery atherosclerotic lesions. *Stroke.* 2005;36:5–8.
13. Atwood L, Wolf P, Heard-Costa N, et al. Genetic variation in white matter hyperintensity volume in the Framingham study. *Stroke.* 2004;35:1609–1613.
14. Turner S, Fornage M, Jack C, et al. Genomic susceptibility loci for brain atrophy, ventricular volume and leukoaraiosis in hypertensive sibships. *Arch Neurol.* 2009;66:847–857.
15. Carmelli D, DeCarli C, Swan G, et al. Evidence for genetic variance in white matter hyperintensity volume in normal elderly male twins. *Stroke.* 1998;29:1177–1181.
16. Markus HS. Unravelling the genetics of ischaemic stroke. *PLoS Med.* 2010;7:e1000225.
17. Dichgans M. Genetics of ischaemic stroke. *Lancet Neurol.* 2007;6:149–161.
18. Casas JP, Hingorani AD, Bautista LS, Sharma P. Meta-analysis of genetic studies in ischaemic stroke: thirty-two genes involving approximately 18000 cases and 58000 controls. *Arch Neurol.* 2004;61:1652–1661.

19. Gretarsdottir S, Thorleifsson G, Reynisdottir ST, et al. The gene encoding phosphodiesterase 4D confers risk of ischaemic stroke. *Nat Genet.* 2003;353:131–138.
20. Bevan S, Dichgans M, Gschwendtnew A, Kuhlenbaumer G, Ringelstein E, Markus HS. Variation in the *PDE4D* gene and ischaemic stroke risk: a systematic review and meta-analysis on 5200 cases and 6600 controls. *Stroke.* 2008;39:1966–1971.
21. Edwards A, Ritter R, Abel K, Manning A, Panhuysen C, Farrer L. Complement factor H polymorphism and age-related macular degeneration. *Science.* 2005;308:421–424.
22. The Wellcome Trust Case Control Consortium. Genome wide association study of 14,000 cases of seven common diseases and 3,000 shared controls. *Nature.* 2007;447:661–678.
23. Schunkert H, Gotz A, Braund P, et al. Repeated replication and a prospective meta-analysis of the association between chromosome 9p21.3 and coronary artery disease. *Circulation.* 2008;117:1675–1684.
24. Gschwendtner A, Bevan S, Cole J, et al. Sequence variants on chromosome 9p21.3 confer risk for atherosclerotic stroke. *Ann Neurol.* 2009;65:531–539.
25. Gudbjartsson D, Arnar D, Helgadottir A, et al. Variants conferring risk of atrial fibrillation on chromosome 4q25. *Nature.* 2007;448:353–357.
26. Gretarsdottir S, Thorleifsson G, Manolescu A, et al. Risk variants for atrial fibrillation on chromosome 4q25 associate with ischaemic stroke. *Ann Neurol.* 2008;64:402–409.
27. Gudbjartsson D, Holm H, Gretarsdottir S, et al. A sequence variant in ZFHX3 on 16q22 associates with arterial fibrillation and ischaemic stroke. *Nat Genet.* 2009;41:876–878.
28. Matarin M, Brown W, Scholz S, et al. A genome wide genotyping study in patients with ischaemic stroke: initial analysis and data release. *Lancet Neurol.* 2007;6:414–420.
29. Ikram A, Seshadri S, Bis J, et al. Genomewide association studies of stroke. *N Engl J Med.* 2009;360:1718–1728.
30. International Stroke Genetic Consortium, Wellcome Trust Case Control Consortium 2. Failure to validate association between 12p13 variants and ischaemic stroke. *N Engl J Med.* 2010;362:1547–1550.
31. Bellenguez C, Bevan S, Gschwendtnew A, et al. Genetic analysis identifies a new susceptibility locus in HDAC9 for large vessel ischemic stroke, and supports genetic heterogeneity across stroke subtypes. *Nat Genet.* 2012;44:328–333.
32. Holliday EG, Maguire J, Evans T-J, et al. Common variants at 6p21.1 are associated with large artery atherosclerotic stroke. *Nat Genet.* 2012;44:1147–1151.
33. Traylor M, Farrall M, Holliday E, et al. Genetic risk factors for ischaemic stroke and its subtypes (the METASTROKE collaboration): a meta-analysis of genome-wide association studies. *Lancet Neurol.* 2012;11:951–962.
34. Wang J, Klysik E, Sood S, Johnson RL, Wehrens XHT, Martin JF. Pitx2 prevents susceptibility to atrial arrhythmias by inhibiting left-sided pacemaker specification. *Proc Natl Acad Sci U S A.* 2010;107:9753–9758.
35. Motterle A, Pu X, Wood H, et al. Functional analyses of coronary artery disease associated variation on chromosome 9p21 in vascualr smooth muscle cells. *Hum Mol Genet.* 2012;21:4021–4029.
36. Markus HS, Makela K-M, Bevan S, et al. Evidence HDAC9 genetic variant associated with ischaemic stroke increases risk via promoting carotid atherosclerosis. *Stroke.* 2013;44:1220–1225.
37. Bowes AJ, Khan MI, Shi Y, Robertson L, Werstuck GH. Valproate attenuates accelerated atherosclerosis in hyperglycemic ApoE deficient mice: evidence in support of a role for endoplasmic reticulum stress and glycogen synthase kinase-3 in lesion development and hepatic stenosis. *Am J Pathol.* 2009;174:330–342.
38. Olesen JB, Abildstrom SZ, Erdal J, et al. Effects of epilepsy and selected antiepileptic drugs on risk of myocardial infarction, stroke and death in patients with or withour previous stroke: a nationwide cohort study. *Pharmacoepidemiol Drug Saf.* 2011;20:964–971.

39. Yang J, Lee S, Goddard M, Visscher P. GCTA: a tool for genome wide complex trait analysis. *Am J Hum Genet.* 2011;88:76–82.
40. Bevan S, Traylor M, Adib-Samii P, et al. Genetic heritability of ischaemic stroke and the contribution of previously reported candidate gene and genomewide associations. *Stroke.* 2012;43:3161–3167.
41. Foround T. Whole exome sequencing on intracranial aneurysm. *Stroke.* 2013;44:S26–S28.
42. Metzker M. Sequencing technologies: the next generation. *Nat Rev Genet.* 2010;11:31–46.
43. Cole JW, Stine OC, Liu XO, et al. Rare variants in ischaemic stroke: an exome pilot study. *PLoS One.* 2012;7:e35591.
44. Kernagis DN, Laskowitz DT. Evolving role of biomarkers in acute cerebrovascualr disease. *Ann Neurol.* 2012;71:289–303.
45. van Empel VPM, De Windt LJ, da Costa Martins PA. Circulating miRNAs: reflecting or affecting cardiovascualr disease? *Curr Hypertens Rep.* 2012;14:498–509.
46. Rink C, Khanna S. MicroRNA in ischaemic stroke etiology and pathology. *Physiol Genomics.* 2011;43:521–528.

6

GENETIC RISK FACTORS OF INTRACEREBRAL HEMORRHAGE

Guido J. Falcone and Jonathan Rosand

Introduction

Intracerebral hemorrhage (ICH) causes approximately 15% of all incident strokes in the United States and as much as 40% in East Asia.[1] The number of ICH cases is expected to increase in coming years as the population ages and the use of antithrombotic therapy among the elderly rises. This condition generates a substantial public health burden; it is the severest form of stroke, with a 90-day mortality that ranges from 30% to 50%. Moreover, only 10% to 25% of survivors achieve functional independence,[2,3] and they are also at increased risk of recurrent ICH. From a therapeutic standpoint, the only treatment demonstrated to decrease ICH risk is appropriate management of hypertension.[4,5] However, current population-attributable risk estimates suggest that only one third of all ICH cases in the elderly would be prevented by control of hypertension.[6] Furthermore, given the severity of ICH when it occurs, no acute therapy is likely to alter clinical outcome substantially on a population basis. Therefore, novel primary and secondary preventive strategies are needed.

Given that there are limited modifiable risk factors for this condition, the identification of genetic variants with a role in ICH is especially urgent, offering the possibility of novel targets for both prevention and treatment of ICH. In recent years, new technologies have revolutionized the field of genetics, offering the possibility of comprehensibly interrogating the genome (DNA), the transcriptome (RNA), and the proteome (proteins). Producing massive amounts of data, these high-throughput approaches have greatly accelerated the pace of identification of associations between phenotypes (outcomes) and variants in genetic sequence, RNA transcript levels, and levels of circulating proteins, yielding scores of new biological pathways for common diseases.

ICH is the final, acute result of a chronic and progressive process that damages the cerebral vasculature.[2] Infrequently, the underlying condition is a vascular malformation. Most of the ICH cases in subjects older than 55 years, however, take place in the context of cerebral small-vessel disease.[2] ICH is categorized based on the location of the bleeding. Lobar ICH corresponds to hemorrhages that occur at the junction of the cortical gray matter and subcortical white matter, and deep (or nonlobar) ICH refers to hematomas located in the thalamus, basal ganglia, brainstem, or cerebellum. In general, each ICH location correlates with a different pathological finding. Because chronic hypertension is the leading risk factor for deep ICH, lipohyalinosis of the small vessels has been found to be the corresponding pathology.[7] Cerebral amyloid angiopathy (CAA), on the other hand, has been identified as the main determinant of lobar ICH, with chronic hypertension having a much more limited role.[8–10]

Role of Genetic Variation in ICH

The relative contribution of genetic variation to risk of a given disease can be estimated by measuring either familial aggregation or heritability. Familial aggregation refers to increased risk in relatives of patients (of the outcome of interest) compared with risk in the general population.[11] Several studies have demonstrated that familial aggregation is elevated in ICH. The Greater Cincinnati/Northern Kentucky study, using a population-based case–control design, found that having a first-degree relative with ICH was strongly related to risk of ICH (odds ratio, 6.3) after adjustment for potential confounding factors. This effect of family history was equally strong in both deep and lobar ICH.[6] In addition, a population-based hospital discharge register in Sweden revealed that sibling history of hemorrhagic stroke more than doubled the incidence of ICH.[12] The effect of family history differed by age; no statistically significant effect was found among those younger than 50 years, whereas the greatest risk was observed in the age group 60 to 69 years.

Heritability for a given condition is defined, formally, as the quotient between the total variability observed and the variability resulting from genes.[13] In other words, it is the proportion of the variation for the disease of interest that is explained by genetic variation. Until recently, heritability could be estimated only through twin studies. Unfortunately, no studies of this sort are available for ICH. Recent advances in the field of statistical genetics, however, now allow the estimation of heritability in unrelated individuals through the analysis of genomewide data.[14] Data from such an analysis for ICH are forthcoming from the International Stroke Genetics Consortium (ISGC).

Familial ICH

Rare mutations in several genes have been identified in families whose members develop ICH at a relatively young age. These disorders cluster within families and follow a clear Mendelian pattern of inheritance, almost always autosomal dominant (one mutated allele is sufficient to cause the disease). Although multiple familial syndromes have been described, each produced by a specific gene mutation, these conditions account for a negligible proportion of all ICH in the general population.

We describe familial disorders that produce ICH by affecting the small vessels of the brain, thus mirroring what happens in sporadic ICH. It should be noted, however, that a few familial disorders produce intracerebral bleeding by contributing to the development of large-vessel vascular malformations, as is the case of familial cerebral cavernous malformations and mutations in the *CCM1* and *CCM2* genes.[15]

FAMILIAL CAA

CAA occurs both as a familial and sporadic disorder, and definitive diagnosis of both forms requires pathological examination. Sporadic CAA, nonetheless, can be diagnosed noninvasively during life combing neuroimaging and clinical data, according to the Boston criteria (Table 6.1).[16]

TABLE 6.1

Boston Criteria for the Diagnosis of Cerebral Amyloid Angiopathy
1. Definite CAA
Full postmortem examination demonstrating
• Lobar, cortical, or corticosubcortical hemorrhage
• Severe CAA with vasculopathy[a]
• Absence of other diagnostic lesion
2. Probable CAA with supporting pathology
Clinical data and pathological tissue (evacuated hematoma or cortical biopsy) demonstrating
• Lobar, cortical, or corticosubcortical hemorrhage
• Some degree of CAA in specimen
• Absence of other diagnostic lesion
3. Probable CAA
Clinical data and MRI or CT demonstrating
• Multiple hemorrhages restricted to lobar, cortical, or corticosubcortical regions (cerebellar hemorrhage allowed)
• Age ≥55 years
• Absence of other cause of hemorrhage[b]
4. Possible CAA
Clinical data and MRI or CT demonstrating:
• Single lobar, cortical, or corticosubcortical hemorrhage
• Age ≥55 years
• Absence of other cause of hemorrhage[b]

CAA, Cerebral Amyloid Angiopathy; MRI, Magnetic Resonance Imaging; CT, Computed Tomography.
Note: International Normalized Ratio 3.0 or other nonspecific laboratory abnormalities are permitted for the diagnosis of possible CAA.
[a]As defined in Von Sattel et al.[17]
[b]Other causes of intracerebral hemorrhage include excessive warfarin dosing (International Normalized Ratio > 3.0), antecedent head trauma or ischemic stroke, central nervous system tumor, vascular malformation, central nervous system vasculitis, blood dyscrasia, and coagulopathy.
CAA, cerebral amyloid angiopathy; CT, computed tomography; MRI, magnetic resonance imaging.

Within this diagnostic framework, a probable diagnosis of CAA can be made, in the absence of pathological examination, based on the tendency of CAA-related hemorrhages (identified through neuroimaging) to be multiple and lobar. The specificity and sensitivity of this diagnostic scheme exceed 90%.[16]

For both forms of CAA—familial and sporadic—the underlying biological mechanism is the deposition of the amyloid beta (Aβ) peptide in small and medium-size vessels within the brain.[8,9] Familial forms follow a Mendelian (usually dominant) pattern of inheritance, present earlier in life, and purport a more severe clinical course as well as an earlier age of death (Table 6.2).[18–22] Most forms of familial CAA are produced by mutations in the Aβ precursor protein (*APP*) gene. All these variants cluster within the Aβ coding region of the gene (exons 16 and 17).[10] The most frequent mechanism of genetic variation is a point mutation within the *APP* gene. Duplication of the *APP* locus, however, has also been described in families with familial early-onset Alzheimer's disease and CAA.[23]

TABLE 6.2

Familial Cerebral Amyloid Angiopathies

Amyloid peptide	Precursor protein	Chromosome	Disease	Features	CAA-ICH
Aβ	APP	21	CAA related to familial AD	Associated with presenilin 1, presenilin 2 and APP mutations	+
Aβ	APP	21	CAA in Down syndrome	Lobar ICH has been reported in some cases	+/–
Aβ	APP	21	CAA in APP duplication	CAA pathology prominent, increased risk of lobar hemorrhage, also causes early-onset autosomal dominant familial AD	+
Aβ	APP	21	Hereditary cerebral hemorrhage with amyloidosis: Dutch type	Described in 2 large families from the Netherlands; age at onset, 50 years; lobar hemorrhages, focal neurological deficits, dementia, and leukoencephalopathy	+
Aβ	APP	21	Hereditary cerebral hemorrhage with amyloidosis: Italian type	Described in 3 Italian families; age at onset, 50 years; lobar hemorrhages and dementia	+
Aβ	APP	21	Hereditary cerebral hemorrhage with amyloidosis: Flemish type	Described in a Dutch family (discovered in Belgium, therefore called *Flemish*) and a British family; age at onset, 45 years; progressive AD-like dementia, in some patients associated with a lobar hemorrhage	+/–
Aβ	APP	21	Hereditary cerebral hemorrhage with amyloidosis: Iowa type	Described in an Iowa family and a Spanish family; age at onset, 50–66 years; memory impairment, expressive language dysfunction, personality changes, myoclonic jerks, short-stepped gait, no clinically manifest ICH (family from Iowa) or lobar hemorrhages (family from Spain)	+/–

Aβ	APP	21	Hereditary cerebral hemorrhage with amyloidosis: Piedmont type	Described in one family from Piedmont, Italy; age at onset, 50–70 years; recurrent lobar hemorrhages, cognitive decline	+
Aβ	APP	21	Hereditary cerebral hemorrhage with amyloidosis: Arctic (Icelandic) type	Described in one family from northern Sweden; age at onset, ~60 years; progressive cognitive decline (no strokes)	–
ACys	Cystatin C	20	Hereditary cerebral hemorrhage with amyloidosis: Icelandic type	Described in 9 subfamilies in Iceland; causes systemic amyloidosis; age at onset, 20–30 years; recurrent lobar hemorrhages	+
ATTR	Transthyretin	18	Meningovascular amyloidosis	Polyneuropathy is the main clinical symptom; rarer findings are ataxia, spasticity, and dementia; systemic amyloidosis	In some families (rare)
AGel	Gelsolin	9	Familial amyloidosis: Finnish Type	Progressive corneal lattice dystrophy, cranial and peripheral neuropathy, cutaneous amyloidosis, systemic amyloidosis	–
PrPSc	Prion protein	20	Gerstmann–Sträussler–Scheinker syndrome	Described in 1 family, progressive cognitive decline	–
ABri	ABri precursor protein	13	Familial British dementia	Described in 4 families; age at onset, 45–50 years; progressive dementia, cerebellar ataxia, spastic tetraparesis	–
ADan	ABri precursor protein	13	Familial Danish dementia	Described in 1 family from Denmark; age at onset, 30 years; cataracts, deafness, progressive ataxia, dementia (previously known as *heredopatia ophthalmo-oto-encephalica*)	–

Aβ, amyloid beta; AD, Alzheimer's disease; APP, amyloid precursor protein; CAA, cerebral amyloid angiopathy; ICH, intracerebral hemorrhage.

Histopathologically, CAA is identified by deposition of a 39- to 43-amino acid proteolytic fragment of amyloid precursor protein (APP) in the vessel walls of capillaries, arterioles, and small and medium-size arteries of the cerebral cortex, leptomeninges, and cerebellum. This "vascular amyloid" is similar to that observed in amyloid plaques in Alzheimer's disease. Involvement ranges from mild (amyloid accumulates at the border of the media and adventitia of the vessel) to severe (there is total replacement of the smooth muscle media with amyloid, accompanied by vasculopathic changes that can include microaneurysm formation, concentric splitting of the vessel wall, chronic inflammatory infiltrates, and fibrinoid necrosis).[9]

Familial CAA can be classified further, depending on the nature and source of the accumulating peptide. Peptide accumulation in cerebral vessels can be found in all familial CAA syndromes (both Aβ and non-Aβ forms), although only in rare instances does lobar ICH represent the main clinical manifestation of non-Aβ CAA (with non-Aβ Icelandic type being the exception). Pleiotropy has been observed for the familial Aβ-CAA mutations; different subjects carrying the same mutation may have different clinical phenotypes. An example can be found for the Iowa mutation (replacement of asparagine for aspartate at position 23), in which one kindred had a history of recurrent ICH whereas a second presented with dementia and leukoaraiosis, but not ICH.[24] These observations demonstrate that additional genetic or environmental factors modify the effect of this mutation, and possibly other forms of familial CAA.[25]

COL4A1-RELATED INTRACEREBRAL HEMORRHAGE

Both familial and sporadic forms of ICH have been described for mutations in the *COL4A1* gene. This gene encodes the *α1* chain of type IV collagen, a subtype of collagen that forms basement membranes of all tissues, including the vasculature, and contributes to their strength. Rare mutations within this gene cause autosomal dominant syndromes manifesting with perinatal intracerebral hemorrhage and porencephaly, adult-onset ICH (all locations), small foci of chronic blood products in normal brain tissue known as *microbleeds*, lacunar strokes, and leukoaraiosis.[26–28] Electron microscopic observations found that mice carrying *COL4A1* mutations have uneven and inconsistent basement membranes, with localized disruptions. Ultimately, these changes lead to increased fragility of vessel walls and ICH.[29]

Most disease-causing mutations in *COL4A1*-related cerebrovascular disease are missense variants affecting a highly conserved hydrophobic glycine residue. This genetic alteration results in inhibition of heterotrimer deposition into the vascular basement membrane, with a consequent alteration of its structural properties. In addition to the ICH-related phenotypes described earlier, the consequences of these structural changes are evident when observing the role of *COL4A1* in determining cerebral vessel tolerance to minor head trauma. Surgical delivery of mouse pups bearing a mutated *COL4A1* allele can prevent the severe perinatal cerebral hemorrhages that occur in spontaneous live births. This finding could have important implications for human disease, because impaired responses to even mild trauma could result in several clinical manifestations that could range from subclinical microbleeds to subarachnoid hemorrhage and ICH.[29]

Sporadic ICH: A Role for Rare and Common Genetic Variants

Both rare and common genetic variants appear to influence risk of ICH without producing the clear familial pattern of Mendelian inheritance. Individuals carrying these variants are at increased risk of sustaining an ICH, but pedigree and genotype data are not enough to predict accurately who will experience an ICH, as is the case with Mendelian disorders. Evidence for this type of non-Mendelian association is generated through candidate gene and genomewide association studies.

CANDIDATE GENE STUDIES

Common genetic variants are those that have a minor allele frequency greater than 5%. These variants presumably have a much smaller effect on disease susceptibility than rare mutations that cause familial (Mendelian) diseases; as a result, they are found in both affected and unaffected individuals. Candidate gene association studies aim to assess the hypothesis that a particular common genetic variant—or a limited number of them—is related statistically to the outcome of interest. The key to the success of candidate gene studies is prescient selection of the genetic variant to be evaluated. Selection strategies usually pursued examination of common variants at loci known to cause Mendelian forms of the outcome, extrapolation of evidence from animal models, and selection of genes known to participate in biological pathways related to the phenotype of interest (e.g. testing association with ICH of common variants for genes that encode proteins involved in the coagulation cascade). Candidate gene studies have yielded mostly negative results in ICH—as is the case for many other complex diseases. Moreover, most of the associations published have been not replicated in subsequent studies.[30] This is probably a result of the limitations observed in these studies: small sample size, application of p value thresholds that are insufficiently stringent, and inability to account for confounding as a result of population structure.

APOLIPOPROTEIN E AND RISK OF SPORADIC CAA

An association that has proved robust in candidate gene studies is that for apolipoprotein E, *APOE*, and sporadic ICH related to CAA—a finding that reflects the biological overlap with Alzheimer's disease. In the population-based, Greater Cincinnati/Northern Kentucky study, possession of the *APOE* ε2 or ε4 allele accounted for the largest proportion of lobar ICH cases, with a population-attributable risk of 30%. Moreover, multiple studies have described associations between the ε2 and ε4 alleles of the *APOE* gene and CAA-ICH.[31–33] Until recently, the small size and, perhaps, the lack of control for confounding resulting from population stratification of all candidate gene studies of *APOE* and CAA-ICH yielded inconsistent results.[34,35]

In 2010, the ISGC was able to accumulate a sample of sufficient size, as well as apply methods to control for population structure, to establish an association between *APOE* variants and lobar ICH at the level needed to account for testing of all common variants across the human genome. In this multicenter meta-analysis, which included more than 2000 patients with ICH and more than 4000 control subjects,[36] both the ε2 and ε4 alleles were associated with lobar ICH risk at genomewide significance levels ($p < 5 \times 10^{-8}$). This association was strengthened when the analysis was restricted to subjects with probable CAA (based on Boston criteria)—a reflection of the link between *APOE* ε2 and ε4 and CAA. In addition to influencing risk of first ICH, both ε2 and ε4 have also been shown to be associated with risk of recurrent ICH,[37] whereas ε2 alone increases the volume of ICH at presentation,[38] as well as the risk of contrast extravasation on neuroimaging (i.e., the "spot sign", see Figure 6.1.)[39] and ICH expansion.[40] These results are in line with previous pathological studies of *APOE* and ICH related to CAA. These reports provided evidence for a distinct role of the ε2 allele in increasing the risk of CAA-related bleeding, possibly through increased damage to small-vessel walls.[41,42] Of note, *APOE* alleles ε2 and ε4 have a very limited relationship with disease risk and clinical evolution over time in familial CAA—a finding that may reflect the overwhelming effect of rare (Mendelian) mutation in causing amyloid accumulation.

COLLAGEN TYPE 4, α1

The role of variation in *COL4A1* in sporadic (nonfamilial) forms of ICH was investigated recently by a sequencing study that followed the candidate gene approach. All coding and flanking intervening sequences at this locus were sequenced in 96 patients with sporadic ICH and 145 ethnically matched control individuals. The study identified two mutations that were present only in patients with ICH: *COL4A1*^{P352L} and *COL4A1*^{R538G}. These variants resulted in missense changes in amino acids that are highly conserved across species.[43]

Collagen type IV, α1 (the product of *COL4A1*), is related structurally and functionally to the collagen type IV, α2, encoded by *COL4A2*. Leveraging this functional relation, another recent study assessed the effect of variants at the *COL4A2* locus on the risk of ICH. All coding and flanking regions of *COL4A2* were sequenced in 96 patients with sporadic ICH and 145 control individuals. Three rare, nonsynonymous coding variants affecting evolutionary conserved amino acids were observed in four patients that were not present in any of the control subjects. The same study showed, using cellular assays, that these variants caused intracellular accumulation of COL4A1 and COL4A2 at the expense of their secretion, providing additional support for their pathogenic role.[44] Of note, a similar approach, examining the role of *APP* mutations in sporadic CAA-related ICH did not identify any mutations.[45]

COMPLEMENT RECEPTOR 1

Identification of the complement receptor 1, or *CR1*, gene as a risk factor for ICH related to CAA arose through the examination of loci that have been implicated in Alzheimer's disease. Accumulated evidence suggests that rs6656401, a common variant within the *CR1* gene, known to increase risk for Alzheimer's disease, influences Aβ amyloid deposition in brain tissue.[46] Prompted by the biological overlap between Alzheimer's disease and CAA, a recent study investigated whether rs6656401 increases the risk of first and recurrent CAA-related ICH in 89 individuals with CAA-related ICH and 324 ICH-free control subjects. rs6656401 was associated with CAA-ICH (odds ratio, 1.61; $p = 8.0 \times 10^{-4}$) as well as with the risk of recurrent CAA-ICH (hazard ratio, 1.35; $p = .02$).[47] (p. 1)

GENOMEWIDE ASSOCIATION STUDIES

Genomewide association studies are comprehensive, unbiased searches for common genetic variants that affect specific traits or diseases. They are now possible because of the availability of affordable high-throughput technologies for genomewide genotyping, specific statistical tools, and publicly available data on single nucleotide polymorphisms (SNPs) and other forms of common genetic variation (HapMap and 1000 Genomes projects).[48–50] Investigators applying this study design make no a priori assumptions about the location or causal role of the genetic variants being interrogated. The combination of available genotyping technologies with advanced imputation techniques allows the evaluation of several million SNPs known to exist within the human genome.

Fundamental to the success of recent whole-genome association studies has been the assembly of large numbers of well-characterized patients by collaborating groups of investigators. Although a number of genomewide association scans have been reported for ischemic stroke, no such study aimed specifically at assessing ICH (or hemorrhagic stroke) has yet been completed. A large, international, multicenter genomewide study of ICH is currently being undertaken by the ISGC. An interim analysis of this study failed to identify loci associated with ICH at a genomewide level of significance (5.0×10^{-8}), but genotyping and analyses are ongoing.[51]

Magnetic Resonance Imaging-Detectable White Matter Hyperintensities: A Potential Endophenotype for ICH

Endophenotypes are measurable traits that are hypothesized to be along the causal pathway from genetic variation to disease expression.[52] Identification of endophenotypes can facilitate the study of genetic risk factors because they are more frequent and easy to identify than the final outcome of interest. Potential endophenotypes for ICH can be obtained by observing other forms of brain injury related to the small-vessel pathologies responsible for ICH. Notable among these are white matter hyperintensities (WMHs; also known as *leukoaraiosis*), which are white matter rarefactions detected sensitively by computed tomography or magnetic resonance imaging. WMHs are common in the aging population, readily quantifiable through neuroimaging, and are strongly heritable, with estimates that range from 55% to 80%.[53–55] More important, WMH is associated with symptomatic ICH in both lobar and nonlobar locations.[56–58]

WMHs can be observed in almost all familial forms of ICH attributable to small-vessel disease. One such example is cerebral autosomal dominant arteriopathy with subcortical infarcts and leukoencephalopathy (CADASIL), a monogenic, autosomal dominant disorder caused by mutations in the *NOTCH3* gene. The protein encoded by *NOTCH3* seems to have a role in blood vessel development and corresponds to a cell-surface receptor expressed on the surface of vascular smooth muscle cells. The majority of mutations associated with CADASIL modify the number of cysteine residues within the extracellular domain of the protein. Mutations at this locus cause a familiar syndrome characterized by migraines with aura, recurrent strokes, progressive cognitive impairment, psychiatric disturbances, and, occasionally, ICH. It should be noted, however, that this condition produces mainly small, usually asymptomatic, microhemorrhages, and that the occurrence of clinically evident ICH is infrequent. From a radiological standpoint, the distinctive findings of CADASIL include microbleeds and diffuse WMH, with preferential, bilateral involvement of the external capsule and anterior temporal lobes (Figure 6.1).

Common genetic variants can also influence WMH burden in a non-Mendelian fashion. A recently completed genomewide association study identified six WMH-associated SNPs on one locus on chromosome 17q25. This locus encompasses six genes: *WBP2, TRIM65, TRIM47, MRPL38, FBF1*, and *ACOX1*. Variant alleles at this locus conferred a small increase in WMH burden—4% to 8% of the overall mean WMH burden in the sample.[59] These genes, together with their corresponding cellular processes, are appealing targets to be assessed for association with ICH and are being actively explored.

Clinical Implications

Recent genetic discoveries in ICH raise the promise of clinical applications.[60] Recognition of subjects carrying rare mutations that cause Mendelian diseases is crucial. These Mendelian

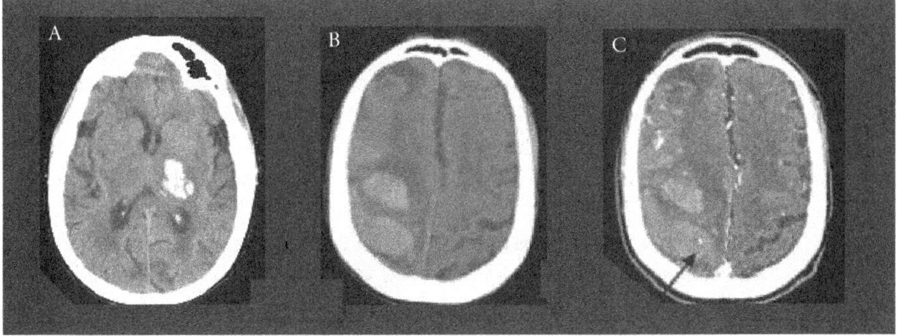

FIGURE 6.1 Radiological findings in intracerebral hemorrhage (ICH). (A) Deep ICH. (B) Lobar ICH. (C) Contrast extravasation within the intracranial hematoma—the "spot sign" (arrow).

conditions can be recognized by their clear pattern of familial aggregation and, in terms of ICH, by a younger age of onset, more severe clinical course, and higher rate of recurrence. Identification of subjects carrying these mutations is important to provide appropriate genetic counseling. In addition, making an accurate genetic diagnosis may improve clinical care, because specific preventive measures can be implemented based on the known natural evolution of each disease. It should be noted, however, that when the possibility of a Mendelian disease has been considered, clinical management should probably be deferred to a geneticist, because genetic testing is not always indicated, and to ensure optimal genetic counseling if the disease is confirmed.

A second important application of genetics to ICH may be in decision making for chronic anticoagulation. Use of warfarin increases both the frequency and the severity of ICH. Thus, even at the annual rate of 0.2% to 0.6% observed in randomized trials of conventional-intensity anticoagulation,[61] warfarin-related ICH exerts a major effect on clinical decision making. Therefore, it is plausible that even relatively weak risk factors for patients with ICH on warfarin might sway the balance in favor of or against treatment. In this regard, an important discovery has been that as much as 35% of the variability observed in the response to warfarin is related to common genetic variants occurring at the *VKORC1*[62] and *CYP2C9*[63] genes.[64–66] Based on these findings, in 2010 the U.S. Food and Drug Administration included in the warfarin product label dose recommendations based on the *CYP2C9* and *VKORC1* genotypes.

Several warfarin pharmacogenetic algorithms that combine clinical and genetic factors are currently available.[64,65] These approaches have already demonstrated their superiority, when compared with standard management, in estimating the correct dosing scheme at the beginning of anticoagulation.[67] Furthermore, the results of a recently published randomized study showed for the first time that warfarin pharmacogenetic algorithms also provide benefit in terms of clinical outcome.[68] In that study, the proportion of serious adverse events at 3 months was 4.5% versus 9.4% for the pharmacogenetic-guided and standard approaches, respectively. Four other clinical trials currently underway will provide important additional information to complement these findings.[69]

Future Directions

The genetic underpinnings of ICH are likely to emerge in the coming years from ongoing studies of related phenotypes as well as ICH itself. A large meta-analysis of genomewide association studies of blood pressure levels has revealed that the burden of these variants is associated with both ischemic and hemorrhagic stroke.[70] This same approach is likely to be applied to other ICH risk factors and endophenotypes for which common genetic variants have been identified, such as body mass index, alcohol abuse, and WMH.

Genomewide data for ICH will soon be available from the ISGC[71] as well as the Risk Assessment of Cerebrovascular Events study. In addition to offering the promise of novel genetic discoveries, these data will be used to estimate ICH heritability; assess, through pathway analysis, the role of specific metabolic and functional cellular pathways; and evaluate interactions between genes and medication exposure.

Genetic risk factors for ICH are available from birth, constant over time, and easy to measure reliably. In the end, the combination of genetic and clinical information is likely to lead to a more precise stratification of ICH risk, aiding in identifying high-risk individuals who may benefit from specific forms of prevention. Furthermore these risk factors are likely to highlight entirely new biological pathways, yielding just the kind of mechanistic insights necessary for the development of effective treatments.

Acknowledgment

Supported by the National Institute of Neurological Disorders and Stroke (R01NS059727, U01 NS069208, U01NS069763, R01NS063925).

REFERENCES

1. Qureshi AI, Tuhrim S, Broderick JP, et al. Spontaneous intracerebral hemorrhage. *N Engl J Med.* 2001;344:1450–1460.
2. Qureshi AI, Mendelow AD, Hanley DF. Intracerebral haemorrhage. *Lancet.* 2009;373:1632–1644.
3. van Asch CJ, Luitse MJ, Rinkel GJ, et al. Incidence, case fatality, and functional outcome of intracerebral haemorrhage over time, according to age, sex, and ethnic origin: a systematic review and meta-analysis. *Lancet Neurol.* 2010;9:167–176.
4. Morgenstern LB, Hemphill JC 3rd, Anderson C, et al. Guidelines for the management of spontaneous intracerebral hemorrhage: a guideline for healthcare professionals from the American Heart Association/American Stroke Association. *Stroke.* 2010;41:2108–2129.
5. Arima H, Tzourio C, Anderson C, et al. Effects of perindopril-based lowering of blood pressure on intracerebral hemorrhage related to amyloid angiopathy: the PROGRESS trial. *Stroke.* 2010;41(2):394–396.
6. Woo D, Sauerbeck LR, Kissela BM, et al. Genetic and environmental risk factors for intracerebral hemorrhage: preliminary results of a population-based study. *Stroke.* 2002;33:1190–1195.
7. Fisher CM. Lacunar strokes and infarcts: a review. *Neurology.* 1982;32:871–876.
8. Vinters HV, Gilbert JJ. Cerebral amyloid angiopathy: incidence and complications in the aging brain. II: the distribution of amyloid vascular changes. *Stroke.* 1983;14:924–928.
9. Vinters HV. Cerebral amyloid angiopathy. a critical review. *Stroke.* 1987;18:311–324.
10. Zhang-Nunes SX, Maat-Schieman MLC, van Duinen SG, et al. The cerebral beta-amyloid angiopathies: hereditary and sporadic. *Brain Pathol.* 2006;16:30–39.
11. Balding DJ, Bishop M, Cannings C. *Handbook of statistical genetics.* Chichester, UK. Wiley, 2001.
12. Sundquist K, Li X, Hemminki K. Familial risk of ischemic and hemorrhagic stroke: a large-scale study of the Swedish population. *Stroke.* 2006;37:1668–1673.
13. Visscher PM, Hill WG, Wray NR. Heritability in the genomics era: concepts and misconceptions. *Nat Rev Genet.* 2008;9(4):255–266.
14. Visscher PM, Medland SE, Ferreira MAR, et al. Assumption-free estimation of heritability from genome-wide identity-by-descent sharing between full siblings. *PLoS Genet.* 2006;2:e41.
15. Brouillard P, Vikkula M. Genetic causes of vascular malformations. *Hum Mol Genet.* 2007;16:R140–R149.
16. Knudsen KA, Rosand J, Karluk D, Greenberg SM. Clinical diagnosis of cerebral amyloid angiopathy: validation of the Boston criteria. *Neurology.* 2001;56:537–539.
17. Von Sattel JP, Myers RH, Hedley-Whyte ET, Ropper AH, Bird ED, Richardson EP Jr. Cerebral amyloid angiopathy without and with cerebral hemorrhages: a comparative histological study. Ann Neurol 1991;30:637–649.
18. Palsdottir A, Snorradottir AO, Thorsteinsson L. Hereditary cystatin C amyloid angiopathy: genetic, clinical, and pathological aspects. *Brain Pathol.* 2006;16:55–59.
19. Bornebroek M, De Jonghe C, Haan J, et al. Hereditary cerebral hemorrhage with amyloidosis Dutch type (AbetaPP 693): decreased plasma amyloid-beta 42 concentration. *Neurobiol Dis.* 2003;14:619–623.
20. De Jonghe C, Zehr C, Yager D, et al. Flemish and Dutch mutations in amyloid beta precursor protein have different effects on amyloid beta secretion. *Neurobiol Dis.* 1998;5:281–286.

21. Farzan M, Schnitzler CE, Vasilieva N, Leung D, Choe H. BACE2, a beta-secretase homolog, cleaves at the beta site and within the amyloid-beta region of the amyloid-beta precursor protein. *Proc Natl Acad Sci U S A.* 2000;97(17):9712–9717.
22. Haass C, Hung AY, Selkoe DJ, Teplow DB. Mutations associated with a locus for familial Alzheimer's disease result in alternative processing of amyloid beta-protein precursor. *J Biol Chem.* 1994;269:17741–17748.
23. Rovelet-Lecrux A, Hannequin D, Raux G, et al. APP locus duplication causes autosomal dominant early-onset Alzheimer disease with cerebral amyloid angiopathy. *Nat Genet.* 2006;38:24–26.
24. Van Nostrand WE, Melchor JP, Cho HS, Greenberg SM, Rebeck GW. Pathogenic effects of D23N Iowa mutant amyloid beta-protein. *J Biol Chem.* 2001;276:32860–32866.
25. Greenberg SM, Shin Y, Grabowski TJ, et al. Hemorrhagic stroke associated with the Iowa amyloid precursor protein mutation. *Neurology.* 2003;60:1020–1022.
26. Vahedi K, Boukobza M, Massin P, et al. Clinical and brain MRI follow-up study of a family with COL4A1 mutation. *Neurology.* 2007;69:1564–1568.
27. van der Knaap MS, Smit LME, Barkhof F, et al. Neonatal porencephaly and adult stroke related to mutations in collagen IV A1. *Ann Neurol.* 2006;59:504–511.
28. McCarron MO, Nicoll JA, Stewart J, et al. The apolipoprotein E epsilon2 allele and the pathological features in cerebral amyloid angiopathy-related hemorrhage. *J Neuropathol Exp Neurol.* 1999;58:711–718.
29. Gould DB, Phalan FC, van Mil SE, et al. Role of COL4A1 in small-vessel disease and hemorrhagic stroke. *N Engl J Med.* 2006;354:1489–1496.
30. Hirschhorn JN, Lohmueller K, Byrne E, Hirschhorn K. A comprehensive review of genetic association studies. *Genet Med.* 2002;4:45–61.
31. Sudlow C, Martínez González NA, Kim J, Clark C. Does apolipoprotein E genotype influence the risk of ischemic stroke, intracerebral hemorrhage, or subarachnoid hemorrhage? Systematic review and meta-analyses of 31 studies among 5961 cases and 17,965 controls. *Stroke.* 2006;37:364–370.
32. Peck G, Smeeth L, Whittaker J, et al. The genetics of primary haemorrhagic stroke, subarachnoid haemorrhage and ruptured intracranial aneurysms in adults. *PLoS One.* 2008;3:e3691.
33. Bertram L, McQueen MB, Mullin K, Blacker D, Tanzi RE. Systematic meta-analyses of Alzheimer disease genetic association studies: the AlzGene database. *Nat Genet.* 2007;39:17–23.
34. Garcia C, Pinho e Melo T, Rocha L, Lechner MC. Cerebral hemorrhage and apoE. *J Neurol.* 1999;246:830–834.
35. Seifert T, Lechner A, Flooh E, et al. Lack of association of lobar intracerebral hemorrhage with apolipoprotein E genotype in an unselected population. *Cerebrovasc Dis.* 2006;21:266–270.
36. Biffi A, Sonni A, Anderson CD, et al. Variants at APOE influence risk of deep and lobar intracerebral hemorrhage. *Ann Neurol.* 2010;68:934–943.
37. O'Donnell HC, Rosand J, Knudsen KA, et al. Apolipoprotein E genotype and the risk of recurrent lobar intracerebral hemorrhage. *N Engl J Med.* 2000;342:240–245.
38. Biffi A, Anderson CD, Jagiella JM, et al. APOE genotype and extent of bleeding and outcome in lobar intracerebral haemorrhage: a genetic association study. *Lancet Neurol.* 2011;10:702–709.
39. Brouwers HB, Biffi A, McNamara KA, et al. Apolipoprotein E genotype is associated with CT angiography spot sign in lobar intracerebral hemorrhage. *Stroke* 2012;43:2120–2125.
40. Brouwers HB, Biffi A, Ayres AM, et al. Apolipoprotein E genotype predicts hematoma expansion in lobar intracerebral hemorrhage. *Stroke.* 2012. Available at: http://www.ncbi.nlm.nih.gov/pubmed/22535266 (accessed May 14, 2012).
41. McCarron MO, Nicoll JA. Apolipoprotein E genotype and cerebral amyloid angiopathy-related hemorrhage. *Ann N Y Acad Sci.* 2000;903:176–179.

42. Greenberg SM, Vonsattel JP, Segal AZ, et al. Association of apolipoprotein E epsilon2 and vasculopathy in cerebral amyloid angiopathy. *Neurology.* 1998;50:961–965.
43. Weng Y-C, Sonni A, Labelle-Dumais C, et al. *COL4A1* mutations in patients with sporadic late-onset intracerebral hemorrhage. *Ann Neurol.* 2012;71:470–477.
44. Jeanne M, Labelle-Dumais C, Jorgensen J, et al. *COL4A2* mutations impair COL4A1 and COL4A2 secretion and cause hemorrhagic stroke. *Am J Hum Genet.* 2012;90:91–101.
45. Biffi A, Plourde A, Shen Y, et al. Screening for familial APP mutations in sporadic cerebral amyloid angiopathy. *PLoS One.* 2010;5:e13949.
46. Chibnik LB, Shulman JM, Leurgans SE, et al. CR1 is associated with amyloid plaque burden and age-related cognitive decline. *Ann Neurol.* 2011;69:560–569.
47. Biffi A, Shulman JM, Jagiella JM, et al. Genetic variation at CR1 increases risk of cerebral amyloid angiopathy. *Neurology.* 2012;78:334–341.
48. Anonymous. The International HapMap Project. *Nature.* 2003;426:789–796.
49. The International HapMap Consortium. A haplotype map of the human genome. *Nature.* 2005;437:1299–1320.
50. Consortium T1000 GP. A map of human genome variation from population-scale sequencing. *Nature.* 2010;467:1061–1073.
51. Brown WM, Biffi A, Jagiella JM, et al. Genome-wide association study of intracerebral hemorrhage. *Stroke.* 2011;42:e218.
52. John B, Lewis KR. Chromosome variability and geographic distribution in insects. *Science.* 1966;152:711–721.
53. Atwood LD, Wolf PA, Heard-Costa NL, et al. Genetic variation in white matter hyperintensity volume in the Framingham study. *Stroke.* 2004;35:1609–1613.
54. Turner ST, Jack CR, Fornage M, et al. Heritability of leukoaraiosis in hypertensive sibships. *Hypertension.* 2004;43:483–487.
55. Carmelli D, DeCarli C, Swan GE, et al. Evidence for genetic variance in white matter hyperintensity volume in normal elderly male twins. *Stroke.* 1998;29:1177–1181.
56. Smith EE, Gurol ME, Eng JA, et al. White matter lesions, cognition, and recurrent hemorrhage in lobar intracerebral hemorrhage. *Neurology.* 2004;63:1606–1612.
57. Smith EE, Rosand J, Knudsen KA, Hylek EM, Greenberg SM. Leukoaraiosis is associated with warfarin-related hemorrhage following ischemic stroke. *Neurology.* 2002;59:193–197.
58. Neumann-Haefelin T, Hoelig S, Berkefeld J, et al. Leukoaraiosis is a risk factor for symptomatic intracerebral hemorrhage after thrombolysis for acute stroke. *Stroke.* 2006;37:2463–2466.
59. Fornage M, Debette S, Bis JC, et al. Genome-wide association studies of cerebral white matter lesion burden: the CHARGE Consortium. *Ann Neurol.* 2011;69:928–939.
60. Collins FS. Reengineering translational science: the time is right. *Sci Transl Med.* 2011;3:90cm17.
61. Singer DE, Albers GW, Dalen JE, et al. Antithrombotic therapy in atrial fibrillation: the Seventh ACCP Conference on Antithrombotic and Thrombolytic Therapy. *Chest.* 2004;126(Suppl):429S–4 56S.
62. Rieder MJ, Reiner AP, Gage BF, et al. Effect of VKORC1 haplotypes on transcriptional regulation and warfarin dose. *N Engl J Med.* 2005;352:2285–2293.
63. Aithal GP, Day CP, Kesteven PJ, Daly AK. Association of polymorphisms in the cytochrome P450 CYP2C9 with warfarin dose requirement and risk of bleeding complications. *Lancet.* 1999;353:717–719.
64. Gage BF, Eby C, Johnson JA, et al. Use of pharmacogenetic and clinical factors to predict the therapeutic dose of warfarin. *Clin Pharmacol Ther.* 2008;84:326–331.
65. Klein TE, Altman RB, Eriksson N, et al. Estimation of the warfarin dose with clinical and pharmacogenetic data. *N Engl J Med.* 2009;360:753–764.

66. Limdi NA, Wadelius M, Cavallari L, et al. Warfarin pharmacogenetics: a single VKORC1 polymorphism is predictive of dose across 3 racial groups. *Blood.* 2010;115:3827–3834.
67. Finkelman BS, Gage BF, Johnson JA, Brensinger CM, Kimmel SE. Genetic warfarin dosing: tables versus algorithms. *J Am Coll Cardiol.* 2011;57:612–618.
68. Anderson JL, Horne BD, Stevens SM, et al. A randomized and clinical effectiveness trial comparing two pharmacogenetic algorithms and standard care for individualizing warfarin dosing (CoumaGen-II): clinical perspective. *Circulation.* 2012;125:1997–2005.
69. Johnson JA, Gong L, Whirl-Carrillo M, et al. Clinical Pharmacogenetics Implementation Consortium guidelines for CYP2C9 and VKORC1 genotypes and warfarin dosing. *Clin Pharmacol Ther.* 2011;90:625–629.
70. Ehret GB, Munroe PB, Rice KM, et al. Genetic variants in novel pathways influence blood pressure and cardiovascular disease risk. *Nature.* 2011;478:103–109.
71. Anonymous. www.strokegenetics.org (accessed May 25, 2012).

7

RELEVANCE FOR STROKE OF GENES ASSOCIATED WITH OTHER VASCULAR PHENOTYPES

Rainer Malik and Martin Dichgans

Introduction

This chapter provides an overview of genes that have been identified for established phenotypes in cardiovascular disease (CVD), whether the specific genes or loci are also implicated in stroke, and whether shared mechanisms between vascular phenotypes can be determined.

It has long been thought that stroke and other CVD phenotypes, and especially arterial disease, share a common etiology.[1,2] Genomewide association studies (GWASs) have been highly successful in identifying susceptibility loci for coronary artery disease (CAD) and myocardial infarction (MI). However, for stroke and other arterial diseases, these efforts have not been as successful so far—mostly because of small sample size and, more important, reduced power to detect associations in subtypes for stroke. This is especially important, because it has been established that genetic risk loci are specific to certain stroke subtypes.[3–7] In this chapter, we highlight the successes in related phenotypes and show how these findings could be related to stroke. We also discuss how to further GWASs to increase the number of risk loci for stroke.

We focus primarily on GWAS findings in predominantly white populations. When this is not the case, either for candidate gene studies or GWASs in nonwhite populations, this is noted in the text.

Coronary Artery Disease

CAD has been the most intensely studied cardiovascular phenotype with regard to GWASs. Pathologically, CAD is characterized by atheromatous plaques in the coronary arteries, with the end point of MI after plaque rupture. It has been speculated that CAD and stroke, and here, especially, the Trial of Org 10172 in Acute Stroke Treatment (TOAST) subtype of large-artery stroke (LAS), share a common etiology because the pathophysiological mechanisms of these diseases both encompass—to varying degrees—the formation and rupture of atherosclerotic plaques with a misbalanced lipid profile and a pathological immune response.

Key risk factors for CAD are elevated cholesterol levels, smoking, diabetes, and hypertension,[8] and have been well established over time.[9] Less established risk factors such as homocysteine levels, triglyceride levels, C-reactive protein, and others have not proved to be useful indicators of CAD so far.

Recently, a large number of risk loci for CAD have been discovered through GWASs and have been replicated stably over time.[10–21] During past years, the number of patients and control subjects in GWASs has grown steadily so that even variants affecting CAD risk with only moderate impact have been discovered. The major loci for CAD, the associated genes, and their respective references are listed in Table 7.1.

TABLE 7.1

Overview of Coronary Artery Disease/Myocardial Infarction-Associated Loci

Locus	Gene/nearest gene	Additional cardiovascular phenotypes showing association
1q21.3	*IL6R*	AAA[22]
1p32.3	*PCSK9*	—
1p32.2	*PPAP2B*	—
1p13.3	*SORT1*	AAA[23]
1q41	*MIA3*	—
2q33.1	*WDR12*	—
2q22.3	*ZEB2-AC074093.1*	—
2p24.1	*APOB*	—
2p21	*ABCG5-ABCG8*	—
2p11.2	*VAMP5-VAMP8- GGCX*	—
3q22.3	*MRAS*	—
4q32.1	*GUCY1A3*	—
4q31.23	*EDNRA*	ICA[24]
5q31.1	*SLC22A4-SLC22A5*	—
6q25.3	*PLG*	—
6q25.3	*SLC22A3/LPAL2/LPA*	—
6q23.2	*TCF21*	—
6p24.1	*PHACTR1*	—
6p21.31	*ANKS1A*	—
6p21.2	*KCNK5*	—
7q32.2	*ZC3HC1*	—
7p21.1	*HDAC9*	LAS[3,25]
7q22	*7q22*	—
8q24.13	*TRIB1*	—
8p21.3	*LPL*	—
9q34.2	*ABO*	LAS, CES, IS26

TABLE 7.1

Continued

Locus	Gene/nearest gene	Additional cardiovascular phenotypes showing association
9p21.3	*CDKN2BAS*	LAS, PAD, ICA[5,24,27]
10q24.32	*CYP17A1/CNNM2/NT5C2*	ICA[28]
10q23.31	*LIPA*	—
10q11.21	*CXCL12*	—
10p11.23	*KIAA1462*	—
11q23.3	*ZNF259/APO5A/APOA1*	—
11q22.3	*PDGFD*	—
12q24.12	*chr12q24/SH2B3*	—
13q34	*COL4A1/COL4A2*	—
13q12.2	*FLT1*	—
14q32.2	*HHIPL1*	—
15q26.1	*FURIN-FES*	—
15q25.1	*ADAMTS7*	—
17q21.32	*UBE2Z*	—
17p13.3	*SMG6*	—
17p11.2	*RAI1-PEMT-RASD1*	—
19p13.2	*LDLR/SMARCA4*	PAD[27]
19q13.32	*ApoE-ApoC1*	—
21q22.11	gene_desert/*KCNE2*	—

Note: Data from CARDIoGRAMplusC4D Consortium.[21] These should be considered the most stable risk loci for coronary artery disease/myocardial infarction.
AAA, abdominal aortic aneurysm; CES, cardioembolic stroke; ICA, intracranial aneurysm; IS, ischemic stroke; LAS, large-artery stroke; PAD, peripheral artery disease.

One of the most intriguing findings associated with CAD is a locus at chromosome 9p21. The first discovery of this locus dates back to 2007.[12] The same region on chromosome 9 was found subsequently also to be associated with diabetes,[29–31] glioma,[32,33] and open-angle glaucoma.[34,35] Throughout the years, this finding has been replicated in various related CVDs (as discussed later) as well as in other CAD studies.[13,14,17–19,36,37] This locus shows a strong association consistently with CAD and other CVD phenotypes, and also mediates the largest effect on CAD risk, normally being reported in the range of an elevated risk per allele (odds ratio) of 1.2 to 1.4. As is the case for all GWAS findings, the clarification of the impact of this risk locus on certain pathways leading to onset or progression of atherosclerosis is a daunting task.

To elicit the biological role of this locus further, biochemical and molecular biology evidence has been published on how this locus might affect CVD risk through interferon-γ signaling.[38] This work has shown that the 9p21 region encompasses a cluster of transcriptional enhancers, with the GWAS signals for CAD in this region being located in one of the enhancers. It has also shown that, in human vascular endothelial cells, the enhancer interval containing the CAD risk locus interacts physically with *CDKN2A/B* (the main transcript at the risk locus), the *MTAP* gene, and an interval downstream of interferon-α.[21] In addition, it is suggested that interferon-γ activation strongly affects the structure of the chromatin and the transcriptional regulation in the 9p21 locus, including STAT1 binding, long-range enhancer interactions, and altered expression of neighboring genes.

Furthermore, different variants of *ANRIL*, a long, noncoding RNA that is found at the 9p21 locus, can affect different sets of genes[39] independent of *CDKN2A/B*. Different variants of *ANRIL* affect downstream targets, most notably *CHD5, HBEGF, BCL2A1*, and *SERPINE1*. These genes are important in mechanisms related to apoptosis and proliferation—both pathways thought to be involved in atherosclerotic processes. *ANRIL* is also known to inhibit *CDKN2B* transcription epigenetically, painting a picture of an intricate genomic interplay between *CDKN2A/B, ANRIL*, and downstream targets affecting multiple mechanisms related to atherosclerosis and subsequent CAD.[40]

These data provide a first view of this genomic locus and the pathways that may act downstream of these variants. Because all these findings are novel, they need to be refined, and the true meaning and exact molecular genetic mechanism of this risk locus in CAD needs to be elicited even further before diagnostic or even therapeutic consequences can be drawn.

For stroke, the association of the 9p21 region could be replicated. Associations have been found with all ischemic stroke (IS),[41–43] as well as with LAS, specifically.[5] However, for IS some investigators have also reported no association with 9p21.[44] This is most likely a result of the fact that the 9p21 risk region is subtype specific to LAS. The normal prevalence of LAS cases in an IS cohort is around 20%[45] and, given the suggestive subtype-specific association, it does not come as a surprise that the association is not observed for all ISs when the subtype distribution is biased against LAS. There is, indeed, evidence that the 9p21 locus is specific to LAS; however, correlated effects over other stroke subtypes cannot be ruled out.[3] Hence, it seems possible that the 9p21 locus is a region associated with other stroke subtypes, but given current sample sizes, the clearest association is observed for LAS. Similarly, a CAD risk region at another locus on chromosome 9 (*ABO*) was also shown to be associated with IS and, interestingly, several stroke subtypes.[26] This is the first demonstration of genetic variants showing evidence of association with multiple subtypes of stroke (LAS and cardioembolic stroke [CES]). ABO is the main component that determines the blood type in humans and is also implicated in many other disease phenotypes[46–48] (Table 7.2[49–71]).

In the opposite direction—LAS risk variants in CAD—single nucleotide polymorphisms near *HDAC9* that were first found to be associated significantly with LAS in a subtype-specific manner[3,25] have also now been observed and replicated for CAD.[21] Together, these findings lead to a novel study investigating the shared genetic component of CAD and IS/LAS[72] using all available GWAS results from IS/LAS and CAD. Here, signals could be identified that are thought to be shared between the two phenotypes but have not been associated with stroke on a genomewide level, most likely as a result of the absence of power to detect these signals. Of note, variants in the *CYP17A1/CNNM2/NT5C2* region on chromosome 10, variants in the *RAI1-PEMT-RASD1* region on chromosome 17, and variants in a risk region for multiple related diseases on chromosome 12 were associated significantly with both CAD and IS, or both CAD and LAS, or all three phenotypes. It was made clear in the study that the genetic overlap between CAD and IS/LAS is, indeed, significant. It will be exciting to see in the near future if—given extended sample sizes—these proposed risk regions will be discovered for IS/LAS at the genomewide level.

In contrast to the discussed CAD risk loci, other risk regions found in CAD GWAS efforts are often identified, not for the CAD phenotype itself, but rather for risk factors for CAD. It can be concluded that these loci do not affect risk for CAD independently, but rather act as confounders through mechanisms affecting risk factors for CAD. Many GWAS loci identified in CVD show a high degree of pleiotropy, meaning the gene affected has influence on multiple diseases that are not necessarily related. As an example, one locus identified at chromosome 11q23 (*ZNF259*; Table 7.2) is also associated significantly with elevated low-density lipoprotein cholesterol levels. It is, therefore,

TABLE 7.2

Association of Coronary Artery Disease Loci with Cardiovascular Disease-Related Risk Factors

Chromosome	Gene	Association with other cardiovascular phenotypes
1p13.3	*SORT1*	LDL cholesterol[49–53]
1p32.3	*PCSK9*	LDL cholesterol[50,51,54]
2p24.1	*APOB*	Total cholesterol[51] and lipid metabolism[55]
2p21	*ABCG5-ABCG8*	Total cholesterol[51,56] and lipid metabolism[55]
4q32.1	*GUCY1A3*	Diastolic blood pressure[57]
6q25.3	*SLC22A3/LPAL2/LPA*	Lipoprotein(a) levels and LDL cholesterol[51,58,59]
8q24.13	*TRIB1*	Total cholesterol[51]
8p21.3	*LPL*	HDL cholesterol[51] and lipid metabolism[55]
9q34.2	ABO	Venous thromboembolism, ACE enzyme activity, plasma E–selectin level, and plasma vWF level, among others[13,51,60–65]
10q24.32	CYP17A1, CNNM2, NT5C2	Systolic blood pressure[66]
11q23.3	ZNF259/APO5A/APOA1	Triglycerides and HDL cholesterol[49,50,67]
12q24.12	chr12q24/SH2B3	Diastolic blood pressure, platelet count, and plasma eosinophil count, among others[66,68,69]
15q26.1	FURIN-FES	Diastolic blood pressure[57]
19p13.2	LDLR/SMARCA4	LDL cholesterol[50–53,56,70,71]
19q13.32	ApoE-ApoC1	Total cholesterol,[51] among others

ACE, angiotensin-converting enzyme; HDL, high-density lipoprotein; LDL, low-density lipoprotein; vWF, von Willebrand factor.

easy to speculate that the increased risk of developing CAD is mediated through this risk factor. Another example is a locus at chromosome 10q24 (*CYP17A1*; Table 7.2), which is associated significantly with hypertension, and thus the risk for CAD may be conferred via high blood pressure.

A summary of variants found in CAD associated with confounders (adapted from Voight et al.[73] and Schunkert et al.[13]) can be seen in Table 7.2. From here it becomes visible that a moderate percentage of loci are associated with either lipoprotein (cholesterol) levels or hypertension—two of the main risk factors for CAD. However, many loci found to be associated with CAD are not associated with a related disease, so these may act independently of risk factors or through mechanisms not yet fully understood. It will be paramount in the future to dissect the dependent from the independent loci to broaden our understanding of mechanisms contributing to CAD and, subsequently, to IS/LAS.

In a recent publication,[21] the first efforts have been conducted to unravel the pathways associated with CAD, incorporating all found genomewide signals. The top three pathways—atherosclerosis signaling, liver X receptor/retinoid X receptor (RXR) activation, and farnesoid X receptor/RXR activation—all harbor genes involved in lipid metabolism, including 10 CAD risk loci. Notably, three of the top four pathways also contain genes involved in inflammation. In addition to the atherosclerosis signaling and liver X receptor/RXR activation pathways, the acute phase response signaling pathway, which includes four CAD risk loci (*APOA1, MRAS*, interleukin 6 receptor [*IL-6R*], and *PLG*), is involved in inflammation and, more specifically, the rapid inflammatory response that is triggered, among other factors, by tissue injury.

Myocardial Infarction

MI has often been studied together with CAD because MI is the direct clinical end point of CAD. Therefore, GWASs aimed directly at MI are scarce,[36,54] and most loci are also reported for CAD alone or for a combined CAD/MI phenotype (as mentioned earlier).

Recently, there has been a large-scale effort to study whether variants associated specifically with MI are also relevant in IS.[74] The authors selected 11 loci previously associated with MI and tried to replicate these findings in an independent stroke cohort.

They found that, for IS, two loci (*PCSK9* at 1p32.3 and *SH2B3* at 12q24.12) show evidence of association, but statistical significance was found to be nominal. Furthermore, they also evaluated the association of MI genes in stroke subtypes and found that the previously identified CAD risk gene (Table 7.1), *MRAS*, is associated with CES, *MIA3* is associated with small-vessel stroke, and *SH2B3* is associated with strokes stemming from an unknown origin, although the associations are, again, at a nominal level only. Their study, although limited by a lack of power, still can serve as an interesting design for future efforts to discover shared disease mechanisms, similar to the study performed on IS/LAS and CAD.[72]

Peripheral Artery Disease

Peripheral artery disease (PAD) affects large arteries supplying the limbs or internal organs. A clinically usefully diagnostic criterion is the ankle–brachial pressure index, which is also used as an endophenotype in GWAS analyses. PAD has a prevalence of around 6%in the general population.[75] Because atherosclerosis is also a hallmark of PAD, risk factors are similar to CAD/MI and include smoking, diabetes, dyslipidemia, obesity, and hypertension.[76,77]

Murabito et al.[27] have recently shown that the 9p21 locus also plays a large role in PAD. In addition, they report that another suggestive CAD-related gene (*LDLR*; Table 7.1) shows borderline genomewide associations with PAD.

Other GWASs have shown that a variant in the neuronal acetylcholine receptor subunit $\alpha 3$, or *CHRNA3*, gene (a nicotinic acetylcholine receptor) is associated with PAD, but this association is most likely mediated by smoking behavior,[78] the main risk factor for PAD and not exclusive to PAD itself. The variant rs7025486 in the disabled homolog 2 interacting protein isoform (*DAB2IP*) gene also showed suggestive association with PAD[79] in a study for a whole array of CVDs. This region, however, shows a more significant association with abdominal aortic aneurysms (AAAs; discussed later).

A classic approach in genetics—complementary to GWAS—is the study of candidate genes, usually genes situated in pathways relevant to the disease phenotype. Zintzaras and Zdoukopoulos[80] show, in their extensive review of candidate gene studies in PAD, that variants in 22 potential PAD genes show a consistent effect over all studies (Table 7.3). They classified the genes in their study according to the biological pathway to which they belong. Pathways considered are the coagulation cascade (factor V Leiden, factor II Leiden), the folate–homocysteine pathway (methylenetetrahydrofolate reductase [MTHFR]), the renin–angiotensin system pathway (angiotensin-converting enzyme [ACE], angiotensinogen), the leukocyte transendothelial migration pathway (matrix metalloproteinase 9 [MMP9], intercellular adhesion molecule 1, and the cytokine–cytokine receptor interaction pathway (IL-6), all of which have been implicated for CVD in general.

Because the threshold for statistical significance is lower for candidate gene studies and, usually, the sample size in candidate gene studies is significantly smaller, these findings need to be confirmed independently using a case–control setup and more markers being tested. However, they still can serve as a good starting point for future studies. MMP9 is of special interest for stroke genetics

TABLE 7.3

Genes Identified for Peripheral Artery Disease Using a Candidate Gene Approach

Gene symbol	Full name	Pathway
F5	Coagulation factor V	Coagulation cascade
F2	Prothrombin	Coagulation cascade
MTHFR	Methylenetetrahydrofolate reductase	Folate pathway
ITGB3	Integrin, β3	Extracellular matrix receptor interaction pathway
ACE	Angiotensin-converting enzyme	Renin–angiotensin system pathway
AGT	Angiotensinogen	Renin–angiotensin system pathway
IL-6	Interleukin 6	Cytokine–cytokine receptor interaction pathway
ICAM1	Intercellular adhesion molecule 1	Leukocyte transendothelial migration pathway
MMP9	Matrix metalloproteinase 9	Leukocyte transendothelial migration pathway
CHRNA3	Neuronal acetylcholine receptor subunit α3	Other

because it is a prognostic marker for poor outcome after stroke,[81] probably through activation of neutrophils in the ischemic brain.[82]

In a different approach using previously discovered regions implicated in telomere length, Raschenberger et al.[83] showed in patients with PAD that their mean telomere length is significantly shorter than in their healthy counterparts. This phenomenon has been already reported for CAD[84] and other CVDs, but no evidence exists to date that this is also true for IS.

Another interesting finding that was communicated by Khandanpour et al.[85] is that elevated homocysteine levels mediated by a variant in the *MTHFR* gene are associated with PAD. As stated earlier, the role of homocysteine levels in stroke and other CVDs is disputed, and the effects might also be restricted to low-folate populations.[86] This is, indeed, a very active area of research and will, hopefully, lead to a complete picture on how folate levels affect stroke risk.

Apart from the 9p21 locus, no gene associated with PAD has been associated with stroke, as is stated specifically for *DAB2IP*[79] and *CHRNA3*.[87]

Intracranial Aneurysm

Intracranial aneurysms (ICAs) occur in up to 6% of the general population, in which subarachnoid hemorrhage after aneurysm rupture is a potentially fatal event. ICAs can occur in every brain artery, but are most common in the anterior cerebral artery and the anterior communicating artery. IS (and here, specifically, LAS), CAD/MI, and PAD on the one side and ICA on the other side are thought to have distinct etiologies, with atherosclerosis being considered a risk factor for the former group, but not for the latter (ICA).[88–90] Therefore, risk loci are not thought to overlap between those two categories. Nevertheless, it is also important to mention that risk factors for ICA overlap with those of stroke and other atherosclerotic diseases—namely, smoking[91] and hypertension[92]—possibly leading to a weakening of the vessel walls and potentially promoting aneurysm rupture in ICA. In summary, risk loci identified for both ICA and IS might affect a broader phenotype of arterial disease and not necessarily via atherosclerotic mechanisms.

This is signified by the 9p21 locus, which also has been identified as a risk region for ICA.[93,94] Furthermore, the *SOX17* cluster on chromosome 8 has also been replicated stably and can be associated with ICA.[28,93] *SOX17* encodes for a member of the Sry-related HMG box transcription factor family and has been implicated in vascular biology and angiogenesis.[95,96] It is of special interest because it ensures endothelial integrity. Suggestive evidence in an Asian population was also found at a region on chromosome 2, namely for a locus encompassing the *BOLL* and *PLCL1* genes.[93] In this work, the authors state that the *PLCL1* gene is of interest because it has significant homology to phospholipase C, which lies downstream of VEGFR2 signaling, suggesting a role in endothelial mechanisms because VEGFR2 plays an essential role in the regulation of angiogenesis, vascular development, vascular permeability, and embryonic hematopoiesis.

In a purely Japanese population, the *EDNRA* gene has been identified as a risk gene for ICA.[97] *EDNRA* is a known and potent mediator of vasoconstriction,[98] and the same locus has also been associated with plaque size in an analysis of carotid intima media thickness and atherosclerotic plaques.[99] In addition, it was also found to be a major risk locus for CAD (Table 7.1).

Yasuno et al[28] identified three novel risk loci for a mixed European and Japanese population, with variants near *RBBP8, STARD13/klotho* (a locus associated with renal failure and arterial stiffening), and *CNNM2* (a CAD risk locus; Table 7.1) being associated with the phenotype. They state that these candidates are implicated in cell cycle progression, potentially affecting the proliferation and senescence of progenitor cell populations that are responsible for vascular formation and repair.

In a recent publication, a variant in the *PRDM6* gene was found to be associated with ICA, but this association is mediated through hypertension and, more specifically, through elevated systolic blood pressure.[100] This comes as no surprise, because PRDM6, a histone methyltransferase that acts as a transcriptional repressor of smooth muscle gene expression, could potentially predispose to elevated systolic blood pressure by an altered vascular wall structure.

The latest and biggest meta-analysis of ICA,[24] using 32,000 patients and 84,000 control subjects, confirmed the assumption that chromosome 9p21, the *SOX17* cluster, and *EDNRA* are the most reliable risk regions for ICA. Interestingly, two of the three major loci are also known to be risk regions for CAD. Other loci could not be replicated. Using a complementary approach, van't Hof et al.[101] showed that a genetic risk profile composed of risk variants for hypertension is associated with ICA, but other, related risk profiles for lipids and CAD are not.

Abdominal Aortic Aneurysm

AAAs are dilations in the abdominal aorta. Ninety percent of these aneurysms occur infrarenally and may spread to the pelvic arteries. Similar to ICAs, they are potentially lethal when aneurysm rupture occurs. Regarding etiology, AAA is thought to occur more frequently in patients with atherosclerosis. It is still debatable whether this association is causal or the result of common risk factors, with most studies suggesting that AAA formation is independent of atherosclerosis.[102,103] The other main risk factors for AAA include advanced age, male gender, smoking, and family history.[104]

As stated earlier, the *DAB2IP* gene[79] and the 9p21 locus[94] have both been associated with AAA, suggesting partly overlapping disease-causing mechanisms related to atherosclerosis. The association of *DAB2IP* with AAA was the most convincing compared with other CVD phenotypes, and therefore should be considered the main risk locus for AAA. DAB2IP is a suppressor for the PI3K-Akt and RAS pathways, and an enhancer of apoptosis. The Akt pathway is known to act in vascular homeostasis and angiogenesis.[105] Furthermore, DAB2IP is also thought to affect VEGFR2-mediated signaling (as mentioned earlier).[106]

In a recent study,[107] an association of variants within the *LRP1* gene with AAA was found. Because LRP1 is a binding partner of apolipoprotein E, a gene implicated primarily in lipid metabolism and a risk candidate for a plethora of CVDs, it would be an ideal candidate also to mediate stroke risk. Apolipoprotein E has proved to be a risk gene for hemorrhagic stroke,[108] but the evidence for IS is still unreliable.[109] Another known CAD risk gene (*SORT1*) was also found to be an independent genetic risk factor for AAA.[23]

A region at chromosome 3p12 near *CNTN3*[110] was identified as an additional risk variant for AAA. This contactin 3-gene product is responsible for cell surface interactions during nervous system development. This finding might also be an indicator of a confounder for smoking behavior, as the authors state in their publication.[110]

In a recent publication, Harrison et al.[22] found that variants in *IL-6R* associate significantly with AAA. One specific variant is responsible for an amino acid shift (Asp358Ala) in IL-6R, leading to a lower risk of AAA. Variants in *IL-6R* have also been reported as increasing risk for CAD (Table 7.1).

Thompson et al.[111] hypothesize in a candidate gene study that gene products in the transforming growth factor β pathway might play a role in AAA, and this was further replicated independently.[112] Transforming growth factor β research has a long-standing tradition in stroke genetics because it has been proved to play a role in angiogenesis after stroke[113] and to act as a neuroprotective agent.[114] Interestingly, associations with *MMP9, ACE,* and *MTHFR* have been show by Thompson et al.[111] also to be associated with AAA through meta-analysis of candidate gene studies. Because these are also thought to be associated with PAD (as discussed earlier), this points toward a broader arterial mechanism involved.

In the same mold, Jones et al.[115] have performed a candidate gene study and found a nonsynonymous single nucleotide polymorphism in the angiotensin II receptor type 1, or *AGTR1*, gene, which belongs to the angiotensin–renin system similar to *ACE* and angiotensinogen in PAD. This is of interest because the angiotensin system, and especially angiotensin II, is the major causative factor of cerebrovascular effects of hypertension.[116] The renin–angiotensin system is thought to have some influence on stroke, but not solely via hypertension; the exact mechanisms are not known thus far. Renin–angiotensin inhibitors have shown some previous success in stroke treatment.[117]

Interestingly, genetic risk profiles of lipid factors and CAD show an association with AAA, but not with ICA—the reverse of what is shown for genetic risk profiles of hypertension.[101] This could lead to the conclusion that genetic variants in these pathways all contribute with small effects toward the risk phenotype.

Conclusion

The chromosome 9p21 locus represents a major risk locus associated with a range of CVDs. Efforts are already being made to elicit further the role of this locus in a broader vascular disease model with regard to the actual biochemical and biological processes involved. There are multiple other candidate loci, many of them plausible biologically, that should be examined further in the future, regardless of whether they also serve as regions implicated in stroke. Most notable, the overlap between CAD and LAS risk variants is encouraging and might lead to the discovery of shared genetic risk regions in the future. Similarly, other related CVDs also show genetic overlap with CAD to some extent (Table 7.1), leading to the hypothesis that these genetic risk factor act on a broader vascular phenotype implicated in several disease etiologies.

One reason why some of these risk regions are, to date, not found as risk regions in stroke could be that stroke, as a complex CVD, is a much more heterogeneous phenotype. Most risk regions identified for stroke (9p21, 6p21 and 7p21 for LAS, and 4q25 and 16q22 for CES) have been identified for subphenotypes only, making it more likely that different stroke subphenotypes have distinct, nonoverlapping genetic risk profiles. One risk region for stroke (*ABO*) is currently the only one identified for multiple subtypes of stroke.[26] These distinct etiologies may share greater similarities with related CVD phenotypes, as is the case, for example, with LAS and CAD. As an additional point, this division into stroke subphenotypes decreases drastically the number of patients studied. With a more homogenous phenotype like CAD, patient numbers of 100,000 are reached in the largest studies, such as CARDIoGRAMplusC4D.[21] These numbers have not been reached yet in the stroke field, with the METASTROKE[25] study being the biggest so far, with 12,000 stroke patients. When studying subphenotypes, this number gets continuously lower, and therefore the discovery of novel risk regions is hampered. Thus, the numbers of cases in each subphenotype needs to be increased dramatically in the future.

Another reason might be the existence of rare variants in the regions identified for related CVD phenotypes. It is still disputed whether the majority of genetic heritability is captured via common variants (frequency, >1%–3% in the general population) or low-frequency/rare variants (frequency, <1%–3%). It could be that rare variants in similar genes/pathways like the ones identified for related diseases play a role in stroke. Therefore, new methods such as targeted deep sequencing, exome sequencing, or even whole-genome sequencing are needed to test these hypotheses further and to identify more risk variants for stroke.

Using these approaches, several risk loci found for related diseases, and especially CAD, might prove to be bona-fide risk regions for IS or its subtypes.

REFERENCES

1. Pasternak RC, Criqui MH, Benjamin EJ, et al. Atherosclerotic vascular disease conference: Writing group I: epidemiology. *Circulation*. 2004;109:2605–2612.
2. Adams RJ, Chimowitz MI, Alpert JS, et al. Coronary risk evaluation in patients with transient ischemic attack and ischemic stroke: a scientific statement for healthcare professionals from the Stroke Council and the Council on Clinical Cardiology of the American Heart Association/American Stroke Association. *Circulation*. 2003;108:1278–1290.
3. Bellenguez C, Bevan S, Gschwendtner A, et al. Genome-wide association study identifies a variant in HDAC9 associated with large vessel ischemic stroke. *Nat Genet*. 2012;44:328–333.
4. Holliday EG, Maguire JM, Evans TJ, et al. Common variants at 6p21.1 are associated with large artery atherosclerotic stroke. *Nat Genet*. 2012;44:1147–1151.
5. Gschwendtner A, Bevan S, Cole JW, et al. Sequence variants on chromosome 9p21.3 confer risk for atherosclerotic stroke. *Ann Neurol*. 2009;65:531–539.
6. Gudbjartsson DF, Holm H, Gretarsdottir S, et al. A sequence variant in ZFHX3 on 16q22 associates with atrial fibrillation and ischemic stroke. *Nat Genet*. 2009;41:876–878.
7. Gretarsdottir S, Thorleifsson G, Manolescu A, et al. Risk variants for atrial fibrillation on chromosome 4q25 associate with ischemic stroke. *Ann Neurol*. 2008;64:402–409.
8. Wilson PW, D'Agostino RB, Levy D, Belanger AM, Silbershatz H, Kannel WB. Prediction of coronary heart disease using risk factor categories. *Circulation*. 1998;97:1837–1847.
9. Berry JD, Dyer A, Cai X, et al. Lifetime risks of cardiovascular disease. *N Engl J Med*. 2012;366:321–329.
10. Erdmann J, Grosshennig A, Braund PS, et al. New susceptibility locus for coronary artery disease on chromosome 3q22.3. *Nat Genet*. 2009;41:280–282.
11. Erdmann J, Willenborg C, Nahrstaedt J, et al. Genome-wide association study identifies a new locus for coronary artery disease on chromosome 10p11.23. *Eur Heart J*. 2011;32:158–168.
12. McPherson R, Pertsemlidis A, Kavaslar N, et al. A common allele on chromosome 9 associated with coronary heart disease. *Science*. 2007;316:1488–1491.
13. Schunkert H, Konig IR, Kathiresan S, et al. Large-scale association analysis identifies 13 new susceptibility loci for coronary artery disease. *Nat Genet*. 2011;43:333–338.

14. Samani NJ, Erdmann J, Hall AS, et al. Genomewide association analysis of coronary artery disease. *N Engl J Med.* 2007;357:443–453.
15. Banerjee A, Silver LE, Heneghan C, et al. Relative familial clustering of cerebral versus coronary ischemic events. *Circulation.* 2011;4:390–396.
16. Davies RW, Wells GA, Stewart AF, et al. A genome-wide association study for coronary artery disease identifies a novel susceptibility locus in the major histocompatibility complex. *Circulation.* 2012;5:217–225.
17. Wild PS, Zeller T, Schillert A, et al. A genome-wide association study identifies lipa as a susceptibility gene for coronary artery disease. *Circulation.* 2011;4:403–412.
18. Coronary Artery Disease (C4D) Genetics Consortium. A genome-wide association study in Europeans and South Asians identifies five new loci for coronary artery disease. *Nat Genet.* 2011;43:339–344.
19. Gongora-Rivera F, Labreuche J, Jaramillo A, Steg PG, Hauw JJ, Amarenco P. Autopsy prevalence of coronary atherosclerosis in patients with fatal stroke. *Stroke.* 2007;38:1203–1210.
20. O'Donnell CJ, Kavousi M, Smith AV, et al. Genome-wide association study for coronary artery calcification with follow-up in myocardial infarction. *Circulation.* 2011;124:2855–2864.
21. CARDIoGRAMplusC4D Consortium, Deloukas P, Kanoni S, et al. Large-scale association analysis identifies new risk loci for coronary artery disease. *Nat Genet.* 2013;45:25–33.
22. Harrison SC, Smith AJ, Jones GT, et al. Interleukin-6 receptor pathways in abdominal aortic aneurysm. *Eur Heart J.* 2013;34:3707–3716.
23. Jones GT, Bown MJ, Gretarsdottir S, et al. A sequence variant associated with sortilin-1 (SORT1) on 1p13.3 is independently associated with abdominal aortic aneurysm. *Hum Mol Genet.* 2013;22:2941–2947.
24. Alg VS, Sofat R, Houlden H, Werring DJ. Genetic risk factors for intracranial aneurysms: a meta-analysis in more than 116,000 individuals. *Neurology.* 2013;80:2154–2165.
25. Traylor M, Farrall M, Holliday EG, et al. Genetic risk factors for ischaemic stroke and its subtypes (the METASTROKE collaboration): a meta-analysis of genome-wide association studies. *Lancet Neurol.* 2012;11:951–962.
26. Williams FM, Carter AM, Hysi PG, et al. Ischemic stroke is associated with the ABO locus: the Euroclot study. *Ann Neurol.* 2013;73:16–31.
27. Murabito JM, White CC, Kavousi M, et al. Association between chromosome 9p21 variants and the ankle-brachial index identified by a meta-analysis of 21 genome-wide association studies. *Circ Cardiovasc Genet.* 2012;5:100–112.
28. Yasuno K, Bilguvar K, Bijlenga P, et al. Genome-wide association study of intracranial aneurysm identifies three new risk loci. *Nat Genet.* 2010;42:420–425.
29. Scott LJ, Mohlke KL, Bonnycastle LL, et al. A genome-wide association study of type 2 diabetes in Finns detects multiple susceptibility variants. *Science.* 2007;316:1341–1345.
30. Saxena R, Voight BF, Lyssenko Vet al. Genome-wide association analysis identifies loci for type 2 diabetes and triglyceride levels. *Science.* 2007;316:1331–1336.
31. Zeggini E, Scott LJ, Saxena R, et al. Meta-analysis of genome-wide association data and large-scale replication identifies additional susceptibility loci for type 2 diabetes. *Nat Genet.* 2008;40:638–645.
32. Shete S, Hosking FJ, Robertson LB, et al. Genome-wide association study identifies five susceptibility loci for glioma. *Nat Genet.* 2009;41:899–904.
33. Wrensch M, Jenkins RB, Chang JS, et al. Variants in the CDKN2B and RTEL1 regions are associated with high-grade glioma susceptibility. *Nat Genet.* 2009;41:905–908.
34. Nakano M, Ikeda Y, Tokuda Y, et al. Common variants in CDKN2B-AS1 associated with optic-nerve vulnerability of glaucoma identified by genome-wide association studies in Japanese. *PloS One.* 2012;7:e33389.

35. Osman W, Low SK, Takahashi A, Kubo M, Nakamura Y. A genome-wide association study in the Japanese population confirms 9p21 and 14q23 as susceptibility loci for primary open angle glaucoma. *Hum Mol Genet.* 2012;21:2836–2842.
36. Helgadottir A, Thorleifsson G, Manolescu A, et al. A common variant on chromosome 9p21 affects the risk of myocardial infarction. *Science.* 2007;316:1491–1493.
37. Slavin TP, Feng T, Schnell A, Zhu X, Elston RC. Two-marker association tests yield new disease associations for coronary artery disease and hypertension. *Hum Genet.* 2011;130:725–733.
38. Harismendy O, Notani D, Song X, et al. 9p21 DNA variants associated with coronary artery disease impair interferon-gamma signalling response. *Nature.* 2011;470:264–268.
39. Congrains A, Kamide K, Katsuya T, et al. CVD-associated non-coding RNA, anril, modulates expression of atherogenic pathways in VSMC. *Biochem Biophys Res Commun.* 2012;419:612–616.
40. Yap KL, Li S, Munoz-Cabello AM, et al. Molecular interplay of the noncoding RNA anril and methylated histone H3 lysine 27 by polycomb CBX7 in transcriptional silencing of INK4A. *Mol Cell.* 2010;38:662–674.
41. Smith JG, Melander O, Lovkvist H, et al. Common genetic variants on chromosome 9p21 confers risk of ischemic stroke: a large-scale genetic association study. *Circulation.* 2009;2:159–164.
42. Anderson CD, Biffi A, Rost NS, Cortellini L, Furie KL, Rosand J. Chromosome 9p21 in ischemic stroke: population structure and meta-analysis. *Stroke.* 2010;41:1123–1131.
43. Matarin M, Brown WM, Singleton A, Hardy JA, Meschia JF. Whole genome analyses suggest ischemic stroke and heart disease share an association with polymorphisms on chromosome 9p21. *Stroke.* 2008;39:1586–1589.
44. Lemmens R, Abboud S, Robberecht W, et al. Variant on 9p21 strongly associates with coronary heart disease, but lacks association with common stroke. *Eur J Hum Genet.* 2009;17:1287–1293.
45. Seshadri S, Wolf PA. Lifetime risk of stroke and dementia: current concepts, and estimates from the Framingham study. *Lancet Neurol.* 2007;6:1106–1114.
46. Tang W, Teichert M, Chasman DI, et al. A genome-wide association study for venous thromboembolism: the extended Cohorts for Heart and Aging Research in Genomic Epidemiology (CHARGE) Consortium. *Genet Epidemiol.* 2013;37:512–521.
47. van der Harst P, Zhang W, Mateo Leach I, et al. Seventy-five genetic loci influencing the human red blood cell. *Nature.* 2012;492:369–375.
48. Tang W, Schwienbacher C, Lopez LM, et al. Genetic associations for activated partial thromboplastin time and prothrombin time, their gene expression profiles, and risk of coronary artery disease. *Am J Hum Genet.* 2012;91:152–162.
49. Grallert H, Dupuis J, Bis JC, et al. Eight genetic loci associated with variation in lipoprotein-associated phospholipase A2 mass and activity and coronary heart disease: meta-analysis of genome-wide association studies from five community-based studies. *Eur Heart J.* 2012;33:238–251.
50. Waterworth DM, Ricketts SL, Song K, et al. Genetic variants influencing circulating lipid levels and risk of coronary artery disease. *Arterioscler Thromb Vasc Biol.* 2010;30:2264–2276.
51. Teslovich TM, Musunuru K, Smith AV, et al. Biological, clinical and population relevance of 95 loci for blood lipids. *Nature.* 2010;466:707–713.
52. Kathiresan S, Melander O, Guiducci C, et al. Six new loci associated with blood low-density lipoprotein cholesterol, high-density lipoprotein cholesterol or triglycerides in humans. *Nat Genet.* 2008;40:189–197.
53. Sabatti C, Service SK, Hartikainen AL, et al. Genome-wide association analysis of metabolic traits in a birth cohort from a founder population. *Nat Genet.* 2009;41:35–46.
54. Kathiresan S, Voight BF, Purcell S, et al. Genome-wide association of early-onset myocardial infarction with single nucleotide polymorphisms and copy number variants. *Nat Genet.* 2009;41:334–341.

55. Chasman DI, Pare G, Mora S, et al. Forty-three loci associated with plasma lipoprotein size, concentration, and cholesterol content in genome-wide analysis. *PLoS Genet.* 2009;5:e1000730.
56. Aulchenko YS, Ripatti S, Lindqvist I, et al. Loci influencing lipid levels and coronary heart disease risk in 16 European population cohorts. *Nat Genet.* 2009;41:47–55.
57. Ehret GB, Munroe PB, Rice KM, et al. Genetic variants in novel pathways influence blood pressure and cardiovascular disease risk. *Nature.* 2011;478:103–109.
59. Clarke R, Peden JF, Hopewell JC, et al. Genetic variants associated with lp(a) lipoprotein level and coronary disease. *N Engl J Med.* 2009;361:2518–2528.
59. Ober C, Nord AS, Thompson EE, et al. Genome-wide association study of plasma lipoprotein(a) levels identifies multiple genes on chromosome 6q. *J Lipid Res.* 2009;50:798–806.
60. Reilly MP, Li M, He J, et al. Identification of ADAMTS7 as a novel locus for coronary atherosclerosis and association of ABO with myocardial infarction in the presence of coronary atherosclerosis: two genome-wide association studies. *Lancet.* 2011;377:383–392.
61. Germain M, Saut N, Greliche N, et al. Genetics of venous thrombosis: insights from a new genome wide association study. *PloS One.* 2011;6:e25581.
62. Chung CM, Wang RY, Chen JW, et al. A genome-wide association study identifies new loci for ace activity: potential implications for response to ace inhibitor. *Pharmacogenom J.* 2010;10:537–544.
63. Paterson AD, Lopes-Virella MF, Waggott D, et al. Genome-wide association identifies the ABO blood group as a major locus associated with serum levels of soluble E-selectin. *Arterioscler Thromb Vasc Biol.* 2009;29:1958–1967.
64. Amundadottir L, Kraft P, Stolzenberg-Solomon RZ, et al. Genome-wide association study identifies variants in the ABO locus associated with susceptibility to pancreatic cancer. *Nat Genet.* 2009;41:986–990.
65. Chambers JC, Zhang W, Sehmi J, et al. Genome-wide association study identifies loci influencing concentrations of liver enzymes in plasma. *Nat Genet.* 2011;43:1131–1138.
66. Newton-Cheh C, Johnson T, Gateva V, et al. Genome-wide association study identifies eight loci associated with blood pressure. *Nat Genet.* 2009;41:666–676.
67. Kim YJ, Go MJ, Hu C, et al. Large-scale genome-wide association studies in East Asians identify new genetic loci influencing metabolic traits. *Nat Genet.* 2011;43:990–995.
68. Ehret GB, Munroe PB, Rice KM, et al. Genetic variants in novel pathways influence blood pressure and cardiovascular disease risk. *Nature.* 2011;478:103–109.
69. Gudbjartsson DF, Bjornsdottir US, Halapi E, et al. Sequence variants affecting eosinophil numbers associate with asthma and myocardial infarction. *Nat Genet.* 2009;41:342–347.
70. Kathiresan S, Willer CJ, Peloso GM, et al. Common variants at 30 loci contribute to polygenic dyslipidemia. *Nat Genet.* 2009;41:56–65.
71. Willer CJ, Sanna S, Jackson AU, et al. Newly identified loci that influence lipid concentrations and risk of coronary artery disease. *Nat Genet.* 2008;40:161–169.
72. Dichgans M, Malik R, König IR, et al. Shared genetic susceptibility to ischemic stroke and coronary artery disease: a genome-wide analysis of common variants. Stroke. 2014;45:24–36.
73. Voight BF, Kang HM, Ding J, et al. The metabochip, a custom genotyping array for genetic studies of metabolic, cardiovascular, and anthropometric traits. *PLoS Genet.* 2012;8:e1002793.
74. Cheng YC, Anderson CD, Bione S, et al. Are myocardial infarction-associated single-nucleotide polymorphisms associated with ischemic stroke? *Stroke.* 2012;43:980–986.
75. Pande RL, Perlstein TS, Beckman JA, Creager MA. Secondary prevention and mortality in peripheral artery disease: National Health and Nutrition Examination Study, 1999 to 2004. *Circulation.* 2011;124:17–23.
76. Shammas NW. Epidemiology, classification, and modifiable risk factors of peripheral arterial disease. *Vasc Health and Risk Manage.* 2007;3:229–234.

77. Ouriel K. Peripheral arterial disease. *Lancet*. 2001;358:1257–1264.
78. Thorgeirsson TE, Geller F, Sulem P, et al. A variant associated with nicotine dependence, lung cancer and peripheral arterial disease. *Nature*. 2008;452:638–642.
79. Gretarsdottir S, Baas AF, Thorleifsson G, et al. Genome-wide association study identifies a sequence variant within the DAB2IP gene conferring susceptibility to abdominal aortic aneurysm. *Nat Genet*. 2010;42:692–697.
80. Zintzaras E, Zdoukopoulos N. A field synopsis and meta-analysis of genetic association studies in peripheral arterial disease: the CUMAGAS-PAD database. *Am J Epidemiol*. 2009;170:1–11.
81. Graham CA, Chan RW, Chan DY, Chan CP, Wong LK, Rainer TH. Matrix metalloproteinase 9 mRNA: an early prognostic marker for patients with acute stroke. *Clin Biochem*. 2012;45:352–355.
82. Gidday JM, Gasche YG, Copin JC, et al. Leukocyte-derived matrix metalloproteinase-9 mediates blood–brain barrier breakdown and is proinflammatory after transient focal cerebral ischemia. *Am J Physiol*. 2005;289:H558–H568.
83. Raschenberger J, Kollerits B, Hammerer-Lercher A, et al. The association of relative telomere length with symptomatic peripheral arterial disease: results from the CAVASIC study. *Atherosclerosis*. 2013;229:469–474.
84. Samani NJ, van der Harst P. Biological ageing and cardiovascular disease. *Heart*. 2008;94:537–539.
85. Khandanpour N, Willis G, Meyer FJ, et al. Peripheral arterial disease and methylenetetrahydrofolate reductase (*MTHFR*) c677t mutations: a case–control study and meta-analysis. *J Vasc Surg*. 2009;49:711–718.
86. Holmes MV, Newcombe P, Hubacek JA, et al. Effect modification by population dietary folate on the association between *MTHFR* genotype, homocysteine, and stroke risk: a meta-analysis of genetic studies and randomised trials. *Lancet*. 2011;378:584–594.
87. Kaur-Knudsen D, Bojesen SE, Tybjaerg-Hansen A, Nordestgaard BG. Nicotinic acetylcholine receptor polymorphism, smoking behavior, and tobacco-related cancer and lung and cardiovascular diseases: a cohort study. *J Clin Oncol*. 2011;29:2875–2882.
88. Clarke M. Systematic review of reviews of risk factors for intracranial aneurysms. *Neuroradiology*. 2008;50:653–664.
89. Feigin VL, Rinkel GJ, Lawes CM, et al. Risk factors for subarachnoid hemorrhage: an updated systematic review of epidemiological studies. *Stroke*. 2005;36:2773–2780.
90. Vlak MH, Algra A, Brandenburg R, Rinkel GJ. Prevalence of unruptured intracranial aneurysms, with emphasis on sex, age, comorbidity, country, and time period: a systematic review and meta-analysis. *Lancet Neurol*. 2011;10:626–636.
91. Juvela S. Natural history of unruptured intracranial aneurysms: risks for aneurysm formation, growth, and rupture. *Acta Neurochir Suppl*. 2002;82:27–30.
92. Inci S, Spetzler RF. Intracranial aneurysms and arterial hypertension: a review and hypothesis. *Surg Neurol*. 2000;53:530–540; discussion, 540–532.
93. Bilguvar K, Yasuno K, Niemela M, et al. Susceptibility loci for intracranial aneurysm in European and Japanese populations. *Nat Genet*. 2008;40:1472–1477.
94. Helgadottir A, Thorleifsson G, Magnusson KP, et al. The same sequence variant on 9p21 associates with myocardial infarction, abdominal aortic aneurysm and intracranial aneurysm. *Nat Genet*. 2008;40:217–224.
95. Matsui T, Kanai-Azuma M, Hara K, et al. Redundant roles of SOX17 and SOX18 in postnatal angiogenesis in mice. *J Cell Sci*. 2006;119:3513–3526.
96. Sakamoto Y, Hara K, Kanai-Azuma M, et al. Redundant roles of SOX17 and SOX18 in early cardiovascular development of mouse embryos. *Biochem Biophys Res Commun*. 2007;360:539–544.
97. Low SK, Takahashi A, Cha PC, et al. Genome-wide association study for intracranial aneurysm in the Japanese population identifies three candidate susceptible loci and a functional genetic variant at *EDNRA*. *Hum Mol Genet*. 2012;21:2102–2110.

98. Zhang Y, Oliver JR, Horowitz JD. Endothelin B receptor-mediated vasoconstriction induced by endothelin a receptor antagonist. *Cardiovasc Res.* 1998;39:665–673.
99. Bis JC, Kavousi M, Franceschini N, et al. Meta-analysis of genome-wide association studies from the CHARGE Consortium identifies common variants associated with carotid intima media thickness and plaque. *Nat Genet.* 2011;43:940–947.
100. Gaal EI, Salo P, Kristiansson K, et al. Intracranial aneurysm risk locus 5q23.2 is associated with elevated systolic blood pressure. *PLoS Genet.* 2012;8:e1002563.
101. van't Hof FN, Ruigrok YM, Baas AF, et al. Impact of inherited genetic variants associated with lipid profile, hypertension, and coronary artery disease on the risk of intracranial and abdominal aortic aneurysms. *Circulation.* 2013;6:264–270.
102. Golledge J, Norman PE. Atherosclerosis and abdominal aortic aneurysm: cause, response, or common risk factors? *Arterioscler Thromb Vasc Biol.* 2010;30:1075–1077.
103. Johnsen SH, Forsdahl SH, Singh K, Jacobsen BK. Atherosclerosis in abdominal aortic aneurysms: a causal event or a process running in parallel? The Tromso study. *Arterioscler Thromb Vasc Biol.* 2010;30:1263–1268.
104. Crawford CM, Hurtgen-Grace K, Talarico E, Marley J. Abdominal aortic aneurysm: an illustrated narrative review. *J Manipulative Physiol Ther.* 2003;26:184–195.
105. Shiojima I, Walsh K. Role of Akt signaling in vascular homeostasis and angiogenesis. *Circulation Res.* 2002;90:1243–1250.
106. Zhang H, He Y, Dai S, et al. AIP1 functions as an endogenous inhibitor of VEGFR2-mediated signaling and inflammatory angiogenesis in mice. *J Clin Invest.* 2008;118:3904–3916.
107. Bown MJ, Jones GT, Harrison SC, et al. Abdominal aortic aneurysm is associated with a variant in low-density lipoprotein receptor-related protein 1. *Am J Hum Genet.* 2011;89:619–627.
108. Biffi A, Anderson CD, Jagiella JM, et al. APOE genotype and extent of bleeding and outcome in lobar intracerebral haemorrhage: a genetic association study. *Lancet Neurol.* 2011;10:702–709.
109. Sudlow C, Martinez Gonzalez NA, Kim J, Clark C. Does apolipoprotein E genotype influence the risk of ischemic stroke, intracerebral hemorrhage, or subarachnoid hemorrhage? Systematic review and meta-analyses of 31 studies among 5961 cases and 17,965 control subjects. *Stroke.* 2006;37:364–370.
110. Elmore JR, Obmann MA, Kuivaniemi H, et al. Identification of a genetic variant associated with abdominal aortic aneurysms on chromosome 3p12.3 by genome wide association. *J Vasc Surg.* 2009;49:1525–1531.
111. Thompson AR, Cooper JA, Jones GT, et al. Assessment of the association between genetic polymorphisms in transforming growth factor beta, and its binding protein (LTBP), and the presence, and expansion, of abdominal aortic aneurysm. *Atherosclerosis.* 2010;209:367–373.
112. Biros E, Norman PE, Jones GT, et al. Meta-analysis of the association between single nucleotide polymorphisms in TGF-beta receptor genes and abdominal aortic aneurysm. *Atherosclerosis.* 2011;219:218–223.
113. Krupinski J, Kumar P, Kumar S, Kaluza J. Increased expression of TGF-beta 1 in brain tissue after ischemic stroke in humans. *Stroke.* 1996;27:852–857.
114. Dhandapani KM, Brann DW. Transforming growth factor-beta: a neuroprotective factor in cerebral ischemia. *Cell Biochem Biophys.* 2003;39:13–22.
115. Jones GT, Thompson AR, van Bockxmeer FM, et al. Angiotensin II type 1 receptor 1166c polymorphism is associated with abdominal aortic aneurysm in three independent cohorts. *Arterioscler Thromb Vasc Biol.* 2008;28:764–770.
116. Iadecola C, Gorelick PB. Hypertension, angiotensin, and stroke: beyond blood pressure. *Stroke.* 2004;35:348–350.
117. Marcheselli S, Micieli G. Renin–angiotensin system and stroke. *Neurol Sci.* 2008;29(Suppl):S277–S278.

8

GENES ASSOCIATED WITH RARE SUBTYPES OF STROKE

Cervical Artery Dissection

Stéphanie Debette

Introduction

Cervical artery dissection (CeAD) is one of the most common causes of ischemic stroke (IS) in young and middle-age adults,[1] occurring at a mean age of 44 years.[2,3] Although the disease can occur in children as well, it is very rare beyond age 65. Carotid dissections are more common than vertebral dissections, with a ratio of approximately 1.7:1 in populations of European origin.[3] A predominance of vertebral dissection has been described in Asian cohorts.[4,5] A slight male predominance was reported in European cohorts (53%–57%).[6] Men more often have carotid dissection and are, on average, 5 years older when CeAD occurs.[6–8]

In the general population, the incidence of CeAD is relatively low—estimated between 2.6/100,00 per year and 3/100,000 per year,[3,9] which makes it a major challenge to study large samples of patients with this disorder. Pathologically, CeAD is associated with a hematoma in the wall of a cervical artery (carotid or vertebral), secondary either to an intimal tear or to direct bleeding within the arterial wall from ruptured vasa vasorum. The most severe complication of CeAD is intraluminal thrombus formation, leading to cerebral—or more seldom retinal—ischemia. CeAD can also present with "local" symptoms or signs only, including headache, cervical pain, Horner's syndrome, and cranial nerve compression, or can be asymptomatic.

Although mechanisms and risk factors of CeAD are poorly understood, neck trauma is an important predisposing factor for CeAD. Rarely, CeAD can occur with major penetrating or non-penetrating traumas.[10] Often, patients with CeAD report a minor trauma,[11–13] such as chiropractic manipulation, whiplash injury, or extreme neck movements, in the days or weeks preceding the dissection. However, a causal relationship is often difficult to establish, reported traumas are often trivial, occurring very often in a lifetime, and many cases of CeAD occur without any trauma at all, suggesting that there must be other susceptibility factors. Recently, hypertension was shown to be associated with a moderately increased risk of CeAD,[14,15] whereas hypercholesterolemia and overweight appear to be associated inversely with the disease.[7,16] Other putative risk factors include recent infection,[17,18] hyperhomocysteinemia,[19–21] and migraine.[22,23]

A number of arguments suggest that patients with CeAD could have an underlying arterial wall weakness, and that genetic factors may play a role in the pathophysiology of CeAD (Figure 8.1). Indeed, various concomitant structural and functional arterial abnormalities were described in association with CeAD, including larger aortic root diameter,[24] increased carotid stiffness,[25] endothelial dysfunction,[26–28] and arterial redundancies.[29] Pathological changes predominating at the media–adventitia border, including vacuolar degeneration, capillary neoangiogenesis, and erythrocyte extravasation, were detected in temporal arteries of patients with CeAD, but not in control subjects.[30] There is also an intriguing overlap of CeAD with other nonatherosclerotic vasculopathies, such as fibromuscular dysplasia[31–33] or reversible cerebral vasoconstriction syndrome.[34–36] Moreover, a number of arguments suggest that this putative underlying arterial wall weakness could reflect, more largely, a weakness of the connective tissue (Figure 8.1). Indeed, more than half of patients with CeAD have ultrastructural skin connective tissue abnormalities on electron microscopy, the most common pattern being Ehlers-Danlos type III-like composite collagen fibrils and fragmentation of elastic fibers.[37] Skin biopsies performed in healthy relatives of index patients with CeAD have suggested that these connective tissue changes may be inherited according to an autosomal dominant pattern.[38] In addition, CeAD is a classic complication of some rare inherited disorders of connective tissue, as detailed next.

Monogenic Disorders and CeAD

In rare instances, CeAD can occur as part of a known monogenic disorder.[39] Arterial dissection is, indeed, a common feature of certain rare inherited disorders of connective tissue, such as vascular Ehlers-Danlos syndrome (vEDS), Marfan syndrome (MFS), or Loeys-Dietz syndrome (LDS).[40]

VASCULAR EHLERS-DANLOS SYNDROME

vEDS is a rare autosomal dominant disease, resulting from a mutation in the *COL3A1* gene on chromosome 2q31 (OMIM 130050). The prevalence is estimated at 0.2 to 1/100,000,[41] and the median survival is 48 years (in older series).[42] The diagnosis is suggested clinically by the presence of at least two of four major clinical criteria[43]: easy bruising, thin skin with visible veins, characteristic facial features, and rupture of arteries, uterus, or intestines. In addition, the diagnosis must be confirmed by the demonstration of either an abnormal type III procollagen synthesis or of a mutation in the *COL3A1* gene. Phenotypic features can be subtle, and most patients are unaware of the diagnosis at the time of their first major complication.[42] The latter usually occurs at a young age, before age 40 years in 80% of patients.[42] Neurological complications of vEDS are essentially cerebrovascular,[44] including CeAD, carotid cavernous fistula, intracranial aneurysms, and arterial rupture. The mean age at occurrence of the first cerebrovascular complication was reported to be 28 years (range, 17–48 years).[44] In the two largest, partly overlapping, series of biologically confirmed patients with vEDS, 2% of them had a history of CeAD (of note, only carotid and not vertebral artery dissections were reported in the most recent study).[42,44] The reported frequency of vEDS cases in large published series of consecutive patients with CeAD is very low, around 0.5% to 2%.[45–48]

Although vEDS seems to be extremely rare among patients with CeAD at the general population level, being aware of and screening for the main clinical diagnostic criteria are important. Indeed, diagnosing vEDS has major consequences for the patient's management. Endovascular investigations are contraindicated in patients with vEDS, given the high risk of iatrogenic arterial dissection and rupture, resulting from the vulnerability of the arterial wall. To prevent primary or recurrent ischemic

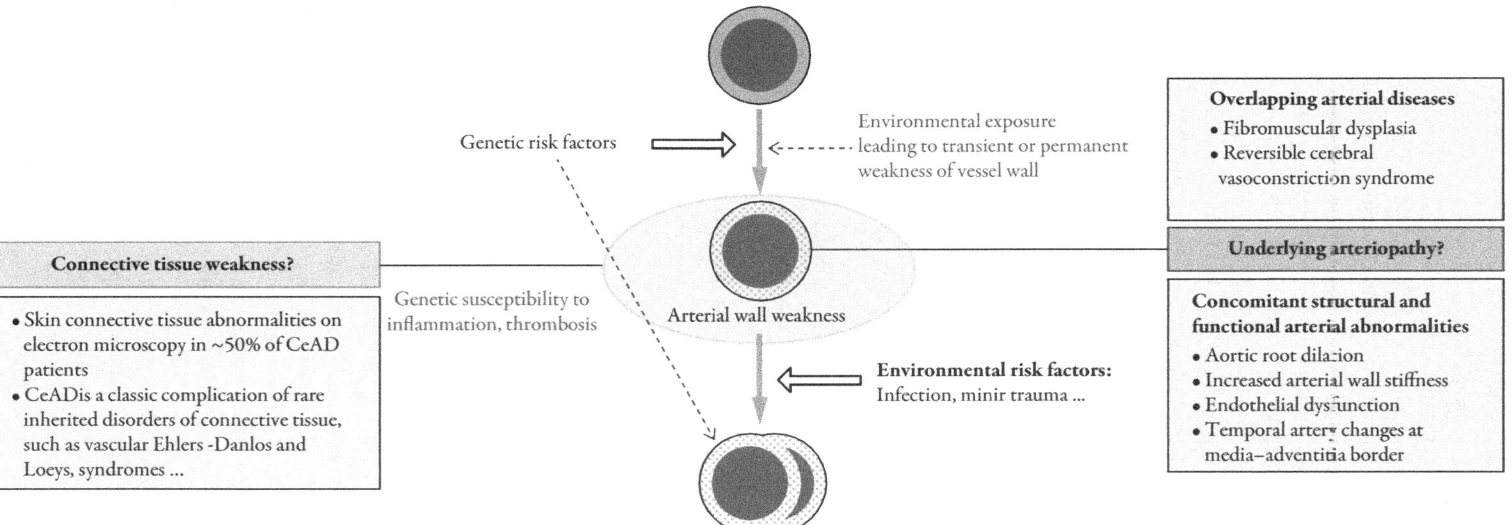
Connective tissue weakness?
• Skin connective tissue abnormalities on electron microscopy in ~50% of CeAD patients
• CeADis a classic complication of rare inherited disorders of connective tissue, such as vascular Ehlers -Danlos and Loeys, syndromes ...
Genetic susceptibility to inflammation, thrombosis
Genetic risk factors
Environmental exposure leading to transient or permanent weakness of vessel wall
Arterial wall weakness
Environmental risk factors:
Infection, minir trauma ...
Cervical artery dissection
Overlapping arterial diseases
• Fibromuscular dysplasia
• Reversible cerebral vasoconstriction syndrome
Underlying arteriopathy?
Concomitant structural and functional arterial abnormalities
• Aortic root dilation
• Increased arterial wall stiffness
• Endothelial dysfunction
• Temporal artery changes at media–adventitia border

FIGURE 8.1 Pathophysiology of cervical artery dissection (CeAD), a multifactorial model.

events, either anticoagulants or antiplatelet agents are prescribed at the acute phase of CeAD, in the general population; their efficacy has not been compared in a randomized trial.[6,48,49] In patients with vEDS, antiplatelet agents might perhaps be the preferred treatment, because fatal bleeding may occur with anticoagulants.[41] Prophylactic treatment with celiprolol is also recommended for patients with vEDS, to prevent recurrences of dissection or arterial rupture.[50]

MARFAN SYNDROME

MFS is an autosomal dominant disease resulting from a mutation in the *fibrillin-1*, or *FBN1*, gene on chromosome 15q21.1 (OMIM 154700). The prevalence is estimated at 1/5000.[51] Clinical signs of MFS include musculoskeletal, ocular, and cardiac complications with aortic and mitral valve anomalies; aortic aneurysms; and dissections conditioning the outcome. The diagnostic criteria have been revised recently.[52] Large series of consecutive patients with CeAD report very low frequencies of MFS (0.6%–0.9%)[2,45,48] without details on how the diagnosis of MFS was confirmed. Many large series do not report any patient with MFS. In patients with a proven diagnosis of MFS, spontaneous CeAD seems to be exceptional and must be differentiated from proximal aortic dissections extending into the brachiocephalic arteries. In a retrospective analysis of neurovascular complications in 513 patients with MFS, not a single case of CeAD was found.[53]

LOEYS-DIETZ SYNDROME

LDS is a recently identified group of extremely rare autosomal dominant disorders (OMIM 609192, OMIM 610380, OMIM 610168, OMIM 608967) caused by mutations in the *transforming growth factor β receptor 1* (*TGFBR1*) and *2* (*TGFBR2*) genes (chromosome 9q22 and 3p22), of unknown prevalence,[54] the phenotypes of which overlap with MFS and vEDS.[55] Three quarters of affected individuals have LDS type I with craniofacial manifestations (ocular hypertelorism, bifid uvula and cleft palate, craniosynostosis); the remaining quarter have LDS type II with cutaneous manifestations (velvety and translucent skin; easy bruising; widened, atrophic scars).[55] The disease is characterized by aggressive arterial aneurysms and a high incidence of pregnancy-related complications, including uterine rupture and death.[55,56] Arterial tortuosity involving head and neck vessels is frequent in patients with LDS. CeAD is a classic complication of LDS, although aortic dissections are more common.[57]

OTHER MONOGENIC DISORDERS

A number of observations have suggested an association of CeAD with other monogenic conditions, including alpha$_1$-antitrypsin deficiency, arterial tortuosity syndrome, osteogenesis imperfecta, autosomal dominant polycystic kidney disease, or hereditary hemochromatosis,[34,58–66] as well as with rare chromosomal disorders such as Turner's syndrome[67,68] or William's syndrome.[69] It is, however, unclear whether the simultaneous occurrence of these disorders is more common than would be expected by chance, and these conditions may not be risk factors for CeAD at the community level.

Last, it cannot be formally excluded that some patients with CeAD have mild forms of inherited disorders of connective tissue with incomplete penetrance or CeAD as the first isolated symptom,[6,70] because patients were not screened systematically for mutations in genes such as *COL3A1, FBN1, TGFBR1*, or *TGFRB2*, which are responsible for vEDS,[42] MFS,[52] and LDS.[55] In earlier studies, a systematic search for mutations in *COL3A1* among 53 patients with CeAD,[71–74] and in *TGFBR1* and *TGFBR2* among 56 consecutive patients with CeAD,[70] identified potentially deleterious mutations in *COL3A1* among two cousins with CeAD,[71] and in *TGFBR2* in two unrelated patients with

CeAD,[70] but none of them fulfilled the clinical diagnostic criteria of vEDS or LDS, possibly pointing to mutations with incomplete penetrance.[43,55,75] Whether identifying such mutations is clinically relevant—especially in terms of risk for CeAD recurrence, other vascular complications, and familial risk—is unclear to date.

Genetic Predisposition to CeAD

In the majority of CeAD cases, there is no clinical evidence for an underlying monogenic disease, and CeAD is believed to occur as part of a multifactorial predisposition (Figure 8.1).[39] Heritability estimates are not available. In one single-center study that addressed the frequency of family history of CeAD systematically, in 200 patients with CeAD,[76] 10 patients from 8 families had a family history of dissection. Of these, five patients (2.5%) from three families (1.5%) had a family history of dissection in the cervical arteries (the remaining being in the intracranial arteries, aorta or renal artery), and in four patients the family history of CeAD was in a first-degree relative (2.0%).[76] Another study, of 181 patients with CeAD, reported the presence of a family history of CeAD in less than 4 (2.2%) of their patients,[77] but familial occurrence of CeAD was not the main scope of that article, thus no details are provided on the degree of relatedness of affected individuals. On the one hand, these scarce reports of family history of CeAD could be an overestimation resulting from recruitment bias through tertiary referral centers, and because several CeAD cases from multiple affected families were included. On the other hand, a family history of CeAD is likely to be underreported because CeAD can be asymptomatic, or clinical signs can be subtle and the diagnosis tricky, especially before magnetic resonance imaging became widely available. Overall, even though familial occurrence of CeAD seems to be rare, it is slightly more common than would be expected by chance given the low incidence of the disease.[78] Familial cases of CeAD usually do not appear to occur in the context of a known, inherited connective tissue disorder.

Genetic factors could, theoretically, predispose to CeAD at various levels, such as (a) by contributing to a weakening of the vessel wall (on top of which environmental factors such as trauma or acute infection could act as triggers); (b) by increasing vulnerability to environmental factors that could have an impact on vascular wall integrity, such as by modulating inflammatory response to infection; and (c) by influencing the occurrence of environmental susceptibility factors of CeAD, such as hypertension, low lipid levels, and body mass.

Different approaches have been used to identify genetic variants contributing to CeAD risk. It should be noted that genetic susceptibility variants for multifactorial diseases such as CeAD usually have modest effects, with odds ratios typically less than 1.5.[79] The main objective, when searching for genetic risk factors of a complex, multifactorial disease, is to improve our understanding of the molecular mechanisms involved in the pathophysiology of this disease and thereby identify novel potential drug targets and optimize preventive strategies.

LINKAGE STUDIES

Linkage studies are family based and consist of testing whether genetic markers cosegregate with a given disease (in this case, CeAD) within families. This is done by examining simultaneously the transmission across generations of both CeAD and marker alleles, either genomewide or in a specific genomic region. Although linkage studies are particularly suited to discover genes causing monogenic disorders, they have also been implemented in some instances to identify genes contributing to complex diseases in family-based studies. Linkage studies for CeAD have been limited by the small number of large families with several members affected by the disease. They have not identified any significant linkage peak to date, but their power was limited.[39] One linkage analysis was performed in a family including three individuals affected by CeAD, using markers flanking the *COL3A1* locus.[74] Other linkage studies have been performed in families with only one member affected by CeAD, but several members presenting skin connective tissue abberrations described as being associated with CeAD.[38,80,81] These studies used microsatellite markers for candidates genes involved in the synthesis of extracellular matrix components,[80,81] and one study performed a whole-genome linkage analysis.[38] Despite some suggestive findings, none of these studies could confirm formally the presence of genetic linkage.

GENETIC ASSOCIATION STUDIES

Genetic association studies consist of comparing the frequency of genetic variants between patients and control subjects. Until recently, genetic association studies were candidate gene based (i.e., genetic variants were selected through a priori hypotheses about the underlying pathophysiology of the disease). One or more genetic variants (usually single nucleotide polymorphisms) from a candidate gene were genotyped in a group of unrelated patients and control subjects, and the association of allele frequencies was compared between patients and control subjects.

In total, 18 genetic association studies testing the association of CeAD with candidate genetic variants have been published, on relatively small samples.[39,82,83] Of these, five have reported significant associations with three different candidate genes: *ICAM-1* (rs5498),[84] *COL3A1* (3′ UTR 2-bp deletion),[74] and *MTHFR* (*MTHFR*-C677T).[20,21,85] The first two were not replicated.[39] Three studies, of which two overlap, found a positive association between the *MTHFR* 677TT genotype and CeAD,[20,21,85] whereas four others did not report any association.[19,83,86,87] A meta-analysis of these studies (comprising 440 patients with CeAD) suggested an overall significant association of the *MTHFR* 677TT genotype with an increased risk of CeAD.[39] However, given the small sample size of individual studies and the publication bias favoring candidate gene studies with significant results, it seems crucial to replicate this finding in a larger, independent sample. The *MTHFR* 677TT genotype is associated with elevated homocysteine levels,[19–21,87] which may contribute to endothelial damage or influence elastic properties of the arterial wall.[20]

Overall, published candidate gene association studies have been markedly underpowered, mainly as a result of the low prevalence of CeAD, which made it difficult to reach sufficient sample sizes. Moreover, candidate gene association studies are unable to identify novel genetic variants involved in unsuspected pathways, because they are based on what is already known or suspected about the pathophysiology of the disease.[79]

Definitive data can be obtained only from much larger multicenter genetic association studies, with replication of positive associations in independent samples.[88] International efforts, as part of the CADISP consortium (www.cadisp.com),[89] have recently enabled the collection of DNA samples from close to 2000 patients with CeAD, and have led to the first genomewide association study (GWAS) of CeAD. GWASs offer an unbiased approach, consisting of genotyping very large numbers of genetic variants (100,000–5,000,000) distributed across the chromosomes using high-throughput genotyping, without requiring any a priori hypothesis. During the past few years, this approach has been applied to a number of complex diseases with major successes, leading to the identification of hundreds of novel genes conferring increased risk of many complex diseases, including stroke (see Chapter 5).[90–92]

Conclusion and Perspectives

To summarize, apart from exceptional cases of CeAD occurring as a complication of rare inherited disorders of connective tissue, and apart from very rare familial cases (<3%), CeAD appears to be mostly a multifactorial disorder. Despite important efforts, no consistent, robustly replicated genetic association with CeAD has been identified to date. Published studies have been markedly underpowered. Results of the first GWAS of CeAD are awaited.

Additional GWASs on larger samples will likely be needed to expand the search further for genetic susceptibility factors of CeAD, if additional patients can be recruited during the coming years. Collecting large samples of dissection patients of non-European ethnicity will also be important to refine our understanding of the genetic architecture of CeAD. Indeed, so far, most genetic studies have been performed in populations of European descent. Interestingly, clinical and demographic characteristics of CeAD differ in part in other ethnic groups.[88,93]

As has been experienced with other complex diseases, GWASs will likely identify only a minor proportion of genetic susceptibility factors for CeAD, even when much larger samples can be collected in the future. Indeed, GWASs focus mostly on single nucleotide polymorphisms, and more recently also on small insertions and deletions. Investigating other types of genetic variation, such as copy number variants, rare variants, or epigenetic modifications, will be another important step. Efforts are already underway to explore these types of variation in CeAD, leveraging available data from existing data sets.

Last, further insight into the biological pathways underlying CeAD may be obtained by exploring the pleiotropy, or shared genetic variation, between CeAD and other arterial diseases showing important phenotypic correlation, such as fibromuscular dysplasia[31,32] or reversible cerebral vasoconstriction syndrome.[35,36]

REFERENCES

1. Leys D, Bandu L, Henon H, et al. Clinical outcome in 287 consecutive young adults (15 to 45 years) with ischemic stroke. *Neurology*. 2002;59:26–33.
2. Touze E, Gauvrit JY, Moulin T, Meder JF, Bracard S, Mas JL. Risk of stroke and recurrent dissection after a cervical artery dissection: A multicenter study. *Neurology*. 2003;61:1347–1351.
3. Lee VH, Brown RD Jr, Mandrekar JN, Mokri B. Incidence and outcome of cervical artery dissection: A population-based study. *Neurology*. 2006;67:1809–1812.
4. Huang YC, Chen YF, Wang YH, Tu YK, Jeng JS, Liu HM. Cervicocranial arterial dissection: experience of 73 patients in a single center. *Surg Neurol*. 2009;72(Suppl 2):S20–S27; discussion, S27.
5. Nakajima S, Tsukahara T, Minematsu K. A study of vertebrobasilar artery dissection with subarachnoid hemorrhage. *Acta Neurochir Suppl*. 2010;107:45–49.
6. Debette S, Leys D. Cervical-artery dissections: predisposing factors, diagnosis, and outcome. *Lancet Neurol*. 2009;8:668–678.
7. Debette S, Grond-Ginsbach C, Bodenant M, et al. Differential features of carotid and vertebral artery dissections: the CADISP study. *Neurology*. 2011;77:1174–1181.
8. Metso AJ, Metso TM, Debette S, et al. Gender and cervical artery dissection. *Eur J Neurol*. 2012;19:594–602.
9. Bejot Y, Daubail B, Debette S, Durier J, Giroud M. Incidence and outcome of cerebrovascular events related to cervical artery dissection: The Dijon Stroke Registry. *Int J Stroke*. 2014;9:879–882.
10. Biffl WL, Ray CE Jr, Moore EE, et al. Treatment-related outcomes from blunt cerebrovascular injuries: importance of routine follow-up arteriography. *Ann Surg*. 2002;235:699–706; discussion, 706–697.
11. Engelter ST, Grond-Ginsbach C, Metso TM, et al. Cervical artery dissection: trauma and other potential mechanical trigger events. *Neurology*. 2013;80:1950–1957.

12. Dittrich R, Rohsbach D, Heidbreder A, et al. Mild mechanical traumas are possible risk factors for cervical artery dissection. *Cerebrovasc Dis*. 2007;23:275–281.
13. Haldeman S, Kohlbeck FJ, McGregor M. Risk factors and precipitating neck movements causing vertebrobasilar artery dissection after cervical trauma and spinal manipulation. *Spine*. 1999;24:785–794.
14. Debette S, Metso T, Pezzini A, et al. Association of vascular risk factors with cervical artery dissection and ischemic stroke in young adults. *Circulation*. 2011;123:1537–1544.
15. Pezzini A, Caso V, Zanferrari C, et al. Arterial hypertension as risk factor for spontaneous cervical artery dissection: a case–control study. *J Neurol Neurosurg Psychiatry*. 2006;77:95–97.
16. Arnold M, Pannier B, Chabriat H, et al. Vascular risk factors and morphometric data in cervical artery dissection: a case–control study. *J Neurol Neurosurg Psychiatry*. 2009;80:232–234.
17. Grond-Ginsbach C, Giossi A, Aksay SS, et al. Elevated peripheral leukocyte counts in acute cervical artery dissection. *Eur J Neurol*. 2013;20:1405–1410.
18. Grau AJ, Buggle F, Ziegler C, et al. Association between acute cerebrovascular ischemia and chronic and recurrent infection. *Stroke*. 1997;28:1724–1729.
19. Gallai V, Caso V, Paciaroni M, et al. Mild hyperhomocyst(e)inemia: a possible risk factor for cervical artery dissection. *Stroke*. 2001;32:714–718.
20. Pezzini A, Del Zotto E, Archetti S, et al. Plasma homocysteine concentration, c677t *MTHFR* genotype, and 844ins68bp *CBS* genotype in young adults with spontaneous cervical artery dissection and atherothrombotic stroke. *Stroke*. 2002;33:664–669.
21. Arauz A, Hoyos L, Cantu C, et al. Mild hyperhomocysteinemia and low folate concentrations as risk factors for cervical arterial dissection. *Cerebrovasc Dis*. 2007;24:210–214.
22. Metso TM, Tatlisumak T, Debette S, et al. Migraine in cervical artery dissection and ischemic stroke patients. *Neurology*. 2012;78:1221–1228.
23. Tzourio C, Benslamia L, Guillon B, et al. Migraine and the risk of cervical artery dissection: a case–control study. *Neurology*. 2002;59:435–437.
24. Tzourio C, Cohen A, Lamisse N, Biousse V, Bousser MG. Aortic root dilatation in patients with spontaneous cervical artery dissection. *Circulation*. 1997;95:2351–2353.
25. Calvet D, Boutouyrie P, Touze E, Laloux B, Mas JL, Laurent S. Increased stiffness of the carotid wall material in patients with spontaneous cervical artery dissection. *Stroke*. 2004;35:2078–2082.
26. Lucas C, Lecroart JL, Gautier C, et al. Impairment of endothelial function in patients with spontaneous cervical artery dissection: evidence for a general arterial wall disease. *Cerebrovasc Dis*. 2004;17:170–174.
27. Baumgartner RW, Lienhardt B, Mosso M, Gandjour J, Michael N, Georgiadis D. Spontaneous and endothelial-independent vasodilation are impaired in patients with spontaneous carotid dissection: a case–control study. *Stroke*. 2007;38:405–406.
28. Baracchini C, Tonello S, Vitaliani R, Giometto B, Meneghetti G, Ballotta E. Vasomotion in multiple spontaneous cervical artery dissections. *Stroke*. 2008;39:1148–1151.
29. Barbour PJ, Castaldo JE, Rae-Grant AD, et al. Internal carotid artery redundancy is significantly associated with dissection. *Stroke*. 1994;25:1201–1206.
30. Volker W, Dittrich R, Grewe S, et al. The outer arterial wall layers are primarily affected in spontaneous cervical artery dissection. *Neurology*. 2011;76:1463–1471.
31. Kim ES, Olin JW, Froehlich JB, et al. Clinical manifestations of fibromuscular dysplasia vary by patient sex: a report of the United States Registry for FMD. *J Am Coll Cardiol*. 2013;62:2026–2028.
32. Olin JW, Froehlich J, Gu X, et al. The United States Registry for Fibromuscular Dysplasia: results in the first 447 patients. *Circulation*. 2012;125:3182–3190.
33. de Bray JM, Marc G, Pautot V, et al. Fibromuscular dysplasia may herald symptomatic recurrence of cervical artery dissection. *Cerebrovasc Dis*. 2007;23:448–452.

34. Southerland AM, Meschia JF, Worrall BB. Shared associations of nonatherosclerotic, large-vessel, cerebrovascular arteriopathies: considering intracranial aneurysms, cervical artery dissection, Moyamoya disease and fibromuscular dysplasia. *Curr Opin Neurol.* 2013;26:13–28.
35. Ducros A. Reversible cerebral vasoconstriction syndrome. *Lancet Neurol.* 2012;11:906–917.
36. Mawet J, Boukobza M, Franc J, et al. Reversible cerebral vasoconstriction syndrome and cervical artery dissection in 20 patients. *Neurology.* 2013;81:821–824.
37. Brandt T, Orberk E, Weber R, et al. Pathogenesis of cervical artery dissections: association with connective tissue abnormalities. *Neurology.* 2001;57:24–30.
38. Wiest T, Hyrenbach S, Bambul P, et al. Genetic analysis of familial connective tissue alterations associated with cervical artery dissections suggests locus heterogeneity. *Stroke.* 2006;37:1697–1702.
39. Debette S, Markus HS. The genetics of cervical artery dissection: a systematic review. *Stroke.* 2009;40:e459–e466.
40. Debette S, Germain DP. Neurologic manifestations of inherited disorders of connective tissue. *Handb Clin Neurol.* 2014;119:565–576.
41. Germain DP. Ehlers-Danlos syndrome type IV. *Orphanet J Rare Dis.* 2007;2:32.
42. Pepin M, Schwarze U, Superti-Furga A, Byers PH. Clinical and genetic features of Ehlers-Danlos syndrome type IV, the vascular type. *N Engl J Med.* 2000;342:673–680.
43. Beighton P, De Paepe A, Steinmann B, Tsipouras P, Wenstrup RJ. Ehlers-Danlos syndromes: revised nosology, Villefranche, 1997: Ehlers-Danlos National Foundation (USA) and Ehlers-Danlos Support Group (UK). *Am J Med Genet.* 1998;77:31–37.
44. North KN, Whiteman DA, Pepin MG, Byers PH. Cerebrovascular complications in Ehlers-Danlos syndrome type IV. *Ann Neurol.* 1995;38:960–964.
45. Arnold M, Bousser MG, Fahrni G, et al. Vertebral artery dissection: Presenting findings and predictors of outcome. *Stroke.* 2006;37:2499–2503.
46. Leys D, Moulin T, Stojkovic T, et al. Follow-up of patients with history of cervical artery dissection. *Cerebrovasc Dis.* 1995;5:43–49.
47. Schievink WI, Mokri B, O'Fallon WM. Recurrent spontaneous cervical-artery dissection. *N Engl J Med.* 1994;330:393–397.
48. Beletsky V, Nadareishvili Z, Lynch J, Shuaib A, Woolfenden A, Norris JW. Cervical arterial dissection: time for a therapeutic trial? *Stroke.* 2003;34:2856–2860.
49. Engelter ST, Brandt T, Debette S, et al. Antiplatelets versus anticoagulation in cervical artery dissection. *Stroke.* 2007;38:2605–2611.
50. Ong KT, Perdu J, De Backer J, et al. Effect of celiprolol on prevention of cardiovascular events in vascular Ehlers-Danlos syndrome: a prospective randomised, open, blinded-endpoints trial. *Lancet.* 2010;376:1476–1484.
51. Gray JR, Bridges AB, West RR, et al. Life expectancy in British Marfan syndrome populations. *Clin Genet.* 1998;54:124–128.
52. Loeys BL, Dietz HC, Braverman AC, et al. The revised Ghent nosology for the Marfan syndrome. *J Med Genet.* 2010;47:476–485.
53. Wityk RJ, Zanferrari C, Oppenheimer S. Neurovascular complications of Marfan syndrome: a retrospective, hospital-based study. *Stroke.* 2002;33:680–684.
54. Loeys BL, Schwarze U, Holm T, et al. Aneurysm syndromes caused by mutations in the TGF-beta receptor. *N Engl J Med.* 2006;355:788–798.
55. Loeys BL, Dietz HC. Loeys-Dietz syndrome. In: Pagon RA, Bird TC, Dolan CR, Stephens K, eds. Seattle, WA: University of Washington.
56. Van Hemelrijk C, Renard M, Loeys B. The Loeys-Dietz syndrome: an update for the clinician. *Curr Opin Cardiol.* 2010;25:546–551.
57. Rodrigues VJ, Elsayed S, Loeys BL, Dietz HC, Yousem DM. Neuroradiologic manifestations of Loeys-Dietz syndrome type 1. *AJNR Am J Neuroradiol.* 2009;30:1614–1619.

58. Schievink WI, Prakash UB, Piepgras DG, Mokri B. Alpha 1-antitrypsin deficiency in intracranial aneurysms and cervical artery dissection. *Lancet.* 1994;343:452–453.
59. Dittrich R, Heidbreder A, Rohsbach D, et al. Connective tissue and vascular phenotype in patients with cervical artery dissection. *Neurology.* 2007;68:2120–2124.
60. Gallerini S, Morelli N, Chiti A, et al. Spontaneous bilateral carotid artery dissection and hereditary haemochromatosis: what relationship? *Neurol Sci.* 2006;27:291–292.
61. Veltkamp R, Veltkamp C, Hartmann M, Schonffeldt-Varas P, Schwaninger M. [Symptomatic dissection of the internal carotid artery: a rare manifestation of autosome dominant polycystic kidney disease?]. *Nervenarzt.* 2004;75:149–152. [in German].
62. Bobrie G, Brunet-Bourgin F, Alamowitch S, et al. Spontaneous artery dissection: is it part of the spectrum of autosomal dominant polycystic kidney disease? *Nephrol Dial Transplant.* 1998;13:2138–2141.
63. Padberg M, Rinkel GJ, Hene RJ, Rabelink TJ. A winking warning. *Nephrol Dial Transplant.* 1998;13:3263–3264.
64. Pezzini A, Magoni M, Corda L, et al. Alpha-1-antitrypsin deficiency-associated cervical artery dissection: report of three cases. *Eur Neurol.* 2002;47:201–204.
65. Plaschke M, Auer D, Trapp T, Trenkwalder P, Trenkwalder C. Severe spontaneous carotid artery dissection and multiple aneurysmal dilatations: a case report. *Angiology.* 1996;47:919–923.
66. Konrad C, Nabavi DG, Junker R, Dziewas R, Henningsen H, Stogbauer F. Spontaneous internal carotid artery dissection and alpha-1-antitrypsin deficiency. *Acta Neurol Scand.* 2003;107:233–236.
67. Fuentes K, Silveira DC, Papamitsakis NI. Spontaneous carotid artery dissection in a patient with turner syndrome. *Cerebrovasc Dis.* 2007;24:543–544.
68. Muscat P, Lidov M, Nahar T, Tuhrim S, Weinberger J. Vertebral artery dissection in Turner's syndrome: diagnosis by magnetic resonance imaging. *J Neuroimaging.* 2001;11:50–54.
69. Vanacker P, Thijs V. Spontaneous cervical artery dissection in adult Williams syndrome. *Cerebrovasc Dis.* 2009;27:309–310.
70. Pezzini A, Drera B, Del Zotto E, et al. Mutations in *TGFBR2* gene cause spontaneous cervical artery dissection. *J Neurol Neurosurg Psychiatry.* 2011;82:1372–1374.
71. Martin JJ, Hausser I, Lyrer P, et al. Familial cervical artery dissections: clinical, morphologic, and genetic studies. *Stroke.* 2006;37:2924–2929.
72. Kuivaniemi H, Prockop DJ, Wu Y, et al. Exclusion of mutations in the gene for type III collagen (COL3A1) as a common cause of intracranial aneurysms or cervical artery dissections: results from sequence analysis of the coding sequences of type III collagen from 55 unrelated patients. *Neurology.* 1993;43:2652–2658.
73. van den Berg JS, Limburg M, Kappelle LJ, Pals G, Arwert F, Westerveld A. The role of type III collagen in spontaneous cervical arterial dissections. *Ann Neurol.* 1998;43:494–498.
74. von Pein F, Valkkila M, Schwarz R, et al. Analysis of the COL3A1 gene in patients with spontaneous cervical artery dissections. *J Neurol.* 2002;249:862–866.
75. De Paepe A, Malfait F. The Ehlers-Danlos syndrome: a disorder with many faces. *Clin Genet.* 2012;82:1–11.
76. Schievink WI, Mokri B, Piepgras DG, Kuiper JD. Recurrent spontaneous arterial dissections: risk in familial versus nonfamilial disease. *Stroke.* 1996;27:622–624.
77. Baumgartner RW, Arnold M, Baumgartner I, et al. Carotid dissection with and without ischemic events: local symptoms and cerebral artery findings. *Neurology.* 2001;57:827–832.
78. Grond-Ginsbach C, Debette S. The association of connective tissue disorders with cervical artery dissections. *Curr Mol Med.* 2009;9:210–214.
79. Zondervan KT, Cardon LR. Designing candidate gene and genome-wide case–control association studies. *Nat Protoc.* 2007;2:2492–2501.

80. Grond-Ginsbach C, Klima B, Weber R, et al. Exclusion mapping of the genetic predisposition for cervical artery dissections by linkage analysis. *Ann Neurol.* 2002;52:359–364.
81. Kuhlenbaumer G, Muller US, Besselmann M, et al. Neither collagen 8A1 nor 8A2 mutations play a major role in cervical artery dissection: a mutation analysis and linkage study. *J Neurol.* 2004;251:357–359.
82. Buss A, Pech K, Roelver S, Bloemeke B, Klotzsch C, Breuer S. Functional polymorphisms in matrix metalloproteinases -1, -3, -9 and -12 in relation to cervical artery dissection. *BMC Neurol.* 2009;9:40.
83. Jara-Prado A, Alonso ME, Martinez Ruano L, et al. *MTHFR* c677t, *FII* g20210a, FV Leiden g1691a, NOS3 intron 4 VNTR, and APOE epsilon4 gene polymorphisms are not associated with spontaneous cervical artery dissection. *Int J Stroke.* 2010;5:80–85.
84. Longoni M, Grond-Ginsbach C, Grau AJ, et al. The ICAM-1 e469k gene polymorphism is a risk factor for spontaneous cervical artery dissection. *Neurology.* 2006;66:1273–1275.
85. Pezzini A, Grassi M, Del Zotto E, et al. Migraine mediates the influence of c677t *MTHFR* genotypes on ischemic stroke risk with a stroke-subtype effect. *Stroke.* 2007;38:3145–3151.
86. Kloss M, Wiest T, Hyrenbach S, et al. *MTHFR* 677tt genotype increases the risk for cervical artery dissections. *J Neurol Neurosurg Psychiatry.* 2006;77:951–952.
87. Konrad C, Muller GA, Langer C, et al. Plasma homocysteine, *MTHFR* c677t, *CBS* 844ins68bp, and *MTHFD1* g1958a polymorphisms in spontaneous cervical artery dissections. *J Neurol.* 2004;251:1242–1248.
88. Dichgans M, Markus HS. Genetic association studies in stroke: Methodological issues and proposed standard criteria. *Stroke.* 2005;36:2027–2031.
89. Debette S, Metso TM, Pezzini A, et al. CADISP-genetics: an international project searching for genetic risk factors of cervical artery dissections. *Int J Stroke.* 2009;4:224–230.
90. Traylor M, Farrall M, Holliday EG, et al. Genetic risk factors for ischaemic stroke and its subtypes (the METASTROKE collaboration): a meta-analysis of genome-wide association studies. *Lancet Neurol.* 2012;11:951–962.
91. Ikram MA, Seshadri S, Bis JC, et al. Genomewide association studies of stroke. *N Engl J Med.* 2009;360:1718–1728.
92. Holliday EG, Maguire JM, Evans TJ, et al. Common variants at 6p21.1 are associated with large artery atherosclerotic stroke. *Nat Genet.* 2012;44:1147–1151.
93. Arauz A, Hoyos L, Espinoza C, Cantu C, Barinagarrementeria F, Roman G. Dissection of cervical arteries: long-term follow-up study of 130 consecutive cases. *Cerebrovasc Dis.* 2006;22:150–154.

9

GENES ASSOCIATED WITH RARE SUBTYPES OF STROKE

Cerebral Venous Thrombosis

Thomas Marjot and Pankaj Sharma

Introduction

Cerebral venous thrombosis (CVT) is a rare form of cerebrovascular disease that accounts for less than 1% of all cases of stroke. The condition was first recognized by French physician Ribes back in the early 19th century[1] and was largely regarded as arising from local or systemic septic conditions. Clinically, CVT was traditionally believed to follow a reliable course of rapidly progressing focal neurological deficit, seizures, coma, and inevitable death. Even up until the middle of the 20th century, CVT remained a postmortem diagnosis, with confident diagnosis based on clinical grounds alone emerging only during the 1940s. Now our understanding of this complex condition has broadened substantially. Modern magnetic resonance imaging and computed tomography have allowed more rapid confirmation of diagnosis and have paved the way for investigation into the treatment, prognosis, and risk factors for this disease.

Anatomy

The venous drainage of the cerebrum can be separated broadly into deep and superficial systems. The superficial system, which lies on the surface of the brain, is composed of venous sinuses, the walls of which are composed of dura mater as opposed to venous endothelium, The superior sagittal sinus is the largest contributor to the superficial system and runs posteriorly and inferiorly toward the confluence of sinuses. Two transverse sinuses travel laterally and inferiorly from this confluence and twist into an S shape, where they form the sigmoid sinuses before ultimately becoming the internal jugular veins bilaterally. The deep venous system is composed of vessels lined by traditional endothelium and has branches that penetrate the deep cerebral structures. These branches come together behind the midbrain to form the vein of Galen. At this point, the vein of Galen joins the inferior sagittal sinus, becoming the straight sinus, which then enters to the confluence of sinuses, the junction where deep and superficial systems meet. Thrombosis within any of these drainage structures constitutes a diagnosis of CVT, and it is therefore not surprising that this disease presents with a wide-ranging variety of signs and symptoms. An important clinical correlate of the venous anatomy is that bilateral cerebral involvement is not infrequent. For example, deep venous thrombosis can cause bilateral thalamic damage and reduced consciousness with little focal neurological deficit. Similarly, bilateral motor impairment is often found in sagittal sinus thrombosis in which the circulatory dysfunction may affect both hemispheres.

Diagnosis and Treatment

Definitive diagnosis relied traditionally on autopsy investigation, which revealed that venous thrombosis often coexisted with hemorrhagic lesions, which for a long time was thought to contraindicate the therapeutic use of heparin. However, recent guidelines, compiled largely from Cochrane reviewed evidence, state that concomitant intracranial hemorrhage is not a contraindication for anticoagulants. Body weight-adjusted, subcutaneous low-molecular weight heparin or dose-adjusted intravenous heparin is now used first line in acute CVT management.[2] The rationale for anticoagulation is to recanalize the occluded sinus or vein, to prevent further development of the thrombus, and, possibly in some cases, to reduce the risk of thromboembolic events elsewhere, such as pulmonary embolism (PE) or deep vein thrombosis (DVT).

CVT is thought to cause neurological damage via two distinguishable mechanisms: (a) thrombosis of the cerebral veins, which leads to local effects caused by venous obstruction; and (b) thrombosis of the major sinuses, which triggers intracranial hypertension.[3] The lasting damage these two processes cause has been largely unappreciated, and robust evidence evaluating long-term prognosis has only become available during the past 10 years. The large, prospective International Study on Cerebral Vein and Dural Sinus Thrombosis (ISCVT) containing 642 adult cases has proved invaluable in this respect because it documents patients' clinical profile over time.[4] Although the study offers a much less fatalistic impression of CVT than early case reports—for example, more than half of patients had no symptoms present at 16 months—there was still a significant proportion of patients (13%) who met the primary outcome of death or dependence at the end of follow-up.[4]

Despite accumulating literature and vast improvements in our understanding of the pathology, treatment, and prognosis of CVT, the disease still remains a diagnostic and therapeutic challenge. Mortality is still significant—hovering consistently around 10%—the disorder may worsen occasionally despite optimal anticoagulation, and any age group can be affected. CVT in neonatal and pediatric groups is of increasing scientific and clinical interest. Compared with adult CVT, neonatal and pediatric CVT is estimated to bring about far more severe long-term neurological outcomes, including developmental delay, cerebral palsy, and lasting seizure disorders.[5] It is also more common, with rates as high as 26 cases per 1 million, as opposed to 4 per 1 million in the adult population.

Diagnostic testing and safe/effective treatment still remain to be evaluated systematically for neonatal/pediatric patients, and current guidelines, unfortunately, are based on scant evidence. Etiology and pathophysiology of CVT in these groups is also still poorly understood, although two prospective studies have concluded that the prevalence of prothrombotic risk factors varied between 41% and 56.4%.[6,7]

More concerning, despite the ascendency of neuroimaging techniques during the past 25 years, CVT is still commonly overlooked, largely as a result of the diversity of clinical presentation and its multifactorial etiology.[8] Traditionally, CVT was regarded as occurring secondary to local or systemic infection, with the remaining proportion being regarded as "idiopathic." During the past 30 years, and although infection remains an important underlying pathology, the causes of CVT have broadened significantly to include surgery, hematologic diseases, vasculitis, pregnancy and puerperium, arteriovenous malformations, cancer, acquired prothrombotic disorders, and oral contraceptive pill (OCP) use. Interestingly, OCPs seems to have altered the demographics of who is susceptible to CVT. Up until the 1970s, men and women were equally affected; however, since then, a definite female preponderance has developed. Both evidence from laboratory analysis[9] and the associations found in CVT case–control studies[10,11] lead us to hypothesize that increasing OCP use may have driven such a distinct epidemiological shift.

Etiology

Numerous etiology-minded case reports also exist that point to the influence of various underlying risk factors, including spontaneous intracranial hypotension,[12] thalidomide use in multiple myeloma,[13] inflammatory bowel disease,[14] altitude,[15] tamoxifen,[16] erythropoietin,[17] and phytoestrogens.[18] In addition, a systematic review has recently been conducted that evaluated a causal association between hyperthyroidism and acute venous thrombotic complications, of which CVT seems to be a particularly common manifestation.[19] As a result of the increasing realization of the numerous possible risk factors involved in CVT, the proportion of cases with no identified risk factors, what might be considered idiopathic, has reduced from ~35% in the year 2000[20] to less than 15% in the more recent and comprehensive ISCVT study.[4] The ISCVT study's "etiological workup" also showed that multiple predisposing conditions were present in 38% of patients, suggesting that risk factor interactions are likely to be important in CVT etiology. One potentially major underlying risk factor believed to predispose an individual to CVT, when a second risk factor is encountered, is that of a genetic thrombophilia.

Genetics

It is now approximated that inherited thrombophilias constitute 22.4% of CVT cases.[4] Genetic thrombophilias should, especially, be considered in the diagnostic workup of any patient with recurrent venous thrombosis, in those with a family history of venous thromboembolism, in the young, and in those with no obvious acquired risk factor. The diversity of proteins involved in the complex coagulation cascade and fibrinolytic system has led to numerous possible substrates being responsible for thromboembolic disease. Deficiency in antithrombin III was first discovered in 1965,[21] followed later by deficiencies of protein C[22] and protein S[23] in 1981 and 1984, respectively. In 1993, resistance to activated protein C was identified as the most common cause of inherited thrombophilia,[24] and 1 year later, a specific polymorphism in Factor V was acknowledged as the major cause for this resistance.[25] The polymorphism was identified as a substitution event in the factor V gene (G1691A), which caused the arginine in residue 506 to be replaced by glutamine (Arg506Glu/R506Q), yielding a protein known as *factor V Leiden* (FVL). Aberrant FVL reduces the rate of inactivation of factor Va by activated protein C, which leads to an increased production of thrombin and, ultimately, clot formation. The FVL genotype has been found to be highly prevalent within the general population, ranging from 0.45% in Asian Americans to more than 5% in white Americans.[26] In 1996, a mutation in the prothrombin (*PT*) gene (G20210A) was found to be a common genetic factor predisposing to thrombosis. The G20210A mutation was found to enhance blood prothrombin activity, thus augmenting thrombin generation. Meta-analysis has shown that both factor V and *PT* polymorphisms appear to be significant in the development of DVT and PE, and also in CVT.[27,28] In CVT, FVL conferred an odds ratio (OR) of 2.40 (95% confidence interval [CI], 1.75–3.30), and prothrombin G20210A an OR of 5.48 (95% CI, 3.88–7.74). These ORs for risk, however, are very different from those found in peripheral venous thrombosis—namely, DVT and PE—with the PT mutation having a far greater impact on CVT than peripheral venous thrombosis. The inverse is true for FVL; this gene variant has a greater impact on peripheral, as opposed to cerebral, venous thrombosis. In this way, there seems to be region-specific mechanisms for thrombosis, with different vascular beds having their own unique susceptibility to the prothrombotic effects of certain gene variants.

Meta-analysis has also confirmed FVL and *PT* G20210A gene variants as being associated significantly with neonatal and pediatric CVT.[29] Kenet et al.[29] demonstrated an OR for risk from the FVL gene variant of 2.74 (95% CI, 1.73–4.34), which is comparable with adult studies. The *PT* G20210A polymorphism, however, had an OR of 1.95 (95% CI, 0.93–4.07) in pediatric CVT, which is markedly smaller than the association observed in adult populations. It may be that birth-related complications and greater incidence of sepsis may make CVT during early stages of life a more environmentally determined condition, with genes such as *PT* G20210A emerging only as predominant in adulthood.

Another established prothrombotic genetic risk factor involves alterations to the methylenetetrahydrofolate reductase (*MTHFR*) gene. The C677T polymorphism, leading to an exchange of alanine to valine, has long been implicated in ischemic heart disease and DVT.[30] Furthermore, meta-analysis has tried to evaluate risk specifically for the development of CVT.[31] In 2009, Gouveia and Canhao[31] found a nonsignificant OR, with considerable heterogeneity between individual studies. They concluded that there was insufficient data to support the risk of C677T *MTHFR* mutation. A 2011 meta-analysis that included five additional case–control studies showed similar conclusions, with no overall association being proved, and interpretations being limited by significant interstudy heterogeneity. Removal of one study, however, which corrected heterogeneity, did give a revised OR of 2.30 (95% CI, 1.20–4.42), suggesting that the *MTHFR* C677T gene variant should not be excluded completely as a genetic risk factor for CVT. In addition, the potential role of the novel *MTHFR* A1298C variant in CVT has recently been explored and has been shown to correlate positively with the disease (OR, 10.25; 95% CI, 5.6–18.7) in a small Tunisian cohort of patients.[32] MTHFR is of particular interest because of its role in homocysteine metabolism. MTHFR is necessary for the conversion of homocysteine to methionine, a less toxic amino acid. Increased blood homocysteine levels have been found to have a significant association with CVT (OR, 4.07),[33] thus providing a plausible etiologic link between *MTHFR* mutation and CVT. In 2005, a technique of "Mendelian randomization" was used to try and ascertain the causal relationships between MTHFR, homocysteine, and stroke.[34] It was noted that the observed increase in risk of stroke conferred by a homozygous *MTHFR* C677T mutation was close to the risk predicted by homocysteine-level changes conferred by such a mutation. These findings were consistent with a causal relationship between MTHFR, homocysteine, and ischemic stroke. These principles and meta-analytical techniques have been applied to CVT, in part using data linking homocysteine levels with DVT, and there is some statistical evidence to suggest causality between *MTHFR* C677T and CVT.

The quest for a more complete understanding of genetics in prothrombotic conditions, including CVT, has given rise to a host of other single nucleotide polymorphisms (SNPs) worthy of consideration. Plasma glutathione peroxidase (*Gpx-3*) T927C,[35,36] protein Z G79A,[37,38] and thrombin activatable fibrinolysis inhibition factor G438A, A505G, and C1040T[39] have all been postulated as conferring a risk for CVT, but no statistical evidence of association has emerged as yet. Several studies have shown a positive correlation of the *PAI-1* 4G allele with thrombotic disease such as DVT,[27,40] PE,[27] myocardial infarction,[41] and atherothrombotic stroke.[42] The 4G allele has been shown to have a gene–dose effect on circulating levels of *PAI-1*, a serine–protease responsible for inhibiting tissue plasminogen activator and urokinase, which together activate plasminogen and, hence, fibrinolysis. Studies in CVT populations, however, have yet to show any statistically significant association.[28,43–47] A gain-of-function mutation in the gene encoding the tyrosine–protein kinase, Janus kinase 2, is typically associated with myeloproliferative disorders, including polycythemia rubra vera, essential thrombocythemia, and primary myelofibrosis. Evidence is accumulating to support the JAK2 mutation as a novel risk factor for thromboembolic disease, which would correlate with the major burden of mortality and morbidity in myeloproliferative disorders being accounted for by vascular events. Patients with CVT have been found to carry the *JAK2* mutation regardless of blood count,[48] and recently *JAK2* status was found to be an independent risk factor for CVT (OR, 5.47; 95% CI, 1.06–28.27) without overt myeloproliferative disorders in an Indian cohort.[49] In a similar Indian case series, the tissue factor pathway inhibitor, or *TFPI*, T33C gene variant is the only polymorphism shown to confer protection against the development of CVT (OR, 0.19; 95% CI, 0.04–0.98).[50] This gene variant is associated strongly with increased tissue factor pathway inhibitor levels, and therefore increased inhibition of factor Xa and thrombin in the coagulation cascade.

Determining accurately the contribution of genetic polymorphisms to vascular thrombosis has had its pitfalls. During the past three decades, there has been wide variation in the number and type of genetic tests available, and many case series have had limited and incomplete thrombophilia workups. Furthermore, thrombophilia testing is expensive and may not specifically guide treatment acutely. There is increasing evidence, however, that an understanding of the genetic susceptibility of a patient to thrombosis will allow clinicians to counsel patients regarding future exposure to environmental risk factors such as the OCP. Martinelli et al.[51] showed that the combination of the *PT* mutation and OCP use conferred a substantially greater risk for CVT (OR, 149.3; 95% CI, 31.0–711.0) than for the *PT* mutation alone (OR, 10.2; 95% CI, 2.3–31.0).

Candidate gene case–control models have formed the bulk of CVT genetic research, but many have failed to recruit sufficient numbers of patients with CVT to draw reliable conclusions of association. Repeated meta-analysis allows pooling of all available data and has provided better insight into the etiology of several vascular disorders.[27,52] Modern genetic epidemiological research must be placed within the context of genomewide association studies (GWAS). These studies are made possible by increasingly sophisticated gene-chip technology, which allows sequencing of more than 1 million SNPs simultaneously. The SNP profiles are then compared, and if one gene variant is more frequent in patients than in control subjects, it is said to be "associated" with the disease phenotype. In contrast to the candidate gene approach, the whole genome is investigated and, as a result, there is greater scope to identify novel polymorphisms that may confer risk for pathology. These SNPs may not necessarily fall within coding regions of known coagulation cascade proteins. Indeed, recent GWAS investigation into DVT and PE confirmed disease risk association with the ABO blood group loci as well as with the well-documented FVL gene variant,[53] whereas an international collaborative genomewide association study (Biorepository to Establish the Aetiology of Sinovenous Thrombosis, or BEAST) is currently underway. A GWAS of this kind in CVT is likely to advance substantially our understanding of the genetics of this type of stroke, guide risk stratification, and offer possible areas for therapeutic intervention.

REFERENCES

1. Ribes MF. Des recherches faites sur la phlébite. *Rev Méd Franç Etrangère J Clin l'Hôtel-Dieu Charité Paris.* 1825;3:5–41.
2. Einhaupl K, Bousser MG, de Bruijn SF, et al. EFNS guideline on the treatment of cerebral venous and sinus thrombosis. *Eur J Neurol.* 2006;13:553–559.
3. Stam J. Thrombosis of the cerebral veins and sinuses. *N Engl J Med.* 2005;352:1791–1798.
4. Ferro JM, Canhao P, Stam J, Bousser MG, Barinagarrementeria F, ISCVT investigators. Prognosis of cerebral vein and dural sinus thrombosis: results of the International Study on Cerebral Vein and Dural Sinus Thrombosis (ISCVT). *Stroke.* 2004;35:664–670.

5. Roach ES, Golomb MR, Adams R, et al. Management of stroke in infants and children: a scientific statement from a special writing group of the American Heart Association Stroke Council and the Council on Cardiovascular Disease in the Young. *Stroke.* 2008;39:2644–2691.
6. deVeber G, Andrew M, Adams C, et al. Cerebral sinovenous thrombosis in children. *N Engl J Med.* 2001;345:417–423.
7. Heller C, Heinecke A, Junker R, et al. Cerebral venous thrombosis in children: a multifactorial origin. *Circulation.* 2003;108:1362–1367.
8. Bousser MG, Ferro JM. Cerebral venous thrombosis: an update. *Lancet Neurol.* 2007;6:162–170.
9. Vandenbroucke JP, Rosing J, Bloemenkamp KW, et al. Oral contraceptives and the risk of venous thrombosis. *N Engl J Med.* 2001;344:1527–1535.
10. Martinelli I, Sacchi E, Landi G, Taioli E, Duca F, Mannucci PM. High risk of cerebral-vein thrombosis in carriers of a prothrombin-gene mutation and in users of oral contraceptives. *N Engl J Med.* 1998;338:1793–1797.
11. de Bruijn SF, Stam J, Koopman MM, Vandenbroucke JP. Case–control study of risk of cerebral sinus thrombosis in oral contraceptive users and in who are [sic] carriers of hereditary prothrombotic conditions. The Cerebral Venous Sinus Thrombosis Study Group. *BMJ.* 1998;316:589–592.
12. Berroir S, Grabli D, Heran F, Bakouche P, Bousser MG. Cerebral sinus venous thrombosis in two patients with spontaneous intracranial hypotension. *Cerebrovasc Dis.* 2004;17:9–12.
13. Lenz RA, Saver J. Venous sinus thrombosis in a patient taking thalidomide. *Cerebrovasc Dis.* 2004;18:175–177.
14. De Cruz P, Lust M, Trost N, Wall A, Gerraty R, Connell WR. Cerebral venous thrombosis associated with ulcerative colitis. *Intern Med J.* 2008;38:865–867.
15. Skaiaa SC, Stave H. Recurrent sagittal sinus thrombosis occurring at high altitude during expeditions to Cho Oyu. *Wilderness Environ Med.* 2006;17:132–136.
16 Masjuan J, Pardo J, Callejo JM, Andres MT, Alvarez-Cermeno JC. Tamoxifen: a new risk factor for cerebral sinus thrombosis. *Neurology.* 2004;62:334–335.
17. Finelli PF, Carley MD. Cerebral venous thrombosis associated with epoetin alfa therapy. *Arch Neurol.* 2000;57:260–262.
18. Guimaraes J, Azevedo E. Phytoestrogens as a risk factor for cerebral sinus thrombosis. *Cerebrovasc Dis.* 2005;20:137–138.
19. Franchini M, Lippi G, Targher G. Hyperthyroidism and venous thrombosis: a casual or causal association? A systematic literature review. *Clin Appl Thromb Hemost.* 2011;17:387–392.
20. Bousser MG. Cerebral venous thrombosis: diagnosis and management. *J Neurol.* 2000;247:252–258.
21. Egeberg O. Inherited antithrombin deficiency causing thrombophilia. *Thromb Diath Haemorrh.* 1965;13:516–530.
22. Griffin JH, Evatt B, Zimmerman TS, Kleiss AJ, Wideman C. Deficiency of protein C in congenital thrombotic disease. *J Clin Invest.* 1981;68:1370–1373.
23. Comp PC, Esmon CT. Recurrent venous thromboembolism in patients with a partial deficiency of protein S. *N Engl J Med.* 1984;311:1525–1528.
24. Dahlback B, Carlsson M, Svensson PJ. Familial thrombophilia due to a previously unrecognized mechanism characterized by poor anticoagulant response to activated protein C: prediction of a cofactor to activated protein C. *Proc Natl Acad Sci U S A.* 1993;90:1004–1008.
25. Bertina RM, Koeleman BP, Koster T, et al. Mutation in blood coagulation factor V associated with resistance to activated protein C. *Nature.* 1994;369:64–67.
26. Ridker PM, Miletich JP, Hennekens CH, Buring JE. Ethnic distribution of factor V Leiden in 4047 men and women: implications for venous thromboembolism screening. *JAMA.* 1997;277:1305–1307.

27. Gohil R, Peck G, Sharma P. The genetics of venous thromboembolism: a meta-analysis involving approximately 120,000 cases and 180,000 controls. *Thromb Haemost.* 2009;102:360–370.
28. Marjot T, Yadav S, Hasan N, Bentley P, Sharma P. Genes associated with adult cerebral venous thrombosis. *Stroke.* 2011;42:913–918.
29. Kenet G, Lutkhoff LK, Albisetti M, et al. Impact of thrombophilia on risk of arterial ischemic stroke or cerebral sinovenous thrombosis in neonates and children: a systematic review and meta-analysis of observational studies. *Circulation.* 2010;121:1838–1847.
30. Wald DS, Law M, Morris JK. Homocysteine and cardiovascular disease: evidence on causality from a meta-analysis. *BMJ.* 2002;325:1202.
31. Gouveia LO, Canhao P. MTHFR and the risk for cerebral venous thrombosis: a meta-analysis. *Thromb Res.* 2010;125:e153–e158.
32. Fekih-Mrissa N, Klai S, Mrad M, et al. Role of methylenetetrahydrofolate reductase A1298C polymorphism in cerebral venous thrombosis. *Blood Coagul Fibrinolysis.* 2013;24:118–119.
33. Dentali F, Crowther M, Ageno W. Thrombophilic abnormalities, oral contraceptives, and risk of cerebral vein thrombosis: a meta-analysis. *Blood.* 2006;107:2766–2773.
34. Casas JP, Bautista LE, Smeeth L, Sharma P, Hingorani AD. Homocysteine and stroke: evidence on a causal link from Mendelian randomisation. *Lancet.* 2005;365:224–232.
35. Voetsch B, Jin RC, Bierl C, et al. Role of promoter polymorphisms in the plasma glutathione peroxidase (GPx-3) gene as a risk factor for cerebral venous thrombosis. *Stroke.* 2008;39:303–307.
36. Grond-Ginsbach C, Arnold ML, Lichy C, Grau A, Reuner K. No association of the plasma glutathione peroxidase (GPx-3) gene with cerebral venous thrombosis in the German population. *Stroke.* 2009;40:e24; author reply, e25.
37. Le Cam-Duchez V, Bagan-Triquenot A, Barbay V, Mihout B, Borg JY. The G79A polymorphism of protein Z gene is an independent risk factor for cerebral venous thrombosis. *J Neurol.* 2008;255:1521–1525.
38. Lichy C, Dong-Si T, Reuner K, et al. Risk of cerebral venous thrombosis and novel gene polymorphisms of the coagulation and fibrinolytic systems. *J Neurol.* 2006;253:316–320.
39. Tokgoz S, Zamani AG, Durakbasi-Dursun HG, et al. *TAFI* gene polymorphisms in patients with cerebral venous thrombosis. *Acta Neurol Belg.* 2013;113:291–297.
40. Akhter MS, Biswas A, Ranjan R, et al. Plasminogen activator inhibitor-1 (PAI-1) gene 4G/5G promoter polymorphism is seen in higher frequency in the Indian patients with deep vein thrombosis. *Clin Appl Thromb Hemost.* 2010;16:184–188.
41. Onalan O, Balta G, Oto A, et al. Plasminogen activator inhibitor-1 4G4G genotype is associated with myocardial infarction but not with stable coronary artery disease. *J Thromb Thrombolysis.* 2008;26:211–217.
42. Wiklund PG, Nilsson L, Ardnor SN, et al. Plasminogen activator inhibitor-1 4G/5G polymorphism and risk of stroke: replicated findings in two nested case–control studies based on independent cohorts. *Stroke.* 2005;36:1661–1665.
43. Ringelstein M, Jung A, Berger K, et al. Promoter polymorphisms of plasminogen activator inhibitor-1 and other thrombophilic genotypes in cerebral venous thrombosis: a case–control study in adults. *J Neurol.* 2012;259:2287–2292.
44. Junker R, Nabavi DG, Wolff E, et al. Plasminogen activator inhibitor-1 4G/4G-genotype is associated with cerebral sinus thrombosis in factor V Leiden carriers. *Thromb Haemost.* 1998;80:706–707.
45. Lichy C, Kloss M, Reismann P, Genius J, Grau A, Reuner K. No evidence for plasminogen activator inhibitor 1 4G/4G genotype as risk factor for cerebral venous thrombosis. *J Neurol.* 2007;254:1124–1125.

46. Miller SP, Wu YW, Lee J, et al. Candidate gene polymorphisms do not differ between newborns with stroke and normal controls. *Stroke.* 2006;37:2678–2683.
47. Ozyurek E, Balta G, Degerliyurt A, Parlak H, Aysun S, Gurgey A. Significance of factor V, prothrombin, MTHFR, and PAI-1 genotypes in childhood cerebral thrombosis. *Clin Appl Thromb Hemost.* 2007;13:154–160.
48. Passamonti SM, Biguzzi E, Cazzola M, et al. The JAK2 V617F mutation in patients with cerebral venous thrombosis. *J Thromb Haemost.* 2012;10:998–1003.
49. De T, Prabhakar P, Nagaraja D, Christopher R. Janus kinase (JAK)2 V617F mutation in Asian Indians with cerebral venous thrombosis and without overt myeloproliferative disorders. *J Neurol Sci.* 2012;323:178–182.
50. Prabhakar P, De T, Nagaraja D, Christopher R. The intron 7-33T>C polymorphism in *TFPI* gene and cerebral venous thrombosis: evidence for a protective role. *Thromb Res.* 2012;130:687–689.
51. Martinelli I, Sacchi E, Landi G, Taioli E, Duca F, Mannucci PM. High risk of cerebral-vein thrombosis in carriers of a prothrombin-gene mutation and in users of oral contraceptives. *N Engl J Med.* 1998;338:1793–1797.
52. Peck G, Smeeth L, Whittaker J, Casas JP, Hingorani A, Sharma P. The genetics of primary haemorrhagic stroke, subarachnoid haemorrhage and ruptured intracranial aneurysms in adults. *PLoS One.* 2008;3:e3691.
53. Tregouet DA, Heath S, Saut N, et al. Common susceptibility alleles are unlikely to contribute as strongly as the FV and ABO loci to VTE risk: results from a GWAS approach. *Blood.* 2009;113:5298–5303.

10

GENETIC RISK FACTORS FOR MRI MARKERS OF CEREBRAL SMALL-VESSEL DISEASE

Ganesh Chauhan, Christophe Tzourio, and Stéphanie Debette

Introduction

Cerebral small-vessel disease (SVD) refers to damage to small vessels of the brain.[1] SVD is a leading cause for stroke, dementia, cognitive decline, and other age-related disabilities.[2–6] Only a fraction of SVD manifests as clinically overt disease such as stroke or dementia.[7] A far greater proportion of SVD remains clinically covert and is highly prevalent in the general population, particularly in older individuals, as has been revealed by brain imaging in large population-based samples.[8] Clinically "covert" SVD is often associated with subtle cognitive and motor dysfunction, and heralds an increased risk of future stroke and dementia.[2,3,9–12]

Parenchymal lesions on magnetic resonance imaging (MRI), which are thought to be caused by damage to cerebral small vessels, are being studied as markers of SVD.[1] Cerebral MRI is currently the best approach to visualize these lesions. MRI measures such as white matter hyperintensities (WMHs), small subcortical brain infarcts (SSBIs), and cerebral microbleeds are most commonly used.[13] Because factors leading to common SVD are largely unknown beyond aging and high blood pressure,[14–16] identifying genetic risk factors for MRI markers of SVD may help unravel molecular pathways and biological processes involved in SVD.

A detailed description of MRI markers of SVD is provided in Chapter 21. Briefly, WMHs correspond to signal abnormalities of variable size in the white matter, appearing as hyperintensities on T2-weighted or fluid-attenuated inversion recovery images, without cavitations.[13] Pathological correlates include myelin degeneration or rarefaction, proliferative astrogliosis, fibrinoid changes, and fibrosis to the vessel walls.[17,18] The underlying mechanisms are poorly understood, with chronic hypoperfusion of the white matter and disruption of the blood–brain barrier leading to chronic leakage of plasma into the white matter being the prevailing hypotheses.[2,13] WMHs are highly prevalent in older community persons, affecting 90% of individuals older than 80 years,[2] and up to 50% of middle-age persons (44–48 years).[19] Lesion volume is highly variable, ranging between 0.3 cm^3 and 10 cm^3 or more in community persons age 45 to 75 years, on average.[19,20] It can be measured quantitatively using automated algorithms, or semiquantitatively based on visual scales.[21–24]

Brain infarcts (BIs) are hypointense foci (usually >3–4 mm) on MRI T1-weighted sequences, appearing hyperintense on T2-weighted sequences and hyper- or hypointense on fluid-attenuated inversion recovery sequences, in a vascular distribution.[25] Among BIs, SSBIs correspond to neuroimaging evidence of infarction in the territory of one perforating arteriole (i.e., <15 mm, and as large as 20 mm in some studies) located in the basal ganglia, the white matter, or the brainstem.[13] SSBIs are believed to reflect SVD primarily, and to account for 60% to 70% of all BIs.[13,26] The vast majority of BIs are "covert" (i.e., not associated with symptoms of acute clinical stroke).[7,27] Their frequency ranges between 10% and 30% in older community persons.[28]

Cerebral microbleeds are small (usually 2–5 mm and as large as 10 mm) hypointense lesions on gradient echo—T2*—or susceptibility-weighted images.[10,29,30] These correspond to hemosiderin deposits and likely represent small foci of blood cell leakage. In the general population, their frequency ranges between 5% and 15%, and increases with age, systolic blood pressure, and smoking.[31–35] They are frequently observed (~60%) in persons with a history of intracerebral hemorrhage (ICH).[32]

Evidence for Genetic Contribution to MRI Markers of Cerebral SVD

Evidence for a genetic basis of MRI markers of SVD, mainly for WMH burden and BIs, comes from heritability estimates based on twin and family studies, and from the observation of monogenic diseases causing SVD.[36,37]

HERITABILITY ESTIMATES FROM TWIN AND FAMILY STUDIES

Heritability of a complex trait can be measured by comparing the similarity of a trait among relatives, and by estimating to what extent differences in incidence are the result of genetic variation or environmental differences. Twin studies, comparing monozygotic and dizygotic twins, are best suited to separate genetic influences from environmental ones (Chapter 4). High heritability estimates suggest that a trait is influenced significantly by genetic factors, making it a compelling target for more specific genetic analyses. A study of older male twins (74 monozygotic vs. 71 dizygotic) found that the heritability of WMH burden was 71% (95% confidence interval, 66–76), after adjusting for age and head size.[38] The heritability for WMH burden remained high after adjustment for a family history score for stroke.[39] High heritability estimates for WMH burden have also been reported in the Framingham Heart Study (55%, $p < .0001$), in Mexican Americans from the San Antonio Family Heart Study (72 ± 11%, $p = 1.0 \times 10^{-14}$), and in hypertensive siblings from the Genetic Epidemiology Network of Arteriopathy (GENOA) study (80 ± 10%, $p < .0001$; and 67 ± 11%, $p < .0001$ after adjusting for sex, age, systolic blood pressure, and brain volume).[40–42] The observation that individuals whose parents or siblings have had stroke are at increased risk for BIs also supports the role of genetic factors in SSBI occurrence.[43,44]

MONOGENIC DISORDERS CAUSING SVD

Several monogenic disorders display phenotypes similar to that of sporadically occurring SVD. The main monogenic diseases causing SVD are listed in Table 10.1[45–66] and are described in greater detail in Chapter 3 and Chapter 6. Genes underlying these disorders could also harbor genetic variants influencing sporadic forms of SVD, as has been observed for other diseases such as type 2 diabetes and obesity.[67]

TABLE 10.1

Monogenic Diseases Causing Small-Vessel Disease

Disease	Prevalence	Mode of inheritance	Causal gene	Reference
Cerebral autosomal dominant arteriopathy with subcortical infarcts and leukoencephalopathy, or CADASIL	1–9/100,000	Autosomal dominant	*NOTCH3*	Joutel et al.,[45] Chabriat et al.[46]
Cerebral autosomal recessive arteriopathy with subcortical infarcts and leukoencephalopathy, or CARASIL	Exceptionally rare	Autosomal recessive	*HTRA1*	Hara et al.,[47] Fukutake et al.[48]
Autosomal dominant retinal vasculopathy with cerebral leukodystrophy, or RVCL	Exceptionally rare	Autosomal dominant	*TREX1*	Jen et al.,[49] Terwindt et al.,[50] Ophoff et al.,[51] Richards et al.[52]
Hereditary cerebral amyloid angiopathy, or H-CAA	Rare	Autosomal dominant	*APP*	Revesz et al.,[53,54] Biffi et al.[55]
COL4A1 syndrome	Rare	Autosomal dominant	*COL4A1*	Gould et al.,[56] Volonghi et al.,[57] Lanfranconi et al.[58]
Fabry disease	1–5/10,000	X-linked recessive	*GLA*	Germain,[59] Pastores et al.,[60] Rolfs et al.,[61] Sims et al.[62]
Mitochondrial encephalopathy with lactic acidosis and strokelike episodes, or MELAS	Unknown	Mitochondrial inheritance	Mitochondrial DNA	Clayton et al.,[63] Hirano et al.,[64] Sproule et al.,[65] Majamaa et al.[66]

Linkage Studies

Linkage analyses are used to map genetic loci by use of observations of related individuals.[68] They are family based and test whether genetic markers cosegregate with a given disease within families. Although they are particularly suited to discover genes causing monogenic disorders, they also have been implemented in some instances to identifying genes contributing to complex traits in family-based studies. At least five studies have performed whole-genome linkage analysis for WMH burden.[42,69–72] Significant logarithm of odds scores for linkage with WMH burden have been reported only for the chromosome 4p16 region by the Framingham Heart Study in older community persons of European ancestry.[70,71] The 4p16 region harbors the gene for Huntington disease (*HTT*), a gene that has been associated with hypertension (*GRK4*) and also genes responsible for mitochondrial functioning. Chromosomal regions that have shown suggestive evidence for linkage include chromosomes 1, 5, and 11.[42,69,72] Interestingly, using bivariate whole-genome linkage analyses, two studies have found an indication of shared genetic loci for WMH volume and blood pressure measurements—the GENOA study and the San Antonio Family Heart Study—suggesting that genes with pleiotropic effects may be underlying both traits.[40,73] Overall, linkage studies are, however, much less powerful than genetic association studies for discovering genetic risk variants for complex diseases.[74]

Candidate Gene-Based Association Studies

Candidate gene association studies test the association of a disease with genetic variants selected through a priori hypotheses about the underlying pathophysiology. They consist of genotyping one or more genetic variants (usually single nucleotide polymorphisms [SNPs]) from a candidate gene in a group of unrelated persons, and test the association of their allelic frequencies with case–control status or with a quantitative trait. Numerous candidate gene-based association studies have been performed for WMH burden and MRI-defined BIs. Very few candidate genes have been studied in association with microbleeds.

Rather than presenting a comprehensive overview of all published candidate gene studies in association with MRI SVD, we provide a summary of the most robust findings in the text. All genes and variants that have shown significant association with one or more MRI markers of SVD in at least one publication are listed in Tables 10.2[75–93] and 10.3.[94–100]

CANDIDATE GENE-BASED STUDIES FOR WMH BURDEN

Genes of Cholesterol Regulation

Apolipoprotein E (APOE) is involved in the transport of cholesterol and other hydrophobic molecules. Common variants of *APOE* are well-established risk factors for dyslipidemia, cardiovascular disorders, ICH, and late-onset Alzheimer's disease (AD), as well.[55,101–106] The ε4 allele of *APOE* is associated with late-onset AD in a dosage-dependent manner. *APOE* ε4 has been investigated in a number of studies for association with WMH burden, but results were not conclusive. In 2009, a meta-analysis of 46 studies (19,000 subjects)[78] found no convincing evidence for association of *APOE* ε4 with WMH burden. A more recent, larger meta-analysis of 42 studies (29,965 participants), including unpublished data, found that *APOE* ε4 is associated with increased WMH burden.[88] Interestingly, this meta-analysis also found that the less frequent *APOE* ε2 allele, which is protective for AD but a risk factor for lobar ICH and ICH volume progression,[52,55,106] was associated with increased WMH burden. Variants in other genes involved in cholesterol regulation (mainly,

TABLE 10.2

Candidate Gene Studies for WMH Burden

Gene	HGNC symbol	Pathway	Polymorphism	Sample size	Reference	Ethnicity	p Value (WMH GWAS)[a]
Calpain10	*CAPN10*	Arteriosclerosis and related pathways	rs7571442	777	Smith et al.[75]	European	NA
Coagulation factor III	*F3*	Arteriosclerosis and related pathways	rs3917643	777	Smith et al.[75]	European	NA
Intercellular adhesion molecule 1	*ICAM1*	Arteriosclerosis and related pathways	rs5498 (K469E)		Han et al.[76]	Chinese	.006
Kit Ligand	*KITLG*	Arteriosclerosis and related pathways	rs995029	777	Smith et al.[75]	European	.99
Matrix metalloproteinase 2	*MMP2*	Arteriosclerosis and related pathways	rs9928731	777	Smith et al.[75]	European	.37
Matrix metalloproteinase 3	*MMP3*	Arteriosclerosis and related pathways	rs679620 (K45E)	756	Fornage et al.[77]	European	.2
Matrix metalloproteinase 9	*MMP9*	Arteriosclerosis and related pathways	rs2250889 (P574R)	756, 671	Fornage et al.[77]	African and European	.12
Angiotensin-converting enzyme	*ACE*	Blood pressure	rs1799752 (I/D)		Paternoster et al.[78]		.62
Adducin 1	*ADD1*	Blood pressure	rs4961 (Gly460Trp)	1018	van Rijn et al.[79]	European	.68
Angiotensinogen	*AGT*	Blood pressure	rs699 (M235T)		Paternoster et al.[78]		.01
Angiotensin II receptor 1	*AGTR1*	Blood pressure	rs5186 (A1166 C)	231	Taylor et al.[80]	European	NA
Angiotensin II receptor 2	*AGTR2*	Blood pressure		231	Taylor et al.[80]	European	NA
Aldosterone synthase	*CYP11B2*	Blood pressure	rs1799998 (−344C/T)	510, 829	Brenner et al.,[81] Verpillat et al.[82]	European	.07

(*continued*)

TABLE 10.2

Continued

Gene	HGNC symbol	Pathway	Polymorphism	Sample size	Reference	Ethnicity	p Value (WMH GWAS)[a]
Methylenetetrahydrofolate reductase	*MTHFR*	Homocysteine metabolism	rs1801133 (C677T), rs1801131	68	Hassan et al.,[83] Kohara et al.,[84] Szolnoki et al.,[85] Paternoster et al.,[78] Linnebank et al.[86]		.73
Interleukin 6	*IL6*	Inflammation	rs1800795	532, 2905	Fornage et al.[87]	African and European	.09
Apolipoprotein E	*APOE*	Lipid metabolism	APOE ε4, APOE ε3, APOE ε2, rs7412, rs429358		Paternoster et al.,[78] Schilling et al.[88]		NA
Cholesteryl ester transfer protein	*CETP*	Lipid metabolism	rs1800775 (C-629A)	452	Qureischie et al.[89]	European	.66
Endothelial nitric oxide synthase	*NOS3*	Oxidative stress	rs1799983	93	Henskens et al.[90]	European	.19
Paraoxanase 1	*PON1*	Oxidative stress	rs854560	264	Schmidt et al.[91]	European	.47
Brain-derived neurotrophic factor	*BDNF*	Regeneration	rs6265 (Val66Met)	312	Taylor et al.[92]	European	NA
NA	*NOTCH3*	Vascular dysfunction	rs10404382	877	Schmidt et al.[93]	European	NA

[a] *p* Values for the association with WMH burden in the GWAS by Fornage et al.[20] are presented.
GWAS, genomewide association study; HGNC, HUGO Gene Nomenclature Committee; I/D, insertions/deletions; NA, not applicable; WMH, white matter hyperintensity.

TABLE 10.3

Candidate Gene Studies for BI

Gene	HGNC symbol	Pathway	Polymorphisms	Sample size	Reference	Ethnicity	p Value (BI GWAS)[a]
Apolipoprotein E	*APOE*	Lipid metabolism	APOE ε2		Schilling et al.[88]		NA
Lipoprotein lipase	*LPL*	Lipid metabolism	rs328 (S447X)	197/964	Morrison et al.[94]	Europeans	.50
Angiotensin I converting enzyme	*ACE*	Blood pressure	rs1799752 (I/D)		Paternoster et al.[78]		.60
Angiotensinogen	*AGT*	Blood pressure	rs699 (M235T)		Paternoster et al.[78]		.70
Adducin 1, alpha	*ADD1*	Blood pressure	rs4961 (Gly460Trp)		van Rijn et al.[95]		.40
Nitric oxide synthase	*NOS3*	Oxidative stress	786T>C, 4a4b, 894G>T	269/234	Song et al.[96]	South Koreans	NA
Interleukin 6	*IL6*	Inflammation	rs1800795, rs1800796	233/465, 2905	Jenny et al.,[97] Fornage et al.[87]	Europeans	.60/.80
Protein kinase C, eta	*PRKCH*	Vascular dysfunction	rs3783799 rs2230500	295/497	Serizawa et al.[98]	Japanese	NA
Fibrinogen gamma chain and alpha chain	*FGG, FGA, FGB*	Clotting	rs2066860, rs2066861, rs1049636, rs2070011, rs2070014, rs2070016, rs6050, rs1800787	213/864	van Oijen et al.[99]	Europeans	0.02–0.80
Micro RNAs	*miR-146a, miR-149, miR-196a2, miR-499*	Micro RNAs	miR-146aG, miR-149T, miR-196a2C, miR-499G	373/553	Jeon et al.[100]	South Korean	NA

[a] *p* Values for the association with the presence of BIs in the GWAS by Debette et al.[26] are presented.

BI, brain infarct; GWAS, genomewide association study; HGNC, HUGO Gene Nomenclature Committee; NA, not applicable.

rs1800775, *CETP*) have shown weak evidence of association with WMH burden in a small, single sample ($N = 452$), with no replication to date.[89]

Genes Involved in Blood Pressure Regulation

Elevated blood pressure is one of the most important known risk factors for WMH burden. Hence, genes that play an important role in blood pressure regulation could influence risk for WMH burden. Angiotensin-converting enzyme (ACE) and angiotensinogen (AGT) are part of the renin–angiotensin system, a major regulator of systemic blood pressure. The *ACE* insertions/deletions polymorphisms (rs1799752) and *AGT* Met235Thr polymorphism (rs699) have been examined in multiple studies for association with WMH burden, with heterogeneous findings. A meta-analysis of nine studies found that the *ACE* DD homozygote genotype was associated significantly with increased risk for WMH burden, whereas no association with *AGT* Met235Thr polymorphism (rs699) was observed in aggregate.[78] The latter polymorphism was, however, associated with WMH burden at a nominal significance level ($p = .01$) in a recent genomewide association study (GWAS) of WMH burden (see Section 10.5).[20] Aldosterone plays an important role in maintaining intravascular volume and blood pressure. Mutations in the aldosterone synthase gene (*CYP11B2*) cause either hypertension or hypotension. The TT genotype of the *CYP11B2* polymorphism rs1799998 was found to be associated with WMH burden in two relatively small, separate studies ($N = 510$ and $N = 829$), independent of hypertension.[81,82]

Genes Involved in Arteriosclerosis and Related Pathways

It has been hypothesized that hypertension might affect WMH burden by accelerating age-related processes such as arteriosclerosis. The GENOA study showed that matrix metalloproteinase (MMP) 3 (*MMP3*) variants were associated with WMH burden in Europeans, and *MMP9* variants with WMH burden in both Europeans and Americans (756 Europeans and 671 blacks).[77] Later, the GENOA study genotyped 1649 SNPs from genes known or hypothesized to be involved in arteriosclerosis and related pathways in 777 European individuals. The study revealed an association for variants in *F3, KITLG, CAPN10,* and *MMP2* variants with WMH burden.[75] A Chinese study has also revealed an association of a genetic variant (rs5498) in *ICAM1* with WMH burden,[76] and this association was replicated at a nominal significance level ($p = .006$) in a recent GWAS of WMH burden (see Section 10.5).[20]

Genes of Homocysteine Metabolism

Serum homocysteine levels have been shown to be correlated positively with WMH burden, whereas folate levels are correlated inversely[107] This has led to the investigation of methylenetetrahydrofolate reductase (*MTHFR*) gene polymorphisms with WMH burden, as the polymorphisms (rs1801133 and rs1801131) of *MTHFR* are associated with homocysteine levels. Three studies have shown an association of the variant rs1801133 (C677T) with WMH burden when comparing the homozygotes carriers of the T allele with the rest.[83,84,108] However a meta-analysis of these three studies for allele-based associations (additive model) did not find any significant association.[78]

Genes Involved in Vascular Dysfunction

NOTCH3 plays a key role in the functional and structural integrity of small arteries, and mutations in *NOTCH3* are causal for cerebral autosomal dominant arteriopathy with subcortical infarcts and leukoencephalopathy, a monogenic form of SVD. Schmidt et al.[109] sequenced all the 33 exons, promoter, and 3′ untranslated region of this gene in a subset of 277 subjects of ASPS.

They showed that four (rs1043994, rs10404382, rs10423702, and rs1043997) of the nine common variants detected by them were associated with WMH burden in subjects with hypertension ($N = 877$, present in their entire cohort), and replicated their most significantly associated SNP (rs10404382) in the Cohorts for Heart and Ageing Research in Genomic Epidemiology (CHARGE) Consortium, comprising 4773 individuals with hypertension who were stroke free. They also showed that subjects with severe WMH burden more often have *NOTCH3* nonsynonymous SNPs predicted to be deleterious.[109]

Most important, most candidate gene association studies were performed in small samples and did not include a preplanned replication in independent samples. Systematic reviews and meta-analyses have not been able to confirm associations of most candidate genes,[78,110] as has been the case for all complex traits.[111]

CANDIDATE GENE-BASED STUDIES FOR BIS

Because WMHs and SSBIs share common risk factors, especially age and hypertension, some of the candidate genes investigated in association with SSBIs overlap with those investigated in association with WMHs. Of note, several studies have examined associations with all BIs and not specifically SSBIs (a marker of SVD), although the latter represents a vast majority (>70%) of BIs in the general population (Table 10.3).

Genes of Cholesterol Regulation

A recent, large-scale meta-analysis of published and two unpublished studies has reported association of the *APOE* ε2 allele with all BIs.[88] The same meta-analysis did not observe any significant association of *APOE* ε4 with all BIs. Results on SSBIs were not available.

Genes Involved in Blood Pressure Regulation

Variants in *ACE, AGT,* and *ADD1* have been shown to be associated with BIs.[79,85,95,112,113] However a meta-analysis of these studies gives little support for the association of these genes with BIs and suggests publication bias resulting from small sample sizes.[110]

Genes Involved in Vascular Dysfunction

A study investigated associations of polymorphisms in *PRKCH* with BIs in a Japanese population (295 patients with BIs vs. 497 control subjects, no replication) and found the associations to be significant under a dominant model of inheritance.[98] *PRKCH* polymorphisms were also shown earlier to be associated with the SVD subtype of ischemic stroke in a Japanese population.[114] However, a recent, large-scale meta-analysis by the METASTROKE consortium[115] failed to replicate the association of *PRKCH* polymorphisms with the SVD subtype of ischemic stroke in populations of European origin. The association of *PRKCH* polymorphisms with MRI-defined SSBIs has not yet been verified in independent Asian and non-Asian samples, to our knowledge.

Genes Involved in Clotting

Fibrinogen has both inflammatory and hemostatic properties, and its higher plasma levels have been associated with an increased risk of coronary artery disease, ischemic stroke, and dementia.[116,117] In the Rotterdam scan study, one haplotype spanning seven common polymorphisms in the fibrinogen genes (*FGG* and *FGA,* "GATAGTG") was found to be more frequent in 213 subjects with MRI-defined BIs than in 864 control subjects.[99] One variant in this haplotype (rs2066861) reached nominal significance ($p = .04$) in association with MRI-defined BIs in a GWAS of MRI-defined BIs (see Section 10.5).[28]

MicroRNA Genes

MicroRNAs (miRNAs) are a class of endogenous, small, noncoding RNAs that play an important role in gene regulation. Four polymorphisms in four miRNAs (miR-146aG, miR-149T, miR-196a2C, and miR-499G) have been shown to be associated with cancer and Moyamoya disease,[118–121] and to affect response to vascular damage.[122–125] A study investigated association of these four polymorphisms with silent BIs in a South Korean population (373 patients with SSBI vs. 553 control subjects).[100] Although none of the four polymorphisms was associated with BIs individually, combinations of their alleles into a genetic risk score was associated with BIs. This result has not yet been confirmed.

CANDIDATE GENE-BASED STUDIES FOR CEREBRAL MICROBLEEDS

Two large meta-analyses have found the *APOE* ε4 allele to be associated strongly with the risk of cerebral microbleeds.[88,126] This association was stronger for microbleeds in the lobar region of the brain and is in agreement with the strong association of the *APOE* ε4 locus with ICH and cerebral amyloid angiopathy.[101,106,127–129] Large studies on the association of other genetic variants with microbleeds are lacking. Homozygous carrier status of variant alleles in four SNPs (rs1699102, rs3824968, rs2282649, and rs1010159) near *SORL1*, another gene in the amyloid pathway, was found to be associated with microbleeds in a small family-based sample from a genetically isolated Dutch population ($N = 129$), but these findings have not yet been replicated.[130]

Genomewide Association Studies of SVD

Candidate gene association studies are unable to identify novel genetic variants involved in unsuspected pathways because they are based on what is already known or suspected about the pathophysiology of a disease.[131] GWASs offer a solution to this problem by genotyping large numbers of SNPs (up to 5 million) distributed across the chromosomes without requiring any a priori hypothesis. During the past 7 years, they have been applied to a number of complex diseases and they enabled the identification of thousands of robust genetic associations with more than 300 complex diseases and traits, including various age-related neurological disorders.[115,132–135] Some of these discoveries have also resulted in the identification of drug targets and in improved disease classification, although clinical applications are still limited.[136,137] This new approach may be equally well suited to MRI markers of SVD, if sufficiently large populations can be collected. So far, only two GWASs of MRI markers of SVD have been completed—one on BIs and another on WMH burden.[20,26]

The GWAS meta-analysis on BIs included 9401 participants (1822 patients with BI vs. 7579 control subjects) from seven population-based cohorts of European origin participating in the CHARGE Consortium.[26] This first GWAS meta-analysis of MRI-defined BIs did not include specific analyses of SSBIs. This GWAS identified variants with suggestive association on chromosome 20p12. The index SNP in the locus 20p12 (rs2208454) is located in intron 3 of the MACRO domain containing 2, or *MACROD2*, and is downstream of fibronectin leucine-rich transmembrane protein 3, or *FLRT3*. However, the association of rs2208454 was not replicated in an independent sample of Europeans and blacks. Four SNPs in weak LD with rs2208454 were associated nominally with BIs in the independent black sample.[26]

The GWAS meta-analysis of WMH burden was also performed on the same seven population-based cohorts as the BI GWAS and included 9361 study participants.[20] Because WMH burden was estimated on different scales (microliters or unitless grades) in the various cohorts, the association statistics of individual studies were combined using random effect meta-analysis. This GWAS identified variants on chromosome 17q25 to be associated significantly with WMH burden ($p = 4 \times 10^{-15}$) and replicated the same successfully in two independent cohorts comprising 3024 subjects. Three other studies (two of European subjects and one of Japanese participants) have shown the same variants in this locus to be associated with WMH burden.[138–140] The 100-kb region of the 17q25 locus that is associated with WMH burden has several genes of various functions. The index SNP rs3744028 of this region is located in intron 2 of the tripartite motif-containing 65 gene, or *TRIM65*. Gene expression studies on HapMap lymphoblastoid cells have shown that the index SNP in this locus is associated with the expression of *TRIM47*.[140] The RING domain of TRIM47 has protein ubiquitination properties that promote proteolysis and cellular homestasis.[141] Ubiquitin–proteasome pathways play an important role in cerebral ischemic injury mechanisms and WMH expression profiles.[142,143] Other genes of interest in the 17q25 locus include *ACOX1* and *UNC13D*, which are associated with rare white matter diseases.[144] Fine mapping of the region (e.g., through targeted sequencing), as well as functional studies, are needed to dissect further the mechanisms underlying the relation between the chromosome 17q25 locus and WMH burden.

Of note, in this first GWAS of WMH burden, associations with 22 previously described candidate genetic variants were explored, in a much larger sample size than the original studies ($N = 9361$). This approach provided only weak evidence for replication of *AGT* polymorphism rs699 ($p = .01$) and *ICAM1* polymorphism rs5498 ($p = .006$), which did not withstand correction for multiple testing.

Lessons Learned, Future Perspectives, and Implications

Despite high heritability estimates, so far only a few genes have been identified that show robust associations with MRI markers of SVD. The lack of large, well-planned studies with preplanned replication, and heterogeneity in defining the phenotype, may have contributed to inconsistent findings across studies. Recently, this has prompted international expert panels to provide a uniform definition and terminology for MRI markers of SVD.[13]

Large collaborative efforts are ongoing as part of large consortia (CHARGE Consortium, International Stroke Genetic Consortium) to expand the search for common and rare variants associated with MRI markers of SVD. These efforts include additional GWASs on large samples, including cohorts of non-European ethnicity, as well as analyses of associations with rare variants through exome-chip genotyping and next-generation sequencing. Structural variants such as insertions/deletions, copy number variations, and repeat polymorphisms have been shown to be involved in many neurological conditions and should not be neglected as MRI markers of SVD. Last, exploring the genetic determinants of novel, cutting-edge MRI markers of SVD—such as subtle changes in white matter microstructure on diffusion tensor imaging or burden of dilated perivascular spaces, including in younger populations that have had less exposure to environmental risk factors—may provide important additional insight into the genetics of MRI markers of SVD.

REFERENCES

1. Pantoni L. Cerebral small vessel disease: from pathogenesis and clinical characteristics to therapeutic challenges. *Lancet Neurol.* 2010;9:689–701.
2. Debette S, Markus HS. The clinical importance of white matter hyperintensities on brain magnetic resonance imaging: systematic review and meta-analysis. *BMJ.* 2010;341:c3666.

3. Vermeer SE, Longstreth WT Jr, Koudstaal PJ. Silent brain infarcts: a systematic review. *Lancet Neurol.* 2007;6:611–619.
4. Norrving B. Lacunar infarcts: no black holes in the brain are benign. *Pract Neurol.* 2008;8:222–228.
5. Gorelick PB, Scuteri A, Black SE, et al. Vascular contributions to cognitive impairment and dementia: a statement for healthcare professionals from the American Heart Association/American Stroke Association. *Stroke.* 2011;42:2672–2713.
6. van der Flier WM, van Straaten EC, Barkhof F, et al. Small vessel disease and general cognitive function in nondisabled elderly: the LADIS study. *Stroke.* 2005;36:2116–2120.
7. Longstreth WT Jr. Brain vascular disease overt and covert. *Stroke.* 2005;36:2062–2063.
8. Launer LJ. Epidemiology of white matter lesions. *Top Magn Reson Imaging.* 2004;15:365–367.
9. Zhu YC, Dufouil C, Soumare A, Mazoyer B, Chabriat H, Tzourio C. High degree of dilated Virchow-Robin spaces on MRI is associated with increased risk of dementia. *J Alzheimers Dis.* 2010;22:663–672.
10. Greenberg SM, Vernooij MW, Cordonnier C, et al. Cerebral microbleeds: a guide to detection and interpretation. *Lancet Neurol.* 2009;8:165–174.
11. Poels MM, Ikram MA, van der Lugt A, et al. Cerebral microbleeds are associated with worse cognitive function: the Rotterdam Scan Study. *Neurology.* 2012;78:326–333.
12. Vermeer SE, Prins ND, den Heijer T, Hofman A, Koudstaal PJ, Breteler MM. Silent brain infarcts and the risk of dementia and cognitive decline. *N Engl J Med.* 2003;348:1215–1222.
13. Wardlaw JM, Smith EE, Biessels GJ, et al. Neuroimaging standards for research into small vessel disease and its contribution to ageing and neurodegeneration. *Lancet Neurol.* 2013;12:822–838.
14. Kovacs KR, Czuriga D, Bereczki D, Bornstein NM, Csiba L. Silent brain infarction: a review of recent observations. *Int J Stroke.* 2013;8:334–347.
15. Bernick C, Kuller L, Dulberg C, et al. Silent MRI infarcts and the risk of future stroke: the Cardiovascular Health Study. *Neurology.* 2001;57:1222–1229.
16. Vermeer SE, Den Heijer T, Koudstaal PJ, Oudkerk M, Hofman A, Breteler MM. Incidence and risk factors of silent brain infarcts in the population-based Rotterdam Scan Study. *Stroke.* 2003;34:392–396.
17. Fazekas F, Kleinert R, Offenbacher H, et al. Pathologic correlates of incidental MRI white matter signal hyperintensities. *Neurology.* 1993;43:1683–1689.
18. Pantoni L, Garcia JH. Pathogenesis of leukoaraiosis: a review. *Stroke.* 1997;28:652–659.
19. Wen W, Sachdev PS, Li JJ, Chen X, Anstey KJ. White matter hyperintensities in the forties: their prevalence and topography in an epidemiological sample aged 44–48. *Hum Brain Mapp.* 2009;30:1155–1167.
20. Fornage M, Debette S, Bis JC, et al. Genome-wide association studies of cerebral white matter lesion burden: the CHARGE Consortium. *Ann Neurol.* 2011;69:928–939.
21. Maillard P, Delcroix N, Crivello F, et al. An automated procedure for the assessment of white matter hyperintensities by multispectral (T1, T2, PD) MRI and an evaluation of its between-centre reproducibility based on two large community databases. *Neuroradiology.* 2008;50:31–42.
22. Scheltens P, Barkhof F, Leys D, et al. A semiquantative rating scale for the assessment of signal hyperintensities on magnetic resonance imaging. *J Neurol Sci.* 1993;114:7–12.
23. Fazekas F, Kapeller P, Schmidt R, Offenbacher H, Payer F, Fazekas G. The relation of cerebral magnetic resonance signal hyperintensities to Alzheimer's disease. *J Neurol Sci.* 1996;142:121–125.
24. Gottesman RF, Coresh J, Catellier DJ, et al. Blood pressure and white-matter disease progression in a biethnic cohort: Atherosclerosis Risk in Communities (ARIC) study. *Stroke.* 2010;41:3–8.
25. Fisher CM. Lacunes: small, deep cerebral infarcts. *Neurology.* 1965;15:774–784.
26. Seshadri S, Beiser A, Pikula A, et al. Parental occurrence of stroke and risk of stroke in their children: the Framingham study. *Circulation.* 2010;121:1304–1312.

27. Saini M, Ikram K, Hilal S, Qiu A, Venketasubramanian N, Chen C. Silent stroke: not listened to rather than silent. *Stroke.* 2012;43:3102–3104.
28. Debette S, Bis JC, Fornage M, et al. Genome-wide association studies of MRI-defined brain infarcts: meta-analysis from the CHARGE Consortium. *Stroke.* 2010;41:210–217.
29. Fazekas F, Kleinert R, Roob G, et al. Histopathologic analysis of foci of signal loss on gradient-echo T2*-weighted MR images in patients with spontaneous intracerebral hemorrhage: evidence of microangiopathy-related microbleeds. *AJNR Am J Neuroradiol.* 1999;20:637–642.
30. Fiehler J. Cerebral microbleeds: old leaks and new haemorrhages. *Int J Stroke.* 2006;1:122–130.
31. Jeerakathil T, Wolf PA, Beiser A, et al. Cerebral microbleeds: prevalence and associations with cardiovascular risk factors in the Framingham study. *Stroke.* 2004;35:1831–1835.
32. Cordonnier C, Al-Shahi Salman R, Wardlaw J. Spontaneous brain microbleeds: systematic review, subgroup analyses and standards for study design and reporting. *Brain.* 2007;130:1988–2003.
33. Sveinbjornsdottir S, Sigurdsson S, Aspelund T, et al. Cerebral microbleeds in the population based Ages–Reykjavik study: prevalence and location. *J Neurol Neurosurg Psychiatry.* 2008;79:1002–1006.
34. Ikram MA, van der Lugt A, Niessen WJ, et al. The Rotterdam Scan Study: design and update up to 2012. *Eur J Epidemiol.* 2011;26:811–824.
35. Akoudad S, Ikram MA, Koudstaal PJ, Hofman A, van der Lugt A, Vernooij MW. Cerebral microbleeds and the risk of mortality in the general population. *Eur J Epidemiol.* 2013;28:815–821.
36. Assareh A, Mather KA, Schofield PR, Kwok JB, Sachdev PS. The genetics of white matter lesions. *CNS Neurosci Ther.* 2011;17:525–540.
37. Bersano A, Debette S, Zanier ER, et al. The genetics of small-vessel disease. *Curr Med Chem.* 2012;19:4124–4141.
38. Carmelli D, DeCarli C, Swan GE, et al. Evidence for genetic variance in white matter hyperintensity volume in normal elderly male twins. *Stroke.* 1998;29:1177–1181.
39. Reed T, Kirkwood SC, DeCarli C, et al. Relationship of family history scores for stroke and hypertension to quantitative measures of white-matter hyperintensities and stroke volume in elderly males. *Neuroepidemiology.* 2000;19:76–86.
40. Turner ST, Jack CR, Fornage M, Mosley TH, Boerwinkle E, de Andrade M. Heritability of leukoaraiosis in hypertensive sibships. *Hypertension.* 2004;43:483–487.
41. Atwood LD, Wolf PA, Heard-Costa NL, et al. Genetic variation in white matter hyperintensity volume in the Framingham study. *Stroke.* 2004;35:1609–1613.
42. Kochunov P, Glahn D, Winkler A, et al. Analysis of genetic variability and whole genome linkage of whole-brain, subcortical, and ependymal hyperintense white matter volume. *Stroke.* 2009;40:3685–3690.
43. Leistner S, Huebner N, Faulstich A, et al. Increased prevalence of microangiopathic brain lesions among siblings of patients with lacunar stroke: a prospective multicenter study. *Eur Neurol.* 2008;59:143–147.
44. Morrison AC, Fornage M, Liao D, Boerwinkle E. Parental history of stroke predicts subclinical but not clinical stroke: the Atherosclerosis Risk in Communities study. *Stroke.* 2000;31:2098–2102.
45. Joutel A, Corpechot C, Ducros A, et al. *Notch3* mutations in CADASIL, a hereditary adult-onset condition causing stroke and dementia. *Nature.* 1996;383:707–710.
46. Chabriat H, Joutel A, Dichgans M, Tournier-Lasserve E, Bousser MG. CADASIL. *Lancet Neurol.* 2009;8:643–653.
47. Hara K, Shiga A, Fukutake T, et al. Association of *HTRA1* mutations and familial ischemic cerebral small-vessel disease. *N Engl J Med.* 2009;360:1729–1739.
48. Fukutake T. Cerebral autosomal recessive arteriopathy with subcortical infarcts and leukoencephalopathy (CARASIL): from discovery to gene identification. *J Stroke Cerebrovasc Dis.* 2011;20:85–93.

49. Jen J, Cohen AH, Yue Q, et al. Hereditary endotheliopathy with retinopathy, nephropathy, and stroke (HERNS). *Neurology.* 1997;49:1322–1330.
50. Terwindt GM, Haan J, Ophoff RA, et al. Clinical and genetic analysis of a large Dutch family with autosomal dominant vascular retinopathy, migraine and Raynaud's phenomenon. *Brain.* 1998;121:303–316.
51. Ophoff RA, DeYoung J, Service SK, et al. Hereditary vascular retinopathy, cerebroretinal vasculopathy, and hereditary endotheliopathy with retinopathy, nephropathy, and stroke map to a single locus on chromosome 3p21.1-p21.3. *Am J Hum Genet.* 2001;69:447–453.
52. Richards A, van den Maagdenberg AM, Jen JC, et al. C-terminal truncations in human 3′-5′ DNA exonuclease *TREX1* cause autosomal dominant retinal vasculopathy with cerebral leukodystrophy. *Nat Genet.* 2007;39:1068–1070.
53. Revesz T, Ghiso J, Lashley T, et al. Cerebral amyloid angiopathies: a pathologic, biochemical, and genetic view. *J Neuropathol Exp Neurol.* 2003;62:885–898.
54. Revesz T, Holton JL, Lashley T, et al. Genetics and molecular pathogenesis of sporadic and hereditary cerebral amyloid angiopathies. *Acta Neuropathol.* 2009;118:115–130.
55. Biffi A, Anderson CD, Jagiella JM, et al. APOE genotype and extent of bleeding and outcome in lobar intracerebral haemorrhage: a genetic association study. *Lancet Neurol.* 2011;10:702–709.
56. Gould DB, Phalan FC, van Mil SE, et al. Role of COL4A1 in small-vessel disease and hemorrhagic stroke. *N Engl J Med.* 2006;354:1489–1496.
57. Volonghi I, Pezzini A, Del Zotto E, et al. Role of COL4A1 in basement-membrane integrity and cerebral small-vessel disease: the COL4A1 stroke syndrome. *Curr Med Chem.* 2010;17:1317–1324.
58. Lanfranconi S, Markus HS. COL4A1 mutations as a monogenic cause of cerebral small vessel disease: a systematic review. *Stroke.* 2010;41:e513–e518.
59. Germain DP. Fabry disease. *Orphanet J Rare Dis.* 2010;5:30.
60. Pastores GM, Lien YH. Biochemical and molecular genetic basis of Fabry disease. *J Am Soc Nephrol.* 2002;13(Suppl 2):S130–S133.
61. Rolfs A, Bottcher T, Zschiesche M, et al. Prevalence of Fabry disease in patients with cryptogenic stroke: a prospective study. *Lancet.* 2005;366:1794–1796.
62. Sims K, Politei J, Banikazemi M, Lee P. Stroke in Fabry disease frequently occurs before diagnosis and in the absence of other clinical events: natural history data from the Fabry Registry. *Stroke.* 2009;40:788–794.
63. Clayton DA, Vinograd J. Circular dimer and catenate forms of mitochondrial DNA in human leukaemic leucocytes. *Nature.* 1967;216:652–657.
64. Hirano M, Ricci E, Koenigsberger MR, et al. MELAS: an original case and clinical criteria for diagnosis. *Neuromuscul Disord.* 1992;2:125–135.
65. Sproule DM, Kaufmann P. Mitochondrial encephalopathy, lactic acidosis, and strokelike episodes: basic concepts, clinical phenotype, and therapeutic management of MELAS syndrome. *Ann N Y Acad Sci.* 2008;1142:133–158.
66. Majamaa K, Turkka J, Karppa M, Winqvist S, Hassinen IE. The common MELAS mutation a3243g in mitochondrial DNA among young patients with an occipital brain infarct. *Neurology.* 1997;49:1331–1334.
67. McCarthy MI. Genomics, type 2 diabetes, and obesity. *N Engl J Med.* 2010;363:2339–2350.
68. Dawn Teare M, Barrett JH. Genetic linkage studies. *Lancet.* 2005;366:1036–1044.
69. Turner ST, Fornage M, Jack CR Jr, et al. Genomic susceptibility loci for brain atrophy in hypertensive sibships from the Genoa study. *Hypertension.* 2005;45:793–798.
70. DeStefano AL, Atwood LD, Massaro JM, et al. Genome-wide scan for white matter hyperintensity: the Framingham Heart Study. *Stroke.* 2006;37:77–81.
71. Seshadri S, DeStefano AL, Au R, et al. Genetic correlates of brain aging on MRI and cognitive test measures: a genome-wide association and linkage analysis in the Framingham study. *BMC Med Genet.* 2007;8(Suppl 1):S15.

72. Turner ST, Fornage M, Jack CR Jr, et al. Genomic susceptibility loci for brain atrophy, ventricular volume, and leukoaraiosis in hypertensive sibships. *Arch Neurol.* 2009;66:847–857.
73. Kochunov P, Glahn D, Lancaster J, et al. Whole brain and regional hyperintense white matter volume and blood pressure: overlap of genetic loci produced by bivariate, whole-genome linkage analyses. *Stroke.* 2010;41:2137–2142.
74. Risch N, Merikangas K. The future of genetic studies of complex human diseases. *Science.* 1996;273:1516–1517.
75. Smith JA, Turner ST, Sun YV, et al. Complexity in the genetic architecture of leukoaraiosis in hypertensive sibships from the Genoa study. *BMC Med Genom.* 2009;2:16.
76. Han JH, Huang YY, Luo YM, Ding D, Hong Z. Association between intercellular adhesion molecule-1 K469E polymorphism and white matter lesions in asymptomatic elderly people. *Chin J Neurol.* 2005;38:23.
77. Fornage M, Mosley TH, Jack CR, et al. Family-based association study of matrix metalloproteinase-3 and -9 haplotypes with susceptibility to ischemic white matter injury. *Hum Genet.* 2007;120:671–680.
78. Paternoster L, Chen W, Sudlow CL. Genetic determinants of white matter hyperintensities on brain scans: a systematic assessment of 19 candidate gene polymorphisms in 46 studies in 19,000 subjects. *Stroke.* 2009;40:2020–2026.
79. van Rijn MJ, Bos MJ, Yazdanpanah M, et al. Alpha-adducin polymorphism, atherosclerosis, and cardiovascular and cerebrovascular risk. *Stroke.* 2006;37:2930–2934.
80. Taylor WD, Steffens DC, Ashley-Koch A, et al. Angiotensin receptor gene polymorphisms and 2-year change in hyperintense lesion volume in men. *Mol Psychiatry.* 2010;15:816–822.
81. Brenner D, Labreuche J, Pico F, et al. The renin–angiotensin–aldosterone system in cerebral small vessel disease. *J Neurol.* 2008;255:993–1000.
82. Verpillat P, Alperovitch A, Cambien F, Besancon V, Desal H, Tzourio C. Aldosterone synthase (cyp11b2) gene polymorphism and cerebral white matter hyperintensities. *Neurology.* 2001;56:673–675.
83. Hassan A, Hunt BJ, O'Sullivan M, et al. Homocysteine is a risk factor for cerebral small vessel disease, acting via endothelial dysfunction. *Brain.* 2004;127:212–219.
84. Kohara K, Fujisawa M, Ando F, et al. *MTHFR* gene polymorphism as a risk factor for silent brain infarcts and white matter lesions in the Japanese general population: the NILS-LSA study. *Stroke.* 2003;34:1130–1135.
85. Szolnoki Z, Somogyvari F, Kondacs A, Szabo M, Fodor L. Evaluation of the roles of common genetic mutations in leukoaraiosis. *Acta Neurol Scand.* 2001;104:281–287.
86. Linnebank M, Moskau S, Jurgens A, et al. Association of genetic variants of methionine metabolism with methotrexate-induced CNS white matter changes in patients with primary CNS lymphoma. *Neurol Oncol.* 2009;11:2–8.
87. Fornage M, Chiang YA, O'Meara ES, et al. Biomarkers of inflammation and MRI-defined small vessel disease of the brain: the Cardiovascular Health Study. *Stroke.* 2008;39:1952–1959.
88. Schilling S, DeStefano AL, Sachdev PS, et al. APOE genotype and MRI markers of cerebrovascular disease: systematic review and meta-analysis. *Neurology.* 2013;81:292–300.
89. Qureischie H, Heun R, Popp J, et al. Association of CETP polymorphisms with the risk of vascular dementia and white matter lesions. *J Neural Transm.* 2009;116:467–472.
90. Henskens LH, Kroon AA, van Boxtel MP, Hofman PA, de Leeuw PW. Associations of the angiotensin II type 1 receptor a1166c and the endothelial NO synthase g894t gene polymorphisms with silent subcortical white matter lesions in essential hypertension. *Stroke.* 2005;36:1869–1873.
91. Schmidt R, Schmidt H, Fazekas F, et al. MRI cerebral white matter lesions and paraoxonase PON1 polymorphisms: three-year follow-up of the Austrian Stroke Prevention Study. *Arterioscler Thromb Vasc Biol.* 2000;20:1811–1816.

92. Taylor WD, Zuchner S, McQuoid DR, et al. The brain-derived neurotrophic factor Val66Met polymorphism and cerebral white matter hyperintensities in late-life depression. *Am J Geriatr Psychiatry*. 2008;16:263–271.
93. Schmidt H, Zeginigg M, Wiltgen M, et al. Genetic variants of the *Notch3* gene in the elderly and magnetic resonance imaging correlates of age-related cerebral small vessel disease. *Brain*. 2011;134:3384–3397.
94. Morrison AC, Ballantyne CM, Bray M, Chambless LE, Sharrett AR, Boerwinkle E. LPl polymorphism predicts stroke risk in men. *Genet Epidemiol*. 2002;22:233–242.
95. van Rijn MJ, Bos MJ, Isaacs A, et al. Polymorphisms of the renin–angiotensin system are associated with blood pressure, atherosclerosis and cerebral white matter pathology. *J Neurol Neurosurg Psychiatry*. 2007;78:1083–1087.
96. Song J, Kim OJ, Kim HS, et al. Endothelial nitric oxide synthase gene polymorphisms and the risk of silent brain infarction. *Int J Mol Med*. 2010;25:819–823.
97. Jenny NS, Tracy RP, Ogg MS, et al. In the elderly, interleukin-6 plasma levels and the -174g>c polymorphism are associated with the development of cardiovascular disease. *Arteriosd Thromb Vasc Biol*. 2002;22:2066–2071.
98. Serizawa M, Nabika T, Ochiai Y, et al. Association between *PRKCH* gene polymorphisms and subcortical silent brain infarction. *Atherosclerosis*. 2008;199:340–345.
99. van Oijen M, Cheung EY, Geluk CE, et al. Haplotypes of the fibrinogen gene and cerebral small vessel disease: the Rotterdam Scan Study. *J Neurol Neurosurg Psychiatry*. 2008;79:799–803.
100. Jeon YJ, Kim OJ, Kim SY, et al. Association of the miR-146a, miR-149, miR-196a2, and miR-499 polymorphisms with ischemic stroke and silent brain infarction risk. *Arterioscler Thromb Vasc Biol*. 2013;33:420–430.
101. Tzourio C, Arima H, Harrap S, et al. APOE genotype, ethnicity, and the risk of cerebral hemorrhage. *Neurology*. 2008;70:1322–1328.
102. Boyle PA, Buchman AS, Wilson RS, Kelly JF, Bennett DA. The APOE epsilon4 allele is associated with incident mild cognitive impairment among community-dwelling older persons. *Neuroepidemiology*. 2010;34:43–49.
103. Ken-Dror G, Talmud PJ, Humphries SE, Drenos F. APOE/c1/c4/c2 gene cluster genotypes, haplotypes and lipid levels in prospective coronary heart disease risk among UK healthy men. *Mol Med*. 2010;16:389–399.
104. Schmidt H, Schmidt R, Fazekas F, et al. Apolipoprotein E ε4 allele in the normal elderly: neuropsychologic and brain MRI correlates. *Clin Genet*. 1996;50:293–299.
105. Ballard C, Gauthier S, Corbett A, Brayne C, Aarsland D, Jones E. Alzheimer's disease. *Lancet*. 2011;377:1019–1031.
106. Biffi A, Sonni A, Anderson CD, et al. Variants at APOE influence risk of deep and lobar intracerebral hemorrhage. *Ann Neurol*. 2010;68:934–943.
107. Sachdev P, Parslow R, Salonikas C, et al. Homocysteine and the brain in midadult life: evidence for an increased risk of leukoaraiosis in men. *Arch Neurol*. 2004;61:1369–1376.
108. Szolnoki Z, Somogyvari F, Kondacs A, et al. Specific Apo E genotypes in combination with the ACE D/D or MTHFR 677tt mutation yield an independent genetic risk of leukoaraiosis. *Acta Neurol Scand*. 2004;109:222–227.
109. Schmidt H, Zeginigg M, Wiltgen M, et al. Genetic variants of the *Notch3* gene in the elderly and magnetic resonance imaging correlates of age-related cerebral small vessel disease. *Brain*. 2011;134:3384–3397.
110. Markus HS. Genes, endothelial function and cerebral small vessel disease in man. *Exp Physiol*. 2008;93:121–127.
111. Hirschhorn JN, Lohmueller K, Byrne E, Hirschhorn K. A comprehensive review of genetic association studies. *Genet Med*. 2002;4:45–61.

112. Schmidt H, Fazekas F, Kostner GM, van Duijn CM, Schmidt R. Angiotensinogen gene promoter haplotype and microangiopathy-related cerebral damage: results of the Austrian Stroke Prevention Study. *Stroke.* 2001;32:405–412.
113. Schmidt R, Schmidt H, Fazekas F, et al. Angiotensinogen polymorphism m235t, carotid atherosclerosis, and small-vessel disease-related cerebral abnormalities. *Hypertension.* 2001;38:110–115.
114. Kubo M, Hata J, Ninomiya T, et al. A nonsynonymous SNP in PRKCH (protein kinase C eta) increases the risk of cerebral infarction. *Nat Genet.* 2007;39:212–217.
115. Traylor M, Farrall M, Holliday EG, et al. Genetic risk factors for ischaemic stroke and its subtypes (the METASTROKE collaboration): a meta-analysis of genome-wide association studies. *Lancet Neurol.* 2012;11:951–962.
116. Danesh J, Lewington S, Thompson SG, et al. Plasma fibrinogen level and the risk of major cardiovascular diseases and nonvascular mortality: an individual participant meta-analysis. *JAMA.* 2005;294:1799–1809.
117. van Oijen M, Witteman JC, Hofman A, Koudstaal PJ, Breteler MM. Fibrinogen is associated with an increased risk of Alzheimer disease and vascular dementia. *Stroke.* 2005;36:2637–2641.
118. Ryan BM, Robles AI, Harris CC. Genetic variation in microRNA networks: the implications for cancer research. *Nat Rev Cancer.* 2010;10:389–402.
119. Min KT, Kim JW, Jeon YJ, et al. Association of the miR-146AC>G, 149C>T, 196A2C>T, and 499A>G polymorphisms with colorectal cancer in the Korean population. *Mol Carcinog.* 2012;51(Suppl 1):E65–E73.
120. Park YS, Jeon YJ, Lee BE, et al. Association of the miR-146AC>G, miR-196A2C>T, and miR-499A>G polymorphisms with Moyamoya disease in the Korean population. *Neurosci Lett.* 2012;521:71–75.
121. Wang AX, Xu B, Tong N, et al. Meta-analysis confirms that a common G/C variant in the pre-miR-146a gene contributes to cancer susceptibility and that ethnicity, gender and smoking status are risk factors. *Genet Mol Res.* 2012;11:3051–3062.
122. Luthra R, Singh RR, Luthra MG, et al. MicroRNA-196a targets annexin A1: a microRNA-mediated mechanism of annexin A1 downregulation in cancers. *Oncogene.* 2008;27:6667–6678.
123. El Gazzar M, Church A, Liu T, McCall CE. MicroRNA-146a regulates both transcription silencing and translation disruption of TNF-alpha during TLR4-induced gene reprogramming. *J Leukoc Biol.* 2011;90:509–519.
124. Yang B, Chen J, Li Y, et al. Association of polymorphisms in pre-miRNA with inflammatory biomarkers in rheumatoid arthritis in the Chinese Han population. *Hum Immunol.* 2012;73:101–106.
125. Wu C, Gong Y, Sun A, et al. The human MTHFR rs4846049 polymorphism increases coronary heart disease risk through modifying miRNA binding. *Nutr Metab Cardiovasc Dis.* 2013;23:693–698.
126. Maxwell SS, Jackson CA, Paternoster L, et al. Genetic associations with brain microbleeds: systematic review and meta-analyses. *Neurology.* 2011;77:158–167.
127. Premkumar DR, Cohen DL, Hedera P, Friedland RP, Kalaria RN. Apolipoprotein E-epsilon4 alleles in cerebral amyloid angiopathy and cerebrovascular pathology associated with Alzheimer's disease. *Am J Pathol.* 1996;148:2083–2095.
128. Sudlow C, Martinez Gonzalez NA, Kim J, Clark C. Does apolipoprotein E genotype influence the risk of ischemic stroke, intracerebral hemorrhage, or subarachnoid hemorrhage? Systematic review and meta-analyses of 31 studies among 5961 cases and 17,965 controls. *Stroke.* 2006;37:364–370.
129. Peck G, Smeeth L, Whittaker J, Casas JP, Hingorani A, Sharma P. The genetics of primary haemorrhagic stroke, subarachnoid haemorrhage and ruptured intracranial aneurysms in adults. *PLoS One.* 2008;3:e3691.

130. Schuur M, van Swieten JC, Schol-Gelok S, et al. Genetic risk factors for cerebral small-vessel disease in hypertensive patients from a genetically isolated population. *J Neurol Neurosurg Psychiatry.* 2011;82:41–44.
131. Zondervan KT, Cardon LR. Designing candidate gene and genome-wide case–control association studies. *Nat Protoc.* 2007;2:2492–2501.
132. McCarthy MI, Abecasis GR, Cardon LR, et al. Genome-wide association studies for complex traits: consensus, uncertainty and challenges. *Nat Rev Genet.* 2008;9:356–369.
133. Mowry BJ, Gratten J. The emerging spectrum of allelic variation in schizophrenia: current evidence and strategies for the identification and functional characterization of common and rare variants. *Mol Psychiatry.* 2013;18:38–52.
134. Visscher PM, Brown MA, McCarthy MI, Yang J. Five years of GWAS discovery. *Am J Hum Genet.* 2012;90:7–24.
135. Lambert JC, Ibrahim-Verbaas CA, Harold D, et al. Meta-analysis of 74,046 individuals identifies 11 new susceptibility loci for Alzheimer's disease. *Nat Genet.* 2013;45:1452–1458.
136. Okada Y, Wu D, Trynka G, et al. Genetics of rheumatoid arthritis contributes to biology and drug discovery. *Nature.* 2014;506:376–381.
137. Manolio TA. Bringing genome-wide association findings into clinical use. *Nat Rev Genet.* 2013;14:549–558.
138. Verhaaren BF, de Boer R, Vernooij MW, et al. Replication study of chr17q25 with cerebral white matter lesion volume. *Stroke.* 2011;42:3297–3299.
139. Tabara Y, Igase M, Okada Y, et al. Association of chr17q25 with cerebral white matter hyperintensities and cognitive impairment: the J-SHIPP Study. *Eur J Neurol.* 2013;20:860–862.
140. Adib-Samii P, Rost N, Traylor M, et al. 17q25 locus is associated with white matter hyperintensity volume in ischemic stroke, but not with lacunar stroke status. *Stroke.* 2013;44:1609–1615.
141 Di Napoli M, McLaughlin B. The ubiquitin–proteasome system as a drug target in cerebrovascular disease: therapeutic potential of proteasome inhibitors. *Curr Opin Investig Drugs.* 2005;6:686–699.
142. Meroni G, Diez-Roux G. TRIM/RBCC, a novel class of "single protein ring finger" e3 ubiquitin ligases. *Bioessays.* 2005;27:1147–1157.
143. Simpson JE, Hosny O, Wharton SB, et al. Microarray RNA expression analysis of cerebral white matter lesions reveals changes in multiple functional pathways. *Stroke.* 2009;40:369–375.
144. Aggarwal NT, De Jager PL. Uncovering the genetic architecture of white matter disease. *Ann Neurol.* 2011;69:907–908.

III

Environmental Risk Factors

11

INTRODUCTION TO ENVIRONMENTAL RISK FACTORS FOR CEREBROVASCULAR DISEASE

Didier Leys

DESPITE MAJOR IMPROVEMENTS made during the past 30 years in stroke prevention, overall stroke incidence is still increasing.[1] The major explanations are the longer life expectancy and increased survival rate after myocardial infarction and first-ever stroke. However, even after adjusting for age, the incidence of stroke is still increasing for ischemic stroke in men.[1] Besides genetic factors that cannot be modified, two categories of modifiable risk factors influence the incidence of stroke: (a) factors that can be modified by patients and physicians, and (b) environmental factors that can be influenced by the society.

Factors related to the patient, are the so-called "modifiable vascular risk factors." High blood pressure, diabetes mellitus, dyslipidemia, tobacco consumption, metabolic syndrome, obesity, excessive alcohol consumption, and estrogen therapy are the most important ones. These factors are major contributors to the occurrence of stroke, and their treatment is usually associated with a reduction of vascular events (i.e., stroke, coronary events, and vascular death). Interestingly, there are some indications that, for a few of these risks factors, their treatment is also associated with a reduction in stroke severity in case of such an event.[2] The management of these risk factors is the basis of primary and of secondary stroke prevention. In low-income countries, these factors can often be treated at a low cost. The effect of an optimal management of these factors is not dramatic at the individual level, and needs months or years to become statistically significant in trials. However, in the long-term, their management is probably the easiest, safest, and cheapest way to reduce the risk of both ischemic and hemorrhagic strokes. Unfortunately, many subjects in the population are not treated correctly, even after a first event.[3]

Factors related to the environment are diet, pollution, passive smoking, and climate. Individuals have almost no possibility of influencing these factors, but politicians can. For instance, campaigns against smoking, laws to prevent excessive intake of sugar in soft drinks, and campaigns promoting physical exercise are long-term measures that are supposed to prevent vascular events. The efficacy of these measures cannot be proved directly by randomized trials, but only by historical comparisons, and cannot have the greatest degree of evidence. However, they are probably the most effective to prevent vascular events on a large scale at the population level.

These so-called *environmental factors* are important because they are the most important targets for vascular prevention. However, similar risk factors do not have the same effect in each of us. This effect depends, probably, on the interaction of modifiable risk factors with many other factors that cannot be modified, such as genetic factors, ethnicity, age, and their association.

Currently, many strokes can be prevented by optimal management of modifiable vascular risk factors. The decision to treat or not to treat a risk factor is currently based on large trials performed in subjects at risk or in the general population. In the future, a more personalized approach could be used, taking into account not only the risk factor that should—or should not—be treated, but also the combination with other risk factors and the presence of nonmodifiable risk factors. This is the domain of personalized medicine.

REFERENCES

1. Khellaf M, Quantin C, d'Athis P, et al. Age-period-cohort analysis of stroke incidence in Dijon from 1985 to 2005. *Stroke*. 2010;41:2762–2767.
2. Deplanque D, Masse I, Lefebvre C, Libersa C, Leys D, Bordet R. Prior TIA, lipid-lowering drug use, and physical activity decrease ischemic stroke severity. *Neurology*. 2006;24;67:1403–1410.
3. Kotseva K, Wood D, De Backer G, et al. EUROASPIRE III: a survey on the lifestyle, risk factors and use of cardioprotective drug therapies in coronary patients from 22 European countries. *Eur J Cardiovasc Prev Rehabil*. 2009;16:121–137.

12

HYPERTENSION

The Major Risk Factor for Stroke

Jennifer L. Dearborn and Rebecca F. Gottesman

Introduction

Hypertension affects millions of individuals worldwide and is a growing epidemic in middle- and low-income countries, as well as in the United States and Europe.[1–3] In the United States alone, approximately 30% of adults are diagnosed with hypertension.[4,5] We now recognize that hypertension is the single most important modifiable risk factor for cerebrovascular disease, including ischemic stroke, hemorrhagic stroke, and small-vessel disease. Because almost three quarters of the world's population with hypertension live in resource-limited settings, low awareness of health risks related to elevated blood pressure is of increasing concern.[6] This knowledge gap emphasizes the need to create health systems to identify and treat hypertension, particularly given its close links with cerebrovascular disease.

The ancient Egyptians observed how to palpate pulses, but it was not until the middle of the 18th century that blood pressure was measured, through the experiments of Stephen Hales.[7] As a veterinarian, he performed a set of experiments during which observations were made about the variation in pulse pressure using a glass tube inserted into the artery of a horse. Hundreds of years later, using a standard sphygmomanometer, we now better understand the risk that blood pressure poses for the spectrum of vascular disease—from myocardial infarction and heart failure to stroke. Many large-scale prospective studies have helped to establish the link between elevated blood pressure and cerebrovascular disease. In this chapter, we discuss mechanisms of hypertension leading to stroke, and review major results from observational studies, meta-analyses, and clinical trials, incorporating data about intracranial hemorrhage and subclinical cerebrovascular disease.

Population Impact of Hypertension and Stroke

Hypertension is exceedingly common. In the years 2005 to 2008, 68 million adults older than 18 years in the United States were diagnosed with hypertension, which represents a prevalence of 31%.[5] Worldwide, about 639 million adults with hypertension live in developing countries, and this number is expected to increase.[6] In the United States, 70% of patients with hypertension are receiving treatment for hypertension, but only 48% (31 million) have their condition controlled.[5] Elevated blood pressure is linked closely to all stroke subtypes. Thus, it is likely that the growing rate of hypertension in this country is a large contributor to the 795,000 people in the United States who experience a new stroke each year.[8, 9]

EVIDENCE LINKING HYPERTENSION AND STROKE

Hypertension is the risk factor for stroke with the largest population-attributable risk (PAR).[10] The PAR is the proportion of a cohort with the outcome (in this case stroke) that is caused by a specific risk factor (in this case, hypertension). It is therefore a good estimate of the burden that the risk factor places on a population attributable to the disease in question. In the case of hypertension, the adjusted PAR for ischemic stroke has been estimated at 26%, with a 95% confidence interval (CI) of 12 to 41. As a comparison, the risk factor with the second highest PAR is history of prior transient ischemic attack (TIA), which carries a PAR of 14% (95% CI, 11–17).[10] The evidence demonstrating associations between hypertension and stroke is reviewed in the next section; trials of antihypertensive treatment are reviewed later in this chapter.

OBSERVATIONAL STUDIES

Starting in 1949, a population-based sample of adults age 30 to 69 years on enrollment were recruited into the Framingham cohort; members were monitored for the development of cardiovascular outcomes.[11] Over 50 years, stroke incidence declined but lifetime risk did not, which could be attributed to increased life expectancy.[12] In 1970, a 14-year interim analysis showed that stroke was more common in subjects with hypertension than in those without[11,13] and, more important, there was no blood pressure threshold critical to risk of developing stroke. As other studies have shown, as blood pressure increased (either systolic or diastolic), there was a log-linear increase in the relative risk for stroke.[14,15] These initial and, at that time, somewhat unexpected data, were reproduced in several studies and meta-analyses.[16,17] It is now estimated that for every 9/5 mmHg increase in usual blood pressure, there is approximately a one-third increase in stroke rate, and this holds for persons with hypertension as well as persons with lower blood pressures that would not reach a threshold of hypertension.[14] This emphasizes that there was no critical threshold of "safe" blood pressure, and that relative risk of stroke increases with higher blood pressures (in the entire blood pressure range studied).[15]

One of the most important meta-analyses in this area was the Prospective Trials Collaboration, which combined data on 1 million adults with vascular risk factors from 61 trials to evaluate associations between blood pressure and mortality.[18] This study of adults age 40 to 69 years found a two-fold difference in the stroke death rate for every 20 mmHg higher systolic blood pressure (SBP), and further confirmed that there was no threshold of increased risk, at least above the lower limit of SBP greater than 115 mmHg. This has important treatment implications, because it suggests there may be some benefit to lower blood pressure for preventing stroke mortality, even in normotensive adults. Trends are similar in the Asia Pacific region, as examined in a meta-analysis of 41 cohorts in which 82% of the subjects were Asian. There was a log-linear relationship between hypertension and stroke that closely paralleled the relationship between hypertension and cardiovascular disease.[19]

A controversy emerged when other observational studies demonstrated that a low diastolic blood pressure (DBP) was associated with increased risk of stroke. These data described a J-shaped curve between DBP and the risk of stroke—meaning, risk of stroke declined, before it increased again, as blood pressure increased, with the greatest risk of stroke at the extreme values of DBP. It was shown in the Rotterdam study that, in the subset of older adults (>55 years) who had treated hypertension, there was an increased risk of stroke in the lowest category of blood pressure.[20] The authors postulated that advanced atherosclerosis and stiff blood vessels could account for this difference, which was found only in the treated group; however, this relationship still held even with adjustment for cardiovascular risk factors, such as prior myocardial infarction. Several other small cohorts replicated this finding.[21] To address this discrepancy between studies showing a J curve and others that consistently showed a linear relationship, several meta-analyses were performed. One comprehensive meta-analysis of more than 48,000 subjects performed in 1991 showed there was not a consistent J-shaped relationship between DBP and stroke.[22] SBP components, however, have not been examined consistently across studies. A recent analysis found that all-cause vascular mortality followed a J curve with hypertension; however, the relationship between SBP and stroke did not follow this trend.[23] The current prevailing theory, as of the date of publication, is that the J curve may not hold for associations between blood pressure and stroke, and that there is not enough evidence of a critical threshold of blood pressure control beyond which harm is caused.[24]

COMPONENTS OF BLOOD PRESSURE IN RELATION TO STROKE

The Framingham cohort also elucidated that, although SBP and DBP are related to stroke incidence, DBP did not add any additional risk over that measured by the SBP if the DBP was less than 95 mmHg.[25] In fact, in subjects with elevated SBP, there was no increased risk conferred by DBP in men, and in women there was only a modest increased risk. The case is different, however, for those with isolated diastolic hypertension. The Perindopril Protection against Recurrent Stroke Study (PROGRESS) trial evaluated 923 individuals with a prior cerebrovascular event (defined as prior stroke or TIA, discussed later), of whom 315 had isolated diastolic hypertension.[26] Lowering blood pressure in those with diastolic hypertension prevented stroke recurrence. This is in accordance with data for other cardiovascular disease, for which it has been shown that the combination of SBP and DBP is superior in predicting the risk of cardiovascular disease than either component alone.[27]

The pulse pressure (PP) and the mean arterial pressure (MAP) are alternative means of expressing blood pressure. The PP is the SBP less DBP, or the pressure required to create the pulse. In younger subjects, a higher PP usually means that the left ventricular ejection fraction is increased, but in older subjects it can be a surrogate marker of arterial stiffness.[28] Blood pressure can also be understood as a steady component (the MAP), which is unchanged from heart beat to beat, and a variable component (the PP), which varies from beat to beat. The MAP is usually defined as the cardiac output times the systemic vascular resistance, which can be calculated directly by $\text{MAP} = \text{DBP} + \frac{1}{3(\text{SBP} - \text{DBP})}$.

There is some debate about whether the PP or the MAP, alone or together, are better predictors of stroke risk than SBP and DBP, and the data seem to suggest that the MAP may be a better measure for assessing risk of cerebrovascular disease than PP. In one study, however, the combination of the PP and the MAP was more robust in predicting cardiovascular disease than the PP, the MAP, SBP, or DBP alone. It was, however, only equivalent to SBP plus DBP in predicting risk.[27] The PP, however, may have an inverse correlation with stroke in women, and was not correlated significantly with stroke in men.[29] In another study, the PP and the MAP were associated independently with ischemic stroke, and the predictive value of the PP depended on the MAP.[30] One might expect that if the PP was, indeed, a good surrogate for arterial stiffness, or vascular disease, it would be more predictive of increased risk of stroke, but this was not the case. Instead, it is the steady-state component that seems to contribute more to the overall risk of stroke.

Blood pressure variability may also be important in increasing an individual's risk of stroke. Variability is measured as differences in mean blood pressure over time (residual standard deviation), often described as visit-to-visit variability and average differences in adjacent blood pressure readings (successive variation).[31] This definition highlights that some patients have episodic hypertension, and some guidelines recommend 24-hour ambulatory monitoring when variability is detected.[32,33] An increased hazard of stroke has been shown both in studies of variability as detected by ambulatory blood pressure monitoring as well as visit-to-visit variability, and has been independent of mean SBP.[34] More specifically, certain patterns of blood pressure variability may increase risk the most: the "morning surge" in blood pressure has been associated with stroke risk,[35] as has variation in the standard nocturnal dip in blood pressure seen in most individuals (either extreme dipping or lack of nocturnal dipping).[36] Orthostatic hypotension, defined as a decrease in SBP by at least 20 mmHg or a decrease in DBP by at least 10 mmHg, has also been associated with a twofold higher hazard of stroke in observational cohorts, independent of other stroke risk factors.[37] Last, differences in the visit-to-visit variability of blood pressure may account for differences in outcomes seen among trials comparing different antihypertensive agents.[38] Taken together, these data suggest that current methods of following mean blood pressure may miss a subpopulation of patients with high variability, in whom stroke risk is also increased.

OTHER CHARACTERISTICS OF BLOOD PRESSURE ASSOCIATED WITH INCREASED RISK OF STROKE

A longer length of exposure to hypertension increases the likelihood of having a stroke.[39] There is an interesting interaction between hypertension and age, however, with the odds ratio of stroke (at some point in a given individual's life) being about 5 at younger ages (50 years) if a person is hypertensive. This decreases gradually until 90 years of age, until there is no increase in risk conferred by hypertension.[10] These data would suggest that there is little benefit, in terms of stroke prevention, to treating hypertension in the very elderly. It may be that "the damage is already done"; clinical trials, however, do not clearly show the lack of a benefit in elderly patients (details discussed later).

Blacks in the United States have higher rates of hypertension than white Americans, and are at a greater risk than the general population of having negative outcomes from hypertension, including stroke.[40] It is particularly important to identify and treat, either through lifestyle modification or drug therapy, hypertension throughout the life span in this population, to reduce the burden of disease including stroke. In the United States, the rates of stroke in Native Americans, multiracial persons, and blacks are greater than those of white Americans, Asian Americans, or Hispanics. Black Americans had a threefold greater rate of lacunar strokes than white Americans.[8]

BLOOD PRESSURE AMONG INDIVIDUALS WITH HISTORY OF STROKE

There is evidence that hypertension is just as tightly tied to recurrent stroke as primary stroke, and that lowering blood pressure in this group is equally important as it is in individuals without history of stroke.[14] An analysis of a large cohort in the UK TIA and aspirin trial showed that each 10-mmHg decrease in SBP and 5-mmHg decrease in DBP after minor stroke or TIA was associated with about one third fewer recurrent strokes (34%; standard deviation, 7%).[41] This is a different result from several small studies that have shown a J-shaped relationship with blood pressure and recurrent stroke,[14] suggesting that a low blood pressure after stroke could actually increase risk for subsequent infarction.

These contradictory findings may be because the studies looked at different populations. It is also possible that low blood pressure immediately after stroke is detrimental to certain stroke subtypes, such as patients with a larger area of infarction, who are at risk of hypoperfusion to areas supplied by collateral blood flow. In addition, hypotension may be a marker of a more critically ill patient with a greater recurrent stroke risk because of underlying comorbidities. A typical TIA patient would not have any of these risks. Thus, in major stroke, it may be that low blood pressure is detrimental during the acute period (supported by the lack of a benefit in acute blood pressure lowering in stroke[42]), but in TIA or smaller volume strokes, or over a longer time period, there is a more linear relationship between blood pressure and stroke.

Stroke patients with major vessel intracranial stenosis are a unique subgroup who may have different blood pressure requirements for secondary prevention of stroke both acutely and long term. A decrease in blood pressure may, theoretically, cause hypoperfusion to a large territory of the brain, and therefore these patients may require a higher baseline blood pressure as their cerebral autoregulatory mechanisms are altered. How antihypertensives should be used in this population is uncertain. A meta-analysis of several trials has suggested that, although SBP is associated with recurrent stroke in moderate artery stenosis, this association disappeared with severe large-vessel stenosis (>70%).[43] This being said, an analysis of patients who received intravenous thrombolysis for acute stroke revealed that withholding antihypertensive therapy in known hypertensives in the 7 days immediately after stroke was associated with poor outcome.[44] All together, long-term blood pressure lowering in patients with prior stroke prevents recurrence, and how soon to initiate this therapy in certain subgroups remains to be determined.

Mechanisms of Hypertension and Stroke

There are different theories of how hypertension predisposes persons to an increased lifetime risk of stroke. Central to many of these theories is the idea that increased intraluminal pressure causes endothelial changes that lead to processes such as accelerated atherosclerosis, microthrombi formation, and structural changes in the blood–brain barrier.[45] Structural remodeling from chronic hypertension reduces the external diameter of the cerebral arterioles, which are characterized by a thickened media, a reduced lumen, and increased extracellular matrix.[46,47] Systemic hypertension induces structural changes that are manifest by increased expression of growth factors such as transforming growth factor β1, vasoactive factors such as angiotensin II, and matrix proteins collagenase and elastase.[47] In addition, the vasculature may have impaired relaxation responses as a result of changes in the endothelium-mediated vasodilation.[48]

Much of these data come from studies of two genetic breeds of rats: the stroke-prone spontaneously hypertensive rat (SHRSP) and the Wistar–Kyoto rat (WKY).[46] Stroke in the SHRSP rat is thought to be similar to clinical stroke in humans,[49] whereas the WKY rat is a normotensive strain. From these rats, we have learned that chronic hypertension does not simply reduce the internal lumen of blood vessels, but rather both the internal and external diameters (Figure 12.1). The result is impaired vasodilation from a hypertrophic vessel and, in addition, a smaller total vessel volume from vascular remodeling. A smaller vessel volume could lead to a greater predisposition to embolization or plaque formation, predisposing the cerebral tissue to global hypoperfusion and impaired oxygenation.

The vasodilator response is mediated by the endothelium, leading to release of a variety of growth factors and cytokines. In the SHRSP rat, the vasculature did not have a robust vasodilatory response to acetylcholine, adenosine diphosphate, or serotonin when compared with the WKY rat, suggesting that, likely secondary to remodeling, a different endothelial milieu exists.[46] From these rats we have also learned there is a difference in collateral blood vessel formation, which may relate to cerebral perfusion, and risk of surrounding cell death and ischemia in an infarct territory. With middle cerebral

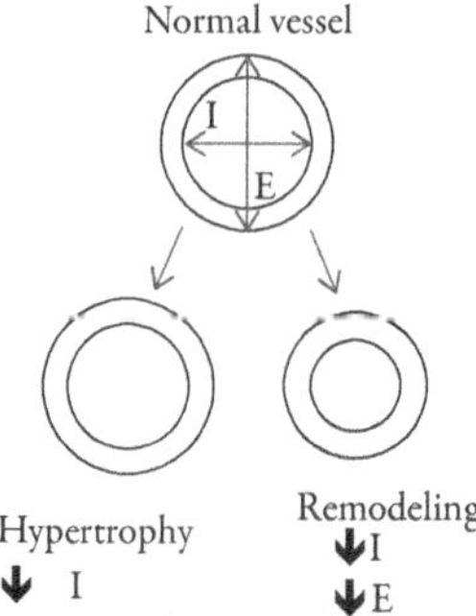

FIGURE 12.1 **In hypertrophy, as the vessel wall thickens, the vessel diameter stays constant externally and reduces internally. In chronic hypertension, remodeling occurs, which causes a narrowing of the internal and external vessel diameter, effectively changing the flow dynamics and autoregulatory curve of the cerebral vasculature. E, external diameter; I, internal diameter.**

Adapted from Heistad DD, Mayhan WG, Coyle P, Baumbach GL. Impaired dilatation of cerebral arterioles in chronic hypertension. *Blood Vessels* 1990;27:258–262.

artery ligation, the SHRSP rat has a larger territory infarct that progresses faster than the WKY rat,[50] which could be due to decreased blood flow from collaterals to the ischemic penumbra. The decrease in luminal size of these end vessels may also contribute to this finding.[51] The acute response to elevated blood pressure may be increased vessel permeability, leading to plasma leakage and edema. This process releases cytokines and growth factors, which, as described earlier, may lead to vascular remodeling in the long term. Studies of hypertensive rats support that, in the setting of hypertension, strokes could result from hyperplastic blood vessels, reduced collaterals, and thrombotic lesions.[49]

Cerebrovascular autoregulation is a process by which the brain vasculature carefully regulates intracranial blood flow so that the brain can operate at a range of systemic blood pressures. The high metabolic demand of the brain requires steady cerebral perfusion. This control is maintained by the constriction or dilation of small arteries or arterioles that respond to changes in pressure.[52] Regulation of this complex process occurs by the sympathetic nervous system, interactions with brain carbon dioxide and other brain metabolites, and neurovascular coupling. In normotension, this response occurs at approximately 60 to 160 mmHg SBP; but, in patients with hypertension, this range may be shifted to higher pressures.[53] Thus, this exquisitely sensitive system is "tuned" by chronic exposure to hypertension to respond at a higher range of blood pressure. This is further evidence that the "hypertensive brain" is structurally different from that of normotensive persons.

In humans, little about the vascular structure of the hypertensive brain is known. In one small, cerebral positron emission tomographic study, there were differences found in regional cerebral blood flow in patients with mild hypertension compared with normotensive patients, with patients with mild hypertension having reduced blood flow in the frontal cortex and basal ganglia.[54] Extrapolating from rats and from in vitro data, it seems that a constellation of vascular remodeling, impaired vasodilation from an altered endothelial response, and a shifted autoregulatory curve may begin to account for the mechanism of hypertension increasing one's risk of stroke.

Treatment Trials for Prevention of Stroke

PRIMARY PREVENTION

Given the clear association between hypertension and increased risk of stroke, there has been much interest in pharmacological management to reduce hypertension, and in whether this is associated with a resulting decrease in stroke rates. Studies have covered both the issue of whether *any* antihypertensive treatment reduces risk of stroke, as well as whether there are differences between specific blood pressure regimens. Many of the trials that reviewed in this chapter examined all cardiovascular outcomes, with stroke outcomes as a subgroup analysis. Because of the large size and randomized design of many of the trials, there is still much knowledge to be gained from them about cerebrovascular disease specifically. Most of the primary studies discussed are summarized in Table 12.1.[55–66]

ANTIHYPERTENSIVE USE (IN GENERAL) AND STROKE

Several meta-analyses including large numbers of patients have shown that blood pressure reduction reduces the risk of stroke significantly, regardless of initial blood pressure.[67-69] These meta-analyses included selected trials that were required to have examined either antihypertensive drugs versus placebo, groups of different blood pressure goals, or comparisons of different classes of antihypertensive drugs. Some of the studies included in this analysis, such as the Antihypertensive and Lipid-Lowering Treatment to Prevent Heart Attack Trial and PROGRESS are also discussed separately.

The results of one collaboration showed that greater blood pressure reductions produced greater reductions in the risk of cardiovascular events or stroke. Calcium channel blockers (CCBs) reduced the risk of recurrent stroke compared with placebo (38% reduction; 95% CI, 18–53), as did angiotensin-converting enzyme inhibitors (ACE-Is), which were associated with a 28% risk reduction (95% CI, 19–36). Blood pressure lowering by any agent reduced the risk of recurrent stroke. Side-by-side comparisons of different regimens reached borderline significance, with ACE-I appearing to be inferior to beta blockers or CCB; however, these differences were most likely the result of differences in blood pressure management, and efficacy in blood pressure control between agents.[69] Later analysis confirmed that, although CCBs, appeared to reduce the risk of stroke preferentially (discussed further later), this effect was accounted for by interindividual variation in blood pressure reduction between agents,[68] or by the fact that the effect size was small and perhaps clinically insignificant with some regimens.[67]

ANGIOTENSIN-CONVERTING ENZYME INHIBITORS

Some of the motivation for evaluating distinct antihypertensive medication regimens evolved from the cardiac literature. For systolic heart failure, for example, there is benefit from ACE-I for reduction in mortality and symptomatic improvement.[70] The Heart Outcomes Prevention Evaluation was a trial designed to evaluate the effect of the ACE-I ramipril on cardiovascular events in patients without left ventricular dysfunction.[56] Individuals at high risk of cardiovascular disease were randomized to ramipril or placebo for 5 years. The major outcome showed that ramipril reduced the rate of death, myocardial infarction, or stroke; the relative risk of stroke was 0.68 ($p < .001$) in the treatment group.

ANGIOTENSIN RECEPTOR BLOCKERS

Another trial looked at angiotensin receptor blockers (ARBs) and their impact on cardiovascular mortality compared with beta blockers. The Losartan Intervention for Endpoint Reduction trial selected subjects with hypertension and left ventricular hypertrophy by electrocardiogram.[57] They were monitored for at least 4 years after randomization to a losartan-based or an atenolol-based regimen. Losartan prevented cardiovascular mortality compared with atenolol, and the relative risk for stroke was 0.75 ($p = .001$) in the losartan-based group. In another study, the ARB telmisartan showed no difference in effect compared with the ACE-I ramipril, or the combination of both medications, in terms of cardiovascular mortality.[65]

TABLE 12.1

Important Studies in Primary Stroke Prevention

Study	Year of publication	Type of study	Subjects	Intervention	Duration of follow-up	Outcome related to stroke
SHEP[55]	1991	Randomized, double-blind, placebo-controlled, step-care design	4736 persons age 60 years and older with hypertension	Diuretic (chlorthalidone), then beta blocker (atenolol) vs. placebo	Average follow-up, 4.5 years	Diuretic reduced risk of stroke by 36% compared with placebo.
Heart Outcomes Prevention Evaluation[56]	2000	Randomized, placebo-controlled, two-by-two factorial design	9297 individuals older than 55 years with vascular disease or diabetes plus one other risk factor, who do not have low ejection fraction or heart failure	ACE-I (ramipril) or placebo, monitored for 5 years	Average follow-up, 5 years	ACE-I reduced the rate of stroke or TIA (RR, 0.68) as well as overall death and myocardial infarction.
Losartan Intervention for Endpoint Reduction trial[57]	2002	Double-masked, randomized, parallel group	9193 participants ages 55 to 90 years with hypertension and left ventricular hypertrophy by electrocardiogram	ARB (losartan)-based or beta blocker (atenolol)-based treatment, monitored for 4 years	Average follow-up, 4.8 years	ARB therapy reduced the rate of stroke compared with beta blocker-based therapy (RR, 0.75).
Antihypertensive and Lipid-Lowering Treatment to Prevent Heart Attack Trial[58]	2002	Randomized, double-blind, active controlled	33,353 patients age 55 years and older with at least one cardiovascular risk factor and hypertension	CCB or ACE-I vs. diuretic (chlorthalidone) vs. CCB (amlodipine) vs. ACE-I (lisinopril)	Average follow-up, 4.9 years	ACE-I therapy had a 15% greater risk of stroke than the diuretic arm. There was no difference in stroke in the CCB vs. the diuretic arm.

Treatment Trials Collaboration[59]	2003	7 sets of prospectively designed overviews of 29 treatment trials	162,341 patients, mainly with hypertension or diabetes, vascular disease, heart disease or cerebrovascular disease	ACE-I, CCB, diuretics, and beta blockers (various)	Range of follow-up, 2–8.4 years	There were some differences in cerebrovascular treatment among medication types; however, these trends only approached significance and were primarily the result of differences in blood pressure.
Health outcomes of various antihypertensives[60]	2003	Network meta-analysis of long–term, randomized, controlled clinical trials from 1995 to 2002	41 trials that included 192,478 patients randomized to 7 treatment strategies	Diuretics vs. placebo, diuretics vs. CCBs, diuretics vs. ACE-I, diuretics vs. beta blockers, diuretics vs. alpha blockers	Variable	Low-dose diuretics were superior to placebo (RR of stroke, 0.71). None of the other agents were better than diuretics for any outcome.
CONVINCE[61]	2003	Randomized, double blind	16,602 individuals with hypertension and more than one cardiovascular risk factor	Randomized to CCB (verapamil) or investigators' choice of beta blocker (atenolol) or diuretic (hydrochlorothiazide) titrated	Median follow-up, 3 years	There were no significant differences in stroke among treatment groups, but nonischemic hemorrhage was increased in the CCB-based group.
Anglo-Scandinavian Cardiac Outcomes–Blood Pressure Lowering Arm[62,63]	2005	Randomized, step care, active treatment	19,257 patients with hypertension age 40 to 70 years who had at least 3 other vascular risk factors but no previous history of CAD	Randomized to CCB (amlodipine) +/– ACE-I (perindopril) vs. beta blocker (atenolol) +/– diuretic (adding bendroflumethiazide)	Follow-up, 5.5 years	Significantly lower rates of stroke in the CCB arm than in the beta blocker arm. After multivariate adjustment for differences in blood pressure, the residuals were no longer significant.

(*continued*)

TABLE 12.1

Continued

Study	Year of publication	Type of study	Subjects	Intervention	Duration of follow-up	Outcome related to stroke
Beta blockers and the treatment of primary hypertension[64]	2005	Meta-analysis of randomized, controlled trials	13 trials ($N = 105,951$), patients with hypertension compared treatment with beta blockers with other antihypertensive drugs, 7 studies ($N = 27,433$) compared beta blockers vs. placebo or no treatment in patients with hypertension	Beta blockers vs. other treatment or beta blockers vs. placebo	Variable	RR of stroke was 16% greater for beta blockers than for other drugs. Beta blockers had a 19% reduced risk of stroke compared with that of placebo or no treatment.
ONTARGET[65]	2008	Randomized, double-blind treatment trial, after a 3-week single, blind run-in period	17,118 patients with vascular disease or diabetes	ARB (telmisartan) vs. ACE-I (ramipril) vs. combination	Median follow-up, 56 months	There was no significant difference in stroke between groups.
ACCOMPLISH[66]	2008	Randomized, double blind	11,506 patients with hypertension at risk for cardiovascular events	ACE-I, CCB combination (benazepril–amlodipine) vs. ACE-I, diuretic (benazepril–hydrochlorothiazide)	Average follow-up, 30 months	There were no significant differences in stroke outcome.

ACCOMPLISH, avoiding cardiovascular events in combination therapy in patients living with systolic hypertension; ACE-I, angiotensin-converting enzyme inhibitor; ARB, angiotensin receptor blocker; CAD, coronary artery disease; CCB, calcium channel blocker; CONVINCE, controlled onset verapamil investigation of cardiovascular endpoints; ONTARGET, ongoing telmisartan alone and in combination with ramipril global endpoint trial; RR, relative risk; SHEP, systolic hypertension in the elderly program; TIA, transient ischemic attack.

DIURETICS

The Antihypertensive and Lipid-Lowering Treatment to Prevent Heart Attack Trial examined the effect of diuretics versus other regimens on cardiovascular mortality.[58] In this large trial, patients 55 years or older with at least one cardiovascular risk factor and hypertension were randomized to chlorthalidone (thiazide diuretic), amlodipine (CCB), or lisinopril (ACE-I). This study showed a clear benefit from diuretics in reducing cardiovascular end points and stroke with no difference in all-cause mortality. The risk of stroke was increased by 15% in the ACE-I (lisinopril) group compared with the diuretic arm ($p = .02$). This provided convincing data for the use of thiazide diuretics, which are inexpensive and well tolerated. These data were supported by another study showing that chlorthalidone reduced the risk of stroke compared with placebo in adults with hypertension age 60 years and older.[55] A meta-analysis performed in 2003 selected 42 trials of first-line antihypertensive therapy with cardiovascular outcomes as end points.[60] More important, this study also showed that low-dose diuretics were superior to placebo for all cardiovascular outcomes, including stroke. There was no other agent that was superior to diuretics.

CALCIUM CHANNEL BLOCKERS

CCBs seem to be neutral in comparison with other agents, showing neither increased benefit nor decrement associated with their use. The Anglo-Scandinavian Cardiac Outcomes–Blood Pressure Lowering Arm trial examined the effect of randomization of subjects between the CCB-based regimen (amlodipine) and an beta blocker-based regimen (atenolol) in subjects with hypertension and risk factors for cardiovascular disease.[62] The results showed a significantly lower rate of stroke in the CCB arm, but this was not significant after adjustment for blood pressure. Another trial showed a lack of effect with the CCB verapamil versus investigators' choice of blood pressure treatment for primary and secondary outcomes.[63] A comparison of combination regimens of the ACE-I benazopril with amlodipine versus benazopril with the diuretic hydrochlorothiazide showed no difference in outcome for stroke.[71] Specific hypotheses about the potential benefit of CCBs are based on the observed stroke risk associated with SBP variability, in that increased SBP variability is associated with greater risk of stroke. CCBs appear to be modestly more effective than other medications (particularly beta blockers) in reduction of SBP variability and thus may be more effective in stroke prevention in particular patients.[38,72]

BETA BLOCKERS

Beta blockers may not only fail to show a clear benefit, but also may be inferior first-line agents for hypertension treatment for primary prevention of stroke. A meta-analysis of 13 randomized, controlled trials showed a 16% increase in the rate of stroke (95% CI, 4–30) when beta blockers were used as primary therapy for hypertension compared with other agents.[64] This has helped to shape guidelines for antihypertensive selection.

From these trials, several important points have been learned, which are well summarized in a 2009 Cochrane review of first-line drugs for hypertension, for primary prevention.[73] This review compiled data from 57 trials of hypertension and cardiovascular outcomes, including 58,040 patients. Its results highlighted that there is evidence for low-dose thiazide diuretics as first-line therapy for hypertension, based on reduced mortality, cardiovascular disease, and stroke risk. It differentiated low-dose diuretics from high-dose diuretics, which do not have the same benefit in terms of cardiovascular disease. This meta-analysis also summarized that there seems to be less benefit to beta blockers (atenolol in all five trials) compared with low-dose thiazides, and suggested they should not be used as first-line therapy. No difference was detected between groups for comparisons of ACE-I and CCBs with thiazides; but, independently, both classes reduced the risk of stroke.

MANAGEMENT OF HYPERTENSION IN OTHER PATIENT GROUPS

As discussed earlier in this chapter, data are less clear on the benefits of treating hypertension in older adults. A trial performed in persons older than 60 years showed a 15% (95% CI, 1–32) increase in stroke rate for every 10-mmHg increase in blood pressure, suggesting there is still an association in older adults.[74] The Prospective Studies Collaboration showed that increased blood pressure in the age group 80 to 89 years was still correlated positively with an increase in stroke mortality.[18] Treating blood pressure in the elderly was shown to have benefit in one trial of subjects older than 80 years. The Hypertension in the Very Elderly Study examined effects of treating subjects older than 80 years and was stopped prematurely because of a reduction in all-cause mortality in the treatment group. In this study, active treatment was associated with a 39% reduction in the risk of death from stroke (95% CI, 1–62).[75] These data support early and long-term treatment of hypertension even in the elderly.[76]

Despite these clinical trial results, the treatment target for blood pressure lowering in persons older than 60 year, and particularly in persons older than 80 years, is somewhat controversial. Recently released Joint National Committee on the Detection, Prevention Evaluation and Treatment of High Blood Pressure (JNC) 8 criteria[77] suggest that a more relaxed threshold of 150 mmHg systolic, rather than 140 mmHg systolic, may be a sufficient goal in older adults without diabetes or chronic kidney disease, although in persons who have achieved a lower blood pressure and have no treatment-related side effects, no change in treatment is recommended.

Data are also less clear on the benefit of treatment of mild hypertension for primary prevention of stroke. A Cochrane Database review from 2012 of 8912 total participants from four clinical trials demonstrated that short-term (4–5 years) use of any antihypertensive medication in individuals with mild hypertension (SBP, 140–159 mmHg, or DBP, 90–99 mmHg) was not clearly associated with a reduction in stroke risk (relative risk, 0.51; 95% CI, 0.24–1.08).[78] This may have been a result of the relatively short follow-up interval, because it might be hypothesized that risk of stroke is only increased substantially over a long-term interval in individuals with more modest increases in blood pressure. The Systolic Blood Pressure Intervention Trial is a large, ongoing study of primary prevention, randomizing individuals 55 years and older with borderline systolic hypertension (≥130 mmHg) and at least one cardiovascular risk factor to either "standard" blood pressure management (goal SBP, <140 mmHg) versus "intensive" blood pressure management (goal SBP, <120 mmHg). Enrollment for this study was ongoing at the time of publication of this chapter, but it is likely that results from this study, with a primary outcome including stroke as part of a composite cardiovascular outcome, will help elucidate optimal management in individuals with borderline or mild hypertension.

SECONDARY PREVENTION

Two studies in the 1990s provided the first evidence that reducing blood pressure in patients with stroke prevented recurrent cerebrovascular disease. The Poststroke Antihypertensive Study (PATS) was a study of 5665 Chinese persons with prior stroke or TIA who were randomized to placebo or the treatment group with the diuretic indapamide.[79] Blood pressure reduction of only 5/2 mmHg reduced recurrent stroke by 29% in the treatment group. Another collaboration, the Individual Data Analysis of Antihypertensive Intervention Trials, also showed benefit to blood pressure lowering for secondary prevention of stroke.[80]

Other trials examining the role of long-term blood pressure management in individuals with a history of stroke (Table 12.2[81–85]) have generally shown that lowering blood pressure is beneficial for

TABLE 12.2

Important Studies in Secondary Stroke Prevention

Study	Year	Type of study	Subjects	Intervention	Duration of follow-up	Outcome
Poststroke Antihypertensive Study[91]	1995	Randomized, double blind, placebo controlled	5,665 Chinese patients with prior stroke or TIA	Diuretic (indapamide) vs. placebo	Average follow-up, 2 years	A blood pressure reduction of only 5/2 mmHg by a diuretic reduced recurrent stroke by 29%.
Individual Data Analysis of Antihypertensive Intervention Trials[92]	1997	Meta-analysis of randomized, controlled trials	9 trials involving 6752 patients with prior stroke or TIA	Various antihypertensive strategies vs. placebo	Variable	The recurrent stroke rate was reduced in the treatment group (RR, 0.72).
Perindopril Protection against Recurrent Stroke Study[93]	2001	Randomized, placebo controlled	6105 individuals with prior stroke or TIA (both hypertensive and nonhypertensive)	ACE-I (perindopril) based therapy +/– diuretic (indapamide) vs. placebo	Average follow-up, 3.9 years	Treatment reduced risk of stroke in all subjects. The combination of ACE-I and a diuretic produced larger risk reductions (by 43%).
Blood pressure reduction and secondary prevention of stroke[93]	2003	Systematic review and meta regression of randomized, controlled trials	7 trials with 8 comparison groups of patients with prior ischemic or hemorrhagic stroke, or TIA	Diuretic, ACE-I, beta blocker, ACE-I and diuretic	Range of follow-up, 2–5 years	Lowering blood pressure reduced stroke (OR, 0.76). ACE-I and diuretics, especially together, as well as separately, reduced stroke; beta blockers had no discernible effect.
Morbidity and Mortality after Stroke, Eprosartan Compared with Nitrendipine for Secondary Prevention study[77]	2005	Randomized treatment trial	1405 patients with hypertension with a cerebral event in the previous 24 months	ARB (eprosartan) vs. CCB (nitrendipine)	Follow-up, 2.5 years	Cerebrovascular events were significantly lower in the ARB group ($n = 102$ vs. $n = 134$)

(continued)

TABLE 12.2

Continued

Study	Year	Type of study	Subjects	Intervention	Duration of follow-up	Outcome
Prevention Regimen for Effectively Avoiding Second Strokes[94]	2008	Randomized, placebo controlled	20,332 patients who recently had an ischemic stroke	ARB (telmisartan) vs. placebo	Follow-up, 2.5 years	ARB did not reduce the rate of stroke.
Secondary Prevention of Small Subcortical Strokes study[95]	2013	Randomized, open label	3020 patients with recent symptomatic lacunar stroke randomized to 2 blood pressure targets (130–149 mmHg and <130 mmHg)	Various antihypertensive strategies to meet goal	Average follow-up, 3.7 years	There were nonsignificant reductions in stroke and vascular events.

ACE-I, angiotensin-converting enzyme inhibitor; ARB, angiotensin receptor blocker; CCB, calcium channel blocker; OR, odds ratio; RR, relative risk; TIA, transient ischemic attack.

secondary prevention after stroke. In PROGRESS, subjects who were hypertensive and nonhypertensive with a prior stroke or TIA were randomized to perindopril (ACE-I), with a physician choice to add indapamide (a diuretic), versus placebo.[86] The treatment arm had a significant reduction in recurrent stroke, even in patients without hypertension, and active treatment reduced major vascular events in those with isolated diastolic hypertension by 32% (95% CI, 17–45). This study is a persuasive one for future treatment studies aimed at reducing stroke rates in individuals with a history of stroke or TIA. A meta-analysis of seven trials confirmed that ACE-Is reduced secondary stroke risk, and they were especially synergistic with diuretics.

As a follow-up to PROGRESS, because of the hypothesis that inhibition of the renin–angiotensin system might reduce stroke recurrence in particular, ARBs were studied in relation to recurrent stroke. The Prevention Regimen for Effectively Avoiding Second Strokes investigated the effect of telmisartan versus placebo in patients who recently had a stroke or TIA,[87] with nearly three fourths of enrollees having a history of hypertension. In the follow-up of more than 2.5 years, telmisartan reduced the rate of recurrent stroke, but this difference was not statistically significant. The difference in blood pressure reduction between the two groups was also small. Other cardiovascular studies have showed no difference in stroke rates in patients on ARB therapy.[88–89]

A post hoc analysis of this trial evaluated whether there was a threshold of blood pressure that was "too low," in that it increased risk of stroke. Surprisingly, among these patients with noncardioembolic stroke, "low normal" blood pressure (<120 mmHg systolic) increased the risk of recurrent stroke.[90] This is evidence that, unlike in primary prevention, in a population with prior stroke the J-shaped relationship may indeed hold, suggestive of possible harm in lowering systolic blood pressure to less than 120 mmHg in this population. In contrast with this finding, however, the Secondary Prevention of Small Subcortical Strokes trial of patients with lacunar stroke found a trend toward fewer strokes in the "lower" blood pressure arm (<130 mmHg), compared with the arm less than 150 mmHg, but this difference did not reach statistical significance.[91] If there is, indeed, an optimal threshold for blood pressure in recurrent stroke, this needs to be confirmed in future studies so that accurate guidelines can be established.

The Morbidity and Mortality after Stroke, Eprosartan Compared with Nitrendipine for Secondary Prevention study examined the effects of the ARB eprosartan with the CCB nitrendipine.[92] Cardiovascular and cerebrovascular events were reduced in the eprosartan arm, although there were similar rates of blood pressure control between the two groups, suggesting a benefit to treatment for secondary prevention with an ARB over a CCB.

Taken together, these data support that lowering blood pressure is an effective intervention in secondary stroke prevention. It is less clear how soon after stroke this should be initiated, because there is the potential for harm or no benefit if implemented immediately after an acute stroke in certain patients.[42] The recurrent rate of stroke may be reduced by as much as 27% (95% CI, 14–38) with adequate treatment.[56] Although the combination of an ACE-I and a thiazide diuretic seems to be beneficial in secondary prevention, data are lacking to allow recommendation of particular drug classes.

CURRENT GUIDELINES FOR BLOOD PRESSURE AND STROKE

In 2003, the guidelines for blood pressure management from the *Seventh Report on the Joint National Committee on the Detection, Prevention Evaluation and Treatment of High Blood Pressure (JNC7)* were released.[93] This report detailed new definitions of blood pressure and, for the first time, detailed a treatment goal of less than 140/90 mmHg, and for those with diabetes or renal disease, of less than 130/80 mmHg. This was a change from the previous blood pressure treatment goals that did not define blood pressures from 120 to 140 mmHg as prehypertensive. The JNC7 recommendations included the results of PROGRESS, which compared ACE-I-based therapy (perindopril) with or without a diuretic (indapamide) compared with placebo. Previous stroke or TIA was included as a "compelling indication" for agent-specific therapy. Based on this trial, a diuretic inhibitor or ACE-I is recommended as first-line therapy for those with prior stroke or TIA (Table 12.3[93,77]).

Results of the recently released JNC8 guidelines are more controversial, mostly secondary to the relaxed blood pressure guidelines in older adults.[77,94] The newer guidelines maintain previous recommendations for patients 60 years or younger, people with diabetes, and individuals with chronic kidney disease. They suggest a more relaxed blood pressure goal, for patients older than 60 years, of less than 150/90 mmHg, maintaining that if such patients are treated to lower than this goal without side effects, current treatment should be continued. The main dissenting opinion was that there was no clear evidence that the more strict goals were harmful, although relaxing blood pressure goals in the frail elderly, such as patients older than 80 years, may be warranted.

The American Heart Association's 2011 guidelines for the primary prevention of stroke mirror the JNC7 recommendations, as level Ia evidence.[95] Regular blood pressure screening, lifestyle modification, and, if necessary, appropriate pharmacological treatment are emphasized. The goal blood pressure set forth for primary stroke prevention is less than 140 mmHg systolic and less than 90 mmHg diastolic. For patients with diabetes or renal disease, the goal is less than 130 mmHg systolic and 80 mmHg diastolic.

TABLE 12.3

JNC7 and JNC8 Recommendations for Blood Pressure Management

Classification	SBP	DBP		
JNC7			Treatment without a compelling indication	Treatment with prior stroke
Normotensive	<120	And <80	None	None
Prehypertension	120–139	Or 80–89	none	Diuretic or ACE-I
Stage 1 hypertension	140–159	Or 90–99	Thiazide diuretic for most, may consider ACE-I, CCB, beta blocker, or combination	Diuretic or ACE-I, other classes as needed
Stage 2 hypertension	≥160	Or ≥100	2-drug combination for most, usually thiazide diuretic and ACE-I or ARB, or CCB or beta blocker	Diuretic or ACE-I, other classes as needed
JNC8			Nonblack	Black
≥60 years	<150; if treatment to <140/90 is without side effects, do not adjust	<90	Initiate therapy with thiazide diuretic, CCB, ACE-I, or ARB	Initiate therapy with thiazide diuretic or CCB
<60 years	<140	<90	Same	Same

Note: Data from Chobanian et al.[93] and James et al.[77]
ACE-I, angiotensin-converting enzyme inhibitor; ARB, angiotensin receptor blocker; CCB, calcium channel blocker; DBP, diastolic blood pressure; SBP, systolic blood pressure.

Guidelines put forth by the American Heart Association in 2006[96] and updated in 2010 are the current standard for treatment of hypertension in patients with stroke.[97] These guidelines provided standard evidence levels to the current recommendations. In the 2010 guidelines, there was level Ia evidence for the following two recommendations: (a) antihypertensive therapy is recommended for those who have had a stroke or TIA for secondary prevention beyond the first 24 hours and (b) some data support the primary use of diuretics or ACE-I as primary drug therapy for patients who have had a stroke or TIA; however, the optimal regimen is uncertain. There is level IIb evidence for treating patients without documented hypertension but with a stroke or TIA with a blood pressure-lowering regimen, if it is deemed safe. Less definitive than the JNC7 report, the recommendations provide level IIb evidence saying that the specific blood pressure goal is uncertain, but reductions of 10/5 mmHg blood pressure are effective in reducing risk, with normotension defined as less than 120/80 mmHg.

Intracerebral Hemorrhage

Intracerebral hemorrhage (ICH) accounts for 15% to 30% of all strokes, and has a high mortality rate compared with ischemic stroke, with only 38% surviving the first year.[98] Hypertension may be the greatest risk factor for ICH, and has consistently shown an association in many case–control and cohort studies.[99] Similar to ischemic stroke, there is a linear increase in risk of hemorrhage for each level of SBP.[43] A study performed during the 1980s found retrospectively that 45% of patients with ICH had preexisting hypertension,[100] and the prevalence is now thought to be as high as 75%.[101] Hypertension results in an almost fourfold greater risk of developing lifetime ICH.[102] Primary ICH accounts for 78% to 88% of all ICH, and is the subtype most associated with hypertension.[98] Hypertension is much more common in nonlobar hemorrhage than in lobar hemorrhage, which has unique risk factors, such as cerebral amyloid angiopathy or underlying metastasis.[103]

One study showed that mortality in ICH was greater in subjects with hypertension who had ceased their blood pressure medication regimen, suggesting that those subjects may be especially prone to vessel rupture, possibly from changes in blood pressure induced by starting or stopping therapy.[104] ICH is often included in total stroke incidence and prevalence estimates, and total stroke risk has been noted to be reduced with antihypertensive therapy.[55,98] PROGRESS showed that, in addition to total stroke, the ICH recurrence rate was also reduced with blood pressure treatment with an ACE-I.[86,105]

Primary ICH occurs when a blood vessel ruptures, which is weakened from the long-term effects of hypertension, and can represent falling off the upper end of the cerebral autoregulatory curve, or can be the result of another intrinsic vascular process such as cerebral amyloid angiopathy. The long-term exposure to higher blood pressures may weaken the arterial wall through a process of lipohyalinosis, especially in smaller blood vessels, which are more prone to rupture in hypertension-related ICH.[101] This explains the predilection of hemorrhage related to hypertension to occur in small penetrating branches of the middle cerebral artery, the paramedian penetrators of the basilar artery, or the branches coming off the posterior cerebral artery, commonly involving subcortical structures such as the thalamus, basal ganglia, brainstem, and cerebellum.[105] Electron microscopy of vessels involved in ICH show a weakened vessel wall, which typically is near the branch points of vessels. This was first described as Charcot-Bouchard microaneurysms in 1868, as a pathological leakage from a damaged vessel at the site with a dilation in the vessel wall.[98] The current thinking is that this pathological change is secondary to the chronic effects of hypertension. We know that the cerebral autoregulatory curve is disordered in acute ICH, and it is possible that derangements in cerebral vasodilation from chronic hypertension predispose to the hemorrhagic event.[106]

White Matter Disease

With the use of magnetic resonance images becoming standard in the treatment and care of patients, white matter hyperintensities, or leukoaraiosis, which is used interchangeably in this chapter, is recognized more frequently (Figure 12.2). Leukoaraiosis is a word that originates from the Greek stem *leuko*, meaning "white," and *araiosis*, meaning "rarified."[107] The term was originally introduced 20 years ago, and today the cause is better understood. It is best understood as a part of the spectrum of small-vessel disease, and is often seen surrounding lacunar infarcts. One mechanism suggested for this is ischemia from continued hypoperfusion. This is observed through techniques such as magnetic resonance perfusion, but it is difficult to prove as a primary rather than a secondary effect. Another theory invokes breakdown of the blood–brain barrier, leading to leakage of toxic serum proteins that elicit a cytotoxic response. Last, there may be endothelial interactions that lead to altered blood flow patterns and breakdown of the blood–brain barrier, causing white matter changes.[107]

Some of the evidence for a vascular etiology of white matter changes is the observed strong association in the epidemiological literature between blood pressure and leukoaraiosis. In addition, greater white matter hyperintensity burden is associated with a greater burden of small-vessel stroke.[108] The Framingham Risk Score was related to white matter hyperintensities, suggesting a similar risk factor profile in both diseases.[109] Hypertension is strongly associated with subclinical infarcts detected on imaging.[110] Similarly, blood pressure has shown a strong association with leukoaraiosis, with higher blood pressures leading to a greater amount of white matter hyperintensities[111] or their progression.[112,113] One study showed a twofold increase in white matter lesions in subjects with moderate to high blood pressure variability in midlife.[114] Both SBP and DBP measured 20 years before imaging were associated with white matter changes, and this relationship was J shaped.[115] This suggests that aggressive blood pressure management may not be beneficial in some subgroups with underlying vascular disease in which the autoregulatory curve has been shifted.

The benefit of antihypertensive treatment in reducing progression of white matter lesions is less clear than these relationships. Although in the study on cognition and prognosis in the elderly (SCOPE, Study on Cognition and Prognosis in the Elderly), in which elderly normotensive subjects

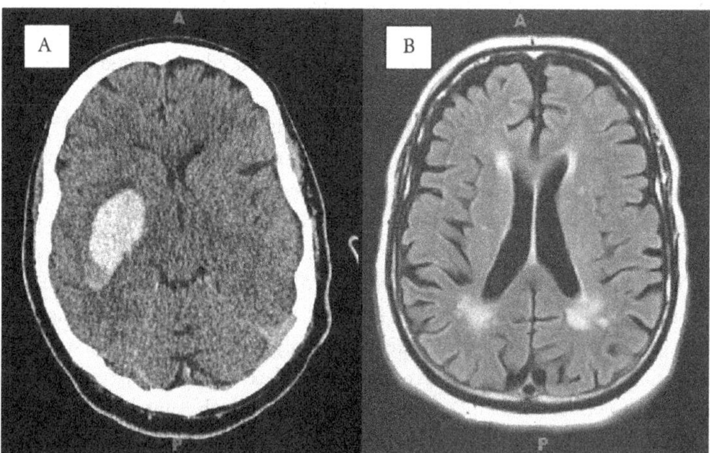

FIGURE 12.2 (A). Head computed tomographic scan showing right intracranial hemorrhage originating in the basal ganglia and extending into the temporal lobe. (B) Magnetic resonance imaging fluid-attenuated inversion recovery sequence demonstrating white matter changes surrounding the lateral ventricles and corona radiata as evidence of small vessel disease, or leukoaraiosis.

were randomized to candesartan therapy or placebo, the placebo group had a greater progression in white matter volume when compared with the candesartan group.[116] The recently published Prevention Regimen for Effectively Avoiding Second Strokes failed to show a difference in white matter lesion progression in individuals treated with telmisartan compared with placebo.[117] This trial had a very short follow-up, however, which might account for lack of a benefit because overall leukoaraiosis progression in both groups was minimal in this study. The PROGRESS trial, with a slightly longer follow-up, did find that individuals in the active antihypertensive arm had less extensive progression of white matter hyperintensities.[118] Despite these conflicting data, it is apparent that leukoaraiosis may be a magnetic resonance imaging marker that can be used to measure the impact of chronic hypertension on the brain, and its underlying causes may be similar to small-vessel stroke.

Conclusion

Hypertension is the greatest risk factor for all subtypes of stroke, including small-vessel stroke, embolic stroke, and hemorrhagic stroke. In addition, it is a significant risk factor for leukoaraiosis, which may represent a spectrum of microvascular disease in the brain. The contribution of hypertension is significant across all populations studied, and is a significant public health concern in developing countries, where access to consistent primary care may be variable. Epidemiological studies show that, although SBP and DBP contribute to the risk of stroke, there may be more to learn from the combination of the MAP and the PP or SBP and DBP in terms of predictive power for stroke. Lowering blood pressure at any level reduces risk of stroke, and there is no critical threshold below which one is "protected" from the log-linear risk of blood pressure and stroke.

Evidence supports the use of low-dose thiazide diuretics for primary prevention of stroke, and low-dose thiazides combined with ACE-I are shown to reduce recurrent stroke. All blood pressure agents reduce risk of stroke, but beta blockers may be less effective than other agents and thus, in the absence of other indications for beta blockers specifically, are not an ideal first-line therapy. The most recent JNC8 blood pressure guidelines maintain the previous JNC7 guidelines for a lower blood pressure goal in patients with diabetes and persons younger than 60 years (≤140/90 mmHg), but allows for a greater threshold in those older than 60 years and, as discussed earlier, this recommendation in older persons is controversial.

Understanding the autoregulatory curve in cerebral blood vessels is key to understanding the lifetime effect of hypertension on the vascular supply of the brain. As we move ahead in research, developing modulators of vascular remodeling may help mitigate the chronic effects on hypertension and the brain. Moving forward, we must integrate the solid epidemiological base of knowledge to target therapy in primary and secondary prevention. As is described, fewer large-scale trials exist in the secondary prevention of stroke, and optimal blood pressure regimens and timing of their initiation still remain to be determined. Hypertension may be the largest risk factor for stroke, but it is modifiable, and creating systems of care that allow for detection and treatment will continue to lower worldwide rates of stroke.

REFERENCES

1. Chow CK, Teo KK, Rangarajan S, et al. Prevalence, awareness, treatment, and control of hypertension in rural and urban communities in high-, middle-, and low-income countries. *JAMA*. 2013;310:959–968.
2. Lawes CM, Vander Hoorn S, Rodgers A, International Society of Hypertension. Global burden of blood-pressure-related disease, 2001. *Lancet*. 2008;371:1513–1518.

3. Wolf-Maier K, Cooper RS, Banegas JR, et al. Hypertension prevalence and blood pressure levels in 6 European countries, Canada, and the United States. *JAMA*. 2003;289:2363–2369.
4. Egan BM, Zhao Y, Axon R. US trends in prevalence, awareness, treatment, and control of hypertension, 1988–2008. *JAMA*. 2010;303:2043–2050.
5. Gillepsie C, Kuklina EV, Briss PA, et al. Vital signs: prevalence, treatment, and control of hypertension: United States, 1999–2002 and 2005–2008. *Morbid Mortal Wkly Rep*. 2011;60:102–108.
6. Ibrahim MM, Damasceno A. Hypertension in developing countries. *Lancet*. 2012;380:611–619.
7. Booth J. A short history of blood pressure measurement. *Proc R Soc Med*. 1977;70:793–799.
8. Rosamond W, Flegal K, Furie K, et al. Heart disease and stroke statistics: 2008 update. *Circulation*. 2008;117:e25–e25-146.
9. Go AS, Mozaffarian D, Roger VL, et al. Heart disease and stroke statistics: 2013 update: a report from the American Heart Association. *Circulation*. 2013;127:e6–e245.
10. Whisnant JP. Modeling of risk factors for ischemic stroke. *Stroke*. 1997;28:1840–1844.
11. Dawber TR, Kannel WB, McNamara PM and Cohen ME. An epidemiologic study of apoplexy ("strokes"). Observations in 5,209 adults in the Framingham Study on Association of Various Factors in the Development of Apoplexy. *Transactions of the American Neurological Association*. 1965;90:237–240.
12. Carandang R, Seshadri S, Beiser A, et al. Trends in incidence, lifetime risk, severity, and 30-day mortality of stroke over the past 50 years. *JAMA*. 2006;296:2939–2946.
13. Kannel WB. Wolf PA, Verter J, McNamara PM. Epidemiologic assessment of the role of blood pressure in stroke: the Framingham study. *JAMA*. 1970;214:301–310.
14. MacMahon S. Blood pressure and the prevention of stroke. *J Hypertens*. 1996;14:S39–S46.
15. MacMahon S, Peto R, Collins R, et al. Blood pressure, stroke, and coronary heart disease: part 1. Prolonged differences in blood pressure: prospective observational studies corrected for the regression dilution bias. 1990;335:765–774.
16. Blood pressure, cholesterol, and stroke in eastern Asia. Eastern Stroke and Coronary Heart Disease Collaborative Research Group. *Lancet*. 1998;352:1801–1807.
17. Cholesterol, diastolic blood pressure, and stroke: 13,000 strokes in 450,000 people in 45 prospective cohorts: Prospective studies collaboration. *Lancet*. 1995;346:1647–1653.
18. Lewington S, Clarke R, Qizilbash N, et al. Age-specific relevance of usual blood pressure to vascular mortality: a meta-analysis of individual data for one million adults in 61 prospective studies. *Lancet*. 2002;360:1903–1913.
19. Nakamura K, Barzi F, Lam T-H, et al. Cigarette smoking, systolic blood pressure, and cardiovascular diseases in the Asia–Pacific region. *Stroke*. 2008;39:1694–1702.
20. Vokó Z, Bots ML, Hofman A, Koudstaal PJ, Witteman JCM, Breteler MMB. J-shaped relation between blood pressure and stroke in treated hypertensives. *Hypertension*. 1999;34:1181–1185.
21. Reshef S, Reshef D. Following the heart: the history of the J-curve in stroke risk. *Am J Pharmacol Toxicol*. 2008;3:185–192.
22. Mulrow FL. The J-curve phenomenon and the treatment of hypertension: is there a point beyond which pressure reduction is dangerous? *JAMA*. 1991;265:489–495.
23. Dorresteijn JAN, van der Graaf Y, Spiering W, Grobbee DE, Bots ML, Visseren FLJ. Relation between blood pressure and vascular events and mortality in patients with manifest vascular disease. *Hypertension*. 2012;59:14–21.
24. Chrysant SG, Chrysant GS. Effectiveness of lowering blood pressure to prevent stroke versus to prevent coronary events. *Am J Cardiol*. 2010;106:825–829.
25. Kannel WB Wolf PA, McGee DL, Dawber TR, McNamara P, Castelli WP. Systolic blood pressure, arterial rigidity, and risk of stroke: the Framingham study. *JAMA*. 1981;245:1225–1229.
26. Arima H, Anderson C, Omae T, et al. Effects of blood pressure lowering on major vascular events among patients with isolated diastolic hypertension. *Stroke*. 2011;42:2339–2341.

27. Franklin SS, Lopez VA, Wong ND, et al. Single versus combined blood pressure components and risk for cardiovascular disease. *Circulation*. 2009;119:243–250.
28. Safar ME, St Laurent S, Safavian AL, Pannier BM, London GM. Pulse pressure in sustained essential hypertension: a haemodynamic study. *J Hypertens*. 1987;5:213–218.
29. Darne B, Girerd X, Safar M, Cambien F, Guize L. Pulsatile versus steady component of blood pressure: a cross-sectional analysis and a prospective analysis on cardiovascular mortality. *Hypertension*. 1989;13:392–400.
30. Zheng L, Sun Z, Li J, et al. Pulse pressure and mean arterial pressure in relation to ischemic stroke among patients with uncontrolled hypertension in rural areas of China. *Stroke*. 2008;39:1932–1937.
31. Rothwell PM. Limitations of the usual blood-pressure hypothesis and importance of variability, instability, and episodic hypertension. *Lancet*. 2010;375:938–948.
32. Pickering TG, Hall JE, Appel LJ, et al. Recommendations for blood pressure measurement in humans and experimental animals. Part 1: blood pressure measurement in humans: a statement for professionals from the Subcommittee of Professional and Public Education of the American Heart Association Council on High Blood Pressure Research. *Hypertension*. 2005;45:142–161.
33. Mancia G, Fagard R, Narkiewicz K, et al. 2013 ESH/ESC guidelines for the management of arterial hypertension: the task force for the management of arterial hypertension of the European Society of Hypertension (ESH) and of the European Society of Cardiology (ESC). *Eur Heart J*. 2013;34:2159–2219.
34. Rothwell PM, Howard SC, Dolan E, et al. Prognostic significance of visit-to-visit variability, maximum systolic blood pressure, and episodic hypertension. *Lancet*. 2010;375:895–905.
35. Kario K, Pickering TG, Umeda Y, et al. Morning surge in blood pressure as a predictor of silent and clinical cerebrovascular disease in elderly hypertensives. *Circulation*. 2003;107:1401–1406.
36. Kario K, Pickering TG, Matsuo T, Hoshide S, Schwartz JE, Shimada K. Stroke prognosis and abnormal nocturnal blood pressure falls in older hypertensives. *Hypertension*. 2001;38:852–857.
37. Eigenbrodt ML, Rose KM, Couper DJ, Arnett DK, Smith R, Jones D. Orthostatic hypotension as a risk factor for stroke. *Stroke*. 2000;31:2307–2313.
38. Rothwell PM, Howard SC, Dolan E, et al. Effects of β blockers and calcium-channel blockers on within-individual variability in blood pressure and risk of stroke. *Lancet Neurol*. 2010;9:469–480.
39. Seshadri S, Wolf PA, Beiser A, et al. Elevated midlife blood pressure increases stroke risk in elderly persons: the Framingham study. *Arch Intern Med*. 2001;161:2343–2350.
40. Douglas J, Bakris GL, Epstein M et al. Management of high blood pressure in African Americans: consensus statement of the Hypertension in African Americans Working Group of the International Society on Hypertension in Blacks. *Arch Intern Med*. 2003:525–541.
41. Rodgers A, MacMahon S, Gamble G, Slattery J, Sandercock P, Warlow C. Blood pressure and risk of stroke in patients with cerebrovascular disease. *BMJ* 1996;313:147.
42. He J, Zhang Y, Xu T, et al. Effects of immediate blood pressure reduction on death and major disability in patients with acute ischemic stroke: the CATIS randomized clinical trial. *JAMA*. 2013;311:479–489.
43. Arima H. Blood pressure-lowering treatment for primary and secondary prevention of different types of stroke. *Ex Rev Cardiovasc Ther*. 2009;7:627–636.
44. Ahmed N, Wahlgren N, Brainin M, et al. Relationship of blood pressure, antihypertensive therapy, and outcome in ischemic stroke treated with intravenous thrombolysis. *Stroke*. 2009;40:2442–2449.
45. Johansson BB. Hypertension Mechanisms Causing Stroke. *Clin Exp Pharmacol Physiol*. 1999;26:563–565.
46. Heistad DD, Mayhan WG, Coyle P, Baumbach GL. Impaired dilatation of cerebral arterioles in chronic hypertension. *Blood Vessels*. 1990;27:258–262.
47. Gibbons GH, Dzau VJ. The emerging concept of vascular remodeling. *N Engl J Med*. 1994;330:1431–1438.

48. Panza JA, Quyyumi AA, Brush JE Jr, Epstein SE. Abnormal endothelium-dependent vascular relaxation in patients with essential hypertension. *N Engl J Med.* 1990;323:22–27.
49. Henning EC, Warach S, Spatz M. Hypertension-induced vascular remodeling contributes to reduced cerebral perfusion and the development of spontaneous stroke in aged SHRSP rats. *J Cereb Blood Flow Metab.* 2010;30:827–836.
50. McCabe C, Gallagher L, Gsell W, Graham D, Dominiczak AF, Macrae IM. Differences in the evolution of the ischemic penumbra in stroke-prone spontaneously hypertensive and Wistar-Kyoto rats. *Stroke.* 2009;40:3864–3868.
51. Coyle P, Heistad DD. Blood flow through cerebral collateral vessels in hypertensive and normotensive rats. *Hypertension.* 1986;8:II67–II71.
52. Paulson OB, Strandgaard S, Fau-Edvinsson L, Edvinsson L. Cerebral autoregulation. *Cerebrovasc Brain Metab Rev.* 1990;2:161–192.
53. Dickinson CJ. Why are strokes related to hypertension? Classic studies and hypotheses revisited. *J Hypertens.* 2001;19:1515–1521.
54. Fujishima M, Ibayashi S, Fujii K, Mori S. Cerebral blood flow and brain function in hypertension. *Hypertens Res.* 1995;18:111–117.
55. Prevention of stroke by antihypertensive drug treatment in older persons with isolated systolic hypertension: final results of the Systolic Hypertension in the Elderly Program (SHEP): SHEP Cooperative Research Group. *JAMA.* 1991;265:3255–3264.
56. Yusuf S, Sleight P, Pogue J, Bosch J, Davies R, Dagenais G. Effects of an angiotensin-converting-enzyme inhibitor, ramipril, on cardiovascular events in high-risk patients: the Heart Outcomes Prevention Evaluation Study Investigators. *N Engl J Med.* 2000;342:145–153.
57. Dahlöf B, Devereux RB, Kjeldsen SE, et al. Cardiovascular morbidity and mortality in the Losartan Intervention for Endpoint Reduction in Hypertension Study (LIFE): a randomised trial against atenolol. *Lancet.* 2002;359:995–1003.
58. The Allhat Officers, Coordinators for the Allhat Collaborative Research Group. Major outcomes in high-risk patients with hypertension randomized to angiotensin-converting enzyme inhibitor or calcium channel blocker vs diuretic: the Antihypertensive and Lipid-Lowering Treatment to Prevent Heart Attack Trial (ALLHAT). *JAMA.* 2002;288:2981–2997.
59. Turnbull F, Blood Pressure Lowering Treatment Trialists Collaboration. Effects of different blood-pressure-lowering regimens on major cardiovascular events: results of prospectively-designed overviews of randomised trials. *Lancet.* 2003;362:1527–1535.
60. Psaty BM, Lumley T, Furberg CD, et al. Health outcomes associated with various antihypertensive therapies used as first-line agents: a network meta-analysis. *JAMA.* 2003;289:2534–2544.
61. Black HR, Elliott WJ, Grandits G, et al. Principal results of the Controlled Onset Verapamil Investigation of Cardiovascular End Points (CONVINCE) trial. *JAMA.* 2003;289:2073–2082.
62. Poulter NR, Wedel H, Dahlöf B, et al. Role of blood pressure and other variables in the differential cardiovascular event rates noted in the Anglo-Scandinavian Cardiac Outcomes Trial–Blood Pressure Lowering Arm (ASCOT-BPLA). *Lancet.* 2005;366:907–913.
63. Dahlöf B, Sever PS, Poulter NR, et al. Prevention of cardiovascular events with an antihypertensive regimen of amlodipine adding perindopril as required versus atenolol adding bendroflumethiazide as required, in the Anglo-Scandinavian Cardiac Outcomes Trial–Blood Pressure Lowering Arm (ASCOT-BPLA): a multicentre randomised controlled trial. *Lancet.* 2005;366:895–906.
64. Lindholm LH, Carlberg B, Samuelsson O. Should β blockers remain first choice in the treatment of primary hypertension? A meta-analysis. *Lancet.* 2005;366:1545–1553.
65. Ontarget Investigators, Yusuf S, Teo KK, et al. Telmisartan, ramipril, or both in patients at high risk for vascular events. *N Engl J Med.* 2008;358:1547–1559.

66. Jamerson K, Weber MA, Bakris GL, et al. Benazepril plus amlodipine or hydrochlorothiazide for hypertension in high-risk patients. *N Engl J Med.* 2008;359:2417–2428.
67. Law MR, Morris JK, Wald NJ. Use of blood pressure lowering drugs in the prevention of cardiovascular disease: meta-analysis of 147 randomised trials in the context of expectations from prospective epidemiological studies. *BMJ.* 2009;338:b1665.
68. Webb AJ, Fischer U, Mehta Z, Rothwell PM. Effects of antihypertensive-drug class on interindividual variation in blood pressure and risk of stroke: a systematic review and meta-analysis. *Lancet.* 2010;375:906–915.
69. Turnbull F, Blood Pressure Lowering Treatment Trialists Collaboration. Effects of different blood-pressure-lowering regimens on major cardiovascular events: results of prospectively-designed overviews of randomised trials. *Lancet.* 2003;362:1527–1535.
70. Sharpe DN, Murphy J, Coxon R, Hannan SF. Enalapril in patients with chronic heart failure: a placebo-controlled, randomized, double-blind study. *Circulation.* 1984;70:271–278.
71. Jamerson K, Weber MA, Bakris GL, et al. Benazepril plus amlodipine or hydrochlorothiazide for hypertension in high-risk patients. *N Engl J Med.* 2008;359:2417–2428.
72. Webb AJS, Rothwell PM. Effect of dose and combination of antihypertensives on interindividual blood pressure variability. *Stroke.* 2011;42:2860–2865.
73. Wright JM, Musini VM. First-line drugs for hypertension. *Cochrane Database Syst Rev.* 2009;(3):CD001841.
74. Davis BR, Vogt T, Frost PH, et al. Risk factors for stroke and type of stroke in persons with isolated systolic hypertension. *Stroke.* 1998;29:1333–1340.
75. Beckett NS, Peters R, Fletcher AE, et al. Treatment of hypertension in patients 80 years of age or older. *N Engl J Med.* 2008;358:1887–1898.
76. Beckett N, Peters R, Tuomilehto J, et al. Immediate and late benefits of treating very elderly people with hypertension: results from active treatment extension to hypertension in the very elderly randomised controlled trial. *BMJ.* 2011;344:d7541.
77. James PA, Oparil S, Carter BL, et al. Evidence-based guideline for the management of high blood pressure in adults: report from the panel members appointed to the Eighth Joint National Committee (JNC 8). *JAMA.* 2014 5;311:507–520.
78. Diao D, Wright JM, Cundiff DK, Gueyffier F. Pharmacotherapy for mild hypertension. *Cochrane Database Syst Rev.* 2012;8:CD006742.
79. Progress Collaborative Group. Post-stroke antihypertensive treatment study: a preliminary result. *Chin Med J.* 1995;108:710–717.
80. Gueyffier F, Boissel J-P, Boutitie F, et al. Effect of antihypertensive treatment in patients having already suffered from stroke. *Stroke.* 1997;28:2557–2562.
81. Gueyffier F, Boissel J-P, Boutitie F, et al. Effect of antihypertensive treatment in patients having already suffered from stroke. *Stroke.* 1997;28:2557–2562.
82. Progress Collaborative Group. Randomised trial of a perindopril-based blood-pressure-lowering regimen among 6105 individuals with previous stroke or transient ischaemic attack. *Lancet.* 2001;358:1033–1041.
83. Rashid P, Leonardi-Bee J, Bath P. Blood pressure reduction and secondary prevention of stroke and other vascular events. *Stroke.* 2003;34:2741–2748.
84. Schrader J, Lüders S, Kulschewski A, et al. Morbidity and mortality after stroke:eprosartan compared with nitrendipine for secondary prevention. *Stroke.* 2005;36:1218–1224.
85. Yusuf S, Diener H-C, Sacco RL, et al. Telmisartan to prevent recurrent stroke and cardiovascular events. *N Engl J Med.* 2008;359:1225–1237.
86. PROGRESS Collaborative Group. Randomised trial of a perindopril-based blood-pressure-lowering regimen among 6105 individuals with previous stroke or transient ischaemic attack. *Lancet.* 2001;358:1033–1041.

87. Yusuf S, Diener H-C, Sacco RL, et al. Telmisartan to prevent recurrent stroke and cardiovascular events. *N Engl J Med.* 2008;359:1225–1237.
88. Telmisartan Randomised AssessmeNt Study in ACEiswcDI, Yusuf S, Teo K, et al. Effects of the angiotensin-receptor blocker telmisartan on cardiovascular events in high-risk patients intolerant to angiotensin-converting enzyme inhibitors: a randomised controlled trial. *Lancet.* 2008;372:1174–1183.
89. Investigators AI, Yusuf S, Healey JS, et al. Irbesartan in patients with atrial fibrillation. *N Engl J Med.* 2011;364:928–938.
90. Ovbiagele B, Diener HC, Yusuf S, et al. Level of systolic blood pressure within the normal range and risk of recurrent stroke. *JAMA.* 2011;306:2137–2144.
91. Group SPSS, Benavente OR, Coffey CS, et al. Blood-pressure targets in patients with recent lacunar stroke: the SPS3 randomised trial. *Lancet.* 2013;382:507–515.
92. Schrader J, Lüders S, Kulschewski A, et al. Morbidity and mortality after stroke: eprosartan compared with nitrendipine for secondary prevention. *Stroke.* 2005;36:1218–1224.
93. Chobanian AV, Bakris GL, Black HR, et al. The Seventh Report of the Joint National Committee on Prevention, Detection, Evaluation, and Treatment of High Blood Pressure: the JNC 7 report. *JAMA.* 2003;289:2560–2572.
94. Wright JT Jr, Fine LJ, Lackland DT, Ogedegbe G, Dennison Himmelfarb CR. Evidence supporting a systolic blood pressure goal of less than 150 mm Hg in patients aged 60 years or older: the minority view. *Ann Intern Med.* 2014.;160:499–503.
95. Goldstein LB, Bushnell CD, Adams RJ, et al. Guidelines for the primary prevention of stroke. *Stroke.* 2011;42:517–584.
96. Sacco RL, Adams R, Albers G, et al. Guidelines for prevention of stroke in patients with ischemic stroke or transient ischemic attack. *Stroke.* 2006;37:577–617.
97. Furie KL, Kasner SE, Adams RJ, et al. Guidelines for the prevention of stroke in patients with stroke or transient ischemic attack: a guideline for healthcare professionals from the American Heart Association/American Stroke Association. *Stroke.* 2011;42:227–276.
98. Qureshi AI, Tuhrim S, Broderick JP, Batjer HH, Hondo H, Hanley DF. Spontaneous intracerebral hemorrhage. *N Engl J Med.* 2001;344:1450–1460.
99. Sessa M. Intracerebral hemorrhage and hypertension. *Neurol Sci.* 2008;29(Suppl 2):S258–S259.
100. Brott T, Thalinger K, Hertzberg V. Hypertension as a risk factor for spontaneous intracerebral hemorrhage. *Stroke.* 1986;17:1078–1083.
101. Aguilar MI, Freeman WD. Spontaneous intracerebral hemorrhage. *Semin Neurol.* 2010;30:555–564.
102. Ariesen MJ, Claus SP, Rinkel GJE, Algra A. Risk factors for intracerebral hemorrhage in the general population. *Stroke.* 2003;34:2060–2065.
103. Matsukawa H, Shinoda M, Fujii M, et al. Factors associated with lobar vs. non-lobar intracerebral hemorrhage. *Acta Neurol Scand.* 2012;126:116–121.
104. Thrift AG, McNeil JJ, Forbes A, Donnan GA. Three important subgroups of hypertensive persons at greater risk of intracerebral hemorrhage. *Hypertension.* 1998;31:1223–1229.
105. Dubow J, Fink ME. Impact of hypertension on stroke. *Curr Atheroscler Rep.* 2011;13:298–305.
106. Diedler J, Sykora M, Rupp A, et al. Impaired cerebral vasomotor activity in spontaneous intracerebral hemorrhage. *Stroke.* 2009;40:815–819.
107. O'Sullivan M. Leukoaraiosis. *Pract Neurol.* 2008;8:26–38.
108. Rost NS, Rahman RM, Biffi A, et al. White matter hyperintensity volume is increased in small vessel stroke subtypes. *Neurology.* 2010;75:1670–1677.
109. Jeerakathil T, Wolf PA, Beiser A, et al. Stroke risk profile predicts white matter hyperintensity volume. *Stroke.* 2004;35:1857–1861.

110. Prabhakaran S, Wright CB, Yoshita M, et al. Prevalence and determinants of subclinical brain infarction. *Neurology*. 2008;70:425–430.
111. Liao D, Cooper L, Cai J, et al. Presence and severity of cerebral white matter lesions and hypertension, its treatment, and its control. *Stroke*. 1996;27:2262–2270.
112. Gottesman RF, Coresh J, Catellier DJ, et al. Blood pressure and white-matter disease progression in a biethnic cohort: Atherosclerosis Risk in Communities (ARIC) study. *Stroke*. 2010;41:3–8.
113. van Dijk EJ, Prins ND, Vrooman HA, Hofman A, Koudstaal PJ, Breteler MMB. Progression of cerebral small vessel disease in relation to risk factors and cognitive consequences. *Stroke*. 2008;39:2712–2719.
114. Havlik RJ, Foley DJ, Sayer B, Masaki K, White L, Launer LJ. Variability in midlife systolic blood pressure is related to late-life brain white matter lesions. *Stroke*. 2002;33:26–30.
115. de Leeuw FE, de Groot JC, Oudkerk M, et al. A follow-up study of blood pressure and cerebral white matter lesions. *Ann Neurol*. 1999;46:827–833.
116. Firbank M, Wiseman R, Burton E, Saxby B, O'Brien J, Ford G. Brain atrophy and white matter hyperintensity change in older adults and relationship to blood pressure. Berlin: Springer, 2007:713–721.
117. Weber R, Weimar C, Blatchford J, et al. Telmisartan on top of antihypertensive treatment does not prevent progression of cerebral white matter lesions in the Prevention Regimen for Effectively Avoiding Second Strokes (PRoFESS) MRI substudy. *Stroke*. 2012;43:2336–2342.
118. Dufouil C, Chalmers J, Coskun O, et al. Effects of blood pressure lowering on cerebral white matter hyperintensities in patients with stroke. *Circulation*. 2005;112:1644–1650.

13

DYSLIPIDEMIA AND RISK OF STROKE AND CEREBROVASCULAR DISEASE

Sabrina Schilling, Christophe Tzourio, and Stéphanie Debette

Introduction

Dyslipidemia refers to abnormal lipid levels, including high levels of low-density lipoprotein cholesterol (LDL-C), total cholesterol (TC), or triglycerides (TGs), and low levels of high-density lipoprotein cholesterol (HDL-C).[1] The definition of thresholds for abnormal levels varies according to the number of associated vascular risk factors and history of vascular disease.[1–3] The lifetime risk for developing dyslipidemia in individuals age 50 years or older is 50% for high LDL-C, 25% (women) and 65% (men) for low HDL-C, and between 20% and 50% for both low HDL-C and high LDL-C.[4] Dyslipidemia, especially elevated LDL-C, is an important risk factor for cardiovascular disease.[5,6] Recent stroke guidelines also consider that dyslipidemia is a well-documented and modifiable risk factor for stroke,[3] but the relationship is less straightforward than for cardiovascular disease.[3,7] Indeed, in observational studies, LDL-C and TC appear less strongly associated with stroke and covert magnetic resonance imaging-defined cerebrovascular disease (CVD) than with coronary artery disease. This could be explained in part by the heterogeneity of stroke and the differential associations of lipid fractions with stroke subtypes, as high levels of LDL-C and TC have been reported as risk factors for ischemic stroke and protective factors for hemorrhagic stroke (intracerebral hemorrhage [ICH]).[8–12] Despite the weakness and complexity of associations between LDL-C and stroke in epidemiological studies, randomized controlled trials (RCTs) have demonstrated that reducing LDL-C reduces the risk of stroke.[13] Less data are available for the relationship of other lipid fractions (TG, HDL-C, non-HDL-C, and so on) with stroke, and on the relationship of dyslipidemia with covert MRI-defined CVD.

In this chapter, we review the literature on the association between lipid fractions or lipid-lowering therapy and CVD, including stroke and MRI markers of CVD.

Epidemiological Studies on LDL-C and Stroke

In contrast with coronary heart disease, which is associated strongly with high LDL-C, epidemiological studies have often failed to show a significant relationship between LDL-C and risk of stroke.[14–16] There are several potential explanations for this. First, heterogeneity of stroke may play a role because associations diverge between ischemic stroke and hemorrhagic stroke, and between ischemic stroke subtypes, as detailed below. Second, a survival effect resulting from competing risks cannot be excluded because individuals exposed to a high risk of vascular disease related to high LDL-C levels, such as myocardial infarction, may have died prematurely, thus attenuating associations with stroke, which often occurs later in life than coronary heart disease. Third, the length of exposure and the age at which exposure is measured may matter. Lipid levels measured in late life can decrease as a result of behavioral changes or because of the presence of comorbidities, as well as a result of the initiation of lipid-lowering drugs. Midlife lipid levels seem to reflect exposure to dyslipidemia over a life span more fully.[17,18]

The epidemiological evidence for an association of high LDL-C with an increased risk of ischemic stroke is relatively weak. The largest meta-analysis, comprising nine cohort studies (N = 688,367) and published 10 years ago, found that low LDL-C levels are associated with a significant reduction in the risk of ischemic stroke (by 15% per 1.0 mmol/L of LDL-C).[19] However, individual study results, including those in more recent studies, have been less consistent. The Prospective Epidemiological Study of Myocardial Infarction (PRIME) study, a large, multicenter, prospective cohort study in healthy European middle-age men (N = 9711), did not find any significant association between LDL-C and incident ischemic stroke during a 10-year period.[16] In the Northern Manhattan Study (NOMAS) study, among 2940 community-dwelling stroke-free individuals (mean age, 68.8 years), baseline LDL-C as a continuous variable was not associated with an increased risk of ischemic stroke after 7.5 years on average,[15] but LDL-C greater than 130 mg/dL predicted an increased risk of stroke (hazard ratio [HR] = 3.81; 95% confidence interval [CI], 1.53–9.51). In a cross-sectional analysis of baseline data from the Fenofibrate Intervention and Event Lowering in Diabetes (FIELD) trial, carried out in 9795 patients with type 2 diabetes, high LDL-C at baseline was an independent risk factor for ischemic stroke or stroke of unknown type (HR = 1.14; 95% CI, 1.02–1.27).[20] When considering ischemic stroke subtypes, several studies have shown a significant association of elevated LDL-C with ischemic stroke resulting from large-artery atheroma,[16,21,22] and not with cardioembolic ischemic stroke.[14,21,22] The Etude du Profil Génétique de l'Infarctus Cérébral (GENIC) case–control study (N = 984) also reported a significant association of LDL-C with lacunar (small-vessel disease [SVD]) stroke (odds ratio [OR] per standard deviation [SD] increase = 2.71; 95% CI, 1.60–4.55).[22]

Regarding ICH, a recent meta-analysis of four observational studies (N = 124,498) showed a significant association between high levels of LDL-C (>3.62 mmol/L or 140 mg/dL) and a 38% reduction in risk of ICH.[23] An earlier meta-analysis of nine cohort studies examining the effect of statins (N = 688,376) reached a comparable conclusion, stating that a 1.0-mmol/L reduction in LDL-C was associated with a significant 19% increase in hemorrhagic stroke risk.[19] A meta-analysis of observational studies did not find an increased risk of recurrent ICH in patients with previous lobar hemorrhage receiving statins (N = 117,948).[24]

RCTs of LDL-C Management and Risk of Stroke

STATINS

Despite the lack of strong epidemiological associations of high LDL-C with ischemic stroke, and even indications of an increased risk of ICH in individuals with low LDL-C levels,[11,12,25] RCTs have shown that reducing LDL-C levels reduces significantly the risk of all stroke, both in primary and secondary prevention. Statins are inhibitors of the 3-hydroxy-3-methyl-glutaryl-CoA reductase enzyme and are the most widely used drugs to lower LDL-C. Standard or low-potency statins (such as simvastatin 40 mg/day) reduce LDL-C by about 41% and TG by 21%, and increase HDL-C by 6%. Higher doses or high-potency statins (such as atorvastatin 40–80 mg/day or rosuvastatin 10–20 mg/day) decrease LDL-C by 41% to 63% and TG by 10% to 35%, and increase HDL C by around 10%, although for the latter the results are variable.[12,26] Interestingly, it was suggested that statins may also have other properties beyond their impact on lipid level reduction,[13] such as atherosclerotic plaque stabilization, decreased inflammation, improved endothelial function, altered thrombogenicity,[13,27,28] and neuroprotective effects.[29]

Primary Prevention

Numerous RCTs have explored the effect of lipid-lowering drugs on the risk of stroke, mostly as secondary end points, with the primary end point often being a composite of vascular events. Most RCTs were performed primarily in individuals without a history of stroke. Overall, recent comprehensive meta-analyses of these RCTs, testing the effect of lipid-lowering drugs against placebo, usual care, or less intensive therapy, reported a significant 4.5% reduction of stroke incidence per 10-mg/dL reduction in LDL-C (N = 195,488),[30] or a 4% relative risk reduction for 10% reduction in LDL-C (N = 266,973).[7] Statins were associated with a 22% reduction in total stroke (fatal and nonfatal combined) in a population free of cardiovascular disease,[31] and with a 15% to 18% reduction in total stroke (n = 130,443–182,803) in populations without such restrictions.[13,24,32] Moreover, another recent meta-analysis of 47 RCTs (N = 175,232) using a Bayesian mixed-treatment comparison to combine direct and indirect (vs. placebo) comparisons of statin doses, showed that high statin doses (leading to an expected minimum of a 40% decrease in LDL-C) were associated significantly with a decreased stroke risk compared with low statin doses (leading to an expected maximum of a 30% decrease in LDL-C).[33] The beneficial effect of statin intake was significant only for nonfatal stroke, with a 19% (95% CI, 4%–32%) reduction (N = 80,711),[34] whereas no significant association was reported between statin intake and risk of fatal stroke.[12,31,34] This pattern did not seem to be modified by statin subtype when performing indirect comparisons between high-potency statins (rosuvastatin and atorvastatin) versus low-potency statins (pravastatin, simvastatin, fluvastatin, and lovastatin).[34]

When focusing on ischemic stroke, statin intake was associated with a significant 17% reduction in ischemic stroke risk in a large meta-analysis of RCTs of 130,443 participants.[24] Moreover, in a meta-analysis of RCTs in high-risk populations with coronary artery disease (N = 39,612), a more aggressive statin therapy (40–80 mg/day atorvastatin or 10–20 mg/day rosuvastatin) was associated with a significant 16% reduction in ischemic stroke when compared with less intensive therapy (20–40 mg/day simvastatin).[12] Intensive statin therapy was, however, also shown to be associated with a greater rate of adverse events, especially elevated liver enzymes and creatine kinase.[33,35]

Regarding hemorrhagic stroke, a subanalysis of a large meta-analysis revealed that statins had no effect on intracranial hemorrhage in a population free of cardiovascular disease (two RCTs, N = 25,634).[31] No significant association with ICH was found in large meta-analyses with and without individuals with preexisting history of cardiovascular disease (23 RCTs, N = 130,443, of which one was exclusively of patients with stroke or transient ischemic attack [TIA]; and 31 RCTs, N = 182,803, of which 11% had a history of stroke).[24,32] One of these meta-analyses also examined the relationship between degree of LDL-C reduction or achieved LDL-C level and ICH risk, showing no association[32] (Table 13.1[36–114]).

TABLE 13.1

RCTs and Meta-analyses Reporting Associations between LDL-Cholesterol or Statins and Stroke

Author/name of study	Year	*N*	Mean age, yr	Men, %	Follow-up duration, yr	Treatment	Effect estimate for all strokes
Primary prevention: RCT							
Baigent et al.[36]/ SHARP	2011	9270	62	63	4.9	Simvastatin, placebo	Rate ratio = 0.81; 95% CI, 0.66–0.99; p = .04
Ruggenenti et al.[37]/ ESPLANADE	2010	87/93	51	76	0.5	Fluvastatin 40–80 mg + benazepril–valsartan, benazepril–valsartan	Information not found in the article
Fassett et al.[38]/ LORD	2010	58/65	60	65	2.5	Atorvastatin 10 mg	RR = 0.22; 95% CI, 0.01–4.57; p = .33[a]
Fellström et al.[39]/ AURORA	2009	1389/1384	64	62	3.8	Rosuvastatin 10 mg, placebo	HR = 1.17; 95% CI, 0.79–1.75; p = .42, for nonfatal stroke
Armitage et al.[40]/ SEARCH	2009	6031/6033	64	83	6.7	Simvastatin 80 mg, simvastatin 20 mg	RR = 0.91; 95% CI, 0.77–1.08; p = .3
Ridker et al.[41]/ JUPITER	2008	8901/8901	66	62	1.9	Rosuvastatin 20 mg, placebo	HR = 0.52; 95% CI, 0.34–0.79; p = .002
Tavazzi et al.[42]/ GISSI-HF	2008	2285/2289	68	77	3.9	Rosuvastatin 10 mg, placebo	HR = 1.23 (0.89, 1.70), p = .21
Sato et al.[43]/OACIS lipid	2008	176/177	63.2	76.7	0.7	Pravastatin 10 mg, standard acute myocardial infarction therapy without pravastatin	p (article) = .252 RR = 0.20; 95% CI, 0.01–4.16; p = 0.30[a]
Bone et al.[44]	2007	604	59	0	1.1	Atorvastatin, placebo	RR = 2.93; 95% CI, 0.12–71.13; p = 0.51[a] (1 hemorrhagic stroke in the atorvastatin 80 group compared with none in placebo group)

(*continued*)

TABLE 13.1

Continued

Author/name of study	Year	N	Mean age, yr	Men, %	Follow-up duration, yr	Treatment	Effect estimate for all strokes
Kjekshus et al.[45]/ CORONA	2007	2514/2497	73	76	2.7	Rosuvastatin, placebo	RR = 0.89; 95% CI, 0.69–1.15; p = .38[a]
Deedwania et al.[46]/ SAGE	2007	446/445	72.5	69.4	1.0	Atorvastatin 80 mg, pravastatin 40 mg	RR = 0.33; 95% CI, 0.03–3.18; p = .34[a]
Knopp et al.[47]/ ASPEN	2006	1211/1199	61	66	4.0	Atorvastatin 10 mg, placebo	RR = 0.89; 95% CI, 0.56–1.40; p = .60[a]
Nakamura et al.[48]/ MEGA	2006	3866/3966	58	32	5.3	Pravastatin 10–20 mg, usual care	HR = 0.83; 95% CI, 0.57–1.21; p = .33
Amarenco et al.[49]/ SPARCL	2006	2365/2366	63	60	4.9	Atorvastatin 80 mg, placebo	HR = 0.84; 95% CI, 0.71–0.99; p = .03
Schmermund et al.[50]	2006	234/233	61.5	74.5	1.0	Atorvastatin 80 mg, atorvastatin 10 mg	RR = 0.33; 95% CI, 0.01–8.11; p = .50[a]
Sakamoto et al.[51]/ MUSUASHI-AMI	2006	237/244	64	80	2.0	Any statin, usual care	RR = 1.54; 95% CI, 0.26–9.16; p = .63[a]
Pedersen et al.[52]/ IDEAL	2005	4439/4449	62	81	4.8	Atorvastatin 80 mg, simvastatin 20 mg	HR = 0.87; 95% CI, 0.70–1.08; p = .20
LaRosa et al.[53]/TNT	2005	4995/5006	61	81	4.9	Atorvastatin 80 mg, atorvastatin 10 mg	HR = 0.75; 95% CI, 0.59–0.96; p = .02
Wanner et al.[54]/4D	2005	1254	66	54	3.9	Atorvastatin 20 mg, placebo	RR = 1.33; 95% CI, 0.90–1.97; p = .15
Anderssen et al.[55]/ HYRIM	2005	283/285	57	100	4	Fluvastatin 40 mg	NS
Yokoi et al.[56]/ ATHEROMA	2005	182/179	59	83	3.0	Pravastatin 10–20 mg, usual care	RR = 1.23; 95% CI, 0.34–4.50; p = .75[a]
Makuuchi et al.[57]/ PCABG	2005	152/151	59	84	4.5	Pravastatin 10–20 mg, usual care	RR = 0.20; 95% CI, 0.02–1.68; p = .14[a]

Stone et al.[58]	2005	96/103	—	86	1.0	Atorvastatin 80 mg, lovastatin 5 mg	RR = 1.07; 95% CI, 0.07–16.91; $p = .96^a$
Koren and Hunninghake[59]/ ALLIANCE	2004	1217/1225	61	82	4.7	Atorvastatin 10–80 mg, usual care	HR = 0.87; 95% CI, 0.55–1.38; $p = .55$
Colhoun et al.[60]/ CARDS	2004	1428/1410	62	68	3.9	Atorvastatin 10 mg, placebo	HR = 0.52; 95% CI, 0.31–0.89
Cannon et al.[61]/ PROVE-IT	2004	2099/2063	58	78	2.0	Atorvastatin 80 mg, pravastatin 40 mg	Risk reduction = −9%, NS
De Lemos et al.[62]/A to Z	2004	2265/2232	61	76	2.0	Simvastatin 80 mg, simvastatin 20 mg	HR = 0.79; 95% CI, 0.48–1.30; $p = .36$
Asselbergs et al.[63]/ PREVEND-IT	2004	864	51	64.5	3.8	Pravastatin 40 mg, placebo	RR = 1.74; 95% CI, 0.51–5.91; $p = .37^a$
Zanchetti et al.[64]/ PHYLLIS	2004	254/254	58	40	2.6	Pravastatin 40 mg, placebo	RR = 3.00; 95% CI, 0.12–73.30; $p = .50^a$
Muldoon et al.[65]	2004	96/93/94	53.6	48	0.5	Simvastatin 10 mg, simvastatin 40 mg, placebo	RR = 3.03; 95% CI, 0.12–73.48; $p = .49^a$
Nakagawa et al.[66]/ PCS	2004	54/66	60	92	5.0	Pravastatin 10 mg, usual care	RR = 0.92; 95% CI, 0.21–3.92; $p = .91^a$
Nissen et al.[67]/ REVERSAL	2004	327/327	56.2	72	1.5	Atorvastatin 80 mg, pravastatin 40 mg	RR = 1.00; 95% CI, 0.06–15.92; $p = 1.00^a$
Bae et al.[68]	2004	105/100	60.0	67.8	0.5	Atorvastatin 10 mg, usual care	RR = 0.95; 95% CI, 0.06–15.02; $p = .97^a$
Sever et al.[69]/ ASCOT-LLA	2003	5168/5137	63	81	3.3	Atorvastatin 10 mg, placebo	HR = 0.73; 95% CI, 0.56–0.93; $p = .024$
Holdaas et al.[70]/ ALERT	2003	2102	50	66	5.1	Fluvastatin 40 mg, placebo	RR = 1.16; 95% CI, 0.83–1.63; for cerebrovascular event (fatal and nonfatal stroke, TIA, reversible ischemic neurological deficit, subarachnoid hemorrhage)

(continued)

TABLE 13.1

Continued

Author/name of study	Year	N	Mean age, yr	Men, %	Follow-up duration, yr	Treatment	Effect estimate for all strokes
Mohler et al.[71]	2003	120/120/114	68.0	77	1.0	Atorvastatin 80 mg, atorvastatin 10 mg, placebo	RR = 2.05; 95% CI, 0.10–42.29; p = 0.64[a]
Olsson et al.[72]/3T	2003	556/537	62.8	75.4	1.0	Atorvastatin 30 mg, simvastatin 35mg	RR = 2.90; 95% CI, 0.12–70.97; p = 0.51[a]
Scanu et al. / ALLHAT-LLT[73]	2002	5170/5185	66	51	4.8	Pravastatin 40 mg, usual care	RR = 0.91; 95% CI, 0.75–1.09; p = 0.31
Athyros et al.[74]/ GREACE	2002	800/800	59	79	3.0	Atorvastatin 10–80 mg, usual care	RR = 0.53; 95% CI, 0.30–0.82; p = .034
Liem et al.[75]/ FLORIDA	2002	265/275	60.5	83	1.0	Fluvastatin 80 mg, placebo	RR = 2.07; 95% CI, 0.19–22.75; p = .55[a] (all fatal stroke)
Craig et al. / HPS[76]	2002	10,269/10,267	65	75	5.0	Simvastatin 40 mg, placebo	Rate ratio = 0.75; 95% CI, 0.66–0.85; p < .0001
Taylor et al.[77]/ ARBITER	2002	79/82	60	71	1.0	Atorvastatin 80 mg, pravastatin 40 mg	RR = 3.11; 95% CI, 0.13–75.28; p = .48[a]
Shepherd et al.[78]/ PROSPER	2002	2891/2913	75	48	3.2	Pravastatin 40 mg, placebo	HR = 1.03; 95% CI, 0.81–1.31; p = .81
Serruys et al.[79]/LIPS	2002	844/833	60	83.8	3.9	Fluvastatin 80 mg, placebo	RR = 1.97; 95% CI, 0.18–21.73; p = .58[a]
Schwartz et al.[80]/ MIRACL	2001	1538/1548	65	65	0.3	Atorvastatin, placebo	RR = 0.50; 95% CI, 0.26–0.99; p = .045
Ito et al.[81]/PATE	2001	331/334	73	21	3.9	Pravastatin 10–20 mg; low dose, 5 mg	RR = 0.64; 95% CI, 0.31–1.29; p = .21[a]
Hedblad et al.[82]/ BCAPS	2001	198/199	61.9	46.8	3.0	Fluvastatin 40 mg, placebo	N = 8 strokes (the article does not distinguish between the 2 groups)

Brown et al.[83]/ HATS	2001	160	53.0	87.0	3.0	Simvastatin 10–20 mg, niacin (+/–antioxidants), placebo or antioxidants	RR = 0.11; 95% CI, 0.01–2.03; $p = .14^{a}$
Schaefer et al. / GISSI-P[84]	2000	2138/2133	60	86	1.9	Pravastatin 20 mg, usual care	RR = 1.05; 95% CI, 0.56–1.96; $p = .88^{a}$
Arntz et al.[85]/ L-CAD	2000	70/56	57	80	2.0	Pravastatin 20–40 mg, usual care	RR = 1.60; 95% CI, 0.15–17.19; $p = .70^{a}$
Teo et al.[86]/SCAT	2000	230/230	61.0	89	4.0	Simvastatin 30 mg, placebo	RR = 0.57; 95% CI, 0.17–1.92; $p = .37^{a}$
Kleemann et al.[87]/ CLAPT	1999	112/114	54	100	2.0	Lovastatin 20-80 mg, usual care	RR = 0.34; 95% CI, 0.01–8.24; $p = .51^{a}$
Downs et al.[88]/ AFCAPS-TexCAPS	1998	3304/3301	58	85	5.2	Lovastatin 20–40 mg, placebo	RR = 0.82; 95% CI, 0.41–1.66; $p = .59^{a}$
Joy et al. / LIPID[89]	1998	4512/4502	62	83	6.1	Pravastatin 40 mg, placebo	Risk reduction = 19%; 95% CI, $p = .048$
Barter et al. / Post-CABG[90]	1997	676/675	62	92	4.3	Lovastatin 40–80 mg, lovastatin 2.5–5 mg	$p = .15$ (article data); RR = 1.12; 95% CI, 0.58–2.18; p
Bertrand et al.[91]/ PREDICT	1997	347/348	58.3	83.7	0.5	Pravastatin 40 mg, placebo	RR = 3.01; 95% CI, 0.12–73.60; $p = 0.50^{a}$
Besterhorn et al.[92]/ CIS	1997	254	49.3	100	2.3	Simvastatin 40 mg, placebo	No stroke
Sacks et al.[93]/CARE	1996	2081/2078	59	86	5.0	Pravastatin 40 mg, placebo	Risk reduction = 31% (3–52), $p = .03$
Shepherd et al.[94]/ WOSCOPS	1995	3302/3293	55	100	4.9	Pravastatin 40 mg, placebo	Risk reduction = 11% (–33 to 40)
Crouse et al.[95]/ PLAC-II	1995	75/76	63	85	3.0	Pravastatin 10–40 mg, placebo	RR = 0.51; 95% CI, 0.05–5.47; $p = .57^{a}$
Salonen et al.[96]/ KAPS	1995	244/223	57	100	3.0	Pravastatin 40 mg, placebo	RR = 0.50; 95% CI, 0.09–2.69; $p = .42^{a}$
Jukema et al.[97]/ REGRESS	1995	450/434	56.2	100	2.0	Pravastatin 40 mg, placebo	RR = 0.58; 95% CI, 0.14–2.41; $p = .45^{a}$

(continued)

TABLE 13.1

(Continued)

Author/name of study	Year	N	Mean age, yr	Men, %	Follow-up duration, yr	Treatment	Effect estimate for all strokes
Pitt et al.[98]/PLAC1	1995	206/202	57.0	77.5	3.0	Pravastatin 40 mg, placebo	RR = 0.20; 95% CI, 0.01–4.06; p = .29[a]
Vermeer et al. / SSSS[99]	1994	2221/2223	58.6	82	5.4	Simvastatin 40 mg, placebo	RR = 0.70; 95% CI, 0.52–0.96; p = .024 for cerebrovascular events (stroke + TIA)
Furberg et al.[100]/ ACAPS	1994	919	62	52	2.8	Lovastatin 20 mg (+1 mg warfarin), placebo	RR = 0.09; 95% CI, 0.005–1.64; p = .10[a]
MAAS investigators[101] / MAAS	1994	193/188	55	89	4.0	Simvastatin 20 mg, placebo	RR = 0.49; 95% CI, 0.04–5.33; p = .56[a]
Waters et al.[102]/ CCAIT	1994	165/166	53	81	2.0	Lovastatin 20 mg, placebo	RR = 3.02; 95% CI, 0.12–73.55; p = .50[a]
Weintraub et al.[103]/ LR	1994	203/201	62.0	72	0.5	Lovastatin 80 mg, placebo	RR = 0.33; 95% CI, 0.01–8.05; p = .50[a]
Kato et al. / PMSG[104]	1993	530/532	55.0	76.5	0.5	Pravastatin 30 mg, placebo	RR = 0.14; 95% CI, 0.01–2.77; p = .20[a]
Blankenhorn et al.[105]/MARS	1993	134/136	58	91	2.2	Lovastatin 80 mg, placebo	RR = 0.14; 95% CI, 0.01–2.78; p = .20[a]
Bradford et al.[106]/ EXCEL	1991	6582/1663	55.8	59	0.9	Lovastatin 20–80 mg, placebo	N = 11 strokes, of which one was fatal; information not detailed in the article
Brown et al.[107]/ FATS	1990	83/81	66	32	2.7	Pravastatin 10 mg, usual care	No stroke
Primary prevention: MA							
Ribeiro et al.[33] (MA)	2013	175,232	49–74 (range, means)	—	3.0	Statins	High-dose statin intake was associated with a decreased risk in stroke (OR, 0.83; 95% CI, 0.68–0.99) compared with low dose (N = 79,515 for this analysis)

Taylor et al.[31] (Cochrane review)	2013	56,934/free of CVD	—	—	>0.5	Statins	-Statin intake was associated with a 22% (95% CI, 11%–32%) reduction in total stroke. -Statin intake had no influence on fatal stroke. -Statin intake had no effect on ICH
McKinney and Kostis[32] (MA)	2012	182,803	62.6 ± 5.2	67	—	Statins	-Statin intake was associated with a 16% (95% CI, 9%–22%) reduction in total stroke. -Statin intake was not associated with ICH incidence. -There was no association between the degree of LDL-C reduction or achieved LDL-C and hemorrhagic stroke risk.
Hackam et al.[24] (MA)	2011	130,443	—	—	3.9 (median)	Statins	Statin intake was associated with -15% (95% CI, 7%–22%) reduction in total stroke -17% (95% CI, 8%–25%) reduction in ischemic stroke risk Statin intake was not associated with ICH (median LDL-C reduction, 1.03 mmol/L).
Tonelli et al.[34] (MA)	2011	60,841	51–76 (range)	—	2 (median)	Statins	-Statin intake was associated with a 19% (95% CI, 4%–32%) reduction in nonfatal stroke. -Statin intake had no influence on fatal stroke.

(continued)

TABLE 13.1

(Continued)

Author/name of study	Year	N	Mean age, yr	Men, %	Follow-up duration, yr	Treatment	Effect estimate for all strokes
Baigent et al.[12]/CTT (MA)	2010	169,138	—	—	—	Statins	-Overall, the risk reduction in the incidence of stroke was 16% (95% CI, 11% – 21%) and was 21% (95% CI, 15% – 26%) for ischemic stroke for a reduction of 1.0 mmol/L of LDL-C, with no significant excess of hemorrhagic stroke. -A 1.0-mmol/L reduction in LDL-C was associated with a 23% (95% CI, 15% – 30%) reduction in first nonfatal ischemic stroke. -No effect on deaths resulting from stroke (ischemic, hemorrhagic, unknown, all strokes)
De Caterina et al.[7] (MA)	2010	266,973	—	—	3.5	Cholesterol-lowering treatment	-Statin intake was associated with a 15% (95% CI, 8% – 22%) reduction in the risk of stroke -4% reduction in RR of stroke incidence for 10% reduction in LDL-C
Labreuche et al.[30] (MA)	2010	195,488	—	—	—	Lipid-modifying drugs	4.5% (95% CI, 1.7% – 7.2%) reduction in stroke incidence for 10 mg/dL reduction in LDL-C
Amarenco and Lebreuche[13] (MA)	2009	165,792 (high risk for stroke)	55 – 75 (range, means)	31 – 100 (range)	0.3 – 6.7 (range)	Statins	18% (95% CI, 13% – 23%) reduction in all stroke incidence, no increase in hemorrhagic stroke
Amarenco and Lebreuche[13] (MA)	2009	83,205	58 – 66 (range,means)	31 – 86 (range)	0.3 – 6.1 (range)	Statins	Primary prevention of hemorrhagic stroke (RR = 0.81; 95% CI, 0.60 – 1.08)

Silva et al.[35] (MA)	2007	27,548	58.2 – 61.7 (range,means)	75.5 – 81.0 (range)	3.4	Atorvastatin or simvastatin 80 mg	-Intensive statin therapy is associated with a decreased stroke risk (OR, 0.82; 95% CI, 0.72 – 0.94). - Intensive statin therapy is associated with the risk of statin-induced adverse events[b] (OR, 1.44; 95% CI, 1.33 – 1.55) and with adverse events requiring discontinuation of therapy (OR, 1.28; 95% CI, 1.18 – 1.39).
Secondary prevention: RCT							
Nagai et al.[108] J-STARS	2014	1578	66.2	68.8	5.0	Pravastatin 10 mg, no statin	Ongoing trial of patients with noncardioembolic ischemic stroke
Milionis et al.[109]/ Athenian Stroke Registry	2009	794	67.0	68.4	10	Statins	Statin therapy after discharge is associated inversely with 10-year stroke recurrence (HRa= 0.65; 95% CI, 0.39 – 0.97)
Kennedy et al.[110]/ FASTER	2007	392	68.1	52.7	0.25	Aspirin, aspirin + clopidogrel, aspirin + simvastatin, aspirin + clopidogrel + simvastatin	RR = 1.5, $p = .25$ (for all strokes and TIAs)
Amarenco et al.[49]/ SPARCL	2006	4731 (stroke or TIA), 2365 (atorvastatin), 2366 (placebo)	63.0 (atorvastatin group), 62.5 (placebo group)	59.7	4.9 (median)	Atorvastatin 80 mg	Statin intake is associated with a 16% (95%CI, 1% – 29%) reduction in stroke recurrence.
Collins et al.[111]/HPS	2004	3280 (CVD)	40 – 80 (range)	75.0	5.0	Simvastatin 40 mg	91% (95% CI, – 8% to 395%) increase in hemorrhagic stroke risk, no effect of statins on stroke recurrence
White et al.[112]/ LIPID	1998/ 2000	369	31 – 75 (range)	83	6.0	Pravastatin 40 mg, placebo	Not available in the article (subanalysis)

(continued)

TABLE 13.1

(Continued)

Author/name of study	Year	*N*	Mean age, yr	Men, %	Follow-up duration, yr	Treatment	Effect estimate for all strokes
Sacks et al.[93]/CARE	1996	333	21 – 75 (range)	86	5.0	Pravastatin 40 mg, placebo	Not available in the article (subanalysis)
Secondary prevention: reviews and MA							
Feher et al.[28] (review)	2011	—	—	—	—	Statins	Marginal reduction of stroke recurrence with statin therapy
Amarenco and Labreuche[13] (MA)	2009	4731 (stroke or TIA) 8,011 (SPARCL + HPS)	63.0/62.5 (atorvastatin group / placebo group) 63.0/62.5 (atorvastatin group / placebo group, for SPARCL) – 40 – 80 (range for HPS)	59.7 59.7 – 75.0	4.9 (median) 4.9 (SPARCL) – 5.0 (HPS)	Atorvastatin 80 mg Atorvastatin, simvastatin	67% (95% CI, 9% – 156%) increase in hemorrhagic stroke risk (SPARCL) 73% (95% CI,19% – 150%) increase in hemorrhagic stroke risk (SPARCL + HPS)

Manktelow and Potter[113] (Cochrane review, MA)	2009	9224 (history of stroke or TIA), 8011 (history of stroke or TIA) (SPARCL + HPS)	18 + 63.0/62.5 (atorvastatin group / placebo group, for SPARCL) – 40 – 80 (range for HPS)	53 – 86 59.7 – 75.0	0.25 – 6.0 (range) 4.9 (SPARCL) – 5.0 (HPS)	Atorvastatin, pravastatin, simvastatin Atorvastatin, simvastatin	Statin intake was associated marginally with decreased stroke recurrence risk (OR, 0.88; 95% CI, 0.77 – 1.00). Statin intake was associated with decreased ischemic stroke recurrence risk (OR, 0.78; 95% CI, 0.67 – 0.92).
Bersano et al.[114] (review)	2008	—	—	—	—	Statins	- Statins reduce the risk of stroke occurrence in high-risk patients and also seem to reduce stroke recurrence. - The low incidence and reversibility of their adverse effects, and the unclear association with hemorrhagic events, support the safe use of these drugs.

[a]Calculated by authors based on the information provided in the article.
[b]Elevation in creatine kinase 10 or more times the upper limit of normal; elevation in alanine or aspartate aminotransferase three times or more the upper limit of normal; rhabdomyolysis; drug-induced adverse events requiring discontinuation; drug-induced events.
3T, Treat-to-Target; 4D, Deutsche Diabetes Dialyse Studie; 4S, Scandinavian Simvastatin Survival Study; A to Z, Aggrastat to Zocar phases; ACAPS, Asymptomatic Carotid Artery Progression Study; AFCAPS-TexCAPS, Air Force – Texas Coronary Atherosclerosis Prevention Study; ALERT, Assessment of Lescol in Renal Transplantation; ALLHAT-LLT, Antihypertensive and Lipid-Lowering Treatment to Prevent Heart Attack Trial; ARBITER, Arterial Biology for the Investigation of the Treatment Effects of Reducing Cholesterol; ASCOT-LLA,

(*continued*)

TABLE 13.1

(Continued)

Anglo-Scandinavian Cardiac Outcomes Trial – Lipid Lowering Arm; ALLIANCE, Aggressive Lipid-Lowering Initiation Abates New Cardiac Events; ASPEN, Atorvastatin Study for Prevention of Coronary Heart Disease Endpoints in Non-Insulin-Dependent Diabetes Mellitus; ATHEROMA, Angiographic Intervention Trial Using an HMG-CoA Reductase Inhibitor to Evaluate the Retardation of Obstructive Multiple Atheroma; AURORA, Study to Evaluate the Use of Rosuvastatin in Subjects on Regular Hemodialysis: An Assessment of Survival and Cardiovascular Events; BCAPS, β-Blocker Cholesterol-Lowering Asymptomatic Plaque Study; CARDS, Collaborative Atorvastatin Diabetes Study; CARE, Cholesterol and Recurrent Events; CCAIT, Canadian Coronary Atherosclerosis Intervention Trial; CI, confidence interval; CIS, Coronary Intervention Study; CLAPT, Cholesterol Lowering Atherosclerosis PTCA Trial; CORONA, Controlled Rosuvastatin Multinational Trial in Heart Failure; CTT, Cholesterol Treatment Trialists; ESPLANADE, European Study for Preventing by Lipid-Lowering Agents and ACE-Inhibitors Dialysis Endpoints; EXCEL, Expanded Clinical Evaluation of Lovastatin; FATS, Familial Atherosclerosis Treatment Study; FLORIDA, Fluvastatin on Risk Diminishment after Acute Myocardial Infarction; GISSI, Gruppo Italino per lo Studio della Sopravvivenza nell' Infarcto Miocardico (-P, Prevenzione; -HF, Heart Failure); GREACE, Greek Atorvastatin and Coronary-Heart-Disease Evaluation; HATS, HDL-Atherosclerosis Treatment Study; HPS, Heart Protection Study; HR, hazard ratio; HRa, adjusted hazard ratio; HYRIM, Hypertension High Risk Management Trial; ICH, intracerebral hemorrhage; IDEAL, Incremental Decrease in End Points Through Aggressive Lipid Lowering; JUPITER, Justification for the Use of Statins in Prevention: an Intervention Trial Evaluating Rosuvastatin; KAPS, Kuopio Atherosclerosis Prevention Study; L-CAD, Lipid Coronary Artery Disease; LDL-C, low-density lipoprotein cholesterol; LIPID, Long-Term Intervention with Pravastatin in Ischemic Disease; LIPS, Lescol Intervention Prevention Study; LORD, Lipid Lowering and Onset of Renal Disease; LR, Lovastatin Restenosis Trial; MA, meta-analysis; MAAS, Multicenter Anti-Atheroma Study; MARS, Monitored Atherosclerosis Regression Study; MEGA, Management of Elevated Cholesterol in the Primary Prevention Group of Adult Japanese; MIRACL, Myocardial Ischemia Reduction with Aggressive Cholesterol Lowering; MUSUASHI-AMI, Multicenter Study for Aggressive Lipid-Lowering Strategy by HMG-CoA Reductase Inhibitors in Patients with Acute Myocardial Infarction; NS, not significant; OACIS-LIPID, Osaka Acute Coronary Insufficiency Study- LIPID; OR: odds ratio; PATE, Pravastatin Anti-Atherosclerosis Trial in the Elderly; PCABG, Pravastatin Coronary Artery Bypass Graft Study; PCS, Prevention of Coronary Sclerosis; PHYLLIS, Plaque Hypertension Lipid-Lowering Italian Study; PLAC-1, Pravastatin Limitation of Atherosclerosis in the Coronary Arteries; PLAC-2, Pravastatin, Lipids, and Atherosclerosis in the Carotids; PMSG, Pravastatin Mutinational Study Group for Cardiac Risk Patients; Post-CABG, Post-Coronary Artery Bypass Grafting; PREDICT, Prevention of Restenosis by Elisor after Transluminal Coronary Angioplasty; PREVEND-IT, Prevention of Renal and Vascular Endstage Disease Intervention Trial; PROSPER, Prospective Study of Pravastatin in the Elderly at Risk; PROVE-IT, Pravastatin or Atorvastatin Evaluation and Infection Therapy; RCT, randomized, controlled trial; REGRESS, Regression Growth Evaluation Statin Study; REVERSAL, Reversal of Atherosclerosis with Aggressive Lipid Lowering; RR, risk ratio; SAGE, Study Assessing Goals in the Elderly; SCAT, Simvastatin/Enalapril Coronary Atherosclerosis Trial; SEARCH, Study of the Effectiveness of Additional Reductions in Cholesterol and Homocysteine; SHARP, Study of Heart and Renal Protection; SPARCL, Stroke Prevention by Aggressive Reduction in Cholesterol Levels; TIA, transient ischemic attack; TNT, Treating to New Targets; WOSCOPS, West of Scotland Coronary Prevention Study; yr, year.

Secondary Prevention

A few RCTs have focused on the effect of lipid-lowering drugs in individuals with a history of stroke. A meta-analysis of four RCTs (N = 8713) on individuals with prior noncardioembolic stroke, TIA, or CVD found that statin intake was associated with a significantly reduced risk of stroke recurrence (risk ratio [RR] = 0.88; 95% CI, 0.78–0.99).[13] A Cochrane meta-analysis of five RCTs (N = 9224) of individuals with a history of stroke or TIA reported a marginal association between statin intake and a decreased risk in stroke recurrence (OR= 0.88; 95% CI, 0.77–1.00), which was more pronounced for ischemic stroke (OR= 0.78; 95% CI, 0.67–0.92; two RCTs, N = 8011).[113] The Stroke Prevention by Aggressive Reduction in Cholesterol Levels (SPARCL) trial was designed to evaluate the effects of atorvastatin 80 mg/day in 4731 patients who experienced a noncardioembolic stroke or TIA in the previous 6 months (but who have no known coronary heart disease), and is the only completed trial that focuses exclusively on patients with a history of stroke. This RCT reported a 16% (95% CI, 1%–29%) reduction in stroke recurrence in patients in the statin arm compared with patients in the placebo arm,[49] which was found consistently in all age groups,[115] genders,[116] and stroke subtypes (the cardioembolic subtype being excluded in this RCT).[117]

In the SPARCL trial (N = 4731) and in a subanalysis of 3280 participants from the Heart Protection Study (HPS) (N = 20,536; comparing 40 mg simvastatin daily vs. placebo in patients with coronary disease, other occlusive arterial disease, or diabetes) with a history of cerebrovascular disease,[111] an increase in risk of hemorrhagic stroke was observed in patients randomized to statin treatment of, respectively, 67% (95% CI, 9%–156%) and 91% (95% CI, −8% to 395%); and this increase in risk was 73% (95 % CI, 19%–150%) when combining SPARCL and HPS (Table 13.1).[13] In the SPARCL trial, this finding remained significant even after adjusting for age, male gender, presentation with hemorrhagic stroke at inclusion, and uncontrolled hypertension.[25] This result was found to be stronger in the subgroup with ischemic stroke resulting from SVD as a qualifying event.[25] However, in these patients, the significant reduction in ischemic stroke risk associated with atorvastatin therapy offset the risk of hemorrhagic stroke, and the benefit in terms of all stroke risk remained significant.[25,117] There is no clear evidence concerning the beneficial effect on stroke recurrence related to statin intake in patients with previous hemorrhagic stroke.[28]

The benefit and safety of more intensive lipid-lowering drug regimens in secondary stroke prevention is currently being evaluated in the Treat Stroke to Target RCT, in which the usual target of 100 mg/dL LDL-C is compared with LDL-C less than 70 mg/dL in individuals with a recent ischemic stroke (<3 months).

EZETIMIBE

Ezetimibe is a cholesterol transporter inhibitor in the small intestine directly targeting Niemann-Pick C1-like 1, which is highly expressed at the surface of absorptive jejunal enterocytes.[118] It is prescribed to lower LDL-C levels when patients are intolerant to statins or do not achieve targeted LDL-C levels.[119] Ezetimibe (10 mg/day) was reported to reduce LDL-C by approximately 20% and TG by around 8%, and to increase HDL-C by approximately 5%.[118] It was tested in combination with statin therapy to obtain a more aggressive lipid-modifying effect, but although no adverse event was observed, the additional benefit of this combination and the effect of ezetimibe alone on clinical outcomes remain unproved.[120,121]

Guidelines for LDL-C management in primary or secondary stroke prevention are shown in Boxes 13.1[122] and 13.2.[123–125]

BOX 13.1

GUIDELINES FOR THE MANAGEMENT OF LOW-DENSITY LIPOPROTEIN CHOLESTEROL AND STATIN THERAPY IN STROKE

Currently, low-density lipoprotein cholesterol (LDL-C) is the only lipid fraction that has an acknowledged guideline in stroke with precise aims.

Primary Prevention

- For patients with coronary heart disease (CHD) or high-risk conditions such as diabetes, statin therapy should be initiated, as well as therapeutic lifestyle modifications to reach fasting LDL-C goals as detailed in the National Cholesterol Education Program—Adult Treatment Panel III[2,3]:
  - No or one risk factor: ≤160 mg/dL
  - More than two risk factors (10-year Framingham CHD risk, ≤20%): <130 mg/dL
  - High-risk patients (CHD or CHD risk equivalents, 10-year Framingham CHD risk, >20%): <100 mg/dL
- In patients with diabetes, especially if they have additional risk factors, statin therapy should be initiated to decrease the risk of first stroke.[3]

Secondary Prevention

- According to the American Heart Association/American Stroke Association, statin therapy should be initiated in patients with ischemic stroke or transient ischemic attack (TIA) with evidence of atherosclerosis but without known CHD if LDL-C is ≥100 mg/dL.[122]
- Reduction of LDL-C levels of at least 50% (or target, <70 mg/dL) is recommended for patients with atherosclerotic ischemic stroke or TIA and without known CHD.[122]
- For patients with ischemic stroke or TIA who have high cholesterol levels or comorbid coronary artery disease, the National Cholesterol Education Program—Adult Treatment Panel III guidelines should be followed: lifestyle modifications, dietary guidelines, medication recommendation.[122]

Other Lipid Fractions and Stroke

Although the focus so far has been mainly on LDL-C lowering and statins, other lipid fractions have recently gained interest in association with stroke risk.

EPIDEMIOLOGICAL STUDIES

Total Cholesterol

TC corresponds to the sum of LDL-C, HDL-C, and very low-density lipoprotein. However, the biggest component of TC being LDL-C, associations of TC with stroke risk largely resemble those of LDL-C. In a meta-analysis of 45 prospective studies including 450,000 individuals, TC was not associated with an increased risk of stroke.[126]

Focusing on ischemic stroke, there was a significant association of the latter with TC levels of 7.0 mmol/L or more, in 28,519 stroke-free male smokers age 50 to 69 years,[10] and a trend toward

BOX 13.2
GUIDELINES CONCERNING LIPID-LOWERING DRUGS OTHER THAN STATINS IN STROKE MANAGEMENT, ACCORDING TO THE AMERICAN HEART ASSOCIATION/AMERICAN STROKE ASSOCIATION[a]

Primary Stroke Prevention

- The use of fibrates alone might be considered for patients with diabetes to decrease the risk of first stroke, but usefulness and efficacy are not well established.[3]
- The use of fibrates in combination with a statin therapy in patients with diabetes is not useful.[3]
- Fibric acid derivatives might be considered for patients with hypertriglyceridemia, but their efficacy in the prevention of ischemic stroke is not established.[3]
- Niacin might be considered for patients with low high-density lipoprotein cholesterol levels or high lipoprotein a levels, but their efficacy is not established for the prevention of ischemic stroke in these patients.[3]
- The use of niacin, fibric acid derivatives, bile acid sequestrants, and ezetimibe in the prevention of ischemic stroke might be considered in patients who do not achieve targeted lows-density lipoprotein cholesterol levels or who are intolerant to statins, but there is a lack of evidence concerning their efficacy in decreasing the risk of stroke.[3]

Secondary Stroke Prevention

- Gemfibrozil, a fibrate acid agent, or niacin might be considered for patients with ischemic stroke or transient ischemic attack and who have low levels of high-density lipoprotein cholesterol, but their usefulness or efficacy is not well established.[122]

[a]Of note, these recommendations have not been updated yet after the publication of two recent negative niacin trials.[123–125]

a positive association with TC was reported in a meta-analysis of 18 Asian cohorts comprising 124,774 participants.[127] When considering ischemic stroke subtypes, a consistent association between TC and both the large-artery disease and the SVD subtypes has been described,[21,22,128,129] and no association[21,22] or even an inverse association has been noted between TC and cardioembolic stroke.[128]

A meta-analysis of 17 observational studies (N = 1,285,222) yielded a significant association between increasing TC and decreased hemorrhagic stroke risk, with an increase of 1 mmol/L TC being associated with a significant 15% reduction in the relative risk of hemorrhagic stroke, especially ICH, but not subarachnoid hemorrhage.[23]

Recent meta-analyses of 78 RCTs (N = 266,973; mean follow-up, 3.5 years), of which 49 tested the efficacy of statins and the remaining 33 tested various lipid-lowering drugs (13 on fibrates, 7 on dietary interventions, 12 on other drugs, and 1 on partial ileal bypass surgery), reported a significant association between reduction in TC and reduction in overall stroke risk, yielding a 0.8% relative risk reduction for each 1% reduction of TC (mostly a result of LDL-C reduction) in a population comprising 3.4% of patients with a history of stroke and 27% of patients with a history of myocardial infarction[7] (Table 13.2[130–149]).

TABLE 13.2

RCTs Studying the Association between Lipid-Lowering Drugs (Other Than Statins) and Stroke

Author/name of study	Year	*N*	Mean age, yr	Men, %	Mean follow-up duration	Treatment	Results
Fibrates: RCT							
Ginsberg et al.[130]/ACCORD study	2010	2765/2753	62	69	4.7 yr	Fenofibrate 160 mg, placebo	RR (95%CI) = 1.06 (0.72, 1.56)
Whitney et al.[131]/AFREGS	2005	71/72	62	92	2.5 yr	Gemfibrozil 600 mg, placebo	RR (95%CI) = 0.90 (0.73, 1.12)
Keech et al.[132]/FIELD study	2005	4895/4900	63	63	5.0 yr	Fenofibrate 200 mg, placebo	RR (95%CI) = 0.20 (0.01, 4.15)
Meade et al.[133]/LEADER study	2002	783/785	68	100	55.2 mo	Bezafibrate 400 mg, placebo	RR (95%CI) = 1.23 (0.85, 1.77)
Diabetes Atherosclerosis Intervention Study Investigators / DAIS[134]	2001	207/211	56.8	73	3.3 yr	Fenofibrate 200 mg, placebo	Not available in the article (*N* = 12 strokes)
BIP Study Group / BIP [135]	2000	1548/1542	60	91	6.2 yr	Bezafibrate 400 mg, placebo	RR (95%CI) = 0.93 (0.68, 1.27)
Rubins et al.[136]/VA-HIT	1999	1264/1267	64	100	5.1 yr	Gemfibrozil 1.2 g, placebo	RR (95%CI) = 0.73 (0.53, 1.00)
Frick et al.[137]/Helsinki Heart Study	1993	311/317	48.6	100	5.0 yr	Gemfibrozil 1.2 g daily, placebo	RR (95%CI)= 1.02 (0.06, 16.22), $p = .99$[a]
Frick et al.[138]/Helsinki Heart Study	1987	2051/2030	47.3	100	5.0 yr	Gemfibrozil 1.2 g, placebo	RR (95%CI) = 1.10 (0.58, 2.07), $p = 0.77$[a]
Acheson et al.[139]	1972	95	NR	68	8.7/7.6 yr	Clofibrate 1–2 g, corn oil then placebo	RR (95%CI) = 1.07 (0.70, 1.63)

Veteran Administration Cooperative Study Group[140]	1973	268/264	NR	100	4.6 yr	Clofibrate 2 g, placebo	RR (95%CI) = 1.58 (0.97, 2.59)
Coronary Drug Project Research Group[141]	1975	3892	NR	100	6.2 yr	Clofibrate 1.8 g, placebo	RR (95%CI) = 1.11 (0.92, 1.34)
Committee of Principal Investigators[142] /	1978	5331/5296	46	100	5.3 yr	Clofibrate 1.6 g, olive oil placebo	RR (95%CI) = 1.18 (0.71, 1.96)
Research Committee of the Scottish Society of Physicians / Scottish[143]	1971	350/367	52.1	82.7	3.4 yr	Clofibrate 1.6 g or 2 g, placebo	Not available in the article (*N* = 5 strokes); secondary prevention trial
Fibrates: MA							
Zhou et al.[144] (MA)	2013	37,791	46–68 (range, means)	63–100 (range)	2.5–8.7 yr (range)	Fibrates	No association between fibrate intake and stroke risk; decrease in fatal stroke risk in patients with diabetes, cardiovascular disease, or stroke (RR (95%CI) = 0.49; 0.26, 0.93)
De Caterina et al.[7] (MA)	2010	39,890	45.9–68.2 (range, means)	—	2.5–6.2 yr (range)	Fibrates	No association between fibrate and stroke risk
Jun et al.[145] (MA)	2010	19,935	—	63–100 (range)	1.8–8.7 yr (range)	Fibrates	No association between fibrate intake and stroke risk (RR (95%CI) = 1.03; 0.91, 1.16)

(continued)

TABLE 13.2

(Continued)

Author/name of study	Year	N	Mean age, yr	Men, %	Mean follow-up duration	Treatment	Results
Niacin: RCT							
Guyton et al.[146]	2008	676/272	57	50	0.5 yr	Niacin 0.5–2 g + ezetimibe 10 mg + simvastatin 20 mg/ ezetimibe 10 mg + simvastatin 20 mg	OR (95%CI), 0.03 (0.00, 2.33); as reported in MA[149]
Whitney et al.[131]/AFREGS	2005	71/72	63	92	2.5 yr	Niacin 0.25–3 g + gemfibrozil 1.2 g + cholestyramine 2 g, placebo	Difference (percentage points) = 2.8 (−5.2 to 13.5); $p > .2$; OR (95%CI), 0.14 (0.01, 2.18); as reported in MA[149]
Taylor et al.[147]/ARBITER-2	2004	87/80	67	91	1.0 yr	Niacin 0.5–1.0 g + any statin, placebo + any statin	OR (95%CI), 0.12 (0.00, 6.27); as reported in MA[149]
Brown et al.[83]/HATS	2001	38/38	53	87	3.0 yr	Niacin 1–4 g + simvastatin 10–20 mg, placebo	OR (95%CI), 0.13 (0.01, 2.15); as reported in MA[149]
Carlson and Rosenhamer[148]/ STOCKHOLM	1988	279/276	60	80	5.0 yr	Niacin 3 g + clofibrate 2 g, usual care	OR (95%CI), 1.19 (0.36, 3.92); as reported in MA[149]
CDP[140]	1975	1119/2789	44	100	6.2 yr	Niacin 3 g, placebo	OR (95%CI), 0.75 (0.60, 0.94); as reported in MA[149]

Niacin: MA							
Bruckert et al.[149] (MA)	2010	6015	36–67 (range, means)	43–100 (range)	0.5–6.2 yr (range)	Niacin alone or in combination	26% (95%CI) (8–41%) reduction in stroke risk
HDL-C: MA							
De Caterina et al.[7] (MA)	2010	224,835	—	—	3.5 yr	—	No effect of HDL-C level change on stroke risk
TG: MA							
De Caterina et al.[7] (MA)	2010	243,875	—	—	3.5 yr	—	Inconsistent results
Labreuche et al.[30] (MA)	2010	96,807/98,681 placebo	34–72 (range, means)	0–100 (range)	1.0–6.2 yr (range)	—	No association with stroke incidence
TC: MA							
De Caterina et al.[7] (MA)	2010	266,973	—	—	3.5 yr	—	1% reduction in TC levels is associated with a 0.8% reduction in relative risk of stroke

[a] calculated by authors based on the information provided in the article; [b] according to raw data provided in [30]ACCORD: Action to Control Cardiovascular Risks in Diabetes; AFREGS, Armed Forces Regression Study; ARBITER-2, Arterial Biology for the Investigation of the Treatment Effects of Reducing Cholesterol 2; BIP, Bezafibrate Infarction Prevention; CI, confidence interval; DAIS, Diabetes Atherosclerosis Invervention Study; FIELD: Fenofibrate Intervention and Event Lowering in Diabetes; HATS, HDL-Atherosclerosis Treatment Study; HDL-C, high-density lipoprotein cholesterol; LEADER, Lowering Extremity Arterial Disease Event Reduction; MA, meta-analysis; mo, month; NR, not recorded; OR, odds ratio; RCT, randomized, controlled trial; RR, risk ratio; Stockholm CDP, Stockholm Coronary Drug Project; TC, total cholesterol; TG, triglyceride; VA-HIT, Veterans Affairs High-Density Lipoprotein Cholesterol Intervention Trial; yr, year.

Triglycerides

TGs are a complex lipid fraction, the levels of which vary considerably, and studies examining their association with stroke have yielded inconsistent results.[120]

A systematic review of epidemiological studies reported that high TG levels were associated with an increased risk of stroke (RR per 1 SD = 1.10; 95% CI, 1.07–1.13).[150] Similarly, in a large meta-analysis of RCTs (N = 195,488), a 10-mg/dL increase in baseline TG levels was associated with a significant increase in the risk of all strokes by 5.5%.[30] When focusing on ischemic stroke, a large meta-analysis of prospective studies carried out in individuals without coronary heart disease did not find any significant association between TG level and ischemic stroke (N = 302,430).[151] Interestingly, although TGs are generally measured in a fasting state, some studies found a significant association of higher nonfasting TG levels (but not fasting TG levels) with increased risk of stroke and ischemic stroke.[152] High levels of nonfasting triglycerides indicate the presence of increased levels of remnants from chylomicrons and very low-density lipoproteins; these may penetrate the arterial endothelium and promote the development of atherosclerosis. No clear differential association with ischemic stroke subtypes has emerged from two case–control studies comparing ischemic stroke patients with control subjects,[21,22] although one retrospective analysis conducted on 1049 patients with ischemic stroke or TIA reported that TG levels were associated with the large-artery disease subtype of ischemic stroke compared with other subtypes of ischemic stroke (OR = 2.69; 95% CI, 1.44–5.2; when comparing the highest TG quartile with the lowest).[153]

No strong association between reduction of TG levels through interventions and reduction of stroke risk has been shown.[135,144] A meta-analysis of RCTs reported inconsistent associations between change in TG levels and stroke reduction (70 RCTs, N = 243,875), although most of the tested multivariable models were in favor of a significant association between TG reduction and stroke risk reduction.[7] Another meta-analysis of RCTs did not report any association between TG change and stroke incidence (64 RCTs, n = 96,807 in the active group and n = 98,681 in the control group),[30] but did observe a trend for an association between TG lowering in fibrate and niacin trials and decreased risk of stroke[30] (Table 13.2).

When focusing on hemorrhagic stroke, large epidemiological studies revealed that low TG levels were a significant risk factor for incident ICH in several population-based studies, including in the 3C-Study (HR for TG ≤0.94 mmol/L = 2.35; 95% CI, 1.18–4.70; N = 8393),[154] and in a pooled analysis of the Cardiovascular Health Study (CHS) and the Atherosclerosis Risk in Communities (ARIC) Study (relative rate for increasing TG = 0.45; 95% CI, 0.30–0.67; N = 21,680).[11] Similar nonsignificant associations were observed in other studies.[155–157] Of note, an earlier large meta-analysis of Asian prospective studies did not report any significant association between TG and the risk of hemorrhagic stroke (26 studies, N = 96,224).[158] In the SPARCL trial, there was no association between baseline TG level and risk of ICH in 4731 patients with previous stroke or TIA.[159]

High-Density Lipoprotein Cholesterol

A large systematic review of 18 studies on the relationship between HDL-C and risk of stroke found that 8 of 10 cohort studies and 3 of 8 case–control studies were in favor of an association between high HDL-C levels and decreased risk of stroke.[160] In prospective studies, an average increase of 10 mg/dL in HDL-C was associated with an 11% to 15% decrease in stroke risk.[160] When considering ischemic stroke, none of the 10 prospective cohort studies reported a significant association with HDL-C.[160] However, three of the eight case–control studies reported an inverse association between HDL-C levels and ischemic stroke, and two reported that increasing HDL-C levels were a significant risk factor for ischemic stroke.[160] There are more limited data and a lack of consistency regarding associations of HDL-C with ischemic stroke subtypes. Increasing HDL-C was reported to be associated significantly with a reduced risk of SVD ischemic stroke (RR per SD = 0.62; 95% CI, 0.48–0.79)[161] and cardioembolic stroke (RR per SD = 0.65; 95% CI, 0.50–0.84)[161] in the ARIC study, a prospective, multicenter, population-based cohort study (*N* = 14,488). In a health maintenance organization-based case–control study from the Group Health Cooperative (*N* = 1555 stroke patients and 6455 control subjects),[129] the top quartile of HDL-C was reported to be associated significantly with a reduced risk of large-artery disease ischemic stroke (OR = 0.4; 95% CI, 0.2–0.7).[129]

Concerning hemorrhagic stroke, in a large systematic review of 18 studies, only limited data from one prospective cohort study and three case–control studies were available on the relationship between HDL-C and hemorrhagic stroke, none of which reported a significant association.[160]

A recent meta-analysis of 78 RCTs (*N* = 266,973), of which 49 tested the efficacy of statins and the remaining 33 tested various lipid-lowering drugs (13 on fibrates, 7 on dietary interventions, 12 on other drugs and 1 on partial ileal bypass surgery), reported no association of change in HDL-C levels with stroke risk (*N* =224,835) in a population comprising 3.4% of patients with a history of stroke and 27% of patients with a history of myocardial infarction.[7] (Table 13.2)

Others

ATHEROGENIC DYSLIPIDEMIA

Atherogenic dyslipidemia refers to the concomitant presence of low HDL-C (<40 mg/dL) and high TG levels, with exact thresholds varying across definitions for TG (>200 mg/dL or >150 mg/dL).[162] The definition may also include the presence of small and dense low-density lipoprotein particles.[163,164] Both low HDL-C and high TG levels have been associated with cardiovascular disease, but their combination might be even worse, by promoting a proinflammatory state and oxidative stress.[165,166] This condition is mostly seen in patients who are obese and have metabolic syndrome, insulin resistance, and type 2 diabetes.[167–169] In a cohort of 1471 patients with previous TIA or minor stroke, atherogenic dyslipidemia was associated significantly with a 4.8% increased risk of recurrent stroke after 90 days.[166] However, data are scarce and there are currently no specific therapeutic recommendations for this group.

NON-HDL CHOLESTEROL

Non-HDL-C corresponds to the measure of all atherogenic apolipoprotein B-containing lipoproteins, including LDL-C, very low-density lipoprotein, intermediate density lipoprotein, and lipoprotein a [Lp(a)].[170] It was reported to be associated with cardiovascular disease incidence and mortality in the general population,[151,171–173] and in individuals with diabetes. [174–176] A secondary analysis of the Cholesterol and Recurrent Events (CARE) trial, evaluating the effect of pravastatin in 2078 patients with myocardial infarction, revealed that baseline non-HDL-C was the only lipid marker that was associated significantly with the risk of incident stroke or TIA (HR = 1.76; 95% CI, 1.05–2.54).[177] Focusing on ischemic stroke, a large meta-analysis—carried out in 302,430 participants from prospective studies without known vascular disease—reported a significant association between non-HDL-C and ischemic stroke risk, but none with hemorrhagic stroke.[151] In a cohort of 1049 patients with ischemic stroke or TIA, the highest non-HDL-C levels were associated with the large-artery atherosclerotic subtype of ischemic stroke compared with all other subtypes (OR = 2.39; 95% CI, 1.40–4.11).[153] In summary, there are accumulating data suggesting an important role of non-HDL-C for the risk of stroke, but additional research is needed to characterize this relationship further and the impact of lipid-lowering therapy in patients with high non-HDL-C.

LIPOPROTEIN(A)

Lp(a) is a low-density lipoproteinlike particle that contains apolipoprotein B-100 linked to the glycoprotein apolipoprotein(a) by a unique disulfide bond. It was reported that Lp(a) has atherogenic properties, possibly related to the plasminogenlike structure of apolipoprotein(a).[178–180] It has been known for a long time that Lp(a) is a risk factor for coronary heart disease and myocardial infarction,[181] which was largely confirmed by several subsequent meta-analyses.[182,183] A meta-analysis of 31 studies of fatal and nonfatal CVD (56,010 subjects, 4609 strokes) showed that high levels of Lp(a) are a risk factor for stroke when conducting a meta-analysis of 23 case–controls studies (N = 19,530, of which 2600 were strokes). The standardized mean difference was 0.39 (95% CI, 0.23–0.54) in studies using means and SD, and the OR was 2.39 (95% CI, 1.57–3.63) for studies using dichotomous values of Lp(a) (either considering the atherogenic threshold of 30 mg/dL or comparing the highest quintile vs. the lowest).[184] This was also the case when combining five prospective cohort studies (N = 37,098, with >1645 incident strokes): the RR was 1.22 (95% CI, 1.04–1.43) comparing the highest tertile of Lp(a) with the lowest one.[184] When considering stroke subtypes, increasing levels of Lp(a) were found to be associated with a significantly increased risk of ischemic stroke (RR = 1.11; 95% CI, 1.02–1.20; per 3.5-fold higher Lp(a) levels), but not hemorrhagic stroke (RR = 1.06; 95% CI, 0.90–1.26), in a large meta-analysis of prospective studies (1.3 million person-years at risk with 1903 incident ischemic strokes and 338 incident hemorrhagic strokes).[185] When focusing on ischemic stroke subtypes, in the ARIC study (N = 14,488), levels of Lp(a) greater than 174 µg/mL were a significant risk factor for nonlacunar stroke (RR = 1.42; 95% CI, 1.10–1.83; $p < .01$), but not for lacunar or cardioembolic subtypes.[161] In summary, available data suggest that high Lp(a) levels may increase the risk of stroke, particularly ischemic stroke, but there are currently no validated cutoffs to define abnormal levels of Lp(a) or intervention thresholds.

DRUGS AIMED AT REDUCING PRIMARILY OTHER LIPID FRACTIONS THAN LDL-C

Several studies report that patients treated with lipid-lowering drugs (mostly statins) do not achieve normal lipid levels.[5,163,186] Therefore, other lipid-modifying drugs have received increasing attention, with the objective to reduce the residual risk defined as the presence of high TG levels or low HDL-C levels despite the lowering of LDL-C levels with statin therapy to provide additional vascular protection.[5,163,187]

Fibrates

Fibrates are agonists of the peroxisome proliferator receptor-α (PPAR-α), increasing the transcription of genes involved in cholesterol metabolism, including fatty acid binding proteins. These proteins increase lipolysis and induce fatty acid uptake by the liver, thus reducing TG production and increasing HDL-C production.[121,187–189] On average, fibrates are reported to reduce TC by 15% to 20%, TG by 32% to 45%, and LDL-C by 3% to 20%, and to increase HDL-C by 6% to 16% in patients with dyslipidemia.[121,190,191] In addition, fibrates were reported to have anti-inflammatory properties, which could confer vascular protection.[192] Fibrates were not associated significantly with stroke risk reduction in recent meta-analyses of RCTs[7,144] carried out respectively in populations comprising 3.4% of patients with a history of stroke and 27% of patients with a history of myocardial infarction,[7] and in patients with previous diabetes, cardiovascular disease, or stroke.[144,145] Noteworthy, in subgroup analyses, fibrate intake decreased significantly the risk of fatal stroke[144] (Table 13.2). In addition to statin therapy, fibrates were reported to be most beneficial for cardiovascular risk in patients with atherogenic dyslipidemia or high TG levels.[193]

Niacin

Niacin (or nicotinic acid) increases HDL-C levels by 30%, reduces TG and LDL by 20% on average,[162] and is the only available drug that modulates Lp(a).[149] A meta-analysis of 11 RCTs ($N = 6616$, mainly with a history of myocardial infarction or with established or suspected coronary heart disease) reported a significant 26% reduction in stroke risk in the treated group[149] (Table 13.2). However, two subsequent RCTs were negative. The Atherothrombosis Intervention in Metabolic Syndrome with Low HDL/High Triglycerides: Impact on Global Health Outcomes (AIM-HIGH) trial randomized 3414 patients, of whom 720 had a history of stroke or CVD, to receive 1500 mg or 2000 mg niacin or placebo, and was interrupted prematurely because of the lack of benefit.[123] The Treatment of HDL to Reduce the Incidence of Vascular Events (HPS2-THRIVE) trial randomized 25,673 patients, of whom 8170 had a history of CVD or placebo, without significant benefit on the occurrence of major vascular events, and with various side effects, especially increased risk of myopathy in association with statins.[124,125]

Bile Acid Sequestrants

Bile acid sequestrants (e.g., cholestyramine) prevent bile acid reabsorption and reduce its recirculation to the liver, thus increasing transformation of cholesterol into bile acid through the LDL-C pathway, leading to a decrease in circulating LDL-C.[121] On average, bile acid sequestrants provide a decrease of 14% in TC and 21% in LDL-C, and a 3% increase in HDL-C and 2% to 5% in TG. It was suggested that bile acid sequestrants have a positive effect on clinical outcomes, but few studies have been carried out, and they have been restricted to coronary heart disease outcomes. Data concerning its effectiveness when associated with statins are lacking.[121] Moreover, they are not commonly prescribed because of numerous drug interactions and low patient tolerance, with mainly gastrointestinal side effects, leading to drug discontinuation.[121]

Other options were, until now, studied unsuccessfully because of major side effects. Other PPAR modulators that might help to reduce the residual risk associated with high TG levels in addition to LDL-C reduction belong to this category.[30,165,189] More specifically PPAR-γ agonists (the thiazolidinediones family, including rosiglitazone and pioglitazone), which were initially approved as antidiabetic treatments, were associated with an increased risk of congestive heart failure and myocardial infarction.[194,195] Cholesteryl ester transfer protein inhibitors, including torcetrapib, have been proposed to increase HDL-C levels.[30,196] However, torcetrapib—which raised HDL-C by approximately 70% and decreased LDL-C by approximately 24%—was associated with a paradoxical increase in major cardiovascular diseases and death of any cause, and increased blood pressure. [196,197] Moreover, the benefit of this molecule on atherosclerosis could not be established.[196,198,199] Other cholesteryl ester transfer protein inhibitors such as dalcetrapib or anacetrapib might be more promising, but their efficacy and safety remain to be proved.[196]

Dyslipidemia and MRI Markers of CVD

MRI markers of CVD, including MRI-defined WMHs, brain infarcts (BIs), and cerebral microbleeds (CMBs), are powerful predictors of stroke, both ischemic stroke and ICH.[200,201] These intermediate markers, which are mainly markers of SVD, are highly prevalent in the general population; more than 80% of community-dwelling adults have some degree of WMHs after 65 years of age, 8% to 28% have BIs in populations age 59 to 75 years on average, and 3.1% to 24.4% have some CMBs in populations age 52.9 to 60 years or more.[202–205] All these MRI markers of "covert" CVD predict an increased risk of stroke and dementia.[202,203,206,207] In this section, data are derived mainly from epidemiological studies and some post hoc analyses within RCTs.

EPIDEMIOLOGICAL STUDIES

MRI Markers of Ischemic CVD

LOW-DENSITY LIPOPROTEIN CHOLESTEROL

Heterogeneous results have been published regarding the association of LDL-C with MRI markers of ischemic CVD, with positive associations being reported mostly in very small samples, which are therefore exposed to false discovery and publication biases. A small study in the general population reported LDL-C as a significant risk factor for deep WMHs (N = 106, r = 0.24, $p < .05$), but not for periventricular WMHs.[208] Two other small studies reported an association of LDL-C with BI, in the Seiryo Clin Study, a cohort of healthy Japanese men (N = 324; OR = 2.54; 95% CI, 1.03–6.27)[209] and in persons with essential hypertension (oxidized LDL subfraction, n = 100).[210] In the Leukoaraiosis and Disability (LADIS) study, carried out in nondisabled to mildly disabled elderly (N = 396) recruited in a hospital-based setting, no association between LDL-C and WMH progression or new lacunes was reported after 3 years of follow-up.[211] Similarly, in 349 volunteers free of neuropsychiatric disease age 50 to 70 years, from the Austrian Stroke Prevention Study (ASPS), LDL-C was not associated with MRI-defined ischemic CVD, a combination of deep WMHs and BIs.[212] LDL-C levels were associated inversely with worsening of WMH grade in 1919 community persons age 65 years or older from the CHS (OR = 0.81; 95% CI, 0.68–0.96),[213] but not with incident BIs after 5 years (N = 1433).[214] In line with these findings, recent analyses in the Three-City-Dijon (3C-Dijon) study and the Epidemiology of Vascular Aging (EVA) study—two large, prospective population-based studies in late-middle-age and older community persons—revealed a borderline significant inverse relationship between higher LDL-C levels and WMH volume (N = 2608; metaregression coefficient, −0.0243 ± 0.0122; p = .047), which was no longer significant after adjusting for other vascular risk factors, and there was no association between lacunar infarcts and LDL-C.[215]

Of note, in the CHS, statin intake was also associated with accelerated WMH progression (by one grade or more) in the group with severe WMHs at baseline (OR = 1.94; 95% CI, 1.06–3.58; N = 538),[213] and with a fourfold decrease in risk of silent infarct (N = 1730).[216] These results should be interpreted with caution, given the observational design.

Overall, available studies do not suggest a consistent association of LDL-C with MRI markers of ischemic CVD.

TOTAL CHOLESTEROL

A study reported a significant inverse association between hyperlipidemia (defined by hypercholesterolemia, hypertriglyceridemia, or use of lipid-lowering drugs) and WMH severity in 1135 acute ischemic stroke patients from two independent hospital-based cohorts, [217] which was confirmed by the LADIS study, reporting hypercholesterolemia as a significant protective factor against severe, age-related white matter changes (including BIs and WMHs) evaluated on MRI (N = 639; OR = 0.56; 95% CI, 0.34–0.94).[218] No association was observed between TC and WMH progression or new lacunes in the LADIS study.[211] In summary, data on the association of TC with MRI markers of ischemic CVD are scarce, but seem to be consistent with a trend toward an inverse association between LDL-C and MRI markers of ischemic CVD. Confirmation from large, population-based studies is lacking.

TRIGLYCERIDES

Several large, community-based studies have found significant associations of higher TG levels with larger WMH volume, although others have not confirmed this association. A study carried out in healthy Japanese volunteers reported a significant association of hypertriglyceridemia with larger WMH burden (N = 1030; OR = 1.94; 95% CI, 1.37–2.73),[219] as did the National

Heart, Lung, and Blood Institute Twin Study (N = 1028, r = 0.22, p < .05).[220] The LADIS study (N = 396) found an association of increasing TG levels with greater risk of new lacunar infarct (OR = 1.2; 95% CI, 1.0–1.5; p < .05), but not with WMH burden.[211] In the population-based 3C-Dijon and EVA studies (N = 2608), higher TG levels were associated with larger WMH volume (metaregression coefficient, = 0.0810 ± 0.0300; p = .007) and with lacunar infarcts (meta-OR = 1.54; 95% CI, 1.04–2.28; p = .03), after adjusting for vascular risk factors.[215] Increased inflammation,[221,222] as well as blood–brain barrier dysfunction, were suggested as possible explanations for these results.[223] Of note, other population-based studies (ASPS, N = 349,119; CHS, N = 1,433,121) did not report any significant association with WMH burden or BIs, respectively, but they were performed either on a smaller sample or did not focus specifically on lacunar BIs—a less heterogeneous phenotype than all BIs, which is believed to reflect mostly cerebral SVD. Hence, although a formal meta-analysis of published data is needed to draw a conclusion, data from several independent studies suggest an association of increasing TG levels with MRI markers of ischemic SVD.

HIGH-DENSITY LIPOPROTEIN CHOLESTEROL

Published results of associations between HDL-C and WMHs are heterogeneous. In the National Heart, Lung, and Blood Institute Twin Study, greater midlife HDL-C levels were associated with a lower WMH burden (N = 514, r = −0.20, p < .05).[220] In the LADIS study (N = 396), there was no association between HDL-C and WMH progression, but there was a significant inverse one with new lacunes (OR = 0.6; 95% CI, 0.5–0.8).[211] In contrast, in the CHS, increased late-life HDL-C was reported as a significant risk factor for WMH progression (N = 1919; OR = 1.24; 95% CI, 1.05–1.48).[213] In the ARIC study (N = 14,488), HDL-C was not associated with silent brain infarcts.[224] Similarly, in the 3C-Dijon and EVA studies (N = 2608), no association was found between HDL-C measured in late life and WMHs or lacunar infarcts.[215] In summary, large population-based studies in older individuals do not support a protective effect of high HDL-C on MRI-defined CVD. Additional data in younger and larger samples are needed.

MRI Marker of Hemorrhagic CVD (CMBs)

LOW-DENSITY LIPOPROTEIN CHOLESTEROL

Available literature seems to agree on the absence of a relationship between LDL-C and CMBs. No association was observed in community participants age 55 years and older from the Rotterdam study.[225] Similarly, in a nested MRI substudy of the Prospective Study of Pravastatin in the Elderly at Risk (PROSPER) trial, an RCT designed to examine the effect of cholesterol-lowering therapy on vascular events, LDL-C was not associated with CMBs (N = 439).[226] Two small studies have examined the relation of LDL-C with CMBs in patients with ICH ($N \leq 163$). Both found no significant association,[227,228] but one of them described an association of statin intake with the presence and increased number of CMBs (OR = 2.72; 95% CI, 1.02–7.22), especially corticosubcortical CMBs, which are associated with cerebral amyloid angiopathy (OR = 4.15; 95% CI, 1.54–11.20); N = 163).[228] Again, caution is required in interpreting this finding, given the observational design of this study.

TOTAL CHOLESTEROL

In the Rotterdam study, a significant inverse association between higher TC levels and decreased risk of deep or infratentorial incident microbleeds (OR = 0.66; 95% CI, 0.44–0.98) was reported,[205] as well as an association between a TC level less than 4.42 mmol/L and risk of CMBs (OR = 2.01; 95% CI, 1.24–3.26; N = 1062).[229] In contrast, no association was found in the Framingham Heart Study or in the nested MRI substudy of the PROSPER study.[211,215] A study carried out in 105 persons with ICH also did not reveal any significant associations between TC and CMB.[227] In a Korean study of 172 patients with stroke (n = 107) or other neurological diseases (n = 65), TC was a risk factor for CMBs (OR = 10.91; 95% CI, 3.98–25.57).[230] Overall, available data are inconsistent. Additional studies are needed to explore the relation of TC with CMBs overall and according to their lobar or deep location.

TRIGLYCERIDES

Literature reports on the association between TGs and CMBs is scarce and conflicting. The Rotterdam study reported a significant inverse relationship between high levels of TG and risk of deep or infratentorial CMBs (OR = 0.37; 95% CI, 0.14–0.96), but not for lobar CMB.[225] However, in the nested MRI substudy of the PROSPER trial, TGs were not associated with CMBs.[226] Similarly, a small study carried out in persons with ICH did not show any significant association between TG and CMB (N = 105).[227]

HIGH-DENSITY LIPOPROTEIN CHOLESTEROL

HDL-C was not associated with CMBs in the population-based Framingham Heart Study,[231] the Rotterdam study,[225] or the PROSPER study.[226] Similarly, a study carried out in persons with ICH did not show any significant associations between HDL-C and CMBs (N = 105).[227] In a Korean study of 172 patients with stroke (n = 107) or other neurological disease (n = 65), HDL-C levels greater than the 75th percentile (=1.47 mmol/L) were reported as a significant risk factor for CMBs (OR = 3.46; 95% CI, 1.45–8.29).[230] Hence, except for one small study in an high-risk Asian population, available studies seem to agree on the absence of a relationship between HDL-C and CMBs at the community level.

RCTs TESTING THE IMPACT OF LIPID-LOWERING DRUGS ON MRI MARKERS OF SVD

No trial to date has been designed specifically to test the impact of lipid-lowering drugs on MRI markers of CVD. However, post hoc ancillary studies of the Regression of Cerebral Artery Stenosis (ROCAS) and PROSPER trials have looked at the association of simvastatin and pravastatin intake on progression of ischemic lesions on brain MRI.

In the ROCAS trial (N = 208), which aimed at evaluating the impact of a 20-mg/day simvastatin intake on the progression of asymptomatic middle cerebral artery stenosis in stroke-free individuals, simvastatin intake was associated significantly with a reduced progression of WMHs in individuals who already had severe WMHs at baseline (regression coefficient, −0.214; p = .043),[232] and with less incident infarcts (N = 227; OR = 0.09; 95% CI, 0.01–0.82),[233] after 2 years of follow up. The PROSPER trial (N = 535) did not find a significant association between a 40-mg/day pravastatin intake and progression of ischemic lesion load after 3 years of follow-up.[234]

Given the lack of robust data from randomized trials, there are currently no available guidelines on how to manage dyslipidemia in individuals with MRI SVD.

Conclusions

Overall, despite inconsistent associations in epidemiological studies, there is strong evidence that lowering LDL-C reduces the risk of stroke—mainly, ischemic stroke. Despite a modest increase in a risk of ICH when lowering LDL-C, the overall benefit in terms of all-stroke prevention remains significant. Statins are currently the only drug recommended in primary and secondary stroke prevention, validated in large RCTs. The optimal therapeutic target (LDL-C

< 0.7 mmol/L vs. <1.0 mmol/L) is currently under evaluation. Their benefit is not demonstrated in patients with a history of ICH. Although there is mounting evidence for a residual risk of stroke associated with high TG levels and low HDL-C levels, it is currently unclear whether therapeutic interventions aiming at modifying TGs and HDL-C have a significant impact on the risk of stroke, and which drug category would be most appropriate. More trials are needed to address this important issue. Another area of uncertainty is the relation of lipid fractions with MRI markers of covert CVD, and whether lipid-lowering drugs should be prescribed in persons with such lesions and no history of clinical vascular disease. No consistent association has been described between most lipid fractions and MRI markers of CVD, although several studies seem to report an increased burden of ischemic SVD in individuals with high TG levels. Additional studies and meta-analyses of published results are needed to understand these associations more fully and to evaluate whether information of MRI markers of SVD should be incorporated in therapeutic algorithms for management of dyslipidemia to reduce the burden of CVD and cognitive decline at the population level.

REFERENCES

1. Steinberg H, Anderson MS, Musliner T, Hanson ME, Engel SS. Management of dyslipidemia and hyperglycemia with a fixed-dose combination of sitagliptin and simvastatin. *Vasc Health Risk Manage.* 2013;9:273–282.
2. Third report of the National Cholesterol Education Program (NCEP) expert panel on detection, evaluation, and treatment of high blood cholesterol in adults (Adult Treatment Panel III) final report. *Circulation.* 2002;106:3143–3421.
3. Goldstein LB, Bushnell CD, Adams RJ, et al. Guidelines for the primary prevention of stroke: a guideline for healthcare professionals from the American Heart Association/American Stroke Association. *Stroke.* 2011;42:517–584.
4. Cobain MR, Pencina MJ, D'Agostino RB Sr, Vasan RS. Lifetime risk for developing dyslipidemia: the Framingham offspring study. *Am J Med.* 2007;120:623–630.
5. Ferrieres J, Amber V, Crisan O, Chazelle F, Junger C, Wood D. Total lipid management and cardiovascular disease in the Dyslipidemia International Study. .*Cardiology.* 2013;125:154–163
6. Stamler J, Vaccaro O, Neaton JD, Wentworth D. Diabetes, other risk factors, and 12-yr cardiovascular mortality for men screened in the Multiple Risk Factor Intervention Trial. *Diabetes Care.* 1993;16:434–444.
7. De Caterina R, Scarano M, Marfisi R, et al. Cholesterol-lowering interventions and stroke: insights from a meta-analysis of randomized controlled trials. *J Am Coll Cardiol.* 2010;55:198–211.
8. Segal AZ, Chiu RI, Eggleston-Sexton PM, Beiser A, Greenberg SM. Low cholesterol as a risk factor for primary intracerebral hemorrhage: a case–control study. *Neuroepidemiology.* 1999;18:185–193.
9. Woo D, Kissela BM, Khoury JC, et al. Hypercholesterolemia, HMG-CoA reductase inhibitors, and risk of intracerebral hemorrhage: a case–control study. *Stroke.* 2004;35:1360–1364.
10. Leppala JM, Virtamo J, Fogelholm R, Albanes D, Heinonen OP. Different risk factors for different stroke subtypes: association of blood pressure, cholesterol, and antioxidants. *Stroke.* 1999;30:2535–2540.
11. Sturgeon JD, Folsom AR, Longstreth WT Jr, Shahar E, Rosamond WD, Cushman M. Risk factors for intracerebral hemorrhage in a pooled prospective study. *Stroke.* 2007;38:2718–2725.
12. Baigent C, Blackwell L, Emberson J, et al. Efficacy and safety of more intensive lowering of LDL cholesterol: a meta-analysis of data from 170,000 participants in 26 randomised trials. *Lancet.* 2010;376:1670–1681.

13. Amarenco P, Labreuche J. Lipid management in the prevention of stroke: review and updated meta-analysis of statins for stroke prevention. *Lancet Neurol.* 2009;8:453–463.
14. Imamura T, Doi Y, Arima H, et al. LDL cholesterol and the development of stroke subtypes and coronary heart disease in a general Japanese population: the Hisayama study. *Stroke.* 2009;40:382–388.
15. Willey JZ, Xu Q, Boden-Albala B, et al. Lipid profile components and risk of ischemic stroke: the Northern Manhattan Study (NOMAS). *Arch Neurol.* 2009;66:1400–1406.
16. Canoui-Poitrine F, Luc G, Bard JM, et al. Relative contribution of lipids and apolipoproteins to incident coronary heart disease and ischemic stroke: the Prime study. *Cerebrovasc Dis.* 2010;30:252–259.
17. Debette S, Seshadri S. Vascular risk factors and dementia revisited. *J Neurol Neurosurg Psychiatry.* 2009;80:1183–1184.
18. Stewart R, White LR, Xue QL, Launer LJ. Twenty-six-year change in total cholesterol levels and incident dementia: the Honolulu–Asia Aging Study. *Arch Neurol.* 2007;64:103–107.
19. Law MR, Wald NJ, Rudnicka AR. Quantifying effect of statins on low density lipoprotein cholesterol, ischaemic heart disease, and stroke: systematic review and meta-analysis. *BMJ.* 2003;326:1423.
20. Hankey GJ, Anderson NE, Ting RD, et al. Rates and predictors of risk of stroke and its subtypes in diabetes: a prospective observational study. *J Neurol Neurosurg Psychiatry.* 2013;84:281–287.
21. Laloux P, Galanti L, Jamart J. Lipids in ischemic stroke subtypes. *Acta Neurol Belg.* 2004;104:13–19.
22. Amarenco P, Labreuche J, Elbaz A, et al. Blood lipids in brain infarction subtypes. *Cerebrovasc Dis.* 2006;22:101–108.
23. Wang X, Dong Y, Qi X, Huang C, Hou L. Cholesterol levels and risk of hemorrhagic stroke: a systematic review and meta-analysis. *Stroke.* 2013;44:1833–1839.
24. Hackam DG, Woodward M, Newby LK, et al. Statins and intracerebral hemorrhage: collaborative systematic review and meta-analysis. *Circulation.* 2011;124:2233–2242.
25. Goldstein LB, Amarenco P, Szarek M, et al. Hemorrhagic stroke in the Stroke Prevention by Aggressive Reduction in Cholesterol Levels study. *Neurology.* 2008;70:2364–2370.
26. Davidson MH, Stein EA, Dujovne CA, et al. The efficacy and six-week tolerability of simvastatin 80 and 160 mg/day. *Am J Cardiol.* 1997;79:38–42.
27. Mills EJ, Rachlis B, Wu P, Devereaux PJ, Arora P, Perri D. Primary prevention of cardiovascular mortality and events with statin treatments: a network meta-analysis involving more than 65,000 patients. *J Am Coll Cardiol.* 2008;52:1769–1781.
28. Feher A, Pusch G, Koltai K, et al. Statin therapy in the primary and the secondary prevention of ischaemic cerebrovascular diseases. *Int J Cardiol.* 2011;148:131–138.
29. Amarenco P, Moskowitz MA. The dynamics of statins: from event prevention to neuroprotection. *Stroke.* 2006;37:294–296.
30. Labreuche J, Deplanque D, Touboul PJ, Bruckert E, Amarenco P. Association between change in plasma triglyceride levels and risk of stroke and carotid atherosclerosis: systematic review and meta-regression analysis. *Atherosclerosis.* 2010;212:9–15.
31. Taylor F, Huffman MD, Macedo AF, et al. Statins for the primary prevention of cardiovascular disease. *Cochrane Database Syst Rev.* 2013;1:CD004816.
32. McKinney JS, Kostis WJ. Statin therapy and the risk of intracerebral hemorrhage: a meta-analysis of 31 randomized controlled trials. *Stroke.* 2012;43:2149–2156.
33. Ribeiro RA, Ziegelmann PK, Duncan BB, et al. Impact of statin dose on major cardiovascular events: a mixed treatment comparison meta-analysis involving more than 175,000 patients. *Int J Cardiol.* 2013;166:431–439.
34. Tonelli M, Lloyd A, Clement F, et al. Efficacy of statins for primary prevention in people at low cardiovascular risk: a meta-analysis. *CMAJ.* 2011;183:E1189–E1202.

35. Silva M, Matthews ML, Jarvis C, et al. Meta-analysis of drug-induced adverse events associated with intensive-dose statin therapy. *Clin Ther.* 2007;29:253–260.
36. Baigent C, Landray MJ, Reith C, et al. The effects of lowering LDL cholesterol with simvastatin plus ezetimibe in patients with chronic kidney disease (study of heart and renal protection): a randomised placebo-controlled trial. *Lancet.* 2011;377:2181–2192.
37. Ruggenenti P, Perna A, Tonelli M, et al. Effects of add-on fluvastatin therapy in patients with chronic proteinuric nephropathy on dual renin–angiotensin system blockade: the Esplanade trial. *Clin J Am Soc Nephrol.* 2010;5:1928–1938.
38. Fassett RG, Robertson IK, Ball MJ, Geraghty DP, Coombes JS. Effect of atorvastatin on kidney function in chronic kidney disease: a randomised double-blind placebo-controlled trial. *Atherosclerosis.* 2010;213:218–224.
39. Fellstrom BC, Jardine AG, Schmieder RE, et al. Rosuvastatin and cardiovascular events in patients undergoing hemodialysis. *N Engl J Med.* 2009;360:1395–1407.
40. Armitage J, Bowman L, Wallendszus K, et al. Intensive lowering of LDL cholesterol with 80 mg versus 20 mg simvastatin daily in 12,064 survivors of myocardial infarction: a double-blind randomised trial. *Lancet.* 2010;376:1658–1669.
41. Ridker PM, Danielson E, Fonseca FA, et al. Rosuvastatin to prevent vascular events in men and women with elevated C-reactive protein. *N Engl J Med.* 2008;359:2195–2207.
42. Tavazzi L, Maggioni AP, Marchioli R, et al. Effect of rosuvastatin in patients with chronic heart failure (the GISSI-HF trial): a randomised, double-blind, placebo-controlled trial. *Lancet.* 2008;372:1231–1239.
43. Sato H, Kinjo K, Ito H, et al. Effect of early use of low-dose pravastatin on major adverse cardiac events in patients with acute myocardial infarction: the OACIS-Lipid study. *Circ J.* 2008;72:17–22.
44. Bone HG, Kiel DP, Lindsay RS, et al. Effects of atorvastatin on bone in postmenopausal women with dyslipidemia: a double-blind, placebo-controlled, dose-ranging trial. *J Clin Endocrinol Metab.* 2007;92:4671–4677.
45. Kjekshus J, Apetrei E, Barrios V, et al. Rosuvastatin in older patients with systolic heart failure. *N Engl J Med.* 2007;357:2248–2261.
46. Deedwania P, Stone PH, Bairey Merz CN, et al. Effects of intensive versus moderate lipid-lowering therapy on myocardial ischemia in older patients with coronary heart disease: results of the study assessing goals in the elderly (SAGE). *Circulation.* 2007;115:700–707.
47. Knopp RH, d'Emden M, Smilde JG, Pocock SJ. Efficacy and safety of atorvastatin in the prevention of cardiovascular end points in subjects with type 2 diabetes: the Atorvastatin Study for Prevention of Coronary Heart Disease Endpoints in Non-insulin-Dependent Diabetes Mellitus (ASPEN). *Diabetes Care.* 2006;29:1478–1485.
48. Nakamura H, Arakawa K, Itakura H, et al. Primary prevention of cardiovascular disease with pravastatin in Japan (Mega Study): a prospective randomised controlled trial. *Lancet.* 2006;368:1155–1163.
49. Amarenco P, Bogousslavsky J, Callahan A 3rd, et al. High-dose atorvastatin after stroke or transient ischemic attack. *N Engl J Med.* 2006;355:549–559.
50. Schmermund A, Achenbach S, Budde T, et al. Effect of intensive versus standard lipid-lowering treatment with atorvastatin on the progression of calcified coronary atherosclerosis over 12 months: a multicenter, randomized, double-blind trial. *Circulation.* 2006;113:427–437.
51. Sakamoto T, Kojima S, Ogawa H, et al. Effects of early statin treatment on symptomatic heart failure and ischemic events after acute myocardial infarction in Japanese. *Am J Cardiol.* 2006;97:1165–1171.
52. Pedersen TR, Faergeman O, Kastelein JJ, et al. High-dose atorvastatin vs usual-dose simvastatin for secondary prevention after myocardial infarction: the ideal study: a randomized controlled trial. *JAMA.* 2005;294:2437–2445.

53. LaRosa JC, Grundy SM, Waters DD, et al. Intensive lipid lowering with atorvastatin in patients with stable coronary disease. *N Engl J Med.* 2005;352:1425–1435.
54. Wanner C, Krane V, Marz W, et al. Atorvastatin in patients with type 2 diabetes mellitus undergoing hemodialysis. *N Engl J Med.* 2005;353:238–248.
55. Anderssen SA, Hjelstuen AK, Hjermann I, Bjerkan K, Holme I. Fluvastatin and lifestyle modification for reduction of carotid intima-media thickness and left ventricular mass progression in drug-treated hypertensives. *Atherosclerosis.* 2005;178:387–397.
56. Yokoi H, Nobuyoshi M, Mitsudo K, Kawaguchi A, Yamamoto A. Three-year follow-up results of angiographic intervention trial using an HMG-CoA reductase inhibitor to evaluate retardation of obstructive multiple atheroma (Atheroma) study. *Circ J.* 2005;69:875–883.
57. Makuuchi H, Furuse A, Endo M, et al. Effect of pravastatin on progression of coronary atherosclerosis in patients after coronary artery bypass surgery. *Circ J.* 2005;69:636–643.
58. Stone PH, Lloyd-Jones DM, Kinlay S, et al. Effect of intensive lipid lowering, with or without antioxidant vitamins, compared with moderate lipid lowering on myocardial ischemia in patients with stable coronary artery disease: the Vascular Basis for the Treatment of Myocardial Ischemia Study. *Circulation.* 2005;111:1747–1755.
59. Koren MJ, Hunninghake DB. Clinical outcomes in managed-care patients with coronary heart disease treated aggressively in lipid-lowering disease management clinics: the Alliance study. *J Am Coll Cardiol.* 2004;44:1772–1779.
60. Colhoun HM, Betteridge DJ, Durrington PN, et al. Primary prevention of cardiovascular disease with atorvastatin in type 2 diabetes in the Collaborative Atorvastatin Diabetes Study (CARDS): multicentre randomised placebo-controlled trial. *Lancet.* 2004;364:685–696.
61. Cannon CP, Braunwald E, McCabe CH, et al. Intensive versus moderate lipid lowering with statins after acute coronary syndromes. *N Engl J Med.* 2004;350:1495–1504.
62. de Lemos JA, Blazing MA, Wiviott SD, et al. Early intensive vs a delayed conservative simvastatin strategy in patients with acute coronary syndromes: phase Z of the A to Z Trial. *JAMA.* 2004;292:1307–1316.
63. Asselbergs FW, Diercks GF, Hillege HL, et al. Effects of fosinopril and pravastatin on cardiovascular events in subjects with microalbuminuria. *Circulation.* 2004;110:2809–2816.
64. Zanchetti A, Crepaldi G, Bond MG, et al. Different effects of antihypertensive regimens based on fosinopril or hydrochlorothiazide with or without lipid lowering by pravastatin on progression of asymptomatic carotid atherosclerosis: principal results of phyllis: a randomized double-blind trial. *Stroke.* 2004;35:2807–2812.
65. Muldoon MF, Ryan CM, Sereika SM, Flory JD, Manuck SB. Randomized trial of the effects of simvastatin on cognitive functioning in hypercholesterolemic adults. *Am J Med.* 2004;117:823–829.
66. Nakagawa T, Kobayashi T, Awata N, et al. Randomized, controlled trial of secondary prevention of coronary sclerosis in normocholesterolemic patients using pravastatin: final 5-year angiographic follow-up of the Prevention of Coronary Sclerosis (PCS) study. *Int J Cardiol.* 2004;97:107–114.
67. Nissen SE, Tuzcu EM, Schoenhagen P, et al. Effect of intensive compared with moderate lipid-lowering therapy on progression of coronary atherosclerosis: a randomized controlled trial. *JAMA.* 2004;291:1071–1080.
68. Bae JH, Bassenge E, Kim KY, Synn YC, Park KR, Schwemmer M. Effects of low-dose atorvastatin on vascular responses in patients undergoing percutaneous coronary intervention with stenting. *J Cardiovasc Pharmacol Ther.* 2004;9:185–192.
69. Sever PS, Dahlof B, Poulter NR, et al. Prevention of coronary and stroke events with atorvastatin in hypertensive patients who have average or lower-than-average cholesterol concentrations, in the Anglo-Scandinavian Cardiac Outcomes Trial–Lipid Lowering Arm (ASCTO-LLA): a multicentre randomised controlled trial. *Lancet.* 2003;361:1149–1158.

70. Holdaas H, Fellstrom B, Jardine AG, et al. Effect of fluvastatin on cardiac outcomes in renal transplant recipients: a multicentre, randomised, placebo-controlled trial. *Lancet.* 2003;361:2024–2031.
71. Mohler ER 3rd, Hiatt WR, Creager MA. Cholesterol reduction with atorvastatin improves walking distance in patients with peripheral arterial disease. *Circulation.* 2003;108:1481–1486.
72. Olsson AG, Eriksson M, Johnson O, et al. A 52-week, multicenter, randomized, parallel-group, double-blind, double-dummy study to assess the efficacy of atorvastatin and simvastatin in reaching low-density lipoprotein cholesterol and triglyceride targets: the Treat-to-Target (3T) study. *Clin Ther.* 2003;25:119–138.
73. ALLHAT Officers and Coordinators for the ALLHAT Collaborative Research Group. Major outcomes in moderately hypercholesterolemic, hypertensive patients randomized to pravastatin vs usual care: the Antihypertensive and Lipid-Lowering Treatment to Prevent Heart Attack Trial (ALLHAT-LLT). *JAMA.* 2002;288:2998–3007.
74. Athyros VG, Papageorgiou AA, Mercouris BR, et al. Treatment with atorvastatin to the National Cholesterol Educational Program goal versus "usual" care in secondary coronary heart disease prevention: the Greek Atorvastatin and Coronary-Heart-Disease Evaluation (GREACE) study. *Curr Med Res Opin.* 2002;18:220–228.
75. Liem AH, van Boven AJ, Veeger NJ, et al. Effect of fluvastatin on ischaemia following acute myocardial infarction: a randomized trial. *Eur Heart J.* 2002;23:1931–1937.
76. MRC/BHF Heart Protection Study of cholesterol lowering with simvastatin in 20,536 high-risk individuals: a randomised placebo-controlled trial. *Lancet.* 2002;360:7–22.
77. Taylor AJ, Kent SM, Flaherty PJ, Coyle LC, Markwood TT, Vernalis MN. ARBITER: Arterial Biology for the Investigation of the Treatment Effects of Reducing Cholesterol: a randomized trial comparing the effects of atorvastatin and pravastatin on carotid intima medial thickness. *Circulation.* 2002;106:2055–2060.
78. Shepherd J, Blauw GJ, Murphy MB, et al. Pravastatin in elderly individuals at risk of vascular disease (PROSPER): a randomised controlled trial. *Lancet.* 2002;360:1623–1630.
79. Serruys PW, de Feyter P, Macaya C, et al. Fluvastatin for prevention of cardiac events following successful first percutaneous coronary intervention: a randomized controlled trial. *JAMA.* 2002;287:3215–3222.
80. Schwartz GG, Olsson AG, Ezekowitz MD, et al. Effects of atorvastatin on early recurrent ischemic events in acute coronary syndromes: the MIRACL study: a randomized controlled trial. *JAMA.* 2001;285:1711–1718.
81. Ito H, Ouchi Y, Ohashi Y, et al. A comparison of low versus standard dose pravastatin therapy for the prevention of cardiovascular events in the elderly: the Pravastatin Anti-atherosclerosis Trial in the Elderly (PATE). *J Atheroscler Thromb.* 2001;8:33–44.
82. Hedblad B, Wikstrand J, Janzon L, Wedel H, Berglund G. Low-dose metoprolol CR/XL and fluvastatin slow progression of carotid intima-media thickness: main results from the beta-blocker cholesterol-lowering asymptomatic plaque study (BCAPS). *Circulation.* 2001;103:1721–1726.
83. Brown BG, Zhao XQ, Chait A, et al. Simvastatin and niacin, antioxidant vitamins, or the combination for the prevention of coronary disease. *N Engl J Med.* 2001;345:1583–1592.
84. GISSI Prevenzione investigators (Gruppo Italiano per lo Studio della Sopravvivenza nell'Infarto Miocardico). Results of the low-dose (20 mg) pravastatin GISSI Prevenzione Trial in 4271 patients with recent myocardial infarction: do stopped trials contribute to overall knowledge?. *Ital Heart J.* 2000;1:810–820.
85. Arntz HR, Agrawal R, Wunderlich W, et al. Beneficial effects of pravastatin (+/–colestyramine/niacin) initiated immediately after a coronary event (the randomized Lipid–Coronary Artery Disease [L-CAD] study). *Am J Cardiol.* 2000;86:1293–1298.

86. Teo KK, Burton JR, Buller CE, et al. Long-term effects of cholesterol lowering and angiotensin-converting enzyme inhibition on coronary atherosclerosis: the Simvastatin/Enalapril Coronary Atherosclerosis Trial (SCAT). *Circulation*. 2000;102:1748–1754.
87. Kleemann A, Eckert S, von Eckardstein A, et al. Effects of lovastatin on progression of non-dilated and dilated coronary segments and on restenosis in patients after PTCA: the Cholesterol Lowering Atherosclerosis PTCA Trial (CLAPT). *Eur Heart J*. 1999;20:1393–1406.
88. Downs JR, Clearfield M, Weis S, et al. Primary prevention of acute coronary events with lovastatin in men and women with average cholesterol levels: results of AFCAPS/TEXCAPS: Air Force/Texas Coronary Atherosclerosis Prevention Study. *JAMA*. 1998;279:1615–1622.
89. The Long-Term Intervention with Pravastatin in Ischaemic Disease (LIPID) Study Group. Prevention of cardiovascular events and death with pravastatin in patients with coronary heart disease and a broad range of initial cholesterol levels. *N Engl J Med*. 1998;339:1349–1357.
90. Post Coronary Artery Bypass Graft Trial Investigators. The effect of aggressive lowering of low-density lipoprotein cholesterol levels and low-dose anticoagulation on obstructive changes in saphenous-vein coronary-artery bypass grafts. *N Engl J Med*. 1997;336:153–162.
91. Bertrand ME, McFadden EP, Fruchart JC, et al. Effect of pravastatin on angiographic restenosis after coronary balloon angioplasty: the PREDICT trial investigators: prevention of restenosis by elisor after transluminal coronary angioplasty. *J Am Coll Cardiol*. 1997;30:863–869.
92. Bestehorn HP, Rensing UF, Roskamm H, et al. The effect of simvastatin on progression of coronary artery disease: the multicenter Coronary Intervention Study (CIS). *Eur Heart J*. 1997;18:226–234.
93. Sacks FM, Pfeffer MA, Moye LA, et al. The effect of pravastatin on coronary events after myocardial infarction in patients with average cholesterol levels. *N Engl J Med*. 1996;335:1001–1009.
94. Shepherd J, Cobbe SM, Ford I, et al. Prevention of coronary heart disease with pravastatin in men with hypercholesterolemia. *N Engl J Med*. 1995;333:1301–1307.
95. Crouse JR 3rd, Byington RP, Bond MG, et al. Pravastatin, Lipids, and Atherosclerosis in the Carotid Arteries (PLAC-II). *Am J Cardiol*. 1995;75:455–459.
96. Salonen R, Nyyssonen K, Porkkala E, et al. Kuopio Atherosclerosis Prevention Study (KAPS): a population-based primary preventive trial of the effect of LDL lowering on atherosclerotic progression in carotid and femoral arteries. *Circulation*. 1995;92:1758–1764.
97. Jukema JW, Bruschke AV, van Boven AJ, et al. Effects of lipid lowering by pravastatin on progression and regression of coronary artery disease in symptomatic men with normal to moderately elevated serum cholesterol levels: the Regression Growth Evaluation Statin Study (REGRESS). *Circulation*. 1995;91:2528–2540.
98. Pitt B, Mancini GB, Ellis SG, Rosman HS, Park JS, McGovern ME. Pravastatin limitation of atherosclerosis in the coronary arteries (PLAC I): reduction in atherosclerosis progression and clinical events. *J Am Coll Cardiol*. 1995;26:1133–1139.
99. Scandinavian Simvastatin Survival Study Group. Randomised trial of cholesterol lowering in 4444 patients with coronary heart disease. *Lancet*. 1994;344:1383–1389.
100. Furberg CD, Adams HP Jr, Applegate WB, et al. Effect of lovastatin on early carotid atherosclerosis and cardiovascular events. Asymptomatic Carotid Artery Progression Study (ACAPS) Research Group. *Circulation*. 1994;90:1679–1687.
101. MAAS Investigators. Effect of simvastatin on coronary atheroma: The multicentre anti-atheroma study (maas). *Lancet*. 1994;344:633–638
102. Waters D, Higginson L, Gladstone P, et al. Effects of monotherapy with an HMG-CoA reductase inhibitor on the progression of coronary atherosclerosis as assessed by serial quantitative arteriography: the Canadian Coronary Atherosclerosis Intervention Trial. *Circulation*. 1994;89:959–968.
103. Weintraub WS, Boccuzzi SJ, Klein JL, et al. Lack of effect of lovastatin on restenosis after coronary angioplasty. *N Engl J Med*. 1994;331:1331–1337.

104. The Pravastatin Multinational Study Group for Cardiac Risk Patients. Effects of pravastatin in patients with serum total cholesterol levels from 5.2 to 7.8 mmol/liter (200 to 300 mg/dL) plus two additional atherosclerotic risk factors. *Am J Cardiol.* 1993;72:1031–1037.
105. Blankenhorn DH, Azen SP, Kramsch DM, et al. Coronary angiographic changes with lovastatin therapy: the Monitored Atherosclerosis Regression Study (MARS). *Ann Intern Med.* 1993;119:969–976.
106. Bradford RH, Shear CL, Chremos AN, et al. Expanded Clinical Evaluation of Lovastatin (EXCEL) study results: I. Efficacy in modifying plasma lipoproteins and adverse event profile in 8245 patients with moderate hypercholesterolemia. *Arch Intern Med.* 1991;151:43–49.
107. Brown G, Albers JJ, Fisher LD, et al. Regression of coronary artery disease as a result of intensive lipid-lowering therapy in men with high levels of apolipoprotein B. *N Engl J Med.* 1990;323:1289–1298.
108. Nagai Y, Kohriyama T, Origasa H, et al. Rationale, design, and baseline features of a randomized controlled trial to assess the effects of statin for the secondary prevention of stroke: the Japan Statin Treatment Against Recurrent Ctroke (J-STARS). *Int J Stroke.* 2014;9:232–239.
109. Milionis HJ, Giannopoulos S, Kosmidou M, et al. Statin therapy after first stroke reduces 10-year stroke recurrence and improves survival. *Neurology.* 2009;72:1816–1822.
110. Kennedy J, Hill MD, Ryckborst KJ, Eliasziw M, Demchuk AM, Buchan AM. Fast Assessment of Stroke and Transient Ischaemic Attack to Prevent Early Recurrence (FASTER): a randomised controlled pilot trial. *Lancet Neurol.* 2007;6:961–969.
111. Collins R, Armitage J, Parish S, Sleight P, Peto R. Effects of cholesterol-lowering with simvastatin on stroke and other major vascular events in 20536 people with cerebrovascular disease or other high-risk conditions. *Lancet.* 2004;363:757–767.
112. White HD, Simes RJ, Anderson NE, et al. Pravastatin therapy and the risk of stroke. *N Engl J Med.* 2000;343:317–326.
113. Manktelow BN, Potter JF. Interventions in the management of serum lipids for preventing stroke recurrence. *Cochrane Database Syst Rev.* 2009 Jul 8;(3):CD002091.
114. Bersano A, Ballabio E, Lanfranconi S, Mazzucco S, Candelise L, Monaco S. Statins and stroke. *Curr Med Chem.* 2008;15:2380–2392.
115. Chaturvedi S, Zivin J, Breazna A, et al. Effect of atorvastatin in elderly patients with a recent stroke or transient ischemic attack. *Neurology.* 2009;72:688–694.
116. Goldstein LB, Amarenco P, Lamonte M, et al. Relative effects of statin therapy on stroke and cardiovascular events in men and women: secondary analysis of the Stroke Prevention by Aggressive Reduction in Cholesterol Levels (SPARCL) study. *Stroke.* 2008;39:2444–2448.
117. Amarenco P, Benavente O, Goldstein LB, et al. Results of the Stroke Prevention by Aggressive Reduction in Cholesterol Levels (SPARCL) trial by stroke subtypes. *Stroke.* 2009;40:1405–1409.
118. Miura S, Saku K. Ezetimibe, a selective inhibitor of the transport of cholesterol. *Intern Med.* 2008;47:1165–1170.
119. Yamaoka-Tojo M, Tojo T, Takahira N, Masuda T, Izumi T. Ezetimibe and reactive oxygen species. *Curr Vasc Pharmacol.* 2011;9:109–120.
120. Endres M, Heuschmann PU, Laufs U, Hakim AM. Primary prevention of stroke: blood pressure, lipids, and heart failure. *Eur Heart J.* 2011;32:545–552.
121. Schuck RN, Mendys PM, Simpson RJ Jr. Beyond statins: lipid management to reduce cardiovascular risk. *Pharmacotherapy.* 2013;33:754–764.
122. Furie KL, Kasner SE, Adams RJ, et al. Guidelines for the prevention of stroke in patients with stroke or transient ischemic attack: a guideline for healthcare professionals from the American Heart Association/American Stroke Association. *Stroke.* 2011;42:227–276.
123. Boden WE, Probstfield JL, Anderson T, et al. Niacin in patients with low HDL cholesterol levels receiving intensive statin therapy. *N Engl J Med.* 2011;365:2255–2267.

124. Al-Hijji M, Martin SS, Joshi PH, Jones SR. Effect of equivalent on-treatment apolipoprotein levels on outcomes (from the AIM-HIGH and HPS2-THRIVE). *Am J Cardiol.* 2013;112:1697–1700.
125. HPS2-THRIVE Collaborative Group. HPS2-THRIVE randomized placebo-controlled trial in 25,673 high-risk patients of ER niacin/laropiprant: trial design, pre-specified muscle and liver outcomes, and reasons for stopping study treatment. *Eur Heart J.* 2013;34:1279–1291.
126. Cholesterol, diastolic blood pressure, and stroke: 13,000 strokes in 450,000 people in 45 prospective cohorts: prospective studies collaboration. *Lancet.* 1995;346:1647–1653.
127. Eastern Stroke and Coronary Heart Disease Collaborative Research Group. Blood pressure, cholesterol, and stroke in eastern Asia. *Lancet.* 1998;352:1801–1807.
128. Schulz UG, Rothwell PM. Differences in vascular risk factors between etiological subtypes of ischemic stroke: importance of population-based studies. *Stroke.* 2003;34:2050–2059.
129. Tirschwell DL, Smith NL, Heckbert SR, Lemaitre RN, Longstreth WT Jr, Psaty BM. Association of cholesterol with stroke risk varies in stroke subtypes and patient subgroups. *Neurology.* 2004;63:1868–1875.
130. Ginsberg HN, Elam MB, Lovato LC, et al. Effects of combination lipid therapy in type 2 diabetes mellitus. *N Engl J Med.* 2010;362:1563–1574.
131. Whitney EJ, Krasuski RA, Personius BE, et al. A randomized trial of a strategy for increasing high-density lipoprotein cholesterol levels: effects on progression of coronary heart disease and clinical events. *Ann Intern Med.* 2005;142:95–104.
132. Keech A, Simes RJ, Barter P, et al. Effects of long-term fenofibrate therapy on cardiovascular events in 9795 people with type 2 diabetes mellitus (the FIELD study): randomised controlled trial. *Lancet.* 2005;366:1849–1861.
133. Meade T, Zuhrie R, Cook C, Cooper J. Bezafibrate in men with lower extremity arterial disease: randomised controlled trial. *BMJ.* 2002;325:1139.
134. Diabetes Atherosclerosis Intervention Study Investigators. Effect of fenofibrate on progression of coronary-artery disease in type 2 diabetes. *Lancet.* 2001;357:905–910.
135. The Bezafibrate Infarction Prevention (BIP) Study Group. Secondary prevention by raising HDL cholesterol and reducing triglycerides in patients with coronary artery disease. *Circulation.* 2000;102:21–27.
136. Rubins HB, Robins SJ, Collins D, et al. Gemfibrozil for the secondary prevention of coronary heart disease in men with low levels of high-density lipoprotein cholesterol. *N Engl J Med.* 1999;341:410–418.
137. Frick MH, Heinonen OP, Huttunen JK, Koskinen P, Manttari M, Manninen V. Efficacy of gemfibrozil in dyslipidaemic subjects with suspected heart disease: an ancillary study in the Helsinki Heart Study frame population. *Ann Med.* 1993;25:41–45.
138. Frick MH, Elo O, Haapa K, et al. Helsinki Heart Study: primary-prevention trial with gemfibrozil in middle-aged men with dyslipidemia: safety of treatment, changes in risk factors, and incidence of coronary heart disease. *N Engl J Med.* 1987;317:1237–1245.
139. Acheson J, Hutchinson EC. Controlled trial of clofibrate in cerebral vascular disease. *Atherosclerosis.* 1972;15:177–183.
140. The Veterans Administration Cooperative Study Group. The treatment of cerebrovascular disease with clofibrate. *Stroke.* 1973;4:684–693.
141. Clofibrate and niacin in coronary heart disease. *JAMA.* 1975;231:360–381.
142. Oliver MF, Heady JA, Morris JN, Cooper J. A co-operative trial in the primary prevention of ischaemic heart disease using clofibrate: report from the committee of principal investigators. *Br Heart J.* 1978;40:1069–1118.
143. Research Committee of the Scottish Society of Physicians. Ischaemic heart disease: a secondary prevention trial using clofibrate. *Br Med J.* 1971;4:775–784.
144. Zhou YH, Ye XF, Yu FF, et al. Lipid management in the prevention of stroke: a meta-analysis of fibrates for stroke prevention. *BMC Neurol.* 2013;13:1.

145. Jun M, Foote C, Lv J, et al. Effects of fibrates on cardiovascular outcomes: a systematic review and meta-analysis. *Lancet*. 2010;375:1875–1884.
146. Guyton JR, Brown BG, Fazio S, Polis A, Tomassini JE, Tershakovec AM. Lipid-altering efficacy and safety of ezetimibe/simvastatin coadministered with extended-release niacin in patients with type IIa or type IIb hyperlipidemia. *J Am Coll Cardiol*. 2008;51:1564–1572.
147. Taylor AJ, Sullenberger LE, Lee HJ, Lee JK, Grace KA. Arterial Biology for the Investigation of the Treatment Effects of Reducing Cholesterol (ARBITER) 2: a double-blind, placebo-controlled study of extended-release niacin on atherosclerosis progression in secondary prevention patients treated with statins. *Circulation*. 2004;110:3512–3517.
148. Carlson LA, Rosenhamer G. Reduction of mortality in the Stockholm Ischaemic Heart Disease Secondary Prevention Study by combined treatment with clofibrate and nicotinic acid. *Acta Med Scand*. 1988;223:405–418.
149. Bruckert E, Labreuche J, Amarenco P. Meta-analysis of the effect of nicotinic acid alone or in combination on cardiovascular events and atherosclerosis. *Atherosclerosis*. 2010;210:353–361.
150. Labreuche J, Touboul PJ, Amarenco P. Plasma triglyceride levels and risk of stroke and carotid atherosclerosis: a systematic review of the epidemiological studies. *Atherosclerosis*. 2009;203:331–345.
151. Di Angelantonio E, Sarwar N, Perry P, et al. Major lipids, apolipoproteins, and risk of vascular disease. *JAMA*. 2009;302:1993–2000.
152. Freiberg JJ, Tybjaerg-Hansen A, Jensen JS, Nordestgaard BG. Nonfasting triglycerides and risk of ischemic stroke in the general population. *JAMA*. 2008;300:2142–2152.
153. Bang OY, Saver JL, Liebeskind DS, Pineda S, Ovbiagele B. Association of serum lipid indices with large artery atherosclerotic stroke. *Neurology*. 2008;70:841–847.
154. Bonaventure A, Kurth T, Pico F, et al. Triglycerides and risk of hemorrhagic stroke vs. ischemic vascular events: the Three-City Study. *Atherosclerosis*. 2010;210:243–248.
155. Patel A, Woodward M, Campbell DJ, et al. Plasma lipids predict myocardial infarction, but not stroke, in patients with established cerebrovascular disease. *Eur Heart J*. 2005;26:1910–1915.
156. Psaty BM, Anderson M, Kronmal RA, et al. The association between lipid levels and the risks of incident myocardial infarction, stroke, and total mortality: the Cardiovascular Health Study. *J Am Geriatr Soc*. 2004;52:1639–1647.
157. Nakaya N, Kita T, Mabuchi H, et al. Large-scale cohort study on the relationship between serum lipid concentrations and risk of cerebrovascular disease under low-dose simvastatin in Japanese patients with hypercholesterolemia: sub-analysis of the Japan Lipid Intervention Trial (J-LIT). *Circ J*. 2005;69:1016–1021.
158. Patel A, Barzi F, Jamrozik K, Lam TH, et al. Serum triglycerides as a risk factor for cardiovascular diseases in the Asia-Pacific region. *Circulation*. 2004;110:2678–2686.
159. Amarenco P, Goldstein LB, Callahan A 3rd, et al. Baseline blood pressure, low- and high-density lipoproteins, and triglycerides and the risk of vascular events in the Stroke Prevention by Aggressive Reduction in Cholesterol Levels (SPARCL) trial. *Atherosclerosis*. 2009;204:515–520.
160. Amarenco P, Labreuche J, Touboul PJ. High-density lipoprotein-cholesterol and risk of stroke and carotid atherosclerosis: a systematic review. *Atherosclerosis*. 2008;196:489–496.
161. Ohira T, Shahar E, Chambless LE, Rosamond WD, Mosley TH Jr, Folsom AR. Risk factors for ischemic stroke subtypes: the atherosclerosis risk in communities study. *Stroke*. 2006;37:2493–2498.
162. Rothwell PM, Algra A, Amarenco P. Medical treatment in acute and long-term secondary prevention after transient ischaemic attack and ischaemic stroke. *Lancet*. 2011;377:1681–1692.
163. Tenenbaum A, Fisman EZ. Fibrates are an essential part of modern anti-dyslipidemic arsenal: spotlight on atherogenic dyslipidemia and residual risk reduction. *Cardiovasc Diabetol*. 2012;11:125.
164. Austin MA, King MC, Vranizan KM, Krauss RM. Atherogenic lipoprotein phenotype: a proposed genetic marker for coronary heart disease risk. *Circulation*. 1990;82:495–506.

165. Fruchart JC, Sacks F, Hermans MP, et al. The residual risk reduction initiative: a call to action to reduce residual vascular risk in patients with dyslipidemia. *Am J Cardiol.* 2008;102:1K–34K.
166. Sirimarco G, Deplanque D, Lavallee PC, et al. Atherogenic dyslipidemia in patients with transient ischemic attack. *Stroke.* 2011;42:2131–2137.
167. Reaven GM, Chen YD, Jeppesen J, Maheux P, Krauss RM. Insulin resistance and hyperinsulinemia in individuals with small, dense low density lipoprotein particles. *J Clin Invest.* 1993;92:141–146.
168. Kathiresan S, Otvos JD, Sullivan LM, et al. Increased small low-density lipoprotein particle number: a prominent feature of the metabolic syndrome in the Framingham Heart Study. *Circulation.* 2006;113:20–29.
169. Musunuru K. Atherogenic dyslipidemia: cardiovascular risk and dietary intervention. *Lipids.* 2010;45:907–914.
170. Executive summary of the third report of the National Cholesterol Education Program (NCEP) Expert Panel on Detection, Evaluation, and Treatment of High Blood Cholesterol in Adults (Adult Treatment Panel III). *JAMA.* 2001;285:2486–2497.
171. Cui Y, Blumenthal RS, Flaws JA, et al. Non-high-density lipoprotein cholesterol level as a predictor of cardiovascular disease mortality. *Arch Intern Med.* 2001;161:1413–1419.
172. Farwell WR, Sesso HD, Buring JE, Gaziano JM. Non-high-density lipoprotein cholesterol versus low-density lipoprotein cholesterol as a risk factor for a first nonfatal myocardial infarction. *Am J Cardiol.* 2005;96:1129–1134.
173. Liu J, Sempos CT, Donahue RP, Dorn J, Trevisan M, Grundy SM. Non-high-density lipoprotein and very-low-density lipoprotein cholesterol and their risk predictive values in coronary heart disease. *Am J Cardiol.* 2006;98:1363–1368.
174. Li C, Ford ES, Tsai J, Zhao G, Balluz LS, Gidding SS. Serum non-high-density lipoprotein cholesterol concentration and risk of death from cardiovascular diseases among U.S. adults with diagnosed diabetes: the Third National Health and Nutrition Examination Survey Linked Mortality Study. *Cardiovasc Diabetol.* 2011;10:46.
175. Jiang R, Schulze MB, Li T, et al. Non-HDL cholesterol and apolipoprotein B predict cardiovascular disease events among men with type 2 diabetes. *Diabetes Care.* 2004;27:1991–1997.
176. Liu J, Sempos C, Donahue RP, Dorn J, Trevisan M, Grundy SM. Joint distribution of non-HDL and LDL cholesterol and coronary heart disease risk prediction among individuals with and without diabetes. *Diabetes Care.* 2005;28:1916–1921.
177. Mahajan N, Ference BA, Arora N, et al. Role of non-high-density lipoprotein cholesterol in predicting cerebrovascular events in patients following myocardial infarction. *Am J Cardiol.* 2012;109:1694–1699.
178. Gaubatz JW, Heideman C, Gotto AM Jr, Morrisett JD, Dahlen GH. Human plasma lipoprotein [a]: structural properties. *J Biol Chem.* 1983;258:4582–4589.
179. Loscalzo J. Lipoprotein(a): a unique risk factor for atherothrombotic disease. *Arteriosclerosis.* 1990;10:672–679.
180. Scanu AM, Lawn RM, Berg K. Lipoprotein(a) and atherosclerosis. *Ann Intern Med.* 1991;115:209–218.
181. Rhoads GG, Dahlen G, Berg K, Morton NE, Dannenberg AL. Lp(a) lipoprotein as a risk factor for myocardial infarction. *JAMA.* 1986;256:2540–2544.
182. Danesh J, Collins R, Peto R. Lipoprotein(a) and coronary heart disease: meta-analysis of prospective studies. *Circulation.* 2000;102:1082–1085.
183. Craig WY, Neveux LM, Palomaki GE, Cleveland MM, Haddow JE. Lipoprotein(a) as a risk factor for ischemic heart disease: metaanalysis of prospective studies. *Clin Chem.* 1998;44:2301–2306.
184. Smolders B, Lemmens R, Thijs V. Lipoprotein (a) and stroke: a meta-analysis of observational studies. *Stroke.* 2007;38:1959–1966.

185. Erqou S, Kaptoge S, Perry PL, et al. Lipoprotein(a) concentration and the risk of coronary heart disease, stroke, and nonvascular mortality. *JAMA*. 2009;302:412–423.
186. Strang AC, Kaasjager HA, Basart DC, Stroes ES. Prevalence of dyslipidaemia in patients treated with lipid-modifying drugs in the Netherlands: part of the Dyslipidaemia International Survey. *Neth J Med*. 2010;68:168–174.
187. Lee M, Saver JL, Towfighi A, Chow J, Ovbiagele B. Efficacy of fibrates for cardiovascular risk reduction in persons with atherogenic dyslipidemia: a meta-analysis. *Atherosclerosis*. 2011;217:492–498.
188. Abourbih S, Filion KB, Joseph L, et al. Effect of fibrates on lipid profiles and cardiovascular outcomes: a systematic review. *Am J Med*. 2009;122:962.e1–8.
189. Fruchart JC. Peroxisome proliferator-activated receptor-alpha (PPARalpha): at the crossroads of obesity, diabetes and cardiovascular disease. *Atherosclerosis*. 2009;205:1–8.
190. Knopp RH, Brown WV, Dujovne CA, et al. Effects of fenofibrate on plasma lipoproteins in hypercholesterolemia and combined hyperlipidemia. *Am J Med*. 1987;83:50–59.
191. Schaefer EJ, Lamon-Fava S, Cole T, et al. Effects of regular and extended-release gemfibrozil on plasma lipoproteins and apolipoproteins in hypercholesterolemic patients with decreased HDL cholesterol levels. *Atherosclerosis*. 1996;127:113–122.
192. Staels B, Koenig W, Habib A, et al. Activation of human aortic smooth-muscle cells is inhibited by PPARalpha but not by PPARgamma activators. *Nature*. 1998;393:790–793.
193. Bruckert E, Labreuche J, Deplanque D, Touboul PJ, Amarenco P. Fibrates effect on cardiovascular risk is greater in patients with high triglyceride levels or atherogenic dyslipidemia profile: a systematic review and meta-analysis. *J Cardiovasc Pharmacol*. 2011;57:267–272.
194. Lago RM, Singh PP, Nesto RW. Congestive heart failure and cardiovascular death in patients with prediabetes and type 2 diabetes given thiazolidinediones: a meta-analysis of randomised clinical trials. *Lancet*. 2007;370:1129–1136.
195. Nissen SE, Wolski K. Effect of rosiglitazone on the risk of myocardial infarction and death from cardiovascular causes. *N Engl J Med*. 2007;356:2457–2471.
196. Joy T, Hegele RA. The end of the road for CETP inhibitors after torcetrapib? *Curr Opin Cardiol*. 2009;24:364–371.
197. Barter PJ, Caulfield M, Eriksson M, et al. Effects of torcetrapib in patients at high risk for coronary events. *N Engl J Med*. 2007;357:2109–2122.
198. Bots ML, Visseren FL, Evans GW, et al. Torcetrapib and carotid intima-media thickness in mixed dyslipidaemia (Radiance 2 Study): a randomised, double-blind trial. *Lancet*. 2007;370:153–160.
199. Nissen SE, Tardif JC, Nicholls SJ, et al. Effect of torcetrapib on the progression of coronary atherosclerosis. *N Engl J Med*. 2007;356:1304–1316.
200. Greenberg SM. Small vessels, big problems. *N Engl J Med*. 2006;354:1451–1453.
201. Bokura H, Saika R, Yamaguchi T, et al. Microbleeds are associated with subsequent hemorrhagic and ischemic stroke in healthy elderly individuals. *Stroke*. 2011;42:1867–1871.
202. Debette S, Markus HS. The clinical importance of white matter hyperintensities on brain magnetic resonance imaging: systematic review and meta-analysis. *BMJ*. 2010;341:c3666.
203. Vermeer SE, Longstreth WT Jr, Koudstaal PJ. Silent brain infarcts: a systematic review. *Lancet Neurol*. 2007;6:611–619.
204. Tsushima Y, Tanizaki Y, Aoki J, Endo K. MR detection of microhemorrhages in neurologically healthy adults. *Neuroradiology*. 2002;44:31–36.
205. Poels MM, Ikram MA, van der Lugt A, et al. Incidence of cerebral microbleeds in the general population: the Rotterdam Scan Study. *Stroke*. 2011;42:656–661.
206. Vermeer SE, Prins ND, den Heijer T, Hofman A, Koudstaal PJ, Breteler MM. Silent brain infarcts and the risk of dementia and cognitive decline. *N Engl J Med*. 2003;348:1215–1222.

207. Poels MM, Ikram MA, van der Lugt A, et al. Cerebral microbleeds are associated with worse cognitive function: the Rotterdam Scan Study. *Neurology.* 2012;78:326–333.
208. Murray AD, Staff RT, Shenkin SD, Deary IJ, Starr JM, Whalley LJ. Brain white matter hyperintensities: relative importance of vascular risk factors in nondemented elderly people. *Radiology.* 2005;237:251–257.
209. Asumi M, Yamaguchi T, Saito K, et al. Are serum cholesterol levels associated with silent brain infarcts? The Seiryo Clinic Study. *Atherosclerosis.* 2010;210:674–677.
210. Kato T, Inoue T, Yamagishi S, Morooka T, Okimoto T, Node K. Low-density lipoprotein subfractions and the prevalence of silent lacunar infarction in subjects with essential hypertension. *Hypertens Res.* 2006;29:303–307.
211. Gouw AA, van der Flier WM, Fazekas F, et al. Progression of white matter hyperintensities and incidence of new lacunes over a 3-year period: the Leukoaraiosis and Disability Study. *Stroke.* 2008;39:1414–1420.
212. Schmidt R, Fazekas F, Hayn M, et al. Risk factors for microangiopathy-related cerebral damage in the Austrian Stroke Prevention Study. *J Neurol Sci.* 1997;152:15–21.
213. Longstreth WT Jr, Arnold AM, Beauchamp NJ Jr, et al. Incidence, manifestations, and predictors of worsening white matter on serial cranial magnetic resonance imaging in the elderly: the Cardiovascular Health Study. *Stroke.* 2005;36:56–61.
214. Longstreth WT Jr, Dulberg C, Manolio TA, et al. Incidence, manifestations, and predictors of brain infarcts defined by serial cranial magnetic resonance imaging in the elderly: the Cardiovascular Health Study. *Stroke.* 2002;33:2376–2382.
215. Schilling S, Tzourio C, Dufouil C, et al. Plasma lipids and cerebral small vessel disease. *Neurology.* 2014;83:1844–1852.
216. Bernick C, Katz R, Smith NL, et al. Statins and cognitive function in the elderly: the Cardiovascular Health Study. *Neurology.* 2005;65:1388–1394.
217. Jimenez-Conde J, Biffi A, Rahman R, et al. Hyperlipidemia and reduced white matter hyperintensity volume in patients with ischemic stroke. *Stroke.* 2010;41:437–442.
218. Basile AM, Pantoni L, Pracucci G, et al. Age, hypertension, and lacunar stroke are the major determinants of the severity of age-related white matter changes. The LADIS (Leukoaraiosis and Disability in the Elderly) study. *Cerebrovasc Dis.* 2006;21:315–322.
219. Park K, Yasuda N, Toyonaga S, et al. Significant association between leukoaraiosis and metabolic syndrome in healthy subjects. *Neurology.* 2007;69:974–978.
220. Carmelli D, Swan GE, Reed T, Wolf PA, Miller BL, DeCarli C. Midlife cardiovascular risk factors and brain morphology in identical older male twins. *Neurology.* 1999;52:1119–1124.
221. Ridker PM, Buring JE, Cook NR, Rifai N. C-reactive protein, the metabolic syndrome, and risk of incident cardiovascular events: an 8-year follow-up of 14,719 initially healthy American women. *Circulation.* 2003;107:391–397.
222. Satizabal CL, Zhu YC, Mazoyer B, Dufouil C, Tzourio C. Circulating IL-6 and CRP are associated with MRI findings in the elderly: the 3C-Dijon study. *Neurology.* 2012;78:720–727.
223. Wardlaw JM, Doubal F, Armitage P, et al. Lacunar stroke is associated with diffuse blood–brain barrier dysfunction. *Ann Neurol.* 2009;65:194–202.
224. Howard G, Wagenknecht LE, Cai J, Cooper L, Kraut MA, Toole JF. Cigarette smoking and other risk factors for silent cerebral infarction in the general population. *Stroke.* 1998;29:913–917.
225. Wieberdink RG, Poels MM, Vernooij MW, et al. Serum lipid levels and the risk of intracerebral hemorrhage: the Rotterdam study. *Arterioscler Thromb Vasc Biol.* 2011;31:2982–2989.
226. van Es AC, van der Grond J, de Craen AJ, Admiraal-Behloul F, Blauw GJ, van Buchem MA. Risk factors for cerebral microbleeds in the elderly. *Cerebrovasc Dis.* 2008;26:397–403.

227. Orken DN, Kenangil G, Uysal E, Gundogdu L, Erginoz E, Forta H. Lack of association between cerebral microbleeds and low serum cholesterol in patients with acute intracerebral hemorrhage. *Clin Neurol Neurosurg.* 2010;112:668–671.
228. Haussen DC, Henninger N, Kumar S, Selim M. Statin use and microbleeds in patients with spontaneous intracerebral hemorrhage. *Stroke.* 2012;43:2677–2681.
229. Vernooij MW, van der Lugt A, Ikram MA, et al. Prevalence and risk factors of cerebral microbleeds: the Rotterdam Scan Study. *Neurology.* 2008;70:1208–1214.
230. Lee SH, Bae HJ, Yoon BW, Kim H, Kim DE, Roh JK. Low concentration of serum total cholesterol is associated with multifocal signal loss lesions on gradient-echo magnetic resonance imaging: analysis of risk factors for multifocal signal loss lesions. *Stroke.* 2002;33:2845–2849.
231. Jeerakathil T, Wolf PA, Beiser A, et al. Cerebral microbleeds: prevalence and associations with cardiovascular risk factors in the Framingham study. *Stroke.* 2004;35:1831–1835.
232. Mok VC, Lam WW, Fan YH, et al. Effects of statins on the progression of cerebral white matter lesion: post hoc analysis of the ROCAS (Regression of Cerebral Artery Stenosis) study. *J Neurol.* 2009;256:750–757.
233. Fu JH, Mok V, Lam W, et al. Effects of statins on progression of subclinical brain infarct. *Cerebrovasc Dis.* 2010;30:51–56.
234. ten Dam VH, van den Heuvel DM, van Buchem MA, et al. Effect of pravastatin on cerebral infarcts and white matter lesions. *Neurology.* 2005;64:1807–1809.

14

METABOLIC DYSFUNCTION AS A RISK FACTOR FOR STROKE

Obesity, Metabolic Syndrome, and Diabetes Mellitus

Erica C. S. Camargo and Lenore J. Launer

Introduction

In this chapter, we discuss diabetes mellitus, metabolic syndrome, and obesity as they pertain to the development of ischemic and hemorrhagic stroke. We begin with an overview of these conditions, then their pathophysiology in relation to stroke, stroke risk and outcomes in persons with these disorders, and management decisions to decrease the risk of stroke. We do not discuss individually, other related stroke risk factors such as hypertension, dyslipidemia, and smoking.

DIABETES MELLITUS

Diabetes is a chronic disease characterized by ongoing hyperglycemia resulting from either glucose intolerance/peripheral resistance to insulin or insufficient levels of insulin. Its definition requires a fasting plasma glucose level of 126 mg/dL or more (≥7 mmol/L) or, according to the World Health Organization (WHO), impaired glucose tolerance as defined by a 2-hour postglucose load test level of 199 mg/dL or more (≥11 mmol/L). In addition, a glycated hemoglobin level of 6.5% or more also determines diabetes. These tests should be replicated at least once to confirm the diagnosis.[1,2] Diabetes is preceded by prediabetes—a prolonged, presymptomatic stage characterized by mild hyperglycemia, insulin resistance, and early decrease in insulin secretion. Prediabetes is determined by a fasting plasma glucose level of 100 to 125 mg/dL (5.6–6.9 mmol/L) or a glycated hemoglobin level of 5.7% to 6.4%.[2]

Type 1 Diabetes

Type 1 diabetes accounts for approximately 5% to 10% of all cases of diabetes and is accompanied by extensive long-term clinical complications, given its lifelong duration. Most cases of type 1 diabetes are the result of a cell-mediated immune response against pancreatic β cells, leading to an absolute or near-absolute deficiency of insulin. Genetic susceptibility mediated mainly through human leukocyte antigen DR and DQ genotypes plays a role in its pathogenesis, as do environmental triggers that alter immune function, such as viral infections, environmental toxins, and exposure to certain foods early in life. A strong indication that environmental factors play an etiologic role in this disease is the observation that migrant populations carry the same incidence of type 1 diabetes as that of the local population.[3]

Type 2 Diabetes

Type 2 diabetes is caused by relative insulin deficiency resulting from impaired insulin production in addition to peripheral insulin resistance. Type 2 diabetes accounts for 90% of all cases of diabetes and has a strong genetic component. A family history of type 2 diabetes increases the risk of disease 2.4 times. Sedentary lifestyle, obesity, and overeating may also trigger disease onset; therefore, environmental factors are fundamental in the pathogenesis of this disease.[1] Type 2 diabetes is often associated with other metabolic abnormalities, including hypertension, dyslipidemia, and metabolic syndrome. Frequently, type 2 diabetes develops gradually over a prolonged period of time with nonspecific symptoms, thus leading to underdiagnosis of this condition.[1]

METABOLIC SYNDROME (SYNDROME X OR INSULIN RESISTANCE SYNDROME)

Metabolic syndrome is comprised of a combination of disease states that lead to a significantly increased risk for cardiovascular disease, stroke, and diabetes. A recent consensus to define metabolic syndrome was determined using definition points from the WHO, the National Cholesterol Education Program's Adult Treatment Panel III, and the International Diabetes Federation. It includes three or more of the following: (a) central obesity (waist circumference ≥102 cm in men or ≥88 cm in women for white populations, or waist circumference ≥94 cm in men or ≥80 cm in women for nonwhite populations), (b) hypertriglyceridemia (triglycerides ≥150 mg/dL or medication use), (c) low high-density lipoprotein (HDL) cholesterol (<40 mg/dL in men and <50 mg/dL in women or medication use), (d) hypertension (blood pressure [BP] ≥35/85 mmHg or antihypertensive use), and (e) a fasting plasma glucose level of 100 mg/dL or more, or medication use.[4] When three of these risk factors are present, the risk of cardiovascular disease and diabetes is increased 1.5 to 2 times. Insulin resistance, promoted mainly by excess free fatty acids and visceral obesity, is key in the role of metabolic syndrome as a risk factor for cardiovascular disease.[5]

OBESITY

Obesity is a chronic pathological condition characterized by the accumulation of excess adipose tissue. It is associated with an increased risk of multiple morbidities and mortality. Obesity is a consequence of a neurochemical imbalance and can be defined operationally by the body mass index (BMI), which is a ratio of weight to height. Normal BMIs range from 18.5 to 24.9 kg/m^2, overweight BMIs range from 25 to 29.9 kg/m^2, and the obesity BMI is 30 kg/m^2 or more. Additional factors weigh into the relevance to health of an individual's weight status, such as age, stability of the BMI, activity level, and distribution of adiposity. Cardiovascular risk is increased with a higher BMI at an earlier age, an increasing BMI, low physical activity, and central adiposity as measured by the waist circumference. Obesity is associated with decreased life expectancy and a higher risk of mortality, diabetes, insulin resistance, and metabolic syndrome.[6]

Epidemiology

Diabetes and metabolic syndrome have become worldwide epidemics, with an impressive impact on cardiovascular disease burden and healthcare costs across the globe. Furthermore, these diseases, once considered mainly conditions of adulthood, have been seen progressively in children and teenagers as well, increasing the magnitude of the epidemic.

DIABETES MELLITUS

According to WHO, there are approximately 346 million people worldwide with diabetes (type 1 and type 2 combined). Diabetes has a very high impact on mortality; there were 3.4 million deaths in 2004 attributed to diabetes, of which 80% were in middle- to lower income nations.[7] A large systematic analysis of national heath surveys and epidemiological studies involving 370 country-years and 2.7 million participants showed an age-standardized prevalence of diabetes of 9.8% in men and 9.2% in women (yielding approximately 173 million affected persons worldwide of each sex), indicating an increase of nearly 194 million cases of diabetes from 1980 to 2008. The countries with the highest fasting plasma glucose levels and highest prevalence of diabetes were in Oceania, North Africa, the Middle East, and the Caribbean. Seventy percent of the additional cases of diabetes from 1980 to 2008 are the result of population growth and aging, and the remainder is a result of an increase in age-specific prevalence.[8] It is also estimated that many patients with diabetes are undiagnosed. In the United States, data from NHANES suggests that 2.2% of noninstitutionalized Americans have undiagnosed diabetes.[9]

The healthcare costs associated with diabetes are significant and, unfortunately, escalating. Persons with diabetes use two to three times more healthcare resources than persons without diabetes, which in some countries can amount to 15% of healthcare expenditures.[10] According to a statement from the American Diabetes Association, in 2007, U.S. healthcare costs attributed to diabetes were US$ 176 billion, of which US$ 116 billion were the result of excess medical expenditure (50% from hospitalizations) and US$ 58 billion were from reduced national productivity (US$ 27 billion from loss of lifetime productivity resulting from early mortality).[9]

Type 1 Diabetes

Type 1 diabetes is considered a disease of the young, with 50% to 60% of cases diagnosed before 16 to 18 years of age and, subsequently, continuing at low incidence rates through adulthood. Unfortunately, the global incidence of type 1 diabetes has also been increasing steadily at about 2% to 5%/year.[3] Based on a Swedish population study, the annual incidence rate of type 1 diabetes was reported to be 16.4/100,000 in men and 8.9/100,000 in women. The incidence decreased by 1%/year of increasing age.[11] These data underscore the known susceptibility to type 1 diabetes of postpubertal men compared with postpubertal women, also reported in other studies (with male-to-female ratios of 1.2–2.1). In addition, there also appears to be a seasonal variation in disease incidence, with a larger number of cases reported in autumn, winter, and early spring.[11]

Type 2 Diabetes

Estimates of the world prevalence of type 2 diabetes indicate approximately 141.9 million persons in the year 2000, corresponding to a crude prevalence of 3.8% of adults older than 20 years. It is estimated that in 2025, there will be 285.4 million persons with type 2 diabetes worldwide.[12]

Type 2 diabetes affects both sexes equally. It presents predominantly in middle and late life, with prevalence rates higher in patients older than 65 years. However, the proportion of middle-age individuals with type 2 diabetes has increased in the United States during the past 20 years.[9,13] In the Framingham Heart Study, during a 30-year period there was a near doubling of the prevalence of type 2 diabetes in individuals age 40 to 55 years. Compared with the 1970s, the age- and sex-adjusted odds ratio for diabetes during the 1980s was 1.40 (95% confidence interval [CI] 0.89–2.22), and 2.05 (95% CI, 1.33–3.14) during the 1990s (*p* value for trend = .0006). Most of the persons who developed type 2 diabetes had BMIs greater than 30 kg/m^2, highlighting the importance of obesity and lifestyle in the disease pathogenesis.[14] Hispanics and blacks are at particularly high risk for type 2 diabetes.[9] It is estimated that the net number of people with diagnosed diabetes in the United States is growing by 1 million each year.[9] From 1988 to 2008 there has been an increase in the incidence of type 2 diabetes in Mexican Americans and other Hispanic populations in the United States, whereas the incidence has decreased in non-Hispanic whites. In 2008, the prevalence of diabetes in the United States was 6.1% for non-Latino whites, 11.6% for Mexican-Americans, and 12.6% for blacks. In addition, Hispanics and blacks with type 2 diabetes were 50% more likely to have worse glycemic control than non-Hispanic whites.[13] Native Americans are also at a very high risk for type 2 diabetes, with reported estimates of disease prevalence ranging from 47% to 73%.[15] Regarding control of vascular risk factors, 54% of persons with type 2 diabetes in the United States maintained poor control of two or more associated cardiovascular risk factors.[13]

METABOLIC SYNDROME

As with diabetes, metabolic syndrome is also becoming a worldwide epidemic, with great variation in prevalence in different countries and according to race. It appears to affect both sexes equally in whites, but women are affected more commonly among blacks and Hispanics.[16] As an example, reported prevalences in men vary from 8% in India to 39% in the United States; and in women, from 7% in France to 43% in Iran. The disease affects more Mexican-Americans than non-Hispanic whites. The prevalence also increases significantly with age, especially in the 60- to 69-year age group. Because the disease is linked directly to obesity, it is becoming more frequent in obese children and teenagers; its prevalence has been reported, in different populations, to affect up to 50% of severely obese children.[5,17]

OBESITY

Initially a disease of developed nations, obesity has become a worldwide epidemic affecting both adults and children.[18] In the United States, the prevalence of obesity was 16.9% in children and 35.5% among adult men and 35.8% among adult women in 2009/2010, according to data from NHANES.[6,19,20] Furthermore, more than two thirds of Americans are overweight or obese. Worldwide, 23.2% of adults are overweight and 9.8% are obese. It is projected there will be 1.35 billion overweight and 537 million obese adults worldwide in 2030.[21] More females are overweight than males at any given age, and obesity increases with age. Interestingly, obesity has increased more in younger than older women, whereas the reverse has occurred in men. Hispanics and blacks have a greater prevalence of obesity than whites.[6]

Pathophysiology of Metabolic Dysfunction and Stroke

DIABETES

Hyperglycemia may contribute to stroke and worsened stroke outcomes through various mechanisms. Hyperglycemia has been shown to be associated with larger infarcts in animal models. Similarly, in humans there is reduced penumbral salvage in acute stroke patients who are hyperglycemic on admission.[22,23] Hyperglycemia may impair arterial recanalization via abnormalities in the coagulation cascade and impaired fibrinolysis, mediated through higher levels of PAI-1 and tissue-type plasminogen activator antigen. Furthermore, chronic hyperglycemia may lead to reduced efficacy of pharmacological fibrinolysis, abnormal blood flow patterns, and impaired vascular reactivity. Other potential mechanisms for worse stroke outcomes include increased reperfusion injury and increased risk of hemorrhagic complications after thrombolysis.[23] Diabetes is known to promote atherosclerosis in the cervical and coronary arteries. Furthermore, diabetes is associated with a 40% increased risk of atrial fibrillation.[24]

METABOLIC SYNDROME

The key aspect of metabolic syndrome, leading to its contribution to cardiovascular disease and stroke, is insulin resistance. The interplay between insulin resistance and obesity leads to the pathogenesis of metabolic syndrome, in which one condition contributes to the other in this complex disease state. Excess free fatty acids increase hepatic glucose production, modify downstream signaling of insulin metabolism, and inhibit insulin effectiveness in decreasing local glucose production. Furthermore, insulin is an important mediator of antilipolysis, which is impaired significantly in insulin resistance. In the setting of increased influx of free fatty acids to the liver, in obese individuals there is an increase in apolipoprotein B-containing, triglyceride-rich very low-density lipoprotein (LDL). Insulin resistance also furthers an increase in triglycerides by promoting hepatic synthesis and by decreasing the concentrations of lipoprotein lipase in the adipose tissues. These lead to additional changes to the lipid profile. In the presence of excess triglycerides, the composition of HDL is modified, and there is an increased clearance of circulating HDL, leading to lower levels of HDL. Similarly, LDL experiences changes to its structure in the presence of elevated levels of triglycerides with greater circulating levels of small, dense LDLs, felt to be more atherogenic than normal circulating LDL. Increasing and prolonged exposure to free fatty acids leads to decreased pancreatic insulin secretion. Insulin resistance also contributes to the development of hypertension—one of the components of metabolic syndrome. The mechanisms by which this occurs are related to the action of insulin as a vasodilator, which is lost in insulin resistance. Insulin also promotes sodium reabsorption and activates the sympathetic nervous system, both of which are still preserved in insulin resistance. Insulin resistance can also contribute to atherogenesis via other mechanisms, including its association with increased uric acid, fibrinogen, PAI-1, asymmetric dimethylarginine, homocysteine, proinflammatory cytokines, microalbuminuria, and obstructive sleep apnea.[5]

OBESITY AND NONOBESE PHENOTYPES

Adipose tissue has various functions in energy homeostasis, including glucose uptake and conversion, lipogenesis, lipolysis, and fatty acid oxidation. Adipocytes may contribute to cardiovascular disease and diabetes via the secretion of lipid and hormonal products termed *adipokines*, and by retaining toxic lipid species. Leptin is an adipokine excreted in proportion to the amount of adipocyte fat content. It acts on the hypothalamus by inhibiting food intake, increasing metabolic rate and energy expenditure, and regulating insulin and glucose homeostasis. Paradoxically, obese individuals have high levels of leptin and, as such, it is postulated that obesity leads to leptin resistance in the brain. Excess leptin decreases vasorelaxation and is linked to endothelial dysfunction.[25] Leptin has been shown to be associated independently with first-ever hemorrhagic stroke, and also with inflammatory markers, procoagulant factors, and insulin resistance.[26,27] Adiponectin, another adipokine, acts as an insulin sensitizer in the liver. It has anti-inflammatory effects and protects cardiac and pancreatic β cells. Its secretion by adipose tissue decreases in obesity, especially in central obesity. Low adiponectin levels are associated with insulin resistance and hypertension.[25] Low adiponectin levels have been shown to be associated with stroke in case–control studies, but the same has not been observed in prospective cohort studies, although associations with diabetes, hyperglycemia, hypertension, and obesity were noted.[28–30] Adiponectin is associated with increased carotid intima media thickness, but not with carotid plaques, in healthy subjects.[31] Interleukin 6, also secreted by adipocytes, promotes insulin resistance by interfering with insulin receptor signal transduction.[32] Resistin regulates glucose homeostasis and insulin metabolism. It may dysregulate endothelial functioning and is implicated in atherosclerosis via endothelial inflammation. Resistin has been associated with ischemic stroke in postmenopausal women and is a predictor of composite outcomes of cerebral and cardiac events.[33,34]

Despite obesity's contribution to cardiovascular disease, as discussed in the section on metabolic syndrome, there are some circumstances in which it may have protective effects. An "obesity paradox" has been described in which obese subjects with cardiovascular disease may survive longer than nonobese control subjects with cardiovascular disease and stroke. The reasons for such a phenomenon are still unclear, but could be the expression of an epidemiological bias. As an example, obese patients may experience stroke subtypes associated with lower recurrence risk, obese patients may receive more aggressive therapy, or the paradox may reflect a survival bias in which patients who are obese and who have survived until their event have metabolically benign obesity.[35] Conversely, there are nonobese subjects who may have high-risk metabolic derangements. Described as *metabolically obese normal weight*, these subjects have hyperinsulinemia, insulin resistance, and hypertriglyceridemia, and are prone to develop diabetes. They may have a normal BMI but a high body fat content and are similarly subject to coronary disease and cardiovascular mortality.[36,37] Another group of patients termed *sarcopenic obese*, have a high body fat content in addition to low lean body mass, and display reduced cardiorespiratory fitness, physical function, and mobility, and experience premature mortality. With this condition, improved fitness levels lead to better cardiovascular outcomes.[38,39] Hemiparetic stroke may exacerbate the metabolic abnormalities of sarcopenic obesity, not only through reduced physical activity but also via changes in skeletal muscle constitution, leading to increased oxidative injury, inflammation, and insulin resistance. This finding may contribute to the very high prevalence (up to 75%) of insulin resistance and diabetes in stroke survivors.[35]

Stroke Risk

Insulin resistance—one of the underlying mechanisms of diabetes, metabolic syndrome, and obesity—has been shown to be an independent risk factor for stroke. Insulin resistance, as measured by plasma insulin concentrations or steady-state plasma glucose levels, carries a relative risk (RR) of ischemic stroke ranging from 1.5 to 2.1 for subjects without diabetes in the highest 20% to 25% of insulin resistance.[40]

DIABETES

Stroke risk has been shown consistently to be increased in subjects with diabetes. In a large meta-analysis of prospective studies involving nearly 700,000 subjects, the hazard ratio (HR) in persons with diabetes compared with control subjects was 2.24 (95% CI, 1.94–2.59) for ischemic stroke and 1.56 (95% CI, 1.19–2.05) for hemorrhagic stroke after adjusting for various cardiovascular risk factors. HRs were greater for younger subjects (HR = 3.74; 95% CI, 3.06–4.58) age 40 to 59 years, and for women compared with men (HR = 2.83; 95% CI, 2.35–3.40). The diabetes-attributable risk of stroke was calculated at 12%.[41] The risk of ischemic stroke is higher in blacks compared with whites with diabetes, with the greatest risk occurring in younger blacks age 35 to 44 years.[42] In the Northern Manhattan Stroke Study, diabetes accounted for 10% and 14% of strokes in Hispanics and blacks, respectively.[43] Duration of diabetes is also important in determining ischemic stroke risk, which increases 3%/year and triples after 10 years of diabetes.[44] Interestingly, in the Northern Manhattan Stroke Study, the risk of stroke was increased only in subjects with fasting blood glucose levels of 126 mg/dL or more, thus suggesting that tight glucose control may ameliorate stroke risk.[45] Among persons with diabetes, microalbuminuria—measured using the albumin-to-creatinine ratio (normal range, 1–2.5 mg/mmol)—of more than 2.5 conferred twice the risk of a stroke compared with those without microalbuminuria.[46]

Differences have been noted in the stroke risk for subjects with type 1 diabetes compared to persons with type 2 diabetes. In the Nurses' Health Study, the RR for ischemic stroke in women age 30 to 55 years who were monitored for 24 years was 6.3 (95% CI, 4.0–9.8) for type 1 diabetes and 2.3 (95% CI, 2.0–2.6) for type 2 diabetes. The risk of hemorrhagic stroke was increased for type 1 diabetes (RR = 3.8; 95% CI, 1.2–11.8) but not for type 2 diabetes. Ischemic stroke subtype risks also varied and were greater for thrombotic, large-vessel, and lacunar stroke in type 1 diabetes (RRs= 6.4 [95% CI, 3.9–10.5], 7.2 [95% CI, 3.2–16.2], and 7.2 [95% CI, 3.2–16.1], respectively).[47] Another large epidemiological study noted that, among young ischemic stroke patients, those with diabetes were more likely to have small-vessel strokes compared with subjects without diabetes. Patients with type 1 diabetes had more associated coronary and peripheral arterial disease, whereas patients with type 2 diabetes were more commonly older and male, and had more associated obesity, peripheral arterial disease, transient ischemic attack, and stroke.[48]

Regarding stroke subtype, patients with type 2 diabetes are at greater risk for lacunar stroke. The ARIC study demonstrated this, showing a risk ratio for incident lacunar stroke of 3.23 after adjusting for multiple risk factors. Diabetes carried a population-attributable fraction of 26.3% for lacunar strokes. The same study also showed that the risk of cardioembolic stroke is elevated in persons with diabetes, with a risk ratio of 2.63 and a population-attributable fraction of 20.7% for cardioembolic stroke.[49] Furthermore, the ARIC study also demonstrated that very small lacunes (diameter, <3 mm) were associated with diabetes compared with larger lacunes.[50] Interestingly, an association between diabetes and atrial fibrillation has been observed in many studies, although the cause of this correlation remains unknown. A large meta-analysis involving approximately 1.6 million subjects showed that diabetes is associated with a 34% increased risk of atrial fibrillation, with a population-attributable risk of atrial fibrillation from diabetes of 2.5%.[24]

METABOLIC SYNDROME

Metabolic syndrome is associated with an increased risk for vascular events and stroke, with an HR for stroke ranging from 1.57 to 2.10.[51] Metabolic syndrome confers a greater stroke risk in women than in men (HR = 2.0; 95% CI, 1.3–3.1 vs. HR = 1.1; 95% CI, 0.6–1.9; respectively). This effect is likely the result of greater overall and central obesity in women compared with men.[52] Furthermore, stroke risk is greater in Hispanics (HR = 2.0; 95% CI, 1.2–3.4) compared with blacks and whites, and also in non-Hispanic blacks compared with non-Hispanic whites.[52,53] It is estimated that elimination of metabolic syndrome would result in a 19% reduction in stroke overall, a 30% reduction of stroke in women, and a 35% reduction of stroke among Hispanics.[52] Metabolic syndrome contributes to cardiovascular and stroke risk in an additive fashion, according to the number of its components.[54,55] However, even after adjusting for these individual components, metabolic syndrome itself is an independent risk factor for stroke.[56,57] It is felt that obesity is the key component of this syndrome that confers stroke risk. Considering stroke subtypes, metabolic syndrome appears to be associated more strongly with intracranial rather than extracranial atherosclerosis.[58] Increased silent brain infarcts and white matter hyperintensities have also been reported in older subjects with metabolic syndrome.[59]

OBESITY

Obesity has been established as a risk factor for stroke. When using BMI for the determination of obesity, men with a BMI of 30 kg/m^2 or more have double the risk of stroke compared with men with a BMI less than 23 kg/m^2. For each unit increase in BMI, there is a 6% increase in stroke risk (RR = 6%; 95% CI, 4–8).[60] Using the waist-to-hip ratio definition of obesity, those in the highest tertile of WHR have a 65% increased risk of stroke compared with those in the lowest tertile. The population-attributable risk of stroke resulting from increased waist-to-hip ratio is 26.5%.[61] In women, each unit increase of waist circumference is associated with a 2% increased stroke risk.[62] Regarding specific stroke subtypes, overweight and obesity are associated with ischemic stroke; in a large meta-analysis, individuals who were overweight and obese had an increased risk for ischemic stroke of 22% and 64%, respectively, compared with normal-weight individuals. This did not differ according to sex or degree of hypertension, but these findings were more significant in Europeans and North Americans than in Asians. Hemorrhagic stroke, however, was associated weakly with overweight status, and approached statistical significance only for obese subjects compared with normal-weight individuals (RR = 1.24; 95% CI, 0.99–1.54; p = .059).[63]

Short- and Long-Term Stroke Outcomes

DIABETES

Diabetes contributes to mortality after stroke. Reports vary regarding the timing of mortality in patients with diabetes with stroke, but most studies do not report an increased mortality during the first 3 months after stroke in persons with diabetes compared with others, although persons with diabetes had longer hospital stays. However, mortality is slightly increased 1 year poststroke (HR = 1.2; 95% CI, 1.1–1.2).[64] Over 10 years, both type 1 and type 2 diabetes are strong predictors of all-cause mortality, with cumulative risks of 33.5% (95% CI, 17–50%) and 25.4% (95% CI, 13.1–37.7%), respectively.[48] Stroke patients with diabetes also have worse functional outcomes than patients without; they were less able to ambulate at discharge and were more likely to be discharged to a skilled nursing facility or to inpatient acute rehabilitation. Diabetes was also observed to be an independent risk factor for worse health-related quality of life 1 year poststroke.[64,65]

Diabetes also affects patient outcomes after stroke negatively. It is unclear whether this is a result of diabetes being a marker of systemic illness or the effects of persistent hyperglycemia.[40] Part of the increased morbidity in stroke patients with diabetes may be explained by the effects of diabetes on cognition. In children, early-onset diabetes has been associated with worse cognitive outcomes, which persist through adulthood.[66] This is likely a result of the adverse effects of metabolic abnormalities on the developing brain. Adults who develop type 2 diabetes later in life also have more cognitive impairment compared with adults without diabetes. The cognitive domains involved are mainly psychomotor efficiency, executive function, learning, and memory. The risks for Alzheimer's disease (RR = 1.5–2.0) and vascular dementia (RR = 2.0–2.5) are increased in individuals with diabetes. Thus, diabetes could have an attributable risk for dementia of 7% to 13%.[66] Older adults with diabetes also have more pronounced brain atrophy, lacunar infarcts, and a modest increase in white matter hyperintensity volumes.[66]

Diabetes is a strong predictor of recurrent stroke, with 9.1% (95% CI, −2.0 to 20.2) of recurrences attributable to diabetes.[67] This risk seems to be even greater in patients younger than 50 years old.[48]

METABOLIC SYNDROME

Metabolic syndrome is associated with poor outcome after cardiovascular disease, with increased cardiovascular mortality (RR = 2.40; 95% CI, 1.87–3.08) and all-cause mortality (RR = 1.58; 95% CI, 1.39–1.78).[68] It has also been associated with cognitive impairment and increased risk of dementia, primarily in elderly subjects with high levels of inflammation.[69] Multiple cognitive domains can be affected, including executive function, memory, visuospatial function, processing speed, and global intellectual functioning.[59] Some of the individual components of metabolic syndrome, such as hypertension, have been shown to contribute individually to the risk of mild cognitive impairment and dementia. Furthermore, the longer the exposure to these components of metabolic syndrome, the greater the risk of developing mild cognitive impairment or dementia later in life. There is no clear evidence that treatment of metabolic syndrome yields significant reductions in the risk of cognitive impairment.[70]

OBESITY

Obesity is also an independent predictor of poor outcome after stroke. BMI predicts mortality from stroke with a 40% increased risk of vascular death for each 5-kg/m^2 increase in BMI.[71] Obesity has also been shown to affect cognition even at an early age, with deficits in executive functioning, attention, and intelligence quotient in children who are obese.[59]

Management and Impact on Stroke

DIABETES MELLITUS

Lifestyle Modifications

Persons with diabetes who have potentially modifiable associated cardiovascular risk factors such as smoking, obesity, inactivity, excessive alcohol intake, and unhealthy diet should be counseled on smoking and alcohol cessation, and adherence to a heart-healthy diet and exercise program/weight loss. One study that addressed specifically the issue of risk factor modification in more than 2000 Japanese men and women with type 2 diabetes showed a significantly decreased incidence of stroke when adhering to lifestyle modification recommendations in addition to receiving usual medical care compared with usual medical care alone (HR = 0.62; 95% CI, 0.39–0.98; p = .04).[72] However, conflicting results have come from the Look Action for Health in Diabetes research group. These investigators reported initially that persons with type 2 diabetes receiving intensive lifestyle interventions were able to achieve 5% to 10% weight loss with exercise and caloric-goal diet modification. Compared with the routine care group, the intervention group had significant improvements in cardiovascular disease risk factors after 1 year.[73] However, after a median follow-up of 9.6 years, the Look Action for Health in Diabetes Trial was stopped early on the basis of futility because the primary outcome (composite of cardiovascular death, nonfatal myocardial infarction, nonfatal stroke, or hospitalization for angina) was similar in both groups despite sustained greater weight loss and greater reductions in glycated hemoglobin (HbA1c) levels in the intervention group (HR = 0.95; 95% CI, 0.83–1.09; p = .51). There was also no significant reduction in the risk of stroke with the intervention (HR = 1.05; 95% CI, 0.77–1.42; p = .78). The authors postulated that the lack of significant differences in outcomes could be the result of more aggressive management of diabetes in the control group and improved risk factor modification in these patients. In addition, there was reduced use of cardioprotective drugs in the intervention group, and the effect of the intervention on weight loss and all other cardiovascular risk factors decreased after the first few years of the study.[74,75] Further studies may be warranted to verify these findings.

Glucose-Lowering Treatments

Intensive versus standard glucose-lowering therapies in diabetes has been the subject of several trials. The United Kingdom Prospective Diabetes Study (UKPDS) group randomized newly diagnosed patients with type 2 diabetes to conventional diabetic management with dietary restriction alone versus intensive glucose-lowering therapy with sulfonylureas or insulin, or metformin in patients with diabetes who were overweight. After 10 years there were no significant differences in HbA1c levels among groups. However, patients with diabetes on sulfonylurea–insulin or metformin had significant risk reductions for any diabetes-related end point, myocardial infarction, and death from any cause compared with the standard-therapy group. In addition, in the sulfonylurea–insulin group there was a significant reduction in the rate of microvascular disease.[76] Converse results were seen in the Action to Control Cardiovascular Risk in Diabetes (ACCORD) trial, which included patients with diabetes with longstanding disease who were at high risk for a cerebrovascular disease-related event and a median HbA1c level of 8.1%. Participants were randomized to intensive glucose-lowering therapy (goal HbA1c level, <6.0%) or standard therapy (target HbA1c level, 7%–7.9%). After 3.5 years, there was no difference in the two groups in the risk of a composite end point of nonfatal myocardial infarction, nonfatal stroke, or cardiovascular death, but there was a significantly greater risk of death in the intensive-therapy group (HR = 1.22; 95% CI, 1.01–1.46; $p = .04$). In addition, there were significantly higher rates of hypoglycemia and weight gain in the intensive-therapy group. The intensive therapy was stopped prematurely because of the higher death rate, and participants in that arm were transitioned to the standard-therapy protocol; the other interventions embedded in the glycemia trial were continued to the planned end. Reasons for the higher mortality rate remain unclear. There were no differences in the risk of stroke between groups.[77] A large meta-analysis of studies of intensive glucose-lowering therapies in type 2 diabetes concluded that the benefit-to-risk ratio for preventing macrovascular and microvascular events remained inconclusive, and the harm associated with hypoglycemia could offset the benefits of therapy. There was no reduction in the rates of all strokes or nonfatal strokes with intensive glucose-lowering therapy.[78]

For patients with type 1 diabetes, intensive glucose-lowering therapy (i.e., three or more daily insulin injections or insulin pump, four or more daily measurements for goal glucose levels of 70–120 mg/dL premeal or <180 mg/dL postmeal, and a goal HbA1c level of <6.05%) compared with conventional therapy (management of hypo-/hyperglycemia and one to two daily injections of insulin) had beneficial effects. After 6.5 years of treatment and 17 years of follow-up, intensive therapy reduced the risk of any cardiovascular event by 42% and risk of nonfatal myocardial infarction, stroke, or cardiovascular death by 57% (both, $p = .02$). Reductions in HbA1c values were associated with the positive effects on reduction of cardiovascular disease. There were very few strokes in both groups to draw conclusions regarding therapy and risk of stroke in type 1 patients with diabetes.[79]

Antihypertensive Treatment

Hypertension has a prevalence of 40% to 60% in patients with diabetes. It increases the risk of cardiovascular complications associated with the disease and promotes microalbuminuria and retinopathy. In the UKPDS, treatment of patients with hypertension with diabetes with an angiotensin-converting enzyme inhibitor or a beta blocker with goal BP of less than 150/85 mmHg reduced substantially the risk of death and complications resulting from diabetes and led to a 44% reduction in the risk of stroke (95% CI, 11–65; $p = .013$).[80] In the ACCORD study, an intensive BP therapeutic trial was embedded in the glycemic trial and showed that decreasing BP further in patients with diabetes to the goal systolic BP of less than 120 mmHg compared with less than 140 mmHg was not associated with reduced risk of fatal or nonfatal cardiovascular events, but did confer a significant risk reduction for stroke (HR = 0.59; 95% CI, 0.39–0.89; $p = .01$). However, this was at the expense of a significantly greater risk of serious adverse events ($p < .001$).[81] A recent meta-analysis concluded that a target systolic BP of 130 to 135 mmHg in patients with type 2 diabetes is acceptable, but that lowering BP further confers no benefit for macrovascular complications other than stroke, and it increases the risk of serious adverse events to 40%.[82] In the LIFE study, losartan was compared with atenolol in patients with diabetes with hypertension and left ventricular hypertrophy. Compared with atenolol, losartan use was associated with a significant decrease in the risk of cardiovascular morbidity and mortality (RR = 0.76; 95% CI, 0.58–0.98; $p = .031$) as well as all-cause mortality, independent of the level of BP control obtained. However, there was no difference in the risk of all-fatal or nonfatal strokes (HR = 0.79; 95% CI, 0.55–1.14; $p = .20$).[83] An alternative approach was sought in the ADVANCE study, in which patients with type 2 diabetes with known cardiovascular disease or cardiovascular risk factors were randomized to combination angiotensin-converting enzyme inhibitor and diuretic (perindopril plus indapamide) or to placebo regardless of baseline BP or use of other antihypertensives. Patients with diabetes on combination therapy had a 9% RR reduction of macrovascular or microvascular complications (HR = 0.91; 95% CI, 0.83–1.00; $p = .04$), and an 18% RR reduction of cardiovascular death (HR = 0.82; 95% CI, 0.68–0.98; $p = .03$). There was no significant effect on the risk of stroke.[84] Unfortunately, the benefits of antihypertensive therapy in patients with type 2 diabetes for reduction of all macrovascular complications, including stroke, were not sustained after 10 years in the UKPDS when between-group differences in BP were lost. Thus, good BP control is necessary to maintain the benefits of antihypertensives in patients with type 2 diabetes.[85]

Lipid-Lowering Therapies

Patients with diabetes commonly have high levels of triglycerides and low levels of HDL, although total cholesterol and LDL levels may not, necessarily, be elevated significantly. The Heart Protection Study aimed to test whether simvastatin could reduce the risk of cardiovascular disease and stroke in patients with diabetes. In this study, 5963 patients with type 1 and type 2 diabetes were allocated randomly to simvastatin 40 mg daily or placebo. Patients receiving simvastatin had a significant 22% rate reduction in cardiovascular events (95% CI, 13–30; $p < .0001$) compared with placebo, and this was present even in the absence of known arterial occlusive disease or with a baseline LDL level of less than 116 mg/dL. Furthermore, the risk of a first fatal or nonfatal stroke was reduced by 24% (95% CI, 6–39; $p = .01$) in the simvastatin group compared with placebo. This reduction was mainly the result of a 28% reduction in ischemic stroke and no difference in hemorrhagic stroke risk. The study authors concluded that statin therapy should be offered to all patients with diabetes at significant risk of cardiovascular disease regardless of their initial lipid profile.[86] Similarly, in the Collaborative Atorvastatin Diabetes Study, atorvastatin 10 mg daily was compared with placebo for primary prevention of cardiovascular disease in patients with diabetes with LDL levels of 75 mg/dL or less, triglyceride levels of 122 mg/dL or less, and hypertension, smoking, or signs of microvascular disease. There was a 37% rate reduction in cardiovascular events (95% CI, −52 to −17; $p = .001$) and a 48% reduction in the rate of stroke (95% CI, −69 to −11; $p = .001$) in the atorvastatin arm compared with placebo.[87] Additional studies explored fibrates, which increase HDL, for the reduction of cardiovascular disease. Compared with placebo, fenofibrate 200 mg daily did not lead to a significant reduction in cardiovascular events in patients with type 2 diabetes with normal total cholesterol and triglyceride levels. There was also no significant reduction in the rate of stroke with fenofibrate therapy.[88] Furthermore, in ACCORD, the combination of fenofibrate and simvastatin did not reduce significantly the rate of cardiovascular disease or stroke when compared with simvastatin plus placebo.[89]

Antithrombotics

The use of antithrombotics for the primary prevention of cardiovascular disease in patients with diabetes has been the subject of a Japanese randomized controlled trial. In that study, the use of aspirin

(ASA) 81 TO 100 mg daily in patients with type 2 diabetes did not reduce the risk of cardiovascular disease, cardiovascular death, transient ischemic attack, fatal stroke, and nonfatal ischemic stroke (HR = 0.93; 95% CI, 0.52–1.66; p = .80) after a median 4.4 years of follow-up.[90] A large meta-analysis explored this issue further and also found no benefit for the use of aspirin for primary prevention of stroke in patients with diabetes.[91] In an antithrombotic trialist's collaboration, secondary prevention of cardiovascular events was assessed in patients receiving antithrombotic medication. In patients with diabetes, there was a reduction of cardiovascular events (including ischemic stroke) similar to that observed in patients without diabetes. Despite the relatively low risk reduction obtained, antiplatelets are still recommended for secondary prevention of cardiovascular disease and stroke in patients with diabetes.[92]

Diabetes is also a risk factor for atrial fibrillation. As such, patients with diabetes with atrial fibrillation should be either on full-dose anticoagulation or antiplatelet therapy, according to their CHA_2DS_2-VAS score, for primary or secondary stroke prevention.[93]

Summary Management Recommendations

The American Diabetes Association recommends screening for diabetes in the following situation: age more than 45 years, or earlier in subjects with additional cardiovascular risk factors. Most important, for subjects with sustained BP greater than 135/80 mmHg, screening is advocated for asymptomatic patients because the targets for BP control change after a diagnosis of diabetes is made.[2] American Diabetes Association management guidelines recommend a goal HBA1c of less than 7.0%, a goal BP of less than 130/80 mmHg, and a goal LDL level of less than 100 mg/dL.[94] Similarly, the National Cholesterol Education Program's Adult Treatment Panel III guidelines suggest a goal total cholesterol of less than 200 mg/dL and an LDL level of less than 100 mg/ dL.[95]

OBESITY

Weight loss is recommended for all overweight or obese people with or without diabetes, with the use of low-carbohydrate, low-fat, calorie-restricted, or Mediterranean diets. In addition, given the risk associated with sarcopenic obesity, behavioral management and physical activity are recommended.[96] A lifestyle modification program that aims at diet modification, exercise, and weight loss prevented the development of type 2 diabetes in obese subjects with glucose intolerance over a follow-up period of 3.2 years.[97] A similar study showed that both lifestyle interventions and metformin use are effective in the prevention of type 2 diabetes, with numbers needed to treat of 6.9/3 years and 13.9/3 years, respectively.[98] Unfortunately, there are no studies to date addressing the issue of weight loss and its impact on stroke risk in purely obese subjects. However, given the linear increase in stroke risk with increases in BMI, it is reasonable to aim for a goal BMI of 22 to 25 kg/m^2.[35]

Guidelines usually recommend an initial weight loss of 5% to 10% of body weight. More can be recommended if the patient is willing, especially if there are abnormal cardiovascular parameters. To achieve weight loss, counseling is recommended initially, with best results obtained from multidisciplinary programs with lifestyle coaching, one-on-one programs with physical activity recommendations, and prepared meals.[99,100] Moderate aerobic physical activity at least five times per week is generally recommended for all adults age 18 to 65 years, but it usually does not result in a significant weight loss as does dietary modification.[101] Medications can be given to help promote weight loss as second-line therapy after diet, exercise, and behavioral modification. As a last option, bariatric surgery (adjustable gastric banding or roux-en-Y gastric bypass) has been shown in clinical trials to promote significant weight loss (up to 21% of body mass), remission of diabetes in up to 75% of subjects, reduction in BP and vascular inflammation, and improved quality of life.[35]

METABOLIC SYNDROME

Metabolic syndrome carries a high risk for cardiovascular disease and type 2 diabetes. These risks can be short-term or may occur over the longer term (>10 years). Thus, all subjects with metabolic syndrome should undergo 10-year risk assessment (e.g., with the Framingham Risk Score) for evaluation of their cardiovascular risk and potential need for pharmacotherapy.[5]

The primary goal in the treatment of metabolic syndrome is to address its modifiable risk factors and thus delay the onset of diabetes and complications of atherogenic dyslipidemia. As with obesity, behavioral approaches should be initiated to promote behavioral modifications aimed at weight loss (goal, loss of 7%–10% body mass in 1 year). Dietary modifications should include low intake of saturated fats, transfats, cholesterol, and simple sugars; and an increased intake of fruits, vegetables, and whole grains.[5] Physical inactivity should be addressed as well, because sustained physical activity improves all the risk factors comprising metabolic syndrome. In subjects in whom atherogenic cardiovascular disease or diabetes are present, pharmacological therapy should be initiated to address each of the components of metabolic syndrome, as discussed in the section on therapy for diabetes. In the treatment of atherogenic dyslipidemia, statins should be used initially to reach the goal LDL. Only thereafter should other therapies (fenofibrates, niacin) be added to address low HDL and elevated triglyceride levels. Antithrombotics are also recommended in metabolic syndrome to counter the associated hypercoagulable state.[5,51]

REFERENCES

1. Stumvoll M, Goldstein BJ, van Haeften TW. Type 2 diabetes: Principles of pathogenesis and therapy. *Lancet.* 2005;365:1333–1346.
2. Inzucchi SE. Clinical practice: Diagnosis of diabetes. *N Engl J Med.* 2012;367:542–550.
3. Daneman D. Type 1 diabetes. *Lancet.* 2006;367:847–858.
4. Alberti KG, Eckel RH, Grundy SM, et al. Harmonizing the metabolic syndrome: a joint interim statement of the International Diabetes Federation Task Force on Epidemiology and Prevention; National Heart, Lung, and Blood Institute; American Heart Association; World Heart Federation; International Atherosclerosis Society; and International Association for the Study of Obesity. *Circulation.* 2009;120:1640–1645.
5. Eckel RH, Grundy SM, Zimmet PZ. The metabolic syndrome. *Lancet.* 2005;365:1415–1428.
6. Bray GA, Bellanger T. Epidemiology, trends, and morbidities of obesity and the metabolic syndrome. *Endocrine.* 2006;29:109–117.
7. World Health Organization. Diabetes. Media centre fact sheet no. 312. 2013.
8. Danaei G, Finucane MM, Lu Y, et al. National, regional, and global trends in fasting plasma glucose and diabetes prevalence since 1980: systematic analysis of health examination surveys and epidemiological studies with 370 country-years and 2.7 million participants. *Lancet.* 2011;378:31–40.
9. Economic costs of diabetes in the U.S. in 2007. *Diabetes Care.* 2008;31:596–615
10. World Health Organization. Global status report on noncommunicable diseases. 2010:9–32.
11. Ostman J, Lonnberg G, Arnqvist HJ, et al. Gender differences and temporal variation in the incidence of type 1 diabetes: results of 8012 cases in the nationwide Diabetes Incidence Study in Sweden 1983–2002. *J Intern Med.* 2008;263:386–394.
12. Green A, Christian Hirsch N, Pramming SK. The changing world demography of type 2 diabetes. *Diabetes Metab Res Rev.* 2003;19:3–7.
13. Chatterji P, Joo H, Lahiri K. Racial/ethnic- and education-related disparities in the control of risk factors for cardiovascular disease among individuals with diabetes. *Diabetes Care.* 2012;35:305–312.

14. Fox CS, Pencina MJ, Meigs JB, Vasan RS, Levitzky YS, D'Agostino RB Sr. Trends in the incidence of type 2 diabetes mellitus from the 1970s to the 1990s: the Framingham Heart Study. *Circulation.* 2006;113:2914–2918.
15. Zhang Y, Galloway JM, Welty TK, et al. Incidence and risk factors for stroke in American Indians: the Strong Heart Study. *Circulation.* 2008;118:1577–1584.
16. Ford ES, Giles WH, Dietz WH. Prevalence of the metabolic syndrome among US adults: findings from the Third National Health and Nutrition Examination Survey. *JAMA.* 2002;287:356–359.
17. McCullough AJ. Epidemiology of the metabolic syndrome in the USA. *J Dig Dis.* 2011;12:333–340.
18. Tanner RM, Brown TM, Muntner P. Epidemiology of obesity, the metabolic syndrome, and chronic kidney disease. *Curr Hypertens Rep.* 2012;14:152–159.
19. Ogden CL, Carroll MD, Kit BK, Flegal KM. Prevalence of obesity and trends in body mass index among US children and adolescents, 1999–2010. *JAMA.* 2012;307:483–490.
20. Flegal KM, Carroll MD, Kit BK, Ogden CL. Prevalence of obesity and trends in the distribution of body mass index among US adults, 1999–2010. *JAMA.* 2012;307:491–497.
21. Kelly T, Yang W, Chen CS, Reynolds K, He J. Global burden of obesity in 2005 and projections to 2030. *Int J Obes (Lond).* 2008;32:1431–1437.
22. Parsons MW, Barber PA, Desmond PM, et al. Acute hyperglycemia adversely affects stroke outcome: a magnetic resonance imaging and spectroscopy study. *Ann Neurol.* 2002;52:20–28.
23. Luitse MJ, Biessels GJ, Rutten GE, Kappelle LJ. Diabetes, hyperglycaemia, and acute ischaemic stroke. *Lancet Neurol.* 2012;11:261–271.
24. Huxley RR, Filion KB, Konety S, Alonso A. Meta-analysis of cohort and case–control studies of type 2 diabetes mellitus and risk of atrial fibrillation. *Am J Cardiol.* 2011;108:56–62.
25. Savopoulos C, Michalakis K, Apostolopoulou M, Miras A, Hatzitolios A. Adipokines and stroke: a review of the literature. *Maturitas.* 2011;70:322–327.
26. Soderberg S, Ahren B, Stegmayr B, et al. Leptin is a risk marker for first-ever hemorrhagic stroke in a population-based cohort. *Stroke.* 1999;30:328–337.
27. Wannamethee SG, Tchernova J, Whincup P, et al. Plasma leptin: associations with metabolic, inflammatory and haemostatic risk factors for cardiovascular disease. *Atherosclerosis.* 2007;191:418–426.
28. Chen MP, Tsai JC, Chung FM, et al. Hypoadiponectinemia is associated with ischemic cerebrovascular disease. *Arterioscler Thromb Vasc Biol.* 2005;25:821–826.
29. Jaleel A, Aqil S, Jaleel S, Jaleel F. Adipocytokines in subjects with and without ischemic cerebrovascular disease. *Acta Neurol Belg.* 2010;110:234–238.
30. Ogorodnikova AD, Wassertheil-Smoller S, Mancuso P, et al. High-molecular-weight adiponectin and incident ischemic stroke in postmenopausal women: a women's health initiative study. *Stroke.* 2010;41:1376–1381.
31. Iglseder B, Mackevics V, Stadlmayer A, Tasch G, Ladurner G, Paulweber B. Plasma adiponectin levels and sonographic phenotypes of subclinical carotid artery atherosclerosis: data from the SAPHIR study. *Stroke.* 2005;36:2577–2582.
32. Elmquist JK, Scherer PE. The cover: neuroendocrine and endocrine pathways of obesity. *JAMA.* 2012;308:1070–1071.
33. Rajpathak SN, Kaplan RC, Wassertheil-Smoller S, et al. Resistin, but not adiponectin and leptin, is associated with the risk of ischemic stroke among postmenopausal women: results from the Women's Health Initiative. *Stroke.* 2011;42:1813–1820.
34. Krecki R, Krzeminska-Pakula M, Peruga JZ, et al. Elevated resistin opposed to adiponectin or angiogenin plasma levels as a strong, independent predictive factor for the occurrence of major adverse cardiac and cerebrovascular events in patients with stable multivessel coronary artery disease over 1-year follow-up. *Med Sci Monit.* 2011;17:CR26–CR32.

35. Kernan WN, Inzucchi SE, Sawan C, Macko RF, Furie KL. Obesity: a stubbornly obvious target for stroke prevention. *Stroke.* 2013;44:278–286.
36. Conus F, Rabasa-Lhoret R, Peronnet F. Characteristics of metabolically obese normal-weight (MONW) subjects. *Appl Physiol Nutr Metab.* 2007;32:4–12.
37. Romero-Corral A, Somers VK, Sierra-Johnson J, et al. Normal weight obesity: a risk factor for cardiometabolic dysregulation and cardiovascular mortality. *Eur Heart J.* 2010;31:737–746.
38. Fogelholm M. Physical activity, fitness and fatness: relations to mortality, morbidity and disease risk factors: a systematic review. *Obes Rev.* 2010;11:202–221.
39. Zamboni M, Mazzali G, Zoico E, et al. Health consequences of obesity in the elderly: a review of four unresolved questions. *Int J Obes (Lond).* 2005;29:1011–1029.
40. Kissela B, Air E. Diabetes: impact on stroke risk and poststroke recovery. *Semin Neurol.* 2006;26:100–107.
41. Sarwar N, Gao P, Seshasai SR, et al. Diabetes mellitus, fasting blood glucose concentration, and risk of vascular disease: a collaborative meta-analysis of 102 prospective studies. *Lancet.* 2010;375:2215–2222.
42. Kissela BM, Khoury J, Kleindorfer D, et al. Epidemiology of ischemic stroke in patients with diabetes: the Greater Cincinnati/Northern Kentucky Stroke Study. *Diabetes Care.* 2005;28:355–359.
43. Sacco RL, Boden-Albala B, Abel G, et al. Race–ethnic disparities in the impact of stroke risk factors: The Northern Manhattan Stroke Study. *Stroke.* 2001;32:1725–1731.
44. Banerjee C, Moon YP, Paik MC, et al. Duration of diabetes and risk of ischemic stroke: the Northern Manhattan Study. *Stroke.* 2012;43:1212–1217.
45. Boden-Albala B, Cammack S, Chong J, et al. Diabetes, fasting glucose levels, and risk of ischemic stroke and vascular events: findings from the Northern Manhattan Study (NOMAS). *Diabetes Care.* 2008;31:1132–1137.
46. Hitman GA, Colhoun H, Newman C, et al. Stroke prediction and stroke prevention with atorvastatin in the Collaborative Atorvastatin Diabetes Study (CARDS). *Diabet Med.* 2007;24:1313–1321.
47. Janghorbani M, Hu FB, Willett WC, et al. Prospective study of type 1 and type 2 diabetes and risk of stroke subtypes: the Nurses' Health Study. *Diabetes Care.* 2007;30:1730–1735.
48. Putaala J, Liebkind R, Gordin D, et al. Diabetes mellitus and ischemic stroke in the young: clinical features and long-term prognosis. *Neurology.* 2011;76:1831–1837.
49. Ohira T, Shahar E, Chambless LE, Rosamond WD, Mosley TH Jr, Folsom AR. Risk factors for ischemic stroke subtypes: the Atherosclerosis Risk in Communities study. *Stroke.* 2006;37:2493–2498.
50. Bezerra DC, Sharrett AR, Matsushita K, et al. Risk factors for lacune subtypes in the Atherosclerosis Risk in Communities (ARIC) study. *Neurology.* 2012;78:102–108.
51. Towfighi A, Ovbiagele B. Metabolic syndrome and stroke. *Curr Diab Rep.* 2008;8:37–41.
52. Boden-Albala B, Sacco RL, Lee HS, et al. Metabolic syndrome and ischemic stroke risk: Northern Manhattan Study. *Stroke.* 2008;39:30–35.
53. Ninomiya JK, L'Italien G, Criqui MH, Whyte JL, Gamst A, Chen RS. Association of the metabolic syndrome with history of myocardial infarction and stroke in the Third National Health and Nutrition Examination Survey. *Circulation.* 2004;109:42–46.
54. Chen HJ, Bai CH, Yeh WT, Chiu HC, Pan WH. Influence of metabolic syndrome and general obesity on the risk of ischemic stroke. *Stroke.* 2006;37:1060–1064.
55. Chen K, Lindsey JB, Khera A, et al. Independent associations between metabolic syndrome, diabetes mellitus and atherosclerosis: observations from the Dallas Heart Study. *Diab Vasc Dis Res.* 2008;5:96–101.
56. Najarian RM, Sullivan LM, Kannel WB, Wilson PW, D'Agostino RB, Wolf PA. Metabolic syndrome compared with type 2 diabetes mellitus as a risk factor for stroke: the Framingham Offspring Study. *Arch Intern Med.* 2006;166:106–111.

57. Wang J, Ruotsalainen S, Moilanen L, Lepisto P, Laakso M, Kuusisto J. The metabolic syndrome predicts incident stroke: a 14-year follow-up study in elderly people in Finland. *Stroke.* 2008;39:1078–1083.
58. Bang OY, Kim JW, Lee JH, et al. Association of the metabolic syndrome with intracranial atherosclerotic stroke. *Neurology.* 2005;65:296–298.
59. Yates KF, Sweat V, Yau PL, Turchiano MM, Convit A. Impact of metabolic syndrome on cognition and brain: a selected review of the literature. *Arterioscler Thromb Vasc Biol.* 2012;32:2060–2067.
60. Kurth T, Gaziano JM, Berger K, et al. Body mass index and the risk of stroke in men. *Arch Intern Med.* 2002;162:2557–2562.
61. O'Donnell MJ, Xavier D, Liu L, et al. Risk factors for ischaemic and intracerebral haemorrhagic stroke in 22 countries (the Interstroke Study): a case–control study. *Lancet.* 2010;376:112–123.
62. Zhang X, Shu XO, Gao YT, Yang G, Li H, Zheng W. General and abdominal adiposity and risk of stroke in Chinese women. *Stroke.* 2009;40:1098–1104.
63. Strazzullo P, D'Elia L, Cairella G, Garbagnati F, Cappuccio FP, Scalfi L. Excess body weight and incidence of stroke: meta-analysis of prospective studies with 2 million participants. *Stroke.* 2010;41:e418–e426.
64. Kamalesh M, Shen J, Eckert GJ. Long term postischemic stroke mortality in diabetes: a veteran cohort analysis. *Stroke.* 2008;39:2727–2731.
65. Reeves MJ, Vaidya RS, Fonarow GC, et al. Quality of care and outcomes in patients with diabetes hospitalized with ischemic stroke: findings from Get with the Guidelines—Stroke. *Stroke.* 2010;41:e409–e417.
66. Biessels GJ, Deary IJ, Ryan CM. Cognition and diabetes: a lifespan perspective. *Lancet Neurol.* 2008;7:184–190.
67. Hillen T, Coshall C, Tilling K, Rudd AG, McGovern R, Wolfe CD. Cause of stroke recurrence is multifactorial: patterns, risk factors, and outcomes of stroke recurrence in the South London Stroke Register. *Stroke.* 2003;34:1457–1463.
68. Mottillo S, Filion KB, Genest J, et al. The metabolic syndrome and cardiovascular risk: a systematic review and meta-analysis. *J Am Coll Cardiol.* 2010;56:1113–1132.
69. Yaffe K, Kanaya A, Lindquist K, et al. The metabolic syndrome, inflammation, and risk of cognitive decline. *JAMA.* 2004;292:2237–2242.
70. Panza F, Frisardi V, Capurso C, et al. Metabolic syndrome and cognitive impairment: current epidemiology and possible underlying mechanisms. *J Alzheimers Dis.* 2010;21:691–724.
71. Whitlock G, Lewington S, Sherliker P, et al. Body-mass index and cause-specific mortality in 900,000 adults: collaborative analyses of 57 prospective studies. *Lancet.* 2009;373:1083–1096.
72. Sone H, Tanaka S, Iimuro S, et al. Long-term lifestyle intervention lowers the incidence of stroke in Japanese patients with type 2 diabetes: a nationwide multicentre randomised controlled trial (the Japan Diabetes Complications Study). *Diabetologia.* 2010;53:419–428.
73. Wing RR, Lang W, Wadden TA, et al. Benefits of modest weight loss in improving cardiovascular risk factors in overweight and obese individuals with type 2 diabetes. *Diabetes Care.* 2011;34:1481–1486.
74. Look Ahead Research Group, Wing RR, Bolin P, et al. Cardiovascular effects of intensive lifestyle intervention in type 2 diabetes. *N Engl J Med.* 2013;369:145–154.
75. Gerstein HC. Do lifestyle changes reduce serious outcomes in diabetes? *N Engl J Med.* 2013;369:189–190.
76. Holman RR, Paul SK, Bethel MA, Matthews DR, Neil HA. 10-Year follow-up of intensive glucose control in type 2 diabetes. *N Engl J Med.* 2008;359:1577–1589.
77. Gerstein HC, Miller ME, Byington RP, et al. Effects of intensive glucose lowering in type 2 diabetes. *N Engl J Med.* 2008;358:2545–2559.
78. Boussageon R, Bejan-Angoulvant T, Saadatian-Elahi M, et al. Effect of intensive glucose lowering treatment on all cause mortality, cardiovascular death, and microvascular events in type 2 diabetes: meta-analysis of randomised controlled trials. *BMJ.* 2011;343:d4169.

79. Nathan DM, Cleary PA, Backlund JY, et al. Intensive diabetes treatment and cardiovascular disease in patients with type 1 diabetes. *N Engl J Med.* 2005;353:2643–2653.
80. Tight blood pressure control and risk of macrovascular and microvascular complications in type 2 diabetes: UKPDS 38: UK Prospective Diabetes Study Group. *BMJ.* 1998;317:703–713.
81. Cushman WC, Evans GW, Byington RP, et al. Effects of intensive blood-pressure control in type 2 diabetes mellitus. *N Engl J Med.* 2010;362:1575–1585.
82. Bangalore S, Kumar S, Lobach I, Messerli FH. Blood pressure targets in subjects with type 2 diabetes mellitus/impaired fasting glucose: observations from traditional and Bayesian random-effects meta-analyses of randomized trials. *Circulation.* 2011;123:2799–2810.
83. Lindholm LH, Ibsen H, Dahlof B, et al. Cardiovascular morbidity and mortality in patients with diabetes in the Losartan Intervention for Endpoint Reduction in Hypertension Study (LIFE): a randomised trial against atenolol. *Lancet.* 2002;359:1004–1010.
84. Patel A, MacMahon S, Chalmers J, et al. Effects of a fixed combination of perindopril and indapamide on macrovascular and microvascular outcomes in patients with type 2 diabetes mellitus (the Advance trial): a randomised controlled trial. *Lancet.* 2007;370:829–840.
85. Holman RR, Paul SK, Bethel MA, Neil HA, Matthews DR. Long-term follow-up after tight control of blood pressure in type 2 diabetes. *N Engl J Med.* 2008;359:1565–1576.
86. Collins R, Armitage J, Parish S, Sleigh P, Peto R. MRC/BHF heart protection study of cholesterol-lowering with simvastatin in 5963 people with diabetes: a randomised placebo-controlled trial. *Lancet.* 2003;361:2005–2016.
87. Colhoun HM, Betteridge DJ, Durrington PN, et al. Primary prevention of cardiovascular disease with atorvastatin in type 2 diabetes in the Collaborative Atorvastatin Diabetes Study (CARDS): multicentre randomised placebo-controlled trial. *Lancet.* 2004;364:685–696.
88. Keech A, Simes RJ, Barter P, et al. Effects of long-term fenofibrate therapy on cardiovascular events in 9795 people with type 2 diabetes mellitus (the Field study): Randomised controlled trial. *Lancet.* 2005;366:1849–1861.
89. Ginsberg HN, Elam MB, Lovato LC, et al. Effects of combination lipid therapy in type 2 diabetes mellitus. *N Engl J Med.* 2010;362:1563–1574.
90. Ogawa H, Nakayama M, Morimoto T, et al. Low-dose aspirin for primary prevention of atherosclerotic events in patients with type 2 diabetes: a randomized controlled trial. *JAMA.* 2008;300:2134–2141.
91. De Berardis G, Sacco M, Strippoli GF, et al. Aspirin for primary prevention of cardiovascular events in people with diabetes: meta-analysis of randomised controlled trials. *BMJ.* 2009;339:b4531.
92. Antithrombotic Trialists' Collaboration. Collaborative meta-analysis of randomised trials of antiplatelet therapy for prevention of death, myocardial infarction, and stroke in high risk patients. *BMJ.* 2002;324:71–86.
93. Lip GY, Nieuwlaat R, Pisters R, Lane DA, Crijns HJ. Refining clinical risk stratification for predicting stroke and thromboembolism in atrial fibrillation using a novel risk factor-based approach: the Euro Heart Survey on atrial fibrillation. *Chest.* 2010;137:263–272.
94. American Diabetes Association. Standards of medical care in diabetes: 2009. *Diabetes Care.* 2009;32(Suppl 1):S13–S61.
95. Executive summary of the third report of the National Cholesterol Education Program (NCEP) Expert Panel on Detection, Evaluation, and Treatment of High Blood Cholesterol in Adults (Adult Treatment Panel III). *JAMA.* 2001;285:2486–2497.
96. Florez H, Castillo-Florez S. Beyond the obesity paradox in diabetes: fitness, fatness, and mortality. *JAMA.* 2012;308:619–620.
97. Tuomilehto J, Lindstrom J, Eriksson JG, et al. Prevention of type 2 diabetes mellitus by changes in lifestyle among subjects with impaired glucose tolerance. *N Engl J Med.* 2001;344:1343–1350.

98. Knowler WC, Barrett-Connor E, Fowler SE, et al. Reduction in the incidence of type 2 diabetes with lifestyle intervention or metformin. *N Engl J Med.* 2002;346:393–403.
99. Appel LJ, Clark JM, Yeh HC, et al. Comparative effectiveness of weight-loss interventions in clinical practice. *N Engl J Med.* 2011;365:1959–1968.
100. Wadden TA, Volger S, Sarwer DB, et al. A two-year randomized trial of obesity treatment in primary care practice. *N Engl J Med.* 2011;365:1969–1979.
101. Haskell WL, Lee IM, Pate RR, et al. Physical activity and public health: updated recommendation for adults from the American College of Sports Medicine and the American Heart Association. *Circulation.* 2007;116:1081–1093.

15

LIFESTYLE FACTORS AND THE RISK OF STROKE

Claudia L. Satizabal

Introduction

There are several risk factors for stroke that involve our everyday health choices and the environment that surrounds us, and the objective of this chapter is to review several of these lifestyle risk factors for stroke. We briefly highlight data on the effect that factors such as smoking, alcohol consumption, dietary habits, physical activity, obstructive sleep apnea, exposure to air pollution and use of illicit substances may have in increasing or reducing the risk of stroke. Because these relationships are heterogeneous, we attempt to describe how they differ by gender, age groups and stroke subtypes, as well as the potential biological mechanisms explaining these associations.

Smoking

The various adverse health effects of cigarette smoking are well recognized, and one of these is an increased risk of stroke. Consistent results across populations of diverse origins have shown smoking to be an independent risk factor for all types of strokes.

The Framingham Heart Study was one of the first epidemiological studies to explore this link.[1] In their study, Wolf et al. showed not only that smoking was associated independently with the risk of stroke over 26 years of follow-up (with a hazard ratio [HR] = 1.6 in women and HR = 1.4 in men), but also that the risk increased in a dose-dependent manner. Heavy smokers consuming more than 40 cigarettes per day had a twofold increased risk of stroke compared with light smokers consuming less than 10 cigarettes per day. Furthermore, the study estimated that, 5 years after smoking cessation, former smokers experienced the same risk of stroke as nonsmokers.

Multiple studies have since noted similar findings in other populations. In the MONICA Risk, Genetics, Archiving and Monograph Project, which included 18 populations in eight European countries,[2] it was estimated that smoking doubled the risk of stroke (HR = 2.0 in women and HR = 1.8 in men) during a follow-up of about 13 years. The Strong Heart Study[3] found that current (HR = 2.4) and previous smoking (HR = 1.6) were each related to an increased risk of stroke compared with never-smokers in 4549 participants belonging to 13 Native American tribes. There have also been several large studies conducted in Asian populations. In the Japan Public Health Center—which studied 19,782 men and 21,500 women age 40 to 59 years who were free of prior diagnosis of stroke, coronary heart disease, or cancer and were monitored for up to 11 years—smokers had a 30% greater risk of all strokes compared with nonsmokers, smoking increased the risk for most stroke subtypes (except intracerebral hemorrhage), and a dose-dependent relationship was again noted.[4] Similarly, the risk of stroke increased in a dose-dependent relationship in a representative sample of 169,871 Chinese women and men smoking 1 to 19 cigarettes per day (HR = 1.21) versus more than 20 cigarettes per day (HR = 1.40)[5] when each group was compared with nonsmokers. Last, the Asia Pacific Cohort Studies Collaboration, which included 40 studies from the Asian-Pacific region,[6] estimated the risk of stroke to be 40% greater among current smokers compared with never-smokers, also displaying a dose-dependent relationship association between the number of cigarettes smoked and an increased risk of stroke.

In high-income countries, the recent decrease in stroke mortality noted is, in part, attributed to a lower prevalence of smoking.[7] Worldwide, the number of new smokers is increasing faster in low- and middle-income countries than in high-income countries, and among women compared with men,[8,9] although smokers are still more likely to be men than women. Smoking rates are projected to peak among women from low- to middle-income countries during the next few years,[10,11] and therefore it is important to assess whether the harmful effects of cigarette smoking might differ between genders as they do for some other cardiovascular risk factors. The excess risk of stroke attributable to cigarette smoking, however, does not seem to differ between women and men. These findings have been summarized in a meta-analysis that pooled results from 81 cohort studies.[12] No differences were found between women and men when comparing the risk of stroke, regardless of stroke subtype, among current smokers versus nonsmokers or never-smokers. Further exploration of the dose-dependent association and the beneficial effects of smoking cessation on the risk of stroke did not differ, either, among the sexes. The only estimate that differed was that of women who currently smoke compared with female nonsmokers, showing a 17% increased risk of total hemorrhagic stroke compared with men, in whom the risk of hemorrhagic stroke was not significantly greater in current smokers compared with nonsmokers.

Concerning stroke subtypes, results from several studies have established the role of cigarette smoking as a risk factor for ischemic stroke and subarachnoid hemorrhage; nevertheless, the findings have been less consistent for intracerebral hemorrhage.[13–15] In the Japan Public Health Center study discussed earlier,[4] multivariate relative risks (RR; 95% confidence intervals [CIs]) for current smokers compared with never-smokers after adjustment for cardiovascular risk factors were 1.27 (95% CI, 1.05–1.54) for total stroke, 1.66 (95% CI, 1.25–2.20) for ischemic stroke, 0.72 (95% CI, 0.49–1.07) for intracerebral hemorrhage, and 3.60 (95% CI, 1.62–8.01) for subarachnoid hemorrhage. The respective multivariate RRs among women were 1.98 (95% CI, 1.42–2.77), 1.57 (95% CI, 0.86–2.87), 1.53 (95% CI, 0.86–4.25), and 2.70 (95% CI, 1.45–5.02).

There are several established biological mechanisms that link smoking and stroke. Exposure to cigarette smoking has been shown to promote arterial wall damage and progression of atherosclerotic disease,[16] increase fibrinogen levels,[17] elevate blood pressure and induce vasoconstriction,[18] all of which can increase the risk of an ischemic stroke. Cigarette smoking has also been shown to be a risk factor for the formation, growth, and rupture of intracranial aneurysms,[19–21] which constitute a primary cause of subarachnoid hemorrhage. Increased blood pressure[18] and vascular wall damage[16] caused by smoking could also contribute to intracerebral hemorrhage.

It should be acknowledged that not only are smokers at an increased risk of stroke, but also those exposed to second-hand smoke experience similar harmful effects. In a pooled analysis including 20 studies from across the United States, Asia, and the United Kingdom, a 25% increased risk of stroke was observed among nonsmokers exposed to second-hand smoke compared with nonexposed individuals. Furthermore, the study showed a dose-dependent relationship, in which individuals exposed to 5, 10, 15, and 40 cigarettes per day had an increased risk of stroke of 16%, 31%, 45%, and 56%, respectively, compared with those not exposed to second-hand smoke.[22]

The reduction in the risk of stroke seen after 5 years of smoking cessation is encouraging, and governments are urged to reinforce public policies to reduce the prevalence of smoking among societies through education, taxation, regulation, and other means; to reinforce preventive strategies targeted at children and young adults (most smokers start smoking in their teens or 20s); and to encourage smokers to stop smoking, including providing them with the incentives and the medical, societal, and psychological support to quit.

Alcohol Consumption

The effects of alcohol consumption on the risk of stroke are less straightforward than those seen for smokers. Heavy drinking has been recognized as a major risk factor for the risk for both ischemic and hemorrhagic stroke; however, the effects of light drinking seem to differ depending on the stroke subtype.

The definition of the amount of alcohol intake varies from one study to the other and according to geographic regions. Broadly, light drinking has been set to a consumption of less than one to two drinks per day (or the equivalent of about 12–24 g/day) whereas heavy drinking is considered to be the intake of more than five drinks per day (or, equivalently, about 60 g/day).[23]

There seems to be a linear, dose-dependent relationship between the amount of alcohol intake and the risk of hemorrhagic stroke.[24] The Honolulu Heart Program was one of the first cohorts to report this association in men, in whom the risk of hemorrhagic stroke doubled in light and moderate drinkers, and tripled in heavy drinkers compared with nondrinkers.[25] A recent meta-analysis suggests, however, that the shape of this relationship might be J shaped for women, in whom light drinking could confer a protective effect for nonfatal hemorrhagic stroke.[26] The aggravating effects of alcohol drinking for hemorrhagic stroke have been attributed to alcohol-induced hypertension,[27] and alterations in homeostatic function leading to impaired fibrinolytic potential[28] that may promote the rupture of aneurysms or small vessels.

As for the risk of ischemic stroke, its association with alcohol intake appears to behave in a J-shaped relationship for both women and men. Compared with nondrinkers, light drinkers have a reduced risk of ischemic stroke whereas heavy drinkers show an increased risk.[24] Interestingly, a potential effect modification by the apolipoprotein E, or *APOE*, gene on the association of alcohol with risk of ischemic stroke has been suggested by the Cardiovascular Health Study,[29] in which the protective effect of light drinking was attenuated in elderly *APOE* ε4 carriers. However, this finding has not been replicated in other populations.[30] The beneficial effects on the cardiovascular system conferred by the light to moderate consumption of alcohol might be mediated by the increase in high-density lipoprotein cholesterol and apolipoprotein A1 levels, as well as a reduction in platelet aggregation and fibrinogen levels.[31] These biological effects might thus confer some protection against ischemic stroke. However, in light of the many detrimental health effects attributable to heavy alcohol use and alcohol abuse, the overall recommendation from the stroke community is for nondrinkers to continue avoidance of alcohol, and for low to moderate consumption by those who already consume alcohol.

Diet

The relation between nutrition and stroke is complex because diet can affect, in different ways, other stroke risk factors such as hypertension, hypercholesterolemia, or diabetes.

A healthy diet may confer protective effects against vascular events. For instance, adherence to a Mediterranean diet has been associated with reduced mortality from cardiovascular diseases.[32] This diet is based on the frequent consumption of plant-based foods (i.e., seasonal fruits and vegetables, breads, cereals, potatoes, beans, nuts, and seeds) and olive oil as the main source of dietary fat; and low to moderate consumption of dairy products (i.e., cheese and yogurt), fish, poultry eggs, and wine; keeping red meat, saturated fats, processed foods, and sweets to a minimum.[33] In the Nurses' Health Study, following a Mediterranean diet was related to a 13% stroke risk reduction among white women, with the greatest adherence after 20 years of follow-up.[34] Another population-based study conducted in a multiethnic population of Hispanic, black, and white persons living in northern Manhattan found that a Mediterranean diet was associated with a 20% risk reduction in the combined end point of ischemic stroke, myocardial infarction, and vascular death after 9 years of follow-up.[35] Other studies have analyzed individual components of diet in relation to stroke. Frequent consumption of fruits, vegetables, grains, and fish has been associated with a reduced risk of stroke. Pooled results from cohort studies conducted in the United States, Japan, and Europe have shown a reduction of 11% in the risk of stroke among individuals consuming three to five portions of fruit and vegetables per day, and a reduction of 26% in the risk of stroke among those consunming more than five portions of fruit and vegetables per day.[36] Results from another meta-analysis suggested a marginally significant reduction of 17% in the risk of stroke in individuals consuming whole grains more frequently.[37] As for fish intake, a meta-analysis including studies from Europe, the United States, Japan, and China found that the consumption of three servings of fish per week was associated with a reduction of 6% in the risk of total stroke and 10% for ischemic as well as hemorrhagic stroke.[38]

The beneficial effects in reducing the risk of stroke are probably mediated by all of the essential vitamins, minerals, fiber, and fats that a varied, healthy diet provides. Results from epidemiological studies often support this concept, although clinical trials do not always confirm these findings. Dietary intake of vitamin C has been related to a reduction in the risk of stroke in prospective cohorts,[39, 40] although these results have not been replicated in clinical trials.[41,42] Greater levels of carotenoids have been associated with a decrease in the risk of stroke in men.[43–45] Results from a meta-analysis of prospective cohorts have shown that a greater intake of flavonols is associated with a reduced risk of stroke.[46] Results for vitamin E are conflicting; clinical trials indicate that vitamin E increases the risk of hemorrhagic stroke by 22% and reduces that of ischemic stroke by 10%.[47] As for vitamin D, results from observational studies have shown that reduced levels are related to an increased risk of stroke.[48,49] Last, greater intake of omega-3 polyunsaturated fatty acids, eicosapentaenoic acid, and docosahexaenoic acid found in fish and certain seeds has been shown to reduce the risk of stroke in women.[50]

In contrast to the Mediterranean diet, the so-called "western diet" has been associated with increased risk of stroke. This dietary pattern seen in industrialized countries is based on the consumption of red and processed meats, refined grains, fried foods, soft drinks, and sweets. After 14 years of follow-up, white women adhering to a western dietary pattern had an increased risk of total (58%) and ischemic (56%) stroke.[51] Another study evaluating racial and regional differences in stroke across the United States found that greater adherence to a southern dietary pattern (close to the western diet, conceptually) was associated with a 30% increased risk of stroke.[52]

Greater consumption of salt is another marker of increased stroke risk, given its widespread and direct relation to hypertension.[53] Indeed, it has been estimated that greater intake of sodium is associated with a 24% increase in risk of stroke and 63% increase in stroke death.[54] In contrast to sodium, greater potassium intake, found in certain fresh fruits and vegetables, has been shown to decrease blood pressure. A meta-analysis including 10 prospective studies found that for every 1000-mg/day increase in potassium, there was a decrease of 11% in the risk of total and ischemic stroke.[55]

Last, some studies have investigated the intake of common beverages in relation to the risk of stroke. Moderate consumption of coffee (three to four cups per day) has been associated with a reduction of 17% in the risk of stroke,[56] whereas the consumption three or more cups per day of either black or green tea reduced the risk of stroke by 21%.[57] Sugar-sweetened beverages, in contrast, have been related to an increased risk of stroke, and diet sodas appear to have a similar adverse impact. One or more servings of sugar-sweetened or even low-calorie soda per day has been associated with an increased risk of stroke, especially in women.[58]

Physical Activity

Regular physical activity has numerous benefits in reducing all-cause mortality and cardiovascular disease, and improves individual well-being and brain health.[59] Several epidemiological studies have shown the protective effect conferred by physical activity in reducing the risk of stroke.[60] Compared with the more sedentary group, moderately or highly physically active individuals had a 20% to 30% reduction in the risk of stroke.[61] Specifically, the risk of ischemic stroke was reduced by 24% in women and 27% in men; and the risk of hemorrhagic stroke was reduced by 8% in women and 40% in men.[62] Benefits are also evident for occupational physical activity, for which risk reductions of 43% for ischemic, 69% hemorrhagic, and 26% total stroke have been noted in individuals who are active in the workplace compared with persons in inactive occupations.[63] In the Nurses' Health Study, greater physical activity in women was associated with a lower risk of ischemic stroke, with a dose–response effect such that, across quintiles of increasing physical activity, the RRs were 1.00, 0.87, 0.83, 0.76, and 0.52 (p for trend = .003), respectively.[64]

Physical activity is also an important component of the "low-risk lifestyle." In a prospective cohort study involving the participants of the Nurses' and Health Professionals Studies, the combination of modest exercise (≥30 minutes/day), not smoking, maintaining a normal weight (body mass index, <25 kg/m^2), light to modest alcohol consumption, and a healthy diet was associated with a reduced risk of total and ischemic stroke in persons with all five low-risk factors, with RRs of 0.21 (95% CI, 0.12–0.36) and 0.31 (95% CI, 0.19–0.53), respectively, compared with persons who had none of these beneficial factors.[65]

Cardiovascular exercise may even be beneficial in improving outcomes after stroke onset. A pooled analysis of clinical trials found that aerobic exercise improved aerobic capacity, walking speed, and endurance in individuals after mild and moderate stroke.[66]

The mechanisms by which physical activity confers protection are multifactorial. Exercise can have a beneficial impact in reducing other vascular risk factors for stroke such as hypertension, obesity, metabolic syndrome, or diabetes.[67] However, benefits may go beyond the reduction of vascular risk factors, because studies adjusting for them still show significant protective effects. Therefore, physical activity may confer a general improvement of vascular functioning. Results from experimental studies have shown a series of beneficial functional changes such as vascular remodeling through angiogenesis and arteriogenesis, improvement in the regulation of coronary tone and vasodilatory capacity, upregulation of antioxidant defense mechanisms in several tissues (e.g., heart, liver, kidney, skeletal muscle), and downregulation of long-term inflammatory responses—associated strongly with the progression of atherosclerosis.[68] Levels of the brain-derived neurotrophic factor are increased by physical activity, and the brain-derived neurotrophic factor in turn appears to mitigate the adverse effects of ischemia on the brain.

Sleep Apnea

Sleep-related breathing disorders have been related increasingly to cardiovascular diseases.[69] Specifically, results from several studies suggest not only that obstructive sleep apnea (OSA) is frequent in stroke and transient ischemic attack patients,[70] but also that OSA is a risk factor for stroke.

Because OSA is frequently present with comorbidities such as obesity, diabetes, or hypertension,[69] it is important to consider adjustment for vascular risk factors when interpreting results. Epidemiological studies relating OSA and stroke come from retrospective analyses in consecutive patients and population-based studies. In the Wisconsin Sleep Cohort Study, it was found that an apnea–hypopnea index of 20 or more was associated independently with a threefold increase in prevalent stroke.[71] Yaggi et al.[72] investigated the association between OSA and first stroke or all-cause mortality in patients referred to the Yale Center for Sleep Medicine. They showed that, compared with patients without the syndrome, the composite end point almost doubled in patients with OSA after 3.4 years of follow-up, independent of other vascular risk factors.[72] Last, a large, prospective study including 5422 participants of the Sleep Heart Health Study found that men with moderately severe OSA were at an increased risk of ischemic stroke by almost threefold after 8 years of follow-up. This association was not seen in women after adjusting for multiple risk factors.[73]

The mechanisms by which the repetitive reduction or cessation of airflow during sleep may cause stroke are diverse. As mentioned earlier, OSA is associated with other risk factors for stroke, which together may exacerbate the risk of cerebrovascular disease.[69] Additional mechanisms include increased variability in heart rate and blood pressure as a result of a sympathetic hyperactivity[74]; intermittent hypoxemia and changes in cerebral blood flow velocity leading to hypoperfusion and a reduced vasomotor reactivity, which predispose to nocturnal cerebral ischemia[75]; and the activation of proinflammatory responses mediated by oxidative stress that, consequently, may promote endothelial dysfunction and atherogenesis.[76]

Air Pollution

Exposure to outdoor air pollution has been associated with an increased risk of stroke and cardiovascular diseases, especially in individuals at greater risk of developing these conditions and in the elderly.[77] Harmful air pollutants include gases and particulate matter (PM). Airborne PM has been studied most intensively because PM levels of less than 10 μm in aerodynamic diameter (PM_{10}) can penetrate the airways and thus have the most adverse health effects.[78,79]

Several epidemiological studies have found both short- as well as long-term associations with ischemic stroke, although associations with hemorrhagic stroke are less consistent.[80,81] A case–crossover study conducted in Canada found that poor air quality—measured as increased concentrations of ozone, fine PM of less than 2.5 μm in aerodynamic diameter ($PM_{2.5}$), and nitrogen dioxide—was associated with more emergency visits for ischemic stroke during the warm-weather months.[82] Another study investigating the short-term effects of air pollution in Boston found a 34% increase in risk of ischemic stroke after 24-hour periods with a moderately high $PM_{2.5}$ compared with periods with good $PM_{2.5}$ levels.[83] Long-term air pollution exposure and risk of stroke was investigated in the Women's Health Initiative. In this prospective cohort, a 10-μg/m³ increase in $PM_{2.5}$ levels was associated with a 35% and 83% increased risk of nonfatal and fatal stroke, respectively, after 6 years of follow-up in women.[84] Another study conducted in Japan showed that exposure to traffic-related air pollution up to 3 years earlier, measured by a 10-μg/m³ elevation in nitrogen dioxide concentrations, was associated with an increased risk of death from intracerebral hemorrhage (31%) and ischemic stroke (33%).[81]

The pathophysiological pathways by which exposure to air pollutants increases the risk of stroke may involve pulmonary and systemic inflammatory responses, which promote oxidative stress, endothelial dysfunction, and immune activation, including greater levels of acute-phase reactants and coagulation factors.[85] Results from experimental studies have shown, for example, that ultrafine PM can enter cells and damage organelles such as the mitochondria, generating reactive oxygen species[86,87] and promoting vascular calcification by the activation of inflammatory pathways.[88] Additional exposure to diesel exhaust has been related to increased thrombus formation and platelet activation in healthy men.[89] Another potential mechanism involves the stimulation of the sympathetic nervous system, which induces higher blood pressure, arrhythmias, and vasoconstriction.[90] All these changes might predispose to plaque rupture and thrombosis, increasing the risk of ischemic stroke.[85]

Consumption of Illicit Substances

Because of its illegality, the implementation of epidemiological studies addressing the association between drug use and stroke independent of other risk factors has been challenging. Nevertheless, the use of illicit substances has been suggested as a cause of both ischemic and hemorrhagic stroke, particularly among young adults, from whom most of the evidence comes in descriptive case reports.[91]

Cocaine use has been associated with stroke. It has been reported that hemorrhagic and ischemic stroke are equally frequent in individuals consuming cocaine in its alkaloid form (also known as *crack*), whereas the hemorrhagic subtype was more frequent in those using cocaine in its hydrochloride or inhaled form.[92] In a case–control study using data from the Kaiser Permanente program, it was shown that women consuming cocaine had almost 14 times greater odds of having a stroke.[93] The mechanisms underlying the occurrence of ischemic stroke include elevation of blood pressure, arrhythmia, and cerebral vasospasm in the short term, and endothelial dysfunction and accelerated atherosclerosis may occur in the long term.[94] As for hemorrhagic stroke, possible mechanisms include aneurysm rupture as a consequence of increased blood pressure, vasoconstriction, vasculitis, and poor cerebrovascular regulation.[92,95,96]

Studies assessing the use of cannabis in relation to stroke are inconclusive, because it is often difficult to dissect the impact of this exposure from that of other drugs and risk factors. For instance, results from a study of consecutive patients from New Zealand found that the odds of having an ischemic stroke/transient ischemic attack were almost doubled among cannabis users; however, this association was no longer significant after adjusting for cigarette smoking.[97] However, a recent study using hospital admission data in Texas reported a 76% increase in odds of ischemic stroke among cannabis users after controlling for potential confounders.[98] Putative mechanisms explaining this finding include multifocal intracranial vasoconstriction[99] and impaired regulation of cerebral blood flow.[100]

The consumption of other illicit substances such as amphetamines, ecstasy, heroin, and doping substances used in sports has also been related to an increase risk of stroke,[94] and these associations are discussed in more detail in Chapter 16.

Conclusions

This chapter briefly summarizes the current evidence linking several lifestyle factors with the risk of stroke. Cigarette smoking increases the risk of ischemic stroke and subarachnoid hemorrhage in a dose-dependent manner and has a less consistent adverse impact on the risk of intracerebral hemorrhage. Concerning alcohol use, the risk of stroke depends on the dose and differs by stroke subtype. Alcohol intake is associated linearly with an increased risk of hemorrhagic stroke, whereas the relationship with ischemic stroke is J-shaped. As for diet, the intake of healthy foods such as those in a Mediterranean diet has been associated with a reduced risk of stroke. In contrast, the consumption of a western-type diet is associated with an increased risk of stroke. Moderate to vigorous physical activity is an important factor that confers protective effects against both ischemic and hemorrhagic stroke. Obstructive sleep apnea and exposure to air pollution have been related increasingly to a greater risk of stroke. Lastly, the consumption of illicit drugs such as cocaine, cannabis, and other psychoactive substances are related to an increased risk of both hemorrhagic and ischemic stroke.

Lifestyle risk factors often cluster in individuals who tend to choose patterns of healthy or unhealthy lifestyles, and thus we see synergistic interactions among the multiple risk factors discussed in this chapter. Although effective behavioral changes might be challenging, modifications in the factors described above represent potential preventive strategies in the fight to lower the burden of stroke across populations.

REFERENCES

1. Wolf PA, D'Agostino RB, Kannel WB, Bonita R, Belanger AJ. Cigarette smoking as a risk factor for stroke: the Framingham study. *JAMA*. 1988;259:1025–1029.
2. Asplund K, Karvanen J, Giampaoli S, et al. Relative risks for stroke by age, sex, and population based on follow-up of 18 European populations in the Morgam Project. *Stroke*. 2009;40:2319–2326.
3. Zhang Y, Galloway JM, Welty TK, et al. Incidence and risk factors for stroke in American Indians: the Strong Heart Study. *Circulation*. 2008;118:1577–1584.
4. Mannami T, Iso H, Baba S, et al. Cigarette smoking and risk of stroke and its subtypes among middle-aged Japanese men and women: the JPHC Study Cohort I. *Stroke*. 2004;35:1248–1253.
5. Kelly TN, Gu D, Chen J, et al. Cigarette smoking and risk of stroke in the Chinese adult population. *Stroke*. 2008;39:1688–1693.
6. Woodward M, Lam TH, Barzi F, et al. Smoking, quitting, and the risk of cardiovascular disease among women and men in the Asia–Pacific region. *Int J Epidemiol*. 2005;34:1036–1045.
7. Lackland DT, Roccella EJ, Deutsch AF, et al. Factors influencing the decline in stroke mortality: a statement from the American Heart Association/American Stroke Association. *Stroke*. 2014;45:315–353.
8. Thun MJ, Carter BD, Feskanich D, et al. 50-Year trends in smoking-related mortality in the United States. *N Engl J Med*. 2013;368:351–364.
9. Peto R. Smoking and death: the past 40 years and the next 40. *BMJ*. 1994;309:937–939.
10. Samet JM, Yoon S-Y. Gender, women and the tobacco epidemic. World Health Organization. 2010. Available at: http://whqlibdoc.who.int/publications/2010/9789241599511_eng.pdf (accessed January 5, 2014).
11. Amos A, Greaves L, Nichter M, Bloch M. Women and tobacco: a call for including gender in tobacco control research, policy and practice. *Tob Control*. 2012;21:236–243.
12. Peters SA, Huxley RR, Woodward M. Smoking as a risk factor for stroke in women compared with men: a systematic review and meta-analysis of 81 cohorts, including 3,980,359 individuals and 42,401 strokes. *Stroke*. 2013;44:2821–2828.
13. Kurth T, Kase CS, Berger K, et al. Smoking and risk of hemorrhagic stroke in women. *Stroke*. 2003;34:2792–2795.
14. Kurth T, Kase CS, Berger K, et al. Smoking and the risk of hemorrhagic stroke in men. *Stroke*. 2003;34:1151–1155.
15. Sturgeon JD, Folsom AR, Longstreth WT Jr, et al. Risk factors for intracerebral hemorrhage in a pooled prospective study. *Stroke*. 2007;38:2718–2725.

16. Howard G, Wagenknecht LE, Burke GL, et al. Cigarette smoking and progression of atherosclerosis: the Atherosclerosis Risk in Communities (ARIC) study. *JAMA.* 1998;279:119–124.
17. Kannel WB, D'Agostino RB, Belanger AJ. Fibrinogen, cigarette smoking, and risk of cardiovascular disease: insights from the Framingham study. *Am Heart J.* 1987;113:1006–1010.
18. Trap-Jensen J. Effects of smoking on the heart and peripheral circulation. *Am Heart J.* 1988;115:263–267.
19. Juvela S, Hillbom M, Numminen H, Koskinen P. Cigarette smoking and alcohol consumption as risk factors for aneurysmal subarachnoid hemorrhage. *Stroke.* 1993;24:639–646.
20. Juvela S. Natural history of unruptured intracranial aneurysms: risks for aneurysm formation, growth, and rupture. *Acta Neurochir Suppl.* 2002;82:27–30.
21. Ellamushi HE, Grieve JP, Jager HR, Kitchen ND. Risk factors for the formation of multiple intracranial aneurysms. *J Neurosurg.* 2001;94:728–732.
22. Oono IP, Mackay DF, Pell JP. Meta-analysis of the association between secondhand smoke exposure and stroke. *J Public Health (Oxf).* 2011;33:496–502.
23. Turner C. How much alcohol is in a "standard drink?" An analysis of 125 studies. *Br J Addict.* 1990;85:1171–1175.
24. Reynolds K, Lewis B, Nolen JD, et al. Alcohol consumption and risk of stroke: a meta-analysis. *JAMA.* 2003;289:579–588.
25. Donahue RP, Abbott RD, Reed DM, Yano K. Alcohol and hemorrhagic stroke: the Honolulu Heart Program. *JAMA.* 1986;255:2311–2314.
26. Patra J, Taylor B, Irving H, et al. Alcohol consumption and the risk of morbidity and mortality for different stroke types: a systematic review and meta-analysis. *BMC Public Health.* 2014 Oct 14;9(10):e109634. doi:10.1371/journal.pone.0109634. eCollection 2014.
27. Puddey IB, Beilin LJ. Alcohol is bad for blood pressure. *Clin Exp Pharmacol Physiol.* 2006;33:847–852.
28. Mukamal KJ, Jadhav PP, D'Agostino RB, et al. Alcohol consumption and hemostatic factors: analysis of the Framingham offspring cohort. *Circulation.* 2001;104:1367–1373.
29. Mukamal KJ, Chung H, Jenny NS, et al. Alcohol use and risk of ischemic stroke among older adults: the Cardiovascular Health Study. *Stroke.* 2005;36:1830–1834.
30. Djousse L, Himali JJ, Beiser A, Kelly-Hayes M, Wolf PA. Apolipoprotein E, alcohol consumption, and risk of ischemic stroke: the Framingham Heart Study revisited. *J Stroke Cerebrovasc Dis.* 2009;18:384–388.
31. Rimm EB, Williams P, Fosher K, Criqui M, Stampfer MJ. Moderate alcohol intake and lower risk of coronary heart disease: meta-analysis of effects on lipids and haemostatic factors. *BMJ.* 1999;319:1523–1528.
32. Sofi F, Cesari F, Abbate R, Gensini GF, Casini A. Adherence to Mediterranean diet and health status: meta-analysis. *BMJ.* 2008;337:a1344.
33. Willett WC, Sacks F, Trichopoulou A, et al. Mediterranean diet pyramid: a cultural model for healthy eating. *Am J Clin Nutr.* 1995;61:1402S–1406S.
34. Fung TT, Rexrode KM, Mantzoros CS, et al. Mediterranean diet and incidence of and mortality from coronary heart disease and stroke in women. *Circulation.* 2009;119:1093–1100.
35. Gardener H, Wright CB, Gu Y, et al. Mediterranean–style diet and risk of ischemic stroke, myocardial infarction, and vascular death: the Northern Manhattan Study. *Am J Clin Nutr.* 2011;94:1458–1464.
36. He FJ, Nowson CA, MacGregor GA. Fruit and vegetable consumption and stroke: meta-analysis of cohort studies. *Lancet.* 2006;367:320–326.
37. Mellen PB, Walsh TF, Herrington DM. Whole grain intake and cardiovascular disease: a meta-analysis. *Nutr Metab Cardiovasc Dis.* 2008;18:283–290.

38. Larsson SC, Orsini N. Fish consumption and the risk of stroke: a dose–response meta-analysis. *Stroke*. 2011;42:3621–3623.
39. Voko Z, Hollander M, Hofman A, Koudstaal PJ, Breteler MM. Dietary antioxidants and the risk of ischemic stroke: the Rotterdam study. *Neurology*. 2003;61:1273–1275.
40. Kubota Y, Iso H, Date C, et al. Dietary intakes of antioxidant vitamins and mortality from cardiovascular disease: the Japan Collaborative Cohort (JACC) study. *Stroke*. 2011;42:1665–1672.
41. Cook NR, Albert CM, Gaziano JM, et al. A randomized factorial trial of vitamins C and E and beta carotene in the secondary prevention of cardiovascular events in women: results from the Women's Antioxidant Cardiovascular Study. *Arch Intern Med*. 2007;167:1610–1618.
42. Sesso HD, Buring JE, Christen WG, et al. Vitamins E and C in the prevention of cardiovascular disease in men: the Physicians' Health Study II randomized controlled trial. *JAMA*. 2008;300:2123–2133.
43. Rissanen TH, Voutilainen S, Nyyssonen K, et al. Low serum lycopene concentration is associated with an excess incidence of acute coronary events and stroke: the Kuopio Ischaemic Heart Disease Risk Factor Study. *Br J Nutr*. 2001;85:749–754.
44. Karppi J, Laukkanen JA, Sivenius J, Ronkainen K, Kurl S. Serum lycopene decreases the risk of stroke in men: a population-based follow-up study. *Neurology*. 2012;79:1540–1547.
45. Hak AE, Ma J, Powell CB, et al. Prospective study of plasma carotenoids and tocopherols in relation to risk of ischemic stroke. *Stroke*. 2004;35:1584–1588.
46. Hollman PC, Geelen A, Kromhout D. Dietary flavonol intake may lower stroke risk in men and women. *J Nutr*. 2010;140:600–604.
47. Schurks M, Glynn RJ, Rist PM, Tzourio C, Kurth T. Effects of vitamin E on stroke subtypes: meta-analysis of randomised controlled trials. *BMJ*. 2010;341:c5702.
48. Kojima G, Bell C, Abbott RD, et al. Low dietary vitamin D predicts 34-year incident stroke: the Honolulu Heart Program. *Stroke*. 2012;43:2163–2167.
49. Pilz S, Dobnig H, Fischer JE, et al. Low vitamin D levels predict stroke in patients referred to coronary angiography. *Stroke*. 2008;39:2611–2613.
50. Larsson SC, Orsini N, Wolk A. Long-chain omega-3 polyunsaturated fatty acids and risk of stroke: a meta-analysis. *Eur J Epidemiol*. 2012;27:895–901.
51. Fung TT, Stampfer MJ, Manson JE, et al. Prospective study of major dietary patterns and stroke risk in women. *Stroke*. 2004;35:2014–2019.
52. Judd SE, Gutierrez OM, Newby PK, et al. Dietary patterns are associated with incident stroke and contribute to excess risk of stroke in black Americans. *Stroke*. 2013;44:3305–3311.
53. Frohlich ED. The salt conundrum: a hypothesis. *Hypertension*. 2007;50:161–166.
54. Aburto NJ, Ziolkovska A, Hooper L, et al. Effect of lower sodium intake on health: systematic review and meta-analyses. *BMJ*. 2013;346:f1326.
55. Larsson SC, Orsini N, Wolk A. Dietary potassium intake and risk of stroke: a dose–response meta-analysis of prospective studies. *Stroke*. 2011;42:2746–2750.
56. Larsson SC, Orsini N. Coffee consumption and risk of stroke: a dose–response meta-analysis of prospective studies. *Am J Epidemiol*. 2011;174:993–1001.
57. Arab L, Liu W, Elashoff D. Green and black tea consumption and risk of stroke: a meta-analysis. *Stroke*. 2009;40:1786–1792.
58. Bernstein AM, de Koning L, Flint AJ, Rexrode KM, Willett WC. Soda consumption and the risk of stroke in men and women. *Am J Clin Nutr*. 2012;95:1190–1199.
59. McKee AC, Daneshvar DH, Alvarez VE, Stein TD. The neuropathology of sport. *Acta Neuropathol*. 2014;127:29–51.
60. Kiely DK, Wolf PA, Cupples LA, Beiser AS, Kannel WB. Physical activity and stroke risk: the Framingham study. *Am J Epidemiol*. 1994;140:608–620.

61. Lee CD, Folsom AR, Blair SN. Physical activity and stroke risk: a meta-analysis. *Stroke.* 2003;34:2475–2481.
62. Reimers CD, Knapp G, Reimers AK. Exercise as stroke prophylaxis. *Dtsch Arztebl Int.* 2009;106:715–721.
63. Wendel-Vos GC, Schuit AJ, Feskens EJ, et al. Physical activity and stroke: a meta-analysis of observational data. *Int J Epidemiol.* 2004;33:787–798.
64. Hu FB, Stampfer MJ, Colditz GA, et al. Physical activity and risk of stroke in women. *JAMA.* 2000;283:2961–2967.
65. Chiuve SE, Rexrode KM, Spiegelman D, et al. Primary prevention of stroke by healthy lifestyle. *Circulation.* 2008;118:947–954.
66. Pang MY, Eng JJ, Dawson AS, Gylfadottir S. The use of aerobic exercise training in improving aerobic capacity in individuals with stroke: a meta-analysis. *Clin Rehabil.* 2006;20:97–111.
67. Yung LM, Laher I, Yao X, et al. Exercise, vascular wall and cardiovascular diseases: an update (part 2). *Sports Med.* 2009;39:45–63.
68. Leung FP, Yung LM, Laher I, et al. Exercise, vascular wall and cardiovascular diseases: an update (part 1). *Sports Med.* 2008;38:1009–1024.
69. Somers VK, White DP, Amin R, et al. Sleep apnea and cardiovascular disease: an American Heart Association/American College of Cardiology Foundation scientific statement from the American Heart Association Council for High Blood Pressure Research Professional Education Committee, Council on Clinical Cardiology, Stroke Council, and Council on Cardiovascular Nursing: in collaboration with the National Heart, Lung, and Blood Institute National Center on Sleep Disorders Research (National Institutes of Health). *Circulation.* 2008;118:1080–1111.
70. Johnson KG, Johnson DC. Frequency of sleep apnea in stroke and TIA patients: a meta-analysis. *J Clin Sleep Med.* 2010;6:131–137.
71. Arzt M, Young T, Finn L, Skatrud JB, Bradley TD. Association of sleep-disordered breathing and the occurrence of stroke. *Am J Respir Crit Care Med.* 2005;172:1447–1451.
72. Yaggi HK, Concato J, Kernan WN, et al. Obstructive sleep apnea as a risk factor for stroke and death. *N Engl J Med.* 2005;353:2034–2041.
73. Redline S, Yenokyan G, Gottlieb DJ, et al. Obstructive sleep apnea–hypopnea and incident stroke: the Sleep Heart Health Study. *Am J Respir Crit Care Med.* 2010;182:269–277.
74. Friedman O, Logan AG. The price of obstructive sleep apnea–hypopnea: hypertension and other ill effects. *Am J Hypertens.* 2009;22:474–483.
75. Franklin KA. Cerebral haemodynamics in obstructive sleep apnoea and Cheyne-Stokes respiration. *Sleep Med Rev.* 2002;6:429–441.
76. Yamauchi M, Kimura H. Oxidative stress in obstructive sleep apnea: putative pathways to the cardiovascular complications. *Antioxid Redox Signal.* 2008;10:755–768.
77. Brook RD, Rajagopalan S, Pope CA 3rd, et al. Particulate matter air pollution and cardiovascular disease: an update to the scientific statement from the American Heart Association. *Circulation.* 2010;121:2331–2378.
78. Oberdorster G. Pulmonary effects of inhaled ultrafine particles. *Int Arch Occup Environ Health.* 2001;74:1–8.
79. Martinelli N, Olivieri O, Girelli D. Air particulate matter and cardiovascular disease: a narrative review. *Eur J Intern Med.* 2013;24:295–302.
80. Wellenius GA, Schwartz J, Mittleman MA. Air pollution and hospital admissions for ischemic and hemorrhagic stroke among Medicare beneficiaries. *Stroke.* 2005;36:2549–2553.
81. Yorifuji T, Kashima S, Tsuda T, et al. Long-term exposure to traffic-related air pollution and the risk of death from hemorrhagic stroke and lung cancer in Shizuoka, Japan. *Sci Total Environ.* 2013;443:397–402.

82. Chen L, Villeneuve PJ, Rowe BH, Liu L, Stieb DM. The air quality health index as a predictor of emergency department visits for ischemic stroke in Edmonton, Canada. *J Expo Sci Environ Epidemiol.* 2014;24:358–364.
83. Wellenius GA, Burger MR, Coull BA, et al. Ambient air pollution and the risk of acute ischemic stroke. *Arch Intern Med.* 2012;172:229–234.
84. Miller KA, Siscovick DS, Sheppard L, et al. Long-term exposure to air pollution and incidence of cardiovascular events in women. *N Engl J Med.* 2007;356:447–458.
85. Brook RD, Franklin B, Cascio W, et al. Air pollution and cardiovascular disease: a statement for healthcare professionals from the Expert Panel on Population and Prevention Science of the American Heart Association. *Circulation.* 2004;109:2655–2671.
86. Marchini T, Magnani N, D'Annunzio V, et al. Impaired cardiac mitochondrial function and contractile reserve following an acute exposure to environmental particulate matter. *Biochim Biophys Acta.* 2013;1830:2545–2552.
87. Moller P, Jacobsen NR, Folkmann JK, et al. Role of oxidative damage in toxicity of particulates. *Free Radic Res.* 2010;44:1–46.
88. Li R, Mittelstein D, Kam W, et al. Atmospheric ultrafine particles promote vascular calcification via the NF-kappab signaling pathway. *Am J Physiol Cell Physiol.* 2013;304:C362–C369.
89. Lucking AJ, Lundback M, Mills NL, et al. Diesel exhaust inhalation increases thrombus formation in man. *Eur Heart J.* 2008;29:3043–3051.
90. Pieters N, Plusquin M, Cox B, et al. An epidemiological appraisal of the association between heart rate variability and particulate air pollution: a meta-analysis. *Heart.* 2012;98:1127–1135.
91. Sloan MA, Kittner SJ, Rigamonti D, Price TR. Occurrence of stroke associated with use/abuse of drugs. *Neurology.* 1991;41:1358–1364.
92. Levine SR, Brust JC, Futrell N, et al. A comparative study of the cerebrovascular complications of cocaine: alkaloidal versus hydrochloride: a review. *Neurology.* 1991;41:1173–1177.
93. Petitti DB, Sidney S, Quesenberry C, Bernstein A. Stroke and cocaine or amphetamine use. *Epidemiology.* 1998;9:596–600.
94. Fonseca AC, Ferro JM. Drug abuse and stroke. *Curr Neurol Neurosci Rep.* 2013;13:325.
95. Oyesiku NM, Colohan AR, Barrow DL, Reisner A. Cocaine-induced aneurysmal rupture: an emergent negative factor in the natural history of intracranial aneurysms? *Neurosurgery.* 1993;32:518–525; discussion, 525–516.
96. Kibayashi K, Mastri AR, Hirsch CS. Cocaine induced intracerebral hemorrhage: analysis of predisposing factors and mechanisms causing hemorrhagic strokes. *Hum Pathol.* 1995;26:659–663.
97. Barber PA, Pridmore HM, Krishnamurthy V, et al. Cannabis, ischemic stroke, and transient ischemic attack: a case–control study. *Stroke.* 2013;44:2327–2329.
98. Westover AN, McBride S, Haley RW. Stroke in young adults who abuse amphetamines or cocaine: a population-based study of hospitalized patients. *Arch Gen Psychiatry.* 2007;64:495–502.
99. Wolff V, Lauer V, Rouyer O, et al. Cannabis use, ischemic stroke, and multifocal intracranial vasoconstriction: a prospective study in 48 consecutive young patients. *Stroke.* 2011;42:1778–1780.
100. Wolff V, Armspach JP, Lauer V, et al. Cannabis-related stroke: myth or reality? *Stroke.* 2013;44:558–563.

16

RISK FACTORS OF STROKE SPECIFIC TO YOUNG ADULTS

Jukka Putaala, Terttu Heikinheimo-Connell, and Turgut Tatlisumak

Introduction

Approximately 5% of all ischemic strokes occur in individuals younger than 45 years of age and 10% occur in those younger than 50 years of age. The age cutoff to define young adults in stroke medicine is arbitrary (it varies from 40–55 years in the literature), but has a rationale that is based on differences of stroke etiology and risk factors between young patients and older patients. The major etiologic subgroups of ischemic stroke in the elderly—namely, large-artery atherosclerosis, atrial fibrillation, and small-vessel occlusion—are infrequent among the young, because most major risk factors predisposing to these outcomes (such as hypertension, diabetes, and dyslipidemia) are either less common or less severe, or have not yet caused substantial damage to the cardiovascular system. Thus, stroke risk factors in the young are distinct and need to be examined carefully.

Another feature related to risk factors that distinguishes younger patients from the elderly is that, even after thorough clinical and laboratory examination, many young patients with ischemic stroke remain without a definite etiologic classification. Furthermore, a number of patients remain without a single detected, well-documented risk factor. Many of these individuals harbor, however, less well-documented risk factors for ischemic stroke, such as heavy alcohol consumption, obstructive sleep apnea, or clotting abnormalities.

Risk factors considered rather specific to young adults include genetic and acquired thrombophilia, illicit drug use, migraine with aura, cardiac interatrial abnormalities, heavy drinking, binge drinking, inflammation and infections, sickle cell disease, and, in women, oral contraceptive use, gravidity, and postpartum status. Although many of these risk factors can also predispose to stroke at older ages, the rationale to regard them as age specific include the following: (a) the factor can exist only at young age (e.g., reproductive health-related factors); (b) the factor can exist at all ages, but the association is stronger statistically at younger ages (e.g., patent foramen ovale [PFO], migraine with aura, infections); or (b) the factor is related to modifiable risk behavior in a population that is more common at younger ages (e.g., illicit drug use, heavy drinking, binge drinking habit, smoking, obesity).

This chapter reviews studies investigating the strength of the association of risk factors particularly in young stroke patients, and overviews the risk factor frequencies with a focus on age-specific differences and gender differences at younger ages. Risk factors considered specific to young adults but not covered elsewhere in this book are discussed in detail here, including cardiac interatrial abnormalities, antiphospholipid antibodies (aPLs), illicit drug use, and chronic and acute infections.

Well-Documented Risk Factors among Young Adults

STRENGTH OF ASSOCIATION OF NONMODIFIABLE RISK FACTORS

A case–control study by MacClellan et al.[1] showed a pronounced aggregation of young-onset stroke in families. Siblings of stroke patients had a fourfold risk for stroke compared with siblings of control subjects.[1] Furthermore, mothers of stroke patients harbored a twofold greater risk for stroke compared with mothers of control subjects. This aggregation was even more profound with decreasing age. For example, odds ratios (ORs) for positive family history for women age 15 to 24 years, 25 to 34 years, and 35 to 49 years were 2.5, 1.6, and 1.5, respectively. Another study including a southeast Asian population showed a statistically strong correlation between stroke family history and stroke in young adults (adjusted OR, 16.15; 95% CI confidence interval [CI] 1.71–151.82),[2] whereas some studies found no such association.[3] In one study, male sex was associated with a greater risk of stroke at a young age.[4]

Even in patients younger than 50 years, increasing age is linked virtually exponentially to increasing risk of ischemic stroke. The risk increases steeply in early midlife and the curve is markedly steeper for males (Figure 16.1).[5] Regarding racial differences among the young, blacks and Hispanics have greater stroke incidence.[6,7]

STRENGTH OF ASSOCIATION OF MODIFIABLE, WELL-DOCUMENTED RISK FACTORS

Rather few case–control studies have assessed the strength of association of traditional modifiable risk factors for ischemic stroke in young adults in nonselected patient populations. Several studies involving multiple ethnicities have confirmed the association of hypertension (OR range, 1.6–8.9)[2,4,8–12] and smoking (OR range, 1.6–7.7)[4,8–13] with stroke risk. Love et al.[13] demonstrated a cumulative dose effect with risk of ischemic stroke increasing with each additional pack-year of smoking and no heterogeneity between etiologic subtypes. Fewer studies found an association of diabetes or elevated fasting blood glucose (OR range, 3.3–22.9)[8,9,11,12] or heart disease (OR range, 2.7–3.3)[10–12] with stroke at younger ages. In a study by Rohr et al.,[8] diabetes appeared to be a stronger risk factor for young white men (OR, 22.9) than for young black men (OR, 4.2), whereas smoking and hypertension were more important risk factors among blacks of both genders. In women age 30 to 55 years, the relative risk of ischemic stroke was sixfold for type 1 diabetes and twofold for type 2 diabetes in another study.[14] However, there are scarce data on the risk difference between diabetes subtypes for stroke, particularly at young ages.

We found only one study that investigated the strength of association between physical inactivity and stroke at a young age. In that study, which involved a Thai population age 18 to 45 years, history of no or irregular exercise increased stroke risk eightfold after adjusting for confounders (OR, 8.06; 95% CI, 1.12–57.60), with the odds being a similar magnitude for hypertension in that population.[2]

An association between low high-density lipoprotein cholesterol and ischemic stroke at a young age has been demonstrated.[2,4,9] Furthermore, the presence of three or more components of metabolic syndrome was associated strongly with stroke in an Indian study comparing ischemic stroke patients

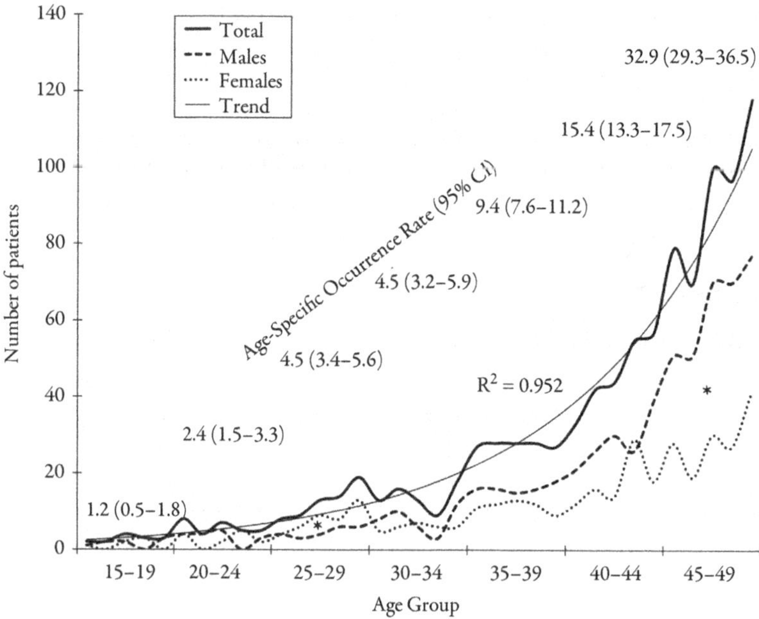

FIGURE 16.1 Incidence of ischemic stroke in patients younger than 50 years stratified according to 5-year age bands in the Helsinki Young Stroke Registry. CI, confidence interval. Number of patients according to age and age-specific occurrence rates per 100 000. R indicates correlation coefficient of the trend line illustrating the exponential increase in occurrence as a function of age. $^{*}P < 0.001$ in comparison of age-specific proportions between genders by Chi-Sq test.

with both community and hospital control subjects (OR, 4.76; 95% CI, 1.93–11.76; OR, 2.09; 95% CI, 1.06–4.13, respectively).[9] Some studies have suggested that lipoprotein(a) concentration increases the risk of ischemic stroke at young age.[15] No such association was found in a study focused on young women only.[16]

The associations of long-term[12] and recent heavy drinking[11,17,18] and ischemic stroke have been confirmed in young adults. Acute heavy drinking or so-called *binge drinking* clearly differentiates young patients from their older counterparts—a risk factor for both ischemic and hemorrhagic stroke considered specific to young adults.[19] There are, however, probably marked cultural variations in drinking habits.

Among a cohort of 6520 Danish men, obesity (body mass index, ≥30 kg/m^2) was associated with a threefold (OR, 3.0; 95% CI, 2.3–4.0) risk of having been diagnosed with any of the following: type 2 diabetes mellitus, hypertension, myocardial infarction, stroke or venous thromboembolism, or death before the age of 55.[20] However, obesity was associated strongly with all individual outcomes as well, except stroke. We found no studies assessing other markers of obesity, dietary habits, or psychosocial stress and the risk of stroke specifically at a young age.

RISK FACTOR PREVALENCE

Table 16.1 summarizes the risk factor frequencies in the three largest data sets to date on ischemic stroke in young adults.[5,21,22] A recent analysis based on pooled data from existing registries in 15 European centers showed that, among patients age 18 to 49 years, the three most frequent risk factors were current smoking (49%), dyslipidemia (46%), and hypertension (36%).[21] The recent, prospective

TABLE 16.1

Comparison of Risk Factor Prevalence in the Three Largest Nonselected Data Sets of Ischemic Cerebrovascular Events at Young Age

	Helsinki Young Stroke Registry (N = 1008)	15 Cities Young Stroke Study (N = 3944[a])	Stroke in Young Fabry Patients (n = 4467[b])
Well-documented, nonmodifiable risk factors			
Mean (SD) or median (IQR) age	41.3 (7.6)	43 (36–46)	47 (40–51)
Male gender	62.3	56.6	59.4
Family history of any stroke	12.7	16.4	17.0
Well-documented, modifiable risk factors			
Dyslipidemia	59.5	45.8	34.9
Cigarette smoking	44.2	48.7	55.5
Hypertension	39.1	35.9	46.6
Obesity (BMI ≥30 kg/m²)	10.6	NA	22.3
Atrial fibrillation	4.2	3.7	2.4
Cardiovascular disease	10.2	NA	9.2
Coronary heart disease	4.9	6.0	4.2
Heart failure	4.8	3.7	1.2
Myocardial infarction	3.7	NA	3.1
Peripheral arterial disease	1.8	2.7	2.2
Valvular disease	NA	NA	2.3
History of TIA	8.9	8.4	9.3
Diabetes mellitus	10.4	8.0	10.3
Type 1	4.4	NA	NA
Type 2	6.0	NA	NA
Hormone replacement therapy	1.7	NA	NA
Nonmodifiable risk factors			
History of migraine	17.2	NA	26.5
Heavy drinking	14.2	NA	33.0
PFO with or without ASA	10.5	NA	NA
Oral contraceptive use	6.7	NA	NA
Obstructive sleep apnea syndrome	3.8	NA	3.3
Genetic thrombophilia	7.0	NA	NA
Acquired thrombophilia	6.2	NA	NA
Active malignancy	1.6	NA	NA
Recent illicit drug use	1.3	NA	NA
Gravidity or postpartum period	1.0	NA	NA

Note. Data are percentages unless indicated otherwise.
[a]The database includes patients from the Helsinki Young Stroke Registry.
[b]Includes 3396 with ischemic stroke and 1071 with TIA.
ASA, atrial septal aneurysm; BMI, body mass index; IQR, interquartile range; NA, not available; PFO, patent foramen ovale; SD, standard deviation; TIA, transient ischemic attack.

Stroke in Young Fabry Patients study, which included 4467 patients age 18 to 55 years with ischemic stroke or transient ischemic attack, demonstrated that the most frequent, well-documented risk factors were smoking (56%), physical inactivity (48%), arterial hypertension (47%), dyslipidemia (35%), and obesity (22%).[22] Diabetes mellitus was found in 8.0% to 10% of participants in these three studies. Only the Finnish study[22] differentiated between type 1 and type 2 diabetes. Of note, the relative proportions may differ in other countries; the prevalence of type 1 diabetes in Finland is one of the highest in the world.[23]

DEMOGRAPHIC DIFFERENCES IN RISK FACTOR PREVALENCE

In the 15 Cities Young Stroke Study,[21] males were older than females and more often had dyslipidemia or coronary heart disease, or were smokers, than females. In both genders, frequency of family history of stroke, dyslipidemia, smoking, hypertension, diabetes mellitus, coronary heart disease, peripheral arterial disease, and atrial fibrillation correlated positively with age. The study found no difference in the risk factor prevalence among southern, central, and northern European patient populations after adjusting for age and gender.

The Stroke in Young Fabry Patients study demonstrated a clustering of multiple risk factors, particularly in males and with increasing age (Figure 16.2).[22] Specifically, dyslipidemia, smoking, hypertension, cardiovascular disease, diabetes mellitus, and high-risk alcohol consumption accumulated among males. With respect to dyslipidemia and cardiovascular disease, the gender disparity was particularly apparent in the age group of 35 years or older. That study showed increasing prevalence with increasing age of physical inactivity, arterial hypertension, dyslipidemia, obesity, and diabetes mellitus. In contrast, females were more often physically inactive at younger ages (<35 years). Female patients frequently were abdominally obese at the age of 25 years or older. More important, a Danish study including stroke patients across a wide age range showed that lifestyle-related risk factors—smoking, alcohol, and obesity—were indeed more common in younger patients (<60 years), with declining relative importance with increasing age.[24]

Cardiac Interatrial Abnormalities

PFO is a remnant of fetal circulatory bypass of the lungs. The foramen ovale remains patent in approximately 25% of adults, based on autopsy studies.[25] PFO is a slitlike communication between the right and left atrium, which is bounded by two thin membranes—the septum secundum on the right atrial side and the septum primum on the left atrial side—in the cranial part of the fossa ovalis. In most individuals, PFO remains closed most of the time by the positive left-to-right pressure gradient that presses the septal membranes together. In some circumstances, such as during an activity inducing a Valsalva maneuver, right atrial pressure can exceed left atrial pressure and thus cause opening of the PFO and a transient right-to-left shunt. Anatomy of atrial septal abnormalities ranges from an atrial septal defect with spontaneous right-to-left shunt, to large to small PFOs with or without atrial septal aneurysm (ASA). ASA is diagnosed when a fixed displacement or a mobile excursion of the fossa ovalis bulges toward the right or left atrium (or both), exceeding 10 mm from the midline.[26]

PFO has long been linked to ischemic stroke with different postulated mechanisms, of which the so-called *paradoxical embolism* is the most prevailing. This link arose from case descriptions in which a thrombosis from the venous circulation was demonstrated passing through the PFO, as seen during autopsy or via echocardiography.[27,28] Nevertheless, concurrent venous thrombosis in the setting of presumed paradoxical embolism is, in fact, detected only rarely and often is clinically silent.[29] The most typical case in which PFO is thought to play a role is a case in which, after an extensive workup

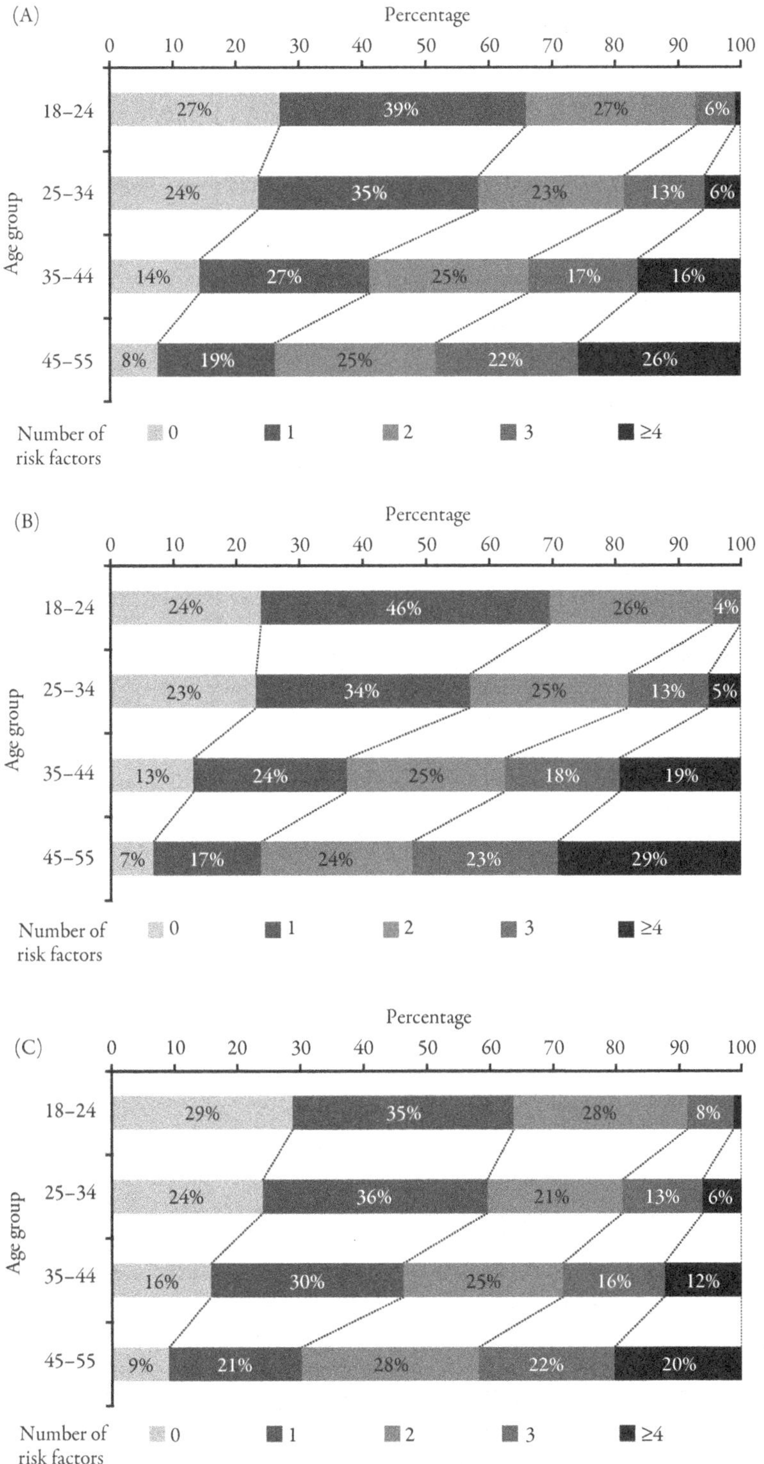

FIGURE 16.2 (A–C) Frequencies of all patients (A), male patients (B), and female patients (C) with none, one, two, three, and four or more well-documented risk factors according to gender.[22]

and the stroke etiology remains unknown, a PFO is demonstrable and, as a result of uncertainty regarding causality, a possible PFO-related stroke is considered a cryptogenic event.

Nevertheless, a meta-analysis has shown an association between PFO, ASA, and PFO with concomitant ASA and ischemic stroke in younger patients.[30] Younger age as a factor clearly increases the odds for these associations. In a recent systematic meta-analysis, Alsheikh-Ali et al.[31] estimated the probability for PFO to be incidental (i.e., not causally related to the stroke) in patients with cryptogenic stroke. They concluded that in studies including stroke patients across a wide age range, the probability that PFO is incidental is 33%, reduced to approximately 20% in younger (<55 years) patients, but is 48% in older patients (≥55 years). These estimates support the view that PFO is an age-dependent risk factor for ischemic stroke, but leave a considerable (at least two-to-five) chance that, even in younger individuals with stroke, it is just an innocent bystander.

PFO characteristics that increase stroke risk include PFO size, length of the PFO tunnel, magnitude of the shunt, and the presence of concomitant ASA.[32] The association of PFO and cryptogenic stroke has been demonstrated in older patients (age ≥55 years) as well. Compared with patients with a known stroke etiology, the OR for having a PFO was 4.7 (95% CI, 1.9–11.7) among younger patients (<55 years) and 2.9 (95% CI, 1.7–5.0) among older patients (≥55 years) with unknown stroke etiology. Similarly, the presence of PFO with ASA in ischemic stroke patients with cryptogenic stroke versus stroke of known etiology was found to be 13.4% versus 2.0% (OR, 7.36; 95% CI, 1.01–326.60; $p = .049$) among younger patients and 15.2% versus 4.4% (OR, 3.88; 95% CI, 1.78–8.46; $p < .001$) among older patients.[33]

Important predisposing factors in PFO-related stroke in which a paradoxical embolism is presumed are concomitant conditions leading to a prothrombotic state, such as inherited thrombophilia,[34,35] and all factors increasing the risk for venous thrombosis.[36] Other possible mechanisms of PFO- or ASA-related stroke include in situ thrombosis in the PFO channel or in the ASA,[28] and predisposition to left atrial dysfunction possibly leading to vulnerability to atrial fibrillation.[37]

The current evidence around PFO as a risk factor for ischemic stroke in the young is supported by meta-analyses of case–control studies, but the mechanisms regarding how this risk increment occurs and how best to prevent recurrent stroke in this setting needs to be investigated more thoroughly. The three recently completed randomized trials on transcatheter PFO closure showed that, in nonselected patients with a nonselected device, the procedure does not reduce the risk for recurrent events compared with best medical treatment.[38] Tools for scoring PFO as potentially pathogenic have been developed recently to guide secondary prevention strategies and to avoid unnecessary closure of PFO.[39]

Antiphospholipid Antibodies

As a result of autoimmune activation, aPLs react against proteins that bind to anionic phospholipids on plasma membranes. Antiphospholipid syndrome (APS) is a condition with at least one clinical event out of (a) arterial, venous, or small-vessel thrombosis in any tissue or organ or (b) pregnancy-related complications such as preeclampsia or miscarriages, associated with two positive blood tests at least 12 weeks apart showing the presence of lupus anticoagulant (LA), anticardiolipin antibodies of immunoglobulin G and/or M isotype in medium or high titer (>40 IgG antiphospholipid units/mL (GPL) or IgM antiphospholipid units/mL (MPL), or more than the 99th percentile), or anti-β_2-glycoprotein I antibodies.[40] In addition, antibodies to plasma protein prothrombin are commonly tested. APS is more prevalent in young women compared with the general population,[41] and can be classified as secondary, if occurring in the setting of systemic lupus erythematosus (SLE) or other collagen vascular disorder, and primary in the absence of SLE.

aPLs can exist in the absence of the criteria for APS. Earlier case–control studies, although with rather small sample sizes, have been able to establish fairly well the role of aPLs as a risk factor for first ischemic stroke at young age in patients mostly free from SLE.[42–47] In older individuals, the association is far more controversial, with studies showing both positive and negative associations.[48] aPLs also contribute to the risk of cerebral venous thrombosis.[49]

A recent analysis based on a comparison of 175 women younger than 50 years with a first ischemic stroke and 628 healthy control subjects demonstrated an OR for ischemic stroke of 43.1 (95% CI, 12.2–152.0) in women having LA and an OR of 2.3 (95% CI, 1.4–3.7) for women having anti-β_2-glycoprotein I antibodies (cutoff, 90th percentile of control subjects).[50] In this study, the risk of ischemic stroke was not affected by the presence of anticardiolipin or antiprothrombin antibodies, possibly as a result of the rather small number of patients with ischemic stroke harboring these antibodies ($n = 26$ and $n = 38$, respectively).[50] More important, the OR for ischemic stroke increased to 201.0 (95% CI, 22.1–1828.0) in women with LA using oral contraceptives and increased to 87.0 (95% CI, 14.5–523.0) in those who were smokers. The association of anticardiolipin and antiprothrombin antibodies with ischemic stroke remains to be elucidated in a larger study, and investigation of the relevance of aPLs in men is warranted.

It seems that aPLs may necessitate a local trigger or additional systemic risk factors to participate in the thrombotic process.[51] In addition to in situ thrombosis at any arterial site (or in the venous bed, resulting in paradoxical embolism or cerebral venous thrombosis), the mechanisms of how aPLs contribute to stroke risk include accelerated atherosclerosis[52] and cardioembolism resulting from valvular disease (a variety of lesions have been described, with the most classic form being Libman-Sacks endocarditis).[53–55] All these conditions may be aggravated by concomitant chronic comorbidities impairing the endothelium and vascular bed,[50] and the induction of aPL production triggered by transient factors such as infections.[56]

Illicit Drug Use

Illicit drug use refers to recreational use of prohibited substances. Illicit drugs include illegal drugs (e.g., cannabis and cocaine), pharmaceutical drugs when used for nonmedical reasons (e.g., sedatives and opiates), and inappropriate use of other substances (e.g., certain inhalants). Illicit drug use and dependence have important consequences and costs. The U.S. Department of Justice noted, in its 2011 report, that the cost of illicit drug use totaled more than $193 billion in 2007 in the United States alone.[57] In the United States, 9% of individuals age 12 years or older have tried an illicit drug within the past month. Approximately 20 million people worldwide have drug use disorders, with significant geographic differences. Industrialized countries and metropolitan cities are most affected, along with illicit drug-producing regions. The majority of users are young, with approximately one fourth being underage individuals.

Infections are the most common complications of injection drug use, presenting as septicemia, systemic fungal infections, hepatitis B, hepatitis C, and human immunodeficiency virus (HIV) infections as well as right-side endocarditis. HIV infection among intravenous drug users worldwide has been reported to reach up to 20%. Stroke, in turn, is a rare but serious complication and occurs mainly in the young, and mostly in males, reflecting the age and gender distribution of users. Polysubstance abuse is also found predominantly among men. Illicit drug use epidemics differ from one city or country to another. Some hospital-based series reported that illicit drug use has been implicated causally in as many as 6% of all ischemic strokes[58] and in 15% to 40% of ischemic stroke in young patients.[59] The same researchers reported later that, among 422 ischemic stroke patients age 15 to 44 years, 12.1% had used an illicit drug recently, and the illicit drug was the likely cause in 4.7% of the patients.[60] In contrast, illicit drug use was, very rarely, the underlying cause of ischemic stroke in young ischemic stroke patients from the greater Helsinki region.[5] The link between stroke and illicit drug use is strong for cocaine and amphetamines, but is less clear for other illicit drugs. Among young abusers, stroke risk was up to 6.5-fold compared with nonusers.[61]

AMPHETAMINES AND RELATED SUBSTANCES

Several amphetaminelike substances (e.g., methamphetamine, methylphenidate, phenylpropanolamine, and ephedrine) are used as central nervous system stimulants, decongestants, and appetite suppressants. A population-based study covering all hospital admissions in Texas between 2000 and 2003 showed that amphetamine abuse was associated with a fivefold increased risk of hemorrhagic stroke, but not with ischemic stroke, and that amphetamine abuse almost tripled hemorrhagic stroke mortality.[62] Amphetamine use was associated with all strokes in young women, with an OR of 3.8 in a population-based study.[63]

Experimental studies in rats and monkeys demonstrated that single or repeated intravenous injections of methamphetamine or methylphenidate led to cerebral vasculiticlike changes.[64] Hemorrhagic strokes after amphetamine use are attributable to acute hypertensive crisis, vasospasm, and drug-induced hemorrhage, sometimes with preexisting arteriovenous malformation or aneurysms. In addition, amphetamine use increases the risk of toxic vasculitis, cardiomyopathy, and heart failure, leading to ischemic stroke.[65]

Methamphetamine is known as crystal, ice, or speed, and can be taken through various routes. It is the most potent of all amphetamines and is the one most frequently abused. It has a similar stroke spectrum as amphetamine. Phenylpropanolamine use in women was associated with increased risk of hemorrhagic stroke, more strongly when used as an appetite suppressant, but also when used as a cough or cold remedy.[66]

Ecstasy (3,4-methylenedioxymethamphetamine), a hallucinogen derivate of amphetamine, was associated with both hemorrhagic and ischemic stroke.[67] Ephedra use showed a trend toward an increased risk of hemorrhagic stroke in a case–control study that led to a ban of its sale and use as a dietary supplement.[68]

COCAINE

Cocaine is the secondmost commonly used illicit drug after marijuana and leads to half of the emergency department visits related to illicit drug abuse. Cocaine can be taken orally, intranasally, or intravenously, whereas crack cocaine is smoked. Cocaine is a local anesthetic, vasoconstrictor, and central nervous system stimulant. In a large population-based study from Texas, cocaine abuse was associated with both hemorrhagic (OR $\cong$ 2.3) and ischemic (OR $\cong$ 2.0) stroke, but not with increased stroke mortality.[62] Cocaine-associated stroke may have several mechanisms, such as acute hypertensive crisis, vasospasm, platelet activation and aggregation with thrombus formation, accelerated atherosclerosis, cardioembolism via arrhythmias and endocarditis, and vasculitis.[65] Cocaine is the most common cause of stroke related to illicit drug use. Arterial constrictions could be demonstrated in cocaine users as early as 20 minutes after intravenous injection, and in a dose-dependent fashion.[69] Several hundred patients with cocaine-related hemorrhagic or ischemic stroke have been reported since 1977.[70] Ischemic and hemorrhagic stroke occurs in roughly equal proportions, and both in anterior and posterior territories.[71]

OPIATES

Heroin, derived from opium, can be snorted, smoked, or injected intravenously or subcutaneously. Hallmarks of heroin overdose are coma, respiratory depression, and pinpoint pupils. Acute toxic leukoencephalopathy has been described after inhalation of heroin ("chasing the dragon").[72] Cerebral hypoxia may stem from hypoventilation and/or hypotension. Most strokes are ischemic. Cardioembolism in the setting of infective endocarditis is a potential mechanism. Foreign-body embolization with talc and cellulose crystals occurs when oral tablets (e.g., pentazocine) are crushed, suspended in water, and injected intravenously. Vasculitides were also reported in heroin users. Stroke as a consequence of heroin use was first described in 1976 in nine young heroin addicts.[73]

CANNABIS

Cannabis is the most widely used illicit drug worldwide. The *Cannabis sativa* plant produces more than 60 different chemicals called *cannabinoids*, of which the most important is Δ-tetrahydrocannabinol, which is absorbed rapidly when smoked and leads to euphoria, self-confidence, and relaxation. It is still controversial whether cannabis use leads to stroke, although there is a temporal relationship between cannabis use and stroke in case series and population-based studies. Most reported cases are in men with ischemic stroke.[74]

REVERSIBLE CEREBRAL VASOCONSTRICTION SYNDROME IN THE SETTING OF DRUG ABUSE

Cannabis, cocaine, methylenedioxymethamphetamine, amphetamines, and lysergic acid diethylamide can lead to reversible cerebral vasoconstriction (RCVS). The general feature of RCVS is a sudden, severe headache (thunderclap), with demonstrated widespread cerebral artery vasospasm with alternating areas of arterial constriction and dilatation in multiple vascular beds—so-called *string-and-beads appearance*. Neurological symptoms and signs differ or may be absent. Hypertension is a frequent feature. Most patients are young to middle-age females. Other causes of thunderclap headache (subarachnoid hemorrhage, dissection, or cerebral venous thrombosis) must be ruled out. Beading of cerebral arteries is common and lasts several days to weeks, but disappears usually within 12 weeks. Cerebrospinal fluid examination is almost always normal or near normal and helps in distinguishing RCVS from vasculitis. The course of RCVS is usually benign, but severe neurological syndromes and even death have been reported. In addition to ischemic changes, intracerebral hemorrhage is also frequent, particularly in patients with extreme blood pressures.[75]

Chronic and Acute Infections

Chronic infections may increase the risk of acute ischemic stroke through the following mechanisms: (a) the vascular endothelium can be damaged by increased systemic inflammation; (b) recurrent bacteremia triggers platelet activation and creates a procoagulant state; (c) long-standing infections can have an influence on risk factors, such as serum lipids, toward a more proatherogenic profile; and (c) chronic infections may also be risk factors that act together with conventional risk factors and a genetic predisposition.[76]

Chronic dental infections seem to be associated with ischemic stroke in the young.[77,78] HIV has the potential to cause ischemic stroke, especially in young stroke patients.[79,80] Several studies have found that, as in coronary heart disease, chronic, active *Chlamydia pneumoniae* infection and its elevated antibodies are prevalent in young stroke patients.[81–83] Other pathogens of chronic infection have not been studied systematically in young stroke patients.

A transient increase in the risk of a vascular event is associated with acute preceding infections occurring within 4 weeks, regardless of the patient's age. In ischemic stroke, acute respiratory tract infections are the most common type of preceding infection.[84–86] In some studies, preceding infections have been linked in particular to large-vessel and cardioembolic ischemic strokes, particularly in patients with no other risk factors.[87,88] A retrospective analysis of 681 patients age 15 to 49 years with ischemic stroke diagnosed within 2 years from symptom onset showed a 10.7% frequency of preceding infections within 4 weeks before stroke.[89] The majority of these infections were upper respiratory tract infections (54%), followed by gastrointestinal (13%), chest (11%), and skin or mucous membrane (11%) infections.

There is a dearth of research on the pathogens causing the acute preceding infection; preceding respiratory infections are mostly of bacterial origin.[85] Viral infections, such as *Varicella zoster* infection, have proved to be potential risk factors for acute ischemic stroke during childhood,[90] but their role is yet to be elucidated in young-adult stroke.

The mechanisms correlating acute infections with stroke involve broadly alterations in immunohematologic mechanisms and systemic manifestations of inflammation, such as elevated anticardiolipin antibody levels, reduced concentrations of circulating antithrombotic proteins, increased concentrations of C-reactive protein, proinflammatory cytokines, or interleukins. These can, in turn, participate, for example, in the initiation of an extrinsic coagulation pathway, can modulate an anticoagulant pathway, or can increase platelet reactivity.[91] Interestingly, even minor acute infections can cause endothelial dysfunction in healthy children.[92] This finding provides evidence that the endothelium and its infection-triggered dysregulation may play a central role in the initiation of thrombotic processes. There also is a significant association between recent infection and cervical artery dissection,[93] which is the most frequent cause of ischemic stroke in young adults. In addition, vessel wall inflammation has been demonstrated by contrast-enhanced high-resolution magnetic resonance imaging and positron emission tomography–computed tomography in patients with cervical artery dissection.[94]

Conclusion

Young patients with ischemic stroke usually have serious and even multiple vascular risk factors and, contrary to customary belief, classic vascular risk factors are commonly present. Identification of these risk factors and implementation of precisely tailored preventive strategies may have a significant impact on long-term prognosis.

Acknowledgments

The authors are supported by grants from the Helsinki University Central Hospital Research Funds (TT, JP), the Diabetes Research Foundation (JP), the Diabetes Wellness Finland (JP), the Finnish Medical Foundation (JP), the Academy of Finland (TT), the Sigrid Juselius Foundation (TT), the Maire Taponen Foundation (TT), the European Union (TT), Biocenter Finland (TT), Biocentrum Helsinki (TT), and Liv och Hälsa Foundation (TT).

REFERENCES

1. MacClellan LR, Mitchell BD, Cole JW, et al. Familial aggregation of ischemic stroke in young women: the Stroke Prevention in Young Women Study. *Genet Epidemiol.* 2006;30:602–608.
2. Bandasak R, Narksawat K, Tangkanakul C, Chinvarun Y, Siri S. Association between hypertension and stroke among young Thai adults in Bangkok, Thailand. *Southeast Asian J Trop Med Public Health.* 2011;42:1241–1248.

3. Siegerink B, Rosendaal FR, Algra A. Family history differs between young women with myocardial infarction and ischemic stroke: results from the RATIO case–control study. *Atherosclerosis.* 2012;223:235–238.
4. Albucher JF, Ferrieres J, Ruidavets JB, Guiraud-Chaumeil B, Perret BP, Chollet F. Serum lipids in young patients with ischaemic stroke: a case–control study. *J Neurol Neurosurg Psychiatry.* 2000;69:29–33.
5. Putaala J, Metso AJ, Metso TM, et al. Analysis of 1008 consecutive patients aged 15 to 49 with first-ever ischemic stroke: the Helsinki Young Stroke Registry. *Stroke.* 2009;40:1195–1203.
6. Jacobs BS, Boden-Albala B, Lin IF, Sacco RL. Stroke in the young in the Northern Manhattan Stroke Study. *Stroke.* 2002;33:2789–2793.
7. Pathak EB, Sloan MA. Recent racial/ethnic disparities in stroke hospitalizations and outcomes for young adults in Florida, 2001–2006. *Neuroepidemiology.* 2009;32:302–311.
8. Rohr J, Kittner S, Feeser B, et al. Traditional risk factors and ischemic stroke in young adults: the Baltimore–Washington Cooperative Young Stroke Study. *Arch Neurol.* 1996;53:603–607.
9. Lipska K, Sylaja PN, Sarma PS, et al. Risk factors for acute ischaemic stroke in young adults in South India. *J Neurol Neurosurg Psychiatry.* 2007;78:959–963.
10. Naess H, Nyland HI, Thomassen L, Aarseth J, Myhr KM. Etiology of and risk factors for cerebral infarction in young adults in western Norway: a population-based case–control study. *Eur J Neurol.* 2004;11:25–30.
11. Haapaniemi H, Hillbom M, Juvela S. Lifestyle-associated risk factors for acute brain infarction among persons of working age. *Stroke.* 1997;28:26–30.
12. You RX, McNeil JJ, O'Malley HM, Davis SM, Thrift AG, Donnan GA. Risk factors for stroke due to cerebral infarction in young adults. *Stroke.* 1997;28:1913–1918.
13. Love BB, Biller J, Jones MP, Adams HP Jr, Bruno A. Cigarette smoking: a risk factor for cerebral infarction in young adults. *Arch Neurol.* 1990;47:693–698.
14. Janghorbani M, Hu FB, Willett WC, et al. Prospective study of type 1 and type 2 diabetes and risk of stroke subtypes: the Nurses' Health Study. *Diabetes Care.* 2007;30:1730–1735.
15. Nagayama M, Shinohara Y, Nagayama T. Lipoprotein(a) and ischemic cerebrovascular disease in young adults. *Stroke.* 1994;25:74–78.
16. Wityk RJ, Kittner SJ, Jenner JL, et al. Lipoprotein (a) and the risk of ischemic stroke in young women. *Atherosclerosis.* 2000;150:389–396.
17. Hillbom M, Kaste M. Does ethanol intoxication promote brain infarction in young adults? *Lancet.* 1978;2:1181–1183.
18. Hillbom M, Numminen H, Juvela S. Recent heavy drinking of alcohol and embolic stroke. *Stroke.* 1999;30:2307–2312.
19. Taylor JR, Combs-Orme T. Alcohol and strokes in young adults. *Am J Psychiatry.* 1985;142:116–118.
20. Schmidt M, Johannesdottir SA, Lemeshow S, et al. Obesity in young men, and individual and combined risks of type 2 diabetes, cardiovascular morbidity and death before 55 years of age: a Danish 33-year follow-up study. *BMJ Open.* 2013;3:e002698 (this is electronic).
21. Putaala J, Yesilot N, Waje-Andreassen U, et al. Demographic and geographic vascular risk factor differences in European young adults with ischemic stroke: the 15 Cities Young Stroke Study. *Stroke.* 2012;43:2624–2630.
22. von Sarnowski B, Putaala J, Grittner U, et al. Lifestyle risk factors for ischemic stroke and transient ischemic attack in young adults in the Stroke in Young Fabry Patients study. *Stroke.* 2013;44:119–125.
23. Harjutsalo V, Sjoberg L, Tuomilehto J. Time trends in the incidence of type 1 diabetes in Finnish children: a cohort study. *Lancet.* 2008;371:1777–1782.

24. Andersen KK, Andersen ZJ, Olsen TS. Age- and gender-specific prevalence of cardiovascular risk factors in 40,102 patients with first-ever ischemic stroke: a Nationwide Danish Study. *Stroke.* 2010;41:2768–2774.
25. Hagen PT, Scholz DG, Edwards WD. Incidence and size of patent foramen ovale during the first 10 decades of life: an autopsy study of 965 normal hearts. *Mayo Clin Proc.* 1984;59:17–20.
26. Pepi M, Evangelista A, Nihoyannopoulos P, et al. Recommendations for echocardiography use in the diagnosis and management of cardiac sources of embolism: European Association of Echocardiography (EAE) (a registered branch of the ESC). *Eur J Echocardiogr.* 2010;11:461–476.
27. Gleysteen JJ, Silver D. Paradoxical arterial embolism: collective review. *Am Surg.* 1970;36:47–54.
28. Thanigaraj S, Zajarias A, Valika A, Lasala J, Perez JE. Caught in the act: serial, real time images of a thrombus traversing from the right to left atrium across a patent foramen ovale. *Eur J Echocardiogr.* 2006;7:179–181.
29. Lethen H, Flachskampf FA, Schneider R, et al. Frequency of deep vein thrombosis in patients with patent foramen ovale and ischemic stroke or transient ischemic attack. *Am J Cardiol.* 1997;80:1066–1069.
30. Overell JR, Bone I, Lees KR. Interatrial septal abnormalities and stroke: a meta-analysis of case–control studies. *Neurology.* 2000;55:1172–1179.
31. Alsheikh-Ali AA, Thaler DE, Kent DM. Patent foramen ovale in cryptogenic stroke: incidental or pathogenic? *Stroke.* 2009;40:2349–2355.
32. Goel SS, Tuzcu EM, Shishehbor MH, et al. Morphology of the patent foramen ovale in asymptomatic versus symptomatic (stroke or transient ischemic attack) patients. *Am J Cardiol.* 2009;103:124–129.
33. Handke M, Harloff A, Olschewski M, Hetzel A, Geibel A. Patent foramen ovale and cryptogenic stroke in older patients. *N Engl J Med.* 2007;357:2262–2268.
34. Botto N, Spadoni I, Giusti S, Ait-Ali L, Sicari R, Andreassi MG. Prothrombotic mutations as risk factors for cryptogenic ischemic cerebrovascular events in young subjects with patent foramen ovale. *Stroke.* 2007;38:2070–2073.
35. Karttunen V, Hiltunen L, Rasi V, Vahtera E, Hillbom M. Factor V Leiden and prothrombin gene mutation may predispose to paradoxical embolism in subjects with patent foramen ovale. *Blood Coagul Fibrinolysis.* 2003;14:261–268.
36. Cramer SC, Rordorf G, Maki JH, et al. Increased pelvic vein thrombi in cryptogenic stroke: results of the Paradoxical Emboli from Large Veins in Ischemic Stroke (PELVIS) study. *Stroke.* 2004;35:46–50.
37. Rigatelli G, Aggio S, Cardaioli P, et al. Left atrial dysfunction in patients with patent foramen ovale and atrial septal aneurysm: an alternative concurrent mechanism for arterial embolism? *JACC Cardiovasc Interv.* 2009;2:655–662.
38. Ntaios G, Papavasileiou V, Makaritsis K, Michel P. PFO closure vs. medical therapy in cryptogenic stroke or transient ischemic attack: a systematic review and meta-analysis. *Int J Cardiol.* 2013;169:101–105.
39. Kent DM, Ruthazer R, Weimar C, et al. An index to identify stroke-related vs incidental patent foramen ovale in cryptogenic stroke. *Neurology.* 2013;81:619–625.
40. Miyakis S, Lockshin MD, Atsumi T, et al. International consensus statement on an update of the classification criteria for definite antiphospholipid syndrome (APS). *J Thromb Haemost.* 2006;4:295–306.
41. Cervera R, Khamashta MA, Font J, et al. Morbidity and mortality in systemic lupus erythematosus during a 10-year period: a comparison of early and late manifestations in a cohort of 1,000 patients. *Medicine (Baltimore).* 2003;82:299–308.

42. Brey RL, Hart RG, Sherman DG, Tegeler CH. Antiphospholipid antibodies and cerebral ischemia in young people. *Neurology.* 1990;40:1190–1196.
43. Brey RL, Stallworth CL, McGlasson DL, et al. Antiphospholipid antibodies and stroke in young women. *Stroke.* 2002;33:2396–2400.
44. Nencini P, Baruffi MC, Abbate R, Massai G, Amaducci L, Inzitari D. Lupus anticoagulant and anticardiolipin antibodies in young adults with cerebral ischemia. *Stroke.* 1992;23:189–193.
45. Toschi V, Motta A, Castelli C, Paracchini ML, Zerbi D, Gibelli A. High prevalence of antiphosphatidylinositol antibodies in young patients with cerebral ischemia of undetermined cause. *Stroke.* 1998;29:1759–1764.
46. Blohorn A, Guegan-Massardier E, Triquenot A, et al. Antiphospholipid antibodies in the acute phase of cerebral ischaemia in young adults: a descriptive study of 139 patients. *Cerebrovasc Dis.* 2002;13:156–162.
47. Singh K, Gaiha M, Shome DK, Gupta VK, Anuradha S. The association of antiphospholipid antibodies with ischaemic stroke and myocardial infarction in young and their correlation: a preliminary study. *J Assoc Physicians India.* 2001;49:527–529.
48. Brey RL. Antiphospholipid antibodies in young adults with stroke. *J Thromb Thrombolysis.* 2005;20:105–112.
49. Carhuapoma JR, Mitsias P, Levine SR. Cerebral venous thrombosis and anticardiolipin antibodies. *Stroke.* 1997;28:2363–2369.
50. Urbanus RT, Siegerink B, Roest M, Rosendaal FR, de Groot PG, Algra A. Antiphospholipid antibodies and risk of myocardial infarction and ischaemic stroke in young women in the RATIO study: a case–control study. *Lancet Neurol.* 2009;8:998–1005.
51. Mackworth-Young CG. Antiphospholipid syndrome: multiple mechanisms. *Clin Exp Immunol.* 2004;136:393–401.
52. Vaarala O. Antiphospholipid antibodies and myocardial infarction. *Lupus.* 1998;7(Suppl 2): S132–S134.
53. Ford SE, Lillicrap D, Brunet D, Ford P. Thrombotic endocarditis and lupus anticoagulant: a pathogenetic possibility for idiopathic “rheumatic type” valvular heart disease. *Arch Pathol Lab Med.* 1989;113:350–353.
54. Khamashta MA, Cervera R, Asherson RA, et al. Association of antibodies against phospholipids with heart valve disease in systemic lupus erythematosus. *Lancet.* 1990;335:1541–1544.
55. Lonnebakken MT, Gerdts E. Libman-Sacks endocarditis and cerebral embolization in antiphospholipid syndrome. *Eur J Echocardiogr.* 2008;9:192–193.
56. Gharavi AE, Pierangeli SS. Origin of antiphospholipid antibodies: induction of aPL by viral peptides. *Lupus.* 1998;7(Suppl 2):S52–S54.
57. U.S. Department of Justice. The economic impact of illicit drug use on American Society. Report no. 2011-Q0317-002. Available at: www.justice.gov/archive/ndic/pubs44/44731/44731p.pdf (accessed June 13, 2013).
58. Sloan MA, Kittner SJ, Rigamonti D, Price TR. Occurrence of stroke associated with use/abuse of drugs. *Neurology.* 1991;41:1358–1364.
59. Sloan M. Toxicity/substance abuse. In: Welch K, Caplan L, Reis D, et al., eds. *Primer on cerebrovascular diseases.* San Diego, CA: Academic Press, 1997:413–416.
60. Sloan MA, Kittner SJ, Feeser BR, et al. Illicit drug-associated ischemic stroke in the Baltimore–Washington Young Stroke Study. *Neurology.* 1998;50:1688–1693.
61. Kaku DA, Lowenstein DH. Emergence of recreational drug abuse as a major risk factor for stroke in young adults. *Ann Intern Med.* 1990;113:821–827.
62. Westover AN, McBride S, Haley RW. Stroke in young adults who abuse amphetamines or cocaine: a population-based study of hospitalized patients. *Arch Gen Psychiatry.* 2007;64:495–502.

63. Petitti DB, Sidney S, Quesenberry C, Bernstein A. Stroke and cocaine or amphetamine use. *Epidemiology*. 1998;9:596–600.
64. Rumbaugh CL, Fang HC, Higgins RE, Bergeron RT, Segall HD, Teal JS. Cerebral microvascular injury in experimental drug abuse. *Invest Radiol*. 1976;11:282–294.
65. Neiman J, Haapaniemi HM, Hillbom M. Neurological complications of drug abuse: pathophysiological mechanisms. *Eur J Neurol*. 2000;7:595–606.
66. Kernan WN, Viscoli CM, Brass LM, et al. Phenylpropanolamine and the risk of hemorrhagic stroke. *N Engl J Med*. 2000;343:1826–1832.
67. Schifano F, Oyefeso A, Webb L, Pollard M, Corkery J, Ghodse AH. Review of deaths related to taking Ecstasy, England and Wales, 1997–2000. *BMJ*. 2003;326:80–81.
68. Morgenstern LB, Viscoli CM, Kernan WN, et al. Use of Ephedra–containing products and risk for hemorrhagic stroke. *Neurology*. 2003;60:132–135.
69. Kaufman MJ, Levin JM, Ross MH, et al. Cocaine-induced cerebral vasoconstriction detected in humans with magnetic resonance angiography. *JAMA*. 1998;279:376–380.
70. Brust JC, Richter RW. Stroke associated with cocaine abuse? *N Y State J Med*. 1977;77:1473–1475.
71. Daras M, Tuchman AJ, Koppel BS, Samkoff LM, Weitzner I, Marc J. Neurovascular complications of cocaine. *Acta Neurol Scand*. 1994;90:124–129.
72. Kriegstein AR, Shungu DC, Millar WS, et al. Leukoencephalopathy and raised brain lactate from heroin vapor inhalation ("chasing the dragon"). *Neurology*. 1999;53:1765–1773.
73. Brust JC, Richter RW. Stroke associated with addiction to heroin. *J Neurol Neurosurg Psychiatry*. 1976;39:194–199.
74. Barber PA, Pridmore HM, Krishnamurthy V, et al. Cannabis, ischemic stroke, and transient ischemic attack: a case–control study. *Stroke*. 2013;44:2327–2329.
75. Ducros A. Reversible cerebral vasoconstriction syndrome. *Lancet Neurol*. 2012;11:906–917.
76. Lindsberg PJ, Grau AJ. Inflammation and infections as risk factors for ischemic stroke. *Stroke*. 2003;34:2518–2532.
77. Syrjanen J, Peltola J, Valtonen V, Iivanainen M, Kaste M, Huttunen JK. Dental infections in association with cerebral infarction in young and middle-aged men. *J Intern Med*. 1989;225:179–184.
78. Grau AJ, Becher H, Ziegler CM, et al. Periodontal disease as a risk factor for ischemic stroke. *Stroke*. 2004;35:496–501.
79. Benjamin LA, Bryer A, Emsley HC, Khoo S, Solomon T, Connor MD. HIV infection and stroke: current perspectives and future directions. *Lancet Neurol*. 2012;11:878–890.
80. Heikinheimo T, Chimbayo D, Kumwenda JJ, Kampondeni S, Allain TJ. Stroke outcomes in Malawi, a country with high prevalence of HIV: a prospective follow-up study. *PLoS One*. 2012;7:e33765.
81. Anzini A, Cassone A, Rasura M, et al. *Chlamydia pneumoniae* infection in young stroke patients: a case–control study. *Eur J Neurol*. 2004;11:321–327.
82. Bandaru VC, Boddu DB, Laxmi V, Neeraja M, Kaul S. Seroprevalence of *Chlamydia pneumoniae* antibodies in stroke in young. *Can J Neurol Sci*. 2009;36:725–730.
83. Piechowski-Jozwiak B, Mickielewicz A, Gaciong Z, Berent H, Kwiecinski H. Elevated levels of anti-*Chlamydia pneumoniae* IgA and IgG antibodies in young adults with ischemic stroke. *Acta Neurol Scand*. 2007;116:144–149.
84. Grau AJ, Buggle F, Heindl S, et al. Recent infection as a risk factor for cerebrovascular ischemia. *Stroke*. 1995;26:373–379.
85. Syrjanen J, Valtonen VV, Iivanainen M, Kaste M, Huttunen JK. Preceding infection as an important risk factor for ischaemic brain infarction in young and middle aged patients. *Br Med J (Clin Res Ed)*. 1988;296:1156–1160.
86. Zurru MC, Alonzo C, Brescacin L, et al. Recent respiratory infection predicts atherothrombotic stroke: case–control study in a Buenos Aires healthcare system. *Stroke*. 2009;40:1986–1990.

87. Nencini P, Sarti C, Innocenti R, Pracucci G, Inzitari D. Acute inflammatory events and ischemic stroke subtypes. *Cerebrovasc Dis.* 2003;15:215–221.
88. Paganini-Hill A, Lozano E, Fischberg G, et al. Infection and risk of ischemic stroke: differences among stroke subtypes. *Stroke.* 2003;34:452–457.
89. Heikinheimo T, Broman J, Haapaniemi E, Kaste M, Tatlisumak T, Putaala J. Preceding and poststroke infections in young adults with first-ever ischemic stroke: effect on short-term and long-term outcomes. *Stroke.* 2013;44:3331–3337.
90. Askalan R, Laughlin S, Mayank S, et al. Chickenpox and stroke in childhood: a study of frequency and causation. *Stroke.* 2001;32:1257–1262.
91. Emsley HC, Hopkins SJ. Acute ischaemic stroke and infection: recent and emerging concepts. *Lancet Neurol.* 2008;7:341–353.
92. Charakida M, Donald AE, Terese M, et al. Endothelial dysfunction in childhood infection. *Circulation.* 2005;111:1660–1665.
93. Grau AJ, Brandt T, Buggle F, et al. Association of cervical artery dissection with recent infection. *Arch Neurol.* 1999;56:851–856.
94. Pfefferkorn T, Saam T, Rominger A, et al. Vessel wall inflammation in spontaneous cervical artery dissection: a prospective, observational positron emission tomography, computed tomography, and magnetic resonance imaging study. *Stroke.* 2011;42:1563–1568.

17

SEX-SPECIFIC RISK FACTORS FOR STROKE IN WOMEN

Starla M. Wise and Cheryl D. Bushnell

Introduction

The incidence of stroke in women varies over the course of life and increases with advancing age. Factors and situations that occur exclusively in the female sex can confer both protective effects and unique risks with regard to stroke. Estrogen, pregnancy and its complications, the postpartum period, menopause, and exogenous hormones represent some of these sex-specific issues.

Traditional Stroke Risk Factors

Typical risk factors for stroke include hypertension, hyperlipidemia, tobacco abuse, atrial fibrillation, and diabetes mellitus, which may be present in both men and women. However, recent cohort studies have demonstrated a definite difference between men and women regarding specific risk factors for stroke. For example, female stroke patients are more likely to have a history of atrial fibrillation and hypertension.[1–4] Di Carlo et al.[1] found a female predominance for prestroke institutionalization as well. The fact that women typically experience strokes at an older age compared with men may explain the increased prevalence of these risk factors, which tend to develop with advancing age. Men are more likely to have a history of tobacco and alcohol use, as well as a history of myocardial infarction and diabetes mellitus.[1,3] Data from the National Health and Nutrition Examination Survey suggest that cholesterol levels in women increase with each decade of life, but remain the same in men, therefore leading to higher cholesterol levels in women by 55 to 64 years.[5] However, a Canadian study found that women are less likely than men to be treated for hyperlipidemia with statin drugs.[4]

Metabolic syndrome is a cluster of risk factors that have demonstrated increasing importance with regard to cardiovascular and cerebrovascular risk.[6] The presence and implications of various components of metabolic syndrome vary among men and women. For example, with regard to the diagnosis of metabolic syndrome, waist circumference and low high-density lipoprotein levels were major contributors for the diagnosis in women, whereas hypertension was the major contributor in men.[7] Certain combinations of risk factors have been shown to act synergistically. One such combination is hypertension and low high-density lipoprotein cholesterol, which yields a greater than expected risk of developing atherosclerosis than either condition alone, particularly in women.[8] Furthermore, women with any single metabolic syndrome factor or combination of factors averaged twice the risk of developing atherosclerosis compared with men.[8] Another study[9] assessed for early atherosclerosis by measuring intima media thickness and the extent of plaques in carotid arteries of men and women with metabolic syndrome and found that women had a greater likelihood of developing atherosclerosis compared with men.

Increased body mass index (BMI) has been associated with increased stroke risk in a near-linear fashion.[10] In a Korean study,[10] the trend was associated more strongly with young women (<50 years) and an ischemic-type stroke.[10] Even when correcting for comorbidities such as cholesterol, glucose, and hypertension, the association remained, indicating that BMI is, in fact, an independent stroke risk factor.[10]

Migraine with aura is a stroke risk factor that is more common in women than in men. A history of migraine headache with aura has been associated with a greater risk for subclinical cerebellar posterior circulation infarcts compared with the general population. In addition, women with a history of migraine with aura had more deep white matter lesions than men.[11] The risk of ischemic stroke increases with a frequency of more than 12 migraine (with aura) attacks per year.[12] The mechanisms leading to ischemic stroke are likely a combination of several factors, including vasospasm, endothelial dysfunction, hypercoagulability, oxidative stress, and cortical-spreading depression.[13] Another consideration is the strong association between migraine with aura and a patent foramen ovale, which together confer a greater risk of stroke than migraine alone.[13] The management of patent foramen ovale in the setting of stroke and migraine has been a controversial topic for several years. Routine patent foramen ovale closure for patients with migraine with aura and cryptogenic stroke is not supported by currently available data.[14,15]

Polycystic ovarian syndrome (PCOS) is a female-specific risk factor for cardiovascular disease. PCOS affects 5% to 10% of adolescent girls and young adult women, and is characterized by two of the following three criteria: hyperandrogenism, oligomenorrhea or amenorrhea, and polycystic ovaries.[16] A case–control study reported that women with PCOS evaluated for subclinical risk factors of vascular disease were more likely than control subjects to have classic stroke risk factors, including glucose intolerance, dyslipidemia, and inflammatory markers as well as decreased vasodilation during reactive hyperemia, indicating early atherosclerosis.[17]

The Effect of Estrogen on Stroke Risk

ENDOGENOUS HORMONES

Many observational studies have demonstrated that women have a lower risk of stroke and cardiovascular disease compared with men of the same age until around age 85, when the incidence of stroke increases among women.[18] An analysis from the Framingham Heart Study found that women with natural menopause before age 42 years had twice the risk for ischemic stroke compared with women who experienced natural menopause after the age of 42.[19] These findings suggest that early depletion in levels of circulating estrogens, specifically 17 β-estradiol (E2) leads to a loss of the protective effect against stroke during a woman's premenopausal years. Estrogen has been studied carefully in both animal models and clinical studies, with efforts made to uncover possible mechanisms behind estrogen's cardio- and cerebrovascular protective effects. Even with the vast amount of research in this area, our knowledge of these mechanisms remains incomplete. A better understanding will enable developments of new therapeutic interventions for the treatment, and prevention of cardiovascular and cerebrovascular disease.[20]

The cerebral circulation is unique in its composition and functionality. It is specialized with tight junctions between endothelial cells, forming the blood–brain barrier and allowing for a very controlled environment. Autoregulatory functions allow for constant blood flow even in response to changing pressures and volume. Estrogen has demonstrated various protective effects on cerebral blood vasculature, including vasodilation, suppression of inflammation, and increased mitochondrial efficiency.

Vasodilation, or decreased vascular tone, is dependent on an intact endothelium. Endothelium-derived relaxing factors, including nitric oxide, prostacyclin, and endothelium-derived hyperpolarizing factor, are produced by the endothelium to mediate vasodilation. In the cerebral circulation, nitric oxide and prostacyclin are potentiated by estrogen, leading to decreased vascular tone in these specific vascular beds, which can help to prevent vascular injury resulting from shear forces.[21] Nitric oxide is the most potent of the endothelium-derived relaxing factors. Estrogen increases nitric oxide production through stimulation of endothelial nitric oxide synthase (eNOS). This occurs both through immediate effects on the plasma membrane, which enhances eNOS production through eNOS phosphorylation, as well as long-term transcriptional effects, leading to an increase in eNOS messenger RNA and protein levels.[21,22] Cerebrovascular endothelial cells have estrogen receptors (ERs; ERα and ERβ), which mediate these effects. ERα has been shown to be the primary mediator of transcriptional effects because ERα knockout mice do not demonstrate increased eNOS activity with chronic exposure to estrogen.[23] Vasomotor reactivity is dependent on a healthy endothelium that has a balance between the endothelium-derived relaxing factors. Various cardiovascular risk factors including hypertension, diabetes, smoking, and hyperlipidemia cause endothelial dysfunction through decreased bioavailability of vasodilating factors—specifically, nitric oxide. This leads to increased production of vasoconstricting factors such as endothelin, vasoconstricting prostanoids, and angiotensin II.[24] Under these pathologic conditions, endothelium-dependent changes in vascular tone are suspected to indicate early atherosclerosis.

Estrogen levels vary throughout a woman's life and fluctuate during the menstrual cycle, leading to measurable effects on vascular physiology. For example, Diomedi et al.[25] evaluated the vascular reactivity of the right middle cerebral artery to hypercapnia with transcranial Doppler ultrasonography in men and women. There was no difference in vasomotor reactivity in women during their menstrual phase compared with men. However, cerebral vasomotor reactivity was increased significantly in women during their ovulatory phase, when estrogen levels peak.[25]

Estrogen has also demonstrated effects on mitochondrial efficiency and oxidative stress, enabling increased energy production and, at the same time, decreasing reactive oxygen species, a by-product of this process. ERα has been demonstrated in cerebrovascular mitochondria, illustrating the important actions associated with ischemic stroke.[22] Specifically, estrogen increases the level of several mitochondrial proteins, including cytochrome *c*, which results in increased energy production and manganese–superoxide dismutase, a superoxide-converting enzyme. Estrogen increases the degree of vasoprotection through this mechanism during an ischemic stroke, enabling increased energy reserves and decreased reactive oxygen species during reperfusion to maximize preservation of the blood–brain barrier while minimizing edema and influx of inflammatory cells.[22]

Cerebrovascular inflammation after cerebral ischemia or injury is believed to contribute to secondary brain injury through the promotion of leukocyte infiltration into the brain, breakdown of the blood–brain barrier, hyperemia, edema, and increased intracerebral pressures. Estrogen-treated animals have lower levels of cyclooxygenase 2, which is an important enzyme that potentiates this inflammatory cascade.[23] Geary et al.[23] demonstrated a decreased acute cerebrovascular inflammatory response to experimental stroke in animals treated with estrogen compared with ovariectomized animals, and also showed that these anti-inflammatory effects are ER mediated. Despite these beneficial effects of estrogen (mostly from animal studies), no studies have shown evidence that premenopausal women have better outcome after stroke than men.

A shorter lifetime exposure to estrogen may be associated with an increased risk of ischemic stroke.[26] One Japanese study found that girls with late-onset menarche (>17 years) had a greater risk of mortality from stroke than those who experienced the onset of menarche at younger ages.[27] Another case–control study demonstrated that a shorter estrogenic lifetime (<34 years) was an independent risk factor for stroke, yielding a 51% greater lifetime stroke risk in these individuals.[26] On the other hand, this same study found that a younger age (<13 years) at menarche was also associated with increased risk for stroke.[26] The Adventist Health Study looked specifically at stroke mortality and age at menarche and found that patients with early menarche (<11 years) experienced a greater risk of mortality with stroke.[28] The biological mechanisms surrounding these findings are poorly understood. Some theorize that these findings may be the result of excess levels of estrogen that accumulate over a lifetime and cause detrimental effects, similar to that seen with hormone replacement therapy suggesting a U-shaped association wherein in excess or insufficient estrogen exposure both increase risk of stroke.[26] Another theory suggests that estrogen exposure may be deleterious in a young, physiologically unprepared individual.[26] One population study by Kivimäki et al.[29] suggested that age at menarche is simply a marker of BMI. A greater BMI before menarche was associated with earlier age at menarche and both were associated with a greater BMI in adulthood.[29]

EXOGENOUS HORMONES: ORAL CONTRACEPTION

Exogenous hormones—specifically, oral contraceptive pills—increase the risk of stroke in young women. The hormonal dosage and an individual's preexisting comorbidities modify this risk. The dosage of estrogen seems to be associated directly with the risk of stroke, although progesterone-only birth control medications may also confer a mildly increased risk of stroke.[13] The use of low-dose oral contraception in the absence of other risk factors has not been proved to cause an increased risk of stroke and probably is not associated with an increased risk of stroke in this instance.[13] The overall risk of stroke in users of oral contraceptive pills is two times the risk of nonusers.[30] Because the overall risk of stroke is low in this age group, however, the absolute risk is only about 8 per 100,000 women.[30]

Comorbidities that are associated with a synergistically increased risk of stroke in combination with exogenous hormones include migraine with aura, tobacco abuse, thrombophilias, obesity, and hypertension.[13]

In general, oral contraception is contraindicated in the setting of migraine with aura but should be safe in women who have migraine without aura. Women with migraine with aura who use oral contraception have an eightfold greater risk of stroke than with either risk factor alone, and a 16-fold greater risk of stroke compared to women with neither risk factor.[31] When a woman with migraine also uses tobacco products and oral contraception, a synergistic increase in stroke risk is observed. This combination of factors is associated with an odds ratio (OR) of 34.4 compared with individuals possessing none of these risk factors.[31] Use of low-estrogen-containing or progestin-only oral contraceptive formulations should be considered for women with a history of migraine with aura.[32,33]

Oral contraception alters mechanisms of coagulation, and therefore patients with an underlying thrombophilia are at an increased risk for thrombotic events. This is well documented for venous thrombosis; however, few studies have evaluated the association between stroke and the use of oral contraception in the setting of an underlying prothrombotic condition. The Risk of Arterial Thrombosis in Relation to Oral Contraceptives study evaluated 193 women age 20 to 49 years with ischemic stroke and compared them with 767 control patients. The study found that patients with factor V Leiden mutation and the MTHFR mutation (677T variant) were 1.8 times more likely to have had a stroke compared with those who lacked these mutations. Carriers of the MTHFR mutation 677T variant who used oral contraceptive pills demonstrated a fivefold increased risk of stroke compared with women with neither risk factor. Carriers of the factor V Leiden mutation who took oral contraception demonstrated an 11-fold increased risk compared with women with neither risk factor.[34]

EXOGENOUS HORMONES: OVARIAN HYPERSTIMULATION SYNDROME

Ovarian hyperstimulation syndrome (OHSS) is a life-threatening complication of in vitro fertilization. Severe OHSS results in massive ovarian enlargement, ascites, pleural effusion, oliguria, electrolyte imbalance, hemoconcentration, and thromboembolism.[35] The exact pathophysiology behind OHSS is unknown. The current understanding is that inflammatory mediators including prostaglandins, histamine, the renin–angiotensin system, and vascular endothelial growth factor result in increased vascular permeability. Proteinaceous fluid from the vasculature leaks into extravascular spaces, resulting in pleural, pericardial, and peritoneal effusions.[36] Thromboembolism resulting in either venous or arterial thrombosis is the most serious complication and is hypothesized to result from a combination of factors. Hemoconcentration may result from reduced circulating blood volumes, immobility may result from ascites, and decreased venous return may result from enlarged ovaries.[35] Most thromboses (75%) are of venous origin[35]; the remaining 25% are arterial thromboses and may affect cerebral, mesenteric, or peripheral arteries, resulting in severe morbidity.[35]

EXOGENOUS HORMONES: HORMONE REPLACEMENT THERAPY

The average age of a woman at menopause is 51, with a range in age from 40 to 60 years.[37] Clinical trials evaluating the safety and efficacy of hormone replacement therapy in postmenopausal women demonstrated that 10 years or more after menopause, hormone replacement therapy seems to cause more harm than benefit.[38]

Some studies have suggested that exogenous estrogen exhibits a differential effect on women after menopause, which varies by age—a concept known as the *timing hypothesis* or *window of opportunity hypothesis*.[13] This may actually have more to do with the level of atherosclerosis rather than age (Figure 17.1). In one animal study, no benefit of estrogen was shown in mice deficient in apolipoprotein E with mature atherosclerotic plaques. Treatment with estrogen did not slow or prevent progression of mature plaques.[39] Benefit was seen, however, in mice with less advanced atherosclerosis after treatment with estrogen. These mice demonstrated fewer signs of initial atherosclerosis, such as fatty streaks.[39] This study suggests that, during the early stages of atherosclerosis, endothelial dysfunction can be improved with estrogen replacement. In the setting of more advanced atherosclerotic lesions, however, the prothrombotic and inflammatory effects of exogenous hormones is likely to lead to progression and instability of mature atherosclerotic lesions.

The largest study of hormone replacement therapy for the prevention of cardiovascular disease and stroke was the Women's Health Initiative (WHI), a randomized trial of 16,608 healthy postmenopausal women. It demonstrated that combination estrogen and progestin replacement increased ischemic stroke by 44% (hazard ratio [HR], 1.44; 95% confidence interval [CI], 1.09–1.90).[19,40] Another arm of the study assessed 10,739 women after hysterectomy and found that women who used conjugated equine estrogen alone also had an increased risk of stroke compared with placebo (HR, 1.39; 95% CI, 1.10–1.77).[41] Subgroup analyses of these two WHI trials suggested that there was a nonsignificant reduction in the risk of coronary heart disease (CHD) in women less than 10 years postmenopause (HR, 0.76; 95% CI, 0.50–1.16) versus placebo. However, there was an increased risk of

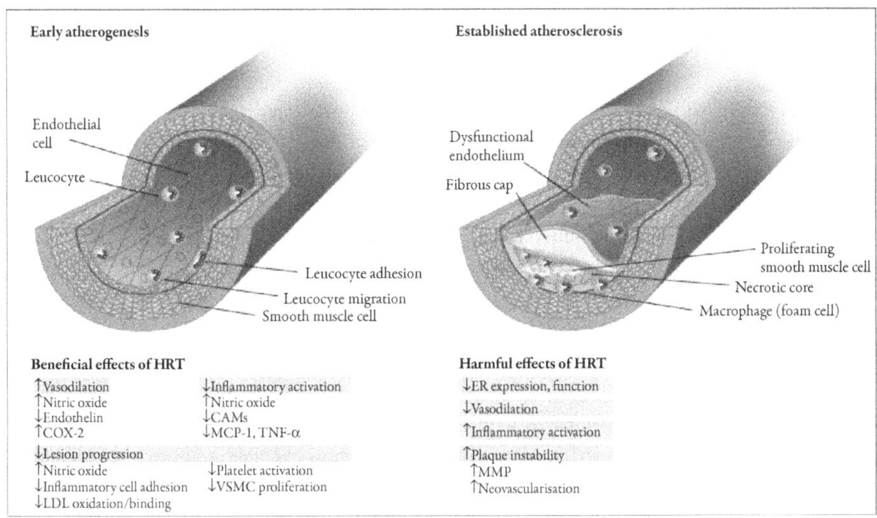

FIGURE 17.1 **Hormone replacement therapy use with early versus late atherosclerosis.** Effects of hormone replacement therapy use with early vs late atherosclerosis; reproduced with permission from: Mendelsohn and Karas. Molecular and cellular basis of cardiovascular gender differences. Science 2005; 308:1583-7.

stroke with hormone therapy (HR, 1.77; 95% CI, 1.05–2.98) in women less than 10 years since menopause.[38] In women age 50 to 59 years at the time of randomization, there was no significant benefit for hormone replacement therapy against CHD (HR, 0.93; 95% CI, 0.65–1.33) or stroke (HR, 1.13; 95% CI, 0.73–1.76).[38] The results of the WHI's assessment of the timing hypothesis showed that there may be a trend toward benefit for CHD with hormone therapy early after menopause, but not for stroke.

Another randomized clinical trial, the Heart and Estrogen/Progestin Replacement Study demonstrated that hormone replacement therapy yielded an increased risk of thromboembolic events without benefit with regard to cardiovascular disease prevention.[42] The Women's Estrogen for Stroke Trial looked at estradiol for secondary prevention of stroke and concluded that it did not reduce recurrent nonfatal stroke (relative risk [RR], 1.0; 95% CI, 0.7–1.4) or mortality alone (RR, 1.2; 95% CI, 0.8–1.8).[43] In fact, women randomized to the estradiol group experienced greater mortality secondary to stroke (RR, 2.9; 95% CI, 0.9–9.0) compared with the placebo group. In addition, the estradiol group was noted to have slightly worse outcomes regarding functional and neurological deficits.[43]

The use of exogenous hormones after premature menopause is not recommended by the American Heart Association for the primary prevention of cardiovascular disease or stroke, primarily because of the WHI results.[19] Additional studies, including the Kronos Early Estrogen Prevention Study as well as the Early Versus Late Intervention Trial with Estradiol. may provide insight regarding the timing of exogenous estrogen treatment with regard to menopause.[44,45]

Stroke Risk over a Lifetime

CHILDHOOD

During childhood, the overall risk of stroke is low, regardless of gender. Two large studies assessing gender ratios in childhood stroke found that boys had a greater overall risk ratio of stroke compared with girls (1.29–1.49).[46,47] A California study of childhood stroke demonstrated a higher mortality rate among boys with ischemic stroke compared with girls, but demonstrated no gender differences with regard to mortality rates for intracerebral hemorrhage or subarachnoid hemorrhage in these groups.[48]

Increased risk of stroke and poorer stroke outcomes in boys have been demonstrated in clinical observational studies as well as in animal models. Hypotheses for these increased risks include hormonal effects, neuroprotective mechanisms in response to cellular injury, and behavioral differences. Regarding hormonal effects, estrogen levels are higher in girls than boys throughout childhood, even in the years preceding puberty.[49] It is well known that estrogen exerts vasodilatory and anti-inflammatory effects on the vascular system; however, the fact that gender differences have been observed in stroke risk and outcome during childhood prompted further research with animal-based models to explore other possible explanations for these innate sexual differences.

Estrogen has been shown to exert a protective effect on brain tissue in the setting of various types of cell injury. For example, astrocytes derived from female neonatal rats were more resistant to oxygen–glucose deprivation compared with astrocytes derived from male rats of the same age.[50] The study was performed in a growth medium that lacked estrogen. Female astrocytes had enhanced aromatase activity, which is the mechanism through which astrocytes produce local estradiol. An aromatase inhibitor resulted in the absence of sex differences in response to oxygen–glucose deprivation, and supplementation with 17 β-estradiol conferred protection from injury in both female and male astrocytes.[50] Another study evaluated male and female rat neurons and their response to various toxins independent of circulating estradiol and found that male neurons were more susceptible to certain types of cytotoxic agents (nitrosative stress and exocytotoxicity) compared with female neurons.[51] This gender difference is secondary theoretically to the inability of XY neurons to maintain reduced glutathione intracellularly. Glutathione plays a role in cell detoxification after various injuries, including those caused by Parkinson's disease, traumatic brain injury, and cerebral ischemia.[51] A third hypothesis regarding gender differences and childhood stroke is behavioral differences—namely, physical activity. This is in light of the strikingly greater rates of stroke resulting from cervical dissection among boys compared with girls. Fullerton et al.[48] demonstrated that boys made up 74% of the total anterior cervical artery dissections (i.e., extra- and intracerebral carotid) and 87% of the posterior cervical artery dissections (i.e., vertebral). Findings from the International Pediatric Stroke Study demonstrated a similar trend.[46] Even after adjusting for dissections resulting from trauma, however, males still demonstrated a significant predominance in the incidence of spontaneous dissection, suggesting that boys may be more susceptible to dissection than girls.[46,48]

PREGNANCY AND STROKE

Epidemiology

Pregnancy and the postpartum period are associated with an increased risk of all stroke, including ischemic stroke, intracerebral hemorrhage, and subarachnoid hemorrhage. Several epidemiological studies have attempted to determine the incidence and RR of stroke during pregnancy and the postpartum period, as well as to identify specific periods when stroke risk is greatest. The incidence of stroke varies, ranging from 4.3 to 18 per 100,000 deliveries for ischemic stroke and 4.6 to 11.6 per 100,000 deliveries for hemorrhagic stroke.[52] One study by Kittner et al.[53] used discharge diagnosis codes from 46 hospitals in the Baltimore–Washington, DC, area and concluded that there is no increased risk of ischemic stroke during pregnancy, but that the risk of all stroke— intracerebral hemorrhage, in particular—was increased in the 6 weeks after delivery. The RR of ischemic stroke was 8.7 during the first 6 weeks postpartum. The RR of intracerebral hemorrhage during pregnancy was 2.5, but increased substantially to 28.3 during the 6 weeks after delivery.[53] This trend—demonstrating only modest increases in the risk of stroke during the early stages of pregnancy, yet substantial increases in risk surrounding delivery and the postpartum period—has been found in other studies as well (Figure 17.2).[54] A French study, which evaluated the pregnancy period and 2 weeks postpartum, revealed greater risks of all strokes during the postpartum period compared with pregnancy.[55] A separate study of pregnancy-related intracerebral hemorrhage in 423 subjects found that most of the increased risk was attributable to the postpartum period.[56]

Pathophysiology

The exact mechanism for this preponderance of stroke during the postpartum period is not known definitively, but thromboembolic stroke risk is likely associated with the relative hypercoagulable state of pregnancy. This change in hemostasis leads to increased levels of clotting factors and fibrinogen, along with decreased anticoagulants and fibrinolytic activity reaching a peak level of hypercoagulability around delivery and immediately postpartum. Most of the coagulation factors increase throughout the course of pregnancy. Factor VII reaches up to 10 times the levels present in nonpregnant females by the end of pregnancy.[57]. Fibrinogen is present in double the amounts by the end of gestation compared with nonpregnant levels, even when accounting for increased plasma volume.[57] Protein S decreases and activated protein C resistance increases during pregnancy.[57] In addition, the decrease in tissue plasminogen activator along with increased levels of endothelial-derived plasminogen activator inhibitor 1, placenta-derived plasminogen activator inhibitor 2, and thrombin activatable fibrinolysis inhibitor result in an overall decrease in fibrinolysis.[57] These changes gradually return to the nonpregnant state around 4 weeks postpartum.[57] Hemostatic changes are probably related to hormonal changes during pregnancy to protect against fatal hemorrhage at the time of placental separation.[57]

The etiology of intracerebral (excluding subarachnoid and subdural) hemorrhage in pregnant and postpartum females is often related to severe hypertension in the setting of preeclampsia and eclampsia. Hemodynamic changes may also contribute to this increased risk—particularly around delivery, when elevations in venous blood pressure cause increased cardiac output and increased arterial

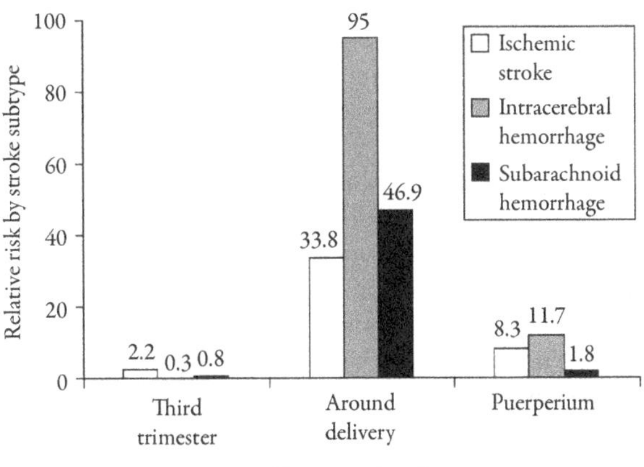

FIGURE 17.2 **Risk of stroke in women during the third trimester and the peri- and postpartum periods versus risk of nonpregnant women and women in their first two trimesters.**[54]

HRT-hormone-replacement therapy. CAMs-cell adhesion molecules. COX-2-cyclooxygenase-2. MCP-1-monocyte chemotactic protein 1. TNF-α-tumor necrosis factor α. VSMC-vascular smooth muscle cell. LDL-low-density lipoprotein. ER-oestrogen receptor. MMP-matrix metalloproteinase protein. Reproduced from Mendelsohn and Karas,[67] by permission of the American Association for the Advancement of Science.

pressures.[52] These hemodynamic changes return to nonpregnant norms around 2 to 6 weeks postpartum.[52] The increased venous and arterial pressures may increase the risk of hemorrhagic stroke, particularly in the setting of underlying pathology such as a cerebrovascular malformation or an aneurysm.[52]

Mechanisms and Risk Factors

Causes of stroke unique to pregnancy include preeclampsia, eclampsia, peripartum cardiomyopathy, postpartum cerebral angiopathy, amniotic fluid embolism, air embolism, and choriocarcinoma.[52] Postpartum cardiomyopathy is a cause of cardioembolic or watershed stroke specific to pregnancy and is defined as unexplained cardiac failure during the ninth month of gestation or the 5 months after delivery.[58] It is rare in the United States overall, affecting about 1 in 3000 to 4000 pregnancies. Within the United States, black and multiparous women are more commonly affected.[52,58] The incidence of postpartum cardiomyopathy is much more common among Haitians, affecting 1 in 350 to 400 deliveries.[59] The exact pathophysiology of postpartum cardiomyopathy is currently not known, but several studies have identified antibodies against cardiac tissue implicating a possible autoimmune mechanism.[59] The condition is associated with high mortality and recurrence with subsequent pregnancies.[60]

Amniotic fluid and air emboli are rare causes of stroke. An amniotic fluid embolism develops when amniotic fluid is forced into the maternal circulation from uterine veins. Rather than focal ischemic infarction, this results more commonly in an acute hemodynamic collapse and disseminated intravascular coagulation, causing global cerebral hypoperfusion.[52,58] However rarely, an amniotic fluid embolus or air embolus may cause a focal ischemic stroke by crossing from the venous to the arterial system via a patent foramen ovale.[52,58] Air embolus can develop at any point during pregnancy but is more common during delivery, particularly via cesarean section.[52,58]

Choriocarcinoma is an important but rare cause of hemorrhagic stroke, which occurs most commonly in molar pregnancies but also may occur in live births, or ectopic or terminated pregnancies.[58] These tumors are highly vascular and arise from gestational trophoblasts. Choriocarcinoma commonly metastasizes to the lungs, liver, and brain.[58] They tend to bleed as a result of their vascular nature and tend to cause subarachnoid hemorrhage or intraparenchymal hemorrhage.[58] In the brain, the tumor typically metastasizes to the gray–white junction, resulting in an intraparenchymal hemorrhage that may be mistaken easily for hemorrhagic transformation of ischemic stroke.[52]

Preeclampsia and eclampsia not only confer an increased risk of both ischemic and hemorrhagic stroke throughout the course of a pregnancy, but also increase the risk of ischemic stroke remote from pregnancy.[61] Preeclampsia is defined as new-onset hypertension (diastolic blood pressure, ≥90 mmHg) with proteinuria (>300 mg protein in a 24-hour period) after 20 weeks' gestation.[62] Preeclampsia is described as severe when the systolic blood pressure is at least 160 mmHg and/or the diastolic blood pressure is 110 mmHg along with proteinuria of 5 g per day or more.[61] About 1% to 2% of patients with severe preeclampsia will develop generalized tonic clonic seizures, meeting the criteria for eclampsia.[61] In addition to hypertension and proteinuria, preeclampsia may affect multiple organ systems, resulting in hemolysis, elevated liver enzymes, and low platelets (HELLP) syndrome; disseminated intravascular coagulation; acute pulmonary edema; and acute renal failure.[61] Fetal complications can accompany the maternal effects, resulting in fetal growth restriction, small size for gestational age, reduced amniotic fluid, and placental insufficiency, which may result in fetal hypoxia and hypoperfusion.[62] Aside from ischemic and hemorrhagic stroke, complications of preeclampsia and eclampsia include reversible posterior leukoencephalopathy syndrome or posterior reversible encephalopathy syndrome characterized by vasogenic edema in the occipital or parietal lobes, which can be identified easily on cerebral imaging.[61] Clinical symptoms include seizures, encephalopathy, or visual field deficit resulting from occipital lobe involvement. Reversible cerebral vasoconstriction syndrome is another syndrome caused by preeclampsia. The unique clinical feature is thunderclap headache with or without focal neurological deficits. Neuroimaging reveals vasoconstriction that affects medium and large arteries that may or may not cause infarction. These vessel abnormalities typically reverse after about 12 weeks.[63]

Women with preeclampsia and eclampsia during pregnancy are four times more likely to develop hypertension after delivery and have a twofold greater risk for both ischemic heart disease and stroke later in life.[61] Some studies have demonstrated earlier onset of menopause in women with preeclampsia compared with those without preeclampsia, as well as greater levels of biomarkers that indicate endothelial dysfunction.[64] Persistent endothelial dysfunction has been demonstrated in women with a history of preeclampsia in studies using brachial artery flow-mediated dilation responses evident 1 year after delivery.[65]

Aspirin for the Prevention of Preeclampsia during Pregnancy

A recent meta-analysis assessed the effectiveness of low-dose aspirin for the prevention of preeclampsia in high-risk women. The criteria used to identify women who were at high risk included previous history of preeclampsia, preexisting hypertension, family history of preeclampsia or vascular disorders, maternal age younger than 20 years or older than 40 years, and gestational diabetes mellitus, as well as those patients who were identified to be at high risk with Doppler ultrasonography, the roll-over test, or the angiotensin II sensitivity test.[66] Overall, these women benefited from low-dose aspirin (<100 mg/day) with a 21% reduction in the risk of preeclampsia (RR, 0.79; 95% CI, 0.65–0.97).[66] In women with low risk for the development of preeclampsia, no risk reduction was observed. One systematic review and meta-analysis of the major randomized controlled trials in this subject found similar results with no benefit in the low-risk group (RR, 0.95; 95% CI, 0.81–1.11), but modest benefit in the high-risk group (RR, 0.87; 95% CI, 0.79–0.96) with low-dose aspirin.[67] Another study found a reduction in preeclampsia (OR, 0.86; 95% CI, 0.76–0.96), perinatal death (OR, 0.79; 95% CI, 0.64–0.96), spontaneous preterm birth (OR, 0.86; 95% CI, 0.79–0.94), and increased mean birth weight without increased risk of placental abruption, fetal hemorrhage, or other neonatal bleeding in patients treated with low-dose aspirin.[68]

Stroke Prevention during Pregnancy

There are scant data available regarding preventative therapies for stroke during pregnancy. Aspirin during pregnancy, particularly during the first trimester, has been associated with an increased risk of congenital anomalies and malformations in both human and animal studies. Because of the limited information available and absence of randomized controlled trials, guidelines vary regarding stroke prevention during pregnancy. The American Heart Association/American Stroke Association recommends consideration of low-molecular weight heparin or unfractionated heparin during the first trimester, followed by a low-dose aspirin in women who would benefit from antiplatelet therapy outside of pregnancy.[69] Guidelines regarding treatment of thrombophilia during pregnancy by the American College of Chest Physicians recommend low-dose aspirin in combination with prophylactic or intermediate-dose unfractionated heparin exclusively for women with antiphospholipid antibody syndrome.[70] They also recommend no prophylaxis for women with inherited thrombophilia or prior miscarriages without antiphospholipid antibody syndorme.[70] Regarding treatment of high-risk thromboembolic conditions, including thrombophilias and mechanical heart valves, the American Heart Association/American Stroke Association recommends low-molecular weight heparin or unfractionated heparin throughout pregnancy.[69] Alternatively, patients may be treated with low-molecular weight heparin or unfractionated heparin during their first trimester, transition to warfarin during the second trimester through the middle of the third trimester, then convert back to using unfractionated heparin or low-molecular weight heparin until they deliver.[69]

Tissue Plasminogen Activator Use During Pregnancy

Recombinant tissue plasminogen activator is listed as category C regarding its safety in use during pregnancy. It has not demonstrated teratogenicity in animal studies and does not cross the placenta. Although pregnancy is a relative contraindication for administration of recombinant tissue plasminogen activator because of the risk of systemic bleeding, there have been several reports of its successful use during pregnancy. Overall, it appears that thrombolytics generally yield positive results when used during pregnancy; however, the risks and benefits must be weighed carefully in each case.[71] The safety and efficacy of mechanical thrombectomy in pregnancy has not been studied formally; however, case studies have demonstrated positive outcomes in this popuation.[71]

MENOPAUSE AND STROKE RISK

The perimenopausal transitional period is characterized by various endocrine and biological changes, resulting in clinical manifestations and eventually leading to the permanent cessation of menstruation. Menopause is defined formally by the absence of a menstrual period for 1 year and typically affects women ages 40 to 60 years with a mean age of 51 years.[37] During menopause, levels of sex hormones decline. Specifically, estradiol levels decline by about 60%.[37] Levels of testosterone decrease by about 50% between 20 to 40 years of age, but remain stable throughout the perimenopausal period and may even increase after menopause, leading to a relative androgen excess.[72,73] These hormonal changes, characterized by the loss of estrogen and the excess of androgens, likely contribute to other accumulated risk factors for stroke, leading to an overall increased risk of stroke during the postmenopausal years. Although the role of age at menopause is still controversial,[37] two studies suggest this might be an important risk factor for stroke. The first analysis was from the Framingham Heart Study, which showed that women with menopause at age 42 or younger had twice the risk of stroke.[19] A second study comes from the Multi-Ethnic Study of Atherosclerosis, which demonstrated that women with menopause onset at age 46 or younger had a twofold increased risk for both stroke and CHD.[74] More research is needed to understand more completely the reasons for earlier menopausal transitions and how they might be tied to stroke risk.[19]

Primary Prevention and Stroke Therapies

Multiple studies demonstrated that men are more likely to be on antiplatelet therapy before experiencing a stroke.[1,3] This may be a result of their propensity for myocardial infarction before stroke. Among stroke survivors, men older than 85 years were more likely than women to receive aspirin, whereas both genders received similar treatment between the ages of 65 years and 84 years in a Canadian–based study.[3] Regarding primary prevention for stroke, a meta-analysis of studies of men only, women only, and both genders showed that aspirin was associated with a 17% reduction in stroke events with no effect on myocardial infarction in women, whereas men had a 32% reduction in myocardial infarction but no impact on stroke risk.[75]

Several recent studies have demonstrated discrepancies among stroke treatment between genders. Several studies have demonstrated no difference regarding treatment with anticoagulants between the sexes despite the increased frequency of atrial fibrillation among women.[1,3,76,77] Gender differences have also been found with regard to the risk of thromboembolism and bleeding complications.[78] The Canadian Registry of Atrial Fibrillation found that women were older at the time of presentation, with faster heart rates in atrial fibrillation. They were half as likely to receive anticoagulant therapy but twice as likely to be treated with aspirin. Of the patients who were treated with warfarin, women were 3.4 times more likely to experience a major bleeding complication than men.[78]

Another secondary prevention treatment that is performed more commonly in men than in women is carotid endarterectomy.[4,79,80] One study found that male stroke survivors were more likely to have carotid atherosclerosis. When restricting the analysis to patients with carotid disease, no gender difference was found, indicating that these gender disparities may be the result of fundamental differences in the pathophysiology of stroke among males and females.[79]

Sex Differences in Stroke Outcomes

Overall, the age-adjusted risk for stroke is greater in men compared with women. Throughout the course of an entire lifetime, however, strokes occur more commonly, cause greater disability, and result in greater mortality in women. Studies evaluating disability after stroke revealed that, even after controlling for age, race, education, and marital status, women were more likely to require assistance with their activities of daily living compared with men.[1,18,81] In general, mortality rates are similar in men and women. However, because of longer life spans in women, this population makes up 60% of the total deaths resulting from stroke.[19] These factors underscore the importance of stroke prevention and risk factor modification in women, particularly as they age.

Conclusion

In conclusion, there are several factors unique to women with regard to stroke. Understanding gender differences in stroke pathophysiology as well as stroke risk factors that are unique to women will enable physicians to provide individualized care. Further research is warranted to enable a better understanding of the roles of estrogen and exogenous hormone therapy, pregnancy, and menopause to develop the best prevention strategies for women across their life span.

REFERENCES

1. Di Carlo A, Lamassa M, Baldereschi M, et al. Sex differences in the clinical presentation, resource use, and 3-month outcome of acute stroke in Europe: data from a multicenter multinational hospital-based registry. *Stroke.* 2003;34:1114–1119.
2. Roquer J, Campello AR, Gomis M. Sex differences in first-ever acute stroke. *Stroke.* 2003;34:1581–1585.
3. Holroyd-Leduc JM, Kapral MK, Austin PC, Tu JV. Sex differences and similarities in the management and outcome of stroke patients. *Stroke.* 2000;31:1833–1837.
4. Kapral MK, Degani N, Hall R, et al. Gender differences in stroke care and outcomes in Ontario. *Womens Health Issues.* 2011;21:171–176.
5. Towfighi A, Saver JL, Engelhardt R, Ovbiagele B. A midlife stroke surge among women in the United States. *Neurology.* 2007;69:1898–1904.
6. Grundy SM, Cleeman JI, Daniels SR, et al. Diagnosis and management of the metabolic syndrome: an American Heart Association/National Heart, Lung, and Blood Institute scientific statement. *Circulation.* 2005;112:2735–2752.
7. Dallongeville J, Cottel D, Arveiler D, et al. The association of metabolic disorders with the metabolic syndrome is different in men and women. *Ann Nutr Metab.* 2004;48:43–50.

8. Hanefeld M, Koehler C, Gallo S, Benke I, Ott P. Impact of the individual components of the metabolic syndrome and their different combinations on the prevalence of atherosclerotic vascular disease in type 2 diabetes: the Diabetes in Germany (DIG) study. *Cardiovasc Diabetol.* 2007;6:13.
9. Iglseder B, Cip P, Malaimare L, Ladurner G, Paulweber B. The metabolic syndrome is a stronger risk factor for early carotid atherosclerosis in women than in men. *Stroke.* 2005;36:1212–1217.
10. Park JW, Lee S-Y, Kim SY, Choe H, Jee SH. BMI and stroke risk in Korean women. *Obesity (Silver Spring).* 2008;16:396–401.
11. Kruit MC, van Buchem MA, Hofman PA, et al. Migraine as a risk factor for subclinical brain lesions. *JAMA.* 2004;291:427–434.
12. MacClellan LR, Giles W, Cole J, et al. Probable migraine with visual aura and risk of ischemic stroke: the Stroke Prevention in Young Women Study. *Stroke.* 2007;38:2438–2445.
13. Salisbury M, Pfeffer G, Yip S. Stroke in young women. *Can J Neurol Sci.* 2011;38:404–410.
14. Dowson A, Mullen MJ, Peatfield R, et al. Migraine intervention with STARFlex technology (MIST) trial: a prospective, multicenter, double-blind, sham-controlled trial to evaluate the effectiveness of patent foramen ovale closure with STARFlex septal repair implant to resolve refractory migraine headache. *Circulation.* 2008;117:1397–1404.
15. Carpenter DA, Ford AL, Lee J-M. Patent foramen ovale and stroke: should PFOs be closed in otherwise cryptogenic stroke? *Curr Atheroscler Rep.* 2010;12:251–258.
16. Shannon M, Wang Y. Polycystic ovary syndrome: a common but often unrecognized condition. *J Midwifery Womens Health.* 2012;57:221–230.
17. Battaglia C, Mancini F, Cianciosi A, et al. Vascular risk in young women with polycystic ovary and polycystic ovary syndrome. *Obstet Gynecol.* 2008;111:385–395.
18. Petrea RE, Beiser AS, Seshadri S, Kelly-Hayes M, Kase CS, Wolf PA. Gender differences in stroke incidence and poststroke disability in the Framingham Heart Study. *Stroke.* 2009;40:1032–1037.
19. Roger VL, Go AS, Lloyd-Jones DM, et al. Heart disease and stroke statistics: 2012 update: a report from the American Heart Association. *Circulation.* 2012;125:e2–e220.
20. Bushnell CD, Hurn P, Colton C, et al. Advancing the study of stroke in women: summary and recommendations for future research from an NINDS-sponsored multidisciplinary working group. *Stroke.* 2006;37:2387–2399.
21. Duckles SP, Krause DN Cerebrovascular effects of oestrogen: multiplicity of action. *Clin Exp Pharmacol Physiol.* 2007;34:801–808.
22. Duckles SP, Krause DN. Mechanisms of cerebrovascular protection: oestrogen, inflammation and mitochondria. *Acta Physiol (Oxf).* 2011;203:149–154.
23. Geary GG, McNeill AM, Ospina JA, Krause DN, Korach KS, Duckles SP. Selected contribution: cerebrovascular NOS and cyclooxygenase are unaffected by estrogen in mice lacking estrogen receptor-α. *J Appl Physiol.* 2001;91:2391–2399.
24. Huang A, Vita J. Effects of systemic inflammation on endothelium-dependent vasodilation. *Trends Cardiovasc Med.* 2006;16:15–20.
25. Diomedi M, Cupini LM, Rizzato B, Ferrante F, Giacomini P, Silvestrini M. Influence of physiologic oscillation of estrogens on cerebral hemodynamics. *J Neurol Sci.* 2001;185:49–53.
26. de Lecinana MA, Egido JA, Casado I, et al. Risk of ischemic stroke and lifetime estrogen exposure. *Neurology.* 2007;68:33–38.
27. Cui R, Iso H, Toyoshima H, et al. Relationships of age at menarche and menopause, and reproductive year with mortality from cardiovascular disease in Japanese postmenopausal women: the JACC study. *J Epidemiol.* 2006;16:177–184.
28. Jacobsen BK, Oda K, Knutsen SF, Fraser GE. Age at menarche, total mortality and mortality from ischaemic heart disease and stroke: the Adventist Health Study, 1976–88. *Int J Epidemiol.* 2009;38:245–252.

29. Kivimäki M, Lawlor DA, Smith GD, et al. Association of age at menarche with cardiovascular risk factors, vascular structure, and function in adulthood: the Cardiovascular Risk in Young Finns study. *Am J Clin Nutr.* 2008;87:1876–1882.
30. Bushnell CD. Stroke in women: risk and prevention throughout the lifespan. *Neurol Clin.* 2008;26:1161–1176.
31. Chang CL, Donaghy M, Poulter N. Migraine and stroke in young women: case–control study. *BMJ.* 1999;318:13–18.
32. Bousser M-G. Stroke in women: the 1997 Paul Dudley White international lecture. *Circulation.* 1999;99:463–467.
33. Bousser M-G. Estrogens, migraine, and stroke. *Stroke.* 2004;35:2652–2656.
34. Slooter AJC, Rosendaal FR, Tanis BC, Kemmeren JM, van der Graaf Y, Algra A. Prothrombotic conditions, oral contraceptives, and the risk of ischemic stroke. *J Thromb Haemost.* 2005;3:1213–1217.
35. Sadek MME, Amer MK, Fahmy M. Acute cerebrovascular accidents with severe ovarian hyperstimulation syndrome. *Hum Reprod.* 1998;13:1793–1795.
36. Elchalal U, Schenker JG. The pathophysiology of ovarian hyperstimulation syndrome: views and ideas. *Hum Reprod.* 1997;12:1129–1137.
37. Lisabeth L, Bushnell C. Stroke risk in women: the role of menopause and hormone therapy. *Lancet Neurol.* 2012;11:82–91.
38. Rossouw JE, Prentice RL, Manson JE, et al. Postmenopausal hormone therapy and risk of cardiovascular disease by age and years since menopause. *JAMA.* 2007;297:1465–1477.
39. Rosenfeld ME, Kauser K, Martin-McNulty B, Polinsky P, Schwartz SM, Rubanyi GM. Estrogen inhibits the initiation of fatty streaks throughout the vasculature but does not inhibit intra-plaque hemorrhage and the progression of established lesions in apolipoprotein E deficient mice. *Atherosclerosis.* 2002;164:251–259.
40. Wassertheil-Smoller SHS. Effect of estrogen plus progestin on stroke in postmenopausal women: the Women's Health Initiative: a randomized trial. *JAMA.* 2003;289:2673–2684.
41. Anderson GL, Limacher M, Assaf AR, et al. Effects of conjugated equine estrogen in postmenopausal women with hysterectomy: the Women's Health Initiative randomized controlled trial. *JAMA.* 2004;291:1701–1712.
42. Hulley S, Grady D, Bush T, et al. Randomized trial of estrogen plus progestin for secondary prevention of coronary heart disease in postmenopausal women: Heart and Estrogen/Progestin Replacement Study (HERS) Research Group. *JAMA.* 1998;280:605–613.
43. Viscoli CM, Brass LM, Kernan WN, Sarrel PM, Suissa S, Horwitz RI. A clinical trial of estrogen-replacement therapy after ischemic stroke. *N Engl J Med.* 2001;345:1243–1249.
44. Harman SM, Brinton EA, Cedars M, et al. KEEPS: the Kronos Early Estrogen Prevention Study. *Climacteric.* 2005;8:3–12.
45. Henderson VW. Aging, estrogens, and episodic memory in women. *Cogn Behav Neurol.* 2009;22:205–214.
46. Golomb MR, Fullerton HJ, Nowak-Gottl U, deVeber G. Male predominance in childhood ischemic stroke findings from the International Pediatric Stroke Study. *Stroke.* 2009;40:52–57.
47. Fullerton HJ, Wu YW, Zhao S, Johnston SC. Risk of stroke in children ethnic and gender disparities. *Neurology.* 2003;61:189–194.
48. Fullerton HJ, Johnston SC, Smith WS. Arterial dissection and stroke in children. *Neurology.* 2001;57:1155–1160.
49. Janfaza M, Sherman TI, Larmore KA, Brown-Dawson J, Klein KO. Estradiol levels and secretory dynamics in normal girls and boys as determined by an ultrasensitive bioassay: a 10 year experience. *J Pediatr Endocrinol Metab.* 2006;19:901–909.

50. Liu M, Hurn PD, Roselli CE, Alkayed NJ. Role of P450 aromatase in sex-specific astrocytic cell death. *J Cereb Blood Flow Metab.* 2006;27:135.
51. Du L, Bayir H, Lai Y, et al. Innate gender-based proclivity in response to cytotoxicity and programmed cell death pathway. *J Biol Chem.* 2004;279:38563–38570.
52. Helms AK, Kittner SJ. Pregnancy and stroke. *CNS Spectr.* 2005;10:580–587.
53. Kittner SJ, Stern BJ, Feeser BR, et al. Pregnancy and the risk of stroke. *N Engl J Med.* 1996;335:768–774.
54. Rosamond W, Flegal K, Friday G, et al. Heart disease and stroke statistics: 2007 update: a report from the American Heart Association Statistics Committee and Stroke Statistics Subcommittee. *Circulation.* 2007;115:e69–e171.
55. Sharshar T, Lamy C, Mas JL. Incidence and causes of strokes associated with pregnancy and puerperium: a study in public hospitals of Ile de France. *Stroke.* 1995;26:930–936.
56. Bateman BT, Schumacher HC, Bushnell CD, et al. Intracerebral hemorrhage in pregnancy: frequency, risk factors, and outcome. *Neurology.* 2006;67:424–429.
57. Franchini M. Haemostasis and pregnancy. *Thromb Haemost.* 2006;95:401–413.
58. Davie CA, O'Brien P. Stroke and pregnancy. *J Neurol Neurosurg Psychiatry.* 2008;79:240–245.
59. Fett JD. Peripartum cardiomyopathy: insights from Haiti regarding a disease of unknown etiology. *Minn Med.* 2002;85:46–48.
60. Elkayam U, Tummala PP, Rao K, et al. Maternal and fetal outcomes of subsequent pregnancies in women with peripartum cardiomyopathy. *N Engl J Med.* 2001;344:1567–1571.
61. Bushnell C, Chireau M. Preeclampsia and stroke: risks during and after pregnancy. *Stroke Res Treat.* 2011;2011:1–9.
62. Milne F. The Pre-eclampsia Community Guideline (PRECOG): how to screen for and detect onset of pre-eclampsia in the community. *BMJ.* 2005;330:576–580.
63. Calabrese LH, Dodick DW, Schwedt TJ, Singhal AB. Narrative review: reversible cerebral vasoconstriction syndromes. *Ann Intern Med.* 2007;146:34–44.
64. Sattar N, Ramsay J, Crawford L, Cheyne H, Greer IA. Classic and novel risk factor parameters in women with a history of preeclampsia. *Hypertension.* 2003;42:39–42.
65. Chambers JC, Fusi L, Malik IS, Haskard DO, De Swiet M, Kooner JS. Association of maternal endothelial dysfunction with preeclampsia. *JAMA.* 2001;285:1607–1612.
66. Trivedi NA. A meta-analysis of low-dose aspirin for prevention of preeclampsia. *J Postgrad Med.* 2011;57:91–95.
67. Ruano R, Fontes RS, Zugaib M. Prevention of preeclampsia with low-dose aspirin: a systematic review and meta-analysis of the main randomized controlled trials. *Clinics (Sao Paulo)* 2005;60:407–414.
68. Coomarasamy A, Honest H, Papaioannou S, Gee H, Khan KS. Aspirin for prevention of preeclampsia in women with historical risk factors: a systematic review. *Obstet Gynecol.* 2003;101:1319–1332.
69. Furie KL, Kasner SE, Adams RJ, et al. Guidelines for the prevention of stroke in patients with stroke or transient ischemic attack: a guideline for healthcare professionals from the American Heart Association/American Stroke Association. *Stroke.* 2011;42:227–276.
70. Bates SM, Greer IA, Middeldorp S, et al. VTE, thrombophilia, antithrombotic therapy, and pregnancy: Antithrombotic Therapy and Prevention of Thrombosis, 9th ed: American College of Chest Physicians Evidence-Based Clinical Practice Guidelines. *Chest.* 2012;141:e691S–e736S.
71. Tate J, Bushnell C. Pregnancy and stroke risk in women. *Women's Health.* 2011;7:363–374.
72. Burger HG, Dudley EC, Robertson DM, Dennerstein L. Hormonal changes in the menopause transition. *Recent Prog Horm Res.* 2002;57:257–275.

73. Liu Y, Ding J, Bush TL, et al. Relative androgen excess and increased cardiovascular risk after menopause: a hypothesized relation. *Am J Epidemiol.* 2001;154:489–494.
74. Wellons M, Ouyang P, Schreiner PJ, Herrington DM, Vaidya D. Early menopause predicts future coronary heart disease and stroke: the Multi-ethnic Study of Atherosclerosis. *Menopause.* 2012;19:1081–1087.
75. Berger JS. Aspirin for the primary prevention of cardiovascular events in women and men: a sex-specific meta-analysis of randomized controlled trials. *JAMA.* 2006;295:306–313.
76. Marini C, De Santis F, Sacco S, et al. Contribution of atrial fibrillation to incidence and outcome of ischemic stroke results from a population-based study. *Stroke.* 2005;36:1115–1119.
77. Hart RG, Pearce LA, McBride R, Rothbart RM, Asinger RW. Factors associated with ischemic stroke during aspirin therapy in atrial fibrillation: analysis of 2012 participants in the SPAF I–III clinical trials. *Stroke.* 1999;30:1223–1229.
78. Humphries KH, Westendorp IC, Bots ML, et al. New-onset atrial fibrillation: sex differences in presentation, treatment, and outcome. *Circulation.* 2001;103:2365–2370.
79. Patrick SJ, Concato J, Viscoli C, Chyatte D, Brass LM. Sex differences in the management of patients hospitalized with ischemic cerebrovascular disease. *Stroke.* 1995;26:577–580.
80. Ramani S, Byrne-Logan S, Freund KM, et al. Gender differences in the treatment of cerebrovascular disease. *J Am Geriatr Soc.* 2000;48:741–745.
81. Löfmark U, Hammarström A. Evidence for age-dependent education-related differences in men and women with first-ever stroke: results from a community-based incidence study in northern Sweden. *Neuroepidemiology.* 2007;28:135–141.

18

MIGRAINE AND RISK OF CEREBROVASCULAR DISEASE AND STROKE

Alessandro Pezzini

Introduction

Migraine is a common, chronic, multifactorial neurovascular disease affecting between 10% and 20% of the population. The clinical presentation is heterogeneous and includes recurrent headache attacks, associated symptoms of vegetative disturbance, and hypersensitivity of various functional responses of the nervous system.[1,2] About one third of migraineurs experience additional transient neurological symptoms, mostly involving the visual system before or during a migraine attack, which are known as *migraine aura*.[2] The International Headache Society (IHS) has established gold-standard criteria for the diagnosis of migraine.[3] Although migraine with aura (MA) and migraine without aura (MO) are the most common forms, the IHS also acknowledges, for example, certain forms lacking one diagnostic criterion as probable migraine as well as rare familial monogenetic forms. Neurological aura symptoms (MA) are present in a percentage of patients that varies, according to the ascertainment criteria and the study design, from up to one third in population-based studies to a lower frequency in clinic-based studies.[3–5]

Although migraine attacks may be acutely disabling, the traditional view is that they do not result in long-term consequences to the brain. Contrary to this assumption, new data have emerged that emphasize the high prevalence of migraine among young individuals with stroke as well as a dysfunction of cerebral arteries during migraine attacks and the finding of silent infarctlike brain lesions in migraineurs, thus leading to the hypothesis that a comorbidity between migraine and cerebral ischemia exists.[6] Despite this, a careful evaluation of the existing data on the relation between migraine and stroke raises more questions than provides a clear picture.

Migraine as a Risk Factor for Ischemic Stroke

Apart from historical anecdotal reports pointing toward a unidirectional causal relation,[7] the first epidemiological suggestion that migraine may be an independent risk factor for stroke came from the Collaborative Group for the Study of Stroke in Young Women, published in 1975,[8] which showed a doubling of the relative risk (RR) of stroke in persons with migraine compared with control subjects. Since then, the association of migraine with the risk of stroke has been investigated in a number of clinic-based and population-based studies (Table 18.1) and three meta-analyses,[9–11] the most recent of which included 13 case–control studies and 8 cohort studies.[11] All the 21 observational studies included in this meta-analysis addressed the potential confounding effect of age and sex in effect estimates. Some studies also addressed the potential confounding effects of hypertension (19 studies), smoking (16 studies), oral contraceptive use (10 studies), cholesterol (9 studies), cardiac disease (8 studies), family history of migraine or stroke (3 studies), and postmenopausal hormone therapy (2 studies).

According to this meta-analysis, the pooled, adjusted odds ratio (OR) of ischemic stroke among patients with any type of migraine is 2.04 (95% confidence interval [CI], 1.72–2.43). The ORs for people with MA and MO are 2.25 (95% CI, 1.53–3.33) and 1.24 (95% CI, 0.86–1.79), respectively, whereas the pooled, adjusted OR for ischemic stroke in studies of women migraineurs only versus nonmigraineurs was 2.89 (95% CI, 2.42–3.45). These results are in apparent disagreement with those of the previous study by Etminan et al.,[9] which reported a statistically significant, although less strong than for MA, risk of stroke for MO (pooled RR, 1.83; 95% CI, 1.06–3.15), and instead support the findings of Schurks et al.[10] (Table 18.2).

The discrepancy with the first meta-analysis is likely the result of the differential inclusion of a large study by Stang et al.,[12] which reported a negative association with ischemic stroke in patients with migraine. Overall, based on these findings, it seems at least unlikely that MA and MO are equally associated with ischemic stroke. Currently, because the association is not as robust, whether MO should be considered a stroke risk factor remains unclear. Similarly, because the prevalence of migraine is three times lower in men than in women, the association is more uncertain in men. There are also strong arguments to hypothesize that the risk of brain ischemia is greater for those with a greater frequency of migraine attack[13,14] and for women with MA who smoke cigarettes and use oral contraceptives.[15]

Is this enough to conclude that migraine is a risk factor for stroke? As pointed out by many authors, most of these studies are subject to several limitations.

First, a consistent definition for migraine is often lacking. Accurate diagnosis of migraine is important to avoid nondifferential misclassification of exposure, which would bias the risk estimate toward showing no association. If this is the case, however, we cannot but assume that the increased risk of stroke emerging from the pooled analysis of data from observational studies is rather an underestimation of the effect. As such, it should be retained as an argument in favor of the reported association between migraine and stroke. Furthermore, in case–control studies an interviewer bias and a recall bias can arise as possible consequences of the retrospective design.

Second, potential bias in the selection of patients should be taken into account. At least theoretically, a referral bias may exist if stroke patients with migraine were referred to the recruiting centers more frequently than stroke cases without migraine, or if the investigators were more prone to include stroke patients with migraine than without migraine. A further bias could be the consequence of a stroke–migraine misdiagnosis. Because transient ischemic attacks are sometimes difficult to distinguish from an attack of MA, especially when the aura occurs without headache, and migraine with

TABLE 18.1

In Epidemiological Studies, Risk of Ischemic Stroke According to Type of Migraine

Authors, year	Methodology	Population	Subjects' characteristics	Patients with migraine		Migraine Status		Adjustment for covariates and confounders	Notes
				ischaemic stroke cases (%): controls (%)	Any RR (95% CI)	MA RR (95% CI)	MO RR (95% CI)		
Collaborative Group for the Study of Stroke in Young Woman, 1975	Case-control study	Women aged 14-44yrs	430 stroke cases, 429 hospital control subjects and 451 neighborhood control subjects	48(34.2) : 234(26.5)	2.0 (1.2 to 3.3)*	NS	NS	Age, contraceptives, smoking	* RR calculated for ischemic stroke using neighbor controls for comparison
Henrich, 1989	Case-control study	Men and women aged 15-65 yrs	89 ischemic stroke cases, 178 hospital controls	17(19.1) : 20(11.2)	1.8 (0.9 to 3.6)	2.6 (1.1 to 6.6)	1.3 (0.5 to 3.6)	NS	
Marini et al, 1993	Case-control study	Men and women aged 15-44 yrs	308 ischemic stroke or TIA cases, 308 hospital controls and 308 population controls	46(14.9) : 57(9.2)*	1.91 (1.05 to 3.5)	14.85 (1.8 to 124)	1.6 (0.9 to 3.0)	Diet, obesity, alcohol, smoking, contraceptives, hypertension, diabetes, paroxysmal disorders, hematocrit, cholesterol, triglycerides, HDL, cardiac and carotid abnormalities	* from ischemic stroke and TIA cases
Tzourio et al, 1993	Case-control study	Men and women aged 18-80 yrs	212 ischemic stroke cases, 212 hospital controls	41(19.3) : 34(16)	1.3 (0.8 to 2.3)	1.3 (0.5 to 3.8)	0.8 (0.4 to 1.5)	NS	

Lidegaard, 1995	Case-control study	Women aged 15-44 yrs	497 stroke cases, 1,370 population controls	64(12.9) : 66(4.8)	2.8 *	NS	NS	Hypertension, other predisposing diseases	* 95% CI not reported; p< 0.01;
Tzourio et al, 1995	Case-control study	Women aged <45yrs	72 ischemic stroke cases, 173 hospital controls	43(59.7) : 52(30)	3.5 (1.8 to 6.4)	6.2 (2.1 to 18)	3.0 (1.5 to 5.8)	Age, smoking, hypertension, contraceptives	
Carolei et al, 1996	Case-control study	Men and women aged 15-44 yrs	308 ischemic stroke or TIA cases, 591 hospital controls and population controls	24(13.9) : 34(10.3)	1.3 (0.7 to 2.4)	1.0 (0.5 to 2.0)	8.6 (1.0 to 75)	Obesity, alcohol, smoking, hypercholesterolaemia, hypertrigliceridaemia, low HDL-cholesterol, age, contraceptives, hypertension, diabetes	
Haapaniemi et al, 1997	Case-control study	Men and women aged 16-60 yrs	506 ischemic stroke cases, 345 hospital controls	86(17) : 42(12.2)	2.1 (1.05 to 2.9)*	NS	NS	Hypertension, cardiac disease, current smoking, diabetes, alcohol, age, body mass index	* RR reported for male subgroup
Chang et al, 1999	Case-control study	Women aged 20-44 yrs	291 ischemic, hemorragic or unclassified arterial stroke cases, 736 hospital controls	26(30.2) : 26(11.8)	3.5 (1.3 to 9.6)	3.81 (1.3 to 11.5)	2.9 (0.7 to 13.5)	Hypertension, smoking, education, family history of migraine, alcohol, social class	
Donaghy et al, 2002	Case-control study	Women aged 20-44 yrs	86 ischemic stroke cases, 214 hospital controls	26(30.2) : 26(12.1)	NS	8.4 (2.3 to 30.1)	2.2 (0.5 to 10.1)	NS	

(*continued*)

TABLE 18.1

Continued

Authors, year	Methodology	Population	Subjects' characteristics	Patients with migraine		Migraine Status		Adjustment for covariates and confounders	Notes
				ischaemic stroke cases (%): controls (%)	Any RR (95% CI)	MA RR (95% CI)	MO RR (95% CI)		
Schwaag et al, 2003	Case-control study	Men and women aged <46 yrs	160 ischemic stroke and TIA cases, 160 hospital controls	37(23.1) : 20(12.5)*	2.1 (1.2 to 3.8)*	NS	NS	NS	* from ischemic stroke and TIA cases
Nightingale et al, 2004	Nested case-control study	Women aged 15-49 yrs	190 ischemic stroke cases, 1,129 population controls	16(8.4) :44(3.9)	2.3 (1.04 to 5.2)	NS	NS	NS	
MacClellan et al, 2007	Case-control study	Women aged 15-49 yrs	386 ischemic stroke cases, 614 population controls	180(47) : 254(42)	NS	1.5 (1.1 to 2.0)	1.0 (0.6 to 1.5)	Age, race, geographic region, study period	
Naess et al, 2004	Case-control study	Men and women aged 15-49 yrs	232 ischemic stroke cases, 217 population controls	187(33) : 217(25)	1.7 (0.9 to 3.2)	NS	NS	NS	
Becker et al, 2007	Cohort study	Poulation from UK/ General Practice Research Database aged 79 yrs or younger	103,376 subjects (51,688 migraine sufferers)	NS	2.85 (1.88 to 4.30)	NS	NS	Age, gender, general practice, calendar time, body mass index, smoking status, diabetes mellitus, hypertension, and dyslipidemia.	

Buring et al, 1995	Cohort study	Male physicians aged 40-84 yrs participants of the Physicians' Health Study	22,071 subjects (1,479 migraine sufferers)	17(1.1) : 154(0.7)	2.0 (1.1 to 3.6)	NS	NS	Age, smoking, elevated cholesterol, diabetes, hystory of angina, body mass index, parental hystory of premature MI, alcohol consumption, excercise, randomized treatment assignment, hypertension	
Merikangas et al, 1997	Cross sectional study	Population-based national-probability sample	12,220 subjects (1,109 migraine sufferers)	NS	2.1 (1.5 to 2.9)*	NS	NS	Age, sex, smoking, hypertension, diabetres, cholesterol, heart condition, alcohol	* from all stroke cases
Velentgas et al, 2004	Cohort study	Population from United Health Care	260,822 (13,0411 migraine sufferers)	216(0.16) : 98(0.07)*	1.6 (1.3 to 2.1)*	NS	NS	Age, sex, year of cohort entry, comorbidities in years prior to study entry, oral contraceptive, estrogen replacement therapy	* from all stroke cases
Hall et al, 2004	Cohort study	Popoulations from General Practice Research Database	14,0814 subjects (63,575 migraine sufferers)	71(0.11) : 31(0.04)	2.5 (1.6 to 3.8)	NS	NS	Hypertension, diabetes, cardiac disease, obesity, hypercholesterolemia, oral contraceptive, smoking	

(*continued*)

TABLE 18.1

Continued

Authors, year	Methodology	Population	Subjects' characteristics	Patients with migraine		Migraine Status		Adjustment for covariates and confounders	Notes
				ischaemic stroke cases (%): controls (%)	Any RR (95% CI)	MA RR (95% CI)	MO RR (95% CI)		
Kurth et al, 2005	Cohort study	Women aged 45 yrs or older partecipants of the Women's Health Study (WHS)	39,754 subjects (385 ischemic, hemorragic or unclassified stroke cases)	41(13.2) : 5126(13)	1.4 (0.97 to 1.9)*	1.7 (1.1 to 2.7)*	1.1 (0.7 to 1.8)*	Age, hypertension, menopausal status, oral contraceptives use, alcohol consumption, randomized aspirin assignment, exercise, body mass index, smoking status, postmenopausal hormone therapy, diabetes, cholesterol	* calculated as Hazard Ratio (95%CI) for ischemic stroke

Stang et al, 2005	Cohort study	Men and women aged 45-64 yrs participants of the Atherosclerosis Risk in the Communities(ARIC) Study	12,750 subjects (1,015 migraine sufferers)	NS	NS	2.8 (1.6 to 4.9)	0.8 (0.4 to 1.7)	Age, sex, race/ center, hypertension medication use, aspirin use, NSAID use, systolic blood pressure, diabetes, parental hystory of migraines, smoking, pack-years of smoking, cholesterol	
Kurth et al, 2007	Cohort study	Men aged 40-84 yrs participants of the Physicians' Health Study	20,084 subjects (1,449 migraine sufferers)	51(3.5): 699(3.7)	1.1 (0.8 to 1.5)*	NS	NS	Age, hypertension, diabetes, smoking, exercise, body mass index, alcohol, cholesterol, parental hystory of MI before age 60 yrs, randomized treatment assignments	* calculated as Hazard Ratio (95%CI) for ischemic stroke

CI, confidence interval; HDL, high-density lipoprotein; MA, migraine with aura; MI, myocardial infarction; MO, migraine without aura; NS, not specified; NSAID, nonsteroidal anti-inflammatory drug; RR, relative risk; TIA, transient ischemic attack.

TABLE 18.2

Summary of the Relative Risk (95% confidence interval) between Migraine and Ischemic Stroke in Three Meta-analyses of Observational Studies

	Etminan et al [9]	Schurks et al [10]	Spector et al [11]
Overall Migraine	2.16 (1.89 – 2.48)	1.73 (1.31 to 2.29)	2.04 (1.72 – 2.43)
Migraine with aura	2.27 (1.61 – 3.19)	2.16 (1.53 – 3.03)	2.25 (1.53 – 3.33)
Migraine without aura	1.83 (1.06 – 3.15)	1.23 (0.90 – 1.69)	1.24 (0.86 – 1.79)

prolonged neurological aura (lasting longer than 24 hours) may mimic stroke, the end results of such misclassifications would be an overestimation of the prevalence of migraine in patients and, therefore, an overestimation of the risk.

Third, in some of the studies the influence of several confounders on the final results was not considered, whereas others were not controlled for. Actually, a number of factors might influence the risk of stroke in people with migraine. For example, migraine has been associated with an increased prevalence of traditional cardiovascular risk factors in several studies,[16–18] although more recent analyses have shown consistently that the increased risk of ischemic stroke in people with MA is seen mainly in those with a favorable vascular risk profile.[15,19–21] Furthermore, the use of medications with a potential effect on stroke risk (i.e., antihypertensive agents) or the presence of risk factors for both migraine and stroke, such as antiphospholipid antibodies, could also be factors affecting the observed association of migraine with stroke.

Fourth, most studies are limited to younger individuals (age 45 years or younger), leaving the association between migraine and stroke among the elderly unclear and ignoring the fact that migraine may start later in life. In these regards, although the available data provide arguments to support the assumption that migraine may have some influence on stroke risk even in older subgroups, effect modification by age appears evident from prospective studies, the risk of stroke in persons with migraine being greater in younger age groups and decreasing over time, with only a modest increase of risk among the elderly (age 60 years or older). Whether this is the consequence of the greater effect of other major risk factors for ischemic stroke with increasing age or of the influence of these factors on the mechanisms by which migraine may lead to stroke remains to be determined.

The association between migraine and increased prevalence of cardiovascular risk factors, and the observation that the vascular dysfunction of migraine may also extend to coronary arteries,[22–24] has led recently to speculation that migraine, especially MA, may not only be associated with increased risk of stroke, but also with other vascular events. To address this specific issue, data from two large-scale prospective cohorts of apparently healthy subjects, one including women age 45 years or older participating in the Women's Health Study (WHS), and the other including men age 40 to 84 years participating in the Physicians' Health Study, were analyzed recently. Data from the 27,840 women included in the WHS indicated an association between overall migraine and major ischemic cardiovascular disease after a mean of 10 years of follow-up. Such an increased risk for any ischemic vascular event was only apparent for women with MA, and turned out to be approximately twofold greater compared with that observed in women who did not report any history of migraine, after adjusting for traditional cardiovascular risk factors. In contrast, no increased risk for any ischemic vascular event was observed in women who reported MO.[23] With regard to men, data from the 20,084 male physicians included in the Physicians' Health Study indicated an association between overall migraine and major cardiovascular disease. Compared with nonmigraineurs, men who reported migraine had an increased risk for major cardiovascular disease, including ischemic stroke, myocardial infarction, coronary revascularization, angina, and ischemic cardiovascular death. Men who were younger than 55 years of age had increased risk of stroke that was not apparent in the older age group,[25] thus confirming the age-dependent effect of migraine on disease risk. At least theoretically, it cannot be excluded that the relation between migraine and stroke might be just one aspect of a more generalized effect of chronic, nonspecific headache. Actually, the evaluation of cross-sectional data from the first U.S. National Health and Nutrition Examination Survey showed a 1.5-fold increased risk of stroke in both patients with migraine and patients with severe nonspecific headache compared with subjects without these conditions.[26] More recently, in a prospective cohort study derived from the FINRISK study, Jousilahti et al.[27] found a significant association between chronic nonspecific headache and stroke among men. However, because of the diagnostic criteria adopted in the National Health and Nutrition Examination Survey, it is likely that most cases of severe nonspecific headache actually experienced migraine. Similarly, the lack of a precise definition of migraine represents a major limitation for a correct interpretation of the data proposed by Jousilahti et al.[27] These drawbacks, in association with recent data from large, prospective cohorts that show no association between nonmigraine headache and stroke, make the hypothesis of a major effect of any nonspecific headache on the risk of cerebral ischemia very unlikely.

Classification of Migraine-Related Stroke

One of the most relevant drawbacks in unraveling the complex relation between migraine and cerebral ischemia is the lack of consistency in the definition of migraine-related stroke. In the attempt to categorize this entity, four major situations might be considered.[28] First, cerebral ischemia can occur in the course of an attack of MA, causing true migraine-induced infarction. Second, migraine and stroke share a common underlying disorder that increases the risk of both diseases. Third, migraine might cause stroke because of the interactions with other risk factors involved in stroke pathogenesis. Fourth, stroke may mimic migraine.

MIGRAINE-INDUCED STROKE: THE MIGRAINOUS INFARCTION

It has long been recognized that, although a rare event, stroke may occur during the course of a migraine attack with aura. This phenomenon suggests a causal relationship between migraine and stroke. According to the IHS migraine classification, "migrainous infarction" is defined as a stroke occurring during a typical attack of MA.[3] Patients have a history of MA and the neurological deficits occur in the same vascular distribution as the aura, and are associated with an ischemic brain lesion in a suitable territory demonstrated by neuroimaging. A major criterion of this cause of infarction is that other possible causes are excluded by appropriate investigations. However, which investigations should be done and when are not clear, and the absence of causes other than migraine does not necessarily imply that migraine is the cause, given that about half of the ischemic strokes in young adults have no detectable cause. Furthermore, stroke has been reported in people experiencing MO, and in two large series this was more common than infarcts during attacks of MA.[29,30] Criteria for true migraine-induced stroke should include potentially modifying risk factors that might be present and that are critical to understanding the mechanisms. Last, the definition of migrainous stroke, with the stipulation that the current MA attack is typical of previous attacks, is also biased toward infarcts in the posterior cerebral artery territory, because most auras are visual in nature. According to large series, the incidence of migrainous infarction varies between 0.5% to 1.5% of all ischemic strokes, and between 10% to 14% of ischemic strokes in young patients.[26,30–33] The incidence of migraine-related infarction (per 100,000 persons per year) was estimated at 1.44 (95% CI, 0–3.07) from the Oxfordshire Community Stroke Project prospective registry, and at 1.7 from a retrospective review of Mayo Clinic records from nearly 5000 migraineurs younger than 50 years.[34,35] In series published since the introduction of the IHS criteria, the percentage of stroke in persons younger than 45 years attributed to migrainous infarction ranges from 1.2% to 14%.[31,32,36,37] Clinical features that were described to be associated with migrainous stroke include female sex, mean age in the low to mid 30s, a history of cigarette smoking, and ischemic involvement of the posterior cerebral artery territory.[31] In summary, IHS criteria might be too strict for a correct diagnosis of migrainous infarction. Despite the limitations inherent in the diagnostic criteria and the consequent weakness of the epidemiological studies, it seems reasonable to assume that migrainous infarction does not account for all strokes occurring during migraine attacks, and, overall, it is responsible for only a minority of migraine-related infarcts.

MIGRAINE AND STROKE SHARE A COMMON CAUSE (SYMPTOMATIC MIGRAINE)

Ischemic stroke and migraine are major clinical features of some specific syndromes, such as cerebral autosomal dominant arteriopathy with subcortical infarcts and leukoencephalopathy (CADASIL); mitochondrial myopathy, encephalopathy, lactic acidosis, and strokelike episodes (MELAS), and retinal vasculopathy with cerebral leukodystrophy (RVCL). The coexistence of ischemic stroke and migraine in the context of a syndrome characterized by a peculiar phenotype, proven inherited background, and chronic alterations of the wall of small cerebral arteries suggests a common pathogenic mechanism shared by these two conditions.

CADASIL is an autosomal dominant disease of vascular and smooth muscle cells due to Notch3 mutations,[38] characterized by leukoencephalopathy; small, deep infarcts; and subcortical dementia. MA is usually the first manifestation, presenting about 15 years before stroke and before the appearance of magnetic resonance imaging (MRI) signal abnormalities. MA is present in one third of symptomatic subjects and its frequency can vary greatly within the affected pedigrees. In 40% of families, more than 60% of symptomatic subjects had a history of MA,[39,40] and within some families, MA is the most important clinical aspect of the phenotype. The frequency of attacks of basilar migraine, hemiplegic migraine, migraine with prolonged aura, or isolated aura, according to the IHS diagnostic criteria, is noticeably high.[40,41] The mechanism underlying MA in CADASIL is not clear. Because it occurs before ischemic manifestations, MA is not the consequence of subcortical infarcts. In CADASIL, the absence of difference in the frequency and distribution of white matter abnormalities between patients with and without MA suggests that chronic subcortical hypoperfusion is also unlikely. Another hypothesis is that MA relates directly to dysfunction of smooth muscle cells of meningeal and cortical vessels, triggering cortical-spreading depression (CSD).[42] Furthermore, if the cell signaling abnormalities (resulting from the mutation) extend and reach neurons, the resulting hyperexcitable membrane instability could predispose to CSD.

Retinal vasculopathy with cerebral leukodystrophy is a rare inherited condition characterized by a primary microangiopathy of the brain in combination with vascular retinopathy. Migraine is a clinical finding in some cases, also including progressive visual loss, seizures, focal neurological deficits of sudden onset, cognitive worsening, renal insufficiency, and proteinuria.

Mitochondrial myopathy, encephalopathy, lactic acidosis, and strokelike episodes is associated to several mutations in mitochondrial DNA. The phenotypic expression is highly variable, ranging from an asymptomatic state to severe childhood multisystem disease with lactic acidosis. Recurrent episodes of headache (mostly migraine) are part of the clinical spectrum.

Migraine is also part of the clinical spectrum of other mitochondrial disorders, such as Leber's hereditary optic neuropathy and myoclonic epilepsy with ragged-red fibers,[43,44] and of hereditary hemorrhagic telangiectasia (Osler-Weber-Rendu disease), an autosomal dominant vascular dysplasia characterized by a high prevalence of vascular malformations in various organs, including lung, liver, kidney, and brain, as well as by mucocutaneous teleangiectasias.[45]

MA is related classically to cerebral arteriovenous malformations (AVMs). In most cases, MA ceasing after removal of an AVM has been documented, consistent with the definition of symptomatic migraine, but there are also sparse reports of cases unchanged after surgery.[46] The possibility of a causal relation is supported indirectly by the side of aura, contralateral to the AVMs, and the side of headache, ipsilateral to the AVMs, as well as by the coexistence of MA and arteriovenous shunts in leptomeningeal angiomatosis (Sturge-Weber syndrome).[47] Besides these conditions, a number of other local or systemic vascular and blood disorders are associated with both MA and stroke, such as Moyamoya disease,[48] antiphospholipid antibody syndrome,[49] Sneddon syndrome,[50] systemic lupus erythematosus,[51] cardiac myxoma,[52] and other rare diseases[53–55] (Table 18.3).

However, as opposed to CADASIL, MA is often infrequent and sometimes probably coincidental in these disorders, and the mechanism by which they increase brain susceptibility to aura remains to be elucidated.

MIGRAINE MIMIC: MIGRAINE AS A CONSEQUENCE OF ISCHEMIC STROKE

Stroke resulting from acute structural disease is accompanied by headache and neurological signs and symptoms indistinguishable from those of migraine. This entity might be termed a *migraine*

TABLE 18.3

Disorders Associated with Stroke and with Migraine with Aura

Disorders with brain vessel wall abnormalities
CADASIL (NOTCH3 mutations)
Brain arteriovenous malformations98
Leptomeningeal angiomatosis (Sturge-Weber syndrome)
Moyamoya syndrome
Hereditary haemorrhagic telangiectasia (Osler-Weber-Rendu disease)
Sneddon syndrome
Mitochondrial disorders (i.e, MEALS)
Disorders related to COL4A1/COL4A2 mutations
Retinal vasculopathy with cerebral leukodystrophy (RVCL)
Cardiac disorders
Patent foramen ovale
Cardiac myxoma
Blood disorders
Antiphospholipid antibody syndrome
Systemic lupus erythematosus
Essential thrombocythaemia
Polycythaemia

mimic. These symptomatic migraine attacks might be more common than migraine-induced ischemic insults.[56] Cerebral infarction can thus present with migraine attacks at onset, which should not be confused with migrainous infarction. The reported frequency of stroke-related headache ranges from 7% to 65%.[57,58] A stronger association was observed among younger female individuals whose ischemic event was located in the vertebrobasilar territory, and with a personal history of migraine. Unfortunately, no precise data are available on the specific frequency of migraine cases caused by cerebral infarction.

COEXISTING ISCHEMIC STROKE AND MIGRAINE

Because of the high frequency of migraine in young adults, the possibility that this condition can coexist with ischemic stroke without contributing to stroke occurrence cannot be ruled out, despite the apparent increased risk of stroke in migraineurs. Because the etiology of these strokes is probably multifactorial, identification and management of other established risk factors should be pursued with particular vigilance in all patients with migraine.

Diffuse White Matter Lesions in Migraineurs

Abnormalities of uncertain clinical significance are frequent findings on brain magnetic resonance images of patients with migraine. The most common abnormality is white matter lesions (WMLs)—typically, multiple, small punctate hyperintensities occurring in the deep or periventricular white matter and often seen on T2-weighted or fluid-attenuated inversion recovery images. Not infrequently, these WMLs may cause uncertainty for physicians and anxiety for patients, and can lead to a variety of diagnostic tests and treatments.[59] In a small minority of cases, the number, distribution, and location of WMLs may lead to the diagnosis of an underlying disease of which migraine may be but one symptomatic manifestation (Table 18.4).

Clinical history, presence or absence of cardiovascular risk factors, family history, physical examination, and specific neuroimaging features assist clinicians in narrowing the differential diagnosis in these cases, whereas, in select circumstances, specific biochemical and genetic testing, and further neuroimaging are necessary. WMLs are common in the general population, occurring in approximately 10% of individuals in the fourth decade of life and up to 80% of individuals in the eighth decade.[60] Several reports suggest that the prevalence and the number of WMLs on brain MRI increase with advancing age, vascular risk factors (diabetes, smoking, hypercholesterolemia, hypertension), cardiovascular disease, stroke, and dementia.[61,62] The prevalence of WMLs in migraine ranges from 6% to 40%.[60,63] Suggested variables that might influence this association are the quality of MRI equipment and the sequences used, patient age, migraine type and frequency, and the presence or absence of vascular risk factors. Results of a recent meta-analysis showed a fourfold increased prevalence of WMLs on MRI in patients with migraine in contrast to nonmigraineur age- and sex-matched control subjects. The risk of WMLs in migraineurs appears to be independent of age and vascular risk factors.[64] The results of the Cerebral Abnormalities in Migraine, an Epidemiological Risk Analysis study support the observation that some migraineurs are at increased risk for subclinical infarctlike brain lesions. This cross-sectional prevalence study evaluated a population-based sample of Dutch adults age 30 to 60 years. Randomly selected patients with MA or MO, and age- and sex-matched control subjects underwent brain MRI. Overall, there was no significant difference between patients with migraine and control subjects in prevalence of infarctlike lesions (8.1% vs. 5.0%). However, patients with migraine had a greater prevalence of such lesions in the cerebellum

TABLE 18.4

Differential Diagnosis of Multifocal White Matter Lesions

Hypoxic/ischemic
Acquired
Small vessel ischemic disease (hypertension, diabetes)
Embolic: cardiac, atheromatous
Unknown mechanism: Alzheimer disease, migraine
Hereditary
Cerebral autosomal dominant arteriopathy with subcortical in farcts (CADASIL)
Mitochondrial encephalaopathy with lactic acidosis and stroke (MELAS)
Fabry's disease
Cerebrotendineous xanthomatosis
Familial hyperlipidemia
Phenylketonuria
Adrenoleukodystrophy
Inflammatory
Multiple sclerosis and variants
Primary CNS vasculitis
Secondary CNS vasculitis (lupus, antiphospholipid antibody syndrome, Sjogren syndrome, Bechet syndrome)
Sarcoidosis
Susac's syndrome
Infectious/post-infectious
Viral: HIV, progressive multifocal leucoencephal omyelopathy (PML)
Spirochetal: Lyme disease, syphilis
Acute demyelinating encephalmyelopathy (ADEM), subacute sclerosing postinfectious encephalitis (SSPE)
Granulomatous (tubercolosis)
Fungal (coccidiomycosis)
Toxic/metabolic
Central pontine myelinolysis
Carbon monoxide intoxication
Radiation-induced
Inhaled solvents, heroin
Vitamin B12 deficiency
Neoplastic
Primary central nervous system malignancy
Metastatic disease
Lymphoma
Other
Prominent Virchow-Robin spaces

than control subjects (5.4% vs. 0.7%, $p = .02$; adjusted OR, 7.1; 95% CI, 0.9–55.0). The adjusted OR was greater for individuals with MA and migraine attack frequency of one or more per month (OR, 15.8; 95% CI, 1.8–140). The study found no association between severity of periventricular WMLs and migraine, regardless of sex, migraine frequency, or migraine subtype. An increased risk for deep WML load was observed in women (OR, 2.1; 95% CI, 1.0–4.1) and in subjects with an attack frequency of one or more per month. Conversely, the prevalence of deep WMLs in male migraineurs did not differ from control subjects.[65] Overall, the study showed that patients with MA have a 12-fold increased risk of cerebellar infarctlike lesions, and that female migraineurs had more supratentorial deep WMLs than nonmigraineurs. The risk of lesions increased with attack frequency, independent of cardiovascular risk factors. Further analyses of the infarctlike lesions observed in the Cerebral Abnormalities in Migraine, an Epidemiological Risk Analysis study were performed subsequently in which topographic details of these parenchymal defects were characterized systematically to define their pathophysiology more completely.[66,67] In line with these findings, a study from Iceland found that women with migraine in mid life had an increased risk of infarctlike lesions in the cerebellum in late life.[68] In contrast, a recent population-based study of individuals age 65 years and older from France showed an association between MA and infarct lesions located mainly outside the cerebellum and the brainstem.[69]

Overall, the combination of vascular distribution, deep border zone location, shape, size, and imaging characteristics on MRI makes it likely that these lesions are, indeed, brain infarcts. However, because there are no postmortem studies identifying the pathology of these MRI findings, their etiology is unknown. Interestingly, patients with migraine who developed what appeared to be cerebellar infarcts on MRI, but whose lesions vanished on repeat imaging, have been reported,[70] thus questioning the hypothesis of an ischemic origin of these lesions.

Is Migraine a Progressive Disorder?

The evidence of WMLs in migraineurs opens the issue of whether migraine may be a *progressive* disorder in some way, rather than simply an episodic disorder. The natural history of migraine is to decrease in severity and to abate and disappear in later life, suggesting a nonprogressive course. However, in a population sample, Scher et al.[71] showed that, throughout the course of 1 year, 3% of individuals with episodic headache (headache frequency, 2–104 days per year) progressed to chronic daily headache (attack frequency, >80 days per year). This population-based result is compatible with findings from a case–control study and numerous clinic-based observation studies.[72] Imaging findings suggesting progressive brain changes in migraine are particularly interesting in light of these epidemiological results. However, these data should be interpreted cautiously because numerous factors, other than the presumed progressive course of the disease, may contribute to "chronification" of episodic migraine. Among them, one of the most common modifiable factors for transformation, occurring in approximately one third of patients developing chronic daily headache, is analgesic overuse. The evidence that chronic daily headache may revert spontaneously to episodic in some cases is a further argument against the hypothesis of migraine as a progressive disorder.[72] Last, because the migraine–stroke relation seems to be subtype specific, the influence being prominent for MA and negligible for MO, one might speculate that migraine is a progressive disorder only in a specific subgroup of subjects. Therefore, whether migraine causes permanent, progressive brain lesions is not established definitively and there are no data for whether lesions in the brain produce chronic migraine. To complicate this issue further, a recent population-based study in women suggested that MA also increases the risk of hemorrhagic stroke (RR, 2.25; 95% CI, 1.11–4.54),[73] supporting the initial evidence from two case–control studies.[74,75] Contrasted with ischemic stroke, this association seems to be more apparent in the elderly.

How Can Migraine Lead to Ischemic Stroke?

Although the relationship between migraine and stroke remains one of the most perplexing problems for neurologists, a pathogenic relation between these two entities is plausible biologically. So far, no fully convincing evidence has been produced to explain the exact mechanism of the increased risk of stroke in migraine. Numerous hypotheses have been raised, including vasospasm, endothelial dysfunction, congenital thrombophilia, platelet hyperaggregability, and association with cardiac abnormalities, among others.

A first hypothesis is that stroke can occur during the course of MAs. Migraine is considered to be a neurovascular disorder in which arterial constriction and decreased blood flow to the posterior circulation are consequences of a spreading wave of neuronal depression in the cerebral cortex. In this regard, CSD may induce short-lived increases in cerebral blood flow and tissue hyperoxia,[76] followed by a more profound oligemia and consequent increased intraparenchymal vascular resistance.[77] Thus, low flow in major intracerebral vessels may be the result of increased downstream resistance, not major intracranial arterial vasospasm. Essentially, a low cerebral blood flow and neuronally mediated vasodilatation could cause sluggish flow in large intracerebral vessels during the aura of migraine. Spreading oligemia persists for 1 to 2 hours and corresponds to a 20% to 30% reduction in cerebral blood flow, well above the ischemic threshold. CSD can be evoked easily in animals by many acute triggers, such as electrical or mechanical stimulation, hypoxia, ischemia, emboli without ischemia, local changes in ion concentration, and various substances including air bubbles, cholesterol crystals, or endothelin.[78–81] Similarly, in human beings, the aura can be triggered acutely by focal ischemia[82]; small, cortical subarachnoid hemorrhages[83]; cerebral venous thrombosis[84]; focal hypoperfusion without ischemia[85]; and emboli or substances reaching the brain in patients with right-to-left shunts, such as a patent foramen ovale (PFO)[86]; and during the Valsalva maneuver,[86] diving,[87] or sclerosing treatment of varicose veins in the legs.[88] When oligemia is combined with factors predisposing to coagulopathy, such as dehydration, hyperviscosity, or intravascular thrombosis, migraine-induced cerebral infarction could occur, although rarely. Neurogenically mediated inflammatory responses accompanying vasodilation of extraparenchymal vessels caused by release of vasoactive peptides, nitric oxide, activation of cytokines, and upregulation of adhesion molecules also predispose to intravascular thrombosis.[89] This could explain why migraine-induced stroke usually respects intracranial arterial territories whereas aura involves more widespread brain regions. In addition, frequent aura, if a result of CSD, could induce cytotoxic cell damage and gliosis based on glutamate release or excess intracellular calcium accumulation.[90] Thus, a persistent neurological deficit could be the result of selective neuronal necrosis. Last, vasospasm, the result of the release of vasoconstrictive molecules (including endothelin and serotonin) once thought to be the mechanism of migraine aura, has been implicated in migrainous infarction, although documented cases are rare.

Experimental data also point toward activation of the thrombotic cascade during the course of a migraine attack. In fact, platelets and mast cells have been shown to release platelet-activating factor, a potent inducer of platelet activation and aggregation also involved in the release of von Willebrand factor, and are involved indirectly in the activation of the platelet IIb/IIIa receptor, crucial for binding fibrinogen, thus leading to primary hemostasis.[91] Increased plasma levels of these molecules have been observed during the course of migraine attacks compared with those in the interictal phases. Despite their biological validity, these mechanisms hold only for the so-called *migrainous stroke*, which—as defined by IHS criteria—is a rare event and cannot explain the increased risk of stroke in migraine. Furthermore, ischemic strokes occur mostly between migraine attacks.[92,93]

A second hypothesis is that the migraine–ischemic stroke pathway is modulated by the intervention of common risk factors. In this regard, different case–control studies have observed that PFO is significantly more common in patients who experience MAs than in patients without migraine.[94,95] Similarly, in patients with ischemic stroke, MA is twice as prevalent in patients with PFO than in those without.[96,97] Several observational studies, from both single- and multi-center experiences, suggest that PFO closure could reduce the frequency of migraine attacks. In particular, among migraineurs, this might be proposed for those patients in the MA subgroup and might reduce indirectly the risk of stroke, despite the small stroke-predisposing effect of PFO and some recent findings indicating no stronger association between MA and ischemic stroke among women with PFO compared with women without.[15] However, these reports present some limitations, including retrospective design, which implicates recall bias; absence of a control group; placebo effect, which can result in up to a 70% reduction of attack frequency[98,99]; administration of aspirin after PFO closure; and its potential prophylactic effect.[100] Paradoxical embolism is suggested to be the causal link between migraine and PFO, but insufficient data are available to substantiate the hypothesis that migraine frequency (and, indirectly, ischemic stroke risk) is reduced by PFO closure. The only way to address this issue is by randomization. Currently, only one prospective, randomized, double-blind trial on the therapeutic effect of PFO device closure in MA patients compared with sham has been conducted—the Migraine Intervention with STARFlex Technology (MIST) trial. In the MIST trial, 73 patients underwent a sham operation and 74 patients had their PFO closed. The primary end point of the study, complete elimination of headache, was not achieved; three patients in the treatment group versus three patients in the sham group had complete resolution of migraine. In contrast, one of the preplanned secondary end points of the MIST trial showed that patients who underwent PFO closure had a 37% reduction in median total migraine headache days compared with 26% in the sham group ($p = .027$), apparently suggesting some benefits of treatment.[101] However, correction for multiple comparison was not applied, making such findings unsubstantiated.[102] A more comprehensive analysis of current data is desirable to provide information about how to identify patients who may have an improvement of their migraine, and a large number of patients with longer follow-up is necessary. Based on all these findings, the possibility of a PFO–migraine–ischemic stroke triangular association remains a matter of speculation.

Although unproved, these observations support the hypothesis that migraine might be a predisposing condition for specific pathogenic subtypes of ischemic stroke, particularly in young patients. In past years, some observations have suggested that migraine may predispose to spontaneous cervical artery dissection (sCeAD), the most common cause of stroke in young adults. In a meta-analysis of five case–control studies,[103] migraine in general was twice as common in patients with dissection as in control subjects, with a further increased risk in patients with multiple dissections. A recent case–control analysis from the Cervical Artery Dissection and Ischemic Stroke Patients study confirmed these findings, also showing that the association was stronger for migraine without aura.[104] The mechanism by which migraine may affect the risk of sCeAD is unknown. A common, generalized vascular disorder is hypothesized to be a predisposing condition for both diseases. Recent observations of increased activity of serum elastase, a metallopeptidase that degrades specific elastin-type amino acid sequences, in migraineurs suggest a possible extracellular matrix degradation,[105] which might facilitate sCeAD occurrence. Furthermore, in line with previous observations of altered common carotid artery distensibility in patients with sCeAD,[106] Lucas et al.[107] recently reported that the endothelium-dependent vasodilatation assessed in the brachial artery is impaired significantly in these subjects. Similar vascular changes have been observed in migraine patients during interictal periods[108] and have been replicated in a recent cross-sectional study in migraineurs of recent onset, thus excluding the possibility of bias resulting from a long-standing history of migraine and repeated exposure to vasoconstricting drugs.[109] Last, analysis of a small number of families has shown that the structural abnormalities related to sCeAD might be familial and follow an autosomal dominant pattern of inheritance.[110,111] This implies that genetically determined alterations of the extracellular matrix may play a crucial pathogenic role and that candidate genes involved in the regulation of endothelial and vessel wall function might increase susceptibility to both conditions.[112,113]

A third hypothesis is that a number of predisposing conditions may be operating to increase the risk of ischemic stroke in migraine, particularly in young women. Hormonal status seems to play a pathogenic role in the development of MO, but not of MA, which is associated with a greater ischemic stroke incidence.[114] Inconsistent results have also been found for the various biological or clinical markers of thrombotic risk studied so far,[115,116] such as platelet activation, factor V Leiden mutation,[116] von Willebrand factor,[117] prothrombin factor 1.2,[118] platelet leukocyte aggregation,[119] antiphospholipid antibodies,[49] and livedo reticularis.[120] In contrast, there is mounting evidence that migraine may be a risk factor for endothelial dysfunction, which may represent a link to ischemic stroke and heart disease. Endothelial dysfunction is characterized by a reduction in the bioavailability of a vasodilator (such as nitric oxide), an increase in endothelial-derived contracting factors, and consequent impairment of the reactivity of the microvasculature. It also comprises endothelial activation, characterized by a procoagulant, proinflammatory, and proliferative state, which, in turn, predisposes to ischemia. Endothelial dysfunction is mediated by increased oxidative stress, an important promoter of the inflammatory process,[121] which has been proposed in the pathogenesis of migraine. In fact, compared with migraine-free control subjects, oxidative stress markers have been found to be higher in migraineurs, even during the interictal period, thus yielding support to the association.

A fourth hypothesis is that the migraine–stroke link is caused by the effects of specific medications. Actually, drugs used in migraine, such as triptans and ergot alkaloids, have been investigated as a possible risk factor for ischemic events. Cardiovascular safety of migraine treatments has been brought forward by their vasoconstrictive action and by reported cases of stroke, myocardial infarction, and ischemic heart disease after triptan and ergotamine use.[122,123] Moreover, an increased number of white matter abnormalities[65] and increased mortality[124] have been found in patients taking ergotamine. During past years, large-scale studies have investigated the risk of ischemic events and death in patients with triptan- and ergotamine-treated migraine. Data from General Practice Research Database in the United Kingdom showed that, in general practice, triptan treatment did not increase the risk of ischemic events.[125] This finding was confirmed by a wide retrospective cohort study from a health care provider in the United States.[124] This study also investigated the rates of vascular events in relation to ergotamine use and found no association. Recently, a retrospective, nested case–control study using data from the PHARMO Record Linkage System, conducted in the Netherlands, investigated whether overuse of triptans and ergotamine is associated with an increased risk of ischemic events.[126] Results showed that overuse of triptans did not increase the risk of cerebral, cardiovascular, or peripheral ischemic events, neither in the general populations nor in those using cardiovascular drugs. In contrast, ergotamine overuse was associated with a significantly increased risk of ischemic complications (OR, 2.55; 95% CI, 1.22–5.36), especially in patients using cardiovascular drugs concomitantly (OR, 8.52; 95% CI, 2.57–28.2). Therapeutic doses of either triptans or ergotamines were not associated with an increased risk of ischemic vascular events. Overall, these findings suggest that triptan use and even triptan overuse is safe in general, whereas ergotamine overuse exposes one to an increased risk of ischemic complications, likely in relation to its greater vasoconstrictive properties.

Although none of the reported mechanisms fully explain the migraine–stroke relation, a unifying hypothesis has been put forward of a continuum between MA and cerebral infarction through hypoxic ischemic episodes that would trigger an MA attack when brief, and an infarct when prolonged, in a subset of patients who have hereditary or acquired comorbid vascular disorders that lower the CSD threshold.[81,85]

GENETIC INFLUENCE ON THE MIGRAINE–STROKE RELATION

Migraine and cerebral ischemia might be linked via genetic pathways. During past years, evidence from twin and family history studies, although not entirely consistent, have supported the notion that genetic predisposition plays a major role in the occurrence of both migraine and ischemic stroke.[127]

MONOGENIC FORMS OF MIGRAINE

Although many chromosomal regions have been reported to be possibly involved in migraine occurrence, the mutations in three genes for familial hemiplegic migraine (FHM) represent the only established monogenic cause of migraine so far. FHM is a subtype of MA characterized by an autosomal dominant pattern of inheritance and at least some degree of weakness (hemiparesis) during the aura. Despite these clinical markers, broad variability is the rule. Age at onset, frequency, duration, and features of attacks may be different from one patient to another, even among affected members from a given family who carry the same mutation in the same gene.[128,129] Less frequent features such as cerebellar ataxia, which occurs in some families, minor head trauma as triggering factor, and severe attacks with impairment of consciousness have been also reported. Furthermore, the majority of patients with FHM also experience attacks of typical MA and MO. Thus, it seems reasonable to assume that FHM represents one side of the spectrum that, at the other end, is marked by the common forms of migraine. Hence, FHM is likely a valid model to study genetic factors for migraine in general as well as the relation between migraine and ischemic stroke. To date, three different genes responsible for different subtypes of FHM have been identified. FHM1 is caused by mutations in the *CACNA1A* gene, located on chromosome 19p13, encoding the pore-forming α_{1A} subunit of $Ca_v2.1$ (P/Q type) voltage-gated neuronal calcium channels.[130] FHM2 is caused by mutations in the *ATP1A2* gene, located on chromosome 1q23,[131] encoding the α_2 subunit of sodium–potassium pump adenosine triphosphatases. FHM3 is caused by mutations in the *SCN1A* gene, located on chromosome 2q24,[132] encoding the $\alpha 1$ subunit of the neuronal voltage-gated sodium channel $Na_v1.1$ that is crucial in the generation and propagation of action potentials.

Overall, the common consequence of FHM1, FHM2, and FHM3 mutations seems to lead to increased levels of glutamate and potassium in the synaptic cleft, causing an increased propensity to CSD. Whether this might also increase the propensity to cerebral ischemia is unknown.

Similarly, the contribution of FHM genes in common forms of migraine (MO and MA) remains unclear. A recent study showed no linkage to the *CACNA1A* and *ATP1A2* genes in families with an apparently autosomal dominant mode of inheritance of MA,[133] whereas a case–control study investigating the role of the *ATP1A2* gene in MA did not find evidence for an association.[134] Transgenic mice that carry a missense mutation in the *CACNA1A* FHM gene appeared to have an increased susceptibility to ischemia, according to a recent report.[135] This supports the hypothesis that the low threshold for CSD that characterizes the brain in MA also lowers the threshold for cerebral ischemia. Despite the obvious biological interest of these observations, however, it should be noted that, in humans, cerebral infarction is extremely rare in FHM.[136,137]

POLYGENIC FORMS OF MIGRAINE

The recent diffusion of robust new technologies of gene analysis along with the possibility to use informatics resources that provide genomewide sequence and variant data have fostered an effective and challenging approach to complex diseases. Among them, genetic association studies are retained as a powerful instrument to identify small RRs. Based on the results of such analyses, several specific genetic variants have been implicated in migraine susceptibility, which can be gathered into three main streams.[138] The first group includes genes involved in the neurotransmitter-related pathway, such as genes encoding for dopamine D2 receptor (DRD2), human serotonin transporter (HSERT), catechol-O-methyltransferase (COMT), and dopamine β-hydroxylase (DBH). The second group includes genes involved in vascular function, such as 5,10-methylene-tetrahydrofolate reductase (MTHFR), angiotensin I-converting enzyme (ACE) and endothelin type A (ETA) receptor. The third group includes genes involved in hormonal function, such as estrogen receptor 1 (ESR1), progesterone receptor (PGR) and androgen receptor (AR).

Several candidate genes for migraine are also good candidates for cerebral ischemia. The C677T polymorphism of the MTHFR gene and the deletion/insertion polymorphism of the ACE gene seem particularly promising because of their potential effect on ischemic stroke risk. Pooled analyses of 13 studies indicated that the MTHFR 677TT genotype is associated with a 48% increased risk for MA (pooled OR, 1.48; 95% CI, 1.02–2.13), but not MO. In contrast, pooled results from nine studies indicated that the ACE II genotype is associated with a reduced risk for MA (pooled OR, 0.71; 95% CI, 0.55–0.93) and MO (pooled OR, 0.84; 95% CI, 0.70–0.99).[139] Although linkage studies and genomewide association studies (GWASs) gave some conflicting results, likely a reflection of the genetic heterogeneity of migraine,[140,141] recent GWASs have led to the identification of multiple, novel risk variants for migraine, which could be robustly replicated.[141–144] Interestingly, the results of a GWAS conducted on subjects included in the Women's Genome Health Study (WGHS), a subpopulation of the WHS with genomewide genetic data, provided some suggestion that five single nucleotide polymorphisms (SNPs) at different loci might be implicated in the relation between migraine and stroke. Two of the SNPs suggested an association with ischemic stroke (rs7698623 in *MEPE*, rs4975709 in *IRX4*), one with major cardiovascular disease (rs2143678 close to *MDF1*) and one with death caused by cardiovascular disease (rs1406961, intergenic) among women with MA. In addition, rs10479641 in *BACE1* appeared to be associated with death caused by cardiovascular disease among women with any migraine. It should be noted, however, that none of the 339,596 SNPs analyzed are associated with cerebrovascular disease events among migraineurs at the genomewide level.[113]

Practical Implications

The identification of susceptibility factors linking migraine to ischemic stroke is still in its early stages and, thus, in the short term, it will be impossible to stratify migraineurs and identify those at greatest risk of stroke occurrence. Currently, available data support the following recommendations:

1. An emphasis on identifying and treating modifiable vascular risk factors, such as smoking, hypertension, diabetes, and hypercholesterolemia, is warranted in migraineurs, especially those with MA.
2. Because of the potential synergistic effect of several migraine-specific drugs with vasoconstrictive action, including triptans, and traditional predisposing conditions in increasing the risk of ischemic stroke, subjects with major cardiovascular risk factors should be encouraged to adopt migraine prophylactic strategies. This approach should also be recommended to those subjects with a personal history of prior ischemic (cerebral and/or myocardial) disease. Drugs that can decrease the risk of stroke (i.e., antihypertensives) are valid pharmacological options in these cases, whereas nonsteroidal anti-inflammatory drugs or combination analgesics should be considered an alternative acute treatment approach. Triptans are also contraindicated in patients with hemiplegic and basilar migraine.
3. Estrogen-containing oral contraceptives should not be prescribed to women with MA, particularly when they have major vascular risk factors or are 35 years old or older.
4. There is no direct evidence that PFO closure is effective for MA prophylaxis and, indirectly, for primary prevention of stroke. As a consequence, this procedure cannot be recommended for MA prophylaxis. Positive results from small observational studies need to be confirmed in the setting of a randomized, unbiased, placebo-controlled study with adequate power. Whether antiplatelet agents might be an effective preventive measure in these subjects remains to be determined.
5. Patients with migrainous stroke should undergo the same diagnostic workup and receive the same pharmacological treatment of any ischemic stroke in the young, both during the acute phase and at follow-up.

6. The possibility that migraine may be conceptualized not just as an episodic disorder but as a chronic–episodic and sometimes chronic–progressive disorder currently remains an attractive hypothesis. If proved, this shift in conceptualization would implicate that the goals of treatment may also shift. Preventing disease progression in migraine has already been added to the traditional goals of relieving pain and restoring patients' ability to function.[145] If the brain lesions of migraineurs have a significant clinical correlate, preventing the accumulation of brain lesions may become an additional goal of treatment. The association of stroke with frequency of migraine attacks suggests that migraine, especially MA, prophylaxis may actually reduce migraine-related stroke risk, and opens the issue of whether prophylactic drugs that decrease such a risk (i.e., antihypertensives) might be the best option in these cases. Currently, data are too limited to recommend the use of antiplatelet drugs to reduce the risk of stroke in migraineurs. Emerging treatment strategies to prevent disease progression, including risk factor modification, preventive therapies, and the early use of acute treatments, will be an important focus for future investigations.[142]

Conclusions

Strong arguments support the hypothesis that the relationship between stroke and migraine is more than coincidental. The link between MA and cerebral ischemia, indicated by epidemiological observations, appears to be stronger among the young, but may persist in the elderly. In contrast, the evidence is very weak for MO. Although recent findings suggest the hypothesis of migraine as a progressive brain disorder, data are still too scarce to draw any conclusion. Identifying the population with migraine at greatest risk of stroke should be the first step toward risk reduction and the goal of future research. Currently, from the available data, the overall absolute risk of stroke among young patients with migraine seems to be fairly low.

REFERENCES

1. Haut SR, Bigal ME, Lipton RB. Chronic disorders with episodic manifestations: focus on epilepsy and migraine. *Lancet Neurol.* 2006;5:148–157.
2. Silberstein SD. Migraine. *Lancet.* 2004;363:381–391.
3. Headache Classification Committee of the International Headache Society. The international classification of headache disorders, 2nd ed. *Cephalalgia.* 2004;24:1–160.
4. Lipton RB, Stewart WF, Diamond S, Diamond ML, Reed M. Prevalence and burden of migraine in the United States: data from the American Migraine Study II. *Headache.* 2001;41:646–657.
5. Launer LJ, Terwindt GM, Ferrari MD. The prevalence and characteristics of migraine in a population-based cohort: the GEM study. *Neurology.* 1999;53:537–542.
6. Lipton RB, Silberstein SD. Why study the comorbidity of migraine? *Neurology.* 1994;44(Suppl 7):S4–S5.
7. Fere C. Note sur un cas de migraine ophtalmique a acces repetes suivis de mort. *Rev Med (Paris).* 1883;3:194–201.
8. Collaborative Group of the Study of Stroke in Young Women. Oral contraceptives and stroke in young women. *JAMA.* 1975;231:718–722.
9. Etminan M, Takkouche B, Isorna FC, Samii A. Risk of ischaemic stroke in people with migraine: systematic review and meta-analysis of observational studies. *BMJ.* 2005;330:63.

10. Schurks M, Rist PM, Bigal ME, Buring JE, Lipton RB, Kurth T. Migraine and cardiovascular disease: systematic review and meta-analysis. *BMJ*. 2009;339:b3914.
11. Spector JT, Kahn SR, Jones MR, Jayakumar M, Dalal D, Nazarian S. Migraine headache and ischemic stroke risk: an updated meta-analysis. *Am J Med*. 2010;123:612–624.
12. Stang PE, Carson AP, Rose KM, et al. Headache, cerebrovascular symptoms, and stroke: the Atherosclerosis Risk in Communities Study. *Neurology*. 2005;64:1573–1577.
13. Donaghy M, Chang CL, Poulter N. Duration, frequency, recency, and type of migraine and the risk of ischaemic stroke in women of childbearing age. *J Neurol Neurosurg Psychiatry*. 2002;73:747–750.
14. Kurth T, Schurks M, Logroscino G, Buring JE. Migraine frequency and risk of cardiovascular disease in women. *Neurology*. 2009;73:581–588.
15. MacClellan LR, Giles W, Cole J, et al. Probable migraine with visual aura and risk of ischemic stroke: the Stroke Prevention in Young Women Study. *Stroke*. 2007;38:2438–2445.
16. Scher AI, Terwindt GM, Picavet HS, Verschuren WM, Ferrari MD, Launer LJ. Cardiovascular risk factors and migraine: the GEM population-based study. *Neurology*. 2005;64:614–620.
17. Bigal ME, Kurth T, Hu H, Santanello N, Lipton RB. Migraine and cardiovascular disease: possible mechanisms of interaction. *Neurology*. 2009;72:1864–1871.
18. Rist PM, Tzourio C, Kurth T. Associations between lipid levels and migraine: cross-sectional analysis in the Epidemiology of Vascular Ageing Study. *Cephalalgia*. 2011;31:1459–1465.
19. Henrich JB, Horwitz RI. A controlled study of ischemic stroke risk in migraine patients. *J Clin Epidemiol*. 1989;42:773–780.
20. Kurth T, Schurks M, Logroscino G, Gaziano JM, Buring JE. Migraine, vascular risk, and cardiovascular events in women: prospective cohort study. *BMJ*. 2008;337:a636.
21. Pezzini A, Grassi M, Lodigiani C, et al. Predictors of migraine subtypes in young adults with ischemic stroke: the Italian Project on Stroke in Young Adults. *Stroke*. 2010;42:17–21.
22. Uyarel H, Erden I, Cam N. Acute migraine attack, angina-like chest pain with documented ST-segment elevation and slow coronary flow. *Acta Cardiol*. 2005;60:221–223.
23. Kurth T, Gaziano JM, Cook NR, Logroscino G, Diener HC, Buring JE. Migraine and risk of cardiovascular disease in women. *JAMA*. 2006;296:283–291.
24. Bigal ME, Kurth T, Santanello N, et al. Migraine and cardiovascular disease: a population-based study. *Neurology*. 2010;74:628–635.
25. Kurth T, Gaziano JM, Cook NR, et al. Migraine and risk of cardiovascular disease in men. *Arch Intern Med*. 2007;167:795–801.
26. Merikangas KR, Fenton BT, Cheng SH, Stolar MJ, Rish N. Association between migraine and stroke in a large-scale epidemiological study of the United States. *Arch Neurol*. 1997;54:362–368.
27. Jousilahti P, Tuomilehto J, Rastenyte D, Vartiainen E. Headache and the risk of stroke: a prospective observational cohort study among 35,056 Finnish men and women. *Arch Intern Med*. 2003;163:1058–1062.
28. Welch KMA. Stroke and migraine: the spectrum of cause and effect. *Funct Neurol*. 2003;18:121–126.
29. Migraine and stroke: a review of the cerebral blood flow [general discussion]. *Cephalalgia*. 1998;18:22–25.
30. Linetsky E, Leker RR, Ben-Hur T. Headache characteristics in patients after migrainous stroke. *Neurology*. 2001;57:130–132.
31. Arboix A, Massons J, Garcia-Eroles L, Oliveres M, Balcells M, Targa C. Migrainous cerebral infarction in the Sagrat Cor Hospital of Barcelona Stroke Registry. *Cephalalgia*. 2003;23:389–394.
32. Kittner SJ, Stern BJ, Wozniak M, et al. Cerebral infarction in young adults: the Baltimore–Washington Cooperative Young Stroke Study. *Neurology*. 1998;50:890–894.
33. Sochurkova D, Moreau T, Lemesle M, Menassa M, Giroud M, Dumas R. Migraine history and migraine-induced stroke in the Dijon Stroke Registry. *Neuroepidemiology*. 1999;18:85–91.

34. Henrich JB, Sandercock PAG, Warlow CP, Jones LN. Stroke and migraine in the Oxfordshire Community Stroke Project. *J Neurol.* 1986;23:257–262.
35. Broderick JP, Swanson JW. Migraine-related stroke: clinical profile and prognosis in 20 patients. *Arch Neurol.* 1987;44:868–871.
36. Sacquegna T, Andreoli A, Baldrati A, et al. Ischemic stroke in young adults: the relevance of migrainous infarction. *Cephalalgia.* 1989;9:255–258.
37. Kristensen B, Malm J, Carlberg B, et al. Epidemiology and etiology of ischemic stroke in young adults aged 18 to 44 years in northern Sweden. *Stroke.* 1997;28:1702–1709.
38. Joutel A, Corpechot C, Ducros A, et al. Notch 3 mutations in CADASIL, a hereditary adult-onset condition causing stroke and dementia. *Nature.* 1996;383:707–710.
39. Chabriat H, Vahedi K, Iba-Zizen MT, et al. Clinical spectrum of CADASIL: a study of 7 families. *Lancet.* 1995;346:934–939.
40. Verin M, Rolland Y, Landgraf F, et al. New phenotype of the cerebral autosomal dominant arteriopathy mapped to chromosome 19: migraine as the prominent clinical feature. *J Neurol Neurosurg Psychiatry.* 1995;59:579–585.
41. Chabriat H, Tournier-Lasserve E, Vahedi K, et al. Autosomal dominant migraine with MRI white-matter abnormalities mapping to the CADASIL locus. *Neurology.* 1995;45:1086–1091.
42. Vahedi K, Chabriat H, Levy C, Joutel A, Tournier-Lasserve E, Bousser MG. Migraine with aura and brain magnetic resonance imaging in patients with CADASIL. *Arch Neurol.* 2004;61:1237–1240.
43. Ferrari MD, Haan J. The genetics of headache. In: Silberstein SD, Lipton RB, Dalessio DJ, eds. Wolff's headache and other head pain, 7th ed. New York: Oxford University Press, 2001:73–84.
44. Haan J, Terwindt GM, Ferrari MD. Genetics of migraine. *Neurol Clin.* 1997;15:43–60.
45. Guttmacher AE, Marchuk DA, White RI. Hereditary hemorrhagic telangiectasia. *N Engl J Med.* 1995;333:918–924.
46. Has DC. Arteriovenous malformations and migraine: case reports and analysis of the relationship. *Headache.* 1991;31:509–513.
47. Chabriat H, Pappata S, Traykov L, Kurtz A, Bousser MG. Angiomatose de Sturge-Weber responsible d'une hémiplégie sans infarctus cérébral en fin de grossesse. *Rev Neurol.* 1996;152:536–541.
48. Park-Matsumoto YC, Tazawa T, Shimizu J. Migraine with aura-like headache associated with Moyamoya disease. *Acta Neurol Scand.* 1999;100:119–121.
49. Krause I, Lev S, Fraser A, et al. Close association between valvar heart disease and central nervous system manifestations in the antiphospholipid syndrome. *Ann Rheum Dis.* 2005;64:1490–1493.
50. Tietjen GE, Al-Qasmi MM, Gunda P, Herial NA. Sneddon's syndrome: another migraine–stroke association? *Cephalalgia.* 2006;26:225–232.
51. Tjensvoll AB, Harboe E, Goransson LG, et al. Migraine is frequent in patients with systemic lupus erythematosus: a case–control study. *Cephalalgia.* 2011;31:401–408.
52. de Ceuster L, van Diepen T, Koehler PJ. Migraine with aura triggered by cardiac myxoma: case report and literature review. *Cephalalgia.* 2010;30:1396–1399.
53. Stam AH, Haan J, van den Maagdenberg AM, Ferrari MD, Terwindt GM. Migraine and genetic and acquired vasculopathies. *Cephalalgia.* 2009;29:1006–1017.
54. Michiels JJ, Berneman Z, Schroyens W, et al. Platelet-mediated erythromelalgic, cerebral, ocular and coronary microvascular ischemic and thrombotic manifestations in patients with essential thrombocythemia and polycythemia vera: a distinct aspirin-responsive and Coumadin-resistant arterial thrombophilia. *Platelets.* 2006;17:528–544.
55. Volonghi I, Pezzini A, Del Zotto E, et al. Role of COL4A1 in basement-membrane integrity and cerebral small-vessel disease: the COL4A1 stroke syndrome. *Curr Med Chem.* 2010;17:1317–1324.
56. Olesen J, Friberg I, Olsen TS, et al. Ischemia-induced (symptomatic) migraine attacks may be more frequent than migraine-induced ischemic insults. *Brain.* 1993;116:187–202.

57. Grau AJ, Weimer C, Buggle F, et al. Risk factors, outcome, and treatment in subtypes of ischemic stroke: the German Stroke Data Bank. *Stroke.* 2001;32:2559–2566.
58. Kolominsky-Rabas PL, Weber M, Gefeller O, Neundoerfer B, Heuschmann PU. Epidemiology of ischemic stroke subtypes according to TOAST criteria: incidence, recurrence, and long-term survival in ischemic stroke subtypes: a population-based study. *Stroke.* 2001;32:2735–2740.
59. McDonald IG, Daly J, Jelinek VM, Panetta F, Gutman JM. Opening Pandora's box: the unpredictability of reassurance by a normal test result. *BMJ.* 1996;313:329–332.
60. Fazekas F, Koch M, Schmidt R, et al. The prevalence of cerebral damage varies with migraine type: a MRI study. *Headache.* 1992;32:287–291.
61. de Groot JC, de Leeuw FE, Oudkerk M, et al. Cerebral white matter lesions and cognitive function: the Rotterdam Scan Study. *Ann Neurol.* 2000;47:145–151.
62. Vermeer SE, Prins ND, den Heijer T, et al. Silent brain infarcts and the risk of dementia and cognitive decline. *N Engl J Med.* 2003;348:1215–1222.
63. Gozke E, Ore O, Dortcan N, Unal Z, Cetinkaya M. Cranial magnetic resonance imaging findings in patients with migraine. *Headache.* 2004;44:166–169.
64. Swartz RH, Kern RZ. Migraine is associated with MRI white matter abnormalities: a meta-analysis. *Arch Neurol.* 2004;61:1366–1368.
65. Kruit MC, van Buchem MA, Hofman PA, et al. Migraine as a risk factor for subclinical brain lesions. *JAMA.* 2004;291:427–434.
66. Kruit MC, Launer LJ, Ferrari MD, van Buchem MA. Infarcts in the posterior circulation territory in migraine: the population-based MRI CAMERA study. *Brain.* 2005;128:2068–2077.
67. Kruit MC, Launer LJ, Ferrari MD, van Buchem MA. Brain stem and cerebellar hyperintense lesions in migraine. *Stroke.* 2006;37:1109–1112.
68. Scher AI, Gudmundsson LS, Sigurdsson S, et al. Migraine headache in middle age and late-life brain infarcts. *JAMA.* 2009;301:2563–2570.
69. Kurth T, Mohamed S, Maillard P, et al. Headache, migraine, and structural brain lesions and function: population based Epidemiology of Vascular Ageing-MRI study. *BMJ.* 2011;342:c7357.
70. Rozen TD. Vanishing cerebellar infarcts in a migraine patient. *Cephalalgia.* 2007;27:557–560.
71. Scher AI, Steward WF, Ricci JA, Lipton RB. Factors associated with the onset and remission of chronic daily headache in a population-based study. *Pain.* 2003;106:81–89.
72. Scher AI, Lipton RB, Steward W. Risk factors for chronic daily headache. *Curr Pain Headache Rep.* 2002,6:486–491.
73. Kurth T, Kase CS, Schurks M, Tzourio C, Buring JE. Migraine and risk of haemorrhagic stroke in women: prospective cohort study. *BMJ.* 2010;341:c3659.
74. Chang CL, Donaghy M, Poulter N. Migraine and stroke in young women: case–control study: the World Health Organisation Collaborative Study of Cardiovascular Disease and Steroid Hormone Contraception. *BMJ.* 1999;318:13–18.
75. Oral contraceptives and stroke in young women: associated risk factors. *JAMA.* 1975;231:718–722.
76. Cao Y, Welch KM, Aurora S, Vikingstad EM. Functional MRI-BOLD of visually triggered headache in patients with migraine. *Arch Neurol.* 1999;56:548–554.
77. Cutrer FM, Sorensen AG, Weisskoff RM, et al. Perfusion-weighted imaging defects during spontaneous migrainous aura. *Ann Neurol.* 1998;43:25–31.
78. Lauritzen M, Dreier JP, Fabricius M, Hartings JA, Graf R, Strong AJ. Clinical relevance of cortical spreading depression in neurological disorders: migraine, malignant stroke, subarachnoid and intracranial hemorrhage, and traumatic brain injury. *J Cereb Blood Flow Metab.* 2011;31:17–35.
79. Dreier JP. The role of spreading depression, spreading depolarization and spreading ischemia in neurological disease. *Nat Med.* 2011;17:439–447.

80. Dreier JP, Kleeberg J, Petzold G, et al. Endothelin-1 potently induces Leao's cortical spreading depression in vivo in the rat: a model for an endothelial trigger of migrainous aura? *Brain.* 2002;125:102–112.
81. Nozari A, Dilekoz E, Sukhotinsky I, et al. Microemboli may link spreading depression, migraine aura, and patent foramen ovale. *Ann Neurol.* 2010;67:221–229.
82. Olesen J, Friberg L, Olsen TS, et al. Ischaemia-induced (symptomatic) migraine attacks may be more frequent than migraine-induced ischaemic insults. *Brain.* 1993;116:187–202.
83. Izenberg A, Aviv RI, Demaerschalk BM, et al. Crescendo transient aura attacks: a transient ischemic attack mimic caused by focal subarachnoid hemorrhage. *Stroke.* 2009;40:3725–3729.
84. Newman DS, Levine SR, Curtis VL, Welch KM. Migraine-like visual phenomena associated with cerebral venous thrombosis. *Headache.* 1989;29:82–85.
85. Dalkara T, Nozari A, Moskowitz MA. Migraine aura pathophysiology: the role of blood vessels and microembolisation. *Lancet Neurol.* 2011;9:309–317.
86. Wilmshurst PT, Nightingale S, Walsh KP, Morrison WL. Effect on migraine of closure of cardiac right-to-left shunts to prevent recurrence of decompression illness or stroke or for haemodynamic reasons. *Lancet.* 2000;356:1648–1651.
87. Bousser MG. Patent foramen ovale and migraine: evidence for a link? *Headache Currents.* 2006;3:44–51.
88. Ratinahirana H, Benigni JP, Bousser MG. Injection of polidocanol foam (PF) in varicose veins as a trigger for attacks of migraine with visual aura. *Cephalalgia.* 2003;23:850–851.
89. Bolay H, Reuter U, Dunn AK, Huang Z, Boas DA, Moskowitz MA. Intrinsic brain activity triggers trigeminal meningeal afferents in migraine model. *Nat Med.* 2002;8:136–142.
90. Welch KMA, Ramadan NM. Mitochondria, magnesium and migraine. *J Neurol Sci.* 1995;134:9–14.
91. McCrary JK, Nolasco LH, Hellums JD, Kroll MH, Turner NA, Moake JL. Direct demonstration of radiolabeled von Willebrand factor binding to platelet glycoprotein Ib and IIb-IIIa in the presence of shear stress. *Ann Biomed Eng.* 1995;23:787–793.
92. Tzourio C, Iglesias S, Hubert JB, et al. Migraine and risk of ischemic stroke: a case–control study. *BMJ.* 1993;307:289–292.
93. Tzourio C, Tehindrazanarivelo A, Iglesias S, et al. Case–control study of migraine and risk of ischemic stroke in young women. *BMJ.* 1995;310:380–383.
94. Anzola GP, Magoni M, Guindani M, Rozzini L, Dalla Volta G. Potential source of cerebral embolism in migraine with aura: a transcranial Doppler study. *Neurology.* 1999;52:1622–1625.
95. Del Sette M, Angeli S, Leandri M, Ferriero GL, Finocchi C, Gandolfo C. Migraine with aura and right-to-left shunt on transcranial Doppler: a case–control study. *Cerebrovasc Dis.* 1998;8:327–330.
96. Lamy C, Giannesini C, Zuber M, et al. Clinical and imaging findings in cryptogenic stroke patients with and without patent foramen ovale: the PFO-ASA study. *Stroke.* 2002;33:706–711.
97. Sztajzel R, Genoud D, Roth S, Mermillod B, Floch-Rohr J. Patent foramen ovale, a possible cause of symptomatic migraine: a study of 74 patients with acute ischemic stroke. *Cerebrovasc Dis.* 2002;13:102–106.
98. Migraine-Nimodipine European Study Group. European multicenter trial of nimodipine in the prophylaxis of common migraine (migraine without aura). *Headache.* 1989;29:633–638.
99. Migraine-Nimodipine European Study Group. European multicenter trial of nimodipine in the prophylaxis of classic migraine (migraine with aura). *Headache.* 1989;29:639–642.
100. Diener HC, Hartung E, Chrubasik J, et al. A comparative study of acetylsalicylic acid and metoprolol for the prophylactic treatment of migraine: a randomized, controlled, double-blind, parallel group phase III study. *Cephalalgia.* 2001;21:120–128.
101. Dowson A, Mullen MJ, Peatfield R, et al. Migraine Intervention with STARFlex Technology (MIST) trial: a prospective, multicenter, double-blind, sham-controlled trial to evaluate the effectiveness of patent foramen ovale closure with STARFlex septal repair implant to resolve refractory migraine headache. *Circulation.* 2008;117:1397–1404.

102. Tepper SJ, Sheftell FD, Bigal ME. The patent foramen ovale–migraine question. *Neurol Sci.* 2007;28:S118–S123.
103. Rist PM, Diener HC, Kurth T, Schurks M. Migraine, migraine aura, and cervical artery dissection: a systematic review and meta-analysis. *Cephalalgia.* 2011;31:886–896.
104. Metso TM, Tatlisumak T, Debette S, et al. Migraine in cervical artery dissection and ischemic stroke patients. *Neurology.* 2012;78:1221–1228.
105. Tzourio C, El Amrani M, Robert L, Alperovitch A. Serum elastase activity is elevated in migraine. *Ann Neurol.* 2000;47:648–651.
106. Guillon B, Tzourio C, Biousse V, Adrai V, Bousser MG, Touboul PJ. Arterial wall properties in carotid artery dissection: an ultrasound study. *Neurology.* 2000;55:663–666.
107. Lucas C, Lecroart JL, Gautier C, et al. Impairment of endothelial function in patients with spontaneous cervical artery dissection: evidence for a general arterial wall disease. *Cerebrovasc Dis.* 2004;17:170–174.
108. de Hoon JN, Willigers JM, Troost J, Struijker-Boudier HA, Van Bortel LM. Cranial and peripheral interictal vascular changes in migraine patients. *Cephalalgia.* 2003;23:96–104.
109. Vanmolkot FH, Van Bortel LM, de Hoon JN. Altered arterial function in migraine of recent onset. *Neurology.* 2007;68:1563–1570.
110. Grond-Ginsbach C, Klima B, Weber R, et al. Exclusion mapping of the genetic predisposition for cervical artery dissection by linkage analysis. *Ann Neurol.* 2002;52:359–364.
111. Hausser I, Muller U, Engelter S, et al. Different types of connective tissue alterations associated with cervical artery dissection. *Acta Neuropathol.* 2004;107:509–514.
112. Pezzini A, Grassi M, Del Zotto E, et al. Migraine mediates the influence of the C677T MTHFR genotypes on ischemic stroke risk with a stroke-subtype effect. *Stroke.* 2007;38:3145–3151.
113. Schürks M, Buring JE, Ridker PM, Chasman DI, Kurth T. Genetic determinants of cardiovascular events among women with migraine: a genome-wide association study. *PLoS One.* 2011;6:e22106.
114. Bousser MG. Estrogens, migraine and stroke. *Stroke.* 2004;35:2652–2656.
115. Crassard, I, Conard J, Bousser MG. Migraine and haemostasis. *Cephalalgia.* 2001;21:630–636.
116. Kern RZ. Migraine-stroke: a causal relationship, but which direction? *Can J Neurol Sci.* 2004;31:451–459.
117. Soriani S, Borgna-Pignatti C, Trabetti E, Casartelli A, Montagna P, Pignatti PF. Frequency of factor V Leiden in juvenile migraine with aura. *Headache.* 1998;38:779–781.
118. Hering-Hanit R, Friedman Z, Schlesinger I, Ellis M. Evidence for activation of the coagulation system in migraine with aura. *Cephalalgia.* 2001;21:137–139.
119. Zeller JA, Frahm K, Baron R, Stingele R, Deuschl G. Platelet–leukocyte interaction and platelet activation in migraine: a link to ischemic stroke? *J Neurol Neurosurg Psychiatry.* 2004;75:984–987.
120. Tietjen GE, Al Qasmi MM, Shukairy MS. Livedo reticularis and migraine: a marker for stroke risk? *Headache.* 2002;42:352–355.
121. Bonetti PO, Lerman LO, Lerman A. Endothelial dysfunction: a marker of atherosclerotic risk. *Arterioscler Thromb Vasc Biol.* 2003;23:168–175.
122. Tfelt-Hansen P, Saxena PR, Dahlöf C, et al. Ergotamine in the acute treatment migraine: a review and European consensus. *Brain.* 2000;123:9–18.
123. Mueller L, Gallagher RM, Ciervo CA. Vasospasm-induced myocardial infarction with sumatriptan. *Headache.* 1996;97:162–164.
124. Velentgas P, Cole JA, Mo J, Sikers CR, Walker AM. Severe vascular events in migraine patients. *Headache.* 2004;44:642–651.
125. Hall GC, Brown MM, Mo J, MacRae KD. Triptans in migraine: the risk of stroke, cardiovascular disease, and death in practice. *Neurology.* 2004;62:563–568.
126. Wammes-van der Heijden EA, Rahimtoola H, Leufkens HGM, Tijssen CC, Egberts AC. Risk of ischemic complications related to the intensity of triptan and ergotamine use. *Neurology.* 2006;67:1128–1134.

127. Ferrari MD. Heritability of migraine: genetic findings. *Neurology.* 2003;60(Suppl 2):S15–S20.
128. Ducros A, Denier C, Joutel A, et al. The clinical spectrum of familial hemiplegic migraine associated with mutations in a neuronal calcium channel. *N Engl J Med.* 2001;345:17–24.
129. Terwindt GM, Ophoff RA, Haan J, et al. Variable clinical expression of mutations in the P/Q-type calcium channel gene in familial hemiplegic migraine. *Neurology.* 1998;50:1105–1110.
130. Ophoff RA, Terwindt GM, Vergouwe MN, et al. Familial hemiplegic migraine and episodic ataxia type-2 are caused by mutations in the Ca^{2+} channel gene CACNL1A4. *Cell.* 1996;87:543–552.
131. De Fusco M, Marconi R, Silvestri L, et al. Haploinsufficiency of ATP1A2 encoding Na^+/K^+ pump alpha2 subunit associated with familial hemiplegic migraine type 2. *Nat Genet.* 2003;33:192–196.
132. Dichgans M, Freilinger T, Eckstein G. Mutation in the neuronal voltage-gated sodium channel SCN1A in familial hemiplegic migraine. *Lancet.* 2005;336:371–377.
133. Kirchmann M, Thomsen LL, Olesen J. The CACNA1A and ATP1A2 genes are not involved in dominantly inherited migraine with aura. *Am J Med Genet B Neuropsychiatry Genet.* 2006;141;250–256.
134. Netzer C, Todt U, Heinze A, et al. Haplotype-based systematic association studies of ATPA1A2 in migraine with aura. *Am J Med Genet B Neuropsychiatry Genet.* 2006;141;257–260.
135. van den Maagdenberg AM, Pizzorusso T, Kaja S, et al. High cortical spreading depression susceptibility and migraine-associated symptoms in Ca(v)2.1 S218L mice. *Ann Neurol.* 2010;67:85–98.
136. Russell MB, Ducros A. Sporadic and familial hemiplegic migraine: pathophysiological mechanisms, clinical characteristics, diagnosis, and management. *Lancet Neurol.* 2011; 10:457–470.
137. Knierim E, Leisle L, Wagner C, et al. Recurrent stroke due to a novel voltage sensor mutation in Cav2.1 responds to verapamil. *Stroke.* 2011;42:e14–e17.
138. Colson NJ, Fernandez F, Lea RA, Griffiths LR. The search for migraine genes: an overview of current knowledge. *Cell Mol Life Sci.* 2007;64:331–344.
139. Schurks M, Rist PM, Kurth T. MTHFR 677 C/T and ACE D/I polymorphisms in migraine: a systematic review and metaanalysis. *Headache.* 2010;50:588–599.
140. Schürks M. Genetics of migraine in the age of genome-wide association studies. *J Headache Pain.* 2012;13:1–9.
141. Freilinger T, Anttila V, de Vries B, et al. Genome-wide association analysis identifies susceptibility loci for migraine without aura. *Nat Genet.* 2012;44:777–782.
142. Anttila V, Winsvold BS, Gormley P, et al. Genome-wide meta-analysis identifies new susceptibility loci for migraine. *Nat Genet.* 2013; 45:912–917.
143. Chasman DI, Schürks M, Anttila V, et al. Genome-wide association study reveals three susceptibility loci for common migraine in the general population. *Nat Genet.* 2011;43:695–698.
144. Anttila V, Stefansson H, Kallela M, et al. Genome-wide association study of migraine implicates a common susceptibility variant on 8q22.1. *Nat Genet.* 2010;42:869–873.
145. Loder E, Biondi D. Disease modification in migraine: a concept that has come of age? *Headache.* 2003;43:135–143.

19

ETHNIC, RACIAL, AND GEOGRAPHIC VARIATIONS IN STROKE RISK, AND RISK FACTORS ASSOCIATED WITH STROKE

Herbert A. Manosalva and Thomas Jeerakathil

The Global Burden of Stroke

It is estimated that in 2005 there were 16 million first-ever strokes worldwide, and this number is projected to increase to 18 million by 2015 and 23 million by 2030.[1] It is also estimated that stroke is responsible for 10% of the 59 million deaths that occur yearly around the world. It is particularly concerning that the World Health Organization estimates that of the almost 6 million persons yearly who die of stroke, 87% live in low-income or middle-income countries that can ill-afford the best treatments for stroke.[1]

According to the Global Burden of Disease Study 2010, cerebrovascular disorders are the second leading cause of death and premature death in the world.[2] The same report describes how cerebrovascular disease has moved from being the fifth most important cause of loss of disability-adjusted life years (DALYs) in the world to the third most important cause in the interval between 1990 and 2010.

Variations in Stroke Occurrence and Mortality by Racial Group and Geography

There is substantial variation in stroke occurrence, stroke subtypes, and mortality by country and racial group. With regard to stroke mortality, the difference between countries is striking (Figure 19.1) with eastern European countries experiencing the highest mortality rate worldwide, and with Europe and North America experiencing lower stroke mortality.[3]

However, to assume that the average stroke mortality for a country is representative of the risk of all or even most of its citizens may be misleading. Even within economically advantaged, developed countries such as the United States, there is impressive variability in stroke mortality across different regions. Since the 1940s a region of the southeastern United States has experienced stroke mortality

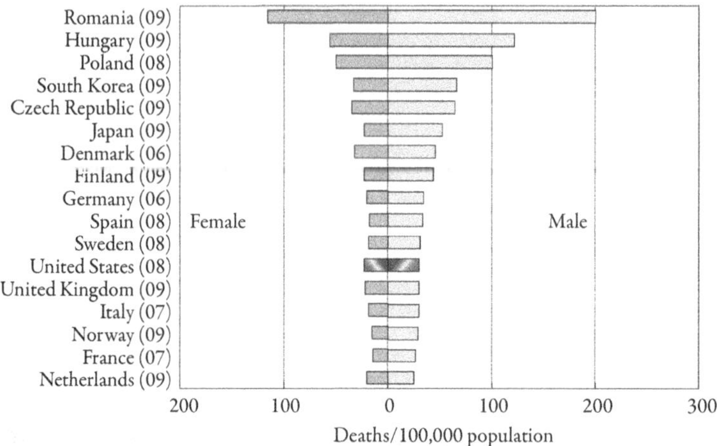

FIGURE 19.1 Variation in Stroke Mortality by Country and Gender in those Aged 35–74. (From 2012 NHLBI Morbidity and Mortality Chart Book, Chart 3-64; with permission)[3]

20% greater than the rest of the nation, and has been labeled the *stroke belt* (Figure 19.2).[4] In more recent years, the central portion of this belt along the coastal plain of North and South Carolina and Georgia has been observed to have even greater stroke mortality (40% greater than the rest of the United States) and has been referred to as the *stroke buckle.* Similar geographic variability has been reported within other countries, such as India (discussed later).

In the United States, there have been consistently greater stroke occurrence rates for non-Hispanic blacks than for whites over time, and recently the Greater Cincinnati/Northern Kentucky Stroke Study reinforced this pattern.[5] Reporting on data from 1993 to 2005, researchers found that the stroke rate for blacks was 1.7-fold greater than for whites, and this ratio was stable over time. An overall decline in stroke occurrence was the result of a statistically significant decline in ischemic stroke occurrence in whites but not blacks. There was no decline in hemorrhagic stroke occurrence in either population.

Stroke mortality has traditionally been higher for non-Hispanic blacks than whites, and this pattern continues to the current day. In the United States, all racial groups have experienced declines in stroke mortality during the past several decades. Although this decline plateaued during the mid to late 1990s, the decline resumed again from the year 2000 onward. Furthermore, although blacks may have experienced a slightly lower annualized decline during the past 10 years than whites (approximately 4.1% compared with 5%, respectively) the trajectory of decline has been similar for blacks and whites (Figure 19.3.[3] Hispanics, North American aboriginals, and Asians appear to be at slightly lower mortality than whites overall, from National Heart, Lung, and Blood Institute data; however, there may be underreporting for the latter two groups (Figure 19.4).[3]

The inaccuracy of stroke mortality reporting for North American aboriginal populations is apparent when studies make more vigorous attempts at case capture. Harwell et al.[6] examined the relative risk for heart disease and stroke for Native Americans compared with whites in Montana and found a 1.5-fold increase in stroke mortality for both men and women compared with whites. It was particularly striking that both the discrepancy in stroke mortality was increasing over time and that most of the excess mortality was in those younger than 65 years (Figure 19.5).[6]

Another population originally thought to have a low rate of stroke is the South Asian population consisting of persons from the Indian subcontinent, including India, Sri Lanka, Pakistan, Nepal, and Bangladesh. The absence of high-quality population-based studies impairs our understanding

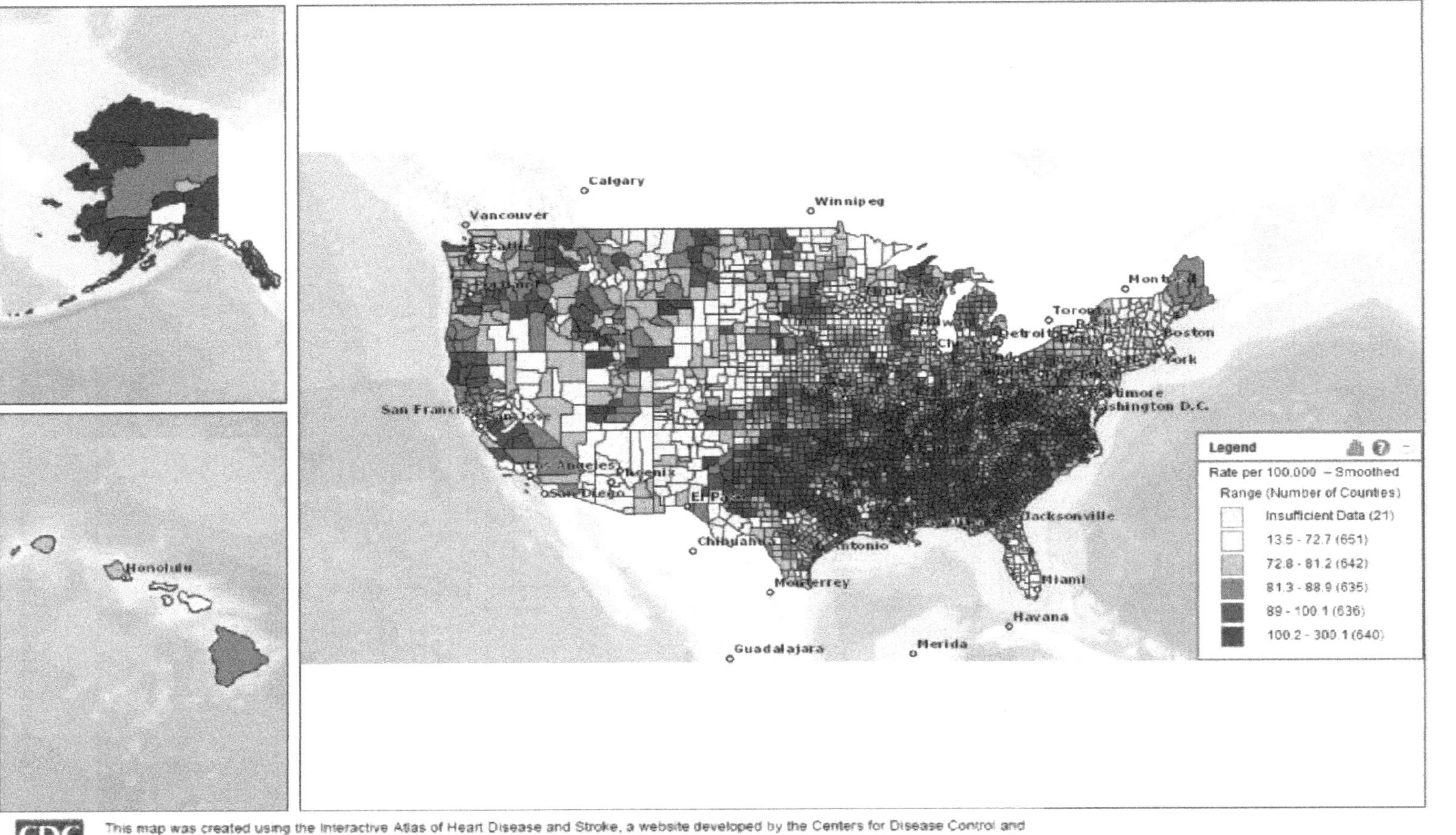

FIGURE 19.2 Stroke Mortality Rates by Region. (From Heart Disease and Stroke Statistics--2014 Update: A Report From the American Heart Association. Chapter 14. Chart 14.7; with permission)[4]

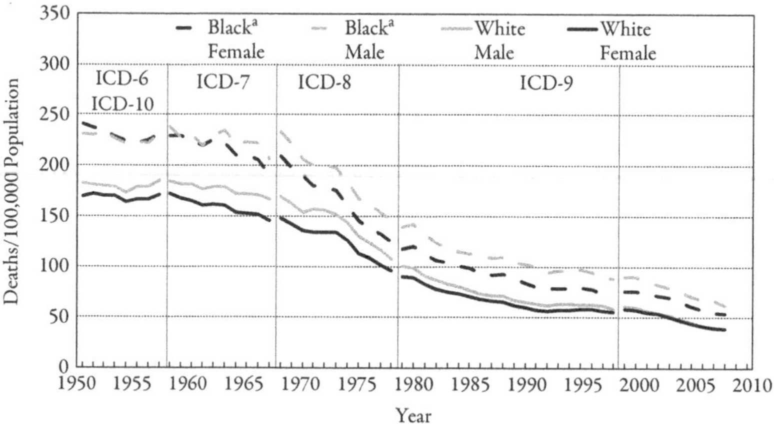

FIGURE 19.3 Age-Adjusted Death Rates for Stroke by Race & Sex, U.S., 1950–2008 (Adapted from from 2012 NHLBI Morbidity and Mortality Chart Book, Chart 3-56; with permission)[3]
[a]Nonwhite from 1950 to 1967. ICD, International Classification of Diseases.

of the true risk for stroke in this population. Early studies examining mostly prevalence rates in India suggested lower prevalence than western industrialized countries.[7] Indeed, the literature is quite inconsistent for South Asians, reporting variably lower and higher rates of stroke compared with western populations and other ethnic groups. However, more rigorous prospective studies performed in recent years in India and incorporating age standardization to the world population demonstrate annual stroke incidence rates that are 50% to 120% higher than western industrialized countries.[7] However, there is evidence of variation within the country of India itself, although studies are hampered by differences in methodology and age strata of the populations sampled. A fairly

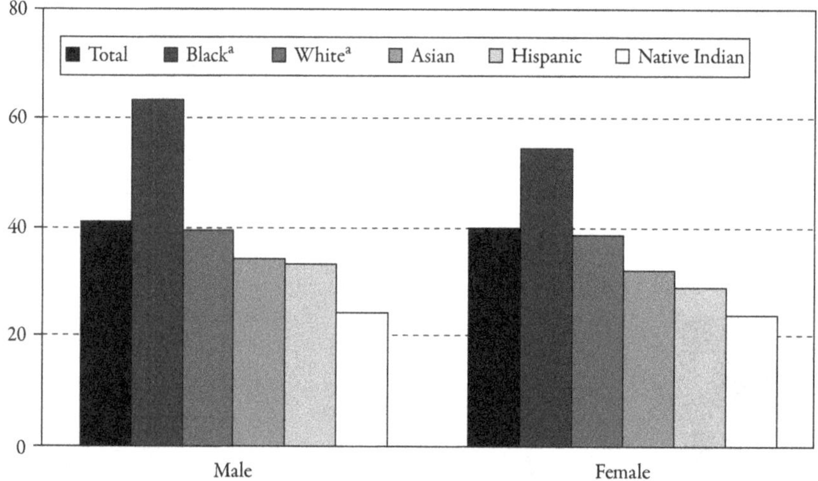

FIGURE 19.4 Age-Adjusted Death Rates for Stroke by Race/Ethnicity and Sex, U.S., 2008 (Adapted from 2012 NHLBI Morbidity and Mortality Chart Book, Chart 3-60; with permission)[3]

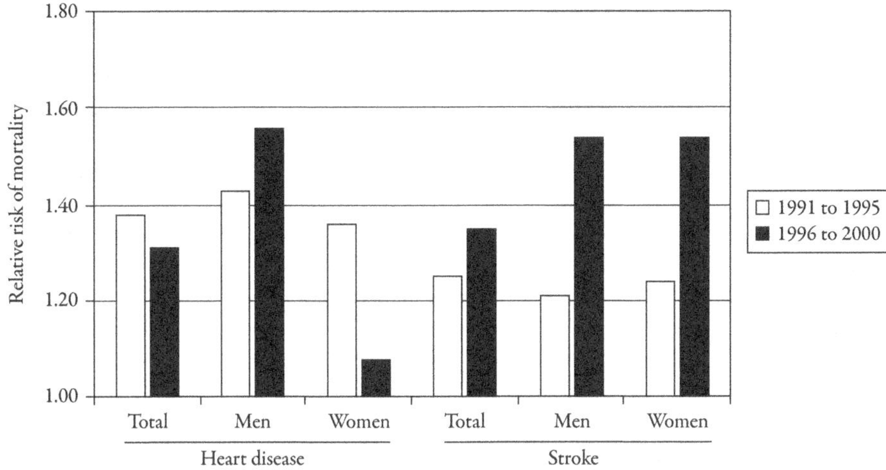

FIGURE 19.5 Relative risk of mortality from heart disease and stroke in American Indians and whites, Montana, 1991 to 1995 and 1996 to 2000. (from Harwell TS, Oser CS, Okon NJ et al. Defining Disparities in Cardiovascular Disease for American Indians: Trends in Heart Disease and Stroke Mortality Among American Indians and Whites in Montana, 1991 to 2000. *Circulation*. 2005;112:2263–2267; originally published online October 3, 2005; doi: 10.1161/CIRCULATIONAHA.105.560607; with permission)[6]

consistent finding is an excess stroke risk in urban and metropolitan populations compared with rural populations.[8]

Although the stroke incidence rates are likely greater for South Asians than for western industrialized populations, the persistent finding of lower stroke prevalence in South Asians requires further explanation. There is evidence for greater stroke case fatality in South Asians than other ethnic groups, which could result in low prevalence as a result of diminished survival. The Kolkata Study took place in a large metropolitan city in India and reported a 30-day case fatality rate for stroke of 42%, which is clearly in excess of that reported for most other countries, with the exception of Eastern Europe.[9] Furthermore, standardized mortality ratios for stroke in migrant South Asian populations in the United Kingdom were 55% greater for males and 41% greater for females compared with the general population.[8] Secular trends in mortality in this population are hard to determine, given the limitations of available data, but suggest either increasing stroke mortality during the past several decades or a substantially lower decline than that observed in western industrialized populations.[7,8]

Race and Stroke Occurrence by Subtypes

Some racial/ethnic groups appear to be more prone to specific subtypes of stroke than others, but a full picture of these discrepancies emerges only when studies of stroke incidence also report stroke classification using a system such as the Trial of Org 10172 in Acute Stroke Treatment (TOAST) classification or the Oxfordshire classification.[10,11] The lack of availability of brain imaging with computed tomography or magnetic resonance imaging is a major limitation to understanding stroke subtypes in much of the developing world.

In an effort to identify the main risk factors operating in the different countries of high, medium, and low income and their ethnic groups, and to estimate the associated population-attributable risks (PARs) for the main subtypes of stroke, ischemic or hemorrhagic, an international multicenter case–control study, the INTERSTROKE study, was developed in 22 countries.[12] Patients having a cerebrovascular event with neurological deficits lasting more than 24 hours were included. The study included neuroimaging (computed tomography or magnetic resonance imaging) and baseline electrocardiography. The patients were classified according to the Oxford Community Stroke Project classification and the study enrolled 6000 participants. In the multiethnic sample overall, the most frequent subtype of stroke was ischemic (78%), with hemorrhagic stroke occurring in 22%, and these proportions establish a reasonable baseline for an "average" global population.[11,12]

An analysis looking at the incidence of the first-ever ischemic stroke in the population examined in the South London Stroke Register study showed that the overall incidence ratio for ischemic stroke (rate ratio, 1.26) was significantly greater among black Caribbeans relative to whites.[13] The rate of small-vessel occlusive stroke was greater for both Caribbean blacks (rate ratio, 1.98) and African blacks (rate ratio, 2.14). Researchers found that both Caribbean and African blacks had a greater proportion of small-vessel occlusion compared with whites (42% for blacks overall compared with 22% for whites).

The Greater Cincinnati/Northern Kentucky Stroke study, which compared first-ever stroke incidence in two different races, showed similar results, with almost twice the incidence of small-vessel strokes and strokes of undetermined etiology in blacks compared with whites.[14] However, the increased incidence of these stroke subtypes parallels the increased incidence of all stroke in American black populations. When stroke subtype is examined as a proportion of total stroke, there are similarities between whites and blacks for small-vessel, large-vessel, and undetermined stroke types. Whites appear to have a slightly greater proportion of cardioembolic strokes (22% vs. 15%).

The Sino–MONICA–Beijing study in China showed a greater incidence of hemorrhagic stroke in Chinese compared with other countries.[15] The most important risk factor explaining the difference is probably the greater incidence of hypertension, but other lifestyle and genetic factors cannot be excluded. A diet producing very low cholesterol levels has been put forward as a potential risk factor for hemorrhagic stroke.

In the United States, a population study at the Mayo Clinic in Rochester, Minnesota, showed that patients from Asia and the Pacific Islands had increased risk of hemorrhagic transformation after intravenous tissue plasminogen activator treatment for ischemic stroke (odds ratio [OR], 2.01; 95% confidence interval [CI], 1.91–2.11) compared with Hispanic, black, and white ethnic groups.[16] One small, uncontrolled trial from Japan has demonstrated reasonable outcomes and an acceptable hemorrhage rate by decreasing the intravenous tissue plasminogen activator dose from 0.9 mg/kg to 0.6 mg/kg, when treating ischemic stroke.[17]

Race, Ethnicity Specific Differences in Impact of Traditional Stroke Risk Factors

HYPERTENSION

Hypertension is the most important risk factor for atherosclerosis and stroke, and a major risk factor for vascular dementia.[18] It is an important risk factor for atherosclerosis. A 10-mmHg increase in arterial pressure may increase the odds for atherosclerosis (ruptured plaque, protruding atheroma) in major vessels, including the aorta, by 43% and, for stroke specifically, by 40%. On the other hand, a 10-mmHg decrease in systolic blood pressure reduces the risk for stroke by 30%. Hypertension is the major risk factor for lacunar ischemic strokes and leukoaraiosis (brain white matter disease). In the INTERSTROKE study, hypertension was the strongest risk factor for hemorrhagic stroke including microbleeds and parenchymal hematomas.[12]

In the provinces of Alberta and British Columbia in Canada, the incidence of hypertension in South Asians (Pakistan, India or Bangladesh origin) is greater compared with whites and Chinese (East Asians from China, Taiwan, or Hong Kong).[19] This is of particular relevance considering that

East Asian populations tend to have a greater incidence of hypertension than the general population in the first place.

The Greater Cincinnati/Northern Kentucky Stroke Study comparing first-ever stroke incidence in two different races showed that hypertension was significantly higher in the black population, and the rate of small-vessel occlusive strokes, which have a particularly strong relationship to hypertension, was almost as twice as high in blacks compared with whites.[14] Along the same lines, the South London Stroke Register study in an urban population in London showed that hypertension was the most frequent risk factor for stroke in black Africans, followed by black Caribbeans, compared with whites.[20]

The Global Burden of Disease 2010 report listed hypertension as the risk factor that has the biggest impact worldwide in regard to DALYs lost.[2] The DALY incorporates both premature mortality and disability, and amounts to years of healthy life lost as a result of a disease or a risk factor. With regard to regional variability, hypertension ranges from being the most important risk factor for stroke in high-income countries in the Asia-Pacific, East Asia (including China and Japan), Central Europe, tropical Latin America, Southeast Asia, Central Asia, North Africa, and the Middle East to ranking as low as the sixth most important risk factor in western Sub-Saharan Africa. Across every geographic region, hypertension exerts substantial influence as a cause of death and disability after stroke.

Smoking

Smoking is a risk factor for all the different subtypes of ischemic stroke (small-vessel occlusion, large-artery atherosclerosis, and cardioembolic stroke) and, unlike many other risk factors, it has the advantage of being completely preventable. In the Greater Cincinnati/Northern Kentucky Stroke Study, current smoking had a significantly greater prevalence in the black population.[14] Black persons smoking more than 1 pack of cigarettes per day were at a four times greater risk for developing an ischemic stroke compared with nonsmokers, and there seems to be little differential effect of smoking as a risk factor across racial groups.[21] The same high prevalence of smoking is true for aboriginal populations in Canada.[22] For Canadian First Nations persons, smoking prevalence ranged from 30% off-reserve to as high as 49% on-reserve, which is considerably greater than the general population of Canada. In a European study in Norway, current smoking was the most important risk factor along with dyslipidemia (OR, 2.06; 95% CI, 1.04–4.08) for the occurrence of small-vessel occlusion.[23]

Smoking was second only to hypertension in importance as a cause of DALYs lost worldwide.[2] The importance of smoking in terms of the proportion of total DALYs lost has been decreasing in the developed world and increasing in the developing world during the past 10 years. Smoking rates vary even between different countries in the developed world, with greater rates on average in western European countries than in North America. Similarly, in the developing world there is substantial variability, with relatively low smoking rates on most of the African continent and very high rates in Asia and Eastern Europe.[24]

Dyslipidemia

Dyslipidemia has a complex relationship with stroke risk, with both low and high levels of lipids conveying some risk for different stroke subtypes. In the multicenter INTERSTROKE study, the ratio of nonhigh-density lipoprotein (non-HDL) cholesterol to HDL cholesterol, increased levels of apolipoprotein B, and, in particular, the ratio of apolipoprotein B to apolipoprotein A1 were associated strongly with ischemic stroke.[12] Similarly, in a study from Norway, a cholesterol level greater than 193.4 mg/dL and a low-density lipoprotein level greater than 116 mg/dL were the main risk factors for large-artery atherosclerosis and small-vessel occlusive ischemic stroke.[23]

However, in the Multiple-Risk Factor Intervention Trial(MRFIT) research, black men with cholesterol less than 160 mg/dL with a diastolic blood pressure of more than 90 mmHg were found to be at risk for hemorrhagic stroke.[25] The observation of the increased risk for intracerebral hemorrhage from low lipid levels has been replicated in multiple populations, including rural Japanese, whites in the Multiple-Risk Factor Intervention Trial, and Hawaiian Japanese, and the relationship is strongest in those with high diastolic blood pressures.[26,27] In the Rotterdam study, a population-based cohort of community-dwelling elderly persons from the Netherlands, it was demonstrated that it is the triglyceride fraction that, when low, predisposes to intracerebral hemorrhage, and there was no independent relationship between low-density lipoprotein or HDL levels and hemorrhage risk.[28] Researchers have postulated that low lipid levels somehow produce weakening of the blood vessel endothelium, predisposing the vessel to rupture.

Obesity and Diabetes

Obesity, impaired glucose tolerance, and hypertriglyceridemia produce morbidity as individual risk factors but also occur together in a cluster of risk factors referred to as *metabolic syndrome*. Although these three risk factors contribute to death and disability globally, there is disparity across regions and ethnic groups in their relative importance.

The Global Burden of Disease project reports that diabetes has moved from the 21st to the 14th most important disease with regard to years of healthy life lost, and it ranks as one of the top 10 diseases in the world for mortality.[2] High fasting blood sugar is a risk factor that incorporates diabetes as well as impaired glucose tolerance, and ranks as the seventh most important risk factor globally with regard to DALYs lost.[2] With regard to years lived with disability, the same study reports wide variation in the relative importance of diabetes by region of the world. Diabetes is the fourth leading disease that causes years lived with disability in Oceania (Micronesia, Melanesia, Polynesia, and Central and South Pacific), but it drops to the 29th leading cause in Central and Sub-Saharan Africa.

Similarly, obesity or high body mass index (BMI) ranks sixth globally in terms of DALYs lost and is the leading risk factor in Australasia, South and Latin America, and Central and Latin America. High BMI is the second or third leading risk factor in Western Europe, North America, Central Europe, North Africa, and the Middle East, and several other global regions.[29] However, in Southeast Asia and East, Central, and West Sub-Saharan Africa, it is a much less important risk factor, ranking from 14th to 18th in importance. The contrast within Africa itself is striking; obesity ranks third in importance for southern Sub-Saharan Africa.

Obesity is a risk factor for dyslipidemia, hypertension, and diabetes, and in European populations risk increases consistently at a BMI of more than 30 kg/m^2. Although it is recognized that adverse risk factor profiles and cardiovascular disease seem to occur at lower BMIs in populations in East and South Asia, the World Health Organization has been reluctant to support different specific cut points for obesity for different ethnic groups. An important study published in 2007 determined, using factor analysis, the BMI cut points for South Asians, Chinese, Europeans, and aboriginals that were associated with adverse risk profiles for dyslipidemia, hypertension, and hyperglycemia.[30] The investigators found a wide range of cut points for specific risk factors, which varied by group (Table 19.1). However, in general, South Asians, aboriginals, and Chinese had adverse glucose profiles at relatively low BMIs. South Asians also had adverse lipid profiles at low BMIs, suggesting that, even at low BMIs, they are particularly at risk as a result of this "double clustering" of risk factors. Chinese and aboriginal subjects had adverse lipid profiles at intermediate BMIs, but still at much lower BMIs than

TABLE 19.1

A Comparison of BMI Cut Points Related to Adverse Cardiovascular Risk Factor Clusters in a Multiethnic Population

	BMI Cut Point for Specific Risk Factor Clusters		
Ethnic group	Dyslipidemia	Hyperglycemia	Hypertension
European	30	30	30
South Asian	22.5	21.0	28.8
Chinese	25.9	20.6	25.3
Aboriginal	26.1	21.8	NS

Note: Adapted from Razak et al.[30]
BMI, body mass index; NS, not significant.

Europeans. Chinese subjects were at risk for high blood pressure at BMIs greater than 25.3, but this relationship was not as strong for South Asians and was not present for aboriginals.[30]

Cardiac Causes

The Miami Stroke Registry compared the prevalence of vascular risk factors and subtypes of ischemic strokes in blacks, Caribbean blacks, Hispanics, and whites.[31] The prevalence of cardioembolism was greatest in whites (OR, 3.02; 95% CI, 1.42–6.42). Moreover, atrial fibrillation is known as the most frequent cause for cardioembolic stroke and has a greater prevalence in the white population compared with African/Caribbean blacks and South Asians.[32] This was confirmed in the South London Stroke Register study, in which the prevalence of atrial fibrillation was found to be 0.63% overall in 2011 and 1.2% in whites, 0.4% in black African/Caribbeans, and 0.2% in South Asians (India, Pakistan, and Bangladesh origin) (Figure 19.6).[33]

In contrast to atrial fibrillation, which is far more common in the elderly, valvular heart disease from rheumatic fever affects mostly children and young adults. It is estimated that there are more than 16 million persons worldwide burdened by this condition, and the greatest prevalence by far (5.7%) is in Sub-Saharan Africa.[34] Given that valvular heart disease from rheumatic fever is preventable with appropriate treatment, developing countries experience a much higher burden of the disease than developed countries. One exception to this rule is the situation of Australian aborigines who, despite living in an economically advantaged country, have among the highest rates of rheumatic fever in the world. The underlying reasons are not known with certainty, but they may involve routes of infection other than streptococcal pharyngitis.[34]

Nontraditional Risk Factors and Conditions Predisposing to Stroke

Strokes of undetermined cause may occur in as much as 40% of cerebrovascular events in the young population.[35] Some of these individuals may have an underlying genetic disorder, and there is evidence for variability in the occurrence of these conditions across different ethnic groups.

CEREBRAL AUTOSOMAL DOMINANT ARTERIOPATHY WITH SUBCORTICAL INFARCTS AND LEUKOENCEPHALOPATHY

Cerebral autosomal dominant arteriopathy with subcortical infarcts and leukoencephalopathy is an autosomal dominant disorder characterized by migraines with aura, small-vessel occlusion ischemic

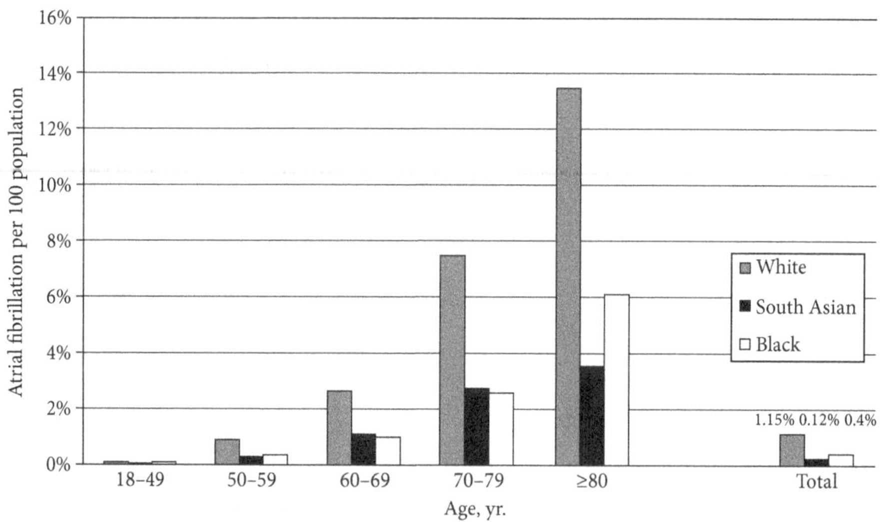

FIGURE 19.6 Prevalence of atrial fibrillation by age and ethnic group. (From Mathur R., Pollara E., Hull S., Schofield P. Ashworth M., et al. Ethnicity and stroke risk in patients with atrial fibrillation. *Heart*. 2013;99:1087–1092; Figure 1; with permission)[33]

strokes, leukoencephalopathy, mood disorder, apathy, and dementia by the sixth decade. Both genders can be affected, but mortality may occur 6 years earlier in men.[36] The underlying genetic disorder is a missense mutation in the *NOTCH3* gene. It has been described in Europeans and South Asians.[37] Cerebral autosomal dominant arteriopathy with subcortical infarcts and leukoencephalopathy has been reported more frequently in Europeans among French, German, and Italian communities.[38] The disease has been identified worldwide, including Arabic families.[39,40]

CEREBRAL AUTOSOMAL RECESSIVE ARTERIOPATHY WITH SUBCORTICAL INFARCTS AND LEUKOARAIOSIS

Cerebral Autosomal Recessive Arteriopathy with Subcortical Infarcts and Leukoaraiosis (CARASIL) is a rare, autosomal recessive disorder characterized by premature baldness, frequent episodes of back pain, migraine, psychiatric disorders such as emotional liability, dementia, and strokes between the third and fourth decade. Patients may develop small-vessel occlusion strokes in the thalamus and basal ganglia, and diffuse white mater disease. This condition is the result of mutations in the *HTRA1* gene. This disorder has been described originally in Japanese and Chinese ethnic groups.[41]

HOMOCYSTINURIA

Homocystinuria was described by McCully[42] in 1969 in autopsies of children who died from a vascular event: cerebrovascular, pulmonary embolism, or ischemic cardiac. Patients develop prematurely severe atherosclerosis of large arteries, such as the carotid arteries, myocardial infarction, or venous thrombosis. Experimental animal models using vitamin B6 could prevent the development of venous thrombosis, but not the progression of the atherosclerotic plaques. Typically, patients have a marfanoid appearance, with ectopia lentis and mental retardation, and may develop hemidystonia, large-artery atherosclerosis ischemic strokes, and venous thromboembolic disease.[42] This is an autosomal recessive disorder, with deficiency in the enzyme cystathionine β-synthase, which has vitamin

B6 as a cofactor, leading to the accumulation of homocysteine (>100 µmol/L) and methionine in plasma, and urine excretion of organic acids. These patients may benefit from vitamin B6 and folic acid. This is an autosomal recessive disorder resulting from mutations in the CBS gene.[43] Allele studies have shown that the frequency of having at least one abnormal allele of this gene is greater in the black population, followed by whites, and is low in East Asians.[44] White patients with homocystinuria homozygous for mutation I278T had a vitamin B6 responsive phenotype, as has been described in Europeans and Americans, whereas black descendants homozygous for mutation T353M had a vitamin B6 nonresponsive phenotype.[45]

HYPERHOMOCYSTEINEMIA

Patients who are homozygous or compound heterozygous for the polymorphism 677 C T, and for whom fasting homocysteine blood levels are greater than 50 µmol/L, may have an increased risk for stroke. This polymorphism is the result of a thermolabile enzyme with 50% reduced activity. It can be seen in 10% of European and 25% of Asian populations. In countries that fortify food with folic acid, the risk turns insignificant.[46]

Homocysteine blood levels can be increased in nutritional vitamin B deficiencies, consumption of animal proteins rich in methionine, increased age, smoking, sedentary lifestyle, postmenopausal state, and decreased renal failure, or provoked by medications such as anticonvulsants, methotrexate, cyclosporine, or cholesterol-lowering medications.[47] Typically, fasting homocysteine levels appear around 15 to 30 µmol/L. The multicenter study VITATOPS, conducted on four continents, showed that supplementation with vitamins in this population was no more effective than placebo in preventing major vascular events.[48]

SICKLE CELL DISEASE

There is a high prevalence of sickle cell disease in the black race. It is an autosomal recessive condition in which there is a mutation in the *HBB* gene, replacing the amino acid glutamic acid for valine in the sixth position of the polypeptide chain. As part of natural selection, people with sickle red blood cells survived the big pandemics of malaria in Africa from the past, because of the inability of the parasite to survive invading a sickle-shaped erythrocyte. The disease begins as hemolytic episodes with vaso-occlusive events in childhood and may affect the brain, eyes, bones, kidney, liver, joints, and spleen. Stroke episodes typically occur during systemic sickle cell crises. These strokelike events may be overlooked in 25% of cases, and the first noticeable neurological symptom may then be cognitive decline, developmental delay, seizures, or abnormal movement disorders such as hemidystonic posturing.[49] In the Northern Manhattan study, the racial/ethnic group at greatest risk for developing stroke resulting from sickle cell disease was, as expected, blacks, followed by Hispanic people—Dominicans in particular.[50] Stroke resulting from sickle cell disease is more common among populations in Africa, the Mediterranean, parts of India, and the Middle East.

MOYAMOYA DISEASE AND FIBROMUSCULAR DYSPLASIA

In Asia, Moyamoya disease can present with steno-occlusive ischemic vascular events, and the first strokes may occur early in childhood. Over time, patients may develop aneurysms and hemorrhagic stroke. Patients typically develop an angiographic picture of a "puff of smoke" (which translates in Japanese to *moyamoya*). The prevalence is higher in Asiatic countries, particularly in Japan and Korea, but is lower in non-Asian populations.[51] A study in California showed that the prevalence of this disease was greatest in Asian Americans (0.28/100,000 person-years), followed by blacks

(0.13/100,000 person-years), then whites (0.06/100,000 person-years), and, last, Hispanic Americans (0.03/100,000 person-years).[52] One reason for the ethnic differences may be genetic. Recently, a mutation (4576G>A) in the ring-finger protein 213 gene, *RNF213*, on chromosome 17 was found to be associated with Moyamoya disease, and this variant is more common in Japanese and Koreans compared with Han Chinese.[53]

Fibromuscular dysplasia can be noticeable in adolescence or early youth, predominantly in white women, affecting large-artery blood vessels such as the carotid or renal arteries, with associated stroke, abdominal angina, or vascular claudication. The disease can present frequently later in life, as well, and is a risk factor for cervical artery dissection and subsequent stroke. Occasionally, this condition may be detected in asymptomatic people during routine angiographies, with the typical appearance of a "string of beads."[54]

A Summary of the Differences in Risk Factor Profile for Stroke by Racial Group and Geography

The South London Stroke Register study examined the PAR for stroke for a number of risk factors in a multiethnic population (Figure 19.7).[20] In this study white patients had the greatest PAR from ischemic heart disease on electrocardiogram (56%) and from obesity (49%), followed by hypertension (36%) and smoking (31%). Black Caribbean patients had an even greater PAR from ischemic heart disease on electrocardiogram (66%) and from hypertension (46%) and diabetes (29%), but less from

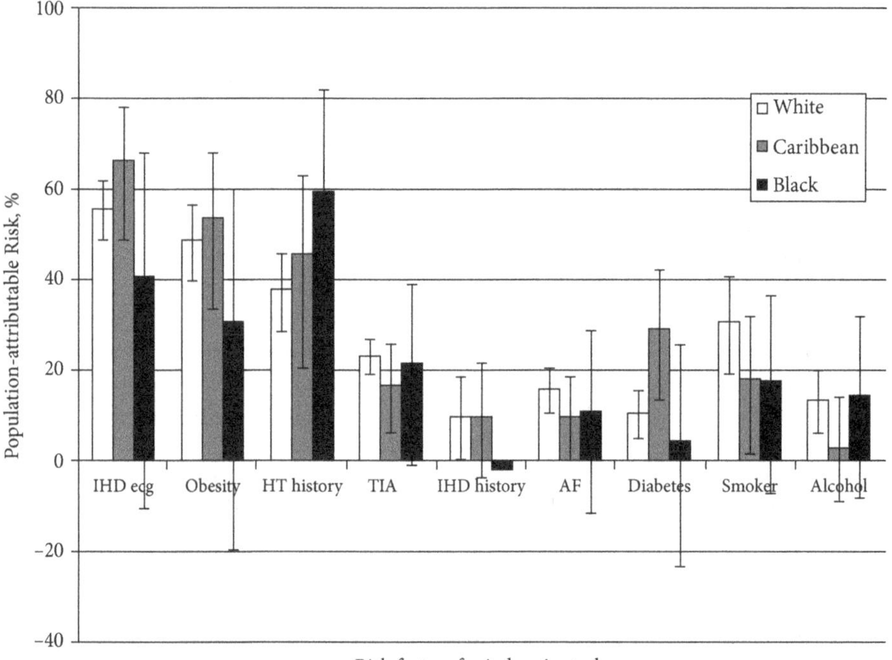

FIGURE 19.7 Population attributable risk for risk factors by ethnic group. (From Hajat C., Tilling K., Stewart J., Lemic-Stojcevic N., Wolfe C. Ethnic differences in risk factors for ischemic stroke: a European case-control study. *Stroke*. 2004;35:1562–1567; Figure; with permission)[20]

AF, atrial fibrillation; HT, hypertension; TIA, transient ischemic attack.

smoking, obesity, and atrial fibrillation. African blacks had the greatest PAR for hypertension (59%) and less for obesity, diabetes, and atrial fibrillation than whites.

In general, East Asian populations, such as those in China and Japan, have lower rates of dyslipidemia and obesity than white populations, but they have greater rates of hypertension. These populations also tend to have greater rates of intracranial arterial stenosis as opposed to the extracranial stenosis that occurs in whites, and much greater rates of stroke and lower rates of myocardial infarction than whites.

In contrast, South Asian populations appear to have a high risk of both stroke and myocardial infarction, with both dyslipidemia and abnormal glucose metabolism occurring at a lower BMI than whites. North American aboriginal populations are developing greater rates of obesity and diabetes than the general population, and also have higher rates of smoking.

Risk factors for stroke remain prevalent around the globe, with adverse trends in a number of regions providing some explanation for why stroke has increased in importance between 2000 and 2010 as a cause of death and disability. Both the developing world and the developed world bear the burden of stroke. Health professionals and policymakers involved in stroke prevention need to understand the specific risk profiles of the regions and racial/ethnic groups they serve to focus their interventions to combat the growing threat of stroke.

REFERENCES

1. Strong K, Mathers C, Bonita R. Preventing stroke: saving lives around the world. *Lancet Neurol.* 2007;6:182–187.
2. Institute for Health Metrics and Evaluation. *The global burden of disease: generating evidence, guiding policy.* Seattle, WA: Institute for Health Metrics and Evaluation, 2013.
3. National Heart Lung and Blood Institute. Morbidity and mortality: 2012 chartbook on cardiovascular, lung, and blood diseases. 2012. National Heart and Lung and Blood Institute, Bethesda, MD.
4. Go AS, Mozaffarian D, Roger VL, et al. In: Heart disease and stroke statistics—2014 update: a report from the American Heart Association. *Circulation.* 2014;129:399–410.
5. Kleindorfer D, Khoury J, Moomaw C, et al. Stroke incidence is decreasing in whites but not in blacks: a population-based estimate of temporal trends in stroke incidence from the Greater Cincinnati/Northern Kentucky Stroke Study. *Stroke.* 2010;41:1326–1331.
6. Harwell TS, Oser CS, Okon NJ, et al. Defining disparities in cardiovascular disease for American Indians: trends in heart disease and stroke mortality among American Indians and whites in Montana, 1991 to 2000. *Circulation.* 2005;112:2263–2267.
7. Das SK, Banerjee TK. Stroke: Indian scenario. *Circulation.* 2008;118:2719–2724.
8. Gunarathne A, Patel JV, Gammon B, Gill PS, Hughes EA, Lip GYH. Ischemic stroke in south Asians: a review of the epidemiology, pathophysiology, and ethnicity-related clinical features. *Stroke.* 2009;40:e415–e423.
9. Das SK, Banerjee TK, Biswas A, et al. A prospective community-based study of stroke in Kolkata, India. *Stroke.* 2007;38:906–910.
10. Adams H, Bendixen B, Kappelle L, et al. Classification of subtype of acute ischemic stroke: definitions for use in a multicenter clinical trial: TOAST: Trial of Org 10172 in acute stroke treatment. *Stroke.* 1993;24:35–41.
11. Bamforth J, Sandercock P, Dennis M, Warlow C, Burn J. Classification and natural history of clinically identifiable subtypes of cerebral infarction. *Lancet.* 1991;337:1521–1526.
12. O'Donnell M, Xavier D, Liu L, et al. Risk factors for ischemic and intracerebral haemorrhagic stroke in 22 countries (the INTERSTROKE study): a case–control study. *Lancet.* 2010;376:112–123.

13. Hajat C, Heuschmann P, Coshall C, et al. Incidence of aetiological subtypes of stroke in a multi-ethnic population based study: the South London Stroke Register. *J Neurol Neurosurg Psychiatry*. 2011;82:527–533.
14. Schneider A, Kissela B, Woo D, et al. Ischemic stroke subtypes: a population-based study of incidence rates among blacks and whites. *Stroke*. 2004;35:1552–1556.
15. Chen D, Roman G, Wu G, et al. Stroke in China (Sino-MONICA-Beijing study) 1984–1986. *Neuroepidemiology*. 1992;11:15–23.
16. Nasr D, Brinjikji W, Cloft H, Rabinstein A. Racial and ethnic disparities in the use of intravenous recombinant tissue plasminogen activator and outcomes for acute ischemic stroke. *J Stroke Cerebrovasc Dis*. 2013;22:154–160.
17. Yamaguchi T, Mori E, Minematsu K, et al. Alteplase at 0.6 mg/kg for acute ischemic stroke within 3 hours of onset: Japan Alteplase Clinical Trial (J-ACT). *Stroke*. 2006;37:1810–1815.
18. Faraco G, Iadecola C. Hypertension: a harbinger of stroke and dementia. *Hypertension*. 2013;62:810–817.
19. Quan H, Chen G, Walker R, et al. Incidence, cardiovascular complications and mortality of hypertension by sex and ethnicity. *Heart*. 2013;99:715–721.
20. Hajat C, Tilling K, Stewart J, Lemic-Stojcevic N, Wolfe C. Ethnic differences in risk factors for ischemic stroke: a European case–control study. *Stroke*. 2004;35:1562–1567.
21. Gillum RF. Risk factors for stroke in blacks: a critical review. *Am J Epidemiol*. 1999;150:1266–1274.
22. Public Health Agency of Canada. Tracking heart disease and stroke in Canada 2009. Ottawa.
23. Ihle-Hansen H, Thommessen B, Wyller T, Engedal K, Fure B. Risk factors for and incidence of subtypes of ischemic stroke. *Funct Neurol*. 2012;27:35–40.
24. Institute for Health Metrics and Evaluation. *Global smoking prevalence and cigarette consumption 1980–2012*. Seattle, WA: Institute for Health Metrics and Evaluation, 2014.
25. Neaton J, Wentworth D, Cutler J, et al. Risk factors for death from different types of stroke: Multiple Risk Factor Intervention Trial research group. *Ann Epidemiol*. 1993;3:493–499.
26. Jeerakathil TJ, Wolf PA. Epidemiology and stroke risk factors. In: Samuels MA, Feske SK, eds. *Office practise of neurology*, 2nd ed. New York: Churchill Livingstone, 2003:252–268.
27. Wolf PA, Cobb JL, D'Agostino RB. Epidemiology of stroke. In: Barnett HJM, Mohr JP, Stein BM, Yatsu FM, eds. *Stroke: pathophysiology, diagnosis, and management*, 2nd ed. New York: Churchill Livingstone, 1992:3–27.
28. Wieberdink RG, Poels MM, Vernooij MW, et al. Serum lipid levels and the risk of intracerebral hemorrhage: the Rotterdam Study. *Arterioscler Thromb Vasc Biol*. 2011;31:2982–2989.
29. Institute for Health Metrics and Evaluation. Global burden of disease 2010 leading causes and risks by region heat map. Available at: http://www.healthmetricsandevaluation.org/gbd/visualizations/gbd-2010-leading-causes-and-risks-region-heat-map/ (accessed February 2, 2014).
30. Razak F, Anand S, Shannon H, et al. Defining obesity cut points in a multiethnic population. *Circulation*. 2007;115:2111–2118.
31. Gutierrez J, Koch S, Dong C, et al. Racial and ethnic disparities in stroke subtypes: a multiethnic sample of patients with stroke. *Neurol Sci*. 2014;35:577–582.
32. Gill P, Calvert M, Davis R, et al. Prevalence of heart failure and atrial fibrillation in minority ethnic subjects: the Ethnic-Echocardiographic Heart of England Screening Study (E-ECHOES). *PLoS One*. 2011;6:e26710.
33. Mathur R, Pollara E, Hull S, et al. Ethnicity and stroke risk in patients with atrial fibrillation. *Heart*. 2013;99:1087–1092.
34. Nkomo VT. Epidemiology and prevention of valvular heart diseases and infective endocarditis in Africa. *Heart*. 2007;93:1510–1519.
35. Jacob B, Boden-Albala B, Lin I, Sacco R. Stroke in young in the Northern Manhattan Stroke Study. *Stroke*. 2002;33:2789–2793.

36. Opherk C, Peters N, Herzog J, Luedtke R, Dichgans M. Long term prognosis and causes of death in CADASIL: a retrospective study in 411 patients. *Brain.* 2004;127:2533–2539.
37. Pankaj S, Yadav S, Meschia J. Genetics of ischemic stroke. *J Neurol Neurosurg Psychiatry.* 2013;84:1302–1308.
38. Desmond D, Moroney J, Lynch T, Chan S, Chin S, Mohr J. The natural history of CADASIL: a pooled analysis of previously published cases. *Stroke.* 1999;30:1230–1233.
39. Yamamoto Y, Craggs L, Baumannt M, Kalimo H, Kalaria R. Review: molecular genetics and pathology of hereditary small vessel diseases of the brain. *Neuropathol Appl Neurobiol.* 2011;37:94–113.
40. Bohlega S, Shubili A, Edris A, et al. CADASIL in Arabs: clinical and genetic findings. *BMC Med Genet.* 2007;8:1–5.
41. Fukutake T. Cerebral autosomal recessive arteriopathy with subcortical infarcts and leukoencephalopathy (CARASIL): from discovery to gene identification. *J Stroke Cerebrovasc Dis.* 2011;20:85–93.
42. McCully KS. Vascular pathology of homocysteinemia: implications for the pathogenesis of arteriosclerosis. *Am J Pathol.* 1969;56:111–128.
43. Picker J, Harvey L. Homocystinuria caused by cystathionine β-synthase deficiency. Gene Reviews, April 26, 2011. Available at: http://www.ncbi.nlm.nih.gov/books/NBK1524/ (accessed February 20, 2014).
44. Zoossmann-Diskin A, Gazit E, Peleg L, Shohat M, Turner D. 844ins68 in the cystathionine β-synthase gene in Israel and review of its distribution in the world. *Anthropologischer Anzeiger.* 2004;62:147–155.
45. Kruger W, Wang L, Jhee K, Singh R, Elsas I. Cystathionine β-synthase deficiency in Georgia (USA): correlation of clinical and biochemical phenotype with genotype. *Hum Mutat.* 2003;22:434–441.
46. Holmes MV, Newcombe P, Hubacek JA, et al. Effect modification by population dietary folate on the association between MTHFR genotype, homocysteine, and stroke risk: a meta-analysis of genetic studies and randomised trials. *Lancet.* 2011;378:584–594.
47. Lonn E. Homocysteine in the prevention of ischemic heart disease, stroke and venous thromboembolism: therapeutic target or just another distraction? *Curr Opin Hematol.* 2007;14:481–487.
48. VITATOPS Trial Study Group. B vitamins in patients with recent transient ischaemic attack or stroke in the VITAmins TO Prevent Stroke (VITATOPS) trial: a randomised, double-blind, parallel, placebo-controlled trial. *Lancet Neurol.* 2010;9:855–865.
49. Bender M, Hobbs W. Sickle cell disease. Gene Reviews, May 17, 2012. Available at: http://www.ncbi.nlm.nih.gov/books/NBK1377/ (accessed January 15, 2014).
50. Siddiqui S, Schunk K, Batista M, et al. Awareness of sickle cell among people of reproductive age: Dominicans and African Americans in northern Manhattan. *J Urban Health.* 2011;89:53–58.
51. Fukui M. Commentary. *Surg Neurol.* 2002;57:62.
52. Uchino K, Johnston C, Becker K, Tirschwell D. Moyamoya disease in Washington state and California. *Neurology.* 2005;65:956–958.
53. Miyatake S, Miyake N, Touho H, et al. Homozygous c.14576G>A variant of RNF213 predicts early-onset and severe form of Moyamoya disease. *Neurology.* 2012;78:803–810.
54. Sperati J, Aggarwal N, Arepally A, Atta G. Fibromuscular dysplasia. *Kidney Int.* 2009;75:333–336.

IV

Integrative Approach

20

CAROTID DISEASE AS AN INTERMEDIATE MARKER OF STROKE RISK

David Della-Morte and Tatjana Rundek

Physiopathology of Carotid Atherosclerosis Disease

Atherosclerosis is the underlying process that causes most cardiovascular disease (CVD), death, and disability worldwide.[1] It is the cause of myocardial infarction (MI), peripheral artery disease, and stroke. About 10% to 20% of ischemic strokes are the result of large-artery atherosclerosis.[2] The atherosclerotic process leads to luminal stenosis with flow restriction and plaque rupture, causing CVD and stroke.[3] Atherosclerosis is a chronic inflammatory process that involves endothelial injury, activation and recruitment of immunoinflammatory cells, smooth muscle cell proliferation, and the influx of lipoprotein.[4] Various mediators such as chemokines, cytokines, growth factors, proteases, adhesion molecules, and hemostasis regulators, and their interactions are involved in the process of atherosclerosis. Proinflammatory signaling is triggered by oxidized low-density lipoprotein (LDL) or by alterations and remodeling in the extracellular matrix.[5,6] This process leads to different plaque composition and its susceptibility for rupture, with variable vascular risk resulting from artery-to-artery embolization.[7]

Atherosclerosis develops predominantly at specific vascular sites, mainly in areas with altered blood flow, such as carotid bifurcations and areas of vessel curvature. Mass transport and shear stress are two mechanical mechanisms proposed to regulate flow and contribute to atherosclerosis. A low or disturbed blood flow results in an increased uptake of bioactive substances into the vessel wall. Mechanical forces of blood flow on the vessel wall, called *shear stress*, also play an important role in the local development of plaque as well as in protection of endothelium.[6] Atherosclerotic lesions develop mainly in areas of low shear stress. The presence of areas of the arterial tree with different wall shear stress may explain, in part, the different localization of atherosclerotic lesions.

Age, sex, lipid, smoking, blood pressure (BP), diabetes, obesity, and race/ethnicity, among others, are all well-established risk factors for atherosclerosis and CVD.[8] They contribute, with different impacts and mechanisms, to the development of atherosclerosis. There are a number of ways to determine the future risk of CVD based on levels of these risk factors. The Framingham Risk Score (FRS)[9] is one of the best known and widely used models to predict CVD. Although these scoring systems are useful to predict risk in the populations, their accuracy in predicting cardiovascular risk for individuals varies considerably across populations.[10] Ultrasound methods for quantifying burden of atherosclerosis have been proposed for use in prediction models with a hope to increase the prediction accuracy of CVD beyond traditional vascular risk factors. In a recent study, researchers demonstrated that traditional vascular risk factors explain only 21% of the variance in total carotid plaque (CP) burden.[11] Variation in carotid atherosclerosis is, therefore, largely unexplained by known vascular risk factors, suggesting that other unaccounted factors—both environmental and genetic—play an important role in the determination of carotid atherosclerosis.

Surrogate or Intermediate Markers of Carotid Atherosclerosis

The development of noninvasive ultrasound methods capable of evaluating atherosclerosis quantitatively has improved our ability to design studies of the natural history, progression, and determinants of atherosclerosis, as well as to evaluate the effects of various therapies and preventive measures. According to the National Institutes of Health Definition Working Group, surrogate markers act as a substitute for a clinical end point and should be able to predict the desired clinical benefit and the lack of benefit, or harm, based on epidemiological, therapeutic, pathophysiological, or other scientific evidence.[12] The most validated ultrasound surrogate or intermediate markers of atherosclerosis include carotid intima media thickness (cIMT), CP, and carotid stiffness (STIFF), and are discussed in the following sections.

CAROTID INTIMA MEDIA THICKNESS

First described by Pignoli et al.[13] in 1986, cIMT is defined as the measured distance between the luminal–intimal interface and the media–adventitial interface of the common carotid artery (CCA). More specifically, the intima media thickness (IMT) is the double-line pattern visualized by B-mode vascular ultrasonography formed by the two parallel lines of (a) the junction of the vessel lumen with the intima and (b) the junction of the media with the adventitia (Figure 20.1).[14]

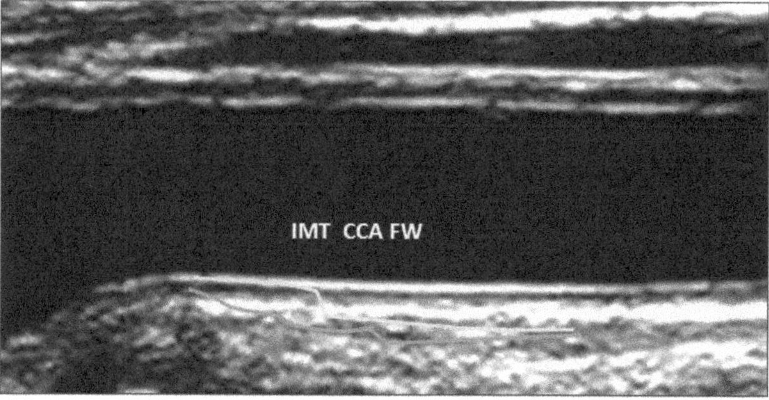

FIGURE 20.1 The double-line pattern of intima media thickness (IMT) in the far wall (FW) of the common carotid artery (CCA). The junction of the lumen (black) and intima is yellow, and that of the media and adventitia is green.

Because of the discrepancies reported in major IMT clinical trials, caused mostly by the use of different scanning and measurement protocols, in 2004 a consensus panel gathered in Mannheim, Germany, to review the cIMT assessment protocols.[15] The large studies reported different associations between cIMT and risk of stroke or MI, depending on whether cIMT was measured in the CCA or in the internal carotid artery (ICA).[16] The Mannheim consensus[17] has recommended that the most reliable cIMT measurements are obtained from the distal 2 cm of the CCA, proximal to the bifurcation, and preferably in a wall region free of plaque. The lower variability of IMT in CCA is one of the advantages of measuring IMT at this level, because the CCA lies close and runs relatively parallel to the skin. Also, plaque formation is less common in the CCA than either the bulb or the ICA, making measurements of IMT easier. The ICA, on the other hand, is less superficial, does not run parallel to the skin of the neck, and is often positioned high in the neck, near the angle of the jaw. These factors make the ICA more difficult to image and leads to a greater variability of IMT in the ICA. Therefore, the incorporation of ICA measurement into the overall cIMT measure produces more variability in the reported IMT results across studies.

For technical aspects, the Mannheim consensus has recommended the use of B-mode transducers with a minimum frequency of 7 MHz, ideally greater than 10 MHz for optimal scanning characteristics. An optimal focus depth of 30 to 40 mm should be used, and frame rates greater than 15 Hz should be obtained. A minimum 10-mm arterial length should be captured within the longitudinal scanning view.[17] Subsequently, other consensus statements for the use of cIMT in assessment of CVD risk in asymptomatic adults have been published by the American Heart Association,[18] the American Society of Echocardiography,[19] the U.S. Preventive Services Task Force,[20] the Society of Atherosclerosis Imaging and Prevention and the International Atherosclerosis Society,[21] and the Society for Vascular Surgery.[22] These professional organizations, in general, agree regarding the use of the standardized and validated IMT protocols for research and call for performing cIMT measurements in certified ultrasound laboratories.

Normal cIMT values in the general populations are reported by several large epidemiology studies.[23–26] The average cIMT varies by age, ranging from 0.50 mm in young individuals to 0.80 mm in the elderly. The upper range of normal is often taken as the 75th percentile of cIMT distribution for a given age, sex, and race/ethnicity of an individual, and values greater than this threshold are indicative of increased cardiovascular risk. By most experts, a cIMT greater than 1.0 mm is considered a value associated with increased vascular risk.

CAROTID PLAQUE

The Mannheim consensus defined CP as a focal extrusion into the arterial lumen of at least 0.5 mm or 50% of the surrounding cIMT value, or a thickness of more than 1.5 mm when measured in the same fashion as cIMT.[15] If CP is identified, the individual is considered to be at risk for future cardiovascular events, and no further cIMT imaging is necessary. Recently, the maximal CP thickness and carotid plaque area (CPA) have been measured by tracing the perimeter of the two-dimensional (2D) longitudinal images of CPs (Figure 20.2). These measures have been associated with a greater risk of stroke and vascular events.[27]

CPA is usually defined as the sum of the 2D areas of all plaques in the carotid arteries.[28] CPA is measured semimanually by tracing the plaque boundaries with electronic cursors or by automated computer-assisted edge detection programs, which are now available commercially (Figure 20.2). Recently, CPA has been demonstrated to be more predictive of stroke than cIMT.[29]

During the early 1990s, Fenster and colleagues began to obtain three-dimensional (3D) images of the carotid arteries[30] and to measure the volume of CP.[31–33] Currently, various, optimized 3D acquisition protocols exist, capturing ~30 slices/s of cross-sectional images of the carotid artery, which are stacked and reconstructed into a 3D image.[27] Although, the current evidence supports the good

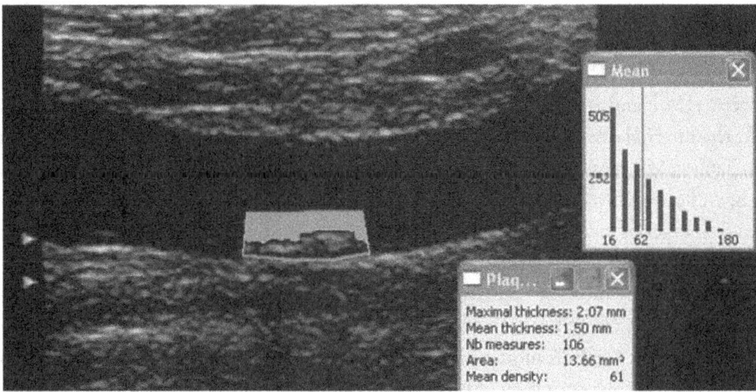

FIGURE 20.2 **Carotid plaque (located in grey area) measurements of maximal plaque thickness of 2.07 mm and area of 13.66 mm² (bottom legend).**

reproducibility of 3D ultrasound for the evaluation of CP volume,[33] there is high heterogeneity between studies. The superiority of 3D over 2D ultrasound in the identification of the vulnerable CP in clinical settings is yet to be established.

CP has been defined as "complicated" if it is associated with ipsilateral neurological symptoms and exhibits common ultrasonic characteristics of being predominately echolucent (soft) or heterogeneous (mixed).[7] In contrast, "uncomplicated" plaques are often asymptomatic, tend to be of uniform consistency, and have no evidence of ulceration.[7] Different classifications of CP ultrasonic appearance have been proposed. CP has been classified as homogenous and heterogeneous. Homogeneous plaques are those with "uniformly bright echoes" that are known as uniformly hyperechoic,[34] as dense and soft,[35] and as echolucent and echogenic based on their overall level of echo characteristics.[36]

The ultrasonographic grayscale densitometry index or grayscale median has been introduced recently as a new parameter to evaluate CP echogenicity. It is calculated as an average (or median) density of the reflecting grayscale signals from the normalized ultrasound image of plaque.[37] The grayscale densitometry index may reflect the content (morphology) of plaque, and therefore may represent a clinically useful marker of vascular risk and a novel tool for monitoring of the effects of antiatherosclerotic therapies.[37]

CAROTID STIFFNESS

STIFF is a measure of the vessel wall's tendency to resist deformation by systolic BP during the cardiac cycle, and is considered a parameter of arterial distensibility (inverse of stiffness).[38] STIFF is greater among people with manifest atherosclerosis, and is considered an early predictor of stroke and CVD.[39] Functional properties of the arterial wall preceding the clinical stage of atherosclerosis have been investigated in peripheral arteries (femoral and brachial) and in the aorta for many years by using different methodologies, such as measurement of pulse wave velocity. Recent development of high-resolution and high-definition ultrasonography has focused new investigations of STIFF on the carotid arteries.

Although an increased STIFF was considered intrinsic to the aging process of the artery,[40] it has been demonstrated that a number of vascular risk factors contribute to the stiffening of the arterial tree.[41] There is no consensus on the gold standard for measuring arterial STIFF. Several methods, including ultrasound, applanation tonometry, and pulse wave velocity, have been recommended by the First International Consensus Conference on the Clinical Applications of Arterial Stiffness[42] and by the European Network for Noninvasive Investigation of Large Arteries.[43] STIFF can be assessed noninvasively using B- or M-mode imaging, or wall track techniques, by measuring changes in lumen diameter during the cardiac cycle and relating them to the differences in systolic and diastolic blood pressure (BP).[44] In the Northern Manhattan Study (NOMAS), STIFF was a metric calculated as $\frac{In(Systolic\ BP - Diastolic\ BP)}{Strain}$, where Strain is defined as the amount of deformation relative to the unstressed state and is expressed as percent change in the arterial diameter: $\frac{Systolic\ Diameter - Diastolic\ Diameter}{Diastolic\ Diameter}$.[44] New methods, such as noninvasive vascular ultrasound elastography, were introduced recently to assess the mechanical properties (strain or elasticity) of peripheral vessel walls. Noninvasive vascular ultrasound elastography uses the Lagrangian estimator to compute vascular elastograms and was found to be quite accurate and reproducible.[45]

Recently, researchers reported racial/ethnic differences in STIFF and arterial diameter in the NOMAS population,[46] with greater carotid artery diameter and STIFF in Hispanics. These findings may offer a possible explanation for disparities in stroke morbidity and mortality in Hispanics in comparison with blacks and whites.

Markers of Carotid Atherosclerosis and Risk of Stroke in Epidemiological Studies

CAROTID INTIMA MEDIA THICKNESS AND RISK OF STROKE

cIMT has been used increasingly as a surrogate end point of vascular outcomes in epidemiological studies and clinical trials aimed at determining the success of interventions that lower risk factors for atherosclerosis and associated vascular disease.[17] The relative risk of high cIMT in comparison with low cIMT in the CCA, adjusted for age and sex, ranged from 2.3 to 3.5 for stroke and 2.3 to 4.0 for total CVD.[47] In a systematic review and meta-analysis, Lorenz et al.[48] reviewed eight observational studies conducted on 37,197 subjects with carotid ultrasound data who were monitored for a mean of 5.5 years. For an absolute cIMT difference of 0.1 mm, the future risk of stroke increased by 13% to 18%.[48] Most studies reported cIMT to be an independent but relatively modest predictor of coronary heart disease (CHD). cIMT may be a better predictor for stroke than for CHD,[47] although this is not reported consistently across studies.

Despite this evidence from epidemiological studies, the enthusiasm for the use of IMT in risk prediction has decreased recently after the results were published of a meta-analysis of 41 trials with 18,307 participants. cIMT regression or slowed progression induced by cardiovascular drug therapies did not translate into the reduction of cerebrovascular events.[49] In addition, prediction of stroke risk varied across the different carotid segments where cIMT was measured. For example, in 1975 participants from the Framingham Offspring Study, cIMT in the ICA, but not in the CCA, was associated with a greater prevalence of magnetic resonance imaging-defined cerebral infarcts.[50] However, a study conducted of 5056 individuals enrolled in the Carotid Atherosclerosis Progression Study demonstrated that cIMT measured in the CCA, bifurcation, and the ICA was highly predictive of stroke even after adjusting for age, sex, and vascular risk factors. Its predictive value was at least as high in younger subjects as in older subjects.[51] In the Atherosclerosis Risk in Communities (ARIC) study, a large population-based study of 13,123 participants with a mean follow-up of 8 years, the absolute annual stroke risk associated with cIMT, measured at the carotid bifurcation, ICA, and CCA, more than 1.0 mm was 0.5% for both men and women.[52] Interestingly, findings from the Progression Intima Media Thickness (PROG-IMT) Study suggested that estimation of cIMT progression may be more useful in predicting CVD than the singular, one-time-point cIMT measurement.[53]

It is important to note that increased cIMT may represent pathological changes of arterial medial hypertrophy or intimal thickening in the absence of atherosclerosis, in which case cIMT is not a real representation of atherosclerosis. However, because the pathological changes and atherosclerosis share common underlying mechanisms, cIMT may be an indicator of the overall vascular risk in an individual.[54]

CP AND RISK OF STROKE

Atherosclerotic plaques that are prone to rupture as a result of their intrinsic composition of a large lipid core, thin fibrous cap, and intraplaque hemorrhage are associated with thromboembolic ischemic events.[55] The presence of stenotic atherosclerotic CP is a well-established risk factor for ischemic stroke.[56]

Small nonstenotic plaque has also been associated with an increased risk of vascular disease. In NOMAS, subclinical CP was a strong predictor of vascular outcomes[57] and beyond the effect of the traditional FRS. In addition, CP with an irregular surface increased the risk of ischemic stroke threefold.[3] The cumulative 5-year ischemic stroke risk among individuals with an irregular plaque surface was more than 8%, whereas those with regular plaque had a stroke risk of less than 3%. These data suggest that plaque surface irregularity, even after adjusting for degree of stenosis and plaque thickness, is an independent predictor of stroke. The data from NOMAS are in agreement with the Rotterdam study,[58] in which the presence of CP increased the risk of stroke and cerebral infarction 1.5-fold, regardless of plaque location.

There is conflicting evidence about the effect of calcified CP on cardiovascular events.[59] Individuals with calcified or echodense plaque are less likely to have symptomatic disease.[60] In contrast, the studies conducted in NOMAS showed that calcified CP was an independent predictor of combined vascular events, defined as ischemic stroke, MI, or vascular death.[61] Moreover, it was demonstrated that people with maximum CP thickness greater than 1.9 mm had a 2.8-fold increased risk of combined vascular events in comparison with subjects without CP.[3] Interestingly, in this study, the amount of atherosclerosis overall was greater among whites and blacks than among Hispanics; but, if CP was present, it had a significant impact on vascular risk only among Hispanics. In fact, in fully adjusted models, the association between CP and vascular events was significant among Hispanics only, suggesting a role of race/ethnicity in the CP-related risk of CVD. Calcified plaque appeared to be a significant predictor of combined vascular outcomes when compared with the absence of plaque and after adjusting for demographics, mean cIMT, education, and risk factors. In agreement with this study, the presence of CP was associated with a twofold increased risk of ischemic stroke in the ARIC study.[62]

New evidence suggests that total CPA is the strongest CVD predictor among the ultrasound phenotypes of subclinical atherosclerosis, including plaque presence, thickness, or cIMT. In the Tromso study, a large population-based study, total CPA was a stronger predictor for incident ischemic stroke than cIMT.[29] In 3240 men and 3444 women, ultrasonographic assessment of plaque area resulted in a significant hazard ratio (HR) of 1.23 in men and 1.19 in women for 1-standard deviation increase in square root-transformed plaque area when adjusted for other cardiovascular risk factors. The multivariable-adjusted HR in the highest quartile of plaque area versus no plaque was 1.73 in men and 1.62 in women.

Taken together, these data support a strong association between the presence of small nonstenotic CP and stroke. However, comparison of the results from various populations must be considered with caution. Differences in demographics and risk factor profiles across different study populations, and use of different measurements of subclinical atherosclerosis may have contributed to varying plaque burden and its associated risk of cerebrovascular events.

STIFF AND RISK OF STROKE

Although study populations, designs, and methods used in different reports have been inconsistent, increased STIFF has been associated with an increased risk of vascular disease. Evidence for a relation of STIFF with future CVD in population-based studies is, however, limited. In a sample of 79 patients with end-stage renal disease patients who were monitored for a mean of 25 months, increased STIFF was associated with a 6.4-fold increased risk of CVD and all-cause mortality, including stroke, independent of other prognostic factors such as diastolic BP and the total cholesterol-to-high-density lipoprotein ratio.[63] In a case–control study conducted in 267 stroke patients, carotid distensibility (inverse of STIFF) was significantly lower in stroke patients than in control subjects even after adjusting for BP, and diastolic carotid diameter and height. Each 1-standard deviation decreased in the carotid distensibility increased the likelihood of stroke independently by 167%.[64] Data from the Second Manifestations of Arterial Disease study confirmed these findings.[65] In 420 participants with carotid stenosis of 50% or greater, the risk of ischemic stroke or transient ischemic attack in the highest quartile of STIFF relative to the lowest quartile was doubled after adjusting for age, sex, systolic BP, minimal diameter of the carotid artery, and degree of carotid artery stenosis.[66]

Several mechanisms may explain the association between increased STIFF and stroke. STIFF may favor the occurrence of CVD through an increase in central pulse pressure that influences arterial remodeling at the sites of both the extracranial and intracranial arteries, increasing the development of carotid artery stenosis and the likelihood of plaque ulceration and rupture. Furthermore, STIFF may be associated with cerebral microvascular processes important in stroke pathogenesis.[39]

In contrast, the Rotterdam study[67] reported no association between carotid distensibility (inverse of STIFF) and stroke. Different populations, methods, and analyses may explain the lack of replication of the study results. Nonetheless, similar to the other markers of subclinical atherosclerosis, the genetic component may play an important role in STIFF.

Table 20.1[68–71] reports some of the principal epidemiological studies that evaluated the impact of subclinical carotid atherosclerosis (cIMT, CP, and STIFF) on the risk of stroke and CVD.

Carotid Plaque (CP) Versus Carotid Intima Media Thickness (cIMT) in the Prediction of CVD

CP is a focal manifestation of atherosclerosis and largely a biologically and genetically different phenotype from cIMT.[27,68] This is not a generally accepted concept, although the supporting evidence that they are distinct markers of vascular disease has been accumulating. cIMT is related mainly to hypertension, resulting in hypertrophy of the media layer of the vessel wall.[15] There is evidence of different genetic contributions to cIMT than to CP, which seems to be influenced more strongly by environmental factors.[72] Traditional vascular risk factors explain only 15% to 17% of the variance in cIMT,[72–74] but account for 52% of the variance in total CPA.[75] Furthermore, although the two processes—cIMT and plaque formation—share some common risk factors, their overlap is partial, and their predictive power for CVD differs. CP seems to be a stronger predictor of CVD than cIMT in large population-based studies (Table 20.2).[76] Nevertheless, the differentiation of early plaque formation from increased cIMT depends on the definition of plaque. Various studies have adopted different plaque definitions, but most include thickness of plaque in the calculation of cIMT.[77]

Atherosclerosis, including plaque formation, represents a dynamic process involving a complex cascade of inflammatory events from lipid deposition to plaque calcification.[78] The combination of cIMT and CP has been shown to improve the prediction of CVD compared with cIMT or CP alone.[79] The comparison of the predictive power of cIMT and CP across various studies, however, is limited as a result of (a) the site of cIMT used (the far wall or the far and near wall combined, the

TABLE 20.1

Principal Epidemiological Studies That Evaluated the Impact of Subclinical Carotid Atherosclerosis on Stroke and Cardiovascular Disease

Study	Subclinical atherosclerosis Measures	n	Follow-up, y	Age, y	Combined vascular events[a] hazard ratio (95% CI)	MI hazard ratio (95% CI)	Stroke hazard ratio (95% CI)
NOMAS[3]	CP	2189	6.9	68 ± 10	2.76 (2.10–3.63)	2.87 (1.73–4.78)	1.79 (1.11–2.90)
Tromsø[34]	cIMT and CP	6584	9.6	25–84	NR	NR	cIMT 1.08 (0.95–1.22) in men, 1.24 (1.05–1.48) in women, TCPA 1.73 (1.19–2.52) in men, 1.62 (1.04–2.53) in women
CAPS[53]	cIMT	5056	4.2	50.1	1.45 (1.38–1.52)	1.43 (1.35–1.51)	1.47 (1.35–1.60)
ARIC[52]	cIMT	14,214	7.5	45–64	NR	NR	2.0 (1.20–3.20) in men, 3.3 (1.90–5.80) in women
Rotterdam[58]	CP	4217	5.2	68 ± 8	NR	NR	2.44 (1.42–4.20)
SMART[65]	STIFF and cIMT	570	11.5	59 ± 12	STIFF, HR = 0.23 (0.17–0.27); cIMT, 1.37 (1.15–1.60)	NR	NR
Rotterdam[67]	STIFF	2835	4.1	71 ± 6	2.40 (1.51–3.83)	2.45 (1.29–4.66)	2.28 (1.05–4.96)
Framingham[69]	cIMT and CP	2965	7.2	58 ± 10	cIMT, 1.13 (1.02–1.24); CP, 0.014 (0.003–0.025)	NR	NR
REACH[70]	cIMT	2317	2	68 ± 10	2.09 (1.07–4.10)	1.71 (1.10–2.67)	1.73 (1.31–2.27)
MESA[71]	cIMT	6698	5.3	45–84	1.62 (1.372–1.874)	2.3 (1.5–3.7)	3.5 (1.9–6.6)

[a]MI, stroke, and vascular death.

ARIC, Atherosclerosis Risk in Communities; CAPS, Carotid Atherosclerosis Progression Study; CI, confidence interval; cIMT, carotid intima media thickness; CP, carotid plaque; MESA, Multi-Ethnic Study of Atherosclerosis; MI: myocardial infarction; NOMAS, Northern Manhattan Study; NR, not reported; REACH, Reduction of Atherothrombosis for Continued Health; SMART, Second Manifestations of Arterial Disease; STIFF, carotid stiffness; TCPA, total carotid plaque area.

TABLE 20.2

Plaque Is a "Better" Predictor of CVD than cIMT

Ultrasound measure of subclinical atherosclerosis	Hazard ratio[a]
IMT >1.0 mm	1.5
Plaque presence	1.8
Plaque thickness	2.0
Plaque area	3.0

[a]Approximate average from various studies.
cIMT, carotid intima media thickness; CVD, cardiovascular disease; IMT, intima media thickness.

single CCA or a combined measure of CCA with bifurcation and ICA), (b) the inconstant incorporation of CP in the cIMT measure, (c) the use of mean or maximum cIMT, (d) different CP phenotypes (presence, thickness, area, calcification, ulceration), (e) the arbitrary cutoff point to evaluate cIMT ability to predict risk, and (f) the generalizability of the prognostic value of cIMT, obtained mainly in middle-age and elderly populations, to younger individuals when data are insufficient. Therefore, further studies are needed to clarify more completely the biological and genetic mechanisms underlying cIMT and CP, and their role in CVD in various populations.

Added Value of Intermediate Markers of Carotid Atherosclerosis on Prediction of Stroke by Risk Factors

Subclinical markers of carotid atherosclerosis may provide additional prognostic information to that of traditional risk factors. Besides traditional vascular risk factors such as high BP, diabetes, smoking, stress, obesity, and metabolic syndrome, there is a growing list of less traditional factors such as high LDL or low high-density lipoprotein, C-reactive protein (CRP), lipoprotein(a), homocysteine, LDL particle size, Lp-PLA2, apolipoprotein B/apolipoprotein A.[80] Most of them have been combined with vascular risk scores such as FRS. However, FRS remains the primarily recommended risk prediction tool in preventive guidelines to identify individuals at risk and their targets for preventive therapy.[81]

In the recent analysis from the ARIC study of 13,145 subjects, approximately 23% individuals were reclassified into a different risk category group after adding information on cIMT and CP.[79] Adding cIMT to traditional risk factors provided the most improvement in the area under the receiver–operating characteristic curve, which increased from 0.74 to 0.77. Adding CP to cIMT and traditional risk factors had, however, the best net reclassification index of 10% in the overall population. In the Cardiovascular Health Study,[82] of 5888 participants, an elevated CRP level was associated with increased risk for CVD and stroke only among those individuals who had increased cIMT and plaque detectable on carotid ultrasound. Despite these significant associations with CVD, CRP, cIMT, and plaque improved only modestly the prediction of CVD outcomes, after accounting for the traditional risk factors. Addition of CRP or subclinical carotid atherosclerosis to conventional risk factors resulted in a modest increase in the ability to predict CVD.

In NOMAS, the presence of CP contributed considerably to the better estimation of 10-year FRS.[3] More than a half of the individuals in low and moderate FRS categories were reclassified into the higher risk category if CP was present, and about 30% to 40% were reclassified if the CP thickness was greater than 1.9 mm (bold type in the Table 20.3).

TABLE 20.3

Carotid Plaque Presence and Thickness Reclassifies More Than 30% of Subjects into a Greater FRS Stroke Category in the General Multiethnic Population

	Low FRS		Moderate FRS		High FRS	
Carotid Measures	*N* or *n* (%)	10Year risk, %	*N* or *n* (%)	10-Year risk, %	*N* or *n* (%)	10-Year risk, %
Overall	505 (26)	11.4	920 (47)	15.6	541 (27)	26.0
No plaque	285 (26)	5.8	402 (44)	11.5	178 (33)	27.6
MCPT ≥1.9mm	**62 (12)**	**24.7**	**173 (19)**	**25.1**	157 (29)	30.7
***p* Value**		.004		.002		.319

Note: Adapted from Rundek et al.[3]
FRS, Framingham Risk Score; MCPT, maximum carotid plaque thickness. Cells in bold indicate participant subgroups wherein carotid data significantly modified risk prediction based on the FRS.

Other studies, such as the Carotid Atherosclerosis Progression Study,[83] the Paroi Artérielle et Risque Cardio-vasculaire (PARC) study,[84] and the Framingham Offspring Study,[69] showed that cIMT measurements may have a favorable impact on selecting and targeting subjects at intermediate FRS risk in primary prevention. Traditional CVD risk prediction schemes need further improvement and assessment of cIMT, and CP may add to risk stratification with a direct implication for intervention in vascular preventive programs.

Clinical Utility of Detecting Carotid Atherosclerosis in Prevention of Stroke: Who Should Be Really Screened?

A major challenge associated with the primary prevention of stroke involves the early and accurate detection of subclinical atherosclerosis in an asymptomatic population at risk. Delay in identifying at-risk individuals may result in a missed opportunity to prevent CVD. Therefore, early detection of subclinical carotid atherosclerosis could help CVD prevention and reduce substantially death and disability attributable to stroke. This goal may be furthered by developing and disseminating the standardized and validated noninvasive ultrasound diagnostic techniques for the identification of individuals at risk in the general population. It has been reported that when subclinical disease develops, the traditional risk factors appear to have a lesser association with the subsequent development of clinical disease, although the traditional risk factors are the primary determinants of subclinical disease.[85] Recently, in NOMAS, researchers demonstrated that traditional vascular risk factors explain only 21% of the variance in the total carotid plaque burden.[11]

With increasing incidence of CVD and stroke, it is important to identify high-risk patients with subclinical manifestation of disease who will benefit from early and aggressive therapy. The Mannheim cIMT consensus states that there is no need to "treat IMT values" nor to monitor IMT values in individual patients apart from a few exceptions.[17] The current American Heart Association guideline for the use of cIMT in the assessment of cardiovascular risk in asymptomatic adults gives cIMT a class IIa rank with a level B for evidence for asymptomatic adults at intermediate risk. It emphasizes the importance of following clear recommendations on the use of appropriate scanning and reading imaging ultrasound methodology.[18] Accordingly, the American Society of Echocardiography recommends that the use of cIMT assessment be reserved for individuals with

Appropriate indications:	Inappropriate:
Intermediate risk patients	Serial testing
Metabolic syndrome	Low risk patients
Older patients	Very high-risk patients

FIGURE 20.3 Appropriate Clinical Use of cIMT.

intermediate cardiovascular risk (e.g., a 6% to 20% 10-year risk of CVD according to FRS). Because some high-risk groups might not be addressed by this approach, there are additional clinical circumstances that should be considered: (a) family history of premature CVD in a first-degree relative (men, <55 years old; women, <65 years old); (b) individuals younger than 60 years with severe abnormalities in a single risk factor (e.g., genetic dyslipidemia) who otherwise would not be candidates for pharmacotherapy, or (c) women younger than 60 years with at least two CVD risk factors.[19]

Appropriate use of measuring cIMT in the clinical setting was examined recently by the Society of Atherosclerosis Imaging and Prevention and the International Atherosclerosis Society.[21] To prevent either under- or overuse of IMT measurements, common clinical scenarios—including risk assessment in the absence of known CHD, risk assessment in patients with known CHD, and serial cIMT imaging for monitoring of CHD risk status—were rated. The conclusion of these professional organizations was that appropriate indications for the use of cIMT should be reserved for individuals without CHD with intermediate risk, older individuals, and individuals with metabolic syndrome. The testing of low-risk or very high-risk individuals with CHD as well as serial cIMT testing is currently considered inappropriate for use in clinical practice (Figure 20.3).

Future Perspectives: Genetics of Subclinical Atherosclerosis and cIMT Progression

GENETICS OF SUBCLINICAL CAROTID ATHEROSCLEROSIS

Genetic and environmental factors underlying subclinical atherosclerosis are of great importance for successful prevention of stroke and CVD, and are in the major focus for future investigations. Genetic contribution also seems to play a pivotal role in the mechanism of cIMT.[86,87] In the Family Study of Stroke Risk and Carotid Atherosclerosis, a high heritability of cIMT was reported in Caribbean Hispanics, and ranged from 0.41 to 0.65 across the different carotid segments. In that study, significant linkage was reported for cIMT on chromosome 7p and 14q.[88,89] Moreover, in a recent cIMT fine-mapping study conducted on the same families, several loci comprising genes strongly related with inflammation were identified.[88] In a candidate gene study conducted in a sample from NOMAS, associations between cIMT and 702 single nucleotide polymorphisms (SNPs) were found for 145 candidate genes involved in the pathophysiology of atherosclerosis,[30] predominantly in hemostasis (PLAT, THBS1), extracellular matrix remodeling (MMP3, MMP12, TGFB2), inflammation (*CXCL12, PTGS2*), antioxidation (*PON1*), endothelium function (*NOS1, SELP*), and the renin–angiotensin system (*SCNN1B, ACE, REN*).[70] In addition, variants in stromelysin 1, interleukin 6, and hepatic lipase genes were associated with cIMT in an earlier study from NOMAS.[90]

Recently in NOMAS, a modest but significant heritability of 0.50 for CP presence and 0.17 for plaque area was reported.[91] The National Heart, Lung, and Blood Institute Family Heart Study[92] reported a heritability of 0.52 for CP, and the San Antonio Family Heart Study[93] showed a heritability of 0.23 for CP. The Diabetes Heart Study[94] found a heritability of 0.40 for calcified CP in white Americans.

In linkage analyses, researchers identified four regions with multipoint LOD scores of 2.00 or more on chromosomes 7q36, 11p15, 14q32, and 15q23 (Figure 20.4). Genetic variants in genes related to inflammation, endothelial function, lipid metabolism, and oxidative stress have been reported to be associated with CP phenotypes.[95,96] These results call for further fine mapping and sequencing of interesting regions, as well as validation in other cohorts.

Other epidemiological studies have taken similar approaches to genetic investigations of subclinical atherosclerosis. Most have reported candidate gene associations, and a few performed linkage analyses and/or fine mapping. In the National Heart, Lung, and Blood Institute Offspring Cohort of the Framingham Heart Study, 11 SNPs with associations at p values less than 10^{-5} were identified for maximum internal cIMT, and five SNPs with associations at p values less than 10^{-5} were identified by family-based association testing for mean common cIMT. In addition, several regions of linkage to internal cIMT were identified on chromosome 12, confirming previous results from the same population.[97]

Recently, the CHARGE consortium[98] reported genomewide association results of cIMT in a sample of 31,211 participants from nine population-based studies and a follow-up analysis that included 11,273 participants from seven independent studies. For common cIMT, they found three independent loci that achieved the genomewide significance threshold ($p < 5 \times 10^{-8}$) in the combined meta-analysis of discovery and follow-up studies. The strongest association was for rs11781551, close to *ZHX2*, and for rs445925, close to *APOC1*. However, scant information exists regarding the function and the proteins encoded by these genes, and their relationships to CVD. No SNP achieved a significance threshold in the follow-up analyses of internal cIMT. For CP, two independent loci achieved the genomewide significance threshold in the combined meta-analysis. The most significant signal was for rs17398575, near *PIK3CG*, which plays an important role in maintaining the structural and functional integrity of endothelium. The second signal was centered at rs1878406, near *EDNRA*, a target for pharmacological treatments to reduce BP. Moreover, SNPs in *EDNRA* were associated with both CP and CHD.

One of the main reasons for the inconsistent results for cIMT and CP may be that multiple genes are likely to influence carotid atherosclerosis, which could account for some of the variation in findings

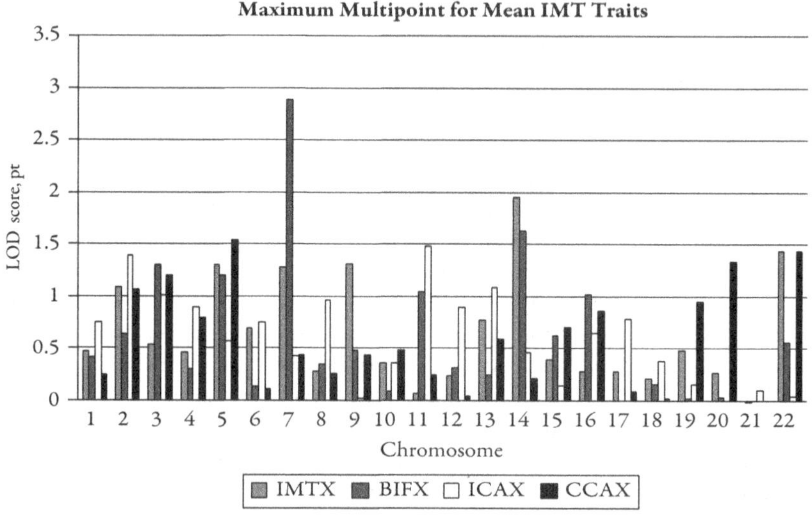

FIGURE 20.4 Maximum multipoint linkage results for mean intima media thickness traits. Multipoint (Logarithm of Odds) LOD scores by chromosome. The most significant results are seen on chromosomes 7 and 14.

IMTX, carotid IMT; BIFX, IMT at carotid bifurcation; ICAX, IMT on internal carotid artery; CCAX, IMT on common carotid artery

among genetic studies. In addition, each segment of carotid artery has its own unique anatomy and hemodynamic environment, and therefore is prone to different pathophysiological mechanisms.[87]. Genetic studies of stroke due to large artery atherosclerosis are discussed in Chapter 5. Collaborative efforts to extend our knowledge of genetic risk factors for subclinical markers of atherosclerosis, and atherosclerosis in relation with stroke, are currently ongoing within various consortia such as CHARGE, the National Institute of Neurological Disorders and Stroke–Ischemic Stroke Genetic Network, the International Stroke Genetic Consortium, and the Genomics and Randomized Trials Network.[99]

Understanding the complexity of the pathogenesis of atherosclerosis will be essential in considering the interaction between genetic and environmental risk factors. Currently, these interactions are poorly understood. Ultimately, the prediction of the disease risk for individuals will be determined by their genotypic and environmental exposures.

PROGRESSION OF CIMT

Recently a collaborative effort has been made by the cIMT Progression Study Group to predict cardiovascular events in the general population (the PROG-IMT collaborative project),[77] a team of international experts in the field of atherosclerosis aiming to test the association between changes in cIMT and cardiovascular risk. In a meta-analysis conducted of 36,984 participants, in whom cIMT progression was derived from two ultrasound visits 2 to 7 years (median, 4 years) apart, the mean cIMT of the baseline as well as of the repeated ultrasound scan was associated positively and robustly with cardiovascular risk, including stroke (HR for the combined end point, 1.16; 95% confidence interval, 1.10–1.22, adjusted for age, sex, mean common cIMT progression, and vascular risk factors).[77] However, cIMT progression calculated from the two visits was not found to be associated significantly with the risk of vascular events. According to the PROG-IMT, the association between cIMT progression assessed from two ultrasound scans and CVD risk in the general population remains unproved. Furthermore, no conclusion can be derived for the use of cIMT progression as a surrogate measure in clinical trials. More frequent cIMT measurements could increase the precision of the assessment of cIMT progression and, therefore, better predict the risk for stroke and CVD. The use of repeated assessment of cIMT in CVD risk assessment still awaits its clinical validation.

Conclusion

In conclusion, subclinical phenotypes of carotid atherosclerosis are significant predictors of vascular events. Ultrasound measures of cIMT, CP, and STIFF are noninvasive, inexpensive tools to detect individuals with increased atherosclerotic burden and risk of CVD and stroke, evaluate the effects of current and novel therapies, and investigate new contributing factors. However, more research is needed to understand more fully the genetic and environmental factors associated with these markers in various populations to develop more efficient and targeted preventive therapies.

REFERENCES

1. Roger VL, Go AS, Lloyd-Jones DM, et al. Heart disease and stroke statistics—2012 update: a report from the American Heart Association. *Circulation*. 2012;125:e2–e220.
2. Prabhakaran S, Rundek T, Ramas R, et al. Carotid plaque surface irregularity predicts ischemic stroke: the Northern Manhattan Study. *Stroke*. 2006;37:2696–2701.
3. Rundek T, Arif H, Boden-Albala B, et al. Carotid plaque, a subclinical precursor of vascular events: the Northern Manhattan Study. *Neurology*. 2008;70:1200–1207.

4. Krupinski J, Font A, Luque A, Turu M, Slevin M. Angiogenesis and inflammation in carotid atherosclerosis. *Front Biosci.* 2008;13:6472–6482.
5. Tardif JC, Heinonen T, Orloff D, Libby P. Vascular biomarkers and surrogates in cardiovascular disease. *Circulation.* 2006;113:2936–2942.
6. Warboys CM, Amini N, de Luca A, Evans PC. The role of blood flow in determining the sites of atherosclerotic plaques. *F1000 Med Rep.* 2011;3:5.
7. Carotid artery plaque composition: relationship to clinical presentation and ultrasound B-mode imaging: European Carotid Plaque Study Group. *Eur J Vasc Endovasc Surg.* 1995;10:23–30.
8. Creager MA, Belkin M, Bluth EI, et al. 2012 ACCF/AHA/ACR/SCAI/SIR/STS/SVM/SVN/SVS key data elements and definitions for peripheral atherosclerotic vascular disease: a report of the American College of Cardiology Foundation/American Heart Association Task Force on Clinical Data Standards (Writing Committee to Develop Clinical Data Standards for Peripheral Atherosclerotic Vascular Disease). *Circulation.* 2012;125:395–467.
9. D'Agostino RB Sr, Vasan RS, Pencina MJ, et al. General cardiovascular risk profile for use in primary care: the Framingham Heart Study. *Circulation.* 2008;117:743–753.
10. Brindle P, Beswick A, Fahey T, Ebrahim S. Accuracy and impact of risk assessment in the primary prevention of cardiovascular disease: a systematic review. *Heart.* 2006;92: 1752–1759.
11. Kuo F, Gardener H, Dong C, et al. Traditional cardiovascular risk factors Explain the minority of the variability in carotid plaque. *Stroke.* 2012;43:1755–1760
12. Atkinson AJ, Colburn WA, DeGruttola VG, et al. Biomarkers and surrogate endpoints: preferred definitions and conceptual framework. *Clin Pharmacol Ther.* 2001;69:89–95.
13. Pignoli P, Tremoli E, Poli A, Oreste P, Paoletti R. Intimal plus medial thickness of the arterial wall: a direct measurement with ultrasound imaging. *Circulation.* 1986;74:1399–1406.
14. Wikstrand J, Wendelhag I. Methodological considerations of ultrasound investigation of intima-media thickness and lumen diameter. *J Intern Med.* 1994;236:555–559.
15. Touboul PJ, Hennerici MG, Meairs S, et al. Mannheim intima-media thickness consensus. *Cerebrovasc Dis.* 2004;18:346–349.
16. Liviakis L, Pogue B, Paramsothy P, Bourne A, Gill EA. Carotid intima-media thickness for the practicing lipidologist. *J Clin Lipidol.* 2010;4: 24–35.
17. Touboul PJ, Hennerici MG, Meairs S, et al. Mannheim carotid intima-media thickness consensus (2004–2006): an update on behalf of the Advisory Board of the 3rd and 4th Watching the Risk Symposium, 13th and 15th European Stroke Conferences, Mannheim, Germany, 2004, and Brussels, Belgium, 2006. *Cerebrovasc Dis.* 2007;23:75–80.
18. Greenland P, Alpert JS, Beller GA, et al. 2010 ACCF/AHA guideline for assessment of cardiovascular risk in asymptomatic adults: a report of the American College of Cardiology Foundation/American Heart Association Task Force on Practice Guidelines. *J Am Coll Cardiol.* 2010;56:e50–e103.
19. Stein JH, Korcarz CE, Hurst RT, et al. Use of carotid ultrasound to identify subclinical vascular disease and evaluate cardiovascular disease risk: a consensus statement from the American Society of Echocardiography Carotid Intima-Media Thickness Task Force: endorsed by the Society for Vascular Medicine. *J Am Soc Echocardiogr.* 2008;21:93–111; quiz 189–190.
20. U.S. Preventive Services Task Force. Using nontraditional risk factors in coronary heart disease risk assessment: U.S. Preventive Services Task Force recommendation statement. *Ann Intern Med.* 2009;151:474–482.
21. Society of Atherosclerosis Imaging and Prevention developed in collaboration with the International Atherosclerosis Society. Appropriate use criteria for carotid intima media thickness testing. *Atherosclerosis.* 2011;214:43–46.
22. Hobson RW 2nd, Mackey WC, Ascher E, et al. Management of atherosclerotic carotid artery disease: clinical practice guidelines of the Society for Vascular Surgery. *J Vasc Surg.* 2008;48:480–486.

23. O'Leary DH, Polak JF, Kronmal RA, et al. Carotid-artery intima and media thickness as a risk factor for myocardial infarction and stroke in older adults: Cardiovascular Health Study Collaborative Research Group. *N Engl J Med.* 1999;340:14–22.
24. Howard G, Sharrett AR, Heiss G, et al. Carotid artery intimal-medial thickness distribution in general populations as evaluated by B-mode ultrasound: ARIC Investigators. *Stroke.* 1993;24:1297–1304.
25. Tzou WS, Douglas PS, Srinivasan SR, et al. Distribution and predictors of carotid intima-media thickness in young adults. *Prev Cardiol.* 2007;10:181–189.
26. Folsom AR, Kronmal RA, Detrano RC, et al. Coronary artery calcification compared with carotid intima-media thickness in the prediction of cardiovascular disease incidence: the Multi-Ethnic Study of Atherosclerosis (MESA). *Arch Intern Med.* 2008;168:1333–1339.
27. Spence JD. Measurement of intima-media thickness vs. carotid plaque: uses in patient care, genetic research and evaluation of new therapies. *Int J Stroke.* 2006;1:216–221.
28. Spence JD. Technology insight: ultrasound measurement of carotid plaque: patient management, genetic research, and therapy evaluation. *Nat Clin Pract Neurol.* 2006;2:611–619.
29. Mathiesen EB, Johnsen SH, Wilsgaard T, et al. Carotid plaque area and intima-media thickness in prediction of first-ever ischemic stroke: a 10-year follow-up of 6584 men and women: the Tromso Study. *Stroke.* 2011;42:972–978.
30. Picot PA, Rickey DW, Mitchell R, Rankin RN, Fenster A. Three-dimensional colour Doppler imaging. *Ultrasound Med Biol.* 1993;19:95–104.
31. Landry A, Fenster A. Theoretical and experimental quantification of carotid plaque volume measurements made by three-dimensional ultrasound using test phantoms. *Med Phys.* 2002;29:2319–2327.
32. Fenster A, Landry A, Downey DB, Hegele RA, Spence JD. 3D ultrasound imaging of the carotid arteries. *Curr Drug Targets Cardiovasc Haematol Disord.* 2004;4:161–175.
33. Landry A, Spence JD, Fenster A. Measurement of carotid plaque volume by 3-dimensional ultrasound. *Stroke.* 2004;35:864–869.
34. Reilly LM, Lusby RJ, Hughes L, et al. Carotid plaque histology using real-time ultrasonography: clinical and therapeutic implications. *Am J Surg.* 1983;146:188–193.
35. Johnson JM, Kennelly MM, Decesare D, Morgan S, Sparrow A. Natural history of asymptomatic carotid plaque. *Arch Surg.* 1985;120:1010–1012.
36. Widder B, Paulat K, Hackspacher J, et al. Morphological characterization of carotid artery stenoses by ultrasound duplex scanning. *Ultrasound Med Biol.* 1990;16:349–354.
37. Della-Morte D, Moussa I, Elkind MS, Sacco RL, Rundek T. The short-term effect of atorvastatin on carotid plaque morphology assessed by computer-assisted gray-scale densitometry: a pilot study. *Neurol Res.* 2011;33:991–994.
38. Godia EC, Madhok R, Pittman J, et al. Carotid artery distensibility: a reliability study. *J Ultrasound Med.* 2007;26:1157–1165.
39. Bots ML, Dijk JM, Oren A, Grobbee DE. Carotid intima-media thickness, arterial stiffness and risk of cardiovascular disease: current evidence. *J Hypertens.* 2002;20:2317–2325.
40. O'Rourke MF. The arterial pulse in health and disease. *Am Heart J.* 1971;82:687–702.
41. Chirinos JA. Arterial stiffness: basic concepts and measurement techniques. *J Cardiovasc Transl Res.* 2012;5:243–255.
42. Van Bortel LM, Duprez D, Starmans-Kool MJ, et al. Clinical applications of arterial stiffness: task force III: recommendations for user procedures. *Am J Hypertens.* 2002;15:445–452.
43. Laurent S, Cockcroft J, Van Bortel L, et al. Expert consensus document on arterial stiffness: methodological issues and clinical applications. *Eur Heart J.* 2006;27:2588–2605.
44. Della-Morte D, Gardener H, Denaro F, et al. Metabolic syndrome increases carotid artery stiffness: the Northern Manhattan Study. *Int J Stroke.* 2010;5:138–144.

45. Maurice RL, Soulez G, Giroux MF, Cloutier G. Noninvasive vascular elastography for carotid artery characterization on subjects without previous history of atherosclerosis. *Med Phys.* 2008;35:3436–3443.
46. Markert MS, Della-Morte D, Cabral D, et al. Ethnic differences in carotid artery diameter and stiffness: the Northern Manhattan Study. *Atherosclerosis.* 2011;219:827–832.
47. Simon A, Megnien JL, Chironi G. The value of carotid intima-media thickness for predicting cardiovascular risk. *Arterioscler Thromb Vasc Biol.* 2010;30:182–185.
48. Lorenz MW, Markus HS, Bots ML, Rosvall M, Sitzer M. Prediction of clinical cardiovascular events with carotid intima-media thickness: a systematic review and meta-analysis. *Circulation.* 2007;115:459–467.
49. Costanzo P, Perrone-Filardi P, Vassallo E, et al. Does carotid intima-media thickness regression predict reduction of cardiovascular events? A meta-analysis of 41 randomized trials. *J Am Coll Cardiol.* 2010;56:2006–2020.
50. Romero JR, Beiser A, Seshadri S, et al. Carotid artery atherosclerosis, MRI indices of brain ischemia, aging, and cognitive impairment: the Framingham study. *Stroke.* 2009;40:1590–1596.
51. Lorenz MW, von Kegler S, Steinmetz H, Markus HS, Sitzer M. Carotid intima-media thickening indicates a higher vascular risk across a wide age range: prospective data from the Carotid Atherosclerosis Progression Study (CAPS). *Stroke.* 2006;37:87–92.
52. Chambless LE, Folsom AR, Clegg LX, et al. Carotid wall thickness is predictive of incident clinical stroke: the Atherosclerosis Risk in Communities (ARIC) study. *Am J Epidemiol.* 2000;151:478–487.
53. Lorenz MW, Bickel H, Bots ML, et al. Individual progression of carotid intima media thickness as a surrogate for vascular risk (PROG-IMT): rationale and design of a meta-analysis project. *Am Heart J.* 2010;159:730–736, e732.
54. Finn AV, Kolodgie FD, Virmani R. Correlation between carotid intimal/medial thickness and atherosclerosis: a point of view from pathology. *Arterioscler Thromb Vasc Biol.* 2010;30:177–181.
55. Mughal MM, Khan MK, DeMarco JK, et al. Symptomatic and asymptomatic carotid artery plaque. *Exp Rev Cardiovasc Ther.* 2011;9:1315–1330.
56. Bock RW, Gray-Weale AC, Mock PA, et al. The natural history of asymptomatic carotid artery disease. *J Vasc Surg.* 1993;17:160–169; discussion 170–171.
57. Abe Y, Rundek T, Sciacca RR, et al. Ultrasound assessment of subclinical cardiovascular disease in a community-based multiethnic population and comparison to the Framingham score. *Am J Cardiol.* 2006;98:1374–1378.
58. Hollander M, Bots ML, Del Sol AI, et al. Carotid plaques increase the risk of stroke and subtypes of cerebral infarction in asymptomatic elderly: the Rotterdam study. *Circulation.* 2002;105:2872–2877.
59. Seeger JM, Barratt E, Lawson GA, Klingman N. The relationship between carotid plaque composition, plaque morphology, and neurologic symptoms. *J Surg Res.* 1995;58:330–336.
60. Hunt JL, Fairman R, Mitchell ME, et al. Bone formation in carotid plaques: a clinicopathological study. *Stroke.* 2002;33:1214–1219.
61. Prabhakaran S, Singh R, Zhou X, et al. Presence of calcified carotid plaque predicts vascular events: the Northern Manhattan Study. *Atherosclerosis.* 2007;195:e197–e201.
62. Hunt KJ, Evans GW, Folsom AR, et al. Acoustic shadowing on B-mode ultrasound of the carotid artery predicts ischemic stroke: the Atherosclerosis Risk in Communities (ARIC) study. *Stroke.* 2001;32:1120–1126.
63. Blacher J, Pannier B, Guerin AP, et al. Carotid arterial stiffness as a predictor of cardiovascular and all-cause mortality in end-stage renal disease. *Hypertension.* 1998;32:570–574.
64. Tsivgoulis G, Vemmos K, Papamichael C, et al. Common carotid arterial stiffness and the risk of ischaemic stroke. *Eur J Neurol.* 2006;13:475–481.

65. Simons PC, Algra A, Bots ML, Grobbee DE, van der Graaf Y. Common carotid intima-media thickness and arterial stiffness: indicators of cardiovascular risk in high-risk patients: the SMART Study (Second Manifestations of ARTerial disease). *Circulation*. 1999;100:951–957.
66. Dijk JM, van der Graaf Y, Grobbee DE, Bots ML. Carotid stiffness indicates risk of ischemic stroke and TIA in patients with internal carotid artery stenosis: the SMART study. *Stroke*. 2004;35:2258–2262.
67. Mattace-Raso FU, van der Cammen TJ, Hofman A, et al. Arterial stiffness and risk of coronary heart disease and stroke: the Rotterdam study. *Circulation*. 2006;113:657–663.
68. Rundek T, Brook RD, Spence JD. Letter by Rundek et al regarding article, "Prediction of clinical cardiovascular events with carotid intima-media thickness: a systematic review and meta-analysis." *Circulation*. 2007;116:e317; author reply e318.
69. Polak JF, Pencina MJ, Pencina KM, O'Donnell CJ, Wolf PA, D'Agostino RB Sr. Carotid-wall intima-media thickness and cardiovascular events. *N Engl J Med*. 2011;365:213–221.
70. Keo HH1, Baumgartner I, Hirsch AT, et al. Carotid plaque and intima-media thickness and the incidence of ischemic events in patients with atherosclerotic vascular disease. *Vasc Med*. 2011;16:323–330.
71. Polak JF, Szklo M, Kronmal RA, et al. The value of carotid artery plaque and intima-media thickness for incident cardiovascular disease: the multi-ethnic study of atherosclerosis. *J Am Heart Assoc*. 2013;2:e000087.
72. Pollex RL, Hegele R Genetic determinants of carotid ultrasound traits. *Curr Atheroscler Rep*. 2006;8:206–215.
73. O'Leary DH, Polak JF, Kronmal RA, Savage PJ, Borhani NO, et al. Thickening of the carotid wall. A marker for atherosclerosis in the elderly? Cardiovascular Health Study Collaborative Research Group. *Stroke*. 1996;27:224–231.
74. Al-Shali K, House AA, Hanley AJ, et al. Differences between carotid wall morphological phenotypes measured by ultrasound in one, two and three dimensions. *Atherosclerosis*. 2005;178:319–325.
75. Spence JD, Barnett PA, Bulman DE, Hegele RA. An approach to ascertain probands with a non-traditional risk factor for carotid atherosclerosis. *Atherosclerosis*. 1999;144:429–434.
76. Spence JD, Eliasziw M, DiCicco M, et al. Carotid plaque area: a tool for targeting and evaluating vascular preventive therapy. *Stroke*. 2002;33:2916–2922.
77. Lorenz MW, Polak JF, Kavousi M, et al. Carotid intima-media thickness progression to predict cardiovascular events in the general population (the PROG-IMT collaborative project): a meta-analysis of individual participant data. *Lancet*. 2012;379:2053–2062.
78. Fuster V, Moreno PR, Fayad ZA, Corti R, Badimon JJ. Atherothrombosis and high-risk plaque: part I: evolving concepts. *J Am Coll Cardiol*. 2005;46:937–954.
79. Nambi V, Chambless L, Folsom AR, et al. Carotid intima-media thickness and presence or absence of plaque improves prediction of coronary heart disease risk: the ARIC (Atherosclerosis Risk In Communities) study. *J Am Coll Cardiol*. 2010;55:1600–1607.
80. Hackam DG, Anand SS. Emerging risk factors for atherosclerotic vascular disease: a critical review of the evidence. *JAMA*. 2003;290:932–940.
81. Expert Panel on Detection, Evaluation, and Treatment of High Blood Cholesterol in Adults. Executive summary of the third report of the National Cholesterol Education Program (NCEP) Expert Panel on Detection, Evaluation, and Treatment of High Blood Cholesterol in Adults (Adult Treatment Panel III). *JAMA*. 2001;285:2486–2497.
82. Cao JJ, Arnold AM, Manolio TA, et al. Association of carotid artery intima-media thickness, plaques, and C-reactive protein with future cardiovascular disease and all-cause mortality: the Cardiovascular Health Study. *Circulation*. 2007;116:32–38.

83. Lorenz MW, Schaefer C, Steinmetz H, Sitzer M. Is carotid intima media thickness useful for individual prediction of cardiovascular risk? Ten-year results from the Carotid Atherosclerosis Progression Study (CAPS). *Eur Heart J.* 2010;31:2041–2048.
84. Touboul PJ, Vicaut E, Labreuche J, et al. Correlation between the Framingham risk score and intima media thickness: the Paroi Arterielle et Risque Cardio-vasculaire (PARC) study. *Atherosclerosis.* 2007;192:363–369.
85. Kuller L, Borhani N, Furberg C, et al. Prevalence of subclinical atherosclerosis and cardiovascular disease and association with risk factors in the Cardiovascular Health Study. *Am J Epidemiol.* 1994;139:1164–1179.
86. Della-Morte D, Guadagni F, Palmirotta R, et al. Genetics of ischemic stroke, stroke-related risk factors, stroke precursors and treatments. *Pharmacogenomics.* 2012;13:595–613.
87. Sacco RL, Blanton SH, Slifer S, et al. Heritability and linkage analysis for carotid intima-media thickness: the family study of stroke risk and carotid atherosclerosis. *Stroke.* 2009;40:2307–2312.
88. Wang L, Beecham A, Zhuo D, et al. Fine mapping study reveals novel candidate genes for carotid intima-media thickness in Dominican Republican families. *Circ Cardiovasc Genet.* 2011;5:234–241.
89. Liao YC, Lin HF, Rundek T, Cheng R, Guo YC, et al. Segment-specific genetic effects on carotid intima-media thickness: the Northern Manhattan study. *Stroke.* 2008;39:3159–3165.
90. Rundek T, Elkind MS, Pittman J, et al. Carotid intima-media thickness is associated with allelic variants of stromelysin-1, interleukin-6, and hepatic lipase genes: the Northern Manhattan Prospective Cohort Study. *Stroke.* 2002;33:1420–1423.
91. Dong C, Beecham A, Slifer S, et al. Genomewide linkage and peakwide association analyses of carotid plaque in Caribbean Hispanics. *Stroke.* 2010;41:2750–2756.
92. Pankow JS, Heiss G, Evans GW, et al. Familial aggregation and genome-wide linkage analysis of carotid artery plaque: the NHLBI Family Heart Study. *Hum Hered.* 2004;57:80–89.
93. Moskau S, Golla A, Grothe C, et al. Heritability of carotid artery atherosclerotic lesions: an ultrasound study in 154 families. *Stroke.* 2005;36:5–8.
94. Bowden DW, Lehtinen AB, Ziegler JT, et al. Genetic epidemiology of subclinical cardiovascular disease in the diabetes heart study. *Ann Hum Genet.* 2008;72:598–610.
95. Wang L, Yanuck D, Beecham A, et al. A candidate gene study revealed sex-specific association between the OLR1 gene and carotid plaque. *Stroke.* 2011;42:588–592.
96. Dong C, Della-Morte D, Wang L, et al. Association of the sirtuin and mitochondrial uncoupling protein genes with carotid plaque. *PLoS One.* 2011;6:e27157.
97. Fox CS, Cupples LA, Chazaro I, et al. Genomewide linkage analysis for internal carotid artery intimal medial thickness: evidence for linkage to chromosome 12. *Am J Hum Genet.* 2004;74:253–261.
98. Bis JC, Kavousi M, Franceschini N, et al. Meta-analysis of genome-wide association studies from the CHARGE consortium identifies common variants associated with carotid intima media thickness and plaque. *Nat Genet.* 2011;43:940–947.
99. Meschia JF, Worrall BB, Rich SS. Genetic susceptibility to ischemic stroke. *Nat Rev Neurol.* 2011;7:369–378.

21

MAGNETIC RESONANCE IMAGING-BASED MARKERS OF CEREBROVASCULAR DISEASE AND THE RISK OF STROKE

Svetlana Lorenzano and Natalia S. Rost

Introduction

Magnetic resonance imaging (MRI) plays an essential role in the field of cerebrovascular diseases. The number of MRI techniques that enables a better characterization of brain tissue and vessel status is constantly evolving and becoming extensively available to both clinicians and researchers.

In a nonemergency clinical setting, MRI has become a routine modality of choice, used both for inpatient and outpatient investigations, and as a result, the interpretation of incidental MRI findings such as leukoaraiosis or white matter hyperintensity (WMH), silent brain infarcts (SBIs), and cerebral microbleeds (CMBs) has become necessary to understand their pathophysiology and to define their clinical significance. A number of population-based studies have explored the potential role that the MRI findings play as markers of cerebrovascular disease, including ischemic and hemorrhagic stroke.[1,2] These studies have specifically addressed the MRI-based findings that contribute to the risk of first-ever stroke, and have provided the basis for exploratory research on preventative and therapeutic interventions. In the setting of nonacute trials, in large studies on cerebrovascular disease MRI findings of small-vessel disease (WMH, SBIs, CMBs, brain atrophy)—for example, WMH measured on T2-weighted (T2W) magnetic resonance image—have been used particularly as markers of disease progression and vascular cognitive impairment, or as predictors of treatment response and long-term outcome.[3–9]

In the emergency clinical setting, advanced multimodal MRI techniques enable a reliable, noninvasive clinical diagnosis of ischemic stroke and provide insight with regard to the underlying etiology and more appropriate stroke subtype definition. Current MRI-based evaluation of acute cerebral ischemia delivers detailed information on infarct area characteristics such as age, extent and location, vessel status, and brain tissue dynamics within minutes from the onset of an ischemic event. Furthermore, the fate of the cerebral tissue after an acute ischemic injury can be evaluated through the degree of cerebral perfusion and estimates of ischemic penumbra.[10,11] In acute hemorrhagic stroke, MRI is not yet used routinely as part of clinical diagnosis, although studies have demonstrated that sensitivity and accuracy of MRI in differentiating intracerebral hemorrhage (ICH) from acute ischemic stroke is high and at least comparable with those of computed tomography (CT).[12,13] Although CT is still considered the preferred acute ICH diagnostic imaging modality, MRI has proved to be superior to CT for identifying subacute and chronic cerebral hemorrhage. Furthermore, in the emergency setting, MRI data can be crucial in guiding clinicians in early patient management options and risk stratification for individualizing acute therapeutic strategies in both ischemic and hemorrhagic stroke. In addition, it can inform the early steps for secondary prevention planning and serves as a potential surrogate marker of stroke recurrence risk and poststroke outcome.[13] In the setting of acute trials, MRI-based findings have been used as part of eligibility criteria for the enrollment of patients with acute ischemic stroke in neuroprotection and pharmacological/interventional recanalization studies, particularly those designed to extend the conventional therapeutic window of the officially approved thrombolytic treatment with recombinant tissue plasminogen activator or to evaluate the response to new thrombolytic agents.[14-21]

In this chapter, we focus on the most frequently used conventional MRI techniques and their applications in detecting all specific gray and white matter changes that have been accepted in the field as markers of cerebrovascular disease, and we evaluate their role in predicting the risk of stroke. Last, we provide insight into novel, advanced MRI techniques that offer great promise in elucidating the pathophysiology of the broad and complex spectrum of cerebrovascular diseases.

Detection of MRI-Based Cerebrovascular Disease Markers

The properties that make MRI the technical modality of choice for the evaluation of neurovascular diseases are noninvasiveness, optimal soft tissue contrast, and the possibility of simultaneous assessment of multiple structural and functional parameters. The most frequently used conventional and advanced MRI techniques in cerebrovascular diseases are those that assess specifically brain structure, including basic T1-weighted (T1W) and T2W imaging, T2 fluid-attenuated inversion recovery (FLAIR), T2*-gradient-recalled echo (GRE), and susceptibility-weighted imaging; and those that evaluate the brain functional aspects such as diffusion-weighted imaging (DWI) and perfusion-weighted imaging (Figure 21.1).[22,23]

During the past few decades, these conventional and advanced MRI techniques have contributed definitively to our increasing knowledge on neuroimaging markers of cerebrovascular disease and their role in stroke risk stratification, stroke recurrence risk, and prediction of poststroke outcomes. In this chapter, we review the MRI markers that are the most common and well delineated through their association with the risk of stroke, such as WMHs, CMBs, SBIs, dilated perivascular spaces (DPVSs), microinfarcts (MIs), and superficial siderosis (SS).

White Matter Hyperintensity

WMH is a common, nonspecific term used for the radiographic finding of increased signal intensity of the cerebral white matter detected on T2W or FLAIR MRI that describes a multitude of underlying cerebrovascular conditions presenting as asymptomatic WMH, usually observed in the healthy aging population,[24] isolated or in combination with other small-vessel-related pathologies, such as lacunar infarcts detected in patients with stroke and/or vascular dementia and CMBs.[2,25] The term *leukoaraiosis* used interchangeably with WMH was coined by Hachinski et al.[26] to describe the radiographic appearance of diffuse hypodensity of the periventricular and deep white matter found

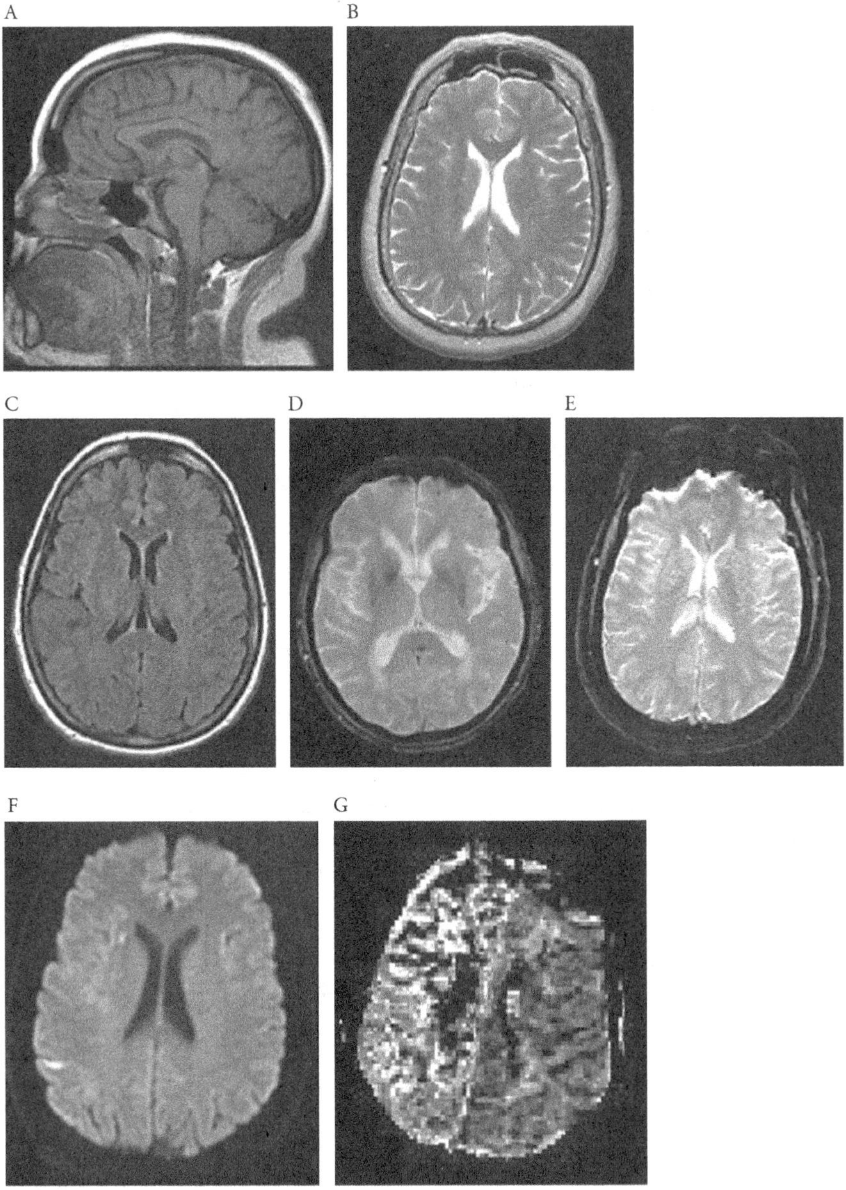

FIGURE 21.1 Magnetic resonance imaging sequences used in study of stroke and cerebrovascular disease. (A) Sagittal T1-weighted image. (B) Axial T2-weighted image. (C) Axial fluid-attenuated inversion recovery image. (D) Axial gradient-recalled echo image. (E) Axial susceptibility weighted image. (F) Axial diffusion-weighted image. (G) Axial perfusion-weighted imaging (mean transit time).

on head CT. Since then, two distinct categories of leukoaraiosis or WMH have been described based on their topography: periventricular WMH (attached and contiguous to the ventricular system) and deep WMH (located in subcortical white matter, apart from the ventricles),[27] giving rise to the ongoing discussion with regard to the potential variability in their respective clinical, histopathological, and pathophysiological correlates.[28]

WMH occurs increasingly with age, and its burden is more severe in the elderly.[29,30] In the general population, WMH prevalence is reported between 11% and 21% in subjects aged 64 years, and is 94% in individuals 82 years old, with the variability explained only in part by different study design, population of interest, and methods adopted for WMH assessment.[1,31–36] The variability in the definitions of WMH as an MRI trait and in its quantification methods have contributed in particular to the heterogeneity of WMH study results reported during the past few decades, and have limited the comparison between individual findings. Early on, semiquantitative visual rating scales became important in the assessment of WMH severity and progression[37,38]; however, the scale and nature of ongoing investigations have demanded a greater precision and high-throughput methodological approaches. Currently, fully automated methods could be considered the gold standard in volumetric assessment of WMH in the context of large, population-based studies.[39] However, semi-automated quantitative methods, which improve measurement specificity and accuracy by using operator-mediated manual correction, have proved to be reliable in ascertaining WMH burden in subjects enrolled in hospital-based studies on acute stroke.[25,40,41] WMH lesion topography detected on MRI, in addition to a total burden of disease, is considered crucial for the potential differentiation of pathophysiology underlying this radiographic trait and in its correlation with the risk of stroke.

MRI APPEARANCE

On T2W MRI, leukoaraiosis is visualized typically as bilateral patchy or confluent areas of hyperintensities, with or without focal, discreet-appearing lesions, distributed in the periventricular, deep, and/or superficial subcortical (juxtacortical) white matter areas. By suppressing the signal from cerebrospinal fluid (CSF) and increasing the signal from white matter changes, FLAIR sequences are conventionally the most sensitive in detecting WMH. As mentioned earlier, WMH also includes subacute and chronic lacunar or nonlacunar infarcts that appear as focal hypointensity on T1W imaging, and hyperintense on FLAIR; but in the case of tissue destruction (e.g., cavities or encephalomalacia), these lesions become hypointense on FLAIR as well and are usually classified as SBIs.

MRI enables one to distinguish different forms and severity of WMHs[42]: (a) periventricular WMH that is usually seen in elderly subjects, including juxtaventricular hyperintensities (i.e., contiguous to the ventricular surface within 3 mm and presenting as thin, hyperintense line—smooth halo) along the lateral ventricles and caps surrounding the horns of the lateral ventricles[43]; (b) irregular periventricular WMH, which is detectable at 3 to 13 mm from the ventricular surface (watershed area)[44–46]; and (c) deep (i.e., subcortical) WMH visualized at approximately 13 mm or farther from the ventricular surface, with multiple punctuate or patchy lesions that may be partially or fully confluent.[47] Last, small WMH lesions located approximately 4 mm apart from the corticomedullary junction can be defined as juxtacortical WMH[42] (Figure 21.2).

HISTOPATHOLOGICAL CORRELATES OF WMH

Histopathological findings corresponding to magnetic resonance-detected WMH can be various based on WMH location (Figures 21.3 and 21.4), possibly reflecting different pathophysiological mechanisms underlying the disease—more specifically, ischemic versus nonischemic (Figure 21.3). In the periventricular caps and smooth halo, areas of demyelination with venous congestion resulting from noninflammatory periventricular venous collagenosis,[48] mild-to-moderate subependymal gliosis, and discontinuity of the ependymal lining that does not have an ischemic origin are observed.[49] No arteriosclerotic vessel changes have been found in these regions.[28] In other cases, areas of irregular periventricular WMH associated with the presence of more severe patchy myelin loss and reactive gliosis of an ischemic nature, including complete microcystic infarcts along with the fibrohyalinotic[50–52] and arteriosclerotic vessels,[50,53] were also observed. Punctuate, early confluent,

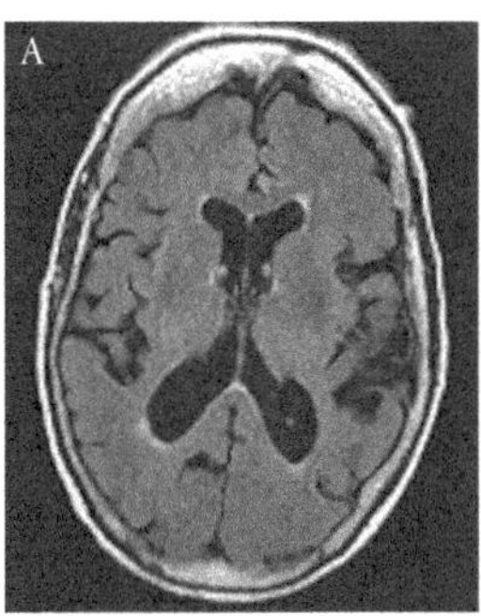

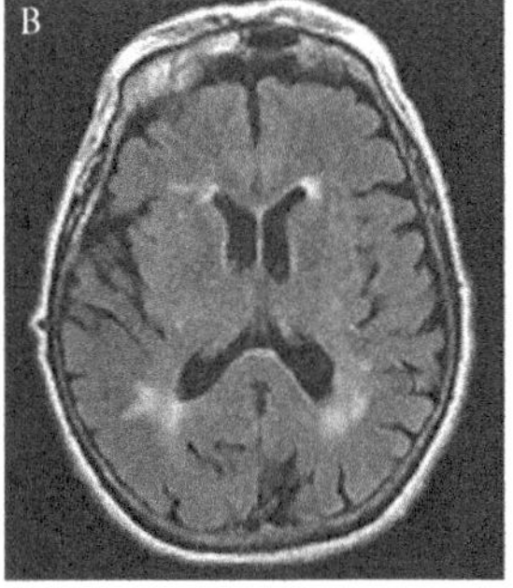

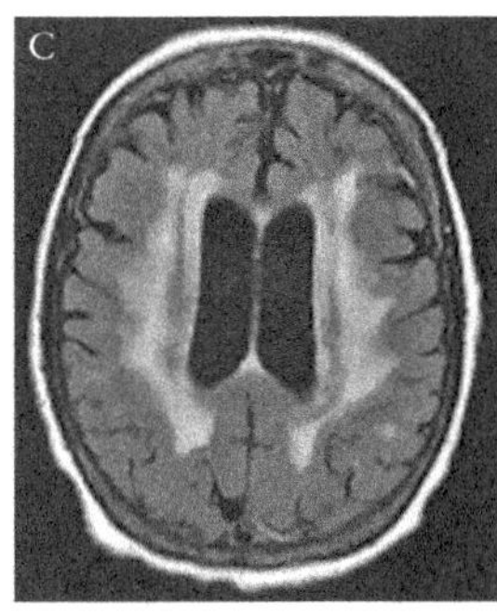

FIGURE 21.2 (A–C) Axial fluid-attenuated inversion recovery (FLAIR) images of mild (A), moderate (B), and severe (C) white matter hyperintensity.

and confluent deep WMH lesions correspond to a degree of progressive tissue changes. In punctuate WMH areas, myelin loss and atrophic neuropil are associated with fibrohyalinotic arterioles and DPVSs. In early confluent deep WMH, myelin sheath rarefaction is combined with loss of axons and astrogliosis. Last, confluent deep WMHs reflect more severe tissue destruction, presenting as loss of

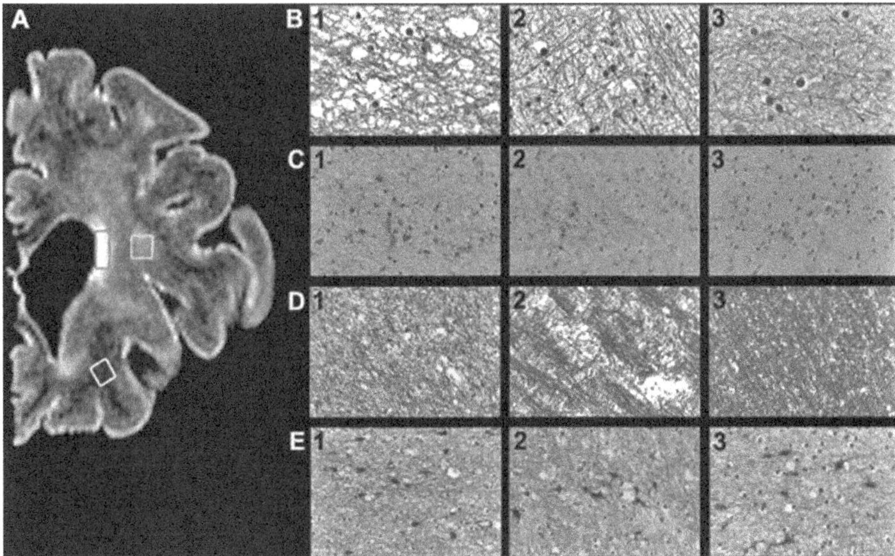

FIGURE 21.3 Histopathological correlates of white matter hyperintensities. (A) Prefrontal coronal fluid-attenuated inversion recovery (FLAIR) image of an 88-year-old woman with Alzheimer's disease. (B–E) Regions of interest represent white matter hyperintensities (WMHs) in the periventricular area (rectangle; B1–E1), WMHs in the deep white matter (upper square; B2–E2), and an area of normal-appearing white matter (NAWM) (lower square, B3–E3). In Bodian Silver-stained sections (B, original magnification ×2003), more lower axonal density was found in WMHs (B1 and B2) than in NAWM (B3). On Human Leukocyte Antigen DR (HLA-DR) immunohistochemical sections (original magnification ×2003), more microglial activation (C) was observed in WMHs (C1 and C2) than in NAWM (C3). In Luxol Fast Blue/Cresyl Violet-stained sections (original magnification ×1003), WMHs also showed more myelin loss (D1 and D2) compared with NAWM (D3). And, in glial fibrillary acidic protein immunostained sections (original magnification ×4003) the severity of astrogliosis (E) was not clearly different between WMHs and NAWM in this patient. (Adapted with permission from Gouw AA et al. *J Neurol Neurosurg Psychiatry* 2011;82:126–135).

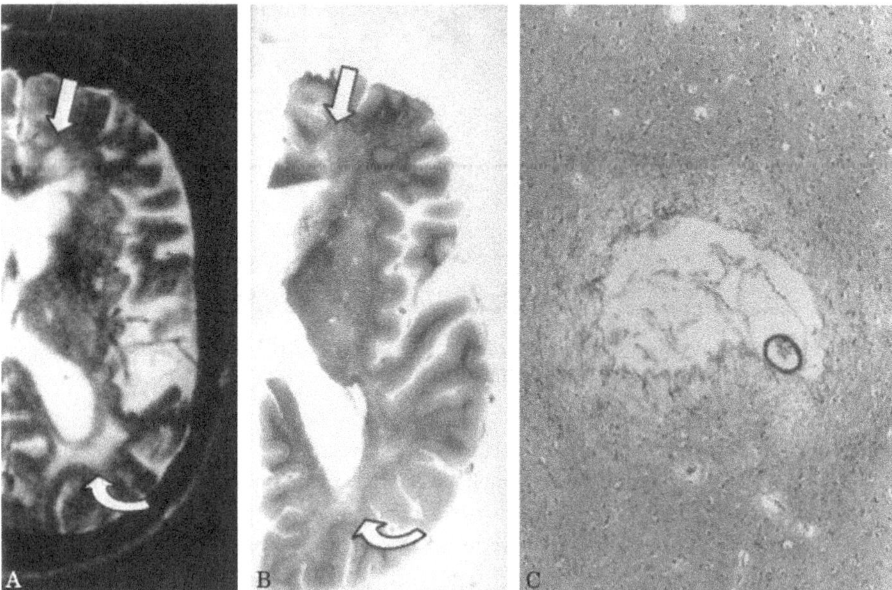

FIGURE 21.4 (A–C) Examples of confluent white matter lesions. Small cavities of tissue destruction are seen within an area of extensive demyelination corresponding to a patchy hyperintensity on premortem (A) and postmortem (B) magnetic resonance imaging (straight arrows in A, B, and magnification of a part of the lesion in C). A large area of myelin pallor is also seen around the posterior horn (curved arrows). (Reprinted with permission in part from Fazekas et al. Pathologic correlates of incidental MRI white matter signal hyperintensities. *Neurology*. 1993;43:1683–1689.)

myelin, axons, and oligodendroglial cells, as well as reactive gliosis associated with DPVSs and areas of complete infarction (Figure 21.4).[28,49,54,55]

PATHOPHYSIOLOGY AND CLINICAL DETERMINANTS OF WMH

Severity and progression of WMH is likely determined by a complex interaction of environmental and genetic factors. WMH has a well-described association with a multitude of cardiovascular risk factors, such as hypertension, diabetes, atherosclerosis, and impaired cerebral blood flow, and it is more common in patients with ischemic stroke and ICH.[31,56–58] WMH is also associated with the development of other important vascular entities such as SBIs[59] and CMBs.[41] However, white matter changes are also a prominent feature in a number of genetic conditions such as mitochondrial encephalomyopathy with lactic acidosis and strokelike episodes caused by mitochondrial DNA mutations[60] and cerebral autosomal dominant arteriopathy with subcortical infarcts and leukoencephalopathy (CADASIL), an autosomal condition caused by mutations of the *NOTCH 3* gene that might represent a basic model for understanding the pathogenesis of the sporadic white matter changes.[61]

The pathological mechanisms underlying WMH are yet to be fully elucidated; however, the most likely hypothesis emphasizes the vascular ischemic origin supported by findings from population-based studies and pathological–radiographic correlation studies.[49] Given the pattern of white matter vascularization as an arterial border zone or watershed area, susceptibility of white matter to damage as a result of a systemic or focal decrease in cerebral blood flow has been implicated as one of the mechanisms of disease in leukoaraiosis.[54,62] Specifically, the irregular periventricular WMH is thought to be more likely the result of chronic hemodynamic dysfunction, corresponding to an area supplied by the noncollateralizing ventriculofugal vessels that arise from subependymal arteries.[44–46] Deep white matter areas are supplied by penetrating medullary arteries arising from the cortical branches of the middle cerebral arteries, also supplying the deep gray matter nuclei, and brainstem, which are areas more prone to small-vessel disease. Hence, deep white matter changes can be caused by pathological alterations of these perforating end arteries,[50,63] and this diseased small vasculature may predispose to the occurrence of both small, as lacunar, subcortical areas of infarctions (which, as mentioned earlier, if not cavitated yet, appear as WMH on T2W and FLAIR imaging and are methodologically difficult to discriminate from other WMH subtypes, unless detected on MRI obtained for the evaluation of acute ischemic stroke) and the more extensive patchy or confluent areas of chronic ischemia. Specifically, two different pathophysiological mechanisms have been proposed in the vascular hypothesis on WMH origin: (a) atherosclerosis of larger perforating arteries leading to bigger lacunar infarcts and (b) diffuse arteriopathic alterations with endothelial dysfunction and blood–brain barrier (BBB) changes causing smaller multiple lacunar infarcts associated with patchy/confluent areas of WMH.[54,64–67] Some of the vessel alterations include replacement of the smooth muscle cells by fibrohyaline material with thickening of the wall and narrowing of the vascular lumen, dysregulation of the blood flow to the white matter, repeated episodes of hypoperfusion and ischemic events that may be associated with BBB disruption—another likely important contributor to white matter changes-leakage of macromolecules from plasma into white matter, and consequent astrocyte activation.[54,68,69] Aging, chronic hypertension, and diabetes could contribute to these changes.[70–72] Activated and swollen astrocytes could be responsible for the specific aspects of white matter changes detected by MRI. Cerebral small-vessel disease also appears to be causative of juxtacortical white matter lesions. Juxtacortical white matter is supplied not only by the long penetrating medullary vessels, but also by short vessels, which cross the white matter and the contiguous gray matter, with U-fibers being usually spared from WMH-related changes.

Of notice, other studies have demonstrated that the only WMH subtype of nonischemic origin may be the one observed in the periventricular caps or halos,[49,73] where disruption of ependymal lining may be linked to increased water reabsorption [27] and leakage of CSF[42] associated with abnormal transependymal flow.

The debate in the field whether WMH detected on MRI represents two distinct categories based on its topography and, thus, related mechanism of disease is still ongoing. The authors who propose that periventricular WMH differs from subcortical white matter lesions by separate vascular etiology support their argument by epidemiological and clinicopathological data.[24,43,49,50,51,74–81] Conversely, segmentation maps of WMH on FLAIR images failed to demonstrate that periventricular and deep WMH behave differently enough to support distinct subtypes. Instead, a unique pattern of WMH topography has been reported in which WMH appears to expand smoothly from around CSF spaces to more distal white matter, with the increase of the total volume of WMH, linking it to a compromised watershed area hypothesis.[39]

Clinically, WMH burden is associated with a wide and complex spectrum of symptoms—gait disturbances, urinary incontinence, depression, cognitive impairment, and dementia—all of them possibly linked to the damage caused by chronic hypoperfusion to the associative connections in frontal and subcortical regions.[82] This anatomic hypothesis is supported further by the increasing severity of clinical dysfunction associated with severity of leukoaraiosis.[82]

WMH AND THE RISK OF STROKE

Advances in WMH assessment using qualitative and quantitative methods for MRI analysis set the stage for a comprehensive evaluation of WMH as a potential marker of clinical cerebrovascular disease and, specifically, for its role in stroke risk stratification. Validated in multiple studies, WMH burden has been proposed as a surrogate end point in clinical trials on stroke prevention.[1,4] Furthermore, WMH location, severity, and progression in longitudinal, prospective studies have been associated reliably with an increased risk of first-ever and recurrent stroke (Tables 20.1 and 20.2).

TABLE 21.1

Summary of Studies That Report Associations between MRI Markers of Cerebrovascular Disease and the Risk of First-Ever and Recurrent Stroke

MRI finding	Author, year	Type of study	n	Mean Age, y	Mean Follow-up, y	Measurement methods and marker definitions	Outcome definition	Risk of stroke
WMH	Kobayashi et al.,[89] 1997	Prospective, general population study	933	57.5	NA (1 to >6)	MRI: 0.15 T, 0.2 T; T1, T2, PD WMH: SQ (PV-WMH, 0 – 4)	All strokes: 19 (14 IS, 4 ICH, 1 SAH)	OR, 4.8 (95% CI. 1.1 – 20.6)[a] with focal WMH PV-WMH was not associated with stroke risk
	Wong et al.,[84] 2002	ARIC study (prospective, longitudinal, population- based study)	1684	62.3	4.7	MRI: 1.5 T; T1, T2, PD WMH: SQ (0 – 9), dichotomized (≥3 vs. <3)	All strokes: 32 (25 IS, 5 ICH, 2 combined) IS: 25	For WMH ≥3 vs. <3: RR, 3.7 (95% CI, 1.7 – 7.8)[b]; RR, 3.4 (95% CI, 1.5 – 7.7)[a] RR, 3.2 (95% CI, 1.2 – 8.3)[a]
	Vermeer et al,[78] 2003	Rotterdam Study (prospective, longitudinal, population- based study)	1077	72	4.2	MRI: 1.5 T; T1, T2, PD PV-WMH-: SQ (0 – 9) D-WMH-: Q, studied as tertiles and as a continuous variable	All strokes: 57 (42 IS, 6 ICH, 9 unspecified)	HR 4.7 (95% CI, 2.0 – 11.2)[a] with 3rd vs. 1st PV-WMH tertile; HR, 1.36 (95% CI, 1.20 – 1.54)[a] per grade increase of PV-WMH; HR, 3.6 (95% CI, 1.4 – 9.2)[a] with 3rd vs. 1st D-WMH tertile

Kuller et al.,[59] 2004	CHS study (prospective, longitudinal, multicenter, population- based study)	3293	75	7	MRI: 1.5 T except for 1 center using 0.35 T; T1, T2, PD WMH: SQ (0 – 9), 6 classes	All strokes: 278 IS: 226	HR, 3.0 (95% CI, 1.9 – 4.7)[a*] with WMH grade ≤5 HR, 2.9 (95% CI, 1.7 – 4.8) for overall IS with WMH grade ≥5; HR, 4.8 (95% CI, 1.7 – 13.8) for cardioembolic IS; HR, 2.8 (95% CI, 1.4 – 6.0) for unknown IS
Bokura et al.,[85] 2006	Prospective, longitudinal, population- based study	2684	57.8	6.3	MRI: 0.15 T, 0.2 T, 1.5 T; T1, T2, PD, FLAIR WMH: SQ (0 – 4 for PV-WMH, 0 – 3 for D-WMH)	All strokes: 102 (56 IS, 21 ICH, 11 SAH, 11 TIA, 3 unspecified)	OR, 2.08 (95% CI, 1.04 – 4.17)[a] with PV-WMH ≥3 vs. <3; OR, 2.73 (95% CI, 1.32 – 5.63)[a] with D-WMH ≥2 vs.<2
Buyck et al.,[86] 2009	3- City Study (prospective, longitudinal, population- based study)	1643	72.3	4.9	MRI: 1.5 T; T1, T2, PD WMH: Q (automated), studied as quartiles and as a continuous variable	All strokes: 25 (20 IS, 4 ICH, 1 unspecified)	HR, 5.7 (95% CI, 2.0 – 16.4)[a] with quartile 4 vs. quartile 1 + 2 of WMH volume; HR, 6.2 (95% CI, 2.0 – 19.5)* with quartile 4 vs. quartile 1 + 2 of PV-WMH volume; HR, 4.1 (95% CI, 1.5 – 11.3)[a] with quartile 4 vs. quartile 1 + 2 of D-WMH volume

(continued)

TABLE 21.1

Continued

MRI finding	Author, year	Type of study	n	Mean Age, y	Mean Follow-up, y	Measurement methods and marker definitions	Outcome definition	Risk of stroke
	Debette et al.,[87] 2010	Framingham Offspring study (prospective, longitudinal, population- based study)	2229	62	5.6	MRI: 1.0 T, 1.5 T; T2 WMH: Q (automated), studied both as a continuous and a dichotomized variable	All strokes: 32 (26 IS, 5 ICH, 1 unspecified)	HR, 1.3 (95% CI, 0.9 – 1.9)[a] with WMH as a continuous variable; HR, 2.3 (95% CI, 1.02 – 5.13)[a] with extensive WMH as a dichotomous variable
	Yamauchi et al.,[98] 2002	Prospective, high- risk population study (subjects with symptomatic lacunar stroke or stroke- free with headache or dizziness)	89	66	4.3	MRI: 0.5 T; T1, T2, PD WMH: SQ, studied as a continuous and a dichotomous (severe vs. mild or absent) variable	All strokes: 7 (5 IS, 2 ICH); proportion of patients with recurrent stroke, NA	RR, 1.6 (95% CI, 1.02 – 2.5)[c] per 1-pt score increase of WMH
	Smith et al.,[101] 2004	Hospital- based study (patients with primary lobar ICH	82	76.3	2.7	CT; MRI: FLAIR WMH: SQ (0 – 9) for PV-WMH, quantitative for D-WMH studied as a continuous variable	Recurrent ICH	HR, 9.0 (95% CI, 1.2 – 67.2)[a] with PV-WMH HR with D-WMH: NA, NS

Appelros et al.,[95] 2005	Hospital- based study (patients with symptomatic lacunar infarct)	81	66.4	5.0	MRI: 1.5 T; T1, T2, PD WMH: SQ, studied as a continuous variable	Recurrent stroke (24): 21 IS (17 lacunar and 4 large-vessel infarcts), 2 ICH, 1 unspecified	HR, 1.7 (95% CI, 1.2 – 2.7)[a]
Fu et al.,[96] 2005	Hospital- based study (patients with acute first- ever stroke)	228	68.3	1.9 (median)	MRI: 1.5 T; T1, T2, FLAIR, DWI WMH: SQ (0 – 3), studied as a continuous variable	Recurrent stroke: 29 (23 IS, 6 ICH)	HR, 4.2 (95% CI, 2.0 – 8.6)[a]
Gerdes et al.,[106] 2006	Hospital- based study (patients with recent [≤6 mo] ischemic stroke, AMI, or peripheral artery disease)	230	62	3.5	MRI: 1.5 T; T1, T2, PD WMH: SQ, studied as dichotomous variable (absence/presence of PV-WMH or D-WMH, and ≥50% vs. <50% of total WMH)	Ischemic stroke: 21 (first ever or recurrent)	HR, 4.4 (95% CI, 1.8 – 11.0) with PV-WMH; HR, 3.2 (95% CI, 1.3 – 8.4)[a] with PV-WMH; HR, 1.5 (95% CI, 0.6 – 3.8) with D-WMH; NS
Naka et al.,[105] 2006	Hospital- based study (patients with stroke)	266	67.2	1.5	MRI: 1 T; T2, T2* WMH: SQ (0 – 3); studied as dichotomous variable (≥2 vs. <2)	All strokes: 26 (16 IS, 10 ICH	HR, 10.7 (95% CI, 2.6 – 43.7)[a] (also adjusted for CMBs) for IS; HR, 0.016 (95% CI, 0.001 – 0.258)[a] (also adjusted for CMBs) for recurrent ICH

(continued)

TABLE 21.1

Continued

MRI finding	Author, year	Type of study	n	Mean Age, y	Mean Follow-up, y	Measurement methods and marker definitions	Outcome definition	Risk of stroke
	Longstreth et al.,[115] 2011	CHS study (population- based, substudy in patients with baseline and follow- up MRI)	1741	NA	9.6	MRI: 1.5 T except for 1 center using 0.35 T; T1, T2, PD WMH: SQ (0 – 9)	All stroke	HR 1.39 (95% CI, 1.02 – 1.88)[a] with WMH progression (if WMH ≥1 at follow-up MRI); after adding WMH grade on the initial scan: HR, 1.35 (95% CI, 1.00 – 1.77)[a] NS anymore
	Conijn et al.,[97] 2011	SMART- MR study (high- risk population study with symptomatic/non symptomatic atherosclerotic disease)	1309	58.6	4.5 (median)	MRI: 1.5 T; T1, T2, FLAIR WMH: Q (automated); studied as a continuous and a dichotomous variable (>4.2 mL upper quintile vs. the 4 lower quintiles)	IS	HR, 1.04 (95% CI, 1.01 – 1.07)[b] per milliliter of WMH volume; HR, 1.04 (95% CI, 1.01 – 1.06)[a] per milliliter of WMH volume; HR, 1.02 (95% CI, 0.99 – 1.05)[d] per milliliter of WMH volume; HR, 3.9 (95% CI, 2.1 – 7.6)[b] with upper quintile; HR, 3.6 (95% CI, 1.9 – 6.9)[a] with upper quintile; HR, 2.6 (95% CI, 1.3 – 4.9)[d] with upper quintile

	Folsom et al.,[88] 2012	ARIC and CHS (population- based studies)	4872	NA, 79% aged ≥65	13	MRI: 1.5 T; T1, T2 WMH: SQ (0 – 9) (4 classes)	ICH: 71	HR, 1.68 (95% CI, 0.86 – 3.30)[a] with WMH grade 2; HR, 3.52 (95% CI, 1.80 – 6.89)[a] with WMH grade 3; HR, 3.96 (95% CI, 1.90 – 8.27)[a] with WMH grades 4 – 9; HR, 1.60 (95% CI, 0.81 – 3.14)[c] with WMH grade 2; NS; HR, 3.19 (95% CI, 1.61 – 6.28)[c] with WMH grade 3; HR, 3.28 (95% CI, 1.53 – 7.04)[c] with WMH grades 4 – 9
SBIs	Kobayashi et al.,[89] 1997	Prospective, general population study	933	57.5	NA (1 to >6)	MRI: 0.15 T, 0.2 T; T1, T2, PD SBI: if diameter 3 – 10 mm	All strokes: 19 (14 IS, 4 ICH, 1 SAH)	OR, 10.5 (95% CI, 3.6 – 30.2)[a]
	Bernick et al.,[170] 2001	Prospective, general population study	3324	≈75	4	MRI: 1.5T	All strokes: 159 (131 IS, 23 ICH, 5 unknown)	HR, 1.80 (95% CI, 1.31 – 2.47)[b] HR, 1.52 (95% CI, 1.10 – 2.10)[a]
	Vermeer et al.,[78] 2003	Rotterdam Study (prospective, longitudinal, population- based study)	1077	72	4.2	MRI: 1.5T; T1, T2, PD SBI: if diameter ≥3 mm	All strokes: 57 (42 IS, 6 ICH, 9 unspecified)	HR, 3.9 (95% CI, 2.3 – 6.8)[a]

(continued)

TABLE 21.1

Continued

MRI finding	Author, year	Type of study	n	Mean Age, y	Mean Follow-up, y	Measurement methods and marker definitions	Outcome definition	Risk of stroke
	Kuller et al.,[59] 2004	CHS study (prospective, longitudinal, multicenter, population- based study)	3293	75	7	MRI: 1.5 T except for 1 center using 0.35 T; SBI: no size definition	All strokes: 278	HR, 4.2 (95% CI, 2.7 – 6.5)[a] in subjects with SBI and WMH = 3; HR, 4.4 (95% CI, 2.6 – 7.4)[a] in subjects with SBI and WMH = 4; HR, 3.7 (95% CI, 2.1 – 6.5)[a] in subjects with SBI WMH ≥5
	Bokura et al.,[85] 2006	Prospective, longitudinal, population- based study	2684	57.8	6.3	MRI: 0.15 T, 0.2 T, 1.5 T; T1, T2, PD, FLAIR SBI: if diameter ≥3 mm	All strokes: 102 (56 IS, 21 ICH, 11 SAH, 11 TIA, 3 unspecified)	OR, 3.66 (95% CI, 2.28 – 5.89)[a]
	Debette et al.,[87] 2010	Framingham Offspring study (prospective, longitudinal, population- based study)	2229	62	5.6	MRI: 1.0 T, 1.5 T; T1, T2, PD SBI: if diameter ≥3 mm	All strokes: 32 (26 IS, 5 ICH, 1 unspecified) ISs: 26	HR, 3.06 (95% CI, 1.44 – 6.51)[b]; HR, 2.84 (95% CI, 1.32 – 6.10)[a]; HR 2.80 (95% CI, 1.29 – 6.06) after adjustment for WMH volume HR, 3.49 (95% CI, 1.54 – 7.91)[a]

Longstreth et al.,[115] 2011	CHS study (population-based, substudy in patients with baseline and follow-up MRI)	1446	NA	9.6	MRI: 1.5 T except for 1 center using 0.35 T; T1, T2, PD SBI: if diameter ≥3 mm	All stroke	HR, 2.11 (95% CI, 1.48 – 3.02)[a] with ≥1 infarct at follow-up MRI; HR, 2.58 (95% CI, 1.53 – 4.36)[a] in 1312 subjects with ≥1 infarct and WMH progression at follow-up imaging
Kang et al.,[175] 2006	Hospital-based, retrospective study (patients with ischemic stroke)	104	74	19.3 mo	MRI: 1.5 T; DWI, FLAIR, early and late SBI: new lesion on DWI at 5 days and 30 – 90 days, respectively, and not associated with clinical events	IS: 8	OR, 6.55 (95% CI, 1.09 – 39.55) (adjusted for age and cardioembolism) with late SBI
Conijn et al.,[97] 2011	SMART-MR study (high-risk population with symptomatic/ not symptomatic atherosclerotic disease)	1309	58.6	4.5 (median)	MRI: 1.5 T; T1, T2, FLAIR; silent LI and symptomatic LI: ≥3 mm	IS	HR, 3.7 (95% CI, 2.0 – 6.7)[b] both silent and symptomatic LI; HR, 3.2 (95% CI, 1.7 – 5.8)[a] both silent and symptomatic LI; HR, 1.5 (95% CI, 0.8 – 3.0)[d] both silent and symptomatic LI; NS
Weber et al.,[174] 2012	PROFESS Imaging substudy (patients with recent, mild noncardioembolic IS)	1014	66.1	2.5	MRI: 1.0 T, 1.5 T; T1, T2, FLAIR SBI: no size definition	All stroke: 24 IS, 3 ICH	OR, 1.42 (95% CI, 0.79 – 2.56)[b]; NS

(continued)

TABLE 21.1

Continued

MRI finding	Author, year	Type of study	n	Mean Age, y	Mean Follow-up, y	Measurement methods and marker definitions	Outcome definition	Risk of stroke
	Folsom et al.,[88] 2012	ARIC and CHS (population- based studies)	4872	NA; 79% aged ≥65	13	MRI: 1.5 T; T1, T2 SBI: if diameter ≥3 mm	ICH: 71	HR, 1.97 (95% CI, 1.10 – 3.54)[a] with 1 SBI; HR, 2.00 (95% CI, 0.83—4.78)[a] with 2 SBIs, NS; HR, 3.12 (95% CI, 1.31 – 7.43)[a] with ≥3 SBIs; HR, 1.72 (95% CI, 0.95 – 3.11)[c] with 1 SBI, NS; HR, 1.49 (95% CI, 0.61 – 3.60)[c] with 2 SBIs, NS; HR, 2.11 (95% CI, 0.87 – 5.14)[c] with ≥3 SBIs, NS
CMBs	Greenberg et al.,[235] 2004	Prospective cohort, hospital- based study of patients with primary lobar ICH	94	47 aged <75, 47 aged ≥75	3	MRI: 1.5 T; GE microhemorrhages: if diameter ≤5 mm; macrohemorrhages: if diameter >5 mm	Symptomatic ICH	HR, 1.5 (95% CI, 1.1 – 2.2) adjusted for vascular risk factors, APOE genotype, and previous ICH
	Soo et al.,[236] 2008	Prospective hospital- based study of patients with IS	908	69.3	26.6 mo	MRI: 1.5 T; T1, T2, T2*-GE, FLAIR CMBs: if diameter 2 – 10 mm	Recurrent stroke (15 ICH, 96 IS)	HR, 5.99 (95% CI, 1.90 – 18.86) adjusted for age; HR, 2.75 (95% CI, 0.50 – 14.99) with 1 CMB, NS; HR, 6.08 (95% CI, 1.35 – 27.42) with 2 – 4 CMBs; HR, 9.81 (95% CI, 2.76 – 34.83) with ≥5 CMBs

Nighoghossian et al.,[247] 2002	Prospective hospital-based study in patients with acute IS	100	60	10 hr	MRI: DWI, T_2, T_2*-GE CMBs: if diameter 2 – 5 mm	All HTs: 26	OR, 7.2 (95% CI, 1.9 – 28.2)[a] (also adjusted for WMH, lacunes, treatment)
Fiehler et al.,[249] 2007	BRASIL study (international, multicenter, nonrandomized analysis of patients with acute IS treated with IV thrombolysis within 6 hr from symptom onset)	570	69	136 min (median)	MRI: DWI, MRA, T_2, T_2*-GE CMBs: if diameter <5 mm	Symptomatic ICH (any ICH associated with >2 pt on NIHSS): 37	OR, 2.23 (95% CI, 0.67 – 6.97) for sICH, NS; ARI 3.1 (95% CI – 2.0 to 8.3) for sICH; OR, 1.61 (95% CI, 0.66 – 3.85) for any ICH, NS; OR, 2.2 (95% CI, 0.6 – 8.0) for patients treated ≤3 hr, NS; OR, 0.1 (95% CI, 0.0 – 23.3) for patients treated from 3 – 6 hr, NS; OR, 2.60 (95% CI, 0.57 – 9.11) with >1 CMBs, NS
Imaizumi et al.,[217] 2004	Prospective hospital-based study on patients with deep ICH or lacunar stroke	337	66	22.5 mo	MRI: T_1-, T_2-, T_2*-weighted, FLAIR, DWI CMBs: if diameter up to 7 mm	All recurrent strokes: 20 (13 deep ICH, 7 lacunar infarcts)	HR, 4.36 (95% CI, 1.72 – 11.0)[a] with ≥5 subcortical CMBs

(continued)

TABLE 21.1

Continued

MRI finding	Author, year	Type of study	n	Mean Age, y	Mean Follow-up, y	Measurement methods and marker definitions	Outcome definition	Risk of stroke
	Viswanathan et al.,[243] 2006	Retrospective hospital- based study of patients with primary ICH	207	74.5 for lobar ICH, 68.4 for deep ICH	10 for lobar ICH, 4 for deep ICH	MRI: 1.5 T; GRE; CMBs: no size definition	Recurrent lobar and deep ICH in patients under antiplatelet therapy during the follow-up period	HR, 0.8 (95% CI, 0.4 – 3.3) for lobar ICH, NS; HR, 1.2 (95% CI, 0.1 – 14.3) for deep ICH, NS (adjusted for CMBs, CT-defined WMH, and APOE genotype)
	Boulanger et al.,[239] 2006	Prospective hospital- based study of patients with TIA and IS	236	68.9	14 mo	MRI: 3 T; T1, T2, FLAIR, GRE, DWI, PWI; CMBs: no size definition	Recurrent stroke: (6 IS, 1 ICH)	HR, 2.8 (95% CI, 1.1 – 7.3) (mostly IS) adjusted for age, other vascular risk factors, and presence of confluent white matter disease
	Ueno et al.,[244] 2008	Prospective hospital- based study of patients with ICH and IS	87	74.5	NA	MRI: 1.5 T; T2*; CMBs: no size definition	Recurrent warfarin- related ICH	OR, 7.38 (95% CI, 1.05 – 51.83) adjusted for age, other vascular risk factors, and advanced WMH
	Lee et al.,[245] 2009	Case – control study of stroke patients with warfarin- related ICH	24	65.0	NA	MRI: 1.5 T; T1, T2, FLAIR, GRE; CMBs: if diameter <5 mm	Recurrent warfarin- related ICH	Adjusted OR, 83.12 (95% CI, 5.96 – 1159.10)

Naka et al.,[105] 2006	Hospital-based study of patients with stroke	266	67.2	1.5	MRI: 1 T; T_2, T_2^*; CMBs: no size definition	All strokes: 26 (16 IS, 10 ICH)	HR, 85.63 (95% CI, 6.34 – 1155.65)[a] (also adjusted for advanced WMH) for recurrent ICH
Kim et al.,[237] 2002	Prospective, hospital-based study of patients with acute IS and ICH	91	64.3	16 mo	MRI: 1.5 T; T_2, T_2^*-GRE CMBs: if diameter ≤5 mm	All strokes	OR, 2.46 (95% CI, 1.38 – 4.39)[b] (also adjusted for lacunae) for ICH (CMBs plus no or mild WMH); OR, 0.99 (95% CI, 0.94 – 1.04)[a] (also adjusted for lacunae) for ICH (CMBs plus advanced WMH)
Kim et al.,[250] 2006	Hospital-based study of patients with acute IS treated with IV thrombolysis within 6 hr of symptom onset	279	67	1–3 days	MRI: 1.5 T; T_1, T_2, FLAIR, T_2^* GRE, DWI, PWI; CMBs: if diameter <5 mm	HT	OR, 1.61 (95% CI, 0.45 – 3.13)[a] NS with CMBs >10
Gregoire et al.,[203] 2010	Case – control study of ICH patients	49	68.7	NA	MRI: 1.5 T; T_2^* GRE, T_1, T_2, FLAIR; CMBs: no size definition	Antiplatelet-related ICH	OR, 1.33 (95% CI, 1.06 – 1.66) with the total number of CMBs (adjusted for the presence of leukoaraiosis); OR, 1.42 (95% CI, 1.07 – 1.89) with lobar CMBs (adjusted for the presence of leukoaraiosis); OR, 5.69 (95% CI, 0.95 – 34.22) with deep CMBs (adjusted for leukoaraiosis), NS

(continued)

TABLE 21.1

Continued

MRI finding	Author, year	Type of study	n	Mean Age, y	Mean Follow-up, y	Measurement methods and marker definitions	Outcome definition	Risk of stroke
	Thijs et al.,[240] 2010	Prospective, hospital-based study of patients with IS or TIA	487	72	2.2	MRI: 1.5 T or 3 T; T1, T2, FLAIR, GRE CMBs: if diameter ≤5 mm	Recurrent stroke: IS (6.6%) and ICH (0.4%)	OR, 2.4 (95% CI, 1.2 – 5.0) (mostly IS) with lobar or mixed CMBs (adjusted for imbalances in WMH and prior history of stroke)
	Biffi et al.,[242] 2010	Prospective, hospital-based study of patients with lobar ICH with a diagnosis of probable/possible CAA	104	72.5	34.3 mo	MRI: 1.5T; GRE; CMBs: if diameter <5 mm	Recurrent ICH: 29 lobar ICH	HR, 2.93 (95% CI, 1.3 – 4.0)[a] with 2 – 4 CMBs; HR, 4.12 (95% CI, 1.6 – 9.3)[a] with ≥5 CMBs (also adjusted per APOE genotype, previous symptomatic hemorrhage)
	Nishikawa et al.,[232] 2009	Prospective, longitudinal, population-based study in healthy elderly subjects	698	66.7	3.5	MRI: 1.5 T; T2; CMBs: if diameter <10 mm	First-ever stroke: 36	HR, 2.87 (95% CI, 1.27 – 6.48)[a] adjusted for age, sex, and hypertension for all stroke; HR, 2.64 (95% CI, 1.34 – 5.19)[a] also adjusted for antithrombotic therapy for all stroke; HR, 1.48 (95% CI, 0.63 – 3.45)[a] also adjusted for antithrombotic therapy for ICH, NS; HR, 11.77 (95% CI, 2.95 – 46.82)[a] also adjusted for antithrombotic therapy for IS

	Bokura et al.,[233] 2011	Prospective, longitudinal, population- based study in healthy elderly subjects	2012	62.1	3.6	MRI: NA; CMBs: no size definition	First-ever stroke: 44	HR, 50.2 (95% CI, 16.7 – 150.9)[a] (also adjusted for SBIs and WMH) for deep ICH associated with deep CMBs; HR, 4.48 (95% CI, 2.20 – 12.2)[a] (also adjusted for SBIs and WMH) for IS
Microinfarcts	Kang et al.,[288] 2012	Prospective, longitudinal study of patients with acute hypertensive ICH	97	59.1	42 mo (median)	MRI: 1.5 T; DWI and GRE MIs: no clear definition is available, authors reported "all the new ischemic lesions"	Recurrent stroke: 5 IS, 3 ICH	HR, 5.87 (95% CI, 1.004 – 34.31)[a] for IS or ICH; HR, 5.00 (95% CI, 1.15 – 21.86)[a] for IS or vascular death; HR, 5.69 (95% CI, 1.36 – 23.70)[a] for IS and ICH, or vascular death

[a] Adjusted for age, sex, and other risk factors.
[b] Adjusted for age and sex.
[c] Adjusted for age, sex, other vascular risk factors, and multiple lacunar infarcts.
[d] Adjusted for age, sex, other vascular risk factors, and presence of non-LI on MRI or history of clinically evident cerebrovascular disease.

AMI, acute myocardial infarction; APOE, apolipoprotein E; ARIC, Atherosclerotic Risk in Communities; ARI, absolute risk increase; CHS, Cardiovascular Health Study; CI, confidence interval; CMBs, cerebral microbleeds; CT, computed tomography; DWI, diffusion-weighted imaging; D-WMH, deep white matter hyperintensity; FLAIR, fluid-attenuated inversion recovery; ICH, intracerebral hemorrhage; GRE, gradient recalled echo; HR, hazard ratio; IS, ischemic stroke; HT, hemorrhagic transformation; ICH, intracerebral hemorrhage; IS, ischemic stroke; IV, intravenous; LI, lacunar infarct; MIs, microinfarcts; MRI, magnetic resonance imaging; NA, not available; NIHSS, National Institutes of Health Stroke Scale; NS, not significant; OR, odds ratio; PD, proton density; PV-WMH, periventricular white matter hyperintensity; PWI, perfusion-weighted imaging; Q, quantitative; RR, relative risk; SAH, subarachnoid hemorrhage; SBI, silent brain infarct; sICH, symptomatic intracerebral hemorrhage; SQ, semiquantitative; TIA, transient ischemic attack; WMH, white matter hyperintensity.

TABLE 21.2

Summary of Studies That Report Associations between Markers of Cerebrovascular Disease and the Risk of Stroke Based on Marker Topography

MRI finding	Author, year	Lesion location/ distribution	Outcome definition	Risk of stroke
WMH	Kobayashi et al.,[89] 1997	PV diffuse WMH	All strokes	Not associated with stroke risk;
		Focal WMH		OR, 4.8 (95% CI, 1.1–20.6)[a]
	Vermeer et al.,[78] 2003	PV-WMH	All strokes	HR, 4.7 (95% CI, 2.0–11.2) with 3rd vs. 1st PV-WMH tertile[a]; HR, 1.36 (95% CI, 1.20–1.54)[a] per grade increase of PVH[a]
		D-WMH: subcortical (deep) WMH		HR, 3.6 (95% CI, 1.4–9.2)[a] with 3rd vs. 1st D-WMH tertile
	Bokura et al.,[85] 2006	PV-WMH	All strokes	OR, 2.08 (95% CI, 1.04–4.17)[a] with PV-WMH ≥3 vs. <3
		D-WMH: subcortical (deep) WMH		OR, 2.73 (95% CI, 1.32–5.63)[a] with D-WMH ≥2 vs. <2
	Buyck et al.,[86] 2009	PV-WMH	All strokes	HR, 6.2 (95% CI, 2.0–19.5)[a] with quartile 4 vs. quartile 1 + 2 of PV-WMH volume
		D-WMH: subcortical (deep) WMH		HR, 4.1 (95% CI, 1.5–11.3)[a] with quartile 4 vs. quartile 1 + 2 of D-WMH volume
	Smith et al.,[101] 2004	PV-WMH	Recurrent ICH	HR, 9.0 (95% CI, 1.2–67.2)[a]
		D-WMH: subcortical (deep) WMH		HR with D-WMH, NA: NS
	Gerdes et al.,[106] 2006	PV-WMH	First ever or recurrent IS	HR, 4.4 (95% CI, 1.8–11.0) HR, 3.2 (95% CI, 1.3–8.4)[a]
		D-WMH: subcortical (deep) WMH		HR, 1.5 (95% CI, 0.6–3.8); NS

(continued)

TABLE 21.2

Continued

MRI finding	Author, year	Lesion location/ distribution	Outcome definition	Risk of stroke
Silent brain infarcts	Bernick et al.,[170] 2001	Cortical	All strokes	HR, 1.36 (95% CI, 0.50–3.72)[b]; NS
		Subcortical		HR, 1.00 (95% CI, 0.37–2.80)[a]; NS
				HR, 1.74 (95% CI, 1.25–2.44)[b]
		Cortical/ subcortical		HR, 1.52 (95% CI, 1.08–2.13)[a]
				HR, 3.18 (95% CI, 1.47–6.88)[b]
				HR, 2.20 (95% CI, 1.00–4.86)[a]
Cerebral microbleeds	Soo et al.,[236] 2008	Mixed cortical–subcortical	Recurrent ICH	HR, 8.87 (95% CI, 3.21–24.52) adjusted for age
	Imaizumi et al.,[217] 2004	Subcortical	Recurrent stroke: deep ICH and lacunar infarcts	HR, 4.36 (95% CI, 1.72–11.0)[a] with ≥5 subcortical CMBs
	Thijs et al.,[240] 2010	Lobar or mixed	Recurrent stroke: IS and ICH	OR, 2.4 (95% CI, 1.2 – 5.0) with lobar or mixed CMBs (adjusted for imbalances in WMH and prior history of stroke)
	Bokura et al.,[233] 2011	Deep	First-ever ICH	HR, 50.2 (95% CI, 16.7 – 150.9)[a] (also adjusted for SBIs and WMH) for deep ICH associated with deep CMBs

[a]Adjusted for age, sex, and other vascular risk factors.
[b]Adjusted for age and sex.
CI, confidence interval; CMBs, cerebral microinfarcts; D, deep; HR, hazard ratio; ICH, intracerebral hemorrhage; IS, ischemic stroke; NA, not available NS, not significant; OR, odds ratio; PV, periventricular; SBIs, silent brain infarcts; WMH, white matter hyperintensity.

WMH and the Risk of First-Ever Stroke

A number of studies have addressed the issue of potential correlation between WMH and the risk of stroke, both in general population and high-risk populations, and in hospital-based cohorts (Table 21.1). This association suggests that WMH may not just be a part of "normal aging" or may be related to generalized, nonspecific vascular changes resulting from an interaction between the broad spectrum of uncontrolled vascular risk factors and age-related changes leading to a symptomatic stroke. But, WMH lesions could serve as a marker for other factors, not yet identified, that could increase the risk of stroke.[1,78] In the general population, the incidence of stroke among healthy, older adults with WMH is increased more than among those without WMH.[83] A number of large prospective, longitudinal, population-based studies[1,59,78,84–86] have demonstrated that WMH, regardless of its location and distribution, is associated independently with the risk of all clinical strokes (ischemic, hemorrhagic, and combined), after adjusting for age, sex, and other vascular risk factors. These studies ranged from 4.2 to 7 years in their follow-up periods and used both semiquantitative and fully quantitative automated methods for MRI analysis of WMH. The hazards ratio (HR) range for the risk of stroke related to WMH was between 2.3 (95% Confidence Interval [CI], 1.02–5.1)[87] and 5.7 (95% CI, 2.0–16.4),[86] independent of WMH distribution. Considering incident ischemic stroke alone, the risk associated with the presence of WMH is equally high and, apparently, irrespective of specific ischemic stroke subtype.[59] The 5-year cumulative incidence of stroke was estimated to be 4% in individuals with white matter lesions.[84] The relative risk of stroke increases with WMH severity, from 0.6% per year in subjects with mild WMH to 2.8% in subjects with more advanced disease, and it is the highest in the patients with a combination of advanced WMH grade and at least one traditional vascular risk factor.[59] Population-based studies using fully automated WMH volumetric assessment methods, which usually provide more sensitive WMH measurements, have confirmed these results, suggesting that stroke incidence is greater with increasing volumes of WMH, reaching a sevenfold greater risk in those with WMH in the higher quartiles of the volume distribution compared with those in the lower quartile, even after controlling for confounding vascular risk factors.[86] Similar data were observed by MRI-based population studies on the risk of first-ever spontaneous ICH over a mean period of 13 years with 79% of subjects aged ≥65 years.[88] The risk increased progressively with the higher grade of WMH (≥3) (for grade 3: HR, 3.52; 95% CI, 1.80–6.89; for grades 4–9: HR, 3.96; 95% CI, 1.90–8.27).[88] The results were confirmed both in a multivariate model including age and all the other vascular risk factors, and in a second model including the presence of MRI-defined SBIs. Moreover, the combination of more severe WMH with silent infarcts was associated with an almost doubled HR for ICH (HR, 4.27; 95% CI, 2.20–8.28) compared with the combination of SBIs with the lower grade of WMH (HR, 3.19; 95% CI, 1.71–5.96).[88] Other studies demonstrated the association with an increased risk of stroke only when WMH volume was considered as a dichotomous rather than a continuous variable, suggestive of a potential threshold effect, because WMH appeared to be related to a greater risk of stroke only beyond a certain volume.[87]

The distribution and location of the white matter lesions can also have a potential role in predicting the overall stroke risk (Table 21.2). Periventricular and deep WMHs often coexist, because both lesion subtypes could be linked through a common pathogenesis.[85] Although there are few conflicting results,[89] most of studies confirmed that subjects with marked periventricular and subcortical WMH burden have approximately a fivefold and fourfold increase in stroke risk, respectively, compared with individuals in the lowest percentiles of the volumes or grades of white matter lesions.[78,85,86] Even stroke-related death prevalence was found to be greater in association with more severe periventricular and deep WMHs[86]; however, the risk estimates for stroke events are greater for periventricular versus subcortical WMH,[86] with marked periventricular WMH being linked more strongly to stroke-related death compared with deep WMH.[85]

Last, a meta-analysis of general population- and high-risk population-based studies confirmed the association of WMH with the risk of ischemic (HR, 3.1; 95% CI, 2.3–4.1, $p < 0.001$; HR, 7.4; 95% CI, 2.4–22.9, $p = 0.001$) and all stroke (HR, 3.5; 95% CI, 2.5–4.9).[1] In combination with the data that link WMH and the risk of stroke in a number of large observational studies on healthy aging adults, high-risk populations, and hospital-based cohorts, this meta-analysis provides convincing evidence that both presence of WMH on brain MRI and its severity represent a validated neuroimaging marker of cerebrovascular disease and a risk factor for stroke.

WMH and the Risk of Recurrent Stroke

In subjects with previous transient ischemic attack (TIA) or stroke, WMH has been linked to the risk of recurrence.[30,54,90–93] A number of early CT-based studies[90–94] demonstrated a twofold increase in recurrent stroke events in patients with prior stroke or TIA, in particular in those with lacunar infarction or widespread leukoaraiosis on head CT, as well as worse outcomes. Despite the differences in characterization of WMH in CT versus MRI, multiple MRI-based studies confirmed the role of WMH severity as an independent predictor of recurrent stroke specifically in patients with symptomatic lacunar infarcts, with stroke recurrence being associated with worse functional outcome (Table 21.1).[95] There was a fourfold increase in 3-year cumulative incidence of recurrent stroke (43.7% vs. 7.8% and 9.3%, respectively, $p = 0.0001$) and a lower survival rate ($p < 0.007$) in patients with severe WMH compared with those with no or mild WMH.[96] In case of either symptomatic nonlacunar[97] or lacunar infarct,[98] the risk of developing recurrent stroke is increased in the presence of severe WMH. In patients with WMH, lacunar infarction and ICH are the most likely recurrent events, suggesting small-vessel disease as a common etiology, as opposed to cortical territorial infarcts usually associated with large-vessel or cardioembolism.[99]

WMH severity has been linked to a greater risk of hemorrhagic transformation of cerebral infarcts in patients treated with warfarin for secondary prevention,[100] of recurrent lobar ICH,[101] as well as symptomatic ICH after intravenous[102,103] or intra-arterial thrombolysis.[104] However, extensive WMH appears to be a strong predictor of recurrent ischemic stroke rather than recurrent ICH.[105]

Topographic distribution of the white matter lesions appears to affect the risk of stroke recurrence (Table 21.2). For example, periventricular WMH was associated with a greater risk of recurrent ischemic stroke (HR, 3.2; 95% CI, 1.3–8.4) compared with deep WMH (HR, 1.5; 95% CI, 0.6–3.8).[106] Similarly, increased risk of recurrent lobar ICH was strongly related to MRI-based periventricular WMH (HR, 9.0; 95% CI, 1.2–67.2).[101]

Progression of WMH and the Risk of Stroke

Longitudinal cohort studies of WMH progression over 4 to 6 years confirmed age as its main predictor.[2,4] The rate of WMH progression varied in different studies. In healthy individuals aged 50 to 75 years, WMH progressed minimally, with a median WMH volume of 0.01 cm^3 (interquartile range, 0.0–0.3) after 3 years[4] versus 0.1 cm^3 (interquartile range, 0.0–0.7) after 6 years.[107] In older subjects with gait dysfunction, a mean (± standard deviation) increase of 1.1 ± 1.8 cm^3 over 4 years was noted[108]; and in the healthy elderly, a change in median WMH volume from 2.5 cm^3 to 6.0 cm^3 ($p < 0.001$) after 5 years[109] was reported.

In addition to age, baseline lesion volume burden seem to be linked more strongly to a greater degree of progression,[110] as opposed to other proposed risk factors including diabetes, hyperlipidemia, body mass index, smoking, and gender, for which study results are conflicting.[111–113] In fact, when stratified by baseline severity, WMH progression demonstrates similar trends toward an increase of the lesion burden starting from more severe baseline WMH, both in healthy adults[4] and in subjects with hypertension within the placebo group of the MRI substudy of the Perindopril Protection Against Recurrent Stroke Study trial.[7]

In addition, WMH progression has been linked to increased risk of stroke. In MRI-/CT-based follow-up studies, WMH progression has been associated significantly with increased stroke risk in patients with no or mild WMH at baseline (Table 21.1).[98,114] In the Cardiovascular Health Study, worsening of WMH independently increased the risk of first-ever stroke in the elderly (adjusted HR, 1.39; 95% CI, 1.02–1.88), but adjusting for a baseline WMH grade removed the effect of WMH progression on stroke risk in this cohort.[115] In patients with symptomatic carotid artery disease, leukoaraiosis has been reported to progress in 31.5% of cases, with an average rate of progression of 5.2% per year, and patients with progressive leukoaraiosis had a higher occurrence (36.0% vs. 23.5%, $p = 0.01$) of one or multiple subsequent stroke events, particularly lacunar strokes.[114] Hence, uncontrolled vascular risk factors were thought to account for WMH deterioration in patients with clinical cerebrovascular disease.[98]

A recent meta-analysis confirmed the association between WMH and risk of stroke in high-vascular risk populations (HR, 7.4; 95% CI, 2.4–22.9) and in an expanded analysis including healthy adults (HR, 3.5; 95% CI, 2.5–4.9).[1] However, heterogeneity of WMH assessment between the studies serves as a limitation in using these data for estimating the individual risk of stroke.

SUMMARY AND FUTURE IMPLICATIONS

WMH is a significant neuroimaging marker that represents a complex underlying pathophysiological process and that is linked strongly to stroke risk in healthy adults and patients with symptomatic cerebrovascular disease. Based on the current understanding of WMH as a pathological entity, its determinants are likely to be complex and interactive, with a large component in its variability being linked to genetic contribution.[116–118] The increasing prevalence and detection of WMH resulting from the increase in life expectancy and the availability of MRI techniques, and its potential impact on cerebrovascular disease in an individual as well as on the population level warrants intense investigation.

Silent Brain Infarcts

The term *silent brain infarct* indicates single or multiple infarctions that are either completely asymptomatic or associated with neurological signs or symptoms that are not recognized by either patients or physicians as stroke.[119] In population studies, more than 90% of SBIs correspond to lacunar infarcts[120,121]; however, even territorial infarcts can be detected incidentally in neuroimaging without known history of stroke in cases when either neurological symptoms were misinterpreted[122] or clinical symptoms were actually absent.[123] In past decades, the introduction of neuroimaging techniques such as CT[124] and subsequently more sophisticated tools such as MRI confirmed this cerebrovascular entity and increased our ability to detect these lesions as incidental findings in the general population,[125] and especially in the apparently healthy elderly.[120,126] Studies on the epidemiology and pathophysiology of SBIs have radically changed the approach to cerebrovascular disease definitions, particularly because these neuroimaging markers have been linked to the risk of clinically overt cerebrovascular disease.

Data on the prevalence[24,120,121,127–132] and incidence[78,133,134] of SBIs varies across the studies according to the population of interest, definition of SBIs, study design, and neuroimaging modalities used in each individual study. Population-based studies reported an overall SBI prevalence of 8% to 28%, with an incidence of 0.3% to 3% per year that increases progressively with age. The presence of SBIs is a strong predictor of the development of new silent infarcts.[121] In high-risk populations, SBIs are more frequent in patients with cardiovascular disease,[135] stroke,[136,137] and dementia,[138] whereas the likelihood of developing new SBIs is greater among patients with TIA at an annual rate of 19%,[139] and in those undergoing carotid endarterectomy[140–142] or carotid artery stenting,[143–145] with a greater proportion of SBIs detected by using DWI in patients treated with endarterectomy.[146] A high prevalence of stroke symptoms has been reported in the general population without prior official diagnosis of stroke or TIA, meaning there is probably a reasonable proportion of subjects with undiagnosed symptomatic cerebrovascular events that are not screened at all for vascular risk factors and do not receive proper preventive treatments.[147] Hence, MRI interpretation of SBIs should be done by experienced physicians with extensive knowledge in neurology.

MRI APPEARANCE

The MRI diagnostic criteria of SBIs have not been unified and vary across methodologies and parameters adopted within different studies. Developing standardized criteria for the diagnosis of SBIs has a potential to improve interpretation and comparison of data between the studies.[148,149]

MRI appearance of SBIs depends on the stage of the infarct evolution. Combination of T1W and T2W images, particularly FLAIR, enables detecting these lesions with a greater sensitivity, and MRI findings usually correspond to relative histopathological studies (Figure 21.5).[150,151] Novel MRI techniques such as DWI allows the detection of acute, silent small strokes.[152] In general, SBIs appear as focal, irregularly shaped, with a heterogeneous T1 hypointensity, becoming hyperintense on T2W images but hypointense on FLAIR sequences, reflecting tissue destruction and cavitation with irregular rim signals related to morphological changes caused by gliosis (Figure 21.6). Topographically, these lesions are located in "silent" areas of the brain typically including basal ganglia, thalamus, cerebral white matter, but also internal capsule, infratentorial regions such as brainstem, particularly pons, and cerebellum, and they have been also found in the cerebral cortex.[153] Lacunar infarcts that might not cavitate depending on the timing of their detection method, location, and time to follow-up[154,155] may appear as T2 or FLAIR hyperintensities with relative T1 hypointensity on MRI,[153] and might be considered as evolving lacunar infarcts or part of the deep WMHs.[156] Hence, specificity of noncavitated lacunar infarcts is low in the presence of WMH,[149] and different pathophysiological mechanisms might be responsible for disease progression of these distinct entities.[28,67] Conversely, cavitated lesions can be located within areas of diffuse WMH, appearing as black "holes" on FLAIR sequences, and they might be interpreted as silent lacunar infarcts.[157]

With regard to lesion size, no clear consensus exists. Although some studies include only focal lesions that are 3 mm or larger, others refer to a maximum diameter of 15 to 20 mm, according to the classic neuropathological definition of lacunar infarcts,[123] and yet other authors include

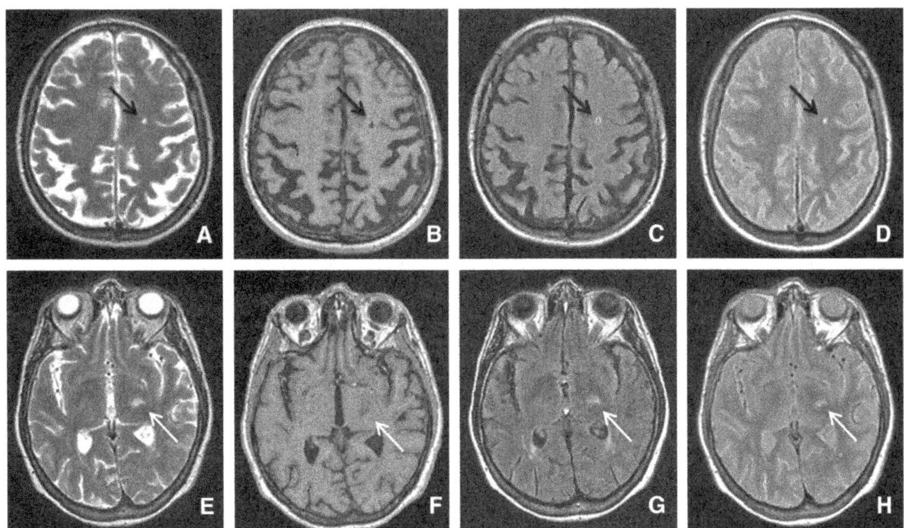

FIGURE 21.5 Main signal characteristics used for defining silent brain infarcts (SBIs) on different magnetic resonance imaging (MRI) sequences. (A–D) A silent brain infarct corresponds to a cerebrospinal fluid (CSF) signal on all MRI sequences (black arrows). (A) Axial T2 weighted (T2W) imaging. (B) Axial T1-weighted (T1W) imaging. (C) Axial fluid-attenuated inversion recovery (FLAIR) imaging. (D) Axial proton density (PD) imaging. (E–H) A hyperintense lesion on T2W images that is moderately hypointense on T1 in the left thalamus (white arrows) is not defined as an SBI in studies defining only cavities containing CSF as infarcts, whereas it is diagnosed as an infarct in studies that simply defined hyperintense T2 and hypointense T1 foci as infarcts. (E) Axial T2W. (F) Axial T1W. (G) Axial FLAIR. (H) Axial PD. (Adapted with permission from Zhu et al. *Stroke.* 2011;42:1140–1145.)

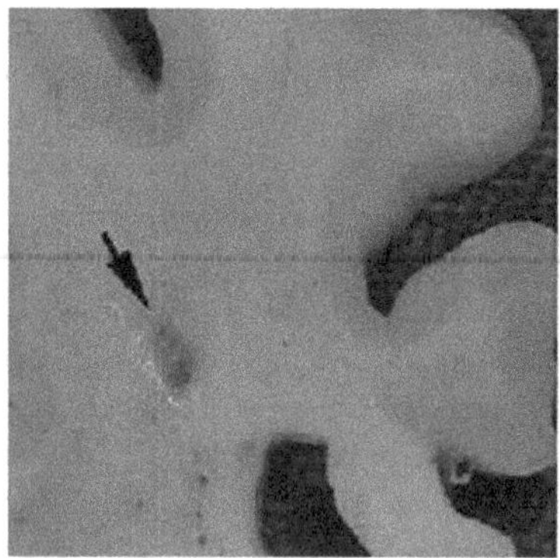

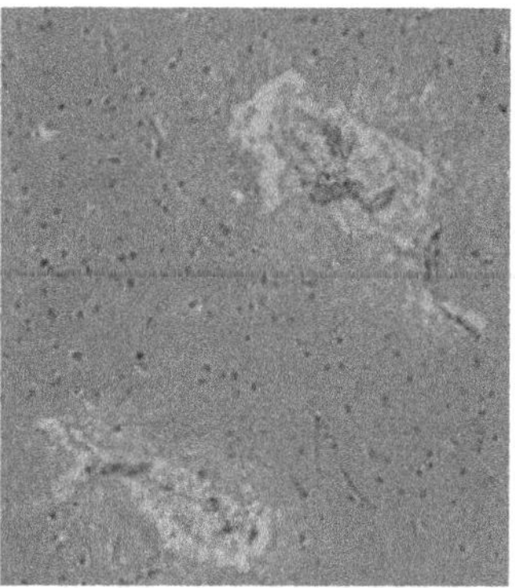

FIGURE 21.6 (A, B) Silent brain infarcts in gross pathology (A) appear as cystic infarcts of 1 cm or less in diameter in the periventricular white matter (arrow), which exhibits softening and discoloration in the surrounding white matter (B). (Adapted with permission from Strozyk et al. *Neurobiol Aging.* 2010;31:1710–1720.)

lesions greater than 25 mm in diameter.[148] Classic MRI studies of healthy individuals reported SBIs as small subcortical infarcts of 3 to 15 mm in diameter[126] and more likely to be located in the basal ganglia.[158] GRE sequences or high-resolution T1W images are particularly helpful in distinguishing SBIs from their mimics, such as DPVSs (état criblé), which are physiological findings surrounding the penetrating arterioles and might be misinterpreted as lacunar infarctions, if enlarged.

HISTOPATHOLOGICAL CORRELATES OF SBIS

Although lacunar infarcts were described for the first time in the 19th century by French neurologists and neuropathologists, Fisher pointed out the common silent nature (up to 77%) of these lesions in clinicopathological studies.[123] The infarcts appear as cystic lesions with ill-defined and irregular margins, the sizes of which are the result of the occluded arterioles. MRI-detected SBIs correspond histologically to irregular cavitations with scattered, fat-laden macrophages and associated surrounding reactive gliosis, myelin, and axonal loss (Figure 21.6).[28,47,123,159,160] With increasing lesion age, the number of macrophages decreases and gliosis becomes more fibrillar,[47,123] whereas other lacunes are found to have selective neuronal loss and relative preservation of glial cells.[123,161]

PATHOPHYSIOLOGY AND CLINICAL DETERMINANTS OF SBIS

SBIs share a similar risk factor profile with symptomatic infarcts, particularly of lacunar subtype, including age; hypertension; diabetes; ischemic heart disease; excessive alcohol consumption; smoking; metabolic syndrome; family history of stroke; symptomatic cerebrovascular diseases; presence of carotid artery stenosis; atrial fibrillation; nocturnal, postprandial, orthostatic hypotension; elevated C-reactive protein; and hyperhomocysteinemia.[119,122,135,153,162,163] In population-based studies, age and hypertension are the strongest predictors of SBIs, whereas other associations remain controversial and may require further validation.[135] To which extent vascular risk factors other than age and hypertension contribute to small-vessel disease and progression to silent lacunar infarction is still unclear.[119,164,165] However, SBIs are associated strongly with WMH,[59,166] and both seem to have synergistic effects[167] on the risk of stroke, suggesting a shared pathophysiology of these distinct MRI entities corresponding to diseased small cerebral vessel state.[54,135]

In younger patients, evidence of SBIs has been associated with type 1 diabetes, obesity, smoking, and increasing age.[168] Genetic factors may also contribute to the risk of SBI development; however, neither the candidate gene association studies (Angiotensin Converting Enzyme [ACE] and endothelial nitric oxide synthase [eNOS] polymorphisms, for example),[153] nor the largest to-date genomewide association studies on MRI-defined brain infarcts in healthy adults[169] have been able to replicate their findings.

SILENT INFARCTS AND THE RISK OF STROKE

The clinical significance of asymptomatic infarcts is still under investigation; nevertheless, prevalence of SBIs will continue to increase as a result of the aging of the population and increased detection, with broader use of advanced neuroimaging. Diagnosis of SBIs may also mark the population that is at high risk for overt cerebrovascular disease (Tables 20.1 and 20.2), as well as recurrent silent infarcts and white matter disease progression, manifesting further risk of brain damage.[167,170,171]

Silent Infarcts and Risk of First-Ever Stroke

In population-based studies, subjects with SBIs have a greater annual incidence of clinical stroke compared with those without (1.8%–2.8% vs. 0.2%–0.9%).[87,89,170] Of these, approximately 74% developed ischemic (mostly lacunar) and 26% hemorrhagic (mostly putaminal hemorrhage) strokes. In extended follow-up, SBIs were associated with a 2- to 10-fold increase in risk of first-ever stroke,[78,89,170] with absolute risk of developing stroke being 11.7% for otherwise healthy adults with SBIs versus 2.3% for those without (adjusted HR, 3.9; 95% CI, 2.3–6.8).[78] In another MRI-based population study of aging adults, not only the risk of first-ever stroke doubled for those persons who had one infarct or more on the follow-up image, but the strength of this association increased when incidence of SBIs was combined with WMH progression.[115] This may explain a recent observation reported in the combined analysis from the Atherosclerosis Risk in Communities study and the Cardiovascular Health Study cohorts that the presence of one or more MRI-defined SBIs, most of them (>80%) lacunar, was associated independently with risk of ICH, and this risk increased progressively with the number of SBIs.[88] Hence, the number of silent infarcts might have a crucial role in modulating the risk of hemorrhagic stroke, as well.[59,78,170] Furthermore, common vascular risk factors such as hypertension may be responsible for variable manifestations of cerebrovascular disease, both silent and symptomatic ischemic and hemorrhagic phenotypes; however, each of these risk factors may demonstrate a different effect size on individual risk of stroke.[78,85,170]

Silent Brain Infarcts and the Risk of Recurrent Stroke

In patients with clinical stroke, SBIs have been linked to stroke recurrence.[172,173] Although there are some conflicting results from small studies,[174] both in CT- and MRI-based studies, patients with TIA or nondisabling symptomatic stroke and evidence of SBI had a greater risk of recurrent atrial fibrillation-related cardioembolism,[173] recurrent acute ischemic stroke predominantly of large-vessel subtype,[175,176] as well as lacunar stroke, or ICH.[97,172,177] SBIs do not seem to account for a greater risk of hemorrhagic transformation in patients treated with intravenous thrombolysis.[176,178] Evidence of SBI after a clinical stroke—either ischemic or hemorrhagic—increases the risk of mortality linked to the index cerebrovascular event (24.3% vs. 10.7%), especially when SBIs are combined with WMH severity.[85]

SUMMARY AND FUTURE IMPLICATIONS

MRI detection of SBIs in the future may reset the current standards of clinical care and ongoing investigations by introducing a sensitive yet reliable approach for cerebrovascular risk assessment.

Although the field may still benefit from standardization of the SBI definition and advancement of neuroimaging techniques to customize an individual image analysis, the use of SBIs, alone or in combination with WMH, may become a centerpiece of stroke risk stratification, targeted treatment approaches, and aggressive prevention strategies in the future.

Cerebral Microbleeds

In addition to silent cerebral ischemia, cerebral small-vessel disease may lead to subclinical hemorrhagic lesions, usually characterized by hemosiderin deposition resulting from blood extravasation from diseased arterioles. These distinct lesions, known as *cerebral microbleeds*, are adjacent to small vessels and are most often asymptomatic; therefore, CMBs are usually detected on MRI as incidental findings.[119,179] First described in the 1990s,[180–182] CMBs are drawing increasing attention both from the clinical and research points of view. Incidental finding of CMBs on the MRIs of apparently healthy individuals as well as patients with stroke depends strongly on the specifics of MRI protocols used. Current data suggest that CMBs are found in up to 6% of the general population, 30% of patients with ischemic stroke, and 60% of patients with primary ICH.[57,183–185] CMBs are associated strongly with age, and CMB incidence ranges between 7% and 23% in various studies.[2,186–190] In the Rotterdam Scan Study, CMBs were found in 18% of individuals aged 60 to 69 years and in 38% of subjects older than 80 years.[190] Based on neuropathological analysis, CMBs in the deep subcortical areas are almost always observed in postmortem brain specimens of subjects aged more than 70 years.[191,192]

MRI APPEARANCE

CMBs can be detected easily using appropriate MRI sequences sensitive to hemoglobin and to its breakdown products,[119] such as T2*-weighted GRE. As a result of the magnetic susceptibility phenomenon exhibited by hemosiderin, CMBs appear as small, homogeneous round or ovoid areas of black signal voids surrounded by brain parenchyma (Figure 21.7.A).[2,188] The adoption of prespecified

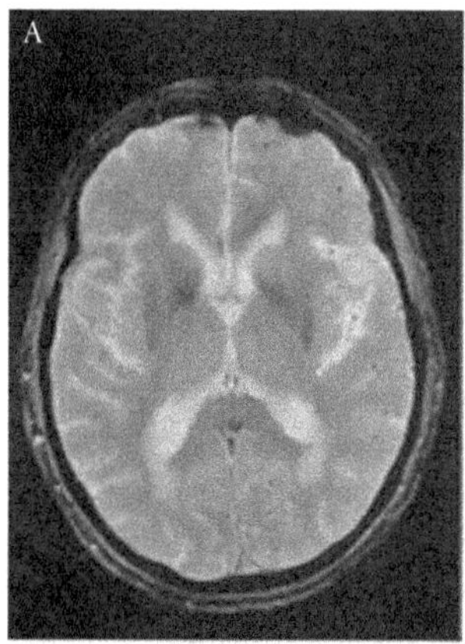

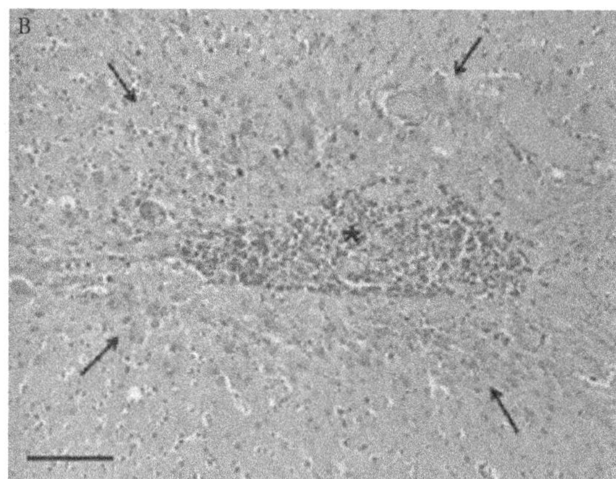

FIGURE 21.7 (A) Axial gradient-recalled echo of microbleeds (A), and histological image of chronic cortical microbleeds using hematoxylin–eosin stain (B). The lesion consists of central hemosiderin accumulation (pigment marked by an asterisk) surrounded by ring-shape astrocytic and microglial proliferation (arrows) with active hemosiderin resorption. Scale bar = 100 μm. Courtesy of Dr. V. Deramecourt. (Figure 7B: Adapted with permission from Cordonnier C et al. *Pract Neurol.* 2010).

MRI parameters such as longer echo time, higher special resolution, lower interslice gap, the use of three-dimensional acquisition, and higher magnetic field can increase the ability to detect CMBs.[193–196]

GRE provides additional information with regard to CMB chronicity as well as their location and overall burden.[122] Cortical CMBs located at the gray–white matter junction and the superficial cortical layers of the parietal, temporal, and occipital lobes are usually associated with cerebral amyloid angiopathy (CAA). The CMBs located in subcortical regions including basal ganglia, thalamus, brainstem, and cerebellum are linked to long-standing arterial hypertension. When multiple CMBs are present, they tend to cluster in the same area.[28,184,197]

Although lesion size cutoffs for CMBs are still debated, a diameter range between 2 mm and 5 to 10 mm is used most frequently.[2,32,185] One proposed diameter cutoff based on bimodal distribution of lesion sizes between micro- and macrohemorrhages was 5.7 mm.[198] However, the more sensitive MRI techniques may increase the number of potentially detectable CMBs,[185,195] as well as possible CMB mimics such as flow voids, cavernous malformations, hemorrhagic transformation of small infarcts, iron deposition, and scattered calcifications that need to be ruled out to improve specificity of CMB detection.[193]

HISTOPATHOLOGICAL CORRELATES OF CMBS

Histological studies correlating brain tissue pathology with neuroimaging confirmed that these hypointense GRE MRI lesions correspond to small hemorrhages, which are usually smaller in size than those apparent on MRI as a result of the blooming effect.[179,199,200] A minority of these lesions may correspond to small lacunes ringed by hemosiderin, vessel wall dissection, or microaneurysm.[200]

On microscopic examination, CMBs correspond to focal hemosiderin deposits containing macrophages in the perivascular space with areas of heme degradation surrounded by inflammatory reaction with activated microglial cells, late complement activation, and apoptosis. Some CMBs are also surrounded by gliosis and ischemic changes. In the walls of the adjacent, ruptured small arterioles, lipohyalinosis-related changes linked to hypertension are usually reported, particularly in CMBs located in basal ganglia, thalamus, and cerebellum.[179] Near CMBs located in the lobar regions, ruptured arteriosclerotic microvessels[201] and CAA-related changes are observed with wall thickening, absence of the muscularis layer, and deposition of β-amyloid (Figure 21.7.B).[179,202]

PATHOPHYSIOLOGY AND CLINICAL DETERMINANTS OF CMBS

As noted earlier, CMBs are detected more frequently in the elderly and are associated strongly with the presence of vascular risk factors such as arterial hypertension,[57,185,193] diabetes mellitus, smoking, or ischemic heart disease, but not with gender.[185] The presence of CMBs and any systolic blood pressure seems to predict the development of new CMBs over a follow-up period of 5.5 years.[203]

CMBs are frequent in patients with CAA, particularly in subjects with hereditary CAA in whom the frequency increases up to 69%.[204] Overall, when compared with healthy subjects and patients with ischemic stroke, prevalence of CMBs has been reported to be greater in patients with both deep and lobar ICH (60.4%–66%).[122,185,188,197] In subjects with primary ICH, age, prior history of stroke, evidence of small-vessel ischemic disease, old hemorrhage on neuroimaging, prior use of antithrombotic drugs, and larger hematoma volume were associated with CMBs.[205,206] Varying reports on prevalence of CMBs in patients with ischemic stroke exist; however, on average, it seems to be approximately 33.5%.[185] CMBs are highly prevalent in patients with lacunar stroke subtype (53.5%–68%),[207] likely reflecting the overlap between cerebral small-vessel disease pathologies. However, CMBs are less common in subjects with atherothrombotic (36%) and cardioembolic (19.4%) stroke subtypes.[185] CMBs have also been associated with other atherosclerosis-related pathological processes, including peripheral artery disease (13%) and ischemic heart disease (4%).[122] CMBs are noted less frequently in patients with TIAs than in those with ischemic stroke.[185,208] Genetic factors influencing vessel wall integrity, such as apolipoprotein E genotype, may play a role in CMB development,[189,190,209] particularly for lobar CMBs in CAA.[210] Moreover, these lesions are also common in Moyamoya disease[211] and small-vessel genetic disorders such as CADASIL, with a prevalence ranging from 25% to 69%.[185,188,197,212,213]

A strong correlation exists between the presence of CMBs and markers of small-vessel disease, including subclinical lacunar infarcts (with a prevalence up to 62.2% in patients with multiple lacunar infarcts),[185] and WMH and its severity.[57,183,186,188,214] Baseline WMH has also been associated with the development of new CMBs in patients with CAA,[41] suggesting that CMBs and WMHs could represent different manifestations of a progressive microangiopathy in the presence of CAA. The link between CMBs and the markers of chronic, poorly controlled hypertension, such as retinal microvascular lesions[215] and left ventricular hypertrophy,[216] is similarly suggestive of the role of underlying high blood pressure in CMB development and burden.

The number of CMBs could mark severity of the microangiopathy,[217] as in patients with CAA in whom vessel thickness related to amyloid deposits correlates with the number of CMBs[198]; however, there is no conclusive evidence on the etiology and significance of a high CMB burden.[185]

The location of CMBs could be particularly important for understanding the underlying mechanisms of disease that contribute to development and progression of these lesions. Their distribution in cortical, but particularly in subcortical areas of the brain (white matter and deep gray matter, such as basal ganglia, particularly putamen; mainly the posterolateral part of the upper putamen and thalamus—lateral nuclei—and infratentorial regions such as brainstem and cerebellum) matching the distribution of small, deep perforating arteries, can be related to hypertensive vasculopathy affecting these vessels.[216] The Rotterdam Scan Study reported systolic blood pressure, severe hypertension, and presence of lacunar infarcts to be associated with deep or infratentorial CMBs.[190] Similarly, CMB distribution and ICH location correspond, so that subjects with deep ICH tend to have more subcortical CMBs compared with those with lobar ICH,[184,197] suggesting hypertensive microangiopathy as an important underlying mechanisms of subcortical CMBs. CMBs located in the lobar regions, particularly in the posterior regions (temporal and occipital lobe),[218] usually in the cortical–subcortical junctions in the distribution territory of the small and medium leptomeningeal and cortical vessels, are often detected in patients with CAA,[188,219] especially in the presence of normotensive subjects with a history of cognitive impairment and recurrent lobar ICH.[220] The CMB lobar distribution in CAA (i.e., in the posterior region [occipital lobe]) has served as an additional radiological marker to the Boston criteria for probable diagnosis of CAA.[202] Hence, hypertensive small-vessel disease and also CAA seem to be the most important pathological entities found to be associated with CMBs. These findings support the hypothesis of a common small-vessel disease-related pathophysiological mechanism.[221] Furthermore, CMBs can also be found in normal aging brains without evidence of cerebral vessel changes related to hypertension or β-amyloid deposition, suggesting the link to aging vessel pathology.[191] Other causative mechanisms, such as transient, mild BBB disruption with blood extravasation from vascular lumen to the parenchyma may explain the pathological finding of CMBs at the level of capillaries.[191,192]

New insights into the pathogenesis of CMBs came from a study of acute ischemic stroke in which new CMBs were noted to appear outside the index infarcted area in 12.7% of cases on the 7-day follow-up MRI. Furthermore, the newly formed CMBs were predicted independently by the presence of baseline CMBs and severe small-vessel disease, but were not associated with thrombolytic or antithrombotic therapy.[222] These findings may support the hypothesis that CMBs could develop acutely as a direct consequence of pathophysiological events after ischemic stroke, such as endothelial dysfunction, BBB disruption, and inflammation.[221] Similarly, acute SBIs detected on DWI of patients with CAA-related ICH [177,223] manifest as a link between ischemic and hemorrhagic stroke, sharing a common pathophysiology on the small-vessel level.[221]

Clinically, although CMBs are often considered silent, small hemorrhagic lesions, a number of studies demonstrated a possible direct effect of CMBs on neurological functions, cognition, and outcome in terms of disability and mortality.[193,224] In patients having CMBs with a CAA-related distribution, stereotyped recurrent, focal neurological symptoms responding to anticonvulsants might be related directly to the CMBs and their location, or to cortex irritation caused by blood products.[225] CMBs, and particularly their burden, could play a role in the development of cognitive impairment, with deterioration of specific cognitive functions such as executive abilities,[2] as has been reported in the presence of multiple lacunar infarcts or WMH.[193] Last, CMBs may also contribute in part to the cognitive impairment observed in patients with Alzheimer's disease, in which they have been detected in 15% to 32% of cases.[185,226–229] However, no direct causative effect of CMBs on cognitive impairment has been demonstrated, with these lesions being most likely a marker of the underlying vasculopathy that leads to cognitive deficits.[230]

MICROBLEEDS AND THE RISK OF STROKE

CMBs have become the center of intense investigations during the past decade, reflecting their potential clinical importance, especially their role in predicting the risk of ICH in patients using anticoagulants or antiplatelet agents. However, no conclusive data exist to date on CMBs as a reliable MRI biomarker of increased risk of stroke, or whether they could be used in clinical decision making (Tables 20.1 and 20.2). This uncertainty arises mostly from the limitations of current studies, including study design, varying definitions of CMBs, imaging protocols adopted to detect CMBs, selection of study populations, and outcomes.[185,231]

Microbleeds and the Risk of First-Ever Stroke

Clinical significance of CMBs has been studied extensively in patients with CAA, in whom it serves as an accurate marker of disease progression, CAA-related ICH, and cognitive impairment.[220] However, the significance of CMBs detected in the apparently healthy general population requires further clarification.[188,193] Limited data are available on the association between CMBs and the risk of first-ever stroke (Table 21.1). In a recent longitudinal study, subjects without history of symptomatic stroke and evidence of CMBs were found to have an approximate threefold increase in the risk of first-ever stroke compared with those without CMBs, even after adjustment for age, sex, hypertension, and antithrombotic therapy (HR, 2.64; 95% CI, 1.34–5.19; $p = 0.005$).[232] Furthermore, evidence of CMBs in these subjects predicted ischemic stroke (HR, 11.77; 95% CI, 2.95–46.82; $p < 0.001$) independently but not hemorrhagic stroke (HR, 1.48; 95% CI, 0.63–3.45; $p = 0.36$).[232] However, in another cohort of individuals at high risk of cerebrovascular disease, CMBs were associated strongly with a greater risk of ICH (HR, 50.2; 95% CI, 16.7–150.9as compared with ischemic stroke (HR, 4.48; 95% CI, 2.20–12.2).[233] Overall, CMBs seem to be more prevalent in patients with recurrent stroke compared with those with first-ever stroke, of any subtype.[185,234]

Microbleeds and the Risk of Recurrent Stroke

Prior studies indicate that CMBs may serve as a reliable MRI marker of recurrent stroke.[235,236] The presence of CMBs increases the risk of recurrent ICH,[105,186,237,238] whereas higher rate of recurrent deep ICH and lacunar infarcts is observed among patients with multiple CMBs and small-vessel disease-related stroke, such as ICH and lacunar stroke.[104,216,217,239,240]

In patients with primary lobar ICH, the total number of hemorrhages on baseline T2*-weighted MRI, including the index ICH and micro- and macrobleeds, predicts cumulative risk of recurrent symptomatic ICH over a 3-year follow-up, and increases with the rising burden of hemorrhages and after adjustment for risk factors, apolipoprotein E genotype, and history of previous ICH (HR, 1.5; 95% CI, 1.1–2.2).[235] Recent studies confirmed the significance of the number of CMBs as an independent predictor of recurrent ICH in patients with primary ICH,[241] and particularly of recurrent lobar ICH in patients with probable/possible CAA (2–4 microbleed: HR, 2.93; 95% CI, 1.3–4.0; $p = 0.041$; ≥5 microbleeds: HR, 4.12; 95% CI, 1.6–9.3; $p = 0.001$).[242] Although it is not yet completely clear whether in these patients recurrent ICH tends to develop at the site of CMBs,[241] both the distribution of new CMBs and the location of recurrent lobar ICH have been reported to be associated with distribution of the baseline CMBs.[218]

The role of CMBs in predicting the risk of hemorrhagic complications in those individuals that use antithrombotic agents is currently under investigation. Symptomatic ICH was reported to be more frequent in aspirin users with multiple CMBs versus aspirin users without CMBs (19 of 21 vs. 7 of 21, $p < 0.001$), and in patients with high CMB loads the risk of ICH may outweigh the benefit of aspirin.[203,236] However, the risk of recurrent cerebral hemorrhagic events associated with antiplatelet use in patients with lobar (HR, 0.8; 95% CI, 0.4–3.3; $p = 0.73$) or deep (HR, 1.2; 95% CI, 0.1–14.3; $p = 0.88$) ICH was not altered.[243] With regard to the risk of warfarin-related ICH, CMBs are associated with ICH independent of an increased international normalized ratio (INR) or hypertension (odds ratio [OR], 7.38; 95% CI, 1.05–51.83).[244] Lobar and basal ganglia CMBs are both likely to be associated with a more brain bleeding-prone status in these patients.[245] In other studies, although the number of CMBs was greater in patients on warfarin compared with control subjects, this difference did not reach statistical significance.[246]

Last, the predictive value of CMBs has been explored with regard to the risk of both spontaneous and thrombolysis-related hemorrhagic transformation in patients with acute ischemic stroke. Some studies found CMBs an independent predictor of all hemorrhagic transformations, both spontaneous and pharmacological, within the infarcted area (OR, 7.2; 95% CI, 1.9–28.2) after adjustment for age, sex, vascular risk factors, treatments, WMH, and lacunes.[247] Other small studies suggested a possible relationship between the presence of CMBs and the risk of new hemorrhage from the CMBs themselves after thrombolytic treatment.[248] Overall, current evidence suggests that thrombolytic treatment appears to be relatively safe in the presence of CMBs,[249,250] but large, prospective studies are warranted to examine this.

PRACTICAL CLINICAL AND RESEARCH IMPLICATIONS

Although the specific clinical significance of CMBs with regard to patient diagnosis and treatment remains unclear, CMBs promise to remain an important MRI marker of ongoing cerebrovascular disease. If validated, detection of CMBs on T2*-weighted MRI may have a particular role in the prediction of hemorrhagic risk in thrombolysis for acute ischemic stroke, as well as in secondary prevention therapy with antithrombotic drugs, both antiplatelets and anticoagulants.[248,251–253] Furthermore, CMBs may be relevant in the prediction of ischemic cerebrovascular events, potentially giving an insight into the underlying pathophysiology of various stroke subtypes and TIA.[236] Last, GRE T2* sequence findings may be used in the future as a marker of small-vessel disease severity and/or to stratify patients based on their hemorrhagic risk as part of selection for clinical trials on antithrombotics, thrombolytics, or antihypertensive agents.[188]

Microinfarcts

With the development of advanced MRI techniques during the past few years, new MRI entities such as MIs emerged as markers of cerebrovascular disease. These lesions are usually clinically silent, like

SBIs, and "invisible" to conventional MRI techniques, but a number of recent studies have demonstrated their possible role in cognitive impairment and dementia.[254,255] MIs likely act synergistically with larger SBIs, and they may represent one of the major, although not yet well-defined, pathophysiological "bridges" between cerebral small-vessel disease and cognitive dysfunction.[256]

MRI APPEARANCE

If MIs were visible on conventional MRI, they probably would be hypointense on FLAIR images and hyperintense on T2W images in their cystic stage, and hyperintense both on FLAIR and T2 in their gliotic stage.[257] The presence of other lesions, particularly those related to small-vessel disease can confound and prevent the detection of MIs, such as WMH, the development toward which MIs may also contribute.[258] MIs could be also confounded with perivascular spaces.[259–261] Increased spatial resolution imaging, such as high-field strength MRI, could detect these microscopic lesions reliably, as shown by a recent postmortem imaging study in patients with CADASIL.[262] In the case of acute MIs, they can be detected with high sensitivity on DWI (Figure 21.8.A).[263,264] As a result of the MRI blooming effect, these lesions may appear larger than they actually are; hence, acute MIs can be classified incorrectly as lacunar infarcts.[256,265]

HISTOPATHOLOGICAL CORRELATES OF MIS

MIs are not visible by the naked eye and on gross macroscopic pathological brain inspection, but they can be detected by light microscopy (Figure 21.8.B).[256,266,267] They appear as microscopic regions of tissue necrosis, which could also be cavitated. The microscopic findings seem to resemble the same pathological characteristics of brain infarcts on a smaller scale; hence, the term *microinfarct*. However,

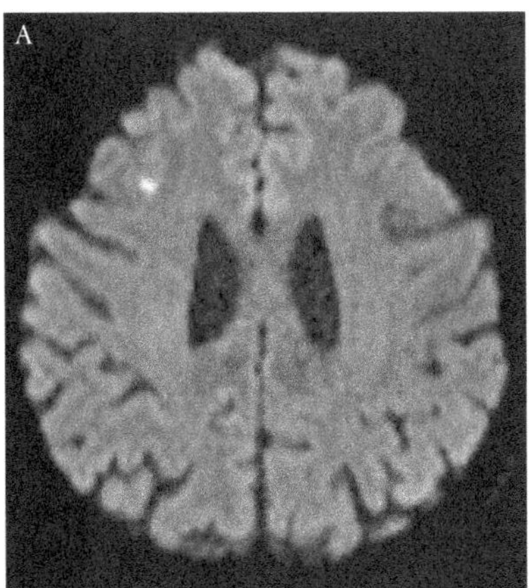

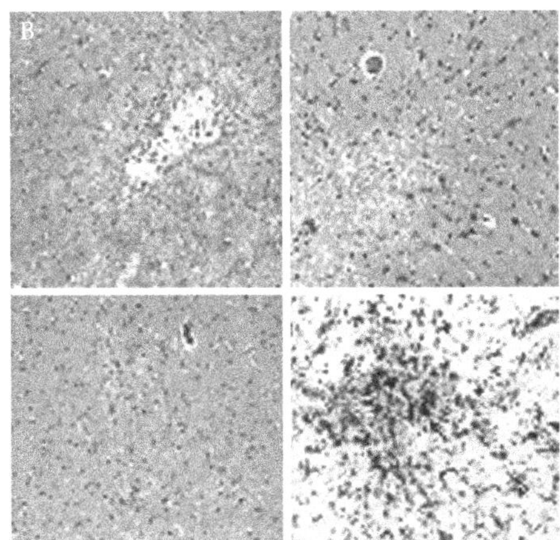

FIGURE 21.8 (A, B) Axial diffusion-weighted imaging of acute microinfarct (A) and histological images of microinfarcts (B). There is a cystic (cavitated) microinfarct (diameter, 600 µm) in the basal ganglia (B, upper left), an incomplete microinfarct without cavitation (diameter, 330 µm) in the midfrontal cortex (B, upper right), a cortical microinfarct with linear scarring (puckering) from the middle temporal cortex (diameter, 120 µm; B, lower left), and immunostaining for major histocompatibility complex II human leukocyte antigen DR3 expression in activated microglia and macrophages in a microinfarct in the basal ganglia (diameter, 320 µm; B, lower right). Images provided by Chunhui Yang (Rush Medical Center, Chicago, IL). (Figure 8B: Adapted with permission from Smith EE et al. *Lancet Neurol.* 2012;11:272–282.)

their pathophysiology is not yet very well defined; thus, areas of incomplete infarction, tissue rarefaction with gliosis, are sometimes erroneously considered MIs.[267–269] The available neuropathological studies, particularly focused on Alzheimer's disease and vascular dementia, are conflicting about the size-based definition of MIs, because some studies have adopted a diameter upper limit of 2 mm,[270] whereas others have an upper limit of 4 mm.[269] Cystic MIs are usually described as larger (up to 5 mm) than noncystic MIs (0.05–0.4 mm).[28,268,271] The mean diameter can have a range from 0.2 to 2.9 mm.[255,272] Another source of variation is represented by the staining methods for the detection of MIs that are not yet standardized.[266] On microscopic examination, MIs appear differently according to their stage. During the acute phase, ischemic red neurons with vacuolization from cytotoxic edema are typically found; during the subacute stage (3–5 days), macrophages surround the infarct area; and later, astrocytosis becomes the prevalent characteristic. Last, during the chronic phase, MIs are reported as having a central area of necrosis or cavitation surrounded by a gliotic reaction.[256] Regarding their location, MIs seem to occur throughout the brain, from cortical to subcortical gray matter and white matter.[257] They are commonly found in the cerebral cortex, at the base or in the superficial layers of gray matter,[268,272] and particularly in the watershed areas of the cerebral cortex.[257] But, their distribution can actually vary from the anterior to posterior white matter, from border zones of major arterial territories [272–274] to the typical location of lacunar infarctions, such as basal ganglia, thalamus, brainstem, and cerebellum, and in this last case they are probably associated with arteriolosclerosis.[256] There are no apparent differences between MIs located in the cortex versus subcortical regions.[257]

PATHOPHYSIOLOGY AND CLINICAL DETERMINANTS OF MIS

Prevalence of MIs on neuropathological examination is extremely heterogeneous, ranging from 3% to 43% in mixed populations with and without dementia, up to 62% in patients with vascular dementia, and up to 78% in patients with dementia and severe CAA.[257] Multiple MIs are present in approximately 6% of subjects without dementia and 31% of patients with dementia[267]—specifically 0 to 4 in patients with different types of dementia,[275] 1 to 37 (with a mean of 6) in patients with severe CAA, 1 to 6 (with a mean of 3) in subjects with mild CAA,[276] and 1 to 4 in each of the watershed zone areas.[274] This variability is mainly a result of the difficulty in detecting these small lesions, which is highly dependent on the thickness of brain tissue slices inspected, favoring semiquantitative methods.[267,270,276,277] In general, among the elderly who died of all causes, MIs are found in 16% to 46%.[256] Because MIs seem to mirror most of the histopathological characteristics of macroscopic infarctions on a smaller scale, they also, in part, share the same risk factor profile. In fact, first of all, these lesions have been associated particularly with markers of small-vessel disease[270] such as lacunar infarcts, leukoaraiosis, ICH,[278,279] CAA,[271,280–283] and CADASIL,[197,284] but also macroinfarcts.[255,278,285,286] However, the underlying pathophysiology of MIs may be more heterogeneous. MIs are commonly observed in the cortical watershed areas, where they may represent the result of intermittent focal ischemic damage from chronic hypoperfusion, particularly in patients with hypertensive microangiopathy or CAA, which is thought to lower the brain's threshold for ischemia.[287] MIs in the brain regions supplied by large arteries may be related to vessel occlusion and thromboembolism.[255,278,285,286] Last, BBB disruption may also contribute to MI development, where the damage is mediated by oxidative stress and inflammation.[256]

Clinically, these lesions are often silent, but it is believed that multiple MIs might play a role in specific clinical syndromes, particularly cognitive impairment, which is likely related to the neuronal loss burden that characterizes these entities, or alterations in neuronal connectivity throughout the brain.[257]

MIS AND THE RISK OF STROKE

Very little evidence exists regarding the link between MIs and risk of stroke (Table 21.1). MIs detected on DWI in patients with acute lacunar infarction or ICH may represent early recurrence of lesions in patients with severe microangiopathy, or may serve as a predictor of future risk of cerebral small-vessel disease. In a study of patients with ICH who underwent repeated DWI, the frequency of acute ischemic lesions was 7.7% at baseline, but increased up to 25% at 5 days.[288] One long-term follow-up study of acute DWI lesions detected during ICH evaluation demonstrated that they predicted independently risk of ischemic stroke or recurrent ICH (HR, 5.87; 95% CI, 1.004–34.31; $p = 0.049$), ischemic stroke or vascular death (HR, 5.00; 95% CI, 1.15–21.86; $p = 0.032$), or both recurrent ischemic stroke and ICH, or vascular death (HR, 5.69; 95% CI, 1.36–23.70; $p = 0.017$).[288] These findings are similar to previously reported associations between SBIs and stroke risk in population-based studies.[78]

PRACTICAL CLINICAL AND RESEARCH IMPLICATIONS

If the initial findings regarding the role of MIs are confirmed in future studies, they may serve as a valuable marker of the risk of cognitive impairment, especially if combined with other MRI features of small-vessel disease.

Dilated Perivascular Spaces

Virchow-Robin spaces are normal physiological structures that surround the wall of vessels (arteries, arterioles, veins, and venules) as they perforate from the subarachnoid spaces through the brain surface and parenchyma. The basic functional role of perivascular spaces is probably to facilitate solute drainage from the brain through the extracellular spaces, in lieu of lymphatic drainage of the nervous system,[289,290] or possibly to facilitate immunological processes.[290–294] When dilated pathologically, these eventually become DPVSs, which were first described in 1843 by Durand-Fardel as "état criblé," in which a multitude of round holes containing small vessels were observed in the hemispheric white matter, thalamus, and basal ganglia.[2,295] DPVSs appear as punctuate, usually less than 3-mm lesions surrounding perforating arteries in the brain parenchyma and arterioles predominantly in the centrum semiovale, basal ganglia, and hippocampus.

MRI APPEARANCE

Signal intensity of DPVSs on MRI is similar to that of CSF; therefore, they appear hyperintense on T2W images and hypointense on FLAIR. When the signal intensity is measured quantitatively, resulting values are lower than that of CSF,[296] possibly because DPVSs represent interstitial fluid trapped in the subpial or interpial space, and/or because of a partial volume effect.[290] In most studies, FLAIR images have been commonly adopted to differentiate DPVSs from lacunes, based on the absence of a hyperintense rim/halo corresponding to morphological changes caused by gliosis[47,119,150,290]; however, astrocytic gliosis has also been observed surrounding DPVSs in postmortem studies.[161,297] Thus, one of the most reliable MRI sequences for DPVS detection is T1W magnetization prepared rapid gradient echo (MPRAGE) (Figure 21.9.A).

For lesions larger than 3 mm, DPVSs can be interpreted erroneously as lacunar infarcts. With the increased use of gradient echo images, which identify CSF, DPVSs have appeared as filled of CSF and not infarcted tissue.[119] Differential diagnosis of DPVSs from lacunar infarction can be based on size (DPVSs are usually less than 3 mm), location, and symmetry (commonly bilateral, located along perforating arteries), and shape (smooth margins, well-demarcated round, linear, or oval).[148,260,290,298–300]

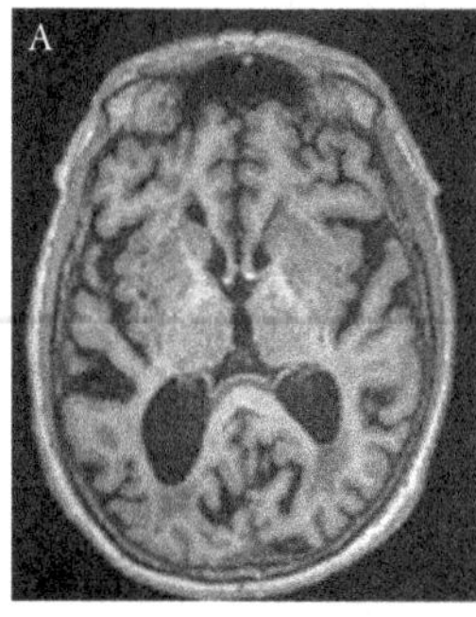

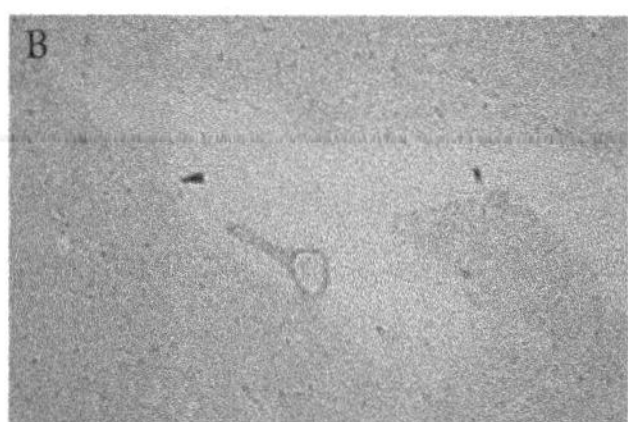

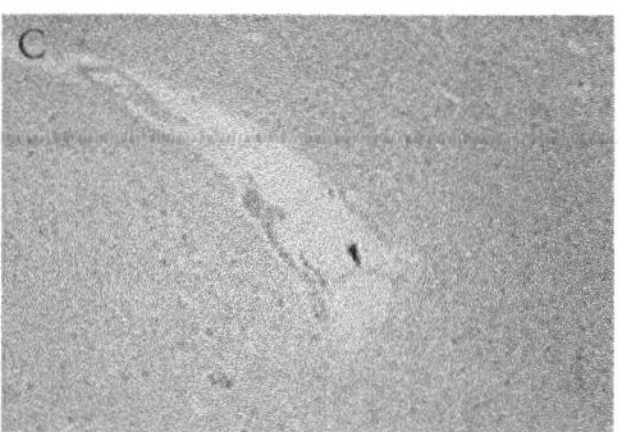

FIGURE 21.9 Dilated perivascular spaces (DPVSs). (A–C) T1-weighted magnetization prepared rapid gradient echo) imaging (MPRAGE) (A) and histological images of DPVSs (B, C), with a photomicrograph showing dilatation of the Virchow-Robin space around an arteriole. A single cell layer (thought to be the inner pial layer) covering the cavity arises at the arteries about 10 mm in diameter (arrowhead) (original magnification ×100). (Figure 9B, C: Adapted with permission from Adachi M et al. *Neuroradiology*. 1998;40:27–31.)

HISTOPATHOLOGICAL CORRELATES OF DPVSS

Pathological studies[299] demonstrate that perivascular spaces do not communicate directly with subarachnoid space,[301–303] but the cortical arteries surrounded by the Virchow-Robin spaces cross from the subarachnoid space through the subpial space into the brain parenchyma (Figure 21.9.B, C).[290] They are bound externally by a layer of pial membrane and internally by the collagen of the arterial adventitia.[302] In contrast, arteries in the basal ganglia are surrounded not by one but by two distinct layers of leptomeninges separated by the Virchow-Robin space.[290]

In histopathological studies, the mean diameter of the arteries incorporated in the DPVSs was 39.0 ± 36.0 μm.[299] The dilation of Virchow-Robin spaces does not seem to be uniform, and some studies reported associated perivascular demyelination, vacuolated myelin sheaths, gliosis,[181,304,305] and arteriolosclerosis.[151]

PATHOPHYSIOLOGY AND CLINICAL DETERMINANTS OF DPVSS

Prevalence of DPVSs depends on the MRI techniques, including field strength and slice thickness adopted for their detection. Overall, DPVS prevalence is low (1.6%–3%) in healthy young individuals,[306,307] but is very common in the aging population.[308]

The pathophysiology of DPVSs is not well understood, but a number of theories have been proposed, including fluid exudation resulting from the increased vessel wall permeability caused by segmental necrotizing angiitis, alterations of interstitial fluid drainage resulting from CSF circulation changes, brain atrophy with a possible ex vacuo phenomenon, perivascular myelin loss, leaking of interstitial fluid from the intracellular compartment to the pial space, fibrosis and obstruction of Virchow-Robin spaces with prevention of fluid drainage, ischemic injury to perivascular tissue, mechanical trauma from pulsation of the CSF, or vascular ectasia resulting from pulsation of elevated blood pressure.[261,290]

MRI-based studies[306] have reported that perivascular spaces are normal anatomic findings in healthy individuals, even if they are dilated. Some studies showed that DPVSs were associated with age, as index of cerebral atrophy, hypertension, and other vascular risk factors, and moreover with cognitive impairment, dementia, and white matter lesions. In some multivariable models, only age remained an independent predictor of DPVSs,[307] whereas others found a significant association between a number of DPVSs and ambulatory blood pressure.[309] Furthermore, DPVSs have been linked to WMH, vascular dementia, depression in the elderly, retinopathy in diabetics, increased BBB permeability in patients with lacunar stroke, migraine,[306,310,311] CADASIL, and CAA.[312–314] In an MRI-based study of patients with different types of dementia, DPVS number and location were sufficiently specific and sensitive in differentiating between vascular and degenerative dementias.[261]

DPVSS AND THE RISK OF STROKE

Clinical relevance of DPVSs is not yet well defined, because there are no systematic data on the association between DPVSs and risk of stroke. A few studies demonstrated that DPVSs correlate strongly with silent brain ischemic lesions and WMH in patients with first-ever symptomatic lacunar stroke,[310] and that a significant association exists between both total and basal ganglia DPVSs with lacunar stroke subtype (β, 0.38; $p = 0.04$; and OR, 3.16; 95% CI, 1.49–6.70, $p = 0.003$), as well as deep and periventricular WMH, even after adjusting for increasing age and other vascular risk factors.[259] Future large, prospective MRI-based studies are warranted to evaluate the true clinical and prognostic value of DPVSs, and their association with the risk of stroke.

Superficial Siderosis

SS is an uncommon and underdiagnosed disorder characterized by chronic, slow, repeated bleeding in subarachnoid spaces.[315] The resulting hemosiderin deposition may be responsible for central nervous system damage, making SS a possible distinct MRI marker of cerebral small-vessel disease.

MRI APPEARANCE

The advent of MRI techniques sensitive to hemosiderin, such as GRE T2*-weighted imaging and susceptibility-weighted imaging[316] has increased detection and diagnosis of SS. It appears on T2*-weighted MRI as a rim of hypointensity that surrounds the surface of cortical sulci (Figure 21.10.A), particularly in cases with prior lobar ICH or possible CAA, or the surface of brainstem, cerebellum, as well as cranial nerves, spinal cord, and, infrequently, along cerebral ventricles.[317] Intra- or extradural fluid collection is often observed along the spinal cord in patients with SS.[316] In most cases, the initial bleeding site is not identified. Cerebellar atrophy, mainly of the superior vermis and of the anterior cerebellar hemispheres, is a common finding and can explain the gait disturbances in subjects with SS.

HISTOPATHOLOGICAL CORRELATES

Theoretically, pathological diagnosis of SS requires the presence of specific glia cells commonly found in the cerebellum, which facilitate the conversion of heme to ferritin and hemosiderin, and possibly mediate the brain damage.[318,319] In vivo imaging and pathological correlations confirmed that the hypointense rim surrounding the surface of cortex, brain, cerebellum, and spinal cord corresponds to hemosiderin deposits.[320] Iron is also observed in subependymal and subpial brain, and spinal cord regions, as well as in endothelial and medial cells of the vessels. Neurons and oligodendroglia do not seem to accumulate iron,[321] but gliosis and neuronal loss associated with hemosiderin deposition are usually observed (Figure 21.10.B).[316] Leptomeninges appear fibrotic, thickened, and with hemosiderin-laden macrophages and astrocytes,[321] together with extracellular iron granules in the

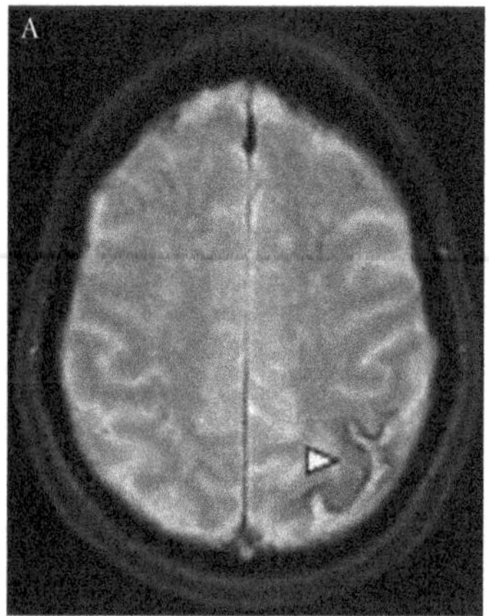

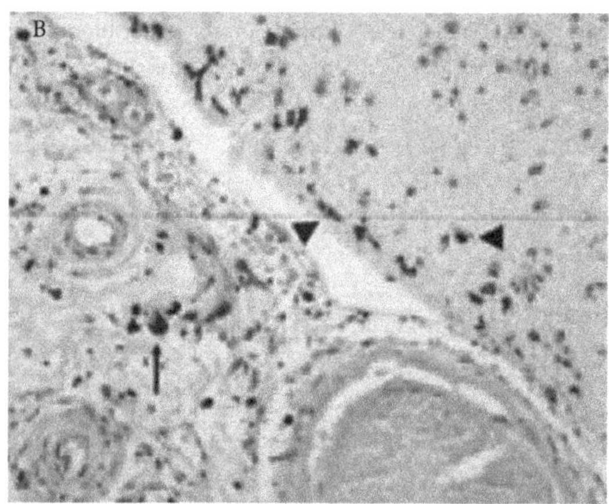

FIGURE 21.10 Superficial siderosis (SS). (A, B) Gradient-recalled echo magnetic resonance imaging of gyriform low signal (arrowheads), corresponding to meningeal siderosis, in the left parietal cortex (A), and a histological image of hemosiderin deposition within macrophages in the subarachnoid space (arrow) and within superficial cortex (arrowheads; B) using Pearl's blue iron staining. (Adapted with permission from Feldman HH et al. *Stroke.* 2008;39:2894–2897.).

subpial brain parenchyma, spinal cord, and cerebellum.[322] Typical histopathological findings of CAA may be associated with SS.[323]

PATHOPHYSIOLOGY AND CLINICAL ASPECTS OF SS

Prevalence of SS on MRI among the general elderly within the Rotterdam Scan Study was 0.7%. Furthermore, SS was found only in subjects with CMBs, particularly lobar ones, supporting the hypothesis of a link with CAA.[324] In patients with definite CAA, SS prevalence was 60.5%.[325]

Most patients with SS have a history of a possible CAA, head or spine injury, ICH, dural pathology, neoplasms, neurosurgical procedures, or have experienced symptoms suggestive of subarachnoid hemorrhage (SAH). In 40% of cases, the source of bleeding remains unknown.[322] Trauma can cause traction of small vessels, which become fragile and prone to rupture, and intradural surgery may cause leakage of blood into the CSF.[317] SS has been also associated with the presence of CSF hypovolemia and craniospinal hypotension, which is usually related to dural defects. The alternate hypothesis of venous hypertension has been proposed given the presence of epidural vein sclerosis resulting from SS.[316] Correlation between SS and CAA might be explained by blood leakage from the superficial CAA-affected vessels from the cerebral parenchyma to the subarachnoid spaces.[326] The association with CMBs can be the result of a clearance disorder of blood product in patients affected by CAA.[324]

SUPERFICIAL SIDEROSIS AND THE RISK OF STROKE

There are a few studies on the association between SS and the risk of stroke, particularly hemorrhagic subtype. SS is a likely marker of CAA-associated focal SAH at the cortical convexity.[323,325–330] Some reports suggested that focal SAH, and hence SS, may predict the risk of future ICH in patients with CAA.[331] Patients with SS and probable or possible CAA followed for a median of 35.3 months demonstrated a high rate of hemorrhagic events (47.1% developed any type of hemorrhage, 35.3% of whom developed ICH; whereas 25.5% developed SAH at the original SS location).[332] Similarly to CMBs, SS might represent the site where vessels are more fragile as a result of a greater deposition of β-amyloid[332,333]; however, this does not explain ICH occurring remotely from the SAH and SS site.[323,325] Moreover, detection of SS in up to 50% of patients with TIA-like syndrome and CAA[225,334–336] suggests cortical localization.

PRACTICAL CLINICAL AND RESEARCH IMPLICATIONS

Future use of SS as an MRI marker of cerebrovascular disease may have important clinical implications, both in diagnosis of CAA and in the decision-making process for patient management regarding the risk/benefit of antiplatelet or anticoagulant therapy.[332] Future studies are required to confirm the current data on the prognostic value of SS and risk of hemorrhagic stroke.

Summary and Conclusions

As a result of the enormous impact of cerebrovascular diseases on health care, economy, and social systems, there is a growing need to understand more fully the specific role of each vascular risk factor and to identify new markers of the disease. Both current and developing MRI techniques facilitate detection, quantification, and characterization of the markers of widespread cerebrovascular disease. During the past few years, new cutting-edge MRI methods, including diffusion tensor imaging (Figure 21.11), magnetization transfer MRI (Figure 21.12), advanced brain perfusion studies, and high-field MRI (Figure 21.13), have advanced our understanding of the underlying mechanisms of cerebrovascular disease. These MRI tools are now expected to translate the data obtained in the research setting into clinical applications that will validate and develop the diagnostic and prognostic value of the MRI markers of cerebrovascular disease. In the future, a total burden of cerebrovascular disease, including both clinical and "silent" manifestations of neurovascular disorders may prove essential to guide risk stratification, diagnostic workflow, and patient selection for acute interventions as well as stroke prevention strategies. Validated MRI markers of cerebrovascular disease may have a radical effect on the direction of clinical research and the development of novel, targeted therapies for stroke, vascular cognitive impairment, and other cerebrovascular diseases.

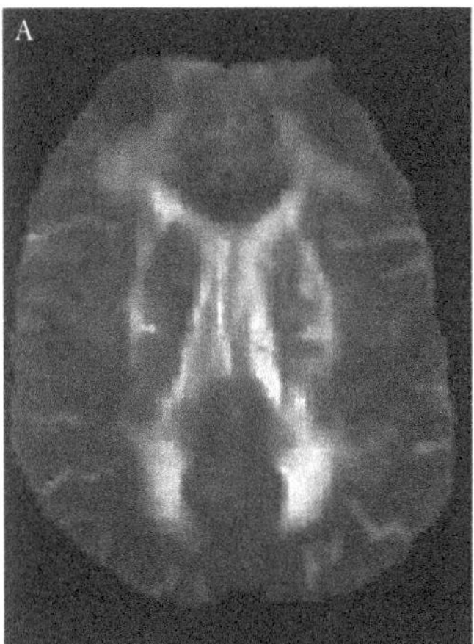

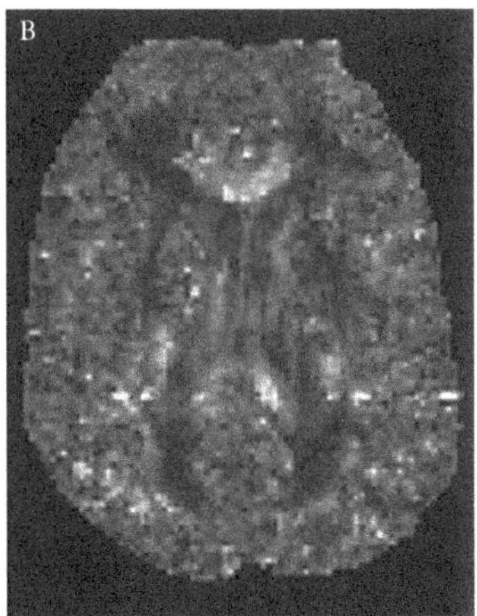

FIGURE 21.11 (A, B) Typical T2-weighted (A) and fractional anisotropy (B) images obtained from a patient. (A) The T2-weighted image shows regions of increased signal intensity adjacent to the horns of the lateral ventricles. (B) The fractional anisotropy image reveals a substantial loss of anisotropy in the regions of leukoaraiosis. (Adapted with permission from Jones DK. *Stroke.* 1999;30:393–397.).

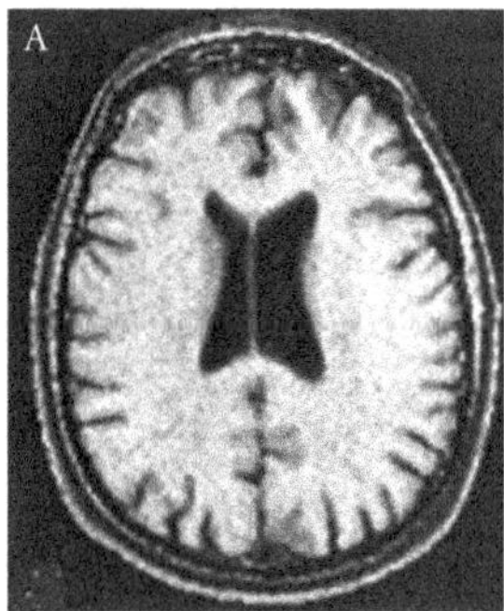

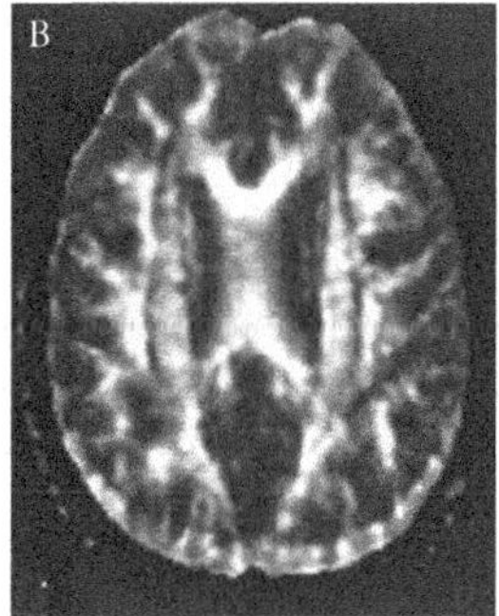

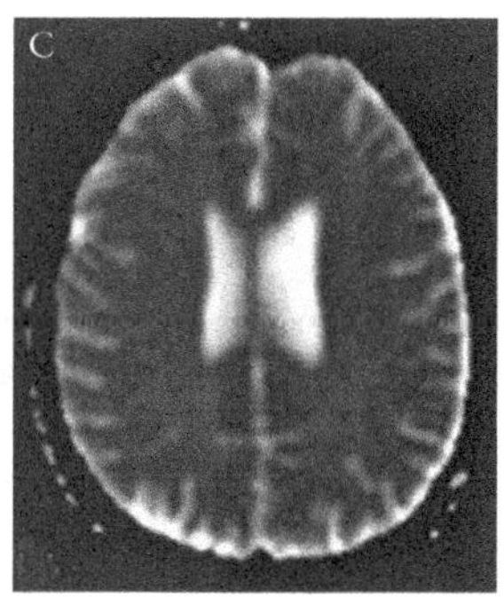

FIGURE 21.12 (A–C) Example of magnetization transfer magnetic resonance imaging (A) compared with fractional anisotropy (B) and mean diffusivity (C). (Adapted with permission from Schiavone F. *J Magn Reson Imag.* 2009;29:23–30.)

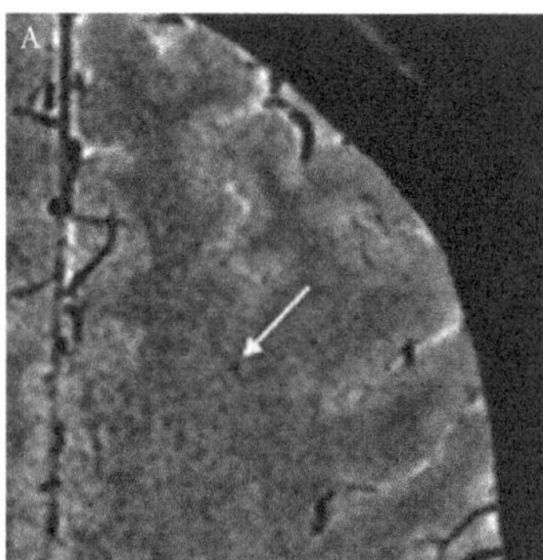

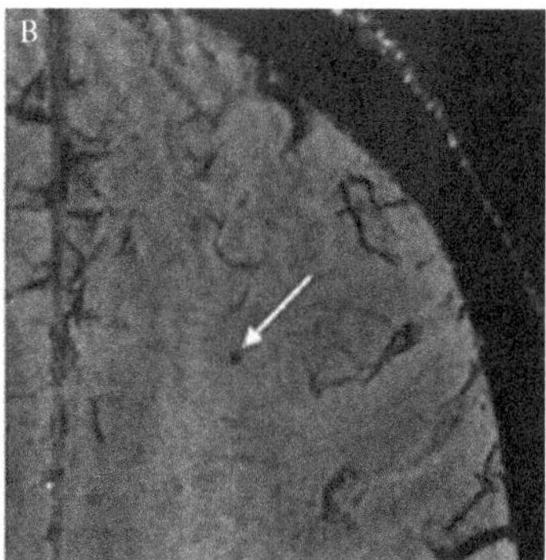

FIGURE 21.13 (A) A 1.5-T magnetic resonance image shows a hypointense lesion (arrow) that was hard to distinguish from noise and was not scored as a microbleed. (B) On 7-T magnetic resonance imaging, this hypointense lesion is visible as a typical microbleed, showing enlargement resulting from the blooming effect. This lesion was scored as a microbleed by two different observers. (Adapted with permission from Conijn MMA. *AJNR Am J Neuroradiol.* 2011;32:1043–1049.)

REFERENCES

1. Debette S, Markus HS. The clinical importance of white matter hyperintensities on brain magnetic resonance imaging: systematic review and meta-analysis. *BMJ.* 2010;341:c3666.
2. Patel B, Markus HS. Magnetic resonance imaging in cerebral small vessel disease and its use as a surrogate disease marker. *Int J Stroke.* 2011;6:47–59.
3. The LADIS Study Group, Poggesi A, Pantoni L, et al. 2001–2011: a decade of the LADIS (Leukoaraiosis And DISability) Study: what have we learned about white matter changes and small-vessel disease? *Cerebrovasc Dis.* 2011;32:577–588.
4. Schmidt R, Scheltens P, Erkinjuntti T, et al. White matter lesion progression: a surrogate endpoint for trials in cerebral small-vessel disease. *Neurology.* 2004;63:139–144.
5. Pantoni L, Basile AM, Pracucci G, et al. Impact of age-related cerebral white matter changes on the transition to disability—the LADIS study: rationale, design and methodology. *Neuroepidemiology.* 2005;24:51–62.

6. Inzitari D, Pracucci G, Poggesi A, et al. Changes in white matter as determinant of global functional decline in older independent outpatients: three year follow-up of LADIS (leukoaraiosis and disability) study cohort. *BMJ*. 2009;339:b2477.
7. Dufouil C, Chalmers J, Coskun O, et al. Effects of blood pressure lowering on cerebral white matter hyperintensities in patients with stroke: the PROGRESS (Perindopril Protection Against Recurrent Stroke Study) Magnetic Resonance Imaging Substudy. *Circulation*. 2005;112:1644–1650.
8. ten Dam VH, van den Heuvel DM, van Buchem MA, et al. Effect of pravastatin on cerebral infarcts and white matter lesions. *Neurology*. 2005;64:1807–1809.
9. Mok VC, Lam WW, Fan YH, et al. Effects of statins on the progression of cerebral white matter lesion: post hoc analysis of the ROCAS (Regression of Cerebral Artery Stenosis) study. *J Neurol*. 2009;256:750–757.
10. Leiva-Salinas C, Hom J, Warach S, Wintermark M. Stroke imaging research road map. *Neuroimaging Clin North Am*. 2011;21:239–245.
11. Kanekar SG, Zacharia T, Roller R. Imaging of stroke: part 2. Pathophysiology at the molecular and cellular levels and corresponding imaging changes. *AJR Am J Roentgenol*. 2012;198:63–74.
12. Kidwell CS, Chalela JA, Saver JL, et al. Comparison of MRI and CT for detection of acute intracerebral hemorrhage. *JAMA*. 2004;292:1823–1830.
13. Burgess RE, Kidwell CS. Use of MRI in the assessment of patients with stroke. *Curr Neurol Neurosci Rep*. 2011;11:28–34.
14. Toth G, Albers GW. Use of MRI to estimate the therapeutic window in acute stroke: is perfusion-weighted imaging/diffusion-weighted imaging mismatch an EPITHET for salvageable ischemic brain tissue? *Stroke*. 2009;40:333–335.
15. Köhrmann M, Jüttler E, Fiebach JB, et al. MRI versus CT-based thrombolysis treatment within and beyond the 3 h time window after stroke onset: a cohort study. *Lancet Neurol*. 2006;5:661–667.
16. Albers GW, Thijs VN, Wechsler L, et al. Magnetic resonance imaging profiles predict clinical response to early reperfusion: the Diffusion and Perfusion Imaging Evaluation for Understanding Stroke Evolution (DEFUSE) study. *Ann Neurol*. 2006;60:508–517.
17. Kakuda W, Lansberg MG, Thijs VN, et al. Optimal definition for PWI/DWI mismatch in acute ischemic stroke patients. *J Cereb Blood Flow Metab*. 2008;28:887–891.
18. Hacke W, Albers G, Al-Rawi Y, et al. The Desmoteplase in Acute Ischemic Stroke Trial (DIAS): a phase II MRI-based 9-hour window acute stroke thrombolysis trial with intravenous desmoteplase. *Stroke*. 2005;36:66–73.
19. Furlan AJ, Eyding D, Albers GW, et al. Dose Escalation of Desmoteplase for Acute Ischemic Stroke (DEDAS): evidence of safety and efficacy 3 to 9 hours after stroke onset. *Stroke*. 2006;37:1227–1231.
20. Davis SM, Donnan GA, Parsons MW, et al. Effects of alteplase beyond 3 h after stroke in the Echoplanar Imaging Thrombolytic Evaluation Trial (EPITHET): a placebo-controlled randomised trial. *Lancet Neurol*. 2008;7:299–309.
21. Parsons MW, Christensen S, McElduff P, et al. Pretreatment diffusion- and perfusion-MR lesion volumes have a crucial influence on clinical response to stroke thrombolysis. *J Cereb Blood Flow Metab*. 2010;30:1214–1225.
22. Savoy RL. Functional magnetic resonance imaging (fMRI). *Encyclopedia of the brain*. 1–21. http://neurosciences.us/courses/systems/FMRI/Savoy_Functional_MRI.pdf
23. Haller S, Pereira VM, Lazeyras F, Vargas MI, Lövblad KO. Magnetic resonance imaging techniques in white matter disease: potentials and limitations. *Top Magn Reson Imaging*. 2009;20:301–312.
24. Ylikoski A, Erkinjuntti T, Raininko R, Sarna S, Sulkava R, Tilvis R. White matter hyperintensities on MRI in the neurologically nondiseased elderly: analysis of cohorts of consecutive subjects aged 55 to 85 years living at home. *Stroke*. 1995;26:1171–1177.

25. Rost NS, Rahman RM, Biffi A, et al. White matter hyperintensity volume is increased in small vessel stroke subtypes. *Neurology*. 2010;75:1670–1677.
26. Hachinski VC, Potter P, Merskey H. Leuko-araiosis. *Arch Neurol*. 1987;44:21–23.
27. Fazekas F, Chawluk JB, Alavi A, Hurtig HI, Zimmerman RA. MR signal abnormalities at 1.5 T in Alzheimer's dementia and normal aging. *AJR Am J Roentgenol*. 1987;149:351–356.
28. Gouw AA, Seewann A, van der Flier WM, et al. Heterogeneity of small vessel disease: a systematic review of MRI and histopathology correlations. *J Neurol Neurosurg Psychiatry*. 2011;82:126–135.
29. Longstreth WT Jr, Arnold AM, Beauchamp NJ Jr, et al. Incidence, manifestations, and predictors of worsening white matter on serial cranial magnetic resonance imaging in the elderly: the Cardiovascular Health Study. *Stroke*. 2005;36:56–61.
30. Pantoni L, Garcia JH. The significance of cerebral white matter abnormalities 100 years after Binswanger's report: a review. *Stroke*. 1995;26:1293–1301.
31. Breteler MM, van Swieten JC, Bots ML, et al. Cerebral white matter lesions, vascular risk factors, and cognitive function in a population-based study: the Rotterdam Study. *Neurology*. 1994;44:1246–1252.
32. de Leeuw FE, de Groot JC, Achten E, et al. Prevalence of cerebral white matter lesions in elderly people: a population based magnetic resonance imaging study: the Rotterdam Scan Study. *J Neurol Neurosurg Psychiatry*. 2001;70:9–14.
33. Hopkins RO, Beck CJ, Burnett DL, Weaver LK, Victoroff J, Bigler ED. Prevalence of white matter hyperintensities in a young healthy population. *J Neuroimaging*. 2006;16:243–251.
34. Launer LJ, Berger K, Breteler MM, et al. Regional variability in the prevalence of cerebral white matter lesions: an MRI study in 9 European countries (CASCADE). *Neuroepidemiology*. 2006;26:23–29.
35. Wen W, Sachdev P. The topography of white matter hyperintensities on brain MRI in healthy 60- to 64-year-old individuals. *Neuroimage*. 2004;22:144–154.
36. Fernando MS, Ince PG, MRC Cognitive Function and Ageing Neuropathology Study Group. Vascular pathologies and cognition in a population-based cohort of elderly people. *J Neurol Sci*. 2004;226:13–17.
37. Scheltens P, Barkhof F, Leys D, et al. A semiquantitative rating scale for the assessment of signal hyperintensities on magnetic resonance imaging. *J Neurol Sci*. 1993;114:7–12.
38. Pantoni L, Simoni M, Pracucci G, Schmidt R, Barkhof F, Inzitari D. Visual rating scales for age-related white matter changes (leukoaraiosis): can the heterogeneity be reduced? *Stroke*. 2002;33:2827–2833.
39. DeCarli C, Fletcher E, Ramey V, Harvey D, Jagust WJ. Anatomical mapping of white matter hyperintensities (WMH): exploring the relationships between periventricular WMH, deep WMH, and total WMH burden. *Stroke*. 2005; 36:50–55.
40. Rost NS, Fitzpatrick K, Biffi A, et al. White matter hyperintensity burden and susceptibility to cerebral ischemia. *Stroke*. 2010;41:2807–2811.
41. Chen YW, Gurol ME, Rosand J, et al. Progression of white matter lesions and hemorrhages in cerebral amyloid angiopathy. *Neurology*. 2006;67:83–87.
42. Kim KW, MacFall JR, Payne ME. Classification of white matter lesions on magnetic resonance imaging in the elderly. *Biol Psychiatry*. 2008;64:273–280.
43. Kertesz A, Black SE, Tokar G, Benke T, Carr T, Nicholson L. Periventricular and subcortical hyperintensities on magnetic resonance imaging: rims, caps, and unidentified bright objects. *Arch Neurol*. 1988;45:404–408.
44. Mayer PL, Kier EL. The controversy of the periventricular white matter circulation: a review of the anatomic literature. *AJNR Am J Neuroradiol*. 1991;12:223–228.
45. Moody DM, Bell MA, Challa VR. Features of the cerebral vascular pattern that predict vulnerability to perfusion or oxygenation deficiency: an anatomic study. *AJNR Am J Neuroradiol*. 1990;11:431–439.

46. Román GC. Senile dementia of the Binswanger type: a vascular form of dementia in the elderly. *JAMA*. 1987;258:1782–1788.
47. Matsusue E, Sugihara S, Fujii S, Ohama E, Kinoshita T, Ogawa T. White matter changes in elderly people: MR–pathologic correlations. *Magn Reson Med Sci*. 2006;5:99–104.
48. Moody DM, Brown WR, Challa VR, Anderson RL. Periventricular venous collagenosis: association with leukoaraiosis. *Radiology*. 1995;194:469–476.
49. Fazekas F, Kleinert R, Offenbacher H, et al. Pathologic correlates of incidental MRI white matter signal hyperintensities. *Neurology*. 1993;43:1683–1689.
50. van Swieten JC, van den Hout JH, van Ketel BA, Hijdra A, Wokke JH, van Gijn J. Periventricular lesions in the white matter on magnetic resonance imaging in the elderly: a morphometric correlation with arteriolosclerosis and dilated perivascular spaces. *Brain*. 1991;114:761–774.
51. Awad IA, Johnson PC, Spetzler RF, Hodak JA. Incidental subcortical lesions identified on magnetic resonance imaging in the elderly: II. Postmortem pathological correlations. *Stroke*. 1986;17:1090–1097.
52. Révész T, Hawkins CP, du Boulay EP, Barnard RO, McDonald WI. Pathological findings correlated with magnetic resonance imaging in subcortical arteriosclerotic encephalopathy (Binswanger's disease). *J Neurol Neurosurg Psychiatry*. 1989;52:1337–1344.
53. Marshall VG, Bradley WG Jr, Marshall CE, Bhoopat T, Rhodes RH. Deep white matter infarction: correlation of MR imaging and histopathologic findings. *Radiology*. 1988;167:517–522.
54. Pantoni L, Garcia JH. Pathogenesis of leukoaraiosis: a review. *Stroke*. 1997;28:652–659.
55. Fazekas F, Schmidt R, Kleinert R, Kapeller P, Roob G, Flooh E. The spectrum of age-associated brain abnormalities: their measurement and histopathological correlates. *J Neural Transm Suppl*. 1998;53:31–39.
56. Firbank MJ, Wiseman RM, Burton EJ, Saxby BK, O'Brien JT, Ford GA. Brain atrophy and white matter hyperintensity change in older adults and relationship to blood pressure: brain atrophy, WMH change and blood pressure. *J Neurol*. 2007;254:713–721.
57. Jeerakathil T, Wolf PA, Beiser A, et al. Stroke risk profile predicts white matter hyperintensity volume: the Framingham Study. *Stroke*. 2004;35:1857–1861.
58. Smith EE, Nandigam KR, Chen YW, et al. MRI markers of small vessel disease in lobar and deep hemispheric intracerebral hemorrhage. *Stroke*. 2010;41:1933–1938.
59. Kuller LH, Longstreth WT Jr, Arnold AM, et al. White matter hyperintensity on cranial magnetic resonance imaging: a predictor of stroke. *Stroke*. 2004;35:1821–1825.
60. Haas R, Dietrich R. Neuroimaging of mitochondrial disorders. *Mitochondrion*. 2004;4:471–490.
61. Dichgans M. Genetics of ischaemic stroke. *Lancet Neurol*. 2007;6:149–161.
62. De Reuck J. The human periventricular arterial blood supply and the anatomy of cerebral infarctions. *Eur Neurol*. 1971;5:321–334.
63. Chabriat H, Mrissa R, Levy C, et al. Brain stem MRI signal abnormalities in CADASIL. *Stroke*. 1999;30:457–459.
64. Fisher CM. Lacunar strokes and infarcts: a review. *Neurology*. 1982;32:871–876.
65. Boiten J, Lodder J, Kessels F. Two clinically distinct lacunar infarct entities? A hypothesis. *Stroke*. 1993;24:652–656.
66. Hassan A, Hunt BJ, O'Sullivan M, et al. Markers of endothelial dysfunction in lacunar infarction and ischaemic leukoaraiosis. *Brain*. 2003;126:424–432.
67. Wardlaw JM, Sandercock PA, Dennis MS, Starr J. Is breakdown of the blood–brain barrier responsible for lacunar stroke, leukoaraiosis, and dementia? *Stroke*. 2003;34:806–812.
68. O'Sullivan M, Lythgoe DJ, Pereira AC, et al. Patterns of cerebral blood flow reduction in patients with ischemic leukoaraiosis. *Neurology*. 2002;59:321–326.
69. Topakian R, Barrick TR, Howe FA, Markus HS. Blood–brain barrier permeability is increased in normal-appearing white matter in patients with lacunar stroke and leucoaraiosis. *J Neurol Neurosurg Psychiatry*. 2010;81:192–197.

70. Furuta A, Ishii N, Nishihara Y, Horie A. Medullary arteries in aging and dementia. *Stroke.* 1991;22:442–446.
71. Ostrow PT, Miller LL. Pathology of small artery disease. *Adv Neurol.* 1993;62:93–123.
72. Alex M, Baron EK, Goldenberg S, Blumenthal HT. An autopsy study of cerebrovascular accident in diabetes mellitus. *Circulation.* 1962;25:663–673.
73. Scheltens P, Barkhof F, Leys D, Wolters EC, Ravid R, Kamphorst W. Histopathologic correlates of white matter changes on MRI in Alzheimer's disease and normal aging. *Neurology.* 1995;45:883–888.
74. Vermeer SE, van Dijk EJ, Koudstaal PJ, et al. Homocysteine, silent brain infarcts, and white matter lesions: the Rotterdam Scan Study. *Ann Neurol.* 2002;51:285–289.
75. de Leeuw FE, De Groot JC, Oudkerk M, et al. Aortic atherosclerosis at middle age predicts cerebral white matter lesions in the elderly. *Stroke.* 2000;31:425–429.
76. de Leeuw FE, de Groot JC, Oudkerk M, et al. Atrial fibrillation and the risk of cerebral white matter lesions. *Neurology.* 2000;54:1795–1801.
77. de Leeuw FE, de Groot JC, Oudkerk M, et al. Hypertension and cerebral white matter lesions in a prospective cohort study. *Brain.* 2002;125:765–772.
78. Vermeer SE, Hollander M, van Dijk EJ, et al. Silent brain infarcts and white matter lesions increase stroke risk in the general population: the Rotterdam Scan Study. *Stroke.* 2003;34:1126–1129.
79. Leifer D, Buonanno FS, Richardson EP Jr. Clinicopathologic correlations of cranial magnetic resonance imaging of periventricular white matter. *Neurology.* 1990;40:911–918.
80. Scarpelli M, Salvolini U, Diamanti L, Montironi R, Chiaromoni L, Maricotti M. MRI and pathological examination of post-mortem brains: the problem of white matter high signal areas. *Neuroradiology.* 1994;36:393–398.
81. Fazekas F, Kleinert R, Offenbacher H, et al. The morphologic correlate of incidental punctate white matter hyperintensities on MR images. *AJNR Am J Neuroradiol.* 1991;12:915–921.
82. Kuo HK, Lipsitz LA. Cerebral white matter changes and geriatric syndromes: is there a link? *J Gerontol A Biol Sci Med Sci.* 2004;59:818–826.
83. Longstreth WT Jr, Diehr P, Manolio TA, et al. Cluster analysis and patterns of findings on cranial magnetic resonance imaging of the elderly: the Cardiovascular Health Study. *Arch Neurol.* 2001;58:635–640.
84. Wong TY, Klein R, Sharrett AR, et al. Atherosclerosis Risk in Communities Study: cerebral white matter lesions, retinopathy, and incident clinical stroke. *JAMA.* 2002;288:67–74.
85. Bokura H, Kobayashi S, Yamaguchi S, et al. Silent brain infarction and subcortical white matter lesions increase the risk of stroke and mortality: a prospective cohort study. *J Stroke Cerebrovasc Dis.* 2006;15:57–63.
86. Buyck JF, Dufouil C, Mazoyer B, et al. Cerebral white matter lesions are associated with the risk of stroke but not with other vascular events: the 3-City Dijon Study. *Stroke.* 2009;40:2327–2331.
87. Debette S, Beiser A, DeCarli C, et al. Association of MRI markers of vascular brain injury with incident stroke, mild cognitive impairment, dementia, and mortality: the Framingham Offspring Study. *Stroke.* 2010;41:600–606.
88. Folsom AR, Yatsuya H, Mosley TH Jr, Psaty BM, Longstreth WT Jr. Risk of intraparenchymal hemorrhage with magnetic resonance imaging-defined leukoaraiosis and brain infarcts. *Ann Neurol.* 2012;71:552–559.
89. Kobayashi S, Okada K, Koide H, Bokura H, Yamaguchi S. Subcortical silent brain infarction as a risk factor for clinical stroke. *Stroke.* 1997;28:1932–1939.
90. Miyao S, Takano A, Teramoto J, Takahashi A. Leukoaraiosis in relation to prognosis for patients with lacunar infarction. *Stroke.* 1992;23:1434–1438.
91. van Swieten JC, Kappelle LJ, Algra A, van Latum JC, Koudstaal PJ, van Gijn J. Hypodensity of the cerebral white matter in patients with transient ischemic attack or minor stroke: influence on the rate of subsequent stroke: Dutch TIA Trial Study Group. *Ann Neurol.* 1992;32:177–183.

92. Streifler JY, Eliasziw M, Benavente OR, et al. Prognostic importance of leukoaraiosis in patients with symptomatic internal carotid artery stenosis. *Stroke.* 2002;33:1651–1655.
93. Hénon H, Vroylandt P, Durieu I, Pasquier F, Leys D. Leukoaraiosis more than dementia is a predictor of stroke recurrence. *Stroke.* 2003;34:2935–2940.
94. Inzitari D, Di Carlo A, Mascalchi M, Pracucci G, Amaducci L. The cardiovascular outcome of patients with motor impairment and extensive leukoaraiosis. *Arch Neurol.* 1995;52:687–691.
95. Appelros P, Samuelsson M, Lindell D. Lacunar infarcts: functional and cognitive outcomes at five years in relation to MRI findings. *Cerebrovasc Dis.* 2005;20:34–40.
96. Fu JH, Lu CZ, Hong Z, Dong Q, Luo Y, Wong KS. Extent of white matter lesions is related to acute subcortical infarcts and predicts further stroke risk in patients with first ever ischaemic stroke. *J Neurol Neurosurg Psychiatry.* 2005;76:793–796.
97. Conijn MM, Kloppenborg RP, Algra A, et al. Cerebral small vessel disease and risk of death, ischemic stroke, and cardiac complications in patients with atherosclerotic disease: the Second Manifestations of ARTerial disease-Magnetic Resonance (SMART-MR) study. *Stroke.* 2011;42:3105–3109.
98. Yamauchi H, Fukuda H, Oyanagi C. Significance of white matter high intensity lesions as a predictor of stroke from arteriolosclerosis. *J Neurol Neurosurg Psychiatry.* 2002;72:576–582.
99. Inzitari D. Leukoaraiosis: an independent risk factor for stroke? *Stroke.* 2003;34:2067–2071.
100. Smith EE, Rosand J, Knudsen KA, Hylek EM, Greenberg SM. Leukoaraiosis is associated with warfarin-related hemorrhage following ischemic stroke. *Neurology.* 2002;59:193–197.
101. Smith EE, Gurol ME, Eng JA, et al. White matter lesions, cognition, and recurrent hemorrhage in lobar intracerebral hemorrhage. *Neurology.* 2004;63:1606–1612.
102. Neumann-Haefelin T, Hoelig S, Berkefeld J, et al. Leukoaraiosis is a risk factor for symptomatic intracerebral hemorrhage after thrombolysis for acute stroke. *Stroke.* 2006;37:2463–2466.
103. Palumbo V, Boulanger JM, Hill MD, Inzitari D, Buchan AM, CASES investigators. Leukoaraiosis and intracerebral hemorrhage after thrombolysis in acute stroke. *Neurology.* 2007;68:1020–1024.
104. Shi ZS, Loh Y, Liebeskind DS, et al. Leukoaraiosis predicts parenchymal hematoma after mechanical thrombectomy in acute ischemic stroke. *Stroke.* 2012;43:1806–1811.
105. Naka H, Nomura E, Takahashi T, et al. Combinations of the presence or absence of cerebral microbleeds and advanced white matter hyperintensity as predictors of subsequent stroke types. *AJNR Am J Neuroradiol.* 2006;27:830–835.
106. Gerdes VE, Kwa VI, ten Cate H, et al. Cerebral white matter lesions predict both ischemic strokes and myocardial infarctions in patients with established atherosclerotic disease. *Atherosclerosis.* 2006;186:166–172.
107. Schmidt R, Enzinger C, Ropele S, Schmidt H, Fazekas F, Austrian Stroke Prevention Study Group. Progression of cerebral white matter lesions: 6-year results of the Austrian Stroke Prevention Study. *Lancet.* 2003;361:2046–2048.
108. Whitman GT, Tang Y, Lin A, Baloh RW. A prospective study of cerebral white matter abnormalities in older people with gait dysfunction. *Neurology.* 2001;57:990–994.
109. Wahlund LO, Almkvist O, Basun H, Julin P. MRI in successful aging: a 5-year follow-up study from the eighth to ninth decade of life. *Magn Reson Imaging.* 1996;14:601–608.
110. Grueter BE, Schulz UG. Age-related cerebral white matter disease (leukoaraiosis): a review. *Postgrad Med J.* 2012;88:79–87.
111. Sachdev P, Wen W, Chen X, Brodaty H. Progression of white matter hyperintensities in elderly individuals over 3 years. *Neurology.* 2007;68:214–222.
112. Gouw AA, van der Flier WM, Fazekas F, et al. Progression of white matter hyperintensities and incidence of new lacunes over a 3-year period: the Leukoaraiosis and Disability study. *Stroke.* 2008;39:1414–1420.

113. van Dijk EJ, Prins ND, Vrooman HA, Hofman A, Koudstaal PJ, Breteler MM. Progression of cerebral small vessel disease in relation to risk factors and cognitive consequences: Rotterdam Scan Study. *Stroke.* 2008;39:2712–2719.
114. Streifler JY, Eliasziw M, Benavente OR, et al. Development and progression of leukoaraiosis in patients with brain ischemia and carotid artery disease. *Stroke.* 2003;34:1913–1916.
115. Longstreth WT Jr, Arnold AM, Kuller LH, et al. Progression of magnetic resonance imaging-defined brain vascular disease predicts vascular events in elderly: the Cardiovascular Health Study. *Stroke.* 2011;42:2970–2972.
116. Atwood LD, Wolf PA, Heard-Costa NL, et al. Genetic variation in white matter hyperintensity volume in the Framingham Study. *Stroke.* 2004;35:1609–1613.
117. Carmelli D, DeCarli C, Swan GE, et al. Evidence for genetic variance in white matter hyperintensity volume in normal elderly male twins. *Stroke.* 1998;29:1177–1181.
118. Kochunov P, Glahn D, Winkler A, et al. Analysis of genetic variability and whole genome linkage of whole-brain, subcortical, and ependymal hyperintense white matter volume. *Stroke.* 2009;40:3685–3690.
119. Yatsu FM, Shaltoni HM. Implications of silent strokes. *Curr Atheroscler Rep.* 2004;6:307–313.
120. Price TR, Manolio TA, Kronmal RA, et al. Silent brain infarction on magnetic resonance imaging and neurological abnormalities in community-dwelling older adults: the Cardiovascular Health Study: CHS Collaborative Research Group. *Stroke.* 1997;28:1158–1164.
121. Vermeer SE, Koudstaal PJ, Oudkerk M, Hofman A, Breteler MM. Prevalence and risk factors of silent brain infarcts in the population-based Rotterdam Scan Study. *Stroke.* 2002;33:21–25.
122. Gállego J, Martínez-Vila E. Asymptomatic cerebrovascular disease and systemic diagnosis in stroke, atherothrombosis as a disease of the vascular tree. *Cerebrovasc Dis.* 2005;20(Suppl 2):1–10.
123. Fisher CM. Lacunes: small, deep cerebral infarcts. *Neurology.* 1965;15:774–784.
124. Kase CS, Wolf PA, Chodosh EH, et al. Prevalence of silent stroke in patients presenting with initial stroke: the Framingham Study. *Stroke.* 1989;20:850–852.
125. Vernooij MW, Ikram MA, Tanghe HL, et al. Incidental findings on brain MRI in the general population. *N Engl J Med.* 2007;357:1821–1828.
126. Kobayashi S, Okada K, Yamashita K. Incidence of silent lacunar lesion in normal adults and its relation to cerebral blood flow and risk factors. *Stroke.* 1991;22:1379–1383.
127. Howard G, Wagenknecht LE, Cai J, Cooper L, Kraut MA, Toole JF. Cigarette smoking and other risk factors for silent cerebral infarction in the general population. *Stroke.* 1998;29:913–917.
128. Kohara K, Fujisawa M, Ando F, et al. *MTHFR* gene polymorphism as a risk factor for silent brain infarcts and white matter lesions in the Japanese general population: the NILS-LSA Study. *Stroke.* 2003;34:1130–1135.
129. Schmidt WP, Roesler A, Kretzschmar K, Ladwig KH, Junker R, Berger K. Functional and cognitive consequences of silent stroke discovered using brain magnetic resonance imaging in an elderly population. *J Am Geriatr Soc.* 2004;52:1045–1050.
130. DeCarli C, Massaro J, Harvey D, et al. Measures of brain morphology and infarction in the Framingham Heart Study: establishing what is normal. *Neurobiol Aging.* 2005;26:491–510.
131. Schmidt R, Schmidt H, Pichler M, et al. C-reactive protein, carotid atherosclerosis, and cerebral small-vessel disease: results of the Austrian Stroke Prevention Study. *Stroke.* 2006;37:2910–2916.
132. Prabhakaran S, Wright CB, Yoshita M, et al. Prevalence and determinants of subclinical brain infarction: the Northern Manhattan Study. *Neurology.* 2008;70:425–430.
133. Longstreth WT Jr, Dulberg C, Manolio TA, et al. Incidence, manifestations, and predictors of brain infarcts defined by serial cranial magnetic resonance imaging in the elderly: the Cardiovascular Health Study. *Stroke.* 2002;33:2376–2382.
134. Schmidt R, Ropele S, Enzinger C, et al. White matter lesion progression, brain atrophy, and cognitive decline: the Austrian Stroke Prevention Study. *Ann Neurol.* 2005;58:610–616.

135. Vermeer SE, Longstreth WT Jr, Koudstaal PJ. Silent brain infarcts: a systematic review. *Lancet Neurol.* 2007;6:611–619.
136. Adachi T, Kobayashi S, Yamaguchi S. Frequency and pathogenesis of silent subcortical brain infarction in acute first-ever ischemic stroke. *Intern Med.* 2002;41:103–108.
137. Mok VC, Wong A, Lam WW, et al. Cognitive impairment and functional outcome after stroke associated with small vessel disease. *J Neurol Neurosurg Psychiatry.* 2004;75:560–566.
138. Bennett DA, Schneider JA, Bienias JL, Evans DA, Wilson RS. Mild cognitive impairment is related to Alzheimer disease pathology and cerebral infarctions. *Neurology.* 2005;64:834–841.
139. Walters RJ, Holmes PA, Thomas DJ. Silent cerebral ischaemic lesions and atrophy in patients with apparently transient cerebral ischaemic attacks. *Cerebrovasc Dis.* 2000;10(Suppl 4):12–13.
140. Barth A, Remonda L, Lövblad KO, Schroth G, Seiler RW. Silent cerebral ischemia detected by diffusion-weighted MRI after carotid endarterectomy. *Stroke.* 2000;31:1824–1828.
141. Feiwell RJ, Besmertis L, Sarkar R, Saloner DA, Rapp JH. Detection of clinically silent infarcts after carotid endarterectomy by use of diffusion-weighted imaging. *AJNR Am J Neuroradiol.* 2001;22:646–649.
142. Forbes KP, Shill HA, Britt PM, Zabramski JM, Spetzler RF, Heiserman JE. Assessment of silent embolism from carotid endarterectomy by use of diffusion-weighted imaging: work in progress. *AJNR Am J Neuroradiol.* 2001;22:650–653.
143. van Heesewijk HP, Vos JA, Louwerse ES, et al. New brain lesions at MR imaging after carotid angioplasty and stent placement. *Radiology.* 2002;224:361–365.
144. Hauth EA, Jansen C, Drescher R, et al. MR and clinical follow-up of diffusion-weighted cerebral lesions after carotid artery stenting. *AJNR Am J Neuroradiol.* 2005;26:2336–2341.
145. Kastrup A, Nägele T, Gröschel K, et al. Incidence of new brain lesions after carotid stenting with and without cerebral protection. *Stroke.* 2006;37:2312–2316.
146. Roh HG, Byun HS, Ryoo JW, et al. Prospective analysis of cerebral infarction after carotid endarterectomy and carotid artery stent placement by using diffusion-weighted imaging. *AJNR Am J Neuroradiol.* 2005;26:376–384.
147. Howard VJ, McClure LA, Meschia JF, Pulley L, Orr SC, Friday GH. High prevalence of stroke symptoms among persons without a diagnosis of stroke or transient ischemic attack in a general population: the REasons for Geographic And Racial Differences in Stroke (REGARDS) study. *Arch Intern Med.* 2006;166:1952–1958.
148. Zhu YC, Dufouil C, Tzourio C, Chabriat H. Silent brain infarcts: a review of MRI diagnostic criteria. *Stroke.* 2011;42:1140–1145.
149. Potter GM, Marlborough FJ, Wardlaw JM. Wide variation in definition, detection, and description of lacunar lesions on imaging. *Stroke.* 2011;42:359–366.
150. Braffman BH, Zimmerman RA, Trojanowski JQ, Gonatas NK, Hickey WF, Schlaepfer WW. Brain MR: pathologic correlation with gross and histopathology: 1. Lacunar infarction and Virchow-Robin spaces. *AJR Am J Roentgenol.* 1988;151:551–558.
151. Révész T, Hawkins CP, du Boulay EP, Barnard RO, McDonald WI. Pathological findings correlated with magnetic resonance imaging in subcortical arteriosclerotic encephalopathy (Binswanger's disease). *J Neurol Neurosurg Psychiatry.* 1989;52:1337–1344.
152. Lövblad KO, Plüschke W, Remonda L, et al. Diffusion-weighted MRI for monitoring neurovascular interventions. *Neuroradiology.* 2000;42:134–138.
153. Lim JS, Kwon HM. Risk of "silent stroke" in patients older than 60 years: risk assessment and clinical perspectives. *Clin Interv Aging.* 2010;5:239–251.
154. Koch S, McClendon MS, Bhatia R. Imaging evolution of acute lacunar infarction: leukoaraiosis or lacune? *Neurology.* 2011;77:1091–1095.
155. Moreau F, Patel S, Lauzon ML, et al. Cavitation after acute symptomatic lacunar stroke depends on time, location, and MRI sequence. *Stroke.* 2012;43:1837–1842.

156. Potter GM, Doubal FN, Jackson CA, et al. Counting cavitating lacunes underestimates the burden of lacunar infarction. *Stroke.* 2010;41:267–272.
157. Pantoni L. Cerebral small vessel disease: from pathogenesis and clinical characteristics to therapeutic challenges. *Lancet Neurol.* 2010;9:689–701.
158. Shinkawa A, Ueda K, Kiyohara Y, et al. Silent cerebral infarction in a community-based autopsy series in Japan: the Hisayama Study. *Stroke.* 1995;26:380–385.
159. Révész T, Hawkins CP, du Boulay EP, Barnard RO, McDonald WI. Pathological findings correlated with magnetic resonance imaging in subcortical arteriosclerotic encephalopathy (Binswanger's disease). *J Neurol Neurosurg Psychiatry.* 1989;52:1337–1344.
160. Strozyk D, Dickson DW, Lipton RB, et al. Contribution of vascular pathology to the clinical expression of dementia. *Neurobiol Aging.* 2010;31:1710–1720.
161. Lammie GA, Brannan F, Wardlaw JM. Incomplete lacunar infarction (type Ib lacunes). *Acta Neuropathol.* 1998;96:163–171.
162. Bokura H, Yamaguchi S, Iijima K, Nagai A, Oguro H. Metabolic syndrome is associated with silent ischemic brain lesions. *Stroke.* 2008;39:1607–1609.
163. Das RR, Seshadri S, Beiser AS, et al. Prevalence and correlates of silent cerebral infarcts in the Framingham Offspring Study. *Stroke.* 2008;39:2929–2935.
164. Nakane H, Ibayashi S, Fujii K, et al. Cerebral blood flow and metabolism in patients with silent brain infarction: occult misery perfusion in the cerebral cortex. *J Neurol Neurosurg Psychiatry.* 1998;65:317–321.
165. Masuda J, Nabika T, Notsu Y. Silent stroke: pathogenesis, genetic factors and clinical implications as a risk factor. *Curr Opin Neurol.* 2001;14:77–82.
166. Longstreth WT Jr, Manolio TA, Arnold A, et al. Clinical correlates of white matter findings on cranial magnetic resonance imaging of 3301 elderly people: the Cardiovascular Health Study. *Stroke.* 1996;27:1274–1282.
167. Norrving B. Lacunar infarcts: no black holes in the brain are benign. *Pract Neurol.* 2008;8:222–228.
168. Putaala J, Kurkinen M, Tarvos V, Salonen O, Kaste M, Tatlisumak T. Silent brain infarcts and leukoaraiosis in young adults with first-ever ischemic stroke. *Neurology.* 2009;72:1823–1829.
169. Debette S, Bis JC, Fornage M, et al. Genome-wide association studies of MRI-defined brain infarcts: meta-analysis from the CHARGE Consortium. *Stroke.* 2010;41:210–217.
170. Bernick C, Kuller L, Dulberg C, et al. Silent MRI infarcts and the risk of future stroke: the Cardiovascular Health Study. *Neurology.* 2001;57:1222–1229.
171. van Zagten M, Boiten J, Kessels F, Lodder J. Significant progression of white matter lesions and small deep (lacunar) infarcts in patients with stroke. *Arch Neurol.* 1996;53:650–655.
172. de Jong G, Kessels F, Lodder J. Two types of lacunar infarcts: further arguments from a study on prognosis. *Stroke.* 2002;33:2072–2076.
173. EAFT Study Group. Silent brain infarction in nonrheumatic atrial fibrillation: European Atrial Fibrillation Trial. *Neurology.* 1996;46:159–165.
174. Weber R, Weimar C, Wanke I, et al. Risk of recurrent stroke in patients with silent brain infarction in the Prevention Regimen for Effectively Avoiding Second Strokes (PRoFESS) imaging substudy. *Stroke.* 2012;43:350–355.
175. Kang DW, Lattimore SU, Latour LL, Warach S. Silent ischemic lesion recurrence on magnetic resonance imaging predicts subsequent clinical vascular events. *Arch Neurol.* 2006;63:1730–1733.
176. Gaillard N, Schmidt C, Costalat V, et al. Hemorrhagic risk of recent silent cerebral infarct on prethrombolysis MR imaging in acute stroke. *AJNR Am J Neuroradiol.* 2012;33:227–231.
177. Kimberly WT, Gilson A, Rost NS, et al. Silent ischemic infarcts are associated with hemorrhage burden in cerebral amyloid angiopathy. *Neurology.* 2009;72:1230–1235.
178. Kobayashi A, Karlinski M, Litwin T, Czlonkowska A. Do silent infarcts modify the effect of thrombolysis for stroke? *Acta Neurol Scand.* 2013;127:227–232.

179. Fazekas F, Kleinert R, Roob G, et al. Histopathologic analysis of foci of signal loss on gradient-echo T2*-weighted MR images in patients with spontaneous intracerebral hemorrhage: evidence of microangiopathy-related microbleeds. *AJNR Am J Neuroradiol.* 1999;20:637–642.
180. Chan S, Kartha K, Yoon SS, Desmond DW, Hilal SK. Multifocal hypointense cerebral lesions on gradient-echo MR are associated with chronic hypertension. *AJNR Am J Neuroradiol.* 1996;17:1821–1827.
181. Greenberg SM, Finklestein SP, Schaefer PW. Petechial hemorrhages accompanying lobar hemorrhage: detection by gradient-echo MRI. *Neurology.* 1996;46:1751–1754.
182. Offenbacher H, Fazekas F, Schmidt R, Koch M, Fazekas G, Kapeller P. MR of cerebral abnormalities concomitant with primary intracerebral hematomas. *AJNR Am J Neuroradiol.* 1996;17:573–578.
183. Fan YH, Mok VC, Lam WW, Hui AC, Wong KS. Cerebral microbleeds and white matter changes in patients hospitalized with lacunar infarcts. *J Neurol.* 2004;251:537–541.
184. Roob G, Lechner A, Schmidt R, Flooh E, Hartung HP, Fazekas F. Frequency and location of microbleeds in patients with primary intracerebral hemorrhage. *Stroke.* 2000;31:2665–2669.
185. Cordonnier C, Al-Shahi Salman R, Wardlaw J. Spontaneous brain microbleeds: systematic review, subgroup analyses and standards for study design and reporting. *Brain.* 2007;130:1988–2003.
186. Kato H, Izumiyama M, Izumiyama K, Takahashi A, Itoyama Y. Silent cerebral microbleeds on T2*-weighted MRI: correlation with stroke subtype, stroke recurrence, and leukoaraiosis. *Stroke.* 2002;33:1536–1540.
187. Hanyu H, Tanaka Y, Shimizu S, et al. Cerebral microbleeds in Binswanger's disease: a gradient-echo T2*-weighted magnetic resonance imaging study. *Neurosci Lett.* 2003;340:213–216.
188. Werring DJ. Cerebral microbleeds: clinical and pathophysiological significance. *J Neuroimaging.* 2007;17:193–203.
189. Sveinbjornsdottir S, Sigurdsson S, Aspelund T, et al. Cerebral microbleeds in the population based AGES-Reykjavik study: prevalence and location. *J Neurol Neurosurg Psychiatry.* 2008;79:1002–1006.
190. Vernooij MW, van der Lugt A, Ikram MA, et al. Prevalence and risk factors of cerebral microbleeds: the Rotterdam Scan Study. *Neurology.* 2008;70:1208–1214.
191. Fisher M. The challenge of mixed cerebrovascular disease. *Ann N Y Acad Sci.* 2010;1207:18–22.
192. Fisher M, French S, Ji P, Kim RC. Cerebral microbleeds in the elderly: a pathological analysis. *Stroke.* 2010;41:2782–2785.
193. Greenberg SM, Vernooij MW, Cordonnier C, et al. Cerebral microbleeds: a guide to detection and interpretation. *Lancet Neurol.* 2009;8:165–174.
194. Tatsumi S, Ayaki T, Shinohara M, Yamamoto T. Type of gradient recalled-echo sequence results in size and number change of cerebral microbleeds. *AJNR Am J Neuroradiol.* 2008;29:e13.
195. Vernooij MW, Ikram MA, Wielopolski PA, Krestin GP, Breteler MM, van der Lugt A. Cerebral microbleeds: accelerated 3D T2*-weighted GRE MR imaging versus conventional 2D T2*-weighted GRE MR imaging for detection. *Radiology.* 2008;248:272–277.
196. Scheid R, Ott DV, Roth H, Schroeter ML, von Cramon DY. Comparative magnetic resonance imaging at 1.5 and 3 Tesla for the evaluation of traumatic microbleeds. *J Neurotrauma.* 2007;24:1811–1816.
197. Viswanathan A, Chabriat H. Cerebral microhemorrhage. *Stroke.* 2006;37:550–555.
198. Greenberg SM, Nandigam RN, Delgado P, et al. Microbleeds versus macrobleeds: evidence for distinct entities. *Stroke.* 2009;40:2382–2386.
199. Tatsumi S, Shinohara M, Yamamoto T. Direct comparison of histology of microbleeds with postmortem MR images: a case report. *Cerebrovasc Dis.* 2008;26:142–146.
200. Schrag M, McAuley G, Pomakian J, et al. Correlation of hypointensities in susceptibility-weighted images to tissue histology in dementia patients with cerebral amyloid angiopathy: a postmortem MRI study. *Acta Neuropathol.* 2010;119:291–302.

201. Tanaka A, Ueno Y, Nakayama Y, Takano K, Takebayashi S. Small chronic hemorrhages and ischemic lesions in association with spontaneous intracerebral hematomas. *Stroke.* 1999;30:1637–1642.
202. Knudsen KA, Rosand J, Karluk D, Greenberg SM. Clinical diagnosis of cerebral amyloid angiopathy: validation of the Boston criteria. *Neurology.* 2001;56:537–539.
203. Gregoire SM, Jäger HR, Yousry TA, Kallis C, Brown MM, Werring DJ. Brain microbleeds as a potential risk factor for antiplatelet-related intracerebral haemorrhage: hospital-based, case–control study. *J Neurol Neurosurg Psychiatry.* 2010;81:679–684.
204. van den Boom R, Bornebroek M, Behloul F, van den Berg-Huysmans AA, Haan J, van Buchem MA. Microbleeds in hereditary cerebral hemorrhage with amyloidosis-Dutch type. *Neurology.* 2005;64:1288–1289.
205. Jeong SW, Jung KH, Chu K, Bae HJ, Lee SH, Roh JK. Clinical and radiologic differences between primary intracerebral hemorrhage with and without microbleeds on gradient-echo magnetic resonance images. *Arch Neurol.* 2004;61:905–909.
206. Lee SH, Kim BJ, Roh JK. Silent microbleeds are associated with volume of primary intracerebral hemorrhage. *Neurology.* 2006;66:430–432.
207. Wardlaw JM, Lewis SC, Keir SL, Dennis MS, Shenkin S. Cerebral microbleeds are associated with lacunar stroke defined clinically and radiologically, independently of white matter lesions. *Stroke.* 2006;37:2633–2636.
208. Werring DJ, Coward LJ, Losseff NA, Jäger HR, Brown MM. Cerebral microbleeds are common in ischemic stroke but rare in TIA. *Neurology.* 2005;65:1914–1918.
209. Kim M, Bae HJ, Lee J, et al. *APOE* epsilon2/epsilon4 polymorphism and cerebral microbleeds on gradient-echo MRI. *Neurology.* 2005;65:1474–1475.
210. Maxwell SS, Jackson CA, Paternoster L, et al. Genetic associations with brain microbleeds: systematic review and meta-analyses. *Neurology.* 2011;77:158–167.
211. Kikuta K, Takagi Y, Nozaki K, et al. Asymptomatic microbleeds in Moyamoya disease: T2*-weighted gradient-echo magnetic resonance imaging study. *J Neurosurg.* 2005;102:470–475.
212. Viswanathan A, Guichard JP, Gschwendtner A, et al. Blood pressure and haemoglobin A1c are associated with microhaemorrhage in CADASIL: a two-centre cohort study. *Brain.* 2006;129:2375–2383.
213. Lesnik Oberstein SA, van den Boom R, van Buchem MA, et al. Cerebral microbleeds in CADASIL. *Neurology.* 2001;57:1066–1070.
214. Roob G, Schmidt R, Kapeller P, Lechner A, Hartung HP, Fazekas F. MRI evidence of past cerebral microbleeds in a healthy elderly population. *Neurology.* 1999;52:991–994.
215. Qiu C, Cotch MF, Sigurdsson S, et al. Retinal and cerebral microvascular signs and diabetes: the Age, Gene/Environment Susceptibility-Reykjavik study. *Diabetes.* 2008;57:1645–1650.
216. Lee SH, Park JM, Kwon SJ, et al. Left ventricular hypertrophy is associated with cerebral microbleeds in hypertensive patients. *Neurology.* 2004;63:16–21.
217. Imaizumi T, Horita Y, Hashimoto Y, Niwa J. Dotlike hemosiderin spots on T2*-weighted magnetic resonance imaging as a predictor of stroke recurrence: a prospective study. *J Neurosurg.* 2004;101:915–920.
218. Rosand J, Muzikansky A, Kumar A, et al. Spatial clustering of hemorrhages in probable cerebral amyloid angiopathy. *Ann Neurol.* 2005;58:459–462.
219. Roob G, Fazekas F. Magnetic resonance imaging of cerebral microbleeds. *Curr Opin Neurol.* 2000;13:69–73.
220. Greenberg SM, O'Donnell HC, Schaefer PW, Kraft E. MRI detection of new hemorrhages: potential marker of progression in cerebral amyloid angiopathy. *Neurology.* 1999;53:1135–1138.

221. Kidwell CS, Greenberg SM. Red meets white: do microbleeds link hemorrhagic and ischemic cerebrovascular disease? *Neurology*. 2009;73:1614–1615.
222. Jeon SB, Kwon SU, Cho AH, Yun SC, Kim JS, Kang DW. Rapid appearance of new cerebral microbleeds after acute ischemic stroke. *Neurology*. 2009;73:1638–1644.
223. Menon RS, Kidwell CS. Neuroimaging demonstration of evolving small vessel ischemic injury in cerebral amyloid angiopathy. *Stroke*. 2009;40:e675–e677.
224. Kwa VI, Franke CL, Verbeeten B Jr, Stam J. Silent intracerebral microhemorrhages in patients with ischemic stroke: Amsterdam Vascular Medicine Group. *Ann Neurol*. 1998;44:372–377.
225. Roch JA, Nighoghossian N, Hermier M, et al. Transient neurologic symptoms related to cerebral amyloid angiopathy: usefulness of T2*-weighted imaging. *Cerebrovasc Dis*. 2005;20:412–414.
226. Nakata Y, Shiga K, Yoshikawa K, et al. Subclinical brain hemorrhages in Alzheimer's disease: evaluation by magnetic resonance T2*-weighted images. *Ann N Y Acad Sci*. 2002;977:169–172.
227. Hanyu H, Tanaka Y, Shimizu S, Takasaki M, Abe K. Cerebral microbleeds in Alzheimer's disease. *J Neurol*. 2003;250:1496–1497.
228. Atri A, Locascio JJ, Lin JM, et al. Prevalence and effects of lobar microhemorrhages in early-stage dementia. *Neurodegener Dis*. 2005;2:305–312.
229. Cordonnier C, van der Flier WM, Sluimer JD, Leys D, Barkhof F, Scheltens P. Prevalence and severity of microbleeds in a memory clinic setting. *Neurology*. 2006;66:1356–1360.
230. Koennecke HC. Cerebral microbleeds on MRI: prevalence, associations, and potential clinical implications. *Neurology*. 2006;66:165–171.
231. Cordonnier C. Brain microbleeds. *Pract Neurol*. 2010;10:94–100.
232. Nishikawa T, Ueba T, Kajiwara M, Fujisawa I, Miyamatsu N, Yamashita K. Cerebral microbleeds predict first-ever symptomatic cerebrovascular events. *Clin Neurol Neurosurg*. 2009;111:825–828.
233. Bokura H, Saika R, Yamaguchi T, et al. Microbleeds are associated with subsequent hemorrhagic and ischemic stroke in healthy elderly individuals. *Stroke*. 2011;42:1867–1871.
234. Naka H, Nomura E, Wakabayashi S, et al. Frequency of asymptomatic microbleeds on T2*-weighted MR images of patients with recurrent stroke: association with combination of stroke subtypes and leukoaraiosis. *AJNR Am J Neuroradiol*. 2004;25:714–719.
235. Greenberg SM, Eng JA, Ning M, Smith EE, Rosand J. Hemorrhage burden predicts recurrent intracerebral hemorrhage after lobar hemorrhage. *Stroke*. 2004;35:1415–1420.
236. Soo YO, Yang SR, Lam WW, et al. Risk vs benefit of anti-thrombotic therapy in ischaemic stroke patients with cerebral microbleeds. *J Neurol*. 2008;255:1679–1686.
237. Kim DE, Bae HJ, Lee SH, Kim H, Yoon BW, Roh JK. Gradient echo magnetic resonance imaging in the prediction of hemorrhagic vs ischemic stroke: a need for the consideration of the extent of leukoariosis. *Arch Neurol*. 2002;59:425–429.
238. Tsushima Y, Aoki J, Endo K. Brain microhemorrhages detected on T2*-weighted gradient-echo MR images. *AJNR Am J Neuroradiol*. 2003;24:88–96.
239. Boulanger JM, Coutts SB, Eliasziw M, et al. Cerebral microhemorrhages predict new disabling or fatal strokes in patients with acute ischemic stroke or transient ischemic attack. *Stroke*. 2006;37:911–914.
240. Thijs V, Lemmens R, Schoofs C, et al. Microbleeds and the risk of recurrent stroke. *Stroke*. 2010;41:2005–2009.
241. Jeon SB, Kang DW, Cho AH, Lee EM, Choi CG, Kwon SU. Initial microbleeds at MR imaging can predict recurrent intracerebral hemorrhage. *J Neurol*. 2007;254:508–512.
242. Biffi A, Halpin A, Towfighi A, et al. Aspirin and recurrent intracerebral hemorrhage in cerebral amyloid angiopathy. *Neurology*. 2010;75:693–698.
243. Viswanathan A, Rakich SM, Engel C, et al. Antiplatelet use after intracerebral hemorrhage. *Neurology*. 2006;66:206–209.

244. Ueno H, Naka H, Ohshita T, et al. Association between cerebral microbleeds on T2*-weighted MR images and recurrent hemorrhagic stroke in patients treated with warfarin following ischemic stroke. *AJNR Am J Neuroradiol.* 2008;29:1483–1486.
245. Lee SH, Ryu WS, Roh JK. Cerebral microbleeds are a risk factor for warfarin-related intracerebral hemorrhage. *Neurology.* 2009;72:171–176.
246. Orken DN, Kenangil G, Uysal E, Forta H. Cerebral microbleeds in ischemic stroke patients on warfarin treatment. *Stroke.* 2009;40:3638–3640.
247. Nighoghossian N, Hermier M, Adeleine P, et al. Old microbleeds are a potential risk factor for cerebral bleeding after ischemic stroke: a gradient-echo T2*-weighted brain MRI study. *Stroke.* 2002;33:735–742.
248. Kidwell CS, Saver JL, Villablanca JP, et al. Magnetic resonance imaging detection of microbleeds before thrombolysis: an emerging application. *Stroke.* 2002;33:95–98.
249. Fiehler J, Albers GW, Boulanger JM, et al. Bleeding Risk Analysis in Stroke Imaging before thromboLysis (BRASIL): pooled analysis of T2*-weighted magnetic resonance imaging data from 570 patients. *Stroke.* 2007;38:2738–2744.
250. Kim HS, Lee DH, Ryu CW, et al. Multiple cerebral microbleeds in hyperacute ischemic stroke: impact on prevalence and severity of early hemorrhagic transformation after thrombolytic treatment. *AJR Am J Roentgenol.* 2006;186:1443–1449.
251. Fan YH, Zhang L, Lam WW, Mok VC, Wong KS. Cerebral microbleeds as a risk factor for subsequent intracerebral hemorrhages among patients with acute ischemic stroke. *Stroke.* 2003;34:2459–2462.
252. Wong KS, Chan YL, Liu JY, Gao S, Lam WW. Asymptomatic microbleeds as a risk factor for aspirin-associated intracerebral hemorrhages. *Neurology.* 2003;60:511–513.
253. Werring DJ, Frazer DW, Coward LJ, et al. Cognitive dysfunction in patients with cerebral microbleeds on T2*-weighted gradient-echo MRI. *Brain.* 2004;127:2265–2275.
254. Matthews FE, Brayne C, Lowe J, McKeith I, Wharton SB, Ince P. Epidemiological pathology of dementia: attributable-risks at death in the Medical Research Council Cognitive Function and Ageing Study. *PLoS Med.* 2009;6:e1000180.
255. Arvanitakis Z, Leurgans SE, Barnes LL, Bennett DA, Schneider JA. Microinfarct pathology, dementia, and cognitive systems. *Stroke.* 2011;42:722–727.
256. Smith EE, Schneider JA, Wardlaw JM, Greenberg SM. Cerebral microinfarcts: the invisible lesions. *Lancet Neurol.* 2012;11:272–282.
257. Brundel M, de Bresser J, van Dillen JJ, Kappelle LJ, Biessels GJ. Cerebral microinfarcts: a systematic review of neuropathological studies. *J Cereb Blood Flow Metab.* 2012;32:425–436.
258. Udaka F, Sawada H, Kameyama M. White matter lesions and dementia: MRI-pathological correlation. *Ann N Y Acad Sci.* 2002;977:411–415.
259. Doubal FN, MacLullich AM, Ferguson KJ, Dennis MS, Wardlaw JM. Enlarged perivascular spaces on MRI are a feature of cerebral small vessel disease. *Stroke.* 2010;41:450–454.
260. Zhu YC, Tzourio C, Soumaré A, Mazoyer B, Dufouil C, Chabriat H. Severity of dilated Virchow-Robin spaces is associated with age, blood pressure, and MRI markers of small vessel disease: a population-based study. *Stroke.* 2010;41:2483–2490.
261. Patankar TF, Mitra D, Varma A, Snowden J, Neary D, Jackson A. Dilatation of the Virchow-Robin space is a sensitive indicator of cerebral microvascular disease: study in elderly patients with dementia. *AJNR Am J Neuroradiol.* 2005;26:1512–1520.
262. Jouvent E, Poupon C, Gray F, et al. Intracortical infarcts in small vessel disease: a combined 7-T postmortem MRI and neuropathological case study in cerebral autosomal-dominant arteriopathy with subcortical infarcts and leukoencephalopathy. *Stroke.* 2011;42:e27–e30.
263. Gass A, Ay H, Szabo K, Koroshetz WJ. Diffusion-weighted MRI for the "small stuff": the details of acute cerebral ischaemia. *Lancet Neurol.* 2004;3:39–45.

264. Romero JM, Schaefer PW, Grant PE, Becerra L, González RG. Diffusion MR imaging of acute ischemic stroke. *Neuroimaging Clin North Am.* 2002;12:35–53.
265. Baird AE, Benfield A, Schlaug G, et al. Enlargement of human cerebral ischemic lesion volumes measured by diffusion-weighted magnetic resonance imaging. *Ann Neurol.* 1997;41:581–589.
266. Vinters HV, Ellis WG, Zarow C, et al. Neuropathologic substrates of ischemic vascular dementia. *J Neuropathol Exp Neurol.* 2000;59:931–945.
267. Sonnen JA, Larson EB, Crane PK, et al. Pathological correlates of dementia in a longitudinal, population-based sample of aging. *Ann Neurol.* 2007;62:406–413.
268. White L, Petrovitch H, Hardman J, et al. Cerebrovascular pathology and dementia in autopsied Honolulu-Asia Aging Study participants. *Ann N Y Acad Sci.* 2002;977:9–23.
269. Kalaria RN, Kenny RA, Ballard CG, Perry R, Ince P, Polvikoski T. Towards defining the neuropathological substrates of vascular dementia. *J Neurol Sci.* 2004;226:75–80.
270. Yip AG, McKee AC, Green RC, et al. APOE, vascular pathology, and the AD brain. *Neurology.* 2005;65:259–265.
271. Haglund M, Passant U, Sjöbeck M, Ghebremedhin E, Englund E. Cerebral amyloid angiopathy and cortical microinfarcts as putative substrates of vascular dementia. *Int J Geriatr Psychiatry.* 2006;21:681–687.
272. Okamoto Y, Ihara M, Fujita Y, Ito H, Takahashi R, Tomimoto H. Cortical microinfarcts in Alzheimer's disease and subcortical vascular dementia. *Neuroreport.* 2009;20:990–996.
273. Miklossy J. Cerebral hypoperfusion induces cortical watershed microinfarcts which may further aggravate cognitive decline in Alzheimer's disease. *Neurol Res.* 2003;25:605–610.
274. Suter OC, Sunthorn T, Kraftsik R, et al. Cerebral hypoperfusion generates cortical watershed microinfarcts in Alzheimer disease. *Stroke.* 2002;33:1986–1992.
275. Erkinjuntti T, Haltia M, Palo J, Sulkava R, Paetau A. Accuracy of the clinical diagnosis of vascular dementia: a prospective clinical and post-mortem neuropathological study. *J Neurol Neurosurg Psychiatry.* 1988;51:1037–1044.
276. Soontornniyomkij V, Lynch MD, Mermash S, et al. Cerebral microinfarcts associated with severe cerebral beta-amyloid angiopathy. *Brain Pathol.* 2010;20:459–467.
277. Schneider JA, Arvanitakis Z, Leurgans SE, Bennett DA. The neuropathology of probable Alzheimer disease and mild cognitive impairment. *Ann Neurol.* 2009;66:200–208.
278. Longstreth WT Jr, Sonnen JA, Koepsell TD, Kukull WA, Larson EB, Montine TJ. Associations between microinfarcts and other macroscopic vascular findings on neuropathologic examination in 2 databases. *Alzheimer Dis Assoc Disord.* 2009;23:291–294.
279. Rossi R, Joachim C, Geroldi C, et al. Association between subcortical vascular disease on CT and neuropathological findings. *Int J Geriatr Psychiatry.* 2004;19:690–695.
280. Okazaki H, Reagan TJ, Campbell RJ. Clinicopathologic studies of primary cerebral amyloid angiopathy. *Mayo Clin Proc.* 1979;54:22–31.
281. Olichney JM, Hansen LA, Lee JH, Hofstetter CR, Katzman R, Thal LJ. Relationship between severe amyloid angiopathy, apolipoprotein E genotype, and vascular lesions in Alzheimer's disease. *Ann N Y Acad Sci.* 2000;903:138–143.
282. Mandybur TI. Cerebral amyloid angiopathy: the vascular pathology and complications. *J Neuropathol Exp Neurol.* 1986;45:79–90.
283. De Reuck J, Deramecourt V, Cordonnier C, Leys D, Maurage CA, Pasquier F. The impact of cerebral amyloid angiopathy on the occurrence of cerebrovascular lesions in demented patients with Alzheimer features: a neuropathological study. *Eur J Neurol.* 2011;18:913–918.
284. Munoz DG. Small vessel disease: neuropathology. *Int Psychogeriatr.* 2003;15(Suppl 1):67–69.
285. Schneider JA, Arvanitakis Z, Bang W, Bennett DA. Mixed brain pathologies account for most dementia cases in community-dwelling older persons. *Neurology.* 2007;69:2197–2204.

286. Troncoso JC, Zonderman AB, Resnick SM, Crain B, Pletnikova O, O'Brien RJ. Effect of infarcts on dementia in the Baltimore longitudinal study of aging. *Ann Neurol.* 2008;64:168–176.
287. Prabhakaran S, Naidech AM. Ischemic brain injury after intracerebral hemorrhage: a critical review. *Stroke.* 2012;43:2258–2263.
288. Kang DW, Han MK, Kim HJ, et al. New ischemic lesions coexisting with acute intracerebral hemorrhage. *Neurology.* 2012;79:848–855.
289. Schley D, Carare-Nnadi R, Please CP, Perry VH, Weller RO. Mechanisms to explain the reverse perivascular transport of solutes out of the brain. *J Theor Biol.* 2006;238:962–974.
290. Kwee RM, Kwee TC. Virchow-Robin spaces at MR imaging. *Radiographics.* 2007;27:1071–186.
291. Weller RO. Pathology of cerebrospinal fluid and interstitial fluid of the CNS: significance for Alzheimer disease, prion disorders and multiple sclerosis. *J Neuropathol Exp Neurol.* 1998;57:885–894.
292. Weller RO, Kida S, Zhang ET. Pathways of fluid drainage from the brain: morphological aspects and immunological significance in rat and man. *Brain Pathol.* 1992;2:277–284.
293. Esiri MM, Gay D. Immunological and neuropathological significance of the Virchow-Robin space. *J Neurol Sci.* 1990;100:3–8.
294. Abbott NJ. Evidence for bulk flow of brain interstitial fluid: significance for physiology and pathology. *Neurochem Int.* 2004;45:545–552.
295. Durand-Fardel M. *Traite du ramollissement du cerveau.* Paris: Balliere, 1843.
296. Oztürk MH, Aydingöz U. Comparison of MR signal intensities of cerebral perivascular (Virchow-Robin) and subarachnoid spaces. *J Comput Assist Tomogr.* 2002;26:902–904.
297. Benhaïem-Sigaux N, Gray F, Gherardi R, Roucayrol AM, Poirier J. Expanding cerebellar lacunes due to dilatation of the perivascular space associated with Binswanger's subcortical arteriosclerotic encephalopathy. *Stroke.* 1987;18:1087–1092.
298. Bokura H, Kobayashi S, Yamaguchi S. Distinguishing silent lacunar infarction from enlarged Virchow-Robin spaces: a magnetic resonance imaging and pathological study. *J Neurol.* 1998;245:116–122.
299. Adachi M, Hosoya T, Haku T, Yamaguchi K. Dilated Virchow-Robin spaces: MRI pathological study. *Neuroradiology.* 1998;40:27–31.
300. Song CJ, Kim JH, Kier EL, Bronen RA. MR imaging and histologic features of subinsular bright spots on T2-weighted MR images: Virchow-Robin spaces of the extreme capsule and insular cortex. *Radiology.* 2000;214:671–677.
301. Hutchings M, Weller RO. Anatomical relationships of the pia mater to cerebral blood vessels in man. *J Neurosurg.* 1986;65:316–325.
302. Zhang ET, Inman CB, Weller RO. Interrelationships of the pia mater and the perivascular (Virchow-Robin) spaces in the human cerebrum. *J Anat.* 1990;170:111–123.
303. Pollock H, Hutchings M, Weller RO, Zhang ET. Perivascular spaces in the basal ganglia of the human brain: their relationship to lacunes. *J Anat.* 1997;191:337–346.
304. Kirkpatrick JB, Hayman LA. White-matter lesions in MR imaging of clinically healthy brains of elderly subjects: possible pathologic basis. *Radiology.* 1987;162:509–511.
305. Shiratori K, Mrowka M, Toussaint A, Spalke G, Bien S. Extreme, unilateral widening of Virchow-Robin spaces: case report. *Neuroradiology.* 2002;44:990–992.
306. Groeschel S, Chong WK, Surtees R, Hanefeld F. Virchow-Robin spaces on magnetic resonance images: normative data, their dilatation, and a review of the literature. *Neuroradiology.* 2006;48:745–754.
307. Heier LA, Bauer CJ, Schwartz L, Zimmerman RD, Morgello S, Deck MD. Large Virchow-Robin spaces: MR–clinical correlation. *AJNR Am J Neuroradiol.* 1989;10:929–936.
308. Zhu YC, Dufouil C, Mazoyer B, et al. Frequency and location of dilated Virchow-Robin spaces in elderly people: a population-based 3D MR imaging study. *AJNR Am J Neuroradiol.* 2011;32:709–713.

309. Klarenbeek P, van Oostenbrugge RJ, Lodder J, Rouhl RP, Knottnerus IL, Staals J. Higher ambulatory blood pressure relates to enlarged Virchow-Robin spaces in first-ever lacunar stroke patients. *J Neurol*. 2013;260:115–121.
310. Rouhl RP, van Oostenbrugge RJ, Knottnerus IL, Staals JE, Lodder J. Virchow-Robin spaces relate to cerebral small vessel disease severity. *J Neurol*. 2008;255:692–696.
311. Wardlaw JM, Doubal F, Armitage P, et al. Lacunar stroke is associated with diffuse blood–brain barrier dysfunction. *Ann Neurol*. 2009;65:194–202.
312. Cumurciuc R, Guichard JP, Reizine D, Gray F, Bousser MG, Chabriat H. Dilation of Virchow-Robin spaces in CADASIL. *Eur J Neurol*. 2006;13:187–190.
313. Chabriat H, Joutel A, Dichgans M, Tournier-Lasserve E, Bousser MG. CADASIL. *Lancet Neurol*. 2009;8:643–653.
314. Roher AE, Kuo YM, Esh C, et al. Cortical and leptomeningeal cerebrovascular amyloid and white matter pathology in Alzheimer's disease. *Mol Med*. 2003;9:112–122.
315. Fearnley JM, Stevens JM, Rudge P. Superficial siderosis of the central nervous system. *Brain*. 1995;118:1051–1066.
316. Kumar N. Neuroimaging in superficial siderosis: an in-depth look. *AJNR Am J Neuroradiol*. 2010;31:5–14.
317. Kumar N, Cohen-Gadol AA, Wright RA, Miller GM, Piepgras DG, Ahlskog JE. Superficial siderosis. *Neurology*. 2006;66:1144–1152.
318. Koeppen AH, Dentinger MP. Brain hemosiderin and superficial siderosis of the central nervous system. *J Neuropathol Exp Neurol*. 1988;47:249–270.
319. Koeppen AH, Dickson AC, Chu RC, Thach RE. The pathogenesis of superficial siderosis of the central nervous system. *Ann Neurol*. 1993;34:646–653.
320. Janss AJ, Galetta SL, Freese A, et al. Superficial siderosis of the central nervous system: magnetic resonance imaging and pathological correlation: case report. *J Neurosurg*. 1993;79:756–760.
321. Koeppen AH, Barron KD. Superficial siderosis of the central nervous system: a histological, histochemical and chemical study. *J Neuropathol Exp Neurol*. 1971;30:448–469.
322. Leussink VI, Flachenecker P, Brechtelsbauer D, et al. Superficial siderosis of the central nervous system: pathogenetic heterogeneity and therapeutic approaches. *Acta Neurol Scand*. 2003;107:54–61.
323. Linn J, Herms J, Dichgans M, et al. Subarachnoid hemosiderosis and superficial cortical hemosiderosis in cerebral amyloid angiopathy. *AJNR Am J Neuroradiol*. 2008;29:184–186.
324. Vernooij MW, Ikram MA, Hofman A, Krestin GP, Breteler MM, van der Lugt A. Superficial siderosis in the general population. *Neurology*. 2009;73:202–205.
325. Linn J, Halpin A, Demaerel P, et al. Prevalence of superficial siderosis in patients with cerebral amyloid angiopathy. *Neurology*. 2010;74:1346–1350.
326. Takeda S, Yamazaki K, Miyakawa T, et al. Subcortical hematoma caused by cerebral amyloid angiopathy: does the first evidence of hemorrhage occur in the subarachnoid space? *Neuropathology*. 2003;23:254–261.
327. Finelli PF. Cerebral amyloid angiopathy as cause of convexity SAH in elderly. *Neurologist*. 2010;16:37–40.
328. Renard D, Castelnovo G, Wacongne A, et al. Interest of CSF biomarker analysis in possible cerebral amyloid angiopathy cases defined by the modified Boston criteria. *J Neurol*. 2012;259:2429–2433.
329. Charidimou A, Gang Q, Werring DJ. Sporadic cerebral amyloid angiopathy revisited: recent insights into pathophysiology and clinical spectrum. *J Neurol Neurosurg Psychiatry*. 2012;83:124–137.
330. Yamada M. Predicting cerebral amyloid angiopathy-related intracerebral hemorrhages and other cerebrovascular disorders in Alzheimer's disease. *Front Neurol*. 2012;3:64.
331. Katoh M, Yoshino M, Asaoka K, et al. A restricted subarachnoid hemorrhage in the cortical sulcus in cerebral amyloid angiopathy: could it be a warning sign? *Surg Neurol*. 2007;68:457–460.

332. Linn J, Wollenweber FA, Lummel N, et al. Superficial siderosis is a warning sign for future intracranial hemorrhage. *J Neurol.* 2013;260:176–181.
333. Dierksen GA, Skehan ME, Khan MA, et al. Spatial relation between microbleeds and amyloid deposits in amyloid angiopathy. *Ann Neurol.* 2010;68:545–548.
334. Izenberg A, Aviv RI, Demaerschalk BM, et al. Crescendo transient aura attacks: a transient ischemic attack mimic caused by focal subarachnoid hemorrhage. *Stroke.* 2009;40:3725–3729.
335. Beitzke M, Gattringer T, Enzinger C, Wagner G, Niederkorn K, Fazekas F. Clinical presentation, etiology, and long-term prognosis in patients with nontraumatic convexal subarachnoid hemorrhage. *Stroke.* 2011;42:3055–3060.
336. Charidimou A, Peeters A, Fox Z, et al. Spectrum of transient focal neurological episodes in cerebral amyloid angiopathy: multicentre magnetic resonance imaging cohort study and meta-analysis. *Stroke.* 2012;43:2324–2330.

22

CIRCULATING BIOMARKERS AND THE RISK OF CEREBROVASCULAR DISEASE AND STROKE

Aleksandra Pikula

Introduction

Cerebrovascular disease is a major public health concern that accounts for a significant proportion of brain aging-related mortality and morbidity. The burden of cerebrovascular disease is attributable largely to well-established vascular risk factors, and genetic and lifestyle differences, but another determinant may be factors that modulate risk and response to ischemic or other vascular brain injury. Therefore, searching for novel biological pathways involved in overt and covert cerebrovascular disease may improve our understanding of disease mechanisms and help facilitate the discovery of new molecular targets for stroke prevention and treatment.

Changes in circulating levels of an increasing number of biological molecules, with varied functions—some specific to the brain and others restricted to the vasculature, liver, blood, or inflammatory pathways—have been associated with an altered risk of stroke.

In this chapter, circulating biomarkers relevant to ischemic cerebrovascular disease are discussed. Based on the plausible biological pathways whereby they might be related to stroke risk, these biomarkers are discussed within pathway-specific categories.

A biomarker has been defined as a characteristic that is measured objectively and evaluated as an indicator of normal biological or pathogenic processes, or of pharmacological responses to a therapeutic intervention. It is thus a marker of a disease "trait, state, or rate." Although biomarkers can include imaging tests and clinical performance characteristics, genetic variants, and cerebrospinal fluid (CSF) levels, in this chapter the term *biomarker* is used to refer to circulating biomarkers only. Biomarkers can have multiple useful functions, permitting more accurate risk prediction, improving prognostication (of recurrence, disability, or mortality after stroke), improving differential diagnosis, and better monitoring of therapeutic interventions.

An ideal biomarker for prediction of vascular risk should be specific and sensitive, but also relatively inexpensive to measure using standardized, precise, reliable, and reproducible assays. Furthermore, it should be independently predictive and additive to already-established vascular risk factors. More important, population-specific normative values should be easily interpretable for clinicians. Biomarkers useful for primary prevention need to have a high specificity to reduce the number of false positives, and need to explain a moderate proportion of disease in the community, in addition to needing evidence that targeting individuals with higher (or lower) levels is superior to conventional risk prevention approaches in preventing stroke. Biomarkers for secondary prevention need to have a high sensitivity to avoid false negatives and are most useful when they influence treatments plans or correlate with disease progression trajectories. Although there are many biomarkers available, markers of endothelial dysfunction and inflammation pathways, such as total homocysteine and high-sensitivity C-reactive protein (CRP), are used more widely in routine clinical practice. All others discussed here are relatively novel biomarkers undergoing validation of their clinical utility in community and clinic-based samples.

Biomarkers of Endothelial Function Pathways

TOTAL HOMOCYSTEINE (THCY)

Homocysteine (tHcy) has been recognized as a marker of endothelial dysfunction and as an independent risk factor for atherosclerosis and cardiovascular disease. The mechanisms by which elevated plasma tHcy concentrations impair vascular function and lead to overt or covert vascular brain injury are not entirely understood. Experimental studies proposed several possible explanations—from endothelial dysfunction leading to an initiation of atherothrombotic mechanisms (oxidation of low-density lipids, activation of monocyte adhesion and inflammatory mechanisms, stimulation of smooth muscle proliferation) to initiation of coagulation cascades with platelet activation, and eventually leading to overt cerebrovascular disease.[1] As an excitatory neurotransmitter, tHcy binds to the N-methyl-D-aspartate (NMDA) receptors resulting in neuronal injury; thus, tHcy is recognized as an important marker of vascular brain injury.[2,3]

Homocysteine is a sulfur-containing amino acid produced by demethylation of the essential amino acid methionine. It is metabolized via two metabolic pathways: (a) remethylation, during which methionine is formed again from a methyl group acquired from methylene tetrahydrofolate or betaine—a process dependent on vitamin B12 and folate—or (b) transsulfuration, during which tHcy is condensed with serine by cystathionine β-synthase to form cystathionine, and this is dependent on vitamin B6. Inherited deficiencies in enzymes necessary for the metabolism of tHcy can result in elevated blood levels of tHcy, as can deficiencies in required cofactors, folate, B12, B6, and betaine.[4]

Blood (plasma or serum) levels of tHcy are measured optimally during the fasting state; serum tHcy concentrations of 5 to 15 μmol/L are considered normal (although for individuals on a folic acid-fortified diet, the upper limit of normal is considered to be 12 μmol/L), and levels more than 15 μmol/L are considered elevated (mildly elevated, 16–30 μmol/L; moderately elevated, 31–100 μmol/L; and severely elevated, >100 μmol/L).[5]

In the general population, deficiency of folic acid, vitamin B12, or vitamin B6 accounts for the majority of persons with elevated tHcy concentrations. Circulating tHcy concentrations increase with age and are elevated in persons with impaired renal function, but are also increased by some medications (carbamazepine, phenytoin, methotrexate), and are elevated in individuals with a gene mutation for methylenetetrahydrofolate reductase.[6]

The "homocysteine hypothesis" of accelerated atherothrombotic vascular disease was proposed in early 1969 by McCully[7] based on his observations of intimal injury, fibrosis, lipid accumulation, and atherothrombosis of the coronary and cerebrovascular vasculature in children with homocystinuria. Similar observations were reported after inducing acute hyperhomocysteinemia with methionine load in older adults.[8] However, the exact role of elevated tHcy in the pathogenesis of cerebrovascular atherosclerosis remains uncertain. Some evidence suggests stroke subtype-specific increased risk for large-artery and small-artery (lacunar) disease compared with cardioembolic stroke and control subjects, but this observation remains inconsistent across studies.[9] There is a strong association between thrombophilia and venous thrombosis in patients with homocystinuria caused by cystathionine β-synthase deficiency.[10] Homocysteine may also contribute to the development of left atrial thrombus in patients with stroke caused by atrial fibrillation, in which the mean tHcy level was greater in patients with thrombus present on transesophageal echocardiography even when the analysis was adjusted for spontaneous echo contrast and atrial dilation (tHcy >15 μmol/L; adjusted odds ratio [OR], 14.25; 95% confidence interval [CI], 2.7–75.1).[11]

After the introduction of folic acid-fortified diet programs, the Framingham study observed that folate status had improved, with the relative reduction of elevated tHcy levels by almost 50%.[12] Since the introduction of folic acid fortification in 1998, there is limited epidemiological data on the relationship of tHcy to overt cerebrovascular disease. Among 1947 elderly Framingham Study participants (mean age, 70 ± 7 years; mean follow-up, 9.9 years; incident stroke events, 165) after adjusting for traditional stroke risk factors, participants with greater baseline tHcy levels (>14.24 μmol/L) compared with those with lower levels (<10 μmol/L) had an increased risk of stroke, with a relative risk (RR) of 1.82 (95% CI, 1.14–2.91).[13] Similar findings were observed among elderly participants from the Rotterdam Study in which the stroke risk by quintiles of tHcy level was increased significantly only in the group with levels greater than 18.6 μmol/L (upper quintile OR, 2.53; 95% CI, 1.19–5.35).[14] Sacco et al.[15] observed that tHcy levels greater than 15 μmol/L are an independent risk factor for ischemic stroke (hazard ratio [HR], 2.01; 95% CI, 1.00–4.05), whereas mild elevations of tHcy of 10 to 15 μmol/L are less predictive. They also found that the vascular effect of tHcy was greatest among whites and Hispanics (HR, 4.04; 95% CI, 0.92–17.62; and HR, 2.42; 95% CI, 0.87–6.76; respectively), but less among blacks (HR, 0.88; 95% CI, 0.24–3.21).[15] tHcy levels of 7.3 μmol/L or more were associated with an elevated OR for stroke of 1.6 (95% CI, 1.1–2.5)l independent of traditional vascular risk factors, vitamin use, and poverty status among young women (age, 15–44 years) in a biracial women study.[16]

In contrast, the Physicians' Health Study (PHS) and a Finnish population study found nonsignificant or borderline significant associations between tHcy and stroke risk.[17,18] There are several possible explanations for this inconsistency. There was a relatively small number of clinical events in the PHS and the Finnish study, limiting power to detect differences due to the overall low prevalence of hyperhomocysteinemia in the Finnish population, and among physicians who were more likely to take dietary and vitamin supplements compared with non-physicians).

In another longitudinal study of 1039 patients with acute stroke (mean age, 75 years), fasting tHcy was measured within 24 hours after admission with acute ischemic stroke, and patients were monitored for up to 15 months for recurrent events. In adjusted analysis, tHcy was an independent predictor of recurrent stroke (OR, 1.3; 95% CI, 1.1–1.5 for each increase in tHcy of 10 μmol/L).[19]

Several studies have also confirmed an association between tHcy concentrations and subclinical vascular brain injury, such as silent/covert brain infarcts[20,21] and white matter hyperintensities.[21–23] In the Framingham Heart Study, 218 participants had an infarct on brain magnetic resonance imaging (MRI). An elevated initial plasma tHcy level was associated with an increased risk of MRI infarct, and similar observations have been made in other epidemiological cohorts.[21]

Despite the relative strength of the association between homocysteine and vascular risk in observational studies, the benefit of tHcy reduction on vascular disease risk is unclear. A meta-analysis projected a reduction of vascular disease by 30% to 40% with greater folic acid intake.[24] Using clinical trials published before August 2012 ($N = 14$, with 54,913 participants) to measure the association between B vitamin supplementation and stroke events, B vitamin supplementation for homocysteine reduction was observed to reduce stroke event rates significantly (RR, 0.93; 95% CI, 0.86–1.00; $p = 0.04$). However, this was not true after the analysis was stratified according to concomitant primary or secondary prevention measures used, ischemic versus hemorrhagic stroke, or occurrence of fatal stroke, although the results remained significant in the stratum of subjects not on dietary folate fortification.[25]

Three large, randomized trials investigated tHcy-lowering vitamin supplement therapy for secondary stroke prevention.[26,27] The Vitamins to Prevent Stroke study included 8000 subjects with recent stroke or transischemic attack (TIA) and studied a combined end point of recurrent stroke, myocardial infarction, and vascular death at 2.5 years, comparing persons on a supplement (2 mg folic acid, 500 μg B12, 50 mg B6) with placebo. This study enrolled a total of 8164 patients who were assigned randomly to receive B vitamins ($n = 4089$) or placebo ($n = 4075$) and were monitored for a median duration of 3.4 years (interquartile range, 2.0–5.5); 616 patients (15%) assigned to B vitamins and 678 (17%) assigned to placebo reached the primary end point, but there was only a marginal reduction in risk (RR, 0.91; 95% CI, 0.82–100; $p = 0.05$). There were no unexpected serious adverse reactions and no significant differences in common adverse effects between the treatment groups. Therefore, daily administration of folic acid, vitamin B6, and vitamin B12 to patients with recent stroke or TIA was safe but did not seem to be more effective than placebo in reducing the incidence of major vascular events.[26] In subsequent subgroup analysis, the Vitamins to Prevent Stroke study group has examined several related questions and found that (a) antiplatelet therapy may amplify the benefits of lowering tHcy levels with B vitamin supplementation such that when comparing persons on supplementation with individuals not on antiplatelet therapy, there was a significant beneficial effect on the primary outcome (123 events in the B vitamins group [17%] vs. 153 events in the placebo group [21%]; HR, 0.76; 95% CI, 0.60–0.96)[28]; (b) B vitamin supplementation did not reduce progression of cerebral small-vessel-related brain lesions measured on brain MRI[29]; and (c) daily supplementation with folic acid, vitamin B6, and vitamin B12 in cognitively unimpaired patients with previous stroke or TIA lowered the mean tHcy level but had no effect on the incidence of cognitive impairment or cognitive decline, as measured by the Mini-Mental State Examination, during a median follow-up of 2.8 years.[30]

The Heart Outcomes Prevention Evaluation trial was a randomized, placebo-controlled trial comparing homocysteine-lowering vitamins (2.5 mg folic acid, 50 mg vitamin B6, 2 mg vitamin B12) or placebo in 5522 patients older than 55 years of age with vascular disease or diabetes, regardless of baseline tHcy level. Subjects were monitored for 5 years for the primary composite outcomes (death resulting from cardiovascular causes, myocardial infarction, or stroke). Almost 12% of the population had a TIA or stroke at study entry. Vitamin therapy did not reduce the risk of the primary end point, but there was a lower risk of stroke (4.0% vs. 5.3%; RR, 0.75; 95% CI, 0.59–0.97; $p = 0.03$) in the active therapy group.[31]

The Vitamins in Stroke Prevention study compared the efficacy of high-dose (2.5 mg folic acid, 400 μg B12, 25 mg B6) and low-dose (200 μg folic acid, 6 μg B12, 0.2 mg B6) vitamin supplementation for secondary prevention of stroke or myocardial infarction in 3600 subjects with recent stroke. Two-year stroke rates were 9.2% in the high-dose arm and 8.8% in the low-dose arm. However, moderate reduction of tHcy after nondisabling stroke had no effect on vascular outcomes during the 2 years of follow-up. Although the study was negative, the authors suggested that the short follow-up could have been insufficient to detect a real difference between the two groups.[27] However, in a hypothesis-driven secondary analysis of a subgroup of patients from the Vitamins in Stroke Prevention study, excluding persons least likely to have experienced lowering of tHcy with the study treatment (those with low or very high serum B12, and those with renal failure, $n = 2155$ patients), there was a significant reduction of stroke, coronary events, and death ($p = 0.049$). When the participants were stratified according to the median entry level of B12 (313 pmol/L), those with high serum

B12 at entry who received high-dose vitamins had a 33% reduction of vascular events compared with those with low B12 who received low-dose vitamins.[32]

Thus current recommendations from the American Heart Association (AHA) regarding secondary stroke prevention strategies concur that folate supplementation reduces levels of tHcy and may be considered for patients with ischemic stroke and hyperhomocysteinemia (class IIb, level of evidence B), although there is no convincing evidence that reducing homocysteine levels prevents stroke recurrence.[33]

ASYMMETRIC DIMETHYLARGININE

Although multiple endogenous products contribute to endothelial homeostasis, endothelium-derived nitric oxide (NO) has been recognized as a key mediator of normal endothelial function and is also called the *endogenous antiatherosclerotic molecule*.[34] However, NO synthesis can be selectively inhibited by competitive blockade of the endothelial NO synthesis active site by asymmetric dimethylarginine (ADMA). Hence, ADMA has been identified as a novel biomarker of endothelial dysfunction and preclinical atherosclerosis.[35]

ADMA is an endogenous molecule produced during the degradation of circulating L-arginine; the substrate for endothelial NO synthesis by the enzyme endothelial NO synthesis. Thus, accumulation of ADMA decreases production of NO. Approximately 90% of ADMA is metabolized in the kidneys and liver by dimethylarginine dimethylaminohydrolase (DDAH), which degrades it to citrulline and methylamine. Pharmacological inhibition of DDAH increases ADMA concentration and reduces NO production. It has also been reported that elevated tHcy concentration, high cholesterol levels, and hyperglycemia could inhibit DDAH activity.[35,36]

ADMA is measured by enzyme-linked immunosorbent assay or high-performance liquid chromatography/liquid chromatography–tandem mass spectrometry—methods that achieve the necessary precision and separation of ADMA from other structural isomers. Although efforts are ongoing to define the normal range of ADMA concentrations in healthy humans in different age and sex groups, elevated plasma ADMA concentrations (defined as higher tertiles, quartiles, or quintiles in the study group) have been observed in patients with hypertension, diabetes, left ventricular hypertrophy, smoking, hypercholesterolemia, and high CRP levels; all well-established risk factors for ischemic stroke.[37–39]

Increased ADMA levels have been associated with an increased risk of atherosclerosis, incident cardiovascular disease, cardiovascular mortality, acute coronary events,[40] and an elevated risk of stroke and TIA.[41,42] Of 52 patients with ischemic stroke and 36 healthy control subjects, Yoo and Lee[41] demonstrated significant differences (p = 0.0001) in ADMA concentrations between those with recurrent strokes (mean, 2.28 μmol/L), index stroke only (mean, 1.46 μmol/L), and control subjects (mean, 0.93 μmol/L). Moreover, levels greater than the 90th percentile of the control group (≥1.43 μmol/L) increased the overall stroke risk in the elderly population studied (OR, 6.05; 95% CI, 2.77–13.3).[41] In the Population Study of Women in Gothenburg, Leong et al.[43] recruited 880 women with baseline ADMA levels and demonstrated that even small increases in ADMA levels over 24 years of follow-up were associated with a 30% greater risk of myocardial infarction or ischemic stroke. Those participants in the highest quintiles of serum ADMA concentrations (>0.71 μmol/L) carried the greatest risk (RR, 1.75; 95% CI 1.18 –2.59] compared with others.[43]

In stroke-free Framingham offspring participants (n = 2013; mean age ± standard deviation [SD], 58 ± 9.5 years; 53% women), baseline plasma ADMA levels were related to subsequent brain MRI measures of subclinical vascular injury such as presence of silent brain infarcts (SBIs). Higher ADMA levels were associated with an increased risk of prevalent SBIs (OR per 1-SD increase in ADMA, 1.16; 95% CI, 1.01–1.33; p = 0.04). Participants in the upper age-specific quartiles (Qs) of plasma ADMA values had an increased prevalence of SBIs (OR for Q2–Q4 vs. Q1, 1.43; 95% CI,

1.00–2.04; $p < 0.05$).[44] Increasing its degradation, DDAH may decrease ADMA levels successfully. Recent data demonstrate that some antidiabetic drugs may lower ADMA levels via regulation of DDAH, thus suggesting that new therapeutic agents should not only target ADMA levels directly, but also perhaps DDAH.[45,46]

Currently, there are no formal recommendations on the value of measuring ADMA concentrations and its use in stroke risk stratification in primary and secondary stroke prevention. However, the literature clearly illustrates that ADMA may be a novel stroke risk factor. Therefore, further studies in larger samples are warranted to validate the clinical significance of elevated circulating ADMA concentrations.

Biomarkers of Inflammatory Pathways

Inflammation plays an important role in the progression of atherosclerosis and in the ulcerating of plaques, resulting in clinical disease such as myocardial infarction and ischemic stroke. Several inflammatory markers have been examined in relation to risk of stroke and stroke outcomes, but most attention has been give to high-sensitivity CRP (hsCRP; CRP measured with a high-sensitivity assay) and lipoprotein-associated phospholipase A2 (Lp-PLA2).

C-REACTIVE PROTEIN

CRP is an acute-phase reactant—a marker of systemic inflammation, produced in liver by interleukin 6, an inflammatory cytokine, but also by endothelial and smooth muscle cells, and by adipose tissue.[47] As a marker of atherosclerosis, CRP is an important predictor for cardiovascular events (myocardial infarction, stroke, peripheral vascular disease, and cardiac death) in individuals without a history of heart disease.[47]

Numerous prospective studies have demonstrated that hsCRP is an independent predictor of stroke in both women and men. During a mean follow-up of 12 to 14 years in 1462 Framingham study subjects (591 men and 871 women free of stroke/TIA; mean age, 69.7 years), CRP was a strong independent predictor of first ischemic stroke or TIA ($n = 196$). In multivariable analysis, after adjustment for traditional stroke risk factors, relative risk of stroke/TIA among participants in the highest compared with the lowest CRP quartile was 2.1 (95% CI 1.19–3.83), but only in women.[48]

In a nested case–control analysis from the Physicians' Health Study comparing 543 apparently healthy men in whom myocardial infarction, stroke, or venous thrombosis subsequently developed with 543 study participants who did not report vascular disease, during a follow-up period exceeding 8 years, persons in the highest CRP quartile had double the risk of ischemic stroke (RR, 1.9; 95% CI, 1.1–3.3, $p = 0.002$) compared with those in the lower two quartiles (Q1–2 vs. Q3–4), independent of other lipid-related and nonlipid-related risk factors.[49]

Studies also demonstrated a strong association between hsCRP concentrations and outcomes after stroke.

In a prospective, observational hospital-based study, Muir et al.[50] examined survival time and cause of death for up to 4 years after the index stroke, and investigated whether the stroke outcomes were related to CRP concentration measured within 72 hours of stroke. Survival in those with a CRP level more than 10.1 mg/L was significantly worse compared with those with CRP ≤10.1 mg/L ($p = 0.00009$). Higher CRP concentration was an independent predictor of mortality (HR, 1.23 per additional log unit; 95% CI, 1.13–1.35; $p = 0.02$), whereas older age, stroke severity, and higher CRP concentrations were independent predictors of mortality during the first 3 months after the index event.[50]

Subsequently, Winbeck et al.[51] examined the association of early serial CRP measurements in hyperacute ischemic stroke with long-term outcomes. A total of 127 patients with a first ischemic stroke (not treated with thrombolysis) were examined within 12 hours after symptom onset and had CRP measurements at admission (CRP 1), within 24 hours (CRP 2), and within 48 hours (CRP 3) after symptom onset. In addition to baseline levels of several vascular risk factors, 1-year outcome and lesion volumes of initial MRI diffusion-weighted images were determined. The CRP concentration increased significantly during the first 48 hours after symptom onset (CRP 1, 0.86 mg/dL [95% CI, 0.69–1.02]; CRP 2, 1.22 mg/dL [95% CI, 0.88–1.55]; CRP 3, 1.75 mg/dL [95% CI, 1.25–2.25]; $p = 0.003$). In multivariable analysis adjusted for vascular risk factors, CRP concentrations obtained within 12 to 48 hours were predictive of an unfavorable outcome (combination of death resulting from any cause and any new nonfatal vascular event such as recurrent stroke, unstable angina, or myocardial infarction [adjusted OR, 3.9; 95% CI, 1.4–10.7; $p = 0.008$]).[51]

Although there is no specific therapy to reduce CRP levels, data from population studies and prospective randomized clinical trials suggest that commonly used agents such as aspirin and 3-hydroxy-3-methylglutaryl-coenzyme A (HMG-CoA) reductase inhibitors (statins) reduce CRP levels. In the PHS study, aspirin decreased the risk of myocardial infarction significantly, but not stroke among men with high CRP concentrations, although there was no clear effect of aspirin on CRP levels.

Among 472 randomly selected participants in the Cholesterol and Recurrent Events trial, CRP levels were measured at baseline and at 5 years. Patients were assigned randomly to pravastatin versus placebo and were monitored for vascular events. Pravastatin use was shown to decrease the risk of vascular events and stroke, and it also decreased CRP levels significantly during the 5-year follow-up, independent of its effect on low-density lipoprotein–cholesterol (LDL-C), whereas in the patients who were on placebo, CRP levels actually increased over this time.[52]

The Justification for the Use of Statins in Prevention: an Intervention Trial Evaluating Rosuvastatin (JUPITER) trial was a double-blind placebo study to investigate whether treatment with rosuvastatin (20 mg daily) versus placebo would decrease the rate of first major cardiovascular events (including any strokes) in patients with normal LDL-C levels but elevated CRP concentrations (>2.0 mg/dL) who also had one additional vascular risk factor for cardiovascular disease. Over a median follow-up of 1.9 years, in participants on rosuvastatin, hsCRP concentrations were decreased by 37% compared with participants on placebo. The JUPITER trial demonstrated a 44% reduction ($p < 0.000001$) of the events in the prespecified primary end point (nonfatal myocardial infarction, nonfatal stroke, hospitalization for unstable angina, coronary revascularization, or cardiovascular death), with no evidence of heterogeneity across geographic regions, a 48% reduction in the risk for nonfatal stroke, and a 51% reduction in risk for ischemic stroke (HR, 0.49; 95% CI, 0.30–0.81; $p = 0.004$).[53] Unlike results from the Stroke Prevention by Aggressive Reduction in Cholesterol Levels trial with atorvastatin for secondary stroke prevention, there was no increase in hemorrhagic stroke with treatment, although the total number of hemorrhagic stroke events was small.[54]

LIPOPROTEIN-ASSOCIATED PHOSPHOLIPASE A2

Lp-PLA2 is a macrophage-derived enzyme belonging to the phospholipase A2 superfamily, is involved in the metabolism of LDL in arterial walls, and is responsible for the release of inflammatory mediators from the vessel wall. Lp-PLA2 plays a significant role in atherogenesis; its inhibition blocks enzyme activity in plasma and within atherosclerotic plaques, thus reducing progression of atherosclerosis. [55] Epidemiological studies demonstrate that relatively high levels of Lp-PLA2 are associated with an increased risk of incident ischemic stroke, independent of hsCRP levels.[56]

In a prospective case–cohort study of 12,762 apparently healthy, middle-aged men and women in the Atherosclerosis Risk in Communities study, during 6 years of follow-up, 194 persons experienced an incident ischemic stroke. After adjusting for traditional stroke risk factors, the highest tertile of Lp-PLA2 concentration was associated with an increased risk of stroke (HR, 2.04; 95% CI, 1.23–3.38, $p < 0.01$). Both Lp-PLA2 and CRP levels in the highest category were also associated with increased stroke risk (HR, 1.91; 95% CI, 1.15–3.18; $p = 0.01$; and HR, 1.87; 95% CI, 1.13–3.10; $p = 0.02$, respectively).[56]

In the Northern Manhattan Stroke study, a population-based study of stroke risk factors, of 467 patients with first ischemic stroke, the authors examined whether levels of hsCRP and Lp-PLA2 predict risk of stroke recurrence, other vascular events, and death. Blood was collected at the time of hospital admission within 72 hours of stroke onset in 391 patients (83.7%) and within 6 days in 420 patients (90.0%). hsCRP, but not Lp-PLA2, was associated with stroke severity. After adjusting for traditional stroke risk factors and hsCRP level, compared with the lowest quartile of Lp-PLA2, those in the highest quartile had an increased risk of recurrent stroke (HR, 2.08; 95% CI, 1.04–4.18) whereas persons with an elevated hsCRP level did not.[57] Subsequently, Elkind et al.[58] demonstrated that hsCRP and Lp-PLA2 measurements collected soon after stroke and myocardial infarction were not reflective of prestroke levels and might be less reliable for long-term risk stratification as a result of the diurnal and acute-phase variability of these biomarkers. Nevertheless, in 2005, the Food and Drug Administration approved the use of Lp-PLA2 for long-term risk prognostication in persons with coronary heart disease or stroke.[58,59]

Current recommendations from the AHA on primary stroke prevention recommends that routine assessment of inflammatory markers such as hsCRP or Lp-PLA2 in patients without cerebrovascular disease be considered to identify patients who might be at increased risk of stroke, although their effectiveness (i.e., usefulness in routine clinical practice) is not well established (class IIb, level of evidence B). Although data remain insufficient to recommend routine use of hsCRP and Lp-PLA2 as additional markers to help determine which stroke patients should be started on statins, such decisions could be based on the Centers for Disease Control and Prevention/AHA guidelines until further data are available.[60]

Biomarkers of Coagulation Pathways

FIBRINOGEN

Fibrinogen is an acute-phase reactant involved in hemostasis and maintenance of blood viscosity. There are 40 different assays to measure fibrinogen, and there are unlimited variations in levels between laboratories; thus, standardization of the assays is important and somewhat lacking.[61]

Nevertheless, several prospective epidemiological studies and recently published meta-analyses recognized strong, independent association between elevated fibrinogen levels and the risk of stroke in individuals with or without a history of prior ischemic event.[62–64]

In a meta-analysis of 154,211 participants in 31 prospective studies, during 1.38 million person-years of follow-up, there were 6944 first nonfatal myocardial infarctions or stroke events and 13,210 deaths. The adjusted HR per 1-g/L increase in fibrinogen level for stroke was 1.75 (95% CI, 1.55–1.98). The association of fibrinogen level with stroke in patients without preexisting cardiovascular disease did not change based on sex, smoking, blood pressure, or blood lipid levels.[64] However, a causal relationship of high fibrinogen levels and stroke risk remains unclear. Only two genetic variants that affect the levels of fibrinogen are related to the risk for ischemic stroke, and a recent Mendelian randomization study suggested that elevations in fibrinogen levels may be consequent to and not causal for atherosclerosis, although this does not rule out the possibility of secondary injury from the elevated fibrinogen levels.[65]

The fibrate class of medications could lower fibrinogen levels. In the large cohort of the Data from an Epidemiological Study on the Insulin Resistance Syndrome study, authors examined the change in fibrinogen concentrations at 3 years of follow-up between individuals who started fibrate (n = 126) or statin (n = 127) treatment during the follow-up and individuals (n = 3906) who were not on treatment during this period. After adjustment for baseline fibrinogen level, age, and sex, and changes in total cholesterol, triglycerides, and alcohol intake, fibrinogen concentration decreased after fibrate treatment, but increased after statin treatment and in those not using lipid-lowering drugs (−0.07 ± 0.54 g/L vs. 0.10 ± 0.54 g/L vs. 0.08 ± 0.52 g/L, respectively; p = 0.01).[66] However, lowering fibrinogen with bezafibrate did not show an effect on reducing stroke risk or even stroke recurrence.[67,68]

Based on these data, use of fibrinogen levels for risk stratification of patients with or without prior cardiovascular disease is not routinely recommended.

Biomarkers of Hemodynamic Stress

BRAIN NATRIURETIC PEPTIDE

B-type or brain natriuretic peptide (BNP) is a natriuretic peptide with strong vasodilatory activities. During hemodynamic stress, BNP is released by cardiomyocytes.[69] As a result of myocardial fibrosis and cardiac hypertrophy, and change in renal function in otherwise healthy elderly persons, BNP levels may be elevated in the older population. BNP levels are used widely in risk stratification of acute coronary syndrome, and are recognized as a strong diagnostic and prognostic marker in patients with chronic congestive heart failure.[70] Elevated levels of BNP are usually observed in individuals with hypertension, left ventricular hypertrophy, diastolic dysfunction, atrial fibrillation, and renal dysfunction.[69] Several population and hospital-based studies observed an association between high BNP levels and the risk of cardioembolic stroke, stroke outcomes, and long-term mortality.

In community-based study of a Japanese population (n = 13,466), during a mean follow-up of 2.8 years, 102 participants (65 males) experienced a first ischemic stroke. In analysis adjusted for traditional stroke risk factors, risk for ischemic stroke was significantly greater in the highest plasma BNP quartile (HR, 2.38; 95% CI, 1.07–5.29), but only for men.[71] In a hospital-based sample of patients (n = 99) with an acute ischemic stroke, after excluding 23 patients with valve disease, heart failure, myocardial infarction, or chronic renal failure, the authors measured BNP levels, ratio of peak early filling velocity to peak atrial systolic velocity, left atrial diameter, and the left atrial appendage flow to examine which of the four measurements was predictive of cardioembolic stroke. Thirty-six patients were diagnosed with cardioembolic stroke. In adjusted analysis, BNP levels and left atrial appendage flow predicted cardioembolic stroke with more than 95% accuracy.[72] Similarly, Montaner et al.[73] examined the diagnostic value of a panel of biochemical markers to differentiate stroke etiologies in acute stroke patients (n = 707). In addition to D-dimer and soluble receptor for advanced glycation end products, high levels of BNP were observed in patients with cardioembolic stroke (p < 0.0001). More important, in addition to atrial fibrillation, a BNP level of more than 76 pg/mL was an independent predictor of cardioembolic stroke, with an OR of 2.3 (95% CI, 1.4–3.7; p = 0.001).[73] Similarly, in patients with cryptogenic stroke, elevated BNP levels (≥360 pg/mL) on admission were highly predictive of development of atrial fibrillation even at 2 years of follow-up (OR, 5.70; 95% CI, 1.11–29.29; p = 0.037), suggesting the initial event may have been cardioembolic.[74]

In a large, prospective hospital-based study, Rost et al.[75] observed that serum levels of BNP were also highly correlated with mortality and long-term functional outcomes (based on the modified Rankin Scale [mRS]) after cardioembolic stroke. Of 569 patients with ischemic stroke (mean age, 67.9 ± 15 years; 46% female), elevated BNP was associated with poor functional outcome (OR, 0.64; 95% CI, 0.41–0.98) and with higher odds of mortality (OR, 1.75; 95% CI, 1.36–2.24). Addition of BNP to multivariate models improved predictive power for functional outcome (p = 0.013) and mortality (p < 0.03) after cardioembolic stroke.

In 3127 stroke-free Framingham offspring (mean age, 59 ± 10 years; 54% female), a panel of eight biomarkers—hsCRP, D-dimer, plasminogen activator inhibitor 1, aldosterone-to-renin ratio, BNP,—tHcy and urinary albumin-to-creatinine ratio were measured and related to risk of stroke/TIA after a median follow-up of 9.2 years. In a backward elimination analysis, higher BNP levels were associated with increased risk of stroke/TIA (HR, 1.39/1-SD increment; $p = 0.002$), and BNP also improved risk prediction when added to a model with the Framingham Stroke Risk Profile alone (Net reclassification index-NRI, 0.109; $p = 0.037$).[76]

Clearly, serum BNP added statistically significant advantage above and beyond the prognostic value of models built using clinical data alone, but further studies are required to validate the value of BNP as a predictor of cardioembolic stroke (vs. other subtypes), functional outcomes, and mortality after stroke.

Biomarkers of Cellular Injury

MATRIX METALLOPROTEINASE 9

Matrix metalloproteinases (MMPs) are a family of zinc- and calcium-dependent endopeptidases involved in the degradation of extracellular matrix proteins, tissue remodeling, inflammation, and angiogenesis. MMPs are regulated by cytokines, chemokines, and growth factors, and are highly destructive when involved in inflammatory processes.[77]

Of all MMPs, plasma levels of MMP-9 have been studied the most in association with acute stroke. Cerebral tissue expression of MMP-9 is normally minimal to undetectable, but plasma levels of MMP-9 are often elevated after acute stroke (ischemic and hemorrhagic) in humans.[78–80] After vascular brain injury, overexpression of MMP-9 and its activity mediates proteolysis and leads to blood–brain barrier leakage and cell death as a result of the destruction of extracellular matrix proteins.[81]

Montaner et al.[79] measured plasma MMP-2 and MMP-9 levels in 39 patients with cardioembolic strokes not treated with tissue plasminogen activator (tPA) to examine the relation of MMPs to infarct volume and risk for hemorrhagic transformation. MMP-9 peaked at admission (<12 hours from onset) and correlated with stroke severity (on the National Institutes of Health Stroke Severity [NIHSS] scale) and infarct volume on computed tomography (CT) at 48 hours. In the same sample, after adjusting for hypertension and lack of vessel recanalization, baseline MMP-9 levels were related to late hemorrhagic transformation (OR, 9; 95% CI, 1.46–55.24; $p = 0.010$).[79]

In 24 patients with acute middle cerebral artery infarction, plasma MMP-9 levels measured on admission/before intravenous tPA therapy were correlated highly with infarct volume as measured with diffusion-weighted MRI ($r = 0.54$, $p = 0.05$). MMP-9 level was also an independent predictor of the lesion growth at 24 hours after thrombolytic therapy (OR, 14; 95% CI, 1.5–131; $p = 0.019$) as assessed on diffusion-weighted MRI.[82]

Serial MMP-2 and MMP-9 measurements obtained in 41 patients with acute stroke who received tPA within 3 hours of stroke onset demonstrated MMP-9 levels to be highest among patients who subsequently developed a parenchymal hematoma when compared with those with or without hemorrhagic infarction. An MMP-9-level threshold of 191.3 ng/mL had a positive predictive value of 67% and a negative predictive value of 100% for subsequent hematoma development. In regression analysis, early (<3 hours) MMP-9 levels were independent predictors of subsequent parenchymal hematoma (OR, 9.62; 95% CI, 1.3–70.3)[83]

Therefore, plasma MMP-9 concentrations measured in an acute stroke setting may predict infarct size and further infarct growth; but, more important, MMP-9 may identify patients who are more likely to develop intracranial hematomas after thrombolytic therapy. Further large-scale research studies are needed to validate utility of MMP-9 as a marker for tPA risk stratification in acute ischemic stroke.

Lipoproteins and Lipid-Related Biomarkers

Numerous studies report inconsistent relationships between lipids and the risk of stroke likely attributable to methodological and sample differences between the studies.[84–94] Several studies found an increased risk of stroke with higher total cholesterol (TC) and lower high-density lipoprotein–cholesterol (HDL-C).[84–88] A large, prospective study from Finland (n = 58,235), during a mean follow-up of 20.1 years, observed 3914 stroke events. In the multivariable-adjusted analysis at different levels of TC (<5 mm/L [reference], 5–5.9 mmol/L, 6–6.9 mmol/L, ≥7.0 mmol/L), HRs were 1.00, 1.05, 1.16, and 1.22 for total stroke (p = 0.036) and 1.00, 1.06, 1.19, and 1.27 for ischemic stroke (p = 0.02) in men. Low levels of HDL-C and a high TC/HDL-C ratio were associated with increased risks of total and ischemic stroke in both men and women, but after further adjustment for body mass index, blood pressure, and history of diabetes, this association diminished for men.[88] The Cardiovascular Health Study found a similar association in men,[92] whereas in the Framingham study, likely as a result of fewer stroke events, only a weak association between HDL-C and stroke was noted.[89] The mechanisms behind this association are complex. Nevertheless, as a strong antiatherogenic lipid molecule with anti-inflammatory properties, HDL-C was established to be more protective for atherosclerotic stroke subtypes.[84–86,95,96]

TC/HDL-C, a ratio between atherogenic and antiatherogenic lipid molecules, is a more potent predictor of cerebrovascular disease than TC, LDL-C, or HDL-C alone,[97,98] but only a few studies have assessed an association between the TC/HDL-C ratio and risk of ischemic stroke.[87,88] In the previously mentioned Finish population, a high TC/HDL-C ratio was associated with increased risk of total and ischemic stroke in both men and women.[88] In the prospective Women's Health Study, of 27,937 U.S. women aged 45 or older, during 11 years of follow-up, 282 ischemic strokes occurred. And in the multivariable-adjusted analysis, HR (95% CI; p value for trend across mean quintile TC/HDL-C ratio values) for ischemic stroke was 1.65 (1.06–2.58; p = 0.02).[87] Therefore, the role of TC/HDL-C definitely deserves further attention in studies evaluating its clinical utility in stratification of patients at risk for ischemic stroke.

Recently, more attention has been give to the relation between nonfasting triglyceride (TG) and risk of ischemic stroke.[94,96] Of 13,956 Copenhagen City Heart Study participants (mean age, 56.5 years), 1529 developed ischemic stroke. Cumulative incidence of ischemic stroke increased with increasing levels of nonfasting TG (log-rank trend, p < 0.001). In multivariate adjusted analysis, men with elevated nonfasting TG levels of 89 to 176 mg/dL had increased risk of stroke, with an HR of 1.3 (95% CI, 0.8–1.9), and for nonfasting TG ≥443 mg/dL, risk was doubled, with an HR of 2.5 (95% CI, 1.3–4.8; 41 events) versus men with nonfasting levels less than 89 mg/dL (HR, 1.0; p < 0.001 for trend). In women, HRs were 1.3 (95% CI, 0.9–1.7) and 3.8 (95% CI, 1.3–11), respectively, versus women with nonfasting TG levels less than 89 mg/dL (HR, 1.0; p < 0.001 for trend). Absolute 10-year risk of ischemic stroke ranged from 2.6% in men younger than 55 years with nonfasting TG levels less than 89 mg/dL to 16.7% in men aged 55 years or older with levels ≥443 mg/dL.[94] The Women's Health Study corroborated the findings of a strong association between elevated nonfasting TG levels and ischemic stroke.[99]

LDL-C, which is highly correlated with TC concentration, is less consistently associated with ischemic stroke.[87,90] Nevertheless, large clinical trials have shown that statin therapy, which through its pleiotropic properties lowers LDL-C levels, also reduced the risk of ischemic stroke in patients with prior stroke/TIA or in high-risk populations.[100] Thus, the underlying mechanism of the previously mentioned associations in primary and secondary stroke prevention remains a subject of great interest for risk stratification in stroke prevention.

New guidelines released by the AHA and the American College of Cardiology have change the standards for who should be taking cholesterol-lowering medications. The panel of experts advises on assessing the overall risk and not focusing on the lipid marker values. Thus, the new guidelines identify four groups of the primary and secondary prevention patients in whom clinicians should focus on the reduction the clinical events, and—based on the individual risk—make recommendations regarding the appropriate "intensity" of statin therapy to achieve relative reductions in LDL cholesterol.[101]

LIPOPROTEIN(A)

Lipoprotein(a) [Lp(a)] is analogous to LDL and is identified by the presence of an additional highly glycosylated protein called *apolipoprotein(a)* that might enhance or inhibit fibrinolysis. However, plasma Lp(a) levels are poorly associated with lipids or fibrinogen levels. Therefore, the mechanism whereby it exerts an influence on vascular pathology remains uncertain. A recent meta-analysis of 31 observational studies including 56,010 subjects with more than 4609 stroke events examined the association of Lp(a) levels with risk of stroke. Unadjusted mean Lp(a) was greater in stroke patients (OR, 2.39; 95% CI, 1.57–3.63), and Lp(a) levels were also more frequently abnormally elevated (defined as Lp(a) levels ≥30 mg/L).[102]

Sensitivity analysis and meta-regression analysis did not find any influence of study design, stroke subtype, age, and sex to explain the substantial heterogeneity between studies ($I^2 = 83.7\%$, $p < 0.001$).

In prospective cohort studies ($n = 5$, >1645 strokes), patients in the highest tertile of Lp(a) distribution versus the lowest tertile had greater risk of stroke (RR, 1.22; 95% CI, 1.04–1.43). There was no publication bias or heterogeneity in the prospective studies ($I^2 = 0.00\%$, $p = 0.67$). In nested case–control studies ($n = 3364$ strokes) Lp(a) was found not to be a risk factor for incident stroke (OR, 1.04; 95% CI, 0.6–1.8).[102] Despite these interesting findings, further large sample studies are needed to examine the strength and independence of the association between Lp(a) and risk for ischemic stroke, and its value as a clinical biomarker.

Growth Factors and Neurotrophins

BRAIN-DERIVED NEUROTROPHIC FACTOR

Brain-derived neurotrophic factor (BDNF) is a major neurotrophin that facilitates neuronal repair by promoting neurogenesis and angiogenesis. BDNF controls differentiation and survival of neurons by binding to its high-affinity tyrosine kinase receptor B.[103] Both BDNF and tyrosine kinase receptor B are widely distributed throughout the brain, but they have also been expressed in nonneuronal cell types such as vascular endothelial cells, activated lymphocytes, vascular smooth muscle cells, and platelets.[104] BDNF may mediate resistance to ischemic injury (neuroprotection).[105] BDNF crosses the blood–brain barrier, and its circulating concentrations are measurable. In a general population study, mean levels remained constant over much of the adult life span, with a gradual decline after age 80.[106]

Low serum BDNF concentrations have been observed in patients with coronary artery disease, type 2 diabetes mellitus, metabolic syndrome, acute coronary syndrome,[107] and physical inactivity[108]—all risk factors associated with cerebrovascular disease.

In 3440 stroke-/TIA-free Framingham study participants (mean age, 65 ± 11 years; 56% women), lower baseline BDNF concentrations were associated with an increased risk of incident stroke/TIA (adjusted HR comparing BDNF Q1 vs. Q2–Q4, 1.47; 95% CI, 1.09–2.00; $p = 0.012$). More important, in reclassification analyses, BDNF when added to a risk assessment model based on traditional stroke risk factors alone (as identified by the Framingham Stroke Risk Profile) resulted in significant improvement of stroke/TIA risk prediction.[109]

In a primate model of lacunar stroke, enhanced production of BDNF was observed in activated glial cells in the white matter ipsilateral to the injury that contributed to tissue repair and regeneration.[110] Therefore, increased expression of BDNF occurring in response to ischemic damage might contribute to "spontaneous" recovery of function in that tissue.[105] In experimental studies, atorvastatin and candesartan appear to be associated with better outcomes after cerebral ischemia as well as induction of BDNF expression.[105,111,112] Yanamoto et al.[113] observed relative resistance to stroke for up to 14 days after the direct intracerebral infusion of recombinant BDNF into the neocortex of experimental animals.

Thus far, one population study has suggested some value for BDNF in stroke prediction, and animal studies have established a positive effect of BDNF on infarct size and on long-term potentiation, neuronal remodeling, and functional motor recovery after induction of an ischemic brain lesion. Therefore, BDNF could have an effect on cerebrovascular disease through its neurotrophic effect or its vascular effect. Further studies are required to confirm whether BDNF will be a useful clinical marker of stroke risk or will help in the prognostication of stroke-related outcomes.

VASCULAR ENDOTHELIAL GROWTH FACTOR

Vascular endothelial growth factor (VEGF) is a vascular permeability factor and specific growth and survival factor for endothelial cells. It promotes vasculogenesis and angiogenesis in physiological and pathophysiological states. VEGF stimulates the synthesis of NO, improves vascular permeability, and stimulates cell growth.[114,115] Biological function of VEGF is mediated via its high-affinity tyrosine kinase receptors; and both (VEGF and its receptors) are expressed not only in vascular tissue, but also in capillary-rich areas of neurons and astrocytes.[114] Experimental data have shown that VEGF and its receptors are upregulated in both neurones and blood vessels in the penumbra after transient or permanent occlusion of the middle cerebral artery.[116] A trophic role of VEGF on neurons has been demonstrated in angiogenesis, neurogenesis, cell survival, and neuronal migration. Thus, under hypoxic and ischemic conditions, VEGF may directly (via inhibition of programmed cell death) or indirectly (via stimulation of angiogenesis, enhancement of blood flow and endothelial permeability, and antioxidant activation) mediate neuroprotective and neuroregenerative effects on neurons.[114,117]

Slevin et al.[118] performed serial measurements of serum VEGF levels (measured on days 0, 1, 3, 7, and 14) in 29 patients with acute ischemic stroke and examined their relationship to stroke subtype and lesion volume. The highest expression of VEGF occurred at day 7 (588 ± 121 pg/mL; $p = 0.005$), and the levels remained significantly elevated at 14 days after stroke. Expression of VEGF correlated with infarct volume, clinical disability (Scandinavian Stroke Scale), and peripheral leukocytosis, and was significantly greater in patients with atherothrombotic large-vessel disease ($p < 0.05$).[118] Subsequently, Lee et al.[119] investigated whether serum VEGF levels in patients with acute ischemic stroke ($n = 188$) with small-vessel disease ($n = 89$; mean age, 63 years; 46% men) and with large-vessel disease ($n = 91$; mean age, 61 years; 47% men) would correlate with long-term prognosis based on the NIHSS scale measured at 24 hours after admission and at 3 months of follow-up. Serum VEGF levels measured within 24 hours of stroke onset were significantly greater in patients with large-vessel disease compared with those with small-vessel infarct. In analysis adjusted for vascular risk factors, higher VEGF levels were correlated with infarct volume ($p = 0.047$). Higher serum VEGF levels in the acute stage were also proportional to an improved NIHSS scale score after 3 months (adjusted OR, 1.57; $p = 0.034$).[119] Interestingly, in a small hospital-based study of 44 patients with suspected ischemic stroke, serum VEGF levels measured on admission and daily for six subsequent days demonstrated a significant increase in VEGF level on the day of symptom onset and at all other time points when compared with healthy control subjects ($p < 0.01$). However, VEGF levels were also elevated in patients with stroke mimics. Therefore, the sensitivity and specificity for diagnosing ischemic stroke with elevated VEGF levels in acute settings was low: 69% and 73%, respectively.[120]

Although circulating VEGF levels are highly heritable,[121] elevated circulating VEGF concentrations were also seen in patients with hypertension, coronary artery disease, type 2 diabetes mellitus, smoking, and obesity.[122] In 3440 stroke-/TIA-free Framingham Heart Study participants (mean age, 65 ± 11 years; 56% women), baseline serum VEGF levels were related to risk of incident stroke/TIA. In analysis adjusted for traditional stroke risk factors, higher serum VEGF levels were associated with an increased risk of stroke/TIA (HR, 1.21/SD increase in VEGF; 95% CI, 1.04–1.40, $p = 0.012$) or stroke alone (HR, 1.23/SD; 95% CI, 1.05–1.46; $p = 0.013$). As mentioned previously for BDNF, the same study observed that BDNF and VEGF levels alone and in combination, when added to a risk assessment model based on traditional stroke risk factors alone (as identified by the Framingham Stroke Risk Profile), resulted in significant improvement of risk prediction (NRI for BDNF Q1 vs. Q2–4, 0.199; 95% CI, 0.023–0.384; NRI for VEGF, 0.234; 95% CI, 0.067–0.401; and NRI for BDNF + VEGF, 0.274; 95% CI, 0.090–0.449).[109] Based on these findings, VEGF along with BDNF represents novel a risk marker that may improve stratification of patients at risk for stroke/TIA; however, further studies are required to support more widespread clinical use of VEGF levels.

Insulin-like Growth Factor 1

Insulin-like growth factor 1 (IGF-1) is a single-chain polypeptide that has structural similarity to proinsulin. It has short-term metabolic and long-term growth factorlike effects on proliferation and differentiation of endothelial cells, neurons, and glial cells during embryonic and postnatal cell development.[123] In plasma and tissue, IGFs are known to associate with specific binding proteins (IGFBPs1–6). The IGFBPs, and in particular IGFBP-3, are known to regulate the bioactivity and release of IGF-1, but also its high affinity to IGF-1 receptor, which is present on practically every cell type.[124] IGF-1 is widely expressed in the brain and it is recognized as a survival factor for both sensory and motor neurons. IGF-1 also modulates brain plasticity by influencing neurite outgrowth, synaptogenesis, neuronal excitability, and neurotransmitter release, and may influence recovery from ischemic brain injury.[125]

Most of the circulating IGF-1 is found in a 150-kDa complex with IGFBP-3. IGF-1 levels in the blood have a wide normal range from 10 to 1000 ng/mL. IGF-1 levels decrease with age, but also with decline in physical functioning, and in persons with atherosclerosis and type 2 diabetes.[126]

Several epidemiological studies have suggested an inverse relationship between plasma IGF-1 levels and risk of stroke. In a prospective, nested case–control study within a Danish follow-up study ("Diet, Cancer, Health") including 57,053 women and men (mean age, 60 years; 61% men), Johnsen et al.[127] examined baseline circulating IGF-1 (mean, 107.1 μg/L) and IGFBP-3 (mean, 3966 μg/L) levels and their association with incident ischemic stroke. During a median follow-up of 3.1 years, there were 266 participants who developed ischemic stroke. When compared with the top two quartiles, participants in the bottom two quartiles of IGF-1 and IGFBP-3 levels were found to have increased risk of ischemic stroke (adjusted OR, 2.06; 95% CI, 1.05–4.03; and OR, 2.29; 95% CI, 1.17–4.49, respectively).[127]

In a case–cohort analysis of older adults (mean age, 73 years) in the Cardiovascular Health Study, during a mean follow-up of 5.6 years, 370 participants experienced incident ischemic stroke, but the authors found no association between circulating levels of IGF-1 and risk of incident ischemic stroke, whereas low IGFBP-3 levels were associated with increased risk of incident coronary events ($p = 0.05$). Although limited by different study designs, it is unclear whether the observed discrepancies in study results could be the result of an effect modification by age of the association between IGF-1 and IGFBP-3 levels and ischemic stroke.[128]

A small case–control study of elderly subjects (mean age, 83 ± 7.4 years; 34% men) admitted with acute ischemic stroke to a geriatric unit found that older subjects with stroke had lower IGF-1 and IGFBP-3 levels then their age- and sex-matched control subjects. The elderly patients with ischemic stroke and lower IGF-1 levels were observed to have poor outcomes (HR for death at 6 months for each 20-ng/mL increase in IGF-1 levels was 0.7; 95% CI, 0.5–0.9).[129]

Recent observations from the Rotterdam study indicated that such associations could be causative. van Rijn et al.[130] examined the relationship between the presence of a 192-bp allele in the IGF-1 promoter region and survival after stroke. They found that noncarriers who also had low plasma IGF-1 levels were at greater mortality risk after stroke compared with gene carriers. Noncarriers had an RR of 0.7 (95% CI, 0.5–1.0) for ischemic stroke, and the RR of death after an ischemic stroke was 1.5 (95% CI, 0.9–2.6).[130]

Interestingly, intravenous tPA treatment in the patients with stroke was shown to increase free serum IGF-1 levels transiently by almost 70%, suggesting that a neuroprotective effect of tPA may be based in part on a neuroprotective effect of IGF-1.[131] Multiple experimental studies of different models of hypoxic or ischemic brain injury have shown a neuroprotective role for IGF-1. Several experimental studies evaluated the effect of exogenous IGF-1 after induction of transient or permanent middle cerebral artery occlusion at 60 minutes or 120 minutes in animal models of stroke. Mode of administration of IGF-1 was different across the studies—from topical IGF-1 applied at the cerebral cortex to intracerebroventricular and intranasal to intravenous. However, all the studies found that, if given within 1 hour or multiple times within 24 hours, the animals receiving IGF-1 had reduced infarct volumes, increased cell survival, improved functional outcomes, and enhanced neurogenesis and neovasculariazation.[132] Despite such convincing findings on its neuroprotective effect, the role of IGF-1 in humans needs to be further clarified prior to its testing in clinical trials. Clearly, IGF-1 shows a promising role in modifying ischemic stroke pathophysiology, but more studies are needed for a better understanding of the role of IGF-1 in risk stratification and stroke outcomes.

Growth Differentiation Factor 15

Growth differentiation factor 15 (GDF-15) is a novel, distant member of the transforming growth factor-β superfamily that is activated in acute-phase responses through a currently unknown receptor. Experimental studies have demonstrated upregulated expression of GDF-15 in atherosclerosis, and have noted that GDF-15 deletion has beneficial effects in early and later atherosclerosis.[133] GDF-15 is widely distributed in the brain and peripheral nervous system.[134] In a mouse model of cerebral ischemia, GDF-15 was highly upregulated after experimental ischemic brain injury.[135]

Worthmann et al.[136] explored an association between circulating levels of GDF-15 and neurological outcome (measured by the mRS) in patients with acute ischemic stroke or TIA. Serial blood samples were measured between 6 hours and 7 days after symptom onset in 57 consecutive patients with acute ischemic stroke ($n = 51$) or TIA ($n = 6$). Six hours after symptom onset, GDF-15 levels were abnormally high (>1200 ng/L) in 68% of the patients, but over the course of 7 days, the levels declined by 8% ($p < 0.001$). Patients with stroke and an mRS score of more than 1 point at 7 days or 90 days had higher circulating levels of GDF-15 at all time points compared with patients with an mRS score of 0 point or 1 point ($p \leq 0.002$). In adjusted analysis, GDF-15 levels measured between 6 hours and 7 days after symptom onset were associated with the mRS at 7 days and 90 days such that patients with higher levels of GDF-15 had poorer functional outcomes.[136]

In a larger sample of 264 patients with acute ischemic stroke (mean age, 70.3 ± 12.7 years; 55.3% male) serum GDF-15 levels were measured at 6 hours and 24 hours of symptom onset to examine its association with functional outcomes measured by the mRS. In adjusted analysis, serum GDF-15 levels were associated independently with an mRS score of ≥2 points after day 90 (OR, 1.03; 95% CI,

1.01–1.05, $p = 0.011$). GDF-15 levels increased with higher NIHSS tertiles ($p = 0.005$). More important, an addition of GDF-15 levels to stroke severity scores (NIHSS) in predicting functional outcomes at 90 days improved the model with modest effect (NRI, 0.044; $p = 0.541$).[137]

Thus far, GDF-15 is emerging as an important prognostic marker in individuals with and without existing cardiovascular disease. In a study of determinants of GDF-15 concentrations that included participants in the Framingham Offspring Study and participants in the Prospective Investigation of the Vasculature in Uppsala Seniors study, GDF-15 was associated positively with age, smoking, antihypertensive treatment, diabetes, kidney function, and use of nonsteroidal anti-inflammatory drugs, but associated negatively with TC and HDL-C. This study suggested that, apart from cardiovascular risk factors, genetic factors might also play an important role in determining circulating GDF-15 concentrations.[138] So, GDF-15 is a promising novel biomarker, and its role in predicting stroke risk and stroke outcomes requires further study.

Brain Tissue-Specific Biomarkers

GLIAL BIOMARKERS OF STROKE

S-100 Beta Protein

S-100 beta protein (S-100B) is an astroglial calcium-mediated protein present in high concentrations in glial and Schwann cells.[139] S-100B is recognized as a marker of generalized blood–brain barrier dysfunction, but also as a biomarker of primary brain injury, including injury consequent to a stroke.[140] S-100B is released into the CSF after neuronal damage. Its concentration in the CSF is much higher than in serum, but because of its excellent stability, serum S-100B protein levels have been studied in experimental and clinical stroke studies.[139]

In studies of experimental stroke, S-100B protein was found to be an excellent surrogate for estimating stroke volume, stroke severity, and long-term neurological outcome, as well as response to thrombolysis.[141,142] Studies demonstrated that serum S-100B concentrations increased significantly after stroke, with peak concentrations occurring within the first 24 hours after cerebral infarction, and subsequent normalization within 48 hours.[143] Missler et al.[144] measured plasma concentrations of S-100B protein on admission, and on days 3, 4, 7, and 14 in 44 patients with acute stroke (mean age, 65.1 years). S-100B protein was found to be a useful indicator of acute lesion volume on CT scan, as well as a marker of prognosis based on the Glasgow Outcome Scale 6 months after the acute event.[144] The National Institute of Neurological Disorders and Stroke (NINDS) tPA Study Group also confirmed association of higher initial S-100B levels with initial stroke severity and larger CT stroke lesion volumes. Higher 24-hour peak concentrations of S-100B were associated with higher NIHSS scores ($r = 0.263$, $p < 0.0001$) and with larger CT lesion volumes ($r = 0.239$, $p < 0.0001$). However, this group did not find an association with functional outcomes.[145]

Subsequent acute stroke studies observed that S-100B might be a useful surrogate of long-term stroke outcomes.[146,147] Foerch et al. measured S-100B concentrations at hospital admission and at 24, 48, 72, 96, 120, and 144 hours after stroke, and assessed functional outcome 6 months after stroke (using the mRS) in 39 patients (mean age, 69.1 years) with acute nonlacunar middle cerebral artery infarction presenting less than 6 hours after symptom onset. They found that a single S-100B value obtained between 48 hours and 72 hours after stroke onset was the best predictor of infarct volume and subsequent functional outcome.

However, elevated S-100B concentrations in the blood are not specific to cerebral infarcts alone. S-100B is also elevated after traumatic brain injury and in extracranial malignancies. More important, S-100B does not differentiate between ischemic and hemorrhagic stroke, and stroke mimics.[148] Thus, its use in clinical practice, although most promising for prognostication of stroke outcomes, remains to be determined in representative large-scale studies.

Glial Fibrillary Acidic Protein

Glial fibrillary acid protein (GFAP) is a monomeric filament protein specific to the brain astrocytes. Studies demonstrate increased serum GFAP concentrations in ischemic stroke patients versus control subjects, with peak concentrations occurring 2 to 4 days after acute symptom onset.[149,150] Herrmann et al.[150] performed a comparative analysis of serum concentrations of GFAP and protein S-100B in patients with acute stroke ($n = 37$) and suggested that postischemic release patterns of GFAP and S-100B protein may help understand the underlying pathophysiology of acute cerebral infarcts. The release of both astroglia-derived proteins varied between different subtypes of stroke such that GFAP was found to be a more sensitive marker of brain damage in patients with smaller lacunar lesions or minor strokes.[150]

In a pilot study assessing 135 stroke patients admitted within 6 hours after symptom onset, Foerch et al.[151] examined whether serum GFAP might help identify intracerebral hemorrhage (ICH) in patients with acute stroke. GFAP was detectable in the serum of 39 patients (34 of 42 [81%] with ICH, and 5 of 93 [5%] with ischemic stroke]. Serum GFAP was higher in patients with ICH (median, 11 ng/L; range, 0–3096 ng/L) compared with patients with ischemic stroke (median, 0 ng/L; range 0–14 ng/L; $p < 0.001$).[151] In a subsequent study, the authors observed that, for the first 24 hours after stroke, median GFAP values in patients with ischemic stroke remained below the detection limit, whereas between 2 hours and 6 hours of stroke onset, serum GFAP was significantly greater in patients with ICH compared with patients with ischemic stroke ($p < 0.001$). More important, 2 hours after stroke onset, serum GFAP values were correlated significantly with ICH volume ($r = 0.755$, $p = 0.007$).[152] Based on these findings, Foerch et al.[153] examined more recently the diagnostic accuracy of plasma GFAP for differentiating ICH versus ischemic stroke in patients with symptoms of acute stroke when a blood sample was collected within 4.5 hours of symptoms onset. They found that (a) GFAP concentrations were increased in patients with ICH compared with patients with ischemic stroke (median, 1.91 mug/L; interquartile range, 0.41–17.66 vs. median, 0.08 mug/L; interquartile range, 0.02–0.14; $p < 0.001$), (b) diagnostic accuracy of GFAP for differentiating ICH from ischemic stroke and stroke mimic was high (area under the curve, 0.915; 95% CI, 0.847–0.982; $p < 0.001$) and (c) a GFAP cutoff of 0.29 mug/L provided a diagnostic sensitivity of 84.2% and a diagnostic specificity of 96.3% for differentiating ICH from ischemic stroke and stroke mimics.[153,154]

The enzyme immunoassays currently available for GFAP measurements are not standardized. Therefore, more data are needed for this promising biomarker that might have a role in early stroke differential diagnosis.

Miscellaneous Biomarkers

PARK7 AND NUCLEOSIDE DIPHOSPHATE KINASE A

PARK7 (also called *DJ-1*) is a multifunction protein that plays a key role in transcriptional regulation and is a molecular chaperone. PARK7 has antioxidative stress and antiapoptotic properties and is highly expressed in reactive central nervous system astrocytes in persons with chronic neurodegenerative disorders such as Parkinson's disease and Alzheimer's disease. Studies have also shown strong immunoreactivity for DJ-1 within reactive astrocytes surrounding incidentally identified infarcts in patients with these neurodegenerative disorders.[155]

Nucleoside diphosphate kinases are ubiquitous and highly conserved enzymes crucial for the cellular homoeostasis of NTPs and nucleoside diphosphates. Nucleoside diphosphate kinase A (NDKA) is expressed in neurons and was found be involved in the ischemic cascade after acute stroke.

Allard et al.[156] recently demonstrated higher plasma PARK7 concentrations in stroke patients compared with control subjects ($p < 0.001$). They used enzyme-linked immunosorbent assay to measure PARK7 and NDKA in plasma in three independent European and North American retrospective studies with a total of 622 stroke patients and 165 control subjects. Increases in both biomarkers were significant, with sensitivities of 54% to 91% for PARK7 and 70% to 90% for NDKA, and specificities of 80% to 97% for PARK7 and 90% to 97% for NDKA. The concentrations of both biomarkers increased within 3 hours of stroke onset.[156] However, PARK7—alone or in combination with NDKA—could not differentiate patients with ischemic stroke from patients with hemorrhagic stroke. Further studies are needed to replicate these findings and clarify the utility of this biomarker.

NMDA RECEPTOR PEPTIDES AND ANTIBODIES

NMDA receptors are major excitatory neuroreceptors that regulate neuronal electrical signals. These receptors are located on the surface of cerebral microvessels and are upregulated by oxidative stress states.[157] NR2 peptide fragments are cleaved rapidly from the NMDA receptors by thrombin-activated serine proteases in acute cerebral ischemic injury.[158] Released into the bloodstream within minutes of onset of acute ischemia via the compromised blood–brain barrier, NR2 peptides remain detectable in the blood for at least 3 days after an event.[159]

In early clinical studies, of 105 patients with stroke or TIA and 255 control subjects NR2 antibodies were identified in significantly greater quantities in the patients with ischemic stroke and TIA compared with control subjects ($p < 0.0001$). At a cutoff point of 2.0 µg/L, test sensitivities for TIA and stroke were 95% and 97%, respectively, and positive predictive values were 86% and 91% for TIA or stroke within 3 hours of symptom onset. However, the assay could not differentiate between hemorrhagic and ischemic stroke in an acute setting, but only after 3 days.[160] Dambinova et al.[159] explored the value of NR2 antibodies in differentiating ischemic stroke from stroke mimics. A total of 192 patients with suspected stroke who presented within 72 hours of symptom onset were enrolled prospectively; clinical diagnosis of ischemic stroke was made in 101 of 192 persons (53%), with a diagnosis of no stroke in 91 subjects (47%). The comparison of NR2 peptide value changed in patients with acute ischemic stroke, and control groups (healthy individuals and persons with well-controlled vascular risk factors) yielded a statistically significant ($p < 0.0001$) increase of NR2 peptide values in persons with acute ischemic stroke. When the NR2 antibody cutoff was set at 1.0 µg/L, this resulted in a sensitivity of 92% and a specificity of 96% to detect ischemic stroke. However, some healthy individuals showed an increase in their NR2 peptide of 1.10 to 1.15 µg/mL.[159] NMDA receptor assays, especially assays measuring NR2 peptide, which is released early into the blood stream after acute ischemic cerebral injury, may prove to be valuable biomarkers to differentiate acute strokes from stroke mimics, but larger scale prospective studies are needed to determine their clinical value.

Multimarker Models

As demonstrated, the literature suggests that several serum biomarkers may be potential predictors for stroke risk stratification, stroke diagnosis, stroke subtype differentiation, or stroke outcome, but currently there are no known individual biomarkers that can be used routinely in these clinical settings.

Most of these biomarkers add only modestly to already existing predictive models; thus, novel techniques such as multimarker approaches to investigate the utility of existing biomarkers have been proposed for better prognostication. To be efficacious, multimarker panels must offer additive information for clinical diagnosis, must be inexpensive, and must be easy to use. They should improve the predictive accuracy of the best available model (representing the standard of care) that also incorporates several known predictors of disease including standard vascular risk factors and biomarkers.[161]

TABLE 22.1

Serum Biomarkers for Ischemic Stroke

Biomarker	Role in stroke pathogenesis	Studied in screening of patients at risk for stroke	Studied in diagnosing acute stroke	Studied in prognostication of stroke outcomes	Studied in clinical trials
Arterial susceptibility					
Endothelial	Endothelial apoptosis	+			+
dysfunction	Oxidative stress	+			
homocysteine	Inflammation				
ADMA	Neuronal injury				
	Endothelial dysfunction				
	Oxidative stress				
	Inflammation				
	Atherosclerotic processes				
Inflammation	Inflammation	+		+	+
C-reactive protein	Atherosclerotic	+			
Lp-PLA2	processes				
	Inflammation				
Atherosclerotic	All markers	+			+
processes	Formation of	+			
TC	atherosclerotic plaque	+			
HDL-C		+			
TC/HDL-C ratio		+			
Triglycerides		+			
LDL-C					
Lp(a)					
Cardiac dysfunction	Hemodynamic stress	+		+	
BNP	Cardiomyocyte damage				
Cell destruction	Inflammation		+	+	+
MMP-9	Degradation of EMPs				
	Angiogenesis				
Blood susceptibility					
Hypercoagulability	Impaired hemostasis	+			+
Fibrinogen	Increase blood	+			
D-Dimer	viscosity				
Fibrinolysis	Decreased fibrinolysis	+			
Dysfunction					
PAI-1					
Growth factors					
BDNF	Neuroprotection	+	+	+	
VEGF	Angiogenesis	+	+	+	
IGF-1	Neuroprotection	+	+	+	
GDF-15	Atherosclerosis	+			

(*continued*)

TABLE 22.1

Continued

Biomarker	Role in stroke pathogenesis	Studied in screening of patients at risk for stroke	Studied in diagnosing acute stroke	Studied in prognostication of stroke outcomes	Studied in clinical trials
Brain susceptibility					
S-100B	Glial damage	+	+	+	
GFAP	Glial damage		+	+	
Miscellaneous markers					
PARK7	Oxidative stress Apoptosis		+		
NDKA	Cellular homeostasis		+		
NMDA receptors	Cell damage		+		

ADMA, asymmetric dimethylarginine; BDNF, brain-derived neurotrophic factor; BNP, brain natriuretic peptide; EMP, Endothelial Microparticle Levels; GDF-15, growth differentiation factor 15; GFAP, glial fibrillary acid protein; HDL-C, high-density lipoprotein–cholesterol; IGF, insulinlike growth factor; LDL-C, low-density lipoprotein–cholesterol; Lp(a), lipoprotein a; Lp-PLA2, lipoprotein-associated phospholipase A2; MMP-9, matrix metalloproteinase 9; NDKA, nucleoside diphosphate kinase A; NMDA, N-methyl-D-aspartate; PARK7, Parkinson Protein 7; S-100B, S-100 beta protein; TC, total cholesterol; VEGF, vascular endothelial growth factor.

The simultaneous association of a biologically plausible panel of biomarkers with stroke/TIA risk was recently examined among 3127 stroke-free Framingham offspring participants (age, 59 ± 10 years; 54% women) as discussed earlier in the section on BNP. A panel of eight biomarkers assessing inflammation (hsCRP), hemostasis (D-dimer and plasminogen activator inhibitor 1), neurohormonal activity (aldosterone-to-renin ratio, BNP, and NTP natriuretic peptides), and endothelial function (tHcy and urinary albumin-to-creatinine ratio) was measured and, in multivariable regression analysis, was examined against the risk of stroke/TIA. During a median follow-up of 9.2 years, 130 participants experienced incident stroke/TIA. The biomarker panel was associated with incident stroke/TIA ($p < 0.05$). As mentioned earlier, in stepwise backward elimination analyses, higher BNP (HR, 1.39/ per 1-SD increment; $p = 0.002$) and urinary albumin-to-creatinine ratio (HR, 1.31/1-SD increment; $p = 0.004$) were associated with increased risk of stroke/TIA; but, more important, both biomarkers improved risk prediction compared with the Framingham Stroke Risk Profile alone (NRI, 0.109; $p = 0.04$).[76] Other statistical techniques such as machine learning are also being applied to identify a parsimonious set of biomarkers that best predict risk of stroke and outcomes after stroke.

Whether serum biomarkers might provide useful information to improve the prediction of outcome after acute ischemic stroke is unclear. Whiteley et al.,[162] in a systematic literature analysis, observed that no study was able to demonstrate that the biomarkers added predictive power to a validated clinical model. Frequent shortcomings of the reviewed studies were small study size, poor selection of the control population, unclear diagnostic cut points, lack of clinical validation of the proposed biomarkers, and choice of reference standard based on inadequate data. Laskowitz et al.,[163] in the Biomarker Rapid Assessment in Ischemic Injury study, examined a panel of biomarkers including D-dimer, CRP, BNP, MMP-9, and S-100B in a total of 1146 patients presenting with neurological symptoms consistent with possible stroke who were enrolled prospectively at 17 different sites. A separate cohort of 343 patients was enrolled independently to validate the multiple biomarker model approach. The multivariate model demonstrated modest discrimination, with an area under the receiver–operating characteristic curve of 0.76 for hemorrhagic stroke and 0.69 for all stroke ($p < 0.001$). When the threshold for the logistic model was set at the first quartile of the markers, this resulted in a sensitivity of 86% for detecting all stroke and a sensitivity of 94% for detecting hemorrhagic stroke, and a specificity to distinguish between stroke and stroke mimics was 37%. Thus, this set of biomarkers was not an optimal panel.[163]

More recently, the Prospective Epidemiological Study on Myocardial Infarction evaluated 14 biomarkers simultaneously from distinct biological pathways for risk prediction of ischemic stroke, including biomarkers of hemostasis, inflammation, and endothelial activation, chemokines, and adipocytokines. The Prospective Epidemiological Study on Myocardial Infarction had a cohort of 9771 healthy men 50 to 59 years of age who were monitored for 10 years for cardiovascular events. In a nested case–control study, 95 patients with ischemic stroke were matched with 190 control subjects. Of those, the authors evaluated the effect of 14 biomarkers on risk of ischemic stroke. In the multivariable analysis adjusted for traditional risk factors, fibrinogen (OR, 1.53; 95% CI, 1.03–2.28), E-selectin (OR, 1.76; 95% CI, 1.06–2.93), interferon-γ-inducible-protein 10 (OR, 1.72; 95% CI, 1.06–2.78), resistin (OR, 2.86; 95% CI, 1.30–6.27), and total adiponectin (OR, 1.82; 95% CI, 1.04–3.19) were associated significantly with ischemic stroke. However, adding E-selectin and resistin to a traditional risk factor model yielded a significant categorical net reclassification improvement of 29.9% ($p = 0.001$) and 28.4% ($p = 0.002$), respectively. Simultaneous inclusion of E-selectin and resistin to the traditional risk factor model increased the area under the receiver–operating characteristic curve to 0.824 (95% CI, 0.770–0.877) and resulted in a net reclassification improvement of 41.4% ($p < 0.001$).[164]

Although there is considerable potential for a panel of biologically plausible biomarkers within a multimarker panel to improve risk stratification and facilitate the initial triage process in acute stroke care, more work is required before such biomarkers can be introduced into routine clinical practice.

Omics Approach

Translational research in stroke holds promising potential because cerebrovascular disease is a complex disorder that manifests by multiple cell–cell interactions in the brain, but also by multiorgan interactions. An omic approach offers the use of targeted, high-throughput large-scale analysis of biological samples (blood, cells, tissue) with the most developed technologies being applied to genomics and proteomics discoveries in stroke research.[165] Omic approaches that are using genes, proteins, and metabolites as potential biomarkers in risk stratification, prediction, and diagnosis of stroke have been criticized for their poor reproducibility and labor-intense methodology that, as a result of large data sets, could produce "noise."[166] Therefore, the future of the omic approach will likely be based on a more meaningful understanding of gene expression achieved through the characterization of the products of that expression, such as RNAs and their regulation (messenger RNA and microRNA), and their respective proteins, which are the essential biological determinants of disease phenotype. Interestingly, the field of biomarkers has recently been enlarged by the availability of array technology to assess messenger RNA, microRNAs, and other newly discovered RNA species.[165] Several experimental and human studies have reported how altered profiles of RNA expression could explain various stroke pathophysiologies.[167,168] Although RNA is induced in minutes and well before a stroke event could be detected using protein markers, at the same time, RNA is unstable and degrades rapidly unless stabilized. As suggested by Sharp et al., developing point-of-care PCR may resolve this problem, but the omic approach is still far from ready for wide use in clinical practice.

System Biology Approach

A system biology approach to biomarker discovery consists of placing biomarkers from plausible pathways discovered with previous experimental analysis in the context of a network of biological interactions, such as gene–gene, gene–protein, or protein–protein interactions, followed by different guilt-by-association analyses.[169] The biological networks are designed from previously published interactions or from computational prediction models by a freely available network visualization tool for integrating biomolecular interaction networks with high-throughput expression data and other molecular states into a unified conceptual framework, such as Cytoscape Web.[170]

REFERENCES

1. Kaul S, Zadeh AA, Shah PK. Homocysteine hypothesis for atherothrombotic cardiovascular disease: not validated. *J Am Coll Cardiol.* 2006;48:914–923.
2. McCully KS. Chemical pathology of homocysteine: IV. Excitotoxicity, oxidative stress, endothelial dysfunction, and inflammation. *Ann Clin Lab Sci.* 2009;39:219–232.
3. Seshadri S. Beauty and the beast: B12, homocysteine, and the brain: a bemusing saga! *Neurology.* 2010;75:1402–1403.
4. Rasmussen K, Moller J. Total homocysteine measurement in clinical practice. *Ann Clin Biochem.* 2000;37:627–648.
5. Refsum H, Smith AD, Ueland PM, et al. Facts and recommendations about total homocysteine determinations: an expert opinion. *Clin Chem.* 2004;50:3–32.
6. Selhub J, Jacques PF, Rosenberg IH, et al. Serum total homocysteine concentrations in the third National Health and Nutrition Examination Survey (1991–1994): population reference ranges and contribution of vitamin status to high serum concentrations. *Ann Intern Med.* 1999;131:331–339.
7. McCully KS. Vascular pathology of homocysteinemia: implications for the pathogenesis of arteriosclerosis. *Am J Pathol* 1969;56:111–128.
8. Bellamy MF, McDowell IF, Ramsey MW, et al. Hyperhomocysteinemia after an oral methionine load acutely impairs endothelial function in healthy adults. *Circulation.* 1998;98:1848–1852.
9. Eikelboom JW, Hankey GJ, Anand SS, Lofthouse E, Staples N, Baker RI. Association between high homocyst(e)ine and ischemic stroke due to large- and small-artery disease but not other etiologic subtypes of ischemic stroke. *Stroke.* 2000;31:1069–1075.
10. Coppola A, Davi G, De Stefano V, Mancini FP, Cerbone AM, Di Minno G. Homocysteine, coagulation, platelet function, and thrombosis. *Semin Thromb Hemostat.* 2000;26:243–254.
11. Ay H, Arsava EM, Tokgozoglu SL, Ozer N, Saribas O. Hyperhomocysteinemia is associated with the presence of left atrial thrombus in stroke patients with nonvalvular atrial fibrillation. *Stroke.* 2003;34:909–912.
12. Jacques PF, Selhub J, Bostom AG, Wilson PW, Rosenberg IH. The effect of folic acid fortification on plasma folate and total homocysteine concentrations. *N Engl J Med.* 1999;340:1449–1454.
13. Bostom AG, Rosenberg IH, Silbershatz H, et al. Nonfasting plasma total homocysteine levels and stroke incidence in elderly persons: the Framingham study. *An Intern Med.* 1999;131:352–355.
14. Bots ML, Launer LJ, Lindemans J, et al. Homocysteine and short-term risk of myocardial infarction and stroke in the elderly: the Rotterdam study. *Arch Intern Med.* 1999;159:38–44.
15. Sacco RL, Anand K, Lee HS, et al. Homocysteine and the risk of ischemic stroke in a triethnic cohort: the Northern Manhattan Study. *Stroke.* 2004;35:2263–2269.
16. Kittner SJ, Giles WH, Macko RF, et al. Homocyst(e)ine and risk of cerebral infarction in a biracial population: the Stroke Prevention in Young Women study. *Stroke.* 1999;30:1554–1560.
17. Verhoef P, Hennekens CH, Malinow MR, Kok FJ, Willett WC, Stampfer MJ. A prospective study of plasma homocyst(e)ine and risk of ischemic stroke. *Stroke.* 1994;25:1924–1930.

18. Alfthan G, Pekkanen J, Jauhiainen M, et al. Relation of serum homocysteine and lipoprotein(a) concentrations to atherosclerotic disease in a prospective finnish population based study. *Atherosclerosis.* 1994;106:9–19.
19. Boysen G, Brander T, Christensen H, Gideon R, Truelsen T. Homocysteine and risk of recurrent stroke. *Stroke.* 2003;34:1258–1261.
20. Matsui T, Arai H, Yuzuriha T, et al. Elevated plasma homocysteine levels and risk of silent brain infarction in elderly people. *Stroke.* 2001;32:1116–1119.
21. Seshadri S, Wolf PA, Beiser AS, et al. Association of plasma total homocysteine levels with subclinical brain injury: cerebral volumes, white matter hyperintensity, and silent brain infarcts at volumetric magnetic resonance imaging in the Framingham Offspring Study. *Arch Neurol.* 2008;65:642–649.
22. Wright CB, Paik MC, Brown TR, et al. Total homocysteine is associated with white matter hyperintensity volume: the Northern Manhattan Study. *Stroke.* 2005;36:1207–1211.
23. Vermeer SE, van Dijk EJ, Koudstaal PJ, et al. Homocysteine, silent brain infarcts, and white matter lesions: the Rotterdam Scan Study. *Ann Neurol.* 2002;51:285–289.
24. Boushey CJ, Beresford SA, Omenn GS, Motulsky AG. A quantitative assessment of plasma homocysteine as a risk factor for vascular disease: probable benefits of increasing folic acid intakes. *JAMA.* 1995;274:1049–1057.
25. Ji Y, Tan S, Xu Y, et al. Vitamin B supplementation, homocysteine levels, and the risk of cerebrovascular disease: a meta-analysis. *Neurology.* 2013;81:1298–1307.
26. The VITATOPS Trial Study Group. B vitamins in patients with recent transient ischaemic attack or stroke in the Vitamins to Prevent Stroke (VITATOPS) trial: a randomised, double-blind, parallel, placebo-controlled trial. *Lancet Neurol.* 2010;9:855–865.
27. Toole JF, Malinow MR, Chambless LE, et al. Lowering homocysteine in patients with ischemic stroke to prevent recurrent stroke, myocardial infarction, and death: the Vitamin Intervention for Stroke Prevention (VISP) randomized controlled trial. *JAMA.* 2004;291:565–575.
28. Hankey GJ, Eikelboom JW, Yi Q, et al. Antiplatelet therapy and the effects of B vitamins in patients with previous stroke or transient ischaemic attack: a post-hoc subanalysis of VITATOPS, a randomised, placebo-controlled trial. *Lancet Neurol.* 2012;11:512–520.
29. Cavalieri M, Schmidt R, Chen C, et al. B vitamins and magnetic resonance imaging-detected ischemic brain lesions in patients with recent transient ischemic attack or stroke: the Vitamins to Prevent Stroke (VITATOPS) MRI-substudy. *Stroke.* 2012;43:3266–3270.
30. Hankey GJ, Ford AH, Yi Q, et al. Effect of B vitamins and lowering homocysteine on cognitive impairment in patients with previous stroke or transient ischemic attack: a prespecified secondary analysis of a randomized, placebo-controlled trial and meta-analysis. *Stroke.* 2013;44:2232–2239.
31. Lonn E, Yusuf S, Arnold MJ, et al. Homocysteine lowering with folic acid and B vitamins in vascular disease. *N Engl J Med.* 2006;354:1567–1577.
32. Spence JD. Perspective on the efficacy analysis of the Vitamin Intervention for Stroke Prevention trial. *Clin Chem Lab Med.* 2007;45:1582–1585.
33. Furie KL, Kasner SE, Adams RJ, et al. Guidelines for the prevention of stroke in patients with stroke or transient ischemic attack: a guideline for healthcare professionals from the American Heart Association/American Stroke Association. *Stroke.* 2011;42:227–276.
34. Cooke JP, Dzau VJ. Nitric oxide synthase: role in the genesis of vascular disease. *Annu Rev Med.* 1997;48:489–509.
35. Boger RH, Bode-Boger SM, Szuba A, et al. Asymmetric dimethylarginine (ADMA): a novel risk factor for endothelial dysfunction: its role in hypercholesterolemia. *Circulation.* 1998;98:1842–1847.
36. Lin KY, Ito A, Asagami T, et al. Impaired nitric oxide synthase pathway in diabetes mellitus: role of asymmetric dimethylarginine and dimethylarginine dimethylaminohydrolase. *Circulation.* 2002;106:987–992.

37. Surdacki A, Nowicki M, Sandmann J, et al. Reduced urinary excretion of nitric oxide metabolites and increased plasma levels of asymmetric dimethylarginine in men with essential hypertension. *J Cardiovasc Pharmacol.* 1999;33:652–658.
38. Abbasi F, Asagmi T, Cooke JP, et al. Plasma concentrations of asymmetric dimethylarginine are increased in patients with type 2 diabetes mellitus. *Am J Cardiol.* 2001;88:1201–1203.
39. Boger RH. Asymmetric dimethylarginine (ADMA) and cardiovascular disease: insights from prospective clinical trials. *Vasc Med.* 2005;10(Suppl 1):S19–S25.
40. Schnabel R, Blankenberg S, Lubos E, et al. Asymmetric dimethylarginine and the risk of cardiovascular events and death in patients with coronary artery disease: results from the Atherogene Study. *Circ Res.* 2005;97:e53–e59.
41. Yoo JH, Lee SC. Elevated levels of plasma homocyst(e)ine and asymmetric dimethylarginine in elderly patients with stroke. *Atherosclerosis.* 2001;158:425–430.
42. Wanby P, Teerlink T, Brudin L, et al. Asymmetric dimethylarginine (ADMA) as a risk marker for stroke and TIA in a Swedish population. *Atherosclerosis.* 2006;185:271–277.
43. Leong T, Zylberstein D, Graham I, et al. Asymmetric dimethylarginine independently predicts fatal and nonfatal myocardial infarction and stroke in women: 24-year follow-up of the Population Study of Women in Gothenburg. *Arterioscl Thromb Vasc Biol.* 2008;28:961–967.
44. Pikula A, Boger RH, Beiser AS, et al. Association of plasma ADMA levels with MRI markers of vascular brain injury: Framingham Offspring Study. *Stroke.* 2009;40:2959–2964.
45. Murray-Rust J, Leiper J, McAlister M, et al. Structural insights into the hydrolysis of cellular nitric oxide synthase inhibitors by dimethylarginine dimethylaminohydrolase. *Nat Struct Biol.* 2001;8:679–683.
46. Li J, Wilson A, Gao X, et al. Coordinated regulation of dimethylarginine dimethylaminohydrolase-1 and cationic amino acid transporter-1 by farnesoid X receptor in mouse liver and kidney and its implication in the control of blood levels of asymmetric dimethylarginine. *J Pharmacol Exp Ther.* 2009;331:234–243.
47. Casas JP, Shah T, Hingorani AD, Danesh J, Pepys MB. C-reactive protein and coronary heart disease: a critical review. *J Intern Med.* 2008;264:295–314.
48. Rost NS, Wolf PA, Kase CS, et al. Plasma concentration of C-reactive protein and risk of ischemic stroke and transient ischemic attack: the Framingham study. *Stroke.* 2001;32:2575–2579.
49. Ridker PM, Cushman M, Stampfer MJ, Tracy RP, Hennekens CH. Inflammation, aspirin, and the risk of cardiovascular disease in apparently healthy men. *N Engl J Med.* 1997;336:973–979.
50. Muir KW, Weir CJ, Alwan W, Squire IB, Lees KR. C-reactive protein and outcome after ischemic stroke. *Stroke.* 1999;30:981–985.
51. Winbeck K, Poppert H, Etgen T, Conrad B, Sander D. Prognostic relevance of early serial C-reactive protein measurements after first ischemic stroke. *Stroke.* 2002;33:2459–2464.
52. Ridker PM, Rifai N, Pfeffer MA, Sacks F, Braunwald E. Long-term effects of pravastatin on plasma concentration of c-reactive protein: the Cholesterol and Recurrent Events (CARE) investigators. *Circulation.* 1999;100:230–235.
53. Ridker PM, Danielson E, Fonseca FA, et al. Rosuvastatin to prevent vascular events in men and women with elevated C-reactive protein. *N Engl J Med.* 2008;359:2195–2207.
54. Amarenco P, Bogousslavsky J, Callahan A 3rd, et al. High-dose atorvastatin after stroke or transient ischemic attack. *N Engl J Med.* 2006;355:549–559.
55. Macphee CH, Nelson JJ, Zalewski A. Lipoprotein-associated phospholipase A2 as a target of therapy. *Curr Opin Lipidol.* 2005;16:442–446.
56. Ballantyne CM, Hoogeveen RC, Bang H, et al. Lipoprotein-associated phospholipase A2, high-sensitivity C-reactive protein, and risk for incident ischemic stroke in middle-aged men and women in the Atherosclerosis Risk in Communities (ARIC) study. *Arch Intern Med.* 2005;165:2479–2484.

57. Elkind MS, Tai W, Coates K, Paik MC, Sacco RL. High-sensitivity C-reactive protein, lipoprotein-associated phospholipase A2, and outcome after ischemic stroke. *Arch Intern Med.* 2006;166:2073–2080.
58. Elkind MS, Leon V, Moon YP, Paik MC, Sacco RL. High-sensitivity C-reactive protein and lipoprotein-associated phospholipase A2 stability before and after stroke and myocardial infarction. *Stroke.* 2009;40:3233–3237.
59. Gorelick PB. Lipoprotein-associated phospholipase A2 and risk of stroke. *Am J Cardiol.* 2008;101:34F–40F.
60. Pearson TA, Mensah GA, Alexander RW, et al. Markers of inflammation and cardiovascular disease: application to clinical and public health practice: a statement for healthcare professionals from the Centers for Disease Control and Prevention and the American Heart Association. *Circulation.* 2003;107:499–511.
61. Tousoulis D, Papageorgiou N, Androulakis E, Briasoulis A, Antoniades C, Stefanadis C. Fibrinogen and cardiovascular disease: genetics and biomarkers. *Blood Rev.* 2011;25:239–245.
62. Kannel WB, Wolf PA, Castelli WP, D'Agostino RB. Fibrinogen and risk of cardiovascular disease: the Framingham study. *JAMA.* 1987;258:1183–1186.
63. Lee AJ, Lowe GD, Woodward M, Tunstall-Pedoe H. Fibrinogen in relation to personal history of prevalent hypertension, diabetes, stroke, intermittent claudication, coronary heart disease, and family history: the Scottish Heart Health Study. *Br Heart J.* 1993;69:338–342.
64. Fibrinogen Studies Collaboration, Danesh J, Lewington S, et al. Plasma fibrinogen level and the risk of major cardiovascular diseases and nonvascular mortality: an individual participant meta-analysis. *JAMA.* 2005;294:1799–1809.

100 000 subjects identifies 23 fibrinogen-associated loci but no strong evidence of a causal association between circulating fibrinogen and cardiovascular disease" journalName="Circulation" vol="128">

65. Sabater-Lleal M, Huang J, Chasman D, et al. Multiethnic meta-analysis of genome-wide association studies in>100 000 subjects identifies 23 fibrinogen-associated loci but no strong evidence of a causal association between circulating fibrinogen and cardiovascular disease. *Circulation.* 2013;128:1310–1324.
66. Maison P, Mennen L, Sapinho D, et al. A pharmacoepidemiological assessment of the effect of statins and fibrates on fibrinogen concentration. *Atherosclerosis.* 2002;160:155–160.
67. Tanne D, Benderly M, Goldbourt U, et al. A prospective study of plasma fibrinogen levels and the risk of stroke among participants in the bezafibrate infarction prevention study. *Am J Med.* 2001;111:457–463.
68. Bezafibrate Infarction Prevention Study. Secondary prevention by raising HDL cholesterol and reducing triglycerides in patients with coronary artery disease. *Circulation.* 2000;102:21–27.
69. Sagnella GA. Practical implications of current natriuretic peptide research. *JRAAS.* 2000;1:304–315.
70. Di Angelantonio E, Chowdhury R, Sarwar N, et al. B-type natriuretic peptides and cardiovascular risk: systematic review and meta-analysis of 40 prospective studies. *Circulation.* 2009;120:2177–2187.
71. Takahashi T, Nakamura M, Onoda T, et al. Predictive value of plasma B-type natriuretic peptide for ischemic stroke: a community-based longitudinal study. *Atherosclerosis.* 2009;207:298–303.
72. Naya T, Yukiiri K, Hosomi N, et al. Brain natriuretic peptide as a surrogate marker for cardioembolic stroke with paroxysmal atrial fibrillation. *Cerebrovasc Dis.* 2008;26:434–440.
73. Montaner J, Perea-Gainza M, Delgado P, et al. Etiologic diagnosis of ischemic stroke subtypes with plasma biomarkers. *Stroke.* 2008;39:2280–2287.
74. Rodriguez-Yanez M, Arias-Rivas S, Santamaria-Cadavid M, Sobrino T, Castillo J, Blanco M. High pro-BNP levels predict the occurrence of atrial fibrillation after cryptogenic stroke. *Neurology.* 2013;81:444–447.
75. Rost NS, Biffi A, Cloonan L, et al. Brain natriuretic peptide predicts functional outcome in ischemic stroke. *Stroke.* 2012;43:441–445.

76. Pikula A, Beiser AS, DeCarli C, et al. Multiple biomarkers and risk of clinical and subclinical vascular brain injury: the Framingham Offspring Study. *Circulation*. 2012;125:2100–2107.
77. Nagase H, Woessner JF Jr. Matrix metalloproteinases. *J Biol Chem*. 1999;274:21491–21494.
78. Rosenberg GA, Navratil M, Barone F, Feuerstein G. Proteolytic cascade enzymes increase in focal cerebral ischemia in rat. *J Cereb Blood Flow Metab*. 1996;16:360–366.
79. Montaner J, Alvarez Sabin J, Molina CA, et al. Matrix metalloproteinase expression is related to hemorrhagic transformation after cardioembolic stroke. *Stroke*. 2001;32:2762–2767.
80. Alvarez-Sabin J, Delgado P, Abilleira S, et al. Temporal profile of matrix metalloproteinases and their inhibitors after spontaneous intracerebral hemorrhage: relationship to clinical and radiological outcome. *Stroke*. 2004;35:1316–1322.
81. Lo EH, Wang X, Cuzner ML. Extracellular proteolysis in brain injury and inflammation: role for plasminogen activators and matrix metalloproteinases. *J Neurosci Res*. 2002;69:1–9.
82. Rosell A, Alvarez-Sabin J, Arenillas JF, et al. A matrix metalloproteinase protein array reveals a strong relation between MMP-9 and MMP-13 with diffusion-weighted image lesion increase in human stroke. *Stroke*. 2005;36:1415–1420.
83. Montaner J, Molina CA, Monasterio J, et al. Matrix metalloproteinase-9 pretreatment level predicts intracranial hemorrhagic complications after thrombolysis in human stroke. *Circulation*. 2003;107:598–603.
84. Sacco RL, Benson RT, Kargman DE, et al. High-density lipoprotein cholesterol and ischemic stroke in the elderly: the Northern Manhattan Stroke study. *JAMA*. 2001;285:2729–2735.
85. Tirschwell DL, Smith NL, Heckbert SR, Lemaitre RN, Longstreth WT Jr, Psaty BM. Association of cholesterol with stroke risk varies in stroke subtypes and patient subgroups. *Neurology*. 2004;63:1868–1875.
86. Amarenco P, Labreuche J, Touboul PJ. High-density lipoprotein–cholesterol and risk of stroke and carotid atherosclerosis: a systematic review. *Atherosclerosis*. 2008;196:489–496.
87. Kurth T, Everett BM, Buring JE, Kase CS, Ridker PM, Gaziano JM. Lipid levels and the risk of ischemic stroke in women. *Neurology*. 2007;68:556–562.
88. Zhang Y, Tuomilehto J, Jousilahti P, Wang Y, Antikainen R, Hu G. Total and high-density lipoprotein cholesterol and stroke risk. *Stroke*. 2012;43:1768–1774.
89. Gordon T, Kannel WB, Castelli WP, Dawber TR. Lipoproteins, cardiovascular disease, and death: the Framingham study. *Arch Intern Medicine*. 1981;141:1128–1131.
90. Willey JZ, Xu Q, Boden-Albala B, et al. Lipid profile components and risk of ischemic stroke: the Northern Manhattan Study (NOMAS). *Arch Neurol*. 2009;66:1400–1406.
91. Shahar E, Chambless LE, Rosamond WD, et al. Plasma lipid profile and incident ischemic stroke: the Atherosclerosis Risk in Communities (ARIC) study. *Stroke*. 2003;34:623–631.
92. Psaty BM, Anderson M, Kronmal RA, et al. The association between lipid levels and the risks of incident myocardial infarction, stroke, and total mortality: the Cardiovascular Health Study. *J Am Geriatr Soc*. 2004;52:1639–1647.
93. Brewer HB Jr. Increasing HDL cholesterol levels. *N Engl J Med*. 2004;350:1491–1494.
94. Freiberg JJ, Tybjaerg-Hansen A, Jensen JS, Nordestgaard BG. Nonfasting triglycerides and risk of ischemic stroke in the general population. *JAMA*. 2008;300:2142–2152.
95. Laloux P, Galanti L, Jamart J. Lipids in ischemic stroke subtypes. *Acta Neurol Belg*. 2004;104:13–19.
96. Kim SJ, Park YG, Kim JH, Han YK, Cho HK, Bang OY. Plasma fasting and nonfasting triglycerides and high-density lipoprotein cholesterol in atherosclerotic stroke: different profiles according to low-density lipoprotein cholesterol. *Atherosclerosis*. 2012;223:463–467.
97. Castelli WP, Anderson K, Wilson PW, Levy D. Lipids and risk of coronary heart disease: the Framingham study. *Ann Epidemiol*. 1992;2:23–28.
98. da Luz PL, Cesena FH, Favarato D, Cerqueira ES. Comparison of serum lipid values in patients with coronary artery disease at <50, 50 to 59, 60 to 69, and>70 years of age. *Am J Cardiol*. 2005;96:1640–1643.

99. Berger JS, McGinn AP, Howard BV, et al. Lipid and lipoprotein biomarkers and the risk of ischemic stroke in postmenopausal women. *Stroke*. 2012;43:958–966.
100. Amarenco P, Goldstein LB, Szarek M, et al. Effects of intense low-density lipoprotein cholesterol reduction in patients with stroke or transient ischemic attack: the Stroke Prevention by Aggressive Reduction in Cholesterol Levels (SPARCL) trial. *Stroke*. 2007;38:3198–3204.
101. Stone NJ, Robinson J, Lichtenstein AH, et al. 2013 ACC/AHA guideline on the treatment of blood cholesterol to reduce atherosclerotic cardiovascular risk in adults: a report of the American College of Cardiology/American Heart Association Task Force on Practice Guidelines. *Circulation*. 2013.
102. Smolders B, Lemmens R, Thijs V. Lipoprotein (a) and stroke: a meta-analysis of observational studies. *Stroke*. 2007;38:1959–1966.
103. Bernd P. The role of neurotrophins during early development. *Gene Exp*. 2008;14:241–250.
104. Yoshii A, Constantine-Paton M. Postsynaptic BDNF-TrKB signaling in synapse maturation, plasticity, and disease. *Dev Neurobiol*. 2010;70:304–322.
105. Wu D. Neuroprotection in experimental stroke with targeted neurotrophins. *NeuroRx*. 2005;2: 120–128.
106. Rosenfeld RD, Zeni L, Haniu M, et al. Purification and identification of brain-derived neurotrophic factor from human serum. *Protein Exp Purific*. 1995;6:465–471.
107. Golden E, Emiliano A, Maudsley S, et al. Circulating brain-derived neurotrophic factor and indices of metabolic and cardiovascular health: data from the Baltimore Longitudinal Study of Aging. *PLoS One*. 2010;5:e10099.
108. Ferris LT, Williams JS, Shen CL. The effect of acute exercise on serum brain-derived neurotrophic factor levels and cognitive function. *Med Sci Sports Exerc*. 2007;39:728–734.
109. Pikula A, Beiser AS, Chen TC, et al. Serum brain-derived neurotrophic factor and vascular endothelial growth factor levels are associated with risk of stroke and vascular brain injury: Framingham study. *Stroke*. 2013;44:2768–2775.
110. Sato Y, Chin Y, Kato T, et al. White matter activated glial cells produce BDNF in a stroke model of monkeys. *Neurosci Res*. 2009;65:71–78.
111. Chen J, Zhang C, Jiang H, et al. Atorvastatin induction of VEFG and BDNF promotes brain plasticity after stroke in mice. *J Cereb Blood Flow Metab*. 2005;25:281–290.
112. Krikov M, Thone-Reineke C, Muller S, Villringer A, Unger T. Candesartan but not ramipril pretreatment improves outcome after stroke and stimulates neurotrophin BDNF/TRKB system in rats. *J Hypertens*. 2008;26:544–552.
113. Yanamoto H, Nagata I, Sakata M, et al. Infarct tolerance induced by intra-cerebral infusion of recombinant brain-derived neurotrophic factor. *Brain Res*. 2000;859:240–248.
114. Pucci S, Mazzarelli P, Missiroli F, Regine F, Ricci F. Neuroprotection: VEGF, IL-6, and clusterin: the dark side of the moon. *Prog Brain Res*. 2008;173:555–573.
115. Rosenstein JM, Krum JM. New roles for VEGF in nervous tissue: beyond blood vessels. *Exp Neurol*. 2004;187:246–253.
116. Plate KH, Beck H, Danner S, Allegrini PR, Wiessner C. Cell type specific upregulation of vascular endothelial growth factor in an MCA-occlusion model of cerebral infarct. *J Neuropathol Exp Neurol*. 1999;58:654–666.
117. Zachary I. Neuroprotective role of vascular endothelial growth factor: signalling mechanisms, biological function, and therapeutic potential. *Neurosignals*. 2005;14:207–221.
118. Slevin M, Krupinski J, Slowik A, Kumar P, Szczudlik A, Gaffney J. Serial measurement of vascular endothelial growth factor and transforming growth factor-beta1 in serum of patients with acute ischemic stroke. *Stroke*. 2000;31:1863–1870.
119. Lee SC, Lee KY, Kim YJ, Kim SH, Koh SH, Lee YJ. Serum VEGF levels in acute ischaemic strokes are correlated with long-term prognosis. *Eur J Neurol*. 2010;17:45–51.

120. Dassan P, Keir G, Jager HR, Brown MM. Value of measuring serum vascular endothelial growth factor levels in diagnosing acute ischemic stroke. *Int J Stroke.* 2012;7:454–459.
121. Debette S, Visvikis-Siest S, Chen MH, et al. Identification of cis- and trans-acting genetic variants explaining up to half the variation in circulating vascular endothelial growth factor levels. *Circ Res.* 2011;109:554–563.
122. Lieb W, Safa R, Benjamin EJ, et al. Vascular endothelial growth factor, its soluble receptor, and hepatocyte growth factor: clinical and genetic correlates and association with vascular function. *Eur Heart J.* 2009;30:1121–1127.
123. Frystyk J, Ledet T, Moller N, Flyvbjerg A, Orskov H. Cardiovascular disease and insulin-like growth factor I. *Circulation.* 2002;106:893–895.
124. Collett-Solberg PF, Cohen P. Genetics, chemistry, and function of the IGF/IGFBP system. *Endocrine.* 2000;12:121–136.
125. Guan J, Miller OT, Waugh KM, McCarthy DC, Gluckman PD. Insulin-like growth factor-1 improves somatosensory function and reduces the extent of cortical infarction and ongoing neuronal loss after hypoxia–ischemia in rats. *Neuroscience.* 2001;105:299–306.
126. Friedrich N, Alte D, Volzke H, et al. Reference ranges of serum IGF-1 and IGFBP-3 levels in a general adult population: results of the Study of Health in Pomerania (SHIP). *Growth Hormon IGF Res.* 2008;18:228–237.
127. Johnsen SP, Hundborg HH, Sorensen HT, et al. Insulin-like growth factor (IGF) I, -II, and IGF binding protein-3 and risk of ischemic stroke. *J Clin Endocrinol Metab.* 2005;90:5937–5941.
128. Kaplan RC, McGinn AP, Pollak MN, et al. Association of total insulin-like growth factor-I, insulin-like growth factor binding protein-1 (IGFBP-1), and IGFBP-3 levels with incident coronary events and ischemic stroke. *J Clin Endocrinol Metab.* 2007;92:1319–1325.
129. Denti L, Annoni V, Cattadori E, et al. Insulin-like growth factor 1 as a predictor of ischemic stroke outcome in the elderly. *Am J Med.* 2004;117:312–317.
130. van Rijn MJ, Slooter AJ, Bos MJ, et al. Insulin-like growth factor I promoter polymorphism, risk of stroke, and survival after stroke: the Rotterdam study. *J Neurol Neurosurg Psychiatry* 2006;77:24–27.
131. Wilczak N, Elting JW, Chesik D, Kema IP, De Keyser J. Intravenous tissue plasminogen activator in patients with stroke increases the bioavailability of insulin-like growth factor-1. *Stroke.* 2006;37:2368–2371.
132. Kooijman R, Sarre S, Michotte Y, De Keyser J. Insulin-like growth factor I: a potential neuroprotective compound for the treatment of acute ischemic stroke? *Stroke.* 2009;40:e83–e88.
133. de Jager SC, Bermudez B, Bot I, et al. Growth differentiation factor 15 deficiency protects against atherosclerosis by attenuating CCR2-mediated macrophage chemotaxis. *J Exp Med.* 2011;208:217–225.
134. Schober A, Bottner M, Strelau J, et al. Expression of growth differentiation factor-15/macrophage inhibitory cytokine-1 (GDF-15/MIC-1) in the perinatal, adult, and injured rat brain. *J Comp Neurol.* 2001;439:32–45.
135. Schindowski K, von Bohlen und Halbach O, Strelau J, et al. Regulation of GDF-15, a distant TGF-beta superfamily member, in a mouse model of cerebral ischemia. *Cell Tissue Res.* 2011;343:399–409.
136. Worthmann H, Kempf T, Widera C, et al. Growth differentiation factor 15 plasma levels and outcome after ischemic stroke. *Cerebrovasc Dis.* 2011;32:72–78.
137. Groschel K, Schnaudigel S, Edelmann F, et al. Growth-differentiation factor-15 and functional outcome after acute ischemic stroke. *J Neurol.* 2012;259:1574–1579.
138. Ho JE, Mahajan A, Chen MH, et al. Clinical and genetic correlates of growth differentiation factor 15 in the community. *Clin Chem.* 2012;58:1582–1591.
139. Persson L, Hardemark HG, Gustafsson J, et al. S-100 protein and neuron-specific enolase in cerebrospinal fluid and serum: markers of cell damage in human central nervous system. *Stroke.* 1987;18:911–918.

140. Korfias S, Stranjalis G, Papadimitriou A, et al. Serum S-100B protein as a biochemical marker of brain injury: a review of current concepts. *Curr Med Chem.* 2006;13:3719–3731.
141. Tanaka Y, Koizumi C, Marumo T, Omura T, Yoshida S. Serum S100B is a useful surrogate marker for long-term outcomes in photochemically-induced thrombotic stroke rat models. *Life Sci.* 2007;81:657–663.
142. Tanaka Y, Marumo T, Omura T, Yoshida S. Serum S100B indicates successful combination treatment with recombinant tissue plasminogen activator and MK-801 in a rat model of embolic stroke. *Brain Res.* 2007;1154:194–199.
143. Wunderlich MT, Wallesch CW, Goertler M. Release of neurobiochemical markers of brain damage is related to the neurovascular status on admission and the site of arterial occlusion in acute ischemic stroke. *J Neurol Sci.* 2004;227:49–53.
144. Missler U, Wiesmann M, Friedrich C, Kaps M. S-100 protein and neuron-specific enolase concentrations in blood as indicators of infarction volume and prognosis in acute ischemic stroke. *Stroke.* 1997;28:1956–1960.
145. Jauch EC, Lindsell C, Broderick J, et al. Association of serial biochemical markers with acute ischemic stroke: the National Institute of Neurological Disorders and Stroke Recombinant Tissue Plasminogen Activator Stroke Study. *Stroke.* 2006;37:2508–2513.
146. Foerch C, du Mesnil de Rochemont R, Singer O, et al. S100B as a surrogate marker for successful clot lysis in hyperacute middle cerebral artery occlusion. *J Neurol Neuros Psychiatry.* 2003;74:322–325.
147. Foerch C, Singer OC, Neumann-Haefelin T, du Mesnil de Rochemont R, Steinmetz H, Sitzer M. Evaluation of serum S100B as a surrogate marker for long-term outcome and infarct volume in acute middle cerebral artery infarction. *Arch Neurol.* 2005;62:1130–1134.
148. Rainer TH, Wong KS, Lam W, Lam NY, Graham CA, Lo YM. Comparison of plasma beta-globin DNA and S-100 protein concentrations in acute stroke. *Clin Chim Acta* 2007;376:190–196.
149. Eng LF, Ghirnikar RS, Lee YL. Glial fibrillary acidic protein: GFAP: thirty-one years (1969–2000). *Neurochem Res.* 2000;25:1439–1451.
150. Herrmann M, Vos P, Wunderlich MT, de Bruijn CH, Lamers KJ. Release of glial tissue-specific proteins after acute stroke: a comparative analysis of serum concentrations of protein S-100B and glial fibrillary acidic protein. *Stroke.* 2000;31:2670–2677.
151. Foerch C, Curdt I, Yan B, et al. Serum glial fibrillary acidic protein as a biomarker for intracerebral haemorrhage in patients with acute stroke. *J Neurol Neurosurg Psychiatry.* 2006;77:181–184.
152. Dvorak F, Haberer I, Sitzer M, Foerch C. Characterisation of the diagnostic window of serum glial fibrillary acidic protein for the differentiation of intracerebral haemorrhage and ischaemic stroke. *Cerebrovasc Dis.* 2009;27:37–41.
153. Foerch C, Niessner M, Back T, et al. Diagnostic accuracy of plasma glial fibrillary acidic protein for differentiating intracerebral hemorrhage and cerebral ischemia in patients with symptoms of acute stroke. *Clin Chem.* 2012;58:237–245.
154. Unden J, Strandberg K, Malm J, et al. Explorative investigation of biomarkers of brain damage and coagulation system activation in clinical stroke differentiation. *J Neurol.* 2009;256:72–77.
155. Mullett SJ, Hamilton RL, Hinkle DA. DJ-1 immunoreactivity in human brain astrocytes is dependent on infarct presence and infarct age. *Neuropathology.* 2009;29:125–131.
156. Allard L, Burkhard PR, Lescuyer P, et al. PARK7 and nucleoside diphosphate kinase A as plasma markers for the early diagnosis of stroke. *Clin Chem.* 2005;51:2043–2051.
157. Betzen C, White R, Zehendner CM, et al. Oxidative stress upregulates the NMDA receptor on cerebrovascular endothelium. *Free Radic Biol Med.* 2009;47:1212–1220.
158. Gappoeva MU, Izykenova GA, Granstrem OK, Dambinova SA. Expression of NMDA neuroreceptors in experimental ischemia. *Biochemistry.* 2003;68:696–702.
159. Dambinova SA, Bettermann K, Glynn T, et al. Diagnostic potential of the NMDA receptor peptide assay for acute ischemic stroke. *PLoS One.* 2012;7:e42362.

160. Dambinova SA, Khounteev GA, Izykenova GA, Zavolokov IG, Ilyukhina AY, Skoromets AA. Blood test detecting autoantibodies to N-methyl-D-aspartate neuroreceptors for evaluation of patients with transient ischemic attack and stroke. *Clin Chem*. 2003;49:1752–1762.
161. Vasan RS. Biomarkers of cardiovascular disease: molecular basis and practical considerations. *Circulation*. 2006;113:2335–2362.
162. Whiteley W, Chong WL, Sengupta A, Sandercock P. Blood markers for the prognosis of ischemic stroke: a systematic review. *Stroke*. 2009;40:e380–e389.
163. Laskowitz DT, Kasner SE, Saver J, Remmel KS, Jauch EC, Group BS. Clinical usefulness of a biomarker-based diagnostic test for acute stroke: the Biomarker Rapid Assessment in Ischemic Injury (BRAIN) study. *Stroke*. 2009;40:77–85.
164. Prugger C, Luc G, Haas B, et al. Multiple biomarkers for the prediction of ischemic stroke: the PRIME study. *Arterioscl Thromb Vasc Biol*. 2013;33:659–666.
165. Sharp FR. Where do omics and markers go next? *Transl Stroke Res*. 2010;1:231–232.
166. Sideso E, Papadakis M, Wright C, et al. Assessing the quality and reproducibility of a proteomic platform for clinical stroke biomarker discovery. *Transl Stroke Res*. 2010;1:304–314.
167. Sharp FR, Jickling GC, Stamova B, et al. Molecular markers and mechanisms of stroke: RNA studies of blood in animals and humans. *J Cereb Blood Flow Metab*. 2011;31:1513–1531.
168. Jickling GC, Stamova B, Ander BP, et al. Profiles of lacunar and nonlacunar stroke. *Ann Neurol*. 2011;70:477–485.
169. Merico D, Gfeller D, Bader GD. How to visually interpret biological data using networks. *Nat Biotechnol*. 2009;27:921–924.
170. Smoot ME, Ono K, Ruscheinski J, Wang PL, Ideker T. Cytoscape 2.8: new features for data integration and network visualization. *Bioinformatics*. 2011;27:431–432.

23

SECULAR TRENDS IN STROKE RISK AND RISK FACTORS FOR STROKE

Raphael A. Carandang

Introduction

The study of secular trends in stroke and stroke risk factors is important (a) to describe the natural history and to quantify the projected burden of disease; (b) to track the progression of known risk factors and identify high-risk populations[1]; (c) to recognize the effect of multiple influences such as the changing demographic characteristics of populations, the development of improved diagnostic techniques and methods, changes in definitions and classifications of disease, as well as the effectiveness of primary and secondary prevention measures and, to a lesser degree, acute stroke therapies; and (d) to provide a basis for evidence-based healthcare planning and direction to public policy and research funding allocation, which are especially relevant as governments and government agencies struggle with economic and political uncertainties and limited resources.[2] The information gathered from studies looking at trends can determine or guide the optimal allocation of resources and impact the burden of disease to a greater extent than any single therapy.

Despite the known limitations and heterogeneity of epidemiological studies such as differences in methods of ascertainment, demographic and geographic variations, differing starting time points and time frames covered, and varying analyses used, epidemiological studies—including cross-sectional studies, but longitudinal cohort studies in particular—are the best methods to study trends because of their long-term follow-up and ability to capture trends over multiple epochs, and their well-established and standardized methods of follow up. Many large cohort studies[3–5] such as the Framingham Heart Study (FHS), Greater Cincinnati/Northern Kentucky Stroke Study (GCNKSS), Atherosclerosis Risk in Communities study, Northern Manhattan Study (NOMAS), Cardiovascular Health Study (CHS) in the United States, and the Oxford Vascular Study (OXVASC) in the United Kingdom; registries such as the World Health Organization Multinational Monitoring of Trends and Determinants of Cardiovascular Disease[6]; and land surveys such as the National Health and

Nutrition Examination Survey (NHANES), among others, have provided and continue to provide important epidemiological information that tracks the incidence, prevalence, severity, mortality, and various other aspects of stroke and stroke risk factors, and provide compelling data that contribute to our understanding of factors influencing the public health burden of stroke and also helps to generate hypotheses, and allows investigation into novel risk factors and assessment of management practices and therapies.

Trends in Prevalence

Given the aging population of the United States and many European industrialized countries, and the improving mortality and 30-day case fatality rates of stroke, particularly ischemic stroke, the prevalence of stroke is expected to increase substantially during the next two decades. Current estimates from the National Health and Nutrition Examination Survey/National Center for Health Statistics (NHANES/NCHS) surveys are that there are 6.8 million Americans with a history of stroke, with an overall prevalence of 2.8%. There is a higher prevalence reported in Native Americans/Alaskans at 5.8%, mixed or other races at 4%, blacks at 3.8%, whites at 3% versus Asian/Pacific Islanders at 1.9% and Hispanics at 1.8% in the Behavioral Risk Factor Surveillance Survey.[5] With the development of better imaging technology, the prevalence of silent ischemic infarcts has also been estimated at 6% to 28% and has been noted to be increasing with age.

A study[7] describing trends in prevalence in the United States between 1973 and 1991 reported an increase in age, race, and sex-adjusted prevalence from 1.41% to 1.87% with an average increase of 7.5% over each 5-year period within these 20 years. However, much of this increase in prevalence was attributable to the aging population. The Centers for Disease Control and Prevention (CDC) *Morbidity and Mortality Weekly Report* describing trends from 2006 to 2010 report an age-adjusted prevalence of stroke of 2.7% in 2006 and 2.6% in 2010. There was a greater prevalence in persons 65 years or older, in Native American and Alaskan natives, and in adults with a lower level of education.[8] Projections to 2030 are that there will be an additional 3.4 million people who will have had a stroke, or an increase of 20.5% in prevalence from 2012.

There was regional variation in prevalence in 2006 ranging from 1.8% in Colorado, Massachusetts, North Dakota, and Vermont to 4.4% in Alabama. In 2010, age-adjusted stroke prevalence ranged from 1.5% in Connecticut to 4.1% in Alabama. From 2006 to 2010, prevalence rates were stable, with only two states having a significant decline: Georgia, from 3.3% to 2.8% (p for trend < 0.01); and South Dakota, from 2.2% to 1.8% (p for trend = 0.04). In 2010, the states with higher stroke prevalence in general were states in the southeastern United States (the so called *stroke belt,* discussed later in the chapter) and Nevada.

A review[9] of nine population-based studies from different countries reports age-standardized prevalence for people aged 65 years or older ranging from 46.1 to 73.3/1000 population. Overall, there was no significant difference in age-standardized prevalence between selected populations in people aged 65 years or more, except in L'Aquila, Italy, and Newcastle, UK, which reported higher prevalences than the other studies.

Analysis of data from the Global Burden of Disease injuries and risk factors study[10] reflect a worldwide prevalence of 33 million in 2010, of which 30% were in those 75 years and older, and of which 52% came from low- to middle-income countries. Prevalence increased significantly with age in all regions, with the most striking increases in prevalence seen in those 75 years old and older, and a steeper increase in prevalence was noted in high-income countries. Stroke prevalence increased significantly (by 27%) in high-income countries but insignificantly (by 8.5%) in low- to middle-income countries from 1990 to 2010.

Prevalence is projected to increase as the demographic characteristics shift to a more elderly population with better survival. Regional and racial differences should concentrate efforts on the southeastern United States and high-risk populations such as blacks, Native Americans, and Hispanics. Global goals should include improving preventive strategies and risk factor prevalence in low- to middle-income countries.

Trends in Incidence

The incidence of stroke increases with age, and one study of populations of European descent found a 9% to 10% increase in relative risk (RR) of stroke with each year in an adult cohort of 93,695 persons aged 19 to 77 years.[11] Age figures prominently in all stroke risk profile scores such as the Framingham Risk Score, and others developed from the CHS, and the Systematic COronary Risk Evaluation (SCORE) risk from the World Health Organization Multinational Monitoring of Trends and Determinants of Cardiovascular Disease project, and it is the most important nonmodifiable risk factor when determining temporal trends because it is a dynamic risk factor that wields its influence on incidence as populations get older, and needs to be adjusted for.

Current estimates from the 2014 American Heart Association statistical updates report, which are extrapolations of incidence estimates from the FHS, the Atherosclerosis Risk in Communities study, the CHS, and the GCNKSS, indicate that each year 795,000 people experience a new or recurrent stroke, which translates to someone having a stroke every 40 seconds in the United States.[5] Of these, 610,000 are first attacks and 185,000 are recurrent attacks. The distribution of stroke subtypes is 87% ischemic, 10% intracerebral hemorrhage (ICH), and 3% subarachnoid hemorrhage (SAH).[5] These estimates have remained fairly stable during the past decade.

Longer term secular trends, however, show that the age-adjusted incidence of stroke has been declining during the last 30 to 50 years in the United States. In Rochester, Minnesota,[12] between 1945 to 1949 and 1975 to 1979, the average annual incidence of stroke declined by 45%, from 209/100,000 population to 115/100,000. The FHS indicated that stroke incidence declined over time in its predominantly white cohort over three epochs that were chosen to mark the onset of widespread use of computed tomographic scanning and magnetic resonance imaging (MRI). Data from 1950 to 1977, 1978 to 1989, and 1990 to 2004 showed that age-adjusted incidence of first stroke per 1000 person-years during each of the three periods was 7.6, 6.2, and 5.3 in men, and 6.2, 5.8, and 5.1 in women, respectively.[13] Numerous studies from Europe and Asia report similar trends in stroke incidence, including studies from China,[14] Denmark,[15] Australia,[16] Japan,[17–19] Finland,[20,21] England,[22] New Zealand,[23] and France[24] reporting either decreasing or stable incidences that are attributed to better treatment of risk factors. A study[25] from Japan suggested a plateau of decline in incidence from 1990 to 2001. In 2010, the worldwide estimate was that there were 16.9 million cases of incident stroke, of which 69% were seen in low- to middle-income countries.[10] There was also an alarming trend of increasing age-standardized incidence in young adults overall, especially in low- to middle-income countries, although not yet significant. Although the mean age of people with stroke is increasing in all countries, the proportion of people younger than 65 years is substantial and is increasing, particularly in the low- to middle-income countries.[10] The current ongoing epidemic of diabetes and increasing prevalence of certain risk factors in young adults, particularly in low- to middle-income countries, constitutes another area of substantial stroke burden globally in addition to the aging population, and requires close surveillance and aggressive strategies for prevention.

There were significant racial differences in the trends of ischemic stroke incidence. In the national Reasons for Geographic and Racial Differences in Stroke[26] cohort, 27,744 participants were monitored for more than 4.4 years (2003–2010), and the overall sex and age-adjusted black/white incidence rate ratio was 1.51. For ages 45 to 54 years, it was 4.02. For those older than 85 years, it was 0.86. Similar trends for a decreasing incidence rate ratio with increasing age were seen in the GCNKSS. The most recent GCNKSS data show that, compared with the 1990s, when stroke incidence rates were stable, stroke incidence in 2005 was decreased for whites, but unfortunately not in blacks.[27] This change was driven by a decrease in ischemic strokes in whites, but there were no changes in the incidence of ischemic strokes in blacks, or for hemorrhagic strokes in blacks or whites. There was also a disturbing trend toward increasing stroke incidence at younger ages, with the mean age at stroke decreasing significantly from 71.2 years to 69.2 years, as well as an increasing proportion of all strokes in those younger than 55 years, with an increase from 12.9% in 1993 to 1994 to 18.6% in 2005. Stroke incidence rates in those aged 20 to 54 years were significantly increasing in both blacks and whites.[28]

The Brain Attack Surveillance in Corpus Christi project demonstrated an increase in the incidence of stroke among Mexican Americans compared with non-Hispanic whites. The crude 3-year cumulative incidence (2000–2002) was 16.8/1000 versus 13.6/1000 in whites. Mexican Americans had a higher cumulative incidence for ischemic stroke at younger ages (45–59 years old: RR, 2.04; 60–74 years old: RR, 1.58), but not at older ages (>75 years old: RR, 1.12). Mexican Americans also had a higher incidence of ICH and SAH than non-Hispanic whites adjusted for age.[29]

The age-adjusted incidence of first ischemic stroke per 1000 was 0.88 for whites, 1.91 for blacks, and 1.49 in Hispanics in NOMAS. Among blacks compared with whites, the relative rate of intracranial atherosclerotic stroke was 5.85; of extracranial atherosclerotic stroke was 3.18; lacunar stroke, 3.09; and cardioembolic stroke, 1.58. Among Hispanics compared with whites, the relative rates for the same categories of stroke were 5.00, 1.71. 2.32, and 1.42 respectively.[30]

Of 4507 Native American participants in the Strong Heart Study in 1989 to 1992, the age-adjusted and sex-adjusted incidence of stroke through 2004 was 6.79/100 person-years, with 86% of incident strokes being ischemic.[31] Blacks, Mexican Americans, and Native Americans are at higher risk, because they have a higher age-adjusted incidence as well as younger age at time of first ischemic stroke.

There were significant gender differences in the secular trends of stroke incidence. Women have a lower age-adjusted stroke incidence than men, but this is modified by age. In the FHS, white women aged 45 to 84 years had a lower stroke risk than white men, but in those older than 85 years this was reversed, with women having an increased stroke risk compared with men.[13] A population-based study from Sweden found stroke incidence to be lower for women than men between ages 55 years and 64 years, but at 75 to 85 years the association reversed. Other studies report a persistent excess risk of stroke for men versus women throughout life, with a diminishment—but no reversal—of the RR.

The decreasing trends in stroke incidence are largely attributable to a decreased incidence of ischemic stroke. ICH, which constitutes 10% of all strokes, has not shown the same decrease. A meta-analysis[32] of 36 studies including 8145 subjects from multiple cohorts all over the world, including Europe, Asia, Australia, South America, and the United States, found no decrease in the incidence of ICH between 1980 and 2008, with an overall incidence of 24.6/100,000 years. Like ischemic stroke, there was a significant increase in incidence with age, but there were no gender differences. There were regional differences in trends; studies from the United Kingdom and Australia reported a decrease from the 1980s to 2001. The Oxfordshire study reported a decrease in incidence of hemorrhage associated with hypertension in those younger than 75 years, but an increase in incidence was associated with antithrombotic treatments in those older than 75 years. Studies from France and Finland reported stable incidences from the 1980 to 2000 and 1980s to 1990s, respectively. A study from Hong Kong noted a stable incidence of ICH but an increasing incidence of hemorrhagic stroke in the younger, 35 to 44–year-old age group, and an overall higher incidence of ICH compared with other countries.[33] Hospital admissions for ICH have increased by 18% during the last 10 years according to a review of published studies and data from clinical trials. This was thought to be secondary to the increase in number of elderly with poor blood pressure control and increasing anticoagulant/antithrombotic use. Mexican, Latin, Native, and black Americans, as well as Chinese and Japanese people have higher incidences than whites. The GCNKSS reported the annual incidence of anticoagulation-associated ICH to be increased from 0.8 to 1.9 to 4.4/100,000 from 1988 to 1993 to 1999. Rates increased from 2.5 to 45.9/100,000 in those older than 80 years.[34]

There are significant differences in incidence between high-income countries versus low-income countries. A systematic review from 2009 analyzed data from population-based studies from 1970 to 2008 and reported a 42% decrease in stroke incidence in high-income countries and a greater than 100% increase in low- to middle-income countries during the past 40 years.[9] Corresponding trends in stroke incidence are observed in younger (<75 years) and older (≥75 years) age groups, although the differences are more pronounced in the older group. In 2000 to 2008, stroke incidence rates in low- to middle-income countries exceeded those in high-income countries by 23%. In high-income countries, there was a greater, albeit nonsignificant, reduction in the incidence of primary ICH compared with ischemic stroke, whereas the incidence of SAH has remained relatively stable during the past four decades. The incidence and proportional frequency of ICH and SAH in low- to middle-income countries are significantly greater than the incidence and frequency in high-income countries.[35] The recent report of the World Health Organization's Global Burden of Disease[10] project confirms that the age-standardized incidence of stroke has declined between 1990 to 2010 by 12% (95% confidence interval [CI], 6–17) in high-income countries, although it increased by 12% (95% CI, −3 to 22) in low-income and middle-income countries, albeit nonsignificantly. Mortality rates decreased significantly in both high income (37%; 95% CI, 31–41) and low-income and middle-income countries (20%; 95% CI, 15–30).

Overall, there has been a decrease in the incidence of stroke driven by a decrease in the incidence of ischemic stroke, which comprises the majority of all strokes, especially among white males. However, there is concern that this declining trend is not as robust in women and has leveled off in blacks. Furthermore, the incidence of hemorrhagic strokes, both cerebral hemorrhage and SAH, has not decreased. Demographic changes in the United States, with an increasing proportion of Hispanics, who have an overall higher risk for stroke, may also adversely affect these trends of declining stroke risk over time. Internationally, the lower income countries have higher and increasing incidences of stroke, and will shape worldwide trends, but we need to establish longitudinal cohort studies for better surveillance of trends in these countries.

Trends in Mortality

There has been a decrease in case fatality and mortality from stroke during the past 50 years. In 1931, stroke ranked second among all causes of death, with a rate of 195/100,000, and this mortality rate was stable until the 1960s. This was followed by a steady decline (−1.2/100,000), which became more rapid in the 1970s to 1980s (−3.3 to −5.6/100,000), but continued, albeit mildly, in the 1990s and moderately into the 2000s (−0.4 to −2.5/100,000). The result is a stroke mortality rate of 40.6/100,000 in 2008, which is an ~75% decrease from the 1930 to 1960 rates.[36] Temporal trends in stroke mortality have either remained stable or declined in most studies from the United States, Europe, Australia, and Japan. The decline in mortality has been attributed to both a decreasing case fatality and a decrease in stroke incidence.[13]

Stroke has now dropped to fourth in rank of all causes of death, behind heart disease, cancer, and chronic lower respiratory disease (CLRD), although part of this is artifactual because of the inclusion of deaths from pneumonia, influenza, and bronchitis as one category in the reclassification of CLRD, which resulted in a dramatic increase in CLRD deaths. The 2011 CDC statistics indicate[37] that, from 1998 to 2008, the annual stroke death rate decreased by 34.8% and the actual number of stroke deaths declined by 19.4%. Despite this decline, stroke continues to be a major cause of mortality, and the

2012 American Heart Association statistical update indicates that every 4 minutes someone dies of a stroke, with stroke accounting for ~1 in every 18 deaths in the United States in 2008. Approximately 54% of stroke deaths occurred outside the hospital in the same year.

Hemorrhagic stroke is more lethal than ischemic stroke. Among persons aged 45 to 64 years, 8% to 12% of ischemic strokes, but more than a third, or 37% to 38%, of hemorrhagic strokes resulted in death within 30 days according to 1987 to 2001 data.[38] In the CHS study from 1989 to 2000 of subjects who were older than 65 years, the 1-month case fatality was 12.6% for all strokes, only 8.1% for ischemic strokes, but 44.6% for hemorrhagic strokes. Hemorrhagic stroke mortality/case fatality has not declined.[39] There is a predilection for greater mortality in women and the elderly. A meta-analysis of 26 study populations reports a median case fatality of 40.4% at 1 month and 54.7% at 1 year, and noted that fatality was higher in women versus men and in those older than 75 years (28.1% vs. 17.8%).[32]

For SAH, the 30-day case fatality did not decline from 1981 to 1986 to 2002 to 2008, but overall mortality from SAH did decline by ~50% in the OXVASC study. After adjusting for age and baseline severity, the authors concluded that patients surviving to the hospital had reduced risk of death and dependency at 12 months during these two decades. A subsequent pooled analysis of 32 studies from 1980 to 2005, seven of which reported temporal trends, observed an unadjusted case fatality decrease of 0.9% per year.[35]

There are significant gender differences in stroke mortality trends, especially at older ages. The 2011 National Health Statistics office reported there were greater declines in stroke death rates in men than in women among people 65 years of age and older than in those who were younger. More women than men die from stroke each year. They accounted for 60.1% of stroke deaths in 2008. In 2002, death certificate data showed that the mean age at stroke death was 79.6 years; however, males had a younger age at stroke death than females, likely because the average age at first stroke is also lower in men.[40] The FHS data did not show a decline in 30-day mortality or case fatality in women—although it did overall—and in men, and this has been reported in other cohort studies from Europe and Japan as well.[13]

There are racial differences in mortality trends that are likely multifactorial in etiology, including a higher incidence of stroke in minorities, and disparities in socioeconomic status and care. These trends are reflected in the geographic disparities in mortality seen in the stroke belt. From 1995 to 1998, age-standardized mortality rates for ischemic stroke, SAH, and ICH were greater among blacks than whites. Among adults 25 to 44 years of age, blacks and Native Americans/Alaskan natives had greater risk ratios than whites for all stroke subtypes. All ethnicities—blacks, Native Americans, Alaskan natives, Asians/Pacific Islanders, and Hispanics—had younger mean ages than whites.[41]

Well-recognized geographic differences have persisted for the past 50 years, with significantly greater stroke death rates seen in the southeastern United States, or the stroke belt, which includes North Carolina, South Carolina, Georgia, Tennessee, Mississippi, Alabama, Louisiana, and Arkansas. Overall stroke mortality is 20% to 40% higher than in the rest of the United States in both whites and blacks. Disparities in incidence are thought to play a substantial role in mortality disparities.[42]

The pattern of changes in stroke incidence rates in high-income and low- to middle-income countries corresponds to those reported in studies of international mortality trends, suggesting that changes in stroke mortality rates are most likely attributable to the corresponding changes in stroke incidence rates. Early stroke case fatality is decreased in both high-income and low- to middle-income countries, and age-standardized mortality decreased by 36% to 38% from 1990 to 2010. However, internationally, disparities continue to exist in many low-income countries, with Sub-Saharan Africa, Central and Latin America, and South Asia continuing to report increasing mortality trends.[10]

Mortality and 30-day case fatality have decreased significantly during the past 50 years overall, and particularly for ischemic stroke. Hemorrhagic stroke mortality continues to be stable, with overall mortality, but not case fatality, improving in SAH. Racial, regional, and gender differences in trends need further investigation and preventive/public health policy formulation. International disparities in stroke mortality are likely related to larger issues of economics, infrastructure, and resources that limit access to high-quality health care, including acute stroke therapies and rehabilitation, as well as secondary stroke prevention.

Trends in Severity and Morbidity

The severity of stroke has remained stable and unchanged during the past 50 years,[13] and stroke continues to be the leading cause of serious long-term disability in the United States.[5] FHS data of ischemic stroke survivors who were more than 65 years of age indicated the following disabilities 6 months poststroke: 50% had hemiparesis, 30% were unable to walk without assistance, 26% were dependent for activities of daily living, 19% had aphasia, 35% had depression, and 26% were institutionalized in nursing homes.[43]

Blacks had greater limitations in ambulation than whites after adjustment for age, sex, and educational attainment, but not for stroke subtype. Blacks were also noted to be younger, had more hemorrhagic strokes, and were more disabled at admission. Blacks and Hispanics also had a poorer functional status at discharge and had less improvement in functional status per inpatient day, but were more likely to be discharged home.[44]

In most studies, women have greater disability after stroke than men. The CHS study found that women were half as likely to be independent in activities of daily living after stroke, even after controlling for age, race, education, and marital status. Another prospective study in Michigan found that women had a 63% lower probability of achieving independence in activities of daily living 3 months after discharge even after controlling for age, race, subtype, prestroke ambulatory status, and other patient characteristics.[45] Women have more strokes secondary to longer life expectancy, have strokes when they are older, and have a higher prevalence of risk factors such as hypertension, atrial fibrillation (AF), and prestroke disability, but have a lower prevalence of lethal risk factors such as heart disease, peripheral vascular disease, smoking, and alcohol use. They are less likely to receive tissue plasminogen activator treatment and lipid testing, and have poorer functional outcomes, more frequent depression and lower quality of life than men.[46]

Trends in Lifetime Risk

Women have a greater lifetime risk of stroke.[47] In the FHS, lifetime risk of stroke for those aged 55 to 75 years was one in five women (20%–21%) and one in six for men (14%–17%). Trends in lifetime risk were studied and compared across three epochs—1950 to 1977, 1978 to 1989, and 1990 to 2004—for incident stroke at 65 years of age and was noted to decrease in the latest data period compared with the first, from 19.5% to 14 % in men and 18% to 16.1 % in women.[13] However, the decrease in lifetime risk did not reach statistical significance. Given that the age-adjusted incidence and 10-year cumulative incidence are both decreasing, the trend in lifetime risk was thought to be secondary to increasing life expectancy, which may offset the decreases in shorter term risk.

Trends in Risk Factors

TRANSIENT ISCHEMIC ATTACK

Transient ischemic attack (TIA) is not often investigated within cross-sectional or longitudinal cohort studies. Precise estimates of incidence and prevalence are not obtainable because of inconsistent criteria used to define TIA in epidemiological studies and problems with accurate ascertainment. Ascertainment and adjudication are problematic in that many people who have had TIAs may not recognize them, and hence may not present to the doctor or hospital. Current estimates come from self-reporting of physician-diagnosed TIA by phone surveys, and they estimate a prevalence of 2.3% or ~5 million,[48] but this is likely an underestimation. The OXVASC study reported that up to 70% of patients do not correctly recognize TIA or minor stroke and 30% delay presentation for medical care for more than 24 hours regardless of age, sex, educational level, or socioeconomic status.[49] The incidence of TIA was reported in the Rochester study[50] in the 1980s and in the GCNKSS in the 1990s, and was estimated at 0.68/1000 and 0.83/1000, respectively. The prevalence of TIA increases with age and varies by sex and race. Men, blacks, and Mexican Americans have greater rates of TIA than their female and non-Hispanic white counterparts.[51]

TIAs confer a substantial short-term risk of stroke, hospitalization for any cardiovascular disease events and death. Of 1707 TIA patients evaluated at the emergency services of Kaiser Permanente, 10% had a stroke within 90 days and 5% had a stroke within 2 days. Predictors of stroke included age older than 60 years, diabetes mellitus (DM), focal neurological symptoms of weakness or speech impairment, and TIA lasting more than 10 minutes. Individuals who survive the initial high-risk period have a 10-year stroke risk of 19% and a combined 10-year stroke, myocardial infarction, and vascular death risk of 43%. Within 1 year of TIA, ~12% of patients will die.[52]

Temporal trends in TIA have been reported only in a few population-based studies from Russia[53] and France,[54] and they report a stable, not decreasing, incidence of TIA in their cohorts.

Because of accumulating data from multiple studies and the development and more widespread use of MRI, the American Heart Association/American Stroke Association has issued a scientific statement endorsing a tissue-based definition, as well as recommendations for workup, diagnosis, and management.[55] The current definition of TIA is a transient episode of neurological dysfunction from focal cerebral, spinal cord, or retinal ischemia *without infarction on imaging*, and the recommended acute imaging modality, preferably undertaken within 24 hours of onset of symptoms, is brain MRI with diffusion weighted imaging sequences. Variability in use of MRI has the potential to impact incidence, and one study estimated that it could result in a 30% reduction in TIA incidence and a 7% increase in ischemic stroke incidence. This will undoubtedly alter the epidemiological data for TIA and ischemic stroke going forward, depending on MRI use. A recent study out of Norway[56] using a prospective registry reported that, with an increase in MRI use for TIA, from 65% in 2006 to 2008 to 89% in 2009 to 2011, there was a significant decrease in proportion of TIAs to ischemic stroke from 12.2% to 8.3%.

HYPERTENSION

Blood pressure is the best-established and most powerful risk factor for both ischemic and hemorrhagic stroke. People with a blood pressure less than 120/80 mmHg have half of the lifetime risk of stroke compared with those with hypertension. Numerous studies, including cohort studies and more than 40 randomized trials with more than 188,000 subjects, have determined that the degree of control has a direct dose–response relationship to risk of stroke, such that each 10-mmHg decrease in blood pressure is associated with an ~33% decrease in risk in subjects 60 to 80 years old regardless of sex, region, stroke subtype, or severity.[57] NHANES statistics[58] suggest that one of three adults in the United States has hypertension, that ~8% of adults have undiagnosed hypertension, and ~76 million Americans have hypertension based on 2008 data. NHANES data[59] describe a favorable trend in blood pressure control from 1988 to 1994 to 2007 to 2008, high blood pressure control rates improved from 27.3% to 50.1%, treatment improved from 54.0% to 73.5%, and the control/treated rates improved from 50.6% to 72.3%. The results of another study looking at only randomized trial data indicated that the benefit of tight blood pressure control is mainly in those without established cardiovascular disease.[60] However, projections show that by 2030, an additional 27 million people could have hypertension, a 9.9% increase in prevalence from 2010, largely as a result of the aging of the population, because the proportion of persons with hypertension increases with increasing age.[61]

There is an overall decreasing trend in age-adjusted incidence of hypertension worldwide, with studies from France, such as the Lausanne Stroke Registry[62]; Portugal[63]; Sweden[64]; Japan[65]; and others all reporting a significant decrease in hypertension in their cohorts.

There is, however, a disturbing trend toward an increasing prevalence of hypertension in children and adolescents in the United States and China. NHANES III, which is a cross-sectional cohort study looking at children and adolescents aged 8 to 17 years, studied trends of systolic and diastolic blood pressure levels between 1988 and 1994, and 1999 and 2000, and found mean systolic blood pressure was 106 mmHg, or 1.4 mmHg higher, and diastolic blood pressure was 61.7 mmHg or 3.3 mmHg higher than in 1988 to 1994. Pressures were higher in blacks and Mexican Americans compared with whites, and these ethnic differences were attenuated when correcting for body mass index (BMI) and obesity.[66] In Shandong, China, the overall prevalence of relatively high blood pressure among children and adolescents aged 7 to 17 years increased from 19.29% (boys) and 14.69% (girls) in 2000 to 26.16% (boys) and 19.77% (girls) in 2010. This was also associated with an increase in obesity and overweight children.[67]

Temporal trends in hypertension appear favorable in most adult cohorts in the United States and worldwide, with a decrease in hypertension and greater use of antihypertensive therapy. There is a concern for the children and adolescents who show an increasing trend in blood pressure in association with greater prevalence of obesity.

DIABETES MELLITUS

Impaired glucose tolerance nearly doubles stroke risk, and DM triples the risk of stroke (see Chapter XX). Age-specific incidence rates and rate ratios show that DM increases ischemic stroke risk at all ages, but is most prominent as a risk factor before age 55 years in blacks and before 65 years in whites. FHS[68] trends show a doubling in the incidence of DM during the past 30 years, most prominently during the 1990s. Of adults 40 to 55 years of age, in each decade of the 1970s, 1980s, and 1990s, the age-adjusted 8-year incidence rates of DM were 2.0%, 3.0%, and 3.7% in women and 2.7%, 3.6%, and 5.8% in men, respectively. Compared with the 1970s, the age- and sex-adjusted odds ratio for DM was 1.40 in the 1980s and 2.05 in the 1990s, with most of the increase in incidence of DM occurring in obese individuals (BMI, >30 kg/m^2).

Racial differences occur in DM incidence in adults.[69] Over 5 years of follow-up in 45- to 84-year-olds, 8.2% of the cohort developed DM. The cumulative incidence was highest in Hispanics (11.3%), followed by black (9.5%), Chinese (7.7%), and white (6.3%) participants. The National Inpatient Survey data from 1997 to 2006 showed that, although stroke incidence decreased, there was trend toward increasing proportion of stroke patients with DM such that one in five to one in three were noted to have DM.[70] According to an international survey[71] and epidemiological data from 2.7 million participants, the prevalence of DM in adults increased from 8.3% (in men) and 7.5% (in women) in 1980 to 9.8% (men) and 9.2% (women) in 2008. The number of individuals affected with DM increased from 153 million in 1980 to 347 million in 2008.

Diabetes appears to be increasing in incidence and prevalence in the United States and is a major risk factor that needs to be addressed to curtail a possible increase in stroke, especially given the increasing incidence of obesity in both children and adults, and changing demographic characteristics in the United States.

OBESITY

Obesity is an epidemic in the United States, with 68% of adults overweight or obese (72% of men and 64% of women). Among men, Mexican Americans and whites were more likely to be overweight or obese than blacks (69%). Among women, blacks (78%) and Mexican Americans (77%) were more likely to be overweight or obese than whites (61%). More than one third (34%) of all adults were obese (32% of men and 36% of women) according to NHANES 2007 to 2008. Among men and women, blacks (37%) and Mexican Americans (36%) were more likely to be obese than whites.[72] Temporal trends as described in the CDC and NHANES data indicate an increasing prevalence of BMI greater than the 95th percentile, at 4% in 1971 to 1974 and increasing to 20% in 2007 to 2008 in children 6 to 11 year olds, and 6% in 1971 to 1974 and increasing to 18% in 2007 to 2008 in adolescents 12 to 19 years old.[73] Compared with 1973 to 1974, the proportion of children 5 to 17 years of age who were obese was five times higher in 2008 to 2009. There was an inverse association with education level, with college graduates having a 20.8% rate of obesity versus those with less than a high school education, of whom 32.9% were obese.

FHS data from 1971 to 2001 showed that among normal-weight white adults between 30 years and 59 years of age, the 4-year rates of becoming overweight varied from 14% to 19% in women and from 26% to 30% in men.[74] The 30-year risk was similar for both sexes, with some variation by age. The age-adjusted prevalence[75] of obesity among adults increased between 1976 to 1980 and between 1988 to 1994, and again between 1988 to 1994 and 1999 to 2000. Obesity prevalence for men was 28% in NHANES 1999 to 2000 (NCHS) and 32% in NHANES 2007 to 2008; for women, obesity prevalence was 33% in 1999 to 2000 and 36% in 2007 to 2008 (Figure 23.1).

Obesity is increasing in children, adolescents, and adults in the United States and other industrialized countries and, like diabetes, needs to be addressed to avoid a costly increase in cardiovascular disease and stroke.

ATRIAL FIBRILLATION

AF is a powerful risk factor for stroke, increasing the risk approximately fivefold independently for all ages. The percentage of strokes secondary to cardioembolism from AF increases steeply from 1.5% at 50 to 59 years to 23.5% at 80 to 89 years.[76] Stroke risk from AF is probably underestimated because AF can often be intermittent and asymptomatic. The prevalence of AF in 2010 ranged from 2.7 million to 6.1 million and is expected to increase as the population ages—to 56 million to 12 million in 40 years. In Olmsted County, Minnesota, the age-adjusted incidence of AF increased by 12.6% from 1980 to 2000. The incidence of AF was greater in men and increased markedly with older age.[77] Blacks, Asians, and Hispanics have a significantly lower adjusted prevalence of AF compared with whites.[78]

HYPERLIPIDEMIA

Hyperlipidemia is a well-accepted risk factor for stroke because of numerous clinical trials and epidemiological data. Current estimates are that there are 31.9. million adults who have hypercholesterolemia, with a prevalence of 13.8%—and possibly 5.6% remain undiagnosed.[5]

The Minnesota Heart Study[79] reported a decline in cholesterol levels from 1980 to 1982 to 2000 to 2002 from an age-adjusted mean total cholesterol of 5.49 mmol/L and 5.38 mmol/L to 5.16 and 5.09 mmol/L. Analyzing NHANES data, there was also a decrease in lipid levels between 1999 to 2000 and 2005 to 2006; the age-adjusted mean total serum cholesterol level decreased from 204 mg/dL to 199 mg/dL and low-density lipoprotein (LDL) cholesterol levels decreased from 129 mg/dL to 123 mg/dL during this period. LDL cholesterol showed a further decrease in 2000 to 2006, from mean levels of 204 mg/dL to 199 mg/dL. The overall prevalence of elevated LDL levels in adults older than 20 years declined by 33% between 1999 to 2006, but this decline was observed mainly for men older than 40 years and for women older than 60 years.[80] There was little change over this time period for other sex/age groups. Lipid-lowering drug use increased significantly for both sexes among those 35 to 74 years of age. Awareness, treatment, and control of hypercholesterolemia have

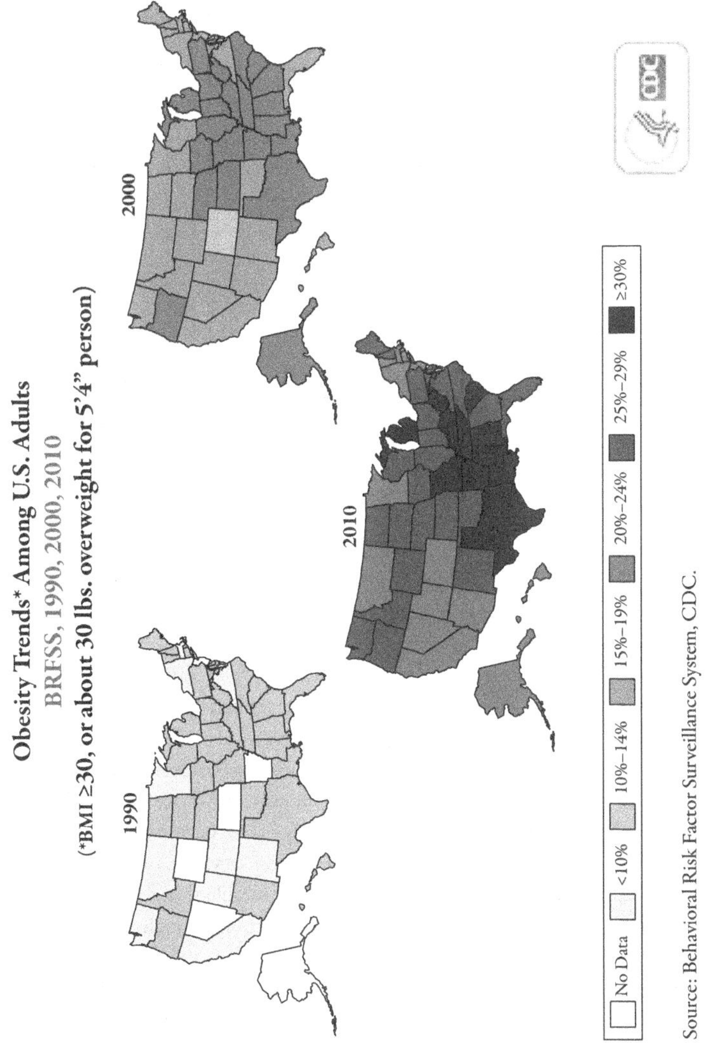

FIGURE 23.1 Obesity trends among U.S. adults over three decades.

increased; however, more than half of those at borderline high risk remain unaware of their condition. Self-reported use of cholesterol-lowering medications increased from 8.2% during 1999 to 2000 to 14.0% during 2005 to 2006.

Cholesterol levels and hyperlipidemia have been decreasing during the past 30 years, and the use of lipid-lowering agents has increased substantially. The improvement in lipid profiles are noted mostly for middle-aged men and women older than 60 years. Future tracking of trends will reveal what kind of impact this improvement in hyperlipidemia will have on stroke.

SMOKING

Cigarette smoking is a well-established, modifiable risk factor for stroke, including ischemic stroke and ICH, and is the most important modifiable risk factor for SAH. Smokers have a two to four times increased risk of stroke compared with nonsmokers or those who have quit for more than 10 years.[81] Data also support a dose–response relationship across old and young age groups. Discontinuation of smoking has been found to reduce stroke risk across sex, age, and race.

From 1998 to 2010, the percentage of U.S. adults who were current cigarette smokers decreased from 24.1% to 19.3%. In 2010, among Americans adults, 21.2% of men and 17.5% of women were current cigarette smokers. From 1998 to 2007, cigarette smoking prevalence among adults decreased in 44 states and the District of Columbia. Six states had no substantial changes in prevalence after controlling for age, sex, and race/ethnicity.[82] The general trend is a decrease in smoking in adults in most states in the United States.

PHYSICAL INACTIVITY

Baseline physical activity has been studied in numerous cohort and case–control studies. FHS investigators found that medium to high levels of physical activity were protective against stroke in men.[83] The CHS results indicated a 5-year mortality benefit in men and women older than 65 years.[84] A meta-analysis found that high levels of physical activity or moderately intense physical activity, both occupational and leisure time activity, were protective (RR, 0.64–0.85) for all stroke, ischemic and hemorrhagic stroke, compared with inactivity.[85] NOMAS study investigators reported a 35% reduction (adjusted HR, 0.37) in ischemic stroke risk with moderate to vigorous exercise in men monitored for up to 9 years.[86] German and Danish studies suggest that recent activity and the timing of activity in relation to stroke were important.[87]

The prevalence of those who engaged in recommended levels of activity increased slightly from 24.3% in 1990 to 25.4% in 1998, and the prevalence of those reporting insufficient activity increased from 45.0% in 1990 to 45.9% in 1998. Those reporting no physical activity decreased from 30.7% in 1990 to 28.7% in 1998. The components of recommended activity remained relatively stable.[88]

A study[89] looking at trends in occupation-related physical activity using U.S. Bureau of Labor statistics and NHANES data from the 1960s concluded that daily occupation-related energy expenditure had decreased by more than 100 calories during the past 50 years.

A 5-year longitudinal study of adolescents reported unfavorable shifts in activity patterns, such as longitudinal decreases in moderate to vigorous physical activity, coupled with longitudinal and secular increases in leisure time computer use.[90]

There is a significant trend[91] toward less physical activity in both adults and adolescents in the long term, although there was a slight decrease in physical inactivity during the early 1990s.

KIDNEY DISEASE

CHS study results indicated that people with a serum creatinine level of more than 1.5 mg/dL were at increased risk of stroke, with an adjusted HR of 1.77, compared with others. Participants in the Reasons for Geographic and Racial Differences in Stroke study with a reduced glomerular filtration rate were also shown to have an increased risk of incident stroke symptoms. The prevalence of end-stage renal disease (ESRD) was reported by the U.S. Renal Data system[92] to be 547,982 cases in 2008 and is projected to increase to 700,000 by 2020.

Overall, during 1995 to 2005, the age-adjusted incidence of ESRD increased from 260.7 per million to 350.9 per million, even as the rate of increase slowed from 1998 to 2005. In the 2000s, compared with the 1990s, the age-adjusted ESRD incidence continued to increase, but at a slower rate among whites and blacks, and has decreased significantly among Native Americans, Asians, and Hispanics.[93]

Prevalence of diabetic kidney disease in the United States increased from 1988 to 2008 in proportion to the prevalence of diabetes. Among persons with diabetes, prevalence of diabetic kidney disease was stable despite increased use of glucose-lowering medications and renin–angiotensin–aldosterone system inhibitors.[94] There is a trend toward overall increasing prevalence of kidney disease and ESRD.

OBSTRUCTIVE SLEEP APNEA

Obstructive sleep apnea was once overlooked but is now a known independent risk factor for stroke. An observational cohort study[95] with 1022 patients, 68% of whom had obstructive sleep apnea, found a significant association with stroke and death (HR, 2.24). After adjusting for age, sex, race, smoking, alcohol consumption, BMI, diabetes, hypertension, AF, and hypertension, the HR was 1.97. Worsening sleep apnea severity is associated with greater stroke risk. Patients with severe sleep apnea have three- to fourfold increased odds of stroke. Continuous positive airway pressure improves a variety of outcomes after stroke. It reduces dramatically the risk of recurrent vascular events among patients with stroke (RR reduction, 81.4%; Number needed to treat-NNT, 3.4). The overall incidence of moderate to severe obstructive sleep apnea for a 5-year period was 11.1% in men and 4.9% in women. Men who had a more than 10-kg weight gain had 5.2-fold odds of increasing their risk of obstructive sleep apnea.[96]

Literature on temporal trends is limited. Given the relationship to weight gain and obesity, the projected trend would be an increase in prevalence.

Summary

Overall, there is a decreasing incidence of stroke, particularly ischemic stroke. Hemorrhagic stroke incidence is stable, and although it comprises a minority of all strokes, it contributes significantly to the mortality and morbidity of stroke. There is a concern that the decreasing trends in stroke incidence and mortality are not as robust in women and blacks. The mortality from stroke has decreased significantly and it now ranks fourth among all causes of death. Mortality from hemorrhagic stroke remains unchanged and has not improved. Severity of stroke is stable, and stroke continues to be the leading neurological cause of long-term morbidity. Women have greater mortality from stroke and poorer recovery, likely a function of having strokes at an older age. Racial and regional differences in mortality exist and need to be addressed with preventive strategies. Lifetime risk of stroke has remained stable despite decreasing stroke incidence and is thought to be secondary to increased life expectancy. Given the aging of the population, decreased mortality, and longer life expectancy, the prevalence of stroke is increasing, and concerns are that it will be a major economic burden to society. Major known risk factors for stroke show divergent trends.[97] Although hypertension, hyperlipidemia, and smoking show decreasing trends in incidence, diabetes, kidney disease, AF, obesity, physical inactivity, and obstructive sleep apnea are increasing, and there are disturbing trends that children and adolescents have increasing blood pressure, obesity, and diabetes. There are composite stroke risk profile scores[98] and American Heart Association recommendations[99] to improve cardiovascular and cerebrovascular health by meeting the metrics: do not smoke; be physically active; have normal blood pressure, blood glucose, and total cholesterol levels; and maintain a healthy weight and eat a healthy diet. These strategies decrease disease and death, but the current success at achieving all these metrics is low. Healthcare planning, policy formulation, and resource allocation should focus on preventive measures, addressed at the population level, for those risk factors that are increasing in prevalence. In addition, investigations of gender, racial, regional, and international differences in care should be instigated.

REFERENCES

1. Ovbiagele B, Nguyen-Huynh M. Stroke epidemiology: advancing our understanding of disease mechanism and therapy. *Neurotherapeutics*. 2011;8:319–329.
2. Feigen VL, Howard G. The importance of epidemiological studies should not be downplayed. *Stroke*. 2008;39:1–2.
3. Wolf PA. Contributions of the Framingham Heart Study to stroke and dementia epidemiological research at 60 years. *Arch Neurol*. 2012;69:567–571.
4. Feigin VL. Lawes CM, Bennett DA, et al. Worldwide stroke incidence and early case fatality reported in 56 population based studies: a systematic review. *Lancet Neurol*. 2009;8:355–369.
5. Go A, Mozaffarian D, Roger V, et al. Heart disease and stroke statistics 2014 update: a report from the American Heart Association. *Circulation*. 2014;129:e28–e292.
6. Thorvaldsen P, Kuulasmaa K, Rajakangas AM, et al. Stroke trends in the WHO MONICA Project. *Stroke*. 1997;28:500–506.
7. Muntner P, Garrett E, Klag M, et al. Trends in stroke prevalence between 1973 and 1991 in the US population 25- to 74 years of age. *Stroke*. 2002;33:1209–1213.
8. Fang J, Shaw K, George M. *MMWR Morb Mortal Wkly Rep*. 2012;61:379–382.
9. Feigin VL, Bennett CM, Anderson CS. Stroke epidemiology: a review of population based studies of incidence, prevalence and case-fatality in the late 20th century. *Lancet Neurol*. 2003;2:42–53.
10. Feigin VL, Forouzanfar H, Krishnamurthi R, et al. Global and regional burden of stroke during 1990–2010: findings from the Global Burden of Disease Study 2010. *Lancet*. 2014;383:245–255.
11. Asplund K, Karvanen J, Giampaoli S, et al. Relative risks for stroke by age, sex and population based on follow up of 18 European populations in the MORGAM project. *Stroke*. 2009;40:2319–2326.
12. Brown RD, Whisnant JP, Sicks RD, O'Fallon WM, Wiebers DO. Stroke incidence, prevalence, and survival: secular trends in Rochester, Minnesota, through 1989. *Stroke*. 1996;27:373–380.
13. Carandang R, Seshadri A, Beiser A, et al. Trends in incidence, lifetime risk, severity and 30-day mortality of stroke over the past 50 years. *JAMA*. 2006;296:2939–2946.
14. Cheng XM, Ziegler DK, Lai YH, et al. Stroke in China, 1986 through 1990. *Stroke*. 1995;26:1990–1994.
15. Thorvaldsen P, Davidsen M, Bronnum-Hansen H, Schroll M, Danish MONICA Study Group. Stable stroke occurrence despite incidence reduction in an aging population: stroke trends in the Danish Monitoring Trends and Determinants in Cardiovascular Disease (MONICA) population. *Stroke*. 1999;30:2529–2535.
16. Jamrozik K, Broadhurst R, Hankey G, Burvill P, Anderson C. Trends in the incidence, severity and short-term outcome of stroke in Perth, Western Australia. *Stroke*. 1999;30:2105–2111.
17. Morikawa Y, Nakagawa H, Naruse Y, et al. Trends in stroke incidence and acute case fatality in a Japanese rural area: the Oyabe Study. *Stroke*. 2000;31:1583–1587.
18. Kubo M, Kiyohara Y, Kato I, et al. Trends in the incidence, mortality, and survival rate of cardiovascular disease in a Japanese community: the Hisayama Study. *Stroke*. 2003;34:2349–2354.
19. Kubo M, Kiyohari Y, Ninomiya T, et al. Decreasing incidence of lacunar vs other types of cerebral infarction in a Japanese population. *Neurology*. 2006;66:1539–1544.
20. Numminen H, Kotila M, Waltimo O, Aho K, Kaste M. Declining incidence and mortality rates of stroke in Finland from 1972 to 1991: results of three population-based stroke registers. *Stroke*. 1996;27:1487–1491.
21. Sivenius J, Tuomilehto P, Immonen-Raiha P, et al. Continuous 15-year decrease in incidence and mortality of stroke in Finland: the FINSTROKE Study. *Stroke*. 2004;35:420–425.
22. Rothwell PM, Coull AJ, Giles MF, et al. Oxford Vascular Study: change in stroke incidence, mortality, case-fatality, severity and risk factors in Oxfordshire, UK from 1981 to 2004 (Oxford Vascular Study). *Lancet*. 2004;363:1925–1933.

23. Anderson CS, Carter KN, Hackett ML, et al. Auckland Regional Community Stroke (ARCOS) Study Group: Trends in stroke incidence in Auckland, New Zealand, during 1981 to 2003. *Stroke.* 2005;36:2087–2093.
24. Benatru I, Rouaud O, Durier J, et al. Stable stroke incidence rates but improved case fatality in Dijon, France, from 1985–2004. *Stroke.* 2006;37:1674–1679.
25. Kita Y, Turin T, Ichikawa M, et al. Trends of stroke incidence in a Japanese population: the Takashima Stroke Registry. *Int J Stroke.* 2009;4:241–249.
26. Howard VJ, McClure LA, Meschia JF, Pulley L, Orr SC, Friday GH. High prevalence of stroke symptoms among persons without a diagnosis of stroke or transient ischemic attack in a general population: the REasons for Geographic And Racial Differences in Stroke (REGARDS) study. *Arch Intern Med.* 2006;166:1952–1958.
27. Kleindorfer DO, Khoury J, Moomaw CJ, et al. Stroke incidence is decreasing in whites but not in blacks: a population-based estimate of temporal trends in stroke incidence from the Greater Cincinnati/Northern Kentucky Stroke Study. *Stroke.* 2010;41:1326–1331.
28. Kissela NM, Khoury JC, Alwell K, et al. Age at stroke: temporal trends in stroke incidence in a large biracial population. *Neurology.* 2012;79:1781–1787.
29. Morgenstern LB, Smith MA, Lisabeth LD, et al. Excess stroke in Mexican Americans compared with non-Hispanic whites: the Brain Attack Surveillance in Corpus Christi Project. *Am J Epidemiol.* 2004;160:376–383.
30. White H, Boden-Albala B, Wang C, et al. Ischemic stroke subtype incidence among whites, blacks, and Hispanics: the Northern Manhattan Study. *Circulation.* 2005;111:1327–1331.
31. Zhang Y, Galloway JM, Welty TK, et al. Incidence and risk factors for stroke in American Indians: the Strong Heart Study. *Circulation.* 2008;118:1577–1584.
32. Van Asch C, Luitse M, Rinkel G, et al. Incidence, case fatality and functional outcome of intracerebral hemorrhage over time, according to age and ethnic origin: a systematic review and meta-analysis. *Lancet Neurol.* 2010;9:167–176.
33. Qureshi AI, Mendelow AD, Hanley DF. Intracerebral haemorrhage. *Lancet.* 2009;373:1632–1644.
34. Flaherty M, Kissela B, Woo D, et al. The increasing incidence of anticoagulant-associated intracerebral hemorrhage. *Neurology.* 2007;68:116–121.
35. Lovelock C, Rinkel G, Rothwell P. Time trends in outcome of subarachnoid hemorrhage. *Neurology.* 2010;74:1494–1501.
36. Towfighi A, Saver J. Stroke declines from third to fourth leading cause of death in the United States: historical perspective and challenges ahead. *Stroke.* 2011;42:2351–2355.
37. Centers for Disease Control and Prevention. Vital statistics public use data files—2008. Available at: http://www.cdc.gov/nchs/data_access/Vitalstatsonline.htm#Mortality_Multiple.
38. Rosamond WD, Folsom AR, Chambless LE, et al. Stroke incidence and survival among middle-aged adults: 9-year follow-up of the Atherosclerosis Risk in Communities (ARIC) cohort. *Stroke.* 1999;30:736–743.
39. El-Saed A, Kuller LH, Newman AB, et al. Geographic variations in stroke incidence and mortality among older populations in four US communities. *Stroke.* 2006;37:1975–1979.
40. National Center for Health Statistics. Health data interactive. 2011. Available at: http://www.cdc.gov/nchs/hdi.htm, accessed December 2012.
41. Centers for Disease Control and Prevention. Disparities in deaths from stroke among persons aged 75 years: United States, 2002. *MMWR Morb Mortal Wkly Rep.* 2005;54:477–481.
42. Casper ML, Barnett E, Williams GI Jr, et al. *Atlas of stroke mortality: racial, ethnic, and geographic disparities in the United States.* Atlanta, GA: Department of Health and Human Services, Centers for Disease Control and Prevention, 2003.
43. Centers for Disease Control and Prevention. Prevalence and most common causes of disability among adults: United States, 2005. *MMWR Morb Mortal Wkly Rep.* 2009;58:421–426.

44. McGruder H, Greenlund K, Croft J, Zheng Z, Centers for Disease Control and Prevention. Differences in disability among black and white stroke survivors: United States, 2000–2001. *MMWR Morb Mortal Wkly Rep.* 2005;54:3–6.
45. Kelly-Hayes M, Beiser A, Kase CS, Scaramucci A, D'Agostino RB, Wolf PA. The influence of gender and age on disability following ischemic stroke: the Framingham study. *J Stroke Cerebrovasc Dis.* 2003;12:119–126.
46. Reeves M, Bushnell C, Howard G, et al. Sex differences in stroke: epidemiology, clinical presentation, medical care and outcomes. *Lancet.* 2008;7:915–926.
47. Seshadri S, Beiser A, Kelly-Hayes M, et al. The lifetime risk of stroke: estimates from the Framingham Study. *Stroke.* 2006;37:345–350.
48. Johnston SC, Fayad PB, Gorelick PB, et al. Prevalence and knowledge of transient ischemic attack among US adults. *Neurology.* 2003;60:1429–1434.
49. Chandratheva A, Lasserson D, Geraghty O, Rothwell P. Population based study of behavior immediately after transient ischemic attack and minor stroke in 1000 consecutive patients. *Stroke.* 2010;41:1108–1114.
50. Brown RD Jr, Petty GW, O'Fallon WM, Wiebers DO, Whisnant JP. Incidence of transient ischemic attack in Rochester, Minnesota, 1985–1989. *Stroke.* 1998;29:2109–2113.
51. Kleindorfer D, Panagos P, Pancioli A, et al. Incidence and short-term prognosis of transient ischemic attack in a population-based study. *Stroke.* 2005;36:720–723.
52. Johnston SC, Gress DR, Browner WS, Sidney S. Short-term prognosis after emergency department diagnosis of TIA. *JAMA.* 2000;284:2901–2906.
53. Feigen VL Shishkin S, Tzirkin GM, et al. Population based study of transient ischemic attack incidence in Novosibirsk, Russia 1987–1988 and 1996–1997. *Stroke.* 2000;31:9–13.
54. Bejot Y, Benatru O, Durier J, et al. Trends in the incidence of transient ischemic attacks, premorbid risk factors and the use of preventive treatments in the population of Dijon, France from 1985 to 2004. *Cerebrovasc Dis.* 2007;23:126–131.
55. Easton JD. Saver JL, Albers G, et al. Definition and evaluation of transient ischemic attack: a scientific statement for health care professionals from the American Heart Association/American Stroke Association Stroke Council. *Stroke.* 2009;40:2276–2239.
56. Kvistad CE, Thomassen L, Waje-Andreassen U, et al. Clinical implications of increased use of MRI in TIA. *Acta Neurol Scan.* 2013;128:32–38.
57. Lawes CM, Bennett DA, Feigin VL, Rogers A. Blood pressure and stroke: an overview of published reviews. *Stroke.* 2004;35:776–785.
58. Fields LE, Burt VL, Cutler JA, Hughes J, Roccella EJ, Sorlie P. The burden of adult hypertension in the United States 1999 to 2000: a rising tide. *Hypertension.* 2004;44:398–404.
59. Egan BM, Zhao Y, Axon RN. US trends in prevalence, awareness, treatment, and control of hypertension, 1988–2008. *JAMA.* 2010;303:2043–2050.
60. Lee M, Saver J, Hong KS, et al. Does achieving intensive versus usual BP level prevent stroke? *Ann Neurol.* 2012;71;133–140.
61. Lloyd-Jones DM, Evans JC, Levy D. Hypertension in adults across the age spectrum: current outcomes and control in the community. *JAMA.* 2005;294:466–472.
62. Periera M. Carreira H, Vales C, et al. Trends in hypertension prevalence and mean blood pressure in Portugal: a systematic review. *Blood Press.* 2012;21:220–226.
63. Carrera E, Maeder-Ingvar M, Bogousslavsky J, et al. Trends in risk factors, patterns, causes in hospitalized strokes over 25 years: the Lausanne Stroke Registry. *Cerebrovasc Dis.* 2007;24:97–103.
64. Eriksson M, Holmgren L, Janlert U, et al Large improvements in major cardiovascular risk factors in the population of northern Sweden: the MONICA study 1986–2009. *J Intern Med.* 2011;269: 219–231.

65. Kubo M, Hata J, Doi Y, et al. Secular trends in the incidence of and risk factors of ischemic stroke and its subtypes in Japanese population. *Circulation.* 2008:118:2672–2678.
66. Muntner P, He J, Cutler JA, et al. Trends in blood pressure among children and adolescents. *JAMA.* 2004;291:2107–2113.
67. Zhang YX, Zhao JS, Sun GZ, Lin M, Chu ZH. Prevalent trends in relatively high blood pressure among children and adolescents in Shandong, China. *Ann Hum Biol.* 2012;39:259–263.
68. Fox CS, Pencina MJ, Meigs JB, Vasan RS, Levitzky YS, D'Agostino RB Sr. Trends in the incidence of type 2 diabetes mellitus from the 1970s to the 1990s: the Framingham Heart Study. *Circulation.* 2006;113:2914–2918.
69. Nettleton JA, Steffen LM, Ni H, Liu K, Jacobs DR Jr. Dietary patterns and risk of incident type 2 diabetes in the Multi-Ethnic Study of Atherosclerosis (MESA). *Diabetes Care.* 2008;31:1777–1782.
70. Towfighi A, Markovic D, Ovbiagele B. Current national patterns of comorbid diabetes among acute ischemic stroke patients. *Cerebrovasc Dis.* 2012;33:411–418.
71. Danaei G, Finucane MM, Lu Y, et al. Global Burden of Metabolic Risk Factors of Chronic Diseases Collaborating Group (Blood Glucose): national, regional, and global trends in fasting plasma glucose and diabetes prevalence since 1980: systematic analysis of health examination surveys and epidemiological studies with 370 country-years and 2.7 million participants. *Lancet.* 2011;378:31–40.
72. Flegal KM, Carroll MD, Ogden CL, Curtin LR. Prevalence and trends in obesity among US adults, 1999–2008. *JAMA.* 2010;303:235–241.
73. Ogden CL, Lamb MM, Carroll MD, Flegal KM. Obesity and socioeconomic status in children and adolescents: United States, 2005–2008. *NCHS Data Brief.* 2010;51:1–8.
74. Ogden CL, Carroll MD, Curtin LR, McDowell MA, Tabak CJ, Flegal KM. Prevalence of overweight and obesity in the United States, 1999–2004. *JAMA.* 2006;295:1549–1555.
75. Centers for Disease Control and Prevention. Estimated prevalence and trends of diabetes and obesity: United States, 2007. *MMWR Morb Mortal Wkly Rep.* 2009;58:1259–1263.
76. Go AS, Hylek EM, Phillips KA, et al. Prevalence of diagnosed atrial fibrillation in adults: national implications for rhythm management and stroke prevention: the Anticoagulation and Risk Factors in Atrial Fibrillation (ATRIA) Study. *JAMA.* 2001;285:2370–2375.
77. Miyasaka Y, Barnes ME, Gersh BJ, et al. Secular trends in incidence of atrial fibrillation in Olmsted County, Minnesota, 1980 to 2000, and implications on the projections for future prevalence. *Circulation.* 2006;114:119–125.
78. Shen AY, Contreras R, Sobnosky S, et al. Racial/ethnic differences in the prevalence of atrial fibrillation among older adults: a cross-sectional study. *J Natl Med Assoc.* 2010;102:906–913.
79. Arnett DK, Jacobs DR Jr, Luepker RV, et al. Twenty year trends in serum cholesterol, hypercholesterolemia and cholesterol medication use: the Minnesota Heart Survey, 1980–82 to 2000–2002. *Circulation.* 2005;112:3884–3891
80. Schober S, Carroll M, Lacher D, Hirsch R. Division of health and nutrition examination surveys: high serum cholesterol: an indicator for monitoring cholesterol lowering efforts US adults, 2005–2006. *NCHS Data Brief.* 2007;2:1–8.
81. Centers for Disease Control and Prevention. Cigarette smoking among adults and trends in smoking cessation: United States, 2008. *MMWR Morb Mortal Wkly Rep.* 2009;58:1227–1232.
82. Kelly N, Gu D, Chen J, et al. Cigarette smoking and risk of stroke in the Chinese adult population. *Stroke.* 2008;39:1688–1693.
83. Kiely DK, Wolf PA, Cupples LA, et al. Physical activity and stroke risk: the Framingham Study. *Am J Epidemiol.* 1994;140:608–620.
84. Grau AJ, Barth C, Geletneky B, et al. Association between recent sports activity, sports activity in young adulthood, and stroke. *Stroke.* 2009;40:426–431.

85. Wendel-Vos G, Schuit A, Feskens E, et al. Physical activity and stroke: a meta-analysis of observational data. *Int J Epidemiol.* 2004;33:787–798.
86. Willey JZ, Moon YP, Paik MC, Boden-Albala B, Sacco RL, Elkind MS. Physical activity and risk of ischemic stroke in the Northern Manhattan Study. *Neurology.* 2009;73:1774–1779.
87. Krarup LH, Truelsen T, Pedersen A, et al. Level of physical activity in the week preceding an ischemic stroke. *Cerebrovasc Dis.* 2007;24:296–300.
88. DiPietro L. Physical activity in aging: changing in patterns and their relationship to health and function. *Am J Gerontol.* 2001;56 (Suppl 2):13–22.
89. Centers for Disease Control and Prevention. Physical activity trends: United States, 2008. *MMWR Morb Mortal Wkly Rep.* 2001;50:166–169.
90. Church TS, Thomas DM, Tudor-Locke C, et al. Trends over 5 decades in U.S. occupation-related physical activity and their associations with obesity. *PLoS One.* 2011;6:e19657.
91. Nelson MC, Neumark-Stzainer D, Hannan PJ, et al. Longitudinal and secular trends in physical activity and sedentary behavior during adolescence. *Pediatrics.* 2006;118:e1627–e1643.
92. US Renal Data System. *USRDS 2010 annual data report: atlas of chronic kidney disease and end-stage renal disease in the United States.* Bethesda, MD: National Institutes of Health, National Institute of Diabetes and Digestive and Kidney Diseases, 2010.
93. Burrows NR, Li Y, Williams DE. Racial and ethnic differences in trends of end-stage renal disease: United States 1995–2005. *Adv Chronic Kidney Dis.* 2008;15:147–152.
94. De Boer I, Rue T, Hall Y, et al. Temporal trends in the prevalence of diabetic kidney disease in the US. *JAMA.* 2011;305:2532–2539.
95. Yaggi HK, Concato J, Kernan WN, et al. Obstructive sleep apnea as a risk factor for stroke and death. *N Engl J Med.* 2005;353:2034–2341.
96. Punjabi N. The epidemiology of adult obstructive sleep apnea. *Proc Am Thorac Soc.* 2008;5:136–143.
97. Borena W, Stocks T, Strohmaier et al. Long-term temporal trends in cardiovascular and metabolic risk factors. *Wein Klin Wochenschr.* 2009;121:623–630.
98. Wolf PA, D'Agostino RB, Belanger AJ, Kannel WB. Probability of stroke: a risk profile from the Framingham study. *Stroke.* 1991;22:312–318.
99. Yang Q, Cogswell ME, Flanders WD, et al. Trends in cardiovascular health metrics and associations with all cause and CVD mortality among US adults. *JAMA.* 2012;307:1273–1283.

Epilogue/Synthesis

STROKE IS A heterogenous entity, but all varieties of stroke share a common etiology of disturbance in the blood supply to the brain. The most common types of ischemic and hemorrhagic stroke share a common substrate of preceding atherosclerotic and arteriosclerotic changes. In this book, genetic variants and a wide range of demographic, lifestyle, and vascular and metabolic characteristics that modify stroke risk have been discussed. We also reviewed circulating biomarkers associated with risk of stroke. Some of these biomarkers likely mediate known associations of lifestyle and vascular risk factors with stroke whereas others appear to point to the involvement of previously unsuspected biological pathways in mediating stroke risk.

Most strokes are predictable and preventable consequences of chronic disease attributable to the impact of risk factors acting over many decades. We can determine the relative impact of addressing various risk factors by estimating a population-attributable risk fraction for each risk factor—a theoretical concept that estimates how much of the disease in a population could be eliminated by the eradication of a specific risk factor—and it depends on both the prevalence of a specific risk factor and the relative risk associated with it. Thus, correcting a common risk factor such as modest elevation in blood pressure would have a greater public health impact than addressing a relatively more rare risk factor such as sickle cell disease, which would reduce risk dramatically for only a few affected persons. Public health strategies to prevent stroke can be categorized as (1) "mass" strategies that focus on health education, legislation, and social, environmental changes, such as cigarette taxes and reducing blood pressure through reduced salt intake; or as (2) "high-risk" strategies that focus on physicians identifying and counseling/treating individual high-risk subjects identified using clinical examination and risk assessment profiles.

The wide range of risk factors discussed in this book do not, of course, act in isolation. Risk factors tend to cluster together, and some of the most frequently observed clusters are recognized as specific conditions with an underlying biological substrate, such as the metabolic syndrome of obesity, hypertension, and dyslipidemia associated with insulin resistance. Moreover, risk factors act synergistically to increase risk. Risk factors most often affect risk in a continuous, graded fashion, extending into the perceived normal range. At any level of each risk factor, stroke risk varies widely, depending on the number and levels of other accompanying risk factors. The Framingham Stroke Risk Profile (FSRP) was developed nearly 25 years ago as a simple risk prediction algorithm to help identify persons at an increased risk of stroke, based only on information from a medical history and physical examination, plus an electrocardiogram. It integrates the effects of age, sex, and baseline measurements of various modifiable vascular risk factors—systolic blood pressure, use of antihypertensive medications, presence or absence of left ventricular hypertrophy on electrocardiography, presence of diabetes, any cardiovascular disease and atrial fibrillation, and smoking status—to arrive at an estimated 10-year probability of stroke. Thus, for a 70-year-old man with elevated levels of one risk factor, a systolic blood pressure of 160 mm Hg, his stroke risk could vary from 8% in the absence of the six other risk factors considered to 85% in the presence of all six. Other composite stroke risk assessment tools have been developed, but the Framingham risk predictor remains the one used most widely to assess risk and to explore the incremental predictive utility of any novel putative risk marker. It has been endorsed and is used in risk stratification and treatment guidelines published by the American Heart Association, and British and European cardiovascular societies. When applied to countries and race/ethnic samples with different baseline risks of stroke, it has required recalibration to the baseline risk of that sample. However, in a wide variety of settings, the FSRP has proved robust, and few newer biomarkers appear to improve risk prediction further.

Among the most promising "new" markers are indicators of subclinical disease such as carotid stenosis, carotid intimal–medial thickness, and magnetic resonance imaging measures of vascular brain injury. This is because existing stroke risk scores use levels of risk factors at the time of risk prediction (current exposure), although the duration and severity of exposure to a risk factor before the time of risk prediction (remote exposure) also determine risk. Measures of subclinical disease are useful markers of past exposure to risk and preexisting injury, and have been described as "signposts on the highway to disease."

Twenty years ago, it was recognized that an average middle-age person would be concerned about his or her risk of stroke beyond the 10-year period for which the FSRP provided an estimate. The concept of a lifetime risk, already well established for estimating the risk of breast and other cancers, was extended to neurological and cardiovascular diseases, including stroke. The lifetime risk of stroke may be defined as the risk that a person, currently free of stroke, would develop at some time before they died; it is based on estimated life expectancy, and age- and sex-specific risks. The various genetic, vascular, lifestyle, and other risk factors discussed in this book alter short-term as well as lifetime risks. Their impact on lifetime risk is greater if they act congruently on both survival and stroke risk. Most factors that increase stroke risk shorten rather than increase life expectancy, so their impact on lifetime risk of stroke is blunted. However, as survival from cancers and other cardiovascular risk factors improves, the impact of these risk factors on stroke risk could increase. Temporal trends in the risk of stroke and of stroke risk factors are discussed in this book. As a consequence of these temporal trends in risk factor prevalence and treatment, the FSRP overestimates stroke risk for contemporaneous populations in Framingham and elsewhere, and a newer risk profile is being developed and validated. Newer circulating and imaging biomarkers and genetic risk variants associated with stroke risk continue to be identified.

Unfortunately despite all these discoveries, risk prediction remains a very inexact science, and despite stroke prevention efforts worldwide, more than 9 million new strokes will occur this year. We hope you, the reader, will expand the knowledge summarized in this book and accelerate its impact on stroke prevention through your own contributions to stroke research and clinical care.

Index

Page numbers followed by *f* and *t* indicate figures and tables, respectively. Numbers followed by *b* indicate boxes.